This thesaurus has been compiled by referring to the Bank of English, a unique database of the English language with examples of over 400 million words enabling Collins lexicographers to analyse how English is actually used today and how it is changing. This is the evidence on which the changes in this thesaurus are based.

The Bank of English was set up as a joint initiative by HarperCollins Publishers and Birmingham University to be a resource for language research and lexicography. It contains a very wide range of material from books, newspapers, radio, TV, magazines, letters and talks reflecting the whole spectrum of English today. Its size and range make it an unequalled resource and the purpose-built software for its analysis is unique to Collins Dictionaries.

This ensures that Collins Dictionaries accurately reflect English as it is used today in a way that is most helpful to the dictionary user as well as including the full range of rarer and historical words and meanings.

FEATURES OF THE BOOK

Entry Word ——————————— **crass** *adjective* <u>INSENSITIVE</u>, boorish, gross, indelicate, oafish, stupid, unrefined, witless

crate *noun* <u>CONTAINER</u>, box, case, packing case, tea chest

crater *noun* <u>HOLLOW</u>, depression, dip

Phrasal Verb ——————————— **crave** *verb* **1** <u>LONG FOR</u>, desire, hanker after, hope for, lust after, want, yearn for **2** *Informal* <u>BEG</u>, ask, beseech, entreat, implore,

Synonym ——————————— petition, plead for, pray for, seek, solicit, supplicate

Most Helpful Synonym ——————————— **craving** *noun* <u>LONGING</u>, appetite, desire, hankering, hope, hunger, thirst, yearning, yen (*informal*)

crawl *verb* **1** <u>CREEP</u>, advance slowly, inch, slither, worm one's way, wriggle, writhe **2** <u>GROVEL</u>, creep,

Sense Number ——————————— fawn, humble oneself, toady **3** <u>BE FULL OF</u>, be alive, be overrun (*slang*), swarm, teem

Part of Speech ——————————— **craze** *noun* <u>FAD</u>, enthusiasm, fashion, infatuation, mania, rage, trend, vogue

crazy *adjective* **1** *Informal* <u>RIDICULOUS</u>, absurd, foolish, idiotic, ill-conceived, ludicrous, nonsensical, preposterous, senseless **2** <u>FANATICAL</u>, devoted, enthusiastic, infatuated, mad, passionate, wild (*informal*)

Usage Label ——————————— **3** <u>INSANE</u>, crazed, demented, deranged, mad, nuts (*slang*), out of one's mind, unbalanced

Idiom ———————————

creak *verb* <u>SQUEAK</u>, grate, grind, groan, scrape, scratch, screech

cream *noun* **1** <u>LOTION</u>, cosmetic, emulsion, essence, liniment, oil, ointment, paste, salve, unguent **2** <u>BEST</u>, *crème de la crème*, elite,

Foreign Word/Phrase ——————————— flower, pick, prime ♦ *adjective* **3** <u>OFF-WHITE</u>, yellowish-white

creamy *adjective* <u>SMOOTH</u>, buttery, milky, rich, soft, velvety

v

EDITORIAL STAFF

A a

abandon *verb* **1** LEAVE, desert,
forsake, strand **2** GIVE UP,
relinquish, surrender, yield ♦ *noun*
3 WILDNESS, recklessness

abandonment *noun* LEAVING,
dereliction, desertion, forsaking

abashed *adjective* EMBARRASSED,
ashamed, chagrined,
disconcerted, dismayed,
humiliated, mortified,
shamefaced, taken aback

abate *verb* DECREASE, decline,
diminish, dwindle, fade, lessen, let
up, moderate, relax, slacken,
subside, weaken

abbey *noun* MONASTERY, convent,
friary, nunnery, priory

abbreviate *verb* SHORTEN, abridge,
compress, condense, contract,
cut, reduce, summarize

abbreviation *noun* SHORTENING,
abridgment, contraction,
reduction, summary, synopsis

abdicate *verb* GIVE UP, abandon,
quit, relinquish, renounce, resign,
step down (*informal*)

abdication *noun* GIVING UP,
abandonment, quitting,
renunciation, resignation,
retirement, surrender

abduct *verb* KIDNAP, carry off, seize,
snatch (*slang*)

abduction *noun* KIDNAPPING,
carrying off, seizure

aberration *noun* ODDITY,
abnormality, anomaly, defect,
irregularity, lapse, peculiarity, quirk

abet *verb* HELP, aid, assist, connive
at, support

abeyance *noun* **in abeyance**
SHELVED, hanging fire, on ice
(*informal*), pending, suspended

abhor *verb* HATE, abominate, detest,
loathe, shrink from, shudder at

abhorrent *adjective* HATEFUL,
abominable, disgusting,
distasteful, hated, horrid,
loathsome, offensive, repulsive

abide *verb* TOLERATE, accept, bear,
endure, put up with, stand, suffer

abide by *verb* OBEY, agree to,
comply with, conform to, follow,
observe, submit to

abiding *adjective* EVERLASTING,
continuing, enduring, lasting,
permanent, persistent,
unchanging

ability *noun* SKILL, aptitude,
capability, competence, expertise,
proficiency, talent

abject *adjective* **1** MISERABLE,
deplorable, forlorn, hopeless,
pitiable, wretched **2** SERVILE,
cringing, degraded, fawning,
grovelling, submissive

ablaze *adjective* ON FIRE, aflame,
alight, blazing, burning, fiery,
flaming, ignited, lighted

able *adjective* CAPABLE,
accomplished, competent,
efficient, proficient, qualified,
skilful

able-bodied *adjective* STRONG, fit,
healthy, robust, sound, sturdy

abnormal *adjective* UNUSUAL,
atypical, exceptional,
extraordinary, irregular, odd,
peculiar, strange, uncommon

abnormality *noun* ODDITY,
deformity, exception, irregularity,
peculiarity, singularity, strangeness

abode *noun* HOME, domicile,
dwelling, habitat, habitation,
house, lodging, pad (*slang*),

quarters, residence

abolish *verb* DO AWAY WITH, annul, cancel, destroy, eliminate, end, eradicate, put an end to, quash, rescind, revoke, stamp out

abolition *noun* ENDING, cancellation, destruction, elimination, end, extermination, termination, wiping out

abominable *adjective* TERRIBLE, despicable, detestable, disgusting, hateful, horrible, horrid, repulsive, revolting, vile

abort *verb* 1 TERMINATE (*a pregnancy*), miscarry 2 STOP, arrest, axe (*informal*), call off, check, end, fail, halt, terminate

abortion *noun* TERMINATION, deliberate miscarriage, miscarriage

abortive *adjective* FAILED, fruitless, futile, ineffectual, miscarried, unsuccessful, useless, vain

abound *verb* BE PLENTIFUL, flourish, proliferate, swarm, swell, teem, thrive

abounding *adjective* PLENTIFUL, abundant, bountiful, copious, full, profuse, prolific, rich

about *preposition* 1 REGARDING, as regards, concerning, dealing with, on, referring to, relating to 2 NEAR, adjacent to, beside, circa (*used with dates*), close to, nearby ◆ *adverb* 3 NEARLY, almost, approaching, approximately, around, close to, more or less, roughly

above *preposition* OVER, beyond, exceeding, higher than, on top of, upon

abrasion *noun Medical* GRAZE, chafe, scrape, scratch, scuff, surface injury

abrasive *adjective* 1 UNPLEASANT, caustic, cutting, galling, grating, irritating, rough, sharp 2 ROUGH, chafing, grating, scraping, scratchy

abreast *adjective* 1 ALONGSIDE, beside, side by side 2 **abreast of** INFORMED ABOUT, acquainted with, *au courant* with, *au fait* with, conversant with, familiar with, in the picture about, in touch with, keeping one's finger on the pulse of, knowledgeable about, up to date with, up to speed with

abridge *verb* SHORTEN, abbreviate, condense, cut, decrease, reduce, summarize

abroad *adverb* OVERSEAS, in foreign lands, out of the country

abrupt *adjective* 1 SUDDEN, precipitate, quick, surprising, unexpected 2 CURT, brusque, gruff, impatient, rude, short, terse

abscond *verb* FLEE, clear out, disappear, escape, make off, run off, steal away

absence *noun* 1 NONATTENDANCE, absenteeism, truancy 2 LACK, deficiency, need, omission, unavailability, want

absent *adjective* 1 MISSING, away, elsewhere, gone, nonexistent, out, unavailable 2 ABSENT-MINDED, blank, distracted, inattentive, oblivious, preoccupied, vacant, vague ◆ *verb* 3 **absent oneself** STAY AWAY, keep away, play truant, withdraw

absent-minded *adjective* VAGUE, distracted, dreaming, forgetful, inattentive, preoccupied, unaware

absolute *adjective* 1 TOTAL, complete, outright, perfect, pure, sheer, thorough, utter 2 SUPREME, full, sovereign, unbounded, unconditional, unlimited, unrestricted

absolutely *adverb* TOTALLY, completely, entirely, fully, one hundred per cent, perfectly, utterly, wholly

absolution noun <u>FORGIVENESS</u>, deliverance, exculpation, exoneration, mercy, pardon, release

absolve verb <u>FORGIVE</u>, deliver, exculpate, excuse, let off, pardon, release, set free

absorb verb 1 <u>SOAK UP</u>, consume, digest, imbibe, incorporate, receive, suck up, take in 2 <u>PREOCCUPY</u>, captivate, engage, engross, fascinate, rivet

absorbed adjective 1 <u>PREOCCUPIED</u>, captivated, engrossed, fascinated, immersed, involved, lost, rapt, riveted, wrapped up 2 <u>DIGESTED</u>, assimilated, incorporated, received, soaked up

absorbent adjective <u>PERMEABLE</u>, porous, receptive, spongy

absorbing adjective <u>FASCINATING</u>, captivating, engrossing, gripping, interesting, intriguing, riveting, spellbinding

absorption noun 1 <u>SOAKING UP</u>, assimilation, consumption, digestion, incorporation, sucking up 2 <u>CONCENTRATION</u>, fascination, immersion, intentness, involvement, preoccupation

abstain verb <u>REFRAIN</u>, avoid, decline, deny (oneself), desist, fast, forbear, forgo, give up, keep from

abstemious adjective <u>SELF-DENYING</u>, ascetic, austere, frugal, moderate, sober, temperate

abstention noun <u>REFUSAL</u>, abstaining, abstinence, avoidance, forbearance, refraining, self-control, self-denial, self-restraint

abstinence noun <u>SELF-DENIAL</u>, abstemiousness, avoidance, forbearance, moderation, self-restraint, soberness, teetotalism, temperance

abstinent adjective <u>SELF-DENYING</u>, abstaining, abstemious, forbearing, moderate, self-controlled, sober, temperate

abstract adjective 1 <u>THEORETICAL</u>, abstruse, general, hypothetical, indefinite, notional, recondite ◆ noun 2 <u>SUMMARY</u>, abridgment, digest, epitome, outline, précis, résumé, synopsis ◆ verb 3 <u>SUMMARIZE</u>, abbreviate, abridge, condense, digest, epitomize, outline, précis, shorten 4 <u>REMOVE</u>, detach, extract, isolate, separate, take away, take out, withdraw

abstraction noun 1 <u>IDEA</u>, concept, formula, generalization, hypothesis, notion, theorem, theory, thought 2 <u>ABSENT-MINDEDNESS</u>, absence, dreaminess, inattention, pensiveness, preoccupation, remoteness, woolgathering

abstruse adjective <u>OBSCURE</u>, arcane, complex, deep, enigmatic, esoteric, recondite, unfathomable, vague

absurd adjective <u>RIDICULOUS</u>, crazy (informal), farcical, foolish, idiotic, illogical, inane, incongruous, irrational, ludicrous, nonsensical, preposterous, senseless, silly, stupid, unreasonable

absurdity noun <u>RIDICULOUSNESS</u>, farce, folly, foolishness, incongruity, joke, nonsense, silliness, stupidity

abundance noun <u>PLENTY</u>, affluence, bounty, copiousness, exuberance, fullness, profusion

abundant adjective <u>PLENTIFUL</u>, ample, bountiful, copious, exuberant, filled, full, luxuriant, profuse, rich, teeming

abuse noun 1 <u>ILL-TREATMENT</u>, damage, exploitation, harm, hurt, injury, maltreatment, manhandling 2 <u>INSULTS</u>, blame, castigation, censure, defamation, derision, disparagement, invective, reproach, scolding, vilification **3** MISUSE, misapplication ♦ *verb* **4** ILL-TREAT, damage, exploit, harm, hurt, injure, maltreat, misuse, take advantage of **5** INSULT, castigate, curse, defame, disparage, malign, scold, vilify

abusive *adjective* **1** INSULTING, censorious, defamatory, disparaging, libellous, offensive, reproachful, rude, scathing **2** HARMFUL, brutal, cruel, destructive, hurtful, injurious, rough

abysmal *adjective* TERRIBLE, appalling, awful, bad, dire, dreadful

abyss *noun* PIT, chasm, crevasse, fissure, gorge, gulf, void

academic *adjective* **1** SCHOLARLY, bookish, erudite, highbrow, learned, literary, studious **2** HYPOTHETICAL, abstract, conjectural, impractical, notional, speculative, theoretical ♦ *noun* **3** SCHOLAR, academician, don, fellow, lecturer, master, professor, tutor

accede *verb* **1** AGREE, accept, acquiesce, admit, assent, comply, concede, concur, consent, endorse, grant **2** INHERIT, assume, attain, come to, enter upon, succeed, succeed to (*as heir*)

accelerate *verb* SPEED UP, advance, expedite, further, hasten, hurry, quicken

acceleration *noun* SPEEDING UP, hastening, hurrying, quickening, stepping up (*informal*)

accent *noun* **1** PRONUNCIATION, articulation, brogue, enunciation, inflection, intonation, modulation, tone **2** EMPHASIS, beat, cadence, force, pitch, rhythm, stress, timbre ♦ *verb* **3** EMPHASIZE, accentuate,

stress, underline, underscore

accentuate *verb* EMPHASIZE, accent, draw attention to, foreground, highlight, stress, underline, underscore

accept *verb* **1** RECEIVE, acquire, gain, get, obtain, secure, take **2** AGREE TO, admit, approve, believe, concur with, consent to, cooperate with, recognize

acceptable *adjective* SATISFACTORY, adequate, admissible, all right, fair, moderate, passable, tolerable

acceptance *noun* **1** ACCEPTING, acquiring, gaining, getting, obtaining, receipt, securing, taking **2** AGREEMENT, acknowledgment, acquiescence, admission, adoption, approval, assent, concurrence, consent, cooperation, recognition

accepted *adjective* AGREED, acknowledged, approved, common, conventional, customary, established, normal, recognized, traditional

access *noun* ENTRANCE, admission, admittance, approach, entry, passage, path, road

accessibility *noun* **1** HANDINESS, availability, nearness, possibility, readiness **2** APPROACHABILITY, affability, cordiality, friendliness, informality **3** OPENNESS, susceptibility

accessible *adjective* **1** HANDY, achievable, at hand, attainable, available, near, nearby, obtainable, reachable **2** APPROACHABLE, affable, available, cordial, friendly, informal **3** OPEN, exposed, liable, susceptible, vulnerable, wide-open

accessory *noun* **1** ADDITION, accompaniment, adjunct, adornment, appendage, attachment, decoration, extra,

supplement, trimming
2 ACCOMPLICE, abettor, assistant, associate (*in crime*), colleague, confederate, helper, partner

accident *noun* **1** MISFORTUNE, calamity, collision, crash, disaster, misadventure, mishap **2** CHANCE, fate, fluke, fortuity, fortune, hazard, luck

accidental *adjective* UNINTENTIONAL, casual, chance, fortuitous, haphazard, inadvertent, incidental, random, unexpected, unforeseen, unlooked-for, unplanned

accidentally *adverb* UNINTENTIONALLY, by accident, by chance, fortuitously, haphazardly, inadvertently, incidentally, randomly, unwittingly

acclaim *verb* **1** PRAISE, applaud, approve, celebrate, cheer, clap, commend, exalt, hail, honour, salute ♦ *noun* **2** PRAISE, acclamation, applause, approval, celebration, commendation, honour, kudos

acclamation *noun* PRAISE, acclaim, adulation, approval, ovation, plaudit, tribute

acclimatization *noun* ADAPTATION, adjustment, habituation, inurement, naturalization

acclimatize *verb* ADAPT, accommodate, accustom, adjust, get used to, habituate, inure, naturalize

accolade *noun* PRAISE, acclaim, applause, approval, commendation, compliment, ovation, recognition, tribute

accommodate *verb* **1** HOUSE, cater for, entertain, lodge, put up, shelter **2** HELP, aid, assist, oblige, serve **3** ADAPT, adjust, comply, conform, fit, harmonize, modify, reconcile, settle

accommodating *adjective* HELPFUL, considerate, cooperative, friendly, hospitable, kind, obliging, polite, unselfish, willing

accommodation *noun* HOUSING, board, digs (*Brit. informal*), house, lodging(s), quarters, shelter

accompaniment *noun*
1 SUPPLEMENT, accessory, companion, complement
2 BACKING MUSIC, backing

accompany *verb* **1** GO WITH, attend, chaperon, conduct, convoy, escort, hold (someone's) hand **2** OCCUR WITH, belong to, come with, follow, go together with, supplement

accompanying *adjective* ADDITIONAL, associated, attached, attendant, complementary, related, supplementary

accomplice *noun* HELPER, abettor, accessory, ally, assistant, associate, collaborator, colleague, henchman, partner

accomplish *verb* DO, achieve, attain, bring about, carry out, complete, effect, execute, finish, fulfil, manage, perform, produce

accomplished *adjective* SKILLED, expert, gifted, masterly, polished, practised, proficient, talented

accomplishment *noun*
1 COMPLETION, bringing about, carrying out, conclusion, execution, finishing, fulfilment, performance **2** ACHIEVEMENT, act, coup, deed, exploit, feat, stroke, triumph

accord *noun* **1** AGREEMENT, conformity, correspondence, harmony, rapport, sympathy, unison ♦ *verb* **2** FIT, agree, conform, correspond, harmonize, match, suit, tally

accordingly *adverb* **1** APPROPRIATELY, correspondingly, fitly, properly, suitably **2** CONSEQUENTLY, as a result, ergo, hence, in consequence, so, therefore, thus

according to *adverb* **1** AS STATED BY, as believed by, as maintained by, in the light of, on the authority of, on the report of **2** IN KEEPING WITH, after, after the manner of, consistent with, in accordance with, in compliance with, in line with, in the manner of

accost *verb* APPROACH, buttonhole, confront, greet, hail

account *noun* **1** DESCRIPTION, explanation, narrative, report, statement, story, tale, version **2** *Commerce* STATEMENT, balance, bill, books, charge, invoice, reckoning, register, score, tally **3** IMPORTANCE, consequence, honour, note, significance, standing, value, worth ♦ *verb* **4** CONSIDER, count, estimate, judge, rate, reckon, regard, think, value

accountability *noun* RESPONSIBILITY, answerability, chargeability, culpability, liability

accountable *adjective* RESPONSIBLE, amenable, answerable, charged with, liable, obligated, obliged

accountant *noun* AUDITOR, bean counter (*informal*), book-keeper

account for *verb* EXPLAIN, answer for, clarify, clear up, elucidate, illuminate, justify, rationalize

accredited *adjective* AUTHORIZED, appointed, certified, empowered, endorsed, guaranteed, licensed, official, recognized

accrue *verb* INCREASE, accumulate, amass, arise, be added, build up, collect, enlarge, flow, follow, grow

accumulate *verb* COLLECT, accrue, amass, build up, gather, hoard, increase, pile up, store

accumulation *noun* COLLECTION, build-up, gathering, heap, hoard, increase, mass, pile, stack, stock,

stockpile, store

accuracy *noun* EXACTNESS, accurateness, authenticity, carefulness, closeness, correctness, fidelity, precision, strictness, truthfulness, veracity

accurate *adjective* EXACT, authentic, close, correct, faithful, precise, scrupulous, spot-on (*Brit. informal*), strict, true, unerring

accurately *adverb* EXACTLY, authentically, closely, correctly, faithfully, precisely, scrupulously, strictly, to the letter, truly, unerringly

accursed *adjective* **1** CURSED, bewitched, condemned, damned, doomed, hopeless, ill-fated, ill-omened, jinxed, unfortunate, unlucky, wretched **2** HATEFUL, abominable, despicable, detestable, execrable, hellish, horrible

accusation *noun* CHARGE, allegation, complaint, denunciation, incrimination, indictment, recrimination

accuse *verb* CHARGE, blame, censure, denounce, impeach, impute, incriminate, indict

accustom *verb* ADAPT, acclimatize, acquaint, discipline, exercise, familiarize, train

accustomed *adjective* **1** USUAL, common, conventional, customary, established, everyday, expected, habitual, normal, ordinary, regular, traditional **2** USED, acclimatized, acquainted, adapted, familiar, familiarized, given to, in the habit of, trained

ace *noun* **1** *Cards, dice, etc.* ONE, single point **2** *Informal* EXPERT, champion, dab hand (*Brit. informal*), master, star, virtuoso, wizard (*informal*) ♦ *adjective* **3** *Informal* EXCELLENT, awesome (*slang*), brilliant, fine, great, outstanding, superb

ache *verb* 1 HURT, pain, pound, smart, suffer, throb, twinge ♦ *noun* 2 PAIN, hurt, pang, pounding, soreness, suffering, throbbing

achieve *verb* ATTAIN, accomplish, acquire, bring about, carry out, complete, do, execute, fulfil, gain, get, obtain, perform

achievement *noun* ACCOMPLISHMENT, act, deed, effort, exploit, feat, feather in one's cap, stroke

acid *adjective* 1 SOUR, acerbic, acrid, pungent, tart, vinegary 2 SHARP, biting, bitter, caustic, cutting, harsh, trenchant, vitriolic

acidity *noun* 1 SOURNESS, acerbity, pungency, tartness 2 SHARPNESS, bitterness, harshness

acknowledge *verb* 1 ACCEPT, admit, allow, concede, confess, declare, grant, own, profess, recognize, yield 2 GREET, address, hail, notice, recognize, salute 3 REPLY TO, answer, notice, react to, recognize, respond to, return

acknowledged *adjective* ACCEPTED, accredited, approved, confessed, declared, professed, recognized, returned

acknowledgment *noun* 1 ACCEPTANCE, admission, allowing, confession, declaration, profession, realization, yielding 2 GREETING, addressing, hail, hailing, notice, recognition, salutation, salute 3 APPRECIATION, answer, credit, gratitude, reaction, recognition, reply, response, return, thanks

acquaint *verb* TELL, disclose, divulge, enlighten, familiarize, inform, let (someone) know, notify, reveal

acquaintance *noun* 1 ASSOCIATE,

colleague, contact 2 KNOWLEDGE, awareness, experience, familiarity, fellowship, relationship, understanding

acquainted with *adjective* FAMILIAR WITH, alive to, apprised of, *au fait* with, aware of, conscious of, experienced in, informed of, knowledgeable about, versed in

acquiesce *verb* AGREE, accede, accept, allow, approve, assent, comply, concur, conform, consent, give in, go along with, submit, yield

acquiescence *noun* AGREEMENT, acceptance, approval, assent, compliance, conformity, consent, giving in, obedience, submission, yielding

acquire *verb* GET, amass, attain, buy, collect, earn, gain, gather, obtain, receive, secure, win

acquisition *noun* 1 POSSESSION, buy, gain, prize, property, purchase 2 ACQUIRING, attainment, gaining, procurement

acquisitive *adjective* GREEDY, avaricious, avid, covetous, grabbing, grasping, predatory, rapacious

acquit *verb* 1 CLEAR, discharge, free, liberate, release, vindicate 2 BEHAVE, bear, comport, conduct, perform

acquittal *noun* CLEARANCE, absolution, deliverance, discharge, exoneration, liberation, release, relief, vindication

acrid *adjective* PUNGENT, bitter, caustic, harsh, sharp, vitriolic

acrimonious *adjective* BITTER, caustic, irascible, petulant, rancorous, spiteful, splenetic, testy

acrimony *noun* BITTERNESS, harshness, ill will, irascibility, rancour, virulence

act noun **1** <u>DEED</u>, accomplishment, achievement, action, exploit, feat, performance, undertaking **2** <u>LAW</u>, bill, decree, edict, enactment, measure, ordinance, resolution, statute **3** <u>PERFORMANCE</u>, routine, show, sketch, turn **4** <u>PRETENCE</u>, affectation, attitude, front, performance, pose, posture, show ♦ verb **5** <u>DO</u>, carry out, enact, execute, function, operate, perform, take effect, work **6** <u>PERFORM</u>, act out, impersonate, mimic, play, play or take the part of, portray, represent

act for verb <u>STAND IN FOR</u>, cover for, deputize for, fill in for, replace, represent, substitute for, take the place of

acting noun **1** <u>PERFORMANCE</u>, characterization, impersonation, performing, playing, portrayal, stagecraft, theatre ♦ adjective **2** <u>TEMPORARY</u>, interim, pro tem, provisional, substitute, surrogate

action noun **1** <u>DEED</u>, accomplishment, achievement, act, exploit, feat, performance **2** <u>LAWSUIT</u>, case, litigation, proceeding, prosecution, suit **3** <u>ENERGY</u>, activity, force, liveliness, spirit, vigour, vim, vitality **4** <u>MOVEMENT</u>, activity, functioning, motion, operation, process, working **5** <u>BATTLE</u>, clash, combat, conflict, contest, encounter, engagement, fight, skirmish, sortie

activate verb <u>START</u>, arouse, energize, galvanize, initiate, mobilize, move, rouse, set in motion, stir

active adjective **1** <u>BUSY</u>, bustling, hard-working, involved, occupied, on the go (informal), on the move, strenuous **2** <u>ENERGETIC</u>, alert, animated, industrious, lively, quick, sprightly, spry, vigorous **3** <u>IN OPERATION</u>, acting, at work, effectual, in action, in force, operative, working

activist noun <u>MILITANT</u>, organizer, partisan

activity noun **1** <u>ACTION</u>, animation, bustle, exercise, exertion, hustle, labour, motion, movement **2** <u>PURSUIT</u>, hobby, interest, pastime, project, scheme

actor noun <u>PERFORMER</u>, actress, luvvie (informal), player, Thespian

actress noun <u>PERFORMER</u>, actor, leading lady, player, starlet, Thespian

actual adjective <u>DEFINITE</u>, concrete, factual, physical, positive, real, substantial, tangible

actually adverb <u>REALLY</u>, as a matter of fact, indeed, in fact, in point of fact, in reality, in truth, literally, truly

acumen noun <u>JUDGMENT</u>, astuteness, cleverness, ingenuity, insight, intelligence, perspicacity, shrewdness

acute adjective **1** <u>SERIOUS</u>, critical, crucial, dangerous, grave, important, severe, urgent **2** <u>SHARP</u>, excruciating, fierce, intense, piercing, powerful, severe, shooting, violent **3** <u>PERCEPTIVE</u>, astute, clever, insightful, keen, observant, sensitive, sharp, smart

acuteness noun **1** <u>SERIOUSNESS</u>, gravity, importance, severity, urgency **2** <u>PERCEPTIVENESS</u>, astuteness, cleverness, discrimination, insight, perspicacity, sharpness

adamant adjective <u>DETERMINED</u>, firm, fixed, obdurate, resolute, stubborn, unbending, uncompromising

adapt verb <u>ADJUST</u>, acclimatize, accommodate, alter, change, conform, convert, modify, remodel, tailor

adaptability noun FLEXIBILITY, changeability, resilience, versatility

adaptable adjective FLEXIBLE, adjustable, changeable, compliant, easy-going, plastic, pliant, resilient, versatile

adaptation noun 1 ACCLIMATIZATION, familiarization, naturalization 2 CONVERSION, adjustment, alteration, change, modification, transformation, variation, version

add verb 1 COUNT UP, add up, compute, reckon, total, tot up 2 INCLUDE, adjoin, affix, append, attach, augment, supplement

addendum noun ADDITION, appendage, appendix, attachment, extension, extra, postscript, supplement

addict noun 1 JUNKIE (informal), fiend (informal), freak (informal) 2 FAN, adherent, buff (informal), devotee, enthusiast, follower, nut (slang)

addicted adjective HOOKED (slang), absorbed, accustomed, dedicated, dependent, devoted, habituated

addiction noun DEPENDENCE, craving, enslavement, habit, obsession

addition noun 1 INCLUSION, adding, amplification, attachment, augmentation, enlargement, extension, increasing 2 EXTRA, addendum, additive, appendage, appendix, extension, gain, increase, increment, supplement 3 COUNTING UP, adding up, computation, totalling, totting up 4 in addition (to) AS WELL (AS), additionally, also, besides, into the bargain, moreover, over and above, to boot, too

additional adjective EXTRA, added, fresh, further, new, other, spare, supplementary

address noun 1 LOCATION, abode, dwelling, home, house, residence, situation, whereabouts 2 SPEECH, discourse, dissertation, lecture, oration, sermon, talk ♦ verb 3 SPEAK TO, approach, greet, hail, talk to 4 address (oneself) to CONCENTRATE ON, apply (oneself) to, attend to, devote (oneself) to, engage in, focus on, take care of

add up verb COUNT UP, add, compute, count, reckon, total, tot up

adept adjective 1 SKILFUL, able, accomplished, adroit, expert, practised, proficient, skilled, versed ♦ noun 2 EXPERT, dab hand (Brit. informal), genius, hotshot (informal), master

adequacy noun SUFFICIENCY, capability, competence, fairness, suitability, tolerability

adequate adjective ENOUGH, competent, fair, satisfactory, sufficient, tolerable, up to scratch (informal)

adhere verb STICK, attach, cleave, cling, fasten, fix, glue, hold fast, paste

adherent noun SUPPORTER, admirer, devotee, disciple, fan, follower, upholder

adhesive adjective 1 STICKY, clinging, cohesive, gluey, glutinous, tenacious ♦ noun 2 GLUE, cement, gum, paste

adieu noun GOODBYE, farewell, leave-taking, parting, valediction

adjacent adjective NEXT, adjoining, beside, bordering, cheek by jowl, close, near, neighbouring, next door, touching

adjoin verb CONNECT, border, join, link, touch

adjoining adjective CONNECTING, abutting, adjacent, bordering, neighbouring, next door, touching

adjourn *verb* POSTPONE, defer, delay, discontinue, interrupt, put off, suspend

adjournment *noun* POSTPONEMENT, delay, discontinuation, interruption, putting off, recess, suspension

adjudicate *verb* JUDGE, adjudge, arbitrate, decide, determine, mediate, referee, settle, umpire

adjudication *noun* JUDGMENT, arbitration, conclusion, decision, finding, pronouncement, ruling, settlement, verdict

adjust *verb* ALTER, accustom, adapt, make conform, modify

adjustable *adjective* ALTERABLE, adaptable, flexible, malleable, modifiable, movable

adjustment *noun* **1** ALTERATION, adaptation, modification, redress, regulation, tuning **2** ACCLIMATIZATION, orientation, settling in

ad-lib *verb* IMPROVISE, busk, extemporize, make up, speak off the cuff, wing it (*informal*)

administer *verb* **1** MANAGE, conduct, control, direct, govern, handle, oversee, run, supervise **2** GIVE, apply, dispense, impose, mete out, perform, provide

administration *noun* MANAGEMENT, application, conduct, control, direction, government, running, supervision

administrative *adjective* MANAGERIAL, directorial, executive, governmental, organizational, regulatory, supervisory

administrator *noun* MANAGER, bureaucrat, executive, official, organizer, supervisor

admirable *adjective* EXCELLENT, commendable, exquisite, fine, laudable, praiseworthy, wonderful, worthy

admiration *noun* REGARD, amazement, appreciation, approval, esteem, praise, respect, wonder

admire *verb* **1** RESPECT, appreciate, approve, esteem, look up to, praise, prize, think highly of, value **2** MARVEL AT, appreciate, delight in, take pleasure in, wonder at

admirer *noun* **1** SUITOR, beau, boyfriend, lover, sweetheart, wooer **2** FAN, devotee, disciple, enthusiast, follower, partisan, supporter

admissible *adjective* PERMISSIBLE, acceptable, allowable, passable, tolerable

admission *noun* **1** ENTRANCE, acceptance, access, admittance, entrée, entry, initiation, introduction **2** CONFESSION, acknowledgment, allowance, declaration, disclosure, divulgence, revelation

admit *verb* **1** CONFESS, acknowledge, declare, disclose, divulge, own, reveal **2** ALLOW, agree, grant, let, permit, recognize **3** LET IN, accept, allow, give access, initiate, introduce, receive, take in

admonish *verb* REPRIMAND, berate, chide, rebuke, scold, slap on the wrist, tell off (*informal*)

adolescence *noun* **1** YOUTH, boyhood, girlhood, minority, teens **2** YOUTHFULNESS, childishness, immaturity

adolescent *adjective* **1** YOUNG, boyish, girlish, immature, juvenile, puerile, teenage, youthful ♦ *noun* **2** YOUTH, juvenile, minor, teenager, youngster

adopt *verb* **1** FOSTER, take in **2** CHOOSE, assume, espouse, follow, maintain, take up

adoption *noun* **1** FOSTERING,

adopting, taking in 2 <u>CHOICE</u>, appropriation, assumption, embracing, endorsement, espousal, selection, taking up

adorable *adjective* <u>LOVABLE</u>, appealing, attractive, charming, cute, dear, delightful, fetching, pleasing

adore *verb* <u>LOVE</u>, admire, cherish, dote on, esteem, exalt, glorify, honour, idolize, revere, worship

adoring *adjective* <u>LOVING</u>, admiring, affectionate, devoted, doting, fond

adorn *verb* <u>DECORATE</u>, array, embellish, festoon

adornment *noun* <u>DECORATION</u>, accessory, embellishment, festoon, frill, frippery, ornament, supplement, trimming

adrift *adjective* 1 <u>DRIFTING</u>, afloat, unanchored, unmoored 2 <u>AIMLESS</u>, directionless, goalless, purposeless ♦ *adverb* 3 <u>WRONG</u>, amiss, astray, off course

adroit *adjective* <u>SKILFUL</u>, adept, clever, deft, dexterous, expert, masterful, neat, proficient, skilled

adulation *noun* <u>WORSHIP</u>, fawning, fulsome praise, servile flattery, sycophancy

adult *noun* 1 <u>GROWN-UP</u>, grown *or* grown-up person (man *or* woman), person of mature age ♦ *adjective* 2 <u>FULLY GROWN</u>, full grown, fully developed, mature, of age, ripe

advance *verb* 1 <u>PROGRESS</u>, come forward, go on, hasten, make inroads, proceed, speed 2 <u>BENEFIT</u>, further, improve, prosper 3 <u>SUGGEST</u>, offer, present, proffer, put forward, submit 4 <u>LEND</u>, pay beforehand, supply on credit ♦ *noun* 5 <u>PROGRESS</u>, advancement, development, forward movement, headway, inroads, onward movement 6 <u>IMPROVEMENT</u>,

breakthrough, gain, growth, progress, promotion, step 7 <u>LOAN</u>, credit, deposit, down payment, prepayment, retainer 8 **advances** <u>OVERTURES</u>, approach, approaches, moves, proposals, proposition ♦ *adjective* 9 <u>PRIOR</u>, beforehand, early, forward, in front 10 **in advance** <u>BEFOREHAND</u>, ahead, earlier, previously

advanced *adjective* <u>FOREMOST</u>, ahead, avant-garde, forward, higher, leading, precocious, progressive

advancement *noun* <u>PROMOTION</u>, betterment, gain, improvement, preferment, progress, rise

advantage *noun* <u>BENEFIT</u>, ascendancy, dominance, good, help, lead, precedence, profit, superiority, sway

advantageous *adjective* 1 <u>BENEFICIAL</u>, convenient, expedient, helpful, of service, profitable, useful, valuable, worthwhile 2 <u>SUPERIOR</u>, dominant, dominating, favourable

adventure *noun* <u>ESCAPADE</u>, enterprise, experience, exploit, incident, occurrence, undertaking, venture

adventurer *noun* 1 <u>MERCENARY</u>, charlatan, fortune-hunter, gambler, opportunist, rogue, speculator 2 <u>HERO</u>, daredevil, heroine, knight-errant, traveller, voyager

adventurous *adjective* <u>DARING</u>, bold, daredevil, enterprising, intrepid, reckless

adversary *noun* <u>OPPONENT</u>, antagonist, competitor, contestant, enemy, foe, rival

adverse *adjective* <u>UNFAVOURABLE</u>, contrary, detrimental, hostile, inopportune, negative, opposing

adversity *noun* <u>HARDSHIP</u>, affliction,

bad luck, disaster, distress, hard times, misfortune, reverse, trouble

advert noun Brit. informal ADVERTISEMENT, ad (informal), announcement, blurb, commercial, notice, plug (informal), poster

advertise verb PUBLICIZE, announce, inform, make known, notify, plug (informal), promote, tout

advertisement noun ADVERT (Brit. informal), ad (informal), announcement, blurb, commercial, notice, plug (informal), poster

advice noun GUIDANCE, counsel, help, opinion, recommendation, suggestion

advisability noun WISDOM, appropriateness, aptness, desirability, expediency, fitness, propriety, prudence, suitability

advisable adjective WISE, appropriate, desirable, expedient, fitting, politic, prudent, recommended, seemly, sensible

advise verb 1 RECOMMEND, admonish, caution, commend, counsel, prescribe, suggest, urge 2 NOTIFY, acquaint, apprise, inform, make known, report, tell, warn

adviser noun GUIDE, aide, confidant, consultant, counsellor, helper, mentor, right-hand man

advisory adjective ADVISING, consultative, counselling, helping, recommending

advocate verb 1 RECOMMEND, advise, argue for, campaign for, champion, commend, encourage, promote, propose, support, uphold ♦ noun 2 SUPPORTER, campaigner, champion, counsellor, defender, promoter, proponent, spokesman, upholder 3 Law LAWYER, attorney, barrister, counsel, solicitor

affable adjective FRIENDLY, amiable, amicable, approachable, congenial, cordial, courteous, genial, pleasant, sociable, urbane

affair noun 1 EVENT, activity, business, episode, happening, incident, matter, occurrence 2 RELATIONSHIP, amour, intrigue, liaison, romance

affect[1] verb 1 INFLUENCE, act on, alter, bear upon, change, concern, impinge upon, relate to 2 MOVE, disturb, overcome, perturb, stir, touch, upset

affect[2] verb PUT ON, adopt, aspire to, assume, contrive, feign, imitate, pretend, simulate

affectation noun PRETENCE, act, artificiality, assumed manners, façade, insincerity, pose, pretentiousness, show

affected adjective PRETENDED, artificial, contrived, feigned, insincere, mannered, phoney or phony (informal), put-on, unnatural

affecting adjective MOVING, pathetic, pitiful, poignant, sad, touching

affection noun FONDNESS, attachment, care, feeling, goodwill, kindness, liking, love, tenderness, warmth

affectionate adjective FOND, attached, caring, devoted, doting, friendly, kind, loving, tender, warm-hearted

affiliate verb JOIN, ally, amalgamate, associate, band together, combine, incorporate, link, unite

affinity noun 1 ATTRACTION, fondness, inclination, leaning, liking, partiality, rapport, sympathy 2 SIMILARITY, analogy, closeness, connection, correspondence, kinship, likeness, relationship, resemblance

affirm verb DECLARE, assert, certify, confirm, maintain, pronounce, state, swear, testify

affirmation noun DECLARATION, assertion, certification, confirmation, oath, pronouncement, statement, testimony

affirmative adjective AGREEING, approving, assenting, concurring, confirming, consenting, corroborative, favourable, positive

afflict verb TORMENT, distress, grieve, harass, hurt, oppress, pain, plague, trouble

affliction noun SUFFERING, adversity, curse, disease, hardship, misfortune, ordeal, plague, scourge, torment, trial, trouble, woe

affluence noun WEALTH, abundance, fortune, opulence, plenty, prosperity, riches

affluent adjective WEALTHY, loaded (slang), moneyed, opulent, prosperous, rich, well-heeled (informal), well-off, well-to-do

afford verb 1 As in **can afford** SPARE, bear, manage, stand, sustain 2 GIVE, offer, produce, provide, render, supply, yield

affordable adjective INEXPENSIVE, cheap, economical, low-cost, moderate, modest, reasonable

affront noun 1 INSULT, offence, outrage, provocation, slap in the face (informal), slight, slur ♦ verb 2 OFFEND, anger, annoy, displease, insult, outrage, provoke, slight

aflame adjective BURNING, ablaze, alight, blazing, fiery, flaming, lit, on fire

afoot adverb GOING ON, abroad, brewing, current, happening, in preparation, in progress, on the

go (informal), up (informal)

afraid adjective 1 SCARED, apprehensive, cowardly, faint-hearted, fearful, frightened, nervous 2 SORRY, regretful, unhappy

afresh adverb AGAIN, anew, newly, once again, once more, over again

after adverb FOLLOWING, afterwards, behind, below, later, subsequently, succeeding, thereafter

aftermath noun EFFECTS, aftereffects, consequences, end result, outcome, results, sequel, upshot, wake

again adverb 1 ONCE MORE, afresh, anew, another time 2 ALSO, besides, furthermore, in addition, moreover

against preposition 1 BESIDE, abutting, facing, in contact with, on, opposite to, touching, upon 2 OPPOSED TO, anti (informal), averse to, hostile to, in defiance of, in opposition to, resisting, versus 3 IN PREPARATION FOR, in anticipation of, in expectation of, in provision for

age noun 1 TIME, date, day(s), duration, epoch, era, generation, lifetime, period, span 2 OLD AGE, advancing years, decline (of life), majority, maturity, senescence, senility, seniority ♦ verb 3 GROW OLD, decline, deteriorate, mature, mellow, ripen

aged adjective OLD, ancient, antiquated, antique, elderly, getting on, grey

agency noun 1 BUSINESS, bureau, department, office, organization 2 Old-fashioned MEDIUM, activity, means, mechanism

agenda noun LIST, calendar, diary, plan, programme, schedule, timetable

agent *noun* **1** REPRESENTATIVE, envoy, go-between, negotiator, rep (*informal*), surrogate **2** WORKER, author, doer, mover, operator, performer **3** FORCE, agency, cause, instrument, means, power, vehicle

aggravate *verb* **1** MAKE WORSE, exacerbate, exaggerate, increase, inflame, intensify, magnify, worsen **2** *Informal* ANNOY, bother, get on one's nerves (*informal*), irritate, nettle, provoke

aggravation *noun* **1** WORSENING, exacerbation, exaggeration, heightening, increase, inflaming, intensification, magnification **2** *Informal* ANNOYANCE, exasperation, gall, grief (*informal*), hassle (*informal*), irritation, provocation

aggregate *noun* **1** TOTAL, accumulation, amount, body, bulk, collection, combination, mass, pile, sum, whole ◆ *adjective* **2** TOTAL, accumulated, collected, combined, composite, cumulative, mixed ◆ *verb* **3** COMBINE, accumulate, amass, assemble, collect, heap, mix, pile

aggression *noun* **1** HOSTILITY, antagonism, belligerence, destructiveness, pugnacity **2** ATTACK, assault, injury, invasion, offensive, onslaught, raid

aggressive *adjective* **1** HOSTILE, belligerent, destructive, offensive, pugnacious, quarrelsome **2** FORCEFUL, assertive, bold, dynamic, energetic, enterprising, militant, pushy (*informal*), vigorous

aggressor *noun* ATTACKER, assailant, assaulter, invader

aggrieved *adjective* HURT, afflicted, distressed, disturbed, harmed, injured, unhappy, wronged

aghast *adjective* HORRIFIED, amazed, appalled, astonished, astounded, awestruck, confounded, shocked, startled, stunned

agile *adjective* **1** NIMBLE, active, brisk, lithe, quick, sprightly, spry, supple, swift **2** ACUTE, alert, bright (*informal*), clever, lively, quick-witted, sharp

agility *noun* NIMBLENESS, litheness, liveliness, quickness, suppleness, swiftness

agitate *verb* **1** UPSET, disconcert, distract, excite, fluster, perturb, trouble, unnerve, worry **2** STIR, beat, convulse, disturb, rouse, shake, toss

agitation *noun* **1** TURMOIL, clamour, commotion, confusion, disturbance, excitement, ferment, trouble, upheaval **2** TURBULENCE, convulsion, disturbance, shaking, stirring, tossing

agitator *noun* TROUBLEMAKER, agent provocateur, firebrand, instigator, rabble-rouser, revolutionary, stirrer (*informal*)

agog *adjective* EAGER, avid, curious, enthralled, enthusiastic, excited, expectant, impatient, in suspense

agonize *verb* SUFFER, be distressed, be in agony, be in anguish, go through the mill, labour, strain, struggle, worry

agony *noun* SUFFERING, anguish, distress, misery, pain, throes, torment, torture

agree *verb* **1** CONSENT, assent, be of the same opinion, comply, concur, see eye to eye **2** GET ON (TOGETHER), coincide, conform, correspond, match, tally

agreeable *adjective* **1** PLEASANT, delightful, enjoyable, gratifying, likable *or* likeable, pleasing, satisfying, to one's taste **2** CONSENTING, amenable, approving, complying, concurring, in accord, onside (*informal*), sympathetic, well-disposed, willing

agreement noun **1** ASSENT, agreeing, compliance, concord, concurrence, consent, harmony, union, unison **2** CORRESPONDENCE, compatibility, conformity, congruity, consistency, similarity **3** CONTRACT, arrangement, bargain, covenant, deal (*informal*), pact, settlement, treaty, understanding

agricultural adjective FARMING, agrarian, country, rural, rustic

agriculture noun FARMING, cultivation, culture, husbandry, tillage

aground adverb BEACHED, ashore, foundered, grounded, high and dry, on the rocks, stranded, stuck

ahead adverb IN FRONT, at an advantage, at the head, before, in advance, in the lead, leading, to the fore, winning

aid noun **1** HELP, assistance, benefit, encouragement, favour, promotion, relief, service, support ◆ verb **2** HELP, assist, encourage, favour, promote, serve, subsidize, support, sustain

aide noun ASSISTANT, attendant, helper, right-hand man, second, supporter

ailing adjective ILL, indisposed, infirm, poorly, sick, under the weather (*informal*), unwell, weak

ailment noun ILLNESS, affliction, complaint, disease, disorder, infirmity, malady, sickness

aim verb **1** INTEND, attempt, endeavour, mean, plan, point, propose, seek, set one's sights on, strive, try ◆ noun **2** INTENTION, ambition, aspiration, desire, goal, objective, plan, purpose, target

aimless adjective PURPOSELESS, directionless, pointless, random, stray

air noun **1** ATMOSPHERE, heavens, sky **2** WIND, breeze, draught, zephyr **3** MANNER, appearance, atmosphere, aura, demeanour, impression, look, mood **4** TUNE, aria, lay, melody, song ◆ verb **5** PUBLICIZE, circulate, display, exhibit, express, give vent to, make known, make public, reveal, voice **6** VENTILATE, aerate, expose, freshen

airborne adjective FLYING, floating, gliding, hovering, in flight, in the air, on the wing

airing noun **1** VENTILATION, aeration, drying, freshening **2** EXPOSURE, circulation, display, dissemination, expression, publicity, utterance, vent

airless adjective STUFFY, close, heavy, muggy, oppressive, stifling, suffocating, sultry

airs plural noun AFFECTATION, arrogance, haughtiness, hauteur, pomposity, pretensions, superciliousness, swank (*informal*)

airy adjective **1** WELL-VENTILATED, fresh, light, open, spacious, uncluttered **2** LIGHT-HEARTED, blithe, cheerful, high-spirited, jaunty, lively, sprightly

aisle noun PASSAGEWAY, alley, corridor, gangway, lane, passage, path

alacrity noun EAGERNESS, alertness, enthusiasm, promptness, quickness, readiness, speed, willingness, zeal

alarm noun **1** FEAR, anxiety, apprehension, consternation, fright, nervousness, panic, scare, trepidation **2** DANGER SIGNAL, alarm bell, alert, bell, distress signal, hooter, siren, warning ◆ verb **3** FRIGHTEN, daunt, dismay, distress, give (someone) a turn (*informal*), panic, scare, startle, unnerve

alarming *adjective* <u>FRIGHTENING</u>, daunting, distressing, disturbing, scaring, shocking, startling, unnerving

alcoholic *noun* **1** <u>DRUNKARD</u>, dipsomaniac, drinker, drunk, inebriate, tippler, toper, wino (*informal*) ♦ *adjective* **2** <u>INTOXICATING</u>, brewed, distilled, fermented, hard, strong

alcove *noun* <u>RECESS</u>, bay, compartment, corner, cubbyhole, cubicle, niche, nook

alert *adjective* **1** <u>WATCHFUL</u>, attentive, awake, circumspect, heedful, observant, on guard, on one's toes, on the lookout, vigilant, wide-awake ♦ *noun* **2** <u>WARNING</u>, alarm, signal, siren ♦ *verb* **3** <u>WARN</u>, alarm, forewarn, inform, notify, signal

alertness *noun* <u>WATCHFULNESS</u>, attentiveness, heedfulness, liveliness, vigilance

alias *adverb* **1** <u>ALSO KNOWN AS</u>, also called, otherwise, otherwise known as ♦ *noun* **2** <u>PSEUDONYM</u>, assumed name, nom de guerre, nom de plume, pen name, stage name

alibi *noun* <u>EXCUSE</u>, defence, explanation, justification, plea, pretext, reason

alien *adjective* **1** <u>FOREIGN</u>, exotic, incongruous, strange, unfamiliar ♦ *noun* **2** <u>FOREIGNER</u>, newcomer, outsider, stranger

alienate *verb* <u>SET AGAINST</u>, disaffect, estrange, make unfriendly, turn away

alienation *noun* <u>SETTING AGAINST</u>, disaffection, estrangement, remoteness, separation, turning away

alight[1] *verb* **1** <u>GET OFF</u>, descend, disembark, dismount, get down **2** <u>LAND</u>, come down, come to rest, descend, light, perch, settle, touch down

alight[2] *adjective* **1** <u>ON FIRE</u>, ablaze, aflame, blazing, burning, fiery, flaming, lighted, lit **2** <u>LIT UP</u>, bright, brilliant, illuminated, shining

align *verb* **1** <u>ALLY</u>, affiliate, agree, associate, cooperate, join, side, sympathize **2** <u>LINE UP</u>, even up, order, range, regulate, straighten

alignment *noun* **1** <u>ALLIANCE</u>, affiliation, agreement, association, cooperation, sympathy, union **2** <u>LINING UP</u>, adjustment, arrangement, evening up, order, straightening up

alike *adjective* **1** <u>SIMILAR</u>, akin, analogous, corresponding, identical, of a piece, parallel, resembling, the same ♦ *adverb* **2** <u>SIMILARLY</u>, analogously, correspondingly, equally, evenly, identically, uniformly

alive *adjective* **1** <u>LIVING</u>, animate, breathing, in the land of the living (*informal*), subsisting **2** <u>IN EXISTENCE</u>, active, existing, extant, functioning, in force, operative **3** <u>LIVELY</u>, active, alert, animated, energetic, full of life, vital, vivacious

all *adjective* **1** <u>THE WHOLE OF</u>, every bit of, the complete, the entire, the sum of, the totality of, the total of **2** <u>EVERY</u>, each, each and every, every one of, every single **3** <u>COMPLETE</u>, entire, full, greatest, perfect, total, utter ♦ *adverb* **4** <u>COMPLETELY</u>, altogether, entirely, fully, totally, utterly, wholly ♦ *noun* **5** <u>WHOLE AMOUNT</u>, aggregate, entirety, everything, sum total, total, totality, utmost

allegation *noun* <u>CLAIM</u>, accusation, affirmation, assertion, charge, declaration, statement

allege *verb* <u>CLAIM</u>, affirm, assert, charge, declare, maintain, state

alleged *adjective* **1** STATED, affirmed, asserted, declared, described, designated **2** SUPPOSED, doubtful, dubious, ostensible, professed, purported, so-called, unproved

allegiance *noun* LOYALTY, constancy, devotion, faithfulness, fidelity, obedience

allegorical *adjective* SYMBOLIC, emblematic, figurative, symbolizing

allegory *noun* SYMBOL, fable, myth, parable, story, symbolism, tale

allergic *adjective* SENSITIVE, affected by, hypersensitive, susceptible

allergy *noun* SENSITIVITY, antipathy, hypersensitivity, susceptibility

alleviate *verb* EASE, allay, lessen, lighten, moderate, reduce, relieve, soothe

alley *noun* PASSAGE, alleyway, backstreet, lane, passageway, pathway, walk

alliance *noun* UNION, affiliation, agreement, association, coalition, combination, confederation, connection, federation, league, marriage, pact, partnership, treaty

allied *adjective* UNITED, affiliated, associated, combined, connected, in league, linked, related

allocate *verb* ASSIGN, allot, allow, apportion, budget, designate, earmark, mete, set aside, share out

allocation *noun* ASSIGNMENT, allotment, allowance, lot, portion, quota, ration, share

allot *verb* ASSIGN, allocate, apportion, budget, designate, earmark, mete, set aside, share out

allotment *noun* **1** PLOT, kitchen garden, patch, tract **2** ASSIGNMENT, allocation, allowance, grant, portion, quota, ration, share, stint

all-out *adjective* TOTAL, complete, exhaustive, full, full-scale, maximum, thoroughgoing, undivided, unremitting, unrestrained

allow *verb* **1** PERMIT, approve, authorize, enable, endure, let, sanction, stand, suffer, tolerate **2** GIVE, allocate, allot, assign, grant, provide, set aside, spare **3** ACKNOWLEDGE, admit, concede, confess, grant, own

allowable *adjective* PERMISSIBLE, acceptable, admissible, all right, appropriate, suitable, tolerable

allowance *noun* **1** PORTION, allocation, amount, grant, lot, quota, ration, share, stint **2** CONCESSION, deduction, discount, rebate, reduction

allow for *verb* TAKE INTO ACCOUNT, consider, make allowances for, make concessions for, make provision for, plan for, provide for, take into consideration

alloy *noun* **1** MIXTURE, admixture, amalgam, blend, combination, composite, compound, hybrid ♦ *verb* **2** MIX, amalgamate, blend, combine, compound, fuse

all right *adjective* **1** SATISFACTORY, acceptable, adequate, average, fair, O.K. *or* okay (*informal*), standard, up to scratch (*informal*) **2** O.K. *or* OKAY (*informal*), healthy, safe, sound, unharmed, uninjured, well, whole

allude *verb* REFER, hint, imply, intimate, mention, suggest, touch upon

allure *noun* **1** ATTRACTIVENESS, appeal, attraction, charm, enchantment, enticement, glamour, lure, persuasion, seductiveness, temptation ♦ *verb* **2** ATTRACT, captivate, charm, enchant, entice, lure, persuade, seduce, tempt, win over

alluring *adjective* <u>ATTRACTIVE</u>, beguiling, captivating, come-hither, fetching, glamorous, seductive, tempting

allusion *noun* <u>REFERENCE</u>, casual remark, hint, implication, innuendo, insinuation, intimation, mention, suggestion

ally *noun* **1** <u>PARTNER</u>, accomplice, associate, collaborator, colleague, friend, helper ♦ *verb* **2** <u>UNITE</u>, associate, collaborate, combine, join, join forces, unify

almighty *adjective* **1** <u>ALL-POWERFUL</u>, absolute, invincible, omnipotent, supreme, unlimited **2** *Informal* <u>GREAT</u>, enormous, excessive, intense, loud, severe, terrible

almost *adverb* <u>NEARLY</u>, about, approximately, close to, just about, not quite, on the brink of, practically, virtually

alone *adjective* <u>BY ONESELF</u>, apart, detached, isolated, lonely, only, on one's tod (*slang*), separate, single, solitary, unaccompanied

aloof *adjective* <u>DISTANT</u>, detached, haughty, remote, standoffish, supercilious, unapproachable, unfriendly

aloud *adverb* <u>OUT LOUD</u>, audibly, clearly, distinctly, intelligibly, plainly

already *adverb* <u>BEFORE NOW</u>, at present, before, by now, by then, even now, heretofore, just now, previously

also *adverb* <u>TOO</u>, additionally, and, as well, besides, further, furthermore, in addition, into the bargain, moreover, to boot

alter *verb* <u>CHANGE</u>, adapt, adjust, amend, convert, modify, reform, revise, transform, turn, vary

alteration *noun* <u>CHANGE</u>, adaptation, adjustment, amendment, conversion, difference, modification, reformation, revision, transformation, variation

alternate *verb* **1** <u>CHANGE</u>, act reciprocally, fluctuate, interchange, oscillate, rotate, substitute, take turns ♦ *adjective* **2** <u>EVERY OTHER</u>, alternating, every second, interchanging, rotating

alternative *noun* **1** <u>CHOICE</u>, option, other (*of two*), preference, recourse, selection, substitute ♦ *adjective* **2** <u>DIFFERENT</u>, alternate, another, other, second, substitute

alternatively *adverb* <u>OR</u>, as an alternative, if not, instead, on the other hand, otherwise

although *conjunction* <u>THOUGH</u>, albeit, despite the fact that, even if, even though, notwithstanding, while

altogether *adverb* **1** <u>COMPLETELY</u>, absolutely, fully, perfectly, quite, thoroughly, totally, utterly, wholly **2** <u>ON THE WHOLE</u>, all in all, all things considered, as a whole, collectively, generally, in general **3** <u>IN TOTAL</u>, all told, everything included, in all, in sum, taken together

altruistic *adjective* <u>SELFLESS</u>, benevolent, charitable, generous, humanitarian, philanthropic, public-spirited, self-sacrificing, unselfish

always *adverb* <u>CONTINUALLY</u>, consistently, constantly, eternally, evermore, every time, forever, invariably, perpetually, repeatedly, without exception

amalgamate *verb* <u>COMBINE</u>, ally, blend, fuse, incorporate, integrate, merge, mingle, unite

amalgamation *noun* <u>COMBINATION</u>, blend, coalition, compound, fusion, joining, merger, mixture, union

amass verb COLLECT, accumulate, assemble, compile, gather, hoard, pile up

amateur noun NONPROFESSIONAL, dabbler, dilettante, layman

amateurish adjective UNPROFESSIONAL, amateur, bungling, clumsy, crude, inexpert, unaccomplished

amaze verb ASTONISH, alarm, astound, bewilder, dumbfound, shock, stagger, startle, stun, surprise

amazement noun ASTONISHMENT, admiration, bewilderment, confusion, perplexity, shock, surprise, wonder

amazing adjective ASTONISHING, astounding, breathtaking, eye-opening, overwhelming, staggering, startling, stunning, surprising

ambassador noun REPRESENTATIVE, agent, consul, deputy, diplomat, envoy, legate, minister

ambiguity noun VAGUENESS, doubt, dubiousness, equivocation, obscurity, uncertainty

ambiguous adjective UNCLEAR, dubious, enigmatic, equivocal, inconclusive, indefinite, indeterminate, obscure, vague

ambition noun 1 ENTERPRISE, aspiration, desire, drive, eagerness, longing, striving, yearning, zeal 2 GOAL, aim, aspiration, desire, dream, hope, intent, objective, purpose, wish

ambitious adjective ENTERPRISING, aspiring, avid, eager, hopeful, intent, purposeful, striving, zealous

ambivalent adjective UNDECIDED, contradictory, doubtful, equivocal, in two minds, uncertain, wavering

amble verb STROLL, dawdle,

meander, mosey (*informal*), ramble, saunter, walk, wander

ambush noun 1 TRAP, lying in wait, waylaying ♦ verb 2 TRAP, attack, bushwhack (*U.S.*), ensnare, surprise, waylay

amenable adjective RECEPTIVE, able to be influenced, acquiescent, agreeable, open, persuadable, responsive, susceptible

amend verb CHANGE, alter, correct, fix, improve, mend, modify, reform, remedy, repair, revise

amendment noun 1 CHANGE, alteration, correction, emendation, improvement, modification, reform, remedy, repair, revision 2 ALTERATION, addendum, addition, attachment, clarification

amends plural noun As in **make amends for** COMPENSATION, atonement, recompense, redress, reparation, restitution, satisfaction

amenity noun FACILITY, advantage, comfort, convenience, service

amiable adjective PLEASANT, affable, agreeable, charming, congenial, engaging, friendly, genial, likable *or* likeable, lovable

amicable adjective FRIENDLY, amiable, civil, cordial, courteous, harmonious, neighbourly, peaceful, sociable

amid, amidst preposition IN THE MIDDLE OF, among, amongst, in the midst of, in the thick of, surrounded by

amiss adverb 1 WRONGLY, erroneously, improperly, inappropriately, incorrectly, mistakenly, unsuitably 2 As in **take (something) amiss** AS AN INSULT, as offensive, out of turn, wrongly ♦ adjective 3 WRONG, awry, faulty, incorrect, mistaken, untoward

ammunition noun MUNITIONS,

armaments, explosives, powder, rounds, shells, shot

amnesty noun GENERAL PARDON, absolution, dispensation, forgiveness, immunity, remission (*of penalty*), reprieve

amok, amuck *adverb As in* run amok MADLY, berserk, destructively, ferociously, in a frenzy, murderously, savagely, uncontrollably, violently, wildly

among, amongst *preposition* **1** IN THE MIDST OF, amid, amidst, in the middle of, in the thick of, surrounded by, together with, with **2** IN THE GROUP OF, in the class of, in the company of, in the number of, out of **3** TO EACH OF, between

amorous *adjective* LOVING, erotic, impassioned, in love, lustful, passionate, tender

amount *noun* QUANTITY, expanse, extent, magnitude, mass, measure, number, supply, volume

amount to *verb* ADD UP TO, become, come to, develop into, equal, mean, total

ample *adjective* PLENTY, abundant, bountiful, copious, expansive, extensive, full, generous, lavish, plentiful, profuse

amplify *verb* **1** EXPLAIN, develop, elaborate, enlarge, expand, flesh out, go into detail **2** INCREASE, enlarge, expand, extend, heighten, intensify, magnify, strengthen, widen

amply *adverb* FULLY, abundantly, completely, copiously, generously, profusely, richly

amputate *verb* CUT OFF, curtail, lop, remove, separate, sever, truncate

amuck see AMOK

amuse *verb* ENTERTAIN, charm, cheer, delight, interest, please, tickle

amusement *noun* **1** ENTERTAINMENT, cheer, enjoyment, fun, merriment, mirth, pleasure **2** ENTERTAINMENT, diversion, game, hobby, joke, pastime, recreation, sport

amusing *adjective* FUNNY, comical, droll, enjoyable, entertaining, humorous, interesting, witty

anaemic *adjective* PALE, ashen, colourless, feeble, pallid, sickly, wan, weak

anaesthetic *noun* **1** PAINKILLER, analgesic, anodyne, narcotic, opiate, sedative, soporific
♦ *adjective* **2** PAIN-KILLING, analgesic, anodyne, deadening, dulling, numbing, sedative, soporific

analogy *noun* SIMILARITY, comparison, correlation, correspondence, likeness, parallel, relation, resemblance

analyse *verb* **1** EXAMINE, evaluate, investigate, research, test, work over **2** BREAK DOWN, dissect, divide, resolve, separate, think through

analysis *noun* EXAMINATION, breakdown, dissection, inquiry, investigation, scrutiny, sifting, test

analytic, analytical *adjective* RATIONAL, inquiring, inquisitive, investigative, logical, organized, problem-solving, systematic

anarchic *adjective* LAWLESS, chaotic, disorganized, rebellious, riotous, ungoverned

anarchist *noun* REVOLUTIONARY, insurgent, nihilist, rebel, terrorist

anarchy *noun* LAWLESSNESS, chaos, confusion, disorder, disorganization, revolution, riot

anatomy *noun* **1** EXAMINATION, analysis, dissection, division, inquiry, investigation, study **2** STRUCTURE, build, composition, frame, framework, make-up

ancestor noun FOREFATHER, forebear, forerunner, precursor, predecessor

ancient adjective OLD, aged, antique, archaic, old-fashioned, primeval, primordial, timeworn

ancillary adjective SUPPLEMENTARY, additional, auxiliary, extra, secondary, subordinate, subsidiary, supporting

and conjunction ALSO, along with, as well as, furthermore, in addition to, including, moreover, plus, together with

anecdote noun STORY, reminiscence, short story, sketch, tale, urban legend, yarn

angel noun 1 DIVINE MESSENGER, archangel, cherub, seraph 2 Informal DEAR, beauty, darling, gem, jewel, paragon, saint, treasure

angelic adjective 1 PURE, adorable, beautiful, entrancing, lovely, saintly, virtuous 2 HEAVENLY, celestial, cherubic, ethereal, seraphic

anger noun 1 RAGE, annoyance, displeasure, exasperation, fury, ire, outrage, resentment, temper, wrath ♦ verb 2 MADDEN, annoy, displease, enrage, exasperate, gall, incense, infuriate, outrage, rile, vex

angle[1] noun 1 INTERSECTION, bend, corner, crook, edge, elbow, nook, point 2 POINT OF VIEW, approach, aspect, outlook, perspective, position, side, slant, standpoint, viewpoint

angle[2] verb FISH, cast

angry adjective FURIOUS, annoyed, cross, displeased, enraged, exasperated, incensed, infuriated, irate, mad (informal), outraged, resentful

angst noun ANXIETY, apprehension, unease, worry

anguish noun SUFFERING, agony, distress, grief, heartache, misery, pain, sorrow, torment, woe

animal noun 1 CREATURE, beast, brute 2 Applied to a person BRUTE, barbarian, beast, monster, savage, wild man ♦ adjective 3 PHYSICAL, bestial, bodily, brutish, carnal, gross, sensual

animate verb 1 ENLIVEN, energize, excite, fire, inspire, invigorate, kindle, move, stimulate ♦ adjective 2 LIVING, alive, alive and kicking, breathing, live, moving

animated adjective LIVELY, ebullient, energetic, enthusiastic, excited, passionate, spirited, vivacious

animation noun LIVELINESS, ebullience, energy, enthusiasm, excitement, fervour, passion, spirit, verve, vivacity, zest

animosity noun HOSTILITY, acrimony, antipathy, bitterness, enmity, hatred, ill will, malevolence, malice, rancour, resentment

annals plural noun RECORDS, accounts, archives, chronicles, history

annex verb 1 SEIZE, acquire, appropriate, conquer, occupy, take over 2 JOIN, add, adjoin, attach, connect, fasten

annihilate verb DESTROY, abolish, eradicate, exterminate, extinguish, obliterate, wipe out

announce verb MAKE KNOWN, advertise, broadcast, declare, disclose, proclaim, report, reveal, tell

announcement noun STATEMENT, advertisement, broadcast, bulletin, communiqué, declaration, proclamation, report, revelation

announcer noun PRESENTER, broadcaster, commentator,

master of ceremonies, newscaster, newsreader, reporter

annoy verb IRRITATE, anger, bother, displease, disturb, exasperate, get on one's nerves (informal), hassle (informal), madden, molest, pester, plague, trouble, vex

annoyance noun **1** IRRITATION, anger, bother, hassle (informal), nuisance, trouble **2** NUISANCE, bore, bother, drag (informal), pain (informal)

annoying adjective IRRITATING, disturbing, exasperating, maddening, troublesome

annual adjective YEARLY, once a year, yearlong

annually adverb YEARLY, by the year, once a year, per annum, per year

annul verb INVALIDATE, abolish, cancel, declare or render null and void, negate, nullify, repeal, retract

anoint verb CONSECRATE, bless, hallow, sanctify

anomalous adjective UNUSUAL, abnormal, eccentric, exceptional, incongruous, inconsistent, irregular, odd, peculiar

anomaly noun IRREGULARITY, abnormality, eccentricity, exception, incongruity, inconsistency, oddity, peculiarity

anonymous adjective UNNAMED, incognito, nameless, unacknowledged, uncredited, unidentified, unknown, unsigned

answer verb **1** REPLY, explain, react, resolve, respond, retort, return, solve ♦ noun **2** REPLY, comeback, defence, explanation, reaction, rejoinder, response, retort, return, riposte, solution

answerable adjective, usually with for or to RESPONSIBLE, accountable, amenable, chargeable, liable, subject, to blame

answer for verb BE RESPONSIBLE FOR, be accountable for, be answerable for, be chargeable for, be liable for, be to blame for

antagonism noun HOSTILITY, antipathy, conflict, discord, dissension, friction, opposition, rivalry

antagonist noun OPPONENT, adversary, competitor, contender, enemy, foe, rival

antagonistic adjective HOSTILE, at odds, at variance, conflicting, incompatible, in dispute, opposed, unfriendly

antagonize verb ANNOY, anger, get on one's nerves (informal), hassle (informal), irritate, offend

anthem noun **1** HYMN, canticle, carol, chant, chorale, psalm **2** SONG OF PRAISE, paean

anthology noun COLLECTION, compendium, compilation, miscellany, selection, treasury

anticipate verb EXPECT, await, foresee, foretell, hope for, look forward to, predict, prepare for

anticipation noun EXPECTATION, expectancy, foresight, forethought, premonition, prescience

anticlimax noun DISAPPOINTMENT, bathos, comedown (informal), letdown

antics plural noun CLOWNING, escapades, horseplay, mischief, playfulness, pranks, tomfoolery, tricks

antidote noun CURE, countermeasure, remedy

antipathy noun HOSTILITY, aversion, bad blood, dislike, enmity, hatred, ill will

antiquated adjective OBSOLETE, antique, archaic, dated, old-fashioned, out-of-date, passé

antique noun 1 PERIOD PIECE, bygone, heirloom, relic ◆ adjective 2 VINTAGE, antiquarian, classic, olden 3 OLD-FASHIONED, archaic, obsolete, outdated

antiquity noun 1 OLD AGE, age, ancientness, elderliness, oldness 2 DISTANT PAST, ancient times, olden days, time immemorial

antiseptic adjective 1 HYGIENIC, clean, germ-free, pure, sanitary, sterile, uncontaminated ◆ noun 2 DISINFECTANT, germicide, purifier

antisocial adjective 1 UNSOCIABLE, alienated, misanthropic, reserved, retiring, uncommunicative, unfriendly, withdrawn 2 DISRUPTIVE, antagonistic, belligerent, disorderly, hostile, menacing, rebellious, uncooperative

antithesis noun OPPOSITE, contrary, contrast, converse, inverse, reverse

anxiety noun UNEASINESS, angst, apprehension, concern, foreboding, misgiving, nervousness, tension, trepidation, worry

anxious adjective 1 UNEASY, apprehensive, concerned, fearful, in suspense, nervous, on tenterhooks, tense, troubled, worried 2 EAGER, desirous, impatient, intent, itching, keen, yearning

apart adverb 1 TO PIECES, asunder, in bits, in pieces, to bits 2 SEPARATE, alone, aside, away, by oneself, isolated, to one side 3 **apart from** EXCEPT FOR, aside from, besides, but, excluding, not counting, other than, save

apartment noun ROOM, accommodation, flat, living quarters, penthouse, quarters, rooms, suite

apathetic adjective UNINTERESTED, cool, indifferent, passive, phlegmatic, unconcerned

apathy noun LACK OF INTEREST, coolness, indifference, inertia, nonchalance, passivity, torpor, unconcern

apex noun HIGHEST POINT, crest, crown, culmination, peak, pinnacle, point, summit, top

apiece adverb EACH, for each, from each, individually, respectively, separately, to each

aplomb noun SELF-POSSESSION, calmness, composure, confidence, level-headedness, poise, sang-froid, self-assurance, self-confidence

apocryphal adjective DUBIOUS, doubtful, legendary, mythical, questionable, unauthenticated, unsubstantiated

apologetic adjective REGRETFUL, contrite, penitent, remorseful, rueful, sorry

apologize verb SAY SORRY, ask forgiveness, beg pardon, express regret

apology noun 1 DEFENCE, acknowledgment, confession, excuse, explanation, justification, plea 2 As in **an apology for** MOCKERY, caricature, excuse, imitation, travesty

apostle noun 1 EVANGELIST, herald, messenger, missionary, preacher 2 SUPPORTER, advocate, champion, pioneer, propagandist, proponent

apotheosis noun DEIFICATION, elevation, exaltation, glorification, idealization, idolization

appal verb HORRIFY, alarm, daunt, dishearten, dismay, frighten, outrage, shock, unnerve

appalling adjective HORRIFYING, alarming, awful, daunting, dreadful, fearful, frightful, horrible, shocking, terrifying

apparatus noun 1 EQUIPMENT, appliance, contraption (*informal*), device, gear, machinery, mechanism, tackle, tools 2 ORGANIZATION, bureaucracy, chain of command, hierarchy, network, setup (*informal*), structure, system

apparent adjective 1 OBVIOUS, discernible, distinct, evident, manifest, marked, unmistakable, visible 2 SEEMING, ostensible, outward, superficial

apparently adverb IT APPEARS THAT, it seems that, on the face of it, ostensibly, outwardly, seemingly, superficially

apparition noun GHOST, chimera, phantom, spectre, spirit, wraith

appeal verb 1 PLEAD, ask, beg, call upon, entreat, pray, request 2 ATTRACT, allure, charm, entice, fascinate, interest, please, tempt ◆ noun 3 PLEA, application, entreaty, petition, prayer, request, supplication 4 ATTRACTION, allure, beauty, charm, fascination

appealing adjective ATTRACTIVE, alluring, charming, desirable, engaging, winsome

appear verb 1 COME INTO VIEW, be present, come out, come to light, crop up (*informal*), emerge, occur, show up (*informal*), surface, turn up 2 LOOK (LIKE or AS IF), occur, seem, strike one as

appearance noun 1 ARRIVAL, coming, emergence, introduction, presence 2 LOOK, demeanour, expression, figure, form, looks, manner, mien (*literary*) 3 IMPRESSION, front, guise, illusion, image, outward show, pretence, semblance

appease verb 1 PACIFY, calm, conciliate, mollify, placate, quiet, satisfy, soothe 2 EASE, allay, alleviate, calm, relieve, soothe

appeasement noun 1 PACIFICATION, accommodation, compromise, concession, conciliation, mollification, placation 2 EASING, alleviation, lessening, relieving, soothing

appendage noun ATTACHMENT, accessory, addition, supplement

appendix noun SUPPLEMENT, addendum, addition, adjunct, appendage, postscript

appetite noun DESIRE, craving, demand, hunger, liking, longing, passion, relish, stomach, taste, yearning

appetizing adjective DELICIOUS, appealing, inviting, mouthwatering, palatable, succulent, tasty, tempting

applaud verb CLAP, acclaim, approve, cheer, commend, compliment, encourage, extol, praise

applause noun OVATION, accolade, approval, big hand, cheers, clapping, hand, praise

appliance noun DEVICE, apparatus, gadget, implement, instrument, machine, mechanism, tool

applicable adjective APPROPRIATE, apt, fitting, pertinent, relevant, suitable, useful

applicant noun CANDIDATE, claimant, inquirer

application noun 1 REQUEST, appeal, claim, inquiry, petition, requisition 2 EFFORT, commitment, dedication, diligence, hard work, industry, perseverance

apply verb 1 REQUEST, appeal, claim, inquire, petition, put in, requisition 2 USE, bring to bear, carry out, employ, exercise, exert, implement, practise, utilize 3 PUT ON, cover with, lay on, paint, place, smear, spread on 4 BE RELEVANT, be applicable, be appropriate, bear upon, be fitting, fit, pertain, refer, relate **5 apply oneself** TRY, be diligent, buckle down (*informal*), commit oneself, concentrate, dedicate oneself, devote oneself, persevere, work hard

appoint verb **1** ASSIGN, choose, commission, delegate, elect, name, nominate, select **2** DECIDE, allot, arrange, assign, choose, designate, establish, fix, set **3** EQUIP, fit out, furnish, provide, supply

appointed adjective **1** ASSIGNED, chosen, delegated, elected, named, nominated, selected **2** DECIDED, allotted, arranged, assigned, chosen, designated, established, fixed, set **3** EQUIPPED, fitted out, furnished, provided, supplied

appointment noun **1** MEETING, arrangement, assignation, date, engagement, interview, rendezvous **2** SELECTION, assignment, choice, election, naming, nomination **3** JOB, assignment, office, place, position, post, situation **4 appointments** FITTINGS, fixtures, furnishings, gear, outfit, paraphernalia, trappings

apportion verb DIVIDE, allocate, allot, assign, dispense, distribute, dole out, ration out, share

apportionment noun DIVISION, allocation, allotment, assignment, dispensing, distribution, doling out, rationing out, sharing

apposite adjective APPROPRIATE, applicable, apt, fitting, pertinent, relevant, suitable, to the point

appraisal noun ASSESSMENT, estimate, estimation, evaluation, judgment, opinion

appraise verb ASSESS, estimate, evaluate, gauge, judge, rate, review, value

appreciable adjective SIGNIFICANT, considerable, definite, discernible, evident, marked, noticeable, obvious, pronounced, substantial

appreciate verb **1** VALUE, admire, enjoy, like, prize, rate highly, respect, treasure **2** BE AWARE OF, perceive, realize, recognize, sympathize with, take account of, understand **3** BE GRATEFUL FOR, be appreciative, be indebted, be obliged, be thankful for, give thanks for **4** INCREASE, enhance, gain, grow, improve, rise

appreciation noun **1** GRATITUDE, acknowledgment, gratefulness, indebtedness, obligation, thankfulness, thanks **2** AWARENESS, admiration, comprehension, enjoyment, perception, realization, recognition, sensitivity, sympathy, understanding **3** INCREASE, enhancement, gain, growth, improvement, rise

appreciative adjective **1** GRATEFUL, beholden, indebted, obliged, thankful **2** AWARE, admiring, enthusiastic, respectful, responsive, sensitive, sympathetic, understanding

apprehend verb **1** ARREST, capture, catch, nick (*slang, chiefly Brit.*), seize, take prisoner **2** UNDERSTAND, comprehend, conceive, get the picture, grasp, perceive, realize, recognize

apprehension noun **1** ANXIETY, alarm, concern, dread, fear, foreboding, suspicion, trepidation, worry **2** ARREST, capture, catching, seizure, taking **3** AWARENESS, comprehension, grasp, perception, understanding

apprehensive adjective ANXIOUS, concerned, foreboding, nervous, uneasy, worried

apprentice noun TRAINEE, beginner, learner, novice, probationer, pupil, student

approach verb 1 MOVE TOWARDS, come close, come near, draw near, near, reach 2 MAKE A PROPOSAL TO, appeal to, apply to, make overtures to, sound out 3 SET ABOUT, begin work on, commence, embark on, enter upon, make a start, undertake ♦ noun 4 COMING, advance, arrival, drawing near, nearing 5 often plural PROPOSAL, advance, appeal, application, invitation, offer, overture, proposition 6 ACCESS, avenue, entrance, passage, road, way 7 WAY, manner, means, method, style, technique 8 LIKENESS, approximation, semblance

approachable adjective 1 FRIENDLY, affable, congenial, cordial, open, sociable 2 ACCESSIBLE, attainable, reachable

appropriate adjective 1 SUITABLE, apt, befitting, fitting, pertinent, relevant, to the point, well-suited ♦ verb 2 SEIZE, commandeer, confiscate, impound, take possession of, usurp 3 STEAL, embezzle, filch, misappropriate, pilfer, pocket 4 SET ASIDE, allocate, allot, apportion, assign, devote, earmark

approval noun 1 CONSENT, agreement, assent, authorization, blessing, endorsement, permission, recommendation, sanction 2 FAVOUR, acclaim, admiration, applause, appreciation, esteem, good opinion, praise, respect

approve verb 1 FAVOUR, admire, commend, have a good opinion of, like, praise, regard highly, respect 2 AGREE TO, allow, assent to, authorize, consent to, endorse, pass, permit, recommend, sanction

approximate adjective 1 CLOSE, near 2 ROUGH, estimated, inexact, loose ♦ verb 3 COME CLOSE, approach, border on, come near, reach, resemble, touch, verge on

approximately adverb ALMOST, about, around, circa (used with dates), close to, in the region of, just about, more or less, nearly, roughly

approximation noun GUESS, conjecture, estimate, estimation, guesswork, rough calculation, rough idea

apron noun PINNY (informal), pinafore

apt adjective 1 INCLINED, disposed, given, liable, likely, of a mind, prone, ready 2 APPROPRIATE, fitting, pertinent, relevant, suitable, to the point 3 GIFTED, clever, quick, sharp, smart, talented

aptitude noun 1 TENDENCY, inclination, leaning, predilection, proclivity, propensity 2 GIFT, ability, capability, faculty, intelligence, proficiency, talent

arable adjective PRODUCTIVE, farmable, fertile, fruitful

arbiter noun 1 JUDGE, adjudicator, arbitrator, referee, umpire 2 AUTHORITY, controller, dictator, expert, governor, lord, master, pundit, ruler

arbitrary adjective RANDOM, capricious, chance, erratic, inconsistent, personal, subjective, whimsical

arbitrate verb SETTLE, adjudicate, decide, determine, judge, mediate, pass judgment, referee, umpire

arbitration noun SETTLEMENT, adjudication, decision, determination, judgment

arbitrator noun JUDGE, adjudicator, arbiter, referee, umpire

arc noun CURVE, arch, bend, bow, crescent, half-moon

arcade noun GALLERY, cloister, colonnade, portico

arcane adjective MYSTERIOUS, esoteric, hidden, occult, recondite, secret

arch[1] noun 1 CURVE, archway, dome, span, vault 2 CURVE, arc, bend, bow, hump, semicircle ♦ verb 3 CURVE, arc, bend, bow, bridge, span

arch[2] adjective PLAYFUL, frolicsome, mischievous, pert, roguish, saucy, sly, waggish

archaic adjective 1 OLD, ancient, antique, bygone, olden (archaic), primitive 2 OLD-FASHIONED, antiquated, behind the times, obsolete, outmoded, out of date, passé

archetypal adjective 1 TYPICAL, classic, ideal, model, standard 2 ORIGINAL, prototypic or prototypical

archetype noun 1 STANDARD, model, paradigm, pattern, prime example 2 ORIGINAL, prototype

architect noun DESIGNER, master builder, planner

architecture noun 1 DESIGN, building, construction, planning 2 STRUCTURE, construction, design, framework, make-up, style

archive noun 1 RECORD OFFICE, museum, registry, repository 2 archives RECORDS, annals, chronicles, documents, papers, rolls

arctic adjective Informal FREEZING, chilly, cold, frigid, frozen, glacial, icy

Arctic adjective POLAR, far-northern, hyperborean

ardent adjective 1 PASSIONATE, amorous, hot-blooded, impassioned, intense, lusty 2 ENTHUSIASTIC, avid, eager, keen, zealous

ardour noun 1 PASSION, fervour, intensity, spirit, vehemence, warmth 2 ENTHUSIASM, avidity, eagerness, keenness, zeal

arduous adjective DIFFICULT, exhausting, fatiguing, gruelling, laborious, onerous, punishing, rigorous, strenuous, taxing, tiring

area noun 1 REGION, district, locality, neighbourhood, zone 2 PART, portion, section, sector 3 FIELD, department, domain, province, realm, sphere, territory

arena noun 1 RING, amphitheatre, bowl, enclosure, field, ground, stadium 2 SPHERE, area, domain, field, province, realm, sector, territory

argue verb 1 DISCUSS, assert, claim, debate, dispute, maintain, reason, remonstrate 2 QUARREL, bicker, disagree, dispute, fall out (informal), fight, squabble

argument noun 1 QUARREL, clash, controversy, disagreement, dispute, feud, fight, row, squabble 2 DISCUSSION, assertion, claim, debate, dispute, plea, questioning, remonstration 3 REASON, argumentation, case, defence, dialectic, ground(s), line of reasoning, logic, polemic, reasoning

argumentative adjective QUARRELSOME, belligerent, combative, contentious, contrary, disputatious, litigious, opinionated

arid adjective 1 DRY, barren, desert, parched, sterile, torrid, waterless 2 BORING, dreary, dry, dull, tedious, tiresome, uninspired, uninteresting

arise verb 1 HAPPEN, begin, emerge, ensue, follow, occur, result, start, stem 2 Old-fashioned GET UP, get to one's feet, go up, rise, stand up, wake up

aristocracy noun UPPER CLASS, elite, gentry, nobility, patricians, peerage, ruling class

aristocrat adjective NOBLE, aristo (*informal*), grandee, lady, lord, patrician, peer, peeress

aristocratic noun UPPER-CLASS, blue-blooded, elite, gentlemanly, lordly, noble, patrician, titled

arm¹ noun UPPER LIMB, appendage, limb

arm² verb *Especially with weapons* EQUIP, accoutre, array, deck out, furnish, issue with, provide, supply

armada noun FLEET, flotilla, navy, squadron

armaments plural noun WEAPONS, ammunition, arms, guns, materiel, munitions, ordnance, weaponry

armed adjective CARRYING WEAPONS, equipped, fitted out, primed, protected

armistice noun TRUCE, ceasefire, peace, suspension of hostilities

armour noun PROTECTION, armour plate, covering, sheathing, shield

armoured adjective PROTECTED, armour-plated, bombproof, bulletproof, ironclad, mailed, steel-plated

arms plural noun 1 WEAPONS, armaments, firearms, guns, instruments of war, ordnance, weaponry 2 HERALDRY, blazonry, crest, escutcheon, insignia

army noun 1 SOLDIERS, armed force, legions, military, military force, soldiery, troops 2 VAST NUMBER, array, horde, host, multitude, pack, swarm, throng

aroma noun SCENT, bouquet, fragrance, odour, perfume, redolence, savour, smell

aromatic adjective FRAGRANT, balmy, perfumed, pungent, redolent, savoury, spicy, sweet-scented, sweet-smelling

around preposition 1 SURROUNDING, about, encircling, enclosing, encompassing, on all sides of, on every side of 2 APPROXIMATELY, about, circa (*used with dates*), roughly ♦ adverb 3 EVERYWHERE, about, all over, here and there, in all directions, on all sides, throughout, to and fro 4 NEAR, at hand, close, close at hand, nearby, nigh (*archaic or dialect*)

arouse verb 1 STIMULATE, excite, incite, instigate, provoke, spur, stir up, summon up, whip up 2 AWAKEN, rouse, waken, wake up

arrange verb 1 PLAN, construct, contrive, devise, fix up, organize, prepare 2 AGREE, adjust, come to terms, compromise, determine, settle 3 PUT IN ORDER, classify, group, line up, order, organize, position, sort 4 ADAPT, instrument, orchestrate, score

arrangement noun 1 often plural PLAN, organization, planning, preparation, provision, schedule 2 AGREEMENT, adjustment, compact, compromise, deal, settlement, terms 3 ORDER, alignment, classification, form, organization, structure, system 4 ADAPTATION, instrumentation, interpretation, orchestration, score, version

array noun 1 ARRANGEMENT, collection, display, exhibition, formation, line-up, parade, show, supply 2 *Poetic* CLOTHING, apparel, attire, clothes, dress, finery, garments, regalia ♦ verb 3 ARRANGE, display, exhibit, group, parade, range, show 4 DRESS, adorn, attire, clothe, deck, decorate, festoon

arrest verb 1 CAPTURE, apprehend, catch, detain, nick (*slang, chiefly Brit.*), seize, take prisoner 2 STOP, block, delay, end, inhibit, interrupt, obstruct, slow, suppress 3 <u>GRIP</u>, absorb, engage, engross, fascinate, hold, intrigue, occupy ♦ *noun* 4 <u>CAPTURE</u>, bust (*informal*), cop (*slang*), detention, seizure 5 <u>STOPPING</u>, blockage, delay, end, hindrance, interruption, obstruction, suppression

arresting *adjective* <u>STRIKING</u>, engaging, impressive, noticeable, outstanding, remarkable, stunning, surprising

arrival *noun* 1 <u>COMING</u>, advent, appearance, arriving, entrance, happening, occurrence, taking place 2 <u>NEWCOMER</u>, caller, entrant, incomer, visitor

arrive *verb* 1 <u>COME</u>, appear, enter, get to, reach, show up (*informal*), turn up 2 *Informal* <u>SUCCEED</u>, become famous, make good, make it (*informal*), make the grade (*informal*)

arrogance *noun* <u>CONCEIT</u>, disdainfulness, haughtiness, high-handedness, insolence, pride, superciliousness, swagger

arrogant *adjective* <u>CONCEITED</u>, disdainful, haughty, high-handed, overbearing, proud, scornful, supercilious

arrow *noun* 1 <u>DART</u>, bolt, flight, quarrel, shaft (*archaic*) 2 <u>POINTER</u>, indicator

arsenal *noun* <u>ARMOURY</u>, ammunition dump, arms depot, ordnance depot, stockpile, store, storehouse, supply

art *noun* <u>SKILL</u>, craft, expertise, ingenuity, mastery, virtuosity

artful *adjective* <u>CUNNING</u>, clever, crafty, shrewd, sly, smart, wily

article *noun* 1 <u>PIECE</u>, composition, discourse, essay, feature, item, paper, story, treatise 2 <u>THING</u>, commodity, item, object, piece, substance, unit 3 <u>CLAUSE</u>, item, paragraph, part, passage, point, portion, section

articulate *adjective* 1 <u>EXPRESSIVE</u>, clear, coherent, eloquent, fluent, lucid, well-spoken ♦ *verb* 2 <u>EXPRESS</u>, enunciate, pronounce, say, speak, state, talk, utter, voice

artifice *noun* 1 <u>TRICK</u>, contrivance, device, machination, manoeuvre, stratagem, subterfuge, tactic 2 <u>CLEVERNESS</u>, ingenuity, inventiveness, skill

artificial *adjective* 1 <u>SYNTHETIC</u>, man-made, manufactured, non-natural, plastic 2 <u>FAKE</u>, bogus, counterfeit, imitation, mock, sham, simulated 3 <u>INSINCERE</u>, affected, contrived, false, feigned, forced, phoney *or* phony (*informal*), unnatural

artillery *noun* <u>BIG GUNS</u>, battery, cannon, cannonry, gunnery, ordnance

artisan *noun* <u>CRAFTSMAN</u>, journeyman, mechanic, skilled workman, technician

artistic *adjective* <u>CREATIVE</u>, aesthetic, beautiful, cultured, elegant, refined, sophisticated, stylish, tasteful

artistry *noun* <u>SKILL</u>, brilliance, craftsmanship, creativity, finesse, mastery, proficiency, virtuosity

artless *adjective* 1 <u>STRAIGHTFORWARD</u>, frank, guileless, open, plain 2 <u>NATURAL</u>, plain, pure, simple, unadorned, unaffected, unpretentious

as *conjunction* 1 <u>WHEN</u>, at the time that, during the time that, just as, while 2 <u>IN THE WAY THAT</u>, in the manner that, like 3 <u>WHAT</u>, that which 4 <u>SINCE</u>, because, considering that, seeing that 5 <u>FOR INSTANCE</u>, like, such as ♦ *preposition* 6 <u>BEING</u>, in the character of, in the role of, under the name of

ascend verb MOVE UP, climb, go up, mount, scale

ascent noun 1 RISE, ascending, ascension, climb, mounting, rising, scaling, upward movement 2 UPWARD SLOPE, gradient, incline, ramp, rise, rising ground

ascertain verb FIND OUT, confirm, determine, discover, establish, learn

ascetic noun 1 MONK, abstainer, hermit, nun, recluse ♦ adjective 2 SELF-DENYING, abstinent, austere, celibate, frugal, puritanical, self-disciplined

ascribe verb ATTRIBUTE, assign, charge, credit, impute, put down, refer, set down

ashamed adjective EMBARRASSED, distressed, guilty, humiliated, mortified, remorseful, shamefaced, sheepish, sorry

ashen adjective PALE, colourless, grey, leaden, like death warmed up (informal), pallid, wan, white

ashore adverb ON LAND, aground, landwards, on dry land, on the beach, on the shore, shorewards, to the shore

aside adverb 1 TO ONE SIDE, apart, beside, on one side, out of the way, privately, separately, to the side ♦ noun 2 INTERPOLATION, parenthesis

asinine adjective STUPID, fatuous, foolish, idiotic, imbecilic, moronic, senseless

ask verb 1 INQUIRE, interrogate, query, question, quiz 2 REQUEST, appeal, beg, demand, plead, seek 3 INVITE, bid, summon

askew adverb 1 CROOKEDLY, aslant, awry, obliquely, off-centre, to one side ♦ adjective 2 CROOKED, awry, cockeyed (informal), lopsided,

oblique, off-centre, skewwhiff (Brit. informal)

asleep adjective SLEEPING, dormant, dozing, fast asleep, napping, slumbering, snoozing (informal), sound asleep

aspect noun 1 FEATURE, angle, facet, side 2 POSITION, outlook, point of view, prospect, scene, situation, view 3 APPEARANCE, air, attitude, bearing, condition, demeanour, expression, look, manner

asphyxiate verb SUFFOCATE, choke, smother, stifle, strangle, strangulate, throttle

aspiration noun AIM, ambition, desire, dream, goal, hope, objective, wish

aspire verb AIM, desire, dream, hope, long, seek, set one's heart on, wish

aspiring adjective HOPEFUL, ambitious, eager, longing, wannabe (informal), would-be

ass noun 1 DONKEY, moke (slang) 2 FOOL, blockhead, halfwit, idiot, jackass, numbskull or numskull, oaf, twit (informal, chiefly Brit.)

assail verb ATTACK, assault, fall upon, lay into (informal), set upon

assailant noun ATTACKER, aggressor, assailer, assaulter, invader

assassin noun MURDERER, executioner, hatchet man (slang), hit man (slang), killer, liquidator, slayer

assassinate verb MURDER, eliminate (slang), hit (slang), kill, liquidate, slay, take out (slang)

assault noun 1 ATTACK, charge, invasion, offensive, onslaught ♦ verb 2 ATTACK, beset, fall upon, lay into (informal), set about, set upon, strike at

assemble verb 1 GATHER, amass, bring together, call together,

collect, come together,
congregate, meet, muster, rally
2 PUT TOGETHER, build up, connect,
construct, fabricate, fit together,
join, piece together, set up

assembly *noun* **1** GATHERING,
collection, company, conference,
congress, council, crowd, group,
mass, meeting **2** PUTTING TOGETHER,
building up, connecting,
construction, piecing together,
setting up

assent *noun* **1** AGREEMENT,
acceptance, approval,
compliance, concurrence,
consent, permission, sanction
♦ *verb* **2** AGREE, allow, approve,
consent, grant, permit

assert *verb* **1** STATE, affirm, declare,
maintain, profess, pronounce,
swear **2** INSIST UPON, claim, defend,
press, put forward, stand up for,
stress, uphold **3 assert oneself** BE
FORCEFUL, exert one's influence,
make one's presence felt, put
oneself forward, put one's foot
down (*informal*)

assertion *noun* **1** STATEMENT, claim,
declaration, pronouncement
2 INSISTENCE, maintenance, stressing

assertive *adjective* CONFIDENT,
aggressive, domineering,
emphatic, feisty (*informal, chiefly
U.S. & Canad.*), forceful, insistent,
positive, pushy (*informal*),
strong-willed

assess *verb* **1** JUDGE, appraise,
estimate, evaluate, rate, size up
(*informal*), value, weigh **2** EVALUATE,
fix, impose, levy, rate, tax, value

assessment *noun* **1** JUDGMENT,
appraisal, estimate, evaluation,
rating, valuation **2** EVALUATION,
charge, fee, levy, rating, toll,
valuation

asset *noun* **1** BENEFIT, advantage,
aid, blessing, boon, feather in
one's cap, help, resource, service

2 assets PROPERTY, capital, estate,
funds, goods, money, possessions,
resources, wealth

assiduous *adjective* DILIGENT,
hard-working, indefatigable,
industrious, persevering,
persistent, unflagging

assign *verb* **1** SELECT, appoint,
choose, delegate, designate,
name, nominate **2** GIVE, allocate,
allot, apportion, consign,
distribute, give out, grant
3 ATTRIBUTE, accredit, ascribe, put
down

assignation *noun* **1** SECRET MEETING,
clandestine meeting, illicit
meeting, rendezvous, tryst
(*archaic*) **2** SELECTION, appointment,
assignment, choice, delegation,
designation

assignment *noun* TASK,
appointment, commission, duty,
job, mission, position, post,
responsibility

assimilate *verb* **1** LEARN, absorb,
digest, incorporate, take in
2 ADJUST, adapt, blend in, mingle

assist *verb* HELP, abet, aid,
cooperate, lend a helping hand,
serve, support

assistance *noun* HELP, aid, backing,
cooperation, helping hand,
support

assistant *noun* HELPER, accomplice,
aide, ally, colleague, right-hand
man, second, supporter

associate *verb* **1** CONNECT, ally,
combine, identify, join, link, lump
together **2** MIX, accompany,
consort, hobnob, mingle, socialize
♦ *noun* **3** PARTNER, collaborator,
colleague, confederate, co-worker
4 FRIEND, ally, companion,
comrade, mate (*informal*)

association *noun* **1** GROUP, alliance,
band, club, coalition, federation,
league, organization, society

2 CONNECTION, blend, combination, joining, juxtaposition, mixture, pairing, union

assorted *adjective* VARIOUS, different, diverse, miscellaneous, mixed, motley, sundry, varied

assortment *noun* VARIETY, array, choice, collection, jumble, medley, mixture, selection

assume *verb* **1** TAKE FOR GRANTED, believe, expect, fancy, imagine, infer, presume, suppose, surmise, think **2** TAKE ON, accept, enter upon, put on, shoulder, take over **3** PUT ON, adopt, affect, feign, imitate, impersonate, mimic, pretend to, simulate

assumed *adjective* **1** FALSE, bogus, counterfeit, fake, fictitious, made-up, make-believe **2** TAKEN FOR GRANTED, accepted, expected, hypothetical, presumed, presupposed, supposed, surmised

assumption *noun* **1** PRESUMPTION, belief, conjecture, guess, hypothesis, inference, supposition, surmise **2** TAKING ON, acceptance, acquisition, adoption, entering upon, putting on, shouldering, takeover, taking up **3** TAKING, acquisition, appropriation, seizure, takeover

assurance *noun* **1** ASSERTION, declaration, guarantee, oath, pledge, promise, statement, vow, word **2** CONFIDENCE, boldness, certainty, conviction, faith, nerve, poise, self-confidence

assure *verb* **1** PROMISE, certify, confirm, declare confidently, give one's word to, guarantee, pledge, swear, vow **2** CONVINCE, comfort, embolden, encourage, hearten, persuade, reassure **3** MAKE CERTAIN, clinch, complete, confirm, ensure, guarantee, make sure, seal, secure

assured *adjective* **1** CONFIDENT, certain, poised, positive,

self-assured, self-confident, sure of oneself **2** CERTAIN, beyond doubt, confirmed, ensured, fixed, guaranteed, in the bag (*slang*), secure, settled, sure

astonish *verb* AMAZE, astound, bewilder, confound, daze, dumbfound, stagger, stun, surprise

astonishing *adjective* AMAZING, astounding, bewildering, breathtaking, brilliant, sensational (*informal*), staggering, stunning, surprising

astonishment *noun* AMAZEMENT, awe, bewilderment, confusion, consternation, surprise, wonder, wonderment

astounding *adjective* AMAZING, astonishing, bewildering, breathtaking, brilliant, impressive, sensational (*informal*), staggering, stunning, surprising

astray *adjective, adverb* OFF THE RIGHT TRACK, adrift, amiss, lost, off, off course, off the mark, off the subject

astute *adjective* INTELLIGENT, canny, clever, crafty, cunning, perceptive, sagacious, sharp, shrewd, subtle

asylum *noun* **1** REFUGE, harbour, haven, preserve, retreat, safety, sanctuary, shelter **2** *Old-fashioned* MENTAL HOSPITAL, hospital, institution, madhouse (*informal*), psychiatric hospital

atheism *noun* NONBELIEF, disbelief, godlessness, heathenism, infidelity, irreligion, paganism, scepticism, unbelief

atheist *noun* NONBELIEVER, disbeliever, heathen, infidel, pagan, sceptic, unbeliever

athlete *noun* SPORTSPERSON, competitor, contestant, gymnast, player, runner, sportsman, sportswoman

athletic *adjective* FIT, active, energetic, muscular, powerful, strapping, strong, sturdy

athletics *plural noun* SPORTS, contests, exercises, gymnastics, races, track and field events

atmosphere *noun* 1 AIR, aerosphere, heavens, sky 2 FEELING, ambience, character, climate, environment, mood, spirit, surroundings, tone

atom *noun* PARTICLE, bit, dot, molecule, speck, spot, trace

atone *verb,* usually with *for* MAKE AMENDS, compensate, do penance, make redress, make reparation, make up for, pay for, recompense, redress

atonement *noun* AMENDS, compensation, penance, recompense, redress, reparation, restitution

atrocious *adjective* 1 CRUEL, barbaric, brutal, fiendish, infernal, monstrous, savage, vicious, wicked 2 *Informal* SHOCKING, appalling, detestable, grievous, horrible, horrifying, terrible

atrocity *noun* 1 CRUELTY, barbarity, brutality, fiendishness, horror, savagery, viciousness, wickedness 2 ACT OF CRUELTY, abomination, crime, evil, horror, outrage

attach *verb* 1 CONNECT, add, couple, fasten, fix, join, link, secure, stick, tie 2 PUT, ascribe, assign, associate, attribute, connect

attached *adjective* 1 SPOKEN FOR, accompanied, engaged, married, partnered 2 **attached to** FOND OF, affectionate towards, devoted to, full of regard for

attachment *noun* 1 FONDNESS, affection, affinity, attraction, liking, regard 2 ACCESSORY, accoutrement, extension, extra, fitting, fixture, supplement

attack *verb* 1 ASSAULT, invade, lay into (*informal*), raid, set upon, storm, strike (at) 2 CRITICIZE, abuse, blame, censure, have a go (at) (*informal*), put down, vilify ♦ *noun* 3 ASSAULT, campaign, charge, foray, incursion, invasion, offensive, onslaught, raid, strike 4 CRITICISM, abuse, blame, censure, denigration, stick (*slang*), vilification 5 BOUT, convulsion, fit, paroxysm, seizure, spasm, stroke

attacker *noun* ASSAILANT, aggressor, assaulter, intruder, invader, raider

attain *verb* ACHIEVE, accomplish, acquire, complete, fulfil, gain, get, obtain, reach

attainment *noun* ACHIEVEMENT, accomplishment, completion, feat

attempt *verb* 1 TRY, endeavour, seek, strive, undertake, venture ♦ *noun* 2 TRY, bid, crack (*informal*), effort, go (*informal*), shot (*informal*), stab (*informal*), trial

attend *verb* 1 BE PRESENT, appear, frequent, go to, haunt, put in an appearance, show oneself, turn up, visit 2 LOOK AFTER, care for, mind, minister to, nurse, take care of, tend 3 PAY ATTENTION, hear, heed, listen, mark, note, observe, pay heed 4 **attend to** APPLY ONESELF TO, concentrate on, devote oneself to, get to work on, look after, occupy oneself with, see to, take care of

attendance *noun* 1 PRESENCE, appearance, attending, being there 2 TURNOUT, audience, crowd, gate, house, number present

attendant *noun* 1 ASSISTANT, aide, companion, escort, follower, guard, helper, servant ♦ *adjective* 2 ACCOMPANYING, accessory, associated, concomitant, consequent, related

attention *noun* 1 CONCENTRATION, deliberation, heed, intentness,

mind, scrutiny, thinking, thought
2 NOTICE, awareness,
consciousness, consideration,
observation, recognition, regard
3 CARE, concern, looking after,
ministration, treatment

attentive adjective **1** INTENT, alert,
awake, careful, concentrating,
heedful, mindful, observant,
studious, watchful **2** CONSIDERATE,
courteous, helpful, kind, obliging,
polite, respectful, thoughtful

attic noun LOFT, garret

attire noun CLOTHES, apparel,
costume, dress, garb, garments,
outfit, robes, wear

attitude noun **1** DISPOSITION,
approach, frame of mind, mood,
opinion, outlook, perspective,
point of view, position, stance
2 POSITION, pose, posture, stance

attract verb APPEAL TO, allure, charm,
draw, enchant, entice, lure, pull
(informal), tempt

attraction noun APPEAL, allure,
charm, enticement, fascination,
lure, magnetism, pull (informal),
temptation

attractive adjective APPEALING,
alluring, charming, fair, fetching,
good-looking, handsome,
inviting, lovely, pleasant, pretty,
tempting

attribute verb **1** ASCRIBE, assign,
charge, credit, put down to, refer,
set down to, trace to ♦ noun
2 QUALITY, aspect, character,
characteristic, facet, feature,
peculiarity, property, trait

attune verb ACCUSTOM, adapt,
adjust, familiarize, harmonize,
regulate

audacious adjective **1** DARING, bold,
brave, courageous, fearless,
intrepid, rash, reckless **2** CHEEKY,
brazen, defiant, impertinent,
impudent, insolent,

presumptuous, shameless

audacity noun **1** DARING, boldness,
bravery, courage, fearlessness,
nerve, rashness, recklessness
2 CHEEK, chutzpah (U.S. & Canad.
informal), effrontery,
impertinence, impudence,
insolence, nerve

audible adjective CLEAR, detectable,
discernible, distinct, hearable,
perceptible

audience noun **1** SPECTATORS,
assembly, crowd, gallery,
gathering, listeners, onlookers,
turnout, viewers **2** INTERVIEW,
consultation, hearing, meeting,
reception

aura noun AIR, ambience,
atmosphere, feeling, mood,
quality, tone

auspicious adjective FAVOURABLE,
bright, encouraging, felicitous,
hopeful, promising

austere adjective **1** STERN,
forbidding, formal, serious, severe,
solemn, strict **2** ASCETIC,
abstemious, puritanical,
self-disciplined, sober, solemn,
strait-laced, strict **3** PLAIN, bleak,
harsh, simple, spare, Spartan, stark

austerity noun **1** STERNNESS,
formality, inflexibility, rigour,
seriousness, severity, solemnity,
stiffness, strictness **2** ASCETICISM,
puritanism, self-denial,
self-discipline, sobriety **3** PLAINNESS,
simplicity, starkness

authentic adjective GENUINE, actual,
authoritative, bona fide,
legitimate, pure, real, true-to-life,
valid

authenticity noun GENUINENESS,
accuracy, certainty, faithfulness,
legitimacy, purity, truthfulness,
validity

author noun **1** WRITER, composer,
creator **2** CREATOR, architect,

designer, father, founder, inventor, originator, producer

authoritarian adjective **1** STRICT, autocratic, dictatorial, doctrinaire, dogmatic, severe, tyrannical ♦ noun **2** DISCIPLINARIAN, absolutist, autocrat, despot, dictator, tyrant

authoritative adjective **1** RELIABLE, accurate, authentic, definitive, dependable, trustworthy, valid **2** COMMANDING, assertive, imperious, imposing, masterly, self-assured

authority noun **1** POWER, command, control, direction, influence, supremacy, sway, weight **2** usually plural POWERS THAT BE, administration, government, management, officialdom, police, the Establishment **3** EXPERT, connoisseur, judge, master, professional, specialist

authorization noun PERMISSION, a blank cheque, approval, leave, licence, permit, warrant

authorize verb **1** EMPOWER, accredit, commission, enable, entitle, give authority to **2** PERMIT, allow, approve, give authority for, license, sanction, warrant

autocracy noun DICTATORSHIP, absolutism, despotism, tyranny

autocrat noun DICTATOR, absolutist, despot, tyrant

autocratic adjective DICTATORIAL, absolute, all-powerful, despotic, domineering, imperious, tyrannical

automatic adjective **1** MECHANICAL, automated, mechanized, push-button, self-propelling **2** INVOLUNTARY, instinctive, mechanical, natural, reflex, spontaneous, unconscious, unwilled

autonomous adjective SELF-RULING, free, independent, self-determining, self-governing, sovereign

autonomy noun INDEPENDENCE, freedom, home rule, self-determination, self-government, self-rule, sovereignty

auxiliary adjective **1** SUPPLEMENTARY, back-up, emergency, fall-back, reserve, secondary, subsidiary, substitute **2** SUPPORTING, accessory, aiding, ancillary, assisting, helping ♦ noun **3** BACKUP, reserve **4** HELPER, assistant, associate, companion, subordinate, supporter

avail verb **1** BENEFIT, aid, assist, be of advantage, be useful, help, profit ♦ noun **2** BENEFIT, advantage, aid, good, help, profit, use

availability noun ACCESSIBILITY, attainability, handiness, readiness

available adjective ACCESSIBLE, at hand, at one's disposal, free, handy, on tap, ready, to hand

avalanche noun **1** SNOW-SLIDE, landslide, landslip **2** FLOOD, barrage, deluge, inundation, torrent

avant-garde adjective PROGRESSIVE, experimental, ground-breaking, innovative, pioneering, unconventional

avarice noun GREED, covetousness, meanness, miserliness, niggardliness, parsimony, stinginess

avaricious adjective GRASPING, covetous, greedy, mean, miserly, niggardly, parsimonious, stingy

avenge verb GET REVENGE FOR, get even for (informal), get one's own back, hit back, punish, repay, retaliate

avenue noun STREET, approach, boulevard, course, drive, passage, path, road, route, way

average noun **1** USUAL, mean,

medium, midpoint, norm, normal, par, standard **2 on average** USUALLY, as a rule, for the most part, generally, normally, typically ♦ *adjective* **3** USUAL, commonplace, fair, general, normal, ordinary, regular, standard, typical **4** MEAN, intermediate, median, medium, middle ♦ *verb* **5** MAKE ON AVERAGE, balance out to, be on average, do on average, even out to

averse *adjective* OPPOSED, disinclined, hostile, ill-disposed, loath, reluctant, unwilling

aversion *noun* HATRED, animosity, antipathy, disinclination, dislike, hostility, revulsion, unwillingness

avert *verb* **1** TURN AWAY, turn aside **2** WARD OFF, avoid, fend off, forestall, frustrate, preclude, prevent, stave off

aviator *noun* PILOT, aeronaut, airman, flyer

avid *adjective* **1** ENTHUSIASTIC, ardent, devoted, eager, fanatical, intense, keen, passionate, zealous **2** INSATIABLE, grasping, greedy, hungry, rapacious, ravenous, thirsty, voracious

avoid *verb* **1** REFRAIN FROM, dodge, duck (out of) (*informal*), eschew, fight shy of, shirk **2** PREVENT, avert **3** KEEP AWAY FROM, bypass, dodge, elude, escape, evade, shun, steer clear of

avoidance *noun* EVASION, dodging, eluding, escape, keeping away, shunning, steering clear

avowed *adjective* **1** DECLARED, open, professed, self-proclaimed, sworn **2** CONFESSED, acknowledged, admitted

await *verb* **1** WAIT FOR, abide, anticipate, expect, look for, look forward to, stay for **2** BE IN STORE FOR, attend, be in readiness for, be

prepared for, be ready for, wait for

awake *adjective* **1** NOT SLEEPING, aroused, awakened, aware, conscious, wakeful, wide-awake **2** ALERT, alive, attentive, aware, heedful, observant, on the lookout, vigilant, watchful ♦ *verb* **3** WAKE UP, awaken, rouse, wake **4** ALERT, arouse, kindle, provoke, revive, stimulate, stir up

awaken *verb* **1** AWAKE, arouse, revive, rouse, wake **2** ALERT, kindle, provoke, stimulate, stir up

awakening *noun* WAKING UP, arousal, revival, rousing, stimulation, stirring up

award *verb* **1** GIVE, bestow, confer, endow, grant, hand out, present ♦ *noun* **2** PRIZE, decoration, gift, grant, trophy

aware *adjective* **1 aware of** KNOWING ABOUT, acquainted with, conscious of, conversant with, familiar with, mindful of **2** INFORMED, enlightened, in the picture, knowledgeable

awareness *noun* KNOWLEDGE, consciousness, familiarity, perception, realization, recognition, understanding

away *adverb* **1** OFF, abroad, elsewhere, from here, from home, hence **2** AT A DISTANCE, apart, far, remote **3** ASIDE, out of the way, to one side **4** CONTINUOUSLY, incessantly, interminably, relentlessly, repeatedly, uninterruptedly, unremittingly ♦ *adjective* **5** NOT PRESENT, abroad, absent, elsewhere, gone, not at home, not here, out

awe *noun* **1** WONDER, admiration, amazement, astonishment, dread, fear, horror, respect, reverence, terror ♦ *verb* **2** IMPRESS, amaze, astonish, frighten, horrify, intimidate, stun, terrify

awesome *adjective* <u>AWE-INSPIRING</u>, amazing, astonishing, breathtaking, formidable, impressive, intimidating, stunning

awful *adjective* **1** <u>TERRIBLE</u>, abysmal, appalling, deplorable, dreadful, frightful, ghastly, horrendous **2** *Obsolete* <u>AWE-INSPIRING</u>, awesome, fearsome, majestic, solemn

awfully *adverb* **1** <u>BADLY</u>, disgracefully, dreadfully, reprehensibly, unforgivably, unpleasantly, woefully, wretchedly **2** *Informal* <u>VERY</u>, dreadfully, exceedingly, exceptionally, extremely, greatly, immensely, terribly

awkward *adjective* **1** <u>CLUMSY</u>, gauche, gawky, inelegant, lumbering, uncoordinated, ungainly **2** <u>UNMANAGEABLE</u>, clunky (*informal*), cumbersome, difficult, inconvenient, troublesome, unwieldy **3** <u>EMBARRASSING</u>, delicate, difficult, ill at ease, inconvenient, uncomfortable

awkwardness *noun* **1** <u>CLUMSINESS</u>, gawkiness, inelegance, ungainliness **2** <u>UNWIELDINESS</u>, difficulty, inconvenience **3** <u>EMBARRASSMENT</u>, delicacy, difficulty, inconvenience

axe *noun* **1** <u>HATCHET</u>, adze, chopper **2** **the axe** *Informal* <u>THE SACK</u> (*informal*), dismissal, termination, the boot (*slang*), the chop (*slang*) ♦ *verb* **3** *Informal* <u>CUT BACK</u>, cancel, dismiss, dispense with, eliminate, fire (*informal*), get rid of, remove, sack (*informal*)

axiom *noun* <u>PRINCIPLE</u>, adage, aphorism, dictum, maxim, precept, truism

axiomatic *adjective* <u>SELF-EVIDENT</u>, accepted, assumed, certain, given, granted, manifest, understood

axis *noun* <u>PIVOT</u>, axle, centre line, shaft, spindle

axle *noun* <u>SHAFT</u>, axis, pin, pivot, rod, spindle

B b

babble verb **1** GABBLE, burble, chatter, jabber, prattle, waffle (*informal, chiefly Brit.*) **2** GIBBER, gurgle ♦ noun **3** GABBLE, burble, drivel, gibberish, waffle (*informal, chiefly Brit.*)

baby noun **1** INFANT, babe, babe in arms, bairn (*Scot.*), child, newborn child ♦ adjective **2** SMALL, little, mini, miniature, minute, teeny-weeny, tiny, wee

babyish adjective CHILDISH, foolish, immature, infantile, juvenile, puerile, sissy, spoiled

back noun **1** REAR, end, far end, hind part, hindquarters, reverse, stern, tail end **2** behind one's back SECRETLY, covertly, deceitfully, sneakily, surreptitiously ♦ verb **3** MOVE BACK, back off, backtrack, go back, retire, retreat, reverse, turn tail, withdraw **4** SUPPORT, advocate, assist, champion, endorse, promote, sponsor ♦ adjective **5** REAR, end, hind, hindmost, posterior, tail **6** PREVIOUS, delayed, earlier, elapsed, former, overdue, past

backbiting noun SLANDER, bitchiness (*slang*), cattiness (*informal*), defamation, disparagement, gossip, malice, scandalmongering, spitefulness

backbone noun **1** *Medical* SPINAL COLUMN, spine, vertebrae, vertebral column **2** STRENGTH OF CHARACTER, character, courage, determination, fortitude, grit, nerve, pluck, resolution

backbreaking adjective EXHAUSTING, arduous, crushing, gruelling, hard, laborious, punishing, strenuous

back down verb GIVE IN, accede, admit defeat, back-pedal, concede, surrender, withdraw, yield

backer noun SUPPORTER, advocate, angel (*informal*), benefactor, patron, promoter, second, sponsor, subscriber

backfire verb FAIL, boomerang, disappoint, flop (*informal*), miscarry, rebound, recoil

background noun HISTORY, circumstances, culture, education, environment, grounding, tradition, upbringing

backing noun SUPPORT, aid, assistance, encouragement, endorsement, moral support, patronage, sponsorship

backlash noun REACTION, counteraction, recoil, repercussion, resistance, response, retaliation

backlog noun BUILD-UP, accumulation, excess, hoard, reserve, stock, supply

back out verb, often with *of* WITHDRAW, abandon, cancel, give up, go back on, resign, retreat

backslide verb RELAPSE, go astray, go wrong, lapse, revert, slip, stray, weaken

backslider noun RELAPSER, apostate, deserter, recidivist, recreant, renegade, turncoat

back up verb SUPPORT, aid, assist, bolster, confirm, corroborate, reinforce, second, stand by, substantiate

backward adjective SLOW, behind, dull, retarded, subnormal, underdeveloped, undeveloped

backwards, backward adverb

TOWARDS THE REAR, behind, in reverse, rearward

bacteria *plural noun* MICROORGANISMS, bacilli, bugs (*slang*), germs, microbes, pathogens, viruses

bad *adjective* 1 INFERIOR, defective, faulty, imperfect, inadequate, poor, substandard, unsatisfactory 2 HARMFUL, damaging, dangerous, deleterious, detrimental, hurtful, ruinous, unhealthy 3 EVIL, corrupt, criminal, immoral, mean, sinful, wicked, wrong 4 NAUGHTY, disobedient, mischievous, unruly 5 ROTTEN, decayed, mouldy, off, putrid, rancid, sour, spoiled 6 UNFAVOURABLE, adverse, distressing, gloomy, grim, troubled, unfortunate, unpleasant

badge *noun* MARK, brand, device, emblem, identification, insignia, sign, stamp, token

badger *verb* PESTER, bully, goad, harass, hound, importune, nag, plague, torment

badinage *noun* WORDPLAY, banter, mockery, pleasantry, repartee, teasing

badly *adverb* 1 POORLY, carelessly, imperfectly, inadequately, incorrectly, ineptly, wrongly 2 UNFAVOURABLY, unfortunately, unsuccessfully 3 SEVERELY, deeply, desperately, exceedingly, extremely, greatly, intensely, seriously

baffle *verb* PUZZLE, bewilder, confound, confuse, flummox, mystify, nonplus, perplex, stump

bag *noun* 1 CONTAINER, receptacle, sac, sack ♦ *verb* 2 CATCH, acquire, capture, kill, land, shoot, trap

baggage *noun* LUGGAGE, accoutrements, bags, belongings, equipment, gear, paraphernalia, suitcases, things

baggy *adjective* LOOSE, bulging, droopy, floppy, ill-fitting, oversize, roomy, sagging, slack

bail *noun Law* SECURITY, bond, guarantee, pledge, surety, warranty

bail out see BALE OUT

bait *noun* 1 LURE, allurement, attraction, decoy, enticement, incentive, inducement, snare, temptation ♦ *verb* 2 TEASE, annoy, bother, harass, hassle (*informal*), hound, irritate, persecute, torment, wind up (*Brit. slang*)

baked *adjective* DRY, arid, desiccated, parched, scorched, seared, sun-baked, torrid

balance *noun* 1 STABILITY, composure, equanimity, poise, self-control, self-possession, steadiness 2 EQUILIBRIUM, correspondence, equity, equivalence, evenness, parity, symmetry 3 REMAINDER, difference, residue, rest, surplus ♦ *verb* 4 STABILIZE, level, match, parallel, steady 5 COMPARE, assess, consider, deliberate, estimate, evaluate, weigh 6 *Accounting* CALCULATE, compute, settle, square, tally, total

balcony *noun* 1 TERRACE, veranda 2 UPPER CIRCLE, gallery, gods

bald *adjective* 1 HAIRLESS, baldheaded, depilated 2 PLAIN, blunt, direct, forthright, straightforward, unadorned, unvarnished

balderdash *noun* NONSENSE, claptrap (*informal*), drivel, garbage (*informal*), gibberish, hogwash, hot air (*informal*), rubbish

baldness *noun* 1 HAIRLESSNESS, alopecia (*Pathology*), baldheadedness 2 PLAINNESS, austerity, bluntness, severity, simplicity

bale out, bail out verb 1 Informal HELP, aid, relieve, rescue, save (someone's) bacon (informal, chiefly Brit.) 2 ESCAPE, quit, retreat, withdraw

balk, baulk verb 1 RECOIL, evade, flinch, hesitate, jib, refuse, resist, shirk, shrink from 2 FOIL, check, counteract, defeat, frustrate, hinder, obstruct, prevent, thwart

ball noun SPHERE, drop, globe, globule, orb, pellet, spheroid

ballast noun COUNTERBALANCE, balance, counterweight, equilibrium, sandbag, stability, stabilizer, weight

balloon verb SWELL, billow, blow up, dilate, distend, expand, grow rapidly, inflate, puff out

ballot noun VOTE, election, poll, polling, voting

ballyhoo noun Informal FUSS, babble, commotion, hubbub, hue and cry, hullabaloo, noise, racket, to-do

balm noun 1 OINTMENT, balsam, cream, embrocation, emollient, lotion, salve, unguent 2 COMFORT, anodyne, consolation, curative, palliative, restorative, solace

balmy adjective MILD, clement, pleasant, summery, temperate

bamboozle verb Informal 1 CHEAT, con (informal), deceive, dupe, fool, hoodwink, swindle, trick 2 PUZZLE, baffle, befuddle, confound, confuse, mystify, perplex, stump

ban verb 1 PROHIBIT, banish, bar, block, boycott, disallow, disqualify, exclude, forbid, outlaw ♦ noun 2 PROHIBITION, boycott, disqualification, embargo, restriction, taboo

banal adjective UNORIGINAL, hackneyed, humdrum, mundane, pedestrian, stale, stereotyped, trite, unimaginative

band[1] noun 1 ENSEMBLE, combo, group, orchestra 2 GANG, body, company, group, party, posse (informal)

band[2] noun STRIP, belt, bond, chain, cord, ribbon, strap

bandage noun 1 DRESSING, compress, gauze, plaster ♦ verb 2 DRESS, bind, cover, swathe

bandit noun ROBBER, brigand, desperado, highwayman, marauder, outlaw, thief

bane noun PLAGUE, bête noire, curse, nuisance, pest, ruin, scourge, torment

bang noun 1 EXPLOSION, clang, clap, clash, pop, slam, thud, thump 2 BLOW, bump, cuff, knock, punch, smack, stroke, whack ♦ verb 3 HIT, belt (informal), clatter, knock, slam, strike, thump 4 EXPLODE, boom, clang, resound, thump, thunder ♦ adverb 5 HARD, abruptly, headlong, noisily, suddenly 6 STRAIGHT, precisely, slap, smack

banish verb 1 EXPEL, deport, eject, evict, exile, outlaw 2 GET RID OF, ban, cast out, discard, dismiss, oust, remove

banishment noun EXPULSION, deportation, exile, expatriation, transportation

banisters plural noun RAILING, balusters, balustrade, handrail, rail

bank[1] noun 1 STOREHOUSE, depository, repository 2 STORE, accumulation, fund, hoard, reserve, reservoir, savings, stock, stockpile ♦ verb 3 SAVE, deposit, keep

bank[2] noun 1 MOUND, banking, embankment, heap, mass, pile, ridge 2 SIDE, brink, edge, margin, shore ♦ verb 3 PILE, amass, heap, mass, mound, stack 4 TILT, camber, cant, heel, incline, pitch, slant, slope, tip

bank³ *noun* ROW, array, file, group, line, rank, sequence, series, succession

bankrupt *adjective* INSOLVENT, broke (*informal*), destitute, impoverished, in queer street, in the red, ruined, wiped out (*informal*)

bankruptcy *noun* INSOLVENCY, disaster, failure, liquidation, ruin

banner *noun* FLAG, colours, ensign, pennant, placard, standard, streamer

banquet *noun* FEAST, dinner, meal, repast, revel, treat

banter *verb* 1 JOKE, jest, kid (*informal*), rib (*informal*), taunt, tease ♦ *noun* 2 JOKING, badinage, jesting, kidding (*informal*), repartee, teasing, wordplay

baptism *noun* Christianity CHRISTENING, immersion, purification, sprinkling

baptize *verb* Christianity PURIFY, cleanse, immerse

bar *noun* 1 ROD, paling, palisade, pole, rail, shaft, stake, stick 2 OBSTACLE, barricade, barrier, block, deterrent, hindrance, impediment, obstruction, stop 3 PUBLIC HOUSE, boozer (*Brit., Austral. & N.Z. informal*), canteen, counter, inn, pub (*informal, chiefly Brit.*), saloon, tavern, watering hole (*facetious slang*) ♦ *verb* 4 FASTEN, bolt, latch, lock, secure 5 OBSTRUCT, hinder, prevent, restrain 6 EXCLUDE, ban, black, blackball, forbid, keep out, prohibit

Bar *noun* **the Bar** *Law* BARRISTERS, body of lawyers, counsel, court, judgment, tribunal

barb *noun* 1 DIG, affront, cut, gibe, insult, sarcasm, scoff, sneer 2 POINT, bristle, prickle, prong,
quill, spike, spur, thorn

barbarian *noun* 1 SAVAGE, brute, yahoo 2 LOUT, bigot, boor, philistine

barbaric *adjective* 1 UNCIVILIZED, primitive, rude, wild 2 BRUTAL, barbarous, coarse, crude, cruel, fierce, inhuman, savage

barbarism *noun* SAVAGERY, coarseness, crudity

barbarous *adjective* 1 UNCIVILIZED, barbarian, brutish, primitive, rough, rude, savage, uncouth, wild 2 BRUTAL, barbaric, cruel, ferocious, heartless, inhuman, monstrous, ruthless, vicious

barbed *adjective* 1 CUTTING, critical, hostile, hurtful, nasty, pointed, scathing, unkind 2 SPIKED, hooked, jagged, prickly, spiny, thorny

bare *adjective* 1 NAKED, nude, stripped, unclad, unclothed, uncovered, undressed, without a stitch on (*informal*) 2 PLAIN, bald, basic, sheer, simple, stark, unembellished 3 SIMPLE, austere, spare, spartan, unadorned, unembellished

barefaced *adjective* 1 OBVIOUS, blatant, flagrant, open, transparent, unconcealed 2 SHAMELESS, audacious, bold, brash, brazen, impudent, insolent

barely *adverb* ONLY JUST, almost, at a push, by the skin of one's teeth, hardly, just, scarcely

bargain *noun* 1 AGREEMENT, arrangement, contract, pact, pledge, promise 2 GOOD BUY, (cheap) purchase, discount, giveaway, good deal, reduction, snip (*informal*), steal (*informal*) ♦ *verb* 3 NEGOTIATE, agree, contract, covenant, promise, stipulate, transact

barge *noun* CANAL BOAT, flatboat, lighter, narrow boat

bark[1] *noun, verb* YAP, bay, growl, howl, snarl, woof, yelp

bark[2] *noun* COVERING, casing, cortex (*Anatomy, botany*), crust, husk, rind, skin

barmy *adjective Slang* INSANE, crazy, daft (*informal*), foolish, idiotic, nuts (*slang*), out of one's mind, stupid

barracks *plural noun* CAMP, billet, encampment, garrison, quarters

barrage *noun* **1** TORRENT, burst, deluge, hail, mass, onslaught, plethora, stream **2** *Military* BOMBARDMENT, battery, cannonade, fusillade, gunfire, salvo, shelling, volley

barren *adjective* **1** INFERTILE, childless, sterile **2** UNPRODUCTIVE, arid, desert, desolate, dry, empty, unfruitful, waste

barricade *noun* **1** BARRIER, blockade, bulwark, fence, obstruction, palisade, rampart, stockade ♦ *verb* **2** BAR, block, blockade, defend, fortify, obstruct, protect, shut in

barrier *noun* **1** BARRICADE, bar, blockade, boundary, fence, obstacle, obstruction, wall **2** HINDRANCE, difficulty, drawback, handicap, hurdle, obstacle, restriction, stumbling block

barter *verb* TRADE, bargain, drive a hard bargain, exchange, haggle, sell, swap, traffic

base[1] *noun* **1** BOTTOM, bed, foot, foundation, pedestal, rest, stand, support **2** BASIS, core, essence, heart, key, origin, root, source **3** CENTRE, camp, headquarters, home, post, settlement, starting point, station ♦ *verb* **4** FOUND, build, construct, depend, derive, establish, ground, hinge **5** PLACE, locate, post, station

base[2] *adjective* **1** DISHONOURABLE, contemptible, despicable, disreputable, evil, immoral, shameful, sordid, wicked **2** COUNTERFEIT, alloyed, debased, fake, forged, fraudulent, impure

baseless *adjective* UNFOUNDED, groundless, unconfirmed, uncorroborated, ungrounded, unjustified, unsubstantiated, unsupported

bash *verb* **1** *Informal* HIT, belt (*informal*), smash, sock (*slang*), strike, wallop (*informal*) ♦ *noun* **2** *Informal* ATTEMPT, crack (*informal*), go (*informal*), shot (*informal*), stab (*informal*), try

bashful *adjective* SHY, blushing, coy, diffident, reserved, reticent, retiring, timid

basic *adjective* ESSENTIAL, elementary, fundamental, key, necessary, primary, vital

basically *adverb* ESSENTIALLY, at heart, fundamentally, inherently, in substance, intrinsically, mostly, primarily

basics *plural noun* ESSENTIALS, brass tacks (*informal*), fundamentals, nitty-gritty (*informal*), nuts and bolts (*informal*), principles, rudiments

basis *noun* FOUNDATION, base, bottom, footing, ground, groundwork, support

bask *verb* LIE IN, laze, loll, lounge, relax, sunbathe, swim in

bass *adjective* DEEP, deep-toned, low, low-pitched, resonant, sonorous

bastard *noun* **1** *Informal, offensive* ROGUE, blackguard, miscreant, reprobate, scoundrel, villain, wretch **2** ILLEGITIMATE CHILD, love child, natural child

bastion *noun* STRONGHOLD, bulwark, citadel, defence, fortress, mainstay, prop, rock, support, tower of strength

bat noun, verb HIT, bang, smack, strike, swat, thump, wallop (*informal*), whack

batch noun GROUP, amount, assemblage, bunch, collection, crowd, lot, pack, quantity, set

bath noun 1 WASH, cleansing, douche, scrubbing, shower, soak, tub ♦ verb 2 WASH, bathe, clean, douse, scrub down, shower, soak

bathe verb 1 SWIM 2 WASH, cleanse, rinse 3 COVER, flood, immerse, steep, suffuse

baton noun STICK, club, crook, mace, rod, sceptre, staff, truncheon, wand

batten verb, usually with *down* FASTEN, board up, clamp down, cover up, fix, nail down, secure, tighten

batter verb BEAT, buffet, clobber (*slang*), pelt, pound, pummel, thrash, wallop (*informal*)

battery noun ARTILLERY, cannon, cannonry, gun emplacements, guns

battle noun 1 FIGHT, action, attack, combat, encounter, engagement, hostilities, skirmish 2 CONFLICT, campaign, contest, crusade, dispute, struggle ♦ verb 3 STRUGGLE, argue, clamour, dispute, fight, lock horns, strive, war

battlefield noun BATTLEGROUND, combat zone, field, field of battle, front

battleship noun WARSHIP, gunboat, man-of-war

batty adjective CRAZY, daft (*informal*), dotty (*slang, chiefly Brit.*), eccentric, mad, odd, peculiar, potty (*Brit. informal*), touched

bauble noun TRINKET, bagatelle, gewgaw, gimcrack, knick-knack, plaything, toy, trifle

baulk see BALK

bawdy adjective RUDE, coarse, dirty, indecent, lascivious, lecherous, lewd, ribald, salacious, smutty

bawl verb 1 CRY, blubber, sob, wail, weep 2 SHOUT, bellow, call, clamour, howl, roar, yell

bay[1] noun INLET, bight, cove, gulf, natural harbour, sound

bay[2] noun RECESS, alcove, compartment, niche, nook, opening

bay[3] verb HOWL, bark, clamour, cry, growl, yelp

bazaar noun 1 FAIR, bring-and-buy, fête, sale of work 2 MARKET, exchange, marketplace

be verb EXIST, be alive, breathe, inhabit, live

beach noun SHORE, coast, sands, seashore, seaside, water's edge

beached adjective STRANDED, abandoned, aground, ashore, deserted, grounded, high and dry, marooned, wrecked

beacon noun SIGNAL, beam, bonfire, flare, lighthouse, sign, watchtower

bead noun DROP, blob, bubble, dot, droplet, globule, pellet, pill

beady adjective BRIGHT, gleaming, glinting, glittering, sharp, shining

beak noun 1 BILL, mandible, neb (*archaic or dialect*), nib 2 Slang NOSE, proboscis, snout

beam noun 1 SMILE, grin 2 RAY, gleam, glimmer, glint, glow, shaft, streak, stream 3 RAFTER, girder, joist, plank, spar, support, timber ♦ verb 4 SMILE, grin 5 RADIATE, glare, gleam, glitter, glow, shine 6 SEND OUT, broadcast, emit, transmit

bear verb 1 SUPPORT, have, hold, maintain, possess, shoulder, sustain, uphold 2 CARRY, bring, convey, hump (*Brit. slang*), move, take, transport **3** PRODUCE, beget, breed, bring forth, engender, generate, give birth to, yield **4** TOLERATE, abide, allow, brook, endure, permit, put up with (*informal*), stomach, suffer

bearable *adjective* TOLERABLE, admissible, endurable, manageable, passable, sufferable, supportable, sustainable

bearer *noun* CARRIER, agent, conveyor, messenger, porter, runner, servant

bearing *noun* **1** usually with *on or upon* RELEVANCE, application, connection, import, pertinence, reference, relation, significance **2** MANNER, air, aspect, attitude, behaviour, demeanour, deportment, posture

bearings *plural noun* POSITION, aim, course, direction, location, orientation, situation, track, way, whereabouts

bear out *verb* SUPPORT, confirm, corroborate, endorse, justify, prove, substantiate, uphold, vindicate

beast *noun* **1** ANIMAL, brute, creature **2** BRUTE, barbarian, fiend, monster, ogre, sadist, savage, swine

beastly *adjective* UNPLEASANT, awful, disagreeable, horrid, mean, nasty, rotten

beat *verb* **1** HIT, bang, batter, buffet, knock, pound, strike, thrash **2** FLAP, flutter **3** THROB, palpitate, pound, pulsate, quake, thump, vibrate **4** DEFEAT, conquer, outdo, overcome, overwhelm, surpass, vanquish ♦ *noun* **5** THROB, palpitation, pulsation, pulse **6** ROUTE, circuit, course, path, rounds, way **7** RHYTHM, accent, cadence, metre, stress, time

beaten *adjective* **1** STIRRED, blended, foamy, frothy, mixed, whipped, whisked **2** DEFEATED, cowed, overcome, overwhelmed, thwarted, vanquished

beat up *verb Informal* ASSAULT, attack, batter, beat the living daylights out of (*informal*), knock about *or* around, thrash

beau *noun* **1** *Chiefly U.S.* BOYFRIEND, admirer, fiancé, lover, suitor, sweetheart **2** DANDY, coxcomb, fop, gallant, ladies' man

beautiful *adjective* ATTRACTIVE, charming, delightful, exquisite, fair, fine, gorgeous, handsome, lovely, pleasing

beautify *verb* MAKE BEAUTIFUL, adorn, decorate, embellish, festoon, garnish, glamorize, ornament

beauty *noun* **1** ATTRACTIVENESS, charm, comeliness, elegance, exquisiteness, glamour, grace, handsomeness, loveliness **2** BELLE, good-looker, lovely (*slang*), stunner (*informal*)

becalmed *adjective* STILL, motionless, settled, stranded, stuck

because *conjunction* SINCE, as, by reason of, in that, on account of, owing to, thanks to

beckon *verb* GESTURE, bid, gesticulate, motion, nod, signal, summon, wave at

become *verb* **1** COME TO BE, alter to, be transformed into, change into, develop into, grow into, mature into, ripen into **2** SUIT, embellish, enhance, fit, flatter, set off

becoming *adjective* **1** APPROPRIATE, compatible, fitting, in keeping, proper, seemly, suitable, worthy **2** FLATTERING, attractive, comely, enhancing, graceful, neat, pretty, tasteful

bed *noun* **1** BEDSTEAD, berth, bunk, cot, couch, divan **2** PLOT, area,

border, garden, patch, row, strip
3 BOTTOM, base, foundation,
groundwork

bedevil *verb* **1** TORMENT, afflict,
distress, harass, plague, trouble,
vex, worry **2** CONFUSE, confound

bedlam *noun* PANDEMONIUM, chaos,
commotion, confusion, furore,
tumult, turmoil, uproar

bedraggled *adjective* MESSY, dirty,
dishevelled, disordered, muddied,
unkempt, untidy

bedridden *adjective* CONFINED TO
BED, confined, flat on one's back,
incapacitated, laid up (*informal*)

bedrock *noun* **1** BOTTOM, bed,
foundation, rock bottom,
substratum, substructure **2** BASICS,
basis, core, essentials,
fundamentals, nuts and bolts
(*informal*), roots

beefy *adjective Informal* BRAWNY,
bulky, hulking, muscular, stocky,
strapping, sturdy, thickset

befall *verb Archaic or literary* HAPPEN,
chance, come to pass, fall, occur,
take place, transpire (*informal*)

befitting *adjective* APPROPRIATE,
apposite, becoming, fit, fitting,
proper, right, seemly, suitable

before *preposition* **1** AHEAD OF, in
advance of, in front of **2** EARLIER
THAN, in advance of, prior to **3** IN
THE PRESENCE OF, in front of ♦ *adverb*
4 PREVIOUSLY, ahead, earlier,
formerly, in advance, sooner **5** IN
FRONT, ahead

beforehand *adverb* IN ADVANCE,
ahead of time, already, before,
earlier, in anticipation, previously,
sooner

befriend *verb* HELP, aid, assist, back,
encourage, side with, stand by,
support, welcome

beg *verb* **1** SCROUNGE, cadge, seek
charity, solicit charity, sponge on,

touch (someone) for (*slang*)
2 IMPLORE, beseech, entreat,
petition, plead, request, solicit

beggar *noun* TRAMP, bag lady
(*chiefly U.S.*), bum (*informal*),
down-and-out, pauper, vagrant

beggarly *adjective* POOR, destitute,
impoverished, indigent, needy,
poverty-stricken

begin *verb* **1** START, commence,
embark on, initiate, instigate,
institute, prepare, set about
2 HAPPEN, appear, arise, come into
being, emerge, originate, start

beginner *noun* NOVICE, amateur,
apprentice, learner, neophyte,
starter, trainee, tyro

beginning *noun* **1** START, birth,
commencement, inauguration,
inception, initiation, onset,
opening, origin, outset **2** SEED,
fount, germ, root

begrudge *verb* RESENT, be jealous,
be reluctant, be stingy, envy,
grudge

beguile *verb* **1** FOOL, cheat, deceive,
delude, dupe, hoodwink, mislead,
take for a ride (*informal*), trick
2 CHARM, amuse, distract, divert,
engross, entertain, occupy

beguiling *adjective* CHARMING,
alluring, attractive, bewitching,
captivating, enchanting,
enthralling, intriguing

behave *verb* **1** ACT, function,
operate, perform, run, work
2 CONDUCT ONESELF PROPERLY, act
correctly, keep one's nose clean,
mind one's manners

behaviour *noun* **1** CONDUCT,
actions, bearing, demeanour,
deportment, manner, manners,
ways **2** ACTION, functioning,
operation, performance

behind *preposition* **1** AFTER, at the
back of, at the heels of, at the rear
of, following, later than **2** CAUSING,

at the bottom of, initiating, instigating, responsible for **3** SUPPORTING, backing, for, in agreement, on the side of ♦ *adverb* **4** AFTER, afterwards, following, in the wake (of), next, subsequently **5** OVERDUE, behindhand, in arrears, in debt ♦ *noun* **6** *Informal* BOTTOM, butt (*U.S. & Canad. informal*), buttocks, posterior

behold *verb Archaic or literary* LOOK AT, observe, perceive, regard, survey, view, watch, witness

beholden *adjective* INDEBTED, bound, grateful, obliged, owing, under obligation

being *noun* **1** EXISTENCE, life, reality **2** NATURE, entity, essence, soul, spirit, substance **3** CREATURE, human being, individual, living thing

belated *adjective* LATE, behindhand, behind time, delayed, late in the day, overdue, tardy

belch *verb* **1** BURP (*informal*), hiccup **2** EMIT, discharge, disgorge, erupt, give off, spew forth, vent

beleaguered *adjective* **1** HARASSED, badgered, hassled (*informal*), persecuted, pestered, plagued, put upon, vexed **2** BESIEGED, assailed, beset, blockaded, hemmed in, surrounded

belief *noun* **1** TRUST, assurance, confidence, conviction, feeling, impression, judgment, notion, opinion **2** FAITH, credo, creed, doctrine, dogma, ideology, principles, tenet

believable *adjective* CREDIBLE, authentic, imaginable, likely, plausible, possible, probable, trustworthy

believe *verb* **1** ACCEPT, be certain of, be convinced of, credit, depend on, have faith in, rely on, swear by, trust **2** THINK, assume, gather, imagine, judge, presume, reckon,

speculate, suppose

believer *noun* FOLLOWER, adherent, convert, devotee, disciple, supporter, upholder, zealot

belittle *verb* DISPARAGE, decry, denigrate, deprecate, deride, scoff at, scorn, sneer at

belligerent *adjective* **1** AGGRESSIVE, bellicose, combative, hostile, pugnacious, unfriendly, warlike, warring ♦ *noun* **2** FIGHTER, combatant, warring nation

bellow *noun, verb* SHOUT, bawl, cry, howl, roar, scream, shriek, yell

belly *noun* **1** STOMACH, abdomen, corporation (*informal*), gut, insides (*informal*), paunch, potbelly, tummy ♦ *verb* **2** SWELL OUT, billow, bulge, fill, spread, swell

bellyful *noun* SURFEIT, enough, excess, glut, plateful, plenty, satiety, too much

belonging *noun* RELATIONSHIP, acceptance, affinity, association, attachment, fellowship, inclusion, loyalty, rapport

belongings *plural noun* POSSESSIONS, accoutrements, chattels, effects, gear, goods, paraphernalia, personal property, stuff, things

belong to *verb* **1** BE THE PROPERTY OF, be at the disposal of, be held by, be owned by **2** BE A MEMBER OF, be affiliated to, be allied to, be associated with, be included in

beloved *adjective* DEAR, admired, adored, darling, loved, pet, precious, prized, treasured, worshipped

below *preposition* **1** LESSER, inferior, subject, subordinate **2** LESS THAN, lower than ♦ *adverb* **3** LOWER, beneath, down, under, underneath

belt *noun* **1** WAISTBAND, band,

cummerbund, girdle, girth, sash
2 *Geography* ZONE, area, district,
layer, region, stretch, strip, tract

bemoan *verb* LAMENT, bewail,
deplore, grieve for, mourn, regret,
rue, weep for

bemused *adjective* PUZZLED, at sea,
bewildered, confused,
flummoxed, muddled,
nonplussed, perplexed

bench *noun* 1 SEAT, form, pew,
settle, stall 2 WORKTABLE, board,
counter, table, trestle table,
workbench 3 **the bench** COURT,
courtroom, judges, judiciary,
magistrates, tribunal

benchmark *noun* REFERENCE POINT,
criterion, gauge, level, measure,
model, norm, par, standard,
yardstick

bend *verb* 1 CURVE, arc, arch, bow,
lean, turn, twist, veer ♦ *noun*
2 CURVE, angle, arc, arch, bow,
corner, loop, turn, twist

beneath *preposition* 1 UNDER,
below, lower than, underneath
2 INFERIOR TO, below, less than
3 UNWORTHY OF, unbefitting
♦ *adverb* 4 UNDERNEATH, below, in a
lower place

benefactor *noun* SUPPORTER, backer,
donor, helper, patron,
philanthropist, sponsor,
well-wisher

beneficial *adjective* HELPFUL,
advantageous, benign,
favourable, profitable, useful,
valuable, wholesome

beneficiary *noun* RECIPIENT, heir,
inheritor, payee, receiver

benefit *noun* 1 HELP, advantage,
aid, asset, assistance, favour,
good, profit ♦ *verb* 2 HELP, aid,
assist, avail, enhance, further,
improve, profit

benevolent *adjective* KIND,
altruistic, benign, caring,

charitable, generous, philanthropic

benign *adjective* 1 KINDLY, amiable,
friendly, genial, kind, obliging,
sympathetic 2 *Medical* HARMLESS,
curable, remediable

bent *adjective* 1 CURVED, angled,
arched, bowed, crooked,
hunched, stooped, twisted 2 **bent
on** DETERMINED TO, disposed to,
fixed on, inclined to, insistent on,
predisposed to, resolved on, set
on ♦ *noun* 3 INCLINATION, ability,
aptitude, leaning, penchant,
preference, propensity, tendency

bequeath *verb* LEAVE, bestow,
endow, entrust, give, grant, hand
down, impart, pass on, will

bequest *noun* LEGACY, bestowal,
endowment, estate, gift,
inheritance, settlement

berate *verb* SCOLD, castigate,
censure, chide, criticize,
harangue, rebuke, reprimand,
reprove, tell off (*informal*), upbraid

bereavement *noun* LOSS, affliction,
death, deprivation, misfortune,
tribulation

bereft *adjective* DEPRIVED, devoid,
lacking, parted from, robbed of,
wanting

berserk *adverb* CRAZY, amok,
enraged, frantic, frenzied, mad,
raging, wild

berth *noun* 1 BUNK, bed, billet,
hammock 2 *Nautical* ANCHORAGE,
dock, harbour, haven, pier, port,
quay, wharf ♦ *verb* 3 *Nautical*
ANCHOR, dock, drop anchor, land,
moor, tie up

beseech *verb* BEG, ask, call upon,
entreat, implore, plead, pray,
solicit

beset *verb* PLAGUE, bedevil, harass,
pester, trouble

beside *preposition* 1 NEXT TO,
abreast of, adjacent to, alongside,

at the side of, close to, near, nearby, neighbouring **2 beside oneself** <u>DISTRAUGHT</u>, apoplectic, at the end of one's tether, demented, desperate, frantic, frenzied, out of one's mind, unhinged

besides *adverb* **1** <u>TOO</u>, also, as well, further, furthermore, in addition, into the bargain, moreover, otherwise, what's more ◆ *preposition* **2** <u>APART FROM</u>, barring, excepting, excluding, in addition to, other than, over and above, without

besiege *verb* **1** <u>SURROUND</u>, blockade, encircle, hem in, lay siege to, shut in **2** <u>HARASS</u>, badger, harry, hassle (*informal*), hound, nag, pester, plague

besotted *adjective* <u>INFATUATED</u>, doting, hypnotized, smitten, spellbound

best *adjective* **1** <u>FINEST</u>, foremost, leading, most excellent, outstanding, pre-eminent, principal, supreme, unsurpassed ◆ *adverb* **2** <u>MOST HIGHLY</u>, extremely, greatly, most deeply, most fully ◆ *noun* **3** <u>FINEST</u>, cream, *crème de la crème*, elite, flower, pick, prime, top

bestial *adjective* <u>BRUTAL</u>, barbaric, beastly, brutish, inhuman, savage, sordid

bestow *verb* <u>PRESENT</u>, award, commit, give, grant, hand out, impart, lavish

bet *noun* **1** <u>GAMBLE</u>, long shot, risk, speculation, stake, venture, wager ◆ *verb* **2** <u>GAMBLE</u>, chance, hazard, risk, speculate, stake, venture, wager

betoken *verb* <u>INDICATE</u>, bode, denote, promise, represent, signify, suggest

betray *verb* **1** <u>BE DISLOYAL</u>, be

treacherous, be unfaithful, break one's promise, double-cross (*informal*), inform on *or* against, sell out (*informal*), stab in the back **2** <u>GIVE AWAY</u>, disclose, divulge, expose, let slip, reveal, uncover, unmask

betrayal *noun* **1** <u>DISLOYALTY</u>, deception, double-cross (*informal*), sell-out (*informal*), treachery, treason, trickery **2** <u>GIVING AWAY</u>, disclosure, divulgence, revelation

better *adjective* **1** <u>SUPERIOR</u>, excelling, finer, greater, higher-quality, more desirable, preferable, surpassing **2** <u>WELL</u>, cured, fully recovered, on the mend (*informal*), recovering, stronger ◆ *adverb* **3** <u>IN A MORE EXCELLENT MANNER</u>, in a superior way, more advantageously, more attractively, more competently, more effectively **4** <u>TO A GREATER DEGREE</u>, more completely, more thoroughly ◆ *verb* **5** <u>IMPROVE</u>, enhance, further, raise

between *preposition* <u>AMIDST</u>, among, betwixt, in the middle of, mid

beverage *noun* <u>DRINK</u>, liquid, liquor, refreshment

bevy *noun* <u>GROUP</u>, band, bunch (*informal*), collection, company, crowd, gathering, pack, troupe

bewail *verb* <u>LAMENT</u>, bemoan, cry over, deplore, grieve for, moan, mourn, regret

beware *verb* <u>BE CAREFUL</u>, be cautious, be wary, guard against, heed, look out, mind, take heed, watch out

bewilder *verb* <u>CONFOUND</u>, baffle, bemuse, confuse, flummox, mystify, nonplus, perplex, puzzle

bewildered *adjective* <u>CONFUSED</u>, at a loss, at sea, baffled, flummoxed, mystified, nonplussed, perplexed, puzzled

bewitch *verb* ENCHANT, beguile, captivate, charm, enrapture, entrance, fascinate, hypnotize

bewitched *adjective* ENCHANTED, charmed, entranced, fascinated, mesmerized, spellbound, under a spell

beyond *preposition* 1 PAST, above, apart from, at a distance, away from, over 2 EXCEEDING, out of reach of, superior to, surpassing

bias *noun* 1 PREJUDICE, favouritism, inclination, leaning, partiality, tendency ♦ *verb* 2 PREJUDICE, distort, influence, predispose, slant, sway, twist, warp, weight

biased *adjective* PREJUDICED, distorted, one-sided, partial, slanted, weighted

bicker *verb* QUARREL, argue, disagree, dispute, fight, row (*informal*), squabble, wrangle

bid *verb* 1 OFFER, proffer, propose, submit, tender 2 SAY, call, greet, tell, wish 3 TELL, ask, command, direct, instruct, order, require ♦ *noun* 4 OFFER, advance, amount, price, proposal, sum, tender 5 ATTEMPT, crack (*informal*), effort, go (*informal*), stab (*informal*), try

bidding *noun* ORDER, beck and call, command, direction, instruction, request, summons

big *adjective* 1 LARGE, enormous, extensive, great, huge, immense, massive, substantial, vast 2 IMPORTANT, eminent, influential, leading, main, powerful, prominent, significant 3 GROWN-UP, adult, elder, grown, mature 4 GENEROUS, altruistic, benevolent, gracious, magnanimous, noble, unselfish

bighead *noun Informal* BOASTER, braggart, know-all (*informal*)

bigheaded *adjective* BOASTFUL, arrogant, cocky, conceited, egotistic, immodest, overconfident, swollen-headed

bigot *noun* FANATIC, racist, sectarian, zealot

bigoted *adjective* INTOLERANT, biased, dogmatic, narrow-minded, opinionated, prejudiced, sectarian

bigotry *noun* INTOLERANCE, bias, discrimination, dogmatism, fanaticism, narrow-mindedness, prejudice, sectarianism

bigwig *noun Informal* IMPORTANT PERSON, big shot (*informal*), celebrity, dignitary, mogul, personage, somebody, V.I.P.

bill[1] *noun* 1 CHARGES, account, invoice, reckoning, score, statement, tally 2 PROPOSAL, measure, piece of legislation, projected law 3 ADVERTISEMENT, bulletin, circular, handbill, handout, leaflet, notice, placard, poster 4 LIST, agenda, card, catalogue, inventory, listing, programme, roster, schedule ♦ *verb* 5 CHARGE, debit, invoice 6 ADVERTISE, announce, give advance notice of, post

bill[2] *noun* BEAK, mandible, neb (*archaic or dialect*), nib

billet *verb* 1 QUARTER, accommodate, berth, station ♦ *noun* 2 QUARTERS, accommodation, barracks, lodging

billow *noun* 1 WAVE, breaker, crest, roller, surge, swell, tide ♦ *verb* 2 SURGE, balloon, belly, puff up, rise up, roll, swell

bind *verb* 1 SECURE, fasten, hitch, lash, stick, strap, tie, wrap 2 OBLIGE, compel, constrain, engage, force, necessitate, require ♦ *noun* 3 *Informal* NUISANCE, bore, difficulty, dilemma, drag (*informal*), pain in the neck (*informal*), quandary, spot (*informal*)

binding *adjective* COMPULSORY, indissoluble, irrevocable, mandatory, necessary, obligatory, unalterable

binge *noun* Informal BOUT, bender (*informal*), feast, fling, orgy, spree

biography *noun* LIFE STORY, account, curriculum vitae, CV, life, memoir, profile, record

birth *noun* 1 CHILDBIRTH, delivery, nativity, parturition 2 ANCESTRY, background, blood, breeding, lineage, parentage, pedigree, stock

bisect *verb* CUT IN TWO, cross, cut across, divide in two, halve, intersect, separate, split

bit[1] *noun* PIECE, crumb, fragment, grain, morsel, part, scrap, speck

bit[2] *noun* CURB, brake, check, restraint, snaffle

bitchy *adjective* Informal SPITEFUL, backbiting, catty (*informal*), mean, nasty, snide, vindictive

bite *verb* 1 CUT, chew, gnaw, nip, pierce, pinch, snap, tear, wound ♦ *noun* 2 WOUND, nip, pinch, prick, smarting, sting, tooth marks 3 SNACK, food, light meal, morsel, mouthful, piece, refreshment, taste

biting *adjective* 1 PIERCING, bitter, cutting, harsh, penetrating, sharp 2 SARCASTIC, caustic, cutting, incisive, mordant, scathing, stinging, trenchant, vitriolic

bitter *adjective* 1 SOUR, acid, acrid, astringent, harsh, sharp, tart, unsweetened, vinegary 2 RESENTFUL, acrimonious, begrudging, hostile, sore, sour, sullen 3 FREEZING, biting, fierce, intense, severe, stinging

bitterness *noun* 1 SOURNESS, acerbity, acidity, sharpness,

tartness 2 RESENTMENT, acrimony, animosity, asperity, grudge, hostility, rancour, sarcasm

bizarre *adjective* STRANGE, eccentric, extraordinary, fantastic, freakish, ludicrous, outlandish, peculiar, unusual, weird, zany

blab *verb* TELL, blurt out, disclose, divulge, give away, let slip, let the cat out of the bag, reveal, spill the beans (*informal*)

black *adjective* 1 DARK, dusky, ebony, jet, raven, sable, swarthy 2 HOPELESS, depressing, dismal, foreboding, gloomy, ominous, sad, sombre 3 ANGRY, furious, hostile, menacing, resentful, sullen, threatening 4 WICKED, bad, evil, iniquitous, nefarious, villainous ♦ *verb* 5 BOYCOTT, ban, bar, blacklist

blacken *verb* 1 DARKEN, befoul, begrime, cloud, dirty, make black, smudge, soil 2 DISCREDIT, defame, denigrate, malign, slander, smear, smirch, vilify

blackguard *noun* SCOUNDREL, bastard (*offensive*), bounder (*old-fashioned Brit. slang*), rascal, rogue, swine, villain

blacklist *verb* EXCLUDE, ban, bar, boycott, debar, expel, reject, snub

black magic *noun* WITCHCRAFT, black art, diabolism, necromancy, sorcery, voodoo, wizardry

blackmail *noun* 1 THREAT, extortion, hush money (*slang*), intimidation, ransom ♦ *verb* 2 THREATEN, coerce, compel, demand, extort, hold to ransom, intimidate, squeeze

blackness *noun* DARKNESS, duskiness, gloom, murkiness, swarthiness

blackout *noun* 1 UNCONSCIOUSNESS, coma, faint, loss of consciousness, oblivion, swoon 2 NONCOMMUNICATION, censorship, radio silence, secrecy, suppression, withholding news

black sheep *noun* DISGRACE, bad egg (*old-fashioned informal*), dropout, ne'er-do-well, outcast, prodigal, renegade, reprobate, wastrel

blame *verb* 1 HOLD RESPONSIBLE, accuse, censure, chide, condemn, criticize, find fault with, reproach ♦ *noun* 2 RESPONSIBILITY, accountability, culpability, fault, guilt, liability, onus

blameless *adjective* INNOCENT, above suspicion, clean, faultless, guiltless, immaculate, impeccable, irreproachable, perfect, unblemished, virtuous

blameworthy *adjective* REPREHENSIBLE, discreditable, disreputable, indefensible, inexcusable, iniquitous, reproachable, shameful

bland *adjective* DULL, boring, flat, humdrum, insipid, tasteless, unexciting, uninspiring, vapid

blank *adjective* 1 UNMARKED, bare, clean, clear, empty, plain, void, white 2 EXPRESSIONLESS, deadpan, empty, impassive, poker-faced (*informal*), vacant, vague ♦ *noun* 3 EMPTY SPACE, emptiness, gap, nothingness, space, vacancy, vacuum, void

blanket *noun* 1 COVER, coverlet, rug 2 COVERING, carpet, cloak, coat, layer, mantle, sheet ♦ *verb* 3 COVER, cloak, coat, conceal, hide, mask, obscure, suppress

blare *verb* SOUND OUT, blast, clamour, clang, resound, roar, scream, trumpet

blarney *noun* FLATTERY, blandishment, cajolery, coaxing, soft soap (*informal*), spiel, sweet talk (*informal*), wheedling

blasé *adjective* INDIFFERENT, apathetic, lukewarm, nonchalant, offhand, unconcerned

blaspheme *verb* CURSE, abuse, damn, desecrate, execrate, profane, revile, swear

blasphemous *adjective* IRREVERENT, godless, impious, irreligious, profane, sacrilegious, ungodly

blasphemy *noun* IRREVERENCE, cursing, desecration, execration, impiety, profanity, sacrilege, swearing

blast *noun* 1 EXPLOSION, bang, burst, crash, detonation, discharge, eruption, outburst, salvo, volley 2 GUST, gale, squall, storm, strong breeze, tempest 3 BLARE, blow, clang, honk, peal, scream, toot, wail ♦ *verb* 4 BLOW UP, break up, burst, demolish, destroy, explode, put paid to, ruin, shatter

blastoff *noun* LAUNCH, discharge, expulsion, firing, launching, liftoff, projection, shot

blatant *adjective* OBVIOUS, brazen, conspicuous, flagrant, glaring, obtrusive, ostentatious, overt

blaze *noun* 1 FIRE, bonfire, conflagration, flames 2 GLARE, beam, brilliance, flare, flash, gleam, glitter, glow, light, radiance ♦ *verb* 3 BURN, fire, flame 4 SHINE, beam, flare, flash, glare, gleam, glow

bleach *verb* WHITEN, blanch, fade, grow pale, lighten, wash out

bleak *adjective* 1 EXPOSED, bare, barren, desolate, unsheltered, weather-beaten, windswept 2 DISMAL, cheerless, depressing, discouraging, dreary, gloomy, grim, hopeless, joyless, sombre

bleary *adjective* DIM, blurred, blurry, foggy, fuzzy, hazy, indistinct, misty, murky

bleed *verb* 1 LOSE BLOOD, flow, gush, ooze, run, shed blood, spurt

2 DRAW *or* TAKE BLOOD, extract, leech **3** *Informal* EXTORT, drain, exhaust, fleece, milk, squeeze

blemish *noun* **1** MARK, blot, defect, disfigurement, fault, flaw, imperfection, smudge, stain, taint ◆ *verb* **2** STAIN, damage, disfigure, impair, injure, mar, mark, spoil, sully, taint, tarnish

blend *verb* **1** MIX, amalgamate, combine, compound, merge, mingle, unite **2** GO WELL, complement, fit, go with, harmonize, suit ◆ *noun* **3** MIXTURE, alloy, amalgamation, combination, compound, concoction, mix, synthesis, union

bless *verb* **1** SANCTIFY, anoint, consecrate, dedicate, exalt, hallow, ordain **2** GRANT, bestow, favour, give, grace, provide

blessed *adjective* HOLY, adored, beatified, divine, hallowed, revered, sacred, sanctified

blessing *noun* **1** BENEDICTION, benison, commendation, consecration, dedication, grace, invocation, thanksgiving **2** APPROVAL, backing, consent, favour, good wishes, leave, permission, sanction, support **3** BENEFIT, favour, gift, godsend, good fortune, help, kindness, service, windfall

blight *noun* **1** CURSE, affliction, bane, contamination, corruption, evil, plague, pollution, scourge, woe **2** DISEASE, canker, decay, fungus, infestation, mildew, pest, pestilence, rot ◆ *verb* **3** FRUSTRATE, crush, dash, disappoint, mar, ruin, spoil, undo, wreck

blind *adjective* **1** SIGHTLESS, eyeless, unseeing, unsighted, visionless **2** UNAWARE OF, careless, heedless, ignorant, inattentive, inconsiderate, indifferent, insensitive, oblivious, unconscious of **3** UNREASONING, indiscriminate, prejudiced ◆ *noun* **4** COVER, camouflage, cloak, façade, feint, front, mask, masquerade, screen, smoke screen

blindly *adverb* **1** THOUGHTLESSLY, carelessly, heedlessly, inconsiderately, recklessly, senselessly **2** AIMLESSLY, at random, indiscriminately, instinctively

blink *verb* **1** WINK, bat, flutter **2** FLICKER, flash, gleam, glimmer, shine, twinkle, wink ◆ *noun* **3 on the blink** *Slang* NOT WORKING (PROPERLY), faulty, malfunctioning, out of action, out of order, playing up

bliss *noun* JOY, beatitude, blessedness, blissfulness, ecstasy, euphoria, felicity, gladness, happiness, heaven, nirvana, paradise, rapture

blissful *adjective* JOYFUL, ecstatic, elated, enraptured, euphoric, happy, heavenly (*informal*), rapturous

blister *noun* SORE, abscess, boil, carbuncle, cyst, pimple, pustule, swelling

blithe *adjective* HEEDLESS, careless, casual, indifferent, nonchalant, thoughtless, unconcerned, untroubled

blitz *noun* ATTACK, assault, blitzkrieg, bombardment, campaign, offensive, onslaught, raid, strike

blizzard *noun* SNOWSTORM, blast, gale, squall, storm, tempest

bloat *verb* PUFF UP, balloon, blow up, dilate, distend, enlarge, expand, inflate, swell

blob *noun* DROP, ball, bead, bubble, dab, droplet, globule, lump, mass

bloc *noun* GROUP, alliance, axis, coalition, faction, league, union

block *noun* **1** PIECE, bar, brick,

chunk, hunk, ingot, lump, mass
2 OBSTRUCTION, bar, barrier,
blockage, hindrance, impediment,
jam, obstacle ♦ verb 3 OBSTRUCT,
bung up (informal), choke, clog,
close, plug, stem the flow, stop up
4 STOP, bar, check, halt, hinder,
impede, obstruct, thwart

blockade noun STOPPAGE, barricade,
barrier, block, hindrance,
impediment, obstacle,
obstruction, restriction, siege

blockage noun OBSTRUCTION, block,
impediment, occlusion, stoppage

blockhead noun IDIOT, chump
(informal), dunce, fool, nitwit,
numbskull or numskull, thickhead,
twit (informal, chiefly Brit.)

bloke noun Informal MAN, chap,
character (informal), fellow, guy
(informal), individual, person

blond, blonde adjective FAIR,
fair-haired, fair-skinned, flaxen,
golden-haired, light, tow-headed

blood noun 1 LIFEBLOOD, gore, vital
fluid 2 FAMILY, ancestry, birth,
descent, extraction, kinship,
lineage, relations

bloodcurdling adjective TERRIFYING,
appalling, chilling, dreadful,
fearful, frightening, hair-raising,
horrendous, horrifying, scaring,
spine-chilling

bloodshed noun KILLING, blood
bath, blood-letting, butchery,
carnage, gore, massacre, murder,
slaughter, slaying

bloodthirsty adjective CRUEL,
barbarous, brutal, cut-throat,
ferocious, gory, murderous,
savage, vicious, warlike

bloody adjective 1 BLOODSTAINED,
bleeding, blood-soaked,
blood-spattered, gaping, raw
2 CRUEL, ferocious, fierce,
sanguinary, savage

bloom noun 1 FLOWER, blossom,

blossoming, bud, efflorescence,
opening (of flowers) 2 PRIME,
beauty, flourishing, freshness,
glow, health, heyday, lustre,
radiance, vigour ♦ verb 3 BLOSSOM,
blow, bud, burgeon, open, sprout
4 FLOURISH, develop, fare well,
grow, prosper, succeed, thrive,
wax

blossom noun 1 FLOWER, bloom,
bud, floret, flowers ♦ verb
2 FLOWER, bloom, burgeon 3 GROW,
bloom, develop, flourish, mature,
progress, prosper, thrive

blot noun 1 SPOT, blotch, mark,
patch, smear, smudge, speck,
splodge 2 STAIN, blemish, defect,
fault, flaw, scar, spot, taint ♦ verb
3 STAIN, disgrace, mark, smirch,
smudge, spoil, spot, sully, tarnish
4 SOAK UP, absorb, dry, take up
5 **blot out a** OBLITERATE, darken,
destroy, eclipse, efface, obscure,
shadow **b** ERASE, cancel, expunge

blow[1] verb 1 CARRY, buffet, drive,
fling, flutter, move, sweep, waft
2 EXHALE, breathe, pant, puff 3 PLAY,
blare, mouth, pipe, sound, toot,
trumpet, vibrate

blow[2] noun 1 KNOCK, bang, clout
(informal), punch, smack, sock
(slang), stroke, thump, wallop
(informal), whack 2 SETBACK,
bombshell, calamity, catastrophe,
disappointment, disaster,
misfortune, reverse, shock

blow out verb 1 PUT OUT,
extinguish, snuff 2 BURST, erupt,
explode, rupture, shatter

blow up verb 1 EXPLODE, blast, blow
sky-high, bomb, burst, detonate,
rupture, shatter 2 INFLATE, bloat,
distend, enlarge, expand, fill, puff
up, pump up, swell 3 Informal LOSE
ONE'S TEMPER, become angry, erupt,
fly off the handle (informal), hit
the roof (informal), rage, see red
(informal)

bludgeon noun **1** CLUB, cosh (*Brit.*), cudgel, truncheon ♦ verb **2** CLUB, beat up, cosh (*Brit.*), cudgel, knock down, strike **3** BULLY, bulldoze (*informal*), coerce, force, railroad (*informal*), steamroller

blue adjective **1** AZURE, cerulean, cobalt, cyan, navy, sapphire, sky-coloured, ultramarine **2** DEPRESSED, dejected, despondent, downcast, low, melancholy, sad, unhappy **3** SMUTTY, indecent, lewd, obscene, risqué, X-rated (*informal*)

blueprint noun PLAN, design, draft, outline, pattern, pilot scheme, prototype, sketch

blues plural noun DEPRESSION, doldrums, dumps (*informal*), gloom, low spirits, melancholy, unhappiness

bluff[1] verb **1** DECEIVE, con, delude, fake, feign, mislead, pretend, pull the wool over someone's eyes ♦ noun **2** DECEPTION, bluster, bravado, deceit, fraud, humbug, pretence, sham, subterfuge

bluff[2] noun **1** PRECIPICE, bank, cliff, crag, escarpment, headland, peak, promontory, ridge ♦ adjective **2** HEARTY, blunt, blustering, genial, good-natured, open, outspoken, plain-spoken

blunder noun **1** MISTAKE, bloomer (*Brit. informal*), clanger (*informal*), faux pas, gaffe, howler (*informal*), indiscretion **2** ERROR, fault, inaccuracy, mistake, oversight, slip, slip-up (*informal*) ♦ verb **3** MAKE A MISTAKE, botch, bungle, err, put one's foot in it (*informal*), slip up (*informal*) **4** STUMBLE, bumble, flounder

blunt adjective **1** DULL, dulled, edgeless, pointless, rounded, unsharpened **2** FORTHRIGHT, bluff, brusque, frank, outspoken, plain-spoken, rude, straightforward, tactless ♦ verb **3** DULL, dampen, deaden, numb, soften, take the edge off, water down, weaken

blur verb **1** MAKE INDISTINCT, cloud, darken, make hazy, make vague, mask, obscure ♦ noun **2** INDISTINCTNESS, confusion, fog, haze, obscurity

blurt out verb EXCLAIM, disclose, let the cat out of the bag, reveal, spill the beans (*informal*), tell all, utter suddenly

blush verb **1** TURN RED, colour, flush, go red (as a beetroot), redden, turn scarlet ♦ noun **2** REDDENING, colour, flush, glow, pink tinge, rosiness, rosy tint, ruddiness

bluster verb **1** ROAR, bully, domineer, hector, rant, storm ♦ noun **2** HOT AIR (*informal*), bluff, bombast, bravado

blustery adjective GUSTY, boisterous, inclement, squally, stormy, tempestuous, violent, wild, windy

board noun **1** PLANK, panel, piece of timber, slat, timber **2** DIRECTORS, advisers, committee, conclave, council, panel, trustees **3** MEALS, daily meals, provisions, victuals ♦ verb **4** GET ON, embark, enter, mount **5** LODGE, put up, quarter, room

boast verb **1** BRAG, blow one's own trumpet, crow, strut, swagger, talk big (*slang*), vaunt **2** POSSESS, be proud of, congratulate oneself on, exhibit, flatter oneself, pride oneself on, show off ♦ noun **3** BRAG, avowal

boastful adjective BRAGGING, cocky, conceited, crowing, egotistical, full of oneself, swaggering, swollen-headed, vaunting

bob verb DUCK, bounce, hop, nod, oscillate, waggle, wobble

bode verb PORTEND, augur, be an omen of, forebode, foretell, predict, signify, threaten

bodily *adjective* <u>PHYSICAL</u>, actual, carnal, corporal, corporeal, material, substantial, tangible

body *noun* **1** <u>PHYSIQUE</u>, build, figure, form, frame, shape **2** <u>TORSO</u>, trunk **3** <u>CORPSE</u>, cadaver, carcass, dead body, remains, stiff (*slang*) **4** <u>ORGANIZATION</u>, association, band, bloc, collection, company, confederation, congress, corporation, society **5** <u>MAIN PART</u>, bulk, essence, mass, material, matter, substance

boffin *noun* Brit. informal <u>EXPERT</u>, brainbox, egghead, genius, intellectual, inventor, mastermind

bog *noun* <u>MARSH</u>, fen, mire, morass, quagmire, slough, swamp, wetlands

bogey *noun* <u>BUGBEAR</u>, bête noire, bugaboo, nightmare

bogus *adjective* <u>FAKE</u>, artificial, counterfeit, false, forged, fraudulent, imitation, phoney *or* phony (*informal*), sham

bohemian *adjective* **1** <u>UNCONVENTIONAL</u>, alternative, artistic, arty (*informal*), left bank, nonconformist, offbeat, unorthodox ♦ *noun* **2** <u>NONCONFORMIST</u>, beatnik, dropout, hippy, iconoclast

boil[1] *verb* <u>BUBBLE</u>, effervesce, fizz, foam, froth, seethe

boil[2] *noun* <u>PUSTULE</u>, blister, carbuncle, gathering, swelling, tumour, ulcer

boisterous *adjective* <u>UNRULY</u>, disorderly, loud, noisy, riotous, rollicking, rowdy, unrestrained, vociferous, wild

bold *adjective* **1** <u>FEARLESS</u>, adventurous, audacious, brave, courageous, daring, enterprising, heroic, intrepid, valiant **2** <u>IMPUDENT</u>, barefaced, brazen, cheeky,

confident, forward, insolent, rude, shameless

bolster *verb* <u>SUPPORT</u>, augment, boost, help, reinforce, shore up, strengthen

bolt *noun* **1** <u>BAR</u>, catch, fastener, latch, lock, sliding bar **2** <u>PIN</u>, peg, rivet, rod ♦ *verb* **3** <u>RUN AWAY</u>, abscond, dash, escape, flee, fly, make a break (for it), run for it **4** <u>LOCK</u>, bar, fasten, latch, secure **5** <u>GOBBLE</u>, cram, devour, gorge, gulp, guzzle, stuff, swallow whole, wolf

bomb *noun* **1** <u>EXPLOSIVE</u>, device, grenade, mine, missile, projectile, rocket, shell, torpedo ♦ *verb* **2** <u>BLOW UP</u>, attack, blow sky-high, bombard, destroy, shell, strafe, torpedo

bombard *verb* **1** <u>BOMB</u>, assault, blitz, fire upon, open fire, pound, shell, strafe **2** <u>ATTACK</u>, assail, beset, besiege, harass, hound, pester

bombardment *noun* <u>BOMBING</u>, assault, attack, barrage, blitz, fusillade, shelling

bombastic *adjective* <u>GRANDILOQUENT</u>, grandiose, high-flown, inflated, pompous, verbose, wordy

bona fide *adjective* <u>GENUINE</u>, actual, authentic, honest, kosher (*informal*), legitimate, real, true

bond *noun* **1** <u>FASTENING</u>, chain, cord, fetter, ligature, manacle, shackle, tie **2** <u>TIE</u>, affiliation, affinity, attachment, connection, link, relation, union **3** <u>AGREEMENT</u>, contract, covenant, guarantee, obligation, pledge, promise, word ♦ *verb* **4** <u>HOLD TOGETHER</u>, bind, connect, fasten, fix together, glue, paste

bondage *noun* <u>SLAVERY</u>, captivity, confinement, enslavement, imprisonment, subjugation

bonus *noun* <u>EXTRA</u>, dividend, gift,

icing on the cake, plus, premium, prize, reward

bony adjective THIN, emaciated, gaunt, lean, scrawny, skin and bone, skinny

book noun 1 WORK, publication, title, tome, tract, volume 2 NOTEBOOK, album, diary, exercise book, jotter, pad ♦ verb 3 RESERVE, arrange for, charter, engage, make reservations, organize, programme, schedule 4 NOTE, enter, list, log, mark down, put down, record, register, write down

booklet noun BROCHURE, leaflet, pamphlet

boom verb 1 BANG, blast, crash, explode, resound, reverberate, roar, roll, rumble, thunder 2 FLOURISH, develop, expand, grow, increase, intensify, prosper, strengthen, swell, thrive ♦ noun 3 BANG, blast, burst, clap, crash, explosion, roar, rumble, thunder 4 EXPANSION, boost, development, growth, improvement, increase, jump, upsurge, upswing, upturn

boon noun BENEFIT, advantage, blessing, favour, gift, godsend, manna from heaven, windfall

boorish adjective LOUTISH, churlish, coarse, crude, oafish, uncivilized, uncouth, vulgar

boost noun 1 HELP, encouragement, praise, promotion 2 RISE, addition, expansion, improvement, increase, increment, jump ♦ verb 3 INCREASE, add to, amplify, develop, enlarge, expand, heighten, raise 4 ADVERTISE, encourage, foster, further, hype, plug (informal), praise, promote

boot verb KICK, drive, drop-kick, knock, punt, put the boot in(to) (slang), shove

booty noun PLUNDER, gains, haul, loot, prey, spoils, swag (slang), takings, winnings

border noun 1 FRONTIER, borderline, boundary, line, march 2 EDGE, bounds, brink, limits, margin, rim, verge ♦ verb 3 EDGE, bind, decorate, fringe, hem, rim, trim

bore[1] verb DRILL, burrow, gouge out, mine, penetrate, perforate, pierce, sink, tunnel

bore[2] verb 1 TIRE, be tedious, fatigue, jade, pall on, send to sleep, wear out, weary ♦ noun 2 NUISANCE, anorak (informal), pain (informal), yawn (informal)

bored adjective FED UP, listless, tired, uninterested, wearied

boredom noun TEDIUM, apathy, ennui, flatness, monotony, sameness, tediousness, weariness, world-weariness

boring adjective UNINTERESTING, dull, flat, humdrum, mind-numbing, monotonous, tedious, tiresome

borrow verb 1 TAKE ON LOAN, cadge, scrounge (informal), touch (someone) for (slang), use temporarily 2 STEAL, adopt, copy, obtain, plagiarize, take, usurp

bosom noun 1 BREAST, bust, chest ♦ adjective 2 INTIMATE, boon, cherished, close, confidential, dear, very dear

boss[1] noun HEAD, chief, director, employer, gaffer (informal, chiefly Brit.), leader, manager, master, supervisor

boss[2] noun STUD, knob, point, protuberance, tip

boss around verb Informal DOMINEER, bully, dominate, oppress, order, push around (slang)

bossy adjective DOMINEERING, arrogant, authoritarian, autocratic, dictatorial, hectoring, high-handed, imperious, overbearing, tyrannical

botch verb 1 SPOIL, blunder, bungle, cock up (Brit. slang), make a pig's ear of (informal), mar, mess up, screw up (informal) ♦ noun 2 MESS, blunder, bungle, cock-up (Brit. slang), failure, hash, pig's ear (informal)

bother verb 1 TROUBLE, alarm, concern, disturb, harass, hassle (informal), inconvenience, pester, plague, worry ♦ noun 2 TROUBLE, difficulty, fuss, hassle (informal), inconvenience, irritation, nuisance, problem, worry

bottleneck noun HOLD-UP, block, blockage, congestion, impediment, jam, obstacle, obstruction, snarl-up (informal, chiefly Brit.)

bottle up verb SUPPRESS, check, contain, curb, keep back, restrict, shut in, trap

bottom noun 1 LOWEST PART, base, bed, depths, floor, foot, foundation 2 UNDERSIDE, lower side, sole, underneath 3 BUTTOCKS, backside, behind (informal), posterior, rear, rump, seat ♦ adjective 4 LOWEST, last

bottomless adjective UNLIMITED, boundless, deep, fathomless, immeasurable, inexhaustible, infinite, unfathomable

bounce verb 1 REBOUND, bob, bound, jump, leap, recoil, ricochet, spring ♦ noun 2 Informal LIFE, dynamism, energy, go (informal), liveliness, vigour, vivacity, zip (informal) 3 SPRINGINESS, elasticity, give, recoil, resilience, spring

bound[1] adjective 1 TIED, cased, fastened, fixed, pinioned, secured, tied up 2 CERTAIN, destined, doomed, fated, sure 3 OBLIGED, beholden, committed, compelled, constrained, duty-bound, forced, pledged, required

bound[2] verb LIMIT, confine, demarcate, encircle, enclose, hem in, restrain, restrict, surround

bound[3] verb, noun LEAP, bob, bounce, gambol, hurdle, jump, skip, spring, vault

boundary noun LIMITS, barrier, border, borderline, brink, edge, extremity, fringe, frontier, margin

boundless adjective UNLIMITED, endless, immense, incalculable, inexhaustible, infinite, unconfined, untold, vast

bounds plural noun BOUNDARY, border, confine, edge, extremity, limit, rim, verge

bountiful adjective Literary 1 PLENTIFUL, abundant, ample, bounteous, copious, exuberant, lavish, luxuriant, prolific 2 GENEROUS, liberal, magnanimous, open-handed, prodigal, unstinting

bounty noun Literary 1 GENEROSITY, benevolence, charity, kindness, largesse or largess, liberality, philanthropy 2 REWARD, bonus, gift, present

bouquet noun 1 BUNCH OF FLOWERS, buttonhole, corsage, garland, nosegay, posy, spray, wreath 2 AROMA, fragrance, perfume, redolence, savour, scent

bourgeois adjective MIDDLE-CLASS, conventional, hidebound, materialistic, traditional

bout noun 1 PERIOD, fit, spell, stint, term, turn 2 FIGHT, boxing match, competition, contest, encounter, engagement, match, set-to, struggle

bow[1] verb 1 BEND, bob, droop, genuflect, nod, stoop 2 GIVE IN, acquiesce, comply, concede, defer, kowtow, relent, submit, succumb, surrender, yield ♦ noun 3 BENDING, bob, genuflexion, kowtow, nod, obeisance

bow[2] noun Nautical PROW, beak,
fore, head, stem

bowels plural noun **1** GUTS, entrails,
innards (informal), insides
(informal), intestines, viscera, vitals
2 DEPTHS, belly, core, deep, hold,
inside, interior

bowl[1] noun BASIN, dish, vessel

bowl[2] verb THROW, fling, hurl, pitch

box[1] noun **1** CONTAINER, carton, case,
casket, chest, pack, package,
receptacle, trunk ♦ verb **2** PACK,
package, wrap

box[2] verb FIGHT, exchange blows,
spar

boxer noun FIGHTER, prizefighter,
pugilist, sparring partner

boy noun LAD, fellow, junior,
schoolboy, stripling, youngster,
youth

boycott verb EMBARGO, ban, bar,
black, exclude, outlaw, prohibit,
refuse, reject

boyfriend noun SWEETHEART,
admirer, beau, date, lover, man,
suitor

boyish adjective YOUTHFUL,
adolescent, childish, immature,
juvenile, puerile, young

brace noun **1** SUPPORT, bolster,
bracket, buttress, prop,
reinforcement, stay, strut, truss
♦ verb **2** SUPPORT, bolster, buttress,
fortify, reinforce, steady,
strengthen

bracing adjective REFRESHING, brisk,
crisp, exhilarating, fresh,
invigorating, stimulating

brag verb BOAST, blow one's own
trumpet, bluster, crow, swagger,
talk big (slang), vaunt

braggart noun BOASTER, bigmouth
(slang), bragger, show-off
(informal)

braid verb INTERWEAVE, entwine,
interlace, intertwine, lace, plait,
twine, weave

brainless adjective STUPID, foolish,
idiotic, inane, mindless, senseless,
thoughtless, witless

brains plural noun INTELLIGENCE,
intellect, sense, understanding

brainwave noun IDEA, bright idea,
stroke of genius, thought

brainy adjective Informal INTELLIGENT,
bright, brilliant, clever, smart

brake noun **1** CONTROL, check,
constraint, curb, rein, restraint
♦ verb **2** SLOW, check, decelerate,
halt, moderate, reduce speed,
slacken, stop

branch noun **1** BOUGH, arm, limb,
offshoot, shoot, spray, sprig
2 DIVISION, chapter, department,
office, part, section, subdivision,
subsection, wing

brand noun **1** LABEL, emblem,
hallmark, logo, mark, marker,
sign, stamp, symbol, trademark
2 KIND, cast, class, grade, make,
quality, sort, species, type, variety
♦ verb **3** MARK, burn, burn in, label,
scar, stamp **4** STIGMATIZE, censure,
denounce, discredit, disgrace,
expose, mark

brandish verb WAVE, display,
exhibit, flaunt, flourish, parade,
raise, shake, swing, wield

brash adjective BOLD, brazen, cocky,
impertinent, impudent, insolent,
pushy (informal), rude

bravado noun SWAGGER, bluster,
boastfulness, boasting, bombast,
swashbuckling, vaunting

brave adjective **1** COURAGEOUS, bold,
daring, fearless, heroic, intrepid,
plucky, resolute, valiant ♦ verb
2 CONFRONT, defy, endure, face,
stand up to, suffer, tackle,
withstand

bravery noun COURAGE, boldness, daring, fearlessness, fortitude, heroism, intrepidity, mettle, pluck, spirit, valour

brawl noun 1 FIGHT, affray (*Law*), altercation, clash, dispute, fracas, fray, melee *or* mêlée, punch-up (*Brit. informal*), rumpus, scuffle, skirmish ♦ verb 2 FIGHT, scrap (*informal*), scuffle, tussle, wrestle

brawn noun MUSCLE, beef (*informal*), might, muscles, power, strength, vigour

brawny adjective MUSCULAR, beefy (*informal*), hefty (*informal*), lusty, powerful, strapping, strong, sturdy, well-built

brazen adjective BOLD, audacious, barefaced, brash, defiant, impudent, insolent, shameless, unabashed, unashamed

breach noun 1 NONOBSERVANCE, contravention, infraction, infringement, noncompliance, transgression, trespass, violation 2 CRACK, cleft, fissure, gap, opening, rift, rupture, split

bread noun 1 FOOD, fare, nourishment, sustenance 2 *Slang* MONEY, cash, dough (*slang*)

breadth noun 1 WIDTH, broadness, latitude, span, spread, wideness 2 EXTENT, compass, expanse, range, scale, scope

break verb 1 SEPARATE, burst, crack, destroy, disintegrate, fracture, fragment, shatter, smash, snap, split, tear 2 DISOBEY, breach, contravene, disregard, infringe, renege on, transgress, violate 3 REVEAL, announce, disclose, divulge, impart, inform, let out, make public, proclaim, tell 4 STOP, abandon, cut, discontinue, give up, interrupt, pause, rest, suspend 5 WEAKEN, demoralize, dispirit, subdue, tame, undermine 6 *Of a record, etc.* BEAT, better, exceed,

excel, go beyond, outdo, outstrip, surpass, top ♦ noun 7 DIVISION, crack, fissure, fracture, gap, hole, opening, split, tear 8 REST, breather (*informal*), hiatus, interlude, intermission, interruption, interval, let-up (*informal*), lull, pause, respite 9 *Informal* STROKE OF LUCK, advantage, chance, fortune, opening, opportunity

breakable adjective FRAGILE, brittle, crumbly, delicate, flimsy, frail, frangible, friable

breakdown noun COLLAPSE, disintegration, disruption, failure, mishap, stoppage

break down verb 1 COLLAPSE, come unstuck, fail, seize up, stop, stop working 2 BE OVERCOME, crack up (*informal*), go to pieces

break-in noun BURGLARY, breaking and entering, robbery

break off verb 1 DETACH, divide, part, pull off, separate, sever, snap off, splinter 2 STOP, cease, desist, discontinue, end, finish, halt, pull the plug on, suspend, terminate

break out verb BEGIN, appear, arise, commence, emerge, happen, occur, set in, spring up, start

breakthrough noun DEVELOPMENT, advance, discovery, find, invention, leap, progress, quantum leap, step forward

break up verb 1 SEPARATE, dissolve, divide, divorce, part, scatter, sever, split 2 STOP, adjourn, disband, dismantle, end, suspend, terminate

breast noun BOSOM, bust, chest, front, teat, udder

breath noun RESPIRATION, breathing, exhalation, gasp, gulp, inhalation, pant, wheeze

breathe verb 1 INHALE AND EXHALE, draw in, gasp, gulp, pant, puff, respire, wheeze 2 WHISPER, murmur, sigh

breather noun Informal REST, break, breathing space, halt, pause, recess, respite

breathless adjective 1 OUT OF BREATH, gasping, gulping, panting, short-winded, spent, wheezing 2 EXCITED, eager, on tenterhooks, open-mouthed, with bated breath

breathtaking adjective AMAZING, astonishing, awe-inspiring, exciting, impressive, magnificent, sensational, stunning (informal), thrilling

breed verb 1 REPRODUCE, bear, bring forth, hatch, multiply, procreate, produce, propagate 2 BRING UP, cultivate, develop, nourish, nurture, raise, rear 3 PRODUCE, arouse, bring about, cause, create, generate, give rise to, stir up ◆ noun 4 VARIETY, pedigree, race, species, stock, strain, type 5 KIND, brand, sort, stamp, type, variety

breeding noun 1 UPBRINGING, ancestry, cultivation, development, lineage, nurture, raising, rearing, reproduction, training 2 REFINEMENT, conduct, courtesy, cultivation, culture, polish, sophistication, urbanity

breeze noun 1 LIGHT WIND, air, breath of wind, current of air, draught, gust, waft, zephyr ◆ verb 2 MOVE BRISKLY, flit, glide, hurry, pass, sail, sweep

breezy adjective 1 WINDY, airy, blowy, blustery, fresh, gusty, squally 2 CAREFREE, blithe, casual, easy-going, free and easy, jaunty, light-hearted, lively, sprightly

brevity noun 1 SHORTNESS, briefness, impermanence, transience, transitoriness 2 CONCISENESS, crispness, curtness, economy, pithiness, succinctness, terseness

brew verb 1 MAKE (beer), boil, ferment, infuse (tea), soak, steep, stew 2 DEVELOP, foment, form, gather, start, stir up ◆ noun 3 DRINK, beverage, blend, concoction, infusion, liquor, mixture, preparation

bribe verb 1 BUY OFF, corrupt, grease the palm or hand of (slang), pay off (informal), reward, suborn ◆ noun 2 INDUCEMENT, allurement, backhander (slang), enticement, kickback (U.S.), pay-off (informal), sweetener (slang)

bribery noun BUYING OFF, corruption, inducement, palm-greasing (slang), payola (informal)

bric-a-brac noun KNICK-KNACKS, baubles, curios, ornaments, trinkets

bridal adjective MATRIMONIAL, conjugal, connubial, marital, marriage, nuptial, wedding

bridge noun 1 ARCH, flyover, overpass, span, viaduct ◆ verb 2 CONNECT, join, link, span

bridle noun 1 CURB, check, control, rein, restraint ◆ verb 2 GET ANGRY, be indignant, bristle, draw (oneself) up, get one's back up, raise one's hackles, rear up

brief adjective 1 SHORT, ephemeral, fleeting, momentary, quick, short-lived, swift, transitory ◆ noun 2 SUMMARY, abridgment, abstract, digest, epitome, outline, précis, sketch, synopsis ◆ verb 3 INFORM, advise, explain, fill in (informal), instruct, keep posted, prepare, prime, put (someone) in the picture (informal)

briefing noun INSTRUCTIONS, conference, directions, guidance, information, preparation, priming, rundown

briefly adverb SHORTLY, concisely, hastily, hurriedly, in a nutshell, in brief, momentarily, quickly

brigade noun GROUP, band, company, corps, force, organization, outfit, squad, team, troop, unit

brigand noun BANDIT, desperado, freebooter, gangster, highwayman, marauder, outlaw, plunderer, robber

bright adjective 1 SHINING, brilliant, dazzling, gleaming, glowing, luminous, lustrous, radiant, shimmering, vivid 2 INTELLIGENT, astute, aware, clever, inventive, quick-witted, sharp, smart, wide-awake 3 SUNNY, clear, cloudless, fair, limpid, lucid, pleasant, translucent, transparent, unclouded

brighten verb MAKE BRIGHTER, gleam, glow, illuminate, lighten, light up, shine

brightness noun 1 SHINE, brilliance, glare, incandescence, intensity, light, luminosity, radiance, vividness 2 INTELLIGENCE, acuity, cleverness, quickness, sharpness, smartness

brilliance, brilliancy noun 1 BRIGHTNESS, dazzle, intensity, luminosity, lustre, radiance, sparkle, vividness 2 TALENT, cleverness, distinction, excellence, genius, greatness, inventiveness, wisdom 3 SPLENDOUR, éclat, glamour, grandeur, illustriousness, magnificence

brilliant adjective 1 SHINING, bright, dazzling, glittering, intense, luminous, radiant, sparkling, vivid 2 SPLENDID, celebrated, famous, glorious, illustrious, magnificent, notable, outstanding, superb 3 INTELLIGENT, clever, expert, gifted, intellectual, inventive, masterly, penetrating, profound, talented

brim noun 1 RIM, border, brink, edge, lip, margin, skirt, verge

◆ verb 2 BE FULL, fill, fill up, hold no more, overflow, run over, spill, well over

bring verb 1 TAKE, bear, carry, conduct, convey, deliver, escort, fetch, guide, lead, transfer, transport 2 CAUSE, contribute to, create, effect, inflict, occasion, produce, result in, wreak

bring about verb CAUSE, accomplish, achieve, create, effect, generate, give rise to, make happen, produce

bring off verb ACCOMPLISH, achieve, carry off, execute, perform, pull off, succeed

bring up verb 1 REAR, breed, develop, educate, form, nurture, raise, support, teach, train 2 MENTION, allude to, broach, introduce, move, propose, put forward, raise

brink noun EDGE, border, boundary, brim, fringe, frontier, limit, lip, margin, rim, skirt, threshold, verge

brisk adjective LIVELY, active, bustling, busy, energetic, quick, sprightly, spry, vigorous

briskly adverb QUICKLY, actively, apace, efficiently, energetically, promptly, rapidly, readily, smartly

bristle noun 1 HAIR, barb, prickle, spine, stubble, thorn, whisker
◆ verb 2 STAND UP, rise, stand on end 3 BE ANGRY, bridle, flare up, rage, see red, seethe

bristly adjective HAIRY, prickly, rough, stubbly

brittle adjective FRAGILE, breakable, crisp, crumbling, crumbly, delicate, frail, frangible, friable

broach verb 1 BRING UP, introduce, mention, open up, propose, raise the subject, speak of, suggest, talk of, touch on 2 OPEN, crack, draw off, pierce, puncture, start, tap, uncork

broad *adjective* 1 <u>WIDE</u>, ample, expansive, extensive, generous, large, roomy, spacious, vast, voluminous, widespread 2 <u>GENERAL</u>, all-embracing, comprehensive, encyclopedic, inclusive, sweeping, wide, wide-ranging

broadcast *noun* 1 <u>TRANSMISSION</u>, programme, show, telecast ♦ *verb* 2 <u>TRANSMIT</u>, air, beam, cable, put on the air, radio, relay, show, televise 3 <u>MAKE PUBLIC</u>, advertise, announce, circulate, proclaim, publish, report, spread

broaden *verb* <u>EXPAND</u>, develop, enlarge, extend, increase, spread, stretch, supplement, swell, widen

broad-minded *adjective* <u>TOLERANT</u>, free-thinking, indulgent, liberal, open-minded, permissive, unbiased, unbigoted, unprejudiced

broadside *noun* <u>ATTACK</u>, assault, battering, bombardment, censure, criticism, denunciation, diatribe

brochure *noun* <u>BOOKLET</u>, advertisement, circular, folder, handbill, hand-out, leaflet, mailshot, pamphlet

broke *adjective Informal* <u>PENNILESS</u>, bankrupt, bust (*informal*), down and out, impoverished, insolvent, in the red, ruined, short, skint (*Brit. slang*)

broken *adjective* 1 <u>SMASHED</u>, burst, fractured, fragmented, ruptured, separated, severed, shattered 2 <u>INTERRUPTED</u>, discontinuous, erratic, fragmentary, incomplete, intermittent, spasmodic 3 <u>NOT WORKING</u>, defective, imperfect, kaput (*informal*), on the blink (*slang*), out of order 4 <u>IMPERFECT</u>, disjointed, halting, hesitating, stammering

brokenhearted *adjective* <u>HEARTBROKEN</u>, desolate, devastated, disconsolate, grief-stricken, inconsolable, miserable, sorrowful, wretched

broker *noun* <u>DEALER</u>, agent, factor, go-between, intermediary, middleman, negotiator

bronze *adjective* <u>REDDISH-BROWN</u>, brownish, chestnut, copper, rust, tan

brood *noun* 1 <u>OFFSPRING</u>, clutch, family, issue, litter, progeny ♦ *verb* 2 <u>THINK UPON</u>, agonize, dwell upon, mope, mull over, muse, ponder, ruminate

brook *noun* <u>STREAM</u>, beck, burn, rill, rivulet, watercourse

brother *noun* 1 <u>SIBLING</u>, blood brother, kin, kinsman, relation, relative 2 <u>MONK</u>, cleric, friar

brotherhood *noun* 1 <u>FELLOWSHIP</u>, brotherliness, camaraderie, companionship, comradeship, friendliness, kinship 2 <u>ASSOCIATION</u>, alliance, community, fraternity, guild, league, order, society, union

brotherly *adjective* <u>KIND</u>, affectionate, altruistic, amicable, benevolent, cordial, fraternal, friendly, neighbourly, philanthropic, sympathetic

browbeat *verb* <u>BULLY</u>, badger, coerce, dragoon, hector, intimidate, ride roughshod over, threaten, tyrannize

brown *adjective* 1 <u>BRUNETTE</u>, auburn, bay, bronze, chestnut, chocolate, coffee, dun, hazel, sunburnt, tan, tanned, tawny, umber ♦ *verb* 2 <u>FRY</u>, cook, grill, sauté, seal, sear

browse *verb* 1 <u>SKIM</u>, dip into, examine cursorily, flip through, glance at, leaf through, look round, look through, peruse, scan, survey 2 <u>GRAZE</u>, eat, feed, nibble

bruise *verb* 1 <u>DISCOLOUR</u>, damage, injure, mar, mark, pound ♦ *noun* 2 <u>DISCOLORATION</u>, black mark, blemish, contusion, injury, mark, swelling

brunt noun FULL FORCE, burden, force, impact, pressure, shock, strain, stress, thrust, violence

brush[1] noun 1 BROOM, besom, sweeper 2 ENCOUNTER, clash, conflict, confrontation, skirmish, tussle ◆ verb 3 CLEAN, buff, paint, polish, sweep, wash 4 TOUCH, flick, glance, graze, kiss, scrape, stroke, sweep

brush[2] noun SHRUBS, brushwood, bushes, copse, scrub, thicket, undergrowth

brush off verb Slang IGNORE, disdain, dismiss, disregard, reject, repudiate, scorn, snub, spurn

brush up verb REVISE, bone up (*informal*), cram, go over, polish up, read up, refresh one's memory, relearn, study

brusque adjective CURT, abrupt, discourteous, gruff, impolite, sharp, short, surly, terse

brutal adjective 1 CRUEL, bloodthirsty, heartless, inhuman, ruthless, savage, uncivilized, vicious 2 HARSH, callous, gruff, impolite, insensitive, rough, rude, severe

brutality noun CRUELTY, atrocity, barbarism, bloodthirstiness, ferocity, inhumanity, ruthlessness, savagery, viciousness

brute noun 1 SAVAGE, barbarian, beast, devil, fiend, monster, sadist, swine 2 ANIMAL, beast, creature, wild animal ◆ adjective 3 MINDLESS, bodily, carnal, fleshly, instinctive, physical, senseless, unthinking

bubble noun 1 AIR BALL, bead, blister, blob, drop, droplet, globule ◆ verb 2 FOAM, boil, effervesce, fizz, froth, percolate, seethe, sparkle 3 GURGLE, babble, burble, murmur, ripple, trickle

bubbly adjective 1 LIVELY, animated, bouncy, elated, excited, happy, merry, sparky 2 FROTHY, carbonated, effervescent, fizzy, foamy, sparkling

buccaneer noun PIRATE, corsair, freebooter, privateer, sea-rover

buckle noun 1 FASTENER, catch, clasp, clip, hasp ◆ verb 2 FASTEN, clasp, close, hook, secure 3 DISTORT, bend, bulge, cave in, collapse, contort, crumple, fold, twist, warp

bud noun 1 SHOOT, embryo, germ, sprout ◆ verb 2 DEVELOP, burgeon, burst forth, grow, shoot, sprout

budding adjective DEVELOPING, beginning, burgeoning, embryonic, fledgling, growing, incipient, nascent, potential, promising

budge verb MOVE, dislodge, push, shift, stir

budget noun 1 ALLOWANCE, allocation, cost, finances, funds, means, resources ◆ verb 2 PLAN, allocate, apportion, cost, estimate, ration

buff[1] adjective 1 YELLOWISH-BROWN, sandy, straw, tan, yellowish ◆ verb 2 POLISH, brush, burnish, rub, shine, smooth

buff[2] noun Informal EXPERT, addict, admirer, aficionado, connoisseur, devotee, enthusiast, fan

buffer noun SAFEGUARD, bulwark, bumper, cushion, fender, intermediary, screen, shield, shock absorber

buffet[1] noun SNACK BAR, brasserie, café, cafeteria, refreshment counter, sideboard

buffet[2] verb BATTER, beat, bump, knock, pound, pummel, strike, thump, wallop (*informal*)

buffoon noun CLOWN, comedian,

comic, fool, harlequin, jester, joker, wag

bug noun 1 Informal ILLNESS, disease, infection, lurgy (informal), virus 2 FAULT, defect, error, flaw, glitch, gremlin ♦ verb 3 Informal ANNOY, bother, disturb, get on one's nerves (informal), hassle (informal), irritate, pester, vex 4 TAP, eavesdrop, listen in, spy

bugbear noun PET HATE, bane, bête noire, bogey, dread, horror, nightmare

build verb 1 CONSTRUCT, assemble, erect, fabricate, form, make, put up, raise ♦ noun 2 PHYSIQUE, body, figure, form, frame, shape, structure

building noun STRUCTURE, domicile, dwelling, edifice, house

build-up noun INCREASE, accumulation, development, enlargement, escalation, expansion, gain, growth

bulbous adjective BULGING, bloated, convex, rounded, swelling, swollen

bulge noun 1 SWELLING, bump, hump, lump, projection, protrusion, protuberance 2 INCREASE, boost, intensification, rise, surge ♦ verb 3 SWELL OUT, dilate, distend, expand, project, protrude, puff out, stick out

bulk noun 1 SIZE, dimensions, immensity, largeness, magnitude, substance, volume, weight 2 MAIN PART, better part, body, lion's share, majority, mass, most, nearly all, preponderance

bulky adjective LARGE, big, cumbersome, heavy, hulking, massive, substantial, unwieldy, voluminous, weighty

bulldoze verb DEMOLISH, flatten, level, raze

bullet noun PROJECTILE, ball, missile, pellet, shot, slug

bulletin noun ANNOUNCEMENT, account, communication, communiqué, dispatch, message, news flash, notification, report, statement

bully noun 1 PERSECUTOR, browbeater, bully boy, coercer, intimidator, oppressor, ruffian, tormentor, tough ♦ verb 2 PERSECUTE, browbeat, coerce, domineer, hector, intimidate, oppress, push around (slang), terrorize, tyrannize

bulwark noun 1 FORTIFICATION, bastion, buttress, defence, embankment, partition, rampart 2 DEFENCE, buffer, guard, mainstay, safeguard, security, support

bumbling adjective CLUMSY, awkward, blundering, bungling, incompetent, inefficient, inept, maladroit, muddled

bump verb 1 KNOCK, bang, collide (with), crash, hit, slam, smash into, strike 2 JERK, bounce, jolt, rattle, shake ♦ noun 3 KNOCK, bang, blow, collision, crash, impact, jolt, thud, thump 4 LUMP, bulge, contusion, hump, nodule, protuberance, swelling

bumper adjective EXCEPTIONAL, abundant, bountiful, excellent, jumbo (informal), massive, whopping (informal)

bumpkin noun YOKEL, country bumpkin, hick (informal, chiefly U.S. & Canad.), hillbilly, peasant, rustic

bumptious adjective COCKY, arrogant, brash, conceited, forward, full of oneself, overconfident, pushy (informal), self-assertive

bumpy adjective ROUGH, bouncy, choppy, jarring, jerky, jolting, rutted, uneven

bunch noun 1 NUMBER, assortment,

batch, bundle, clump, cluster, collection, heap, lot, mass, pile **2** GROUP, band, crowd, flock, gang, gathering, party, team ♦ verb **3** GROUP, assemble, bundle, cluster, collect, huddle, mass, pack

bundle noun **1** BUNCH, assortment, batch, collection, group, heap, mass, pile, stack ♦ verb **2** with *out, off, into, etc.* PUSH, hurry, hustle, rush, shove, throw, thrust

bundle up verb WRAP UP, swathe

bungle verb MESS UP, blow (*slang*), blunder, botch, foul up, make a mess of, muff, ruin, spoil

bungling adjective INCOMPETENT, blundering, cack-handed (*informal*), clumsy, ham-fisted (*informal*), inept, maladroit

bunk, bunkum noun Informal NONSENSE, balderdash, baloney (*informal*), garbage (*informal*), hogwash, hot air (*informal*), moonshine, poppycock (*informal*), rubbish, stuff and nonsense, twaddle

buoy noun **1** MARKER, beacon, float, guide, signal ♦ verb **2 buoy up** ENCOURAGE, boost, cheer, cheer up, hearten, keep afloat, lift, raise, support, sustain

buoyancy noun **1** LIGHTNESS, weightlessness **2** CHEERFULNESS, animation, bounce (*informal*), good humour, high spirits, liveliness

buoyant adjective **1** FLOATING, afloat, light, weightless **2** CHEERFUL, carefree, chirpy (*informal*), happy, jaunty, light-hearted, upbeat (*informal*)

burden noun **1** LOAD, encumbrance, weight **2** TROUBLE, affliction, millstone, onus, responsibility, strain, weight, worry ♦ verb **3** WEIGH DOWN, bother, handicap, load, oppress, saddle with, tax,

worry

bureau noun **1** OFFICE, agency, branch, department, division, service **2** DESK, writing desk

bureaucracy noun **1** GOVERNMENT, administration, authorities, civil service, corridors of power, officials, the system **2** RED TAPE, officialdom, regulations

bureaucrat noun OFFICIAL, administrator, civil servant, functionary, mandarin, officer, public servant

burglar noun HOUSEBREAKER, cat burglar, filcher, pilferer, robber, sneak thief, thief

burglary noun BREAKING AND ENTERING, break-in, housebreaking, larceny, robbery, stealing, theft, thieving

burial noun INTERMENT, entombment, exequies, funeral, obsequies

buried adjective **1** INTERRED, entombed, laid to rest **2** HIDDEN, concealed, private, sequestered, tucked away

burlesque noun **1** PARODY, caricature, mockery, satire, send-up (*Brit. informal*), spoof (*informal*), takeoff (*informal*), travesty ♦ verb **2** SATIRIZE, ape, caricature, exaggerate, imitate, lampoon, make a monkey out of, make fun of, mock, parody, ridicule, send up (*Brit. informal*), spoof (*informal*), take off (*informal*), take the piss out of (*taboo slang*), travesty

burly adjective BRAWNY, beefy (*informal*), big, bulky, hefty, hulking, stocky, stout, sturdy, thickset, well-built

burn verb **1** BE ON FIRE, be ablaze, blaze, flame, flare, glow, go up in flames, smoke **2** SET ON FIRE, char, ignite, incinerate, kindle, light,

parch, scorch, sear, singe, toast
3 BE PASSIONATE, be angry, be
aroused, be inflamed, fume,
seethe, simmer, smoulder

burning *adjective* **1** INTENSE, ardent,
eager, fervent, impassioned,
passionate, vehement **2** CRUCIAL,
acute, compelling, critical,
essential, important, pressing,
significant, urgent, vital **3** BLAZING,
fiery, flaming, flashing, gleaming,
glowing, illuminated, scorching,
smouldering

burnish *verb* POLISH, brighten, buff,
furbish, glaze, rub up, shine,
smooth

burrow *noun* **1** HOLE, den, lair,
retreat, shelter, tunnel ♦ *verb*
2 DIG, delve, excavate, hollow out,
scoop out, tunnel

burst *verb* **1** EXPLODE, blow up,
break, crack, puncture, rupture,
shatter, split, tear apart **2** RUSH,
barge, break, break out, erupt,
gush forth, run, spout ♦ *noun*
3 EXPLOSION, bang, blast, blowout,
break, crack, discharge, rupture,
split **4** RUSH, gush, gust, outbreak,
outburst, outpouring, spate,
spurt, surge, torrent ♦ *adjective*
5 RUPTURED, flat, punctured, rent,
split

bury *verb* **1** INTER, consign to the
grave, entomb, inhume, lay to
rest **2** EMBED, engulf, submerge
3 HIDE, conceal, cover, enshroud,
secrete, stow away

bush *noun* **1** SHRUB, hedge, plant,
shrubbery, thicket **2 the bush** THE
WILD, backwoods, brush, scrub,
scrubland, woodland

bushy *adjective* THICK, bristling,
fluffy, fuzzy, luxuriant, rough,
shaggy, unruly

busily *adverb* ACTIVELY, assiduously,
briskly, diligently, energetically,
industriously, purposefully,
speedily, strenuously

business *noun* **1** TRADE, bargaining,
commerce, dealings, industry,
manufacturing, selling,
transaction **2** ESTABLISHMENT,
company, concern, corporation,
enterprise, firm, organization,
venture **3** PROFESSION, career,
employment, function, job, line,
occupation, trade, vocation, work
4 CONCERN, affair, assignment,
duty, pigeon (*informal*), problem,
responsibility, task

businesslike *adjective* EFFICIENT,
methodical, orderly, organized,
practical, professional, systematic,
thorough, well-ordered

businessman *noun* EXECUTIVE,
capitalist, employer, entrepreneur,
financier, industrialist, merchant,
tradesman, tycoon

bust[1] *noun* BOSOM, breast, chest,
front, torso

bust[2] *Informal* ♦ *verb* **1** BREAK, burst,
fracture, rupture **2** ARREST, catch,
raid, search ♦ *adjective* **3 go bust**
GO BANKRUPT, become insolvent, be
ruined, fail

bustle *verb* **1** HURRY, fuss, hasten,
rush, scamper, scurry, scuttle
♦ *noun* **2** ACTIVITY, ado, commotion,
excitement, flurry, fuss,
hurly-burly, stir, to-do

bustling *adjective* BUSY, active,
buzzing, crowded, full, humming,
lively, swarming, teeming

busy *adjective* **1** OCCUPIED, active,
employed, engaged, hard at
work, industrious, on duty, rushed
off one's feet, working **2** LIVELY,
energetic, exacting, full, hectic,
hustling ♦ *verb* **3** OCCUPY, absorb,
employ, engage, engross,
immerse, interest

busybody *noun* NOSY PARKER
(*informal*), gossip, meddler,
snooper, stirrer (*informal*),
troublemaker

but *conjunction* **1** HOWEVER, further, moreover, nevertheless, on the contrary, on the other hand, still, yet ◆ *preposition* **2** EXCEPT, bar, barring, excepting, excluding, notwithstanding, save, with the exception of ◆ *adverb* **3** ONLY, just, merely, simply, singly, solely

butcher *noun* **1** MURDERER, destroyer, killer, slaughterer, slayer ◆ *verb* **2** SLAUGHTER, carve, clean, cut, cut up, dress, joint, prepare **3** KILL, assassinate, cut down, destroy, exterminate, liquidate, massacre, put to the sword, slaughter, slay

butt[1] *noun* **1** END, haft, handle, hilt, shaft, shank, stock **2** STUB, fag end (*informal*), leftover, tip

butt[2] *noun* TARGET, Aunt Sally, dupe, laughing stock, victim

butt[3] *verb, noun* **1** *With or of the head or horns* KNOCK, bump, poke, prod, push, ram, shove, thrust ◆ *verb* **2 butt in** INTERFERE, chip in (*informal*), cut in, interrupt, intrude, meddle, put one's oar in, stick one's nose in

butt[4] *noun* CASK, barrel

buttonhole *verb* DETAIN, accost, bore, catch, grab, importune, take aside, waylay

buttress *noun* **1** SUPPORT, brace, mainstay, prop, reinforcement, stanchion, strut ◆ *verb* **2** SUPPORT, back up, bolster, prop up, reinforce, shore up, strengthen, sustain, uphold

buxom *adjective* PLUMP, ample, bosomy, busty, curvaceous, healthy, voluptuous, well-rounded

buy *verb* **1** PURCHASE, acquire, get, invest in, obtain, pay for, procure, shop for ◆ *noun* **2** PURCHASE, acquisition, bargain, deal

by *preposition* **1** VIA, by way of, over **2** THROUGH, through the agency of **3** NEAR, along, beside, close to, next to, past ◆ *adverb* **4** NEAR, at hand, close, handy, in reach **5** PAST, aside, away, to one side

bygone *adjective* PAST, antiquated, extinct, forgotten, former, lost, of old, olden

bypass *verb* GO ROUND, avoid, circumvent, depart from, detour round, deviate from, get round, give a wide berth to, pass round

bystander *noun* ONLOOKER, eyewitness, looker-on, observer, passer-by, spectator, viewer, watcher, witness

byword *noun* SAYING, adage, maxim, motto, precept, proverb, slogan

C c

cab noun <u>TAXI</u>, hackney carriage, minicab, taxicab

cabal noun 1 <u>CLIQUE</u>, caucus, conclave, faction, league, party, set 2 <u>PLOT</u>, conspiracy, intrigue, machination, scheme

cabin noun 1 <u>ROOM</u>, berth, compartment, quarters 2 <u>HUT</u>, chalet, cottage, lodge, shack, shanty, shed

cabinet noun <u>CUPBOARD</u>, case, chiffonier, closet, commode, dresser, escritoire, locker

Cabinet noun <u>COUNCIL</u>, administration, assembly, counsellors, ministry

cad noun Old-fashioned, informal <u>SCOUNDREL</u>, bounder (old-fashioned Brit. slang), heel (slang), rat (informal), rotter (slang, chiefly Brit.)

caddish adjective <u>UNGENTLEMANLY</u>, despicable, ill-bred, low, unmannerly

café noun <u>SNACK BAR</u>, brasserie, cafeteria, coffee bar, coffee shop, lunchroom, restaurant, tearoom

cage noun <u>ENCLOSURE</u>, pen, pound

cagey, cagy adjective Informal <u>WARY</u>, careful, cautious, chary, discreet, guarded, noncommittal, shrewd, wily

cajole verb <u>PERSUADE</u>, coax, flatter, seduce, sweet-talk (informal), wheedle

cake noun 1 <u>BLOCK</u>, bar, cube, loaf, lump, mass, slab ♦ verb 2 <u>ENCRUST</u>, bake, coagulate, congeal, solidify

calamitous adjective <u>DISASTROUS</u>, cataclysmic, catastrophic, deadly, devastating, dire, fatal, ruinous, tragic

calamity noun <u>DISASTER</u>, cataclysm, catastrophe, misadventure, misfortune, mishap, ruin, tragedy, tribulation

calculate verb 1 <u>WORK OUT</u>, compute, count, determine, enumerate, estimate, figure, reckon 2 <u>PLAN</u>, aim, design, intend

calculated adjective <u>DELIBERATE</u>, considered, intended, intentional, planned, premeditated, purposeful

calculating adjective <u>SCHEMING</u>, crafty, cunning, devious, Machiavellian, manipulative, sharp, shrewd, sly

calculation noun 1 <u>WORKING OUT</u>, answer, computation, estimate, forecast, judgment, reckoning, result 2 <u>PLANNING</u>, contrivance, deliberation, discretion, foresight, forethought, precaution

calibre noun 1 <u>WORTH</u>, ability, capacity, distinction, merit, quality, stature, talent 2 <u>DIAMETER</u>, bore, gauge, measure

call verb 1 <u>NAME</u>, christen, describe as, designate, dub, entitle, label, style, term 2 <u>CRY</u>, arouse, hail, rouse, shout, yell 3 <u>PHONE</u>, ring up (informal, chiefly Brit.), telephone 4 <u>SUMMON</u>, assemble, convene, gather, muster, rally ♦ noun 5 <u>CRY</u>, hail, scream, shout, signal, whoop, yell 6 <u>SUMMONS</u>, appeal, command, demand, invitation, notice, order, plea, request 7 <u>NEED</u>, cause, excuse, grounds, justification, occasion, reason

call for verb 1 <u>REQUIRE</u>, demand, entail, involve, necessitate, need, occasion, suggest 2 <u>FETCH</u>, collect, pick up

calling noun <u>PROFESSION</u>, career, life's work, mission, trade, vocation

call on verb VISIT, drop in on, look in on, look up, see

callous adjective HEARTLESS, cold, hard-bitten, hardened, hardhearted, insensitive, uncaring, unfeeling

callow adjective INEXPERIENCED, green, guileless, immature, naive, raw, unsophisticated

calm adjective 1 COOL, collected, composed, dispassionate, relaxed, sedate, self-possessed, unemotional 2 STILL, balmy, mild, quiet, serene, smooth, tranquil, windless ♦ noun 3 PEACEFULNESS, hush, peace, quiet, repose, serenity, stillness ♦ verb 4 QUIETEN, hush, mollify, placate, relax, soothe

calmness noun 1 COOLNESS, composure, cool (slang), equanimity, impassivity, poise, sang-froid, self-possession 2 PEACEFULNESS, calm, hush, quiet, repose, restfulness, serenity, stillness, tranquillity

camouflage noun 1 DISGUISE, blind, cloak, concealment, cover, mask, masquerade, screen, subterfuge ♦ verb 2 DISGUISE, cloak, conceal, cover, hide, mask, obfuscate, obscure, screen, veil

camp[1] noun CAMP SITE, bivouac, camping ground, encampment, tents

camp[2] adjective Informal EFFEMINATE, affected, artificial, mannered, ostentatious, posturing

campaign noun OPERATION, attack, crusade, drive, expedition, movement, offensive, push

canal noun WATERWAY, channel, conduit, duct, passage, watercourse

cancel verb 1 CALL OFF, abolish, abort, annul, delete, do away with, eliminate, erase, expunge, obliterate, repeal, revoke 2 **cancel out** MAKE UP FOR, balance out, compensate for, counterbalance, neutralize, nullify, offset

cancellation noun ABANDONMENT, abolition, annulment, deletion, elimination, repeal, revocation

cancer noun GROWTH, corruption, malignancy, pestilence, sickness, tumour

candid adjective HONEST, blunt, forthright, frank, open, outspoken, plain, straightforward, truthful

candidate noun CONTENDER, applicant, claimant, competitor, contestant, entrant, nominee, runner

candour noun HONESTY, directness, forthrightness, frankness, openness, outspokenness, straightforwardness, truthfulness

canker noun DISEASE, bane, blight, cancer, corruption, infection, rot, scourge, sore, ulcer

cannon noun GUN, big gun, field gun, mortar

canny adjective SHREWD, astute, careful, cautious, clever, judicious, prudent, wise

canon noun 1 RULE, criterion, dictate, formula, precept, principle, regulation, standard, statute, yardstick 2 LIST, catalogue, roll

canopy noun AWNING, covering, shade, sunshade

cant[1] noun 1 HYPOCRISY, humbug, insincerity, lip service, pretence, pretentiousness, sanctimoniousness 2 JARGON, argot, lingo, patter, slang, vernacular

cant[2] verb TILT, angle, bevel, incline, rise, slant, slope

cantankerous adjective

BAD-TEMPERED, choleric, contrary, disagreeable, grumpy, irascible, irritable, testy, waspish

canter noun 1 JOG, amble, dogtrot, lope ♦ verb 2 JOG, amble, lope

canvass verb 1 CAMPAIGN, electioneer, solicit, solicit votes 2 POLL, examine, inspect, investigate, scrutinize, study ♦ noun 3 POLL, examination, investigation, scrutiny, survey, tally

cap verb Informal BEAT, better, crown, eclipse, exceed, outdo, outstrip, surpass, top, transcend

capability noun ABILITY, capacity, competence, means, potential, power, proficiency, qualification(s), wherewithal

capable adjective ABLE, accomplished, competent, efficient, gifted, proficient, qualified, talented

capacious adjective SPACIOUS, broad, commodious, expansive, extensive, roomy, sizable or sizeable, substantial, vast, voluminous, wide

capacity noun 1 SIZE, amplitude, compass, dimensions, extent, magnitude, range, room, scope, space, volume 2 ABILITY, aptitude, aptness, capability, competence, facility, genius, gift 3 FUNCTION, office, position, post, province, role, sphere

cape noun HEADLAND, head, peninsula, point, promontory

caper noun 1 ESCAPADE, antic, high jinks, jape, lark (informal), mischief, practical joke, prank, stunt ♦ verb 2 DANCE, bound, cavort, frolic, gambol, jump, skip, spring, trip

capital noun 1 MONEY, assets, cash, finances, funds, investment(s), means, principal, resources, wealth, wherewithal ♦ adjective

2 PRINCIPAL, cardinal, major, prime, vital 3 Old-fashioned FIRST-RATE, excellent, fine, splendid, sterling, superb

capitalism noun PRIVATE ENTERPRISE, free enterprise, laissez faire or laisser faire, private ownership

capitalize on verb TAKE ADVANTAGE OF, benefit from, cash in on (informal), exploit, gain from, make the most of, profit from

capitulate verb GIVE IN, come to terms, give up, relent, submit, succumb, surrender, yield

caprice noun WHIM, fad, fancy, fickleness, impulse, inconstancy, notion, whimsy

capricious adjective UNPREDICTABLE, changeful, erratic, fickle, fitful, impulsive, inconsistent, inconstant, mercurial, variable, wayward, whimsical

capsize verb OVERTURN, invert, keel over, tip over, turn over, turn turtle, upset

capsule noun 1 PILL, lozenge, tablet 2 Botany POD, case, receptacle, seed case, sheath, shell, vessel

captain noun LEADER, boss, chief, commander, head, master, skipper

captivate verb CHARM, allure, attract, beguile, bewitch, enchant, enrapture, enthral, entrance, fascinate, infatuate, mesmerize

captive noun 1 PRISONER, convict, detainee, hostage, internee, prisoner of war, slave ♦ adjective 2 CONFINED, caged, enslaved, ensnared, imprisoned, incarcerated, locked up, penned, restricted, subjugated

captivity noun CONFINEMENT, bondage, custody, detention, imprisonment, incarceration, internment, slavery

capture verb 1 CATCH, apprehend,

arrest, bag, collar (*informal*), secure, seize, take, take prisoner ♦ *noun* **2** CATCHING, apprehension, arrest, imprisonment, seizure, taking, taking captive, trapping

car *noun* **1** VEHICLE, auto (*U.S.*), automobile, jalopy (*informal*), machine, motor, motorcar, wheels (*informal*) **2** *U.S. & Canad.* (RAILWAY) CARRIAGE, buffet car, cable car, coach, dining car, sleeping car, van

carcass *noun* BODY, cadaver (*Medical*), corpse, dead body, framework, hulk, remains, shell, skeleton

cardinal *adjective* PRINCIPAL, capital, central, chief, essential, first, fundamental, key, leading, main, paramount, primary

care *verb* **1** BE CONCERNED, be bothered, be interested, mind ♦ *noun* **2** CAUTION, attention, carefulness, consideration, forethought, heed, management, pains, prudence, vigilance, watchfulness **3** PROTECTION, charge, control, custody, guardianship, keeping, management, supervision **4** WORRY, anxiety, concern, disquiet, perplexity, pressure, responsibility, stress, trouble

career *noun* **1** OCCUPATION, calling, employment, life's work, livelihood, pursuit, vocation ♦ *verb* **2** RUSH, barrel (along) (*informal, chiefly U.S. & Canad.*), bolt, dash, hurtle, race, speed, tear

care for *verb* **1** LOOK AFTER, attend, foster, mind, minister to, nurse, protect, provide for, tend, watch over **2** LIKE, be fond of, desire, enjoy, love, prize, take to, want

carefree *adjective* UNTROUBLED, blithe, breezy, cheerful, easy-going, halcyon, happy-go-lucky, light-hearted

careful *adjective* **1** CAUTIOUS, chary, circumspect, discreet, prudent, scrupulous, thoughtful, thrifty **2** THOROUGH, conscientious, meticulous, painstaking, particular, precise

careless *adjective* **1** SLAPDASH, cavalier, inaccurate, irresponsible, lackadaisical, neglectful, offhand, slipshod, sloppy (*informal*) **2** NEGLIGENT, absent-minded, forgetful, hasty, remiss, thoughtless, unthinking **3** NONCHALANT, artless, casual, unstudied

carelessness *noun* NEGLIGENCE, indiscretion, irresponsibility, laxity, neglect, omission, slackness, sloppiness (*informal*), thoughtlessness

caress *verb* **1** STROKE, cuddle, embrace, fondle, hug, kiss, neck (*informal*), nuzzle, pet ♦ *noun* **2** STROKE, cuddle, embrace, fondling, hug, kiss, pat

caretaker *noun* WARDEN, concierge, curator, custodian, janitor, keeper, porter, superintendent, watchman

cargo *noun* LOAD, baggage, consignment, contents, freight, goods, merchandise, shipment

caricature *noun* **1** PARODY, burlesque, cartoon, distortion, farce, lampoon, satire, send-up (*Brit. informal*), takeoff (*informal*), travesty ♦ *verb* **2** PARODY, burlesque, distort, lampoon, mimic, mock, ridicule, satirize, send up (*Brit. informal*), take off (*informal*)

carnage *noun* SLAUGHTER, blood bath, bloodshed, butchery, havoc, holocaust, massacre, mass murder, murder, shambles

carnal *adjective* SEXUAL, erotic, fleshly, lascivious, lewd, libidinous, lustful, sensual

carnival *noun* FESTIVAL, celebration,

fair, fête, fiesta, gala, holiday, jamboree, jubilee, merrymaking, revelry

carol noun SONG, chorus, ditty, hymn, lay

carp verb FIND FAULT, cavil, complain, criticize, pick holes, quibble, reproach

carpenter noun JOINER, cabinet-maker, woodworker

carriage noun 1 VEHICLE, cab, coach, conveyance 2 BEARING, air, behaviour, comportment, conduct, demeanour, deportment, gait, manner, posture

carry verb 1 TRANSPORT, bear, bring, conduct, convey, fetch, haul, lug, move, relay, take, transfer 2 WIN, accomplish, capture, effect, gain, secure

carry on verb 1 CONTINUE, endure, keep going, last, maintain, perpetuate, persevere, persist 2 Informal MAKE A FUSS, create (slang), misbehave, raise Cain

carry out verb PERFORM, accomplish, achieve, carry through, effect, execute, fulfil, implement, realize

carton noun BOX, case, container, pack, package, packet

cartoon noun 1 DRAWING, caricature, comic strip, lampoon, parody, satire, sketch, takeoff (informal) 2 ANIMATION, animated cartoon, animated film

cartridge noun 1 SHELL, charge, round 2 CONTAINER, capsule, case, cassette, cylinder, magazine

carve verb CUT, chip, chisel, engrave, etch, hew, mould, sculpt, slice, whittle

cascade noun 1 WATERFALL, avalanche, cataract, deluge, downpour, falls, flood, fountain, outpouring, shower, torrent ♦ verb 2 FLOW, descend, fall, flood, gush,

overflow, pitch, plunge, pour, spill, surge, teem, tumble

case[1] noun 1 INSTANCE, example, illustration, occasion, occurrence, specimen 2 SITUATION, circumstance(s), condition, context, contingency, event, position, state 3 Law LAWSUIT, action, dispute, proceedings, suit, trial

case[2] noun 1 CONTAINER, box, canister, carton, casket, chest, crate, holder, receptacle, suitcase, tray 2 COVERING, capsule, casing, envelope, jacket, sheath, shell, wrapper

cash noun MONEY, brass (Northern English dialect), coinage, currency, dough (slang), funds, notes, ready money, silver

cashier[1] noun TELLER, bank clerk, banker, bursar, clerk, purser, treasurer

cashier[2] verb DISMISS, discard, discharge, drum out, expel, give the boot to (slang)

casket noun BOX, case, chest, coffer, jewel box

cast noun 1 ACTORS, characters, company, dramatis personae, players, troupe 2 TYPE, complexion, manner, stamp, style ♦ verb 3 CHOOSE, allot, appoint, assign, name, pick, select 4 GIVE OUT, bestow, deposit, diffuse, distribute, emit, radiate, scatter, shed, spread 5 FORM, found, model, mould, set, shape 6 THROW, fling, hurl, launch, pitch, sling, thrust, toss

caste noun CLASS, estate, grade, order, rank, social order, status, stratum

castigate verb REPRIMAND, berate, censure, chastise, criticize, lambast(e), rebuke, scold

cast-iron adjective CERTAIN,

copper-bottomed, definite, established, fixed, guaranteed, settled

castle noun FORTRESS, chateau, citadel, keep, palace, stronghold, tower

cast-off adjective 1 UNWANTED, discarded, rejected, scrapped, surplus to requirements, unneeded, useless ♦ noun 2 REJECT, discard, failure, outcast, second

castrate verb NEUTER, emasculate, geld

casual adjective 1 CARELESS, blasé, cursory, lackadaisical, nonchalant, offhand, relaxed, unconcerned 2 OCCASIONAL, accidental, chance, incidental, irregular, random, unexpected 3 INFORMAL, non-dressy, sporty

casualty noun VICTIM, death, fatality, loss, sufferer, wounded

cat noun FELINE, kitty (informal), moggy (slang), puss (informal), pussy (informal), tabby

catacombs plural noun VAULT, crypt, tomb

catalogue noun 1 LIST, directory, gazetteer, index, inventory, record, register, roll, roster, schedule ♦ verb 2 LIST, accession, alphabetize, classify, file, index, inventory, register, tabulate

catapult noun 1 SLING, slingshot (U.S.) ♦ verb 2 SHOOT, heave, hurl, pitch, plunge, propel

catastrophe noun DISASTER, adversity, calamity, cataclysm, fiasco, misfortune, tragedy, trouble

catcall noun JEER, boo, gibe, hiss, raspberry, whistle

catch verb 1 SEIZE, clutch, get, grab, grasp, grip, lay hold of, snatch, take 2 CAPTURE, apprehend, arrest, ensnare, entrap, snare 3 DISCOVER, catch in the act, detect, expose,

find out, surprise, take unawares, unmask 4 CONTRACT, develop, get, go down with, incur, succumb to, suffer from 5 MAKE OUT, comprehend, discern, get, grasp, hear, perceive, recognize, sense, take in 6 noun FASTENER, bolt, clasp, clip, latch 7 Informal DRAWBACK, disadvantage, fly in the ointment, hitch, snag, stumbling block, trap, trick

catching adjective INFECTIOUS, communicable, contagious, transferable, transmittable

catch on verb Informal UNDERSTAND, comprehend, find out, get the picture, grasp, see, see through, twig (Brit. informal)

catchword noun SLOGAN, byword, motto, password, watchword

catchy adjective MEMORABLE, captivating, haunting, popular

categorical adjective ABSOLUTE, downright, emphatic, explicit, express, positive, unambiguous, unconditional, unequivocal, unqualified, unreserved

category noun CLASS, classification, department, division, grade, grouping, heading, section, sort, type

cater verb PROVIDE, furnish, outfit, purvey, supply

cattle plural noun COWS, beasts, bovines, livestock, stock

catty adjective SPITEFUL, backbiting, bitchy (informal), malevolent, malicious, rancorous, shrewish, snide, venomous

cause noun 1 ORIGIN, agent, beginning, creator, genesis, mainspring, maker, producer, root, source, spring 2 REASON, basis, grounds, incentive, inducement, justification, motivation, motive, purpose 3 AIM, belief, conviction, enterprise,

ideal, movement, principle ♦ *verb*
4 PRODUCE, bring about, create,
generate, give rise to, incite,
induce, lead to, result in

caustic *adjective* **1** BURNING, acrid,
astringent, biting, corroding,
corrosive, mordant, vitriolic
2 SARCASTIC, acrimonious, cutting,
pungent, scathing, stinging,
trenchant, virulent, vitriolic

caution *noun* **1** CARE, alertness,
carefulness, circumspection,
deliberation, discretion,
forethought, heed, prudence,
vigilance, watchfulness **2** WARNING,
admonition, advice, counsel,
injunction ♦ *verb* **3** WARN,
admonish, advise, tip off, urge

cautious *adjective* CAREFUL, cagey
(*informal*), chary, circumspect,
guarded, judicious, prudent,
tentative, wary

cavalcade *noun* PARADE, array,
march-past, procession, spectacle,
train

cavalier *adjective* HAUGHTY,
arrogant, disdainful, lofty, lordly,
offhand, scornful, supercilious

cavalry *noun* HORSEMEN, horse,
mounted troops

cave *noun* HOLLOW, cavern, cavity,
den, grotto

cavern *noun* CAVE, hollow, pothole

cavernous *adjective* DEEP, hollow,
sunken, yawning

cavity *noun* HOLLOW, crater, dent,
gap, hole, pit

cease *verb* STOP, break off,
conclude, discontinue, end, finish,
halt, leave off, refrain, terminate

ceaseless *adjective* CONTINUAL,
constant, endless, eternal,
everlasting, incessant,
interminable, never-ending,
nonstop, perpetual, unremitting

cede *verb* SURRENDER, concede, hand

over, make over, relinquish,
renounce, resign, transfer, yield

celebrate *verb* **1** REJOICE,
commemorate, drink to, keep, kill
the fatted calf, observe, put the
flags out, toast **2** PERFORM, bless,
honour, solemnize

celebrated *adjective* WELL-KNOWN,
acclaimed, distinguished,
eminent, famous, illustrious,
notable, popular, prominent,
renowned

celebration *noun* **1** PARTY, festival,
festivity, gala, jubilee,
merrymaking, red-letter day,
revelry **2** PERFORMANCE, anniversary,
commemoration, honouring,
observance, remembrance,
solemnization

celebrity *noun* **1** PERSONALITY, big
name, big shot (*informal*),
dignitary, luminary, star,
superstar, V.I.P. **2** FAME, distinction,
notability, prestige, prominence,
renown, reputation, repute,
stardom

celestial *adjective* HEAVENLY, angelic,
astral, divine, ethereal, spiritual,
sublime, supernatural

celibacy *noun* CHASTITY, continence,
purity, virginity

cell *noun* **1** ROOM, cavity, chamber,
compartment, cubicle, dungeon,
stall **2** UNIT, caucus, core, coterie,
group, nucleus

cement *noun* **1** MORTAR, adhesive,
glue, gum, paste, plaster, sealant
♦ *verb* **2** STICK TOGETHER, attach,
bind, bond, combine, glue, join,
plaster, seal, unite, weld

cemetery *noun* GRAVEYARD, burial
ground, churchyard, God's acre,
necropolis

censor *verb* CUT, blue-pencil,
bowdlerize, expurgate

censorious *adjective* CRITICAL,
captious, carping, cavilling,

condemnatory, disapproving, disparaging, fault-finding, hypercritical, scathing, severe

censure noun 1 DISAPPROVAL, blame, condemnation, criticism, obloquy, rebuke, reprimand, reproach, reproof, stick (slang) ◆ verb 2 CRITICIZE, blame, castigate, condemn, denounce, rap over the knuckles, rebuke, reprimand, reproach, scold, slap on the wrist

central adjective 1 MIDDLE, inner, interior, mean, median, mid 2 MAIN, chief, essential, focal, fundamental, key, primary, principal

centralize verb UNIFY, concentrate, condense, incorporate, rationalize, streamline

centre noun 1 MIDDLE, core, focus, heart, hub, kernel, midpoint, nucleus, pivot ◆ verb 2 FOCUS, cluster, concentrate, converge, revolve

ceremonial adjective 1 RITUAL, formal, liturgical, ritualistic, solemn, stately ◆ noun 2 RITUAL, ceremony, formality, rite, solemnity

ceremonious adjective FORMAL, civil, courteous, deferential, dignified, punctilious, solemn, stately, stiff

ceremony noun 1 RITUAL, commemoration, function, observance, parade, rite, service, show, solemnities 2 FORMALITY, ceremonial, decorum, etiquette, niceties, pomp, propriety, protocol

certain adjective 1 SURE, assured, confident, convinced, positive, satisfied 2 KNOWN, conclusive, incontrovertible, irrefutable, true, undeniable, unequivocal 3 INEVITABLE, bound, definite, destined, fated, inescapable, sure 4 FIXED, decided, definite, established, settled

certainly adverb DEFINITELY, assuredly, indisputably, indubitably, surely, truly, undeniably, undoubtedly, without doubt

certainty noun 1 SURENESS, assurance, confidence, conviction, faith, positiveness, trust, validity 2 FACT, reality, sure thing (informal), truth

certificate noun DOCUMENT, authorization, credential(s), diploma, licence, testimonial, voucher, warrant

certify verb CONFIRM, assure, attest, authenticate, declare, guarantee, testify, validate, verify

chafe verb 1 RUB, abrade, rasp, scrape, scratch 2 BE ANNOYED, be impatient, fret, fume, rage, worry

chaff[1] noun WASTE, dregs, husks, refuse, remains, rubbish, trash

chaff[2] verb TEASE, mock, rib (informal), ridicule, scoff, taunt

chain noun 1 LINK, bond, coupling, fetter, manacle, shackle 2 SERIES, progression, sequence, set, string, succession, train ◆ verb 3 BIND, confine, enslave, fetter, handcuff, manacle, restrain, shackle, tether

chairman noun DIRECTOR, chairperson, chairwoman, master of ceremonies, president, speaker, spokesman

challenge noun 1 TEST, confrontation, provocation, question, trial, ultimatum ◆ verb 2 TEST, confront, defy, dispute, object to, question, tackle, throw down the gauntlet

chamber noun 1 ROOM, apartment, bedroom, compartment, cubicle, enclosure, hall 2 COUNCIL, assembly, legislative body, legislature

champion noun 1 WINNER, conqueror, hero, title holder,

victor **2** DEFENDER, backer, guardian, patron, protector, upholder ♦ *verb* **3** SUPPORT, advocate, back, commend, defend, encourage, espouse, fight for, promote, uphold

chance *noun* **1** PROBABILITY, likelihood, odds, possibility, prospect **2** OPPORTUNITY, occasion, opening, time **3** LUCK, accident, coincidence, destiny, fate, fortune, providence **4** RISK, gamble, hazard, jeopardy, speculation, uncertainty ♦ *verb* **5** RISK, endanger, gamble, hazard, jeopardize, stake, try, venture, wager

change *noun* **1** ALTERATION, difference, innovation, metamorphosis, modification, mutation, revolution, transformation, transition **2** VARIETY, break (*informal*), departure, diversion, novelty, variation **3** EXCHANGE, conversion, interchange, substitution, swap, trade ♦ *verb* **4** ALTER, convert, modify, mutate, reform, reorganize, restyle, shift, transform, vary **5** EXCHANGE, barter, convert, interchange, replace, substitute, swap, trade

changeable *adjective* VARIABLE, erratic, fickle, inconstant, irregular, mobile, mutable, protean, shifting, unsettled, unstable, volatile, wavering

channel *noun* **1** ROUTE, approach, artery, avenue, course, means, medium, path, way **2** PASSAGE, canal, conduit, duct, furrow, groove, gutter, route, strait ♦ *verb* **3** DIRECT, conduct, convey, guide, transmit

chant *verb* **1** SING, carol, chorus, descant, intone, recite, warble ♦ *noun* **2** SONG, carol, chorus, melody, psalm

chaos *noun* DISORDER, anarchy, bedlam, confusion, disorganization, lawlessness, mayhem, pandemonium, tumult

chaotic *adjective* DISORDERED, anarchic, confused, deranged, disorganized, lawless, riotous, topsy-turvy, tumultuous, uncontrolled

chap *noun Informal* FELLOW, bloke (*Brit. informal*), character, guy (*informal*), individual, man, person

chaperone *noun* **1** ESCORT, companion ♦ *verb* **2** ESCORT, accompany, attend, protect, safeguard, shepherd, watch over

chapter *noun* SECTION, clause, division, episode, part, period, phase, stage, topic

character *noun* **1** NATURE, attributes, calibre, complexion, disposition, personality, quality, temperament, type **2** REPUTATION, honour, integrity, rectitude, strength, uprightness **3** ROLE, part, persona, portrayal **4** ECCENTRIC, card (*informal*), oddball (*informal*), original **5** SYMBOL, device, figure, hieroglyph, letter, mark, rune, sign

characteristic *noun* **1** FEATURE, attribute, faculty, idiosyncrasy, mark, peculiarity, property, quality, quirk, trait ♦ *adjective* **2** TYPICAL, distinctive, distinguishing, idiosyncratic, individual, peculiar, representative, singular, special, symbolic, symptomatic

characterize *verb* IDENTIFY, brand, distinguish, indicate, mark, represent, stamp, typify

charade *noun* PRETENCE, fake, farce, pantomime, parody, travesty

charge *verb* **1** ACCUSE, arraign, blame, impeach, incriminate, indict **2** RUSH, assail, assault, attack, stampede, storm **3** FILL, load **4** *Formal* COMMAND, bid, commit, demand, entrust, instruct, order, require ♦ *noun* 5 PRICE, amount, cost, expenditure, expense, outlay, payment, rate, toll 6 ACCUSATION, allegation, imputation, indictment 7 RUSH, assault, attack, onset, onslaught, sortie, stampede 8 CARE, custody, duty, office, responsibility, safekeeping, trust 9 WARD 10 INSTRUCTION, command, demand, direction, injunction, mandate, order, precept

charisma *noun* CHARM, allure, attraction, lure, magnetism, personality

charismatic *adjective* CHARMING, alluring, attractive, enticing, influential, magnetic

charitable *adjective* 1 TOLERANT, considerate, favourable, forgiving, humane, indulgent, kindly, lenient, magnanimous, sympathetic, understanding 2 GENEROUS, beneficent, benevolent, bountiful, kind, lavish, liberal, philanthropic

charity *noun* 1 DONATIONS, assistance, benefaction, contributions, endowment, fund, gift, hand-out, help, largesse *or* largess, philanthropy, relief 2 KINDNESS, altruism, benevolence, compassion, fellow feeling, generosity, goodwill, humanity, indulgence

charlatan *noun* FRAUD, cheat, con man (*informal*), fake, impostor, phoney *or* phony (*informal*), pretender, quack, sham, swindler

charm *noun* 1 ATTRACTION, allure, appeal, fascination, magnetism 2 SPELL, enchantment, magic, sorcery 3 TALISMAN, amulet, fetish, trinket ♦ *verb* 4 ATTRACT, allure, beguile, bewitch, captivate, delight, enchant, enrapture, entrance, fascinate, mesmerize, win over

charming *adjective* ATTRACTIVE, appealing, captivating, cute, delightful, fetching, likable *or* likeable, pleasing, seductive, winsome

chart *noun* 1 TABLE, blueprint, diagram, graph, map, plan ♦ *verb* 2 PLOT, delineate, draft, map out, outline, shape, sketch

charter *noun* 1 DOCUMENT, contract, deed, licence, permit, prerogative ♦ *verb* 2 HIRE, commission, employ, lease, rent 3 AUTHORIZE, sanction

chase *verb* 1 PURSUE, course, follow, hunt, run after, track 2 DRIVE AWAY, drive, expel, hound, put to flight ♦ *noun* 3 PURSUIT, hunt, hunting, race

chasm *noun* GULF, abyss, crater, crevasse, fissure, gap, gorge, ravine

chaste *adjective* PURE, immaculate, innocent, modest, simple, unaffected, undefiled, virtuous

chasten *verb* SUBDUE, chastise, correct, discipline, humble, humiliate, put in one's place, tame

chastise *verb* 1 SCOLD, berate, castigate, censure, correct, discipline, upbraid 2 *Old-fashioned* BEAT, flog, lash, lick (*informal*), punish, scourge, whip

chastity *noun* PURITY, celibacy, continence, innocence, maiden-hood, modesty, virginity, virtue

chat *noun* 1 TALK, chatter, chinwag (*Brit. informal*), conversation, gossip, heart-to-heart, natter, tête-à-tête ♦ *verb* 2 TALK, chatter, gossip, jaw (*slang*), natter

chatter *noun* 1 PRATTLE, babble, blather, chat, gab (*informal*), gossip, natter ♦ *verb* 2 PRATTLE, babble, blather, chat, gab (*informal*), gossip, natter, rabbit (on) (*Brit. informal*), schmooze (*slang*)

cheap *adjective* 1 INEXPENSIVE, bargain, cut-price, economical, keen, low-cost, low-priced, reasonable, reduced 2 INFERIOR, common, poor, second-rate, shoddy, tatty, tawdry, two a penny, worthless 3 *Informal* DESPICABLE, contemptible, mean

cheapen *verb* DEGRADE, belittle, debase, demean, denigrate, depreciate, devalue, discredit, disparage, lower

cheat *verb* 1 DECEIVE, beguile, con (*informal*), defraud, double-cross (*informal*), dupe, fleece, fool, mislead, rip off (*slang*), swindle, trick ◆ *noun* 2 DECEIVER, charlatan, con man (*informal*), double-crosser (*informal*), shark, sharper, swindler, trickster 3 DECEPTION, deceit, fraud, rip-off (*slang*), scam (*slang*), swindle, trickery

check *verb* 1 EXAMINE, inquire into, inspect, investigate, look at, make sure, monitor, research, scrutinize, study, test, vet 2 STOP, delay, halt, hinder, impede, inhibit, limit, obstruct, restrain, retard ◆ *noun* 3 EXAMINATION, inspection, investigation, once-over (*informal*), research, scrutiny, test 4 STOPPAGE, constraint, control, curb, damper, hindrance, impediment, limitation, obstacle, obstruction, restraint

cheek *noun Informal* IMPUDENCE, audacity, brass neck (*Brit. informal*), chutzpah (*U.S. & Canad. informal*), disrespect, effrontery, impertinence, insolence, lip (*slang*), nerve, temerity

cheeky *adjective* IMPUDENT, audacious, disrespectful, forward, impertinent, insolent, insulting, pert, saucy

cheer *verb* 1 APPLAUD, acclaim, clap, hail 2 CHEER UP, brighten, buoy up, comfort, encourage, gladden, hearten, uplift ◆ *noun* 3 APPLAUSE, acclamation, ovation, plaudits

cheerful *adjective* HAPPY, buoyant, cheery, chirpy (*informal*), enthusiastic, jaunty, jolly, light-hearted, merry, optimistic, upbeat (*informal*)

cheerfulness *noun* HAPPINESS, buoyancy, exuberance, gaiety, geniality, good cheer, good humour, high spirits, jauntiness, light-heartedness

cheerless *adjective* GLOOMY, bleak, desolate, dismal, drab, dreary, forlorn, miserable, sombre, woeful

cheer up *verb* 1 COMFORT, encourage, enliven, gladden, hearten, jolly along (*informal*) 2 TAKE HEART, buck up (*informal*), perk up, rally

cheery *adjective* CHEERFUL, breezy, carefree, chirpy (*informal*), genial, good-humoured, happy, jovial, upbeat (*informal*)

chemist *noun* PHARMACIST, apothecary (*obsolete*), dispenser

cherish *verb* 1 CLING TO, cleave to, encourage, entertain, foster, harbour, hold dear, nurture, prize, sustain, treasure 2 CARE FOR, comfort, hold dear, love, nurse, shelter, support

chest *noun* BOX, case, casket, coffer, crate, strongbox, trunk

chew *verb* BITE, champ, chomp, crunch, gnaw, grind, masticate, munch

chewy *adjective* TOUGH, as tough as old boots, leathery

chic *adjective* STYLISH, elegant, fashionable, smart, trendy (*Brit. informal*)

chide *verb Old-fashioned* SCOLD, admonish, berate, censure, criticize, lecture, rebuke, reprimand, reproach, reprove, tell off (*informal*)

chief noun 1 HEAD, boss (*informal*), captain, commander, director, governor, leader, manager, master, principal, ruler ♦ *adjective* 2 PRIMARY, foremost, highest, key, leading, main, predominant, pre-eminent, premier, prime, principal, supreme, uppermost

chiefly adverb 1 ESPECIALLY, above all, essentially, primarily, principally 2 MAINLY, in general, in the main, largely, mostly, on the whole, predominantly, usually

child noun YOUNGSTER, babe, baby, bairn (*Scot.*), infant, juvenile, kid (*informal*), offspring, toddler, tot

childbirth noun CHILD-BEARING, confinement, delivery, labour, lying-in, parturition, travail

childhood noun YOUTH, boyhood *or* girlhood, immaturity, infancy, minority, schooldays

childish adjective IMMATURE, boyish *or* girlish, foolish, infantile, juvenile, puerile, young

childlike adjective INNOCENT, artless, guileless, ingenuous, naive, simple, trusting

chill noun 1 COLD, bite, coldness, coolness, crispness, frigidity, nip, rawness, sharpness ♦ *verb* 2 COOL, freeze, refrigerate 3 DISHEARTEN, dampen, deject, depress, discourage, dismay ♦ *adjective* 4 COLD, biting, bleak, chilly, freezing, frigid, raw, sharp, wintry

chilly adjective 1 COOL, brisk, crisp, draughty, fresh, nippy, penetrating, sharp 2 UNFRIENDLY, frigid, hostile, unresponsive, unsympathetic, unwelcoming

chime verb, noun RING, clang, jingle, peal, sound, tinkle, toll

china noun POTTERY, ceramics, crockery, porcelain, service, tableware, ware

chink noun OPENING, aperture, cleft, crack, cranny, crevice, fissure, gap

chip noun 1 SCRATCH, fragment, nick, notch, shard, shaving, sliver, wafer ♦ *verb* 2 NICK, chisel, damage, gash, whittle

chirp verb CHIRRUP, cheep, peep, pipe, tweet, twitter, warble

chivalrous adjective COURTEOUS, bold, brave, courageous, gallant, gentlemanly, honourable, valiant

chivalry noun COURTESY, courage, gallantry, gentlemanliness, knight-errantry, knighthood, politeness

choice noun 1 OPTION, alternative, pick, preference, say 2 SELECTION, range, variety ♦ *adjective* 3 BEST, elite, excellent, exclusive, prime, rare, select

choke verb 1 STRANGLE, asphyxiate, gag, overpower, smother, stifle, suffocate, suppress, throttle 2 BLOCK, bar, bung, clog, congest, constrict, obstruct, stop

choose verb PICK, adopt, designate, elect, opt for, prefer, select, settle upon

choosy adjective Informal FUSSY, discriminating, faddy, fastidious, finicky, particular, picky (*informal*), selective

chop verb CUT, cleave, fell, hack, hew, lop, sever

chore noun TASK, burden, duty, errand, job

chortle verb, noun CHUCKLE, cackle, crow, guffaw

chorus noun 1 CHOIR, choristers, ensemble, singers, vocalists 2 REFRAIN, burden, response, strain 3 UNISON, accord, concert, harmony

christen verb 1 BAPTIZE 2 NAME, call,

designate, dub, style, term, title

Christmas noun FESTIVE SEASON, Noel, Xmas (*informal*), Yule (*archaic*), Yuletide (*archaic*)

chronicle noun 1 RECORD, account, annals, diary, history, journal, narrative, register, story ♦ *verb* 2 RECORD, enter, narrate, put on record, recount, register, relate, report, set down, tell

chubby adjective PLUMP, buxom, flabby, podgy, portly, rotund, round, stout, tubby

chuck verb Informal THROW, cast, fling, heave, hurl, pitch, sling, toss

chuckle verb LAUGH, chortle, crow, exult, giggle, snigger, titter

chum noun Informal FRIEND, companion, comrade, crony, mate (*informal*), pal (*informal*)

chunk noun PIECE, block, dollop (*informal*), hunk, lump, mass, nugget, portion, slab

churlish adjective RUDE, brusque, harsh, ill-tempered, impolite, sullen, surly, uncivil

churn verb STIR UP, agitate, beat, convulse, swirl, toss

cinema noun FILMS, big screen (*informal*), flicks (*slang*), motion pictures, movies, pictures

cipher noun 1 CODE, cryptograph 2 NOBODY, nonentity

circle noun 1 RING, disc, globe, orb, sphere 2 GROUP, clique, club, company, coterie, set, society ♦ *verb* 3 GO ROUND, circumnavigate, circumscribe, encircle, enclose, envelop, ring, surround

circuit noun COURSE, journey, lap, orbit, revolution, route, tour, track

circuitous adjective INDIRECT, labyrinthine, meandering, oblique, rambling, roundabout, tortuous, winding

circular adjective 1 ROUND, ring-shaped, rotund, spherical 2 ORBITAL, circuitous, cyclical ♦ *noun* 3 ADVERTISEMENT, notice

circulate verb 1 SPREAD, broadcast, disseminate, distribute, issue, make known, promulgate, publicize, publish 2 FLOW, gyrate, radiate, revolve, rotate

circulation noun 1 BLOODSTREAM 2 FLOW, circling, motion, rotation 3 DISTRIBUTION, currency, dissemination, spread, transmission

circumference noun BOUNDARY, border, edge, extremity, limits, outline, perimeter, periphery, rim

circumstance noun EVENT, accident, condition, contingency, happening, incident, occurrence, particular, respect, situation

circumstances plural noun SITUATION, means, position, state, state of affairs, station, status

cistern noun TANK, basin, reservoir, sink, vat

citadel noun FORTRESS, bastion, fortification, keep, stronghold, tower

cite verb QUOTE, adduce, advance, allude to, enumerate, extract, mention, name, specify

citizen noun INHABITANT, denizen, dweller, resident, subject, townsman

city noun TOWN, conurbation, metropolis, municipality

civic adjective PUBLIC, communal, local, municipal

civil adjective 1 CIVIC, domestic, municipal, political 2 POLITE, affable, courteous, obliging, refined, urbane, well-mannered

civilization noun 1 CULTURE, advancement, cultivation, development, education, enlightenment, progress, refinement, sophistication **2** SOCIETY, community, nation, people, polity

civilize verb CULTIVATE, educate, enlighten, refine, sophisticate, tame

civilized adjective CULTURED, educated, enlightened, humane, polite, sophisticated, tolerant, urbane

claim verb **1** ASSERT, allege, challenge, insist, maintain, profess, uphold **2** DEMAND, ask, call for, insist, need, require ◆ noun **3** ASSERTION, affirmation, allegation, pretension, privilege, protestation **4** DEMAND, application, call, petition, request, requirement **5** RIGHT, title

clairvoyant noun **1** PSYCHIC, diviner, fortune-teller, visionary ◆ adjective **2** PSYCHIC, extrasensory, second-sighted, telepathic, visionary

clamber verb CLIMB, claw, scale, scrabble, scramble, shin

clammy adjective MOIST, close, damp, dank, sticky, sweaty

clamour noun NOISE, commotion, din, hubbub, outcry, racket, shouting, uproar

clamp noun **1** VICE, bracket, fastener, grip, press ◆ verb **2** FASTEN, brace, fix, make fast, secure

clan noun FAMILY, brotherhood, faction, fraternity, group, society, tribe

clandestine adjective SECRET, cloak-and-dagger, concealed, covert, furtive, private, stealthy, surreptitious, underground

clap verb APPLAUD, acclaim, cheer

clarification noun EXPLANATION, elucidation, exposition,

illumination, interpretation, simplification

clarify verb EXPLAIN, clear up, elucidate, illuminate, interpret, make plain, simplify, throw or shed light on

clarity noun CLEARNESS, definition, limpidity, lucidity, precision, simplicity, transparency

clash verb **1** CONFLICT, cross swords, feud, grapple, lock horns, quarrel, war, wrangle **2** CRASH, bang, clang, clank, clatter, jangle, jar, rattle ◆ noun **3** CONFLICT, brush, collision, confrontation, difference of opinion, disagreement, fight, showdown (informal)

clasp noun **1** FASTENING, brooch, buckle, catch, clip, fastener, grip, hook, pin **2** GRASP, embrace, grip, hold, hug ◆ verb **3** GRASP, clutch, embrace, grip, hold, hug, press, seize, squeeze **4** FASTEN, connect

class noun **1** GROUP, category, division, genre, kind, set, sort, type ◆ verb **2** CLASSIFY, brand, categorize, designate, grade, group, label, rank, rate

classic adjective **1** DEFINITIVE, archetypal, exemplary, ideal, model, quintessential, standard **2** TYPICAL, characteristic, regular, standard, time-honoured, usual **3** BEST, consummate, finest, first-rate, masterly, world-class **4** LASTING, abiding, ageless, deathless, enduring, immortal, undying ◆ noun **5** STANDARD, exemplar, masterpiece, model, paradigm, prototype

classical adjective PURE, elegant, harmonious, refined, restrained, symmetrical, understated, well-proportioned

classification noun CATEGORIZATION, analysis, arrangement, grading, sorting, taxonomy

classify verb CATEGORIZE, arrange, catalogue, grade, pigeonhole, rank, sort, systematize, tabulate

classy adjective Informal HIGH-CLASS, elegant, exclusive, posh (informal, chiefly Brit.), stylish, superior, top-drawer, up-market

clause noun SECTION, article, chapter, condition, paragraph, part, passage

claw noun 1 NAIL, pincer, talon, tentacle ♦ verb 2 SCRATCH, dig, lacerate, maul, rip, scrape, tear

clean adjective 1 PURE, flawless, fresh, immaculate, impeccable, spotless, unblemished, unsullied 2 HYGIENIC, antiseptic, decontaminated, purified, sterile, sterilized, uncontaminated, unpolluted 3 MORAL, chaste, decent, good, honourable, innocent, pure, respectable, upright, virtuous 4 COMPLETE, conclusive, decisive, entire, final, perfect, thorough, total, unimpaired, whole ♦ verb 5 CLEANSE, disinfect, launder, purge, purify, rinse, sanitize, scour, scrub, wash

cleanse verb CLEAN, absolve, clear, purge, purify, rinse, scour, scrub, wash

cleanser noun DETERGENT, disinfectant, purifier, scourer, soap, solvent

clear adjective 1 CERTAIN, convinced, decided, definite, positive, resolved, satisfied, sure 2 OBVIOUS, apparent, blatant, comprehensible, conspicuous, distinct, evident, manifest, palpable, plain, pronounced, recognizable, unmistakable 3 TRANSPARENT, crystalline, glassy, limpid, pellucid, see-through, translucent 4 BRIGHT, cloudless, fair, fine, light, luminous, shining, sunny, unclouded 5 UNOBSTRUCTED, empty, free, open, smooth, unhindered, unimpeded 6 UNBLEMISHED, clean, immaculate, innocent, pure, untarnished ♦ verb 7 UNBLOCK, disentangle, extricate, free, loosen, open, rid, unload 8 PASS OVER, jump, leap, miss, vault 9 BRIGHTEN, break up, lighten 10 CLEAN, cleanse, erase, purify, refine, sweep away, tidy (up), wipe 11 ABSOLVE, acquit, excuse, exonerate, justify, vindicate 12 GAIN, acquire, earn, make, reap, secure

clear-cut adjective STRAIGHTFORWARD, black-and-white, cut-and-dried (informal), definite, explicit, plain, precise, specific, unambiguous, unequivocal

clearly adverb OBVIOUSLY, beyond doubt, distinctly, evidently, markedly, openly, overtly, undeniably, undoubtedly

clergy noun PRIESTHOOD, churchmen, clergymen, clerics, holy orders, ministry, the cloth

clergyman noun MINISTER, chaplain, cleric, man of God, man of the cloth, padre, parson, pastor, priest, vicar

clever adjective INTELLIGENT, bright, gifted, ingenious, knowledgeable, quick-witted, resourceful, shrewd, smart, talented

cleverness noun INTELLIGENCE, ability, brains, ingenuity, quick wits, resourcefulness, shrewdness, smartness

cliché noun PLATITUDE, banality, commonplace, hackneyed phrase, stereotype, truism

client noun CUSTOMER, applicant, buyer, consumer, patient, patron, shopper

clientele noun CUSTOMERS, business, clients, following, market, patronage, regulars, trade

cliff noun ROCK FACE, bluff, crag, escarpment, overhang, precipice, scar, scarp

climactic adjective CRUCIAL, critical, decisive, paramount, peak

climate noun WEATHER, temperature

climax noun CULMINATION, height, highlight, high point, peak, summit, top, zenith

climb verb ASCEND, clamber, mount, rise, scale, shin up, soar, top

climb down verb 1 DESCEND, dismount 2 BACK DOWN, eat one's words, retract, retreat

clinch verb SETTLE, conclude, confirm, decide, determine, seal, secure, set the seal on, sew up (*informal*)

cling verb STICK, adhere, clasp, clutch, embrace, grasp, grip, hug

clinical adjective UNEMOTIONAL, analytic, cold, detached, dispassionate, impersonal, objective, scientific

clip[1] verb 1 TRIM, crop, curtail, cut, pare, prune, shear, shorten, snip ♦ noun, verb 2 *Informal* SMACK, clout (*informal*), cuff, knock, punch, strike, thump, wallop (*informal*), whack

clip[2] verb ATTACH, fasten, fix, hold, pin, staple

clique noun GROUP, cabal, circle, coterie, faction, gang, set

cloak noun 1 CAPE, coat, mantle, wrap ♦ verb 2 COVER, camouflage, conceal, disguise, hide, mask, obscure, screen, veil

clog verb OBSTRUCT, block, congest, hinder, impede, jam

close[1] verb 1 SHUT, bar, block, lock, plug, seal, secure, stop up 2 END, cease, complete, conclude, finish, shut down, terminate, wind up 3 CONNECT, come together, couple,

fuse, join, unite ♦ noun 4 END, completion, conclusion, culmination, denouement, ending, finale, finish

close[2] adjective 1 NEAR, adjacent, adjoining, at hand, cheek by jowl, handy, impending, nearby, neighbouring, nigh 2 INTIMATE, attached, confidential, dear, devoted, familiar, inseparable, loving 3 CAREFUL, detailed, intense, minute, painstaking, rigorous, thorough 4 COMPACT, congested, crowded, dense, impenetrable, jam-packed, packed, tight 5 STIFLING, airless, heavy, humid, muggy, oppressive, stuffy, suffocating, sweltering 6 SECRETIVE, private, reticent, secret, taciturn, uncommunicative 7 MEAN, miserly, stingy

closed adjective 1 SHUT, fastened, locked, out of service, sealed 2 EXCLUSIVE, restricted 3 FINISHED, concluded, decided, ended, over, resolved, settled, terminated

cloth noun FABRIC, material, textiles

clothe verb DRESS, array, attire, cover, drape, equip, fit out, garb, robe, swathe

clothes plural noun CLOTHING, apparel, attire, costume, dress, garb, garments, gear (*informal*), outfit, wardrobe, wear

clothing noun CLOTHES, apparel, attire, costume, dress, garb, garments, gear (*informal*), outfit, wardrobe, wear

cloud noun 1 MIST, gloom, haze, murk, vapour ♦ verb 2 OBSCURE, becloud, darken, dim, eclipse, obfuscate, overshadow, shade, shadow, veil 3 CONFUSE, disorient, distort, impair, muddle, muddy the waters

cloudy adjective 1 DULL, dim, gloomy, leaden, louring *or* lowering, overcast, sombre, sunless 2 <u>OPAQUE</u>, muddy, murky

clout *Informal* ♦ *noun* 1 <u>INFLUENCE</u>, authority, power, prestige, pull, weight ♦ *verb* 2 <u>HIT</u>, clobber (*slang*), punch, sock (*slang*), strike, thump, wallop (*informal*)

clown *noun* 1 <u>COMEDIAN</u>, buffoon, comic, fool, harlequin, jester, joker, prankster ♦ *verb* 2 <u>PLAY THE FOOL</u>, act the fool, jest, mess about

club *noun* 1 <u>ASSOCIATION</u>, company, fraternity, group, guild, lodge, set, society, union 2 <u>STICK</u>, bat, bludgeon, cosh (*Brit*.), cudgel, truncheon ♦ *verb* 3 <u>BEAT</u>, bash, batter, bludgeon, cosh (*Brit*.), hammer, pummel, strike

clue *noun* <u>INDICATION</u>, evidence, hint, lead, pointer, sign, suggestion, suspicion, trace

clueless *adjective* <u>STUPID</u>, dim, dozy (*Brit. informal*), dull, half-witted, simple, slow, thick, unintelligent, witless

clump *noun* 1 <u>CLUSTER</u>, bunch, bundle, group, mass ♦ *verb* 2 <u>STOMP</u>, lumber, plod, thud, thump, tramp

clumsy *adjective* <u>AWKWARD</u>, bumbling, gauche, gawky, ham-fisted (*informal*), lumbering, maladroit, ponderous, uncoordinated, ungainly, unwieldy

cluster *noun* 1 <u>GATHERING</u>, assemblage, batch, bunch, clump, collection, group, knot ♦ *verb* 2 <u>GATHER</u>, assemble, bunch, collect, flock, group

clutch *verb* <u>SEIZE</u>, catch, clasp, cling to, embrace, grab, grasp, grip, snatch

clutches *plural noun* <u>POWER</u>, claws, control, custody, grasp, grip, hands, keeping, possession, sway

clutter *verb* 1 <u>LITTER</u>, scatter, strew ♦ *noun* 2 <u>UNTIDINESS</u>, confusion, disarray, disorder, hotchpotch, jumble, litter, mess, muddle

coach *noun* 1 <u>BUS</u>, car, carriage, charabanc, vehicle 2 <u>INSTRUCTOR</u>, handler, teacher, trainer, tutor ♦ *verb* 3 <u>INSTRUCT</u>, drill, exercise, prepare, train, tutor

coalesce *verb* <u>BLEND</u>, amalgamate, combine, fuse, incorporate, integrate, merge, mix, unite

coalition *noun* <u>ALLIANCE</u>, amalgamation, association, bloc, combination, confederation, conjunction, fusion, merger, union

coarse *adjective* 1 <u>ROUGH</u>, crude, homespun, impure, unfinished, unpolished, unprocessed, unpurified, unrefined 2 <u>VULGAR</u>, earthy, improper, indecent, indelicate, ribald, rude, smutty

coarseness *noun* 1 <u>ROUGHNESS</u>, crudity, unevenness 2 <u>VULGARITY</u>, bawdiness, crudity, earthiness, indelicacy, ribaldry, smut, uncouthness

coast *noun* 1 <u>SHORE</u>, beach, border, coastline, seaboard, seaside ♦ *verb* 2 <u>CRUISE</u>, drift, freewheel, glide, sail, taxi

coat *noun* 1 <u>FUR</u>, fleece, hair, hide, pelt, skin, wool 2 <u>LAYER</u>, coating, covering, overlay ♦ *verb* 3 <u>COVER</u>, apply, plaster, smear, spread

coax *verb* <u>PERSUADE</u>, allure, cajole, entice, prevail upon, sweet-talk (*informal*), talk into, wheedle

cocktail *noun* <u>MIXTURE</u>, blend, combination, mix

cocky *adjective* <u>OVERCONFIDENT</u>, arrogant, brash, cocksure, conceited, egotistical, full of oneself, swaggering, vain

code *noun* 1 <u>CIPHER</u>, cryptograph 2 <u>PRINCIPLES</u>, canon, convention, custom, ethics, etiquette, manners, maxim, regulations, rules, system

cogent *adjective* <u>CONVINCING</u>, compelling, effective, forceful, influential, potent, powerful, strong, weighty

cogitate *verb* <u>THINK</u>, consider, contemplate, deliberate, meditate, mull over, muse, ponder, reflect, ruminate

coherent *adjective* 1 <u>CONSISTENT</u>, logical, lucid, meaningful, orderly, organized, rational, reasoned, systematic 2 <u>INTELLIGIBLE</u>, articulate, comprehensible

coil *verb* <u>WIND</u>, curl, loop, snake, spiral, twine, twist, wreathe, writhe

coin *noun* 1 <u>MONEY</u>, cash, change, copper, silver, specie ♦ *verb* 2 <u>INVENT</u>, create, fabricate, forge, make up, mint, mould, originate

coincide *verb* 1 <u>OCCUR SIMULTANEOUSLY</u>, be concurrent, coexist, synchronize 2 <u>AGREE</u>, accord, concur, correspond, harmonize, match, square, tally

coincidence *noun* 1 <u>CHANCE</u>, accident, fluke, happy accident, luck, stroke of luck 2 <u>COINCIDING</u>, concurrence, conjunction, correlation, correspondence

coincidental *adjective* <u>CHANCE</u>, accidental, casual, fluky (*informal*), fortuitous, unintentional, unplanned

cold *adjective* 1 <u>CHILLY</u>, arctic, bleak, cool, freezing, frigid, frosty, frozen, icy, wintry 2 <u>UNFRIENDLY</u>, aloof, distant, frigid, indifferent, reserved, standoffish ♦ *noun* 3 <u>COLDNESS</u>, chill, frigidity, frostiness, iciness

cold-blooded *adjective* <u>CALLOUS</u>, dispassionate, heartless, ruthless, steely, stony-hearted, unemotional, unfeeling

collaborate *verb* 1 <u>WORK TOGETHER</u>, cooperate, join forces, participate, play ball (*informal*), team up

2 <u>CONSPIRE</u>, collude, cooperate, fraternize

collaboration *noun* <u>TEAMWORK</u>, alliance, association, cooperation, partnership

collaborator *noun* 1 <u>CO-WORKER</u>, associate, colleague, confederate, partner, team-mate 2 <u>TRAITOR</u>, fraternizer, quisling, turncoat

collapse *verb* 1 <u>FALL DOWN</u>, cave in, crumple, fall, fall apart at the seams, give way, subside 2 <u>FAIL</u>, come to nothing, fold, founder, go belly-up (*informal*) ♦ *noun* 3 <u>FALLING DOWN</u>, cave-in, disintegration, falling apart, ruin, subsidence 4 <u>FAILURE</u>, downfall, flop, slump 5 <u>FAINT</u>, breakdown, exhaustion, prostration

collar *verb Informal* <u>SEIZE</u>, apprehend, arrest, capture, catch, grab, nab (*informal*), nail (*informal*)

colleague *noun* <u>FELLOW WORKER</u>, ally, assistant, associate, collaborator, comrade, helper, partner, team-mate, workmate

collect *verb* 1 <u>ASSEMBLE</u>, cluster, congregate, convene, converge, flock together, rally 2 <u>GATHER</u>, accumulate, amass, assemble, heap, hoard, save, stockpile

collected *adjective* <u>CALM</u>, composed, cool, poised, self-possessed, serene, unperturbed, unruffled

collection *noun* 1 <u>ACCUMULATION</u>, anthology, compilation, heap, hoard, mass, pile, set, stockpile, store 2 <u>GROUP</u>, assembly, assortment, cluster, company, crowd 3 <u>CONTRIBUTION</u>, alms, offering, offertory

collective *adjective* <u>COMBINED</u>, aggregate, composite, corporate, cumulative, joint, shared, unified, united

collide *verb* 1 <u>CRASH</u>, clash, come

into collision, meet head-on
2 CONFLICT, clash

collision noun 1 CRASH, accident,
bump, impact, pile-up (informal),
prang (informal), smash
2 CONFLICT, clash, confrontation,
encounter, opposition, skirmish

colloquial adjective INFORMAL,
conversational, demotic,
everyday, familiar, idiomatic,
vernacular

colony noun SETTLEMENT,
community, dependency,
dominion, outpost, possession,
province, satellite state, territory

colossal adjective HUGE, enormous,
gigantic, immense, mammoth,
massive, monumental, prodigious,
vast

colour noun 1 HUE, colorant, dye,
paint, pigment, shade, tint ♦ verb
2 PAINT, dye, stain, tinge, tint
3 BLUSH, flush, redden

colourful adjective 1 BRIGHT,
brilliant, multicoloured,
psychedelic, variegated
2 INTERESTING, distinctive, graphic,
lively, picturesque, rich, vivid

colourless adjective 1 DRAB,
achromatic, anaemic, ashen,
bleached, faded, wan, washed out
2 UNINTERESTING, characterless,
dreary, dull, insipid, lacklustre,
vapid

column noun 1 PILLAR, obelisk, post,
shaft, support, upright 2 LINE,
cavalcade, file, procession, rank,
row

coma noun UNCONSCIOUSNESS,
oblivion, stupor, trance

comb verb 1 UNTANGLE, arrange,
dress, groom 2 SEARCH, forage,
hunt, rake, ransack, rummage,
scour, sift

combat noun 1 FIGHT, action,
battle, conflict, contest,
encounter, engagement, skirmish,

struggle, war, warfare ♦ verb
2 FIGHT, defy, do battle with,
oppose, resist, withstand

combatant noun FIGHTER,
adversary, antagonist, enemy,
opponent, soldier, warrior

combination noun 1 MIXTURE,
amalgamation, blend,
coalescence, composite,
connection, mix 2 ASSOCIATION,
alliance, coalition, confederation,
consortium, federation, syndicate,
union

combine verb JOIN TOGETHER,
amalgamate, blend, connect,
integrate, link, merge, mix, pool,
unite

come verb 1 MOVE TOWARDS,
advance, approach, draw near,
near 2 ARRIVE, appear, enter,
materialize, reach, show up
(informal), turn up (informal)
3 HAPPEN, fall, occur, take place
4 RESULT, arise, emanate, emerge,
flow, issue, originate 5 REACH,
extend 6 BE AVAILABLE, be made, be
offered, be on offer, be produced

come about verb HAPPEN, arise,
befall, come to pass, occur, result,
take place, transpire (informal)

come across verb FIND, bump into
(informal), chance upon, discover,
encounter, meet, notice, stumble
upon, unearth

comeback noun 1 Informal RETURN,
rally, rebound, recovery,
resurgence, revival, triumph
2 RESPONSE, rejoinder, reply,
retaliation, retort, riposte

come back verb RETURN, reappear,
recur, re-enter

comedian noun COMIC, card
(informal), clown, funny man,
humorist, jester, joker, wag, wit

comedown noun 1 DECLINE,
deflation, demotion, reverse
2 Informal DISAPPOINTMENT,

anticlimax, blow, humiliation, letdown

comedy *noun* HUMOUR, farce, fun, hilarity, jesting, joking, light entertainment

comeuppance *noun Informal* PUNISHMENT, chastening, deserts, due reward, recompense, retribution

comfort *noun* 1 LUXURY, cosiness, ease, opulence, snugness, wellbeing 2 RELIEF, compensation, consolation, help, succour, support ◆ *verb* 3 CONSOLE, commiserate with, hearten, reassure, soothe

comfortable *adjective* 1 RELAXING, agreeable, convenient, cosy, homely, pleasant, restful, snug 2 HAPPY, at ease, at home, contented, gratified, relaxed, serene 3 *Informal* WELL-OFF, affluent, in clover (*informal*), prosperous, well-to-do

comforting *adjective* CONSOLING, cheering, consolatory, encouraging, heart-warming, reassuring, soothing

comic *adjective* 1 FUNNY, amusing, comical, droll, farcical, humorous, jocular, witty ◆ *noun* 2 COMEDIAN, buffoon, clown, funny man, humorist, jester, wag, wit

comical *adjective* FUNNY, amusing, comic, droll, farcical, hilarious, humorous, priceless, side-splitting

coming *adjective* 1 APPROACHING, at hand, forthcoming, imminent, impending, in store, near, nigh ◆ *noun* 2 ARRIVAL, advent, approach

command *verb* 1 ORDER, bid, charge, compel, demand, direct, require 2 HAVE AUTHORITY OVER, control, dominate, govern, handle, head, lead, manage, rule, supervise ◆ *noun* 3 ORDER, commandment, decree, demand,

directive, instruction, requirement, ultimatum 4 AUTHORITY, charge, control, government, management, mastery, power, rule, supervision

commandeer *verb* SEIZE, appropriate, confiscate, requisition, sequester, sequestrate

commander *noun* OFFICER, boss, captain, chief, commanding officer, head, leader, ruler

commanding *adjective* CONTROLLING, advantageous, decisive, dominant, dominating, superior

commemorate *verb* REMEMBER, celebrate, honour, immortalize, pay tribute to, salute

commemoration *noun* REMEMBRANCE, ceremony, honouring, memorial service, tribute

commence *verb* BEGIN, embark on, enter upon, initiate, open, originate, start

commend *verb* PRAISE, acclaim, applaud, approve, compliment, extol, recommend, speak highly of

commendable *adjective* PRAISEWORTHY, admirable, creditable, deserving, estimable, exemplary, laudable, meritorious, worthy

commendation *noun* PRAISE, acclaim, acclamation, approbation, approval, credit, encouragement, good opinion, panegyric, recommendation

comment *noun* 1 REMARK, observation, statement 2 NOTE, annotation, commentary, explanation, exposition, illustration ◆ *verb* 3 REMARK, mention, note, observe, point out, say, utter 4 ANNOTATE, elucidate, explain, interpret

commentary *noun* 1 NARRATION,

description, voice-over 2 <u>NOTES</u>, analysis, critique, explanation, review, treatise

commentator *noun* 1 <u>REPORTER</u>, special correspondent, sportscaster 2 <u>CRITIC</u>, annotator, interpreter

commerce *noun* <u>TRADE</u>, business, dealing, exchange, traffic

commercial *adjective* 1 <u>MERCANTILE</u>, trading 2 <u>MATERIALISTIC</u>, mercenary, profit-making

commiserate *verb* <u>SYMPATHIZE</u>, console, feel for, pity

commission *noun* 1 <u>DUTY</u>, errand, mandate, mission, task 2 <u>FEE</u>, cut, percentage, rake-off (*slang*), royalties 3 <u>COMMITTEE</u>, board, commissioners, delegation, deputation, representatives ♦ *verb* 4 <u>APPOINT</u>, authorize, contract, delegate, depute, empower, engage, nominate, order, select

commit *verb* 1 <u>DO</u>, carry out, enact, execute, perform, perpetrate 2 <u>PUT IN CUSTODY</u>, confine, imprison

commitment *noun* 1 <u>DEDICATION</u>, devotion, involvement, loyalty 2 <u>RESPONSIBILITY</u>, duty, engagement, liability, obligation, tie

common *adjective* 1 <u>AVERAGE</u>, commonplace, conventional, customary, everyday, familiar, frequent, habitual, ordinary, regular, routine, standard, stock, usual 2 <u>POPULAR</u>, accepted, general, prevailing, prevalent, universal, widespread 3 <u>COLLECTIVE</u>, communal, popular, public, social 4 <u>VULGAR</u>, coarse, inferior, plebeian

commonplace *adjective* 1 <u>EVERYDAY</u>, banal, common, humdrum, mundane, obvious, ordinary, run-of-the-mill, widespread ♦ *noun* 2 <u>CLICHÉ</u>, banality, platitude, truism

common sense *noun* <u>GOOD SENSE</u>, gumption (*Brit. informal*), horse

sense, level-headedness, native intelligence, prudence, sound judgment, wit

commotion *noun* <u>DISTURBANCE</u>, disorder, excitement, furore, fuss, hue and cry, rumpus, tumult, turmoil, upheaval, uproar

communal *adjective* <u>PUBLIC</u>, collective, general, joint, shared

commune *noun* <u>COMMUNITY</u>, collective, cooperative, kibbutz

commune with *verb* <u>CONTEMPLATE</u>, meditate on, muse on, ponder, reflect on

communicate *verb* <u>MAKE KNOWN</u>, convey, declare, disclose, impart, inform, pass on, proclaim, transmit

communication *noun* 1 <u>PASSING ON</u>, contact, conversation, correspondence, dissemination, link, transmission 2 <u>MESSAGE</u>, announcement, disclosure, dispatch, information, news, report, statement, word

communicative *adjective* <u>TALKATIVE</u>, chatty, expansive, forthcoming, frank, informative, loquacious, open, outgoing, voluble

Communism *noun* <u>SOCIALISM</u>, Bolshevism, collectivism, Marxism, state socialism

Communist *noun* <u>SOCIALIST</u>, Bolshevik, collectivist, Marxist, Red (*informal*)

community *noun* <u>SOCIETY</u>, brotherhood, commonwealth, company, general public, people, populace, public, residents, state

commuter *noun* <u>DAILY TRAVELLER</u>, straphanger (*informal*), suburbanite

compact[1] *adjective* 1 <u>CLOSELY PACKED</u>, compressed, condensed, dense, pressed together, solid, thick 2 <u>BRIEF</u>, compendious, concise, succinct, terse, to the point ♦ *verb*

3 PACK CLOSELY, compress, condense, cram, stuff, tamp

compact[2] *noun* AGREEMENT, arrangement, bargain, bond, contract, covenant, deal, pact, treaty, understanding

companion *noun* **1** FRIEND, accomplice, ally, associate, colleague, comrade, consort, mate (*informal*), partner **2** ESCORT, aide, assistant, attendant, chaperon, squire

companionship *noun* FELLOWSHIP, camaraderie, company, comradeship, conviviality, esprit de corps, friendship, rapport, togetherness

company *noun* **1** BUSINESS, association, concern, corporation, establishment, firm, house, partnership, syndicate **2** GROUP, assembly, band, collection, community, crowd, gathering, party, set **3** GUESTS, callers, party, visitors

comparable *adjective* **1** ON A PAR, a match for, as good as, commensurate, equal, equivalent, in a class with, proportionate, tantamount **2** SIMILAR, akin, alike, analogous, cognate, corresponding, cut from the same cloth, of a piece, related

comparative *adjective* RELATIVE, by comparison, qualified

compare *verb* **1** WEIGH, balance, contrast, juxtapose, set against **2** usually with *with* BE ON A PAR WITH, approach, bear comparison, be in the same class as, be the equal of, compete with, equal, hold a candle to, match **3 compare to** LIKEN TO, correlate to, equate to, identify with, mention in the same breath as, parallel, resemble

comparison *noun* **1** CONTRAST, distinction, juxtaposition **2** SIMILARITY, analogy,

comparability, correlation, likeness, resemblance

compartment *noun* SECTION, alcove, bay, berth, booth, carriage, cubbyhole, cubicle, locker, niche, pigeonhole

compass *noun* RANGE, area, boundary, circumference, extent, field, limit, reach, realm, scope

compassion *noun* SYMPATHY, condolence, fellow feeling, humanity, kindness, mercy, pity, sorrow, tender-heartedness, tenderness, understanding

compassionate *adjective* SYMPATHETIC, benevolent, charitable, humane, humanitarian, kind-hearted, merciful, pitying, tender-hearted, understanding

compatibility *noun* HARMONY, affinity, agreement, concord, empathy, like-mindedness, rapport, sympathy

compatible *adjective* HARMONIOUS, adaptable, congruous, consistent, in harmony, in keeping, suitable

compel *verb* FORCE, coerce, constrain, dragoon, impel, make, oblige, railroad (*informal*)

compelling *adjective* **1** FASCINATING, enchanting, enthralling, gripping, hypnotic, irresistible, mesmeric, spellbinding **2** PRESSING, binding, coercive, imperative, overriding, peremptory, unavoidable, urgent **3** CONVINCING, cogent, conclusive, forceful, irrefutable, powerful, telling, weighty

compensate *verb* **1** RECOMPENSE, atone, make amends, make good, refund, reimburse, remunerate, repay **2** CANCEL (OUT), balance, counteract, counterbalance, make up for, offset, redress

compensation *noun* RECOMPENSE, amends, atonement, damages, reimbursement, remuneration, reparation, restitution, satisfaction

compete verb CONTEND, be in the running, challenge, contest, fight, strive, struggle, vie

competence noun ABILITY, capability, capacity, expertise, fitness, proficiency, skill, suitability

competent adjective ABLE, adequate, capable, fit, proficient, qualified, suitable

competition noun 1 RIVALRY, opposition, strife, struggle 2 CONTEST, championship, event, head-to-head, puzzle, quiz, tournament 3 OPPOSITION, challengers, field, rivals

competitive adjective 1 CUT-THROAT, aggressive, antagonistic, at odds, dog-eat-dog, opposing, rival 2 AMBITIOUS, combative

competitor noun CONTESTANT, adversary, antagonist, challenger, opponent, rival

compilation noun COLLECTION, accumulation, anthology, assemblage, assortment, treasury

compile verb PUT TOGETHER, accumulate, amass, collect, cull, garner, gather, marshal, organize

complacency noun SELF-SATISFACTION, contentment, satisfaction, smugness

complacent adjective SELF-SATISFIED, contented, pleased with oneself, resting on one's laurels, satisfied, serene, smug, unconcerned

complain verb FIND FAULT, bemoan, bewail, carp, deplore, groan, grouse, grumble, lament, moan, whine, whinge (informal)

complaint noun 1 CRITICISM, charge, grievance, gripe (informal), grouse, grumble, lament, moan, protest 2 ILLNESS, affliction, ailment, disease, disorder, malady,

sickness, upset

complement noun 1 COMPLETION, companion, consummation, counterpart, finishing touch, rounding-off, supplement 2 TOTAL, aggregate, capacity, entirety, quota, totality, wholeness ♦ verb 3 COMPLETE, cap (informal), crown, round off, set off

complementary adjective COMPLETING, companion, corresponding, interdependent, interrelating, matched, reciprocal

complete adjective 1 TOTAL, absolute, consummate, outright, perfect, thorough, thoroughgoing, utter 2 FINISHED, accomplished, achieved, concluded, ended 3 ENTIRE, all, faultless, full, intact, plenary, unbroken, whole ♦ verb 4 FINISH, close, conclude, crown, end, finalize, round off, settle, wrap up (informal)

completely adverb TOTALLY, absolutely, altogether, entirely, every inch, fully, hook, line and sinker, in full, lock, stock and barrel, one hundred per cent, perfectly, thoroughly, utterly, wholly

completion noun FINISHING, bitter end, close, conclusion, culmination, end, fruition, fulfilment

complex adjective 1 COMPOUND, composite, heterogeneous, manifold, multifarious, multiple 2 COMPLICATED, elaborate, intricate, involved, labyrinthine, tangled, tortuous ♦ noun 3 STRUCTURE, aggregate, composite, network, organization, scheme, system 4 Informal OBSESSION, fixation, fixed idea, idée fixe, phobia, preoccupation

complexion noun 1 SKIN, colour, colouring, hue, pigmentation, skin tone **2** <u>NATURE</u>, appearance, aspect, character, guise, light, look, make-up

complexity noun <u>COMPLICATION</u>, elaboration, entanglement, intricacy, involvement, ramification

complicate verb <u>MAKE DIFFICULT</u>, confuse, entangle, involve, muddle, ravel

complicated adjective **1** <u>DIFFICULT</u>, involved, perplexing, problematic, puzzling, troublesome **2** <u>INVOLVED</u>, complex, convoluted, elaborate, intricate, labyrinthine

complication noun **1** <u>COMPLEXITY</u>, confusion, entanglement, intricacy, web **2** <u>PROBLEM</u>, difficulty, drawback, embarrassment, obstacle, snag

compliment noun **1** <u>PRAISE</u>, bouquet, commendation, congratulations, eulogy, flattery, honour, tribute ♦ verb **2** <u>PRAISE</u>, commend, congratulate, extol, flatter, pay tribute to, salute, speak highly of

complimentary adjective **1** <u>FLATTERING</u>, appreciative, approving, commendatory, congratulatory, laudatory **2** <u>FREE</u>, courtesy, donated, gratis, gratuitous, honorary, on the house

compliments plural noun <u>GREETINGS</u>, good wishes, regards, remembrances, respects, salutation

comply verb <u>OBEY</u>, abide by, acquiesce, adhere to, conform to, follow, observe, submit, toe the line

component noun **1** <u>PART</u>, constituent, element, ingredient, item, piece, unit ♦ adjective **2** <u>CONSTITUENT</u>, inherent, intrinsic

compose verb **1** <u>PUT TOGETHER</u>, build, comprise, constitute, construct, fashion, form, make, make up **2** <u>CREATE</u>, contrive, devise, invent, produce, write **3** <u>CALM</u>, collect, control, pacify, placate, quiet, soothe **4** <u>ARRANGE</u>, adjust

composed adjective <u>CALM</u>, at ease, collected, cool, level-headed, poised, relaxed, sedate, self-possessed, serene, unflappable

composition noun **1** <u>CREATION</u>, compilation, fashioning, formation, formulation, making, production, putting together **2** <u>DESIGN</u>, arrangement, configuration, formation, layout, make-up, organization, structure **3** <u>ESSAY</u>, exercise, literary work, opus, piece, treatise, work

composure noun <u>CALMNESS</u>, aplomb, equanimity, poise, sang-froid, self-assurance, self-possession, serenity

compound noun **1** <u>COMBINATION</u>, alloy, amalgam, blend, composite, fusion, medley, mixture, synthesis ♦ verb **2** <u>COMBINE</u>, amalgamate, blend, intermingle, mix, synthesize, unite **3** <u>INTENSIFY</u>, add to, aggravate, augment, complicate, exacerbate, heighten, magnify, worsen ♦ adjective **4** <u>COMPLEX</u>, composite, intricate, multiple

comprehend verb <u>UNDERSTAND</u>, apprehend, conceive, fathom, grasp, know, make out, perceive, see, take in

comprehensible adjective <u>UNDERSTANDABLE</u>, clear, coherent, conceivable, explicit, intelligible, plain

comprehension noun <u>UNDERSTANDING</u>, conception, discernment, grasp, intelligence, perception, realization

comprehensive adjective <u>BROAD</u>, all-embracing, all-inclusive, blanket, complete, encyclopedic, exhaustive, full, inclusive, thorough

compress verb SQUEEZE, abbreviate, concentrate, condense, contract, crush, press, shorten, squash

comprise verb 1 BE COMPOSED OF, consist of, contain, embrace, encompass, include, take in 2 MAKE UP, compose, constitute, form

compromise noun 1 GIVE-AND-TAKE, accommodation, adjustment, agreement, concession, settlement, trade-off ♦ verb 2 MEET HALFWAY, adjust, agree, concede, give and take, go fifty-fifty (informal), settle, strike a balance 3 DISHONOUR, discredit, embarrass, expose, jeopardize, prejudice, weaken

compulsion noun 1 URGE, drive, necessity, need, obsession, preoccupation 2 FORCE, coercion, constraint, demand, duress, obligation, pressure, urgency

compulsive adjective IRRESISTIBLE, compelling, driving, neurotic, obsessive, overwhelming, uncontrollable, urgent

compulsory adjective OBLIGATORY, binding, de rigueur, forced, imperative, mandatory, required, requisite

compute verb CALCULATE, add up, count, enumerate, figure out, reckon, tally, total

comrade noun COMPANION, ally, associate, colleague, co-worker, fellow, friend, partner

con Informal ♦ noun 1 SWINDLE, deception, fraud, scam (slang), sting (informal), trick ♦ verb 2 SWINDLE, cheat, deceive, defraud, double-cross (informal), dupe, hoodwink, rip off (slang), trick

concave adjective HOLLOW, indented

conceal verb HIDE, bury, camouflage, cover, disguise, mask, obscure, screen

concede verb 1 ADMIT, accept, acknowledge, allow, confess, grant, own 2 GIVE UP, cede, hand over, relinquish, surrender, yield

conceit noun 1 SELF-IMPORTANCE, arrogance, egotism, narcissism, pride, swagger, vanity 2 Archaic FANCY, fantasy, image, whim, whimsy

conceited adjective SELF-IMPORTANT, arrogant, bigheaded (informal), cocky, egotistical, full of oneself, immodest, narcissistic, too big for one's boots or breeches, vain

conceivable adjective IMAGINABLE, believable, credible, possible, thinkable

conceive verb 1 IMAGINE, believe, comprehend, envisage, fancy, suppose, think, understand 2 THINK UP, contrive, create, design, devise, formulate 3 BECOME PREGNANT, become impregnated

concentrate verb 1 FOCUS ONE'S ATTENTION ON, be engrossed in, put one's mind to, rack one's brains 2 FOCUS, bring to bear, centre, cluster, converge 3 GATHER, accumulate, cluster, collect, congregate, huddle

concentrated adjective 1 INTENSE, all-out (informal), deep, hard, intensive 2 CONDENSED, boiled down, evaporated, reduced, rich, thickened, undiluted

concentration noun 1 SINGLE-MINDEDNESS, absorption, application, heed 2 FOCUSING, bringing to bear, centralization, centring, consolidation, convergence, intensification 3 CONVERGENCE, accumulation, aggregation, cluster, collection, horde, mass

concept noun IDEA, abstraction, conception, conceptualization, hypothesis, image, notion, theory, view

conception noun 1 IDEA, concept, design, image, notion, plan 2 IMPREGNATION, fertilization, germination, insemination

concern noun 1 WORRY, anxiety, apprehension, burden, care, disquiet, distress 2 IMPORTANCE, bearing, interest, relevance 3 BUSINESS, affair, interest, job, responsibility, task 4 BUSINESS, company, corporation, enterprise, establishment, firm, organization ♦ verb 5 WORRY, bother, disquiet, distress, disturb, make anxious, perturb, trouble 6 BE RELEVANT TO, affect, apply to, bear on, interest, involve, pertain to, regard, touch

concerned adjective 1 INVOLVED, active, implicated, interested, mixed up, privy to 2 WORRIED, anxious, bothered, distressed, disturbed, troubled, uneasy, upset

concerning preposition REGARDING, about, apropos of, as regards, on the subject of, re, relating to, respecting, touching, with reference to

concession noun 1 GRANT, adjustment, allowance, boon, compromise, indulgence, permit, privilege, sop 2 CONCEDING, acknowledgment, admission, assent, confession, surrender, yielding

conciliate verb PACIFY, appease, clear the air, mediate, mollify, placate, reconcile, soothe, win over

conciliation noun PACIFICATION, appeasement, mollification, placation, reconciliation, soothing

conciliatory adjective PACIFYING, appeasing, mollifying, pacific, peaceable, placatory

concise adjective BRIEF,

compendious, condensed, laconic, pithy, short, succinct, terse

conclude verb 1 DECIDE, assume, deduce, gather, infer, judge, surmise, work out 2 END, cease, close, complete, finish, round off, terminate, wind up 3 ACCOMPLISH, bring about, carry out, effect, pull off

conclusion noun 1 DECISION, conviction, deduction, inference, judgment, opinion, verdict 2 END, bitter end, close, completion, ending, finale, finish, result, termination 3 OUTCOME, consequence, culmination, end result, result, upshot

conclusive adjective DECISIVE, clinching, convincing, definite, final, irrefutable, ultimate, unanswerable

concoct verb MAKE UP, brew, contrive, devise, formulate, hatch, invent, prepare, think up

concoction noun MIXTURE, blend, brew, combination, compound, creation, preparation

concrete adjective 1 SPECIFIC, definite, explicit 2 REAL, actual, factual, material, sensible, substantial, tangible

concur verb AGREE, acquiesce, assent, consent

condemn verb 1 DISAPPROVE, blame, censure, damn, denounce, reproach, reprove, upbraid 2 SENTENCE, convict, damn, doom, pass sentence on

condemnation noun 1 DISAPPROVAL, blame, censure, denunciation, reproach, reproof, stricture 2 SENTENCE, conviction, damnation, doom, judgment

condensation noun 1 DISTILLATION, liquefaction, precipitate, precipitation 2 ABRIDGMENT, contraction, digest, précis, synopsis **3** <u>CONCENTRATION</u>, compression, consolidation, crystallization, curtailment, reduction

condense *verb* **1** <u>ABRIDGE</u>, abbreviate, compress, concentrate, epitomize, shorten, summarize **2** <u>CONCENTRATE</u>, boil down, reduce, thicken

condensed *adjective* **1** <u>ABRIDGED</u>, compressed, concentrated, shortened, shrunken, slimmed-down, summarized **2** <u>CONCENTRATED</u>, boiled down, reduced, thickened

condescend *verb* **1** <u>PATRONIZE</u>, talk down to **2** <u>LOWER ONESELF</u>, bend, deign, humble *or* demean oneself, see fit, stoop

condescending *adjective* <u>PATRONIZING</u>, disdainful, lofty, lordly, snobbish, snooty (*informal*), supercilious, superior, toffee-nosed (*slang, chiefly Brit.*)

condition *noun* **1** <u>STATE</u>, circumstances, lie of the land, position, shape, situation, state of affairs **2** <u>REQUIREMENT</u>, limitation, prerequisite, proviso, qualification, restriction, rider, stipulation, terms **3** <u>HEALTH</u>, fettle, fitness, kilter, order, shape, state of health, trim **4** <u>AILMENT</u>, complaint, infirmity, malady, problem, weakness ♦ *verb* **5** <u>ACCUSTOM</u>, adapt, equip, prepare, ready, tone up, train, work out

conditional *adjective* <u>DEPENDENT</u>, contingent, limited, provisional, qualified, subject to, with reservations

conditions *plural noun* <u>CIRCUMSTANCES</u>, environment, milieu, situation, surroundings, way of life

condone *verb* <u>OVERLOOK</u>, excuse, forgive, let pass, look the other way, make allowance for, pardon, turn a blind eye to

conduct *noun* **1** <u>BEHAVIOUR</u>, attitude, bearing, demeanour, deportment, manners, ways **2** <u>MANAGEMENT</u>, administration, control, direction, guidance, handling, organization, running, supervision ♦ *verb* **3** <u>CARRY OUT</u>, administer, control, direct, handle, manage, organize, preside over, run, supervise **4** <u>BEHAVE</u>, acquit, act, carry, comport, deport **5** <u>ACCOMPANY</u>, convey, escort, guide, lead, steer, usher

confederacy *noun* <u>UNION</u>, alliance, coalition, confederation, federation, league

confer *verb* **1** <u>DISCUSS</u>, consult, converse, deliberate, discourse, talk **2** <u>GRANT</u>, accord, award, bestow, give, hand out, present

conference *noun* <u>MEETING</u>, colloquium, congress, consultation, convention, discussion, forum, seminar, symposium

confess *verb* **1** <u>ADMIT</u>, acknowledge, come clean (*informal*), concede, confide, disclose, divulge, own up **2** <u>DECLARE</u>, affirm, assert, confirm, profess, reveal

confession *noun* <u>ADMISSION</u>, acknowledgment, disclosure, exposure, revelation, unbosoming

confidant, confidante *noun* <u>CLOSE FRIEND</u>, alter ego, bosom friend, crony, familiar, intimate

confide *verb* **1** <u>TELL</u>, admit, confess, disclose, divulge, impart, reveal, whisper **2** *Formal* <u>ENTRUST</u>, commend, commit, consign

confidence *noun* **1** <u>TRUST</u>, belief, credence, dependence, faith, reliance **2** <u>SELF-ASSURANCE</u>, aplomb, assurance, boldness, courage, firmness, nerve, self-possession **3 in confidence** <u>IN SECRECY</u>, between you and me (and the gatepost), confidentially, privately

confident adjective 1 <u>CERTAIN</u>, convinced, counting on, positive, satisfied, secure, sure 2 <u>SELF-ASSURED</u>, assured, bold, dauntless, fearless, self-reliant

confidential adjective <u>SECRET</u>, classified, hush-hush (informal), intimate, off the record, private, privy

confidentially adverb <u>IN SECRET</u>, behind closed doors, between ourselves, in camera, in confidence, personally, privately, sub rosa

confine verb <u>RESTRICT</u>, cage, enclose, hem in, hold back, imprison, incarcerate, intern, keep, limit, shut up

confinement noun 1 <u>IMPRISONMENT</u>, custody, detention, incarceration, internment, porridge (slang) 2 <u>CHILDBIRTH</u>, childbed, labour, lying-in, parturition

confines plural noun <u>LIMITS</u>, boundaries, bounds, circumference, edge, precincts

confirm verb 1 <u>PROVE</u>, authenticate, bear out, corroborate, endorse, ratify, substantiate, validate, verify 2 <u>STRENGTHEN</u>, buttress, establish, fix, fortify, reinforce

confirmation noun 1 <u>PROOF</u>, authentication, corroboration, evidence, substantiation, testimony, validation, verification 2 <u>SANCTION</u>, acceptance, agreement, approval, assent, endorsement, ratification

confirmed adjective <u>LONG-ESTABLISHED</u>, chronic, dyed-in-the-wool, habitual, hardened, ingrained, inveterate, seasoned

confiscate verb <u>SEIZE</u>, appropriate, commandeer, impound, sequester, sequestrate

confiscation noun <u>SEIZURE</u>, appropriation, forfeiture, impounding, sequestration, takeover

conflict noun 1 <u>OPPOSITION</u>, antagonism, difference, disagreement, discord, dissension, friction, hostility, strife 2 <u>BATTLE</u>, clash, combat, contest, encounter, fight, strife, war ◆ verb 3 <u>BE INCOMPATIBLE</u>, be at variance, clash, collide, differ, disagree, interfere

conflicting adjective <u>INCOMPATIBLE</u>, antagonistic, clashing, contradictory, contrary, discordant, inconsistent, opposing, paradoxical

conform verb 1 <u>COMPLY</u>, adapt, adjust, fall in with, follow, obey, toe the line 2 <u>AGREE</u>, accord, correspond, harmonize, match, suit, tally

conformist noun <u>TRADITIONALIST</u>, stick-in-the-mud (informal), yes man

conformity noun <u>COMPLIANCE</u>, conventionality, observance, orthodoxy, traditionalism

confound verb <u>BEWILDER</u>, astound, baffle, confuse, dumbfound, flummox, mystify, nonplus, perplex

confront verb <u>FACE</u>, accost, challenge, defy, encounter, oppose, stand up to, tackle

confrontation noun <u>CONFLICT</u>, contest, encounter, fight, head-to-head, set-to (informal), showdown (informal)

confuse verb 1 <u>MIX UP</u>, disarrange, disorder, jumble, mingle, muddle, ravel 2 <u>BEWILDER</u>, baffle, bemuse, faze, flummox, mystify, nonplus, perplex, puzzle 3 <u>DISCONCERT</u>, discompose, disorient, fluster, rattle (informal), throw off balance, unnerve, upset

confused *adjective* 1 BEWILDERED, at sea, baffled, disorientated, flummoxed, muddled, nonplussed, perplexed, puzzled, taken aback 2 DISORDERED, chaotic, disorganized, higgledy-piggledy (*informal*), in disarray, jumbled, mixed up, topsy-turvy, untidy

confusing *adjective* BEWILDERING, baffling, contradictory, disconcerting, misleading, perplexing, puzzling, unclear

confusion *noun* 1 BEWILDERMENT, disorientation, mystification, perplexity, puzzlement 2 DISORDER, chaos, commotion, jumble, mess, muddle, shambles, turmoil, untidiness, upheaval

congenial *adjective* 1 PLEASANT, affable, agreeable, companionable, favourable, friendly, genial, kindly 2 COMPATIBLE, kindred, like-minded, sympathetic, well-suited

congenital *adjective* INBORN, immanent, inbred, inherent, innate, natural

congested *adjective* 1 OVERCROWDED, crowded, teeming 2 CLOGGED, blocked-up, crammed, jammed, overfilled, overflowing, packed, stuffed

congestion *noun* 1 OVERCROWDING, crowding 2 CLOGGING, bottleneck, jam, surfeit

congratulate *verb* COMPLIMENT, pat on the back, wish joy to

congratulations *plural noun, interjection* GOOD WISHES, best wishes, compliments, felicitations, greetings

congregate *verb* COME TOGETHER, assemble, collect, convene, converge, flock, gather, mass, meet

congregation *noun* ASSEMBLY, brethren, crowd, fellowship, flock, multitude, throng

congress *noun* MEETING, assembly, conclave, conference, convention, council, legislature, parliament

conjecture *noun* 1 GUESS, hypothesis, shot in the dark, speculation, supposition, surmise, theory ♦ *verb* 2 GUESS, hypothesize, imagine, speculate, suppose, surmise, theorize

conjugal *adjective* MARITAL, bridal, connubial, married, matrimonial, nuptial, wedded

conjure *verb* PERFORM TRICKS, juggle

conjure up *verb* BRING TO MIND, contrive, create, evoke, produce as if by magic, recall, recollect

conjuror, conjurer *noun* MAGICIAN, illusionist, sorcerer, wizard

connect *verb* LINK, affix, attach, couple, fasten, join, unite

connected *adjective* LINKED, affiliated, akin, allied, associated, combined, coupled, joined, related, united

connection *noun* 1 ASSOCIATION, affinity, bond, liaison, link, relationship, relevance, tie-in 2 LINK, alliance, association, attachment, coupling, fastening, junction, tie, union 3 CONTACT, acquaintance, ally, associate, friend, sponsor

connivance *noun* COLLUSION, abetting, complicity, conspiring, tacit consent

connive *verb* 1 CONSPIRE, collude, cook up (*informal*), intrigue, plot, scheme 2 **connive at** TURN A BLIND EYE TO, abet, disregard, let pass, look the other way, overlook, wink at

connoisseur *noun* EXPERT, aficionado, appreciator, authority, buff (*informal*), devotee, judge

conquer *verb* 1 DEFEAT, beat, crush,

get the better of, master, overcome, overpower, overthrow, quell, subjugate, vanquish **2** SEIZE, acquire, annex, obtain, occupy, overrun, win

conqueror noun WINNER, conquistador, defeater, master, subjugator, vanquisher, victor

conquest noun **1** DEFEAT, mastery, overthrow, rout, triumph, victory **2** TAKEOVER, annexation, coup, invasion, occupation, subjugation

conscience noun PRINCIPLES, moral sense, scruples, sense of right and wrong, still small voice

conscientious adjective THOROUGH, careful, diligent, exact, faithful, meticulous, painstaking, particular, punctilious

conscious adjective **1** AWARE, alert, alive to, awake, responsive, sensible, sentient **2** DELIBERATE, calculated, intentional, knowing, premeditated, self-conscious, studied, wilful

consciousness noun AWARENESS, apprehension, knowledge, realization, recognition, sensibility

consecrate verb SANCTIFY, dedicate, devote, hallow, ordain, set apart, venerate

consecutive adjective SUCCESSIVE, in sequence, in turn, running, sequential, succeeding, uninterrupted

consensus noun AGREEMENT, assent, common consent, concord, general agreement, harmony, unanimity, unity

consent noun **1** AGREEMENT, acquiescence, approval, assent, compliance, go-ahead (*informal*), O.K. *or* okay (*informal*), permission, sanction ♦ verb **2** AGREE, acquiesce, allow, approve, assent, concur, permit

consequence noun **1** RESULT, effect,

end result, issue, outcome, repercussion, sequel, upshot **2** IMPORTANCE, account, concern, import, moment, significance, value, weight

consequent adjective FOLLOWING, ensuing, resultant, resulting, subsequent, successive

consequently adverb AS A RESULT, accordingly, ergo, hence, subsequently, therefore, thus

conservation noun PROTECTION, guardianship, husbandry, maintenance, preservation, safeguarding, safekeeping, saving, upkeep

conservative adjective **1** TRADITIONAL, cautious, conventional, die-hard, hidebound, reactionary, sober ♦ noun **2** TRADITIONALIST, reactionary, stick-in-the-mud (*informal*)

Conservative adjective **1** TORY, right-wing ♦ noun **2** TORY, right-winger

conserve verb PROTECT, hoard, husband, keep, nurse, preserve, save, store up, take care of, use sparingly

consider verb **1** THINK, believe, deem, hold to be, judge, rate, regard as **2** THINK ABOUT, cogitate, contemplate, deliberate, meditate, ponder, reflect, ruminate, turn over in one's mind, weigh **3** BEAR IN MIND, keep in view, make allowance for, reckon with, remember, respect, take into account

considerable adjective LARGE, appreciable, goodly, great, marked, noticeable, plentiful, sizable *or* sizeable, substantial

considerably adverb GREATLY, appreciably, markedly, noticeably, remarkably, significantly, substantially, very much

considerate adjective THOUGHTFUL, attentive, concerned, kindly, mindful, obliging, patient, tactful, unselfish

consideration noun 1 THOUGHT, analysis, deliberation, discussion, examination, reflection, review, scrutiny 2 FACTOR, concern, issue, point 3 THOUGHTFULNESS, concern, considerateness, kindness, respect, tact 4 PAYMENT, fee, recompense, remuneration, reward, tip

considering preposition TAKING INTO ACCOUNT, in the light of, in view of

consignment noun SHIPMENT, batch, delivery, goods

consist verb 1 **consist of** BE MADE UP OF, amount to, be composed of, comprise, contain, embody, include, incorporate, involve 2 **consist in** LIE IN, be expressed by, be found or contained in, inhere in, reside in

consistency noun 1 TEXTURE, compactness, density, firmness, thickness, viscosity 2 CONSTANCY, evenness, regularity, steadfastness, steadiness, uniformity

consistent adjective 1 UNCHANGING, constant, dependable, persistent, regular, steady, true to type, undeviating 2 AGREEING, coherent, compatible, congruous, consonant, harmonious, logical

consolation noun COMFORT, cheer, encouragement, help, relief, solace, succour, support

console verb COMFORT, calm, cheer, encourage, express sympathy for, soothe

consolidate verb 1 STRENGTHEN, fortify, reinforce, secure, stabilize 2 COMBINE, amalgamate, federate, fuse, join, unite

consort verb 1 ASSOCIATE, fraternize, go around with, hang about, around or out with, keep company, mix ♦ noun 2 SPOUSE, companion, husband, partner, wife

conspicuous adjective 1 OBVIOUS, blatant, clear, evident, noticeable, patent, salient 2 NOTEWORTHY, illustrious, notable, outstanding, prominent, remarkable, salient, signal, striking

conspiracy noun PLOT, collusion, intrigue, machination, scheme, treason

conspirator noun PLOTTER, conspirer, intriguer, schemer, traitor

conspire verb 1 PLOT, contrive, intrigue, machinate, manoeuvre, plan, scheme 2 WORK TOGETHER, combine, concur, contribute, cooperate, tend

constant adjective 1 CONTINUOUS, ceaseless, incessant, interminable, nonstop, perpetual, sustained, unrelenting 2 UNCHANGING, even, fixed, invariable, permanent, stable, steady, uniform, unvarying 3 FAITHFUL, devoted, loyal, stalwart, staunch, true, trustworthy, trusty

constantly adverb CONTINUOUSLY, all the time, always, continually, endlessly, incessantly, interminably, invariably, nonstop, perpetually

consternation noun DISMAY, alarm, anxiety, distress, dread, fear, trepidation

constituent noun 1 VOTER, elector 2 COMPONENT, element, factor, ingredient, part, unit ♦ adjective 3 COMPONENT, basic, elemental, essential, integral

constitute verb MAKE UP, compose, comprise, establish, form, found, set up

constitution noun 1 HEALTH, build, character, disposition, physique 2 STRUCTURE, composition, form, make-up, nature

constitutional adjective 1 STATUTORY, chartered, vested ♦ noun 2 WALK, airing, stroll, turn

constrain verb 1 FORCE, bind, coerce, compel, impel, necessitate, oblige, pressurize 2 RESTRICT, check, confine, constrict, curb, restrain, straiten

constraint noun 1 RESTRICTION, check, curb, deterrent, hindrance, limitation, rein 2 FORCE, coercion, compulsion, necessity, pressure, restraint

construct verb BUILD, assemble, compose, create, fashion, form, make, manufacture, put together, shape

construction noun 1 BUILDING, composition, creation, edifice 2 Formal INTERPRETATION, explanation, inference, reading, rendering

constructive adjective HELPFUL, positive, practical, productive, useful, valuable

consult verb ASK, compare notes, confer, pick (someone's) brains, question, refer to, take counsel, turn to

consultant noun SPECIALIST, adviser, authority

consultation noun SEMINAR, appointment, conference, council, deliberation, dialogue, discussion, examination, hearing, interview, meeting, session

consume verb 1 EAT, devour, eat up, gobble (up), put away, swallow 2 USE UP, absorb, dissipate, exhaust, expend, spend, squander, waste 3 DESTROY, annihilate, demolish, devastate, lay waste, ravage 4 often passive OBSESS, absorb, dominate, eat up, engross, monopolize, preoccupy

consumer noun BUYER, customer, purchaser, shopper, user

consummate verb 1 COMPLETE, accomplish, conclude, crown, end, finish, fulfil ♦ adjective 2 SKILLED, accomplished, matchless, perfect, polished, practised, superb, supreme 3 COMPLETE, absolute, conspicuous, extreme, supreme, total, utter

consumption noun 1 USING UP, depletion, diminution, dissipation, exhaustion, expenditure, loss, waste 2 Old-fashioned TUBERCULOSIS, T.B.

contact noun 1 COMMUNICATION, association, connection 2 TOUCH, contiguity 3 ACQUAINTANCE, connection ♦ verb 4 GET or BE IN TOUCH WITH, approach, call, communicate with, reach, speak to, write to

contagious adjective INFECTIOUS, catching, communicable, spreading, transmissible

contain verb 1 HOLD, accommodate, enclose, have capacity for, incorporate, seat 2 INCLUDE, comprehend, comprise, consist of, embody, embrace, involve 3 RESTRAIN, control, curb, hold back, hold in, keep a tight rein on, repress, stifle

container noun HOLDER, receptacle, repository, vessel

contaminate verb POLLUTE, adulterate, befoul, corrupt, defile, infect, stain, taint, tarnish

contamination noun POLLUTION, contagion, corruption, defilement, impurity, infection, poisoning, taint

contemplate verb 1 THINK ABOUT, consider, deliberate, meditate, muse over, ponder, reflect upon, ruminate (upon) **2** CONSIDER, envisage, expect, foresee, intend, plan, think of **3** LOOK AT, examine, eye up, gaze at, inspect, regard, stare at, study, survey, view

contemporary *adjective*
1 COEXISTING, concurrent, contemporaneous **2** MODERN, à la mode, current, newfangled, present, present-day, recent, up-to-date ♦ *noun* **3** PEER, fellow

contempt *noun* SCORN, derision, disdain, disregard, disrespect, mockery, neglect, slight

contemptible *adjective* DESPICABLE, detestable, ignominious, measly, paltry, pitiful, shameful, worthless

contemptuous *adjective* SCORNFUL, arrogant, condescending, derisive, disdainful, haughty, sneering, supercilious, withering

contend *verb* **1** COMPETE, clash, contest, fight, jostle, strive, struggle, vie **2** ARGUE, affirm, allege, assert, dispute, hold, maintain

content[1] *noun* **1** MEANING, essence, gist, significance, substance **2** AMOUNT, capacity, load, measure, size, volume

content[2] *adjective* **1** SATISFIED, agreeable, at ease, comfortable, contented, fulfilled, willing to accept ♦ *verb* **2** SATISFY, appease, humour, indulge, mollify, placate, please ♦ *noun* **3** SATISFACTION, comfort, contentment, ease, gratification, peace of mind, pleasure

contented *adjective* SATISFIED, comfortable, content, glad, gratified, happy, pleased, serene, thankful

contentious *adjective* ARGUMENTATIVE, bickering, captious, cavilling, disputatious, quarrelsome, querulous, wrangling

contentment *noun* SATISFACTION, comfort, content, ease, equanimity, fulfilment, happiness, peace, pleasure, serenity

contents *plural noun* CONSTITUENTS, elements, ingredients, load

contest *noun* **1** COMPETITION, game, match, tournament, trial **2** STRUGGLE, battle, combat, conflict, controversy, dispute, fight ♦ *verb* **3** DISPUTE, argue, call in *or* into question, challenge, debate, doubt, object to, oppose, question **4** COMPETE, contend, fight, strive, vie

contestant *noun* COMPETITOR, candidate, contender, entrant, participant, player

context *noun* **1** CIRCUMSTANCES, ambience, conditions, situation **2** FRAME OF REFERENCE, background, connection, framework, relation

contingency *noun* POSSIBILITY, accident, chance, emergency, event, eventuality, happening, incident

continual *adjective* CONSTANT, frequent, incessant, interminable, recurrent, regular, repeated, unremitting

continually *adverb* CONSTANTLY, all the time, always, forever, incessantly, interminably, nonstop, persistently, repeatedly

continuation *noun* **1** CONTINUING, perpetuation, prolongation, resumption **2** ADDITION, extension, furtherance, postscript, sequel, supplement

continue *verb* **1** REMAIN, abide, carry on, endure, last, live on, persist, stay, survive **2** KEEP ON, carry on, go on, maintain, persevere, persist in, stick at, sustain **3** RESUME, carry on, pick up where one left off, proceed, recommence, return to, take up

continuing adjective LASTING, enduring, in progress, ongoing, sustained

continuity noun SEQUENCE, cohesion, connection, flow, progression, succession

continuous adjective CONSTANT, extended, prolonged, unbroken, unceasing, undivided, uninterrupted

contraband noun 1 SMUGGLING, black-marketing, bootlegging, trafficking ♦ adjective 2 SMUGGLED, banned, bootleg, forbidden, hot (informal), illegal, illicit, prohibited, unlawful

contract noun 1 AGREEMENT, arrangement, bargain, commitment, covenant, pact, settlement ♦ verb 2 AGREE, bargain, come to terms, commit oneself, covenant, negotiate, pledge 3 SHORTEN, abbreviate, curtail, diminish, dwindle, lessen, narrow, reduce, shrink, shrivel 4 CATCH, acquire, be afflicted with, develop, get, go down with, incur

contraction noun SHORTENING, abbreviation, compression, narrowing, reduction, shrinkage, shrivelling, tightening

contradict verb DENY, be at variance with, belie, challenge, controvert, fly in the face of, negate, rebut

contradiction noun DENIAL, conflict, contravention, incongruity, inconsistency, negation, opposite

contradictory adjective INCONSISTENT, conflicting, contrary, incompatible, opposed, opposite, paradoxical

contraption noun Informal DEVICE, apparatus, contrivance, gadget, instrument, mechanism

contrary noun 1 OPPOSITE,

antithesis, converse, reverse ♦ adjective 2 OPPOSED, adverse, clashing, contradictory, counter, discordant, hostile, inconsistent, opposite, paradoxical 3 PERVERSE, awkward, cantankerous, difficult, disobliging, intractable, obstinate, stroppy (Brit. slang), unaccommodating

contrast noun 1 DIFFERENCE, comparison, disparity, dissimilarity, distinction, divergence, foil, opposition ♦ verb 2 DIFFERENTIATE, compare, differ, distinguish, oppose, set in opposition, set off

contribute verb 1 GIVE, add, bestow, chip in (informal), donate, provide, subscribe, supply 2 **contribute to** BE PARTLY RESPONSIBLE FOR, be conducive to, be instrumental in, help, lead to, tend to

contribution noun GIFT, addition, donation, grant, input, offering, subscription

contributor noun GIVER, donor, patron, subscriber, supporter

contrite adjective SORRY, chastened, conscience-stricken, humble, penitent, regretful, remorseful, repentant, sorrowful

contrivance noun 1 DEVICE, apparatus, appliance, contraption, gadget, implement, instrument, invention, machine, mechanism 2 PLAN, intrigue, machination, plot, ruse, scheme, stratagem, trick

contrive verb 1 BRING ABOUT, arrange, effect, manage, manoeuvre, plan, plot, scheme, succeed 2 DEVISE, concoct, construct, create, design, fabricate, improvise, invent, manufacture

contrived adjective FORCED, artificial, elaborate, laboured, overdone, planned, strained, unnatural

control noun 1 POWER, authority, charge, command, guidance, management, oversight, supervision, supremacy 2 RESTRAINT, brake, check, curb, limitation, regulation ♦ verb 3 HAVE POWER OVER, administer, command, direct, govern, handle, have charge of, manage, manipulate, supervise 4 RESTRAIN, check, constrain, contain, curb, hold back, limit, repress, subdue

controls plural noun INSTRUMENTS, console, control panel, dash, dashboard, dials

controversial adjective DISPUTED, at issue, contentious, debatable, disputable, open to question, under discussion

controversy noun ARGUMENT, altercation, debate, dispute, quarrel, row, squabble, wrangling

convalescence noun RECOVERY, improvement, recuperation, rehabilitation, return to health

convalescent adjective RECOVERING, getting better, improving, mending, on the mend, recuperating

convene verb GATHER, assemble, bring together, call, come together, congregate, convoke, meet, summon

convenience noun 1 AVAILABILITY, accessibility, advantage, appropriateness, benefit, fitness, suitability, usefulness, utility 2 APPLIANCE, amenity, comfort, facility, help, labour-saving device

convenient adjective 1 USEFUL, appropriate, fit, handy, helpful, labour-saving, serviceable, suitable, timely 2 NEARBY, accessible, at hand, available, close at hand, handy, just round the corner, within reach

convention noun 1 CUSTOM, code, etiquette, practice, propriety, protocol, tradition, usage 2 AGREEMENT, bargain, contract, pact, protocol, treaty 3 ASSEMBLY, conference, congress, convocation, council, meeting

conventional adjective 1 ORDINARY, accepted, customary, normal, orthodox, regular, standard, traditional, usual 2 UNORIGINAL, banal, hackneyed, prosaic, routine, run-of-the-mill, stereotyped

converge verb COME TOGETHER, coincide, combine, gather, join, meet, merge

conversation noun TALK, chat, conference, dialogue, discourse, discussion, gossip, tête-à-tête

converse[1] verb TALK, chat, commune, confer, discourse, exchange views

converse[2] noun 1 OPPOSITE, antithesis, contrary, obverse, other side of the coin, reverse ♦ adjective 2 OPPOSITE, contrary, counter, reverse, reversed, transposed

conversion noun 1 CHANGE, metamorphosis, transformation 2 ADAPTATION, alteration, modification, reconstruction, remodelling, reorganization

convert verb 1 CHANGE, alter, transform, transpose, turn 2 ADAPT, apply, customize, modify, remodel, reorganize, restyle, revise 3 REFORM, convince, proselytize ♦ noun 4 NEOPHYTE, disciple, proselyte

convex adjective ROUNDED, bulging, gibbous, protuberant

convey verb 1 COMMUNICATE, disclose, impart, make known, relate, reveal, tell 2 CARRY, bear, bring, conduct, fetch, guide, move, send, transport

convict *verb* 1 FIND GUILTY, condemn, imprison, pronounce guilty, sentence ♦ *noun* 2 PRISONER, criminal, culprit, felon, jailbird, lag (*slang*)

conviction *noun* 1 BELIEF, creed, faith, opinion, persuasion, principle, tenet, view 2 CONFIDENCE, assurance, certainty, certitude, firmness, reliance

convince *verb* PERSUADE, assure, bring round, prevail upon, satisfy, sway, win over

convincing *adjective* PERSUASIVE, cogent, conclusive, credible, impressive, plausible, powerful, telling

convulse *verb* SHAKE, agitate, churn up, derange, disorder, disturb, twist, work

convulsion *noun* SPASM, contraction, cramp, fit, paroxysm, seizure

cool *adjective* 1 COLD, chilled, chilly, nippy, refreshing 2 CALM, collected, composed, relaxed, sedate, self-controlled, self-possessed, unemotional, unruffled 3 UNFRIENDLY, aloof, distant, indifferent, lukewarm, offhand, standoffish, unenthusiastic, unwelcoming ♦ *verb* 4 CHILL, cool off, freeze, lose heat, refrigerate ♦ *noun* 5 *Slang* CALMNESS, composure, control, poise, self-control, self-discipline, self-possession, temper

cooperate *verb* WORK TOGETHER, collaborate, combine, conspire, coordinate, join forces, pool resources, pull together

cooperation *noun* TEAMWORK, collaboration, combined effort, esprit de corps, give-and-take, unity

cooperative *adjective* 1 HELPFUL,

accommodating, obliging, onside (*informal*), responsive, supportive 2 SHARED, collective, combined, joint

coordinate *verb* BRING TOGETHER, harmonize, integrate, match, organize, synchronize, systematize

cope *verb* 1 MANAGE, carry on, get by (*informal*), hold one's own, make the grade, struggle through, survive 2 **cope with** DEAL WITH, contend with, grapple with, handle, struggle with, weather, wrestle with

copious *adjective* ABUNDANT, ample, bountiful, extensive, full, lavish, plentiful, profuse

copy *noun* 1 REPRODUCTION, counterfeit, duplicate, facsimile, forgery, imitation, likeness, model, replica ♦ *verb* 2 REPRODUCE, counterfeit, duplicate, replicate, transcribe 3 IMITATE, ape, emulate, follow, mimic, mirror, repeat

cord *noun* ROPE, line, string, twine

cordial *adjective* WARM, affable, agreeable, cheerful, congenial, friendly, genial, hearty, sociable

cordon *noun* 1 CHAIN, barrier, line, ring ♦ *verb* 2 **cordon off** SURROUND, close off, encircle, enclose, fence off, isolate, picket, separate

core *noun* CENTRE, crux, essence, gist, heart, kernel, nub, nucleus, pith

corner *noun* 1 ANGLE, bend, crook, joint 2 SPACE, hideaway, hide-out, nook, retreat ♦ *verb* 3 TRAP, run to earth 4 *As in* **corner the market** MONOPOLIZE, dominate, engross, hog (*slang*)

corny *adjective Slang* UNORIGINAL, hackneyed, old-fashioned, old hat, stale, stereotyped, trite

corporation *noun* 1 BUSINESS, association, corporate body, society 2 TOWN COUNCIL, civic

authorities, council, municipal
authorities 3 *Informal* <u>PAUNCH</u>, beer
belly (*informal*), middle-age
spread (*informal*), potbelly, spare
tyre (*Brit. slang*), spread (*informal*)

corps *noun* <u>TEAM</u>, band, company,
detachment, division, regiment,
squadron, troop, unit

corpse *noun* <u>BODY</u>, cadaver, carcass,
remains, stiff (*slang*)

correct *adjective* 1 <u>TRUE</u>, accurate,
exact, faultless, flawless, O.K. *or*
okay (*informal*), precise, right
2 <u>PROPER</u>, acceptable, appropriate,
fitting, kosher (*informal*), O.K. *or*
okay (*informal*), seemly, standard
♦ *verb* 3 <u>RECTIFY</u>, adjust, amend,
cure, emend, redress, reform,
remedy, right 4 <u>PUNISH</u>, admonish,
chasten, chastise, chide,
discipline, rebuke, reprimand,
reprove

correction *noun* 1 <u>RECTIFICATION</u>,
adjustment, alteration,
amendment, emendation,
improvement, modification
2 <u>PUNISHMENT</u>, admonition,
castigation, chastisement,
discipline, reformation, reproof

correctly *adverb* <u>RIGHTLY</u>, accurately,
perfectly, precisely, properly, right

correctness *noun* 1 <u>TRUTH</u>,
accuracy, exactitude, exactness,
faultlessness, fidelity, preciseness,
precision, regularity 2 <u>DECORUM</u>,
civility, good breeding, propriety,
seemliness

correspond *verb* 1 <u>BE CONSISTENT</u>,
accord, agree, conform, fit,
harmonize, match, square, tally
2 <u>COMMUNICATE</u>, exchange letters,
keep in touch, write

correspondence *noun* 1 <u>LETTERS</u>,
communication, mail, post,
writing 2 <u>RELATION</u>, agreement,
coincidence, comparison,
conformity, correlation, harmony,
match, similarity

correspondent *noun* 1 <u>LETTER</u>
<u>WRITER</u>, pen friend *or* pal 2 <u>REPORTER</u>,
contributor, journalist

corresponding *adjective* <u>RELATED</u>,
analogous, answering,
complementary, equivalent,
matching, reciprocal, similar

corridor *noun* <u>PASSAGE</u>, aisle, alley,
hallway, passageway

corroborate *verb* <u>SUPPORT</u>,
authenticate, back up, bear out,
confirm, endorse, ratify,
substantiate, validate

corrode *verb* <u>EAT AWAY</u>, consume,
corrupt, erode, gnaw, oxidize,
rust, wear away

corrosive *adjective* <u>CORRODING</u>,
caustic, consuming, erosive,
virulent, vitriolic, wasting, wearing

corrupt *adjective* 1 <u>DISHONEST</u>, bent
(*slang*), bribable, crooked
(*informal*), fraudulent,
unprincipled, unscrupulous, venal
2 <u>DEPRAVED</u>, debased, degenerate,
dissolute, profligate, vicious
3 <u>DISTORTED</u>, altered, doctored,
falsified ♦ *verb* 4 <u>BRIBE</u>, buy off,
entice, fix (*informal*), grease
(someone's) palm (*slang*), lure,
suborn 5 <u>DEPRAVE</u>, debauch,
pervert, subvert 6 <u>DISTORT</u>, doctor,
tamper with

corruption *noun* 1 <u>DISHONESTY</u>,
bribery, extortion, fraud, shady
dealings (*informal*),
unscrupulousness, venality
2 <u>DEPRAVITY</u>, decadence, evil,
immorality, perversion, vice,
wickedness 3 <u>DISTORTION</u>,
doctoring, falsification

corset *noun* <u>GIRDLE</u>, belt, bodice

cosmetic *adjective* <u>BEAUTIFYING</u>,
nonessential, superficial, surface

cosmic *adjective* <u>UNIVERSAL</u>, stellar

cosmopolitan *adjective*
1 <u>SOPHISTICATED</u>, broad-minded,
catholic, open-minded, universal,

urbane, well-travelled, worldly-wise ♦ *noun* 2 MAN *or* WOMAN OF THE WORLD, jet-setter, sophisticate

cost *noun* 1 PRICE, amount, charge, damage (*informal*), expense, outlay, payment, worth 2 LOSS, damage, detriment, expense, harm, hurt, injury, penalty, sacrifice, suffering ♦ *verb* 3 SELL AT, come to, command a price of, set (someone) back (*informal*) 4 LOSE, do disservice to, harm, hurt, injure

costly *adjective* 1 EXPENSIVE, dear, exorbitant, extortionate, highly-priced, steep (*informal*), stiff 2 DAMAGING, catastrophic, deleterious, disastrous, harmful, loss-making, ruinous

costs *plural noun* EXPENSES, budget, outgoings, overheads

costume *noun* OUTFIT, apparel, attire, clothing, dress, ensemble, garb, livery, uniform

cosy *adjective* SNUG, comfortable, comfy (*informal*), homely, intimate, sheltered, tucked up, warm

cottage *noun* CABIN, chalet, hut, lodge, shack

cough *noun* 1 FROG *or* TICKLE IN ONE'S THROAT, bark, hack ♦ *verb* 2 CLEAR ONE'S THROAT, bark, hack

council *noun* GOVERNING BODY, assembly, board, cabinet, committee, conference, congress, convention, panel, parliament

counsel *noun* 1 ADVICE, direction, guidance, information, recommendation, suggestion, warning 2 LEGAL ADVISER, advocate, attorney, barrister, lawyer, solicitor ♦ *verb* 3 ADVISE, advocate, exhort, instruct, recommend, urge, warn

count *verb* 1 ADD (UP), calculate, compute, enumerate, number, reckon, tally, tot up 2 MATTER, be important, carry weight, rate, signify, tell, weigh 3 CONSIDER, deem, judge, look upon, rate, regard, think 4 TAKE INTO ACCOUNT *or* CONSIDERATION, include, number among ♦ *noun* 5 CALCULATION, computation, enumeration, numbering, poll, reckoning, sum, tally

counter *verb* 1 RETALIATE, answer, hit back, meet, oppose, parry, resist, respond, ward off ♦ *adverb* 2 OPPOSITE TO, against, at variance with, contrariwise, conversely, in defiance of, versus

counteract *verb* ACT AGAINST, foil, frustrate, negate, neutralize, offset, resist, thwart

counterbalance *verb* OFFSET, balance, compensate, make up for, set off

counterfeit *adjective* 1 FAKE, bogus, false, forged, imitation, phoney *or* phony (*informal*), sham, simulated ♦ *noun* 2 FAKE, copy, forgery, fraud, imitation, phoney *or* phony (*informal*), reproduction, sham ♦ *verb* 3 FAKE, copy, fabricate, feign, forge, imitate, impersonate, pretend, sham, simulate

countermand *verb* CANCEL, annul, override, repeal, rescind, retract, reverse, revoke

counterpart *noun* OPPOSITE NUMBER, complement, equal, fellow, match, mate, supplement, tally, twin

countless *adjective* INNUMERABLE, endless, immeasurable, incalculable, infinite, legion, limitless, myriad, numberless, untold

count on *or* **upon** *verb* DEPEND ON, bank on, believe (in), lean on, pin one's faith on, reckon on, rely on, take for granted, take on trust, trust

country noun 1 NATION, commonwealth, kingdom, people, realm, state 2 TERRITORY, land, region, terrain 3 PEOPLE, citizens, community, inhabitants, nation, populace, public, society 4 COUNTRYSIDE, backwoods, farmland, green belt, outback (*Austral. & N.Z.*), provinces, sticks (*informal*)

countryside noun COUNTRY, farmland, green belt, outback (*Austral. & N.Z.*), outdoors, sticks (*informal*)

count up verb ADD, reckon up, sum, tally, total

county noun PROVINCE, shire

coup noun MASTERSTROKE, accomplishment, action, deed, exploit, feat, manoeuvre, stunt

couple noun 1 PAIR, brace, duo, two, twosome ♦ verb 2 LINK, connect, hitch, join, marry, pair, unite, wed, yoke

coupon noun SLIP, card, certificate, ticket, token, voucher

courage noun BRAVERY, daring, fearlessness, gallantry, heroism, mettle, nerve, pluck, resolution, valour

courageous adjective BRAVE, bold, daring, fearless, gallant, gritty, intrepid, lion-hearted, stouthearted, valiant

courier noun 1 GUIDE, representative 2 MESSENGER, bearer, carrier, envoy, runner

course noun 1 CLASSES, curriculum, lectures, programme, schedule 2 PROGRESSION, development, flow, movement, order, progress, sequence, unfolding 3 ROUTE, direction, line, passage, path, road, track, trajectory, way 4 RACECOURSE, cinder track, circuit 5 PROCEDURE, behaviour, conduct, manner, method, mode, plan,

policy, programme 6 PERIOD, duration, lapse, passage, passing, sweep, term, time 7 of course NATURALLY, certainly, definitely, indubitably, needless to say, obviously, undoubtedly, without a doubt ♦ verb 8 RUN, flow, gush, race, speed, stream, surge 9 HUNT, chase, follow, pursue

court noun 1 LAW COURT, bar, bench, tribunal 2 COURTYARD, cloister, piazza, plaza, quad (*informal*), quadrangle, square, yard 3 PALACE, hall, manor 4 ROYAL HOUSEHOLD, attendants, cortege, entourage, retinue, suite, train ♦ verb 5 WOO, date, go (out) with, run after, serenade, set one's cap at, take out, walk out with 6 CULTIVATE, curry favour with, fawn upon, flatter, pander to, seek, solicit 7 INVITE, attract, bring about, incite, prompt, provoke, seek

courteous adjective POLITE, affable, attentive, civil, gallant, gracious, refined, respectful, urbane, well-mannered

courtesy noun 1 POLITENESS, affability, civility, courteousness, gallantry, good manners, graciousness, urbanity 2 FAVOUR, indulgence, kindness

courtier noun ATTENDANT, follower, squire

courtly adjective CEREMONIOUS, chivalrous, dignified, elegant, formal, gallant, polished, refined, stately, urbane

courtyard noun YARD, enclosure, quad, quadrangle

cove noun BAY, anchorage, inlet, sound

covenant noun 1 PROMISE, agreement, arrangement, commitment, contract, pact, pledge ♦ verb 2 PROMISE, agree, contract, pledge, stipulate, undertake

cover verb 1 <u>CLOTHE</u>, dress, envelop, put on, wrap 2 <u>OVERLAY</u>, coat, daub, encase, envelop 3 <u>SUBMERGE</u>, engulf, flood, overrun, wash over 4 <u>CONCEAL</u>, cloak, disguise, enshroud, hide, mask, obscure, shroud, veil 5 <u>TRAVEL OVER</u>, cross, pass through or over, traverse 6 <u>PROTECT</u>, defend, guard, shield 7 <u>REPORT</u>, describe, investigate, narrate, relate, tell of, write up ♦ noun 8 <u>COVERING</u>, canopy, case, coating, envelope, jacket, lid, top, wrapper 9 <u>DISGUISE</u>, façade, front, mask, pretext, screen, smoke screen, veil 10 <u>PROTECTION</u>, camouflage, concealment, defence, guard, shelter, shield 11 <u>INSURANCE</u>, compensation, indemnity, protection, reimbursement

covering adjective 1 <u>EXPLANATORY</u>, accompanying, descriptive, introductory ♦ noun 2 <u>COVER</u>, blanket, casing, coating, layer, wrapping

cover-up noun <u>CONCEALMENT</u>, complicity, conspiracy, front, smoke screen, whitewash (informal)

cover up verb <u>CONCEAL</u>, draw a veil over, hide, hush up, suppress, sweep under the carpet, whitewash (informal)

covet verb <u>LONG FOR</u>, aspire to, crave, desire, envy, lust after, set one's heart on, yearn for

covetous adjective <u>ENVIOUS</u>, acquisitive, avaricious, close-fisted, grasping, greedy, jealous, rapacious, yearning

coward noun <u>WIMP</u> (informal), chicken (slang), scaredy-cat (informal), yellow-belly (slang)

cowardice noun <u>FAINT-HEARTEDNESS</u>, fearfulness, spinelessness, weakness

cowardly adjective <u>FAINT-HEARTED</u>, chicken (slang), craven, fearful, scared, soft, spineless, timorous, weak, yellow (informal)

cowboy noun <u>COWHAND</u>, cattleman, drover, gaucho (S. American), herdsman, rancher, stockman

cower verb <u>CRINGE</u>, draw back, flinch, grovel, quail, shrink, tremble

coy adjective <u>SHY</u>, bashful, demure, modest, reserved, retiring, shrinking, timid

crack verb 1 <u>BREAK</u>, burst, cleave, fracture, snap, splinter, split 2 <u>SNAP</u>, burst, crash, detonate, explode, pop, ring 3 <u>GIVE IN</u>, break down, collapse, give way, go to pieces, lose control, succumb, yield 4 Informal <u>HIT</u>, clip (informal), clout (informal), cuff, slap, smack, whack 5 <u>SOLVE</u>, decipher, fathom, get the answer to, work out ♦ noun 6 <u>SNAP</u>, burst, clap, crash, explosion, pop, report 7 <u>BREAK</u>, chink, cleft, cranny, crevice, fissure, fracture, gap, rift 8 Informal <u>BLOW</u>, clip (informal), clout (informal), cuff, slap, smack, whack 9 Informal <u>JOKE</u>, dig, funny remark, gag (informal), jibe, quip, wisecrack, witticism ♦ adjective 10 Slang <u>FIRST-CLASS</u>, ace, choice, elite, excellent, first-rate, hand-picked, superior, world-class

crackdown noun <u>SUPPRESSION</u>, clampdown, crushing, repression

cracked adjective <u>BROKEN</u>, chipped, damaged, defective, faulty, flawed, imperfect, split

cradle noun 1 <u>CRIB</u>, bassinet, cot, Moses basket 2 <u>BIRTHPLACE</u>, beginning, fount, fountainhead, origin, source, spring, wellspring ♦ verb 3 <u>HOLD</u>, lull, nestle, nurse, rock, support

craft noun 1 <u>OCCUPATION</u>, business, employment, handicraft, pursuit, trade, vocation, work 2 <u>SKILL</u>, ability, aptitude, art, artistry, expertise, ingenuity, know-how (*informal*), technique, workmanship 3 <u>VESSEL</u>, aircraft, boat, plane, ship, spacecraft

craftsman *noun* <u>SKILLED WORKER</u>, artisan, maker, master, smith, technician, wright

craftsmanship *noun* <u>WORKMANSHIP</u>, artistry, expertise, mastery, technique

crafty *adjective* <u>CUNNING</u>, artful, calculating, devious, sharp, shrewd, sly, subtle, wily

crag *noun* <u>ROCK</u>, bluff, peak, pinnacle, tor

cram *verb* 1 <u>STUFF</u>, compress, force, jam, pack in, press, shove, squeeze 2 <u>OVEREAT</u>, glut, gorge, satiate, stuff 3 <u>STUDY</u>, bone up (*informal*), mug up (*slang*), revise, swot

cramp[1] *noun* <u>SPASM</u>, ache, contraction, convulsion, pain, pang, stitch, twinge

cramp[2] *verb* <u>RESTRICT</u>, constrain, hamper, handicap, hinder, impede, inhibit, obstruct

cramped *adjective* <u>CLOSED IN</u>, confined, congested, crowded, hemmed in, overcrowded, packed, uncomfortable

cranny *noun* <u>CREVICE</u>, chink, cleft, crack, fissure, gap, hole, opening

crash *noun* 1 <u>COLLISION</u>, accident, bump, pile-up (*informal*), prang (*informal*), smash, wreck 2 <u>SMASH</u>, bang, boom, clang, clash, clatter, din, racket, thunder 3 <u>COLLAPSE</u>, debacle, depression, downfall, failure, ruin ♦ *verb* 4 <u>COLLIDE</u>, bump (into), crash-land (*an aircraft*), drive into, have an accident, hit, plough into, wreck 5 <u>COLLAPSE</u>, be ruined, fail, fold, fold up, go belly up (*informal*), go bust (*informal*), go to the wall, go under 6 <u>HURTLE</u>,

fall headlong, give way, lurch, overbalance, plunge, topple

crass *adjective* <u>INSENSITIVE</u>, boorish, gross, indelicate, oafish, stupid, unrefined, witless

crate *noun* <u>CONTAINER</u>, box, case, packing case, tea chest

crater *noun* <u>HOLLOW</u>, depression, dip

crave *verb* 1 <u>LONG FOR</u>, desire, hanker after, hope for, lust after, want, yearn for 2 *Informal* <u>BEG</u>, ask, beseech, entreat, implore, petition, plead for, pray for, seek, solicit, supplicate

craving *noun* <u>LONGING</u>, appetite, desire, hankering, hope, hunger, thirst, yearning, yen (*informal*)

crawl *verb* 1 <u>CREEP</u>, advance slowly, inch, slither, worm one's way, wriggle, writhe 2 <u>GROVEL</u>, creep, fawn, humble oneself, toady 3 <u>BE FULL OF</u>, be alive, be overrun (*slang*), swarm, teem

craze *noun* <u>FAD</u>, enthusiasm, fashion, infatuation, mania, rage, trend, vogue

crazy *adjective* 1 *Informal* <u>RIDICULOUS</u>, absurd, foolish, idiotic, ill-conceived, ludicrous, nonsensical, preposterous, senseless 2 <u>FANATICAL</u>, devoted, enthusiastic, infatuated, mad, passionate, wild (*informal*) 3 <u>INSANE</u>, crazed, demented, deranged, mad, nuts (*slang*), out of one's mind, unbalanced

creak *verb* <u>SQUEAK</u>, grate, grind, groan, scrape, scratch, screech

cream *noun* 1 <u>LOTION</u>, cosmetic, emulsion, essence, liniment, oil, ointment, paste, salve, unguent 2 <u>BEST</u>, crème de la crème, elite, flower, pick, prime ♦ *adjective* 3 <u>OFF-WHITE</u>, yellowish-white

creamy *adjective* <u>SMOOTH</u>, buttery, milky, rich, soft, velvety

crease noun **1** LINE, corrugation, fold, groove, ridge, wrinkle ♦ *verb* **2** WRINKLE, corrugate, crumple, double up, fold, rumple, screw up

create *verb* **1** MAKE, compose, devise, formulate, invent, originate, produce, spawn **2** CAUSE, bring about, lead to, occasion **3** APPOINT, constitute, establish, install, invest, make, set up

creation noun **1** MAKING, conception, formation, generation, genesis, procreation **2** SETTING UP, development, establishment, formation, foundation, inception, institution, production **3** INVENTION, achievement, brainchild (*informal*), concoction, handiwork, magnum opus, *pièce de résistance*, production **4** UNIVERSE, cosmos, nature, world

creative *adjective* IMAGINATIVE, artistic, clever, gifted, ingenious, inspired, inventive, original, visionary

creativity noun IMAGINATION, cleverness, ingenuity, inspiration, inventiveness, originality

creator noun MAKER, architect, author, designer, father, inventor, originator, prime mover

creature noun **1** LIVING THING, animal, beast, being, brute **2** PERSON, human being, individual, man, mortal, soul, woman

credentials *plural noun* CERTIFICATION, authorization, document, licence, papers, passport, reference(s), testimonial

credibility noun BELIEVABILITY, integrity, plausibility, reliability, trustworthiness

credible *adjective* **1** BELIEVABLE, conceivable, imaginable, likely, plausible, possible, probable, reasonable, thinkable **2** RELIABLE,

dependable, honest, sincere, trustworthy, trusty

credit noun **1** PRAISE, acclaim, acknowledgment, approval, commendation, honour, kudos, recognition, tribute **2** *As in* **be a credit to** SOURCE OF SATISFACTION *or* PRIDE, feather in one's cap, honour **3** PRESTIGE, esteem, good name, influence, position, regard, reputation, repute, standing, status **4** BELIEF, confidence, credence, faith, reliance, trust **5 on credit** ON ACCOUNT, by deferred payment, by instalments, on hire-purchase, on (the) H.P., on the slate (*informal*), on tick (*informal*) ♦ *verb* **6** BELIEVE, accept, have faith in, rely on, trust **7 credit with** ATTRIBUTE TO, ascribe to, assign to, impute to

creditable *adjective* PRAISEWORTHY, admirable, commendable, honourable, laudable, reputable, respectable, worthy

credulity noun GULLIBILITY, blind faith, credulousness, naïveté

creed noun BELIEF, articles of faith, catechism, credo, doctrine, dogma, principles

creek noun **1** INLET, bay, bight, cove, firth *or* frith (*Scot.*) **2** *U.S., Canad., Austral., & N.Z.* STREAM, bayou, brook, rivulet, runnel, tributary, watercourse

creep *verb* **1** SNEAK, approach unnoticed, skulk, slink, steal, tiptoe **2** CRAWL, glide, slither, squirm, wriggle, writhe ♦ *noun* **3** *Slang* BOOTLICKER (*informal*), crawler (*slang*), sneak, sycophant, toady

creeper noun CLIMBING PLANT, rambler, runner, trailing plant, vine (*chiefly U.S.*)

creeps *plural noun* **give one the creeps** *Informal* DISGUST, frighten, make one's hair stand on end, make one squirm, repel, repulse, scare

creepy *adjective Informal* DISTURBING, eerie, frightening, hair-raising, macabre, menacing, scary (*informal*), sinister

crescent *noun* MENISCUS, new moon, sickle

crest *noun* 1 TOP, apex, crown, highest point, peak, pinnacle, ridge, summit 2 TUFT, comb, crown, mane, plume 3 EMBLEM, badge, bearings, device, insignia, symbol

crestfallen *adjective* DISAPPOINTED, dejected, depressed, despondent, discouraged, disheartened, downcast, downhearted

crevice *noun* GAP, chink, cleft, crack, cranny, fissure, hole, opening, slit

crew *noun* 1 (SHIP'S) COMPANY, hands, (ship's) complement 2 TEAM, corps, gang, posse, squad 3 *Informal* CROWD, band, bunch (*informal*), gang, horde, mob, pack, set

crib *noun* 1 *Informal* TRANSLATION, key 2 CRADLE, bassinet, bed, cot 3 MANGER, rack, stall ◆ *verb* 4 *Informal* COPY, cheat, pirate, plagiarize, purloin, steal

crime *noun* 1 OFFENCE, felony, misdeed, misdemeanour, transgression, trespass, unlawful act, violation 2 LAWBREAKING, corruption, illegality, misconduct, vice, wrongdoing

criminal *noun* 1 LAWBREAKER, convict, crook (*informal*), culprit, felon, offender, sinner, villain ◆ *adjective* 2 UNLAWFUL, corrupt, crooked (*informal*), illegal, illicit, immoral, lawless, wicked, wrong 3 *Informal* DISGRACEFUL, deplorable, foolish, preposterous, ridiculous, scandalous, senseless

cringe *verb* 1 SHRINK, cower, draw back, flinch, recoil, shy, wince 2 GROVEL, bootlick (*informal*), crawl, creep, fawn, kowtow, pander to, toady

cripple *verb* 1 DISABLE, hamstring, incapacitate, lame, maim, paralyse, weaken 2 DAMAGE, destroy, impair, put out of action, put paid to, ruin, spoil

crippled *adjective* DISABLED, handicapped, incapacitated, laid up (*informal*), lame, paralysed

crisis *noun* 1 CRITICAL POINT, climax, crunch (*informal*), crux, culmination, height, moment of truth, turning point 2 EMERGENCY, deep water, dire straits, meltdown (*informal*), panic stations (*informal*), plight, predicament, trouble

crisp *adjective* 1 CRUNCHY, brittle, crispy, crumbly, firm, fresh 2 CLEAN, neat, smart, spruce, tidy, trim, well-groomed, well-pressed 3 BRACING, brisk, fresh, invigorating, refreshing

criterion *noun* STANDARD, bench mark, gauge, measure, principle, rule, test, touchstone, yardstick

critic *noun* 1 JUDGE, analyst, authority, commentator, connoisseur, expert, pundit, reviewer 2 FAULT-FINDER, attacker, detractor, knocker (*informal*)

critical *adjective* 1 CRUCIAL, all-important, decisive, pivotal, precarious, pressing, serious, urgent, vital 2 DISPARAGING, captious, censorious, derogatory, disapproving, fault-finding, nagging, nit-picking (*informal*), scathing 3 ANALYTICAL, discerning, discriminating, fastidious, judicious, penetrating, perceptive

criticism *noun* 1 FAULT-FINDING, bad press, censure, character assassination, disapproval, disparagement, flak (*informal*), stick (*slang*) 2 ANALYSIS, appraisal, appreciation, assessment, comment, commentary, critique, evaluation, judgment

criticize *verb* FIND FAULT WITH, carp, censure, condemn, disapprove of, disparage, knock (*informal*), put down, slate (*informal*)

croak *verb* SQUAWK, caw, grunt, utter *or* speak huskily, wheeze

crook *noun Informal* CRIMINAL, cheat, racketeer, robber, rogue, shark, swindler, thief, villain

crooked *adjective* 1 BENT, curved, deformed, distorted, hooked, irregular, misshapen, out of shape, twisted, warped, zigzag 2 AT AN ANGLE, askew, awry, lopsided, off-centre, skewwhiff (*Brit. informal*), slanting, squint, uneven 3 *Informal* DISHONEST, bent (*slang*), corrupt, criminal, fraudulent, illegal, shady (*informal*), underhand, unlawful

croon *verb* SING, hum, purr, warble

crop *noun* 1 PRODUCE, fruits, gathering, harvest, reaping, vintage, yield ♦ *verb* 2 CUT, clip, lop, pare, prune, shear, snip, trim 3 GRAZE, browse, nibble

crop up *verb Informal* HAPPEN, appear, arise, emerge, occur, spring up, turn up

cross *verb* 1 GO ACROSS, bridge, cut across, extend over, move across, pass over, span, traverse 2 INTERSECT, crisscross, intertwine 3 OPPOSE, block, impede, interfere, obstruct, resist 4 INTERBREED, blend, crossbreed, cross-fertilize, cross-pollinate, hybridize, intercross, mix, mongrelize ♦ *noun* 5 CRUCIFIX, rood 6 CROSSROADS, crossing, intersection, junction 7 MIXTURE, amalgam, blend, combination 8 TROUBLE, affliction, burden, grief, load, misfortune,

trial, tribulation, woe, worry ♦ *adjective* 9 ANGRY, annoyed, grumpy, ill-tempered, in a bad mood, irascible, put out, short 10 TRANSVERSE, crosswise, diagonal, intersecting, oblique

cross-examine *verb* QUESTION, grill (*informal*), interrogate, pump, quiz

cross out *or* **off** *verb* STRIKE OFF *or* OUT, blue-pencil, cancel, delete, eliminate, score off *or* out

crouch *verb* BEND DOWN, bow, duck, hunch, kneel, squat, stoop

crow *verb* GLOAT, blow one's own trumpet, boast, brag, exult, strut, swagger, triumph

crowd *noun* 1 MULTITUDE, army, horde, host, mass, mob, pack, swarm, throng 2 GROUP, bunch (*informal*), circle, clique, lot, set 3 AUDIENCE, attendance, gate, house, spectators ♦ *verb* 4 FLOCK, congregate, gather, mass, stream, surge, swarm, throng 5 SQUEEZE, bundle, congest, cram, pack, pile

crowded *adjective* PACKED, busy, congested, cramped, full, jam-packed, swarming, teeming

crown *noun* 1 CORONET, circlet, diadem, tiara 2 LAUREL WREATH, garland, honour, laurels, prize, trophy, wreath 3 HIGH POINT, apex, crest, pinnacle, summit, tip, top ♦ *verb* 4 HONOUR, adorn, dignify, festoon 5 CAP, be the climax *or* culmination of, complete, finish, perfect, put the finishing touch to, round off, top 6 *Slang* STRIKE, belt (*informal*), biff (*slang*), box, cuff, hit over the head, punch

Crown *noun* 1 MONARCHY, royalty, sovereignty 2 MONARCH, emperor *or* empress, king *or* queen, ruler, sovereign

crucial *adjective* 1 *Informal* VITAL, essential, high-priority, important, momentous, pressing, urgent

2 CRITICAL, central, decisive, pivotal

crucify *verb* EXECUTE, persecute, torment, torture

crude *adjective* **1** PRIMITIVE, clumsy, makeshift, rough, rough-and-ready, rudimentary, unpolished **2** VULGAR, coarse, dirty, gross, indecent, obscene, smutty, tasteless, uncouth **3** UNREFINED, natural, raw, unprocessed

crudely *adverb* VULGARLY, bluntly, coarsely, impolitely, roughly, rudely, tastelessly

crudity *noun* **1** ROUGHNESS, clumsiness, crudeness **2** VULGARITY, coarseness, impropriety, indecency, indelicacy, obscenity, smuttiness

cruel *adjective* **1** BRUTAL, barbarous, callous, hard-hearted, heartless, inhumane, malevolent, sadistic, spiteful, unkind, vicious **2** MERCILESS, pitiless, ruthless, unrelenting

cruelly *adverb* **1** BRUTALLY, barbarously, callously, heartlessly, in cold blood, mercilessly, pitilessly, sadistically, spitefully **2** BITTERLY, deeply, fearfully, grievously, monstrously, severely

cruelty *noun* BRUTALITY, barbarity, callousness, depravity, fiendishness, inhumanity, mercilessness, ruthlessness, spitefulness

cruise *noun* **1** SAIL, boat trip, sea trip, voyage ♦ *verb* **2** SAIL, coast, voyage **3** TRAVEL ALONG, coast, drift, keep a steady pace

crumb *noun* BIT, fragment, grain, morsel, scrap, shred, *soupçon*

crumble *verb* **1** DISINTEGRATE, collapse, decay, degenerate, deteriorate, fall apart, go to pieces, go to wrack and ruin, tumble down **2** CRUSH, fragment, granulate, grind, pound, powder, pulverize

crumple *verb* **1** CRUSH, crease, rumple, screw up, scrumple, wrinkle **2** COLLAPSE, break down, cave in, fall, give way, go to pieces

crunch *verb* **1** CHOMP, champ, chew noisily, grind, munch ♦ *noun* **2** *Informal* CRITICAL POINT, crisis, crux, emergency, moment of truth, test

crusade *noun* CAMPAIGN, cause, drive, movement, push

crush *verb* **1** SQUASH, break, compress, press, pulverize, squeeze **2** OVERCOME, conquer, overpower, overwhelm, put down, quell, stamp out, subdue **3** HUMILIATE, abash, mortify, put down (*slang*), quash, shame ♦ *noun* **4** CROWD, huddle, jam

crust *noun* LAYER, coating, covering, shell, skin, surface

crusty *adjective* **1** CRISPY, hard **2** IRRITABLE, cantankerous, cross, gruff, prickly, short-tempered, testy

cry *verb* **1** WEEP, blubber, shed tears, snivel, sob **2** SHOUT, bawl, bellow, call out, exclaim, howl, roar, scream, shriek, yell ♦ *noun* **3** WEEPING, blubbering, snivelling, sob, sobbing, weep **4** SHOUT, bellow, call, exclamation, howl, roar, scream, screech, shriek, yell **5** APPEAL, plea

cry off *verb* *Informal* BACK OUT, excuse oneself, quit, withdraw

cub *noun* YOUNG, offspring, whelp

cuddle *verb* HUG, bill and coo, cosset, embrace, fondle, pet, snuggle

cudgel *noun* CLUB, baton, bludgeon, cosh (*Brit.*), stick, truncheon

cue *noun* SIGNAL, catchword, hint, key, prompting, reminder, sign, suggestion

cul-de-sac noun DEAD END, blind alley

culminate verb END UP, climax, close, come to a climax, come to a head, conclude, finish, wind up

culmination noun CLIMAX, acme, conclusion, consummation, finale, peak, pinnacle, zenith

culpable adjective BLAMEWORTHY, at fault, found wanting, guilty, in the wrong, to blame, wrong

culprit noun OFFENDER, criminal, evildoer, felon, guilty party, miscreant, transgressor, wrongdoer

cult noun 1 SECT, clique, faction, religion, school 2 DEVOTION, idolization, worship

cultivate verb 1 FARM, plant, plough, tend, till, work 2 DEVELOP, foster, improve, promote, refine 3 COURT, dance attendance upon, run after, seek out

cultivation noun 1 FARMING, gardening, husbandry, planting, ploughing, tillage 2 DEVELOPMENT, encouragement, fostering, furtherance, nurture, patronage, promotion, support

cultural adjective ARTISTIC, civilizing, edifying, educational, enlightening, enriching, humane, liberal

culture noun 1 CIVILIZATION, customs, lifestyle, mores, society, way of life 2 REFINEMENT, education, enlightenment, good taste, sophistication, urbanity 3 FARMING, cultivation, husbandry

cultured adjective REFINED, educated, enlightened, highbrow, sophisticated, urbane, well-informed, well-read

culvert noun DRAIN, channel, conduit, gutter, watercourse

cumbersome adjective AWKWARD, bulky, burdensome, heavy, unmanageable, unwieldy, weighty

cunning adjective 1 CRAFTY, artful, devious, Machiavellian, sharp, shifty, sly, wily 2 SKILFUL, imaginative, ingenious ♦ noun 3 CRAFTINESS, artfulness, deviousness, guile, slyness, trickery 4 SKILL, artifice, cleverness, ingenuity, subtlety

cup noun 1 MUG, beaker, bowl, chalice, goblet, teacup 2 TROPHY

cupboard noun CABINET, press

curb noun 1 RESTRAINT, brake, bridle, check, control, deterrent, limitation, rein ♦ verb 2 RESTRAIN, check, control, hinder, impede, inhibit, restrict, retard, suppress

cure verb 1 MAKE BETTER, correct, ease, heal, mend, relieve, remedy, restore 2 PRESERVE, dry, pickle, salt, smoke ♦ noun 3 REMEDY, antidote, medicine, nostrum, panacea, treatment

curiosity noun 1 INQUISITIVENESS, interest, nosiness (informal), prying, snooping (informal) 2 ODDITY, freak, novelty, phenomenon, rarity, sight, spectacle, wonder

curious adjective 1 INQUIRING, inquisitive, interested, questioning, searching 2 INQUISITIVE, meddling, nosy (informal), prying 3 UNUSUAL, bizarre, extraordinary, mysterious, novel, odd, peculiar, rare, strange, unexpected

curl verb 1 TWIRL, bend, coil, curve, loop, spiral, turn, twist, wind ♦ noun 2 TWIST, coil, kink, ringlet, spiral, whorl

curly adjective CURLING, crinkly, curled, frizzy, fuzzy, wavy, winding

currency noun 1 MONEY, coinage, coins, notes 2 ACCEPTANCE, circulation, exposure, popularity, prevalence, vogue

current adjective 1 PRESENT, contemporary, fashionable, in fashion, in vogue, present-day, trendy (Brit. informal), up-to-date 2 PREVALENT, accepted, common, customary, in circulation, popular, topical, widespread ♦ noun 3 FLOW, course, draught, jet, progression, river, stream, tide, undertow 4 MOOD, atmosphere, feeling, tendency, trend, undercurrent

curse verb 1 SWEAR, blaspheme, cuss (informal), take the Lord's name in vain 2 DAMN, anathematize, excommunicate ♦ noun 3 OATH, blasphemy, expletive, obscenity, swearing, swearword 4 DENUNCIATION, anathema, ban, excommunication, hoodoo (informal), jinx 5 AFFLICTION, bane, hardship, plague, scourge, torment, trouble

cursed adjective DAMNED, accursed, bedevilled, doomed, ill-fated

curt adjective SHORT, abrupt, blunt, brief, brusque, gruff, monosyllabic, succinct, terse

curtail verb CUT SHORT, cut back, decrease, diminish, dock, lessen, reduce, shorten, truncate

curtain noun HANGING, drape (chiefly U.S.)

curve noun 1 BEND, arc, curvature, loop, trajectory, turn ♦ verb 2 BEND, arc, arch, coil, hook, spiral, swerve, turn, twist, wind

curved adjective BENT, arched, bowed, rounded, serpentine, sinuous, twisted

cushion noun 1 PILLOW, beanbag, bolster, hassock, headrest, pad ♦ verb 2 SOFTEN, dampen, deaden, muffle, stifle, suppress

cushy adjective Informal EASY, comfortable, soft, undemanding

custody noun 1 SAFEKEEPING, care, charge, keeping, protection, supervision 2 IMPRISONMENT, confinement, detention, incarceration

custom noun 1 TRADITION, convention, policy, practice, ritual, rule, usage 2 HABIT, practice, procedure, routine, way, wont 3 CUSTOMERS, patronage, trade

customary adjective USUAL, accepted, accustomed, common, conventional, established, normal, ordinary, routine, traditional

customer noun CLIENT, buyer, consumer, patron, purchaser, regular (informal), shopper

customs plural noun DUTY, import charges, tariff, tax, toll

cut verb 1 PENETRATE, chop, pierce, score, sever, slash, slice, slit, wound 2 DIVIDE, bisect, dissect, slice, split 3 TRIM, clip, hew, lop, mow, pare, prune, shave, snip 4 ABRIDGE, abbreviate, condense, curtail, delete, shorten 5 REDUCE, contract, cut back, decrease, diminish, lower, slash, slim (down) 6 SHAPE, carve, chisel, engrave, fashion, form, sculpt, whittle 7 HURT, insult, put down, snub, sting, wound 8 Informal IGNORE, avoid, cold-shoulder, slight, spurn, turn one's back on ♦ noun 9 INCISION, gash, laceration, nick, slash, slit, stroke, wound 10 REDUCTION, cutback, decrease, fall, lowering, saving 11 Informal SHARE, percentage, piece, portion, section, slice 12 STYLE, fashion, look, shape

cutback noun REDUCTION, cut, decrease, economy, lessening, retrenchment

cut down verb 1 FELL, hew, level, lop 2 REDUCE, decrease, lessen, lower

cute adjective APPEALING, attractive,

charming, delightful, engaging, lovable, sweet, winning, winsome

cut in *verb* INTERRUPT, break in, butt in, intervene, intrude

cut off *verb* 1 SEPARATE, isolate, sever 2 INTERRUPT, disconnect, intercept

cut out *verb* STOP, cease, give up, refrain from

cutthroat *adjective* 1 COMPETITIVE, dog-eat-dog, fierce, relentless, ruthless, unprincipled ♦ *noun* 2 MURDERER, assassin, butcher, executioner, hit man (*slang*), killer

cutting *adjective* HURTFUL, acrimonious, barbed, bitter, caustic, malicious, sarcastic, scathing, vitriolic, wounding

cycle *noun* ERA, circle, period, phase, revolution, rotation

cynic *noun* SCEPTIC, doubter, misanthrope, misanthropist, pessimist, scoffer

cynical *adjective* SCEPTICAL, contemptuous, derisive, distrustful, misanthropic, mocking, pessimistic, scoffing, scornful, unbelieving

cynicism *noun* SCEPTICISM, disbelief, doubt, misanthropy, pessimism

D d

dab verb 1 PAT, daub, stipple, tap, touch ♦ noun 2 SPOT, bit, drop, pat, smudge, speck 3 PAT, flick, stroke, tap, touch

dabble verb 1 PLAY AT, dip into, potter, tinker, trifle (with) 2 SPLASH, dip

daft adjective Informal, chiefly Brit. 1 FOOLISH, absurd, asinine, crackpot (informal), crazy, idiotic, silly, stupid, witless 2 CRAZY, crackers (Brit. slang), demented, deranged, insane, nuts (slang), touched, unhinged

dagger noun KNIFE, bayonet, dirk, stiletto

daily adjective 1 EVERYDAY, diurnal, quotidian ♦ adverb 2 EVERY DAY, day by day, once a day

dainty adjective DELICATE, charming, elegant, exquisite, fine, graceful, neat, petite, pretty

dam noun 1 BARRIER, barrage, embankment, obstruction, wall ♦ verb 2 BLOCK UP, barricade, hold back, obstruct, restrict

damage verb 1 HARM, hurt, impair, injure, ruin, spoil, weaken, wreck ♦ noun 2 HARM, destruction, detriment, devastation, hurt, injury, loss, suffering 3 Informal COST, bill, charge, expense

damages plural noun Law COMPENSATION, fine, reimbursement, reparation, satisfaction

damaging adjective HARMFUL, deleterious, detrimental, disadvantageous, hurtful, injurious, ruinous

dame noun NOBLEWOMAN, baroness, dowager, grande dame, lady, peeress

damn verb 1 CONDEMN, blast, censure, criticize, denounce, put down 2 SENTENCE, condemn, doom

damnation noun CONDEMNATION, anathema, damning, denunciation, doom

damned adjective 1 DOOMED, accursed, condemned, lost 2 Slang DETESTABLE, confounded, hateful, infernal, loathsome

damp adjective 1 MOIST, clammy, dank, dewy, drizzly, humid, soggy, sopping, wet ♦ noun 2 MOISTURE, dampness, dankness, drizzle ♦ verb 3 MOISTEN, dampen, wet 4 damp down REDUCE, allay, check, curb, diminish, inhibit, pour cold water on, stifle

dampen verb 1 REDUCE, check, dull, lessen, moderate, restrain, stifle 2 MOISTEN, make damp, spray, wet

damper noun As in **put a damper on** DISCOURAGEMENT, cold water (informal), hindrance, restraint, wet blanket (informal)

dance verb 1 PRANCE, hop, jig, skip, sway, trip, whirl ♦ noun 2 BALL, disco, discotheque, hop (informal), knees-up (Brit. informal), social

dancer noun BALLERINA, Terpsichorean

danger noun PERIL, hazard, jeopardy, menace, pitfall, risk, threat, vulnerability

dangerous adjective PERILOUS, breakneck, chancy (informal), hazardous, insecure, precarious, risky, unsafe, vulnerable

dangerously adverb PERILOUSLY, alarmingly, hazardously, precariously, recklessly, riskily, unsafely

dangle verb 1 <u>HANG</u>, flap, hang down, sway, swing, trail 2 <u>WAVE</u>, brandish, flaunt, flourish

dapper adjective <u>NEAT</u>, natty (informal), smart, soigné or soignée, spruce, spry, trim, well-groomed, well turned out

dare verb 1 <u>RISK</u>, hazard, make bold, presume, venture 2 <u>CHALLENGE</u>, defy, goad, provoke, taunt, throw down the gauntlet ♦ noun 3 <u>CHALLENGE</u>, provocation, taunt

daredevil noun 1 <u>ADVENTURER</u>, desperado, exhibitionist, madcap, show-off (informal), stunt man ♦ adjective 2 <u>DARING</u>, adventurous, audacious, bold, death-defying, madcap, reckless

daring adjective 1 <u>BRAVE</u>, adventurous, audacious, bold, daredevil, fearless, intrepid, reckless, venturesome ♦ noun 2 <u>BRAVERY</u>, audacity, boldness, bottle (Brit. slang), courage, fearlessness, nerve (informal), pluck, temerity

dark adjective 1 <u>DIM</u>, dingy, murky, shadowy, shady, sunless, unlit 2 <u>BLACK</u>, dark-skinned, dusky, ebony, sable, swarthy 3 <u>GLOOMY</u>, bleak, dismal, grim, morose, mournful, sad, sombre 4 <u>EVIL</u>, foul, infernal, sinister, vile, wicked 5 <u>SECRET</u>, concealed, hidden, mysterious ♦ noun 6 <u>DARKNESS</u>, dimness, dusk, gloom, murk, obscurity, semi-darkness 7 <u>NIGHT</u>, evening, nightfall, night-time, twilight

darken verb <u>MAKE DARK</u>, blacken, dim, obscure, overshadow

darkness noun <u>DARK</u>, blackness, duskiness, gloom, murk, nightfall, shade, shadows

darling noun 1 <u>BELOVED</u>, dear, dearest, love, sweetheart, truelove ♦ adjective 2 <u>BELOVED</u>, adored, cherished, dear, precious, treasured

darn verb 1 <u>MEND</u>, cobble up, patch, repair, sew up, stitch ♦ noun 2 <u>MEND</u>, invisible repair, patch, reinforcement

dart verb <u>DASH</u>, fly, race, run, rush, shoot, spring, sprint, tear

dash verb 1 <u>RUSH</u>, bolt, fly, hurry, race, run, speed, sprint, tear 2 <u>THROW</u>, cast, fling, hurl, slam, sling 3 <u>CRASH</u>, break, destroy, shatter, smash, splinter 4 <u>FRUSTRATE</u>, blight, foil, ruin, spoil, thwart, undo ♦ noun 5 <u>RUSH</u>, dart, race, run, sortie, sprint, spurt 6 <u>LITTLE</u>, bit, drop, hint, pinch, soupçon, sprinkling, tinge, touch 7 <u>STYLE</u>, brio, élan, flair, flourish, panache, spirit, verve

dashing adjective 1 <u>BOLD</u>, debonair, gallant, lively, spirited, swashbuckling 2 <u>STYLISH</u>, elegant, flamboyant, jaunty, showy, smart, sporty

data noun <u>INFORMATION</u>, details, facts, figures, statistics

date noun 1 <u>TIME</u>, age, epoch, era, period, stage 2 <u>APPOINTMENT</u>, assignation, engagement, meeting, rendezvous, tryst 3 <u>PARTNER</u>, escort, friend ♦ verb 4 <u>PUT A DATE ON</u>, assign a date to, fix the period of 5 <u>BECOME OLD-FASHIONED</u>, be dated, show one's age 6 **date from** or **date back to** <u>COME FROM</u>, bear a date of, belong to, exist from, originate in

dated adjective <u>OLD-FASHIONED</u>, obsolete, old hat, outdated, outmoded, out of date, passé, unfashionable

daub verb <u>SMEAR</u>, coat, cover, paint, plaster, slap on (informal)

daunting adjective <u>INTIMIDATING</u>, alarming, demoralizing, disconcerting, discouraging, disheartening, frightening,

off-putting (*Brit. informal*),
unnerving

dauntless *adjective* FEARLESS, bold,
doughty, gallant, indomitable,
intrepid, resolute, stouthearted,
undaunted, unflinching

dawdle *verb* WASTE TIME, dally,
delay, drag one's feet *or* heels,
hang about, idle, loaf, loiter, trail

dawn *noun* 1 DAYBREAK, aurora
(*poetic*), cockcrow, crack of dawn,
daylight, morning, sunrise, sunup
2 BEGINNING, advent, birth,
emergence, genesis, origin, rise,
start ♦ *verb* 3 GROW LIGHT, break,
brighten, lighten 4 BEGIN, appear,
develop, emerge, originate, rise,
unfold 5 **dawn on** *or* **upon** HIT,
become apparent, come into
one's head, come to mind, occur,
register (*informal*), strike

day *noun* 1 TWENTY-FOUR HOURS,
daylight, daytime 2 POINT IN TIME,
date, time 3 TIME, age, epoch, era,
heyday, period, zenith

daybreak *noun* DAWN, break of day,
cockcrow, crack of dawn, first
light, morning, sunrise, sunup

daydream *noun* 1 FANTASY, dream,
fancy, imagining, pipe dream,
reverie, wish ♦ *verb* 2 FANTASIZE,
dream, envision, fancy, imagine,
muse

daylight *noun* SUNLIGHT, light of
day, sunshine

daze *verb* 1 STUN, benumb, numb,
paralyse, shock, stupefy ♦ *noun*
2 SHOCK, bewilderment, confusion,
distraction, stupor, trance,
trancelike state

dazed *adjective* SHOCKED,
bewildered, confused,
disorientated, dizzy, muddled,
punch-drunk, staggered, stunned

dazzle *verb* 1 IMPRESS, amaze,
astonish, bowl over (*informal*),
overpower, overwhelm, take one's
breath away 2 BLIND, bedazzle,
blur, confuse, daze ♦ *noun*
3 SPLENDOUR, brilliance, glitter,
magnificence, razzmatazz (*slang*),
sparkle

dazzling *adjective* SPLENDID, brilliant,
glittering, glorious, scintillating,
sensational (*informal*), sparkling,
stunning, virtuoso

dead *adjective* 1 DECEASED, defunct,
departed, extinct, late, passed
away, perished 2 NOT WORKING,
inactive, inoperative, stagnant,
unemployed, useless 3 NUMB,
inert, paralysed 4 TOTAL, absolute,
complete, outright, thorough,
unqualified, utter 5 *Informal*
EXHAUSTED, dead beat (*informal*),
spent, tired, worn out 6 BORING,
dull, flat, uninteresting ♦ *noun*
7 MIDDLE, depth, midst ♦ *adverb*
8 *Informal* EXACTLY, absolutely,
completely, directly, entirely,
totally

deaden *verb* REDUCE, alleviate,
blunt, cushion, diminish, dull,
lessen, muffle, smother, stifle,
suppress, weaken

deadline *noun* TIME LIMIT, cutoff
point, limit, target date

deadlock *noun* IMPASSE, dead heat,
draw, gridlock, stalemate,
standoff, standstill, tie

deadlocked *adjective* EVEN, equal,
level, neck and neck

deadly *adjective* 1 LETHAL,
dangerous, death-dealing,
deathly, fatal, malignant, mortal
2 *Informal* BORING, dull,
mind-numbing, monotonous,
tedious, tiresome, uninteresting,
wearisome

deadpan *adjective* EXPRESSIONLESS,
blank, impassive, inexpressive,
inscrutable, poker-faced,
straight-faced

deaf *adjective* 1 HARD OF HEARING,

stone deaf, without hearing
2 OBLIVIOUS, indifferent,
unconcerned, unhearing,
unmoved

deafen verb MAKE DEAF, din, drown
out, split or burst the eardrums

deafening adjective EAR-PIERCING,
booming, ear-splitting,
overpowering, piercing,
resounding, ringing, thunderous

deal noun 1 Informal AGREEMENT,
arrangement, bargain, contract,
pact, transaction, understanding
2 AMOUNT, degree, extent, portion,
quantity, share ◆ verb 3 SELL,
bargain, buy and sell, do business,
negotiate, stock, trade, traffic

dealer noun TRADER, merchant,
purveyor, supplier, tradesman,
wholesaler

deal out verb DISTRIBUTE, allot,
apportion, assign, dispense, dole
out, give, mete out, share

deal with verb 1 HANDLE, attend to,
cope with, get to grips with,
manage, see to, take care of, treat
2 BE CONCERNED WITH, consider

dear noun 1 BELOVED, angel, darling,
loved one, precious, treasure
◆ adjective 2 BELOVED, cherished,
close, favourite, intimate,
precious, prized, treasured
3 EXPENSIVE, at a premium, costly,
high-priced, overpriced, pricey
(informal)

dearly adverb 1 VERY MUCH,
extremely, greatly, profoundly
2 AT GREAT COST, at a high price

dearth noun SCARCITY, deficiency,
inadequacy, insufficiency, lack,
paucity, poverty, shortage, want

death noun 1 DYING, demise,
departure, end, exit, passing
2 DESTRUCTION, downfall,
extinction, finish, ruin, undoing

deathly adjective DEATHLIKE, ghastly,
grim, pale, pallid, wan

debacle noun DISASTER, catastrophe,
collapse, defeat, fiasco, reversal,
rout

debase verb DEGRADE, cheapen,
devalue, lower, reduce

debatable adjective DOUBTFUL,
arguable, controversial, dubious,
moot, problematical,
questionable, uncertain

debate noun 1 DISCUSSION,
argument, contention,
controversy, dispute ◆ verb
2 DISCUSS, argue, dispute, question
3 CONSIDER, deliberate, ponder,
reflect, ruminate, weigh

debauchery noun DEPRAVITY,
dissipation, dissoluteness, excess,
indulgence, intemperance,
lewdness, overindulgence

debonair adjective ELEGANT,
charming, courteous, dashing,
refined, smooth, suave, urbane,
well-bred

debrief verb INTERROGATE,
cross-examine, examine, probe,
question, quiz

debris noun REMAINS, bits, detritus,
fragments, rubble, ruins, waste,
wreckage

debt noun 1 DEBIT, commitment,
liability, obligation 2 in debt
OWING, in arrears, in the red
(informal), liable

debtor noun BORROWER, mortgagor

debunk verb Informal EXPOSE, cut
down to size, deflate, disparage,
mock, ridicule, show up

debut noun INTRODUCTION,
beginning, bow, coming out,
entrance, first appearance,
initiation, presentation

decadence noun DEGENERATION,
corruption, decay, decline,
deterioration, dissipation,
dissolution

decadent adjective DEGENERATE,

corrupt, decaying, declining,
dissolute, immoral, self-indulgent

decapitate verb BEHEAD, execute,
guillotine

decay verb 1 DECLINE, crumble,
deteriorate, disintegrate, dwindle,
shrivel, wane, waste away, wither
2 ROT, corrode, decompose,
perish, putrefy ♦ noun 3 DECLINE,
collapse, degeneration,
deterioration, fading, failing,
wasting, withering 4 ROT, caries,
decomposition, gangrene,
putrefaction

decease noun Formal DEATH,
demise, departure, dying, release

deceased adjective DEAD, defunct,
departed, expired, former, late,
lifeless

deceit noun DISHONESTY, cheating,
chicanery, deception, fraud, lying,
pretence, treachery, trickery

deceitful adjective DISHONEST,
deceptive, false, fraudulent,
sneaky, treacherous, two-faced,
untrustworthy

deceive verb TAKE IN (informal),
cheat, con (informal), dupe, fool,
hoodwink, mislead, swindle, trick

deceiver noun LIAR, cheat, con man
(informal), double-dealer, fraud,
impostor, swindler, trickster

decency noun RESPECTABILITY, civility,
correctness, courtesy, decorum,
etiquette, modesty, propriety

decent adjective 1 REASONABLE,
adequate, ample, fair, passable,
satisfactory, sufficient, tolerable
2 RESPECTABLE, chaste, decorous,
modest, proper, pure 3 PROPER,
appropriate, becoming, befitting,
fitting, seemly, suitable 4 Informal
KIND, accommodating, courteous,
friendly, generous, gracious,
helpful, obliging, thoughtful

deception noun 1 TRICKERY,
cunning, deceit, fraud, guile,

legerdemain, treachery 2 TRICK,
bluff, decoy, hoax, illusion, lie,
ruse, subterfuge

deceptive adjective MISLEADING,
ambiguous, deceitful, dishonest,
false, fraudulent, illusory,
unreliable

decide verb REACH or COME TO A
DECISION, adjudge, adjudicate,
choose, conclude, determine,
make up one's mind, resolve

decidedly adverb DEFINITELY, clearly,
distinctly, downright, positively,
unequivocally, unmistakably

decimate verb DEVASTATE, ravage,
wreak havoc on

decipher verb FIGURE OUT (informal),
crack, decode, deduce, interpret,
make out, read, solve

decision noun 1 JUDGMENT,
arbitration, conclusion, finding,
resolution, ruling, sentence,
verdict 2 DECISIVENESS,
determination, firmness, purpose,
resolution, resolve, strength of
mind or will

decisive adjective 1 INFLUENTIAL,
conclusive, critical, crucial, fateful,
momentous, significant 2 RESOLUTE,
decided, determined, firm,
forceful, incisive, strong-minded,
trenchant

deck verb DECORATE, adorn, array,
beautify, clothe, dress, embellish,
festoon

declaim verb 1 ORATE, harangue,
hold forth, lecture, proclaim, rant,
recite, speak 2 **declaim against**
PROTEST AGAINST, attack, decry,
denounce, inveigh, rail

declaration noun 1 STATEMENT,
acknowledgment, affirmation,
assertion, avowal, disclosure,
protestation, revelation, testimony
2 ANNOUNCEMENT, edict,
notification, proclamation,
profession, pronouncement

declare verb 1 <u>STATE</u>, affirm, announce, assert, claim, maintain, proclaim, profess, pronounce, swear, utter 2 <u>MAKE KNOWN</u>, confess, disclose, reveal, show

decline verb 1 <u>LESSEN</u>, decrease, diminish, dwindle, ebb, fade, fall off, shrink, sink, wane 2 <u>DETERIORATE</u>, decay, degenerate, droop, languish, pine, weaken, worsen 3 <u>REFUSE</u>, abstain, avoid, reject, say 'no', turn down ♦ noun 4 <u>LESSENING</u>, downturn, drop, dwindling, falling off, recession, slump 5 <u>DETERIORATION</u>, decay, degeneration, failing, weakening, worsening

decode verb <u>DECIPHER</u>, crack, decrypt, interpret, solve, unscramble, work out

decompose verb <u>ROT</u>, break up, crumble, decay, fall apart, fester, putrefy

decor noun <u>DECORATION</u>, colour scheme, furnishing style, ornamentation

decorate verb 1 <u>ADORN</u>, beautify, embellish, festoon, grace, ornament, trim 2 <u>DO UP</u> (informal), colour, furbish, paint, paper, renovate, wallpaper 3 <u>PIN A MEDAL ON</u>, cite, confer an honour on or upon

decoration noun 1 <u>ADORNMENT</u>, beautification, elaboration, embellishment, enrichment, ornamentation, trimming 2 <u>ORNAMENT</u>, bauble, frill, garnish, trimmings 3 <u>MEDAL</u>, award, badge, ribbon, star

decorative adjective <u>ORNAMENTAL</u>, beautifying, fancy, nonfunctional, pretty

decorous adjective <u>PROPER</u>, becoming, correct, decent, dignified, fitting, polite, seemly, well-behaved

decorum noun <u>PROPRIETY</u>, decency, dignity, etiquette, good manners, politeness, protocol, respectability

decoy noun 1 <u>LURE</u>, bait, enticement, inducement, pretence, trap ♦ verb 2 <u>LURE</u>, deceive, ensnare, entice, entrap, seduce, tempt

decrease verb 1 <u>LESSEN</u>, cut down, decline, diminish, drop, dwindle, lower, reduce, shrink, subside ♦ noun 2 <u>LESSENING</u>, contraction, cutback, decline, dwindling, falling off, loss, reduction, subsidence

decree noun 1 <u>LAW</u>, act, command, edict, order, proclamation, ruling, statute ♦ verb 2 <u>ORDER</u>, command, demand, ordain, prescribe, proclaim, pronounce, rule

decrepit adjective 1 <u>WEAK</u>, aged, doddering, feeble, frail, infirm 2 <u>WORN-OUT</u>, battered, beat-up (informal), broken-down, dilapidated, ramshackle, rickety, run-down, tumbledown, weather-beaten

decry verb <u>CONDEMN</u>, belittle, criticize, denigrate, denounce, discredit, disparage, put down, run down

dedicate verb 1 <u>DEVOTE</u>, commit, give over to, pledge, surrender 2 <u>INSCRIBE</u>, address

dedicated adjective <u>DEVOTED</u>, committed, enthusiastic, purposeful, single-minded, wholehearted, zealous

dedication noun 1 <u>DEVOTION</u>, adherence, allegiance, commitment, faithfulness, loyalty, single-mindedness, wholeheartedness 2 <u>INSCRIPTION</u>, address, message

deduce verb <u>CONCLUDE</u>, draw, gather, glean, infer, reason, take to mean, understand

deduct *verb* SUBTRACT, decrease by, knock off (*informal*), reduce by, remove, take away, take off

deduction *noun* 1 SUBTRACTION, decrease, diminution, discount, reduction, withdrawal 2 CONCLUSION, assumption, finding, inference, reasoning, result

deed *noun* 1 ACTION, achievement, act, exploit, fact, feat, performance 2 *Law* DOCUMENT, contract, title

deep *adjective* 1 WIDE, bottomless, broad, far, profound, unfathomable, yawning 2 MYSTERIOUS, abstract, abstruse, arcane, esoteric, hidden, obscure, recondite, secret 3 INTENSE, extreme, grave, great, profound, serious (*informal*), unqualified 4 ABSORBED, engrossed, immersed, lost, preoccupied, rapt 5 DARK, intense, rich, strong, vivid 6 LOW, bass, booming, low-pitched, resonant, sonorous ♦ *noun* 7 **the deep** *Poetic* OCEAN, briny (*informal*), high seas, main, sea

deepen *verb* INTENSIFY, grow, increase, magnify, reinforce, strengthen

deeply *adverb* 1 THOROUGHLY, completely, gravely, profoundly, seriously, severely, to the core, to the heart, to the quick 2 INTENSELY, acutely, affectingly, distressingly, feelingly, mournfully, movingly, passionately, sadly

deface *verb* VANDALIZE, damage, deform, disfigure, mar, mutilate, spoil, tarnish

de facto *adverb* 1 IN FACT, actually, in effect, in reality, really ♦ *adjective* 2 ACTUAL, existing, real

defame *verb* SLANDER, bad-mouth (*slang, chiefly U.S. & Canad.*), cast aspersions on, denigrate, discredit, disparage, knock (*informal*), libel, malign, smear

default *noun* 1 FAILURE, deficiency, dereliction, evasion, lapse, neglect, nonpayment, omission ♦ *verb* 2 FAIL, dodge, evade, neglect

defeat *verb* 1 BEAT, conquer, crush, master, overwhelm, rout, trounce, vanquish, wipe the floor with (*informal*) 2 FRUSTRATE, baffle, balk, confound, foil, get the better of, ruin, thwart ♦ *noun* 3 CONQUEST, beating, overthrow, pasting (*slang*), rout 4 FRUSTRATION, failure, rebuff, reverse, setback, thwarting

defeatist *noun* 1 PESSIMIST, prophet of doom, quitter ♦ *adjective* 2 PESSIMISTIC

defect *noun* 1 IMPERFECTION, blemish, blotch, error, failing, fault, flaw, spot, taint ♦ *verb* 2 DESERT, abandon, change sides, go over, rebel, revolt, walk out on (*informal*)

defection *noun* DESERTION, apostasy, rebellion

defective *adjective* FAULTY, broken, deficient, flawed, imperfect, not working, on the blink (*slang*), out of order

defector *noun* DESERTER, apostate, renegade, turncoat

defence *noun* 1 PROTECTION, cover, guard, immunity, resistance, safeguard, security, shelter 2 SHIELD, barricade, bulwark, buttress, fortification, rampart 3 ARGUMENT, excuse, explanation, justification, plea, vindication 4 *Law* PLEA, alibi, denial, rebuttal, testimony

defenceless *adjective* HELPLESS, exposed, naked, powerless, unarmed, unguarded, unprotected, vulnerable, wide open

defend *verb* 1 PROTECT, cover, guard, keep safe, preserve, safeguard, screen, shelter, shield

2 SUPPORT, champion, endorse, justify, speak up for, stand up for, stick up for (*informal*), uphold, vindicate

defendant *noun* THE ACCUSED, defence, offender, prisoner at the bar, respondent

defender *noun* **1** PROTECTOR, bodyguard, escort, guard **2** SUPPORTER, advocate, champion, sponsor

defensive *adjective* ON GUARD, on the defensive, protective, uptight (*informal*), watchful

defer[1] *verb* POSTPONE, delay, hold over, procrastinate, put off, put on ice, shelve, suspend

defer[2] *verb* COMPLY, accede, bow, capitulate, give in, give way to, submit, yield

deference *noun* RESPECT, attention, civility, consideration, courtesy, honour, politeness, regard, reverence

deferential *adjective* RESPECTFUL, ingratiating, obedient, obeisant, obsequious, polite, reverential, submissive

defiance *noun* RESISTANCE, confrontation, contempt, disobedience, disregard, insolence, insubordination, opposition, rebelliousness

defiant *adjective* RESISTING, audacious, bold, daring, disobedient, insolent, insubordinate, mutinous, provocative, rebellious

deficiency *noun* **1** LACK, absence, dearth, deficit, scarcity, shortage **2** FAILING, defect, demerit, fault, flaw, frailty, imperfection, shortcoming, weakness

deficient *adjective* **1** LACKING, inadequate, insufficient, meagre, scant, scarce, short, skimpy, wanting **2** UNSATISFACTORY,

defective, faulty, flawed, impaired, imperfect, incomplete, inferior, weak

deficit *noun* SHORTFALL, arrears, deficiency, loss, shortage

define *verb* **1** DESCRIBE, characterize, designate, explain, expound, interpret, specify, spell out **2** MARK OUT, bound, circumscribe, delineate, demarcate, limit, outline

definite *adjective* **1** CLEAR, black-and-white, cut-and-dried (*informal*), exact, fixed, marked, particular, precise, specific **2** CERTAIN, assured, decided, guaranteed, positive, settled, sure

definitely *adverb* CERTAINLY, absolutely, categorically, clearly, positively, surely, undeniably, unmistakably, unquestionably, without doubt

definition *noun* **1** EXPLANATION, clarification, elucidation, exposition, statement of meaning **2** SHARPNESS, clarity, contrast, distinctness, focus, precision

definitive *adjective* **1** FINAL, absolute, complete, conclusive, decisive **2** AUTHORITATIVE, exhaustive, perfect, reliable, ultimate

deflate *verb* **1** COLLAPSE, empty, exhaust, flatten, puncture, shrink **2** HUMILIATE, chasten, disconcert, dispirit, humble, mortify, put down (*slang*), squash **3** *Economics* REDUCE, depress, devalue, diminish

deflect *verb* TURN ASIDE, bend, deviate, diverge, glance off, ricochet, swerve, veer

deflection *noun* DEVIATION, bend, divergence, swerve

deform *verb* **1** DISTORT, buckle, contort, gnarl, mangle, misshape, twist, warp **2** DISFIGURE, deface, maim, mar, mutilate, ruin, spoil

deformity *noun* ABNORMALITY,

defect, disfigurement, malformation

defraud verb CHEAT, con (*informal*), diddle (*informal*), embezzle, fleece, pilfer, rip off (*slang*), swindle, trick

deft adjective SKILFUL, adept, adroit, agile, dexterous, expert, neat, nimble, proficient

defunct adjective 1 DEAD, deceased, departed, extinct, gone 2 OBSOLETE, bygone, expired, inoperative, invalid, nonexistent, out of commission

defy verb RESIST, brave, confront, disregard, flout, scorn, slight, spurn

degenerate adjective 1 DEPRAVED, corrupt, debauched, decadent, dissolute, immoral, low, perverted ♦ verb 2 WORSEN, decay, decline, decrease, deteriorate, fall off, lapse, sink, slip

degradation noun 1 DISGRACE, discredit, dishonour, humiliation, ignominy, mortification, shame 2 DETERIORATION, decline, degeneration, demotion, downgrading

degrade verb 1 DISGRACE, debase, demean, discredit, dishonour, humble, humiliate, shame 2 DEMOTE, downgrade, lower

degrading adjective DEMEANING, dishonourable, humiliating, infra dig (*informal*), shameful, undignified, unworthy

degree noun STAGE, grade, notch, point, rung, step, unit

deity noun GOD, divinity, goddess, godhead, idol, immortal, supreme being

dejected adjective DOWNHEARTED, crestfallen, depressed, despondent, disconsolate, disheartened, downcast, glum, miserable, sad

dejection noun LOW SPIRITS, depression, despair, despondency, doldrums, downheartedness, gloom, melancholy, sadness, sorrow, unhappiness

de jure adverb LEGALLY, by right, rightfully

delay verb 1 PUT OFF, defer, hold over, postpone, procrastinate, shelve, suspend 2 HOLD UP, bog down, detain, hinder, hold back, impede, obstruct, set back, slow up ♦ noun 3 PUTTING OFF, deferment, postponement, procrastination, suspension 4 HOLD-UP, hindrance, impediment, interruption, interval, setback, stoppage, wait

delegate noun 1 REPRESENTATIVE, agent, ambassador, commissioner, deputy, envoy, legate ♦ verb 2 ENTRUST, assign, consign, devolve, give, hand over, pass on, transfer 3 APPOINT, accredit, authorize, commission, depute, designate, empower, mandate

delegation noun 1 DEPUTATION, commission, contingent, embassy, envoys, legation, mission 2 DEVOLUTION, assignment, commissioning, committal

delete verb REMOVE, cancel, cross out, efface, erase, expunge, obliterate, rub out, strike out

deliberate adjective 1 INTENTIONAL, calculated, conscious, planned, prearranged, premeditated, purposeful, wilful 2 UNHURRIED, careful, cautious, circumspect, measured, methodical, ponderous, slow, thoughtful ♦ verb 3 CONSIDER, cogitate, consult, debate, discuss, meditate, ponder, reflect, think, weigh

deliberately adverb INTENTIONALLY, by design, calculatingly, consciously, in cold blood, knowingly, on purpose, wilfully, wittingly

deliberation noun 1 <u>CONSIDERATION</u>, calculation, circumspection, forethought, meditation, reflection, thought 2 <u>DISCUSSION</u>, conference, consultation, debate

delicacy noun 1 <u>FINENESS</u>, accuracy, daintiness, elegance, exquisiteness, lightness, precision, subtlety 2 <u>FRAGILITY</u>, flimsiness, frailty, slenderness, tenderness, weakness 3 <u>TREAT</u>, dainty, luxury, savoury, titbit 4 <u>FASTIDIOUSNESS</u>, discrimination, finesse, purity, refinement, sensibility, taste 5 <u>SENSITIVITY</u>, sensitiveness, tact

delicate adjective 1 <u>FINE</u>, deft, elegant, exquisite, graceful, precise, skilled, subtle 2 <u>SUBTLE</u>, choice, dainty, delicious, fine, savoury, tender 3 <u>FRAGILE</u>, flimsy, frail, slender, slight, tender, weak 4 <u>CONSIDERATE</u>, diplomatic, discreet, sensitive, tactful

delicately adverb 1 <u>FINELY</u>, daintily, deftly, elegantly, exquisitely, gracefully, precisely, skilfully, subtly 2 <u>TACTFULLY</u>, diplomatically, sensitively

delicious adjective <u>DELECTABLE</u>, appetizing, choice, dainty, mouthwatering, savoury, scrumptious (informal), tasty, toothsome

delight noun 1 <u>PLEASURE</u>, ecstasy, enjoyment, gladness, glee, happiness, joy, rapture ◆ verb 2 <u>PLEASE</u>, amuse, charm, cheer, enchant, gratify, thrill 3 **delight in** <u>TAKE PLEASURE IN</u>, appreciate, enjoy, feast on, like, love, relish, revel in, savour

delighted adjective <u>PLEASED</u>, ecstatic, elated, enchanted, happy, joyous, jubilant, overjoyed, thrilled

delightful adjective <u>PLEASANT</u>,

agreeable, charming, delectable, enchanting, enjoyable, pleasurable, rapturous, thrilling

delinquent noun <u>CRIMINAL</u>, culprit, lawbreaker, miscreant, offender, villain, wrongdoer

delirious adjective 1 <u>MAD</u>, crazy, demented, deranged, incoherent, insane, raving, unhinged 2 <u>ECSTATIC</u>, beside oneself, carried away, excited, frantic, frenzied, hysterical, wild

delirium noun 1 <u>MADNESS</u>, derangement, hallucination, insanity, raving 2 <u>FRENZY</u>, ecstasy, fever, hysteria, passion

deliver verb 1 <u>CARRY</u>, bear, bring, cart, convey, distribute, transport 2 <u>HAND OVER</u>, commit, give up, grant, make over, relinquish, surrender, transfer, turn over, yield 3 <u>GIVE</u>, announce, declare, present, read, utter 4 <u>RELEASE</u>, emancipate, free, liberate, loose, ransom, rescue, save 5 <u>STRIKE</u>, administer, aim, deal, direct, give, inflict, launch

deliverance noun <u>RELEASE</u>, emancipation, escape, liberation, ransom, redemption, rescue, salvation

delivery noun 1 <u>HANDING OVER</u>, consignment, conveyance, dispatch, distribution, surrender, transfer, transmission 2 <u>SPEECH</u>, articulation, elocution, enunciation, intonation, utterance 3 <u>CHILDBIRTH</u>, confinement, labour, parturition

delude verb <u>DECEIVE</u>, beguile, dupe, fool, hoodwink, kid (informal), mislead, take in (informal), trick

deluge noun 1 <u>FLOOD</u>, cataclysm, downpour, inundation, overflowing, spate, torrent 2 <u>RUSH</u>, avalanche, barrage, flood, spate, torrent ◆ verb 3 <u>FLOOD</u>, douse, drench, drown, inundate, soak, submerge, swamp **4** OVERWHELM, engulf, inundate, overload, overrun, swamp

delusion noun MISCONCEPTION, error, fallacy, false impression, fancy, hallucination, illusion, misapprehension, mistake

de luxe adjective LUXURIOUS, costly, exclusive, expensive, grand, opulent, select, special, splendid, superior

delve verb RESEARCH, burrow, explore, ferret out, forage, investigate, look into, probe, rummage, search

demagogue noun AGITATOR, firebrand, rabble-rouser

demand verb **1** REQUEST, ask, challenge, inquire, interrogate, question **2** REQUIRE, call for, cry out for, entail, involve, necessitate, need, want **3** CLAIM, exact, expect, insist on, order ♦ noun **4** REQUEST, inquiry, order, question, requisition **5** NEED, call, claim, market, requirement, want

demanding adjective DIFFICULT, challenging, exacting, hard, taxing, tough, trying, wearing

demarcation noun DELIMITATION, differentiation, distinction, division, separation

demean verb LOWER, abase, debase, degrade, descend, humble, stoop

demeanour noun BEHAVIOUR, air, bearing, carriage, comportment, conduct, deportment, manner

demented adjective MAD, crazed, crazy, deranged, frenzied, insane, maniacal, unbalanced, unhinged

demise noun **1** FAILURE, collapse, downfall, end, fall, ruin **2** Euphemistic DEATH, decease, departure

democracy noun SELF-GOVERNMENT, mmonwealth, republic

democratic adjective SELF-GOVERNING, autonomous, egalitarian, popular, populist, representative

demolish verb **1** KNOCK DOWN, bulldoze, destroy, dismantle, flatten, level, raze, tear down **2** DEFEAT, annihilate, destroy, overthrow, overturn, undo, wreck

demolition noun KNOCKING DOWN, bulldozing, destruction, explosion, levelling, razing, tearing down, wrecking

demon noun **1** EVIL SPIRIT, devil, fiend, ghoul, goblin, malignant spirit **2** WIZARD, ace (informal), fiend, master

demonic, demoniac, demoniacal adjective **1** DEVILISH, diabolic, diabolical, fiendish, hellish, infernal, satanic **2** FRENZIED, crazed, frantic, frenetic, furious, hectic, maniacal, manic

demonstrable adjective PROVABLE, evident, irrefutable, obvious, palpable, self-evident, unmistakable, verifiable

demonstrate verb **1** PROVE, display, exhibit, indicate, manifest, show, testify to **2** SHOW HOW, describe, explain, illustrate, make clear, teach **3** MARCH, parade, picket, protest, rally

demonstration noun **1** MARCH, mass lobby, parade, picket, protest, rally, sit-in **2** EXPLANATION, description, exposition, presentation, test, trial **3** PROOF, confirmation, display, evidence, exhibition, expression, illustration, testimony

demoralize verb DISHEARTEN, deject, depress, discourage, dispirit, undermine, unnerve, weaken

demote verb DOWNGRADE, degrade, kick downstairs (slang), lower in rank, relegate

demur verb 1 OBJECT, balk, dispute, hesitate, protest, refuse, take exception, waver ♦ noun 2 As in **without demur** OBJECTION, compunction, dissent, hesitation, misgiving, protest, qualm

demure adjective SHY, diffident, modest, reserved, reticent, retiring, sedate, unassuming

den noun 1 LAIR, cave, cavern, haunt, hide-out, hole, shelter 2 Chiefly U.S. STUDY, cubbyhole, hideaway, retreat, sanctuary, sanctum

denial noun 1 NEGATION, contradiction, dissent, renunciation, repudiation, retraction 2 REFUSAL, prohibition, rebuff, rejection, repulse, veto

denigrate verb DISPARAGE, bad-mouth (slang, chiefly U.S. & Canad.), belittle, knock (informal), malign, rubbish (informal), run down, slander, vilify

denomination noun 1 RELIGIOUS GROUP, belief, creed, persuasion, school, sect 2 UNIT, grade, size, value

denote verb INDICATE, betoken, designate, express, imply, mark, mean, show, signify

denounce verb CONDEMN, accuse, attack, censure, denunciate, revile, stigmatize, vilify

dense adjective 1 THICK, close-knit, compact, condensed, heavy, impenetrable, opaque, solid 2 Informal STUPID, dozy (Brit. informal), dull, obtuse, slow-witted, stolid, thick

density noun TIGHTNESS, bulk, compactness, consistency, denseness, impenetrability, mass, solidity, thickness

dent noun 1 HOLLOW, chip, crater, depression, dimple, dip, impression, indentation, pit ♦ verb 2 MAKE A DENT IN, gouge, hollow, press in, push in

deny verb 1 CONTRADICT, disagree with, disprove, rebuff, rebut, refute 2 REFUSE, begrudge, disallow, forbid, reject, turn down, withhold 3 RENOUNCE, disclaim, disown, recant, repudiate, retract

depart verb 1 LEAVE, absent (oneself), disappear, exit, go, go away, quit, retire, retreat, withdraw 2 DEVIATE, differ, digress, diverge, stray, swerve, turn aside, vary, veer

department noun SECTION, branch, bureau, division, office, station, subdivision, unit

departure noun 1 LEAVING, exit, exodus, going, going away, leave-taking, removal, retirement, withdrawal 2 DIVERGENCE, deviation, digression, variation 3 SHIFT, change, difference, innovation, novelty, whole new ball game (informal)

depend verb 1 TRUST IN, bank on, count on, lean on, reckon on, rely upon, turn to 2 BE DETERMINED BY, be based on, be contingent on, be subject to, be subordinate to, hang on, hinge on, rest on, revolve around

dependable adjective RELIABLE, faithful, reputable, responsible, staunch, steady, sure, trustworthy, trusty, unfailing

dependant noun RELATIVE, child, minor, protégé, subordinate

dependent adjective 1 RELYING ON, defenceless, helpless, reliant, vulnerable, weak 2 **dependent on** or **upon** DETERMINED BY, conditional on, contingent on, depending on, influenced by, subject to

depict verb 1 DRAW, delineate, illustrate, outline, paint, picture, portray, sketch 2 DESCRIBE, characterize, narrate, outline, represent

depiction *noun* REPRESENTATION, delineation, description, picture, portrayal, sketch

deplete *verb* USE UP, consume, drain, empty, exhaust, expend, impoverish, lessen, reduce

deplorable *adjective* 1 REGRETTABLE, grievous, lamentable, pitiable, sad, unfortunate, wretched 2 DISGRACEFUL, dishonourable, reprehensible, scandalous, shameful

deplore *verb* DISAPPROVE OF, abhor, censure, condemn, denounce, object to, take a dim view of

deploy *verb* POSITION, arrange, set out, station, use, utilize

deployment *noun* POSITION, arrangement, organization, spread, stationing, use, utilization

deport *verb* 1 EXPEL, banish, exile, expatriate, extradite, oust 2 **deport oneself** BEHAVE, acquit oneself, act, bear oneself, carry oneself, comport oneself, conduct oneself, hold oneself

depose *verb* 1 REMOVE FROM OFFICE, demote, dethrone, dismiss, displace, oust 2 *Law* TESTIFY, avouch, declare, make a deposition

deposit *verb* 1 PUT, drop, lay, locate, place 2 STORE, bank, consign, entrust, lodge ♦ *noun* 3 DOWN PAYMENT, instalment, part payment, pledge, retainer, security, stake 4 SEDIMENT, accumulation, dregs, lees, precipitate, silt

depot *noun* 1 STOREHOUSE, depository, repository, warehouse 2 *Chiefly U.S. & Canad.* BUS STATION, garage, terminus

...ed *adjective* CORRUPT, ...erate, dissolute, evil,

immoral, sinful, vicious, vile, wicked

depravity *noun* CORRUPTION, debauchery, evil, immorality, sinfulness, vice, wickedness

depreciate *verb* 1 DEVALUE, decrease, deflate, lessen, lose value, lower, reduce 2 DISPARAGE, belittle, denigrate, deride, detract, run down, scorn, sneer at

depreciation *noun* 1 DEVALUATION, deflation, depression, drop, fall, slump 2 DISPARAGEMENT, belittlement, denigration, deprecation, detraction

depress *verb* 1 SADDEN, deject, discourage, dishearten, dispirit, make despondent, oppress, weigh down 2 LOWER, cheapen, depreciate, devalue, diminish, downgrade, lessen, reduce 3 PRESS DOWN, flatten, level, lower, push down

depressed *adjective* 1 LOW-SPIRITED, blue, dejected, despondent, discouraged, dispirited, downcast, downhearted, fed up, sad, unhappy 2 POVERTY-STRICKEN, deprived, disadvantaged, needy, poor, run-down 3 LOWERED, cheapened, depreciated, devalued, weakened 4 SUNKEN, concave, hollow, indented, recessed

depressing *adjective* BLEAK, discouraging, disheartening, dismal, dispiriting, gloomy, harrowing, sad, saddening

depression *noun* 1 LOW SPIRITS, dejection, despair, despondency, downheartedness, dumps (*informal*), gloominess, melancholy, sadness, the blues 2 RECESSION, economic decline, hard *or* bad times, inactivity, slump, stagnation 3 HOLLOW, bowl, cavity, dent, dimple, dip, indentation, pit, valley

deprivation *noun* 1 WITHHOLDING, denial, dispossession, expropriation, removal, withdrawal 2 WANT, destitution, distress, hardship, need, privation

deprive *verb* WITHHOLD, bereave, despoil, dispossess, rob, strip

deprived *adjective* POOR, bereft, destitute, disadvantaged, down at heel, in need, lacking, needy

depth *noun* 1 DEEPNESS, drop, extent, measure 2 INSIGHT, astuteness, discernment, penetration, profoundness, profundity, sagacity, wisdom

deputation *noun* DELEGATION, commission, embassy, envoys, legation

deputize *verb* STAND IN FOR, act for, take the place of, understudy

deputy *noun* SUBSTITUTE, delegate, legate, lieutenant, number two, proxy, representative, second-in-command, surrogate

deranged *adjective* MAD, crazed, crazy, demented, distracted, insane, irrational, unbalanced, unhinged

derelict *adjective* 1 ABANDONED, deserted, dilapidated, discarded, forsaken, neglected, ruined ♦ *noun* 2 TRAMP, bag lady, down-and-out, outcast, vagrant

deride *verb* MOCK, disdain, disparage, insult, jeer, ridicule, scoff, scorn, sneer, taunt

derisory *adjective* RIDICULOUS, contemptible, insulting, laughable, ludicrous, outrageous, preposterous

derivation *noun* ORIGIN, beginning, foundation, root, source

derive from *verb* COME FROM, arise from, emanate from, flow from, issue from, originate from, proceed from, spring from, stem from

derogatory *adjective* DISPARAGING, belittling, defamatory, offensive, slighting, uncomplimentary, unfavourable, unflattering

descend *verb* 1 MOVE DOWN, drop, fall, go down, plummet, plunge, sink, subside, tumble 2 SLOPE, dip, incline, slant 3 LOWER ONESELF, degenerate, deteriorate, stoop 4 **be descended** ORIGINATE, be handed down, be passed down, derive, issue, proceed, spring 5 **descend on** ATTACK, arrive, invade, raid, swoop

descent *noun* 1 COMING DOWN, drop, fall, plunge, swoop 2 SLOPE, declivity, dip, drop, incline, slant 3 ANCESTRY, extraction, family tree, genealogy, lineage, origin, parentage 4 DECLINE, degeneration, deterioration

describe *verb* 1 RELATE, depict, explain, express, narrate, portray, recount, report, tell 2 TRACE, delineate, draw, mark out, outline

description *noun* 1 ACCOUNT, depiction, explanation, narrative, portrayal, report, representation, sketch 2 KIND, brand, category, class, order, sort, type, variety

descriptive *adjective* GRAPHIC, detailed, explanatory, expressive, illustrative, pictorial, picturesque, vivid

desert[1] *noun* WILDERNESS, solitude, waste, wasteland, wilds

desert[2] *verb* ABANDON, abscond, forsake, jilt, leave, leave stranded, maroon, quit, strand, walk out on (*informal*)

deserted *adjective* ABANDONED, derelict, desolate, empty, forsaken, neglected, unoccupied, vacant

deserter *noun* DEFECTOR, absconder, escapee, fugitive, renegade, runaway, traitor, truant

desertion noun ABANDONMENT, absconding, apostasy, betrayal, defection, dereliction, escape, evasion, flight, relinquishment

deserve verb MERIT, be entitled to, be worthy of, earn, justify, rate, warrant

deserved adjective WELL-EARNED, due, earned, fitting, justified, merited, proper, rightful, warranted

deserving adjective WORTHY, commendable, estimable, laudable, meritorious, praiseworthy, righteous

design verb 1 PLAN, draft, draw, outline, sketch, trace 2 CREATE, conceive, fabricate, fashion, invent, originate, think up 3 INTEND, aim, mean, plan, propose, purpose ♦ noun 4 PLAN, blueprint, draft, drawing, model, outline, scheme, sketch 5 ARRANGEMENT, construction, form, organization, pattern, shape, style 6 INTENTION, aim, end, goal, object, objective, purpose, target

designate verb 1 NAME, call, dub, entitle, label, style, term 2 APPOINT, assign, choose, delegate, depute, nominate, select

designation noun NAME, description, label, mark, title

designer noun CREATOR, architect, deviser, inventor, originator, planner

desirable adjective 1 WORTHWHILE, advantageous, advisable, beneficial, good, preferable, profitable 2 ATTRACTIVE, adorable, alluring, fetching, glamorous, seductive, sexy (informal)

desire verb 1 WANT, crave, hanker after, hope for, long for, set one's heart on, thirst for, wish for, yearn for ♦ noun 2 WISH, aspiration,

craving, hankering, hope, longing, thirst, want 3 LUST, appetite, libido, passion

desist verb STOP, break off, cease, discontinue, end, forbear, leave off, pause, refrain from

desolate adjective 1 UNINHABITED, bare, barren, bleak, dreary, godforsaken, solitary, wild 2 MISERABLE, dejected, despondent, disconsolate, downcast, forlorn, gloomy, wretched ♦ verb 3 LAY WASTE, depopulate, despoil, destroy, devastate, lay low, pillage, plunder, ravage, ruin 4 DEJECT, depress, discourage, dishearten, dismay, distress, grieve

desolation noun 1 RUIN, destruction, devastation, havoc 2 BLEAKNESS, barrenness, isolation, solitude 3 MISERY, anguish, dejection, despair, distress, gloom, sadness, woe, wretchedness

despair noun 1 DESPONDENCY, anguish, dejection, depression, desperation, gloom, hopelessness, misery, wretchedness ♦ verb 2 LOSE HOPE, give up, lose heart

despairing adjective HOPELESS, dejected, desperate, despondent, disconsolate, frantic, grief-stricken, inconsolable, miserable, wretched

despatch see DISPATCH

desperado noun CRIMINAL, bandit, lawbreaker, outlaw, villain

desperate adjective 1 RECKLESS, audacious, daring, frantic, furious, risky 2 GRAVE, drastic, extreme, urgent

desperately adverb 1 GRAVELY, badly, dangerously, perilously, seriously, severely 2 HOPELESSLY, appallingly, fearfully, frightfully, shockingly

desperation noun 1 RECKLESSNESS,

foolhardiness, frenzy, impetuosity, madness, rashness **2** MISERY, agony, anguish, despair, hopelessness, trouble, unhappiness, worry

despicable *adjective* CONTEMPTIBLE, detestable, disgraceful, hateful, mean, shameful, sordid, vile, worthless, wretched

despise *verb* LOOK DOWN ON, abhor, detest, loathe, revile, scorn

despite *preposition* IN SPITE OF, against, even with, in the face of, in the teeth of, notwithstanding, regardless of, undeterred by

despondency *noun* DEJECTION, depression, despair, desperation, gloom, low spirits, melancholy, misery, sadness

despondent *adjective* DEJECTED, depressed, disconsolate, disheartened, dispirited, downhearted, glum, in despair, sad, sorrowful

despot *noun* TYRANT, autocrat, dictator, oppressor

despotic *adjective* TYRANNICAL, authoritarian, autocratic, dictatorial, domineering, imperious, oppressive

despotism *noun* TYRANNY, autocracy, dictatorship, oppression, totalitarianism

destination *noun* JOURNEY'S END, haven, resting-place, station, stop, terminus

destined *adjective* FATED, bound, certain, doomed, intended, meant, predestined

destiny *noun* FATE, doom, fortune, karma, kismet, lot, portion

destitute *adjective* PENNILESS, down and out, impoverished, indigent, insolvent, moneyless, penurious, poor, poverty-stricken

destroy *verb* RUIN, annihilate, crush, demolish, devastate, eradicate,

shatter, wipe out, wreck

destruction *noun* RUIN, annihilation, demolition, devastation, eradication, extermination, havoc, slaughter, wreckage

destructive *adjective* DAMAGING, calamitous, catastrophic, deadly, devastating, fatal, harmful, lethal, ruinous

detach *verb* SEPARATE, cut off, disconnect, disengage, divide, remove, sever, tear off, unfasten

detached *adjective* **1** SEPARATE, disconnected, discrete, unconnected **2** UNINVOLVED, disinterested, dispassionate, impartial, impersonal, neutral, objective, reserved, unbiased

detachment *noun* **1** INDIFFERENCE, aloofness, coolness, nonchalance, remoteness, unconcern **2** IMPARTIALITY, fairness, neutrality, objectivity **3** *Military* UNIT, body, force, party, patrol, squad, task force

detail *noun* **1** POINT, aspect, component, element, fact, factor, feature, particular, respect **2** FINE POINT, nicety, particular, triviality **3** *Military* PARTY, assignment, body, detachment, duty, fatigue, force, squad ♦ *verb* **4** LIST, catalogue, enumerate, itemize, recite, recount, rehearse, relate, tabulate **5** APPOINT, allocate, assign, charge, commission, delegate, send

detailed *adjective* COMPREHENSIVE, blow-by-blow, exhaustive, full, intricate, minute, particular, thorough

detain *verb* **1** DELAY, check, hinder, hold up, impede, keep back, retard, slow up (*or* down) **2** HOLD, arrest, confine, intern, restrain

detect *verb* **1** NOTICE, ascertain, identify, note, observe, perceive, recognize, spot **2** DISCOVER, find, track down, uncover, unmask

detective *noun* INVESTIGATOR, cop (*slang*), gumshoe (*U.S. slang*), private eye, private investigator, sleuth (*informal*)

detention *noun* IMPRISONMENT, confinement, custody, incarceration, quarantine

deter *verb* DISCOURAGE, dissuade, frighten, inhibit from, intimidate, prevent, put off, stop, talk out of

detergent *noun* CLEANER, cleanser

deteriorate *verb* DECLINE, degenerate, go downhill (*informal*), lower, slump, worsen

determination *noun* TENACITY, dedication, doggedness, fortitude, perseverance, persistence, resolve, single-mindedness, steadfastness, willpower

determine *verb* **1** SETTLE, conclude, decide, end, finish, ordain, regulate **2** FIND OUT, ascertain, detect, discover, learn, verify, work out **3** DECIDE, choose, elect, make up one's mind, resolve

determined *adjective* RESOLUTE, dogged, firm, intent, persevering, persistent, single-minded, steadfast, tenacious, unwavering

deterrent *noun* DISCOURAGEMENT, check, curb, disincentive, hindrance, impediment, obstacle, restraint

detest *verb* HATE, abhor, abominate, despise, dislike intensely, loathe, recoil from

detonate *verb* EXPLODE, blast, blow up, discharge, set off, trigger

detour *noun* DIVERSION, bypass, indirect course, roundabout way

detract *verb* LESSEN, devaluate, diminish, lower, reduce, take away from

detriment *noun* DAMAGE, disadvantage, disservice, harm, hurt, impairment, injury, loss

detrimental *adjective* DAMAGING, adverse, deleterious, destructive, disadvantageous, harmful, prejudicial, unfavourable

devastate *verb* DESTROY, demolish, lay waste, level, ravage, raze, ruin, sack, wreck

devastating *adjective* OVERWHELMING, cutting, overpowering, savage, trenchant, vitriolic, withering

devastation *noun* DESTRUCTION, demolition, desolation, havoc, ruin

develop *verb* **1** ADVANCE, evolve, flourish, grow, mature, progress, prosper, ripen **2** FORM, breed, establish, generate, invent, originate **3** EXPAND, amplify, augment, broaden, elaborate, enlarge, unfold, work out

development *noun* **1** GROWTH, advance, evolution, expansion, improvement, increase, progress, spread **2** EVENT, happening, incident, occurrence, result, turn of events, upshot

deviant *adjective* **1** PERVERTED, kinky (*slang*), sick (*informal*), twisted, warped ♦ *noun* **2** PERVERT, freak, misfit

deviate *verb* DIFFER, depart, diverge, stray, swerve, veer, wander

deviation *noun* DEPARTURE, digression, discrepancy, disparity, divergence, inconsistency, irregularity, shift, variation

device *noun* **1** GADGET, apparatus, appliance, contraption, implement, instrument, machine, tool **2** PLOY, gambit, manoeuvre, plan, scheme, stratagem, trick, wile

devil *noun* **1** the Devil SATAN, Beelzebub, Evil One, Lucifer,

Mephistopheles, Old Nick (*informal*), Prince of Darkness **2** <u>BRUTE</u>, beast, demon, fiend, monster, ogre, terror **3** <u>SCAMP</u>, rascal, rogue, scoundrel **4** <u>PERSON</u>, beggar, creature, thing, wretch

devilish *adjective* <u>FIENDISH</u>, atrocious, damnable, detestable, diabolical, hellish, infernal, satanic, wicked

devious *adjective* **1** <u>SLY</u>, calculating, deceitful, dishonest, double-dealing, insincere, scheming, surreptitious, underhand, wily **2** <u>INDIRECT</u>, circuitous, rambling, roundabout

devise *verb* <u>WORK OUT</u>, conceive, construct, contrive, design, dream up, formulate, invent, think up

devoid *adjective* <u>LACKING</u>, bereft, deficient, destitute, empty, free from, wanting, without

devote *verb* <u>DEDICATE</u>, allot, apply, assign, commit, give, pledge, reserve, set apart

devoted *adjective* <u>DEDICATED</u>, ardent, committed, constant, devout, faithful, loyal, staunch, steadfast, true

devotee *noun* <u>ENTHUSIAST</u>, adherent, admirer, aficionado, buff (*informal*), disciple, fan, fanatic, follower, supporter

devotion *noun* **1** <u>DEDICATION</u>, adherence, allegiance, commitment, constancy, faithfulness, fidelity, loyalty **2** <u>LOVE</u>, affection, attachment, fondness, passion **3** <u>DEVOUTNESS</u>, godliness, holiness, piety, reverence, spirituality **4 devotions** <u>PRAYERS</u>, church service, divine office, religious observance

devour *verb* **1** <u>EAT</u>, consume, gobble, gulp, guzzle, polish off (*informal*), swallow, wolf **2** <u>DESTROY</u>, annihilate, consume, ravage,

waste, wipe out **3** <u>ENJOY</u>, read compulsively *or* voraciously, take in

devout *adjective* <u>RELIGIOUS</u>, godly, holy, orthodox, pious, prayerful, pure, reverent, saintly

dexterity *noun* **1** <u>SKILL</u>, adroitness, deftness, expertise, finesse, nimbleness, proficiency, touch **2** <u>CLEVERNESS</u>, ability, aptitude, ingenuity

diabolical *adjective Informal* <u>DREADFUL</u>, abysmal, appalling, atrocious, hellish, outrageous, shocking, terrible

diagnose *verb* <u>IDENTIFY</u>, analyse, determine, distinguish, interpret, pinpoint, pronounce, recognize

diagnosis *noun* **1** <u>EXAMINATION</u>, analysis, investigation, scrutiny **2** <u>OPINION</u>, conclusion, interpretation, pronouncement

diagonal *adjective* <u>SLANTING</u>, angled, cross, crossways, crosswise, oblique

diagonally *adverb* <u>ASLANT</u>, at an angle, cornerwise, crosswise, obliquely

diagram *noun* <u>PLAN</u>, chart, drawing, figure, graph, representation, sketch

dialect *noun* <u>LANGUAGE</u>, brogue, idiom, jargon, patois, provincialism, speech, vernacular

dialogue *noun* <u>CONVERSATION</u>, communication, conference, discourse, discussion

diary *noun* <u>JOURNAL</u>, appointment book, chronicle, daily record, engagement book, Filofax (*Trademark*)

dicky *adjective Brit. informal* <u>WEAK</u>, fluttery, shaky, unreliable, unsound, unsteady

dictate *verb* **1** <u>SPEAK</u>, read out, say, utter **2** <u>ORDER</u>, command, decree, demand, direct, impose, lay down

the law, pronounce ♦ *noun*
3 COMMAND, decree, demand,
direction, edict, fiat, injunction,
order **4** PRINCIPLE, code, law, rule

dictator *noun* ABSOLUTE RULER,
autocrat, despot, oppressor, tyrant

dictatorial *adjective* **1** ABSOLUTE,
arbitrary, autocratic, despotic,
totalitarian, tyrannical, unlimited,
unrestricted **2** DOMINEERING,
authoritarian, bossy (*informal*),
imperious, oppressive, overbearing

dictatorship *noun* ABSOLUTE RULE,
absolutism, authoritarianism,
autocracy, despotism,
totalitarianism, tyranny

diction *noun* PRONUNCIATION,
articulation, delivery, elocution,
enunciation, fluency, inflection,
intonation, speech

dictionary *noun* WORDBOOK,
glossary, lexicon, vocabulary

die *verb* **1** PASS AWAY, breathe one's
last, croak (*slang*), expire, give up
the ghost, kick the bucket (*slang*),
peg out (*informal*), perish, snuff it
(*slang*) **2** DWINDLE, decay, decline,
fade, sink, subside, wane, wilt,
wither **3** STOP, break down, fade
out *or* away, fail, fizzle out, halt,
lose power, peter out, run down
4 be dying LONG, ache, be eager,
desire, hunger, pine for, yearn

die-hard *noun* REACTIONARY, fanatic,
old fogey, stick-in-the-mud
(*informal*)

diet[1] *noun* **1** FOOD, fare,
nourishment, nutriment,
provisions, rations, sustenance,
victuals **2** REGIME, abstinence, fast,
regimen ♦ *verb* **3** SLIM, abstain, eat
sparingly, fast, lose weight

diet[2] *noun* COUNCIL, chamber,
congress, convention, legislature,
meeting, parliament

differ *verb* **1** BE DISSIMILAR, contradict,
contrast, depart from, diverge,

run counter to, stand apart, vary
2 DISAGREE, clash, contend, debate,
demur, dispute, dissent, oppose,
take exception, take issue

difference *noun* **1** DISSIMILARITY,
alteration, change, contrast,
discrepancy, disparity, diversity,
variation, variety **2** DISAGREEMENT,
argument, clash, conflict,
contretemps, debate, dispute,
quarrel **3** REMAINDER, balance, rest,
result

different *adjective* **1** UNLIKE, altered,
changed, contrasting, disparate,
dissimilar, divergent, inconsistent,
opposed **2** VARIOUS, assorted,
diverse, miscellaneous, sundry,
varied **3** UNUSUAL, atypical,
distinctive, extraordinary,
peculiar, singular, special, strange,
uncommon

differentiate *verb* **1** DISTINGUISH,
contrast, discriminate, make a
distinction, mark off, separate, set
off *or* apart, tell apart **2** MAKE
DIFFERENT, adapt, alter, change,
convert, modify, transform

difficult *adjective* **1** HARD, arduous,
demanding, formidable,
laborious, onerous, strenuous,
uphill **2** PROBLEMATICAL, abstruse,
baffling, complex, complicated,
intricate, involved, knotty,
obscure **3** HARD TO PLEASE,
demanding, fastidious, fussy,
perverse, refractory,
unaccommodating

difficulty *noun* **1** LABORIOUSNESS,
arduousness, awkwardness,
hardship, strain, strenuousness,
tribulation **2** PREDICAMENT,
dilemma, embarrassment, hot
water (*informal*), jam (*informal*),
mess, plight, quandary, trouble
3 PROBLEM, complication,
hindrance, hurdle, impediment,
obstacle, pitfall, snag, stumbling
block

diffidence *noun* SHYNESS,

bashfulness, hesitancy, insecurity, modesty, reserve, self-consciousness, timidity

diffident *adjective* SHY, bashful, doubtful, hesitant, insecure, modest, reserved, self-conscious, timid, unassertive, unassuming

dig *verb* 1 EXCAVATE, burrow, delve, hollow out, mine, quarry, scoop, tunnel 2 INVESTIGATE, delve, dig down, go into, probe, research, search 3 *with out or up* FIND, discover, expose, uncover, unearth, uproot 4 POKE, drive, jab, prod, punch, thrust ♦ *noun* 5 POKE, jab, prod, punch, thrust 6 CUTTING REMARK, barb, crack (*slang*), gibe, insult, jeer, sneer, taunt, wisecrack (*informal*)

digest *verb* 1 INGEST, absorb, assimilate, dissolve, incorporate 2 TAKE IN, absorb, consider, contemplate, grasp, study, understand ♦ *noun* 3 SUMMARY, abridgment, abstract, epitome, précis, résumé, synopsis

digestion *noun* INGESTION, absorption, assimilation, conversion, incorporation, transformation

dignified *adjective* DISTINGUISHED, formal, grave, imposing, noble, reserved, solemn, stately

dignitary *noun* PUBLIC FIGURE, bigwig (*informal*), high-up (*informal*), notable, personage, pillar of society, V.I.P., worthy

dignity *noun* 1 DECORUM, courtliness, grandeur, gravity, loftiness, majesty, nobility, solemnity, stateliness 2 HONOUR, eminence, importance, rank, respectability, standing, status 3 SELF-IMPORTANCE, pride, self-esteem, self-respect

digress *verb* WANDER, depart, deviate, diverge, drift, get off the point *or* subject, go off at a

tangent, ramble, stray

digression *noun* DEPARTURE, aside, detour, deviation, divergence, diversion, straying, wandering

dilapidated *adjective* RUINED, broken-down, crumbling, decrepit, in ruins, ramshackle, rickety, run-down, tumbledown

dilate *verb* ENLARGE, broaden, expand, puff out, stretch, swell, widen

dilatory *adjective* TIME-WASTING, delaying, lingering, procrastinating, slow, sluggish, tardy, tarrying

dilemma *noun* PREDICAMENT, difficulty, mess, plight, problem, puzzle, quandary, spot (*informal*)

dilettante *noun* AMATEUR, aesthete, dabbler, trifler

diligence *noun* APPLICATION, attention, care, industry, laboriousness, perseverance

diligent *adjective* HARD-WORKING, assiduous, attentive, careful, conscientious, industrious, painstaking, persistent, studious, tireless

dilute *verb* 1 WATER DOWN, adulterate, cut, make thinner, thin (out), weaken 2 REDUCE, attenuate, decrease, diffuse, diminish, lessen, mitigate, temper, weaken

dim *adjective* 1 POORLY LIT, cloudy, dark, grey, overcast, shadowy, tenebrous 2 UNCLEAR, bleary, blurred, faint, fuzzy, ill-defined, indistinct, obscured, shadowy 3 *Informal* STUPID, dense, dozy (*Brit. informal*), dull, dumb (*informal*), obtuse, slow on the uptake (*informal*), thick 4 **take a dim view** DISAPPROVE, be displeased, be sceptical, look askance, reject, suspect, take exception, view with disfavour ♦ *verb* 5 DULL, blur, cloud, darken, fade, obscure

dimension *noun,* often plural
MEASUREMENT, amplitude, bulk,
capacity, extent, proportions, size,
volume

diminish *verb* **1** DECREASE, curtail,
cut, lessen, lower, reduce, shrink
2 DWINDLE, decline, die out, recede,
subside, wane

diminutive *adjective* SMALL, little,
mini, miniature, minute, petite,
tiny, undersized

din *noun* **1** NOISE, clamour, clatter,
commotion, crash,
pandemonium, racket, row,
uproar ♦ *verb* **2** **din (something)
into (someone)** INSTIL, drum into,
go on at, hammer into, inculcate,
instruct, teach

dine *verb* EAT, banquet, feast, lunch,
sup

dingy *adjective* DULL, dark, dim,
drab, dreary, gloomy, murky,
obscure, sombre

dinner *noun* MEAL, banquet, feast,
main meal, repast, spread
(*informal*)

dip *verb* **1** PLUNGE, bathe, douse,
duck, dunk, immerse **2** SLOPE,
decline, descend, drop (down),
fall, lower, sink, subside ♦ *noun*
3 PLUNGE, douche, drenching,
ducking, immersion, soaking
4 BATHE, dive, plunge, swim
5 HOLLOW, basin, concavity,
depression, hole, incline, slope
6 DROP, decline, fall, lowering, sag,
slip, slump

dip into *verb* SAMPLE, browse,
glance at, peruse, skim

diplomacy *noun* **1** STATESMANSHIP,
international negotiation,
statecraft **2** TACT, artfulness, craft,
delicacy, discretion, finesse,
savoir-faire, skill, subtlety

diplomat *noun* NEGOTIATOR,
conciliator, go-between,
mediator, moderator, politician,

tactician

diplomatic *adjective* TACTFUL, adept,
discreet, polite, politic, prudent,
sensitive, subtle

dire *adjective* **1** DISASTROUS, awful,
calamitous, catastrophic, horrible,
ruinous, terrible, woeful
2 DESPERATE, critical, crucial, drastic,
extreme, now or never, pressing,
urgent **3** GRIM, dismal, dreadful,
fearful, gloomy, ominous,
portentous

direct *adjective* **1** STRAIGHT, nonstop,
not crooked, shortest, through,
unbroken, uninterrupted
2 IMMEDIATE, face-to-face,
first-hand, head-on, personal
3 HONEST, candid, frank, open,
plain-spoken, straight,
straightforward, upfront (*informal*)
4 EXPLICIT, absolute, blunt,
categorical, downright, express,
plain, point-blank, unambiguous,
unequivocal ♦ *verb* **5** CONTROL,
conduct, guide, handle, lead,
manage, oversee, run, supervise
6 ORDER, bid, charge, command,
demand, dictate, instruct **7** GUIDE,
indicate, lead, point in the
direction of, point the way, show
8 ADDRESS, label, mail, route, send
9 AIM, focus, level, point, train

direction *noun* **1** WAY, aim, bearing,
course, line, path, road, route,
track **2** MANAGEMENT,
administration, charge,
command, control, guidance,
leadership, order, supervision

directions *plural noun* INSTRUCTIONS,
briefing, guidance, guidelines,
plan, recommendation,
regulations

directive *noun* ORDER, command,
decree, edict, injunction,
instruction, mandate, regulation,
ruling

directly *adverb* **1** STRAIGHT, by the
shortest route, exactly, in a

beeline, precisely, unswervingly, without deviation 2 HONESTLY, openly, plainly, point-blank, straightforwardly, truthfully, unequivocally 3 AT ONCE, as soon as possible, forthwith, immediately, promptly, right away, straightaway

director noun CONTROLLER, administrator, chief, executive, governor, head, leader, manager, supervisor

dirge noun LAMENT, dead march, elegy, funeral song, requiem, threnody

dirt noun 1 FILTH, dust, grime, impurity, muck, mud 2 SOIL, clay, earth, loam 3 OBSCENITY, indecency, pornography, sleaze, smut

dirty adjective 1 FILTHY, foul, grimy, grubby, messy, mucky, muddy, polluted, soiled, unclean 2 DISHONEST, crooked, fraudulent, illegal, treacherous, unfair, unscrupulous, unsporting 3 OBSCENE, blue, indecent, pornographic, salacious, sleazy, smutty 4 As in **a dirty look** ANGRY, annoyed, bitter, choked, indignant, offended, resentful, scorching ♦ verb 5 SOIL, blacken, defile, foul, muddy, pollute, smirch, spoil, stain

disability noun 1 HANDICAP, affliction, ailment, complaint, defect, disorder, impairment, infirmity, malady 2 INCAPACITY, inability, unfitness

disable verb 1 HANDICAP, cripple, damage, enfeeble, immobilize, impair, incapacitate, paralyse 2 DISQUALIFY, invalidate, render or declare incapable

disabled adjective HANDICAPPED, crippled, incapacitated, infirm, lame, paralysed, weakened

disadvantage noun 1 HARM, damage, detriment, disservice, hurt, injury, loss, prejudice 2 DRAWBACK, downside, handicap, inconvenience, nuisance, snag, trouble

disagree verb 1 DIFFER (IN OPINION), argue, clash, cross swords, dispute, dissent, object, quarrel, take issue with 2 CONFLICT, be dissimilar, contradict, counter, differ, diverge, run counter to, vary 3 MAKE ILL, bother, discomfort, distress, hurt, nauseate, sicken, trouble, upset

disagreeable adjective 1 NASTY, disgusting, displeasing, distasteful, objectionable, obnoxious, offensive, repugnant, repulsive, unpleasant 2 RUDE, bad-tempered, churlish, difficult, disobliging, irritable, surly, unpleasant

disagreement noun 1 INCOMPATIBILITY, difference, discrepancy, disparity, dissimilarity, divergence, incongruity, variance 2 ARGUMENT, altercation, clash, conflict, dispute, dissent, quarrel, row, squabble

disallow verb REJECT, disavow, dismiss, disown, rebuff, refuse, repudiate

disappear verb 1 VANISH, evanesce, fade away, pass, recede 2 CEASE, die out, dissolve, evaporate, leave no trace, melt away, pass away, perish

disappearance noun VANISHING, departure, eclipse, evanescence, evaporation, going, melting, passing

disappoint verb LET DOWN, disenchant, disgruntle, dishearten, disillusion, dismay, dissatisfy, fail

disappointed adjective LET DOWN, cast down, despondent, discouraged, disenchanted, disgruntled, dissatisfied, downhearted, frustrated

disappointing *adjective* UNSATISFACTORY, depressing, disconcerting, discouraging, inadequate, insufficient, sad, sorry

disappointment *noun* 1 FRUSTRATION, chagrin, discontent, discouragement, disenchantment, disillusionment, dissatisfaction, regret 2 LETDOWN, blow, calamity, choker (*informal*), misfortune, setback

disapproval *noun* DISPLEASURE, censure, condemnation, criticism, denunciation, dissatisfaction, objection, reproach

disapprove *verb* CONDEMN, deplore, dislike, find unacceptable, frown on, look down one's nose at (*informal*), object to, reject, take a dim view of, take exception to

disarm *verb* 1 RENDER DEFENCELESS, disable 2 WIN OVER, persuade, set at ease 3 DEMILITARIZE, deactivate, demobilize, disband

disarmament *noun* ARMS REDUCTION, arms limitation, de-escalation, demilitarization, demobilization

disarming *adjective* CHARMING, irresistible, likable *or* likeable, persuasive, winning

disarrange *verb* DISORDER, confuse, disorganize, disturb, jumble (up), mess (up), scatter, shake (up), shuffle

disarray *noun* 1 CONFUSION, disorder, disorganization, disunity, indiscipline, unruliness 2 UNTIDINESS, chaos, clutter, hotchpotch, jumble, mess, muddle, shambles

disaster *noun* CATASTROPHE, adversity, calamity, cataclysm, misfortune, ruin, tragedy, trouble

disastrous *adjective* TERRIBLE, calamitous, cataclysmic, catastrophic, devastating, fatal, ruinous, tragic

disbelief *noun* SCEPTICISM, distrust, doubt, dubiety, incredulity, mistrust, unbelief

discard *verb* GET RID OF, abandon, cast aside, dispense with, dispose of, drop, dump (*informal*), jettison, reject, throw away *or* out

discharge *verb* 1 RELEASE, allow to go, clear, free, liberate, pardon, set free 2 DISMISS, cashier, discard, expel, fire (*informal*), oust, remove, sack (*informal*) 3 FIRE, detonate, explode, let loose (*informal*), let off, set off, shoot 4 POUR FORTH, dispense, emit, exude, give off, leak, ooze, release 5 CARRY OUT, accomplish, do, execute, fulfil, observe, perform 6 PAY, clear, honour, meet, relieve, satisfy, settle, square up ♦ *noun* 7 RELEASE, acquittal, clearance, liberation, pardon 8 DISMISSAL, demobilization, ejection 9 FIRING, blast, burst, detonation, explosion, report, salvo, shot, volley 10 EMISSION, excretion, ooze, pus, secretion, seepage, suppuration

disciple *noun* FOLLOWER, adherent, apostle, devotee, pupil, student, supporter

disciplinarian *noun* AUTHORITARIAN, despot, martinet, stickler, taskmaster, tyrant

discipline *noun* 1 TRAINING, drill, exercise, method, practice, regimen, regulation 2 PUNISHMENT, castigation, chastisement, correction 3 SELF-CONTROL, conduct, control, orderliness, regulation, restraint, strictness 4 FIELD OF STUDY, area, branch of knowledge, course, curriculum, speciality, subject ♦ *verb* 5 TRAIN, bring up, drill, educate, exercise, prepare 6 PUNISH, bring to book, castigate, chasten, chastise, correct, penalize, reprimand, reprove

disclose verb 1 <u>MAKE KNOWN</u>, broadcast, communicate, confess, divulge, let slip, publish, relate, reveal 2 <u>SHOW</u>, bring to light, expose, lay bare, reveal, uncover, unveil

disclosure noun <u>REVELATION</u>, acknowledgment, admission, announcement, confession, declaration, divulgence, leak, publication

discolour verb <u>STAIN</u>, fade, mark, soil, streak, tarnish, tinge

discomfort noun 1 <u>PAIN</u>, ache, hurt, irritation, malaise, soreness 2 <u>UNEASINESS</u>, annoyance, distress, hardship, irritation, nuisance, trouble

disconcert verb <u>DISTURB</u>, faze, fluster, perturb, rattle (informal), take aback, unsettle, upset, worry

disconcerting adjective <u>DISTURBING</u>, alarming, awkward, bewildering, confusing, distracting, embarrassing, off-putting (Brit. informal), perplexing, upsetting

disconnect verb <u>CUT OFF</u>, detach, disengage, divide, part, separate, sever, take apart, uncouple

disconnected adjective <u>ILLOGICAL</u>, confused, disjointed, incoherent, jumbled, mixed-up, rambling, unintelligible

disconsolate adjective <u>INCONSOLABLE</u>, crushed, dejected, desolate, forlorn, grief-stricken, heartbroken, miserable, wretched

discontent noun <u>DISSATISFACTION</u>, displeasure, envy, regret, restlessness, uneasiness, unhappiness

discontented adjective <u>DISSATISFIED</u>, disaffected, disgruntled, displeased, exasperated, fed up, unhappy, vexed

discontinue verb <u>STOP</u>, abandon, break off, cease, drop, end, give up, quit, suspend, terminate

discord noun 1 <u>DISAGREEMENT</u>, conflict, dissension, disunity, division, friction, incompatibility, strife 2 <u>DISHARMONY</u>, cacophony, din, dissonance, harshness, jarring, racket, tumult

discordant adjective 1 <u>DISAGREEING</u>, at odds, clashing, conflicting, contradictory, contrary, different, incompatible 2 <u>INHARMONIOUS</u>, cacophonous, dissonant, grating, harsh, jarring, shrill, strident

discount verb 1 <u>LEAVE OUT</u>, brush off (slang), disbelieve, disregard, ignore, overlook, pass over 2 <u>DEDUCT</u>, lower, mark down, reduce, take off ◆ noun 3 <u>DEDUCTION</u>, concession, cut, rebate, reduction

discourage verb 1 <u>DISHEARTEN</u>, dampen, deject, demoralize, depress, dispirit, intimidate, overawe, put a damper on 2 <u>PUT OFF</u>, deter, dissuade, inhibit, prevent, talk out of

discouraged adjective <u>PUT OFF</u>, crestfallen, deterred, disheartened, dismayed, dispirited, downcast, down in the mouth, glum

discouragement noun 1 <u>LOSS OF CONFIDENCE</u>, dejection, depression, despair, despondency, disappointment, dismay, downheartedness 2 <u>DETERRENT</u>, damper, disincentive, hindrance, impediment, obstacle, opposition, setback

discouraging adjective <u>DISHEARTENING</u>, dampening, daunting, depressing, disappointing, dispiriting, off-putting (Brit. informal), unfavourable

discourse noun 1 <u>CONVERSATION</u>, chat, communication, dialogue, discussion, seminar, speech, talk

2 SPEECH, dissertation, essay, homily, lecture, oration, sermon, treatise ♦ verb 3 HOLD FORTH, expatiate, speak, talk

discourteous adjective RUDE, bad-mannered, boorish, disrespectful, ill-mannered, impolite, insolent, offhand, ungentlemanly, ungracious

discourtesy noun 1 RUDENESS, bad manners, disrespectfulness, impertinence, impoliteness, incivility, insolence 2 INSULT, affront, cold shoulder, kick in the teeth (slang), rebuff, slight, snub

discover verb 1 FIND, come across, come upon, dig up, locate, turn up, uncover, unearth 2 FIND OUT, ascertain, detect, learn, notice, perceive, realize, recognize, uncover

discovery noun 1 FINDING, detection, disclosure, exploration, location, revelation, uncovering 2 BREAKTHROUGH, find, innovation, invention, secret

discredit verb 1 DISGRACE, bring into disrepute, defame, dishonour, disparage, slander, smear, vilify 2 DOUBT, challenge, deny, disbelieve, discount, dispute, distrust, mistrust, question ♦ noun 3 DISGRACE, dishonour, disrepute, ignominy, ill-repute, scandal, shame, stigma

discreditable adjective DISGRACEFUL, dishonourable, ignominious, reprehensible, scandalous, shameful, unworthy

discreet adjective TACTFUL, careful, cautious, circumspect, considerate, diplomatic, guarded, judicious, prudent, wary

discrepancy noun DISAGREEMENT, conflict, contradiction, difference, disparity, divergence, incongruity, inconsistency, variation

discretion noun 1 TACT, carefulness, caution, consideration, diplomacy, judiciousness, prudence, wariness 2 CHOICE, inclination, pleasure, preference, volition, will

discriminate verb 1 SHOW PREJUDICE, favour, show bias, single out, treat as inferior, treat differently, victimize 2 DIFFERENTIATE, distinguish, draw a distinction, segregate, separate, tell the difference

discriminating adjective DISCERNING, cultivated, fastidious, particular, refined, selective, tasteful

discrimination noun 1 PREJUDICE, bias, bigotry, favouritism, intolerance, unfairness 2 DISCERNMENT, judgment, perception, refinement, subtlety, taste

discuss verb TALK ABOUT, argue, confer, consider, converse, debate, deliberate, examine

discussion noun TALK, analysis, argument, conference, consultation, conversation, debate, deliberation, dialogue, discourse

disdain noun 1 CONTEMPT, arrogance, derision, haughtiness, scorn, superciliousness ♦ verb 2 SCORN, deride, disregard, look down on, reject, slight, sneer at, spurn

disdainful adjective CONTEMPTUOUS, aloof, arrogant, derisive, haughty, proud, scornful, sneering, supercilious, superior

disease noun ILLNESS, affliction, ailment, complaint, condition, disorder, infection, infirmity, malady, sickness

diseased adjective SICK, ailing, infected, rotten, sickly, unhealthy, unsound, unwell, unwholesome

disembark verb <u>LAND</u>, alight, arrive, get off, go ashore, step out of

disenchanted adjective <u>DISILLUSIONED</u>, cynical, disappointed, indifferent, jaundiced, let down, sick of, soured

disenchantment noun <u>DISILLUSIONMENT</u>, disappointment, disillusion, rude awakening

disengage verb <u>RELEASE</u>, disentangle, extricate, free, loosen, set free, unloose, untie

disentangle verb <u>UNTANGLE</u>, disconnect, disengage, extricate, free, loose, unravel

disfavour noun <u>DISAPPROVAL</u>, disapprobation, dislike, displeasure

disfigure verb <u>DAMAGE</u>, blemish, deface, deform, distort, mar, mutilate, scar

disgorge verb <u>VOMIT</u>, discharge, eject, empty, expel

disgrace noun 1 <u>SHAME</u>, degradation, dishonour, disrepute, ignominy, infamy, odium, opprobrium 2 <u>STAIN</u>, blemish, blot, reproach, scandal, slur, stigma ◆verb 3 <u>BRING SHAME UPON</u>, degrade, discredit, dishonour, humiliate, shame, sully, taint

disgraceful adjective <u>SHAMEFUL</u>, contemptible, detestable, dishonourable, disreputable, ignominious, scandalous, shocking, unworthy

disgruntled adjective <u>DISCONTENTED</u>, annoyed, displeased, dissatisfied, grumpy, irritated, peeved, put out, vexed

disguise verb 1 <u>HIDE</u>, camouflage, cloak, conceal, cover, mask, screen, shroud, veil 2 <u>MISREPRESENT</u>, fake, falsify ◆noun 3 <u>COSTUME</u>,

camouflage, cover, mask, screen, veil 4 <u>FAÇADE</u>, deception, dissimulation, front, pretence, semblance, trickery, veneer

disguised adjective <u>IN DISGUISE</u>, camouflaged, covert, fake, false, feigned, incognito, masked, undercover

disgust noun 1 <u>LOATHING</u>, abhorrence, aversion, dislike, distaste, hatred, nausea, repugnance, repulsion, revulsion ◆verb 2 <u>SICKEN</u>, displease, nauseate, offend, put off, repel, revolt

disgusted adjective <u>SICKENED</u>, appalled, nauseated, offended, repulsed, scandalized

disgusting adjective <u>SICKENING</u>, foul, gross, loathsome, nauseating, offensive, repellent, repugnant, revolting

dish noun 1 <u>BOWL</u>, plate, platter, salver 2 <u>FOOD</u>, fare, recipe

dishearten verb <u>DISCOURAGE</u>, cast down, deject, depress, deter, dismay, dispirit, put a damper on

dishevelled adjective <u>UNTIDY</u>, bedraggled, disordered, messy, ruffled, rumpled, tousled, uncombed, unkempt

dishonest adjective <u>DECEITFUL</u>, bent (slang), cheating, corrupt, crooked (informal), disreputable, double-dealing, false, lying, treacherous

dishonesty noun <u>DECEIT</u>, cheating, chicanery, corruption, fraud, treachery, trickery, unscrupulousness

dishonour verb 1 <u>SHAME</u>, debase, debauch, defame, degrade, discredit, disgrace, sully ◆noun 2 <u>SHAME</u>, discredit, disgrace, disrepute, ignominy, infamy, obloquy, reproach, scandal 3 <u>INSULT</u>, abuse, affront, discourtesy, indignity, offence, outrage, sacrilege, slight

dishonourable *adjective*
1 <u>SHAMEFUL</u>, contemptible, despicable, discreditable, disgraceful, ignominious, infamous, scandalous
2 <u>UNTRUSTWORTHY</u>, blackguardly, corrupt, disreputable, shameless, treacherous, unprincipled, unscrupulous

disillusioned *adjective* <u>DISENCHANTED</u>, disabused, disappointed, enlightened, undeceived

disinclination *noun* <u>RELUCTANCE</u>, aversion, dislike, hesitance, objection, opposition, repugnance, resistance, unwillingness

disinclined *adjective* <u>RELUCTANT</u>, averse, hesitating, loath, not in the mood, opposed, resistant, unwilling

disinfect *verb* <u>STERILIZE</u>, clean, cleanse, decontaminate, deodorize, fumigate, purify, sanitize

disinfectant *noun* <u>ANTISEPTIC</u>, germicide, sterilizer

disinherit *verb* *Law* <u>CUT OFF</u>, disown, dispossess, oust, repudiate

disintegrate *verb* <u>BREAK UP</u>, break apart, crumble, fall apart, go to pieces, separate, shatter, splinter

disinterest *noun* <u>IMPARTIALITY</u>, detachment, fairness, neutrality

disinterested *adjective* <u>IMPARTIAL</u>, detached, dispassionate, even-handed, impersonal, neutral, objective, unbiased, unprejudiced

disjointed *adjective* <u>INCOHERENT</u>, confused, disconnected, disordered, rambling

dislike *verb* 1 <u>BE AVERSE TO</u>, despise, detest, disapprove, hate, loathe,

not be able to bear *or* abide *or* stand, object to, take a dim view of ♦ *noun* 2 <u>AVERSION</u>, animosity, antipathy, disapproval, disinclination, displeasure, distaste, enmity, hostility, repugnance

dislodge *verb* <u>DISPLACE</u>, disturb, extricate, force out, knock loose, oust, remove, uproot

disloyal *adjective* <u>TREACHEROUS</u>, faithless, false, subversive, traitorous, two-faced, unfaithful, untrustworthy

disloyalty *noun* <u>TREACHERY</u>, breach of trust, deceitfulness, double-dealing, falseness, inconstancy, infidelity, treason, unfaithfulness

dismal *adjective* <u>GLOOMY</u>, bleak, cheerless, dark, depressing, discouraging, dreary, forlorn, sombre, wretched

dismantle *verb* <u>TAKE APART</u>, demolish, disassemble, strip, take to pieces

dismay *verb* 1 <u>ALARM</u>, appal, distress, frighten, horrify, paralyse, scare, terrify, unnerve 2 <u>DISAPPOINT</u>, daunt, discourage, dishearten, disillusion, dispirit, put off ♦ *noun* 3 <u>ALARM</u>, anxiety, apprehension, consternation, dread, fear, horror, trepidation 4 <u>DISAPPOINTMENT</u>, chagrin, discouragement, disillusionment

dismember *verb* <u>CUT INTO PIECES</u>, amputate, dissect, mutilate, sever

dismiss *verb* 1 <u>SACK</u> (*informal*), axe (*informal*), cashier, discharge, fire (*informal*), give notice to, give (someone) their marching orders, lay off, remove 2 <u>LET GO</u>, disperse, dissolve, free, release, send away 3 <u>PUT OUT OF ONE'S MIND</u>, banish, discard, dispel, disregard, lay aside, reject, set aside

dismissal *noun* THE SACK (*informal*), expulsion, marching orders (*informal*), notice, removal, the boot (*slang*), the push (*slang*)

disobedience *noun* DEFIANCE, indiscipline, insubordination, mutiny, noncompliance, nonobservance, recalcitrance, revolt, unruliness, waywardness

disobedient *adjective* DEFIANT, contrary, disorderly, insubordinate, intractable, naughty, refractory, undisciplined, unruly, wayward

disobey *verb* REFUSE TO OBEY, contravene, defy, disregard, flout, ignore, infringe, rebel, violate

disorder *noun* 1 UNTIDINESS, chaos, clutter, confusion, disarray, jumble, mess, muddle, shambles 2 DISTURBANCE, commotion, riot, turmoil, unrest, unruliness, uproar 3 ILLNESS, affliction, ailment, complaint, disease, malady, sickness

disorderly *adjective* 1 UNTIDY, chaotic, confused, disorganized, higgledy-piggledy (*informal*), jumbled, messy, shambolic (*informal*) 2 UNRULY, disruptive, indisciplined, lawless, riotous, rowdy, tumultuous, turbulent, ungovernable

disorganized *adjective* MUDDLED, chaotic, confused, disordered, haphazard, jumbled, unsystematic

disown *verb* DENY, cast off, disavow, disclaim, reject, renounce, repudiate

disparage *verb* RUN DOWN, belittle, denigrate, deprecate, deride, malign, put down, ridicule, slander, vilify

dispassionate *adjective* 1 UNEMOTIONAL, calm, collected, composed, cool, imperturbable, serene, unruffled 2 OBJECTIVE, detached, disinterested, fair, impartial, impersonal, neutral, unbiased, unprejudiced

dispatch, despatch *verb* 1 SEND, consign, dismiss, hasten 2 CARRY OUT, discharge, dispose of, finish, perform, settle 3 MURDER, assassinate, execute, kill, slaughter, slay ♦ *noun* 4 MESSAGE, account, bulletin, communication, communiqué, news, report, story

dispel *verb* DRIVE AWAY, banish, chase away, dismiss, disperse, eliminate, expel

dispense *verb* 1 DISTRIBUTE, allocate, allot, apportion, assign, deal out, dole out, share 2 PREPARE, measure, mix, supply 3 ADMINISTER, apply, carry out, discharge, enforce, execute, implement, operate 4 **dispense with** a DO AWAY WITH, abolish, brush aside, cancel, dispose of, get rid of b DO WITHOUT, abstain from, forgo, give up, relinquish

disperse *verb* 1 SCATTER, broadcast, diffuse, disseminate, distribute, spread, strew 2 BREAK UP, disband, dissolve, scatter, separate

dispirited *adjective* DISHEARTENED, crestfallen, dejected, depressed, despondent, discouraged, downcast, gloomy, glum, sad

displace *verb* 1 MOVE, disturb, misplace, shift, transpose 2 REPLACE, oust, succeed, supersede, supplant, take the place of

display *verb* 1 SHOW, demonstrate, disclose, exhibit, expose, manifest, present, reveal 2 SHOW OFF, flash (*informal*), flaunt, flourish, parade, vaunt ♦ *noun* 3 EXHIBITION, array, demonstration, presentation, revelation, show 4 SHOW, flourish, ostentation, pageant, parade, pomp, spectacle

displease *verb* ANNOY, anger, irk,

irritate, offend, pique, put out, upset, vex

displeasure noun <u>ANNOYANCE</u>, anger, disapproval, dissatisfaction, distaste, indignation, irritation, resentment

disposable adjective 1 <u>THROWAWAY</u>, biodegradable, nonreturnable 2 <u>AVAILABLE</u>, consumable, expendable

disposal noun 1 <u>THROWING AWAY</u>, discarding, dumping (*informal*), ejection, jettisoning, removal, riddance, scrapping 2 **at one's disposal** <u>AVAILABLE</u>, at one's service, consumable, expendable, free for use

dispose verb <u>ARRANGE</u>, array, distribute, group, marshal, order, place, put

dispose of verb 1 <u>GET RID OF</u>, destroy, discard, dump (*informal*), jettison, scrap, throw out *or* away, unload 2 <u>DEAL WITH</u>, decide, determine, end, finish with, settle

disposition noun 1 <u>CHARACTER</u>, constitution, make-up, nature, spirit, temper, temperament 2 <u>TENDENCY</u>, bent, bias, habit, inclination, leaning, proclivity, propensity 3 <u>ARRANGEMENT</u>, classification, distribution, grouping, ordering, organization, placement

disproportion noun <u>INEQUALITY</u>, asymmetry, discrepancy, disparity, imbalance, lopsidedness, unevenness

disproportionate adjective <u>UNEQUAL</u>, excessive, inordinate, out of proportion, unbalanced, uneven, unreasonable

disprove verb <u>PROVE FALSE</u>, contradict, discredit, expose, give the lie to, invalidate, negate, rebut, refute

dispute noun 1 <u>DISAGREEMENT</u>,

altercation, argument, conflict, feud, quarrel 2 <u>ARGUMENT</u>, contention, controversy, debate, discussion, dissension ♦ verb 3 <u>DOUBT</u>, challenge, contest, contradict, deny, impugn, question, rebut 4 <u>ARGUE</u>, clash, cross swords, debate, quarrel, squabble

disqualification noun <u>BAN</u>, elimination, exclusion, ineligibility, rejection

disqualified adjective <u>INELIGIBLE</u>, debarred, eliminated, knocked out, out of the running

disqualify verb <u>BAN</u>, debar, declare ineligible, preclude, prohibit, rule out

disquiet noun 1 <u>UNEASINESS</u>, alarm, anxiety, concern, disturbance, foreboding, nervousness, trepidation, worry ♦ verb 2 <u>MAKE UNEASY</u>, bother, concern, disturb, perturb, trouble, unsettle, upset, worry

disregard verb 1 <u>IGNORE</u>, brush aside *or* away, discount, make light of, neglect, overlook, pass over, pay no heed to, turn a blind eye to ♦ noun 2 <u>INATTENTION</u>, contempt, disdain, disrespect, indifference, neglect, negligence, oversight

disrepair noun <u>DILAPIDATION</u>, collapse, decay, deterioration, ruination

disreputable adjective <u>DISCREDITABLE</u>, dishonourable, ignominious, infamous, louche, notorious, scandalous, shady (*informal*), shameful

disrepute noun <u>DISCREDIT</u>, disgrace, dishonour, ignominy, ill repute, infamy, obloquy, shame, unpopularity

disrespect noun <u>CONTEMPT</u>, cheek, impertinence, impoliteness, impudence, insolence, irreverence, lack of respect, rudeness, sauce

disrespectful *adjective* CONTEMPTUOUS, cheeky, discourteous, impertinent, impolite, impudent, insolent, insulting, irreverent, rude

disrupt *verb* 1 DISTURB, confuse, disorder, disorganize, spoil, upset 2 INTERRUPT, break up *or* into, interfere with, intrude, obstruct, unsettle, upset

disruption *noun* DISTURBANCE, interference, interruption, stoppage

disruptive *adjective* DISTURBING, disorderly, distracting, troublesome, unruly, unsettling, upsetting

dissatisfaction *noun* DISCONTENT, annoyance, chagrin, disappointment, displeasure, frustration, irritation, resentment, unhappiness

dissatisfied *adjective* DISCONTENTED, disappointed, disgruntled, displeased, fed up, frustrated, unhappy, unsatisfied

dissect *verb* 1 CUT UP *or* APART, anatomize, dismember, lay open 2 ANALYSE, break down, explore, inspect, investigate, research, scrutinize, study

disseminate *verb* SPREAD, broadcast, circulate, disperse, distribute, publicize, scatter

dissension *noun* DISAGREEMENT, conflict, discord, dispute, dissent, friction, quarrel, row, strife

dissent *verb* 1 DISAGREE, differ, object, protest, refuse, withhold assent *or* approval ♦ *noun* 2 DISAGREEMENT, discord, dissension, objection, opposition, refusal, resistance

dissenter *noun* OBJECTOR, dissident,

nonconformist

dissertation *noun* THESIS, critique, discourse, disquisition, essay, exposition, treatise

disservice *noun* BAD TURN, harm, injury, injustice, unkindness, wrong

dissident *adjective* 1 DISSENTING, disagreeing, discordant, heterodox, nonconformist ♦ *noun* 2 PROTESTER, agitator, dissenter, rebel

dissimilar *adjective* DIFFERENT, disparate, divergent, diverse, heterogeneous, unlike, unrelated, various

dissipate *verb* 1 SQUANDER, consume, deplete, expend, fritter away, run through, spend, waste 2 DISPERSE, disappear, dispel, dissolve, drive away, evaporate, scatter, vanish

dissipation *noun* 1 DISPERSAL, disappearance, disintegration, dissolution, scattering, vanishing 2 DEBAUCHERY, dissoluteness, excess, extravagance, indulgence, intemperance, prodigality, profligacy, wantonness, waste

dissociate *verb* 1 BREAK AWAY, break off, part company, quit 2 SEPARATE, detach, disconnect, distance, divorce, isolate, segregate, set apart

dissolute *adjective* IMMORAL, debauched, degenerate, depraved, dissipated, profligate, rakish, wanton, wild

dissolution *noun* 1 BREAKING UP, disintegration, division, parting, separation 2 ADJOURNMENT, discontinuation, end, finish, suspension, termination

dissolve *verb* 1 MELT, deliquesce, fuse, liquefy, soften, thaw 2 END, break up, discontinue, suspend, terminate, wind up

dissuade verb DETER, advise against, discourage, put off, remonstrate, talk out of, warn

distance noun 1 SPACE, extent, gap, interval, length, range, span, stretch 2 RESERVE, aloofness, coldness, coolness, remoteness, restraint, stiffness 3 **in the distance** FAR OFF, afar, far away, on the horizon, yonder ♦ verb 4 **distance oneself** SEPARATE ONESELF, be distanced from, dissociate oneself

distant adjective 1 FAR-OFF, abroad, far, faraway, far-flung, outlying, out-of-the-way, remote 2 APART, dispersed, distinct, scattered, separate 3 RESERVED, aloof, cool, reticent, standoffish, unapproachable, unfriendly, withdrawn

distaste noun DISLIKE, aversion, disgust, horror, loathing, odium, repugnance, revulsion

distasteful adjective UNPLEASANT, disagreeable, objectionable, offensive, repugnant, repulsive, uninviting, unpalatable, unsavoury

distil verb EXTRACT, condense, purify, refine

distinct adjective 1 DIFFERENT, detached, discrete, individual, separate, unconnected 2 DEFINITE, clear, decided, evident, marked, noticeable, obvious, palpable, unmistakable, well-defined

distinction noun 1 DIFFERENTIATION, discernment, discrimination, perception, separation 2 FEATURE, characteristic, distinctiveness, individuality, mark, particularity, peculiarity, quality 3 DIFFERENCE, contrast, differential, division, separation 4 EXCELLENCE, eminence, fame, greatness, honour, importance, merit, prominence, repute

distinctive adjective CHARACTERISTIC, idiosyncratic, individual, original, peculiar, singular, special, typical, unique

distinctly adverb DEFINITELY, clearly, decidedly, markedly, noticeably, obviously, patently, plainly, unmistakably

distinguish verb 1 DIFFERENTIATE, ascertain, decide, determine, discriminate, judge, tell apart, tell the difference 2 CHARACTERIZE, categorize, classify, mark, separate, set apart, single out 3 MAKE OUT, discern, know, perceive, pick out, recognize, see, tell

distinguished adjective EMINENT, acclaimed, celebrated, famed, famous, illustrious, noted, renowned, well-known

distort verb 1 MISREPRESENT, bias, colour, falsify, pervert, slant, twist 2 DEFORM, bend, buckle, contort, disfigure, misshape, twist, warp

distortion noun 1 MISREPRESENTATION, bias, falsification, perversion, slant 2 DEFORMITY, bend, buckle, contortion, crookedness, malformation, twist, warp

distract verb 1 DIVERT, draw away, sidetrack, turn aside 2 AMUSE, beguile, engross, entertain, occupy

distracted adjective AGITATED, at sea, flustered, harassed, in a flap (informal), perplexed, puzzled, troubled

distraction noun 1 DIVERSION, disturbance, interference, interruption 2 ENTERTAINMENT, amusement, diversion, pastime, recreation 3 AGITATION, bewilderment, commotion, confusion, discord, disorder, disturbance

distraught adjective FRANTIC, agitated, beside oneself, desperate, distracted, distressed, out of one's mind, overwrought, worked-up

distress noun 1 WORRY, grief, heartache, misery, pain, sorrow, suffering, torment, wretchedness 2 NEED, adversity, difficulties, hardship, misfortune, poverty, privation, trouble ♦ verb 3 UPSET, disturb, grieve, harass, sadden, torment, trouble, worry

distressed adjective 1 UPSET, agitated, distracted, distraught, tormented, troubled, worried, wretched 2 POVERTY-STRICKEN, destitute, down at heel, indigent, needy, poor, straitened

distressing adjective UPSETTING, disturbing, harrowing, heart-breaking, painful, sad, worrying

distribute verb 1 HAND OUT, circulate, convey, deliver, pass round 2 SHARE, allocate, allot, apportion, deal, dispense, dole out

distribution noun 1 DELIVERY, dealing, handling, mailing, transportation 2 SHARING, allocation, allotment, apportionment, division 3 CLASSIFICATION, arrangement, grouping, organization, placement

district noun AREA, locale, locality, neighbourhood, parish, quarter, region, sector, vicinity

distrust verb 1 SUSPECT, be suspicious of, be wary of, disbelieve, doubt, mistrust, question, smell a rat (informal) ♦ noun 2 SUSPICION, disbelief, doubt, misgiving, mistrust, question, scepticism, wariness

disturb verb 1 INTERRUPT, bother, butt in on, disrupt, interfere with, intrude on, pester 2 UPSET, alarm, distress, fluster, harass, perturb, trouble, unnerve, unsettle, worry 3 MUDDLE, disarrange, disorder

disturbance noun 1 INTERRUPTION, annoyance, bother, distraction, intrusion 2 DISORDER, brawl, commotion, fracas, fray, rumpus

disturbed adjective 1 Psychiatry UNBALANCED, disordered, maladjusted, neurotic, troubled, upset 2 WORRIED, anxious, apprehensive, bothered, concerned, nervous, troubled, uneasy, upset

disturbing adjective WORRYING, alarming, disconcerting, distressing, frightening, harrowing, startling, unsettling, upsetting

disuse noun NEGLECT, abandonment, decay, idleness

ditch noun 1 CHANNEL, drain, dyke, furrow, gully, moat, trench, watercourse ♦ verb 2 Slang GET RID OF, abandon, discard, dispose of, drop, dump (informal), jettison, scrap, throw out or overboard

dither verb 1 Chiefly Brit. VACILLATE, faff about (Brit. informal), hesitate, hum and haw, shillyshally (informal), teeter, waver ♦ noun 2 Chiefly Brit. FLUTTER, flap (informal), fluster, tizzy (informal)

dive verb 1 PLUNGE, descend, dip, drop, duck, nose-dive, plummet, swoop ♦ noun 2 PLUNGE, jump, leap, lunge, nose dive, spring

diverge verb 1 SEPARATE, branch, divide, fork, part, split, spread 2 DEVIATE, depart, digress, meander, stray, turn aside, wander

diverse adjective 1 VARIOUS, assorted, manifold, miscellaneous, of every description, several, sundry, varied 2 DIFFERENT, discrete, disparate, dissimilar, distinct, divergent, separate, unlike, varying

diversify verb VARY, branch out, change, expand, have a finger in every pie, spread out

diversion noun 1 *Chiefly Brit.* DETOUR, departure, deviation, digression 2 PASTIME, amusement, distraction, entertainment, game, recreation, relaxation, sport

diversity noun DIFFERENCE, distinctiveness, diverseness, heterogeneity, multiplicity, range, variety

divert verb 1 REDIRECT, avert, deflect, switch, turn aside 2 DISTRACT, draw *or* lead away from, lead astray, sidetrack 3 ENTERTAIN, amuse, beguile, delight, gratify, regale

diverting adjective ENTERTAINING, amusing, beguiling, enjoyable, fun, humorous, pleasant

divide verb 1 SEPARATE, bisect, cut (up), part, partition, segregate, split 2 SHARE, allocate, allot, deal out, dispense, distribute 3 CAUSE TO DISAGREE, break up, come between, estrange, split

dividend noun BONUS, cut (*informal*), divvy (*informal*), extra, gain, plus, portion, share, surplus

divine adjective 1 HEAVENLY, angelic, celestial, godlike, holy, spiritual, superhuman, supernatural 2 SACRED, consecrated, holy, religious, sanctified, spiritual 3 *Informal* WONDERFUL, beautiful, excellent, glorious, marvellous, perfect, splendid, superlative ◆ verb 4 INFER, apprehend, deduce, discern, guess, perceive, suppose, surmise

divinity noun 1 THEOLOGY, religion, religious studies 2 GOD *or* GODDESS, deity, guardian spirit, spirit 3 GODLINESS, deity, divine nature, holiness, sanctity

divisible adjective DIVIDABLE, separable, splittable

division noun 1 SEPARATION, cutting up, dividing, partition, splitting up 2 SHARING, allotment,

apportionment, distribution 3 PART, branch, category, class, department, group, section 4 DISAGREEMENT, difference of opinion, discord, rupture, split, variance

divorce noun 1 SEPARATION, annulment, dissolution, split-up ◆ verb 2 SEPARATE, disconnect, dissociate, dissolve (*marriage*), divide, part, sever, split up

divulge verb MAKE KNOWN, confess, declare, disclose, let slip, proclaim, reveal, tell

dizzy adjective 1 GIDDY, faint, light-headed, off balance, reeling, shaky, swimming, wobbly, woozy (*informal*) 2 CONFUSED, at sea, befuddled, bemused, bewildered, dazed, dazzled, muddled

do verb 1 PERFORM, accomplish, achieve, carry out, complete, execute 2 BE ADEQUATE, be sufficient, cut the mustard, pass muster, satisfy, suffice 3 GET READY, arrange, fix, look after, prepare, see to 4 SOLVE, decipher, decode, figure out, puzzle out, resolve, work out 5 CAUSE, bring about, create, effect, produce ◆ noun 6 *Informal, chiefly Brit. & N.Z.* EVENT, affair, function, gathering, occasion, party

do away with verb 1 KILL, exterminate, murder, slay 2 GET RID OF, abolish, discard, discontinue, eliminate, put an end to, put paid to, remove

docile adjective SUBMISSIVE, amenable, biddable, compliant, manageable, obedient, pliant

docility noun SUBMISSIVENESS, compliance, manageability, meekness, obedience

dock[1] noun 1 WHARF, harbour, pier, quay, waterfront ◆ verb 2 MOOR, anchor, berth, drop anchor, land, put in, tie up 3 *Of spacecraft* LINK

UP, couple, hook up, join, rendezvous, unite

dock[2] verb 1 DEDUCT, decrease, diminish, lessen, reduce, subtract, withhold 2 CUT OFF, clip, crop, curtail, cut short, shorten

doctor noun 1 G.P., general practitioner, medic (*informal*), medical practitioner, physician ◆ verb 2 CHANGE, alter, disguise, falsify, misrepresent, pervert, tamper with 3 ADD TO, adulterate, cut, dilute, mix with, spike, water down

doctrinaire adjective DOGMATIC, biased, fanatical, inflexible, insistent, opinionated, rigid

doctrine noun TEACHING, article of faith, belief, conviction, creed, dogma, opinion, precept, principle, tenet

document noun 1 PAPER, certificate, record, report ◆ verb 2 SUPPORT, authenticate, certify, corroborate, detail, substantiate, validate, verify

dodge verb 1 DUCK, dart, sidestep, swerve, turn aside 2 EVADE, avoid, elude, get out of, shirk ◆ noun 3 TRICK, device, ploy, ruse, scheme, stratagem, subterfuge, wheeze (*Brit. slang*)

dog noun 1 HOUND, canine, cur, man's best friend, pooch (*slang*) 2 **go to the dogs** Informal GO TO RUIN, degenerate, deteriorate, go down the drain, go to pot ◆ verb 3 TROUBLE, follow, haunt, hound, plague, pursue, track, trail

dogged adjective DETERMINED, indefatigable, obstinate, persistent, resolute, steadfast, stubborn, tenacious, unflagging, unshakable

dogma noun DOCTRINE, belief, credo, creed, opinion, teachings

dogmatic adjective OPINIONATED, arrogant, assertive, doctrinaire, emphatic, obdurate, overbearing

doldrums noun **the doldrums** INACTIVITY, depression, dumps (*informal*), gloom, listlessness, malaise

dole noun 1 Brit. & Austral. informal BENEFIT, allowance, gift, grant, handout ◆ verb 2 **dole out** GIVE OUT, allocate, allot, apportion, assign, dispense, distribute, hand out

dollop noun LUMP, helping, portion, scoop, serving

dolt noun IDIOT, ass, blockhead, chump (*informal*), clot (*Brit. informal*), dope (*informal*), dunce, fool, oaf

domestic adjective 1 HOME, family, household, private 2 HOME-LOVING, domesticated, homely, housewifely, stay-at-home 3 DOMESTICATED, house-trained, pet, tame, trained 4 NATIVE, indigenous, internal ◆ noun 5 SERVANT, char (*informal*), charwoman, daily, help, maid

dominant adjective 1 CONTROLLING, assertive, authoritative, commanding, governing, ruling, superior, supreme 2 MAIN, chief, predominant, pre-eminent, primary, principal, prominent

dominate verb 1 CONTROL, direct, govern, have the whip hand over, monopolize, rule, tyrannize 2 TOWER ABOVE, loom over, overlook, stand head and shoulders above, stand over, survey

domination noun CONTROL, ascendancy, authority, command, influence, power, rule, superiority, supremacy

domineering adjective OVERBEARING, arrogant, authoritarian, bossy (*informal*), dictatorial, high-handed, imperious, oppressive, tyrannical

dominion noun 1 <u>CONTROL</u>, authority, command, jurisdiction, power, rule, sovereignty, supremacy 2 <u>KINGDOM</u>, country, domain, empire, realm, territory

don verb <u>PUT ON</u>, clothe oneself in, dress in, get into, pull on, slip on or into

donate verb <u>GIVE</u>, contribute, make a gift of, present, subscribe

donation noun <u>CONTRIBUTION</u>, gift, grant, hand-out, offering, present, subscription

donor noun <u>GIVER</u>, benefactor, contributor, donator, philanthropist

doom noun 1 <u>DESTRUCTION</u>, catastrophe, downfall, fate, fortune, ruin ♦ verb 2 <u>CONDEMN</u>, consign, damn, destine, sentence

doomed adjective <u>CONDEMNED</u>, bewitched, cursed, fated, hopeless, ill-fated, ill-omened, luckless, star-crossed

door noun <u>OPENING</u>, doorway, entrance, entry, exit

dope noun 1 Slang <u>DRUG</u>, narcotic, opiate 2 Informal <u>IDIOT</u>, dimwit (informal), dunce, fool, nitwit (informal), numbskull or numskull, simpleton, twit (informal, chiefly Brit.) ♦ verb 3 <u>DRUG</u>, anaesthetize, knock out, narcotize, sedate, stupefy

dormant adjective <u>INACTIVE</u>, asleep, hibernating, inert, inoperative, latent, sleeping, slumbering, suspended

dose noun <u>QUANTITY</u>, dosage, draught, measure, portion, potion, prescription

dot noun 1 <u>SPOT</u>, fleck, jot, mark, point, speck, speckle 2 **on the dot** <u>ON TIME</u>, exactly, on the button (informal), precisely, promptly,

punctually, to the minute ♦ verb 3 <u>SPOT</u>, dab, dabble, fleck, speckle, sprinkle, stipple, stud

dotage noun <u>SENILITY</u>, decrepitude, feebleness, imbecility, old age, second childhood, weakness

dote on or **upon** verb <u>ADORE</u>, admire, hold dear, idolize, lavish affection on, prize, treasure

doting adjective <u>ADORING</u>, devoted, fond, foolish, indulgent, lovesick

double adjective 1 <u>TWICE</u>, coupled, dual, duplicate, in pairs, paired, twin, twofold ♦ verb 2 <u>MULTIPLY</u>, duplicate, enlarge, grow, increase, magnify ♦ noun 3 <u>TWIN</u>, clone, dead ringer (slang), Doppelgänger, duplicate, lookalike, replica, spitting image (informal) 4 **at** or **on the double** <u>QUICKLY</u>, at full speed, briskly, immediately, posthaste, without delay

double-cross verb <u>BETRAY</u>, cheat, defraud, hoodwink, mislead, swindle, trick, two-time (informal)

doubt noun 1 <u>UNCERTAINTY</u>, hesitancy, hesitation, indecision, irresolution, lack of conviction, suspense 2 <u>SUSPICION</u>, apprehension, distrust, misgiving, mistrust, qualm, scepticism ♦ verb 3 <u>BE UNCERTAIN</u>, be dubious, demur, fluctuate, hesitate, scruple, vacillate, waver 4 <u>SUSPECT</u>, discredit, distrust, fear, lack confidence in, mistrust, query, question

doubtful adjective 1 <u>UNLIKELY</u>, debatable, dubious, equivocal, improbable, problematic(al), questionable, unclear 2 <u>UNSURE</u>, distrustful, hesitating, in two minds (informal), sceptical, suspicious, tentative, uncertain, unconvinced, wavering

doubtless adverb 1 <u>CERTAINLY</u>, assuredly, indisputably, of course,

surely, undoubtedly,
unquestionably, without doubt
2 PROBABLY, apparently, most likely,
ostensibly, presumably,
seemingly, supposedly

dour adjective GLOOMY, dismal,
dreary, forbidding, grim, morose,
sour, sullen, unfriendly

dowdy adjective FRUMPY, dingy,
drab, frowzy, old-fashioned,
shabby, unfashionable

do without verb MANAGE WITHOUT,
abstain from, dispense with,
forgo, get along without, give up,
kick (informal)

down adjective 1 DEPRESSED,
dejected, disheartened, downcast,
low, miserable, sad, unhappy
♦ verb 2 Informal SWALLOW, drain,
drink (down), gulp, put away, toss
off ♦ noun 3 **have a down on**
Informal BE ANTAGONISTIC or HOSTILE
TO, bear a grudge towards, be
prejudiced against, be set against,
have it in for (slang)

down-and-out noun 1 TRAMP, bag
lady, beggar, derelict, dosser (Brit.
slang), pauper, vagabond, vagrant
♦ adjective 2 DESTITUTE, derelict,
impoverished, on one's uppers
(informal), penniless, short,
without two pennies to rub
together (informal)

downcast adjective DEJECTED,
crestfallen, depressed,
despondent, disappointed,
disconsolate, discouraged,
disheartened, dismayed, dispirited

downfall noun RUIN, collapse,
comeuppance (slang),
destruction, disgrace, fall,
overthrow, undoing

downgrade verb DEMOTE, degrade,
humble, lower or reduce in rank,
take down a peg (informal)

downhearted adjective DEJECTED,
crestfallen, depressed,

despondent, discouraged,
disheartened, dispirited,
downcast, sad, unhappy

downpour noun RAINSTORM,
cloudburst, deluge, flood,
inundation, torrential rain

downright adjective COMPLETE,
absolute, out-and-out, outright,
plain, thoroughgoing, total,
undisguised, unqualified, utter

down-to-earth adjective SENSIBLE,
matter-of-fact, no-nonsense,
plain-spoken, practical, realistic,
sane, unsentimental

downtrodden adjective OPPRESSED,
exploited, helpless, subjugated,
subservient, tyrannized

downward adjective DESCENDING,
declining, earthward, heading
down, sliding, slipping

doze verb 1 NAP, kip (Brit. slang),
nod off (informal), sleep, slumber,
snooze (informal) ♦ noun 2 NAP,
catnap, forty winks (informal), kip
(Brit. slang), shuteye (slang),
siesta, snooze (informal)

drab adjective DULL, dingy, dismal,
dreary, flat, gloomy, shabby,
sombre

draft noun 1 OUTLINE, abstract, plan,
rough, sketch, version 2 ORDER, bill
(of exchange), cheque, postal
order ♦ verb 3 OUTLINE, compose,
design, draw, draw up, formulate,
plan, sketch

drag verb 1 PULL, draw, haul, lug,
tow, trail, tug 2 **drag on** or **out**
LAST, draw out, extend, keep
going, lengthen, persist, prolong,
protract, spin out, stretch out
♦ noun 3 Slang NUISANCE,
annoyance, bore, bother, pain
(informal), pest

dragoon verb FORCE, browbeat,
bully, coerce, compel, constrain,
drive, impel, intimidate, railroad
(informal)

drain noun 1 PIPE, channel, conduit, culvert, ditch, duct, sewer, sink, trench 2 REDUCTION, depletion, drag, exhaustion, sap, strain, withdrawal ♦ verb 3 REMOVE, bleed, draw off, dry, empty, pump off or out, tap, withdraw 4 FLOW OUT, effuse, exude, leak, ooze, seep, trickle, well out 5 DRINK UP, finish, gulp down, quaff, swallow 6 EXHAUST, consume, deplete, dissipate, empty, sap, strain, use up

drama noun 1 PLAY, dramatization, show, stage show 2 THEATRE, acting, dramaturgy, stagecraft 3 EXCITEMENT, crisis, histrionics, scene, spectacle, turmoil

dramatic adjective 1 THEATRICAL, dramaturgical, Thespian 2 POWERFUL, expressive, impressive, moving, striking, vivid 3 EXCITING, breathtaking, climactic, electrifying, melodramatic, sensational, suspenseful, tense, thrilling

dramatist noun PLAYWRIGHT, dramaturge, screenwriter, scriptwriter

dramatize verb EXAGGERATE, lay it on (thick) (slang), overdo, overstate, play to the gallery

drape verb COVER, cloak, fold, swathe, wrap

drastic adjective EXTREME, desperate, dire, forceful, harsh, radical, severe, strong

draught noun 1 BREEZE, current, flow, movement, puff 2 DRINK, cup, dose, potion, quantity

draw verb 1 SKETCH, depict, design, map out, mark out, outline, paint, portray, trace 2 PULL, drag, haul, tow, tug 3 TAKE OUT, extract, pull out 4 ATTRACT, allure, elicit, entice, evoke, induce, influence, invite, persuade 5 DEDUCE, derive, infer, make, take ♦ noun 6 Informal

ATTRACTION, enticement, lure, pull (informal) 7 TIE, dead heat, deadlock, impasse, stalemate

drawback noun DISADVANTAGE, deficiency, difficulty, downside, flaw, handicap, hitch, snag, stumbling block

drawing noun PICTURE, cartoon, depiction, illustration, outline, portrayal, representation, sketch, study

drawn adjective TENSE, haggard, pinched, stressed, tired, worn

draw on verb MAKE USE OF, employ, exploit, extract, fall back on, have recourse to, rely on, take from, use

draw out verb EXTEND, drag out, lengthen, make longer, prolong, protract, spin out, stretch, string out

draw up verb 1 DRAFT, compose, formulate, frame, prepare, write out 2 HALT, bring to a stop, pull up, stop

dread verb 1 FEAR, cringe at, have cold feet (informal), quail, shrink from, shudder, tremble ♦ noun 2 FEAR, alarm, apprehension, dismay, fright, horror, terror, trepidation

dreadful adjective TERRIBLE, abysmal, appalling, atrocious, awful, fearful, frightful, hideous, horrible, shocking

dream noun 1 VISION, delusion, hallucination, illusion, imagination, trance 2 DAYDREAM, fantasy, pipe dream 3 AMBITION, aim, aspiration, desire, goal, hope, wish 4 DELIGHT, beauty, gem, joy, marvel, pleasure, treasure ♦ verb 5 HAVE DREAMS, conjure up, envisage, fancy, hallucinate, imagine, think, visualize 6 DAYDREAM, build castles in the air or in Spain, fantasize, stargaze

dreamer noun IDEALIST, daydreamer,

escapist, fantasist, utopian, visionary, Walter Mitty

dreamy *adjective* 1 VAGUE, absent, abstracted, daydreaming, faraway, pensive, preoccupied, with one's head in the clouds 2 IMPRACTICAL, airy-fairy, fanciful, imaginary, quixotic, speculative

dreary *adjective* DULL, boring, drab, humdrum, monotonous, tedious, tiresome, uneventful, wearisome

dregs *plural noun* 1 SEDIMENT, deposit, dross, grounds, lees, residue, residuum, scum, waste 2 SCUM, good-for-nothings, rabble, ragtag and bobtail, riffraff

drench *verb* SOAK, drown, flood, inundate, saturate, souse, steep, swamp, wet

dress *noun* 1 FROCK, gown, outfit, robe 2 CLOTHING, apparel, attire, clothes, costume, garb, garments, togs ♦ *verb* 3 PUT ON, attire, change, clothe, don, garb, robe, slip on *or* into 4 BANDAGE, bind up, plaster, treat 5 ARRANGE, adjust, align, get ready, prepare, straighten

dressmaker *noun* SEAMSTRESS, couturier, tailor

dribble *verb* 1 RUN, drip, drop, fall in drops, leak, ooze, seep, trickle 2 DROOL, drivel, slaver, slobber

drift *verb* 1 FLOAT, be carried along, coast, go (aimlessly), meander, stray, waft, wander 2 PILE UP, accumulate, amass, bank up, drive, gather ♦ *noun* 3 PILE, accumulation, bank, heap, mass, mound 4 MEANING, direction, gist, import, intention, purport, significance, tendency, thrust

drifter *noun* WANDERER, beachcomber, bum (*informal*), hobo (*U.S.*), itinerant, rolling stone, vagrant

drill *noun* 1 BORING TOOL, bit, borer, gimlet 2 TRAINING, discipline, exercise, instruction, practice, preparation, repetition ♦ *verb* 3 BORE, penetrate, perforate, pierce, puncture, sink in 4 TRAIN, coach, discipline, exercise, instruct, practise, rehearse, teach

drink *verb* 1 SWALLOW, gulp, guzzle, imbibe, quaff, sip, suck, sup 2 BOOZE (*informal*), hit the bottle (*informal*), tipple, tope ♦ *noun* 3 BEVERAGE, liquid, potion, refreshment 4 ALCOHOL, booze (*informal*), hooch *or* hootch (*informal, chiefly U.S. & Canad.*), liquor, spirits, the bottle (*informal*) 5 GLASS, cup, draught

drip *verb* 1 DROP, dribble, exude, plop, splash, sprinkle, trickle ♦ *noun* 2 DROP, dribble, leak, trickle 3 *Informal* WEAKLING, mummy's boy (*informal*), namby-pamby, softie (*informal*), weed (*informal*), wet (*Brit. informal*)

drive *verb* 1 OPERATE, direct, guide, handle, manage, motor, ride, steer, travel 2 GOAD, coerce, constrain, force, press, prod, prompt, spur 3 PUSH, herd, hurl, impel, propel, send, urge 4 PUSH, hammer, ram, thrust ♦ *noun* 5 RUN, excursion, jaunt, journey, outing, ride, spin (*informal*), trip 6 CAMPAIGN, action, appeal, crusade, effort, push (*informal*) 7 INITIATIVE, ambition, energy, enterprise, get-up-and-go (*informal*), motivation, vigour, zip (*informal*)

drivel *noun* 1 NONSENSE, garbage (*informal*), gibberish, hogwash, hot air (*informal*), poppycock (*informal*), rubbish, trash, twaddle, waffle (*informal, chiefly Brit.*) ♦ *verb* 2 BABBLE, blether, gab (*informal*), prate, ramble, waffle (*informal, chiefly Brit.*)

driving *adjective* FORCEFUL, compelling, dynamic, energetic, sweeping, vigorous, violent

drizzle noun 1 FINE RAIN, Scotch mist ♦ verb 2 RAIN, shower, spot or spit with rain, spray, sprinkle

droll adjective AMUSING, comical, entertaining, funny, humorous, jocular, waggish, whimsical

drone verb 1 HUM, buzz, purr, thrum, vibrate, whirr 2 **drone on** SPEAK MONOTONOUSLY, be boring, chant, intone, spout, talk interminably ♦ noun 3 HUM, buzz, murmuring, purr, thrum, vibration, whirring

drool verb 1 DRIBBLE, drivel, salivate, slaver, slobber, water at the mouth 2 **drool over** GLOAT OVER, dote on, gush, make much of, rave about (informal)

droop verb SAG, bend, dangle, drop, fall down, hang (down), sink

drop verb 1 FALL, decline, descend, diminish, plummet, plunge, sink, tumble 2 DRIP, dribble, fall in drops, trickle 3 DISCONTINUE, axe (informal), give up, kick (informal), quit, relinquish ♦ noun 4 DROPLET, bead, bubble, drip, globule, pearl, tear 5 DASH, mouthful, shot (informal), sip, spot, tot, trace, trickle 6 DECREASE, cut, decline, deterioration, downturn, fall-off, lowering, reduction, slump 7 FALL, descent, plunge

drop off verb 1 SET DOWN, deliver, leave, let off 2 Informal FALL ASLEEP, doze (off), have forty winks (informal), nod (off), snooze (informal) 3 DECREASE, decline, diminish, dwindle, fall off, lessen, slacken

drop out verb LEAVE, abandon, fall by the wayside, give up, quit, stop, withdraw

drought noun DRY SPELL, aridity, dehydration, dryness

drove noun HERD, collection,

company, crowd, flock, horde, mob, multitude, swarm, throng

drown verb 1 DRENCH, deluge, engulf, flood, go under, immerse, inundate, sink, submerge, swamp 2 OVERPOWER, deaden, muffle, obliterate, overcome, overwhelm, stifle, swallow up, wipe out

drowsy adjective SLEEPY, dopey (slang), dozy, half asleep, heavy, lethargic, somnolent, tired, torpid

drudge noun MENIAL, dogsbody (informal), factotum, servant, skivvy (chiefly Brit.), slave, toiler, worker

drudgery noun MENIAL LABOUR, donkey-work, fag (informal), grind (informal), hard work, labour, skivvying (Brit.), slog, toil

drug noun 1 MEDICATION, medicament, medicine, physic, poison, remedy 2 DOPE (slang), narcotic, opiate, stimulant ♦ verb 3 DOSE, administer a drug, dope (slang), medicate, treat 4 KNOCK OUT, anaesthetize, deaden, numb, poison, stupefy

drum verb 1 BEAT, pulsate, rap, reverberate, tap, tattoo, throb 2 **drum into** DRIVE HOME, din into, hammer away, harp on, instil into, reiterate

drunk adjective 1 INTOXICATED, drunken, inebriated, legless (informal), merry (Brit. informal), plastered (slang), tipsy, under the influence (informal) ♦ noun 2 DRUNKARD, alcoholic, boozer (informal), inebriate, lush (slang), wino (informal)

drunkard noun DRINKER, alcoholic, dipsomaniac, drunk, lush (slang), tippler, wino (informal)

drunkenness noun INTOXICATION, alcoholism, bibulousness, dipsomania, inebriation, insobriety, intemperance

dry *adjective* **1** DEHYDRATED, arid, barren, desiccated, dried up, parched, thirsty **2** DULL, boring, dreary, monotonous, plain, tedious, tiresome, uninteresting **3** SARCASTIC, deadpan, droll, low-key, sly ◆ *verb* **4** DEHYDRATE, dehumidify, desiccate, drain, make dry, parch, sear

dry out *or* **up** *verb* BECOME DRY, harden, shrivel up, wilt, wither, wizen

dual *adjective* TWOFOLD, binary, double, duplex, duplicate, matched, paired, twin

dubious *adjective* **1** SUSPECT, fishy (*informal*), questionable, suspicious, unreliable, untrustworthy **2** UNSURE, doubtful, hesitant, sceptical, uncertain, unconvinced, undecided, wavering

duck *verb* **1** BOB, bend, bow, crouch, dodge, drop, lower, stoop **2** PLUNGE, dip, dive, douse, dunk, immerse, souse, submerge, wet **3** *Informal* DODGE, avoid, escape, evade, shirk, shun, sidestep

dud *Informal* ◆ *noun* **1** FAILURE, flop (*informal*), washout (*informal*) ◆ *adjective* **2** USELESS, broken, duff (*Brit. informal*), failed, inoperative, worthless

dudgeon *noun* **in high dudgeon** INDIGNANT, angry, choked, fuming, offended, resentful, vexed

due *adjective* **1** EXPECTED, scheduled **2** PAYABLE, in arrears, outstanding, owed, owing, unpaid **3** FITTING, appropriate, deserved, justified, merited, proper, rightful, suitable, well-earned ◆ *noun* **4** RIGHT(S), comeuppance (*slang*), deserts, merits, privilege ◆ *adverb* **5** DIRECTLY, dead, exactly, straight, undeviatingly

duel *noun* **1** SINGLE COMBAT, affair of honour **2** CONTEST, clash, competition, encounter, engagement, fight, head-to-head, rivalry ◆ *verb* **3** FIGHT, clash, compete, contend, contest, lock horns, rival, struggle, vie with

dues *plural noun* MEMBERSHIP FEE, charge, charges, contribution, fee, levy

dull *adjective* **1** BORING, dreary, flat, humdrum, monotonous, plain, run-of-the-mill, tedious, uninteresting **2** STUPID, dense, dim-witted (*informal*), dozy (*Brit. informal*), slow, thick, unintelligent **3** CLOUDY, dim, dismal, gloomy, leaden, overcast **4** LIFELESS, apathetic, blank, indifferent, listless, passionless, unresponsive **5** BLUNT, blunted, unsharpened ◆ *verb* **6** RELIEVE, allay, alleviate, blunt, lessen, moderate, soften, take the edge off

duly *adverb* **1** PROPERLY, accordingly, appropriately, befittingly, correctly, decorously, deservedly, fittingly, rightfully, suitably **2** ON TIME, at the proper time, punctually

dumb *adjective* **1** MUTE, mum, silent, soundless, speechless, tongue-tied, voiceless, wordless **2** *Informal* STUPID, asinine, dense, dim-witted (*informal*), dull, foolish, thick, unintelligent

dumbfounded *adjective* AMAZED, astonished, astounded, flabbergasted (*informal*), lost for words, nonplussed, overwhelmed, speechless, staggered, stunned

dummy *noun* **1** MODEL, figure, form, manikin, mannequin **2** COPY, counterfeit, duplicate, imitation, sham, substitute **3** *Slang* FOOL, blockhead, dunce, idiot, nitwit (*informal*), numbskull *or* numskull, oaf, simpleton ◆ *adjective* **4** IMITATION, artificial, bogus, fake, false, mock, phoney *or* phony (*informal*), sham, simulated

dump verb 1 <u>DROP</u>, deposit, fling down, let fall, throw down 2 <u>GET RID OF</u>, dispose of, ditch (slang), empty out, jettison, scrap, throw away or out, tip, unload ♦ noun 3 <u>RUBBISH TIP</u>, junkyard, refuse heap, rubbish heap, tip 4 Informal <u>PIGSTY</u>, hole (informal), hovel, mess, slum

dunce noun <u>SIMPLETON</u>, blockhead, duffer (informal), dunderhead, ignoramus, moron, nincompoop, numbskull or numskull, thickhead

dungeon noun <u>PRISON</u>, cage, cell, oubliette, vault

duplicate adjective 1 <u>IDENTICAL</u>, corresponding, matched, matching, twin, twofold ♦ noun 2 <u>COPY</u>, carbon copy, clone, double, facsimile, photocopy, replica, reproduction ♦ verb 3 <u>COPY</u>, clone, double, repeat, replicate, reproduce

durability noun <u>DURABLENESS</u>, constancy, endurance, imperishability, permanence, persistence

durable adjective <u>LONG-LASTING</u>, dependable, enduring, hard-wearing, persistent, reliable, resistant, strong, sturdy, tough

duration noun <u>LENGTH</u>, extent, period, span, spell, stretch, term, time

duress noun <u>PRESSURE</u>, coercion, compulsion, constraint, threat

dusk noun <u>TWILIGHT</u>, dark, evening, eventide, gloaming (Scot. or poetic), nightfall, sundown, sunset

dusky adjective 1 <u>DARK</u>, dark-complexioned, sable, swarthy 2 <u>DIM</u>, cloudy, gloomy, murky, obscure, shadowy, shady, tenebrous, twilit

dust noun 1 <u>GRIME</u>, grit, particles, powder ♦ verb 2 <u>SPRINKLE</u>, cover, dredge, powder, scatter, sift, spray, spread

dusty adjective <u>DIRTY</u>, grubby, sooty, unclean, unswept

dutiful adjective <u>CONSCIENTIOUS</u>, devoted, obedient, respectful, reverential, submissive

duty noun 1 <u>RESPONSIBILITY</u>, assignment, function, job, obligation, role, task, work 2 <u>LOYALTY</u>, allegiance, deference, obedience, respect, reverence 3 <u>TAX</u>, excise, levy, tariff, toll 4 **on duty** <u>AT WORK</u>, busy, engaged, on active service

dwarf verb 1 <u>TOWER ABOVE</u> or <u>OVER</u>, diminish, dominate, overshadow ♦ adjective 2 <u>MINIATURE</u>, baby, bonsai, diminutive, small, tiny, undersized ♦ noun 3 <u>MIDGET</u>, Lilliputian, pygmy or pigmy, Tom Thumb

dwell verb Formal, literary <u>LIVE</u>, abide, inhabit, lodge, reside

dwelling noun Formal, literary <u>HOME</u>, abode, domicile, habitation, house, lodging, quarters, residence

dwindle verb <u>LESSEN</u>, decline, decrease, die away, diminish, fade, peter out, shrink, subside, taper off, wane

dye noun 1 <u>COLOURING</u>, colorant, colour, pigment, stain, tinge, tint ♦ verb 2 <u>COLOUR</u>, pigment, stain, tinge, tint

dying adjective <u>EXPIRING</u>, at death's door, failing, in extremis, moribund, not long for this world

dynamic adjective <u>ENERGETIC</u>, forceful, go-ahead, go-getting (informal), high-powered, lively, powerful, vital

dynasty noun <u>EMPIRE</u>, government, house, regime, rule, sovereignty

E e

each adjective **1** EVERY ◆ pronoun **2** EVERY ONE, each and every one, each one, one and all ◆ adverb **3** APIECE, for each, individually, per capita, per head, per person, respectively, to each

eager adjective KEEN, agog, anxious, athirst, avid, enthusiastic, fervent, hungry, impatient, longing

eagerness noun KEENNESS, ardour, enthusiasm, fervour, hunger, impatience, thirst, yearning, zeal

ear noun SENSITIVITY, appreciation, discrimination, taste

early adjective **1** PREMATURE, advanced, forward, untimely **2** PRIMITIVE, primeval, primordial, undeveloped, young ◆ adverb **3** TOO SOON, ahead of time, beforehand, in advance, in good time, prematurely

earmark verb SET ASIDE, allocate, designate, flag, label, mark out, reserve

earn verb **1** MAKE, bring in, collect, gain, get, gross, net, receive **2** DESERVE, acquire, attain, be entitled to, be worthy of, merit, rate, warrant, win

earnest adjective **1** SERIOUS, grave, intent, resolute, resolved, sincere, solemn, thoughtful ◆ noun **2** As in **in earnest** SERIOUSNESS, sincerity, truth

earnings plural noun INCOME, pay, proceeds, profits, receipts, remuneration, salary, takings, wages

earth noun **1** WORLD, globe, orb, planet, sphere **2** SOIL, clay, dirt, ground, land, turf

earthenware noun CROCKERY, ceramics, pots, pottery, terracotta

earthly adjective **1** WORLDLY, human, material, mortal, secular, temporal **2** Informal POSSIBLE, conceivable, feasible, imaginable, likely, practical

earthy adjective CRUDE, bawdy, coarse, raunchy (slang), ribald, robust, uninhibited, unsophisticated

ease noun **1** EASINESS, effortlessness, facility, readiness, simplicity **2** CONTENT, comfort, happiness, peace, peace of mind, quiet, serenity, tranquillity **3** REST, leisure, relaxation, repose, restfulness ◆ verb **4** RELIEVE, alleviate, calm, comfort, lessen, lighten, relax, soothe **5** MOVE CAREFULLY, edge, inch, manoeuvre, slide, slip

easily adverb WITHOUT DIFFICULTY, comfortably, effortlessly, readily, smoothly, with ease, with one hand tied behind one's back

easy adjective **1** NOT DIFFICULT, a piece of cake (informal), child's play (informal), effortless, no trouble, painless, plain sailing, simple, straightforward, uncomplicated, undemanding **2** CAREFREE, comfortable, cushy (informal), leisurely, peaceful, quiet, relaxed, serene, tranquil, untroubled **3** TOLERANT, easy-going, indulgent, lenient, mild, permissive, unoppressive

easy-going adjective RELAXED, carefree, casual, easy, even-tempered, happy-go-lucky, laid-back (informal), nonchalant, placid, tolerant, undemanding

eat verb **1** CONSUME, chew, devour, gobble, ingest, munch, scoff (slang), swallow **2** HAVE A MEAL, dine, feed, take nourishment **3** DESTROY, corrode, decay, dissolve, erode, rot, waste away, wear away

eavesdrop verb LISTEN IN, earwig (*informal*), monitor, overhear, snoop (*informal*), spy

ebb verb 1 FLOW BACK, go out, recede, retire, retreat, subside, wane, withdraw 2 DECLINE, decrease, diminish, dwindle, fade away, fall away, flag, lessen, peter out ◆ noun 3 FLOWING BACK, going out, low tide, low water, retreat, subsidence, wane, withdrawal

eccentric adjective 1 ODD, freakish, idiosyncratic, irregular, outlandish, peculiar, quirky, strange, unconventional ◆ noun 2 CRANK (*informal*), character (*informal*), nonconformist, oddball (*informal*), weirdo or weirdie (*informal*)

eccentricity noun ODDITY, abnormality, caprice, capriciousness, foible, idiosyncrasy, irregularity, peculiarity, quirk

ecclesiastic noun 1 CLERGYMAN, churchman, cleric, holy man, man of the cloth, minister, parson, pastor, priest ◆ adjective 2 Also **ecclesiastical** CLERICAL, divine, holy, pastoral, priestly, religious, spiritual

echo noun 1 REPETITION, answer, reverberation 2 COPY, imitation, mirror image, parallel, reflection, reiteration, reproduction ◆ verb 3 REPEAT, resound, reverberate 4 COPY, ape, imitate, mirror, parallel, recall, reflect, resemble

eclipse noun 1 OBSCURING, darkening, dimming, extinction, shading ◆ verb 2 SURPASS, exceed, excel, outdo, outshine, put in the shade (*informal*), transcend

economic adjective 1 FINANCIAL, commercial, industrial 2 PROFITABLE, money-making, productive, profit-making, remunerative,

viable 3 *Informal Also* **economical** INEXPENSIVE, cheap, low-priced, modest, reasonable

economical adjective 1 THRIFTY, careful, frugal, prudent, scrimping, sparing 2 COST-EFFECTIVE, efficient, money-saving, sparing, time-saving

economize verb CUT BACK, be economical, be frugal, draw in one's horns, retrench, save, scrimp, tighten one's belt

economy noun THRIFT, frugality, husbandry, parsimony, prudence, restraint

ecstasy noun RAPTURE, bliss, delight, elation, euphoria, fervour, joy, seventh heaven

ecstatic adjective RAPTUROUS, blissful, elated, enraptured, entranced, euphoric, in seventh heaven, joyous, on cloud nine (*informal*), overjoyed

eddy noun 1 SWIRL, counter-current, counterflow, undertow, vortex, whirlpool ◆ verb 2 SWIRL, whirl

edge noun 1 BORDER, boundary, brink, fringe, limit, outline, perimeter, rim, side, verge 2 SHARPNESS, bite, effectiveness, force, incisiveness, keenness, point 3 *As in* **have the edge on** ADVANTAGE, ascendancy, dominance, lead, superiority, upper hand 4 **on edge** NERVOUS, apprehensive, edgy, ill at ease, impatient, irritable, keyed up, on tenterhooks, tense ◆ verb 5 BORDER, fringe, hem 6 INCH, creep, ease, sidle, steal

edgy adjective NERVOUS, anxious, ill at ease, irritable, keyed up, on edge, on tenterhooks, restive, tense

edible adjective EATABLE, digestible, fit to eat, good, harmless, palatable, wholesome

edict noun DECREE, act, command, injunction, law, order, proclamation, ruling

edifice noun BUILDING, construction, erection, house, structure

edify verb INSTRUCT, educate, enlighten, guide, improve, inform, nurture, school, teach

edit verb REVISE, adapt, condense, correct, emend, polish, rewrite

edition noun VERSION, copy, impression, issue, number, printing, programme (*TV, Radio*), volume

educate verb TEACH, civilize, develop, discipline, enlighten, improve, inform, instruct, school, train, tutor

educated adjective 1 TAUGHT, coached, informed, instructed, nurtured, schooled, tutored 2 CULTURED, civilized, cultivated, enlightened, knowledgeable, learned, refined, sophisticated

education noun TEACHING, development, discipline, enlightenment, instruction, nurture, schooling, training, tuition

educational adjective INSTRUCTIVE, cultural, edifying, educative, enlightening, improving, informative

eerie adjective FRIGHTENING, creepy (*informal*), ghostly, mysterious, scary (*informal*), spooky (*informal*), strange, uncanny, unearthly, weird

efface verb OBLITERATE, blot out, cancel, delete, destroy, eradicate, erase, rub out, wipe out

effect noun 1 RESULT, conclusion, consequence, end result, event, outcome, upshot 2 OPERATION, action, enforcement, execution, force, implementation 3 IMPRESSION, essence, impact,

sense, significance, tenor ♦ verb 4 BRING ABOUT, accomplish, achieve, complete, execute, fulfil, perform, produce

effective adjective 1 EFFICIENT, active, adequate, capable, competent, productive, serviceable, useful 2 IN OPERATION, active, current, in effect, in force, operative 3 POWERFUL, cogent, compelling, convincing, forceful, impressive, persuasive, telling

effects plural noun BELONGINGS, gear, goods, paraphernalia, possessions, property, things

effeminate adjective WOMANLY, camp (*informal*), feminine, sissy, soft, tender, unmanly, weak, womanish

effervescent adjective 1 BUBBLING, carbonated, fizzy, foaming, frothy, sparkling 2 LIVELY, animated, bubbly, ebullient, enthusiastic, exuberant, irrepressible, vivacious

effete adjective DECADENT, dissipated, enfeebled, feeble, ineffectual, spoiled, weak

efficacious adjective EFFECTIVE, adequate, efficient, operative, potent, powerful, productive, successful, useful

efficiency noun COMPETENCE, adeptness, capability, economy, effectiveness, power, productivity, proficiency

efficient adjective COMPETENT, businesslike, capable, economic, effective, organized, productive, proficient, well-organized, workmanlike

effigy noun LIKENESS, dummy, figure, guy, icon, idol, image, picture, portrait, representation, statue

effluent noun WASTE, effluvium, pollutant, sewage

effort noun 1 EXERTION, application,

elbow grease (*facetious*),
endeavour, energy, pains,
struggle, toil, trouble, work
2 ATTEMPT, endeavour, essay, go
(*informal*), shot (*informal*), stab
(*informal*), try

effortless *adjective* EASY, painless,
plain sailing, simple, smooth,
uncomplicated, undemanding

effrontery *noun* INSOLENCE,
arrogance, audacity, brazenness,
cheek (*informal*), impertinence,
impudence, nerve, presumption,
temerity

effusive *adjective* DEMONSTRATIVE,
ebullient, expansive, exuberant,
gushing, lavish, unreserved,
unrestrained

egg on *verb* ENCOURAGE, exhort,
goad, incite, prod, prompt, push,
spur, urge

egocentric *adjective* SELF-CENTRED,
egoistic, egoistical, egotistic,
egotistical, selfish

egotism, egoism *noun*
SELF-CENTREDNESS, conceitedness,
narcissism, self-absorption,
self-esteem, self-importance,
self-interest, selfishness, vanity

egotist, egoist *noun* EGOMANIAC,
bighead (*informal*), boaster,
braggart, narcissist

egotistic, egotistical, egoistic *or*
egoistical *adjective* SELF-CENTRED,
boasting, conceited, egocentric,
full of oneself, narcissistic,
self-absorbed, self-important, vain

egress *noun Formal* EXIT, departure,
exodus, way out, withdrawal

eject *verb* THROW OUT, banish, drive
out, evict, expel, oust, remove,
turn out

ejection *noun* EXPULSION,
banishment, deportation,
eviction, exile, removal

eke out *verb* BE SPARING WITH,
economize on, husband, stretch
out

elaborate *adjective* 1 DETAILED,
intricate, minute, painstaking,
precise, studied, thorough
2 COMPLICATED, complex, fancy,
fussy, involved, ornamented,
ornate ♦ *verb* 3 EXPAND (UPON), add
detail, amplify, develop,
embellish, enlarge, flesh out

elapse *verb* PASS, glide by, go by,
lapse, roll by, slip away

elastic *adjective* 1 STRETCHY, plastic,
pliable, pliant, resilient, rubbery,
springy, supple, tensile 2 ADAPTABLE,
accommodating, adjustable,
compliant, flexible, supple,
tolerant, variable, yielding

elated *adjective* JOYFUL,
cock-a-hoop, delighted, ecstatic,
euphoric, exhilarated, gleeful,
jubilant, overjoyed

elation *noun* JOY, bliss, delight,
ecstasy, euphoria, exhilaration,
glee, high spirits, jubilation,
rapture

elbow *noun* 1 JOINT, angle ♦ *verb*
2 PUSH, jostle, knock, nudge, shove

elbow room *noun* SCOPE, freedom,
latitude, leeway, play, room, space

elder *adjective* 1 OLDER, first-born,
senior ♦ *noun* 2 OLDER PERSON, senior

elect *verb* CHOOSE, appoint,
determine, opt for, pick, prefer,
select, settle on, vote

election *noun* VOTING,
appointment, choice, judgment,
preference, selection, vote

elector *noun* VOTER, constituent,
selector

electric *adjective* CHARGED, dynamic,
exciting, rousing, stimulating,
stirring, tense, thrilling

electrify *verb* STARTLE, astound,
excite, galvanize, invigorate, jolt,
shock, stir, thrill

elegance noun STYLE, dignity, exquisiteness, grace, gracefulness, grandeur, luxury, refinement, taste

elegant adjective STYLISH, chic, delicate, exquisite, fine, graceful, handsome, polished, refined, tasteful

element noun 1 COMPONENT, constituent, factor, ingredient, part, section, subdivision, unit 2 As in **in one's element** ENVIRONMENT, domain, field, habitat, medium, milieu, sphere

elementary adjective SIMPLE, clear, easy, plain, rudimentary, straightforward, uncomplicated

elements plural noun 1 BASICS, essentials, foundations, fundamentals, nuts and bolts (informal), principles, rudiments 2 WEATHER CONDITIONS, atmospheric conditions, powers of nature

elevate verb 1 RAISE, heighten, hoist, lift, lift up, uplift 2 PROMOTE, advance, aggrandize, exalt, prefer, upgrade

elevated adjective HIGH-MINDED, dignified, exalted, grand, high-flown, inflated, lofty, noble, sublime

elevation noun 1 PROMOTION, advancement, aggrandizement, exaltation, preferment, upgrading 2 ALTITUDE, height

elicit verb 1 BRING ABOUT, bring forth, bring out, bring to light, call forth, cause, derive, evolve, give rise to 2 OBTAIN, draw out, evoke, exact, extort, extract, wrest

eligible adjective QUALIFIED, acceptable, appropriate, desirable, fit, preferable, proper, suitable, worthy

eliminate verb GET RID OF, cut out, dispose of, do away with, eradicate, exterminate, remove, stamp out, take out

elite noun BEST, aristocracy, cream, crème de la crème, flower, nobility, pick, upper class

elitist adjective SNOBBISH, exclusive, selective

elixir noun PANACEA, nostrum

elocution noun DICTION, articulation, declamation, delivery, enunciation, oratory, pronunciation, speech, speechmaking

elongate verb MAKE LONGER, draw out, extend, lengthen, prolong, protract, stretch

elope verb RUN AWAY, abscond, bolt, decamp, disappear, escape, leave, run off, slip away, steal away

eloquence noun EXPRESSIVENESS, expression, fluency, forcefulness, oratory, persuasiveness, rhetoric, way with words

eloquent adjective 1 SILVER-TONGUED, articulate, fluent, forceful, moving, persuasive, stirring, well-expressed 2 EXPRESSIVE, meaningful, suggestive, telling, vivid

elsewhere adverb IN or TO ANOTHER PLACE, abroad, away, hence (archaic), not here, somewhere else

elucidate verb CLARIFY, clear up, explain, explicate, expound, illuminate, illustrate, make plain, shed or throw light upon, spell out

elude verb 1 ESCAPE, avoid, dodge, duck (informal), evade, flee, get away from, outrun 2 BAFFLE, be beyond (someone), confound, escape, foil, frustrate, puzzle, stump, thwart

elusive adjective 1 DIFFICULT TO CATCH, shifty, slippery, tricky 2 INDEFINABLE, fleeting, intangible, subtle, transient, transitory

emaciated adjective SKELETAL,

cadaverous, gaunt, haggard, lean, pinched, scrawny, thin, undernourished, wasted

emanate verb FLOW, arise, come forth, derive, emerge, issue, originate, proceed, spring, stem

emancipate verb FREE, deliver, liberate, release, set free, unchain, unfetter

emancipation noun FREEDOM, deliverance, liberation, liberty, release

embalm verb PRESERVE, mummify

embargo noun 1 BAN, bar, boycott, interdiction, prohibition, restraint, restriction, stoppage ♦ verb 2 BAN, bar, block, boycott, prohibit, restrict, stop

embark verb 1 GO ABOARD, board ship, take ship 2 **embark on** or **upon** BEGIN, commence, enter, launch, plunge into, set about, set out, start, take up

embarrass verb SHAME, discomfit, disconcert, distress, fluster, humiliate, mortify, show up (informal)

embarrassed adjective ASHAMED, awkward, blushing, discomfited, disconcerted, humiliated, mortified, red-faced, self-conscious, sheepish

embarrassing adjective HUMILIATING, awkward, compromising, discomfiting, disconcerting, mortifying, sensitive, shameful, toe-curling (informal), uncomfortable

embarrassment noun 1 SHAME, awkwardness, bashfulness, distress, humiliation, mortification, self-consciousness, showing up (informal) 2 PREDICAMENT, bind (informal), difficulty, mess, pickle (informal), scrape (informal)

embellish verb DECORATE, adorn,

beautify, elaborate, embroider, enhance, enrich, festoon, ornament

embellishment noun DECORATION, adornment, elaboration, embroidery, enhancement, enrichment, exaggeration, ornament, ornamentation

embezzle verb MISAPPROPRIATE, appropriate, filch, misuse, peculate, pilfer, purloin, rip off (slang), steal

embezzlement noun MISAPPROPRIATION, appropriation, filching, fraud, misuse, peculation, pilfering, stealing, theft

embittered adjective RESENTFUL, angry, bitter, disaffected, disillusioned, rancorous, soured, with a chip on one's shoulder (informal)

emblem noun SYMBOL, badge, crest, image, insignia, mark, sign, token

embodiment noun PERSONIFICATION, epitome, example, exemplar, expression, incarnation, representation, symbol

embody verb 1 PERSONIFY, exemplify, manifest, represent, stand for, symbolize, typify 2 INCORPORATE, collect, combine, comprise, contain, include

embolden verb ENCOURAGE, fire, inflame, invigorate, rouse, stimulate, stir, strengthen

embrace verb 1 HUG, clasp, cuddle, envelop, hold, seize, squeeze, take or hold in one's arms 2 ACCEPT, adopt, espouse, seize, take on board, take up, welcome 3 INCLUDE, comprehend, comprise, contain, cover, encompass, involve, take in ♦ noun 4 HUG, clasp, clinch (slang), cuddle, squeeze

embroil verb INVOLVE, enmesh, ensnare, entangle, implicate, incriminate, mire, mix up

embryo noun GERM, beginning, nucleus, root, rudiment

emend verb REVISE, amend, correct, edit, improve, rectify

emendation noun REVISION, amendment, correction, editing, improvement, rectification

emerge verb 1 COME INTO VIEW, appear, arise, come forth, emanate, issue, rise, spring up, surface 2 BECOME APPARENT, become known, come out, come out in the wash, come to light, crop up, transpire

emergence noun COMING, advent, appearance, arrival, development, materialization, rise

emergency noun CRISIS, danger, difficulty, extremity, necessity, plight, predicament, quandary, scrape (*informal*)

emigrate verb MOVE ABROAD, migrate, move

emigration noun DEPARTURE, exodus, migration

eminence noun PROMINENCE, distinction, esteem, fame, greatness, importance, note, prestige, renown, repute

eminent adjective PROMINENT, celebrated, distinguished, esteemed, famous, high-ranking, illustrious, noted, renowned, well-known

emission noun GIVING OFF or OUT, discharge, ejaculation, ejection, exhalation, radiation, shedding, transmission

emit verb GIVE OFF, cast out, discharge, eject, emanate, exude, radiate, send out, transmit

emotion noun FEELING, ardour, excitement, fervour, passion, sensation, sentiment, vehemence, warmth

emotional adjective 1 SENSITIVE, demonstrative, excitable, hot-blooded, passionate, sentimental, temperamental 2 MOVING, affecting, emotive, heart-warming, poignant, sentimental, stirring, touching

emotive adjective SENSITIVE, controversial, delicate, touchy

emphasis noun STRESS, accent, attention, force, importance, priority, prominence, significance, weight

emphasize verb STRESS, accentuate, dwell on, give priority to, highlight, lay stress on, play up, press home, underline

emphatic adjective FORCEFUL, categorical, definite, insistent, positive, pronounced, resounding, unequivocal, unmistakable, vigorous

empire noun KINGDOM, commonwealth, domain, realm

empirical, empiric adjective FIRST-HAND, experiential, experimental, observed, practical, pragmatic

employ verb 1 HIRE, commission, engage, enlist, retain, take on 2 KEEP BUSY, engage, fill, make use of, occupy, take up, use up 3 USE, apply, bring to bear, exercise, exert, make use of, ply, put to use, utilize ♦ noun 4 As in **in the employ of** SERVICE, employment, engagement, hire

employed adjective WORKING, active, busy, engaged, in a job, in employment, in work, occupied

employee noun WORKER, hand, job-holder, staff member, wage-earner, workman

employer noun BOSS (*informal*), company, firm, gaffer (*informal, chiefly Brit.*), owner, patron, proprietor

employment noun 1 <u>TAKING ON</u>, engagement, enlistment, hire, retaining 2 <u>USE</u>, application, exercise, exertion, utilization 3 <u>JOB</u>, line, occupation, profession, trade, vocation, work

emporium noun Old-fashioned <u>SHOP</u>, bazaar, market, mart, store, warehouse

empower verb <u>ENABLE</u>, allow, authorize, commission, delegate, entitle, license, permit, qualify, sanction, warrant

emptiness noun 1 <u>BARENESS</u>, blankness, desolation, vacancy, vacuum, void, waste 2 <u>PURPOSELESSNESS</u>, banality, futility, hollowness, inanity, meaninglessness, senselessness, vanity, worthlessness 3 <u>INSINCERITY</u>, cheapness, hollowness, idleness

empty adjective 1 <u>BARE</u>, blank, clear, deserted, desolate, hollow, unfurnished, uninhabited, unoccupied, vacant, void 2 <u>PURPOSELESS</u>, banal, fruitless, futile, hollow, inane, meaningless, senseless, vain, worthless 3 <u>INSINCERE</u>, cheap, hollow, idle ♦ verb 4 <u>EVACUATE</u>, clear, drain, exhaust, pour out, unload, vacate, void

empty-headed adjective <u>SCATTERBRAINED</u>, brainless, dizzy (informal), featherbrained, harebrained, silly, vacuous

emulate verb <u>IMITATE</u>, compete with, copy, echo, follow, mimic, rival

enable verb <u>ALLOW</u>, authorize, empower, entitle, license, permit, qualify, sanction, warrant

enact verb 1 <u>ESTABLISH</u>, authorize, command, decree, legislate, ordain, order, proclaim, sanction 2 <u>PERFORM</u>, act out, depict, play, play the part of, portray, represent

enamoured adjective <u>IN LOVE</u>, captivated, charmed, enraptured, fond, infatuated, smitten, taken

encampment noun <u>CAMP</u>, base, bivouac, camping ground, campsite, cantonment, quarters, tents

encapsulate verb <u>SUM UP</u>, abridge, compress, condense, digest, epitomize, précis, summarize

enchant verb <u>FASCINATE</u>, beguile, bewitch, captivate, charm, delight, enrapture, enthral, ravish

enchanter noun <u>SORCERER</u>, conjuror, magician, magus, necromancer, warlock, witch, wizard

enchanting adjective <u>FASCINATING</u>, alluring, attractive, bewitching, captivating, charming, delightful, entrancing, lovely, pleasant

enclose verb 1 <u>SURROUND</u>, bound, encase, encircle, fence, hem in, shut in, wall in 2 <u>SEND WITH</u>, include, insert, put in

encompass verb 1 <u>SURROUND</u>, circle, encircle, envelop, ring 2 <u>INCLUDE</u>, admit, comprise, contain, cover, embrace, hold, incorporate, take in

encounter verb 1 <u>MEET</u>, bump into (informal), chance upon, come upon, confront, experience, face, run across ♦ noun 2 <u>MEETING</u>, brush, confrontation, rendezvous 3 <u>BATTLE</u>, clash, conflict, contest, head-to-head, run-in (informal)

encourage verb 1 <u>INSPIRE</u>, buoy up, cheer, comfort, console, embolden, hearten, reassure 2 <u>SPUR</u>, advocate, egg on, foster, promote, prompt, support, urge

encouragement noun <u>INSPIRATION</u>, cheer, incitement, promotion, reassurance, stimulation, stimulus, support

encouraging adjective <u>PROMISING</u>, bright, cheerful, comforting, good, heartening, hopeful, reassuring, rosy

encroach *verb* INTRUDE, impinge, infringe, invade, make inroads, overstep, trespass, usurp

encumber *verb* BURDEN, hamper, handicap, hinder, impede, inconvenience, obstruct, saddle, weigh down

end *noun* 1 EXTREMITY, boundary, edge, extent, extreme, limit, point, terminus, tip 2 FINISH, cessation, close, closure, ending, expiration, expiry, stop, termination 3 CONCLUSION, culmination, denouement, ending, finale, resolution 4 REMNANT, butt, fragment, leftover, oddment, remainder, scrap, stub 5 DESTRUCTION, death, demise, doom, extermination, extinction, ruin 6 PURPOSE, aim, goal, intention, object, objective, point, reason ◆ *verb* 7 FINISH, cease, close, conclude, culminate, stop, terminate, wind up

endanger *verb* PUT AT RISK, compromise, imperil, jeopardize, put in danger, risk, threaten

endearing *adjective* ATTRACTIVE, captivating, charming, cute, engaging, lovable, sweet, winning

endearment *noun* LOVING WORD, sweet nothing

endeavour *Formal* ◆ *verb* 1 TRY, aim, aspire, attempt, labour, make an effort, strive, struggle, take pains ◆ *noun* 2 EFFORT, attempt, enterprise, trial, try, undertaking, venture

ending *noun* FINISH, cessation, close, completion, conclusion, culmination, denouement, end, finale

endless *adjective* ETERNAL, boundless, continual, everlasting, incessant, infinite, interminable,

unlimited

endorse *verb* 1 APPROVE, advocate, authorize, back, champion, promote, ratify, recommend, support 2 SIGN, countersign

endorsement *noun* 1 APPROVAL, advocacy, approbation, authorization, backing, favour, ratification, recommendation, seal of approval, support 2 SIGNATURE, countersignature

endow *verb* PROVIDE, award, bequeath, bestow, confer, donate, finance, fund, give

endowment *noun* PROVISION, award, benefaction, bequest, donation, gift, grant, legacy

endurable *adjective* BEARABLE, acceptable, sufferable, sustainable, tolerable

endurance *noun* 1 STAYING POWER, fortitude, patience, perseverance, persistence, resolution, stamina, strength, tenacity, toleration 2 PERMANENCE, continuity, durability, duration, longevity, stability

endure *verb* 1 BEAR, cope with, experience, stand, suffer, sustain, undergo, withstand 2 LAST, continue, live on, persist, remain, stand, stay, survive

enduring *adjective* LONG-LASTING, abiding, continuing, lasting, perennial, persistent, steadfast, unfaltering, unwavering

enemy *noun* FOE, adversary, antagonist, competitor, opponent, rival, the opposition, the other side

energetic *adjective* VIGOROUS, active, animated, dynamic, forceful, indefatigable, lively, strenuous, tireless

energy *noun* VIGOUR, drive, forcefulness, get-up-and-go (*informal*), liveliness, pep, stamina, verve, vitality

enforce verb IMPOSE, administer, apply, carry out, execute, implement, insist on, prosecute, put into effect

engage verb 1 PARTICIPATE, embark on, enter into, join, set about, take part, undertake 2 OCCUPY, absorb, engross, grip, involve, preoccupy 3 CAPTIVATE, arrest, catch, fix, gain 4 EMPLOY, appoint, enlist, enrol, hire, retain, take on 5 *Military* BEGIN BATTLE WITH, assail, attack, encounter, fall on, join battle with, meet, take on 6 SET GOING, activate, apply, bring into operation, energize, switch on

engaged adjective 1 BETROTHED (*archaic*), affianced, pledged, promised, spoken for 2 OCCUPIED, busy, employed, in use, tied up, unavailable

engagement noun 1 APPOINTMENT, arrangement, commitment, date, meeting 2 BETROTHAL, troth (*archaic*) 3 BATTLE, action, combat, conflict, encounter, fight

engaging adjective CHARMING, agreeable, attractive, fetching (*informal*), likable or likeable, pleasing, winning, winsome

engender verb PRODUCE, breed, cause, create, generate, give rise to, induce, instigate, lead to

engine noun MACHINE, mechanism, motor

engineer verb BRING ABOUT, contrive, create, devise, effect, mastermind, plan, plot, scheme

engrave verb 1 CARVE, chisel, cut, etch, inscribe 2 FIX, embed, impress, imprint, ingrain, lodge

engraving noun CARVING, etching, inscription, plate, woodcut

engross verb ABSORB, engage, immerse, involve, occupy, preoccupy

engrossed adjective ABSORBED, caught up, enthralled, fascinated, gripped, immersed, lost, preoccupied, rapt, riveted

engulf verb IMMERSE, envelop, inundate, overrun, overwhelm, submerge, swallow up, swamp

enhance verb IMPROVE, add to, boost, heighten, increase, lift, reinforce, strengthen, swell

enigma noun MYSTERY, conundrum, problem, puzzle, riddle, teaser

enigmatic adjective MYSTERIOUS, ambiguous, cryptic, equivocal, inscrutable, obscure, puzzling, unfathomable

enjoy verb 1 TAKE PLEASURE IN or FROM, appreciate, be entertained by, be pleased with, delight in, like, relish 2 HAVE, be blessed or favoured with, experience, have the benefit of, own, possess, reap the benefits of, use

enjoyable adjective PLEASURABLE, agreeable, delightful, entertaining, gratifying, pleasant, satisfying, to one's liking

enjoyment noun PLEASURE, amusement, delectation, delight, entertainment, fun, gratification, happiness, joy, relish

enlarge verb 1 INCREASE, add to, amplify, broaden, expand, extend, grow, magnify, swell, widen 2 **enlarge on** EXPAND ON, descant on, develop, elaborate on, expatiate on, give further details about

enlighten verb INFORM, advise, cause to understand, counsel, edify, educate, instruct, make aware, teach

enlightened adjective INFORMED, aware, civilized, cultivated, educated, knowledgeable, open-minded, reasonable, sophisticated

enlightenment *noun*
UNDERSTANDING, awareness,
comprehension, education,
insight, instruction, knowledge,
learning, wisdom

enlist *verb* 1 JOIN UP, enrol, enter
(into), join, muster, register, sign
up, volunteer 2 OBTAIN, engage,
procure, recruit

enliven *verb* CHEER UP, animate,
excite, inspire, invigorate, pep up,
rouse, spark, stimulate, vitalize

enmity *noun* HOSTILITY, acrimony,
animosity, bad blood, bitterness,
hatred, ill will, malice

ennoble *verb* DIGNIFY, aggrandize,
elevate, enhance, exalt, glorify,
honour, magnify, raise

enormity *noun* 1 WICKEDNESS,
atrocity, depravity,
monstrousness, outrageousness,
vileness, villainy 2 ATROCITY,
abomination, crime, disgrace, evil,
horror, monstrosity, outrage
3 *Informal* HUGENESS, greatness,
immensity, magnitude, vastness

enormous *adjective* HUGE, colossal,
gigantic, gross, immense,
mammoth, massive,
mountainous, tremendous, vast

enough *adjective* 1 SUFFICIENT,
abundant, adequate, ample,
plenty ♦ *noun* 2 SUFFICIENCY,
abundance, adequacy, ample
supply, plenty, right amount
♦ *adverb* 3 SUFFICIENTLY, abundantly,
adequately, amply, reasonably,
satisfactorily, tolerably

enquire see INQUIRE

enquiry see INQUIRY

enrage *verb* ANGER, exasperate,
incense, inflame, infuriate,
madden

enrich *verb* 1 ENHANCE, augment,
develop, improve, refine,
supplement 2 MAKE RICH, make
wealthy

enrol *verb* ENLIST, accept, admit,
join up, recruit, register, sign up *or*
on, take on

enrolment *noun* ENLISTMENT,
acceptance, admission,
engagement, matriculation,
recruitment, registration

en route *adverb* ON *or* ALONG THE
WAY, in transit, on the road

ensemble *noun* 1 WHOLE,
aggregate, collection, entirety,
set, sum, total, totality 2 OUTFIT,
costume, get-up (*informal*), suit
3 GROUP, band, cast, chorus,
company, troupe

ensign *noun* FLAG, banner, colours,
jack, pennant, pennon, standard,
streamer

ensue *verb* FOLLOW, arise, come
next, derive, flow, issue, proceed,
result, stem

ensure *verb* 1 MAKE CERTAIN, certify,
confirm, effect, guarantee, make
sure, secure, warrant 2 PROTECT,
guard, make safe, safeguard,
secure

entail *verb* INVOLVE, bring about, call
for, demand, give rise to,
necessitate, occasion, require

entangle *verb* 1 TANGLE, catch,
embroil, enmesh, ensnare, entrap,
implicate, snag, snare, trap 2 MIX
UP, complicate, confuse, jumble,
muddle, perplex, puzzle

enter *verb* 1 COME *or* GO IN *or* INTO,
arrive, make an entrance, pass
into, penetrate, pierce 2 JOIN,
commence, embark upon, enlist,
enrol, set out on, start, take up
3 RECORD, inscribe, list, log, note,
register, set down, take down

enterprise *noun* 1 FIRM, business,
company, concern, establishment,
operation 2 UNDERTAKING,
adventure, effort, endeavour,
operation, plan, programme,
project, venture 3 INITIATIVE,

adventurousness, boldness, daring, drive, energy, enthusiasm, resourcefulness

enterprising *adjective* RESOURCEFUL, adventurous, bold, daring, energetic, enthusiastic, go-ahead, intrepid, spirited

entertain *verb* 1 AMUSE, charm, cheer, delight, please, regale 2 SHOW HOSPITALITY TO, accommodate, be host to, harbour, have company, lodge, put up, treat 3 CONSIDER, conceive, contemplate, imagine, keep in mind, think about

entertaining *adjective* ENJOYABLE, amusing, cheering, diverting, funny, humorous, interesting, pleasant, pleasurable

entertainment *noun* ENJOYMENT, amusement, fun, leisure activity, pastime, pleasure, recreation, sport, treat

enthral *verb* FASCINATE, captivate, charm, enchant, enrapture, entrance, grip, mesmerize

enthusiasm *noun* KEENNESS, eagerness, fervour, interest, passion, relish, zeal, zest

enthusiast *noun* LOVER, aficionado, buff (*informal*), devotee, fan, fanatic, follower, supporter

enthusiastic *adjective* KEEN, avid, eager, fervent, passionate, vigorous, wholehearted, zealous

entice *verb* ATTRACT, allure, cajole, coax, lead on, lure, persuade, seduce, tempt

entire *adjective* WHOLE, complete, full, gross, total

entirely *adverb* COMPLETELY, absolutely, altogether, fully, in every respect, thoroughly, totally, utterly, wholly

entitle *verb* 1 GIVE THE RIGHT TO, allow, authorize, empower,

enable, license, permit 2 CALL, christen, dub, label, name, term, title

entity *noun* THING, being, creature, individual, object, organism, substance

entourage *noun* RETINUE, associates, attendants, company, court, escort, followers, staff, train

entrails *plural noun* INTESTINES, bowels, guts, innards (*informal*), insides (*informal*), offal, viscera

entrance[1] *noun* 1 WAY IN, access, door, doorway, entry, gate, opening, passage 2 APPEARANCE, arrival, coming in, entry, introduction 3 ADMISSION, access, admittance, entrée, entry, permission to enter

entrance[2] *verb* 1 ENCHANT, bewitch, captivate, charm, delight, enrapture, enthral, fascinate 2 MESMERIZE, hypnotize, put in a trance

entrant *noun* COMPETITOR, candidate, contestant, entry, participant, player

entreaty *noun* PLEA, appeal, earnest request, exhortation, petition, prayer, request, supplication

entrenched *adjective* FIXED, deep-rooted, deep-seated, ineradicable, ingrained, rooted, set, unshakable, well-established

entrepreneur *noun* BUSINESSMAN *or* BUSINESSWOMAN, impresario, industrialist, magnate, tycoon

entrust *verb* GIVE CUSTODY OF, assign, commit, confide, delegate, deliver, hand over, turn over

entry *noun* 1 WAY IN, access, door, doorway, entrance, gate, opening, passage 2 COMING IN, appearance, entering, entrance, initiation, introduction 3 ADMISSION, access, entrance, entrée, permission to enter

4 RECORD, account, item, listing, note

entwine *verb* TWIST, interlace, interweave, knit, plait, twine, weave, wind

enumerate *verb* LIST, cite, itemize, mention, name, quote, recite, recount, relate, spell out

enunciate *verb* **1** PRONOUNCE, articulate, enounce, say, sound, speak, utter, vocalize, voice **2** STATE, declare, proclaim, promulgate, pronounce, propound, publish

envelop *verb* ENCLOSE, cloak, cover, encase, encircle, engulf, shroud, surround, wrap

envelope *noun* WRAPPING, case, casing, cover, covering, jacket, wrapper

enviable *adjective* DESIRABLE, advantageous, favoured, fortunate, lucky, privileged, to die for (*informal*)

envious *adjective* COVETOUS, green with envy, grudging, jealous, resentful

environment *noun* SURROUNDINGS, atmosphere, background, conditions, habitat, medium, setting, situation

environmental *adjective* ECOLOGICAL, green

environmentalist *noun* CONSERVATIONIST, ecologist, green

environs *plural noun* SURROUNDING AREA, district, locality, neighbourhood, outskirts, precincts, suburbs, vicinity

envisage *verb* **1** IMAGINE, conceive (of), conceptualize, contemplate, fancy, picture, think up, visualize **2** FORESEE, anticipate, envision, predict, see

envoy *noun* MESSENGER, agent, ambassador, courier, delegate, diplomat, emissary, intermediary, representative

envy *noun* **1** COVETOUSNESS, enviousness, jealousy, resentfulness, resentment ♦ *verb* **2** COVET, be envious (of), begrudge, be jealous (of), grudge, resent

ephemeral *adjective* BRIEF, fleeting, momentary, passing, short-lived, temporary, transient, transitory

epidemic *noun* SPREAD, contagion, growth, outbreak, plague, rash, upsurge, wave

epigram *noun* WITTICISM, aphorism, bon mot, quip

epilogue *noun* CONCLUSION, coda, concluding speech, postscript

episode *noun* **1** EVENT, adventure, affair, escapade, experience, happening, incident, matter, occurrence **2** PART, chapter, instalment, passage, scene, section

epistle *noun* LETTER, communication, message, missive, note

epitaph *noun* MONUMENT, inscription

epithet *noun* NAME, appellation, description, designation, moniker *or* monicker (*slang*), nickname, sobriquet, tag, title

epitome *noun* PERSONIFICATION, archetype, embodiment, essence, quintessence, representation, type, typical example

epitomize *verb* TYPIFY, embody, exemplify, illustrate, personify, represent, symbolize

epoch *noun* ERA, age, date, period, time

equable *adjective* EVEN-TEMPERED, calm, composed, easy-going, imperturbable, level-headed, placid, serene, unflappable (*informal*)

equal *adjective* 1 IDENTICAL, alike, corresponding, equivalent, the same, uniform 2 REGULAR, symmetrical, uniform, unvarying 3 EVEN, balanced, evenly matched, fifty-fifty (*informal*), level pegging (*Brit. informal*) 4 FAIR, egalitarian, even-handed, impartial, just, unbiased 5 **equal to** CAPABLE OF, competent to, fit for, good enough for, ready for, strong enough, suitable for, up to ♦ *noun* 6 MATCH, counterpart, equivalent, rival, twin ♦ *verb* 7 MATCH, amount to, be tantamount to, correspond to, equate, level, parallel, tie with

equality *noun* 1 SAMENESS, balance, correspondence, equivalence, evenness, identity, likeness, similarity, uniformity 2 FAIRNESS, egalitarianism, equal opportunity, parity

equalize *verb* MAKE EQUAL, balance, equal, even up, level, match, regularize, smooth, square, standardize

equate *verb* MAKE *or* BE EQUAL, be commensurate, compare, correspond with *or* to, liken, mention in the same breath, parallel

equation *noun* EQUATING, comparison, correspondence, parallel

equilibrium *noun* STABILITY, balance, equipoise, evenness, rest, steadiness, symmetry

equip *verb* SUPPLY, arm, array, fit out, furnish, kit out, provide, stock

equipment *noun* TOOLS, accoutrements, apparatus, gear, paraphernalia, stuff, supplies, tackle

equitable *adjective* FAIR, even-handed, honest, impartial, just, proper, reasonable, unbiased

equivalence *noun* EQUALITY, correspondence, evenness, likeness, parity, sameness, similarity

equivalent *noun* 1 EQUAL, counterpart, match, opposite number, parallel, twin ♦ *adjective* 2 EQUAL, alike, commensurate, comparable, corresponding, interchangeable, of a piece, same, similar, tantamount

equivocal *adjective* AMBIGUOUS, evasive, indefinite, indeterminate, misleading, oblique, obscure, uncertain, vague

era *noun* AGE, date, day *or* days, epoch, generation, period, time

eradicate *verb* WIPE OUT, annihilate, destroy, eliminate, erase, exterminate, extinguish, obliterate, remove, root out

erase *verb* WIPE OUT, blot, cancel, delete, expunge, obliterate, remove, rub out

erect *verb* 1 BUILD, construct, put up, raise, set up 2 FOUND, create, establish, form, initiate, institute, organize, set up ♦ *adjective* 3 UPRIGHT, elevated, perpendicular, pricked-up, stiff, straight, vertical

erode *verb* WEAR DOWN *or* AWAY, abrade, consume, corrode, destroy, deteriorate, disintegrate, eat away, grind down

erosion *noun* DETERIORATION, abrasion, attrition, destruction, disintegration, eating away, grinding down, wearing down *or* away

erotic *adjective* SEXUAL, amatory, carnal, lustful, seductive, sensual, sexy (*informal*), voluptuous

err *verb* MAKE A MISTAKE, blunder, go wrong, miscalculate, misjudge, mistake, slip up (*informal*)

errand *noun* JOB, charge, commission, message, mission, task

erratic *adjective* <u>UNPREDICTABLE</u>, changeable, inconsistent, irregular, uneven, unreliable, unstable, variable, wayward

erroneous *adjective* <u>INCORRECT</u>, fallacious, false, faulty, flawed, invalid, mistaken, unsound, wrong

error *noun* <u>MISTAKE</u>, bloomer (*Brit. informal*), blunder, howler (*informal*), miscalculation, oversight, slip, solecism

erstwhile *adjective* <u>FORMER</u>, bygone, late, old, once, one-time, past, previous, sometime

erudite *adjective* <u>LEARNED</u>, cultivated, cultured, educated, knowledgeable, scholarly, well-educated, well-read

erupt *verb* 1 <u>EXPLODE</u>, belch forth, blow up, burst out, gush, pour forth, spew forth *or* out, spout, throw off 2 *Medical* <u>BREAK OUT</u>, appear

eruption *noun* 1 <u>EXPLOSION</u>, discharge, ejection, flare-up, outbreak, outburst 2 *Medical* <u>INFLAMMATION</u>, outbreak, rash

escalate *verb* <u>INCREASE</u>, expand, extend, grow, heighten, intensify, mount, rise

escapade *noun* <u>ADVENTURE</u>, antic, caper, prank, scrape (*informal*), stunt

escape *verb* 1 <u>GET AWAY</u>, abscond, bolt, break free *or* out, flee, fly, make one's getaway, run away *or* off, slip away 2 <u>AVOID</u>, dodge, duck, elude, evade, pass, shun, slip 3 <u>LEAK</u>, emanate, exude, flow, gush, issue, pour forth, seep ♦ *noun* 4 <u>GETAWAY</u>, break, break-out, flight 5 <u>AVOIDANCE</u>, circumvention, evasion 6 <u>RELAXATION</u>, distraction, diversion, pastime, recreation 7 <u>LEAK</u>, emanation, emission, seepage

escort *noun* 1 <u>GUARD</u>, bodyguard, convoy, cortege, entourage, retinue, train 2 <u>COMPANION</u>, attendant, beau, chaperon, guide, partner ♦ *verb* 3 <u>ACCOMPANY</u>, chaperon, conduct, guide, lead, partner, shepherd, usher

especial *adjective* Formal <u>EXCEPTIONAL</u>, noteworthy, outstanding, principal, special, uncommon, unusual

especially *adverb* <u>EXCEPTIONALLY</u>, conspicuously, markedly, notably, outstandingly, remarkably, specially, strikingly, uncommonly, unusually

espionage *noun* <u>SPYING</u>, counter-intelligence, intelligence, surveillance, undercover work

espousal *noun* <u>SUPPORT</u>, adoption, advocacy, backing, championing, defence, embracing, promotion, taking up

espouse *verb* <u>SUPPORT</u>, adopt, advocate, back, champion, embrace, promote, stand up for, take up, uphold

essay *noun* 1 <u>COMPOSITION</u>, article, discourse, dissertation, paper, piece, tract, treatise ♦ *verb* 2 *Formal* <u>ATTEMPT</u>, aim, endeavour, try, undertake

essence *noun* 1 <u>FUNDAMENTAL NATURE</u>, being, core, heart, nature, quintessence, soul, spirit, substance 2 <u>CONCENTRATE</u>, distillate, extract, spirits, tincture

essential *adjective* 1 <u>VITAL</u>, crucial, important, indispensable, necessary, needed, requisite 2 <u>FUNDAMENTAL</u>, basic, cardinal, elementary, innate, intrinsic, main, principal ♦ *noun* 3 <u>PREREQUISITE</u>, basic, fundamental, must, necessity, rudiment, *sine qua non*

establish *verb* 1 <u>CREATE</u>, constitute, form, found, ground, inaugurate, institute, settle, set up **2** <u>PROVE</u>, authenticate, certify, confirm, corroborate, demonstrate, substantiate, verify

establishment noun **1** <u>CREATION</u>, formation, foundation, founding, inauguration, installation, institution, organization, setting up **2** <u>ORGANIZATION</u>, business, company, concern, corporation, enterprise, firm, institution, outfit (*informal*) **3 the Establishment** <u>THE AUTHORITIES</u>, ruling class, the powers that be, the system

estate noun **1** <u>LANDS</u>, area, domain, holdings, manor, property **2** *Law* <u>PROPERTY</u>, assets, belongings, effects, fortune, goods, possessions, wealth

esteem noun **1** <u>RESPECT</u>, admiration, credit, estimation, good opinion, honour, regard, reverence, veneration ♦ *verb* **2** <u>RESPECT</u>, admire, love, prize, regard highly, revere, think highly of, treasure, value **3** *Formal* <u>CONSIDER</u>, believe, deem, estimate, judge, reckon, regard, think, view

estimate verb **1** <u>CALCULATE ROUGHLY</u>, assess, evaluate, gauge, guess, judge, number, reckon, value **2** <u>FORM AN OPINION</u>, believe, conjecture, consider, judge, rank, rate, reckon, surmise ♦ *noun* **3** <u>APPROXIMATE CALCULATION</u>, assessment, ballpark figure (*informal*), guess, guesstimate (*informal*), judgment, valuation **4** <u>OPINION</u>, appraisal, assessment, belief, estimation, judgment

estimation noun <u>OPINION</u>, appraisal, appreciation, assessment, belief, consideration, considered opinion, judgment, view

estuary noun <u>INLET</u>, creek, firth, fjord, mouth

et cetera adverb **1** <u>AND SO ON</u>, and

so forth ♦ *noun* **2** <u>AND THE REST</u>, and others, and the like, et al.

etch verb <u>CUT</u>, carve, eat into, engrave, impress, imprint, inscribe, stamp

etching noun <u>PRINT</u>, carving, engraving, impression, imprint, inscription

eternal adjective **1** <u>EVERLASTING</u>, endless, immortal, infinite, never-ending, perpetual, timeless, unceasing, unending **2** <u>PERMANENT</u>, deathless, enduring, immutable, imperishable, indestructible, lasting, unchanging

eternity noun **1** <u>INFINITY</u>, ages, endlessness, immortality, perpetuity, timelessness **2** *Theology* <u>THE AFTERLIFE</u>, heaven, paradise, the hereafter, the next world

ethical adjective <u>MORAL</u>, conscientious, fair, good, honourable, just, principled, proper, right, upright, virtuous

ethics plural noun <u>MORAL CODE</u>, conscience, morality, moral philosophy, moral values, principles, rules of conduct, standards

ethnic, ethnical adjective <u>CULTURAL</u>, folk, indigenous, national, native, racial, traditional

etiquette noun <u>GOOD</u> *or* <u>PROPER</u> <u>BEHAVIOUR</u>, civility, courtesy, decorum, formalities, manners, politeness, propriety, protocol

euphoria noun <u>ELATION</u>, ecstasy, exaltation, exhilaration, intoxication, joy, jubilation, rapture

evacuate verb <u>CLEAR</u>, abandon, desert, forsake, leave, move out, pull out, quit, vacate, withdraw

evade verb **1** <u>AVOID</u>, dodge, duck, elude, escape, get away from, sidestep, steer clear of **2** <u>AVOID</u>

ANSWERING, equivocate, fend off, fudge, hedge, parry

evaluate *verb* ASSESS, appraise, calculate, estimate, gauge, judge, rate, reckon, size up (*informal*), weigh

evaporate *verb* 1 DRY UP, dehydrate, desiccate, dry, vaporize 2 DISAPPEAR, dematerialize, dissolve, fade away, melt away, vanish

evasion *noun* 1 AVOIDANCE, dodging, escape 2 DECEPTION, equivocation, evasiveness, prevarication

evasive *adjective* DECEPTIVE, cagey (*informal*), equivocating, indirect, oblique, prevaricating, shifty, slippery

eve *noun* 1 NIGHT BEFORE, day before, vigil 2 BRINK, edge, point, threshold, verge

even *adjective* 1 LEVEL, flat, horizontal, parallel, smooth, steady, straight, true, uniform 2 REGULAR, constant, smooth, steady, unbroken, uniform, uninterrupted, unvarying, unwavering 3 EQUAL, comparable, fifty-fifty (*informal*), identical, level, like, matching, neck and neck, on a par, similar, tied 4 CALM, composed, cool, even-tempered, imperturbable, placid, unruffled, well-balanced 5 **get even (with)** *Informal* PAY BACK, get one's own back, give tit for tat, reciprocate, repay, requite

evening *noun* DUSK, gloaming (*Scot. or poetic*), twilight

event *noun* 1 INCIDENT, affair, business, circumstance, episode, experience, happening, occasion, occurrence 2 COMPETITION, bout, contest, game, tournament

even-tempered *adjective* CALM, composed, cool, imperturbable, level-headed, placid, tranquil, unexcitable, unruffled

eventful *adjective* EXCITING, active, busy, dramatic, full, lively, memorable, remarkable

eventual *adjective* FINAL, concluding, overall, ultimate

eventuality *noun* POSSIBILITY, case, chance, contingency, event, likelihood, probability

eventually *adverb* IN THE END, after all, at the end of the day, finally, one day, some time, ultimately, when all is said and done

ever *adverb* 1 AT ANY TIME, at all, at any period, at any point, by any chance, in any case, on any occasion 2 ALWAYS, at all times, constantly, continually, evermore, for ever, perpetually

everlasting *adjective* ETERNAL, endless, immortal, indestructible, never-ending, perpetual, timeless, undying

evermore *adverb* FOR EVER, always, eternally, ever, to the end of time

every *adjective* EACH, all, each one

everybody *pronoun* EVERYONE, all and sundry, each one, each person, every person, one and all, the whole world

everyday *adjective* COMMON, customary, mundane, ordinary, routine, run-of-the-mill, stock, usual, workaday

everyone *pronoun* EVERYBODY, all and sundry, each one, each person, every person, one and all, the whole world

everything *pronoun* ALL, each thing, the lot, the whole lot

everywhere *adverb* TO *or* IN EVERY PLACE, all around, all over, far and wide *or* near, high and low, in every nook and cranny, the world over, ubiquitously

evict verb EXPEL, boot out (*informal*), eject, kick out (*informal*), oust, remove, throw out, turf out (*informal*), turn out

evidence noun 1 PROOF, confirmation, corroboration, demonstration, grounds, indication, sign, substantiation, testimony ♦ verb 2 SHOW, demonstrate, display, exhibit, indicate, prove, reveal, signify, witness

evident adjective OBVIOUS, apparent, clear, manifest, noticeable, perceptible, plain, unmistakable, visible

evidently adverb 1 OBVIOUSLY, clearly, manifestly, plainly, undoubtedly, unmistakably, without question 2 APPARENTLY, ostensibly, outwardly, seemingly, to all appearances

evil noun 1 WICKEDNESS, badness, depravity, malignity, sin, vice, villainy, wrongdoing 2 HARM, affliction, disaster, hurt, ill, injury, mischief, misfortune, suffering, woe ♦ adjective 3 WICKED, bad, depraved, immoral, malevolent, malicious, sinful, villainous 4 HARMFUL, calamitous, catastrophic, destructive, dire, disastrous, pernicious, ruinous 5 OFFENSIVE, foul, noxious, pestilential, unpleasant, vile

evoke verb RECALL, arouse, awaken, call, give rise to, induce, rekindle, stir up, summon up

evolution noun DEVELOPMENT, expansion, growth, increase, maturation, progress, unfolding, working out

evolve verb DEVELOP, expand, grow, increase, mature, progress, unfold, work out

exact adjective 1 ACCURATE, correct, definite, faultless, precise, right, specific, true, unerring ♦ verb

2 DEMAND, claim, command, compel, extort, extract, force

exacting adjective DEMANDING, difficult, hard, harsh, rigorous, severe, strict, stringent, taxing, tough

exactly adverb 1 PRECISELY, accurately, correctly, explicitly, faithfully, scrupulously, truthfully, unerringly 2 IN EVERY RESPECT, absolutely, indeed, precisely, quite, specifically, to the letter

exactness noun PRECISION, accuracy, correctness, exactitude, rigorousness, scrupulousness, strictness, veracity

exaggerate verb OVERSTATE, amplify, embellish, embroider, enlarge, overemphasize, overestimate

exaggeration noun OVERSTATEMENT, amplification, embellishment, enlargement, hyperbole, overemphasis, overestimation

exalt verb 1 PRAISE, acclaim, extol, glorify, idolize, set on a pedestal, worship 2 RAISE, advance, elevate, ennoble, honour, promote, upgrade

exaltation noun 1 PRAISE, acclaim, glorification, idolization, reverence, tribute, worship 2 RISE, advancement, elevation, ennoblement, promotion, upgrading

exalted adjective HIGH-RANKING, dignified, eminent, grand, honoured, lofty, prestigious

examination noun 1 INSPECTION, analysis, exploration, interrogation, investigation, research, scrutiny, study, test 2 QUESTIONING, inquiry, inquisition, probe, quiz, test

examine verb 1 INSPECT, analyse, explore, investigate, peruse, scrutinize, study, survey 2 QUESTION, cross-examine, grill

example 175 **exclaim**

(*informal*), inquire, interrogate, quiz, test

example *noun* 1 SPECIMEN, case, illustration, instance, sample 2 MODEL, archetype, ideal, paradigm, paragon, prototype, standard 3 WARNING, caution, lesson

exasperate *verb* IRRITATE, anger, annoy, enrage, incense, inflame, infuriate, madden, pique

exasperation *noun* IRRITATION, anger, annoyance, fury, pique, provocation, rage, wrath

excavate *verb* DIG OUT, burrow, delve, dig up, mine, quarry, tunnel, uncover, unearth

exceed *verb* 1 SURPASS, beat, better, cap (*informal*), eclipse, outdo, outstrip, overtake, pass, top 2 GO OVER THE LIMIT OF, go over the top, overstep

exceedingly *adverb* EXTREMELY, enormously, exceptionally, extraordinarily, hugely, superlatively, surpassingly, unusually, very

excel *verb* 1 BE SUPERIOR, beat, eclipse, outdo, outshine, surpass, transcend 2 **excel in** *or* **at** BE GOOD AT, be proficient in, be skilful at, be talented at, shine at, show talent in

excellence *noun* HIGH QUALITY, distinction, eminence, goodness, greatness, merit, pre-eminence, superiority, supremacy

excellent *adjective* OUTSTANDING, brilliant, exquisite, fine, first-class, first-rate, good, great, superb, superlative, world-class

except *preposition* 1 *Also* **except for** APART FROM, barring, besides, but, excepting, excluding, omitting, other than, saving, with the exception of ♦ *verb* 2 EXCLUDE, leave out, omit, pass over

exception *noun* 1 SPECIAL CASE, anomaly, deviation, freak,

inconsistency, irregularity, oddity, peculiarity 2 EXCLUSION, leaving out, omission, passing over

exceptional *adjective* 1 SPECIAL, abnormal, atypical, extraordinary, irregular, odd, peculiar, strange, unusual 2 REMARKABLE, excellent, extraordinary, marvellous, outstanding, phenomenal, prodigious, special, superior

excerpt *noun* EXTRACT, fragment, part, passage, piece, quotation, section, selection

excess *noun* 1 SURFEIT, glut, overload, superabundance, superfluity, surplus, too much 2 OVERINDULGENCE, debauchery, dissipation, dissoluteness, extravagance, intemperance, prodigality

excessive *adjective* IMMODERATE, disproportionate, exaggerated, extreme, inordinate, overmuch, superfluous, too much, undue, unfair, unreasonable

exchange *verb* 1 INTERCHANGE, barter, change, convert into, swap, switch, trade ♦ *noun* 2 INTERCHANGE, barter, quid pro quo, reciprocity, substitution, swap, switch, tit for tat, trade

excitable *adjective* NERVOUS, emotional, highly strung, hot-headed, mercurial, quick-tempered, temperamental, volatile

excite *verb* AROUSE, animate, galvanize, inflame, inspire, provoke, rouse, stir up, thrill

excitement *noun* AGITATION, action, activity, animation, commotion, furore, passion, thrill

exciting *adjective* STIMULATING, dramatic, electrifying, exhilarating, rousing, sensational, stirring, thrilling

exclaim *verb* CRY OUT, call out,

declare, proclaim, shout, utter, yell

exclamation noun CRY, call, interjection, outcry, shout, utterance, yell

exclude verb 1 KEEP OUT, ban, bar, boycott, disallow, forbid, prohibit, refuse, shut out 2 LEAVE OUT, count out, eliminate, ignore, omit, pass over, reject, rule out, set aside

exclusion noun 1 BAN, bar, boycott, disqualification, embargo, prohibition, veto 2 ELIMINATION, omission, rejection

exclusive adjective 1 SOLE, absolute, complete, entire, full, total, undivided, whole 2 LIMITED, confined, peculiar, restricted, unique 3 SELECT, chic, cliquish, fashionable, posh (informal, chiefly Brit.), restricted, snobbish, up-market

excommunicate verb EXPEL, anathematize, ban, banish, cast out, denounce, exclude, repudiate

excruciating adjective AGONIZING, harrowing, insufferable, intense, piercing, severe, unbearable, violent

exculpate verb ABSOLVE, acquit, clear, discharge, excuse, exonerate, pardon, vindicate

excursion noun TRIP, day trip, expedition, jaunt, journey, outing, pleasure trip, ramble, tour

excusable adjective FORGIVABLE, allowable, defensible, justifiable, pardonable, permissible, understandable, warrantable

excuse noun 1 JUSTIFICATION, apology, defence, explanation, grounds, mitigation, plea, reason, vindication ◆ verb 2 JUSTIFY, apologize for, defend, explain, mitigate, vindicate 3 FORGIVE, acquit, exculpate, exonerate, make allowances for, overlook, pardon, tolerate, turn a blind eye

to 4 FREE, absolve, discharge, exempt, let off, release, relieve, spare

execute verb 1 PUT TO DEATH, behead, electrocute, guillotine, hang, kill, shoot 2 CARRY OUT, accomplish, administer, discharge, effect, enact, implement, perform, prosecute

execution noun 1 CARRYING OUT, accomplishment, administration, enactment, enforcement, implementation, operation, performance, prosecution 2 KILLING, capital punishment, hanging

executioner noun 1 HANGMAN, headsman 2 KILLER, assassin, exterminator, hit man (slang), liquidator, murderer, slayer

executive noun 1 ADMINISTRATOR, director, manager, official 2 ADMINISTRATION, directorate, directors, government, hierarchy, leadership, management ◆ adjective 3 ADMINISTRATIVE, controlling, decision-making, directing, governing, managerial

exemplary adjective 1 IDEAL, admirable, commendable, excellent, fine, good, model, praiseworthy 2 WARNING, cautionary

exemplify verb SHOW, demonstrate, display, embody, exhibit, illustrate, represent, serve as an example of

exempt adjective 1 IMMUNE, excepted, excused, free, not liable, released, spared ◆ verb 2 GRANT IMMUNITY, absolve, discharge, excuse, free, let off, release, relieve, spare

exemption noun IMMUNITY, absolution, discharge, dispensation, exception, exoneration, freedom, release

exercise noun 1 EXERTION, activity,

effort, labour, toil, training, work, work-out **2** TASK, drill, lesson, practice, problem **3** USE, application, discharge, fulfilment, implementation, practice, utilization ♦ *verb* **4** PUT TO USE, apply, bring to bear, employ, exert, use, utilize **5** TRAIN, practise, work out

exert *verb* **1** USE, apply, bring to bear, employ, exercise, make use of, utilize, wield **2 exert oneself** MAKE AN EFFORT, apply oneself, do one's best, endeavour, labour, strain, strive, struggle, toil, work

exertion *noun* EFFORT, elbow grease (*facetious*), endeavour, exercise, industry, strain, struggle, toil

exhaust *verb* **1** TIRE OUT, debilitate, drain, enervate, enfeeble, fatigue, sap, weaken, wear out **2** USE UP, consume, deplete, dissipate, expend, run through, spend, squander, waste

exhausted *adjective* **1** WORN OUT, all in (*slang*), debilitated, done in (*informal*), drained, fatigued, knackered (*slang*), spent, tired out **2** USED UP, consumed, depleted, dissipated, expended, finished, spent, squandered, wasted

exhausting *adjective* TIRING, backbreaking, debilitating, gruelling, laborious, punishing, sapping, strenuous, taxing

exhaustion *noun* **1** TIREDNESS, debilitation, fatigue, weariness **2** DEPLETION, consumption, emptying, using up

exhaustive *adjective* THOROUGH, all-embracing, complete, comprehensive, extensive, full-scale, in-depth, intensive

exhibit *verb* DISPLAY, demonstrate, express, indicate, manifest, parade, put on view, reveal, show

exhibition *noun* DISPLAY,

demonstration, exposition, performance, presentation, representation, show, spectacle

exhilarating *adjective* EXCITING, breathtaking, enlivening, invigorating, stimulating, thrilling

exhort *verb Formal* URGE, advise, beseech, call upon, entreat, persuade, press, spur

exhume *verb Formal* DIG UP, disentomb, disinter, unearth

exigency, exigence *noun* NEED, constraint, demand, necessity, requirement

exile *noun* **1** BANISHMENT, deportation, expatriation, expulsion **2** EXPATRIATE, deportee, émigré, outcast, refugee ♦ *verb* **3** BANISH, deport, drive out, eject, expatriate, expel

exist *verb* **1** BE, be present, endure, live, occur, survive **2** SURVIVE, eke out a living, get along *or* by, keep one's head above water, stay alive, subsist

existence *noun* BEING, actuality, life, subsistence

existent *adjective* IN EXISTENCE, alive, existing, extant, living, present, standing, surviving

exit *noun* **1** WAY OUT, door, gate, outlet **2** DEPARTURE, exodus, farewell, going, goodbye, leave-taking, retreat, withdrawal ♦ *verb* **3** DEPART, go away, go offstage (*Theatre*), go out, leave, make tracks, retire, retreat, take one's leave, withdraw

exodus *noun* DEPARTURE, evacuation, exit, flight, going out, leaving, migration, retreat, withdrawal

exonerate *verb* CLEAR, absolve, acquit, discharge, exculpate, excuse, justify, pardon, vindicate

exorbitant *adjective* EXCESSIVE, extortionate, extravagant, immoderate, inordinate, outrageous, preposterous, unreasonable

exorcise verb DRIVE OUT, cast out, deliver (from), expel, purify

exotic adjective 1 UNUSUAL, colourful, fascinating, glamorous, mysterious, strange, striking, unfamiliar 2 FOREIGN, alien, external, imported, naturalized

expand verb 1 INCREASE, amplify, broaden, develop, enlarge, extend, grow, magnify, swell, widen 2 SPREAD (OUT), diffuse, stretch (out), unfold, unfurl, unravel, unroll 3 **expand on** GO INTO DETAIL ABOUT, amplify, develop, elaborate on, embellish, enlarge on, expatiate on, expound on, flesh out

expanse noun AREA, breadth, extent, range, space, stretch, sweep, tract

expansion noun INCREASE, amplification, development, enlargement, growth, magnification, opening out, spread

expansive adjective 1 WIDE, broad, extensive, far-reaching, voluminous, wide-ranging, widespread 2 TALKATIVE, affable, communicative, effusive, friendly, loquacious, open, outgoing, sociable, unreserved

expatriate adjective 1 EXILED, banished, emigrant, émigré ◆ noun 2 EXILE, emigrant, émigré, refugee

expect verb 1 THINK, assume, believe, imagine, presume, reckon, suppose, surmise, trust 2 LOOK FORWARD TO, anticipate, await, contemplate, envisage, hope for, predict, watch for 3 REQUIRE, call for, demand, insist on, want

expectant adjective 1 EXPECTING, anticipating, apprehensive, eager, hopeful, in suspense, ready, watchful 2 PREGNANT, expecting (informal), gravid

expectation noun 1 PROBABILITY, assumption, belief, conjecture, forecast, likelihood, presumption, supposition 2 ANTICIPATION, apprehension, expectancy, hope, promise, suspense

expediency noun SUITABILITY, advisability, benefit, convenience, pragmatism, profitability, prudence, usefulness, utility

expedient noun 1 MEANS, contrivance, device, makeshift, measure, method, resort, scheme, stopgap ◆ adjective 2 ADVANTAGEOUS, appropriate, beneficial, convenient, effective, helpful, opportune, practical, suitable, useful

expedition noun JOURNEY, excursion, mission, quest, safari, tour, trek, voyage

expel verb 1 DRIVE OUT, belch, cast out, discharge, eject, remove, spew 2 DISMISS, ban, banish, drum out, evict, exclude, exile, throw out, turf out (informal)

expend verb Formal SPEND, consume, dissipate, exhaust, go through, pay out, use (up)

expendable adjective DISPENSABLE, inessential, nonessential, replaceable, unimportant, unnecessary

expenditure noun SPENDING, consumption, cost, expense, outgoings, outlay, output, payment

expense noun COST, charge, expenditure, loss, outlay, payment, spending

expensive adjective DEAR, costly, exorbitant, extravagant, high-priced, lavish, overpriced, steep (*informal*), stiff

experience *noun* **1** KNOWLEDGE, contact, exposure, familiarity, involvement, participation, practice, training **2** EVENT, adventure, affair, encounter, episode, happening, incident, occurrence ♦ *verb* **3** UNDERGO, encounter, endure, face, feel, go through, live through, sample, taste

experienced *adjective* KNOWLEDGEABLE, accomplished, expert, practised, seasoned, tested, tried, veteran, well-versed

experiment *noun* **1** TEST, examination, experimentation, investigation, procedure, proof, research, trial, trial run ♦ *verb* **2** TEST, examine, investigate, put to the test, research, sample, try, verify

experimental *adjective* TEST, exploratory, pilot, preliminary, probationary, provisional, speculative, tentative, trial, trial-and-error

expert *noun* **1** MASTER, authority, connoisseur, dab hand (*Brit. informal*), past master, professional, specialist, virtuoso ♦ *adjective* **2** SKILFUL, adept, adroit, experienced, masterly, practised, professional, proficient, qualified, virtuoso

expertise *noun* SKILL, adroitness, command, facility, judgment, know-how (*informal*), knowledge, mastery, proficiency

expire *verb* **1** FINISH, cease, close, come to an end, conclude, end, lapse, run out, stop, terminate **2** BREATHE OUT, emit, exhale, expel **3** DIE, depart, kick the bucket (*informal*), pass away *or* on, perish

explain *verb* **1** MAKE CLEAR *or* PLAIN, clarify, clear up, define, describe, elucidate, expound, resolve, teach **2** ACCOUNT FOR, excuse, give a reason for, justify

explanation *noun* **1** REASON, account, answer, excuse, justification, motive, vindication **2** DESCRIPTION, clarification, definition, elucidation, illustration, interpretation

explanatory *adjective* DESCRIPTIVE, illustrative, interpretive

explicit *adjective* CLEAR, categorical, definite, frank, precise, specific, straightforward, unambiguous

explode *verb* **1** BLOW UP, burst, detonate, discharge, erupt, go off, set off, shatter **2** DISPROVE, debunk, discredit, give the lie to, invalidate, refute, repudiate

exploit *verb* **1** TAKE ADVANTAGE OF, abuse, manipulate, milk, misuse, play on *or* upon **2** MAKE THE BEST USE OF, capitalize on, cash in on (*informal*), profit by *or* from, use, utilize ♦ *noun* **3** FEAT, accomplishment, achievement, adventure, attainment, deed, escapade, stunt

exploitation *noun* MISUSE, abuse, manipulation

exploration *noun* **1** INVESTIGATION, analysis, examination, inquiry, inspection, research, scrutiny, search **2** EXPEDITION, reconnaissance, survey, tour, travel, trip

exploratory *adjective* INVESTIGATIVE, experimental, fact-finding, probing, searching, trial

explore *verb* **1** INVESTIGATE, examine, inquire into, inspect, look into, probe, research, search **2** TRAVEL, reconnoitre, scout, survey, tour

explosion *noun* **1** BANG, blast, burst, clap, crack, detonation, discharge, report **2** OUTBURST, eruption, fit, outbreak

explosive *adjective* 1 UNSTABLE, volatile 2 VIOLENT, fiery, stormy, touchy, vehement

exponent *noun* 1 ADVOCATE, backer, champion, defender, promoter, proponent, supporter, upholder 2 PERFORMER, player

expose *verb* 1 UNCOVER, display, exhibit, present, reveal, show, unveil 2 MAKE VULNERABLE, endanger, imperil, jeopardize, lay open, leave open, subject

exposed *adjective* 1 UNCONCEALED, bare, on display, on show, on view, revealed, uncovered 2 UNSHELTERED, open, unprotected 3 VULNERABLE, in peril, laid bare, susceptible, wide open

exposure *noun* PUBLICITY, display, exhibition, presentation, revelation, showing, uncovering, unveiling

expound *verb* EXPLAIN, describe, elucidate, interpret, set forth, spell out, unfold

express *verb* 1 STATE, articulate, communicate, declare, phrase, put into words, say, utter, voice, word 2 SHOW, convey, exhibit, indicate, intimate, make known, represent, reveal, signify, stand for, symbolize ◆ *adjective* 3 EXPLICIT, categorical, clear, definite, distinct, plain, unambiguous 4 SPECIFIC, clear-cut, especial, particular, singular, special 5 FAST, direct, high-speed, nonstop, rapid, speedy, swift

expression *noun* 1 STATEMENT, announcement, communication, declaration, utterance 2 INDICATION, demonstration, exhibition, manifestation, representation, show, sign, symbol, token 3 LOOK, air, appearance, aspect, countenance, face 4 PHRASE, idiom, locution, remark, term, turn of phrase, word

expressive *adjective* VIVID, eloquent, moving, poignant, striking, telling

expressly *adverb* 1 DEFINITELY, categorically, clearly, distinctly, explicitly, in no uncertain terms, plainly, unambiguously 2 SPECIFICALLY, especially, particularly, specially

expulsion *noun* EJECTION, banishment, dismissal, eviction, exclusion, removal

exquisite *adjective* 1 BEAUTIFUL, attractive, charming, comely, lovely, pleasing, striking 2 FINE, beautiful, dainty, delicate, elegant, lovely, precious 3 INTENSE, acute, keen, sharp

extempore *adverb, adjective* IMPROMPTU, ad lib, freely, improvised, offhand, off the cuff (*informal*), spontaneously, unpremeditated, unprepared

extend *verb* 1 MAKE LONGER, drag out, draw out, lengthen, prolong, spin out, spread out, stretch 2 LAST, carry on, continue, go on 3 WIDEN, add to, augment, broaden, enhance, enlarge, expand, increase, supplement 4 OFFER, confer, impart, present, proffer

extension *noun* 1 ANNEXE, addition, appendage, appendix, supplement 2 LENGTHENING, broadening, development, enlargement, expansion, increase, spread, widening

extensive *adjective* WIDE, broad, far-flung, far-reaching, large-scale, pervasive, spacious, vast, voluminous, widespread

extent *noun* SIZE, amount, area, breadth, expanse, length, stretch, volume, width

extenuating *adjective* MITIGATING, justifying, moderating, qualifying

exterior noun 1 <u>OUTSIDE</u>, coating, covering, façade, face, shell, skin, surface ♦ adjective 2 <u>OUTSIDE</u>, external, outer, outermost, outward, surface

exterminate verb <u>DESTROY</u>, abolish, annihilate, eliminate, eradicate

external adjective 1 <u>OUTER</u>, exterior, outermost, outside, outward, surface 2 <u>OUTSIDE</u>, alien, extrinsic, foreign

extinct adjective <u>DEAD</u>, defunct, gone, lost, vanished

extinction noun <u>DYING OUT</u>, abolition, annihilation, destruction, eradication, extermination, obliteration, oblivion

extinguish verb 1 <u>PUT OUT</u>, blow out, douse, quench, smother, snuff out, stifle 2 <u>DESTROY</u>, annihilate, eliminate, end, eradicate, exterminate, remove, wipe out

extol verb <u>PRAISE</u>, acclaim, commend, eulogize, exalt, glorify, sing the praises of

extort verb <u>FORCE</u>, blackmail, bully, coerce, extract, squeeze

extortionate adjective <u>EXORBITANT</u>, excessive, extravagant, inflated, outrageous, preposterous, sky-high, unreasonable

extra adjective 1 <u>ADDITIONAL</u>, added, ancillary, auxiliary, further, more, supplementary 2 <u>SURPLUS</u>, excess, leftover, redundant, spare, superfluous, unused ♦ noun 3 <u>ADDITION</u>, accessory, attachment, bonus, extension, supplement ♦ adverb 4 <u>EXCEPTIONALLY</u>, especially, extraordinarily, extremely, particularly, remarkably, uncommonly, unusually

extract verb 1 <u>PULL OUT</u>, draw, pluck out, pull, remove, take out, uproot, withdraw 2 <u>DERIVE</u>, draw,

elicit, glean, obtain ♦ noun 3 <u>PASSAGE</u>, citation, clipping, cutting, excerpt, quotation, selection 4 <u>ESSENCE</u>, concentrate, distillation, juice

extraneous adjective <u>IRRELEVANT</u>, beside the point, immaterial, inappropriate, off the subject, unconnected, unrelated

extraordinary adjective <u>UNUSUAL</u>, amazing, exceptional, fantastic, outstanding, phenomenal, remarkable, strange, uncommon

extravagance noun 1 <u>WASTE</u>, lavishness, overspending, prodigality, profligacy, squandering, wastefulness 2 <u>EXCESS</u>, exaggeration, outrageousness, preposterousness, wildness

extravagant adjective 1 <u>WASTEFUL</u>, lavish, prodigal, profligate, spendthrift 2 <u>EXCESSIVE</u>, outrageous, over the top (slang), preposterous, reckless, unreasonable

extreme adjective 1 <u>MAXIMUM</u>, acute, great, highest, intense, severe, supreme, ultimate, utmost 2 <u>SEVERE</u>, drastic, harsh, radical, rigid, strict, uncompromising 3 <u>EXCESSIVE</u>, fanatical, immoderate, radical 4 <u>FARTHEST</u>, far-off, most distant, outermost, remotest ♦ noun 5 <u>LIMIT</u>, boundary, edge, end, extremity, pole

extremely adverb <u>VERY</u>, awfully (informal), exceedingly, exceptionally, extraordinarily, severely, terribly, uncommonly, unusually

extremist noun <u>FANATIC</u>, die-hard, radical, zealot

extremity noun 1 <u>LIMIT</u>, border, boundary, edge, extreme, frontier, pinnacle, tip 2 <u>CRISIS</u>, adversity, dire straits, disaster, emergency, exigency, trouble 3 **extremities** <u>HANDS AND FEET</u>, fingers and toes, limbs

extricate *verb* <u>FREE</u>, disengage, disentangle, get out, release, remove, rescue, wriggle out of

extrovert *adjective* <u>OUTGOING</u>, exuberant, gregarious, sociable

exuberance *noun* **1** <u>HIGH SPIRITS</u>, cheerfulness, ebullience, enthusiasm, liveliness, spirit, vitality, vivacity, zest **2** <u>LUXURIANCE</u>, abundance, copiousness, lavishness, profusion

exuberant *adjective* **1** <u>HIGH-SPIRITED</u>, animated, cheerful, ebullient, energetic, enthusiastic, lively, spirited, vivacious **2** <u>LUXURIANT</u>, abundant, copious, lavish, plentiful, profuse

exult *verb* <u>BE JOYFUL</u>, be overjoyed, celebrate, jump for joy, rejoice

eye *noun* **1** <u>EYEBALL</u>, optic (*informal*) **2** <u>APPRECIATION</u>, discernment, discrimination, judgment, perception, recognition, taste ♦ *verb* **3** <u>LOOK AT</u>, check out (*informal*), contemplate, inspect, study, survey, view, watch

eyesight *noun* <u>VISION</u>, perception, sight

eyesore *noun* <u>MESS</u>, blemish, blot, disfigurement, horror, monstrosity, sight (*informal*)

eyewitness *noun* <u>OBSERVER</u>, bystander, onlooker, passer-by, spectator, viewer, witness

F f

fable noun 1 STORY, allegory, legend, myth, parable, tale 2 FICTION, fabrication, fantasy, invention, tall story (*informal*), urban legend, yarn (*informal*)

fabric noun 1 CLOTH, material, stuff, textile, web 2 FRAMEWORK, constitution, construction, foundations, make-up, organization, structure

fabricate verb 1 MAKE UP, concoct, devise, fake, falsify, feign, forge, invent, trump up 2 BUILD, assemble, construct, erect, form, make, manufacture, shape

fabrication noun 1 FORGERY, concoction, fake, falsehood, fiction, invention, lie, myth 2 CONSTRUCTION, assembly, building, erection, manufacture, production

fabulous adjective 1 *Informal* WONDERFUL, brilliant, fantastic (*informal*), marvellous, out-of-this-world (*informal*), sensational (*informal*), spectacular, superb 2 ASTOUNDING, amazing, breathtaking, inconceivable, incredible, phenomenal, unbelievable 3 LEGENDARY, apocryphal, fantastic, fictitious, imaginary, invented, made-up, mythical, unreal

façade noun APPEARANCE, exterior, face, front, guise, mask, pretence, semblance, show

face noun 1 COUNTENANCE, features, mug (*slang*), visage 2 EXPRESSION, appearance, aspect, look 3 SCOWL, frown, grimace, pout, smirk 4 FAÇADE, appearance, display, exterior, front, mask, show 5 SIDE, exterior, front, outside, surface 6 SELF-RESPECT, authority, dignity, honour, image, prestige, reputation, standing, status ♦ verb 7 MEET, brave, come up against, confront, deal with, encounter, experience, oppose, tackle 8 LOOK ONTO, be opposite, front onto, overlook 9 COAT, clad, cover, dress, finish

faceless adjective IMPERSONAL, anonymous, remote

facet noun ASPECT, angle, face, part, phase, plane, side, slant, surface

facetious adjective FUNNY, amusing, comical, droll, flippant, frivolous, humorous, jocular, playful, tongue in cheek

face up to verb ACCEPT, acknowledge, come to terms with, confront, cope with, deal with, meet head-on, tackle

facile adjective SUPERFICIAL, cursory, glib, hasty, shallow, slick

facilitate verb PROMOTE, expedite, forward, further, help, make easy, pave the way for, speed up

facility noun 1 SKILL, ability, adroitness, dexterity, ease, efficiency, effortlessness, fluency, proficiency 2 often plural EQUIPMENT, advantage, aid, amenity, appliance, convenience, means, opportunity, resource

facsimile noun COPY, carbon copy, duplicate, fax, photocopy, print, replica, reproduction, transcript

fact noun 1 EVENT, act, deed, *fait accompli*, happening, incident, occurrence, performance 2 TRUTH, certainty, reality

faction noun 1 GROUP, bloc, cabal, clique, contingent, coterie, gang, party, set, splinter group 2 DISSENSION, conflict, disagreement, discord, disunity, division, infighting, rebellion

factor noun ELEMENT, aspect, cause, component, consideration, influence, item, part

factory noun WORKS, mill, plant

factual adjective TRUE, authentic, correct, exact, genuine, precise, real, true-to-life

faculties plural noun POWERS, capabilities, intelligence, reason, senses, wits

faculty noun 1 ABILITY, aptitude, capacity, facility, power, propensity, skill 2 DEPARTMENT, school

fad noun CRAZE, fashion, mania, rage, trend, vogue, whim

fade verb 1 PALE, bleach, discolour, lose colour, wash out 2 DWINDLE, decline, die away, disappear, dissolve, melt away, vanish, wane

faded adjective DISCOLOURED, bleached, dull, indistinct, pale, washed out

fading adjective DECLINING, decreasing, disappearing, dying, on the decline, vanishing

fail verb 1 BE UNSUCCESSFUL, bite the dust, break down, come to grief, come unstuck, fall, fizzle out (informal), flop (informal), founder, miscarry, misfire 2 DISAPPOINT, abandon, desert, forget, forsake, let down, neglect, omit 3 GIVE OUT, conk out (informal), cut out, die, peter out, stop working 4 GO BANKRUPT, become insolvent, close down, fold (informal), go broke (informal), go bust (informal), go into receivership, go out of business, go to the wall, go under ♦ noun 5 **without fail** REGULARLY, conscientiously, constantly, dependably, like clockwork, punctually, religiously, without exception

failing noun 1 WEAKNESS, blemish, defect, deficiency, drawback, fault, flaw, imperfection, shortcoming ♦ preposition 2 IN THE ABSENCE OF, in default of, lacking

failure noun 1 DEFEAT, breakdown, collapse, downfall, fiasco, lack of success, miscarriage, overthrow 2 LOSER, black sheep, dead duck (slang), disappointment, dud (informal), flop (informal), nonstarter, washout (informal) 3 BANKRUPTCY, crash, downfall, insolvency, liquidation, ruin

faint adjective 1 DIM, distant, faded, indistinct, low, muted, soft, subdued, vague 2 SLIGHT, feeble, remote, unenthusiastic, weak 3 DIZZY, exhausted, giddy, light-headed, muzzy, weak, woozy (informal) ♦ verb 4 PASS OUT, black out, collapse, flake out (informal), keel over (informal), lose consciousness, swoon (literary) ♦ noun 5 BLACKOUT, collapse, swoon (literary), unconsciousness

faintly adverb 1 SOFTLY, feebly, in a whisper, indistinctly, weakly 2 SLIGHTLY, a little, dimly, somewhat

fair[1] adjective 1 UNBIASED, above board, equitable, even-handed, honest, impartial, just, lawful, legitimate, proper, unprejudiced 2 LIGHT, blond, blonde, fair-haired, flaxen-haired, towheaded 3 RESPECTABLE, adequate, average, decent, moderate, O.K. or okay (informal), passable, reasonable, satisfactory, tolerable 4 BEAUTIFUL, bonny, comely, handsome, lovely, pretty 5 FINE, bright, clear, cloudless, dry, sunny, unclouded

fair[2] noun CARNIVAL, bazaar, festival, fête, gala, show

fairly adverb 1 MODERATELY, adequately, pretty well, quite, rather, reasonably, somewhat, tolerably 2 DESERVEDLY, equitably, honestly, impartially, justly, objectively, properly, without fear or favour **3** POSITIVELY, absolutely, really

fairness noun IMPARTIALITY, decency, disinterestedness, equitableness, equity, justice, legitimacy, rightfulness

fairy noun SPRITE, brownie, elf, leprechaun, peri, pixie, Robin Goodfellow

fairy tale or **fairy story** noun **1** FOLK TALE, romance **2** LIE, cock-and-bull story (*informal*), fabrication, fiction, invention, tall story, untruth

faith noun **1** CONFIDENCE, assurance, conviction, credence, credit, dependence, reliance, trust **2** RELIGION, belief, church, communion, creed, denomination, dogma, persuasion **3** ALLEGIANCE, constancy, faithfulness, fidelity, loyalty

faithful adjective **1** LOYAL, constant, dependable, devoted, reliable, staunch, steadfast, true, trusty **2** ACCURATE, close, exact, precise, strict, true

faithless adjective DISLOYAL, false, fickle, inconstant, traitorous, treacherous, unfaithful, unreliable

fake verb **1** FORGE, copy, counterfeit, fabricate, feign, pretend, put on, sham, simulate ♦ noun **2** IMPOSTOR, charlatan, copy, forgery, fraud, hoax, imitation, reproduction, sham ♦ adjective **3** ARTIFICIAL, counterfeit, false, forged, imitation, mock, phoney or phony (*informal*), sham

fall verb **1** DESCEND, cascade, collapse, dive, drop, plummet, plunge, sink, subside, tumble **2** DECREASE, decline, diminish, drop, dwindle, go down, lessen, slump, subside **3** BE OVERTHROWN, capitulate, pass into enemy hands,

succumb, surrender **4** DIE, be killed, meet one's end, perish **5** OCCUR, befall, chance, come about, come to pass, happen, take place **6** SLOPE, fall away, incline **7** LAPSE, err, go astray, offend, sin, transgress, trespass ♦ noun **8** DESCENT, dive, drop, nose dive, plummet, plunge, slip, tumble **9** DECREASE, cut, decline, dip, drop, lessening, lowering, reduction, slump **10** COLLAPSE, capitulation, defeat, destruction, downfall, overthrow, ruin **11** LAPSE, sin, transgression

fallacy noun ERROR, delusion, falsehood, flaw, misapprehension, misconception, mistake, untruth

fallible adjective IMPERFECT, erring, frail, ignorant, uncertain, weak

fall out verb ARGUE, clash, come to blows, differ, disagree, fight, quarrel, squabble

fallow adjective UNCULTIVATED, dormant, idle, inactive, resting, unplanted, unused

false adjective **1** INCORRECT, erroneous, faulty, inaccurate, inexact, invalid, mistaken, wrong **2** UNTRUE, lying, unreliable, unsound, untruthful **3** ARTIFICIAL, bogus, counterfeit, fake, forged, imitation, sham, simulated **4** DECEPTIVE, deceitful, fallacious, fraudulent, hypocritical, misleading, trumped up

falsehood noun **1** UNTRUTHFULNESS, deceit, deception, dishonesty, dissimulation, mendacity **2** LIE, fabrication, fib, fiction, story, untruth

falsify verb FORGE, alter, counterfeit, distort, doctor, fake, misrepresent, tamper with

falter verb HESITATE, stammer, stumble, stutter, totter, vacillate, waver

faltering *adjective* HESITANT, broken, irresolute, stammering, tentative, timid, uncertain, weak

fame *noun* PROMINENCE, celebrity, glory, honour, renown, reputation, repute, stardom

familiar *adjective* 1 WELL-KNOWN, accustomed, common, customary, frequent, ordinary, recognizable, routine 2 FRIENDLY, amicable, close, easy, intimate, relaxed 3 DISRESPECTFUL, bold, forward, impudent, intrusive, presumptuous

familiarity *noun* 1 ACQUAINTANCE, awareness, experience, grasp, understanding 2 FRIENDLINESS, ease, informality, intimacy, openness, sociability 3 DISRESPECT, boldness, forwardness, presumption

familiarize *verb* ACCUSTOM, habituate, instruct, inure, school, season, train

family *noun* 1 RELATIONS, folk (*informal*), household, kin, kith and kin, one's nearest and dearest, one's own flesh and blood, relatives 2 CLAN, dynasty, house, race, tribe 3 GROUP, class, genre, network, subdivision, system

famine *noun* HUNGER, dearth, scarcity, starvation

famished *adjective* STARVING, ravenous, voracious

famous *adjective* WELL-KNOWN, acclaimed, celebrated, distinguished, eminent, illustrious, legendary, noted, prominent, renowned

fan[1] *noun* 1 BLOWER, air conditioner, ventilator ♦ *verb* 2 BLOW, air-condition, cool, refresh, ventilate

fan[2] *noun* SUPPORTER, admirer, aficionado, buff (*informal*), devotee, enthusiast, follower, lover

fanatic *noun* EXTREMIST, activist, bigot, militant, zealot

fanatical *adjective* PASSIONATE, bigoted, extreme, fervent, frenzied, immoderate, obsessive, overenthusiastic, wild, zealous

fanciful *adjective* UNREAL, imaginary, mythical, romantic, visionary, whimsical, wild

fancy *adjective* 1 ELABORATE, baroque, decorative, embellished, extravagant, intricate, ornamental, ornate ♦ *noun* 2 WHIM, caprice, desire, humour, idea, impulse, inclination, notion, thought, urge 3 DELUSION, chimera, daydream, dream, fantasy, vision ♦ *verb* 4 SUPPOSE, believe, conjecture, imagine, reckon, think, think likely 5 WISH FOR, crave, desire, hanker after, hope for, long for, thirst for, yearn for 6 *Informal* BE ATTRACTED TO, be captivated by, like, lust after, take a liking to, take to

fantasize *verb* DAYDREAM, dream, envision, imagine

fantastic *adjective* 1 *Informal* EXCELLENT, awesome (*slang*), first-rate, marvellous, sensational (*informal*), superb, wonderful 2 STRANGE, fanciful, grotesque, outlandish 3 UNREALISTIC, extravagant, far-fetched, ludicrous, ridiculous, wild 4 IMPLAUSIBLE, absurd, cock-and-bull (*informal*), incredible, preposterous, unlikely

fantasy *noun* 1 IMAGINATION, creativity, fancy, invention, originality 2 DAYDREAM, dream, flight of fancy, illusion, mirage, pipe dream, reverie, vision

far *adverb* 1 A LONG WAY, afar, a good way, a great distance, deep, miles 2 MUCH, considerably, decidedly, extremely, greatly, incomparably, very much ♦ *adjective* 3 REMOTE, distant, faraway, far-flung, far-off, outlying, out-of-the-way

farce noun **1** COMEDY, buffoonery, burlesque, satire, slapstick **2** MOCKERY, joke, nonsense, parody, sham, travesty

farcical adjective LUDICROUS, absurd, comic, derisory, laughable, nonsensical, preposterous, ridiculous, risible

fare noun **1** CHARGE, price, ticket money **2** FOOD, provisions, rations, sustenance, victuals ♦ verb **3** GET ON, do, get along, make out, manage, prosper

farewell noun GOODBYE, adieu, departure, leave-taking, parting, sendoff (informal), valediction

far-fetched adjective UNCONVINCING, cock-and-bull (informal), fantastic, implausible, incredible, preposterous, unbelievable, unlikely, unrealistic

farm noun **1** SMALLHOLDING, croft (Scot.), farmstead, grange, homestead, plantation, ranch (chiefly North American) ♦ verb **2** CULTIVATE, plant, work

fascinate verb INTRIGUE, absorb, beguile, captivate, engross, enthral, entrance, hold spellbound, rivet, transfix

fascinating adjective GRIPPING, alluring, captivating, compelling, engaging, engrossing, enticing, intriguing, irresistible, riveting

fascination noun ATTRACTION, allure, charm, enchantment, lure, magic, magnetism, pull

fashion noun **1** STYLE, craze, custom, fad, look, mode, rage, trend, vogue **2** METHOD, manner, mode, style, way ♦ verb **3** MAKE, construct, create, forge, form, manufacture, mould, shape

fashionable adjective POPULAR, à la mode, chic, in (informal), in

vogue, modern, stylish, trendy, up-to-date, with it (informal)

fast[1] adjective **1** QUICK, brisk, fleet, flying, hasty, nippy (Brit. informal), rapid, speedy, swift **2** FIXED, close, fastened, firm, immovable, secure, sound, steadfast, tight **3** DISSIPATED, dissolute, extravagant, loose, profligate, reckless, self-indulgent, wanton, wild ♦ adverb **4** QUICKLY, hastily, hurriedly, in haste, like lightning, rapidly, speedily, swiftly **5** SOUNDLY, deeply, firmly, fixedly, securely, tightly

fast[2] verb **1** GO HUNGRY, abstain, deny oneself, go without food ♦ noun **2** FASTING, abstinence

fasten verb FIX, affix, attach, bind, connect, join, link, secure, tie

fat adjective **1** OVERWEIGHT, corpulent, heavy, obese, plump, podgy, portly, rotund, stout, tubby **2** FATTY, adipose, greasy, oily, oleaginous ♦ noun **3** FATNESS, blubber, bulk, corpulence, flab, flesh, obesity, paunch

fatal adjective **1** LETHAL, deadly, final, incurable, killing, malignant, terminal **2** RUINOUS, baleful, baneful, calamitous, catastrophic, disastrous

fatality noun DEATH, casualty, loss, mortality

fate noun **1** DESTINY, chance, divine will, fortune, kismet, nemesis, predestination, providence **2** FORTUNE, cup, horoscope, lot, portion, stars

fated adjective DESTINED, doomed, foreordained, inescapable, inevitable, predestined, preordained, sure, written

fateful adjective **1** CRUCIAL, critical, decisive, important, portentous, significant **2** DISASTROUS, deadly, destructive, fatal, lethal, ominous, ruinous

father noun 1 DADDY (*informal*), dad (*informal*), old man (*informal*), pa (*informal*), papa (*old-fashioned informal*), pater, pop (*informal*) 2 FOREFATHER, ancestor, forebear, predecessor, progenitor 3 FOUNDER, architect, author, creator, inventor, maker, originator, prime mover 4 PRIEST, padre (*informal*), pastor ♦ verb 5 SIRE, beget, get, procreate

fatherland noun HOMELAND, motherland, native land

fatherly adjective PATERNAL, affectionate, benevolent, benign, kindly, patriarchal, protective, supportive

fathom verb UNDERSTAND, comprehend, get to the bottom of, grasp, interpret

fatigue noun 1 TIREDNESS, heaviness, languor, lethargy, listlessness ♦ verb 2 TIRE, drain, exhaust, knacker (*slang*), take it out of (*informal*), weaken, wear out, weary

fatten verb 1 GROW FAT, expand, gain weight, put on weight, spread, swell, thicken 2 often with *up* FEED UP, build up, feed, nourish, overfeed, stuff

fatty adjective GREASY, adipose, fat, oily, oleaginous, rich

fatuous adjective FOOLISH, brainless, idiotic, inane, ludicrous, mindless, moronic, silly, stupid, witless

fault noun 1 FLAW, blemish, defect, deficiency, failing, imperfection, shortcoming, weakness, weak point 2 MISTAKE, blunder, error, indiscretion, lapse, oversight, slip 3 RESPONSIBILITY, accountability, culpability, liability 4 **at fault** GUILTY, answerable, blamable, culpable, in the wrong, responsible, to blame 5 **find fault with** CRITICIZE, carp at, complain, pick holes in, pull to pieces, quibble, take to task 6 **to a fault** EXCESSIVELY, immoderately, in the extreme, overmuch, unduly ♦ verb 7 CRITICIZE, blame, censure, find fault with, hold (someone) responsible, impugn

faultless adjective 1 FLAWLESS, correct, exemplary, foolproof, impeccable, model, perfect, unblemished 2 BLAMELESS, above reproach, guiltless, innocent

faulty adjective DEFECTIVE, broken, damaged, flawed, impaired, imperfect, incorrect, malfunctioning, out of order, unsound

favour noun 1 APPROVAL, approbation, backing, good opinion, goodwill, patronage, support 2 GOOD TURN, benefit, boon, courtesy, indulgence, kindness, service ♦ verb 3 SIDE WITH, indulge, reward, smile upon 4 ADVOCATE, approve, champion, commend, encourage, incline towards, prefer, support

favourable adjective 1 ADVANTAGEOUS, auspicious, beneficial, encouraging, helpful, opportune, promising, propitious, suitable 2 POSITIVE, affirmative, agreeable, approving, encouraging, enthusiastic, reassuring, sympathetic

favourably adverb 1 ADVANTAGEOUSLY, auspiciously, conveniently, fortunately, opportunely, profitably, to one's advantage, well 2 POSITIVELY, approvingly, enthusiastically, helpfully, with approval

favourite adjective 1 PREFERRED, best-loved, choice, dearest, esteemed, favoured ♦ noun 2 DARLING, beloved, blue-eyed boy (*informal*), idol, pet, teacher's pet, the apple of one's eye

fawn[1] verb, often with *on* or *upon*

CURRY FAVOUR, crawl, creep, cringe, dance attendance, flatter, grovel, ingratiate oneself, kowtow, pander to

fawn[2] *adjective* BEIGE, buff, greyish-brown, neutral

fawning *adjective* OBSEQUIOUS, crawling, cringing, deferential, flattering, grovelling, servile, sycophantic

fear *noun* 1 ALARM, apprehensiveness, dread, fright, horror, panic, terror, trepidation 2 BUGBEAR, bête noire, bogey, horror, nightmare, spectre ♦ *verb* 3 BE AFRAID, dread, shake in one's shoes, shudder at, take fright, tremble at 4 **fear for** WORRY ABOUT, be anxious about, feel concern for

fearful *adjective* 1 SCARED, afraid, alarmed, frightened, jumpy, nervous, timid, timorous, uneasy 2 FRIGHTFUL, awful, dire, dreadful, gruesome, hair-raising, horrendous, horrific, terrible

fearfully *adverb* 1 NERVOUSLY, apprehensively, diffidently, timidly, timorously, uneasily 2 VERY, awfully, exceedingly, excessively, frightfully, terribly, tremendously

fearless *adjective* BRAVE, bold, courageous, dauntless, indomitable, intrepid, plucky, unafraid, undaunted, valiant

fearsome *adjective* TERRIFYING, awe-inspiring, daunting, formidable, frightening, horrifying, menacing, unnerving

feasible *adjective* POSSIBLE, achievable, attainable, likely, practicable, reasonable, viable, workable

feast *noun* 1 BANQUET, dinner, repast, spread (*informal*), treat 2 FESTIVAL, celebration, fête, holiday, holy day, red-letter day,

saint's day 3 TREAT, delight, enjoyment, gratification, pleasure ♦ *verb* 4 EAT ONE'S FILL, gorge, gormandize, indulge, overindulge, pig out (*slang*), wine and dine

feat *noun* ACCOMPLISHMENT, achievement, act, attainment, deed, exploit, performance

feathers *plural noun* PLUMAGE, down, plumes

feature *noun* 1 ASPECT, characteristic, facet, factor, hallmark, peculiarity, property, quality, trait 2 HIGHLIGHT, attraction, main item, speciality 3 ARTICLE, column, item, piece, report, story ♦ *verb* 4 SPOTLIGHT, emphasize, foreground, give prominence to, play up, present, star

features *plural noun* FACE, countenance, lineaments, physiognomy

feckless *adjective* IRRESPONSIBLE, good-for-nothing, hopeless, incompetent, ineffectual, shiftless, worthless

federation *noun* UNION, alliance, amalgamation, association, coalition, combination, league, syndicate

fed up *adjective* DISSATISFIED, bored, brassed off (*Brit. slang*), depressed, discontented, down in the mouth, glum, sick and tired (*informal*), tired

fee *noun* CHARGE, bill, payment, remuneration, toll

feeble *adjective* 1 WEAK, debilitated, doddering, effete, frail, infirm, puny, sickly, weedy (*informal*) 2 UNCONVINCING, flimsy, inadequate, insufficient, lame, paltry, pathetic, poor, tame, thin

feebleness *noun* WEAKNESS, effeteness, frailty, infirmity, languor, lassitude, sickliness

feed verb 1 CATER FOR, nourish, provide for, provision, supply, sustain, victual, wine and dine 2 sometimes with on EAT, devour, exist on, live on, partake of ♦ noun 3 FOOD, fodder, pasturage, provender 4 Informal MEAL, feast, nosh (slang), repast, spread (informal)

feel verb 1 TOUCH, caress, finger, fondle, handle, manipulate, paw, stroke 2 EXPERIENCE, be aware of, notice, observe, perceive 3 SENSE, be convinced, intuit 4 BELIEVE, consider, deem, hold, judge, think ♦ noun 5 TEXTURE, finish, surface, touch 6 IMPRESSION, air, ambience, atmosphere, feeling, quality, sense

feeler noun 1 ANTENNA, tentacle, whisker 2 APPROACH, advance, probe

feeling noun 1 EMOTION, ardour, fervour, intensity, passion, sentiment, warmth 2 IMPRESSION, hunch, idea, inkling, notion, presentiment, sense, suspicion 3 OPINION, inclination, instinct, point of view, view 4 SYMPATHY, compassion, concern, empathy, pity, sensibility, sensitivity, understanding 5 SENSE OF TOUCH, perception, sensation 6 ATMOSPHERE, air, ambience, aura, feel, mood, quality

fell verb CUT DOWN, cut, demolish, hew, knock down, level

fellow noun 1 MAN, bloke (Brit. informal), chap (informal), character, guy (informal), individual, person 2 ASSOCIATE, colleague, companion, comrade, partner, peer

fellowship noun 1 CAMARADERIE, brotherhood, companionship, sociability 2 SOCIETY, association, brotherhood, club, fraternity, guild, league, order

feminine adjective WOMANLY, delicate, gentle, ladylike, soft, tender

femme fatale noun SEDUCTRESS, enchantress, siren, vamp (informal)

fen noun MARSH, bog, morass, quagmire, slough, swamp

fence noun 1 BARRIER, barricade, defence, hedge, palisade, railings, rampart, wall ♦ verb 2 often with in or off ENCLOSE, bound, confine, encircle, pen, protect, surround 3 EVADE, dodge, equivocate, flannel (Brit. informal), parry

ferment noun COMMOTION, disruption, excitement, frenzy, furore, stir, tumult, turmoil, unrest, uproar

ferocious adjective 1 FIERCE, predatory, rapacious, ravening, savage, violent, wild 2 CRUEL, bloodthirsty, brutal, ruthless, vicious

ferocity noun SAVAGERY, bloodthirstiness, brutality, cruelty, fierceness, viciousness, wildness

ferret out verb TRACK DOWN, dig up, discover, elicit, root out, search out, trace, unearth

ferry noun 1 FERRY BOAT, packet, packet boat ♦ verb 2 CARRY, chauffeur, convey, run, ship, shuttle, transport

fertile adjective RICH, abundant, fecund, fruitful, luxuriant, plentiful, productive, prolific, teeming

fertility noun FRUITFULNESS, abundance, fecundity, luxuriance, productiveness, richness

fertilizer noun COMPOST, dressing, dung, manure

fervent, fervid adjective ARDENT, devout, earnest, enthusiastic, heartfelt, impassioned, intense, vehement

fervour noun INTENSITY, ardour,

enthusiasm, excitement, passion, vehemence, warmth, zeal

fester *verb* **1** DECAY, putrefy, suppurate, ulcerate **2** INTENSIFY, aggravate, smoulder

festival *noun* **1** CELEBRATION, carnival, entertainment, fête, gala, jubilee **2** HOLY DAY, anniversary, commemoration, feast, fête, fiesta, holiday, red-letter day, saint's day

festive *adjective* CELEBRATORY, cheery, convivial, happy, jovial, joyful, joyous, jubilant, merry

festivity *noun,* often plural CELEBRATION, entertainment, festival, party

festoon *verb* DECORATE, array, deck, drape, garland, hang, swathe, wreathe

fetch *verb* **1** BRING, carry, convey, deliver, get, go for, obtain, retrieve, transport **2** SELL FOR, bring in, earn, go for, make, realize, yield

fetching *adjective* ATTRACTIVE, alluring, captivating, charming, cute, enticing, winsome

fetish *noun* **1** FIXATION, mania, obsession, thing (*informal*) **2** TALISMAN, amulet

feud *noun* **1** HOSTILITY, argument, conflict, disagreement, enmity, quarrel, rivalry, row, vendetta ♦ *verb* **2** QUARREL, bicker, clash, contend, dispute, fall out, row, squabble, war

fever *noun* EXCITEMENT, agitation, delirium, ferment, fervour, frenzy, restlessness

feverish *adjective* **1** HOT, febrile, fevered, flushed, inflamed, pyretic (*Medical*) **2** EXCITED, agitated, frantic, frenetic, frenzied, overwrought, restless

few *adjective* NOT MANY, meagre, negligible, rare, scanty, scarcely

any, sparse, sporadic

fiasco *noun* DEBACLE, catastrophe, cock-up (*Brit. slang*), disaster, failure, mess, washout (*informal*)

fib *noun* LIE, fiction, story, untruth, white lie

fibre *noun* **1** THREAD, filament, pile, strand, texture, wisp **2** ESSENCE, nature, quality, spirit, substance **3** *As in* **moral fibre** RESOLUTION, stamina, strength, toughness

fickle *adjective* CHANGEABLE, capricious, faithless, inconstant, irresolute, temperamental, unfaithful, variable, volatile

fiction *noun* **1** TALE, fantasy, legend, myth, novel, romance, story, yarn (*informal*) **2** LIE, cock and bull story (*informal*), fabrication, falsehood, invention, tall story, untruth, urban legend

fictional *adjective* IMAGINARY, invented, legendary, made-up, nonexistent, unreal

fictitious *adjective* FALSE, bogus, fabricated, imaginary, invented, made-up, make-believe, mythical, untrue

fiddle *verb* **1** FIDGET, finger, interfere with, mess about *or* around, play, tamper with, tinker **2** *Informal* CHEAT, cook the books (*informal*), diddle (*informal*), fix, swindle, wangle (*informal*) ♦ *noun* **3** VIOLIN **4** *Informal* FRAUD, fix, racket, scam (*slang*), swindle **5** **fit as a fiddle** HEALTHY, blooming, hale and hearty, in fine fettle, in good form, in good shape, in rude health, in the pink, sound, strong

fiddling *adjective* TRIVIAL, futile, insignificant, pettifogging, petty, trifling

fidelity *noun* **1** LOYALTY, allegiance, constancy, dependability, devotion, faithfulness, staunchness, trustworthiness

2 ACCURACY, closeness, correspondence, exactness, faithfulness, precision, scrupulousness

fidget verb **1** MOVE RESTLESSLY, fiddle (*informal*), fret, squirm, twitch ♦ *noun* **2 the fidgets** RESTLESSNESS, fidgetiness, jitters (*informal*), nervousness, unease, uneasiness

fidgety adjective RESTLESS, impatient, jittery (*informal*), jumpy, nervous, on edge, restive, twitchy (*informal*), uneasy

field noun **1** MEADOW, grassland, green, lea (*poetic*), pasture **2** COMPETITORS, applicants, candidates, competition, contestants, entrants, possibilities, runners **3** SPECIALITY, area, department, discipline, domain, line, province, territory ♦ *verb* **4** RETRIEVE, catch, pick up, return, stop **5** DEAL WITH, deflect, handle, turn aside

fiend noun **1** DEMON, devil, evil spirit **2** BRUTE, barbarian, beast, ghoul, monster, ogre, savage **3** *Informal* ENTHUSIAST, addict, fanatic, freak (*informal*), maniac

fiendish adjective WICKED, cruel, devilish, diabolical, hellish, infernal, malignant, monstrous, satanic, unspeakable

fierce adjective **1** WILD, brutal, cruel, dangerous, ferocious, fiery, menacing, savage, vicious **2** STRONG, furious, howling, inclement, powerful, raging, stormy, tempestuous, violent **3** INTENSE, cut-throat, keen, relentless, strong

fiercely adverb FEROCIOUSLY, furiously, passionately, savagely, tempestuously, tigerishly, tooth and nail, viciously, with no holds barred

fiery adjective **1** BURNING, ablaze, afire, aflame, blazing, flaming, on fire **2** EXCITABLE, fierce, hot-headed, impetuous, irascible, irritable, passionate

fight verb **1** BATTLE, box, clash, combat, do battle, grapple, spar, struggle, tussle, wrestle **2** OPPOSE, contest, defy, dispute, make a stand against, resist, stand up to, withstand **3** ENGAGE IN, carry on, conduct, prosecute, wage ♦ *noun* **4** CONFLICT, battle, clash, contest, dispute, duel, encounter, struggle, tussle **5** RESISTANCE, belligerence, militancy, pluck, spirit

fighter noun **1** SOLDIER, fighting man, man-at-arms, warrior **2** BOXER, prize fighter, pugilist

fight off verb REPEL, beat off, keep or hold at bay, repress, repulse, resist, stave off, ward off

figure noun **1** NUMBER, character, digit, numeral, symbol **2** AMOUNT, cost, price, sum, total, value **3** SHAPE, body, build, frame, physique, proportions **4** DIAGRAM, design, drawing, illustration, pattern, representation, sketch **5** CHARACTER, big name, celebrity, dignitary, personality ♦ *verb* **6** CALCULATE, compute, count, reckon, tally, tot up, work out **7** usually with *in* FEATURE, act, appear, be featured, contribute to, play a part

figurehead noun FRONT MAN, mouthpiece, puppet, titular or nominal head

figure out verb **1** CALCULATE, compute, reckon, work out **2** UNDERSTAND, comprehend, decipher, fathom, make out, see

filch verb STEAL, embezzle, misappropriate, pilfer, pinch (*informal*), take, thieve, walk off with

file[1] noun **1** FOLDER, case, data, documents, dossier, information, portfolio **2** LINE, column, queue, row ♦ *verb* **3** REGISTER, document, enter, pigeonhole, put in place, record **4** MARCH, parade, troop

file² *verb* SMOOTH, abrade, polish, rasp, rub, scrape, shape

fill *verb* **1** STUFF, cram, crowd, glut, pack, stock, supply, swell **2** SATURATE, charge, imbue, impregnate, pervade, suffuse **3** PLUG, block, bung, close, cork, seal, stop **4** PERFORM, carry out, discharge, execute, fulfil, hold, occupy ♦ *noun* **5 one's fill** SUFFICIENT, all one wants, ample, enough, plenty

filler *noun* PADDING, makeweight, stopgap

fill in *verb* **1** COMPLETE, answer, fill out (*U.S.*), fill up **2** *Informal* INFORM, acquaint, apprise, bring up to date, give the facts *or* background **3** REPLACE, deputize, represent, stand in, sub, substitute, take the place of

filling *noun* **1** STUFFING, contents, filler, inside, insides, padding, wadding ♦ *adjective* **2** SATISFYING, ample, heavy, square, substantial

film *noun* **1** MOVIE, flick (*slang*), motion picture **2** LAYER, coating, covering, dusting, membrane, skin, tissue ♦ *verb* **3** PHOTOGRAPH, shoot, take, video, videotape

filter *noun* **1** SIEVE, gauze, membrane, mesh, riddle, strainer ♦ *verb* **2** PURIFY, clarify, filtrate, refine, screen, sieve, sift, strain, winnow **3** TRICKLE, dribble, escape, exude, leak, ooze, penetrate, percolate, seep

filth *noun* **1** DIRT, excrement, grime, muck, refuse, sewage, slime, sludge, squalor **2** OBSCENITY, impurity, indecency, pornography, smut, vulgarity

filthy *adjective* **1** DIRTY, foul, polluted, putrid, slimy, squalid,

unclean **2** MUDDY, begrimed, blackened, grimy, grubby **3** OBSCENE, corrupt, depraved, impure, indecent, lewd, licentious, pornographic, smutty

final *adjective* **1** LAST, closing, concluding, latest, terminal, ultimate **2** DEFINITIVE, absolute, conclusive, decided, definite, incontrovertible, irrevocable, settled

finale *noun* ENDING, climax, close, conclusion, culmination, denouement, epilogue

finalize *verb* COMPLETE, clinch, conclude, decide, settle, tie up, work out, wrap up (*informal*)

finally *adverb* **1** EVENTUALLY, at last, at length, at long last, in the end, lastly, ultimately **2** IN CONCLUSION, in summary, to conclude

finance *noun* **1** ECONOMICS, accounts, banking, business, commerce, investment, money ♦ *verb* **2** FUND, back, bankroll (*U.S.*), guarantee, pay for, subsidize, support, underwrite

finances *plural noun* RESOURCES, affairs, assets, capital, cash, funds, money, wherewithal

financial *adjective* ECONOMIC, fiscal, monetary, pecuniary

find *verb* **1** DISCOVER, come across, encounter, hit upon, locate, meet, recognize, spot, uncover **2** PERCEIVE, detect, discover, learn, note, notice, observe, realise ♦ *noun* **3** DISCOVERY, acquisition, asset, bargain, catch, good buy

find out *verb* **1** LEARN, detect, discover, note, observe, perceive, realize **2** DETECT, catch, disclose, expose, reveal, uncover, unmask

fine¹ *adjective* **1** EXCELLENT, accomplished, exceptional, exquisite, first-rate, magnificent, masterly, outstanding, splendid, superior 2 <u>SUNNY</u>, balmy, bright, clear, clement, cloudless, dry, fair, pleasant 3 <u>SATISFACTORY</u>, acceptable, all right, convenient, good, O.K. or okay (*informal*), suitable 4 <u>DELICATE</u>, dainty, elegant, expensive, exquisite, fragile, quality 5 <u>SUBTLE</u>, abstruse, acute, hairsplitting, minute, nice, precise, sharp 6 <u>SLENDER</u>, diaphanous, flimsy, gauzy, gossamer, light, sheer, thin

fine² noun 1 <u>PENALTY</u>, damages, forfeit, punishment ♦verb 2 <u>PENALIZE</u>, mulct, punish

finery noun <u>SPLENDOUR</u>, frippery, gear (*informal*), glad rags (*informal*), ornaments, showiness, Sunday best, trappings, trinkets

finesse noun <u>SKILL</u>, adeptness, adroitness, craft, delicacy, diplomacy, discretion, savoir-faire, sophistication, subtlety, tact

finger verb <u>TOUCH</u>, feel, fiddle with (*informal*), handle, manipulate, maul, paw (*informal*), toy with

finish verb 1 <u>STOP</u>, cease, close, complete, conclude, end, round off, terminate, wind up, wrap up (*informal*) 2 <u>CONSUME</u>, devour, dispose of, eat, empty, exhaust, use up 3 <u>DESTROY</u>, bring down, defeat, dispose of, exterminate, overcome, put an end to, put paid to, rout, ruin 4 <u>PERFECT</u>, polish, refine 5 <u>COAT</u>, gild, lacquer, polish, stain, texture, veneer, wax ♦noun 6 <u>END</u>, cessation, close, completion, conclusion, culmination, denouement, finale, run-in 7 <u>DEFEAT</u>, annihilation, curtains (*informal*), death, end, end of the road, ruin 8 <u>SURFACE</u>, lustre, patina, polish, shine, smoothness, texture

finished adjective 1 <u>POLISHED</u>, accomplished, perfected, professional, refined 2 <u>OVER</u>, closed, complete, done, ended,

finalized, through 3 <u>SPENT</u>, done, drained, empty, exhausted, used up 4 <u>RUINED</u>, defeated, done for (*informal*), doomed, lost, through, undone, wiped out

finite adjective <u>LIMITED</u>, bounded, circumscribed, delimited, demarcated, restricted

fire noun 1 <u>FLAMES</u>, blaze, combustion, conflagration, inferno 2 <u>BOMBARDMENT</u>, barrage, cannonade, flak, fusillade, hail, salvo, shelling, sniping, volley 3 <u>PASSION</u>, ardour, eagerness, enthusiasm, excitement, fervour, intensity, sparkle, spirit, verve, vigour ♦verb 4 <u>SHOOT</u>, detonate, discharge, explode, let off, pull the trigger, set off, shell 5 <u>INSPIRE</u>, animate, enliven, excite, galvanize, impassion, inflame, rouse, stir 6 *Informal* <u>DISMISS</u>, cashier, discharge, make redundant, sack (*informal*), show the door

firebrand noun <u>RABBLE-ROUSER</u>, agitator, demagogue, incendiary, instigator, tub-thumper

fireworks plural noun 1 <u>PYROTECHNICS</u>, illuminations 2 <u>RAGE</u>, hysterics, row, storm, trouble, uproar

firm¹ adjective 1 <u>HARD</u>, dense, inflexible, rigid, set, solid, solidified, stiff, unyielding 2 <u>SECURE</u>, embedded, fast, fixed, immovable, rooted, stable, steady, tight, unshakable 3 <u>DEFINITE</u>, adamant, inflexible, resolute, resolved, set on, unbending, unshakable, unyielding

firm² noun <u>COMPANY</u>, association, business, concern, conglomerate, corporation, enterprise, organization, partnership

firmly adverb 1 <u>SECURELY</u>, immovably, like a rock, steadily, tightly, unflinchingly, unshakably

2 <u>RESOLUTELY</u>, staunchly, steadfastly, unchangeably, unwaveringly

firmness noun 1 <u>HARDNESS</u>, inelasticity, inflexibility, resistance, rigidity, solidity, stiffness 2 <u>RESOLVE</u>, constancy, inflexibility, resolution, staunchness, steadfastness

first adjective 1 <u>FOREMOST</u>, chief, head, highest, leading, pre-eminent, prime, principal, ruling 2 <u>EARLIEST</u>, initial, introductory, maiden, opening, original, premier, primordial 3 <u>ELEMENTARY</u>, basic, cardinal, fundamental, key, primary, rudimentary ♦ noun 4 As in **from the first** <u>START</u>, beginning, commencement, inception, introduction, outset, starting point ♦ adverb 5 <u>BEFOREHAND</u>, at the beginning, at the outset, firstly, initially, in the first place, to begin with, to start with

first-rate adjective <u>EXCELLENT</u>, crack (slang), elite, exceptional, first class, outstanding, superb, superlative, top-notch (informal), world-class

fishy adjective 1 Informal <u>SUSPICIOUS</u>, dodgy (Brit., Austral., & N.Z. informal), dubious, funny (informal), implausible, odd, questionable, suspect, unlikely 2 <u>FISHLIKE</u>, piscatorial, piscatory, piscine

fissure noun <u>CRACK</u>, breach, cleft, crevice, fault, fracture, opening, rift, rupture, split

fit[1] verb 1 <u>MATCH</u>, accord, belong, conform, correspond, meet, suit, tally 2 <u>PREPARE</u>, arm, equip, fit out, kit out, provide 3 <u>ADAPT</u>, adjust, alter, arrange, customize, modify, shape, tweak (informal) ♦ adjective 4 <u>APPROPRIATE</u>, apt, becoming, correct, fitting, proper, right, seemly, suitable 5 <u>HEALTHY</u>, able-bodied, hale, in good shape, robust, strapping, trim, well

fit[2] noun 1 <u>SEIZURE</u>, attack, bout, convulsion, paroxysm, spasm 2 <u>OUTBREAK</u>, bout, burst, outburst, spell

fitful adjective <u>IRREGULAR</u>, broken, desultory, disturbed, inconstant, intermittent, spasmodic, sporadic, uneven

fitness noun 1 <u>APPROPRIATENESS</u>, aptness, competence, eligibility, propriety, readiness, suitability 2 <u>HEALTH</u>, good condition, good health, robustness, strength, vigour

fitting adjective 1 <u>APPROPRIATE</u>, apposite, becoming, correct, decent, proper, right, seemly, suitable ♦ noun 2 <u>ACCESSORY</u>, attachment, component, part, piece, unit

fix verb 1 <u>PLACE</u>, embed, establish, implant, install, locate, plant, position, set 2 <u>FASTEN</u>, attach, bind, connect, link, secure, stick, tie 3 <u>DECIDE</u>, agree on, arrange, arrive at, determine, establish, set, settle, specify 4 <u>REPAIR</u>, correct, mend, patch up, put to rights, see to 5 <u>FOCUS</u>, direct 6 Informal <u>MANIPULATE</u>, fiddle (informal), influence, rig ♦ noun 7 Informal <u>PREDICAMENT</u>, difficulty, dilemma, embarrassment, mess, pickle (informal), plight, quandary

fixation noun <u>PREOCCUPATION</u>, complex, hang-up (informal), idée fixe, infatuation, mania, obsession, thing (informal)

fixed adjective 1 <u>PERMANENT</u>, established, immovable, rigid, rooted, secure, set 2 <u>INTENT</u>, resolute, steady, unwavering 3 <u>AGREED</u>, arranged, decided, definite, established, planned, resolved, settled

fix up verb 1 <u>ARRANGE</u>, agree on, fix, organize, plan, settle, sort out 2 often with with <u>PROVIDE</u>, arrange for, bring about, lay on

fizz *verb* <u>BUBBLE</u>, effervesce, fizzle, froth, hiss, sparkle, sputter

fizzy *adjective* <u>BUBBLY</u>, bubbling, carbonated, effervescent, gassy, sparkling

flabbergasted *adjective* <u>ASTONISHED</u>, amazed, astounded, dumbfounded, lost for words, overwhelmed, speechless, staggered, stunned

flabby *adjective* <u>LIMP</u>, baggy, drooping, flaccid, floppy, loose, pendulous, sagging

flag[1] *noun* 1 <u>BANNER</u>, colours, ensign, pennant, pennon, standard, streamer ♦ *verb* 2 <u>MARK</u>, indicate, label, note 3 sometimes with *down* <u>HAIL</u>, signal, warn, wave

flag[2] *verb* <u>WEAKEN</u>, abate, droop, fade, languish, peter out, sag, wane, weary, wilt

flagging *adjective* <u>FADING</u>, declining, deteriorating, faltering, waning, weakening, wilting

flagrant *adjective* <u>OUTRAGEOUS</u>, barefaced, blatant, brazen, glaring, heinous, scandalous, shameless

flagstone *noun* <u>PAVING STONE</u>, block, flag, slab

flail *verb* <u>THRASH</u>, beat, thresh, windmill

flair *noun* 1 <u>ABILITY</u>, aptitude, faculty, feel, genius, gift, knack, mastery, talent 2 <u>STYLE</u>, chic, dash, discernment, elegance, panache, stylishness, taste

flake *noun* 1 <u>WAFER</u>, layer, peeling, scale, shaving, sliver ♦ *verb* 2 <u>BLISTER</u>, chip, peel (off)

flake out *verb* <u>COLLAPSE</u>, faint, keel over, pass out

flamboyant *adjective* 1 <u>EXTRAVAGANT</u>, dashing, elaborate,

florid, ornate, ostentatious, showy, swashbuckling, theatrical 2 <u>COLOURFUL</u>, brilliant, dazzling, glamorous, glitzy (*slang*)

flame *noun* 1 <u>FIRE</u>, blaze, brightness, light 2 *Informal* <u>SWEETHEART</u>, beau, boyfriend, girlfriend, heart-throb (*Brit.*), lover ♦ *verb* 3 <u>BURN</u>, blaze, flare, flash, glare, glow, shine

flaming *adjective* <u>BURNING</u>, ablaze, blazing, fiery, glowing, raging, red-hot

flank *noun* 1 <u>SIDE</u>, hip, loin, thigh 2 <u>WING</u>, side

flap *verb* 1 <u>FLUTTER</u>, beat, flail, shake, thrash, vibrate, wag, wave ♦ *noun* 2 <u>FLUTTER</u>, beating, shaking, swinging, swish, waving 3 *Informal* <u>PANIC</u>, agitation, commotion, fluster, state (*informal*), sweat (*informal*), tizzy (*informal*)

flare *verb* 1 <u>BLAZE</u>, burn up, flicker, glare 2 <u>WIDEN</u>, broaden, spread out ♦ *noun* 3 <u>FLAME</u>, blaze, burst, flash, flicker, glare

flare up *verb* <u>LOSE ONE'S TEMPER</u>, blow one's top (*informal*), boil over, explode, fly off the handle (*informal*), throw a tantrum

flash *noun* 1 <u>BLAZE</u>, burst, dazzle, flare, flicker, gleam, shimmer, spark, streak 2 <u>MOMENT</u>, instant, jiffy (*informal*), second, split second, trice, twinkling of an eye ♦ *adjective* 3 *Informal* <u>OSTENTATIOUS</u>, tacky (*informal*), tasteless, vulgar ♦ *verb* 4 <u>BLAZE</u>, flare, flicker, glare, gleam, shimmer, sparkle, twinkle 5 <u>SPEED</u>, dart, dash, fly, race, shoot, streak, whistle, zoom 6 <u>SHOW</u>, display, exhibit, expose, flaunt, flourish

flashy *adjective* <u>SHOWY</u>, flamboyant, garish, gaudy, glitzy (*slang*), jazzy (*informal*), ostentatious, snazzy (*informal*)

flat[1] *adjective* **1** EVEN, horizontal, level, levelled, low, smooth **2** DULL, boring, dead, lacklustre, lifeless, monotonous, tedious, tiresome, uninteresting **3** ABSOLUTE, categorical, downright, explicit, out-and-out, positive, unequivocal, unqualified **4** PUNCTURED, blown out, burst, collapsed, deflated, empty ♦ *adverb* **5** COMPLETELY, absolutely, categorically, exactly, point blank, precisely, utterly **6 flat out** AT FULL SPEED, all out, at full tilt, for all one is worth, hell for leather (*informal*)

flat[2] *noun* APARTMENT, rooms

flatly *adverb* ABSOLUTELY, categorically, completely, positively, unhesitatingly

flatness *noun* **1** EVENNESS, smoothness, uniformity **2** DULLNESS, monotony, tedium

flatten *verb* LEVEL, compress, even out, iron out, raze, smooth off, squash, trample

flatter *verb* **1** PRAISE, butter up, compliment, pander to, soft-soap (*informal*), sweet-talk (*informal*), wheedle **2** SUIT, become, do something for, enhance, set off, show to advantage

flattering *adjective* **1** BECOMING, effective, enhancing, kind, well-chosen **2** INGRATIATING, adulatory, complimentary, fawning, fulsome, laudatory

flattery *noun* OBSEQUIOUSNESS, adulation, blandishment, fawning, servility, soft-soap (*informal*), sweet-talk (*informal*), sycophancy

flaunt *verb* SHOW OFF, brandish, display, exhibit, flash about, flourish, parade, sport (*informal*)

flavour *noun* **1** TASTE, aroma, flavouring, piquancy, relish, savour, seasoning, smack, tang, zest **2** QUALITY, character, essence, feel, feeling, style, tinge, tone ♦ *verb* **3** SEASON, ginger up, imbue, infuse, leaven, spice

flaw *noun* WEAKNESS, blemish, chink in one's armour, defect, failing, fault, imperfection, weak spot

flawed *adjective* DAMAGED, blemished, defective, erroneous, faulty, imperfect, unsound

flawless *adjective* PERFECT, faultless, impeccable, spotless, unblemished, unsullied

flee *verb* RUN AWAY, bolt, depart, escape, fly, make one's getaway, scarper (*Brit. slang*), take flight, take off (*informal*), take to one's heels, turn tail

fleet *noun* NAVY, armada, flotilla, task force

fleeting *adjective* MOMENTARY, brief, ephemeral, passing, short-lived, temporary, transient, transitory

flesh *noun* **1** MEAT, brawn, fat, tissue, weight **2** HUMAN NATURE, carnality, flesh and blood **3 one's own flesh and blood** FAMILY, blood, kin, kinsfolk, kith and kin, relations, relatives

flexibility *noun* ADAPTABILITY, adjustability, elasticity, give (*informal*), pliability, pliancy, resilience, springiness

flexible *adjective* **1** PLIABLE, elastic, lithe, plastic, pliant, springy, stretchy, supple **2** ADAPTABLE, adjustable, discretionary, open, variable

flick *verb* **1** STRIKE, dab, flip, hit, tap, touch **2 flick through** BROWSE, flip through, glance at, skim, skip, thumb

flicker *verb* **1** TWINKLE, flare, flash, glimmer, gutter, shimmer, sparkle **2** FLUTTER, quiver, vibrate, waver ♦ *noun* **3** GLIMMER, flare, flash, gleam, spark **4** TRACE, breath, glimmer, iota, spark

flight[1] *noun* **1** *Of air travel* JOURNEY, trip, voyage **2** AVIATION, aeronautics, flying **3** FLOCK, cloud, formation, squadron, swarm, unit

flight[2] *noun* ESCAPE, departure, exit, exodus, fleeing, getaway, retreat, running away

flimsy *adjective* **1** FRAGILE, delicate, frail, insubstantial, makeshift, rickety, shaky **2** THIN, gauzy, gossamer, light, sheer, transparent **3** UNCONVINCING, feeble, implausible, inadequate, pathetic, poor, unsatisfactory, weak

flinch *verb* RECOIL, cower, cringe, draw back, quail, shirk, shrink, shy away, wince

fling *verb* **1** THROW, cast, catapult, heave, hurl, propel, sling, toss ♦ *noun* **2** BINGE (*informal*), bash, good time, party, rave-up (*Brit. slang*), spree

flip *verb, noun* TOSS, flick, snap, spin, throw

flippancy *noun* FRIVOLITY, impertinence, irreverence, levity, pertness, sauciness

flippant *adjective* FRIVOLOUS, cheeky, disrespectful, glib, impertinent, irreverent, offhand, superficial

flirt *verb* **1** LEAD ON, chat up (*informal*), make advances, make eyes at, make sheep's eyes at, philander **2** usually with *with* TOY WITH, consider, dabble in, entertain, expose oneself to, give a thought to, play with, trifle with ♦ *noun* **3** TEASE, coquette, heart-breaker, philanderer

flirtatious *adjective* TEASING, amorous, come-hither, coquettish, coy, enticing, flirty, provocative, sportive

float *verb* **1** BE BUOYANT, hang, hover **2** GLIDE, bob, drift, move gently, sail, slide, slip along **3** LAUNCH, get going, promote, set up

floating *adjective* **1** BUOYANT, afloat, buoyed up, sailing, swimming **2** FLUCTUATING, free, movable, unattached, variable, wandering

flock *noun* **1** HERD, colony, drove, flight, gaggle, skein **2** CROWD, collection, company, congregation, gathering, group, herd, host, mass ♦ *verb* **3** GATHER, collect, congregate, converge, crowd, herd, huddle, mass, throng

flog *verb* BEAT, flagellate, flay, lash, scourge, thrash, trounce, whack, whip

flood *noun* **1** DELUGE, downpour, inundation, overflow, spate, tide, torrent **2** ABUNDANCE, flow, glut, profusion, rush, stream, torrent ♦ *verb* **3** IMMERSE, drown, inundate, overflow, pour over, submerge, swamp **4** ENGULF, overwhelm, surge, swarm, sweep **5** OVERSUPPLY, choke, fill, glut, saturate

floor *noun* **1** TIER, level, stage, storey ♦ *verb* **2** KNOCK DOWN, deck (*slang*), prostrate **3** *Informal* BEWILDER, baffle, confound, defeat, disconcert, dumbfound, perplex, puzzle, stump, throw (*informal*)

flop *verb* **1** FALL, collapse, dangle, droop, drop, sag, slump **2** *Informal* FAIL, come unstuck, fall flat, fold (*informal*), founder, go belly-up (*slang*), misfire ♦ *noun* **3** *Informal* FAILURE, debacle, disaster, fiasco, nonstarter, washout (*informal*)

floppy *adjective* DROOPY, baggy, flaccid, limp, loose, pendulous, sagging, soft

floral *adjective* FLOWERY, flower-patterned

florid *adjective* **1** FLUSHED, blowsy, high-coloured, rubicund, ruddy **2** FLOWERY, baroque, flamboyant, fussy, high-flown, ornate, overelaborate

flotsam noun <u>DEBRIS</u>, detritus, jetsam, junk, odds and ends, wreckage

flounder verb <u>FUMBLE</u>, grope, struggle, stumble, thrash, toss

flourish verb 1 <u>PROSPER</u>, bloom, blossom, boom, flower, grow, increase, succeed, thrive 2 <u>WAVE</u>, brandish, display, flaunt, shake, wield ♦ noun 3 <u>WAVE</u>, display, fanfare, parade, show 4 <u>ORNAMENTATION</u>, curlicue, decoration, embellishment, plume, sweep

flourishing adjective <u>SUCCESSFUL</u>, blooming, going places, in the pink, luxuriant, prospering, rampant, thriving

flout verb <u>DEFY</u>, laugh in the face of, mock, scoff at, scorn, sneer at, spurn

flow verb 1 <u>RUN</u>, circulate, course, move, roll 2 <u>POUR</u>, cascade, flood, gush, rush, stream, surge, sweep 3 <u>RESULT</u>, arise, emanate, emerge, issue, proceed, spring ♦ noun 4 <u>TIDE</u>, course, current, drift, flood, flux, outpouring, spate, stream

flower noun 1 <u>BLOOM</u>, blossom, efflorescence 2 <u>ELITE</u>, best, cream, crème de la crème, pick ♦ verb 3 <u>BLOSSOM</u>, bloom, flourish, mature, open, unfold

flowery adjective <u>ORNATE</u>, baroque, embellished, fancy, florid, high-flown

flowing adjective 1 <u>STREAMING</u>, falling, gushing, rolling, rushing, smooth, sweeping 2 <u>FLUENT</u>, continuous, easy, smooth, unbroken, uninterrupted

fluctuate verb <u>CHANGE</u>, alternate, oscillate, seesaw, shift, swing, vary, veer, waver

fluency noun <u>EASE</u>, articulateness, assurance, command, control, facility, readiness, slickness, smoothness

fluent adjective <u>SMOOTH</u>, articulate, easy, effortless, flowing, natural, voluble, well-versed

fluff noun 1 <u>FUZZ</u>, down, nap, pile ♦ verb 2 Informal <u>SPOIL</u>, bungle, make a mess off, mess up (informal), muddle

fluffy adjective <u>SOFT</u>, downy, feathery, fleecy, fuzzy

fluid noun 1 <u>LIQUID</u>, liquor, solution ♦ adjective 2 <u>LIQUID</u>, flowing, liquefied, melted, molten, runny, watery

fluke noun <u>LUCKY BREAK</u>, accident, chance, coincidence, quirk of fate, serendipity, stroke of luck

flurry noun 1 <u>COMMOTION</u>, ado, bustle, disturbance, excitement, flutter, fuss, stir 2 <u>GUST</u>, squall

flush[1] verb 1 <u>BLUSH</u>, colour, glow, go red, redden 2 <u>RINSE OUT</u>, cleanse, flood, hose down, wash out ♦ noun 3 <u>BLUSH</u>, colour, glow, redness, rosiness

flush[2] adjective 1 <u>LEVEL</u>, even, flat, square, true 2 Informal <u>WEALTHY</u>, in the money (informal), moneyed, rich, well-heeled (informal), well-off

flushed adjective <u>BLUSHING</u>, crimson, embarrassed, glowing, hot, red, rosy, ruddy

fluster verb 1 <u>UPSET</u>, agitate, bother, confuse, disturb, perturb, rattle (informal), ruffle, unnerve ♦ noun 2 <u>TURMOIL</u>, disturbance, dither (chiefly Brit.), flap (informal), flurry, flutter, furore, state (informal)

flutter verb 1 <u>BEAT</u>, flap, palpitate, quiver, ripple, tremble, vibrate, waver ♦ noun 2 <u>VIBRATION</u>, palpitation, quiver, shiver, shudder, tremble, tremor, twitching 3 <u>AGITATION</u>, commotion, confusion, dither (chiefly Brit.), excitement, fluster, state (*informal*)

fly *verb* **1** <u>TAKE WING</u>, flit, flutter, hover, sail, soar, wing **2** <u>PILOT</u>, control, manoeuvre, operate **3** <u>DISPLAY</u>, flap, float, flutter, show, wave **4** <u>PASS</u>, elapse, flit, glide, pass swiftly, roll on, run its course, slip away **5** <u>RUSH</u>, career, dart, dash, hurry, race, shoot, speed, sprint, tear **6** <u>FLEE</u>, escape, get away, run for it, skedaddle (*informal*), take to one's heels

flying *adjective* <u>HURRIED</u>, brief, fleeting, hasty, rushed, short-lived, transitory

foam *noun* **1** <u>FROTH</u>, bubbles, head, lather, spray, spume, suds ♦ *verb* **2** <u>BUBBLE</u>, boil, effervesce, fizz, froth, lather

focus *noun* **1** <u>CENTRE</u>, focal point, heart, hub, target ♦ *verb* **2** <u>CONCENTRATE</u>, aim, centre, direct, fix, pinpoint, spotlight, zoom in

foe *noun* <u>ENEMY</u>, adversary, antagonist, opponent, rival

fog *noun* <u>MIST</u>, gloom, miasma, murk, peasouper (*informal*), smog

foggy *adjective* <u>MISTY</u>, cloudy, dim, hazy, indistinct, murky, smoggy, vaporous

foil¹ *verb* <u>THWART</u>, balk, counter, defeat, disappoint, frustrate, nullify, stop

foil² *noun* <u>CONTRAST</u>, antithesis, complement

foist *verb* <u>IMPOSE</u>, fob off, palm off, pass off, sneak in, unload

fold *verb* **1** <u>BEND</u>, crease, double over **2** *Informal* <u>GO BANKRUPT</u>, collapse, crash, fail, go bust (*informal*), go to the wall, go under, shut down ♦ *noun* **3** <u>CREASE</u>, bend, furrow, overlap, pleat, wrinkle

folder *noun* <u>FILE</u>, binder, envelope, portfolio

folk *noun* <u>PEOPLE</u>, clan, family, kin, kindred, race, tribe

follow *verb* **1** <u>COME AFTER</u>, come next, succeed, supersede, supplant, take the place of **2** <u>PURSUE</u>, chase, dog, hound, hunt, shadow, stalk, track, trail **3** <u>ACCOMPANY</u>, attend, escort, tag along **4** <u>OBEY</u>, be guided by, conform, heed, observe **5** <u>UNDERSTAND</u>, appreciate, catch on (*informal*), comprehend, fathom, grasp, realize, take in **6** <u>RESULT</u>, arise, develop, ensue, flow, issue, proceed, spring **7** <u>BE INTERESTED IN</u>, cultivate, keep abreast of, support

follower *noun* <u>SUPPORTER</u>, adherent, apostle, devotee, disciple, fan, pupil

following *adjective* **1** <u>NEXT</u>, consequent, ensuing, later, subsequent, succeeding, successive ♦ *noun* **2** <u>SUPPORTERS</u>, clientele, coterie, entourage, fans, retinue, suite, train

folly *noun* <u>FOOLISHNESS</u>, imprudence, indiscretion, lunacy, madness, nonsense, rashness, stupidity

fond *adjective* **1** <u>LOVING</u>, adoring, affectionate, amorous, caring, devoted, doting, indulgent, tender, warm **2** <u>FOOLISH</u>, deluded, delusive, empty, naive, overoptimistic, vain **3** **fond of** <u>KEEN ON</u>, addicted to, attached to, enamoured of, having a soft spot for, hooked on, into (*informal*), partial to

fondle *verb* <u>CARESS</u>, cuddle, dandle, pat, pet, stroke

fondly *adverb* **1** <u>LOVINGLY</u>, affectionately, dearly, indulgently, possessively, tenderly, with affection **2** <u>FOOLISHLY</u>, credulously, naively, stupidly, vainly

fondness *noun* **1** <u>LIKING</u>, attachment, fancy, love, partiality, penchant, soft spot, taste, weakness 2 DEVOTION, affection, attachment, kindness, love, tenderness

food noun NOURISHMENT, cuisine, diet, fare, grub (*slang*), nutrition, rations, refreshment

fool noun 1 SIMPLETON, blockhead, dunce, halfwit, idiot, ignoramus, imbecile (*informal*), numbskull or numskull, twit (*informal, chiefly Brit.*) 2 DUPE, fall guy (*informal*), laughing stock, mug (*Brit. slang*), stooge (*slang*), sucker (*slang*) 3 CLOWN, buffoon, harlequin, jester ♦ verb 4 DECEIVE, beguile, con (*informal*), delude, dupe, hoodwink, mislead, take in, trick

foolhardy adjective RASH, hot-headed, impetuous, imprudent, irresponsible, reckless

foolish adjective UNWISE, absurd, ill-judged, imprudent, injudicious, senseless, silly

foolishly adverb UNWISELY, idiotically, ill-advisedly, imprudently, injudiciously, mistakenly, stupidly

foolishness noun STUPIDITY, absurdity, folly, imprudence, indiscretion, irresponsibility, silliness, weakness

foolproof adjective INFALLIBLE, certain, guaranteed, safe, sure-fire (*informal*), unassailable, unbreakable

footing noun 1 BASIS, foundation, groundwork 2 RELATIONSHIP, grade, position, rank, standing, status

footling adjective TRIVIAL, fiddling, hairsplitting, insignificant, minor, petty, silly, trifling, unimportant

footstep noun STEP, footfall, tread

forage verb 1 SEARCH, cast about, explore, hunt, rummage, scour, seek ♦ noun 2 *Cattle, etc.* FODDER, feed, food, provender

foray noun RAID, incursion, inroad, invasion, sally, sortie, swoop

forbear verb REFRAIN, abstain, cease, desist, hold back, keep from, restrain oneself, stop

forbearance noun PATIENCE, long-suffering, moderation, resignation, restraint, self-control, temperance, tolerance

forbearing adjective PATIENT, forgiving, indulgent, lenient, long-suffering, merciful, moderate, tolerant

forbid verb PROHIBIT, ban, disallow, exclude, outlaw, preclude, rule out, veto

forbidden adjective PROHIBITED, banned, outlawed, out of bounds, proscribed, taboo, vetoed

forbidding adjective THREATENING, daunting, frightening, hostile, menacing, ominous, sinister, unfriendly

force noun 1 POWER, energy, impulse, might, momentum, pressure, strength, vigour 2 COMPULSION, arm-twisting (*informal*), coercion, constraint, duress, pressure, violence 3 INTENSITY, emphasis, fierceness, vehemence, vigour 4 ARMY, host, legion, patrol, regiment, squad, troop, unit 5 **in force: a** VALID, binding, current, effective, in operation, operative, working **b** IN GREAT NUMBERS, all together, in full strength ♦ verb 6 COMPEL, coerce, constrain, dragoon, drive, impel, make, oblige, press, pressurize 7 BREAK OPEN, blast, prise, wrench, wrest 8 PUSH, propel, thrust

forced adjective 1 COMPULSORY, conscripted, enforced, involuntary, mandatory, obligatory 2 FALSE, affected, artificial, contrived, insincere, laboured, stiff, strained, unnatural, wooden

forceful *adjective* <u>POWERFUL</u>, cogent, compelling, convincing, dynamic, effective, persuasive

forcible *adjective* 1 <u>VIOLENT</u>, aggressive, armed, coercive, compulsory 2 <u>STRONG</u>, compelling, energetic, forceful, potent, powerful, weighty

forebear *noun* <u>ANCESTOR</u>, father, forefather, forerunner, predecessor

foreboding *noun* <u>DREAD</u>, anxiety, apprehension, apprehensiveness, chill, fear, misgiving, premonition, presentiment

forecast *verb* 1 <u>PREDICT</u>, anticipate, augur, divine, foresee, foretell, prophesy ♦ *noun* 2 <u>PREDICTION</u>, conjecture, guess, prognosis, prophecy

forefather *noun* <u>ANCESTOR</u>, father, forebear, forerunner, predecessor

forefront *noun* <u>LEAD</u>, centre, fore, foreground, front, prominence, spearhead, vanguard

foregoing *adjective* <u>PRECEDING</u>, above, antecedent, anterior, former, previous, prior

foreign *adjective* <u>ALIEN</u>, exotic, external, imported, remote, strange, unfamiliar, unknown

foreigner *noun* <u>ALIEN</u>, immigrant, incomer, stranger

foremost *adjective* <u>LEADING</u>, chief, highest, paramount, pre-eminent, primary, prime, principal, supreme

forerunner *noun* <u>PRECURSOR</u>, envoy, harbinger, herald, prototype

foresee *verb* <u>ANTICIPATE</u>, envisage, forecast, foretell, predict, prophesy

foreshadow *verb* <u>PREDICT</u>, augur, forebode, indicate, portend, prefigure, presage, promise, signal

foresight *noun* <u>ANTICIPATION</u>, far-sightedness, forethought, precaution, preparedness, prescience, prudence

foretell *verb* <u>PREDICT</u>, forecast, forewarn, presage, prognosticate, prophesy

forethought *noun* <u>ANTICIPATION</u>, far-sightedness, foresight, precaution, providence, provision, prudence

forever *adverb* 1 <u>EVERMORE</u>, always, for all time, for keeps, in perpetuity, till Doomsday, till the cows come home (*informal*) 2 <u>CONSTANTLY</u>, all the time, continually, endlessly, eternally, incessantly, interminably, perpetually, unremittingly

forewarn *verb* <u>CAUTION</u>, advise, alert, apprise, give fair warning, put on guard, tip off

forfeit *noun* 1 <u>PENALTY</u>, damages, fine, forfeiture, loss, mulct ♦ *verb* 2 <u>LOSE</u>, be deprived of, be stripped of, give up, relinquish, renounce, say goodbye to, surrender

forge *verb* 1 <u>CREATE</u>, construct, devise, fashion, form, frame, make, mould, shape, work 2 <u>FALSIFY</u>, copy, counterfeit, fake, feign, imitate

forgery *noun* 1 <u>FRAUDULENCE</u>, coining, counterfeiting, falsification, fraudulent imitation 2 <u>FAKE</u>, counterfeit, falsification, imitation, phoney *or* phony (*informal*), sham

forget *verb* <u>NEGLECT</u>, leave behind, lose sight of, omit, overlook

forgetful *adjective* <u>ABSENT-MINDED</u>, careless, inattentive, neglectful, oblivious, unmindful, vague

forgive *verb* <u>EXCUSE</u>, absolve, acquit, condone, exonerate, let bygones be bygones, let off (*informal*), pardon

forgiveness *noun* <u>PARDON</u>, absolution, acquittal, amnesty, exoneration, mercy, remission

forgiving adjective MERCIFUL, clement, compassionate, forbearing, lenient, magnanimous, soft-hearted, tolerant

forgo verb GIVE UP, abandon, do without, relinquish, renounce, resign, surrender, waive, yield

forgotten adjective LEFT BEHIND, bygone, lost, omitted, past, past recall, unremembered

fork verb BRANCH, bifurcate, diverge, divide, part, split

forked adjective BRANCHING, angled, bifurcate(d), branched, divided, pronged, split, zigzag

forlorn adjective MISERABLE, disconsolate, down in the dumps (informal), helpless, hopeless, pathetic, pitiful, unhappy, woebegone, wretched

form noun 1 SHAPE, appearance, configuration, formation, pattern, structure 2 TYPE, kind, sort, style, variety 3 CONDITION, fettle, fitness, health, shape, trim 4 PROCEDURE, convention, custom, etiquette, protocol 5 DOCUMENT, application, paper, sheet 6 CLASS, grade, rank ♦ verb 7 MAKE, build, construct, create, fashion, forge, mould, produce, shape 8 ARRANGE, combine, draw up, organize 9 TAKE SHAPE, appear, become visible, come into being, crystallize, grow, materialize, rise 10 DEVELOP, acquire, contract, cultivate, pick up 11 CONSTITUTE, compose, comprise, make up

formal adjective 1 OFFICIAL, ceremonial, ritualistic, solemn 2 CONVENTIONAL, affected, correct, precise, stiff, unbending

formality noun 1 CONVENTION, custom, procedure, red tape, rite, ritual 2 CORRECTNESS, decorum, etiquette, protocol

format noun STYLE, appearance, arrangement, construction, form, layout, look, make-up, plan, type

formation noun 1 ESTABLISHMENT, constitution, development, forming, generation, genesis, manufacture, production 2 PATTERN, arrangement, configuration, design, grouping, structure

formative adjective DEVELOPMENTAL, influential

former adjective PREVIOUS, earlier, erstwhile, one-time, prior

formerly adverb PREVIOUSLY, at one time, before, lately, once

formidable adjective 1 INTIMIDATING, daunting, dismaying, fearful, frightful, menacing, terrifying, threatening 2 IMPRESSIVE, awesome, great, mighty, powerful, redoubtable, terrific, tremendous

formula noun METHOD, blueprint, precept, principle, procedure, recipe, rule

formulate verb 1 DEFINE, detail, express, frame, give form to, set down, specify, systematize 2 DEVISE, develop, forge, invent, map out, originate, plan, work out

forsake verb 1 DESERT, abandon, disown, leave in the lurch, strand 2 GIVE UP, forgo, relinquish, renounce, set aside, surrender, yield

forsaken adjective DESERTED, abandoned, disowned, forlorn, left in the lurch, marooned, outcast, stranded

fort noun 1 FORTRESS, blockhouse, camp, castle, citadel, fortification, garrison, stronghold 2 **hold the fort** STAND IN, carry on, keep things on an even keel, take over the reins

forte noun SPECIALITY, gift, long suit (informal), métier, strength, strong point, talent

forth adverb FORWARD, ahead, away, onward, out, outward

forthcoming adjective
1 APPROACHING, coming, expected, future, imminent, impending, prospective, upcoming
2 ACCESSIBLE, at hand, available, in evidence, obtainable, on tap (informal), ready 3 COMMUNICATIVE, chatty, expansive, free, informative, open, sociable, talkative, unreserved

forthright adjective OUTSPOKEN, blunt, candid, direct, frank, open, plain-spoken, straightforward, upfront (informal)

forthwith adverb AT ONCE, directly, immediately, instantly, quickly, right away, straightaway, without delay

fortification noun 1 DEFENCE, bastion, fastness, fort, fortress, protection, stronghold
2 STRENGTHENING, reinforcement

fortify verb STRENGTHEN, augment, buttress, protect, reinforce, shore up, support

fortitude noun COURAGE, backbone, bravery, fearlessness, grit, perseverance, resolution, strength, valour

fortress noun CASTLE, citadel, fastness, fort, redoubt, stronghold

fortunate adjective 1 LUCKY, favoured, in luck, jammy (Brit. slang), successful, well-off
2 FAVOURABLE, advantageous, convenient, expedient, felicitous, fortuitous, helpful, opportune, providential, timely

fortunately adverb LUCKILY, by a happy chance, by good luck, happily, providentially

fortune noun 1 WEALTH, affluence, opulence, possessions, property, prosperity, riches, treasure 2 LUCK, chance, destiny, fate, kismet,

providence 3 **fortunes** DESTINY, adventures, experiences, history, lot, success

forward adjective 1 LEADING, advance, first, foremost, front, head 2 PRESUMPTUOUS, bold, brash, brazen, cheeky, familiar, impertinent, impudent, pushy (informal) 3 WELL-DEVELOPED, advanced, precocious, premature ♦ adverb 4 AHEAD, forth, on, onward ♦ verb 5 PROMOTE, advance, assist, expedite, further, hasten, hurry 6 SEND, dispatch, post, send on

foster verb 1 PROMOTE, cultivate, encourage, feed, nurture, stimulate, support, uphold 2 BRING UP, mother, nurse, raise, rear, take care of

foul adjective 1 DIRTY, fetid, filthy, malodorous, nauseating, putrid, repulsive, squalid, stinking, unclean 2 OBSCENE, abusive, blue, coarse, indecent, lewd, profane, scurrilous, vulgar 3 OFFENSIVE, abhorrent, despicable, detestable, disgraceful, scandalous, shameful, wicked 4 UNFAIR, crooked, dishonest, fraudulent, shady (informal), underhand, unscrupulous ♦ verb 5 POLLUTE, besmirch, contaminate, defile, dirty, stain, sully, taint

found verb ESTABLISH, constitute, create, inaugurate, institute, organize, originate, set up, start

foundation noun 1 GROUNDWORK, base, basis, bedrock, bottom, footing, substructure, underpinning 2 SETTING UP, endowment, establishment, inauguration, institution, organization, settlement

founder[1] noun INITIATOR, architect, author, beginner, father, inventor, originator

founder[2] verb 1 SINK, be lost, go

down, go to the bottom,
submerge 2 FAIL, break down,
collapse, come to grief, come
unstuck, fall through, miscarry,
misfire 3 STUMBLE, lurch, sprawl,
stagger, trip

foundling noun STRAY, orphan,
outcast, waif

fountain noun 1 JET, font, fount,
reservoir, spout, spray, spring,
well 2 SOURCE, cause, derivation,
fount, fountainhead, origin,
wellspring

foyer noun ENTRANCE HALL,
antechamber, anteroom, lobby,
reception area, vestibule

fracas noun BRAWL, affray (*Law*),
disturbance, melee *or* mêlée, riot,
rumpus, scuffle, skirmish

fraction noun PIECE, part,
percentage, portion, section,
segment, share, slice

fractious adjective IRRITABLE,
captious, cross, petulant,
querulous, refractory, testy,
tetchy, touchy

fracture noun 1 BREAK, cleft, crack,
fissure, opening, rift, rupture, split
♦ verb 2 BREAK, crack, rupture,
splinter, split

fragile adjective DELICATE, breakable,
brittle, dainty, fine, flimsy, frail,
frangible, weak

fragment noun 1 PIECE, bit, chip,
particle, portion, scrap, shred,
sliver ♦ verb 2 BREAK, break up,
come apart, come to pieces,
crumble, disintegrate, shatter,
splinter, split up

fragmentary adjective INCOMPLETE,
bitty, broken, disconnected,
incoherent, partial, piecemeal,
scattered, scrappy, sketchy

fragrance noun SCENT, aroma,
balm, bouquet, fragrancy,
perfume, redolence, smell, sweet
odour

fragrant adjective PERFUMED,
aromatic, balmy, odorous,
redolent, sweet-scented,
sweet-smelling

frail adjective WEAK, delicate, feeble,
flimsy, fragile, infirm,
insubstantial, puny, vulnerable

frailty noun FEEBLENESS, fallibility,
frailness, infirmity, susceptibility,
weakness

frame noun 1 CASING, construction,
framework, shell, structure
2 PHYSIQUE, anatomy, body, build,
carcass 3 **frame of mind** MOOD,
attitude, disposition, humour,
outlook, state, temper ♦ verb
4 CONSTRUCT, assemble, build,
make, manufacture, put together
5 DRAFT, compose, devise, draw
up, formulate, map out, sketch
6 MOUNT, case, enclose, surround

framework noun STRUCTURE,
foundation, frame, groundwork,
plan, shell, skeleton, the bare
bones

frank adjective HONEST, blunt,
candid, direct, forthright, open,
outspoken, plain-spoken, sincere,
straightforward, truthful

frankly adverb 1 HONESTLY, candidly,
in truth, to be honest 2 OPENLY,
bluntly, directly, freely, plainly,
without reserve

frankness noun OUTSPOKENNESS,
bluntness, candour,
forthrightness, openness, plain
speaking, truthfulness

frantic adjective 1 FURIOUS, at the
end of one's tether, berserk,
beside oneself, distracted,
distraught, wild 2 HECTIC,
desperate, fraught (*informal*),
frenetic, frenzied

fraternity noun 1 CLUB, association,
brotherhood, circle, company,
guild, league, union
2 COMPANIONSHIP, brotherhood,

camaraderie, fellowship, kinship

fraternize *verb* ASSOCIATE, consort, cooperate, hobnob, keep company, mingle, mix, socialize

fraud *noun* 1 DECEPTION, chicanery, deceit, double-dealing, duplicity, sharp practice, swindling, treachery, trickery 2 IMPOSTOR, charlatan, fake, fraudster, hoaxer, phoney *or* phony (*informal*), pretender, swindler

fraudulent *adjective* DECEITFUL, crooked (*informal*), dishonest, double-dealing, duplicitous, sham, swindling, treacherous

fray *verb* WEAR THIN, chafe, rub, wear

freak *noun* 1 ODDITY, aberration, anomaly, malformation, monstrosity, weirdo *or* weirdie (*informal*) 2 ENTHUSIAST, addict, aficionado, buff (*informal*), devotee, fan, fanatic, fiend (*informal*), nut (*slang*) ◆ *adjective* 3 ABNORMAL, exceptional, unparalleled, unusual

free *adjective* 1 FOR NOTHING, complimentary, for free (*informal*), free of charge, gratis, gratuitous, on the house, unpaid, without charge 2 AT LIBERTY, at large, footloose, independent, liberated, loose, on the loose, unfettered 3 ALLOWED, able, clear, permitted, unimpeded, unrestricted 4 AVAILABLE, empty, idle, spare, unemployed, unoccupied, unused, vacant 5 GENEROUS, lavish, liberal, unsparing, unstinting ◆ *verb* 6 RELEASE, deliver, let out, liberate, loose, set free, turn loose, unchain, untie 7 EXTRICATE, cut loose, disengage, disentangle, rescue

freedom *noun* 1 LIBERTY, deliverance, emancipation, independence, release 2 OPPORTUNITY, blank cheque, carte blanche, discretion, free rein, latitude, licence

free-for-all *noun* FIGHT, brawl, dust-up (*informal*), fracas, melee *or* mêlée, riot, row, scrimmage

freely *adverb* 1 WILLINGLY, of one's own accord, of one's own free will, spontaneously, voluntarily, without prompting 2 OPENLY, candidly, frankly, plainly, unreservedly, without reserve 3 ABUNDANTLY, amply, copiously, extravagantly, lavishly, liberally, unstintingly

freeze *verb* 1 CHILL, harden, ice over *or* up, stiffen 2 SUSPEND, fix, hold up, inhibit, peg, stop

freezing *adjective* ICY, arctic, biting, bitter, chill, frosty, glacial, raw, wintry

freight *noun* 1 TRANSPORTATION, carriage, conveyance, shipment 2 CARGO, burden, consignment, goods, load, merchandise, payload

French *adjective* GALLIC

frenzied *adjective* FURIOUS, distracted, feverish, frantic, frenetic, rabid, uncontrolled, wild

frenzy *noun* FURY, derangement, hysteria, paroxysm, passion, rage, seizure

frequent *adjective* 1 COMMON, customary, everyday, familiar, habitual, persistent, recurrent, repeated, usual ◆ *verb* 2 VISIT, attend, be found at, hang out at (*informal*), haunt, patronize

frequently *adverb* OFTEN, commonly, habitually, many times, much, not infrequently, repeatedly

fresh *adjective* 1 NEW, different, modern, novel, original, recent, up-to-date 2 ADDITIONAL, added, auxiliary, extra, further, more, other, supplementary 3 INVIGORATING, bracing, brisk, clean, cool, crisp, pure, refreshing, unpolluted **4** LIVELY, alert, energetic, keen, refreshed, sprightly, spry, vigorous **5** NATURAL, unprocessed **6** *Informal* CHEEKY, disrespectful, familiar, forward, impudent, insolent, presumptuous

freshen *verb* REFRESH, enliven, freshen up, liven up, restore, revitalize

freshness *noun* **1** NOVELTY, inventiveness, newness, originality **2** CLEANNESS, brightness, clearness, glow, shine, sparkle, vigour, wholesomeness

fret *verb* WORRY, agonize, brood, grieve, lose sleep over, upset *or* distress oneself

fretful *adjective* IRRITABLE, crotchety (*informal*), edgy, fractious, querulous, short-tempered, testy, touchy, uneasy

friction *noun* **1** RUBBING, abrasion, chafing, grating, rasping, resistance, scraping **2** HOSTILITY, animosity, bad blood, conflict, disagreement, discord, dissension, resentment

friend *noun* **1** COMPANION, buddy (*informal*), chum (*informal*), comrade, mate (*informal*), pal, playmate **2** SUPPORTER, ally, associate, patron, well-wisher

friendliness *noun* KINDLINESS, affability, amiability, congeniality, conviviality, geniality, neighbourliness, sociability, warmth

friendly *adjective* SOCIABLE, affectionate, amicable, close, familiar, helpful, intimate, neighbourly, on good terms, pally (*informal*), sympathetic, welcoming

friendship *noun* GOODWILL, affection, amity, attachment, concord, familiarity, friendliness, harmony, intimacy

fright *noun* FEAR, alarm, consternation, dread, horror, panic, scare, shock, trepidation

frighten *verb* SCARE, alarm, intimidate, petrify, shock, startle, terrify, terrorize, unnerve

frightened *adjective* AFRAID, alarmed, petrified, scared, scared stiff, startled, terrified, terrorized, terror-stricken

frightening *adjective* TERRIFYING, alarming, fearful, fearsome, horrifying, menacing, scary (*informal*), shocking, unnerving

frightful *adjective* TERRIFYING, alarming, awful, dreadful, fearful, ghastly, horrendous, horrible, terrible, traumatic

frigid *adjective* **1** COLD, arctic, frosty, frozen, glacial, icy, wintry **2** FORBIDDING, aloof, austere, formal, unapproachable, unfeeling, unresponsive

frills *plural noun* TRIMMINGS, additions, bells and whistles, embellishments, extras, frippery, fuss, ornamentation, ostentation

fringe *noun* **1** BORDER, edging, hem, trimming **2** EDGE, borderline, limits, margin, outskirts, perimeter, periphery ♦ *adjective* **3** UNOFFICIAL, unconventional, unorthodox

frisk *verb* **1** FROLIC, caper, cavort, gambol, jump, play, prance, skip, trip **2** *Informal* SEARCH, check, inspect, run over, shake down (*U.S. slang*)

frisky *adjective* LIVELY, coltish, frolicsome, high-spirited, kittenish, playful, sportive

fritter away *verb* WASTE, dissipate, idle away, misspend, run through, spend like water, squander

frivolity *noun* FUN, flippancy, frivolousness, gaiety, levity, light-heartedness, silliness, superficiality, triviality

frivolous adjective 1 FLIPPANT, childish, foolish, idle, juvenile, puerile, silly, superficial 2 TRIVIAL, footling (informal), minor, petty, shallow, trifling, unimportant

frolic verb 1 PLAY, caper, cavort, frisk, gambol, lark, make merry, romp, sport ♦ noun 2 REVEL, antic, game, lark, romp, spree

frolicsome adjective PLAYFUL, coltish, frisky, kittenish, lively, merry, sportive

front noun 1 EXTERIOR, façade, face, foreground, frontage 2 FOREFRONT, front line, head, lead, vanguard 3 DISGUISE, blind, cover, cover-up, façade, mask, pretext, show ♦ adjective 4 FIRST, foremost, head, lead, leading, topmost ♦ verb 5 FACE ONTO, look over or onto, overlook

frontier noun BOUNDARY, borderline, edge, limit, perimeter, verge

frost noun HOARFROST, freeze, rime

frosty adjective 1 COLD, chilly, frozen, icy, wintry 2 UNFRIENDLY, discouraging, frigid, off-putting (Brit. informal), standoffish, unenthusiastic, unwelcoming

froth noun 1 FOAM, bubbles, effervescence, head, lather, scum, spume, suds ♦ verb 2 FIZZ, bubble over, come to a head, effervesce, foam, lather

frothy adjective FOAMY, foaming, sudsy

frown verb 1 SCOWL, glare, glower, knit one's brows, look daggers, lour or lower 2 **frown on** DISAPPROVE OF, discourage, dislike, look askance at, take a dim view of

frozen adjective ICY, arctic, chilled, frigid, frosted, icebound, ice-cold, ice-covered, numb

frugal adjective THRIFTY, abstemious, careful, economical, niggardly, parsimonious, prudent, sparing

fruit noun 1 PRODUCE, crop, harvest, product, yield 2 RESULT, advantage, benefit, consequence, effect, end result, outcome, profit, return, reward

fruitful adjective USEFUL, advantageous, beneficial, effective, productive, profitable, rewarding, successful, worthwhile

fruition noun MATURITY, attainment, completion, fulfilment, materialization, perfection, realization, ripeness

fruitless adjective USELESS, futile, ineffectual, pointless, profitless, unavailing, unproductive, unprofitable, unsuccessful, vain

frustrate verb THWART, balk, block, check, counter, defeat, disappoint, foil, forestall, nullify, stymie

frustrated adjective DISAPPOINTED, discouraged, disheartened, embittered, resentful

frustration noun 1 OBSTRUCTION, blocking, circumvention, foiling, thwarting 2 ANNOYANCE, disappointment, dissatisfaction, grievance, irritation, resentment, vexation

fuddy-duddy noun CONSERVATIVE, (old) fogey, square (informal), stick-in-the-mud (informal), stuffed shirt (informal)

fudge verb HEDGE, equivocate, flannel (Brit. informal), stall

fuel noun INCITEMENT, ammunition, provocation

fugitive noun 1 RUNAWAY, deserter, escapee, refugee ♦ adjective 2 MOMENTARY, brief, ephemeral, fleeting, passing, short-lived, temporary, transient, transitory

fulfil verb 1 ACHIEVE, accomplish,

carry out, complete, perform, realise, satisfy **2** COMPLY WITH, answer, conform to, fill, meet, obey, observe

fulfilment noun ACHIEVEMENT, accomplishment, attainment, completion, consummation, implementation, realization

full adjective **1** SATURATED, brimming, complete, filled, loaded, replete, satiated, stocked **2** PLENTIFUL, abundant, adequate, ample, comprehensive, exhaustive, extensive, generous **3** RICH, clear, deep, distinct, loud, resonant, rounded **4** PLUMP, buxom, curvaceous, rounded, voluptuous **5** LOOSE, baggy, capacious, large, puffy, voluminous ♦ noun **6 in full** COMPLETELY, in its entirety, in total, without exception

full-blooded adjective VIGOROUS, hearty, lusty, red-blooded, virile

fullness noun **1** PLENTY, abundance, copiousness, fill, profusion, satiety, saturation, sufficiency **2** RICHNESS, clearness, loudness, resonance, strength

full-scale adjective MAJOR, all-out, comprehensive, exhaustive, in-depth, sweeping, thorough, thoroughgoing, wide-ranging

fully adverb TOTALLY, altogether, completely, entirely, in all respects, one hundred per cent, perfectly, thoroughly, utterly, wholly

fulsome adjective INSINCERE, excessive, extravagant, immoderate, inordinate, sycophantic, unctuous

fumble verb GROPE, feel around, flounder, scrabble

fume verb RAGE, get hot under the collar (informal), rant, see red (informal), seethe, smoulder, storm

fumes plural noun SMOKE, exhaust, gas, pollution, smog, vapour

fumigate verb DISINFECT, clean out or up, cleanse, purify, sanitize, sterilize

fuming adjective ANGRY, enraged, in a rage, incensed, on the warpath (informal), raging, seething, up in arms

fun noun **1** ENJOYMENT, amusement, entertainment, jollity, merriment, mirth, pleasure, recreation, sport **2 make fun of** MOCK, lampoon, laugh at, parody, poke fun at, ridicule, satirize, send up (Brit. informal) ♦ adjective **3** ENJOYABLE, amusing, convivial, diverting, entertaining, lively, witty

function noun **1** PURPOSE, business, duty, job, mission, raison d'être, responsibility, role, task **2** RECEPTION, affair, do (informal), gathering, social occasion ♦ verb **3** WORK, act, behave, do duty, go, operate, perform, run

functional adjective **1** PRACTICAL, hard-wearing, serviceable, useful, utilitarian **2** WORKING, operative

fund noun **1** RESERVE, kitty, pool, stock, store, supply ♦ verb **2** FINANCE, pay for, subsidize, support

fundamental adjective **1** ESSENTIAL, basic, cardinal, central, elementary, key, primary, principal, rudimentary, underlying ♦ noun **2** PRINCIPLE, axiom, cornerstone, law, rudiment, rule

fundamentally adverb ESSENTIALLY, at bottom, at heart, basically, intrinsically, primarily, radically

funds plural noun MONEY, capital, cash, finance, ready money, resources, savings, the wherewithal

funeral noun BURIAL, cremation, inhumation, interment, obsequies

funnel verb CHANNEL, conduct,

convey, direct, filter, move, pass, pour

funny *adjective* **1** HUMOROUS, amusing, comic, comical, droll, entertaining, hilarious, riotous, side-splitting, witty **2** PECULIAR, curious, mysterious, odd, queer, strange, suspicious, unusual, weird

furious *adjective* **1** ANGRY, beside oneself, enraged, fuming, incensed, infuriated, livid (*informal*), raging, up in arms **2** VIOLENT, fierce, intense, savage, turbulent, unrestrained, vehement

furnish *verb* **1** DECORATE, equip, fit out, stock **2** SUPPLY, give, grant, hand out, offer, present, provide

furniture *noun* HOUSEHOLD GOODS, appliances, fittings, furnishings, goods, possessions, things (*informal*)

furore *noun* DISTURBANCE, commotion, hullabaloo, outcry, stir, to-do, uproar

furrow *noun* **1** GROOVE, channel, crease, hollow, line, rut, seam, trench, wrinkle ♦ *verb* **2** WRINKLE, corrugate, crease, draw together, knit

further *adverb* **1** IN ADDITION, additionally, also, besides, furthermore, into the bargain, moreover, to boot ♦ *adjective* **2** ADDITIONAL, extra, fresh, more, new, other, supplementary ♦ *verb* **3** PROMOTE, advance, assist, encourage, forward, help, lend support to, work for

furthermore *adverb* BESIDES, additionally, as well, further, in addition, into the bargain, moreover, to boot, too

furthest *adjective* MOST DISTANT, extreme, farthest, furthermost,

outmost, remotest, ultimate

furtive *adjective* SLY, clandestine, conspiratorial, secretive, sneaky, stealthy, surreptitious, underhand, under-the-table

fury *noun* **1** ANGER, frenzy, impetuosity, madness, passion, rage, wrath **2** VIOLENCE, ferocity, fierceness, force, intensity, savagery, severity, vehemence

fuss *noun* **1** BOTHER, ado, commotion, excitement, hue and cry, palaver, stir, to-do **2** ARGUMENT, complaint, furore, objection, row, squabble, trouble ♦ *verb* **3** WORRY, fidget, flap (*informal*), fret, get worked up, take pains

fussy *adjective* **1** HARD TO PLEASE, choosy (*informal*), difficult, fastidious, finicky, nit-picking (*informal*), particular, pernickety, picky (*informal*) **2** OVERELABORATE, busy, cluttered, overworked, rococo

fusty *adjective* STALE, airless, damp, mildewed, mouldering, musty, stuffy

futile *adjective* USELESS, fruitless, ineffectual, unavailing, unprofitable, unsuccessful, vain, worthless

futility *noun* USELESSNESS, emptiness, hollowness, ineffectiveness

future *noun* **1** HEREAFTER, time to come **2** OUTLOOK, expectation, prospect ♦ *adjective* **3** FORTHCOMING, approaching, coming, fated, impending, later, subsequent, to come

fuzzy *adjective* **1** FLUFFY, downy, frizzy, woolly **2** INDISTINCT, bleary, blurred, distorted, ill-defined, out of focus, unclear, vague

G g

gabble *verb* 1 <u>PRATTLE</u>, babble, blabber, gibber, gush, jabber, spout ♦ *noun* 2 <u>GIBBERISH</u>, babble, blabber, chatter, drivel, prattle, twaddle

gadabout *noun* <u>PLEASURE-SEEKER</u>, gallivanter, rambler, rover, wanderer

gadget *noun* <u>DEVICE</u>, appliance, contraption (*informal*), contrivance, gizmo (*slang, chiefly U.S.*), instrument, invention, thing, tool

gaffe *noun* <u>BLUNDER</u>, bloomer (*informal*), clanger (*informal*), faux pas, howler, indiscretion, lapse, mistake, slip, solecism

gaffer *noun* 1 *Informal* <u>MANAGER</u>, boss (*informal*), foreman, overseer, superintendent, supervisor 2 <u>OLD MAN</u>, granddad, greybeard, old boy (*informal*), old fellow, old-timer (*U.S.*)

gag[1] *verb* 1 <u>SUPPRESS</u>, curb, muffle, muzzle, quiet, silence, stifle, stop up 2 <u>RETCH</u>, heave, puke (*slang*), spew, throw up (*informal*), vomit

gag[2] *noun* <u>JOKE</u>, crack (*slang*), funny (*informal*), hoax, jest, wisecrack (*informal*), witticism

gaiety *noun* 1 <u>CHEERFULNESS</u>, blitheness, exhilaration, glee, high spirits, jollity, light-heartedness, merriment, mirth 2 <u>MERRYMAKING</u>, conviviality, festivity, fun, jollification, revelry

gaily *adverb* 1 <u>CHEERFULLY</u>, blithely, gleefully, happily, joyfully, light-heartedly, merrily 2 <u>COLOURFULLY</u>, brightly, brilliantly, flamboyantly, flashily, gaudily, showily

gain *verb* 1 <u>OBTAIN</u>, acquire, attain, capture, collect, gather, get, land, pick up, secure, win 2 <u>REACH</u>, arrive at, attain, come to, get to 3 **gain on** <u>GET NEARER</u>, approach, catch up with, close, narrow the gap, overtake ♦ *noun* 4 <u>PROFIT</u>, advantage, benefit, dividend, return, yield 5 <u>INCREASE</u>, advance, growth, improvement, progress, rise

gainful *adjective* <u>PROFITABLE</u>, advantageous, beneficial, fruitful, lucrative, productive, remunerative, rewarding, useful, worthwhile

gains *plural noun* <u>PROFITS</u>, earnings, prize, proceeds, revenue, takings, winnings

gainsay *verb* <u>CONTRADICT</u>, contravene, controvert, deny, disagree with, dispute, rebut, retract

gait *noun* <u>WALK</u>, bearing, carriage, pace, step, stride, tread

gala *noun* <u>FESTIVAL</u>, carnival, celebration, festivity, fête, jamboree, pageant

gale *noun* 1 <u>STORM</u>, blast, cyclone, hurricane, squall, tempest, tornado, typhoon 2 *Informal* <u>OUTBURST</u>, burst, eruption, explosion, fit, howl, outbreak, peal, shout, shriek

gall[1] *noun* 1 *Informal* <u>IMPUDENCE</u>, brazenness, cheek (*informal*), chutzpah (*U.S. & Canad. informal*), effrontery, impertinence, insolence, nerve (*informal*) 2 <u>BITTERNESS</u>, acrimony, animosity, bile, hostility, rancour

gall[2] *verb* 1 <u>SCRAPE</u>, abrade, chafe, irritate 2 <u>ANNOY</u>, exasperate, irk, irritate, provoke, rankle, vex

gallant *adjective* 1 BRAVE, bold, courageous, heroic, honourable, intrepid, manly, noble, valiant 2 CHIVALROUS, attentive, courteous, gentlemanly, gracious, noble, polite

gallantry *noun* 1 BRAVERY, boldness, courage, heroism, intrepidity, manliness, spirit, valour 2 ATTENTIVENESS, chivalry, courteousness, courtesy, gentlemanliness, graciousness, nobility, politeness

galling *adjective* ANNOYING, bitter, exasperating, irksome, irritating, provoking, vexatious

gallivant *verb* WANDER, gad about, ramble, roam, rove

gallop *verb* RUN, bolt, career, dash, hurry, race, rush, speed, sprint

galore *adverb* IN ABUNDANCE, all over the place, aplenty, everywhere, in great quantity, in numbers, in profusion, to spare

galvanize *verb* STIMULATE, electrify, excite, inspire, invigorate, jolt, provoke, spur, stir

gamble *verb* 1 BET, game, have a flutter (*informal*), play, punt, wager 2 RISK, chance, hazard, speculate, stick one's neck out (*informal*), take a chance ♦ *noun* 3 RISK, chance, leap in the dark, lottery, speculation, uncertainty, venture 4 BET, flutter (*informal*), punt, wager

gambol *verb* 1 FROLIC, caper, cavort, frisk, hop, jump, prance, skip ♦ *noun* 2 FROLIC, caper, hop, jump, prance, skip

game *noun* 1 PASTIME, amusement, distraction, diversion, entertainment, lark, recreation, sport 2 MATCH, competition, contest, event, head-to-head, meeting, tournament 3 WILD ANIMALS, prey, quarry 4 SCHEME,

design, plan, plot, ploy, stratagem, tactic, trick ♦ *adjective* 5 BRAVE, courageous, gallant, gritty, intrepid, persistent, plucky, spirited 6 WILLING, desirous, eager, interested, keen, prepared, ready

gamut *noun* RANGE, area, catalogue, compass, field, scale, scope, series, sweep

gang *noun* GROUP, band, clique, club, company, coterie, crowd, mob, pack, squad, team

gangling *adjective* TALL, angular, awkward, lanky, rangy, rawboned, spindly

gangster *noun* RACKETEER, crook (*informal*), hood (*U.S. slang*), hoodlum (*chiefly U.S.*), mobster (*U.S. slang*)

gap *noun* 1 OPENING, break, chink, cleft, crack, hole, space 2 INTERVAL, breathing space, hiatus, interlude, intermission, interruption, lacuna, lull, pause, respite 3 DIFFERENCE, disagreement, disparity, divergence, inconsistency

gape *verb* 1 STARE, gawk, gawp (*Brit. slang*), goggle, wonder 2 OPEN, crack, split, yawn

gaping *adjective* WIDE, broad, cavernous, great, open, vast, wide open, yawning

garbage *noun* RUBBISH, refuse, trash (*chiefly U.S.*), waste

garbled *adjective* JUMBLED, confused, distorted, double-Dutch, incomprehensible, mixed up, unintelligible

garish *adjective* GAUDY, brash, brassy, flashy, loud, showy, tacky (*informal*), tasteless, vulgar

garland *noun* 1 WREATH, bays, chaplet, crown, festoon, honours, laurels ♦ *verb* 2 ADORN, crown, deck, festoon, wreathe

garments *plural noun* CLOTHES,

apparel, attire, clothing, costume, dress, garb, gear (*slang*), outfit, uniform

garner verb COLLECT, accumulate, amass, gather, hoard, save, stockpile, store, stow away

garnish verb 1 DECORATE, adorn, embellish, enhance, ornament, set off, trim ♦ noun 2 DECORATION, adornment, embellishment, enhancement, ornamentation, trimming

garrison noun 1 TROOPS, armed force, command, detachment, unit 2 FORT, base, camp, encampment, fortification, fortress, post, station, stronghold ♦ verb 3 STATION, assign, position, post, put on duty

garrulous adjective TALKATIVE, chatty, gossiping, loquacious, prattling, verbose, voluble

gash verb 1 CUT, gouge, lacerate, slash, slit, split, tear, wound ♦ noun 2 CUT, gouge, incision, laceration, slash, slit, split, tear, wound

gasp verb 1 GULP, blow, catch one's breath, choke, pant, puff ♦ noun 2 GULP, exclamation, pant, puff, sharp intake of breath

gate noun BARRIER, door, entrance, exit, gateway, opening, passage, portal

gather verb 1 ASSEMBLE, accumulate, amass, collect, garner, mass, muster, stockpile 2 LEARN, assume, conclude, deduce, hear, infer, surmise, understand 3 PICK, cull, garner, glean, harvest, pluck, reap, select 4 INTENSIFY, deepen, expand, grow, heighten, increase, rise, swell, thicken 5 FOLD, pleat, tuck

gathering noun ASSEMBLY, company, conclave, congress, convention, crowd, group, meeting

gauche adjective AWKWARD, clumsy, ill-mannered, inelegant, tactless, unsophisticated

gaudy adjective GARISH, bright, flashy, loud, showy, tacky (*informal*), tasteless, vulgar

gauge verb 1 MEASURE, ascertain, calculate, check, compute, count, determine, weigh 2 JUDGE, adjudge, appraise, assess, estimate, evaluate, guess, rate, reckon, value ♦ noun 3 INDICATOR, criterion, guide, guideline, measure, meter, standard, test, touchstone, yardstick

gaunt adjective THIN, angular, bony, haggard, lean, pinched, scrawny, skinny, spare

gawky adjective AWKWARD, clumsy, gauche, loutish, lumbering, maladroit, ungainly

gay adjective 1 HOMOSEXUAL, lesbian, queer (*informal, derogatory*) 2 CAREFREE, blithe, cheerful, jovial, light-hearted, lively, merry, sparkling 3 COLOURFUL, bright, brilliant, flamboyant, flashy, rich, showy, vivid ♦ noun 4 HOMOSEXUAL, lesbian

gaze verb 1 STARE, gape, look, regard, view, watch, wonder ♦ noun 2 STARE, fixed look, look

gazette noun NEWSPAPER, journal, news-sheet, paper, periodical

gear noun 1 COG, cogwheel, gearwheel 2 MECHANISM, cogs, machinery, works 3 EQUIPMENT, accoutrements, apparatus, instruments, paraphernalia, supplies, tackle, tools 4 CLOTHING, clothes, costume, dress, garments, outfit, togs, wear ♦ verb 5 EQUIP, adapt, adjust, fit

gelatinous adjective JELLY-LIKE, glutinous, gummy, sticky, viscous

gelid adjective COLD, arctic, chilly, freezing, frigid, frosty, frozen, glacial, ice-cold, icy

gem noun 1 PRECIOUS STONE, jewel, stone 2 PRIZE, jewel, masterpiece, pearl, treasure

general adjective 1 COMMON, accepted, broad, extensive, popular, prevalent, public, universal, widespread 2 IMPRECISE, approximate, ill-defined, indefinite, inexact, loose, unspecific, vague 3 UNIVERSAL, across-the-board, blanket, collective, comprehensive, indiscriminate, miscellaneous, sweeping, total

generally adverb 1 USUALLY, as a rule, by and large, customarily, normally, on the whole, ordinarily, typically 2 COMMONLY, extensively, popularly, publicly, universally, widely

generate verb PRODUCE, breed, cause, create, engender, give rise to, make, propagate

generation noun 1 PRODUCTION, creation, formation, genesis, propagation, reproduction 2 AGE GROUP, breed, crop 3 AGE, epoch, era, period, time

generic adjective COLLECTIVE, blanket, common, comprehensive, general, inclusive, universal, wide

generosity noun 1 CHARITY, beneficence, bounty, kindness, largesse or largess, liberality, munificence, open-handedness 2 UNSELFISHNESS, goodness, high-mindedness, magnanimity, nobleness

generous adjective 1 CHARITABLE, beneficent, bountiful, hospitable, kind, lavish, liberal, open-handed, unstinting 2 UNSELFISH, big-hearted, good, high-minded, lofty, magnanimous, noble 3 PLENTIFUL, abundant, ample, copious, full, lavish, liberal, rich, unstinting

genesis noun BEGINNING, birth, creation, formation, inception, origin, start

genial adjective CHEERFUL, affable, agreeable, amiable, congenial, friendly, good-natured, jovial, pleasant, warm

geniality noun CHEERFULNESS, affability, agreeableness, amiability, conviviality, cordiality, friendliness, good cheer, joviality, warmth

genius noun 1 MASTER, brainbox, expert, hotshot (informal), maestro, mastermind, virtuoso, whiz (informal) 2 BRILLIANCE, ability, aptitude, bent, capacity, flair, gift, knack, talent

genre noun TYPE, category, class, group, kind, sort, species, style

genteel adjective REFINED, courteous, cultured, elegant, gentlemanly, ladylike, polite, respectable, urbane, well-mannered

gentle adjective 1 SWEET-TEMPERED, compassionate, humane, kindly, meek, mild, placid, tender 2 MODERATE, light, mild, muted, slight, soft, soothing 3 GRADUAL, easy, imperceptible, light, mild, moderate, slight, slow 4 TAME, biddable, broken, docile, manageable, placid, tractable

gentlemanly adjective POLITE, civil, courteous, gallant, genteel, honourable, refined, urbane, well-mannered

gentleness noun TENDERNESS, compassion, kindness, mildness, softness, sweetness

gentry noun NOBILITY, aristocracy, elite, upper class, upper crust (informal)

genuine adjective 1 AUTHENTIC, actual, bona fide, legitimate, real, the real McCoy, true, veritable

2 SINCERE, candid, earnest, frank, heartfelt, honest, unaffected, unfeigned

germ noun 1 MICROBE, bacterium, bug (*informal*), microorganism, virus 2 BEGINNING, embryo, origin, root, rudiment, seed, source, spark

germane adjective RELEVANT, apposite, appropriate, apropos, connected, fitting, material, pertinent, related, to the point or purpose

germinate verb SPROUT, bud, develop, generate, grow, originate, shoot, swell, vegetate

gesticulate verb SIGNAL, gesture, indicate, make a sign, motion, sign, wave

gesture noun 1 SIGNAL, action, gesticulation, indication, motion, sign ♦ verb 2 SIGNAL, gesticulate, indicate, motion, sign, wave

get verb 1 OBTAIN, acquire, attain, fetch, gain, land, net, pick up, procure, receive, secure, win 2 CONTRACT, catch, come down with, fall victim to, take 3 CAPTURE, grab, lay hold of, nab (*informal*), seize, take 4 BECOME, come to be, grow, turn 5 UNDERSTAND, catch, comprehend, fathom, follow, perceive, see, take in, work out 6 PERSUADE, convince, induce, influence, prevail upon 7 *Informal* ANNOY, bug (*informal*), gall, irritate, upset, vex

get across verb 1 CROSS, ford, negotiate, pass over, traverse 2 COMMUNICATE, bring home to, convey, impart, make clear or understood, put over, transmit

get at verb 1 GAIN ACCESS TO, acquire, attain, come to grips with, get hold of, reach 2 IMPLY, hint, intend, lead up to, mean, suggest 3 CRITICIZE, attack, blame, find fault with, nag, pick on

getaway noun ESCAPE, break, break-out, flight

get by verb MANAGE, cope, exist, fare, get along, keep one's head above water, make both ends meet, survive

get off verb LEAVE, alight, depart, descend, disembark, dismount, escape, exit

get on verb 1 BOARD, ascend, climb, embark, mount 2 BE FRIENDLY, be compatible, concur, get along, hit it off (*informal*)

get over verb RECOVER FROM, come round, get better, mend, pull through, rally, revive, survive

ghastly adjective HORRIBLE, dreadful, frightful, gruesome, hideous, horrendous, loathsome, shocking, terrible, terrifying

ghost noun 1 SPIRIT, apparition, phantom, soul, spectre, spook (*informal*), wraith 2 TRACE, glimmer, hint, possibility, semblance, shadow, suggestion

ghostly adjective SUPERNATURAL, eerie, ghostlike, phantom, spectral, spooky (*informal*), unearthly, wraithlike

ghoulish adjective MACABRE, disgusting, grisly, gruesome, morbid, sick (*informal*), unwholesome

giant noun 1 OGRE, colossus, monster, titan ♦ adjective 2 HUGE, colossal, enormous, gargantuan, gigantic, immense, mammoth, titanic, vast

gibberish noun NONSENSE, babble, drivel, gobbledegook (*informal*), mumbo jumbo, twaddle

gibe, jibe verb 1 TAUNT, jeer, make fun of, mock, poke fun at, ridicule, scoff, scorn, sneer ♦ noun 2 TAUNT, barb, crack (*slang*), dig, jeer, sarcasm, scoffing, sneer

giddiness noun DIZZINESS, faintness, light-headedness, vertigo

giddy adjective DIZZY, dizzying, faint, light-headed, reeling, unsteady, vertiginous

gift noun 1 DONATION, bequest, bonus, contribution, grant, hand-out, legacy, offering, present 2 TALENT, ability, capability, capacity, flair, genius, knack, power

gifted adjective TALENTED, able, accomplished, brilliant, capable, clever, expert, ingenious, masterly, skilled

gigantic adjective ENORMOUS, colossal, giant, huge, immense, mammoth, stupendous, titanic, tremendous

giggle verb, noun LAUGH, cackle, chortle, chuckle, snigger, titter, twitter

gild verb EMBELLISH, adorn, beautify, brighten, coat, dress up, embroider, enhance, ornament

gimmick noun STUNT, contrivance, device, dodge, ploy, scheme

gingerly adverb CAUTIOUSLY, carefully, charily, circumspectly, hesitantly, reluctantly, suspiciously, timidly, warily

gird verb SURROUND, encircle, enclose, encompass, enfold, hem in, ring

girdle noun 1 BELT, band, cummerbund, sash, waistband
♦ verb 2 SURROUND, bound, encircle, enclose, encompass, gird, ring

girl noun FEMALE CHILD, damsel (*archaic*), daughter, lass, lassie (*informal*), maid (*archaic*), maiden (*archaic*), miss

girth noun CIRCUMFERENCE, bulk, measure, size

gist noun POINT, core, essence, force, idea, meaning, sense,

significance, substance

give verb 1 PRESENT, award, contribute, deliver, donate, grant, hand over *or* out, provide, supply 2 ANNOUNCE, communicate, issue, notify, pronounce, transmit, utter 3 CONCEDE, grant, hand over, relinquish, surrender, yield 4 PRODUCE, cause, engender, make, occasion

give away verb REVEAL, betray, disclose, divulge, expose, leak, let out, let slip, uncover

give in verb ADMIT DEFEAT, capitulate, collapse, concede, quit, submit, succumb, surrender, yield

give off verb EMIT, discharge, exude, produce, release, send out, throw out

give out verb EMIT, discharge, exude, produce, release, send out, throw out

give up verb ABANDON, call it a day *or* night, cease, desist, leave off, quit, relinquish, renounce, stop, surrender

glad adjective 1 HAPPY, contented, delighted, gratified, joyful, overjoyed, pleased 2 PLEASING, cheerful, cheering, gratifying, pleasant

gladden verb PLEASE, cheer, delight, gratify, hearten

gladly adverb HAPPILY, cheerfully, freely, gleefully, readily, willingly, with pleasure

gladness noun HAPPINESS, cheerfulness, delight, gaiety, glee, high spirits, joy, mirth, pleasure

glamorous adjective ELEGANT, attractive, dazzling, exciting, fascinating, glittering, glossy, prestigious, smart

glamour noun CHARM, allure, appeal, attraction, beauty, enchantment, fascination, prestige

glance verb 1 LOOK, glimpse, peek, peep, scan, view 2 GLEAM, flash, glimmer, glint, glisten, glitter, reflect, shimmer, shine, twinkle ♦ noun 3 LOOK, dekko (slang), glimpse, peek, peep, view

glare verb 1 SCOWL, frown, glower, look daggers, lour or lower 2 DAZZLE, blaze, flame, flare ♦ noun 3 SCOWL, black look, dirty look, frown, glower, lour or lower 4 DAZZLE, blaze, brilliance, flame, glow

glaring adjective 1 CONSPICUOUS, blatant, flagrant, gross, manifest, obvious, outrageous, unconcealed 2 DAZZLING, blazing, bright, garish, glowing

glassy adjective 1 TRANSPARENT, clear, glossy, shiny, slippery, smooth 2 EXPRESSIONLESS, blank, cold, dull, empty, fixed, glazed, lifeless, vacant

glaze verb 1 COAT, enamel, gloss, lacquer, polish, varnish ♦ noun 2 COAT, enamel, finish, gloss, lacquer, lustre, patina, polish, shine, varnish

gleam noun 1 GLOW, beam, flash, glimmer, ray, sparkle 2 TRACE, flicker, glimmer, hint, inkling, suggestion ♦ verb 3 SHINE, flash, glimmer, glint, glisten, glitter, glow, shimmer, sparkle

glee noun DELIGHT, elation, exhilaration, exuberance, exultation, joy, merriment, triumph

gleeful adjective DELIGHTED, cock-a-hoop, elated, exuberant, exultant, joyful, jubilant, overjoyed, triumphant

glib adjective SMOOTH, easy, fluent, insincere, plausible, quick, ready, slick, suave, voluble

glide verb SLIDE, coast, drift, float, flow, roll, run, sail, skate, slip

glimmer verb 1 FLICKER, blink, gleam, glisten, glitter, glow, shimmer, shine, sparkle, twinkle ♦ noun 2 GLEAM, blink, flicker, glow, ray, shimmer, sparkle, twinkle 3 TRACE, flicker, gleam, hint, inkling, suggestion

glimpse noun 1 LOOK, glance, peek, peep, sight, sighting ♦ verb 2 CATCH SIGHT OF, espy, sight, spot, spy, view

glint verb 1 GLEAM, flash, glimmer, glitter, shine, sparkle, twinkle ♦ noun 2 GLEAM, flash, glimmer, glitter, shine, sparkle, twinkle, twinkling

glisten verb GLEAM, flash, glance, glare, glimmer, glint, glitter, shimmer, shine, sparkle, twinkle

glitch noun PROBLEM, blip, difficulty, gremlin, hitch, interruption, malfunction, snag

glitter verb 1 SHINE, flash, glare, gleam, glimmer, glint, glisten, shimmer, sparkle, twinkle ♦ noun 2 SHINE, brightness, flash, glare, gleam, radiance, sheen, shimmer, sparkle 3 GLAMOUR, display, gaudiness, pageantry, show, showiness, splendour, tinsel

gloat verb RELISH, crow, drool, exult, glory, revel in, rub it in (informal), triumph

global adjective 1 WORLDWIDE, international, universal, world 2 COMPREHENSIVE, all-inclusive, exhaustive, general, total, unlimited

globe noun SPHERE, ball, earth, orb, planet, world

globule noun DROPLET, bead, bubble, drop, particle, pearl, pellet

gloom noun 1 DARKNESS, blackness, dark, dusk, murk, obscurity, shade, shadow, twilight 2 DEPRESSION, dejection, despondency, low spirits, melancholy, sorrow, unhappiness, woe

gloomy *adjective* **1** DARK, black, dim, dismal, dreary, dull, grey, murky, sombre **2** DEPRESSING, bad, cheerless, disheartening, dispiriting, dreary, sad, sombre **3** MISERABLE, crestfallen, dejected, dispirited, downcast, downhearted, glum, melancholy, morose, pessimistic, sad

glorify *verb* **1** ENHANCE, aggrandize, dignify, elevate, ennoble, magnify **2** WORSHIP, adore, bless, exalt, honour, idolize, pay homage to, revere, venerate **3** PRAISE, celebrate, eulogize, extol, sing *or* sound the praises of

glorious *adjective* **1** FAMOUS, celebrated, distinguished, eminent, honoured, illustrious, magnificent, majestic, renowned **2** SPLENDID, beautiful, brilliant, dazzling, gorgeous, shining, superb **3** DELIGHTFUL, excellent, fine, gorgeous, marvellous, wonderful

glory *noun* **1** HONOUR, dignity, distinction, eminence, fame, praise, prestige, renown **2** SPLENDOUR, grandeur, greatness, magnificence, majesty, nobility, pageantry, pomp ◆ *verb* **3** TRIUMPH, boast, exult, pride oneself, relish, revel, take delight

gloss[1] *noun* SHINE, brightness, gleam, lustre, patina, polish, sheen, veneer

gloss[2] *noun* **1** COMMENT, annotation, commentary, elucidation, explanation, footnote, interpretation, note, translation ◆ *verb* **2** INTERPRET, annotate, comment, elucidate, explain, translate

glossy *adjective* SHINY, bright, glassy, glazed, lustrous, polished, shining, silky

glow *verb* **1** SHINE, brighten, burn,

gleam, glimmer, redden, smoulder ◆ *noun* **2** LIGHT, burning, gleam, glimmer, luminosity, phosphorescence **3** RADIANCE, brightness, brilliance, effulgence, splendour, vividness

glower *verb* **1** SCOWL, frown, give a dirty look, glare, look daggers, lour *or* lower ◆ *noun* **2** SCOWL, black look, dirty look, frown, glare, lour *or* lower

glowing *adjective* **1** BRIGHT, aglow, flaming, luminous, radiant **2** COMPLIMENTARY, adulatory, ecstatic, enthusiastic, laudatory, rave (*informal*), rhapsodic

glue *noun* **1** ADHESIVE, cement, gum, paste ◆ *verb* **2** STICK, affix, cement, fix, gum, paste, seal

glum *adjective* GLOOMY, crestfallen, dejected, doleful, low, morose, pessimistic, sullen

glut *noun* **1** SURFEIT, excess, oversupply, plethora, saturation, superfluity, surplus ◆ *verb* **2** SATURATE, choke, clog, deluge, flood, inundate, overload, oversupply

glutton *noun* GOURMAND, gannet (*slang*), pig (*informal*)

gluttonous *adjective* GREEDY, gormandizing, insatiable, piggish, ravenous, voracious

gluttony *noun* GREED, gormandizing, greediness, voracity

gnarled *adjective* TWISTED, contorted, knotted, knotty, rough, rugged, weather-beaten, wrinkled

gnaw *verb* BITE, chew, munch, nibble

go *verb* **1** MOVE, advance, journey, make for, pass, proceed, set off, travel **2** LEAVE, depart, make tracks, move out, slope off, withdraw **3** FUNCTION, move, operate, perform, run, work **4** CONTRIBUTE, lead to, serve, tend, work towards

5 HARMONIZE, agree, blend, chime, complement, correspond, fit, match, suit **6** ELAPSE, expire, flow, lapse, pass, slip away ♦ *noun* **7** ATTEMPT, bid, crack (*informal*), effort, shot (*informal*), try, turn **8** *Informal* ENERGY, drive, force, life, spirit, verve, vigour, vitality, vivacity

goad *verb* **1** PROVOKE, drive, egg on, exhort, incite, prod, prompt, spur ♦ *noun* **2** PROVOCATION, impetus, incentive, incitement, irritation, spur, stimulus, urge

goal *noun* AIM, ambition, end, intention, object, objective, purpose, target

gobble *verb* DEVOUR, bolt, cram, gorge, gulp, guzzle, stuff, swallow, wolf

gobbledegook *noun* NONSENSE, babble, cant, gabble, gibberish, hocus-pocus, jargon, mumbo jumbo, twaddle

go-between *noun* INTERMEDIARY, agent, broker, dealer, mediator, medium, middleman

godforsaken *adjective* DESOLATE, abandoned, bleak, deserted, dismal, dreary, forlorn, gloomy, lonely, remote, wretched

godlike *adjective* DIVINE, celestial, heavenly, superhuman, transcendent

godly *adjective* DEVOUT, god-fearing, good, holy, pious, religious, righteous, saintly

godsend *noun* BLESSING, boon, manna, stroke of luck, windfall

go for *verb* **1** FAVOUR, admire, be attracted to, be fond of, choose, like, prefer **2** ATTACK, assail, assault, launch oneself at, rush upon, set about *or* upon, spring upon

golden *adjective* **1** YELLOW, blond *or* blonde, flaxen **2** SUCCESSFUL, flourishing, glorious, halcyon,

happy, prosperous, rich **3** PROMISING, excellent, favourable, opportune

gone *adjective* **1** FINISHED, elapsed, ended, over, past **2** MISSING, absent, astray, away, lacking, lost, vanished

good *adjective* **1** PLEASING, acceptable, admirable, excellent, fine, first-class, first-rate, great, satisfactory, splendid, superior **2** PRAISEWORTHY, admirable, ethical, honest, honourable, moral, righteous, trustworthy, upright, virtuous, worthy **3** EXPERT, able, accomplished, adept, adroit, clever, competent, proficient, skilled, talented **4** BENEFICIAL, advantageous, convenient, favourable, fitting, helpful, profitable, suitable, useful, wholesome **5** KIND, altruistic, benevolent, charitable, friendly, humane, kind-hearted, kindly, merciful, obliging **6** VALID, authentic, bona fide, genuine, legitimate, proper, real, true **7** WELL-BEHAVED, dutiful, obedient, orderly, polite, well-mannered **8** FULL, adequate, ample, complete, considerable, extensive, large, substantial, sufficient ♦ *noun* **9** BENEFIT, advantage, gain, interest, profit, use, usefulness, welfare, wellbeing **10** VIRTUE, excellence, goodness, merit, morality, rectitude, right, righteousness, worth **11 for good** PERMANENTLY, finally, for ever, irrevocably, once and for all

goodbye *noun* FAREWELL, adieu, leave-taking, parting

good-for-nothing *noun* **1** LAYABOUT, black sheep, idler, ne'er-do-well, skiver (*Brit. slang*), slacker (*informal*), waster, wastrel ♦ *adjective* **2** WORTHLESS, feckless, idle, irresponsible, useless

goodly *adjective* CONSIDERABLE,

ample, large, significant, sizable *or* sizeable, substantial, tidy (*informal*)

goodness *noun* **1** EXCELLENCE, merit, quality, superiority, value, worth **2** KINDNESS, benevolence, friendliness, generosity, goodwill, humaneness, kind-heartedness, kindliness, mercy **3** VIRTUE, honesty, honour, integrity, merit, morality, probity, rectitude, righteousness, uprightness **4** BENEFIT, advantage, salubriousness, wholesomeness

goods *plural noun* **1** PROPERTY, belongings, chattels, effects, gear, paraphernalia, possessions, things, trappings **2** MERCHANDISE, commodities, stock, stuff, wares

goodwill *noun* FRIENDLINESS, amity, benevolence, friendship, heartiness, kindliness

go off *verb* **1** EXPLODE, blow up, detonate, fire **2** LEAVE, decamp, depart, go away, move out, part, quit, slope off **3** *Informal* ROT, go bad, go stale

go out *verb* **1** LEAVE, depart, exit **2** BE EXTINGUISHED, die out, expire, fade out

go over *verb* EXAMINE, inspect, rehearse, reiterate, review, revise, study, work over

gore[1] *noun* BLOOD, bloodshed, butchery, carnage, slaughter

gore[2] *verb* PIERCE, impale, transfix, wound

gorge *noun* **1** RAVINE, canyon, chasm, cleft, defile, fissure, pass ♦ *verb* **2** OVEREAT, cram, devour, feed, glut, gobble, gulp, guzzle, stuff, wolf

gorgeous *adjective* **1** BEAUTIFUL, dazzling, elegant, magnificent, ravishing, splendid, stunning (*informal*), sumptuous, superb **2** *Informal* PLEASING, delightful, enjoyable, exquisite, fine, glorious, good, lovely

gory *adjective* BLOODTHIRSTY, blood-soaked, bloodstained, bloody, murderous, sanguinary

gospel *noun* **1** TRUTH, certainty, fact, the last word **2** DOCTRINE, credo, creed, message, news, revelation, tidings

gossip *noun* **1** IDLE TALK, blether, chinwag (*Brit. informal*), chitchat, hearsay, scandal, small talk, tittle-tattle **2** BUSYBODY, chatterbox (*informal*), chatterer, gossipmonger, scandalmonger, tattler, telltale ♦ *verb* **3** CHAT, blether, gabble, jaw (*slang*), prate, prattle, tattle

go through *verb* **1** SUFFER, bear, brave, endure, experience, tolerate, undergo, withstand **2** EXAMINE, check, explore, forage, hunt, look, search

gouge *verb* **1** SCOOP, chisel, claw, cut, dig (out), hollow (out) ♦ *noun* **2** GASH, cut, furrow, groove, hollow, scoop, scratch, trench

gourmet *noun* CONNOISSEUR, *bon vivant*, epicure, foodie (*informal*), gastronome

govern *verb* **1** RULE, administer, command, control, direct, guide, handle, lead, manage, order **2** RESTRAIN, check, control, curb, discipline, hold in check, master, regulate, subdue, tame

government *noun* **1** RULE, administration, authority, governance, sovereignty, statecraft **2** EXECUTIVE, administration, ministry, powers-that-be, regime

governor *noun* LEADER, administrator, chief, commander, controller, director, executive, head, manager, ruler

gown *noun* DRESS, costume, frock, garb, garment, habit, robe

grab *verb* SNATCH, capture, catch,

catch *or* take hold of, clutch,
grasp, grip, pluck, seize, snap up

grace *noun* **1** <u>ELEGANCE</u>,
attractiveness, beauty, charm,
comeliness, ease, gracefulness,
poise, polish, refinement,
tastefulness **2** <u>GOODWILL</u>,
benefaction, benevolence, favour,
generosity, goodness, kindliness,
kindness **3** <u>MANNERS</u>, consideration,
decency, decorum, etiquette,
propriety, tact **4** <u>INDULGENCE</u>,
mercy, pardon, reprieve **5** <u>PRAYER</u>,
benediction, blessing, thanks,
thanksgiving ♦ *verb* **6** <u>HONOUR</u>,
adorn, decorate, dignify,
embellish, enhance, enrich,
favour, ornament, set off

graceful *adjective* <u>ELEGANT</u>,
beautiful, charming, comely, easy,
pleasing, tasteful

gracious *adjective* <u>KIND</u>, charitable,
civil, considerate, cordial,
courteous, friendly, polite,
well-mannered

grade *noun* **1** <u>LEVEL</u>, category, class,
degree, echelon, group, rank,
stage ♦ *verb* **2** <u>CLASSIFY</u>, arrange,
class, group, order, range, rank,
rate, sort

gradient *noun* <u>SLOPE</u>, bank,
declivity, grade, hill, incline, rise

gradual *adjective* <u>STEADY</u>, gentle,
graduated, piecemeal,
progressive, regular, slow,
unhurried

gradually *adverb* <u>STEADILY</u>, by
degrees, gently, little by little,
progressively, slowly, step by step,
unhurriedly

graduate *verb* **1** <u>MARK OFF</u>, calibrate,
grade, measure out, proportion,
regulate **2** <u>CLASSIFY</u>, arrange, grade,
group, order, rank, sort

graft *noun* **1** <u>SHOOT</u>, bud, implant,
scion, splice, sprout ♦ *verb*
2 <u>TRANSPLANT</u>, affix, implant,

ingraft, insert, join, splice

grain *noun* **1** <u>CEREALS</u>, corn **2** <u>SEED</u>,
grist, kernel **3** <u>BIT</u>, fragment,
granule, modicum, morsel,
particle, piece, scrap, speck, trace
4 <u>TEXTURE</u>, fibre, nap, pattern,
surface, weave **5** *As in* **go against
the grain** <u>INCLINATION</u>, character,
disposition, humour, make-up,
temper

grand *adjective* **1** <u>IMPRESSIVE</u>,
dignified, grandiose, great,
imposing, large, magnificent,
regal, splendid, stately, sublime
2 <u>EXCELLENT</u>, fine, first-class, great
(*informal*), outstanding, smashing
(*informal*), splendid, wonderful

grandeur *noun* <u>SPLENDOUR</u>, dignity,
magnificence, majesty, nobility,
pomp, stateliness, sublimity

grandiose *adjective* **1** <u>PRETENTIOUS</u>,
affected, bombastic, extravagant,
flamboyant, high-flown,
ostentatious, pompous, showy
2 <u>IMPOSING</u>, grand, impressive,
lofty, magnificent, majestic,
monumental, stately

grant *verb* **1** <u>CONSENT TO</u>, accede to,
agree to, allow, permit **2** <u>GIVE</u>,
allocate, allot, assign, award,
donate, hand out, present **3** <u>ADMIT</u>,
acknowledge, concede ♦ *noun*
4 <u>AWARD</u>, allowance, donation,
endowment, gift, hand-out,
present, subsidy

granule *noun* <u>GRAIN</u>, atom, crumb,
fragment, molecule, particle,
scrap, speck

graphic *adjective* **1** <u>VIVID</u>, clear,
detailed, explicit, expressive,
lively, lucid, striking **2** <u>PICTORIAL</u>,
diagrammatic, visual

grapple *verb* **1** <u>GRIP</u>, clutch, grab,
grasp, seize, wrestle **2** <u>DEAL WITH</u>,
address oneself to, confront, get
to grips with, struggle, tackle, take
on

grasp *verb* **1** GRIP, catch, clasp, clinch, clutch, grab, grapple, hold, lay *or* take hold of, seize, snatch **2** UNDERSTAND, catch on, catch *or* get the drift of, comprehend, get, realize, see, take in ♦ *noun* **3** GRIP, clasp, clutches, embrace, hold, possession, tenure **4** CONTROL, power, reach, scope **5** UNDERSTANDING, awareness, comprehension, grip, knowledge, mastery

grasping *adjective* GREEDY, acquisitive, avaricious, covetous, rapacious

grate *verb* **1** SHRED, mince, pulverize, triturate **2** SCRAPE, creak, grind, rasp, rub, scratch **3** ANNOY, exasperate, get on one's nerves (*informal*), irritate, jar, rankle, set one's teeth on edge

grateful *adjective* THANKFUL, appreciative, beholden, indebted, obliged

gratification *noun* SATISFACTION, delight, enjoyment, fulfilment, indulgence, pleasure, relish, reward, thrill

gratify *verb* PLEASE, delight, give pleasure, gladden, humour, requite, satisfy

grating[1] *adjective* IRRITATING, annoying, discordant, displeasing, harsh, jarring, offensive, raucous, strident, unpleasant

grating[2] *noun* GRILLE, grate, grid, gridiron, lattice, trellis

gratitude *noun* THANKFULNESS, appreciation, gratefulness, indebtedness, obligation, recognition, thanks

gratuitous *adjective* **1** FREE, complimentary, gratis, spontaneous, unasked-for, unpaid, unrewarded, voluntary **2** UNJUSTIFIED, baseless, causeless, groundless, needless, superfluous, uncalled-for, unmerited, unnecessary, unwarranted, wanton

gratuity *noun* TIP, bonus, donation, gift, largesse *or* largess, reward

grave[1] *noun* BURYING PLACE, crypt, mausoleum, pit, sepulchre, tomb, vault

grave[2] *adjective* **1** SOLEMN, dignified, dour, earnest, serious, sober, sombre, unsmiling **2** IMPORTANT, acute, critical, dangerous, pressing, serious, severe, threatening, urgent

graveyard *noun* CEMETERY, burial ground, charnel house, churchyard, necropolis

gravity *noun* **1** IMPORTANCE, acuteness, momentousness, perilousness, seriousness, severity, significance, urgency, weightiness **2** SOLEMNITY, dignity, earnestness, gravitas, seriousness, sobriety

graze[1] *verb* FEED, browse, crop, pasture

graze[2] *verb* **1** TOUCH, brush, glance off, rub, scrape, shave, skim **2** SCRATCH, abrade, chafe, scrape, skin ♦ *noun* **3** SCRATCH, abrasion, scrape

greasy *adjective* FATTY, oily, oleaginous, slimy, slippery

great *adjective* **1** LARGE, big, enormous, gigantic, huge, immense, prodigious, vast, voluminous **2** IMPORTANT, critical, crucial, momentous, serious, significant **3** FAMOUS, eminent, illustrious, noteworthy, outstanding, prominent, remarkable, renowned **4** *Informal* EXCELLENT, fantastic (*informal*), fine, marvellous (*informal*), superb, terrific (*informal*), tremendous (*informal*), wonderful

greatly *adverb* VERY MUCH, considerably, enormously,

exceedingly, hugely, immensely, remarkably, tremendously, vastly

greatness noun 1 IMMENSITY, enormity, hugeness, magnitude, prodigiousness, size, vastness 2 IMPORTANCE, gravity, momentousness, seriousness, significance, urgency, weight 3 FAME, celebrity, distinction, eminence, glory, grandeur, illustriousness, note, renown

greed, greediness noun 1 GLUTTONY, edacity, esurience, gormandizing, hunger, voracity 2 AVARICE, acquisitiveness, avidity, covetousness, craving, desire, longing, selfishness

greedy adjective 1 GLUTTONOUS, gormandizing, hungry, insatiable, piggish, ravenous, voracious 2 GRASPING, acquisitive, avaricious, avid, covetous, craving, desirous, rapacious, selfish

green adjective 1 LEAFY, grassy, verdant 2 ECOLOGICAL, conservationist, environment-friendly, non-polluting, ozone-friendly 3 IMMATURE, gullible, inexperienced, naive, new, raw, untrained, wet behind the ears (informal) 4 JEALOUS, covetous, envious, grudging, resentful ◆ noun 5 LAWN, common, sward, turf

greet verb WELCOME, accost, address, compliment, hail, meet, receive, salute

greeting noun WELCOME, address, reception, salutation, salute

gregarious adjective OUTGOING, affable, companionable, convivial, cordial, friendly, sociable, social

grey adjective 1 PALE, ashen, pallid, wan 2 DISMAL, dark, depressing, dim, drab, dreary, dull, gloomy 3 CHARACTERLESS, anonymous, colourless, dull

gridlock noun STANDSTILL, deadlock, impasse, stalemate

grief noun SADNESS, anguish, distress, heartache, misery, regret, remorse, sorrow, suffering, woe

grievance noun COMPLAINT, axe to grind, gripe (informal), injury, injustice

grieve verb 1 MOURN, complain, deplore, lament, regret, rue, suffer, weep 2 SADDEN, afflict, distress, hurt, injure, pain, wound

grievous adjective 1 PAINFUL, dreadful, grave, harmful, severe 2 DEPLORABLE, atrocious, dreadful, monstrous, offensive, outrageous, shameful, shocking

grim adjective FORBIDDING, formidable, harsh, merciless, ruthless, severe, sinister, stern, terrible

grimace noun 1 SCOWL, face, frown, sneer ◆ verb 2 SCOWL, frown, lour or lower, make a face or faces, sneer

grime noun DIRT, filth, grot (slang), smut, soot

grimy adjective DIRTY, filthy, foul, grubby, soiled, sooty, unclean

grind verb 1 CRUSH, abrade, granulate, grate, mill, pound, powder, pulverize, triturate 2 SMOOTH, polish, sand, sharpen, whet 3 SCRAPE, gnash, grate ◆ noun 4 Informal HARD WORK, chore, drudgery, labour, sweat (informal), toil

grip noun 1 CLASP, hold 2 CONTROL, clutches, domination, influence, possession, power 3 UNDERSTANDING, command, comprehension, grasp, mastery ◆ verb 4 GRASP, clasp, clutch, hold, seize, take hold of 5 ENGROSS, absorb, enthral, entrance, fascinate, hold, mesmerize, rivet

gripping adjective FASCINATING,

compelling, engrossing, enthralling, entrancing, exciting, riveting, spellbinding, thrilling

grisly *adjective* GRUESOME, appalling, awful, dreadful, ghastly, horrible, macabre, shocking, terrifying

grit *noun* 1 GRAVEL, dust, pebbles, sand 2 COURAGE, backbone, determination, fortitude, guts (*informal*), perseverance, resolution, spirit, tenacity ♦ *verb* 3 GRIND, clench, gnash, grate

gritty *adjective* 1 ROUGH, dusty, granular, gravelly, rasping, sandy 2 COURAGEOUS, brave, determined, dogged, plucky, resolute, spirited, steadfast, tenacious

groan *noun* 1 MOAN, cry, sigh, whine 2 *Informal* COMPLAINT, gripe (*informal*), grouse, grumble, objection, protest ♦ *verb* 3 MOAN, cry, sigh, whine 4 *Informal* COMPLAIN, bemoan, gripe (*informal*), grouse, grumble, lament, object

groggy *adjective* DIZZY, confused, dazed, faint, shaky, unsteady, weak, wobbly

groom *noun* 1 STABLEMAN, hostler *or* ostler (*archaic*), stableboy ♦ *verb* 2 SMARTEN UP, clean, preen, primp, spruce up, tidy 3 RUB DOWN, brush, clean, curry, tend 4 TRAIN, coach, drill, educate, make ready, nurture, prepare, prime, ready

groove *noun* INDENTATION, channel, cut, flute, furrow, hollow, rut, trench, trough

grope *verb* FEEL, cast about, fish, flounder, forage, fumble, scrabble, search

gross *adjective* 1 FAT, corpulent, hulking, obese, overweight 2 TOTAL, aggregate, before deductions, before tax, entire, whole 3 VULGAR, coarse, crude, indelicate, obscene, offensive

4 BLATANT, flagrant, grievous, heinous, rank, sheer, unmitigated, utter ♦ *verb* 5 EARN, bring in, make, rake in (*informal*), take

grotesque *adjective* UNNATURAL, bizarre, deformed, distorted, fantastic, freakish, outlandish, preposterous, strange

ground *noun* 1 EARTH, dry land, land, soil, terra firma, terrain, turf 2 STADIUM, arena, field, park (*informal*), pitch 3 *often plural* LAND, estate, fields, gardens, terrain, territory 4 *usually plural* DREGS, deposit, lees, sediment 5 **grounds** REASON, basis, cause, excuse, foundation, justification, motive, occasion, pretext, rationale ♦ *verb* 6 BASE, establish, fix, found, set, settle 7 INSTRUCT, acquaint with, familiarize with, initiate, teach, train, tutor

groundless *adjective* UNJUSTIFIED, baseless, empty, idle, uncalled-for, unfounded, unwarranted

groundwork *noun* PRELIMINARIES, foundation, fundamentals, preparation, spadework, underpinnings

group *noun* 1 SET, band, bunch, cluster, collection, crowd, gang, pack, party ♦ *verb* 2 ARRANGE, bracket, class, classify, marshal, order, sort

grouse *verb* 1 COMPLAIN, bellyache (*slang*), carp, gripe (*informal*), grumble, moan, whine, whinge (*informal*) ♦ *noun* 2 COMPLAINT, grievance, gripe (*informal*), grouch (*informal*), grumble, moan, objection, protest

grove *noun* WOOD, coppice, copse, covert, plantation, spinney, thicket

grovel *verb* HUMBLE ONESELF, abase oneself, bow and scrape, crawl, creep, cringe, demean oneself, fawn, kowtow, toady

grow verb 1 INCREASE, develop, enlarge, expand, get bigger, multiply, spread, stretch, swell 2 ORIGINATE, arise, issue, spring, stem 3 IMPROVE, advance, flourish, progress, prosper, succeed, thrive 4 BECOME, come to be, get, turn 5 CULTIVATE, breed, farm, nurture, produce, propagate, raise

grown-up adjective 1 MATURE, adult, fully-grown, of age ♦ noun 2 ADULT, man, woman

growth noun 1 INCREASE, development, enlargement, expansion, multiplication, proliferation, stretching 2 IMPROVEMENT, advance, expansion, progress, prosperity, rise, success 3 Medical TUMOUR, lump

grub noun 1 LARVA, caterpillar, maggot 2 Slang FOOD, nosh (slang), rations, sustenance, victuals ♦ verb 3 DIG UP, burrow, pull up, root (informal) 4 SEARCH, ferret, forage, hunt, rummage, scour, uncover, unearth

grubby adjective DIRTY, filthy, grimy, messy, mucky, scruffy, seedy, shabby, sordid, squalid, unwashed

grudge verb 1 RESENT, begrudge, complain, covet, envy, mind ♦ noun 2 RESENTMENT, animosity, antipathy, bitterness, dislike, enmity, grievance, rancour

gruelling adjective EXHAUSTING, arduous, backbreaking, demanding, laborious, punishing, severe, strenuous, taxing, tiring

gruesome adjective HORRIFIC, ghastly, grim, grisly, horrible, macabre, shocking, terrible

gruff adjective 1 SURLY, bad-tempered, brusque, churlish, grumpy, rough, rude, sullen, ungracious 2 HOARSE, croaking, guttural, harsh, husky, low, rasping, rough, throaty

grumble verb 1 COMPLAIN, bleat, carp, gripe (informal), grouch (informal), grouse, moan, whine, whinge (informal) 2 RUMBLE, growl, gurgle, murmur, mutter, roar ♦ noun 3 COMPLAINT, grievance, gripe (informal), grouch (informal), grouse, moan, objection, protest 4 RUMBLE, growl, gurgle, murmur, muttering, roar

grumpy adjective IRRITABLE, cantankerous, crotchety (informal), ill-tempered, peevish, sulky, sullen, surly, testy

guarantee noun 1 ASSURANCE, bond, certainty, pledge, promise, security, surety, warranty, word of honour ♦ verb 2 MAKE CERTAIN, assure, certify, ensure, pledge, promise, secure, vouch for, warrant

guard verb 1 WATCH OVER, defend, mind, preserve, protect, safeguard, secure, shield ♦ noun 2 PROTECTOR, custodian, defender, lookout, picket, sentinel, sentry, warder, watch, watchman 3 PROTECTION, buffer, defence, safeguard, screen, security, shield 4 off guard UNPREPARED, napping, unready, unwary 5 on guard PREPARED, alert, cautious, circumspect, on the alert, on the lookout, ready, vigilant, wary, watchful

guarded adjective CAUTIOUS, cagey (informal), careful, circumspect, noncommittal, prudent, reserved, reticent, suspicious, wary

guardian noun KEEPER, champion, curator, custodian, defender, guard, protector, warden

guerrilla noun FREEDOM FIGHTER, partisan, underground fighter

guess verb 1 ESTIMATE, conjecture, hypothesize, predict, speculate, work out 2 SUPPOSE, believe, conjecture, fancy, imagine, judge,

reckon, suspect, think ♦ *noun*
3 <small>PREDICTION,</small> conjecture,
hypothesis, shot in the dark,
speculation, supposition, theory

guesswork *noun* <small>SPECULATION,</small>
conjecture, estimation,
supposition, surmise, theory

guest *noun* <small>VISITOR,</small> boarder, caller,
company, lodger, visitant

guidance *noun* <small>ADVICE,</small> counselling,
direction, help, instruction,
leadership, management, teaching

guide *noun* **1** <small>ESCORT,</small> adviser,
conductor, counsellor, leader,
mentor, teacher, usher **2** <small>MODEL,</small>
example, ideal, inspiration,
paradigm, standard **3** <small>POINTER,</small>
beacon, guiding light, landmark,
lodestar, marker, sign, signpost
4 <small>GUIDEBOOK,</small> Baedeker, catalogue,
directory, handbook, instructions,
key, manual ♦ *verb* **5** <small>LEAD,</small>
accompany, conduct, direct,
escort, shepherd, show the way,
usher **6** <small>STEER,</small> command, control,
direct, handle, manage,
manoeuvre **7** <small>SUPERVISE,</small> advise,
counsel, influence, instruct,
oversee, superintend, teach, train

guild *noun* <small>SOCIETY,</small> association,
brotherhood, club, company,
corporation, fellowship, fraternity,
league, lodge, order,
organization, union

guile *noun* <small>CUNNING,</small> artifice,
cleverness, craft, deceit, slyness,
trickery, wiliness

guilt *noun* **1** <small>CULPABILITY,</small> blame,
guiltiness, misconduct,
responsibility, sinfulness,
wickedness, wrongdoing
2 <small>REMORSE,</small> contrition, guilty
conscience, regret, self-reproach,
shame, stigma

guiltless *adjective* <small>INNOCENT,</small>
blameless, clean (*slang*),
irreproachable, pure, sinless,
spotless, squeaky-clean, untainted

guilty *adjective* **1** <small>RESPONSIBLE,</small> at
fault, blameworthy, culpable,
reprehensible, sinful, to blame,
wrong **2** <small>REMORSEFUL,</small> ashamed,
conscience-stricken, contrite,
regretful, rueful, shamefaced,
sheepish, sorry

guise *noun* <small>FORM,</small> appearance,
aspect, demeanour, disguise,
mode, pretence, semblance, shape

gulf *noun* **1** <small>BAY,</small> bight, sea inlet
2 <small>CHASM,</small> abyss, gap, opening, rift,
separation, split, void

gullibility *noun* <small>CREDULITY,</small>
innocence, naïveté, simplicity

gullible *adjective* <small>NAIVE,</small> born
yesterday, credulous, innocent,
simple, trusting, unsuspecting,
wet behind the ears (*informal*)

gully *noun* <small>CHANNEL,</small> ditch, gutter,
watercourse

gulp *verb* **1** <small>SWALLOW,</small> devour,
gobble, guzzle, quaff, swig
(*informal*), swill, wolf **2** <small>GASP,</small>
choke, swallow ♦ *noun* **3** <small>SWALLOW,</small>
draught, mouthful, swig (*informal*)

gum *noun* **1** <small>GLUE,</small> adhesive,
cement, paste, resin ♦ *verb* **2** <small>STICK,</small>
affix, cement, glue, paste

gumption *noun* <small>RESOURCEFULNESS,</small>
acumen, astuteness, common
sense, enterprise, initiative,
mother wit, savvy (*slang*), wit(s)

gun *noun* <small>FIREARM,</small> handgun, piece
(*slang*), shooter (*slang*)

gunman *noun* <small>TERRORIST,</small> bandit,
gunslinger (*U.S. slang*), killer

gurgle *verb* **1** <small>MURMUR,</small> babble,
bubble, lap, plash, purl, ripple,
splash ♦ *noun* **2** <small>MURMUR,</small> babble,
purl, ripple

guru *noun* <small>TEACHER,</small> authority,
leader, master, mentor, sage,
Svengali, tutor

gush *verb* **1** <small>FLOW,</small> cascade, flood,
pour, run, rush, spout, spurt,

stream 2 ENTHUSE, babble, chatter, effervesce, effuse, overstate, spout ♦ noun 3 STREAM, cascade, flood, flow, jet, rush, spout, spurt, torrent

gust noun 1 BLAST, blow, breeze, puff, rush, squall ♦ verb 2 BLOW, blast, squall

gusto noun RELISH, delight, enjoyment, enthusiasm, fervour, pleasure, verve, zeal

gut noun 1 Informal PAUNCH, belly, potbelly, spare tyre (Brit. slang) 2 guts: a INTESTINES, belly, bowels, entrails, innards (informal), insides (informal), stomach, viscera b Informal COURAGE, audacity, backbone, bottle (slang), daring, mettle, nerve, pluck, spirit ♦ verb 3 DISEMBOWEL, clean 4 RAVAGE, clean out, despoil, empty ♦ adjective 5 As in gut reaction INSTINCTIVE, basic, heartfelt, intuitive,

involuntary, natural, spontaneous, unthinking, visceral

gutsy adjective BRAVE, bold, courageous, determined, gritty, indomitable, plucky, resolute, spirited

gutter noun DRAIN, channel, conduit, ditch, sluice, trench, trough

guttural adjective THROATY, deep, gravelly, gruff, hoarse, husky, rasping, rough, thick

guy noun Informal MAN, bloke (Brit. informal), chap, fellow, lad, person

guzzle verb DEVOUR, bolt, cram, drink, gobble, stuff (oneself), swill, wolf

Gypsy, Gipsy noun TRAVELLER, Bohemian, nomad, rambler, roamer, Romany, rover, wanderer

H h

habit *noun* **1** MANNERISM, custom, practice, proclivity, propensity, quirk, tendency, way **2** ADDICTION, dependence

habitation *noun* **1** DWELLING, abode, domicile, home, house, living quarters, lodging, quarters, residence **2** OCCUPANCY, inhabitance, occupation, tenancy

habitual *adjective* CUSTOMARY, accustomed, familiar, normal, regular, routine, standard, traditional, usual

hack[1] *verb* CUT, chop, hew, lacerate, mangle, mutilate, slash

hack[2] *noun* **1** SCRIBBLER, literary hack, penny-a-liner **2** HORSE, crock, nag

hackneyed *adjective* UNORIGINAL, clichéd, commonplace, overworked, stale, stereotyped, stock, threadbare, tired, trite

hag *noun* WITCH, crone, harridan

haggard *adjective* GAUNT, careworn, drawn, emaciated, pinched, thin, wan

haggle *verb* BARGAIN, barter, beat down

hail[1] *noun* **1** BOMBARDMENT, barrage, downpour, rain, shower, storm, volley ♦ *verb* **2** RAIN DOWN ON, batter, beat down upon, bombard, pelt, rain, shower

hail[2] *verb* **1** GREET, acclaim, acknowledge, applaud, cheer, honour, salute, welcome **2** FLAG DOWN, signal to, wave down **3 hail from** COME FROM, be a native of, be born in, originate in

hair *noun* LOCKS, head of hair, mane, mop, shock, tresses

hairdresser *noun* STYLIST, barber, coiffeur *or* coiffeuse

hair-raising *adjective* FRIGHTENING, alarming, bloodcurdling, horrifying, scary, shocking, spine-chilling, terrifying

hairstyle *noun* HAIRCUT, coiffure, cut, hairdo, style

hairy *adjective* **1** SHAGGY, bushy, furry, hirsute, stubbly, unshaven, woolly **2** *Slang* DANGEROUS, difficult, hazardous, perilous, risky

halcyon *adjective* **1** PEACEFUL, calm, gentle, quiet, serene, tranquil, undisturbed **2** *As in* **halcyon days** HAPPY, carefree, flourishing, golden, palmy, prosperous

hale *adjective* HEALTHY, able-bodied, fit, flourishing, in the pink, robust, sound, strong, vigorous, well

half *noun* **1** EQUAL PART, fifty per cent, hemisphere, portion, section ♦ *adjective* **2** PARTIAL, halved, limited, moderate ♦ *adverb* **3** PARTIALLY, in part, partly

half-baked *adjective* ILL-JUDGED, ill-conceived, impractical, poorly planned, short-sighted, unformed, unthought out *or* through

half-hearted *adjective* UNENTHUSIASTIC, apathetic, indifferent, lacklustre, listless, lukewarm, perfunctory, tame

halfway *adverb* **1** MIDWAY, to *or* in the middle ♦ *adjective* **2** MIDWAY, central, equidistant, intermediate, mid, middle

halfwit *noun* FOOL, airhead (*slang*), dunderhead, idiot, imbecile (*informal*), moron, numbskull *or* numskull, simpleton, twit (*informal, chiefly Brit.*)

hall *noun* **1** ENTRANCE HALL, corridor, entry, foyer, hallway, lobby, passage, passageway, vestibule

2 MEETING PLACE, assembly room, auditorium, chamber, concert hall

hallmark noun **1** SEAL, device, endorsement, mark, sign, stamp, symbol **2** INDICATION, sure sign, telltale sign

hallucination noun ILLUSION, apparition, delusion, dream, fantasy, figment of the imagination, mirage, vision

halo noun RING OF LIGHT, aura, corona, nimbus, radiance

halt verb **1** STOP, break off, cease, come to an end, desist, rest, stand still, wait **2** END, block, bring to an end, check, curb, cut short, nip in the bud, terminate ♦ noun **3** STOP, close, end, pause, standstill, stoppage

halting adjective FALTERING, awkward, hesitant, laboured, stammering, stumbling, stuttering

halve verb BISECT, cut in half, divide equally, share equally, split in two

hammer verb **1** HIT, bang, beat, drive, knock, strike, tap **2** Informal DEFEAT, beat, drub, run rings around (informal), thrash, trounce, wipe the floor with (informal)

hamper verb HINDER, frustrate, hamstring, handicap, impede, interfere with, obstruct, prevent, restrict

hand noun **1** PALM, fist, mitt (slang), paw (informal) **2** HIRED MAN, artisan, craftsman, employee, labourer, operative, worker, workman **3** PENMANSHIP, calligraphy, handwriting, script **4** OVATION, clap, round of applause **5** **at** or **on hand** NEARBY, at one's fingertips, available, close, handy, near, ready, within reach ♦ verb **6** PASS, deliver, hand over

handbook noun GUIDEBOOK, Baedeker, guide, instruction book, manual

handcuff verb SHACKLE, fetter, manacle

handcuffs plural noun SHACKLES, cuffs (informal), fetters, manacles

handful noun FEW, small number, smattering, sprinkling

handicap noun **1** DISADVANTAGE, barrier, drawback, hindrance, impediment, limitation, obstacle, restriction, stumbling block **2** ADVANTAGE, head start **3** DISABILITY, defect, impairment ♦ verb **4** RESTRICT, burden, encumber, hamper, hamstring, hinder, hold back, impede, limit

handicraft noun CRAFTSMANSHIP, art, craft, handiwork, skill, workmanship

handiwork noun CREATION, achievement, design, invention, product, production

handle noun **1** GRIP, haft, hilt, stock ♦ verb **2** HOLD, feel, finger, grasp, pick up, touch **3** CONTROL, direct, guide, manage, manipulate, manoeuvre **4** DEAL WITH, cope with, manage

hand-out noun **1** CHARITY, alms, dole **2** LEAFLET, bulletin, circular, literature (informal), mailshot, press release

handsome adjective **1** GOOD-LOOKING, attractive, comely, dishy (informal, chiefly Brit.), elegant, gorgeous, personable, well-proportioned **2** LARGE, abundant, ample, considerable, generous, liberal, plentiful, sizable or sizeable

handwriting noun PENMANSHIP, calligraphy, hand, scrawl, script

handy adjective **1** AVAILABLE, accessible, at hand, at one's fingertips, close, convenient, nearby, on hand, within reach **2** USEFUL, convenient, easy to use, helpful, manageable, neat, practical, serviceable, user-friendly **3** SKILFUL, adept, adroit, deft, dexterous, expert, proficient, skilled

hang verb **1** SUSPEND, dangle, droop **2** EXECUTE, lynch, string up (*informal*) ♦ noun **3 get the hang of** GRASP, comprehend, understand

hang back verb HESITATE, be reluctant, demur, hold back, recoil

hangdog adjective GUILTY, cowed, cringing, defeated, downcast, furtive, shamefaced, wretched

hangover noun AFTEREFFECTS, crapulence, morning after (*informal*)

hang-up noun PREOCCUPATION, block, difficulty, inhibition, obsession, problem, thing (*informal*)

hank noun COIL, length, loop, piece, roll, skein

hanker verb, with *for* or *after* DESIRE, crave, hunger, itch, long, lust, pine, thirst, yearn

haphazard adjective DISORGANIZED, aimless, casual, hit or miss (*informal*), indiscriminate, slapdash

happen verb **1** OCCUR, come about, come to pass, develop, result, take place, transpire (*informal*) **2** CHANCE, turn out

happening noun EVENT, affair, episode, experience, incident, occurrence, proceeding

happily adverb **1** WILLINGLY, freely, gladly, with pleasure **2** JOYFULLY, blithely, cheerfully, gaily, gleefully, joyously, merrily **3** LUCKILY, fortunately, opportunely, providentially

happiness noun JOY, bliss, cheerfulness, contentment, delight, ecstasy, elation, jubilation, pleasure, satisfaction

happy adjective **1** JOYFUL, blissful, cheerful, content, delighted, ecstatic, elated, glad, jubilant, merry, overjoyed, pleased, thrilled **2** FORTUNATE, advantageous, auspicious, favourable, lucky, timely

happy-go-lucky adjective CAREFREE, blithe, easy-going, light-hearted, nonchalant, unconcerned, untroubled

harangue verb **1** RANT, address, declaim, exhort, hold forth, lecture, spout (*informal*) ♦ noun **2** SPEECH, address, declamation, diatribe, exhortation, tirade

harass verb ANNOY, bother, harry, hassle (*informal*), hound, persecute, pester, plague, trouble, vex

harassed adjective WORRIED, careworn, distraught, hassled (*informal*), strained, tormented, troubled, under pressure, vexed

harassment noun TROUBLE, annoyance, bother, hassle (*informal*), irritation, nuisance, persecution, pestering

harbour noun **1** PORT, anchorage, haven ♦ verb **2** SHELTER, hide, protect, provide refuge, shield **3** MAINTAIN, cling to, entertain, foster, hold, nurse, nurture, retain

hard adjective **1** SOLID, firm, inflexible, rigid, rocklike, stiff, strong, tough, unyielding **2** STRENUOUS, arduous, backbreaking, exacting, exhausting, laborious, rigorous, tough **3** DIFFICULT, complicated, intricate, involved, knotty, perplexing, puzzling, thorny **4** UNFEELING, callous, cold, cruel, hardhearted, pitiless, stern, unkind, unsympathetic **5** PAINFUL, disagreeable, distressing, grievous, intolerable, unpleasant ♦ adverb **6** ENERGETICALLY, fiercely, forcefully, forcibly, heavily, intensely, powerfully, severely, sharply, strongly, vigorously, violently, with all one's might, with might and main **7** DILIGENTLY, doggedly, industriously, persistently, steadily, untiringly

hard-bitten or **hard-boiled** adjective TOUGH, cynical, hard-nosed (informal), matter-of-fact, practical, realistic, unsentimental

harden verb **1** SOLIDIFY, anneal, bake, cake, freeze, set, stiffen **2** ACCUSTOM, habituate, inure, season, train

hardened adjective **1** HABITUAL, chronic, incorrigible, inveterate, shameless **2** ACCUSTOMED, habituated, inured, seasoned, toughened

hard-headed adjective SENSIBLE, level-headed, practical, pragmatic, realistic, shrewd, tough, unsentimental

hardhearted adjective UNSYMPATHETIC, callous, cold, hard, heartless, insensitive, uncaring, unfeeling

hardiness noun RESILIENCE, resolution, robustness, ruggedness, sturdiness, toughness

hardly adverb BARELY, just, only just, scarcely, with difficulty

hardship noun SUFFERING, adversity, difficulty, misfortune, need, privation, tribulation

hard up adjective POOR, broke (informal), impecunious, impoverished, on the breadline, out of pocket, penniless, short, skint (Brit. slang), strapped for cash (informal)

hardy adjective STRONG, robust, rugged, sound, stout, sturdy, tough

harm verb **1** INJURE, abuse, damage, hurt, ill-treat, maltreat, ruin, spoil,

wound ♦ noun **2** INJURY, abuse, damage, hurt, ill, loss, mischief, misfortune

harmful adjective DESTRUCTIVE, damaging, deleterious, detrimental, hurtful, injurious, noxious, pernicious

harmless adjective INNOCUOUS, gentle, innocent, inoffensive, nontoxic, safe, unobjectionable

harmonious adjective **1** MELODIOUS, agreeable, concordant, consonant, dulcet, mellifluous, musical, sweet-sounding, tuneful **2** FRIENDLY, agreeable, amicable, compatible, congenial, cordial, sympathetic

harmonize verb BLEND, chime with, cohere, coordinate, correspond, match, tally, tone in with

harmony noun **1** AGREEMENT, accord, amicability, compatibility, concord, cooperation, friendship, peace, rapport, sympathy **2** TUNEFULNESS, euphony, melody, tune, unison

harness noun **1** EQUIPMENT, gear, tack, tackle ♦ verb **2** EXPLOIT, channel, control, employ, mobilize, utilize

harrowing adjective DISTRESSING, agonizing, disturbing, heart-rending, nerve-racking, painful, terrifying, tormenting, traumatic

harry verb PESTER, badger, bother, chivvy, harass, hassle (informal), molest, plague

harsh adjective **1** RAUCOUS, discordant, dissonant, grating, guttural, rasping, rough, strident **2** SEVERE, austere, cruel, Draconian, drastic, pitiless, punitive, ruthless, stern

harshly adverb SEVERELY, brutally, cruelly, roughly, sternly, strictly

harshness noun SEVERITY, asperity,

austerity, brutality, rigour,
roughness, sternness

harvest *noun* 1 CROP, produce,
yield ♦ *verb* 2 GATHER, mow, pick,
pluck, reap

hash *noun* **make a hash of**
Informal MESS UP, botch, bungle,
make a pig's ear of (*informal*),
mishandle, mismanage, muddle

hassle *noun* 1 ARGUMENT, bickering,
disagreement, dispute, fight,
quarrel, row, squabble 2 TROUBLE,
bother, difficulty, grief (*informal*),
inconvenience, problem ♦ *verb*
3 BOTHER, annoy, badger, bug
(*informal*), harass, hound, pester

haste *noun* 1 SPEED, alacrity,
quickness, rapidity, swiftness,
urgency, velocity 2 RUSH, hurry,
hustle, impetuosity

hasten *verb* RUSH, dash, fly, hurry
(up), make haste, race, scurry,
speed

hastily *adverb* 1 SPEEDILY, promptly,
quickly, rapidly 2 HURRIEDLY,
impetuously, precipitately, rashly

hasty *adjective* 1 SPEEDY, brisk,
hurried, prompt, rapid, swift,
urgent 2 IMPETUOUS, impulsive,
precipitate, rash, thoughtless

hatch *verb* 1 INCUBATE, breed, bring
forth, brood 2 DEVISE, conceive,
concoct, contrive, cook up
(*informal*), design, dream up
(*informal*), think up

hate *verb* 1 DETEST, abhor, despise,
dislike, loathe, recoil from 2 BE
UNWILLING, be loath, be reluctant,
be sorry, dislike, feel disinclined,
shrink from ♦ *noun* 3 DISLIKE,
animosity, antipathy, aversion,
detestation, enmity, hatred,
hostility, loathing

hateful *adjective* DESPICABLE,
abhorrent, detestable, horrible,
loathsome, obnoxious, odious,
offensive, repellent, repugnant,

repulsive

hatred *noun* DISLIKE, animosity,
antipathy, aversion, detestation,
enmity, hate, repugnance,
revulsion

haughty *adjective* PROUD, arrogant,
conceited, contemptuous,
disdainful, imperious, scornful,
snooty (*informal*), stuck-up
(*informal*), supercilious

haul *verb* 1 DRAG, draw, heave, lug,
pull, tug ♦ *noun* 2 GAIN, booty,
catch, harvest, loot, spoils,
takings, yield

haunt *verb* 1 PLAGUE, obsess,
possess, prey on, recur, stay with,
torment, trouble, weigh on ♦ *noun*
2 MEETING PLACE, hangout
(*informal*), rendezvous, stamping
ground

haunted *adjective* 1 POSSESSED,
cursed, eerie, ghostly, jinxed,
spooky (*informal*) 2 PREOCCUPIED,
obsessed, plagued, tormented,
troubled, worried

haunting *adjective* POIGNANT,
evocative, nostalgic, persistent,
unforgettable

have *verb* 1 POSSESS, hold, keep,
obtain, own, retain 2 RECEIVE,
accept, acquire, gain, get, obtain,
procure, secure, take 3 EXPERIENCE,
endure, enjoy, feel, meet with,
suffer, sustain, undergo 4 *Slang*
CHEAT, deceive, dupe, fool, outwit,
swindle, take in (*informal*), trick
5 GIVE BIRTH TO, bear, bring forth,
deliver 6 **have to** BE OBLIGED, be
bound, be compelled, be forced,
have got to, must, ought, should

haven *noun* SANCTUARY, asylum,
refuge, retreat, sanctum, shelter

have on *verb* 1 WEAR, be clothed in,
be dressed in 2 TEASE, deceive, kid
(*informal*), pull someone's leg,
take the mickey, trick, wind up
(*Brit. slang*)

havoc noun DISORDER, chaos, confusion, disruption, mayhem, shambles

haywire adjective As in **go haywire** TOPSY-TURVY, chaotic, confused, disordered, disorganized, mixed up, out of order, shambolic (*informal*)

hazard noun 1 DANGER, jeopardy, peril, pitfall, risk, threat ♦ verb 2 JEOPARDIZE, endanger, expose, imperil, risk, threaten 3 As in **hazard a guess** CONJECTURE, advance, offer, presume, throw out, venture, volunteer

hazardous adjective DANGEROUS, dicey (*informal, chiefly Brit.*), difficult, insecure, perilous, precarious, risky, unsafe

haze noun MIST, cloud, fog, obscurity, vapour

hazy adjective 1 MISTY, cloudy, dim, dull, foggy, overcast 2 VAGUE, fuzzy, ill-defined, indefinite, indistinct, muddled, nebulous, uncertain, unclear

head noun 1 SKULL, crown, loaf (*slang*), nut (*slang*), pate 2 LEADER, boss (*informal*), captain, chief, commander, director, manager, master, principal, supervisor 3 TOP, crest, crown, peak, pinnacle, summit, tip 4 BRAIN, brains (*informal*), intellect, intelligence, mind, thought, understanding 5 **go to one's head** EXCITE, intoxicate, make conceited, puff up 6 **head over heels** UNCONTROLLABLY, completely, intensely, thoroughly, utterly, wholeheartedly ♦ adjective 7 CHIEF, arch, first, leading, main, pre-eminent, premier, prime, principal, supreme ♦ verb 8 LEAD, be or go first, cap, crown, lead the way, precede, top 9 CONTROL, be in charge of, command, direct, govern, guide, lead, manage, run 10 MAKE FOR, aim, go to, make a

beeline for, point, set off for, set out, start towards, steer, turn

headache noun 1 MIGRAINE, head (*informal*), neuralgia 2 PROBLEM, bane, bother, inconvenience, nuisance, trouble, vexation, worry

heading noun TITLE, caption, headline, name, rubric

headlong adverb, adjective 1 HEADFIRST, head-on ♦ adverb 2 HASTILY, heedlessly, helter-skelter, hurriedly, pell-mell, precipitately, rashly, thoughtlessly ♦ adjective 3 HASTY, breakneck, dangerous, impetuous, impulsive, inconsiderate, precipitate, reckless, thoughtless

headstrong adjective OBSTINATE, foolhardy, heedless, impulsive, perverse, pig-headed, self-willed, stubborn, unruly, wilful

headway noun PROGRESS, advance, improvement, progression, way

heady adjective 1 INEBRIATING, intoxicating, potent, strong 2 EXCITING, exhilarating, intoxicating, stimulating, thrilling 3 HASTY, impetuous, rash

heal verb CURE, make well, mend, regenerate, remedy, restore, treat

health noun 1 WELLBEING, fitness, good condition, healthiness, robustness, soundness, strength, vigour 2 CONDITION, constitution, fettle, shape, state

healthy adjective 1 WELL, active, fit, hale and hearty, in fine fettle, in good shape (*informal*), in the pink, robust, strong 2 WHOLESOME, beneficial, hygienic, invigorating, nourishing, nutritious, salubrious, salutary

heap noun 1 PILE, accumulation, collection, hoard, lot, mass, mound, stack 2 often plural A LOT, great deal, load(s) (*informal*), lots (*informal*), mass, plenty, pot(s) (*informal*), stack(s), tons ♦ *verb* **3** PILE, accumulate, amass, collect, gather, hoard, stack **4** CONFER, assign, bestow, load, shower upon

hear *verb* **1** LISTEN TO, catch, overhear **2** LEARN, ascertain, discover, find out, gather, get wind of (*informal*), pick up **3** *Law* TRY, examine, investigate, judge

hearing *noun* INQUIRY, industrial tribunal, investigation, review, trial

hearsay *noun* RUMOUR, gossip, idle talk, report, talk, tittle-tattle, word of mouth

heart *noun* **1** NATURE, character, disposition, soul, temperament **2** BRAVERY, courage, fortitude, pluck, purpose, resolution, spirit, will **3** CENTRE, core, hub, middle, nucleus, quintessence **4 by heart** BY MEMORY, by rote, off pat, parrot-fashion (*informal*), pat, word for word

heartache *noun* SORROW, agony, anguish, despair, distress, grief, heartbreak, pain, remorse, suffering, torment, torture

heartbreak *noun* GRIEF, anguish, desolation, despair, misery, pain, sorrow, suffering

heartbreaking *adjective* TRAGIC, agonizing, distressing, harrowing, heart-rending, pitiful, poignant, sad

heartbroken *adjective* MISERABLE, brokenhearted, crushed, desolate, despondent, disconsolate, dispirited, heartsick

heartfelt *adjective* SINCERE, deep, devout, earnest, genuine, honest, profound, unfeigned, wholehearted

heartily *adverb* ENTHUSIASTICALLY, eagerly, earnestly, resolutely, vigorously, zealously

heartless *adjective* CRUEL, callous, cold, hard, hardhearted, merciless, pitiless, uncaring, unfeeling

heart-rending *adjective* MOVING, affecting, distressing, harrowing, heartbreaking, poignant, sad, tragic

hearty *adjective* **1** FRIENDLY, back-slapping, ebullient, effusive, enthusiastic, genial, jovial, warm **2** SUBSTANTIAL, ample, filling, nourishing, sizable *or* sizeable, solid, square

heat *verb* **1** WARM UP, make hot, reheat ♦ *noun* **2** HOTNESS, high temperature, warmth **3** INTENSITY, excitement, fervour, fury, passion, vehemence

heated *adjective* ANGRY, excited, fierce, frenzied, furious, impassioned, intense, passionate, stormy, vehement

heathen *noun* **1** UNBELIEVER, infidel, pagan ♦ *adjective* **2** PAGAN, godless, idolatrous, irreligious

heave *verb* **1** LIFT, drag (up), haul (up), hoist, pull (up), raise, tug **2** THROW, cast, fling, hurl, pitch, send, sling, toss **3** SIGH, groan, puff **4** VOMIT, be sick, gag, retch, spew, throw up (*informal*)

heaven *noun* **1** PARADISE, bliss, Elysium *or* Elysian fields (*Greek myth*), hereafter, life everlasting, next world, nirvana (*Buddhism, Hinduism*), Zion (*Christianity*) **2** HAPPINESS, bliss, ecstasy, paradise, rapture, seventh heaven, utopia **3 the heavens** SKY, ether, firmament

heavenly *adjective* **1** BEAUTIFUL, blissful, delightful, divine (*informal*), exquisite, lovely, ravishing, sublime, wonderful **2** CELESTIAL, angelic, blessed, divine, holy, immortal

heavily *adverb* **1** PONDEROUSLY,

awkwardly, clumsily, weightily
2 DENSELY, closely, compactly,
thickly 3 CONSIDERABLY, a great deal,
copiously, excessively, to excess,
very much

heaviness noun WEIGHT, gravity,
heftiness, ponderousness

heavy adjective 1 WEIGHTY, bulky,
hefty, massive, ponderous
2 CONSIDERABLE, abundant, copious,
excessive, large, profuse

heckle verb JEER, barrack (informal),
boo, disrupt, interrupt, shout
down, taunt

hectic adjective FRANTIC, animated,
chaotic, feverish, frenetic, heated,
turbulent

hedge noun 1 BARRIER, boundary,
screen, windbreak ♦ verb 2 DODGE,
duck, equivocate, evade, flannel
(Brit. informal), prevaricate,
sidestep, temporize 3 INSURE,
cover, guard, protect, safeguard,
shield

heed noun 1 CARE, attention,
caution, mind, notice, regard,
respect, thought ♦ verb 2 PAY
ATTENTION TO, bear in mind,
consider, follow, listen to, note,
obey, observe, take notice of

heedless adjective CARELESS,
foolhardy, inattentive, oblivious,
thoughtless, unmindful

heel noun Slang SWINE, bounder
(old-fashioned Brit. slang), cad
(Brit. informal), rotter (slang,
chiefly Brit.)

heel over verb LEAN OVER, keel over,
list, tilt

hefty adjective STRONG, big, burly,
hulking, massive, muscular,
robust, strapping

height noun 1 ALTITUDE, elevation,
highness, loftiness, stature,
tallness 2 PEAK, apex, crest, crown,
pinnacle, summit, top, zenith
3 CULMINATION, climax, limit,

maximum, ultimate

heighten verb INTENSIFY, add to,
amplify, enhance, improve,
increase, magnify, sharpen,
strengthen

heir noun SUCCESSOR, beneficiary,
heiress (fem.), inheritor, next in
line

hell noun 1 UNDERWORLD, abyss, fire
and brimstone, Hades (Greek
myth), hellfire, inferno, nether
world 2 TORMENT, agony, anguish,
misery, nightmare, ordeal,
suffering, wretchedness

hellish adjective DEVILISH, damnable,
diabolical, fiendish, infernal

hello interjection WELCOME, good
afternoon, good evening, good
morning, greetings

helm noun 1 TILLER, rudder, wheel
2 **at the helm** IN CHARGE, at the
wheel, in command, in control, in
the driving seat, in the saddle

help verb 1 AID, abet, assist,
cooperate, lend a hand, succour,
support 2 IMPROVE, alleviate,
ameliorate, ease, facilitate,
mitigate, relieve 3 REFRAIN FROM,
avoid, keep from, prevent, resist
♦ noun 4 ASSISTANCE, advice, aid,
cooperation, guidance, helping
hand, support

helper noun ASSISTANT, adjutant,
aide, ally, attendant, collaborator,
helpmate, mate, right-hand man,
second, supporter

helpful adjective 1 USEFUL,
advantageous, beneficial,
constructive, practical, profitable,
timely 2 COOPERATIVE,
accommodating, considerate,
friendly, kind, neighbourly,
supportive, sympathetic

helping noun PORTION, dollop
(informal), piece, plateful, ration,
serving

helpless adjective WEAK, disabled,

impotent, incapable, infirm,
paralysed, powerless

helter-skelter *adjective*
1 HAPHAZARD, confused, disordered,
higgledy-piggledy (*informal*),
hit-or-miss, jumbled, muddled,
random, topsy-turvy ♦ *adverb*
2 CARELESSLY, anyhow, hastily,
headlong, hurriedly, pell-mell,
rashly, recklessly, wildly

hem *noun* **1** EDGE, border, fringe,
margin, trimming ♦ *verb* **2 hem in**
SURROUND, beset, circumscribe,
confine, enclose, restrict, shut in

hence *conjunction* THEREFORE, ergo,
for this reason, on that account,
thus

henchman *noun* ATTENDANT,
associate, bodyguard, follower,
minder (*slang*), right-hand man,
sidekick (*slang*), subordinate,
supporter

henpecked *adjective* BULLIED,
browbeaten, dominated, meek,
subjugated, timid

herald *noun* **1** MESSENGER, crier
2 FORERUNNER, harbinger,
indication, omen, precursor, sign,
signal, token ♦ *verb* **3** INDICATE,
foretoken, portend, presage,
promise, show, usher in

herd *noun* **1** MULTITUDE, collection,
crowd, drove, flock, horde, mass,
mob, swarm, throng ♦ *verb*
2 CONGREGATE, assemble, collect,
flock, gather, huddle, muster, rally

hereafter *adverb* **1** IN FUTURE, from
now on, hence, henceforth,
henceforward ♦ *noun* **2** AFTERLIFE,
life after death, next world

hereditary *adjective* **1** GENETIC,
inborn, inbred, inheritable,
transmissible **2** INHERITED, ancestral,
traditional

heredity *noun* GENETICS,
constitution, genetic make-up,
inheritance

heresy *noun* DISSIDENCE, apostasy,
heterodoxy, iconoclasm,
unorthodoxy

heretic *noun* DISSIDENT, apostate,
dissenter, nonconformist,
renegade, revisionist

heretical *adjective* UNORTHODOX,
heterodox, iconoclastic,
idolatrous, impious, revisionist

heritage *noun* INHERITANCE, bequest,
birthright, endowment, legacy,
tradition

hermit *noun* RECLUSE, anchorite,
eremite, loner (*informal*), monk

hero *noun* **1** IDOL, champion,
conqueror, star, superstar, victor
2 LEADING MAN, protagonist

heroic *adjective* COURAGEOUS, brave,
daring, fearless, gallant, intrepid,
lion-hearted, valiant

heroine *noun* LEADING LADY, diva,
prima donna, protagonist

heroism *noun* BRAVERY, courage,
courageousness, fearlessness,
gallantry, intrepidity, spirit, valour

hesitant *adjective* UNCERTAIN,
diffident, doubtful, half-hearted,
halting, irresolute, reluctant,
unsure, vacillating, wavering

hesitate *verb* **1** WAVER, delay, dither
(*chiefly Brit.*), doubt, hum and
haw, pause, vacillate, wait **2** BE
RELUCTANT, balk, be unwilling,
demur, hang back, scruple, shrink
from, think twice

hesitation *noun* **1** INDECISION, delay,
doubt, hesitancy, irresolution,
uncertainty, vacillation
2 RELUCTANCE, misgiving(s),
qualm(s), scruple(s), unwillingness

hew *verb* **1** CUT, axe, chop, hack,
lop, split **2** CARVE, fashion, form,
make, model, sculpt, sculpture,
shape, smooth

heyday *noun* PRIME, bloom, pink,
prime of life, salad days

hiatus noun PAUSE, break, discontinuity, gap, interruption, interval, respite, space

hidden adjective CONCEALED, clandestine, covert, latent, secret, under wraps, unseen, veiled

hide[1] verb 1 CONCEAL, secrete, stash (informal) 2 GO INTO HIDING, go to ground, go underground, hole up, lie low, take cover 3 DISGUISE, camouflage, cloak, conceal, cover, mask, obscure, shroud, veil 4 SUPPRESS, draw a veil over, hush up, keep dark, keep secret, keep under one's hat, withhold

hide[2] noun SKIN, pelt

hidebound adjective CONVENTIONAL, narrow-minded, rigid, set in one's ways, strait-laced, ultraconservative

hideous adjective UGLY, ghastly, grim, grisly, grotesque, gruesome, monstrous, repulsive, revolting, unsightly

hide-out noun HIDEAWAY, den, hiding place, lair, shelter

hiding noun BEATING, drubbing, licking (informal), spanking, thrashing, walloping (informal), whipping

hierarchy noun GRADING, pecking order, ranking

high adjective 1 TALL, elevated, lofty, soaring, steep, towering 2 EXTREME, excessive, extraordinary, great, intensified, sharp, strong 3 IMPORTANT, arch, chief, eminent, exalted, powerful, superior 4 Informal INTOXICATED, stoned (slang), tripping (informal) 5 HIGH-PITCHED, acute, penetrating, piercing, piping, sharp, shrill, strident ♦ adverb 6 ALOFT, at great height, far up, way up

highbrow noun 1 INTELLECTUAL, aesthete, egghead (informal), scholar ♦ adjective 2 INTELLECTUAL, bookish, cultivated, cultured, sophisticated

high-flown adjective EXTRAVAGANT, elaborate, exaggerated, florid, grandiose, inflated, lofty, overblown, pretentious

high-handed adjective DICTATORIAL, despotic, domineering, imperious, oppressive, overbearing, tyrannical, wilful

highlight noun 1 FEATURE, climax, focal point, focus, high point, high spot, peak ♦ verb 2 EMPHASIZE, accent, accentuate, bring to the fore, show up, spotlight, stress, underline

highly adverb EXTREMELY, exceptionally, greatly, immensely, tremendously, vastly, very, very much

highly strung adjective NERVOUS, edgy, excitable, neurotic, sensitive, stressed, temperamental, tense

hijack verb SEIZE, commandeer, expropriate, take over

hike noun 1 WALK, march, ramble, tramp, trek ♦ verb 2 WALK, back-pack, ramble, tramp 3 **hike up** RAISE, hitch up, jack up, lift, pull up

hilarious adjective FUNNY, amusing, comical, entertaining, humorous, rollicking, side-splitting, uproarious

hilarity noun LAUGHTER, amusement, exhilaration, glee, high spirits, jollity, merriment, mirth

hill noun MOUNT, fell, height, hillock, hilltop, knoll, mound, tor

hillock noun MOUND, hummock, knoll

hilly adjective MOUNTAINOUS, rolling, undulating

hilt noun HANDLE, grip, haft, handgrip

hinder verb OBSTRUCT, block, check, delay, encumber, frustrate, hamper, handicap, hold up or back, impede, interrupt, stop

hindmost adjective LAST, final, furthest, furthest behind, rearmost, trailing

hindrance noun OBSTACLE, barrier, deterrent, difficulty, drawback, handicap, hitch, impediment, obstruction, restriction, snag, stumbling block

hinge verb DEPEND, be contingent, hang, pivot, rest, revolve around, turn

hint noun 1 INDICATION, allusion, clue, implication, innuendo, insinuation, intimation, suggestion 2 ADVICE, help, pointer, suggestion, tip 3 TRACE, dash, suggestion, suspicion, tinge, touch, undertone ♦ verb 4 SUGGEST, imply, indicate, insinuate, intimate

hippy noun BOHEMIAN, beatnik, dropout

hire verb 1 EMPLOY, appoint, commission, engage, sign up, take on 2 RENT, charter, engage, lease, let ♦ noun 3 RENTAL, charge, cost, fee, price, rent

hiss noun 1 SIBILATION, buzz, hissing 2 CATCALL, boo, jeer ♦ verb 3 WHISTLE, sibilate, wheeze, whirr, whiz 4 JEER, boo, deride, hoot, mock

historic adjective SIGNIFICANT, epoch-making, extraordinary, famous, ground-breaking, momentous, notable, outstanding, remarkable

historical adjective FACTUAL, actual, attested, authentic, documented, real

history noun 1 CHRONICLE, account, annals, narrative, recital, record, story 2 THE PAST, antiquity, olden days, yesterday, yesteryear

hit verb 1 STRIKE, bang, beat, clout (informal), knock, slap, smack, thump, wallop (informal), whack 2 COLLIDE WITH, bang into, bump, clash with, crash against, run into, smash into 3 REACH, accomplish, achieve, arrive at, attain, gain 4 AFFECT, damage, devastate, impact on, influence, leave a mark on, overwhelm, touch 5 **hit it off** Informal GET ON (WELL) WITH, be on good terms, click (slang), get on like a house on fire (informal) ♦ noun 6 STROKE, belt (informal), blow, clout (informal), knock, rap, slap, smack, wallop (informal) 7 SUCCESS, sensation, smash (informal), triumph, winner

hit-and-miss adjective HAPHAZARD, aimless, casual, disorganized, indiscriminate, random, undirected, uneven

hitch noun 1 PROBLEM, catch, difficulty, drawback, hindrance, hold-up, impediment, obstacle, snag ♦ verb 2 FASTEN, attach, connect, couple, harness, join, tether, tie 3 Informal HITCHHIKE, thumb a lift 4 **hitch up** PULL UP, jerk, tug, yank

hitherto adverb PREVIOUSLY, heretofore, so far, thus far, until now

hit on verb THINK UP, arrive at, discover, invent, light upon, strike upon, stumble on

hoard noun 1 STORE, accumulation, cache, fund, pile, reserve, stockpile, supply, treasure-trove ♦ verb 2 SAVE, accumulate, amass, collect, gather, lay up, put by, stash away (informal), stockpile, store

hoarse adjective RAUCOUS, croaky, grating, gravelly, gruff, guttural, husky, rasping, rough, throaty

hoax noun 1 TRICK, con (informal), deception, fraud, practical joke,

prank, spoof (*informal*), swindle
♦ *verb* **2** DECEIVE, con (*slang*), dupe,
fool, hoodwink, swindle, take in
(*informal*), trick

hobby *noun* PASTIME, diversion,
(leisure) activity, leisure pursuit,
relaxation

hobnob *verb* SOCIALIZE, associate,
consort, fraternize, hang about,
hang out (*informal*), keep
company, mingle, mix

hoist *verb* **1** RAISE, elevate, erect,
heave, lift ♦ *noun* **2** LIFT, crane,
elevator, winch

hold *verb* **1** OWN, have, keep,
maintain, occupy, possess, retain
2 GRASP, clasp, cling, clutch, cradle,
embrace, enfold, grip **3** RESTRAIN,
confine, detain, impound,
imprison **4** CONSIDER, assume,
believe, deem, judge, presume,
reckon, regard, think **5** CONVENE,
call, conduct, preside over, run
6 ACCOMMODATE, contain, have a
capacity for, seat, take ♦ *noun*
7 GRIP, clasp, grasp **8** FOOTHOLD,
footing, support **9** CONTROL,
influence, mastery

holder *noun* **1** OWNER, bearer,
keeper, possessor, proprietor
2 CASE, container, cover

hold forth *verb* SPEAK, declaim,
discourse, go on, lecture, preach,
spiel (*informal*), spout (*informal*)

hold-up *noun* **1** DELAY, bottleneck,
hitch, setback, snag, stoppage,
traffic jam, wait **2** ROBBERY,
mugging (*informal*), stick-up
(*slang, chiefly U.S.*), theft

hold up *verb* **1** DELAY, detain,
hinder, retard, set back, slow
down, stop **2** SUPPORT, prop, shore
up, sustain **3** ROB, mug (*informal*),
waylay

hold with *verb* APPROVE OF, agree to
or with, be in favour of,
countenance, subscribe to,

support

hole *noun* **1** OPENING, aperture,
breach, crack, fissure, gap, orifice,
perforation, puncture, tear, vent
2 CAVITY, cave, cavern, chamber,
hollow, pit **3** BURROW, den, earth,
lair, shelter **4** *Informal* HOVEL, dive
(*slang*), dump (*informal*), slum
5 *Informal* PREDICAMENT, dilemma,
fix (*informal*), hot water (*informal*),
jam (*informal*), mess, scrape
(*informal*), spot (*informal*), tight
spot

holiday *noun* **1** VACATION, break,
leave, recess, time off **2** FESTIVAL,
celebration, feast, fête, gala

holiness *noun* DIVINITY, godliness,
piety, purity, righteousness,
sacredness, saintliness, sanctity,
spirituality

hollow *adjective* **1** EMPTY, unfilled,
vacant, void **2** REVERBERANT, deep,
dull, low, muted **3** WORTHLESS,
fruitless, futile, meaningless,
pointless, useless, vain ♦ *noun*
4 CAVITY, basin, bowl, crater,
depression, hole, pit, trough
5 VALLEY, dale, dell, dingle, glen
♦ *verb* **6** SCOOP, dig, excavate,
gouge

holocaust *noun* GENOCIDE,
annihilation, conflagration,
destruction, devastation, massacre

holy *adjective* **1** DEVOUT,
god-fearing, godly, pious, pure,
religious, righteous, saintly,
virtuous **2** SACRED, blessed,
consecrated, hallowed,
sacrosanct, sanctified, venerable

homage *noun* RESPECT, adoration,
adulation, deference, devotion,
honour, reverence, worship

home *noun* **1** HOUSE, abode,
domicile, dwelling, habitation,
pad (*slang*), residence **2** BIRTHPLACE,
home town **3 at home: a** IN,
available, present **b** AT EASE,
comfortable, familiar, relaxed

4 bring home to <u>MAKE CLEAR</u>, drive home, emphasize, impress upon, press home ♦ *adjective* **5** <u>DOMESTIC</u>, familiar, internal, local, native

homeland *noun* <u>NATIVE LAND</u>, country of origin, fatherland, mother country, motherland

homeless *adjective* **1** <u>DESTITUTE</u>, displaced, dispossessed, down-and-out ♦ *noun* **2 the homeless** <u>VAGRANTS</u>, squatters

homely *adjective* <u>COMFORTABLE</u>, cosy, friendly, homespun, modest, ordinary, plain, simple, welcoming

homespun *adjective* <u>UNSOPHISTICATED</u>, coarse, homely, home-made, plain, rough

homicidal *adjective* <u>MURDEROUS</u>, deadly, lethal, maniacal, mortal

homicide *noun* **1** <u>MURDER</u>, bloodshed, killing, manslaughter, slaying **2** <u>MURDERER</u>, killer, slayer

homily *noun* <u>SERMON</u>, address, discourse, lecture, preaching

homogeneity *noun* <u>UNIFORMITY</u>, consistency, correspondence, sameness, similarity

homogeneous *adjective* <u>UNIFORM</u>, akin, alike, analogous, comparable, consistent, identical, similar, unvarying

hone *verb* <u>SHARPEN</u>, edge, file, grind, point, polish, whet

honest *adjective* **1** <u>TRUSTWORTHY</u>, ethical, honourable, law-abiding, reputable, scrupulous, truthful, upright, virtuous **2** <u>OPEN</u>, candid, direct, forthright, frank, plain, sincere, upfront (*informal*)

honestly *adverb* **1** <u>ETHICALLY</u>, by fair means, cleanly, honourably, lawfully, legally **2** <u>FRANKLY</u>, candidly, in all sincerity, plainly, straight (out), to one's face, truthfully

honesty *noun* **1** <u>INTEGRITY</u>, honour, incorruptibility, morality, probity, rectitude, scrupulousness, trustworthiness, truthfulness, uprightness, virtue **2** <u>FRANKNESS</u>, bluntness, candour, openness, outspokenness, sincerity, straightforwardness

honorary *adjective* <u>NOMINAL</u>, complimentary, in name *or* title only, titular, unofficial, unpaid

honour *noun* **1** <u>GLORY</u>, credit, dignity, distinction, fame, prestige, renown, reputation **2** <u>TRIBUTE</u>, accolade, commendation, homage, praise, recognition **3** <u>FAIRNESS</u>, decency, goodness, honesty, integrity, morality, probity, rectitude **4** <u>PRIVILEGE</u>, compliment, credit, pleasure ♦ *verb* **5** <u>RESPECT</u>, adore, appreciate, esteem, prize, value **6** <u>FULFIL</u>, be true to, carry out, discharge, keep, live up to, observe **7** <u>ACCLAIM</u>, commemorate, commend, decorate, praise **8** <u>ACCEPT</u>, acknowledge, pass, pay, take

honourable *adjective* <u>RESPECTED</u>, creditable, estimable, reputable, respectable, virtuous

hoodwink *verb* <u>DECEIVE</u>, con (*informal*), delude, dupe, fool, mislead, swindle, trick

hook *noun* **1** <u>FASTENER</u>, catch, clasp, link, peg ♦ *verb* **2** <u>FASTEN</u>, clasp, fix, secure **3** <u>CATCH</u>, ensnare, entrap, snare, trap

hooked *adjective* **1** <u>BENT</u>, aquiline, curved, hook-shaped **2** <u>ADDICTED</u>, devoted, enamoured, obsessed, taken, turned on (*slang*)

hooligan *noun* <u>DELINQUENT</u>, lager lout, ruffian, vandal, yob *or* yobbo (*Brit. slang*)

hooliganism *noun* <u>DELINQUENCY</u>, disorder, loutishness, rowdiness, vandalism, violence

hoop noun RING, band, circlet, girdle, loop, wheel

hoot noun 1 CRY, call, toot 2 CATCALL, boo, hiss, jeer ♦ verb 3 JEER, boo, hiss, howl down

hop verb 1 JUMP, bound, caper, leap, skip, spring, trip, vault ♦ noun 2 JUMP, bounce, bound, leap, skip, spring, step, vault

hope verb 1 DESIRE, aspire, cross one's fingers, long, look forward to, set one's heart on ♦ noun 2 DESIRE, ambition, assumption, dream, expectation, longing

hopeful adjective 1 OPTIMISTIC, buoyant, confident, expectant, looking forward to, sanguine 2 PROMISING, auspicious, bright, encouraging, heartening, reassuring, rosy

hopefully adverb OPTIMISTICALLY, confidently, expectantly

hopeless adjective POINTLESS, futile, impossible, no-win, unattainable, useless, vain

horde noun CROWD, band, drove, gang, host, mob, multitude, pack, swarm, throng

horizon noun SKYLINE, vista

horizontal adjective LEVEL, flat, parallel

horrible adjective 1 TERRIFYING, appalling, dreadful, frightful, ghastly, grim, grisly, gruesome, hideous, repulsive, revolting, shocking 2 UNPLEASANT, awful, cruel, disagreeable, dreadful, horrid, mean, nasty, terrible

horrid adjective 1 UNPLEASANT, awful, disagreeable, dreadful, horrible, terrible 2 Informal UNKIND, beastly (informal), cruel, mean, nasty

horrific adjective TERRIFYING, appalling, awful, dreadful, frightful, ghastly, grisly, horrendous, horrifying, shocking

horrify verb 1 TERRIFY, alarm, frighten, intimidate, make one's hair stand on end, petrify, scare 2 SHOCK, appal, dismay, outrage, sicken

horror noun 1 TERROR, alarm, consternation, dread, fear, fright, panic 2 HATRED, aversion, detestation, disgust, loathing, odium, repugnance, revulsion

horse noun NAG, colt, filly, gee-gee (slang), mare, mount, stallion, steed (archaic or literary)

horseman noun RIDER, cavalier, cavalryman, dragoon, equestrian

horseplay noun BUFFOONERY, clowning, fooling around, high jinks, pranks, romping, rough-and-tumble, skylarking (informal)

hospitable adjective WELCOMING, cordial, friendly, generous, gracious, kind, liberal, sociable

hospitality noun WELCOME, conviviality, cordiality, friendliness, neighbourliness, sociability, warmth

host[1] noun 1 MASTER OF CEREMONIES, entertainer, innkeeper, landlord or landlady, proprietor 2 PRESENTER, anchorman or anchorwoman, compere (Brit.) ♦ verb 3 PRESENT, compere (Brit.), front (informal), introduce

host[2] noun MULTITUDE, army, array, drove, horde, legion, myriad, swarm, throng

hostage noun PRISONER, captive, pawn

hostile adjective 1 OPPOSED, antagonistic, belligerent, contrary, ill-disposed, rancorous 2 UNFRIENDLY, adverse, inhospitable, unsympathetic, unwelcoming

hostilities plural noun WARFARE, conflict, fighting, war

hostility noun OPPOSITION, animosity, antipathy, enmity, hatred, ill will, malice, resentment, unfriendliness

hot adjective 1 HEATED, boiling, roasting, scalding, scorching, searing, steaming, sultry, sweltering, torrid, warm 2 SPICY, biting, peppery, piquant, pungent, sharp 3 FIERCE, fiery, intense, passionate, raging, stormy, violent 4 RECENT, fresh, just out, latest, new, up to the minute 5 POPULAR, approved, favoured, in demand, in vogue, sought-after

hot air noun EMPTY TALK, bombast, claptrap (informal), guff (slang), verbiage, wind

hot-blooded adjective PASSIONATE, ardent, excitable, fiery, impulsive, spirited, temperamental, wild

hotchpotch noun MIXTURE, farrago, jumble, medley, mélange, mess, mishmash, potpourri

hot-headed adjective RASH, fiery, foolhardy, hasty, hot-tempered, impetuous, quick-tempered, reckless, volatile

hound verb HARASS, badger, goad, harry, impel, persecute, pester, provoke

house noun 1 HOME, abode, domicile, dwelling, habitation, homestead, pad (slang), residence 2 FAMILY, household 3 DYNASTY, clan, tribe 4 FIRM, business, company, organization, outfit (informal) 5 ASSEMBLY, Commons, legislative body, parliament 6 **on the house** FREE, for nothing, gratis ◆ verb 7 ACCOMMODATE, billet, harbour, lodge, put up, quarter, take in 8 CONTAIN, cover, keep, protect, sheathe, shelter, store

household noun FAMILY, home, house

householder noun OCCUPANT,

homeowner, resident, tenant

housing noun 1 ACCOMMODATION, dwellings, homes, houses 2 CASE, casing, container, cover, covering, enclosure, sheath

hovel noun HUT, cabin, den, hole, shack, shanty, shed

hover verb 1 FLOAT, drift, flutter, fly, hang 2 LINGER, hang about 3 WAVER, dither (chiefly Brit.), fluctuate, oscillate, vacillate

however adverb NEVERTHELESS, after all, anyhow, but, nonetheless, notwithstanding, still, though, yet

howl noun 1 CRY, bawl, bay, clamour, groan, roar, scream, shriek, wail ◆ verb 2 CRY, bawl, bellow, roar, scream, shriek, wail, weep, yell

howler noun MISTAKE, bloomer (Brit. informal), blunder, boob (Brit. slang), clanger (informal), error, malapropism

hub noun CENTRE, core, focal point, focus, heart, middle, nerve centre

huddle verb 1 CROWD, cluster, converge, flock, gather, press, throng 2 CURL UP, crouch, hunch up ◆ noun 3 Informal CONFERENCE, confab (informal), discussion, meeting, powwow

hue noun COLOUR, dye, shade, tinge, tint, tone

hug verb 1 CLASP, cuddle, embrace, enfold, hold close, squeeze, take in one's arms ◆ noun 2 EMBRACE, bear hug, clasp, clinch (slang), squeeze

huge adjective LARGE, colossal, enormous, gigantic, immense, mammoth, massive, monumental, tremendous, vast

hulk noun 1 WRECK, frame, hull, shell, shipwreck 2 OAF, lout, lubber, lump (informal)

hull noun FRAME, body, casing,

covering, framework

hum verb 1 MURMUR, buzz, drone, purr, throb, thrum, vibrate, whir 2 BE BUSY, bustle, buzz, pulsate, pulse, stir

human adjective 1 MORTAL, manlike ♦noun 2 HUMAN BEING, creature, individual, man or woman, mortal, person, soul

humane adjective KIND, benign, compassionate, forgiving, good-natured, merciful, sympathetic, tender, understanding

humanitarian adjective 1 COMPASSIONATE, altruistic, benevolent, charitable, humane, philanthropic, public-spirited ♦noun 2 PHILANTHROPIST, altruist, benefactor, Good Samaritan

humanity noun 1 HUMAN RACE, Homo sapiens, humankind, man, mankind, people 2 HUMAN NATURE, mortality 3 SYMPATHY, charity, compassion, fellow feeling, kind-heartedness, kindness, mercy, philanthropy

humanize verb CIVILIZE, educate, enlighten, improve, soften, tame

humble adjective 1 MODEST, meek, self-effacing, unassuming, unostentatious, unpretentious 2 LOWLY, mean, modest, obscure, ordinary, plebeian, poor, simple, undistinguished ♦verb 3 HUMILIATE, chasten, crush, disgrace, put (someone) in their place, subdue, take down a peg (informal)

humbug noun 1 FRAUD, charlatan, con man (informal), faker, impostor, phoney or phony (informal), swindler, trickster 2 NONSENSE, baloney (informal), cant, claptrap (informal), hypocrisy, quackery, rubbish

humdrum adjective DULL, banal, boring, dreary, monotonous, mundane, ordinary, tedious, tiresome, uneventful

humid adjective DAMP, clammy, dank, moist, muggy, steamy, sticky, sultry, wet

humidity noun DAMP, clamminess, dampness, dankness, moistness, moisture, mugginess, wetness

humiliate verb EMBARRASS, bring low, chasten, crush, degrade, humble, mortify, put down, put (someone) in their place, shame

humiliating adjective EMBARRASSING, crushing, degrading, humbling, ignominious, mortifying, shaming

humiliation noun EMBARRASSMENT, degradation, disgrace, dishonour, humbling, ignominy, indignity, loss of face, mortification, put-down, shame

humility noun MODESTY, humbleness, lowliness, meekness, submissiveness, unpretentiousness

humorist noun COMEDIAN, card (informal), comic, funny man, jester, joker, wag, wit

humorous adjective FUNNY, amusing, comic, comical, droll, entertaining, jocular, playful, waggish, witty

humour noun 1 FUNNINESS, amusement, comedy, drollery, facetiousness, fun, jocularity, ludicrousness 2 JOKING, comedy, farce, jesting, pleasantry, wisecracks (informal), wit, witticisms 3 MOOD, disposition, frame of mind, spirits, temper ♦verb 4 INDULGE, accommodate, flatter, go along with, gratify, mollify, pander to

hump noun 1 LUMP, bulge, bump, mound, projection, protrusion, protuberance, swelling ♦verb 2 Slang CARRY, heave, hoist, lug, shoulder

hunch noun 1 FEELING, idea,

impression, inkling, intuition, premonition, presentiment, suspicion ♦ *verb* 2 DRAW IN, arch, bend, curve

hunger *noun* 1 FAMINE, starvation 2 APPETITE, emptiness, hungriness, ravenousness 3 DESIRE, ache, appetite, craving, itch, lust, thirst, yearning ♦ *verb* 4 WANT, ache, crave, desire, hanker, itch, long, thirst, wish, yearn

hungry *adjective* 1 EMPTY, famished, peckish (*informal, chiefly Brit.*), ravenous, starved, starving, voracious 2 EAGER, athirst, avid, covetous, craving, desirous, greedy, keen, yearning

hunk *noun* LUMP, block, chunk, mass, nugget, piece, slab, wedge

hunt *verb* 1 STALK, chase, hound, pursue, track, trail 2 SEARCH, ferret about, forage, look, scour, seek ♦ *noun* 3 SEARCH, chase, hunting, investigation, pursuit, quest

hurdle *noun* 1 FENCE, barricade, barrier 2 OBSTACLE, barrier, difficulty, handicap, hazard, hindrance, impediment, obstruction, stumbling block

hurl *verb* THROW, cast, fling, heave, launch, let fly, pitch, propel, sling, toss

hurricane *noun* STORM, cyclone, gale, tempest, tornado, twister (*U.S. informal*), typhoon

hurried *adjective* HASTY, brief, cursory, perfunctory, quick, rushed, short, speedy, swift

hurry *verb* 1 RUSH, dash, fly, get a move on (*informal*), make haste, scoot, scurry, step on it (*informal*) ♦ *noun* 2 URGENCY, flurry, haste, quickness, rush, speed

hurt *verb* 1 HARM, bruise, damage, disable, impair, injure, mar, spoil, wound 2 ACHE, be sore, be tender, burn, smart, sting, throb 3 SADDEN,

annoy, distress, grieve, pain, upset, wound ♦ *noun* 4 DISTRESS, discomfort, pain, pang, soreness, suffering ♦ *adjective* 5 INJURED, bruised, cut, damaged, harmed, scarred, wounded 6 OFFENDED, aggrieved, crushed, wounded

hurtful *adjective* UNKIND, cruel, cutting, damaging, destructive, malicious, nasty, spiteful, upsetting, wounding

hurtle *verb* RUSH, charge, crash, fly, plunge, race, shoot, speed, stampede, tear

husband *noun* 1 PARTNER, better half (*humorous*), mate, spouse ♦ *verb* 2 ECONOMIZE, budget, conserve, hoard, save, store

husbandry *noun* 1 FARMING, agriculture, cultivation, tillage 2 THRIFT, economy, frugality

hush *verb* 1 QUIETEN, mute, muzzle, shush, silence ♦ *noun* 2 QUIET, calm, peace, silence, stillness, tranquillity

hush-hush *adjective* SECRET, classified, confidential, restricted, top-secret, under wraps

husky *adjective* 1 HOARSE, croaky, gruff, guttural, harsh, raucous, rough, throaty 2 *Informal* MUSCULAR, burly, hefty, powerful, rugged, stocky, strapping, thickset

hustle *verb* JOSTLE, elbow, force, jog, push, shove

hut *noun* SHED, cabin, den, hovel, lean-to, shanty, shelter

hybrid *noun* CROSSBREED, amalgam, composite, compound, cross, half-breed, mixture, mongrel

hygiene *noun* CLEANLINESS, sanitation

hygienic *adjective* CLEAN, aseptic, disinfected, germ-free, healthy, pure, sanitary, sterile

hymn *noun* ANTHEM, carol, chant, paean, psalm

hype *noun* <u>PUBLICITY</u>, ballyhoo
(*informal*), brouhaha, plugging
(*informal*), promotion, razzmatazz
(*slang*)

hypnotic *adjective* <u>MESMERIC</u>,
mesmerizing, sleep-inducing,
soothing, soporific, spellbinding

hypnotize *verb* <u>MESMERIZE</u>, put in a
trance, put to sleep

hypocrisy *noun* <u>INSINCERITY</u>, cant,
deceitfulness, deception,
duplicity, pretence

hypocrite *noun* <u>FRAUD</u>, charlatan,
deceiver, impostor, phoney *or*
phony (*informal*), pretender

hypocritical *adjective* <u>INSINCERE</u>,
canting, deceitful, duplicitous,
false, fraudulent, phoney *or* phony
(*informal*), sanctimonious,
two-faced

hypothesis *noun* <u>ASSUMPTION</u>,
postulate, premise, proposition,
supposition, theory, thesis

hypothetical *adjective* <u>THEORETICAL</u>,
academic, assumed, conjectural,
imaginary, putative, speculative,
supposed

hysteria *noun* <u>FRENZY</u>, agitation,
delirium, hysterics, madness, panic

hysterical *adjective* **1** <u>FRENZIED</u>,
crazed, distracted, distraught,
frantic, overwrought, raving
2 *Informal* <u>HILARIOUS</u>, comical,
side-splitting, uproarious

I i

icy *adjective* **1** COLD, biting, bitter, chill, chilly, freezing, frosty, ice-cold, raw **2** SLIPPERY, glassy, slippy (*informal or dialect*) **3** UNFRIENDLY, aloof, cold, distant, frigid, frosty, unwelcoming

idea *noun* **1** THOUGHT, concept, impression, perception **2** BELIEF, conviction, notion, opinion, teaching, view **3** PLAN, aim, intention, object, objective, purpose

ideal *adjective* **1** PERFECT, archetypal, classic, complete, consummate, model, quintessential, supreme ◆ *noun* **2** MODEL, last word, paradigm, paragon, pattern, perfection, prototype, standard

idealist *noun* ROMANTIC, dreamer, Utopian, visionary

idealistic *adjective* PERFECTIONIST, impracticable, optimistic, romantic, starry-eyed, Utopian, visionary

idealize *verb* ROMANTICIZE, apotheosize, ennoble, exalt, glorify, magnify, put on a pedestal, worship

ideally *adverb* IN A PERFECT WORLD, all things being equal, if one had one's way

identical *adjective* ALIKE, duplicate, indistinguishable, interchangeable, matching, twin

identification *noun* **1** RECOGNITION, naming, pinpointing **2** EMPATHY, association, connection, fellow feeling, involvement, rapport, relationship, sympathy

identify *verb* **1** RECOGNIZE, diagnose, make out, name, pick out, pinpoint, place, put one's finger on (*informal*), spot **2** **identify with**

RELATE TO, associate with, empathize with, feel for, respond to

identity *noun* **1** EXISTENCE, individuality, personality, self **2** SAMENESS, correspondence, unity

idiocy *noun* FOOLISHNESS, asininity, fatuousness, imbecility, inanity, insanity, lunacy, senselessness

idiom *noun* **1** PHRASE, expression, turn of phrase **2** LANGUAGE, jargon, parlance, style, vernacular

idiosyncrasy *noun* PECULIARITY, characteristic, eccentricity, mannerism, oddity, quirk, trick

idiot *noun* FOOL, chump, cretin, dunderhead, halfwit, imbecile, moron, nincompoop, numbskull *or* numskull, simpleton, twit (*informal, chiefly Brit.*)

idiotic *adjective* FOOLISH, asinine, crazy, daft (*informal*), foolhardy, harebrained, insane, moronic, senseless, stupid

idle *adjective* **1** INACTIVE, redundant, unemployed, unoccupied, unused, vacant **2** LAZY, good-for-nothing, indolent, lackadaisical, shiftless, slothful, sluggish **3** USELESS, fruitless, futile, groundless, ineffective, pointless, unavailing, unsuccessful, vain, worthless ◆ *verb* **4** often with *away* LAZE, dally, dawdle, kill time, loaf, loiter, lounge, potter

idleness *noun* **1** INACTIVITY, inaction, leisure, time on one's hands, unemployment **2** LAZINESS, inertia, shiftlessness, sloth, sluggishness, torpor

idol *noun* **1** GRAVEN IMAGE, deity, god **2** HERO, beloved, darling, favourite, pet, pin-up (*slang*)

idolatry noun <u>ADORATION</u>, adulation, exaltation, glorification

idolize verb <u>WORSHIP</u>, adore, dote upon, exalt, glorify, hero-worship, look up to, love, revere, venerate

idyllic adjective <u>IDEALIZED</u>, charming, halcyon, heavenly, ideal, picturesque, unspoiled

if conjunction <u>PROVIDED</u>, assuming, on condition that, providing, supposing

ignite verb 1 <u>CATCH FIRE</u>, burn, burst into flames, flare up, inflame, take fire 2 <u>SET FIRE TO</u>, kindle, light, set alight, torch

ignominious adjective <u>HUMILIATING</u>, discreditable, disgraceful, dishonourable, indecorous, inglorious, shameful, sorry, undignified

ignominy noun <u>DISGRACE</u>, discredit, dishonour, disrepute, humiliation, infamy, obloquy, shame, stigma

ignorance noun <u>UNAWARENESS</u>, inexperience, innocence, unconsciousness, unfamiliarity

ignorant adjective 1 <u>UNINFORMED</u>, benighted, inexperienced, innocent, oblivious, unaware, unconscious, unenlightened, uninitiated, unwitting 2 <u>UNEDUCATED</u>, illiterate 3 <u>INSENSITIVE</u>, crass, half-baked (informal), rude

ignore verb <u>OVERLOOK</u>, discount, disregard, neglect, pass over, reject, take no notice of, turn a blind eye to

ill adjective 1 <u>UNWELL</u>, ailing, diseased, indisposed, infirm, off-colour, poorly (informal), sick, under the weather (informal), unhealthy 2 <u>HARMFUL</u>, bad, damaging, deleterious, detrimental, evil, foul, injurious, unfortunate ♦ noun 3 <u>HARM</u>, affliction, hardship, hurt, injury, misery, misfortune, trouble, unpleasantness, woe ♦ adverb 4 <u>BADLY</u>, inauspiciously, poorly, unfavourably, unfortunately, unluckily 5 <u>HARDLY</u>, barely, by no means, scantily

ill-advised adjective <u>MISGUIDED</u>, foolhardy, ill-considered, ill-judged, imprudent, incautious, injudicious, rash, reckless, thoughtless, unwise

ill-disposed adjective <u>UNFRIENDLY</u>, antagonistic, disobliging, hostile, inimical, uncooperative, unwelcoming

illegal adjective <u>UNLAWFUL</u>, banned, criminal, felonious, forbidden, illicit, outlawed, prohibited, unauthorized, unlicensed

illegality noun <u>CRIME</u>, felony, illegitimacy, lawlessness, wrong

illegible adjective <u>INDECIPHERABLE</u>, obscure, scrawled, unreadable

illegitimate adjective 1 <u>UNLAWFUL</u>, illegal, illicit, improper, unauthorized 2 <u>BORN OUT OF WEDLOCK</u>, bastard

ill-fated adjective <u>DOOMED</u>, hapless, ill-omened, ill-starred, luckless, star-crossed, unfortunate, unhappy, unlucky

illicit adjective 1 <u>ILLEGAL</u>, criminal, felonious, illegitimate, prohibited, unauthorized, unlawful, unlicensed 2 <u>FORBIDDEN</u>, clandestine, furtive, guilty, immoral, improper

illiterate adjective <u>UNEDUCATED</u>, ignorant, uncultured, untaught, untutored

ill-mannered adjective <u>RUDE</u>, badly behaved, boorish, churlish, discourteous, impolite, insolent, loutish, uncouth

illness noun <u>DISEASE</u>, affliction, ailment, disorder, infirmity, malady, sickness

illogical *adjective* IRRATIONAL, absurd, inconsistent, invalid, meaningless, senseless, unreasonable, unscientific, unsound

ill-treat *verb* ABUSE, damage, harm, injure, maltreat, mishandle, misuse, oppress

illuminate *verb* 1 LIGHT UP, brighten 2 EXPLAIN, clarify, clear up, elucidate, enlighten, interpret, make clear, shed light on

illuminating *adjective* INFORMATIVE, enlightening, explanatory, helpful, instructive, revealing

illumination *noun* 1 LIGHT, brightness, lighting, radiance 2 ENLIGHTENMENT, clarification, insight, revelation

illusion *noun* 1 FANTASY, chimera, daydream, figment of the imagination, hallucination, mirage, will-o'-the-wisp 2 MISCONCEPTION, deception, delusion, error, fallacy, misapprehension

illusory *adjective* UNREAL, chimerical, deceptive, delusive, fallacious, false, hallucinatory, mistaken, sham

illustrate *verb* DEMONSTRATE, bring home, elucidate, emphasize, explain, point up, show

illustrated *adjective* PICTORIAL, decorated, graphic

illustration *noun* 1 EXAMPLE, case, instance, specimen 2 PICTURE, decoration, figure, plate, sketch

illustrious *adjective* FAMOUS, celebrated, distinguished, eminent, glorious, great, notable, prominent, renowned

ill will *noun* HOSTILITY, animosity, bad blood, dislike, enmity, hatred, malice, rancour, resentment, venom

image *noun* 1 REPRESENTATION, effigy, figure, icon, idol, likeness, picture, portrait, statue 2 REPLICA, counterpart, (dead) ringer (*slang*), Doppelgänger, double, facsimile, spitting image (*informal*) 3 CONCEPT, idea, impression, mental picture, perception

imaginable *adjective* POSSIBLE, believable, comprehensible, conceivable, credible, likely, plausible

imaginary *adjective* FICTIONAL, fictitious, hypothetical, illusory, imagined, invented, made-up, nonexistent, unreal

imagination *noun* 1 CREATIVITY, enterprise, ingenuity, invention, inventiveness, originality, resourcefulness, vision 2 UNREALITY, illusion, supposition

imaginative *adjective* CREATIVE, clever, enterprising, ingenious, inspired, inventive, original

imagine *verb* 1 ENVISAGE, conceive, conceptualize, conjure up, picture, plan, think of, think up, visualize 2 BELIEVE, assume, conjecture, fancy, guess (*informal, chiefly U.S. & Canad.*), infer, suppose, surmise, suspect, take it, think

imbecile *noun* 1 IDIOT, chump, cretin, fool, halfwit, moron, numbskull *or* numskull, thickhead, twit (*informal, chiefly Brit.*) ♦ *adjective* 2 STUPID, asinine, fatuous, feeble-minded, foolish, idiotic, moronic, thick, witless

imbibe *verb* 1 DRINK, consume, knock back (*informal*), quaff, sink (*informal*), swallow, swig (*informal*) 2 *Literary* ABSORB, acquire, assimilate, gain, gather, ingest, receive, take in

imbroglio *noun* COMPLICATION, embarrassment, entanglement, involvement, misunderstanding, quandary

imitate verb COPY, ape, echo, emulate, follow, mimic, mirror, repeat, simulate

imitation noun 1 MIMICRY, counterfeiting, duplication, likeness, resemblance, simulation 2 REPLICA, fake, forgery, impersonation, impression, reproduction, sham, substitution ◆ adjective 3 ARTIFICIAL, dummy, ersatz, man-made, mock, phoney or phony (informal), reproduction, sham, simulated, synthetic

imitative adjective DERIVATIVE, copycat (informal), mimetic, parrot-like, second-hand, simulated, unoriginal

imitator noun IMPERSONATOR, copier, copycat (informal), impressionist, mimic, parrot

immaculate adjective 1 CLEAN, neat, spick-and-span, spotless, spruce, squeaky-clean 2 FLAWLESS, above reproach, faultless, impeccable, perfect, unblemished, unexceptionable, untarnished

immaterial adjective IRRELEVANT, extraneous, inconsequential, inessential, insignificant, of no importance, trivial, unimportant

immature adjective 1 YOUNG, adolescent, undeveloped, unformed, unripe 2 CHILDISH, callow, inexperienced, infantile, juvenile, puerile

immaturity noun 1 UNRIPENESS, greenness, imperfection, rawness, unpreparedness 2 CHILDISHNESS, callowness, inexperience, puerility

immediate adjective 1 INSTANT, instantaneous 2 NEAREST, close, direct, near, next

immediately adverb AT ONCE, directly, forthwith, instantly, now, promptly, right away, straight away, this instant, without delay

immense adjective HUGE, colossal, enormous, extensive, gigantic, great, massive, monumental, stupendous, tremendous, vast

immensity noun SIZE, bulk, enormity, expanse, extent, greatness, hugeness, magnitude, vastness

immerse verb 1 PLUNGE, bathe, dip, douse, duck, dunk, sink, submerge 2 ENGROSS, absorb, busy, engage, involve, occupy, take up

immersion noun 1 DIPPING, dousing, ducking, dunking, plunging, submerging 2 INVOLVEMENT, absorption, concentration, preoccupation

immigrant noun SETTLER, incomer, newcomer

imminent adjective NEAR, at hand, close, coming, forthcoming, gathering, impending, in the pipeline, looming

immobile adjective STATIONARY, at a standstill, at rest, fixed, immovable, motionless, rigid, rooted, static, still, stock-still, unmoving

immobility noun STILLNESS, fixity, inertness, motionlessness, stability, steadiness

immobilize verb PARALYSE, bring to a standstill, cripple, disable, freeze, halt, stop, transfix

immoderate adjective EXCESSIVE, exaggerated, exorbitant, extravagant, extreme, inordinate, over the top (slang), undue, unjustified, unreasonable

immoral adjective WICKED, bad, corrupt, debauched, depraved, dissolute, indecent, sinful, unethical, unprincipled, wrong

immorality noun WICKEDNESS, corruption, debauchery, depravity, dissoluteness, sin, vice, wrong

immortal adjective 1 ETERNAL, deathless, enduring, everlasting, imperishable, lasting, perennial, undying ◆ noun 2 GOD, goddess 3 GREAT, genius, hero

immortality noun 1 ETERNITY, everlasting life, perpetuity 2 FAME, celebrity, glory, greatness, renown

immortalize verb COMMEMORATE, celebrate, exalt, glorify

immovable adjective 1 FIXED, firm, immutable, jammed, secure, set, stable, stationary, stuck 2 INFLEXIBLE, adamant, obdurate, resolute, steadfast, unshakable, unwavering, unyielding

immune adjective EXEMPT, clear, free, invulnerable, proof (against), protected, resistant, safe, unaffected

immunity noun 1 EXEMPTION, amnesty, freedom, indemnity, invulnerability, licence, release 2 RESISTANCE, immunization, protection

immunize verb VACCINATE, inoculate, protect, safeguard

imp noun 1 DEMON, devil, sprite 2 RASCAL, brat, minx, rogue, scamp

impact noun 1 COLLISION, blow, bump, contact, crash, jolt, knock, smash, stroke, thump 2 EFFECT, consequences, impression, influence, repercussions, significance ◆ verb 3 HIT, clash, collide, crash, crush, strike

impair verb WORSEN, blunt, damage, decrease, diminish, harm, hinder, injure, lessen, reduce, undermine, weaken

impaired adjective DAMAGED, defective, faulty, flawed, imperfect, unsound

impart verb 1 COMMUNICATE, convey, disclose, divulge, make known, pass on, relate, reveal, tell 2 GIVE, accord, afford, bestow, confer, grant, lend, yield

impartial adjective NEUTRAL, detached, disinterested, equitable, even-handed, fair, just, objective, open-minded, unbiased, unprejudiced

impartiality noun NEUTRALITY, detachment, disinterestedness, dispassion, equity, even-handedness, fairness, objectivity, open-mindedness

impassable adjective BLOCKED, closed, impenetrable, obstructed

impasse noun DEADLOCK, dead end, stalemate, standoff, standstill

impassioned adjective INTENSE, animated, fervent, fiery, heated, inspired, passionate, rousing, stirring

impatience noun 1 HASTE, impetuosity, intolerance, rashness 2 RESTLESSNESS, agitation, anxiety, eagerness, edginess, fretfulness, nervousness, uneasiness

impatient adjective 1 HASTY, demanding, hot-tempered, impetuous, intolerant 2 RESTLESS, eager, edgy, fretful, straining at the leash

impeach verb CHARGE, accuse, arraign, indict

impeccable adjective FAULTLESS, blameless, flawless, immaculate, irreproachable, perfect, unblemished, unimpeachable

impecunious adjective POOR, broke (informal), destitute, down and out, indigent, insolvent, penniless, poverty-stricken

impede verb HINDER, block, check, disrupt, hamper, hold up, obstruct, slow (down), thwart

impediment noun OBSTACLE, barrier, difficulty, encumbrance, hindrance, obstruction, snag, stumbling block

impel verb <u>FORCE</u>, compel, constrain, drive, induce, oblige, push, require

impending adjective <u>LOOMING</u>, approaching, coming, forthcoming, gathering, imminent, in the pipeline, near, upcoming

impenetrable adjective 1 <u>SOLID</u>, dense, impassable, impermeable, impervious, inviolable, thick 2 <u>INCOMPREHENSIBLE</u>, arcane, enigmatic, inscrutable, mysterious, obscure, unfathomable, unintelligible

imperative adjective <u>URGENT</u>, crucial, essential, pressing, vital

imperceptible adjective <u>UNDETECTABLE</u>, faint, indiscernible, microscopic, minute, slight, small, subtle, tiny

imperfect adjective <u>FLAWED</u>, damaged, defective, faulty, impaired, incomplete, limited, unfinished

imperfection noun <u>FAULT</u>, blemish, defect, deficiency, failing, flaw, frailty, shortcoming, taint, weakness

imperial adjective <u>ROYAL</u>, kingly, majestic, princely, queenly, regal, sovereign

imperil verb <u>ENDANGER</u>, expose, jeopardize, risk

impersonal adjective <u>REMOTE</u>, aloof, cold, detached, dispassionate, formal, inhuman, neutral

impersonate verb <u>IMITATE</u>, ape, do (informal), masquerade as, mimic, pass oneself off as, pose as (informal), take off (informal)

impersonation noun <u>IMITATION</u>, caricature, impression, mimicry, parody, takeoff (informal)

impertinence noun <u>RUDENESS</u>, brazenness, cheek (informal),

disrespect, effrontery, front, impudence, insolence, nerve (informal), presumption

impertinent adjective <u>RUDE</u>, brazen, cheeky (informal), disrespectful, impolite, impudent, insolent, presumptuous

imperturbable adjective <u>CALM</u>, collected, composed, cool, nerveless, self-possessed, serene, unexcitable, unflappable (informal), unruffled

impervious adjective 1 <u>SEALED</u>, impassable, impenetrable, impermeable, resistant 2 <u>UNAFFECTED</u>, immune, invulnerable, proof against, unmoved, untouched

impetuosity noun <u>HASTE</u>, impulsiveness, precipitateness, rashness

impetuous adjective <u>RASH</u>, hasty, impulsive, precipitate, unthinking

impetus noun 1 <u>INCENTIVE</u>, catalyst, goad, impulse, motivation, push, spur, stimulus 2 <u>FORCE</u>, energy, momentum, power

impinge verb 1 <u>ENCROACH</u>, infringe, invade, obtrude, trespass, violate 2 <u>AFFECT</u>, bear upon, have a bearing on, impact, influence, relate to, touch

impious adjective <u>SACRILEGIOUS</u>, blasphemous, godless, irreligious, irreverent, profane, sinful, ungodly, unholy, wicked

impish adjective <u>MISCHIEVOUS</u>, devilish, puckish, rascally, roguish, sportive, waggish

implacable adjective <u>UNYIELDING</u>, inflexible, intractable, merciless, pitiless, unbending, uncompromising, unforgiving

implant verb 1 <u>INSTIL</u>, inculcate, infuse 2 <u>INSERT</u>, fix, graft

implement verb 1 <u>CARRY OUT</u>, bring

about, complete, effect, enforce, execute, fulfil, perform, realize ♦ *noun* 2 TOOL, apparatus, appliance, device, gadget, instrument, utensil

implicate *verb* INCRIMINATE, associate, embroil, entangle, include, inculpate, involve

implication *noun* SUGGESTION, inference, innuendo, meaning, overtone, presumption, significance

implicit *adjective* 1 IMPLIED, inferred, latent, tacit, taken for granted, undeclared, understood, unspoken 2 ABSOLUTE, constant, firm, fixed, full, steadfast, unqualified, unreserved, wholehearted

implied *adjective* UNSPOKEN, hinted at, implicit, indirect, suggested, tacit, undeclared, unexpressed, unstated

implore *verb* BEG, beseech, entreat, importune, plead with, pray

imply *verb* 1 HINT, insinuate, intimate, signify, suggest 2 ENTAIL, indicate, involve, mean, point to, presuppose

impolite *adjective* BAD-MANNERED, discourteous, disrespectful, ill-mannered, insolent, loutish, rude, uncouth

impoliteness *noun* BAD MANNERS, boorishness, churlishness, discourtesy, disrespect, insolence, rudeness

import *verb* 1 BRING IN, introduce ♦ *noun* 2 MEANING, drift, gist, implication, intention, sense, significance, thrust 3 IMPORTANCE, consequence, magnitude, moment, significance, substance, weight

importance *noun* 1 SIGNIFICANCE, concern, consequence, import, interest, moment, substance,

usefulness, value, weight 2 PRESTIGE, distinction, eminence, esteem, influence, prominence, standing, status

important *adjective* 1 SIGNIFICANT, far-reaching, momentous, seminal, serious, substantial, urgent, weighty 2 POWERFUL, eminent, high-ranking, influential, noteworthy, pre-eminent, prominent

importunate *adjective* PERSISTENT, demanding, dogged, insistent, pressing, urgent

impose *verb* 1 ESTABLISH, decree, fix, institute, introduce, levy, ordain 2 INFLICT, appoint, enforce, saddle (someone) with

imposing *adjective* IMPRESSIVE, commanding, dignified, grand, majestic, stately, striking

imposition *noun* 1 APPLICATION, introduction, levying 2 INTRUSION, liberty, presumption

impossibility *noun* HOPELESSNESS, impracticability, inability

impossible *adjective* 1 UNATTAINABLE, impracticable, inconceivable, out of the question, unachievable, unobtainable, unthinkable 2 ABSURD, ludicrous, outrageous, preposterous, unreasonable

impostor *noun* IMPERSONATOR, charlatan, deceiver, fake, fraud, phoney *or* phony (*informal*), pretender, sham, trickster

impotence *noun* POWERLESSNESS, feebleness, frailty, helplessness, inability, incapacity, incompetence, ineffectiveness, paralysis, uselessness, weakness

impotent *adjective* POWERLESS, feeble, frail, helpless, incapable, incapacitated, incompetent, ineffective, paralysed, weak

impoverish *verb* 1 BANKRUPT, beggar, break, ruin 2 DIMINISH, deplete, drain, exhaust, reduce, sap, use up, wear out

impoverished *adjective* POOR, bankrupt, destitute, impecunious, needy, on one's uppers, penurious, poverty-stricken

impracticable *adjective* UNFEASIBLE, impossible, out of the question, unachievable, unattainable, unworkable

impractical *adjective* 1 UNWORKABLE, impossible, impracticable, inoperable, nonviable, unrealistic, wild 2 IDEALISTIC, romantic, starry-eyed, unrealistic

imprecise *adjective* INDEFINITE, equivocal, hazy, ill-defined, indeterminate, inexact, inexplicit, loose, rough, vague, woolly

impregnable *adjective* INVULNERABLE, impenetrable, indestructible, invincible, secure, unassailable, unbeatable, unconquerable

impregnate *verb* 1 SATURATE, infuse, permeate, soak, steep, suffuse 2 FERTILIZE, inseminate, make pregnant

impress *verb* 1 EXCITE, affect, inspire, make an impression, move, stir, strike, touch 2 STRESS, bring home to, emphasize, fix, inculcate, instil into 3 IMPRINT, emboss, engrave, indent, mark, print, stamp

impression *noun* 1 EFFECT, feeling, impact, influence, reaction 2 IDEA, belief, conviction, feeling, hunch, notion, sense, suspicion 3 MARK, dent, hollow, imprint, indentation, outline, stamp 4 IMITATION, impersonation, parody, send-up (*Brit. informal*), takeoff (*informal*)

impressionable *adjective* SUGGESTIBLE, gullible, ingenuous, open, receptive, responsive, sensitive, susceptible, vulnerable

impressive *adjective* GRAND, awesome, dramatic, exciting, moving, powerful, stirring, striking

imprint *noun* 1 MARK, impression, indentation, sign, stamp ♦ *verb* 2 FIX, engrave, etch, impress, print, stamp

imprison *verb* JAIL, confine, detain, incarcerate, intern, lock up, put away, send down (*informal*)

imprisoned *adjective* JAILED, behind bars, captive, confined, incarcerated, in jail, inside (*slang*), locked up, under lock and key

imprisonment *noun* CUSTODY, confinement, detention, incarceration, porridge (*slang*)

improbability *noun* DOUBT, dubiety, uncertainty, unlikelihood

improbable *adjective* DOUBTFUL, dubious, fanciful, far-fetched, implausible, questionable, unconvincing, unlikely, weak

impromptu *adjective* UNPREPARED, ad-lib, extemporaneous, improvised, offhand, off the cuff (*informal*), spontaneous, unrehearsed, unscripted

improper *adjective* 1 INDECENT, risqué, smutty, suggestive, unbecoming, unseemly, untoward, vulgar 2 UNWARRANTED, inappropriate, out of place, uncalled-for, unfit, unsuitable

impropriety *noun* INDECENCY, bad taste, incongruity, vulgarity

improve *verb* 1 ENHANCE, advance, better, correct, help, rectify, touch up, upgrade 2 PROGRESS, develop, make strides, pick up, rally, rise

improvement *noun* 1 ENHANCEMENT, advancement, betterment 2 PROGRESS, development, rally, recovery, upswing

improvident *adjective* IMPRUDENT,

careless, negligent, prodigal, profligate, reckless, short-sighted, spendthrift, thoughtless, wasteful

improvisation noun 1 <u>SPONTANEITY</u>, ad-libbing, extemporizing, invention 2 <u>MAKESHIFT</u>, ad-lib, expedient

improvise verb 1 <u>EXTEMPORIZE</u>, ad-lib, busk, invent, play it by ear (*informal*), speak off the cuff (*informal*), wing it (*informal*) 2 <u>CONCOCT</u>, contrive, devise, throw together

imprudent adjective <u>UNWISE</u>, careless, foolhardy, ill-advised, ill-considered, ill-judged, injudicious, irresponsible, rash, reckless

impudence noun <u>BOLDNESS</u>, audacity, brazenness, cheek (*informal*), effrontery, impertinence, insolence, nerve (*informal*), presumption, shamelessness

impudent adjective <u>BOLD</u>, audacious, brazen, cheeky (*informal*), impertinent, insolent, presumptuous, rude, shameless

impulse noun <u>URGE</u>, caprice, feeling, inclination, notion, whim, wish

impulsive adjective <u>INSTINCTIVE</u>, devil-may-care, hasty, impetuous, intuitive, passionate, precipitate, rash, spontaneous

impunity noun <u>SECURITY</u>, dispensation, exemption, freedom, immunity, liberty, licence, permission

impure adjective 1 <u>UNREFINED</u>, adulterated, debased, mixed 2 <u>CONTAMINATED</u>, defiled, dirty, infected, polluted, tainted 3 <u>IMMORAL</u>, corrupt, indecent, lascivious, lewd, licentious, obscene, unchaste

impurity noun <u>CONTAMINATION</u>, defilement, dirtiness, infection, pollution, taint

imputation noun <u>BLAME</u>, accusation, aspersion, censure, insinuation, reproach, slander, slur

inability noun <u>INCAPABILITY</u>, disability, disqualification, impotence, inadequacy, incapacity, incompetence, ineptitude, powerlessness

inaccessible adjective <u>OUT OF REACH</u>, impassable, out of the way, remote, unapproachable, unattainable, unreachable

inaccuracy noun <u>ERROR</u>, defect, erratum, fault, lapse, mistake

inaccurate adjective <u>INCORRECT</u>, defective, erroneous, faulty, imprecise, mistaken, out, unreliable, unsound, wrong

inactive adjective <u>UNUSED</u>, dormant, idle, inoperative, unemployed, unoccupied

inactivity noun <u>IMMOBILITY</u>, dormancy, hibernation, inaction, passivity, unemployment

inadequacy noun 1 <u>SHORTAGE</u>, dearth, insufficiency, meagreness, paucity, poverty, scantiness 2 <u>INCOMPETENCE</u>, deficiency, inability, incapacity, ineffectiveness 3 <u>SHORTCOMING</u>, defect, failing, imperfection, weakness

inadequate adjective 1 <u>INSUFFICIENT</u>, meagre, scant, sketchy, sparse 2 <u>INCOMPETENT</u>, deficient, faulty, found wanting, incapable, not up to scratch (*informal*), unqualified

inadmissible adjective <u>UNACCEPTABLE</u>, inappropriate, irrelevant, unallowable

inadvertently adverb <u>UNINTENTIONALLY</u>, accidentally, by accident, by mistake, involuntarily, mistakenly, unwittingly

inadvisable *adjective* UNWISE, ill-advised, impolitic, imprudent, inexpedient, injudicious

inane *adjective* SENSELESS, empty, fatuous, frivolous, futile, idiotic, mindless, silly, stupid, vacuous

inanimate *adjective* LIFELESS, cold, dead, defunct, extinct, inert

inapplicable *adjective* IRRELEVANT, inappropriate, unsuitable

inappropriate *adjective* UNSUITABLE, improper, incongruous, out of place, unbecoming, unbefitting, unfitting, unseemly, untimely

inarticulate *adjective* FALTERING, halting, hesitant, poorly spoken

inattention *noun* NEGLECT, absent-mindedness, carelessness, daydreaming, inattentiveness, preoccupation, thoughtlessness

inattentive *adjective* PREOCCUPIED, careless, distracted, dreamy, negligent, unobservant, vague

inaudible *adjective* INDISTINCT, low, mumbling, out of earshot, stifled, unheard

inaugural *adjective* FIRST, initial, introductory, maiden, opening

inaugurate *verb* 1 LAUNCH, begin, commence, get under way, initiate, institute, introduce, set in motion 2 INVEST, induct, install

inauguration *noun* 1 LAUNCH, initiation, institution, opening, setting up 2 INVESTITURE, induction, installation

inauspicious *adjective* UNPROMISING, bad, discouraging, ill-omened, ominous, unfavourable, unfortunate, unlucky, unpropitious

inborn *adjective* NATURAL, congenital, hereditary, inbred, ingrained, inherent, innate, instinctive, intuitive, native

inbred *adjective* INNATE, constitutional, deep-seated, ingrained, inherent, native, natural

incalculable *adjective* COUNTLESS, boundless, infinite, innumerable, limitless, numberless, untold, vast

incantation *noun* CHANT, charm, formula, invocation, spell

incapable *adjective* 1 INCOMPETENT, feeble, inadequate, ineffective, inept, inexpert, insufficient, unfit, unqualified, weak 2 UNABLE, helpless, impotent, powerless

incapacitate *verb* DISABLE, cripple, immobilize, lay up (*informal*), paralyse, put out of action (*informal*)

incapacitated *adjective* INDISPOSED, hors de combat, immobilized, laid up (*informal*), out of action (*informal*), unfit

incapacity *noun* INABILITY, impotence, inadequacy, incapability, incompetency, ineffectiveness, powerlessness, unfitness, weakness

incarcerate *verb* IMPRISON, confine, detain, impound, intern, jail *or* gaol, lock up, throw in jail

incarceration *noun* IMPRISONMENT, captivity, confinement, detention, internment

incarnate *adjective* PERSONIFIED, embodied, typified

incarnation *noun* EMBODIMENT, epitome, manifestation, personification, type

incense *verb* ANGER, enrage, inflame, infuriate, irritate, madden, make one's hackles rise, rile (*informal*)

incensed *adjective* ANGRY, enraged, fuming, furious, indignant, infuriated, irate, maddened, steamed up (*slang*), up in arms

incentive *noun* ENCOURAGEMENT, bait, carrot (*informal*), enticement, inducement, lure, motivation, spur, stimulus

inception *noun* BEGINNING, birth, commencement, dawn, initiation, origin, outset, start

incessant *adjective* ENDLESS, ceaseless, constant, continual, eternal, interminable, never-ending, nonstop, perpetual, unceasing, unending

incessantly *adverb* ENDLESSLY, ceaselessly, constantly, continually, eternally, interminably, nonstop, perpetually, persistently

incident *noun* 1 HAPPENING, adventure, episode, event, fact, matter, occasion, occurrence 2 DISTURBANCE, clash, commotion, confrontation, contretemps, scene

incidental *adjective* SECONDARY, ancillary, minor, nonessential, occasional, subordinate, subsidiary

incidentally *adverb* PARENTHETICALLY, by the bye, by the way, in passing

incinerate *verb* BURN UP, carbonize, char, cremate, reduce to ashes

incipient *adjective* BEGINNING, commencing, developing, embryonic, inchoate, nascent, starting

incision *noun* CUT, gash, notch, opening, slash, slit

incisive *adjective* PENETRATING, acute, keen, perspicacious, piercing, trenchant

incite *verb* PROVOKE, encourage, foment, inflame, instigate, spur, stimulate, stir up, urge, whip up

incitement *noun* PROVOCATION, agitation, encouragement, impetus, instigation, prompting, spur, stimulus

incivility *noun* RUDENESS, bad manners, boorishness, discourteousness, discourtesy, disrespect, ill-breeding, impoliteness

inclement *adjective* STORMY, foul, harsh, intemperate, rough, severe, tempestuous

inclination *noun* 1 TENDENCY, disposition, liking, partiality, penchant, predilection, predisposition, proclivity, proneness, propensity 2 SLOPE, angle, gradient, incline, pitch, slant, tilt

incline *verb* 1 PREDISPOSE, influence, persuade, prejudice, sway 2 SLOPE, lean, slant, tilt, tip, veer ♦ *noun* 3 SLOPE, ascent, descent, dip, grade, gradient, rise

inclined *adjective* DISPOSED, apt, given, liable, likely, minded, predisposed, prone, willing

include *verb* 1 CONTAIN, comprise, cover, embrace, encompass, incorporate, involve, subsume, take in 2 INTRODUCE, add, enter, insert

inclusion *noun* ADDITION, incorporation, insertion

inclusive *adjective* COMPREHENSIVE, across-the-board, all-embracing, blanket, general, global, sweeping, umbrella

incognito *adjective* IN DISGUISE, disguised, under an assumed name, unknown, unrecognized

incoherence *noun* UNINTELLIGIBILITY, disjointedness, inarticulateness

incoherent *adjective* UNINTELLIGIBLE, confused, disjointed, disordered, inarticulate, inconsistent, jumbled, muddled, rambling, stammering, stuttering

income *noun* REVENUE, earnings, pay, proceeds, profits, receipts, salary, takings, wages

incoming *adjective* ARRIVING, approaching, entering,

homeward, landing, new, returning

incomparable *adjective*
UNEQUALLED, beyond compare, inimitable, matchless, peerless, superlative, supreme, transcendent, unmatched, unparalleled, unrivalled

incompatible *adjective*
INCONSISTENT, conflicting, contradictory, incongruous, mismatched, unsuited

incompetence *noun* INEPTITUDE, inability, inadequacy, incapability, incapacity, ineffectiveness, unfitness, uselessness

incompetent *adjective* INEPT, bungling, floundering, incapable, ineffectual, inexpert, unfit, useless

incomplete *adjective* UNFINISHED, deficient, fragmentary, imperfect, partial, wanting

incomprehensible *adjective*
UNINTELLIGIBLE, baffling, beyond one's grasp, impenetrable, obscure, opaque, perplexing, puzzling, unfathomable

inconceivable *adjective*
UNIMAGINABLE, beyond belief, incomprehensible, incredible, mind-boggling (*informal*), out of the question, unbelievable, unheard-of, unthinkable

inconclusive *adjective* INDECISIVE, ambiguous, indeterminate, open, unconvincing, undecided, up in the air (*informal*), vague

incongruity *noun* INAPPROPRIATENESS, conflict, discrepancy, disparity, incompatibility, inconsistency, unsuitability

incongruous *adjective*
INAPPROPRIATE, discordant, improper, incompatible, out of keeping, out of place, unbecoming, unsuitable

inconsiderable *adjective*

INSIGNIFICANT, inconsequential, minor, negligible, slight, small, trifling, trivial, unimportant

inconsiderate *adjective* SELFISH, indelicate, insensitive, rude, tactless, thoughtless, unkind, unthinking

inconsistency *noun*
1 INCOMPATIBILITY, disagreement, discrepancy, disparity, divergence, incongruity, variance
2 UNRELIABILITY, fickleness, instability, unpredictability, unsteadiness

inconsistent *adjective*
1 INCOMPATIBLE, at odds, conflicting, contradictory, discordant, incongruous, irreconcilable, out of step **2** CHANGEABLE, capricious, erratic, fickle, unpredictable, unstable, unsteady, variable

inconsolable *adjective* HEARTBROKEN, brokenhearted, desolate, despairing

inconspicuous *adjective*
UNOBTRUSIVE, camouflaged, hidden, insignificant, ordinary, plain, unassuming, unnoticeable, unostentatious

incontrovertible *adjective*
INDISPUTABLE, certain, established, incontestable, indubitable, irrefutable, positive, sure, undeniable, unquestionable

inconvenience *noun* **1** TROUBLE, awkwardness, bother, difficulty, disadvantage, disruption, disturbance, fuss, hindrance, nuisance ♦ *verb* **2** TROUBLE, bother, discommode, disrupt, disturb, put out, upset

inconvenient *adjective*
TROUBLESOME, awkward, bothersome, disadvantageous, disturbing, inopportune, unsuitable, untimely

incorporate *verb* INCLUDE, absorb,

assimilate, blend, combine, integrate, merge, subsume

incorrect *adjective* FALSE, erroneous, faulty, flawed, inaccurate, mistaken, untrue, wrong

incorrigible *adjective* INCURABLE, hardened, hopeless, intractable, inveterate, irredeemable, unreformed

incorruptible *adjective* 1 HONEST, above suspicion, straight, trustworthy, upright 2 IMPERISHABLE, everlasting, undecaying

increase *verb* 1 GROW, advance, boost, develop, enlarge, escalate, expand, extend, multiply, raise, spread, swell ♦ *noun* 2 GROWTH, development, enlargement, escalation, expansion, extension, gain, increment, rise, upturn

increasingly *adverb* PROGRESSIVELY, more and more

incredible *adjective* 1 IMPLAUSIBLE, beyond belief, far-fetched, improbable, inconceivable, preposterous, unbelievable, unimaginable, unthinkable 2 *Informal* AMAZING, astonishing, astounding, extraordinary, prodigious, sensational (*informal*), wonderful

incredulity *noun* DISBELIEF, distrust, doubt, scepticism

incredulous *adjective* DISBELIEVING, distrustful, doubtful, dubious, sceptical, suspicious, unbelieving, unconvinced

increment *noun* INCREASE, accrual, addition, advancement, augmentation, enlargement, gain, step up, supplement

incriminate *verb* IMPLICATE, accuse, blame, charge, impeach, inculpate, involve

incumbent *adjective* OBLIGATORY, binding, compulsory, mandatory, necessary

incur *verb* EARN, arouse, bring (upon oneself), draw, expose oneself to, gain, meet with, provoke

incurable *adjective* FATAL, inoperable, irremediable, terminal

indebted *adjective* GRATEFUL, beholden, in debt, obligated, obliged, under an obligation

indecency *noun* OBSCENITY, immodesty, impropriety, impurity, indelicacy, lewdness, licentiousness, pornography, vulgarity

indecent *adjective* 1 LEWD, crude, dirty, filthy, immodest, improper, impure, licentious, pornographic, salacious 2 UNBECOMING, in bad taste, indecorous, unseemly, vulgar

indecipherable *adjective* ILLEGIBLE, indistinguishable, unintelligible, unreadable

indecision *noun* HESITATION, dithering (*chiefly Brit.*), doubt, indecisiveness, shilly-shallying (*informal*), uncertainty, vacillation, wavering

indecisive *adjective* HESITATING, dithering (*chiefly Brit.*), faltering, in two minds (*informal*), tentative, uncertain, undecided, vacillating, wavering

indeed *adverb* REALLY, actually, certainly, in truth, truly, undoubtedly

indefensible *adjective* UNFORGIVABLE, inexcusable, unjustifiable, unpardonable, untenable, unwarrantable, wrong

indefinable *adjective* INEXPRESSIBLE, impalpable, indescribable

indefinite *adjective* UNCLEAR, doubtful, equivocal, ill-defined, imprecise, indeterminate, inexact, uncertain, unfixed, vague

indefinitely *adverb* ENDLESSLY, ad

infinitum, continually, for ever

indelible *adjective* PERMANENT, enduring, indestructible, ineradicable, ingrained, lasting

indelicate *adjective* OFFENSIVE, coarse, crude, embarrassing, immodest, risqué, rude, suggestive, tasteless, vulgar

indemnify *verb* 1 INSURE, guarantee, protect, secure, underwrite 2 COMPENSATE, reimburse, remunerate, repair, repay

indemnity *noun* 1 INSURANCE, guarantee, protection, security 2 COMPENSATION, redress, reimbursement, remuneration, reparation, restitution

independence *noun* FREEDOM, autonomy, liberty, self-reliance, self-rule, self-sufficiency, sovereignty

independent *adjective* 1 FREE, liberated, separate, unconstrained, uncontrolled 2 SELF-GOVERNING, autonomous, nonaligned, self-determining, sovereign 3 SELF-SUFFICIENT, liberated, self-contained, self-reliant, self-supporting

independently *adverb* SEPARATELY, alone, autonomously, by oneself, individually, on one's own, solo, unaided

indescribable *adjective* UNUTTERABLE, beyond description, beyond words, indefinable, inexpressible

indestructible *adjective* PERMANENT, enduring, everlasting, immortal, imperishable, incorruptible, indelible, indissoluble, lasting, unbreakable

indeterminate *adjective* UNCERTAIN, imprecise, indefinite, inexact, undefined, unfixed, unspecified, unstipulated, vague

indicate *verb* 1 SIGNIFY, betoken, denote, imply, manifest, point to, reveal, suggest 2 POINT OUT, designate, specify 3 SHOW, display, express, read, record, register

indication *noun* SIGN, clue, evidence, hint, inkling, intimation, manifestation, mark, suggestion, symptom

indicative *adjective* SUGGESTIVE, pointing to, significant, symptomatic

indicator *noun* SIGN, gauge, guide, mark, meter, pointer, signal, symbol

indict *verb* CHARGE, accuse, arraign, impeach, prosecute, summon

indictment *noun* CHARGE, accusation, allegation, impeachment, prosecution, summons

indifference *noun* DISREGARD, aloofness, apathy, coldness, coolness, detachment, inattention, negligence, nonchalance, unconcern

indifferent *adjective* 1 UNCONCERNED, aloof, callous, cold, cool, detached, impervious, inattentive, uninterested, unmoved, unsympathetic 2 MEDIOCRE, moderate, no great shakes (*informal*), ordinary, passable, so-so (*informal*), undistinguished

indigestion *noun* HEARTBURN, dyspepsia, upset stomach

indignant *adjective* RESENTFUL, angry, disgruntled, exasperated, incensed, irate, peeved (*informal*), riled, scornful, up in arms (*informal*)

indignation *noun* RESENTMENT, anger, exasperation, pique, rage, scorn, umbrage

indignity *noun* HUMILIATION, affront, dishonour, disrespect, injury, insult, opprobrium, slight, snub

indirect *adjective* **1** CIRCUITOUS, long-drawn-out, meandering, oblique, rambling, roundabout, tortuous, wandering **2** INCIDENTAL, secondary, subsidiary, unintended

indiscreet *adjective* TACTLESS, impolitic, imprudent, incautious, injudicious, naive, rash, reckless, unwise

indiscretion *noun* MISTAKE, error, faux pas, folly, foolishness, gaffe, lapse, slip

indiscriminate *adjective* RANDOM, careless, desultory, general, uncritical, undiscriminating, unsystematic, wholesale

indispensable *adjective* ESSENTIAL, crucial, imperative, key, necessary, needed, requisite, vital

indisposed *adjective* ILL, ailing, poorly (*informal*), sick, under the weather, unwell

indisposition *noun* ILLNESS, ailment, ill health, sickness

indisputable *adjective* UNDENIABLE, beyond doubt, certain, incontestable, incontrovertible, indubitable, irrefutable, unquestionable

indistinct *adjective* UNCLEAR, blurred, faint, fuzzy, hazy, ill-defined, indeterminate, shadowy, undefined, vague

individual *adjective* **1** PERSONAL, characteristic, distinctive, exclusive, idiosyncratic, own, particular, peculiar, singular, special, specific, unique ♦ *noun* **2** PERSON, being, character, creature, soul, unit

individualist *noun* MAVERICK, freethinker, independent, loner, lone wolf, nonconformist, original

individuality *noun* DISTINCTIVENESS, character, originality, personality, separateness, singularity, uniqueness

individually *adverb* SEPARATELY, apart, independently, one at a time, one by one, singly

indoctrinate *verb* TRAIN, brainwash, drill, ground, imbue, initiate, instruct, school, teach

indoctrination *noun* TRAINING, brainwashing, drilling, grounding, inculcation, instruction, schooling

indolent *adjective* LAZY, idle, inactive, inert, languid, lethargic, listless, slothful, sluggish, workshy

indomitable *adjective* INVINCIBLE, bold, resolute, staunch, steadfast, unbeatable, unconquerable, unflinching, unyielding

indubitable *adjective* CERTAIN, incontestable, incontrovertible, indisputable, irrefutable, obvious, sure, undeniable, unquestionable

induce *verb* **1** PERSUADE, convince, encourage, incite, influence, instigate, prevail upon, prompt, talk into **2** CAUSE, bring about, effect, engender, generate, give rise to, lead to, occasion, produce

inducement *noun* INCENTIVE, attraction, bait, carrot (*informal*), encouragement, incitement, lure, reward

indulge *verb* **1** GRATIFY, feed, give way to, pander to, satisfy, yield to **2** SPOIL, cosset, give in to, go along with, humour, mollycoddle, pamper

indulgence *noun* **1** GRATIFICATION, appeasement, fulfilment, satiation, satisfaction **2** LUXURY, extravagance, favour, privilege, treat **3** TOLERANCE, forbearance, patience, understanding

indulgent *adjective* LENIENT, compliant, easy-going, forbearing, kindly, liberal, permissive, tolerant, understanding

industrialist *noun* CAPITALIST, big businessman, captain of industry, magnate, manufacturer, tycoon

industrious *adjective* HARD-WORKING, busy, conscientious, diligent, energetic, persistent, purposeful, tireless, zealous

industry *noun* **1** BUSINESS, commerce, manufacturing, production, trade **2** EFFORT, activity, application, diligence, labour, tirelessness, toil, zeal

inebriated *adjective* DRUNK, half-cut (*informal*), intoxicated, legless (*informal*), merry (*Brit. informal*), paralytic (*informal*), plastered (*slang*), tight (*informal*), tipsy, under the influence (*informal*)

ineffective *adjective* USELESS, fruitless, futile, idle, impotent, inefficient, unavailing, unproductive, vain, worthless

ineffectual *adjective* WEAK, feeble, impotent, inadequate, incompetent, ineffective, inept

inefficiency *noun* INCOMPETENCE, carelessness, disorganization, muddle, slackness, sloppiness

inefficient *adjective* INCOMPETENT, disorganized, ineffectual, inept, wasteful, weak

ineligible *adjective* UNQUALIFIED, disqualified, ruled out, unacceptable, unfit, unsuitable

inept *adjective* INCOMPETENT, bumbling, bungling, clumsy, inexpert, maladroit

ineptitude *noun* INCOMPETENCE, clumsiness, inexpertness, unfitness

inequality *noun* DISPARITY, bias, difference, disproportion, diversity, irregularity, prejudice, unevenness

inequitable *adjective* UNFAIR, biased, discriminatory, one-sided,

partial, partisan, preferential, prejudiced, unjust

inert *adjective* INACTIVE, dead, dormant, immobile, lifeless, motionless, static, still, unreactive, unresponsive

inertia *noun* INACTIVITY, apathy, immobility, lethargy, listlessness, passivity, sloth, unresponsiveness

inescapable *adjective* UNAVOIDABLE, certain, destined, fated, ineluctable, inevitable, inexorable, sure

inestimable *adjective* INCALCULABLE, immeasurable, invaluable, precious, priceless, prodigious

inevitable *adjective* UNAVOIDABLE, assured, certain, destined, fixed, ineluctable, inescapable, inexorable, sure

inevitably *adverb* UNAVOIDABLY, as a result, automatically, certainly, necessarily, of necessity, perforce, surely, willy-nilly

inexcusable *adjective* UNFORGIVABLE, indefensible, outrageous, unjustifiable, unpardonable, unwarrantable

inexorable *adjective* UNRELENTING, inescapable, relentless, remorseless, unbending, unyielding

inexpensive *adjective* CHEAP, bargain, budget, economical, modest, reasonable

inexperience *noun* UNFAMILIARITY, callowness, greenness, ignorance, newness, rawness

inexperienced *adjective* IMMATURE, callow, green, new, raw, unpractised, untried, unversed

inexpert *adjective* AMATEURISH, bungling, cack-handed (*informal*), clumsy, inept, maladroit, unpractised, unprofessional, unskilled

inexplicable adjective UNACCOUNTABLE, baffling, enigmatic, incomprehensible, insoluble, mysterious, mystifying, strange, unfathomable, unintelligible

inextricably adverb INSEPARABLY, indissolubly, indistinguishably, intricately, irretrievably, totally

infallibility noun PERFECTION, impeccability, omniscience, supremacy, unerringness

infallible adjective FOOLPROOF, certain, dependable, reliable, sure, sure-fire (informal), trustworthy, unbeatable, unfailing

infamous adjective NOTORIOUS, disreputable, ignominious, ill-famed

infancy noun BEGINNINGS, cradle, dawn, inception, origins, outset, start

infant noun BABY, babe, bairn (Scot.), child, toddler, tot

infantile adjective CHILDISH, babyish, immature, puerile

infatuate verb OBSESS, besot, bewitch, captivate, enchant, enrapture, fascinate

infatuated adjective OBSESSED, besotted, bewitched, captivated, carried away, enamoured, enraptured, fascinated, possessed, smitten (informal), spellbound

infatuation noun OBSESSION, crush (informal), fixation, madness, passion, thing (informal)

infect verb CONTAMINATE, affect, blight, corrupt, defile, poison, pollute, taint

infection noun CONTAMINATION, contagion, corruption, defilement, poison, pollution, virus

infectious adjective CATCHING, communicable, contagious, spreading, transmittable, virulent

infer verb DEDUCE, conclude, derive, gather, presume, surmise, understand

inference noun DEDUCTION, assumption, conclusion, presumption, reading, surmise

inferior adjective 1 LOWER, lesser, menial, minor, secondary, subordinate, subsidiary ♦ noun 2 UNDERLING, junior, menial, subordinate

inferiority noun 1 INADEQUACY, deficiency, imperfection, insignificance, mediocrity, shoddiness, worthlessness 2 SUBSERVIENCE, abasement, lowliness, subordination

infernal adjective DEVILISH, accursed, damnable, damned, diabolical, fiendish, hellish, satanic

infertile adjective BARREN, sterile, unfruitful, unproductive

infertility noun STERILITY, barrenness, infecundity, unproductiveness

infest verb OVERRUN, beset, invade, penetrate, permeate, ravage, swarm, throng

infested adjective OVERRUN, alive, crawling, ravaged, ridden, swarming, teeming

infiltrate verb PENETRATE, filter through, insinuate oneself, make inroads (into), percolate, permeate, pervade, sneak in (informal)

infinite adjective NEVER-ENDING, boundless, eternal, everlasting, illimitable, immeasurable, inexhaustible, limitless, measureless, unbounded

infinitesimal adjective MICROSCOPIC, insignificant, minuscule, minute, negligible, teeny, tiny, unnoticeable

infinity noun ETERNITY,

boundlessness, endlessness, immensity, vastness

infirm *adjective* FRAIL, ailing, debilitated, decrepit, doddering, enfeebled, failing, feeble, weak

infirmity *noun* FRAILTY, decrepitude, ill health, sickliness, vulnerability

inflame *verb* ENRAGE, anger, arouse, excite, incense, infuriate, madden, provoke, rouse, stimulate

inflamed *adjective* SORE, fevered, hot, infected, red, swollen

inflammable *adjective* FLAMMABLE, combustible, incendiary

inflammation *noun* SORENESS, painfulness, rash, redness, tenderness

inflammatory *adjective* PROVOCATIVE, explosive, fiery, intemperate, like a red rag to a bull, rabble-rousing

inflate *verb* EXPAND, bloat, blow up, dilate, distend, enlarge, increase, puff up *or* out, pump up, swell

inflated *adjective* EXAGGERATED, ostentatious, overblown, swollen

inflation *noun* EXPANSION, enlargement, escalation, extension, increase, rise, spread, swelling

inflexibility *noun* OBSTINACY, intransigence, obduracy

inflexible *adjective* **1** OBSTINATE, implacable, intractable, obdurate, resolute, set in one's ways, steadfast, stubborn, unbending, uncompromising **2** INELASTIC, hard, rigid, stiff, taut

inflict *verb* IMPOSE, administer, apply, deliver, levy, mete *or* deal out, visit, wreak

infliction *noun* IMPOSITION, administration, perpetration, wreaking

influence *noun* **1** EFFECT, authority, control, domination, magnetism, pressure, weight **2** POWER, clout (*informal*), hold, importance, leverage, prestige, pull (*informal*)
♦ *verb* **3** AFFECT, control, direct, guide, manipulate, sway

influential *adjective* IMPORTANT, authoritative, instrumental, leading, potent, powerful, significant, telling, weighty

influx *noun* ARRIVAL, incursion, inrush, inundation, invasion, rush

inform *verb* **1** TELL, advise, communicate, enlighten, instruct, notify, teach, tip off **2** INCRIMINATE, betray, blow the whistle on (*informal*), denounce, grass (*Brit. slang*), inculpate, shop (*slang, chiefly Brit.*), squeal (*slang*)

informal *adjective* RELAXED, casual, colloquial, cosy, easy, familiar, natural, simple, unofficial

informality *noun* FAMILIARITY, casualness, ease, naturalness, relaxation, simplicity

information *noun* FACTS, data, intelligence, knowledge, message, news, notice, report

informative *adjective* INSTRUCTIVE, chatty, communicative, edifying, educational, enlightening, forthcoming, illuminating, revealing

informed *adjective* KNOWLEDGEABLE, enlightened, erudite, expert, familiar, in the picture, learned, up to date, versed, well-read

informer *noun* BETRAYER, accuser, Judas, sneak, stool pigeon

infrequent *adjective* OCCASIONAL, few and far between, once in a blue moon, rare, sporadic, uncommon, unusual

infringe *verb* BREAK, contravene, disobey, transgress, violate

infringement *noun* CONTRAVENTION,

breach, infraction, transgression, trespass, violation

infuriate verb ENRAGE, anger, exasperate, incense, irritate, madden, provoke, rile

infuriating adjective ANNOYING, exasperating, galling, irritating, maddening, mortifying, provoking, vexatious

ingenious adjective CREATIVE, bright, brilliant, clever, crafty, inventive, original, resourceful, shrewd

ingenuity noun ORIGINALITY, cleverness, flair, genius, gift, inventiveness, resourcefulness, sharpness, shrewdness

ingenuous adjective NAIVE, artless, guileless, honest, innocent, open, plain, simple, sincere, trusting, unsophisticated

inglorious adjective DISHONOURABLE, discreditable, disgraceful, disreputable, ignoble, ignominious, infamous, shameful, unheroic

ingratiate verb PANDER TO, crawl, curry favour, fawn, flatter, grovel, insinuate oneself, toady

ingratiating adjective SYCOPHANTIC, crawling, fawning, flattering, humble, obsequious, servile, toadying, unctuous

ingratitude noun UNGRATEFULNESS, thanklessness

ingredient noun COMPONENT, constituent, element, part

inhabit verb LIVE, abide, dwell, occupy, populate, reside

inhabitant noun DWELLER, citizen, denizen, inmate, native, occupant, occupier, resident, tenant

inhabited adjective POPULATED, colonized, developed, occupied, peopled, settled, tenanted

inhale verb BREATHE IN, draw in, gasp, respire, suck in

inherent adjective INNATE, essential, hereditary, inborn, inbred, inbuilt, ingrained, inherited, intrinsic, native, natural

inherit verb BE LEFT, come into, fall heir to, succeed to

inheritance noun LEGACY, bequest, birthright, heritage, patrimony

inhibit verb RESTRAIN, check, constrain, curb, discourage, frustrate, hinder, hold back or in, impede, obstruct

inhibited adjective SHY, constrained, guarded, repressed, reserved, reticent, self-conscious, subdued

inhibition noun SHYNESS, block, hang-up (*informal*), reserve, restraint, reticence, self-consciousness

inhospitable adjective
1 UNWELCOMING, cool, uncongenial, unfriendly, unreceptive, unsociable, xenophobic 2 BLEAK, barren, desolate, forbidding, godforsaken, hostile

inhuman adjective CRUEL, barbaric, brutal, cold-blooded, heartless, merciless, pitiless, ruthless, savage, unfeeling

inhumane adjective CRUEL, brutal, heartless, pitiless, unfeeling, unkind, unsympathetic

inhumanity noun CRUELTY, atrocity, barbarism, brutality, heartlessness, pitilessness, ruthlessness, unkindness

inimical adjective HOSTILE, adverse, antagonistic, ill-disposed, opposed, unfavourable, unfriendly, unwelcoming

inimitable adjective UNIQUE, consummate, incomparable, matchless, peerless, unparalleled, unrivalled

iniquitous adjective WICKED, criminal, evil, immoral, reprehensible, sinful, unjust

iniquity noun WICKEDNESS, abomination, evil, injustice, sin, wrong

initial adjective FIRST, beginning, incipient, introductory, opening, primary

initially adverb AT FIRST, at or in the beginning, first, firstly, originally, primarily

initiate verb 1 BEGIN, commence, get under way, kick off (informal), launch, open, originate, set in motion, start 2 INDUCT, indoctrinate, introduce, invest 3 INSTRUCT, acquaint with, coach, familiarize with, teach, train ♦ noun 4 NOVICE, beginner, convert, entrant, learner, member, probationer

initiation noun INTRODUCTION, debut, enrolment, entrance, inauguration, induction, installation, investiture

initiative noun 1 FIRST STEP, advantage, first move, lead 2 RESOURCEFULNESS, ambition, drive, dynamism, enterprise, get-up-and-go (informal), leadership

inject verb 1 VACCINATE, inoculate 2 INTRODUCE, bring in, infuse, insert, instil

injection noun 1 VACCINATION, inoculation, jab (informal), shot (informal) 2 INTRODUCTION, dose, infusion, insertion

injudicious adjective UNWISE, foolish, ill-advised, ill-judged, impolitic, imprudent, incautious, inexpedient, rash, unthinking

injunction noun ORDER, command, exhortation, instruction, mandate, precept, ruling

injure verb HURT, damage, harm, impair, ruin, spoil, undermine, wound

injured adjective HURT, broken, damaged, disabled, undermined, weakened, wounded

injury noun HARM, damage, detriment, disservice, hurt, ill, trauma (Pathology), wound, wrong

injustice noun UNFAIRNESS, bias, discrimination, inequality, inequity, iniquity, oppression, partisanship, prejudice, wrong

inkling noun SUSPICION, clue, conception, hint, idea, indication, intimation, notion, suggestion, whisper

inland adjective INTERIOR, domestic, internal, upcountry

inlet noun BAY, bight, creek, firth or frith (Scot.), fjord, passage

inmost or **innermost** adjective DEEPEST, basic, central, essential, intimate, personal, private, secret

innate adjective INBORN, congenital, constitutional, essential, inbred, ingrained, inherent, instinctive, intuitive, native, natural

inner adjective 1 INSIDE, central, interior, internal, inward, middle 2 PRIVATE, hidden, intimate, personal, repressed, secret, unrevealed

innkeeper noun PUBLICAN, host or hostess, hotelier, landlord or landlady, mine host

innocence noun 1 GUILTLESSNESS, blamelessness, clean hands, incorruptibility, probity, purity, uprightness, virtue 2 HARMLESSNESS, innocuousness, inoffensiveness 3 INEXPERIENCE, artlessness, credulousness, gullibility, ingenuousness, naïveté, simplicity, unworldliness

innocent adjective 1 NOT GUILTY,

blameless, guiltless, honest, in the clear, uninvolved **2** HARMLESS, innocuous, inoffensive, unobjectionable, well-intentioned, well-meant **3** NAIVE, artless, childlike, credulous, gullible, ingenuous, open, simple, unworldly

innovation noun MODERNIZATION, alteration, change, departure, introduction, newness, novelty, variation

innuendo noun INSINUATION, aspersion, hint, implication, imputation, intimation, overtone, suggestion, whisper

innumerable adjective COUNTLESS, beyond number, incalculable, infinite, multitudinous, myriad, numberless, numerous, unnumbered, untold

inoffensive adjective HARMLESS, innocent, innocuous, mild, quiet, retiring, unobjectionable, unobtrusive

inoperative adjective OUT OF ACTION, broken, defective, ineffective, invalid, null and void, out of order, out of service, useless

inopportune adjective INCONVENIENT, ill-chosen, ill-timed, inappropriate, unfavourable, unfortunate, unpropitious, unseasonable, unsuitable, untimely

inordinate adjective EXCESSIVE, disproportionate, extravagant, immoderate, intemperate, preposterous, unconscionable, undue, unreasonable, unwarranted

inorganic adjective ARTIFICIAL, chemical, man-made

inquest noun INQUIRY, inquisition, investigation, probe

inquire verb **1** INVESTIGATE, examine, explore, look into, make inquiries, probe, research **2** Also **enquire**

ASK, query, question

inquiry noun **1** INVESTIGATION, examination, exploration, inquest, interrogation, probe, research, study, survey **2** Also **enquiry** QUESTION, query

inquisition noun INVESTIGATION, cross-examination, examination, grilling (*informal*), inquest, inquiry, questioning, third degree (*informal*)

inquisitive adjective CURIOUS, inquiring, nosy (*informal*), probing, prying, questioning

insane adjective **1** MAD, crazed, crazy, demented, deranged, mentally ill, out of one's mind, unhinged **2** STUPID, daft (*informal*), foolish, idiotic, impractical, irrational, irresponsible, preposterous, senseless

insanitary adjective UNHEALTHY, dirty, disease-ridden, filthy, infested, insalubrious, polluted, unclean, unhygienic

insanity noun **1** MADNESS, delirium, dementia, mental disorder, mental illness **2** STUPIDITY, folly, irresponsibility, lunacy, senselessness

insatiable adjective UNQUENCHABLE, greedy, intemperate, rapacious, ravenous, voracious

inscribe verb CARVE, cut, engrave, etch, impress, imprint

inscription noun ENGRAVING, dedication, legend, words

inscrutable adjective **1** ENIGMATIC, blank, deadpan, impenetrable, poker-faced (*informal*) **2** MYSTERIOUS, hidden, incomprehensible, inexplicable, unexplainable, unfathomable, unintelligible

insecure adjective **1** ANXIOUS, afraid, uncertain, unsure **2** UNSAFE, defenceless, exposed, unguarded, unprotected, vulnerable, wide-open

insecurity noun <u>ANXIETY</u>, fear, uncertainty, worry

insensible adjective <u>UNAWARE</u>, impervious, oblivious, unaffected, unconscious, unmindful

insensitive adjective <u>UNFEELING</u>, callous, hardened, indifferent, thick-skinned, tough, uncaring, unconcerned

inseparable adjective 1 <u>INDIVISIBLE</u>, indissoluble 2 <u>DEVOTED</u>, bosom, close, intimate

insert verb <u>ENTER</u>, embed, implant, introduce, place, put, stick in

insertion noun <u>INCLUSION</u>, addition, implant, interpolation, introduction, supplement

inside adjective 1 <u>INNER</u>, interior, internal, inward 2 <u>CONFIDENTIAL</u>, classified, exclusive, internal, private, restricted, secret ♦ adverb 3 <u>INDOORS</u>, under cover, within ♦ noun 4 <u>INTERIOR</u>, contents 5 **insides** Informal <u>STOMACH</u>, belly, bowels, entrails, guts, innards (informal), viscera, vitals

insidious adjective <u>STEALTHY</u>, deceptive, sly, smooth, sneaking, subtle, surreptitious

insight noun <u>UNDERSTANDING</u>, awareness, comprehension, discernment, judgment, observation, penetration, perception, perspicacity, vision

insignia noun <u>BADGE</u>, crest, emblem, symbol

insignificance noun <u>UNIMPORTANCE</u>, inconsequence, irrelevance, meaninglessness, pettiness, triviality, worthlessness

insignificant adjective <u>UNIMPORTANT</u>, inconsequential, irrelevant, meaningless, minor, nondescript, paltry, petty, trifling, trivial

insincere adjective <u>DECEITFUL</u>, dishonest, disingenuous, duplicitous, false, hollow, hypocritical, lying, two-faced, untruthful

insincerity noun <u>DECEITFULNESS</u>, dishonesty, dissimulation, duplicity, hypocrisy, pretence, untruthfulness

insinuate verb 1 <u>IMPLY</u>, allude, hint, indicate, intimate, suggest 2 <u>INGRATIATE</u>, curry favour, get in with, worm or work one's way in

insinuation noun <u>IMPLICATION</u>, allusion, aspersion, hint, innuendo, slur, suggestion

insipid adjective 1 <u>BLAND</u>, anaemic, characterless, colourless, prosaic, uninteresting, vapid, wishy-washy (informal) 2 <u>TASTELESS</u>, bland, flavourless, unappetizing, watery

insist verb 1 <u>DEMAND</u>, lay down the law, put one's foot down (informal), require 2 <u>ASSERT</u>, aver, claim, maintain, reiterate, repeat, swear, vow

insistence noun <u>PERSISTENCE</u>, emphasis, importunity, stress

insistent adjective <u>PERSISTENT</u>, dogged, emphatic, importunate, incessant, persevering, unrelenting, urgent

insolence noun <u>RUDENESS</u>, boldness, cheek (informal), disrespect, effrontery, impertinence, impudence

insolent adjective <u>RUDE</u>, bold, contemptuous, impertinent, impudent, insubordinate, insulting

insoluble adjective <u>INEXPLICABLE</u>, baffling, impenetrable, indecipherable, mysterious, unaccountable, unfathomable, unsolvable

insolvency noun <u>BANKRUPTCY</u>, failure, liquidation, ruin

insolvent *adjective* BANKRUPT, broke (*informal*), failed, gone bust (*informal*), gone to the wall, in receivership, ruined

insomnia *noun* SLEEPLESSNESS, wakefulness

inspect *verb* EXAMINE, check, go over *or* through, investigate, look over, scrutinize, survey, vet

inspection *noun* EXAMINATION, check, checkup, investigation, once-over (*informal*), review, scrutiny, search, survey

inspector *noun* EXAMINER, censor, investigator, overseer, scrutinizer, superintendent, supervisor

inspiration *noun* 1 INFLUENCE, muse, spur, stimulus 2 REVELATION, creativity, illumination, insight

inspire *verb* 1 STIMULATE, animate, encourage, enliven, galvanize, influence, spur 2 AROUSE, enkindle, excite, give rise to, produce

inspired *adjective* 1 BRILLIANT, dazzling, impressive, memorable, outstanding, superlative, thrilling, wonderful 2 UPLIFTED, elated, enthused, exhilarated, stimulated

inspiring *adjective* UPLIFTING, exciting, exhilarating, heartening, moving, rousing, stimulating, stirring

instability *noun* UNPREDICTABILITY, changeableness, fickleness, fluctuation, impermanence, inconstancy, insecurity, unsteadiness, variability, volatility

install *verb* 1 SET UP, fix, lay, lodge, place, position, put in, station 2 INDUCT, establish, inaugurate, institute, introduce, invest 3 SETTLE, ensconce, position

installation *noun* 1 SETTING UP, establishment, fitting, instalment, placing, positioning 2 INDUCTION, inauguration, investiture 3 EQUIPMENT, machinery, plant, system

instalment *noun* PORTION, chapter, division, episode, part, repayment, section

instance *noun* 1 EXAMPLE, case, illustration, occasion, occurrence, situation ♦ *verb* 2 QUOTE, adduce, cite, mention, name, specify

instant *noun* 1 SECOND, flash, jiffy (*informal*), moment, split second, trice, twinkling of an eye (*informal*) 2 JUNCTURE, moment, occasion, point, time ♦ *adjective* 3 IMMEDIATE, direct, instantaneous, on-the-spot, prompt, quick, split-second 4 PRECOOKED, convenience, fast, ready-mixed

instantaneous *adjective* IMMEDIATE, direct, instant, on-the-spot, prompt

instantaneously *adverb* IMMEDIATELY, at once, instantly, in the twinkling of an eye (*informal*), on the spot, promptly, straight away

instantly *adverb* IMMEDIATELY, at once, directly, instantaneously, now, right away, straight away, this minute

instead *adverb* 1 RATHER, alternatively, in lieu, in preference, on second thoughts, preferably 2 **instead of** IN PLACE OF, in lieu of, rather than

instigate *verb* PROVOKE, bring about, incite, influence, initiate, prompt, set off, start, stimulate, trigger

instigation *noun* PROMPTING, behest, bidding, encouragement, incitement, urging

instigator *noun* RINGLEADER, agitator, leader, motivator, prime mover, troublemaker

instil *verb* INTRODUCE, engender, imbue, implant, inculcate, infuse, insinuate

instinct noun INTUITION, faculty, gift, impulse, knack, predisposition, proclivity, talent, tendency

instinctive adjective INBORN, automatic, inherent, innate, intuitive, involuntary, natural, reflex, spontaneous, unpremeditated, visceral

instinctively adverb INTUITIVELY, automatically, by instinct, involuntarily, naturally, without thinking

institute noun 1 SOCIETY, academy, association, college, foundation, guild, institution, school ♦ verb 2 ESTABLISH, fix, found, initiate, introduce, launch, organize, originate, pioneer, set up, start

institution noun 1 ESTABLISHMENT, academy, college, foundation, institute, school, society 2 CUSTOM, convention, law, practice, ritual, rule, tradition

institutional adjective CONVENTIONAL, accepted, established, formal, orthodox

instruct verb 1 ORDER, bid, charge, command, direct, enjoin, tell 2 TEACH, coach, drill, educate, ground, school, train, tutor

instruction noun 1 TEACHING, coaching, education, grounding, guidance, lesson(s), schooling, training, tuition 2 ORDER, command, demand, directive, injunction, mandate, ruling

instructions plural noun ORDERS, advice, directions, guidance, information, key, recommendations, rules

instructive adjective INFORMATIVE, edifying, educational, enlightening, helpful, illuminating, revealing, useful

instructor noun TEACHER, adviser, coach, demonstrator, guide, mentor, trainer, tutor

instrument noun 1 TOOL, apparatus, appliance, contraption (informal), device, gadget, implement, mechanism 2 MEANS, agency, agent, mechanism, medium, organ, vehicle

instrumental adjective ACTIVE, contributory, helpful, influential, involved, useful

insubordinate adjective DISOBEDIENT, defiant, disorderly, mutinous, rebellious, recalcitrant, refractory, undisciplined, ungovernable, unruly

insubordination noun DISOBEDIENCE, defiance, indiscipline, insurrection, mutiny, rebellion, recalcitrance, revolt

insubstantial adjective FLIMSY, feeble, frail, poor, slight, tenuous, thin, weak

insufferable adjective UNBEARABLE, detestable, dreadful, impossible, insupportable, intolerable, unendurable

insufficient adjective INADEQUATE, deficient, incapable, lacking, scant, short

insular adjective NARROW-MINDED, blinkered, circumscribed, inward-looking, limited, narrow, parochial, petty, provincial

insulate verb ISOLATE, close off, cocoon, cushion, cut off, protect, sequester, shield

insult verb 1 OFFEND, abuse, affront, call names, put down, slander, slight, snub ♦ noun 2 ABUSE, affront, aspersion, insolence, offence, put-down, slap in the face (informal), slight, snub

insulting adjective OFFENSIVE, abusive, contemptuous, degrading, disparaging, insolent, rude, scurrilous

insuperable adjective INSURMOUNTABLE, impassable,

invincible, unconquerable

insupportable *adjective*
1 INTOLERABLE, insufferable,
unbearable, unendurable
2 UNJUSTIFIABLE, indefensible,
untenable

insurance *noun* PROTECTION,
assurance, cover, guarantee,
indemnity, safeguard, security,
warranty

insure *verb* PROTECT, assure, cover,
guarantee, indemnify, underwrite,
warrant

insurgent *noun* **1** REBEL,
insurrectionist, mutineer,
revolutionary, rioter ♦ *adjective*
2 REBELLIOUS, disobedient,
insubordinate, mutinous,
revolting, revolutionary, riotous,
seditious

insurmountable *adjective*
INSUPERABLE, hopeless, impassable,
impossible, invincible,
overwhelming, unconquerable

insurrection *noun* REBELLION, coup,
insurgency, mutiny, revolt,
revolution, riot, uprising

intact *adjective* UNDAMAGED,
complete, entire, perfect, sound,
unbroken, unharmed,
unimpaired, unscathed, whole

integral *adjective* ESSENTIAL, basic,
component, constituent,
fundamental, indispensable,
intrinsic, necessary

integrate *verb* COMBINE,
amalgamate, assimilate, blend,
fuse, incorporate, join, merge,
unite

integration *noun* ASSIMILATION,
amalgamation, blending,
combining, fusing, incorporation,
mixing, unification

integrity *noun* **1** HONESTY,
goodness, honour,
incorruptibility, principle, probity,
purity, rectitude, uprightness,

virtue **2** UNITY, coherence,
cohesion, completeness,
soundness, wholeness

intellect *noun* INTELLIGENCE, brains
(*informal*), judgment, mind,
reason, sense, understanding

intellectual *adjective* **1** SCHOLARLY,
bookish, cerebral, highbrow,
intelligent, studious, thoughtful
♦ *noun* **2** THINKER, academic,
egghead (*informal*), highbrow

intelligence *noun* **1** UNDERSTANDING,
acumen, brain power, brains
(*informal*), cleverness,
comprehension, intellect,
perception, sense **2** INFORMATION,
data, facts, findings, knowledge,
news, notification, report

intelligent *adjective* CLEVER, brainy
(*informal*), bright, enlightened,
perspicacious, quick-witted,
sharp, smart, well-informed

intelligentsia *noun* INTELLECTUALS,
highbrows, literati

intelligible *adjective*
UNDERSTANDABLE, clear,
comprehensible, distinct, lucid,
open, plain

intemperate *adjective* EXCESSIVE,
extreme, immoderate, profligate,
self-indulgent, unbridled,
unrestrained, wild

intend *verb* PLAN, aim, have in mind
or view, mean, propose, purpose

intense *adjective* **1** EXTREME, acute,
deep, excessive, fierce, great,
powerful, profound, severe
2 PASSIONATE, ardent, fanatical,
fervent, fierce, heightened,
impassioned, vehement

intensify *verb* INCREASE, add to,
aggravate, deepen, escalate,
heighten, magnify, redouble,
reinforce, sharpen, strengthen

intensity *noun* FORCE, ardour,
emotion, fanaticism, fervour,
fierceness, passion, strength,

vehemence

intensive *adjective* <u>CONCENTRATED</u>, comprehensive, demanding, exhaustive, in-depth, thorough, thoroughgoing

intent *noun* **1** <u>INTENTION</u>, aim, design, end, goal, meaning, object, objective, plan, purpose ◆ *adjective* **2** <u>ATTENTIVE</u>, absorbed, determined, eager, engrossed, preoccupied, rapt, resolved, steadfast, watchful

intention *noun* <u>PURPOSE</u>, aim, design, end, goal, idea, object, objective, point, target

intentional *adjective* <u>DELIBERATE</u>, calculated, intended, meant, planned, premeditated, wilful

intentionally *adverb* <u>DELIBERATELY</u>, designedly, on purpose, wilfully

inter *verb* <u>BURY</u>, entomb, lay to rest

intercede *verb* <u>MEDIATE</u>, arbitrate, intervene, plead

intercept *verb* <u>SEIZE</u>, block, catch, cut off, head off, interrupt, obstruct, stop

interchange *verb* **1** <u>SWITCH</u>, alternate, exchange, reciprocate, swap ◆ *noun* **2** <u>JUNCTION</u>, intersection

interchangeable *adjective* <u>IDENTICAL</u>, equivalent, exchangeable, reciprocal, synonymous

intercourse *noun* **1** <u>COMMUNICATION</u>, commerce, contact, dealings **2** <u>SEXUAL INTERCOURSE</u>, carnal knowledge, coitus, copulation, sex (*informal*)

interest *noun* **1** <u>CURIOSITY</u>, attention, concern, notice, regard **2** <u>HOBBY</u>, activity, diversion, pastime, preoccupation, pursuit **3** <u>ADVANTAGE</u>, benefit, good, profit **4** <u>STAKE</u>, claim, investment, right, share ◆ *verb* **5** <u>INTRIGUE</u>, attract, catch one's eye, divert, engross, fascinate

interested *adjective* **1** <u>CURIOUS</u>, attracted, drawn, excited, fascinated, keen **2** <u>INVOLVED</u>, concerned, implicated

interesting *adjective* <u>INTRIGUING</u>, absorbing, appealing, attractive, compelling, engaging, engrossing, gripping, stimulating, thought-provoking

interface *noun* <u>CONNECTION</u>, border, boundary, frontier, link

interfere *verb* **1** <u>INTRUDE</u>, butt in, intervene, meddle, stick one's oar in (*informal*), tamper **2** *often with* *with* <u>CONFLICT</u>, clash, hamper, handicap, hinder, impede, inhibit, obstruct

interference *noun* **1** <u>INTRUSION</u>, intervention, meddling, prying **2** <u>CONFLICT</u>, clashing, collision, obstruction, opposition

interim *adjective* <u>TEMPORARY</u>, acting, caretaker, improvised, makeshift, provisional, stopgap

interior *noun* **1** <u>INSIDE</u>, centre, core, heart ◆ *adjective* **2** <u>INSIDE</u>, inner, internal, inward **3** <u>MENTAL</u>, hidden, inner, intimate, personal, private, secret, spiritual

interloper *noun* <u>TRESPASSER</u>, gate-crasher (*informal*), intruder, meddler

interlude *noun* <u>INTERVAL</u>, break, breathing space, delay, hiatus, intermission, pause, respite, rest, spell, stoppage

intermediary *noun* <u>MEDIATOR</u>, agent, broker, go-between, middleman

intermediate *adjective* <u>MIDDLE</u>, halfway, in-between (*informal*), intervening, mid, midway, transitional

interment *noun* <u>BURIAL</u>, funeral

interminable *adjective* ENDLESS, ceaseless, everlasting, infinite, long-drawn-out, long-winded, never-ending, perpetual, protracted

intermingle *verb* MIX, blend, combine, fuse, interlace, intermix, interweave, merge

intermission *noun* INTERVAL, break, interlude, pause, recess, respite, rest, stoppage

intermittent *adjective* PERIODIC, broken, fitful, irregular, occasional, spasmodic, sporadic

intern *verb* IMPRISON, confine, detain, hold, hold in custody

internal *adjective* 1 INNER, inside, interior 2 DOMESTIC, civic, home, in-house, intramural

international *adjective* UNIVERSAL, cosmopolitan, global, intercontinental, worldwide

Internet *noun* INFORMATION SUPERHIGHWAY, cyberspace, the net (*informal*), the web (*informal*), World Wide Web

interpose *verb* INTERRUPT, insert, interject, put one's oar in

interpret *verb* EXPLAIN, construe, decipher, decode, elucidate, make sense of, render, translate

interpretation *noun* EXPLANATION, analysis, clarification, elucidation, exposition, portrayal, rendition, translation, version

interpreter *noun* TRANSLATOR, commentator

interrogate *verb* QUESTION, cross-examine, examine, grill (*informal*), investigate, pump, quiz

interrogation *noun* QUESTIONING, cross-examination, examination, grilling (*informal*), inquiry, inquisition, third degree (*informal*)

interrupt *verb* 1 INTRUDE, barge in

(*informal*), break in, butt in, disturb, heckle, interfere (with) 2 SUSPEND, break off, cut short, delay, discontinue, hold up, lay aside, stop

interruption *noun* STOPPAGE, break, disruption, disturbance, hitch, intrusion, pause, suspension

intersection *noun* JUNCTION, crossing, crossroads, interchange

interval *noun* BREAK, delay, gap, interlude, intermission, pause, respite, rest, space, spell

intervene *verb* 1 INVOLVE ONESELF, arbitrate, intercede, interfere, intrude, mediate, step in (*informal*), take a hand (*informal*) 2 HAPPEN, befall, come to pass, ensue, occur, take place

intervention *noun* MEDIATION, agency, interference, intrusion

interview *noun* 1 MEETING, audience, conference, consultation, dialogue, press conference, talk ♦ *verb* 2 QUESTION, examine, interrogate, talk to

interviewer *noun* QUESTIONER, examiner, interrogator, investigator, reporter

intestines *plural noun* GUTS, bowels, entrails, innards (*informal*), insides (*informal*), viscera

intimacy *noun* FAMILIARITY, closeness, confidentiality

intimate[1] *adjective* 1 CLOSE, bosom, confidential, dear, near, thick (*informal*) 2 PERSONAL, confidential, private, secret 3 DETAILED, deep, exhaustive, first-hand, immediate, in-depth, profound, thorough 4 SNUG, comfy (*informal*), cosy, friendly, warm ♦ *noun* 5 FRIEND, close friend, confidant *or* confidante, (constant) companion, crony

intimate[2] *verb* 1 SUGGEST, hint,

imply, indicate, insinuate
2 ANNOUNCE, communicate,
declare, make known, state

intimately *adverb* **1** CONFIDINGLY,
affectionately, confidentially,
familiarly, personally, tenderly,
warmly **2** IN DETAIL, fully, inside out,
thoroughly, very well

intimation *noun* **1** HINT, allusion,
indication, inkling, insinuation,
reminder, suggestion, warning
2 ANNOUNCEMENT, communication,
declaration, notice

intimidate *verb* FRIGHTEN, browbeat,
bully, coerce, daunt, overawe,
scare, subdue, terrorize, threaten

intimidation *noun* BULLYING,
arm-twisting (*informal*),
browbeating, coercion, menaces,
pressure, terrorization, threat(s)

intolerable *adjective* UNBEARABLE,
excruciating, impossible,
insufferable, insupportable,
painful, unendurable

intolerance *noun*
NARROW-MINDEDNESS, bigotry,
chauvinism, discrimination,
dogmatism, fanaticism, illiberality,
prejudice

intolerant *adjective* NARROW-MINDED,
bigoted, chauvinistic, dictatorial,
dogmatic, fanatical, illiberal,
prejudiced, small-minded

intone *verb* RECITE, chant

intoxicated *adjective* **1** DRUNK,
drunken, inebriated, legless
(*informal*), paralytic (*informal*),
plastered (*slang*), tipsy, under the
influence **2** EUPHORIC, dizzy, elated,
enraptured, excited, exhilarated,
high (*informal*)

intoxicating *adjective* **1** ALCOHOLIC,
strong **2** EXCITING, exhilarating,
heady, thrilling

intoxication *noun* **1** DRUNKENNESS,
inebriation, insobriety, tipsiness
2 EXCITEMENT, delirium, elation,
euphoria, exhilaration

intransigent *adjective*
UNCOMPROMISING, hardline,
intractable, obdurate, obstinate,
stiff-necked, stubborn,
unbending, unyielding

intrepid *adjective* FEARLESS,
audacious, bold, brave,
courageous, daring, gallant,
plucky, stouthearted, valiant

intricacy *noun* COMPLEXITY,
complication, convolutions,
elaborateness

intricate *adjective* COMPLICATED,
complex, convoluted, elaborate,
fancy, involved, labyrinthine,
tangled, tortuous

intrigue *verb* **1** INTEREST, attract,
fascinate, rivet, titillate **2** PLOT,
connive, conspire, machinate,
manoeuvre, scheme ♦ *noun* **3** PLOT,
chicanery, collusion, conspiracy,
machination, manoeuvre,
scheme, stratagem, wile **4** AFFAIR,
amour, intimacy, liaison, romance

intriguing *adjective* INTERESTING,
beguiling, compelling, diverting,
exciting, fascinating, tantalizing,
titillating

intrinsic *adjective* INBORN, basic,
built-in, congenital, constitutional,
essential, fundamental, inbred,
inherent, native, natural

introduce *verb* **1** PRESENT, acquaint,
familiarize, make known **2** BRING IN,
establish, found, initiate, institute,
launch, pioneer, set up, start
3 BRING UP, advance, air, broach,
moot, put forward, submit
4 INSERT, add, inject, put in, throw
in (*informal*)

introduction *noun* **1** LAUNCH,
establishment, inauguration,
institution, pioneering **2** OPENING,
foreword, intro (*informal*), lead-in,
preamble, preface, prelude,
prologue

introductory adjective PRELIMINARY, first, inaugural, initial, opening, preparatory

introspective adjective INWARD-LOOKING, brooding, contemplative, introverted, meditative, pensive

introverted adjective INTROSPECTIVE, inner-directed, inward-looking, self-contained, withdrawn

intrude verb INTERFERE, butt in, encroach, infringe, interrupt, meddle, push in, trespass

intruder noun TRESPASSER, gate-crasher (*informal*), infiltrator, interloper, invader, prowler

intrusion noun INVASION, encroachment, infringement, interference, interruption, trespass

intrusive adjective INTERFERING, impertinent, importunate, meddlesome, nosy (*informal*), presumptuous, pushy (*informal*), uncalled-for, unwanted

intuition noun INSTINCT, hunch, insight, perception, presentiment, sixth sense

intuitive adjective INSTINCTIVE, innate, spontaneous, untaught

inundate verb FLOOD, drown, engulf, immerse, overflow, overrun, overwhelm, submerge, swamp

invade verb 1 ATTACK, assault, burst in, descend upon, encroach, infringe, make inroads, occupy, raid, violate 2 INFEST, overrun, permeate, pervade, swarm over

invader noun ATTACKER, aggressor, plunderer, raider, trespasser

invalid[1] adjective 1 DISABLED, ailing, bedridden, frail, ill, infirm, sick ♦ noun 2 PATIENT, convalescent, valetudinarian

invalid[2] adjective NULL AND VOID, fallacious, false, illogical, inoperative, irrational, unfounded, unsound, void, worthless

invalidate verb NULLIFY, annul, cancel, overthrow, undermine, undo

invaluable adjective PRECIOUS, inestimable, priceless, valuable, worth one's *or* its weight in gold

invariably adverb CONSISTENTLY, always, customarily, day in, day out, habitually, perpetually, regularly, unfailingly, without exception

invasion noun 1 ATTACK, assault, campaign, foray, incursion, inroad, offensive, onslaught, raid 2 INTRUSION, breach, encroachment, infraction, infringement, usurpation, violation

invective noun ABUSE, censure, denunciation, diatribe, tirade, tongue-lashing, vilification, vituperation

invent verb 1 CREATE, coin, conceive, design, devise, discover, formulate, improvise, originate, think up 2 MAKE UP, concoct, cook up (*informal*), fabricate, feign, forge, manufacture, trump up

invention noun 1 CREATION, brainchild (*informal*), contraption, contrivance, design, device, discovery, gadget, instrument 2 CREATIVITY, genius, imagination, ingenuity, inventiveness, originality, resourcefulness 3 FICTION, fabrication, falsehood, fantasy, forgery, lie, untruth, yarn

inventive adjective CREATIVE, fertile, imaginative, ingenious, innovative, inspired, original, resourceful

inventor noun CREATOR, architect, author, coiner, designer, maker, originator

inventory noun LIST, account, catalogue, file, record, register, roll, roster

inverse adjective OPPOSITE, contrary, converse, reverse, reversed, transposed

invert verb OVERTURN, reverse, transpose, upset, upturn

invest verb 1 SPEND, advance, devote, lay out, put in, sink 2 EMPOWER, authorize, charge, license, sanction, vest

investigate verb EXAMINE, explore, go into, inquire into, inspect, look into, probe, research, study

investigation noun EXAMINATION, exploration, inquest, inquiry, inspection, probe, review, search, study, survey

investigator noun EXAMINER, inquirer, (private) detective, private eye (informal), researcher, sleuth

investiture noun INSTALLATION, enthronement, inauguration, induction, ordination

investment noun 1 TRANSACTION, speculation, venture 2 STAKE, ante (informal), contribution

inveterate adjective LONG-STANDING, chronic, confirmed, deep-seated, dyed-in-the-wool, entrenched, habitual, hardened, incorrigible, incurable

invidious adjective UNDESIRABLE, hateful

invigilate verb WATCH OVER, conduct, keep an eye on, oversee, preside over, run, superintend, supervise

invigorate verb REFRESH, energize, enliven, exhilarate, fortify, galvanize, liven up, revitalize, stimulate

invincible adjective UNBEATABLE, impregnable, indestructible, indomitable, insuperable, invulnerable, unassailable,

unconquerable

inviolable adjective SACROSANCT, hallowed, holy, inalienable, sacred, unalterable

inviolate adjective INTACT, entire, pure, unbroken, undefiled, unhurt, unpolluted, unsullied, untouched, whole

invisible adjective UNSEEN, imperceptible, indiscernible

invitation noun REQUEST, call, invite (informal), summons

invite verb 1 REQUEST, ask, beg, bid, summon 2 ENCOURAGE, ask for (informal), attract, court, entice, provoke, tempt, welcome

inviting adjective TEMPTING, alluring, appealing, attractive, enticing, mouthwatering, seductive, welcoming

invocation noun APPEAL, entreaty, petition, prayer, supplication

invoke verb 1 CALL UPON, appeal to, beg, beseech, entreat, implore, petition, pray, supplicate 2 APPLY, implement, initiate, put into effect, resort to, use

involuntary adjective UNINTENTIONAL, automatic, instinctive, reflex, spontaneous, unconscious, uncontrolled, unthinking

involve verb 1 ENTAIL, imply, mean, necessitate, presuppose, require 2 CONCERN, affect, draw in, implicate, touch

involved adjective 1 COMPLICATED, complex, confusing, convoluted, elaborate, intricate, labyrinthine, tangled, tortuous 2 CONCERNED, caught (up), implicated, mixed up in or with, participating, taking part

involvement noun CONNECTION, association, commitment, interest, participation

invulnerable *adjective* SAFE, impenetrable, indestructible, insusceptible, invincible, proof against, secure, unassailable

inward *adjective* 1 INCOMING, entering, inbound, ingoing 2 INTERNAL, inner, inside, interior 3 PRIVATE, confidential, hidden, inmost, innermost, personal, secret

inwardly *adverb* PRIVATELY, at heart, deep down, inside, secretly

irate *adjective* ANGRY, annoyed, cross, enraged, furious, incensed, indignant, infuriated, livid

irksome *adjective* IRRITATING, annoying, bothersome, disagreeable, exasperating, tiresome, troublesome, trying, vexing, wearisome

iron *adjective* 1 FERROUS, chalybeate, ferric 2 INFLEXIBLE, adamant, hard, implacable, indomitable, rigid, steely, strong, tough, unbending, unyielding

ironic, ironical *adjective* 1 SARCASTIC, double-edged, mocking, sardonic, satirical, with tongue in cheek, wry 2 PARADOXICAL, incongruous

iron out *verb* SETTLE, clear up, get rid of, put right, reconcile, resolve, smooth over, sort out, straighten out

irony *noun* 1 SARCASM, mockery, satire 2 PARADOX, incongruity

irrational *adjective* ILLOGICAL, absurd, crazy, nonsensical, preposterous, unreasonable

irrefutable *adjective* UNDENIABLE, certain, incontestable, incontrovertible, indisputable, indubitable, sure, unquestionable

irregular *adjective* 1 VARIABLE, erratic, fitful, haphazard, occasional, random, spasmodic, sporadic, unsystematic 2 UNCONVENTIONAL, abnormal,

exceptional, extraordinary, peculiar, unofficial, unorthodox, unusual 3 UNEVEN, asymmetrical, bumpy, crooked, jagged, lopsided, ragged, rough

irregularity *noun* 1 UNCERTAINTY, desultoriness, disorganization, haphazardness 2 ABNORMALITY, anomaly, oddity, peculiarity, unorthodoxy 3 UNEVENNESS, asymmetry, bumpiness, jaggedness, lopsidedness, raggedness, roughness

irrelevant *adjective* UNCONNECTED, beside the point, extraneous, immaterial, impertinent, inapplicable, inappropriate, neither here nor there, unrelated

irreparable *adjective* BEYOND REPAIR, incurable, irremediable, irretrievable, irreversible

irrepressible *adjective* EBULLIENT, boisterous, buoyant, effervescent, unstoppable

irreproachable *adjective* BLAMELESS, beyond reproach, faultless, impeccable, innocent, perfect, pure, unimpeachable

irresistible *adjective* OVERWHELMING, compelling, compulsive, overpowering, urgent

irresponsible *adjective* IMMATURE, careless, reckless, scatterbrained, shiftless, thoughtless, unreliable, untrustworthy

irreverent *adjective* DISRESPECTFUL, cheeky (*informal*), flippant, iconoclastic, impertinent, impudent, mocking, tongue-in-cheek

irreversible *adjective* IRREVOCABLE, final, incurable, irreparable, unalterable

irrevocable *adjective* FIXED, fated, immutable, irreversible, predestined, predetermined, settled, unalterable

irrigate verb WATER, flood, inundate, moisten, wet

irritability noun BAD TEMPER, ill humour, impatience, irascibility, prickliness, testiness, tetchiness, touchiness

irritable adjective BAD-TEMPERED, cantankerous, crotchety (informal), ill-tempered, irascible, oversensitive, prickly, testy, tetchy, touchy

irritate verb 1 ANNOY, anger, bother, exasperate, get on one's nerves (informal), infuriate, needle (informal), nettle, rankle with, try one's patience 2 RUB, chafe, inflame, pain

irritated adjective ANNOYED, angry, bothered, cross, exasperated, nettled, piqued, put out, vexed

irritating adjective ANNOYING, disturbing, infuriating, irksome, maddening, nagging, troublesome, trying

irritation noun 1 ANNOYANCE, anger, displeasure, exasperation, indignation, resentment, testiness, vexation 2 NUISANCE, drag (informal), irritant, pain in the neck (informal), thorn in one's flesh

island noun ISLE, ait or eyot (dialect), atoll, cay or key, islet

isolate verb SEPARATE, cut off, detach, disconnect, insulate, segregate, set apart

isolated adjective REMOTE, hidden, lonely, off the beaten track, outlying, out-of-the-way, secluded

isolation noun SEPARATION, detachment, remoteness, seclusion, segregation, solitude

issue noun 1 TOPIC, bone of contention, matter, point, problem, question, subject 2 OUTCOME, consequence, effect, end result, result, upshot 3 EDITION, copy, number, printing 4 CHILDREN, descendants, heirs, offspring, progeny 5 **take issue** DISAGREE, challenge, dispute, object, oppose, raise an objection, take exception ♦ verb 6 PUBLISH, announce, broadcast, circulate, deliver, distribute, give out, put out, release

isthmus noun STRIP, spit

itch noun 1 IRRITATION, itchiness, prickling, tingling 2 DESIRE, craving, hankering, hunger, longing, lust, passion, yearning, yen (informal) ♦ verb 3 PRICKLE, irritate, tickle, tingle 4 LONG, ache, crave, hanker, hunger, lust, pine, yearn

itching adjective LONGING, avid, eager, impatient, mad keen (informal), raring, spoiling for

itchy adjective IMPATIENT, eager, edgy, fidgety, restive, restless, unsettled

item noun 1 DETAIL, article, component, entry, matter, particular, point, thing 2 REPORT, account, article, bulletin, dispatch, feature, note, notice, paragraph, piece

itinerant adjective WANDERING, migratory, nomadic, peripatetic, roaming, roving, travelling, vagrant

itinerary noun SCHEDULE, programme, route, timetable

J j

jab *verb, noun* <u>POKE</u>, dig, lunge, nudge, prod, punch, stab, tap, thrust

jabber *verb* <u>CHATTER</u>, babble, blether, gabble, mumble, prate, rabbit (on) (*Brit. informal*), ramble, yap (*informal*)

jacket *noun* <u>COVERING</u>, case, casing, coat, sheath, skin, wrapper, wrapping

jackpot *noun* <u>PRIZE</u>, award, bonanza, reward, winnings

jack up *verb* <u>RAISE</u>, elevate, hoist, lift, lift up

jaded *adjective* <u>TIRED</u>, exhausted, fatigued, spent, weary

jagged *adjective* <u>UNEVEN</u>, barbed, craggy, indented, ragged, serrated, spiked, toothed

jail *noun* **1** <u>PRISON</u>, nick (*Brit. slang*), penitentiary (*U.S.*), reformatory, slammer (*slang*) ♦ *verb* **2** <u>IMPRISON</u>, confine, detain, incarcerate, lock up, send down

jailer *noun* <u>GUARD</u>, keeper, warden, warder

jam *verb* **1** <u>PACK</u>, cram, force, press, ram, squeeze, stuff, wedge **2** <u>CROWD</u>, crush, throng **3** <u>CONGEST</u>, block, clog, obstruct, stall, stick ♦ *noun* **4** <u>PREDICAMENT</u>, deep water, fix (*informal*), hole (*slang*), hot water, pickle (*informal*), tight spot, trouble

jamboree *noun* <u>FESTIVAL</u>, carnival, celebration, festivity, fête, revelry

jangle *verb* <u>RATTLE</u>, chime, clank, clash, clatter, jingle, vibrate

janitor *noun* <u>CARETAKER</u>, concierge, custodian, doorkeeper, porter

jar¹ *noun* <u>POT</u>, container, crock, jug, pitcher, urn, vase

jar² *verb* **1** <u>JOLT</u>, bump, convulse, rattle, rock, shake, vibrate **2** <u>IRRITATE</u>, annoy, get on one's nerves (*informal*), grate, irk, nettle, offend ♦ *noun* **3** <u>JOLT</u>, bump, convulsion, shock, vibration

jargon *noun* <u>PARLANCE</u>, argot, idiom, usage

jaundiced *adjective* **1** <u>CYNICAL</u>, sceptical **2** <u>BITTER</u>, envious, hostile, jealous, resentful, spiteful, suspicious

jaunt *noun* <u>OUTING</u>, airing, excursion, expedition, ramble, stroll, tour, trip

jaunty *adjective* <u>SPRIGHTLY</u>, buoyant, carefree, high-spirited, lively, perky, self-confident, sparky

jaw *verb* <u>TALK</u>, chat, chatter, gossip, spout

jaws *plural noun* <u>OPENING</u>, entrance, mouth

jazz up *verb* <u>ENLIVEN</u>, animate, enhance, improve

jazzy *adjective* <u>FLASHY</u>, fancy, gaudy, snazzy (*informal*)

jealous *adjective* **1** <u>ENVIOUS</u>, covetous, desirous, green, grudging, resentful **2** <u>WARY</u>, mistrustful, protective, suspicious, vigilant, watchful

jealousy *noun* <u>ENVY</u>, covetousness, mistrust, possessiveness, resentment, spite, suspicion

jeans *plural noun* <u>DENIMS</u>, Levis (*Trademark*)

jeer *verb* **1** <u>SCOFF</u>, barrack, deride, gibe, heckle, mock, ridicule, taunt ♦ *noun* **2** <u>TAUNT</u>, abuse, boo, catcall, derision, gibe, ridicule

jell *verb* **1** <u>SOLIDIFY</u>, congeal, harden, set, thicken **2** <u>TAKE SHAPE</u>, come together, crystallize, materialize

jeopardize *verb* ENDANGER, chance, expose, gamble, imperil, risk, stake, venture

jeopardy *noun* DANGER, insecurity, peril, risk, vulnerability

jerk *verb, noun* TUG, jolt, lurch, pull, thrust, twitch, wrench, yank

jerky *adjective* BUMPY, convulsive, jolting, jumpy, shaky, spasmodic, twitchy

jerry-built *adjective* RAMSHACKLE, cheap, defective, flimsy, rickety, shabby, slipshod, thrown together

jest *noun* 1 JOKE, bon mot, crack (*slang*), jape, pleasantry, prank, quip, wisecrack (*informal*), witticism ♦ *verb* 2 JOKE, kid (*informal*), mock, quip, tease

jester *noun* CLOWN, buffoon, fool, harlequin

jet¹ *adjective* BLACK, coal-black, ebony, inky, pitch-black, raven, sable

jet² *noun* 1 STREAM, flow, fountain, gush, spout, spray, spring 2 NOZZLE, atomizer, sprayer, sprinkler ♦ *verb* 3 FLY, soar, zoom

jettison *verb* ABANDON, discard, dump, eject, expel, scrap, throw overboard, unload

jetty *noun* PIER, breakwater, dock, groyne, mole, quay, wharf

jewel *noun* 1 GEMSTONE, ornament, rock (*slang*), sparkler (*informal*) 2 RARITY, collector's item, find, gem, humdinger (*slang*), pearl, treasure, wonder

jewellery *noun* JEWELS, finery, gems, ornaments, regalia, treasure, trinkets

jib *verb* REFUSE, balk, recoil, retreat, shrink, stop short

jibe see GIBE

jig *verb* SKIP, bob, bounce, caper, prance, wiggle

jingle *noun* 1 RATTLE, clang, clink, reverberation, ringing, tinkle 2 SONG, chorus, ditty, melody, tune ♦ *verb* 3 RING, chime, clatter, clink, jangle, rattle, tinkle

jinx *noun* 1 CURSE, hex (*U.S. & Canad. informal*), hoodoo (*informal*), nemesis ♦ *verb* 2 CURSE, bewitch, hex (*U.S. & Canad. informal*)

jitters *plural noun* NERVES, anxiety, butterflies (in one's stomach) (*informal*), cold feet (*informal*), fidgets, nervousness, the shakes (*informal*)

jittery *adjective* NERVOUS, agitated, anxious, fidgety, jumpy, shaky, trembling, twitchy (*informal*)

job *noun* 1 TASK, assignment, chore, duty, enterprise, errand, undertaking, venture 2 OCCUPATION, business, calling, career, employment, livelihood, profession, vocation

jobless *adjective* UNEMPLOYED, idle, inactive, out of work, unoccupied

jocular *adjective* HUMOROUS, amusing, droll, facetious, funny, joking, jovial, playful, sportive, teasing, waggish

jog *verb* 1 NUDGE, prod, push, shake, stir 2 RUN, canter, lope, trot

joie de vivre *noun* ENTHUSIASM, ebullience, enjoyment, gusto, relish, zest

join *verb* 1 CONNECT, add, append, attach, combine, couple, fasten, link, unite 2 ENROL, enlist, enter, sign up

joint *adjective* 1 SHARED, collective, combined, communal, cooperative, joined, mutual, united ♦ *noun* 2 JUNCTION, connection, hinge, intersection, nexus, node ♦ *verb* 3 DIVIDE, carve, cut up, dissect, segment, sever

jointly *adverb* <u>COLLECTIVELY</u>, as one, in common, in conjunction, in league, in partnership, mutually, together

joke *noun* **1** <u>JEST</u>, gag (*informal*), jape, prank, pun, quip, wisecrack (*informal*), witticism **2** <u>CLOWN</u>, buffoon, laughing stock ♦ *verb* **3** <u>JEST</u>, banter, kid (*informal*), mock, play the fool, quip, taunt, tease

joker *noun* <u>COMEDIAN</u>, buffoon, clown, comic, humorist, jester, prankster, trickster, wag, wit

jolly *adjective* <u>HAPPY</u>, cheerful, chirpy (*informal*), genial, jovial, merry, playful, sprightly, upbeat (*informal*)

jolt *noun* **1** <u>JERK</u>, bump, jar, jog, jump, lurch, shake, start **2** <u>SURPRISE</u>, blow, bolt from the blue, bombshell, setback, shock ♦ *verb* **3** <u>JERK</u>, jar, jog, jostle, knock, push, shake, shove **4** <u>SURPRISE</u>, discompose, disturb, perturb, stagger, startle, stun

jostle *verb* <u>PUSH</u>, bump, elbow, hustle, jog, jolt, shake, shove

jot *verb* **1** <u>NOTE DOWN</u>, list, record, scribble ♦ *noun* **2** <u>BIT</u>, fraction, grain, morsel, scrap, speck

journal *noun* **1** <u>NEWSPAPER</u>, daily, gazette, magazine, monthly, periodical, weekly **2** <u>DIARY</u>, chronicle, log, record

journalist *noun* <u>REPORTER</u>, broadcaster, columnist, commentator, correspondent, hack, journo (*slang*), newsman *or* newswoman, pressman

journey *noun* **1** <u>TRIP</u>, excursion, expedition, odyssey, pilgrimage, tour, trek, voyage ♦ *verb* **2** <u>TRAVEL</u>, go, proceed, roam, rove, tour, traverse, trek, voyage, wander

jovial *adjective* <u>CHEERFUL</u>, animated, cheery, convivial, happy, jolly, merry, mirthful

joy *noun* <u>DELIGHT</u>, bliss, ecstasy, elation, gaiety, glee, pleasure, rapture, satisfaction

joyful *adjective* <u>DELIGHTED</u>, elated, enraptured, glad, gratified, happy, jubilant, merry, pleased

joyless *adjective* <u>UNHAPPY</u>, cheerless, depressed, dismal, dreary, gloomy, miserable, sad

joyous *adjective* <u>JOYFUL</u>, festive, merry, rapturous

jubilant *adjective* <u>OVERJOYED</u>, elated, enraptured, euphoric, exuberant, exultant, thrilled, triumphant

jubilation *noun* <u>JOY</u>, celebration, ecstasy, elation, excitement, exultation, festivity, triumph

jubilee *noun* <u>CELEBRATION</u>, festival, festivity, holiday

judge *noun* **1** <u>REFEREE</u>, adjudicator, arbiter, arbitrator, moderator, umpire **2** <u>CRITIC</u>, arbiter, assessor, authority, connoisseur, expert **3** <u>MAGISTRATE</u>, beak (*Brit. slang*), justice ♦ *verb* **4** <u>ARBITRATE</u>, adjudicate, decide, mediate, referee, umpire **5** <u>CONSIDER</u>, appraise, assess, esteem, estimate, evaluate, rate, value

judgment *noun* **1** <u>SENSE</u>, acumen, discernment, discrimination, prudence, shrewdness, understanding, wisdom **2** <u>VERDICT</u>, arbitration, decision, decree, finding, ruling, sentence **3** <u>OPINION</u>, appraisal, assessment, belief, diagnosis, estimate, finding, valuation, view

judicial *adjective* <u>LEGAL</u>, official

judicious *adjective* <u>SENSIBLE</u>, astute, careful, discriminating, enlightened, prudent, shrewd, thoughtful, well-judged, wise

jug *noun* <u>CONTAINER</u>, carafe, crock, ewer, jar, pitcher, urn, vessel

juggle verb MANIPULATE, alter, change, manoeuvre, modify

juice noun LIQUID, extract, fluid, liquor, nectar, sap

juicy adjective **1** MOIST, lush, succulent **2** INTERESTING, colourful, provocative, racy, risqué, sensational, spicy (*informal*), suggestive, vivid

jumble noun **1** MUDDLE, clutter, confusion, disarray, disorder, mess, mishmash, mixture ♦ verb **2** MIX, confuse, disorder, disorganize, mistake, muddle, shuffle

jumbo adjective GIANT, gigantic, huge, immense, large, oversized

jump verb **1** LEAP, bounce, bound, hop, hurdle, skip, spring, vault **2** RECOIL, flinch, jerk, start, wince **3** MISS, avoid, evade, omit, skip **4** INCREASE, advance, ascend, escalate, rise, surge ♦ noun **5** LEAP, bound, hop, skip, spring, vault **6** INTERRUPTION, break, gap, hiatus, lacuna, space **7** RISE, advance, increase, increment, upsurge, upturn

jumped-up adjective CONCEITED, arrogant, insolent, overbearing, pompous, presumptuous

jumper noun SWEATER, jersey, pullover, woolly

jumpy adjective NERVOUS, agitated, anxious, apprehensive, fidgety, jittery (*informal*), on edge, restless, tense

junction noun CONNECTION, coupling, linking, union

juncture noun MOMENT, occasion, point, time

junior adjective MINOR, inferior, lesser, lower, secondary, subordinate, younger

junk noun RUBBISH, clutter, debris, litter, odds and ends, refuse, scrap, trash, waste

jurisdiction noun **1** AUTHORITY, command, control, influence, power, rule **2** RANGE, area, bounds, compass, field, province, scope, sphere

just adverb **1** EXACTLY, absolutely, completely, entirely, perfectly, precisely **2** RECENTLY, hardly, lately, only now, scarcely **3** MERELY, by the skin of one's teeth, only, simply, solely ♦ adjective **4** FAIR, conscientious, equitable, fair-minded, good, honest, upright, virtuous **5** PROPER, appropriate, apt, deserved, due, fitting, justified, merited, rightful

justice noun **1** FAIRNESS, equity, honesty, integrity, law, legality, legitimacy, right **2** JUDGE, magistrate

justifiable adjective REASONABLE, acceptable, defensible, excusable, legitimate, sensible, understandable, valid, warrantable

justification noun **1** EXPLANATION, defence, excuse, rationalization, vindication **2** REASON, basis, grounds, warrant

justify verb EXPLAIN, defend, exculpate, excuse, exonerate, support, uphold, vindicate, warrant

justly adverb PROPERLY, correctly, equitably, fairly, lawfully

jut verb STICK OUT, bulge, extend, overhang, poke, project, protrude

juvenile adjective **1** YOUNG, babyish, callow, childish, immature, inexperienced, infantile, puerile, youthful ♦ noun **2** CHILD, adolescent, boy, girl, infant, minor, youth

juxtaposition noun PROXIMITY, closeness, contact, nearness, propinquity, vicinity

K k

kamikaze *adjective* SELF-DESTRUCTIVE, foolhardy, suicidal

keel over *verb* COLLAPSE, black out (*informal*), faint, pass out

keen *adjective* 1 EAGER, ardent, avid, enthusiastic, impassioned, intense, zealous 2 SHARP, cutting, incisive, razor-like 3 ASTUTE, canny, clever, perceptive, quick, shrewd, wise

keenness *noun* EAGERNESS, ardour, enthusiasm, fervour, intensity, passion, zeal, zest

keep *verb* 1 RETAIN, conserve, control, hold, maintain, possess, preserve 2 STORE, carry, deposit, hold, place, stack, stock 3 LOOK AFTER, care for, guard, maintain, manage, mind, protect, tend, watch over 4 SUPPORT, feed, maintain, provide for, subsidize, sustain 5 DETAIN, delay, hinder, hold back, keep back, obstruct, prevent, restrain ♦ *noun* 6 BOARD, food, living, maintenance 7 TOWER, castle

keeper *noun* GUARDIAN, attendant, caretaker, curator, custodian, guard, preserver, steward, warden

keeping *noun* 1 CARE, charge, custody, guardianship, possession, protection, safekeeping 2 *As in* **in keeping with** AGREEMENT, accord, balance, compliance, conformity, correspondence, harmony, observance, proportion

keepsake *noun* SOUVENIR, memento, relic, reminder, symbol, token

keep up *verb* MAINTAIN, continue, keep pace, preserve, sustain

keg *noun* BARREL, cask, drum, vat

kernel *noun* ESSENCE, core, germ, gist, nub, pith, substance

key *noun* 1 OPENER, latchkey 2 ANSWER, explanation, solution ♦ *adjective* 3 ESSENTIAL, crucial, decisive, fundamental, important, leading, main, major, pivotal, principal

key in *verb* TYPE, enter, input, keyboard

keynote *noun* HEART, centre, core, essence, gist, substance, theme

kick *verb* 1 BOOT, punt 2 *Informal* GIVE UP, abandon, desist from, leave off, quit, stop ♦ *noun* 3 *Informal* THRILL, buzz (*slang*), pleasure, stimulation

kick off *verb* *Informal* BEGIN, commence, get the show on the road, initiate, open, start

kick out *verb* DISMISS, eject, evict, expel, get rid of, remove, sack (*informal*)

kid[1] *noun* *Informal* CHILD, baby, bairn, infant, teenager, tot, youngster, youth

kid[2] *verb* TEASE, delude, fool, hoax, jest, joke, pretend, trick, wind up (*Brit. slang*)

kidnap *verb* ABDUCT, capture, hijack, hold to ransom, seize

kill *verb* 1 SLAY, assassinate, butcher, destroy, execute, exterminate, liquidate, massacre, murder, slaughter 2 SUPPRESS, extinguish, halt, quash, quell, scotch, smother, stifle, stop

killer *noun* ASSASSIN, butcher, cut-throat, executioner, exterminator, gunman, hit man (*slang*), murderer, slayer

killing *adjective* 1 *Informal* TIRING, debilitating, exhausting, fatiguing, punishing **2** *Informal* <u>HILARIOUS</u>, comical, ludicrous, uproarious ◆ *noun* **3** <u>SLAUGHTER</u>, bloodshed, carnage, extermination, homicide, manslaughter, massacre, murder, slaying **4** *Informal* <u>BONANZA</u>, bomb (*slang*), cleanup (*informal*), coup, gain, profit, success, windfall

killjoy *noun* <u>SPOILSPORT</u>, dampener, wet blanket (*informal*)

kin *noun* <u>FAMILY</u>, kindred, kinsfolk, relations, relatives

kind[1] *adjective* <u>CONSIDERATE</u>, benign, charitable, compassionate, courteous, friendly, generous, humane, kindly, obliging, philanthropic, tender-hearted

kind[2] *noun* <u>CLASS</u>, brand, breed, family, set, sort, species, variety

kind-hearted *adjective* <u>SYMPATHETIC</u>, altruistic, compassionate, considerate, generous, good-natured, helpful, humane, kind, tender-hearted

kindle *verb* **1** <u>SET FIRE TO</u>, ignite, inflame, light **2** <u>AROUSE</u>, awaken, induce, inspire, provoke, rouse, stimulate, stir

kindliness *noun* <u>KINDNESS</u>, amiability, benevolence, charity, compassion, friendliness, gentleness, humanity, kind-heartedness

kindly *adjective* **1** <u>GOOD-NATURED</u>, benevolent, benign, compassionate, helpful, kind, pleasant, sympathetic, warm ◆ *adverb* **2** <u>POLITELY</u>, agreeably, cordially, graciously, tenderly, thoughtfully

kindness *noun* <u>GOODWILL</u>, benevolence, charity, compassion, generosity, humanity, kindliness, philanthropy, understanding

kindred *adjective* **1** <u>SIMILAR</u>, akin, corresponding, like, matching, related ◆ *noun* **2** <u>FAMILY</u>, kin,

kinsfolk, relations, relatives

king *noun* <u>RULER</u>, emperor, monarch, sovereign

kingdom *noun* <u>COUNTRY</u>, nation, realm, state, territory

kink *noun* **1** <u>TWIST</u>, bend, coil, wrinkle **2** <u>QUIRK</u>, eccentricity, fetish, foible, idiosyncrasy, vagary, whim

kinky *adjective* **1** <u>WEIRD</u>, eccentric, odd, outlandish, peculiar, queer, quirky, strange **2** <u>TWISTED</u>, coiled, curled, tangled

kinship *noun* **1** <u>RELATION</u>, consanguinity, kin, ties of blood **2** <u>SIMILARITY</u>, affinity, association, connection, correspondence, relationship

kiosk *noun* <u>BOOTH</u>, bookstall, counter, newsstand, stall, stand

kiss *verb* **1** <u>OSCULATE</u>, neck (*informal*), peck (*informal*) **2** <u>BRUSH</u>, glance, graze, scrape, touch ◆ *noun* **3** <u>OSCULATION</u>, peck (*informal*), smacker (*slang*)

kit *noun* <u>EQUIPMENT</u>, apparatus, gear, paraphernalia, tackle, tools

kit out *verb* <u>EQUIP</u>, accoutre, arm, deck out, fit out, fix up, furnish, provide with, supply

knack *noun* <u>SKILL</u>, ability, aptitude, capacity, expertise, facility, gift, propensity, talent, trick

knave *noun* <u>ROGUE</u>, blackguard, bounder (*old-fashioned Brit. slang*), rascal, rotter (*slang, chiefly Brit.*), scoundrel, villain

knead *verb* <u>SQUEEZE</u>, form, manipulate, massage, mould, press, rub, shape, work

kneel *verb* <u>GENUFLECT</u>, stoop

knell *noun* <u>RINGING</u>, chime, peal, sound, toll

knickers *plural noun* <u>UNDERWEAR</u>, bloomers, briefs, drawers, panties, smalls

knick-knack noun TRINKET, bagatelle, bauble, bric-a-brac, plaything, trifle

knife noun 1 BLADE, cutter ♦ verb 2 CUT, lacerate, pierce, slash, stab, wound

knit verb 1 JOIN, bind, fasten, intertwine, link, tie, unite, weave 2 WRINKLE, crease, furrow, knot, pucker

knob noun LUMP, bump, hump, knot, projection, protrusion, stud

knock verb 1 HIT, belt (informal), cuff, punch, rap, smack, strike, thump 2 Informal CRITICIZE, abuse, belittle, censure, condemn, denigrate, deprecate, disparage, find fault, run down ♦ noun 3 BLOW, clip, clout (informal), cuff, rap, slap, smack, thump 4 SETBACK, defeat, failure, rebuff, rejection, reversal

knockabout adjective BOISTEROUS, farcical, riotous, rollicking, slapstick

knock about or **around** verb 1 WANDER, ramble, range, roam, rove, travel 2 HIT, abuse, batter, beat up (informal), maltreat, manhandle, maul, mistreat, strike

knock down verb DEMOLISH, destroy, fell, level, raze

knock off verb 1 STOP WORK, clock off, clock out, finish 2 STEAL, nick (slang, chiefly Brit.), pinch, rob, thieve

knockout noun 1 KILLER BLOW, coup de grâce, KO or K.O. (slang) 2 SUCCESS, hit, sensation, smash,

smash hit, triumph, winner

knot noun 1 CONNECTION, bond, joint, ligature, loop, tie 2 CLUSTER, bunch, clump, collection ♦ verb 3 TIE, bind, loop, secure, tether

know verb 1 REALIZE, comprehend, feel certain, notice, perceive, recognize, see, understand 2 BE ACQUAINTED WITH, be familiar with, have dealings with, have knowledge of, recognize

know-how noun CAPABILITY, ability, aptitude, expertise, ingenuity, knack, knowledge, savoir-faire, skill, talent

knowing adjective MEANINGFUL, expressive, significant

knowingly adverb DELIBERATELY, consciously, intentionally, on purpose, purposely, wilfully, wittingly

knowledge noun 1 LEARNING, education, enlightenment, erudition, instruction, intelligence, scholarship, wisdom 2 ACQUAINTANCE, familiarity, intimacy

knowledgeable adjective 1 WELL-INFORMED, au fait, aware, clued-up (informal), cognizant, conversant, experienced, familiar, in the know (informal) 2 INTELLIGENT, educated, erudite, learned, scholarly

known adjective FAMOUS, acknowledged, avowed, celebrated, noted, recognized, well-known

L l

label *noun* 1 TAG, marker, sticker, ticket ♦ *verb* 2 MARK, stamp, tag

laborious *adjective* HARD, arduous, backbreaking, exhausting, onerous, strenuous, tiring, tough, wearisome

labour *noun* 1 WORK, industry, toil 2 WORKERS, employees, hands, labourers, workforce 3 CHILDBIRTH, delivery, parturition ♦ *verb* 4 WORK, endeavour, slave, strive, struggle, sweat (*informal*), toil 5 usually with *under* BE DISADVANTAGED, be a victim of, be burdened by, suffer 6 OVEREMPHASIZE, dwell on, elaborate, overdo, strain

laboured *adjective* FORCED, awkward, difficult, heavy, stiff, strained

labourer *noun* WORKER, blue-collar worker, drudge, hand, manual worker, navvy (*Brit. informal*)

labyrinth *noun* MAZE, intricacy, jungle, tangle

lace *noun* 1 NETTING, filigree, openwork 2 CORD, bootlace, shoelace, string, tie ♦ *verb* 3 FASTEN, bind, do up, thread, tie 4 MIX IN, add to, fortify, spike

lacerate *verb* TEAR, claw, cut, gash, mangle, rip, slash, wound

laceration *noun* CUT, gash, rent, rip, slash, tear, wound

lack *noun* 1 SHORTAGE, absence, dearth, deficiency, need, scarcity, want ♦ *verb* 2 NEED, be deficient in, be short of, be without, miss, require, want

lackadaisical *adjective* 1 LETHARGIC, apathetic, dull, half-hearted, indifferent, languid, listless 2 LAZY, abstracted, dreamy, idle, indolent, inert

lackey *noun* 1 HANGER-ON, flatterer, minion, sycophant, toady, yes man 2 MANSERVANT, attendant, flunky, footman, valet

lacklustre *adjective* FLAT, drab, dull, leaden, lifeless, muted, prosaic, uninspired, vapid

laconic *adjective* TERSE, brief, concise, curt, monosyllabic, pithy, short, succinct

lad *noun* BOY, fellow, guy (*informal*), juvenile, kid (*informal*), youngster, youth

laden *adjective* LOADED, burdened, charged, encumbered, full, weighed down

lady *noun* 1 GENTLEWOMAN, dame 2 WOMAN, female

lady-killer *noun* WOMANIZER, Casanova, Don Juan, heartbreaker, ladies' man, libertine, philanderer, rake, roué

ladylike *adjective* REFINED, elegant, genteel, modest, polite, proper, respectable, sophisticated, well-bred

lag *verb* HANG BACK, dawdle, delay, linger, loiter, straggle, tarry, trail

laggard *noun* STRAGGLER, dawdler, idler, loiterer, slowcoach (*Brit. informal*), sluggard, snail

laid-back *adjective* RELAXED, casual, easy-going, free and easy, unflappable (*informal*), unhurried

lair *noun* NEST, burrow, den, earth, hole

laissez faire *noun* NONINTERVENTION, free enterprise, free trade

lake *noun* POND, lagoon, loch (*Scot.*), lough (*Irish*), mere, reservoir, tarn

lame *adjective* 1 <u>DISABLED</u>, crippled, game, handicapped, hobbling, limping 2 <u>UNCONVINCING</u>, feeble, flimsy, inadequate, pathetic, poor, thin, unsatisfactory, weak

lament *verb* 1 <u>COMPLAIN</u>, bemoan, bewail, deplore, grieve, mourn, regret, sorrow, wail, weep ♦ *noun* 2 <u>COMPLAINT</u>, lamentation, moan, wailing 3 <u>DIRGE</u>, elegy, requiem, threnody

lamentable *adjective* <u>REGRETTABLE</u>, deplorable, distressing, grievous, mournful, tragic, unfortunate, woeful

lampoon *noun* 1 <u>SATIRE</u>, burlesque, caricature, parody, send-up (*Brit. informal*), skit, takeoff (*informal*) ♦ *verb* 2 <u>RIDICULE</u>, caricature, make fun of, mock, parody, satirize, send up (*Brit. informal*), take off (*informal*)

land *noun* 1 <u>GROUND</u>, dry land, earth, terra firma 2 <u>SOIL</u>, dirt, ground, loam 3 <u>COUNTRYSIDE</u>, farmland 4 <u>PROPERTY</u>, estate, grounds, realty 5 <u>COUNTRY</u>, district, nation, province, region, territory, tract ♦ *verb* 6 <u>ARRIVE</u>, alight, come to rest, disembark, dock, touch down 7 <u>END UP</u>, turn up, wind up 8 *Informal* <u>OBTAIN</u>, acquire, gain, get, secure, win

landlord *noun* 1 <u>INNKEEPER</u>, host, hotelier 2 <u>OWNER</u>, freeholder, lessor, proprietor

landmark *noun* 1 <u>FEATURE</u>, monument 2 <u>MILESTONE</u>, turning point, watershed

landscape *noun* <u>SCENERY</u>, countryside, outlook, panorama, prospect, scene, view, vista

landslide *noun* 1 <u>ROCKFALL</u>, avalanche, landslip ♦ *adjective* 2 <u>OVERWHELMING</u>, conclusive, decisive, runaway

lane *noun* <u>ROAD</u>, alley, footpath, passageway, path, pathway, street, way

language *noun* 1 <u>SPEECH</u>, communication, discourse, expression, parlance, talk 2 <u>TONGUE</u>, dialect, patois, vernacular

languid *adjective* 1 <u>LAZY</u>, indifferent, lackadaisical, languorous, listless, unenthusiastic 2 <u>LETHARGIC</u>, dull, heavy, sluggish, torpid

languish *verb* 1 <u>WEAKEN</u>, decline, droop, fade, fail, faint, flag, wilt, wither 2 *often with for* <u>PINE</u>, desire, hanker, hunger, long, yearn 3 <u>BE NEGLECTED</u>, be abandoned, rot, suffer, waste away

lank *adjective* 1 <u>LIMP</u>, lifeless, straggling 2 <u>THIN</u>, emaciated, gaunt, lean, scrawny, skinny, slender, slim, spare

lanky *adjective* <u>GANGLING</u>, angular, bony, gaunt, rangy, spare, tall

lap[1] *noun* <u>CIRCUIT</u>, circle, loop, orbit, tour

lap[2] *verb* 1 <u>RIPPLE</u>, gurgle, plash, purl, splash, swish, wash 2 <u>DRINK</u>, lick, sip, sup

lapse *noun* 1 <u>MISTAKE</u>, error, failing, fault, indiscretion, negligence, omission, oversight, slip 2 <u>INTERVAL</u>, break, breathing space, gap, intermission, interruption, lull, pause 3 <u>DROP</u>, decline, deterioration, fall ♦ *verb* 4 <u>DROP</u>, decline, degenerate, deteriorate, fall, sink, slide, slip 5 <u>END</u>, expire, run out, stop, terminate

lapsed *adjective* <u>OUT OF DATE</u>, discontinued, ended, expired, finished, invalid, run out

large *adjective* 1 <u>BIG</u>, considerable, enormous, gigantic, great, huge, immense, massive, monumental, sizable *or* sizeable, substantial, vast 2 **at large: a** <u>FREE</u>, at liberty, on the loose, on the run, unconfined **b** <u>IN GENERAL</u>, as a whole, chiefly, generally, in the main, mainly **c** <u>AT LENGTH</u>, exhaustively, greatly, in full detail

largely adverb <u>MAINLY</u>, as a rule, by and large, chiefly, generally, mostly, predominantly, primarily, principally, to a great extent

large-scale adjective <u>WIDE-RANGING</u>, broad, extensive, far-reaching, global, sweeping, vast, wholesale, wide

lark noun **1** <u>PRANK</u>, caper, escapade, fun, game, jape, mischief ◆ verb **2 lark about** <u>PLAY</u>, caper, cavort, have fun, make mischief

lash[1] noun **1** <u>BLOW</u>, hit, stripe, stroke, swipe (informal) ◆ verb **2** <u>WHIP</u>, beat, birch, flog, scourge, thrash **3** <u>POUND</u>, beat, buffet, dash, drum, hammer, smack, strike **4** <u>SCOLD</u>, attack, blast, censure, criticize, put down, slate (informal, chiefly Brit.), tear into (informal), upbraid

lash[2] verb <u>FASTEN</u>, bind, make fast, secure, strap, tie

lass noun <u>GIRL</u>, damsel, lassie (informal), maid, maiden, young woman

last[1] adjective **1** <u>HINDMOST</u>, at the end, rearmost **2** <u>MOST RECENT</u>, latest **3** <u>FINAL</u>, closing, concluding, terminal, ultimate ◆ adverb **4** <u>IN THE REAR</u>, after, behind, bringing up the rear, in or at the end

last[2] verb <u>CONTINUE</u>, abide, carry on, endure, keep on, persist, remain, stand up, survive

lasting adjective <u>CONTINUING</u>, abiding, durable, enduring, long-standing, long-term, perennial, permanent

latch noun **1** <u>FASTENING</u>, bar, bolt, catch, hasp, hook, lock ◆ verb **2** <u>FASTEN</u>, bar, bolt, make fast, secure

late adjective **1** <u>OVERDUE</u>, behind, behindhand, belated, delayed, last-minute, tardy **2** <u>RECENT</u>, advanced, fresh, modern, new **3** <u>DEAD</u>, deceased, defunct, departed, former, past ◆ adverb **4** <u>BELATEDLY</u>, at the last minute, behindhand, behind time, dilatorily, tardily

lately adverb <u>RECENTLY</u>, in recent times, just now, latterly, not long ago, of late

lateness noun <u>DELAY</u>, belatedness, tardiness

latent adjective <u>HIDDEN</u>, concealed, dormant, invisible, potential, undeveloped, unrealized

later adverb <u>AFTERWARDS</u>, after, by and by, in a while, in time, later on, subsequently, thereafter

lateral adjective <u>SIDEWAYS</u>, edgeways, flanking

latest adjective <u>UP-TO-DATE</u>, current, fashionable, modern, most recent, newest, up-to-the-minute

lather noun **1** <u>FROTH</u>, bubbles, foam, soapsuds, suds **2** Informal <u>FLUSTER</u>, dither (chiefly Brit.), flap (informal), fuss, state (informal), sweat, tizzy (informal) ◆ verb **3** <u>FROTH</u>, foam, soap

latitude noun <u>SCOPE</u>, elbowroom, freedom, laxity, leeway, liberty, licence, play

latter adjective <u>LAST-MENTIONED</u>, closing, concluding, last, second

latterly adverb <u>RECENTLY</u>, lately, of late

lattice noun <u>GRID</u>, grating, grille, trellis

laudable adjective <u>PRAISEWORTHY</u>, admirable, commendable, creditable, excellent, meritorious, of note, worthy

laugh verb **1** <u>CHUCKLE</u>, be in stitches, chortle, giggle, guffaw, snigger,

split one's sides, titter ♦ *noun*
2 CHUCKLE, chortle, giggle, guffaw,
snigger, titter 3 *Informal* CLOWN,
card (*informal*), entertainer, hoot
(*informal*), scream (*informal*)
4 *Informal* JOKE, hoot (*informal*),
lark, scream (*informal*)

laughable *adjective* RIDICULOUS,
absurd, derisory, farcical,
ludicrous, nonsensical,
preposterous, risible

laughing stock *noun* FIGURE OF FUN,
Aunt Sally (*Brit.*), butt, target,
victim

laugh off *verb* DISREGARD, brush
aside, dismiss, ignore, minimize,
pooh-pooh, shrug off

laughter *noun* AMUSEMENT, glee,
hilarity, merriment, mirth

launch *verb* 1 PROPEL, discharge,
dispatch, fire, project, send off, set
in motion 2 BEGIN, commence,
embark upon, inaugurate, initiate,
instigate, introduce, open, start

laurels *plural noun* GLORY, credit,
distinction, fame, honour, praise,
prestige, recognition, renown

lavatory *noun* TOILET, bathroom,
cloakroom (*Brit.*), latrine, loo (*Brit.*
informal), powder room, (public)
convenience, washroom, water
closet, W.C.

lavish *adjective* 1 PLENTIFUL,
abundant, copious, profuse,
prolific 2 GENEROUS, bountiful, free,
liberal, munificent, open-handed,
unstinting 3 EXTRAVAGANT,
exaggerated, excessive,
immoderate, prodigal,
unrestrained, wasteful, wild ♦ *verb*
4 SPEND, deluge, dissipate, expend,
heap, pour, shower, squander,
waste

law *noun* 1 CONSTITUTION, charter,
code 2 RULE, act, command,
commandment, decree, edict,
order, ordinance, regulation,

statute 3 PRINCIPLE, axiom, canon,
precept

law-abiding *adjective* OBEDIENT,
compliant, dutiful, good, honest,
honourable, lawful, orderly,
peaceable

law-breaker *noun* CRIMINAL,
convict, crook (*informal*), culprit,
delinquent, felon, miscreant,
offender, villain, wrongdoer

lawful *adjective* LEGAL, authorized,
constitutional, legalized,
legitimate, licit, permissible,
rightful, valid, warranted

lawless *adjective* DISORDERLY,
anarchic, chaotic, rebellious,
riotous, unruly, wild

lawlessness *noun* ANARCHY, chaos,
disorder, mob rule

lawsuit *noun* CASE, action, dispute,
industrial tribunal, litigation,
proceedings, prosecution, suit,
trial

lawyer *noun* LEGAL ADVISER,
advocate, attorney, barrister,
counsel, counsellor, solicitor

lax *adjective* SLACK, careless, casual,
lenient, negligent, overindulgent,
remiss, slapdash, slipshod

lay¹ *verb* 1 PLACE, deposit, leave,
plant, put, set, set down, spread
2 ARRANGE, organize, position, set
out 3 PRODUCE, bear, deposit 4 PUT
FORWARD, advance, bring forward,
lodge, offer, present, submit
5 ATTRIBUTE, allocate, allot, ascribe,
assign, impute 6 DEVISE, concoct,
contrive, design, hatch, plan, plot,
prepare, work out 7 BET, gamble,
give odds, hazard, risk, stake,
wager

lay² *adjective* 1 NONCLERICAL, secular
2 NONSPECIALIST, amateur, inexpert,
nonprofessional

layabout *noun* IDLER, couch potato
(*slang*), good-for-nothing, loafer,
lounger, ne'er-do-well, skiver (*Brit.*

slang), wastrel

layer noun TIER, row, seam, stratum, thickness

layman noun AMATEUR, lay person, nonprofessional, outsider

lay-off noun DISMISSAL, discharge, unemployment

lay off verb DISMISS, discharge, let go, make redundant, pay off

lay on verb PROVIDE, cater (for), furnish, give, purvey, supply

layout noun ARRANGEMENT, design, formation, outline, plan

lay out verb 1 ARRANGE, design, display, exhibit, plan, spread out 2 *Informal* SPEND, disburse, expend, fork out (*slang*), invest, pay, shell out (*informal*) 3 *Informal* KNOCK OUT, knock for six (*informal*), knock unconscious, KO or K.O. (*slang*)

laziness noun IDLENESS, inactivity, indolence, slackness, sloth, sluggishness

lazy adjective 1 IDLE, inactive, indolent, inert, slack, slothful, slow, workshy 2 LETHARGIC, drowsy, languid, languorous, sleepy, slow-moving, sluggish, somnolent, torpid

leach verb EXTRACT, drain, filter, percolate, seep, strain

lead verb 1 GUIDE, conduct, escort, pilot, precede, show the way, steer, usher 2 PERSUADE, cause, dispose, draw, incline, induce, influence, prevail, prompt 3 COMMAND, direct, govern, head, manage, preside over, supervise 4 BE AHEAD (OF), blaze a trail, come first, exceed, excel, outdo, outstrip, surpass, transcend 5 LIVE, experience, have, pass, spend, undergo 6 RESULT IN, bring on, cause, contribute, produce ♦ noun 7 FIRST PLACE, precedence, primacy, priority, supremacy, vanguard 8 ADVANTAGE, edge, margin, start

9 EXAMPLE, direction, guidance, leadership, model 10 CLUE, hint, indication, suggestion 11 LEADING ROLE, principal, protagonist, title role ♦ adjective 12 MAIN, chief, first, foremost, head, leading, premier, primary, prime, principal

leader noun PRINCIPAL, boss (*informal*), captain, chief, chieftain, commander, director, guide, head, ringleader, ruler

leadership noun 1 GUIDANCE, direction, domination, management, running, superintendency 2 AUTHORITY, command, control, influence, initiative, pre-eminence, supremacy

leading adjective MAIN, chief, dominant, first, foremost, greatest, highest, primary, principal

lead on verb ENTICE, beguile, deceive, draw on, lure, seduce, string along (*informal*), tempt

lead up to verb INTRODUCE, pave the way, prepare for

leaf noun 1 FROND, blade 2 PAGE, folio, sheet ♦ verb 3 **leaf through** BROWSE, flip, glance, riffle, skim, thumb (through)

leaflet noun BOOKLET, brochure, circular, pamphlet

leafy adjective GREEN, bosky (*literary*), shaded, shady, verdant

league noun 1 ASSOCIATION, alliance, coalition, confederation, consortium, federation, fraternity, group, guild, partnership, union 2 CLASS, category, level

leak noun 1 HOLE, aperture, chink, crack, crevice, fissure, opening, puncture 2 DRIP, leakage, percolation, seepage 3 DISCLOSURE, divulgence ♦ verb 4 DRIP, escape, exude, ooze, pass, percolate, seep, spill, trickle 5 DISCLOSE, divulge, give away, let slip, make known, make public, pass on, reveal, tell

leaky *adjective* <u>PUNCTURED</u>, cracked, holey, leaking, perforated, porous, split

lean[1] *verb* **1** <u>REST</u>, be supported, prop, recline, repose **2** <u>BEND</u>, heel, incline, slant, slope, tilt, tip **3** <u>TEND</u>, be disposed to, be prone to, favour, prefer **4** **lean on** <u>DEPEND ON</u>, count on, have faith in, rely on, trust

lean[2] *adjective* **1** <u>SLIM</u>, angular, bony, gaunt, rangy, skinny, slender, spare, thin, wiry **2** <u>UNPRODUCTIVE</u>, barren, meagre, poor, scanty, unfruitful

leaning *noun* <u>TENDENCY</u>, bent, bias, disposition, inclination, partiality, penchant, predilection, proclivity, propensity

leap *verb* **1** <u>JUMP</u>, bounce, bound, hop, skip, spring ♦ *noun* **2** <u>JUMP</u>, bound, spring, vault **3** <u>INCREASE</u>, escalation, rise, surge, upsurge, upswing

learn *verb* **1** <u>MASTER</u>, grasp, pick up **2** <u>MEMORIZE</u>, commit to memory, get off pat, learn by heart **3** <u>DISCOVER</u>, ascertain, detect, discern, find out, gather, hear, understand

learned *adjective* <u>SCHOLARLY</u>, academic, erudite, highbrow, intellectual, versed, well-informed, well-read

learner *noun* <u>BEGINNER</u>, apprentice, neophyte, novice, tyro

learning *noun* <u>KNOWLEDGE</u>, culture, education, erudition, information, lore, scholarship, study, wisdom

lease *verb* <u>HIRE</u>, charter, let, loan, rent

leash *noun* <u>LEAD</u>, rein, tether

least *adjective* <u>SMALLEST</u>, fewest,

lowest, meanest, minimum, poorest, slightest, tiniest

leathery *adjective* <u>TOUGH</u>, hard, rough

leave[1] *verb* **1** <u>DEPART</u>, decamp, disappear, exit, go away, make tracks, move, pull out, quit, retire, slope off, withdraw **2** <u>FORGET</u>, leave behind, mislay **3** <u>CAUSE</u>, deposit, generate, produce, result in **4** <u>GIVE UP</u>, abandon, drop, relinquish, renounce, surrender **5** <u>ENTRUST</u>, allot, assign, cede, commit, consign, give over, refer **6** <u>BEQUEATH</u>, hand down, will

leave[2] *noun* **1** <u>PERMISSION</u>, allowance, authorization, concession, consent, dispensation, freedom, liberty, sanction **2** <u>HOLIDAY</u>, furlough, leave of absence, sabbatical, time off, vacation **3** <u>PARTING</u>, adieu, departure, farewell, goodbye, leave-taking, retirement, withdrawal

leave out *verb* <u>OMIT</u>, cast aside, disregard, exclude, ignore, neglect, overlook, reject

lecherous *adjective* <u>LUSTFUL</u>, lascivious, lewd, libidinous, licentious, prurient, randy (*informal, chiefly Brit.*), salacious

lecture *noun* **1** <u>TALK</u>, address, discourse, instruction, lesson, speech **2** <u>REBUKE</u>, dressing-down (*informal*), reprimand, reproof, scolding, talking-to (*informal*), telling off (*informal*) ♦ *verb* **3** <u>TALK</u>, address, discourse, expound, hold forth, speak, spout, teach **4** <u>SCOLD</u>, admonish, berate, castigate, censure, reprimand, reprove, tell off (*informal*)

ledge *noun* <u>SHELF</u>, mantle, projection, ridge, sill, step

leer *noun, verb* <u>GRIN</u>, gloat, goggle, ogle, smirk, squint, stare

lees *plural noun* <u>SEDIMENT</u>, deposit,

dregs, grounds

leeway noun <u>ROOM</u>, elbowroom, latitude, margin, play, scope, space

left adjective 1 <u>LEFT-HAND</u>, larboard (*Nautical*), port, sinistral 2 *Of politics* <u>SOCIALIST</u>, leftist, left-wing, radical

leftover noun <u>REMNANT</u>, oddment, scrap

left-wing adjective <u>SOCIALIST</u>, communist, radical, red (*informal*)

leg noun 1 <u>LIMB</u>, lower limb, member, pin (*informal*), stump (*informal*) 2 <u>SUPPORT</u>, brace, prop, upright 3 <u>STAGE</u>, lap, part, portion, section, segment, stretch 4 **pull someone's leg** *Informal* <u>TEASE</u>, fool, kid (*informal*), make fun of, trick, wind up (*Brit. slang*)

legacy noun <u>BEQUEST</u>, estate, gift, heirloom, inheritance

legal adjective 1 <u>LEGITIMATE</u>, allowed, authorized, constitutional, lawful, licit, permissible, sanctioned, valid 2 <u>JUDICIAL</u>, forensic, juridical

legality noun <u>LEGITIMACY</u>, lawfulness, rightfulness, validity

legalize verb <u>ALLOW</u>, approve, authorize, decriminalize, legitimate, legitimize, license, permit, sanction, validate

legation noun <u>DELEGATION</u>, consulate, embassy, representation

legend noun 1 <u>MYTH</u>, fable, fiction, folk tale, saga, story, tale 2 <u>CELEBRITY</u>, luminary, megastar (*informal*), phenomenon, prodigy 3 <u>INSCRIPTION</u>, caption, motto

legendary adjective 1 <u>MYTHICAL</u>, apocryphal, fabled, fabulous, fictitious, romantic, traditional 2 <u>FAMOUS</u>, celebrated, famed, illustrious, immortal, renowned, well-known

legibility noun <u>CLARITY</u>, neatness, readability

legible adjective <u>CLEAR</u>, decipherable, distinct, easy to read, neat, readable

legion noun 1 <u>ARMY</u>, brigade, company, division, force, troop 2 <u>MULTITUDE</u>, drove, horde, host, mass, myriad, number, throng

legislation noun 1 <u>LAWMAKING</u>, enactment, prescription, regulation 2 <u>LAW</u>, act, bill, charter, measure, regulation, ruling, statute

legislative adjective <u>LAW-MAKING</u>, judicial, law-giving

legislator noun <u>LAWMAKER</u>, lawgiver

legislature noun <u>PARLIAMENT</u>, assembly, chamber, congress, senate

legitimate adjective 1 <u>LEGAL</u>, authentic, authorized, genuine, kosher (*informal*), lawful, licit, rightful 2 <u>REASONABLE</u>, admissible, correct, justifiable, logical, sensible, valid, warranted, well-founded ♦ verb 3 <u>AUTHORIZE</u>, legalize, legitimize, permit, pronounce lawful, sanction

legitimize verb <u>LEGALIZE</u>, authorize, permit, sanction

leisure noun <u>SPARE TIME</u>, ease, freedom, free time, liberty, recreation, relaxation, rest

leisurely adjective <u>UNHURRIED</u>, comfortable, easy, gentle, lazy, relaxed, slow

lend verb 1 <u>LOAN</u>, advance 2 <u>ADD</u>, bestow, confer, give, grant, impart, provide, supply 3 **lend itself to** <u>SUIT</u>, be appropriate, be serviceable

length noun 1 *Of linear extent* <u>DISTANCE</u>, extent, longitude, measure, reach, span 2 *Of time* <u>DURATION</u>, period, space, span, stretch, term 3 <u>PIECE</u>, measure, portion, section, segment 4 **at**

length: a <u>IN DETAIL</u>, completely, fully, in depth, thoroughly, to the full **b** <u>FOR A LONG TIME</u>, for ages, for hours, interminably **c** <u>AT LAST</u>, at long last, eventually, finally, in the end

lengthen *verb* <u>EXTEND</u>, continue, draw out, elongate, expand, increase, prolong, protract, spin out, stretch

lengthy *adjective* <u>LONG</u>, drawn-out, extended, interminable, long-drawn-out, long-winded, prolonged, protracted, tedious

leniency *noun* <u>TOLERANCE</u>, clemency, compassion, forbearance, indulgence, mercy, moderation, pity, quarter

lenient *adjective* <u>TOLERANT</u>, compassionate, forbearing, forgiving, indulgent, kind, merciful, sparing

lesbian *adjective* <u>HOMOSEXUAL</u>, gay, sapphic

less *adjective* **1** <u>SMALLER</u>, shorter ♦*preposition* **2** <u>MINUS</u>, excepting, lacking, subtracting, without

lessen *verb* <u>REDUCE</u>, contract, decrease, diminish, ease, lower, minimize, narrow, shrink

lesser *adjective* <u>MINOR</u>, inferior, less important, lower, secondary

lesson *noun* **1** <u>CLASS</u>, coaching, instruction, period, schooling, teaching, tutoring **2** <u>EXAMPLE</u>, deterrent, message, moral

let[1] *verb* **1** <u>ALLOW</u>, authorize, entitle, give permission, give the go-ahead, permit, sanction, tolerate **2** <u>LEASE</u>, hire, rent

let[2] *noun* <u>HINDRANCE</u>, constraint, impediment, interference, obstacle, obstruction, prohibition, restriction

letdown *noun* <u>DISAPPOINTMENT</u>, anticlimax, blow, comedown

(*informal*), setback, washout (*informal*)

let down *verb* <u>DISAPPOINT</u>, disenchant, disillusion, dissatisfy, fail, fall short, leave in the lurch, leave stranded

lethal *adjective* <u>DEADLY</u>, dangerous, destructive, devastating, fatal, mortal, murderous, virulent

lethargic *adjective* <u>SLUGGISH</u>, apathetic, drowsy, dull, languid, listless, sleepy, slothful

lethargy *noun* <u>SLUGGISHNESS</u>, apathy, drowsiness, inertia, languor, lassitude, listlessness, sleepiness, sloth

let off *verb* **1** <u>FIRE</u>, detonate, discharge, explode **2** <u>EMIT</u>, exude, give off, leak, release **3** <u>EXCUSE</u>, absolve, discharge, exempt, exonerate, forgive, pardon, release, spare

let on *verb* <u>REVEAL</u>, admit, disclose, divulge, give away, let the cat out of the bag (*informal*), make known, say

let out *verb* **1** <u>EMIT</u>, give vent to, produce **2** <u>RELEASE</u>, discharge, free, let go, liberate

letter *noun* **1** <u>CHARACTER</u>, sign, symbol **2** <u>MESSAGE</u>, communication, dispatch, epistle, line, missive, note

let-up *noun* <u>LESSENING</u>, break, breathing space, interval, lull, pause, remission, respite, slackening

let up *verb* <u>STOP</u>, abate, decrease, diminish, ease (up), moderate, relax, slacken, subside

level *adjective* **1** <u>HORIZONTAL</u>, flat **2** <u>EVEN</u>, consistent, plain, smooth, uniform **3** <u>EQUAL</u>, balanced, commensurate, comparable, equivalent, even, neck and neck, on a par, proportionate ♦*verb* **4** <u>FLATTEN</u>, even off *or* out, plane, smooth **5** EQUALIZE, balance, even up **6** RAZE, bulldoze, demolish, destroy, devastate, flatten, knock down, pull down, tear down **7** DIRECT, aim, focus, point, train ♦ *noun* **8** POSITION, achievement, degree, grade, rank, stage, standard, standing, status **9 on the level** *Informal* HONEST, above board, fair, genuine, square, straight

level-headed *adjective* STEADY, balanced, calm, collected, composed, cool, sensible, unflappable (*informal*)

lever *noun* **1** HANDLE, bar ♦ *verb* **2** PRISE, force

leverage *noun* INFLUENCE, authority, clout (*informal*), pull (*informal*), weight

levity *noun* LIGHT-HEARTEDNESS, facetiousness, flippancy, frivolity, silliness, skittishness, triviality

levy *verb* **1** IMPOSE, charge, collect, demand, exact **2** CONSCRIPT, call up, mobilize, muster, raise ♦ *noun* **3** IMPOSITION, assessment, collection, exaction, gathering **4** TAX, duty, excise, fee, tariff, toll

lewd *adjective* INDECENT, bawdy, lascivious, libidinous, licentious, lustful, obscene, pornographic, smutty, wanton

lewdness *noun* INDECENCY, bawdiness, carnality, debauchery, depravity, lasciviousness, lechery, licentiousness, obscenity, pornography, wantonness

liability *noun* **1** RESPONSIBILITY, accountability, answerability, culpability **2** DEBT, debit, obligation **3** DISADVANTAGE, burden, drawback, encumbrance, handicap, hindrance, inconvenience, millstone, nuisance

liable *adjective* **1** RESPONSIBLE, accountable, answerable,

obligated **2** VULNERABLE, exposed, open, subject, susceptible **3** LIKELY, apt, disposed, inclined, prone, tending

liaise *verb* LINK, communicate, keep contact, mediate

liaison *noun* **1** COMMUNICATION, connection, contact, hook-up, interchange **2** AFFAIR, amour, entanglement, intrigue, love affair, romance

liar *noun* FALSIFIER, fabricator, fibber, perjurer

libel *noun* **1** DEFAMATION, aspersion, calumny, denigration, smear ♦ *verb* **2** DEFAME, blacken, malign, revile, slur, smear, vilify

libellous *adjective* DEFAMATORY, derogatory, false, injurious, malicious, scurrilous, untrue

liberal *adjective* **1** PROGRESSIVE, libertarian, radical, reformist **2** GENEROUS, beneficent, bountiful, charitable, kind, open-handed, open-hearted, unstinting **3** TOLERANT, broad-minded, indulgent, permissive **4** ABUNDANT, ample, bountiful, copious, handsome, lavish, munificent, plentiful, profuse, rich

liberality *noun* **1** GENEROSITY, beneficence, benevolence, bounty, charity, kindness, largesse *or* largess, munificence, philanthropy **2** TOLERATION, broad-mindedness, latitude, liberalism, libertarianism, permissiveness

liberalize *verb* RELAX, ease, loosen, moderate, modify, slacken, soften

liberate *verb* FREE, deliver, emancipate, let loose, let out, release, rescue, set free

liberation *noun* DELIVERANCE, emancipation, freedom, freeing, liberty, release

liberator *noun* DELIVERER,

emancipator, freer, redeemer, rescuer, saviour

libertine noun REPROBATE, debauchee, lecher, profligate, rake, roué, sensualist, voluptuary, womanizer

liberty noun 1 FREEDOM, autonomy, emancipation, immunity, independence, liberation, release, self-determination, sovereignty 2 IMPERTINENCE, impropriety, impudence, insolence, presumption 3 **at liberty** FREE, on the loose, unrestricted

libidinous adjective LUSTFUL, carnal, debauched, lascivious, lecherous, randy (informal, chiefly Brit.), sensual, wanton

licence noun 1 CERTIFICATE, charter, permit, warrant 2 PERMISSION, authority, authorization, blank cheque, carte blanche, dispensation, entitlement, exemption, immunity, leave, liberty, right 3 LATITUDE, freedom, independence, leeway, liberty 4 LAXITY, excess, immoderation, indulgence, irresponsibility

license verb PERMIT, accredit, allow, authorize, certify, empower, sanction, warrant

licentious adjective PROMISCUOUS, abandoned, debauched, dissolute, immoral, lascivious, lustful, sensual, wanton

lick verb 1 TASTE, lap, tongue 2 Of flames FLICKER, dart, flick, play over, ripple, touch 3 Slang BEAT, defeat, master, outdo, outstrip, overcome, rout, trounce, vanquish ♦ noun 4 DAB, bit, stroke, touch 5 Informal PACE, clip (informal), rate, speed

lie[1] verb 1 FALSIFY, dissimulate, equivocate, fabricate, fib, prevaricate, tell untruths ♦ noun 2 FALSEHOOD, deceit, fabrication, fib, fiction, invention, prevarication, untruth

lie[2] verb 1 RECLINE, loll, lounge, repose, rest, sprawl, stretch out 2 BE SITUATED, be, be placed, exist, remain

life noun 1 BEING, sentience, vitality 2 EXISTENCE, being, lifetime, span, time 3 BIOGRAPHY, autobiography, confessions, history, life story, memoirs, story 4 BEHAVIOUR, conduct, life style, way of life 5 LIVELINESS, animation, energy, high spirits, spirit, verve, vigour, vitality, vivacity, zest

lifeless adjective 1 DEAD, deceased, defunct, extinct, inanimate 2 DULL, colourless, flat, lacklustre, lethargic, listless, sluggish, wooden 3 UNCONSCIOUS, comatose, dead to the world (informal), insensible

lifelike adjective REALISTIC, authentic, exact, faithful, natural, true-to-life, vivid

lifelong adjective LONG-STANDING, enduring, lasting, long-lasting, perennial, persistent

lifetime noun EXISTENCE, career, day(s), span, time

lift verb 1 RAISE, draw up, elevate, hoist, pick up, uplift, upraise 2 REVOKE, annul, cancel, countermand, end, remove, rescind, stop, terminate 3 DISAPPEAR, be dispelled, disperse, dissipate, vanish ♦ noun 4 RIDE, drive, run 5 BOOST, encouragement, fillip, pick-me-up, shot in the arm (informal) 6 ELEVATOR (chiefly U.S.)

light[1] noun 1 BRIGHTNESS, brilliance, glare, gleam, glint, glow, illumination, luminosity, radiance, shine 2 LAMP, beacon, candle, flare, lantern, taper, torch 3 ASPECT, angle, context, interpretation, point of view, slant, vantage point, viewpoint 4 MATCH, flame, lighter ◆ *adjective* 5 BRIGHT, brilliant, illuminated, luminous, lustrous, shining, well-lit 6 PALE, bleached, blond, faded, fair, pastel ◆ *verb* 7 IGNITE, inflame, kindle 8 ILLUMINATE, brighten, light up

light[2] *adjective* 1 INSUBSTANTIAL, airy, buoyant, flimsy, portable, slight, underweight 2 WEAK, faint, gentle, indistinct, mild, moderate, slight, soft 3 INSIGNIFICANT, inconsequential, inconsiderable, scanty, slight, small, trifling, trivial 4 NIMBLE, agile, graceful, lithe, sprightly, sylphlike 5 LIGHT-HEARTED, amusing, entertaining, frivolous, funny, humorous, witty 6 DIGESTIBLE, frugal, modest ◆ *verb* 7 SETTLE, alight, land, perch 8 **light on** *or* **upon** COME ACROSS, chance upon, discover, encounter, find, happen upon, hit upon, stumble on

lighten[1] *verb* BRIGHTEN, become light, illuminate, irradiate, light up

lighten[2] *verb* 1 EASE, allay, alleviate, ameliorate, assuage, lessen, mitigate, reduce, relieve 2 CHEER, brighten, buoy up, lift, perk up, revive

light-headed *adjective* FAINT, dizzy, giddy, hazy, vertiginous, woozy (*informal*)

light-hearted *adjective* CAREFREE, blithe, cheerful, happy-go-lucky, jolly, jovial, playful, upbeat (*informal*)

lightly *adverb* 1 GENTLY, delicately, faintly, slightly, softly 2 MODERATELY, sparingly, sparsely, thinly 3 EASILY, effortlessly, readily, simply 4 CARELESSLY, breezily, flippantly, frivolously, heedlessly, thoughtlessly

lightweight *adjective* UNIMPORTANT, inconsequential, insignificant, paltry, petty, slight, trifling, trivial, worthless

likable, likeable *adjective* ATTRACTIVE, agreeable, amiable, appealing, charming, engaging, nice, pleasant, sympathetic

like[1] *adjective* SIMILAR, akin, alike, analogous, corresponding, equivalent, identical, parallel, same

like[2] *verb* 1 ENJOY, be fond of, be keen on, be partial to, delight in, go for, love, relish, revel in 2 ADMIRE, appreciate, approve, cherish, esteem, hold dear, prize, take to 3 WISH, care to, choose, desire, fancy, feel inclined, prefer, want

likelihood *noun* PROBABILITY, chance, possibility, prospect

likely *adjective* 1 INCLINED, apt, disposed, liable, prone, tending 2 PROBABLE, anticipated, expected, odds-on, on the cards, to be expected 3 PLAUSIBLE, believable, credible, feasible, possible, reasonable 4 PROMISING, hopeful, up-and-coming

liken *verb* COMPARE, equate, match, parallel, relate, set beside

likeness *noun* 1 RESEMBLANCE, affinity, correspondence, similarity 2 PORTRAIT, depiction, effigy, image, picture, representation

likewise *adverb* SIMILARLY, in like manner, in the same way

liking *noun* FONDNESS, affection, inclination, love, partiality, penchant, preference, soft spot, taste, weakness

limb *noun* 1 PART, appendage, arm, extremity, leg, member, wing 2 BRANCH, bough, offshoot, projection, spur

limelight *noun* PUBLICITY, attention, celebrity, fame, prominence, public eye, recognition, stardom, the spotlight

limit noun 1 BREAKING POINT, deadline, end, ultimate 2 BOUNDARY, border, edge, frontier, perimeter ♦ verb 3 RESTRICT, bound, check, circumscribe, confine, curb, ration, restrain

limitation noun RESTRICTION, check, condition, constraint, control, curb, qualification, reservation, restraint

limited adjective RESTRICTED, bounded, checked, circumscribed, confined, constrained, controlled, curbed, finite

limitless adjective INFINITE, boundless, countless, endless, inexhaustible, unbounded, unlimited, untold, vast

limp[1] verb 1 HOBBLE, falter, hop, shamble, shuffle ♦ noun 2 LAMENESS, hobble

limp[2] adjective FLOPPY, drooping, flabby, flaccid, pliable, slack, soft

line noun 1 STROKE, band, groove, mark, score, scratch, streak, stripe 2 WRINKLE, crease, crow's foot, furrow, mark 3 BOUNDARY, border, borderline, edge, frontier, limit 4 STRING, cable, cord, rope, thread, wire 5 TRAJECTORY, course, direction, path, route, track 6 JOB, area, business, calling, employment, field, occupation, profession, specialization, trade 7 ROW, column, file, procession, queue, rank 8 in line for DUE FOR, in the running for ♦ verb 9 MARK, crease, furrow, rule, score 10 BORDER, bound, edge, fringe

lineaments plural noun FEATURES, countenance, face, physiognomy

lined adjective 1 RULED, feint 2 WRINKLED, furrowed, wizened, worn

lines plural noun WORDS, part, script

line-up noun ARRANGEMENT, array, row, selection, team

linger verb 1 STAY, hang around, loiter, remain, stop, tarry, wait 2 DELAY, dally, dawdle, drag one's feet or heels, idle, take one's time

link noun 1 COMPONENT, constituent, element, member, part, piece 2 CONNECTION, affinity, association, attachment, bond, relationship, tie-up ♦ verb 3 FASTEN, attach, bind, connect, couple, join, tie, unite 4 ASSOCIATE, bracket, connect, identify, relate

lip noun 1 EDGE, brim, brink, margin, rim 2 Slang IMPUDENCE, backchat (informal), cheek (informal), effrontery, impertinence, insolence

liquid noun 1 FLUID, juice, solution ♦ adjective 2 FLUID, aqueous, flowing, melted, molten, running, runny 3 Of assets CONVERTIBLE, negotiable

liquidate verb 1 PAY, clear, discharge, honour, pay off, settle, square 2 DISSOLVE, abolish, annul, cancel, terminate 3 KILL, destroy, dispatch, eliminate, exterminate, get rid of, murder, wipe out (informal)

liquor noun 1 ALCOHOL, booze (informal), drink, hard stuff (informal), spirits, strong drink 2 JUICE, broth, extract, liquid, stock

list[1] noun 1 REGISTER, catalogue, directory, index, inventory, record, roll, series, tally ♦ verb 2 TABULATE, catalogue, enter, enumerate, itemize, record, register

list[2] verb 1 LEAN, careen, heel over, incline, tilt, tip ♦ noun 2 TILT, cant, leaning, slant

listen verb 1 HEAR, attend, lend an ear, prick up one's ears 2 PAY ATTENTION, heed, mind, obey, observe, take notice

listless adjective LANGUID, apathetic,

indifferent, indolent, lethargic, sluggish

literacy noun EDUCATION, knowledge, learning

literal adjective **1** EXACT, accurate, close, faithful, strict, verbatim, word for word **2** ACTUAL, bona fide, genuine, plain, real, simple, true, unvarnished

literally adverb STRICTLY, actually, exactly, faithfully, precisely, really, to the letter, truly, verbatim, word for word

literary adjective WELL-READ, bookish, erudite, formal, learned, scholarly

literate adjective EDUCATED, informed, knowledgeable

literature noun WRITINGS, letters, lore

lithe adjective SUPPLE, flexible, limber, lissom(e), loose-limbed, pliable

litigant noun CLAIMANT, party, plaintiff

litigate verb SUE, go to court, press charges, prosecute

litigation noun LAWSUIT, action, case, prosecution

litter noun **1** RUBBISH, debris, detritus, garbage (chiefly U.S.), muck, refuse, trash **2** BROOD, offspring, progeny, young ♦ verb **3** CLUTTER, derange, disarrange, disorder, mess up **4** SCATTER, strew

little adjective **1** SMALL, diminutive, miniature, minute, petite, short, tiny, wee **2** YOUNG, babyish, immature, infant, junior, undeveloped ♦ adverb **3** HARDLY, barely **4** RARELY, hardly ever, not often, scarcely, seldom ♦ noun **5** BIT, fragment, hint, particle, speck, spot, touch, trace

live¹ verb **1** EXIST, be, be alive, breathe **2** PERSIST, last, prevail **3** DWELL, abide, inhabit, lodge, occupy, reside, settle **4** SURVIVE,

endure, get along, make ends meet, subsist, support oneself **5** THRIVE, flourish, prosper

live² adjective **1** LIVING, alive, animate, breathing **2** TOPICAL, burning, controversial, current, hot, pertinent, pressing, prevalent **3** BURNING, active, alight, blazing, glowing, hot, ignited, smouldering

livelihood noun OCCUPATION, bread and butter (informal), employment, job, living, work

liveliness noun ENERGY, animation, boisterousness, dynamism, spirit, sprightliness, vitality, vivacity

lively adjective **1** VIGOROUS, active, agile, alert, brisk, energetic, keen, perky, quick, sprightly **2** ANIMATED, cheerful, chirpy (informal), sparky, spirited, upbeat (informal), vivacious **3** VIVID, bright, colourful, exciting, forceful, invigorating, refreshing, stimulating

liven up verb STIR, animate, brighten, buck up (informal), enliven, perk up, rouse

liverish adjective **1** SICK, bilious, queasy **2** IRRITABLE, crotchety (informal), crusty, disagreeable, grumpy, ill-humoured, irascible, splenetic, tetchy

livery noun COSTUME, attire, clothing, dress, garb, regalia, suit, uniform

livid adjective **1** Informal ANGRY, beside oneself, enraged, fuming, furious, incensed, indignant, infuriated, outraged **2** DISCOLOURED, black-and-blue, bruised, contused, purple

living adjective **1** ALIVE, active, breathing, existing **2** CURRENT, active, contemporary, extant, in use ♦ noun **3** EXISTENCE, being, existing, life, subsistence **4** LIFE STYLE, way of life

load noun **1** CARGO, consignment,

freight, shipment 2 BURDEN,
albatross, encumbrance,
millstone, onus, trouble, weight,
worry ♦ verb 3 FILL, cram, freight,
heap, pack, pile, stack, stuff
4 BURDEN, encumber, oppress,
saddle with, weigh down, worry
5 Of firearms MAKE READY, charge,
prime

loaded adjective 1 WEIGHTED, biased,
distorted 2 TRICKY, artful, insidious,
manipulative, prejudicial 3 Slang
RICH, affluent, flush (informal),
moneyed, wealthy, well-heeled
(informal), well off, well-to-do

loaf[1] noun 1 LUMP, block, cake,
cube, slab 2 Slang HEAD, gumption
(Brit. informal), nous (Brit. slang),
sense

loaf[2] verb IDLE, laze, lie around,
loiter, lounge around, take it easy

loan noun 1 ADVANCE, credit ♦ verb
2 LEND, advance, let out

loath, loth adjective UNWILLING,
averse, disinclined, opposed,
reluctant

loathe verb HATE, abhor, abominate,
despise, detest, dislike

loathing noun HATRED, abhorrence,
antipathy, aversion, detestation,
disgust, repugnance, repulsion,
revulsion

loathsome adjective HATEFUL,
abhorrent, detestable, disgusting,
nauseating, obnoxious, odious,
offensive, repugnant, repulsive,
revolting, vile

lobby noun 1 CORRIDOR, entrance
hall, foyer, hallway, passage,
porch, vestibule 2 PRESSURE GROUP
♦ verb 3 CAMPAIGN, influence,
persuade, press, pressure,
promote, push, urge

local adjective 1 REGIONAL, provincial
2 RESTRICTED (chiefly U.S.), confined,
limited ♦ noun 3 RESIDENT,
inhabitant, native

locality noun 1 NEIGHBOURHOOD,
area, district, neck of the woods
(informal), region, vicinity 2 SITE,
locale, location, place, position,
scene, setting, spot

localize verb RESTRICT, circumscribe,
confine, contain, delimit, limit

locate verb 1 FIND, come across,
detect, discover, pin down,
pinpoint, track down, unearth
2 PLACE, establish, fix, put, seat,
set, settle, situate

location noun POSITION, locale,
place, point, site, situation, spot,
venue

lock[1] noun 1 FASTENING, bolt, clasp,
padlock ♦ verb 2 FASTEN, bolt, close,
seal, secure, shut 3 UNITE, clench,
engage, entangle, entwine, join,
link 4 EMBRACE, clasp, clutch,
encircle, enclose, grasp, hug, press

lock[2] noun STRAND, curl, ringlet,
tress, tuft

lockup noun PRISON, cell, jail or gaol

lock up verb IMPRISON, cage,
confine, detain, incarcerate, jail,
put behind bars, shut up

lodge noun 1 CABIN, chalet, cottage,
gatehouse, hut, shelter 2 SOCIETY,
branch, chapter, club, group
♦ verb 3 STAY, board, room 4 STICK,
come to rest, imbed, implant
5 REGISTER, file, put on record,
submit

lodger noun TENANT, boarder,
paying guest, resident

lodging noun, often plural
ACCOMMODATION, abode,
apartments, digs (Brit. informal),
quarters, residence, rooms, shelter

lofty adjective 1 HIGH, elevated,
raised, soaring, towering 2 NOBLE,
dignified, distinguished, elevated,
exalted, grand, illustrious,
renowned 3 HAUGHTY, arrogant,
condescending, disdainful,
patronizing, proud, supercilious

log noun 1 STUMP, block, chunk, trunk 2 RECORD, account, journal, logbook ♦ verb 3 CHOP, cut, fell, hew 4 RECORD, chart, note, register, set down

loggerheads plural noun **at loggerheads** QUARRELLING, at daggers drawn, at each other's throats, at odds, feuding, in dispute, opposed

logic noun REASON, good sense, sense

logical adjective 1 RATIONAL, clear, cogent, coherent, consistent, sound, valid, well-organized 2 REASONABLE, plausible, sensible, wise

loiter verb LINGER, dally, dawdle, dilly-dally (informal), hang about or around, idle, loaf, skulk

loll verb 1 LOUNGE, loaf, recline, relax, slouch, slump, sprawl 2 DROOP, dangle, drop, flap, flop, hang, sag

lone adjective SOLITARY, one, only, single, sole, unaccompanied

loneliness noun SOLITUDE, desolation, isolation, seclusion

lonely adjective 1 ABANDONED, destitute, forlorn, forsaken, friendless, lonesome 2 SOLITARY, alone, apart, companionless, isolated, lone, single, withdrawn 3 REMOTE, deserted, desolate, godforsaken, isolated, out-of-the-way, secluded, unfrequented, uninhabited

loner noun INDIVIDUALIST, lone wolf, maverick, outsider, recluse

lonesome adjective LONELY, companionless, desolate, dreary, forlorn, friendless, gloomy

long[1] adjective 1 ELONGATED, expanded, extended, extensive, far-reaching, lengthy, spread out, stretched 2 PROLONGED, interminable, lengthy, lingering, long-drawn-out, protracted, sustained

long[2] verb DESIRE, crave, hanker, itch, lust, pine, want, wish, yearn

longing noun DESIRE, ambition, aspiration, craving, hope, itch, thirst, urge, wish, yearning, yen (informal)

long-lived adjective LONG-LASTING, enduring

long shot noun OUTSIDER, dark horse

long-standing adjective ESTABLISHED, abiding, enduring, fixed, long-established, long-lasting, time-honoured

long-suffering adjective UNCOMPLAINING, easy-going, forbearing, forgiving, patient, resigned, stoical, tolerant

long-winded adjective RAMBLING, lengthy, long-drawn-out, prolix, prolonged, repetitious, tedious, tiresome, verbose, wordy

look verb 1 SEE, contemplate, examine, eye, gaze, glance, observe, scan, study, survey, view, watch 2 SEEM, appear, look like, strike one as 3 FACE, front, overlook 4 HOPE, anticipate, await, expect, reckon on 5 SEARCH, forage, hunt, seek ♦ noun 6 VIEW, examination, gaze, glance, glimpse, inspection, observation, peek, sight 7 APPEARANCE, air, aspect, bearing, countenance, demeanour, expression, manner, semblance

look after verb TAKE CARE OF, attend to, care for, guard, keep an eye on, mind, nurse, protect, supervise, take charge of, tend

look down on verb DISDAIN, contemn, despise, scorn, sneer, spurn

look forward to verb ANTICIPATE, await, expect, hope for, long for, look for, wait for

lookout noun 1 VIGIL, guard, readiness, watch 2 WATCHMAN, guard, sentinel, sentry 3 WATCHTOWER, observation post, observatory, post 4 Informal CONCERN, business, worry

look out verb BE CAREFUL, beware, keep an eye out, pay attention, watch out

look up verb 1 RESEARCH, find, hunt for, search for, seek out, track down 2 IMPROVE, get better, perk up, pick up, progress, shape up (informal) 3 VISIT, call on, drop in on (informal), look in on 4 **look up to** RESPECT, admire, defer to, esteem, honour, revere

loom verb APPEAR, bulk, emerge, hover, impend, menace, take shape, threaten

loop noun 1 CURVE, circle, coil, curl, ring, spiral, twirl, twist, whorl ♦ verb 2 TWIST, coil, curl, knot, roll, spiral, turn, wind round

loophole noun LET-OUT, escape, excuse

loose adjective 1 UNTIED, free, insecure, unattached, unbound, unfastened, unfettered, unrestricted 2 SLACK, easy, relaxed, sloppy 3 VAGUE, ill-defined, imprecise, inaccurate, indistinct, inexact, rambling, random 4 PROMISCUOUS, abandoned, debauched, dissipated, dissolute, fast, immoral, profligate ♦ verb 5 FREE, detach, disconnect, liberate, release, set free, unfasten, unleash, untie

loosen verb 1 UNTIE, detach, separate, undo, unloose 2 FREE, liberate, release, set free 3 **loosen up** RELAX, ease up or off, go easy (informal), let up, soften

loot noun 1 PLUNDER, booty, goods, haul, prize, spoils, swag (slang) ♦ verb 2 PLUNDER, despoil, pillage, raid, ransack, ravage, rifle, rob, sack

lopsided adjective CROOKED, askew, asymmetrical, awry, cockeyed, disproportionate, skewwhiff (Brit. informal), squint, unbalanced, uneven, warped

lord noun 1 MASTER, commander, governor, leader, liege, overlord, ruler, superior 2 NOBLEMAN, earl, noble, peer, viscount 3 **Our Lord** or **the Lord** JESUS CHRIST, Christ, God, Jehovah, the Almighty ♦ verb 4 **lord it over** ORDER AROUND, boss around (informal), domineer, pull rank, put on airs, swagger

lordly adjective PROUD, arrogant, condescending, disdainful, domineering, haughty, high-handed, imperious, lofty, overbearing

lore noun TRADITIONS, beliefs, doctrine, sayings, teaching, wisdom

lose verb 1 MISLAY, be deprived of, drop, forget, misplace 2 FORFEIT, miss, pass up (informal), yield 3 BE DEFEATED, come to grief, lose out

loser noun FAILURE, also-ran, dud (informal), flop (informal)

loss noun 1 DEFEAT, failure, forfeiture, mislaying, squandering, waste 2 DAMAGE, cost, destruction, harm, hurt, injury, ruin 3 sometimes plural DEFICIT, debit, debt, deficiency, depletion 4 **at a loss** CONFUSED, at one's wits' end, baffled, bewildered, helpless, nonplussed, perplexed, puzzled, stumped

lost adjective 1 MISSING, disappeared, mislaid, misplaced, vanished, wayward 2 OFF-COURSE, adrift, astray, at sea, disoriented, off-track

lot noun 1 COLLECTION, assortment, batch, bunch (informal), consignment, crowd, group, quantity, set **2** DESTINY, accident, chance, doom, fate, fortune **3 a lot** or **lots** PLENTY, abundance, a great deal, heap(s), load(s) (*informal*), masses (*informal*), piles (*informal*), scores, stack(s)

loth see LOATH

lotion noun CREAM, balm, embrocation, liniment, salve, solution

lottery noun **1** RAFFLE, draw, sweepstake **2** GAMBLE, chance, hazard, risk, toss-up (*informal*)

loud adjective **1** NOISY, blaring, booming, clamorous, deafening, ear-splitting, forte (*Music*), resounding, thundering, tumultuous, vociferous **2** GARISH, brash, flamboyant, flashy, gaudy, glaring, lurid, showy

loudly adverb NOISILY, deafeningly, fortissimo (*Music*), lustily, shrilly, uproariously, vehemently, vigorously, vociferously

lounge verb RELAX, laze, lie about, loaf, loiter, loll, sprawl, take it easy

lout noun OAF, boor, dolt, lummox (*informal*), yob or yobbo (*Brit. slang*)

lovable, loveable adjective ENDEARING, adorable, amiable, charming, cute, delightful, enchanting, likable or likeable, lovely, sweet

love verb **1** ADORE, cherish, dote on, hold dear, idolize, prize, treasure, worship **2** ENJOY, appreciate, delight in, like, relish, savour, take pleasure in ♦ noun **3** PASSION, adoration, affection, ardour, attachment, devotion, infatuation, tenderness, warmth **4** LIKING, devotion, enjoyment, fondness, inclination, partiality, relish, soft spot, taste, weakness **5** BELOVED, darling, dear, dearest, lover, sweetheart, truelove **6 in love**

ENAMOURED, besotted, charmed, enraptured, infatuated, smitten

love affair noun ROMANCE, affair, amour, intrigue, liaison, relationship

lovely adjective **1** ATTRACTIVE, adorable, beautiful, charming, comely, exquisite, graceful, handsome, pretty **2** ENJOYABLE, agreeable, delightful, engaging, nice, pleasant, pleasing

lover noun SWEETHEART, admirer, beloved, boyfriend or girlfriend, flame (*informal*), mistress, suitor

loving adjective AFFECTIONATE, amorous, dear, devoted, doting, fond, tender, warm-hearted

low adjective **1** SMALL, little, short, squat, stunted **2** INFERIOR, deficient, inadequate, poor, second-rate, shoddy **3** COARSE, common, crude, disreputable, rough, rude, undignified, vulgar **4** DEJECTED, depressed, despondent, disheartened, downcast, down in the dumps (*informal*), fed up, gloomy, glum, miserable **5** ILL, debilitated, frail, stricken, weak **6** QUIET, gentle, hushed, muffled, muted, soft, subdued, whispered

lowdown noun Informal INFORMATION, gen (*Brit. informal*), info (*informal*), inside story, intelligence

lower adjective **1** MINOR, inferior, junior, lesser, secondary, second-class, smaller, subordinate **2** REDUCED, curtailed, decreased, diminished, lessened ♦ verb **3** DROP, depress, fall, let down, sink, submerge, take down **4** LESSEN, cut, decrease, diminish, minimize, prune, reduce, slash

low-key adjective SUBDUED, muted, quiet, restrained, toned down, understated

lowly adjective HUMBLE, meek, mild,

modest, unassuming

low-spirited *adjective* DEPRESSED, dejected, despondent, dismal, down, down-hearted, fed up, low, miserable, sad

loyal *adjective* FAITHFUL, constant, dependable, devoted, dutiful, staunch, steadfast, true, trustworthy, trusty, unwavering

loyalty *noun* FAITHFULNESS, allegiance, constancy, dependability, devotion, fidelity, staunchness, steadfastness, trustworthiness

lubricate *verb* OIL, grease, smear

lucid *adjective* 1 CLEAR, comprehensible, explicit, intelligible, transparent 2 TRANSLUCENT, clear, crystalline, diaphanous, glassy, limpid, pellucid, transparent 3 CLEAR-HEADED, all there, *compos mentis*, in one's right mind, rational, sane

luck *noun* 1 FORTUNE, accident, chance, destiny, fate 2 GOOD FORTUNE, advantage, blessing, godsend, prosperity, serendipity, success, windfall

luckily *adverb* FORTUNATELY, favourably, happily, opportunely, propitiously, providentially

luckless *adjective* ILL-FATED, cursed, doomed, hapless, hopeless, jinxed, unfortunate, unlucky

lucky *adjective* FORTUNATE, advantageous, blessed, charmed, favoured, jammy (*Brit. slang*), serendipitous, successful

lucrative *adjective* PROFITABLE, advantageous, fruitful, productive, remunerative, well-paid

lucre *noun* MONEY, gain, mammon, pelf, profit, riches, spoils, wealth

ludicrous *adjective* RIDICULOUS, absurd, crazy, farcical, laughable,

nonsensical, outlandish, preposterous, silly

luggage *noun* BAGGAGE, bags, cases, gear, impedimenta, paraphernalia, suitcases, things

lugubrious *adjective* GLOOMY, doleful, melancholy, mournful, sad, serious, sombre, sorrowful, woebegone

lukewarm *adjective* 1 TEPID, warm 2 HALF-HEARTED, apathetic, cool, indifferent, unenthusiastic, unresponsive

lull *verb* 1 CALM, allay, pacify, quell, soothe, subdue, tranquillize ♦ *noun* 2 RESPITE, calm, hush, let-up (*informal*), pause, quiet, silence

lumber[1] *noun* 1 JUNK, clutter, jumble, refuse, rubbish, trash ♦ *verb* 2 *Informal* BURDEN, encumber, land, load, saddle

lumber[2] *verb* PLOD, shamble, shuffle, stump, trudge, trundle, waddle

lumbering *adjective* AWKWARD, clumsy, heavy, hulking, ponderous, ungainly

luminous *adjective* BRIGHT, glowing, illuminated, luminescent, lustrous, radiant, shining

lump *noun* 1 PIECE, ball, chunk, hunk, mass, nugget 2 SWELLING, bulge, bump, growth, hump, protrusion, tumour ♦ *verb* 3 GROUP, collect, combine, conglomerate, consolidate, mass, pool

lumpy *adjective* BUMPY, knobbly, uneven

lunacy *noun* 1 INSANITY, dementia, derangement, madness, mania, psychosis 2 FOOLISHNESS, absurdity, craziness, folly, foolhardiness, madness, stupidity

lunatic *adjective* 1 IRRATIONAL, crackbrained, crackpot (*informal*), crazy, daft, deranged, insane, mad ♦ *noun* **2** <u>MADMAN</u>, maniac, nutcase (*slang*), psychopath

lunge *noun* **1** <u>THRUST</u>, charge, jab, pounce, spring, swing ♦ *verb* **2** <u>POUNCE</u>, charge, dive, leap, plunge, thrust

lurch *verb* **1** <u>TILT</u>, heave, heel, lean, list, pitch, rock, roll **2** <u>STAGGER</u>, reel, stumble, sway, totter, weave

lure *verb* **1** <u>TEMPT</u>, allure, attract, draw, ensnare, entice, invite, seduce ♦ *noun* **2** <u>TEMPTATION</u>, allurement, attraction, bait, carrot (*informal*), enticement, incentive, inducement

lurid *adjective* **1** <u>SENSATIONAL</u>, graphic, melodramatic, shocking, vivid **2** <u>GLARING</u>, intense

lurk *verb* <u>HIDE</u>, conceal oneself, lie in wait, prowl, skulk, slink, sneak

luscious *adjective* <u>DELICIOUS</u>, appetizing, juicy, mouth-watering, palatable, succulent, sweet, toothsome

lush *adjective* **1** <u>ABUNDANT</u>, dense, flourishing, green, rank, verdant **2** <u>LUXURIOUS</u>, elaborate, extravagant, grand, lavish, opulent, ornate, palatial, plush (*informal*), sumptuous

lust *noun* **1** <u>LECHERY</u>, lasciviousness, lewdness, sensuality **2** <u>APPETITE</u>, craving, desire, greed, longing, passion, thirst ♦ *verb* **3** <u>DESIRE</u>, covet, crave, hunger for *or* after, want, yearn

lustre *noun* **1** <u>SPARKLE</u>, gleam, glint, glitter, gloss, glow, sheen, shimmer, shine **2** <u>GLORY</u>, distinction, fame, honour, prestige, renown

lusty *adjective* <u>VIGOROUS</u>, energetic, healthy, hearty, powerful, robust, strong, sturdy, virile

luxurious *adjective* <u>SUMPTUOUS</u>, comfortable, expensive, lavish, magnificent, opulent, plush (*informal*), rich, splendid

luxury *noun* **1** <u>OPULENCE</u>, affluence, hedonism, richness, splendour, sumptuousness **2** <u>EXTRAVAGANCE</u>, extra, frill, indulgence, treat

lying *noun* **1** <u>DISHONESTY</u>, deceit, mendacity, perjury, untruthfulness ♦ *adjective* **2** <u>DECEITFUL</u>, dishonest, false, mendacious, perfidious, treacherous, two-faced, untruthful

lyrical *adjective* <u>ENTHUSIASTIC</u>, effusive, impassioned, inspired, poetic, rhapsodic

M m

macabre *adjective* GRUESOME, dreadful, eerie, frightening, ghastly, ghostly, ghoulish, grim, grisly, morbid

machiavellian *adjective* SCHEMING, astute, crafty, cunning, cynical, double-dealing, opportunist, sly, underhand, unscrupulous

machine *noun* 1 APPLIANCE, apparatus, contraption, contrivance, device, engine, instrument, mechanism, tool 2 SYSTEM, machinery, organization, setup (*informal*), structure

machinery *noun* EQUIPMENT, apparatus, gear, instruments, tackle, tools

macho *adjective* MANLY, chauvinist, masculine, virile

mad *adjective* 1 INSANE, crazy (*informal*), demented, deranged, *non compos mentis*, nuts (*slang*), of unsound mind, out of one's mind, psychotic, raving, unhinged, unstable 2 FOOLISH, absurd, asinine, daft (*informal*), foolhardy, irrational, nonsensical, preposterous, senseless, wild 3 *Informal* ANGRY, berserk, enraged, furious, incensed, livid (*informal*), wild 4 ENTHUSIASTIC, ardent, avid, crazy (*informal*), fanatical, impassioned, infatuated, wild 5 FRENZIED, excited, frenetic, uncontrolled, unrestrained, wild 6 **like mad** *Informal* ENERGETICALLY, enthusiastically, excitedly, furiously, rapidly, speedily, violently, wildly

madcap *adjective* RECKLESS, crazy, foolhardy, hare-brained, imprudent, impulsive, rash, thoughtless

madden *verb* INFURIATE, annoy, derange, drive one crazy, enrage, incense, inflame, irritate, upset

madly *adverb* 1 INSANELY, crazily, deliriously, distractedly, frantically, frenziedly, hysterically 2 FOOLISHLY, absurdly, irrationally, ludicrously, senselessly, wildly 3 ENERGETICALLY, excitedly, furiously, like mad (*informal*), recklessly, speedily, wildly 4 *Informal* PASSIONATELY, desperately, devotedly, intensely, to distraction

madman *or* **madwoman** *noun* LUNATIC, maniac, nutcase (*slang*), psycho (*slang*), psychopath

madness *noun* 1 INSANITY, aberration, craziness, delusion, dementia, derangement, distraction, lunacy, mania, mental illness, psychopathy, psychosis 2 FOOLISHNESS, absurdity, daftness (*informal*), folly, foolhardiness, idiocy, nonsense, preposterousness, wildness

maelstrom *noun* 1 WHIRLPOOL, vortex 2 TURMOIL, chaos, confusion, disorder, tumult, upheaval

maestro *noun* MASTER, expert, genius, virtuoso

magazine *noun* 1 JOURNAL, pamphlet, periodical 2 STOREHOUSE, arsenal, depot, store, warehouse

magic *noun* 1 SORCERY, black art, enchantment, necromancy, witchcraft, wizardry 2 CONJURING, illusion, legerdemain, prestidigitation, sleight of hand, trickery 3 CHARM, allurement, enchantment, fascination, glamour, magnetism, power
♦ *adjective* 4 *Also* **magical** MIRACULOUS, bewitching, charming, enchanting, entrancing, fascinating, marvellous,

spellbinding

magician noun SORCERER, conjuror or conjuror, enchanter or enchantress, illusionist, necromancer, warlock, witch, wizard

magisterial adjective AUTHORITATIVE, commanding, lordly, masterful

magistrate noun JUDGE, J.P., justice, justice of the peace

magnanimity noun GENEROSITY, benevolence, big-heartedness, largesse or largess, nobility, selflessness, unselfishness

magnanimous adjective GENEROUS, big-hearted, bountiful, charitable, kind, noble, selfless, unselfish

magnate noun TYCOON, baron, captain of industry, mogul, plutocrat

magnetic adjective ATTRACTIVE, captivating, charismatic, charming, fascinating, hypnotic, irresistible, mesmerizing, seductive

magnetism noun CHARM, allure, appeal, attraction, charisma, drawing power, magic, pull, seductiveness

magnification noun INCREASE, amplification, enhancement, enlargement, expansion, heightening, intensification

magnificence noun SPLENDOUR, brilliance, glory, grandeur, majesty, nobility, opulence, stateliness, sumptuousness

magnificent adjective 1 SPLENDID, glorious, gorgeous, imposing, impressive, majestic, regal, sublime, sumptuous 2 EXCELLENT, brilliant, fine, outstanding, splendid, superb

magnify verb 1 ENLARGE, amplify, blow up (informal), boost, dilate, expand, heighten, increase, intensify 2 OVERSTATE, exaggerate,

inflate, overemphasize, overplay

magnitude noun 1 IMPORTANCE, consequence, greatness, moment, note, significance, weight 2 SIZE, amount, amplitude, extent, mass, quantity, volume

maid noun 1 GIRL, damsel, lass, lassie (informal), maiden, wench 2 SERVANT, housemaid, maidservant, serving-maid

maiden noun 1 GIRL, damsel, lass, lassie (informal), maid, virgin, wench ♦ adjective 2 UNMARRIED, unwed 3 FIRST, inaugural, initial, introductory

maidenly adjective MODEST, chaste, decent, decorous, demure, pure, virginal

mail noun 1 POST, correspondence, letters ♦ verb 2 POST, dispatch, forward, send

maim verb CRIPPLE, disable, hurt, injure, mutilate, wound

main adjective 1 CHIEF, central, essential, foremost, head, leading, pre-eminent, primary, principal ♦ noun 2 CONDUIT, cable, channel, duct, line, pipe 3 in the main ON THE WHOLE, for the most part, generally, in general, mainly, mostly

mainly adverb CHIEFLY, for the most part, in the main, largely, mostly, on the whole, predominantly, primarily, principally

mainstay noun PILLAR, anchor, backbone, bulwark, buttress, lynchpin, prop

mainstream adjective CONVENTIONAL, accepted, current, established, general, orthodox, prevailing, received

maintain verb 1 KEEP UP, carry on, continue, perpetuate, preserve, prolong, retain, sustain 2 SUPPORT, care for, look after, provide for, supply, take care of 3 ASSERT, avow, claim, contend, declare, insist, profess, state

maintenance noun 1 CONTINUATION, carrying-on, perpetuation, prolongation 2 UPKEEP, care, conservation, keeping, nurture, preservation, repairs 3 ALLOWANCE, alimony, keep, support

majestic adjective GRAND, grandiose, impressive, magnificent, monumental, regal, splendid, stately, sublime, superb

majesty noun GRANDEUR, glory, magnificence, nobility, pomp, splendour, stateliness

major adjective 1 MAIN, bigger, chief, greater, higher, leading, senior, supreme 2 IMPORTANT, critical, crucial, great, notable, outstanding, serious, significant

majority noun 1 PREPONDERANCE, best part, bulk, greater number, mass, most 2 ADULTHOOD, manhood or womanhood, maturity, seniority

make verb 1 CREATE, assemble, build, construct, fashion, form, manufacture, produce, put together, synthesize 2 PRODUCE, accomplish, bring about, cause, create, effect, generate, give rise to, lead to 3 FORCE, cause, compel, constrain, drive, impel, induce, oblige, prevail upon, require 4 AMOUNT TO, add up to, compose, constitute, form 5 PERFORM, carry out, do, effect, execute 6 EARN, clear, gain, get, net, obtain, win 7 **make it** Informal SUCCEED, arrive (informal), crack it (informal), get on, prosper ◆ noun 8 BRAND, kind, model, sort, style, type, variety

make-believe noun FANTASY, imagination, play-acting, pretence, unreality

make for verb HEAD FOR, aim for, be bound for, head towards

make off verb 1 FLEE, bolt, clear out (informal), run away or off, take to one's heels 2 **make off with** STEAL, abduct, carry off, filch, kidnap, nick (slang, chiefly Brit.), pinch (informal), run away or off with

make out verb 1 SEE, detect, discern, discover, distinguish, perceive, recognize 2 UNDERSTAND, comprehend, decipher, fathom, follow, grasp, work out 3 WRITE OUT, complete, draw up, fill in or out 4 PRETEND, assert, claim, let on, make as if or though 5 FARE, get on, manage

maker noun MANUFACTURER, builder, constructor, producer

makeshift adjective TEMPORARY, expedient, provisional, stopgap, substitute

make-up noun 1 COSMETICS, face (informal), greasepaint (Theatre), paint (informal), powder 2 STRUCTURE, arrangement, assembly, composition, configuration, constitution, construction, format, organization 3 NATURE, character, constitution, disposition, temperament

make up verb 1 FORM, compose, comprise, constitute 2 INVENT, coin, compose, concoct, construct, create, devise, dream up, formulate, frame, originate 3 COMPLETE, fill, supply 4 SETTLE, bury the hatchet, call it quits, reconcile 5 **make up for** COMPENSATE FOR, atone for, balance, make amends for, offset, recompense

making noun CREATION, assembly, building, composition, construction, fabrication, manufacture, production

makings plural noun BEGINNINGS, capacity, ingredients, potential

maladjusted adjective DISTURBED, alienated, neurotic, unstable

maladministration noun
MISMANAGEMENT, corruption,
dishonesty, incompetence,
inefficiency, malpractice, misrule

maladroit adjective CLUMSY,
awkward, cack-handed (informal),
ham-fisted or ham-handed
(informal), inept, inexpert, unskilful

malady noun DISEASE, affliction,
ailment, complaint, disorder,
illness, infirmity, sickness

malaise noun UNEASE, anxiety,
depression, disquiet, melancholy

malcontent noun TROUBLEMAKER,
agitator, mischief-maker, rebel,
stirrer (informal)

male adjective MASCULINE, manly,
virile

malefactor noun WRONGDOER,
criminal, delinquent, evildoer,
miscreant, offender, villain

malevolence noun MALICE, hate,
hatred, ill will, rancour, spite,
vindictiveness

malevolent adjective SPITEFUL,
hostile, ill-natured, malicious,
malign, vengeful, vindictive

malformation noun DEFORMITY,
distortion, misshapenness

malformed adjective MISSHAPEN,
abnormal, crooked, deformed,
distorted, irregular, twisted

malfunction verb 1 BREAK DOWN,
fail, go wrong ◆ noun 2 FAULT,
breakdown, defect, failure, flaw,
glitch

malice noun ILL WILL, animosity,
enmity, evil intent, hate, hatred,
malevolence, spite, vindictiveness

malicious adjective SPITEFUL,
ill-disposed, ill-natured,
malevolent, rancorous, resentful,
vengeful

malign verb 1 DISPARAGE, abuse,
defame, denigrate, libel, run

down, slander, smear, vilify
◆ adjective 2 EVIL, bad, destructive,
harmful, hostile, injurious,
malevolent, malignant,
pernicious, wicked

malignant adjective 1 HARMFUL,
destructive, hostile, hurtful,
malevolent, malign, pernicious,
spiteful 2 Medical UNCONTROLLABLE,
cancerous, dangerous, deadly,
fatal, irremediable

malleable adjective 1 WORKABLE,
ductile, plastic, soft, tensile
2 MANAGEABLE, adaptable, biddable,
compliant, impressionable,
pliable, tractable

malodorous adjective SMELLY, fetid,
mephitic, nauseating, noisome,
offensive, putrid, reeking, stinking

malpractice noun MISCONDUCT,
abuse, dereliction,
mismanagement, negligence

maltreat verb ABUSE, bully, harm,
hurt, ill-treat, injure, mistreat

mammoth adjective COLOSSAL,
enormous, giant, gigantic, huge,
immense, massive, monumental,
mountainous, prodigious

man noun 1 MALE, bloke (Brit.
informal), chap (informal),
gentleman, guy (informal)
2 HUMAN, human being, individual,
person, soul 3 MANKIND, Homo
sapiens, humanity, humankind,
human race, people 4 MANSERVANT,
attendant, retainer, servant, valet
◆ verb 5 STAFF, crew, garrison,
occupy, people

manacle noun 1 HANDCUFF, bond,
chain, fetter, iron, shackle ◆ verb
2 HANDCUFF, bind, chain, fetter, put
in chains, shackle

manage verb 1 ADMINISTER, be in
charge (of), command, conduct,
direct, handle, run, supervise
2 SUCCEED, accomplish, arrange,
contrive, effect, engineer 3 HANDLE,

control, manipulate, operate, use
4 COPE, carry on, get by (*informal*),
make do, muddle through, survive

manageable *adjective* DOCILE,
amenable, compliant, easy,
submissive

management *noun* 1 DIRECTORS,
administration, board, employers,
executive(s) 2 ADMINISTRATION,
command, control, direction,
handling, operation, running,
supervision

manager *noun* SUPERVISOR,
administrator, boss (*informal*),
director, executive, governor,
head, organizer

mandate *noun* COMMAND,
commission, decree, directive,
edict, instruction, order

mandatory *adjective* COMPULSORY,
binding, obligatory, required,
requisite

manfully *adverb* BRAVELY, boldly,
courageously, determinedly,
gallantly, hard, resolutely, stoutly,
valiantly

mangle *verb* CRUSH, deform,
destroy, disfigure, distort,
mutilate, ruin, spoil, tear, wreck

mangy *adjective* SCRUFFY, dirty,
moth-eaten, seedy, shabby,
shoddy, squalid

manhandle *verb* ROUGH UP, knock
about *or* around, maul, paw
(*informal*)

manhood *noun* MANLINESS,
masculinity, virility

mania *noun* 1 MADNESS, delirium,
dementia, derangement, insanity,
lunacy 2 OBSESSION, craze, fad
(*informal*), fetish, fixation, passion,
preoccupation, thing (*informal*)

maniac *noun* 1 MADMAN *or*
MADWOMAN, headcase (*informal*),
lunatic, psycho (*slang*),
psychopath 2 FANATIC, enthusiast,

fan, fiend (*informal*), freak
(*informal*)

manifest *adjective* 1 OBVIOUS,
apparent, blatant, clear,
conspicuous, evident, glaring,
noticeable, palpable, patent ◆ *verb*
2 DISPLAY, demonstrate, exhibit,
expose, express, reveal, show

manifestation *noun* DISPLAY,
demonstration, exhibition,
expression, indication, mark,
show, sign, symptom

manifold *adjective* NUMEROUS,
assorted, copious, diverse, many,
multifarious, multiple, varied,
various

manipulate *verb* 1 WORK, handle,
operate, use 2 INFLUENCE, control,
direct, engineer, manoeuvre

mankind *noun* PEOPLE, Homo
sapiens, humanity, humankind,
human race, man

manliness *noun* VIRILITY, boldness,
bravery, courage, fearlessness,
masculinity, valour, vigour

manly *adjective* VIRILE, bold, brave,
courageous, fearless, manful,
masculine, strapping, strong,
vigorous

man-made *adjective* ARTIFICIAL,
ersatz, manufactured, mock,
synthetic

manner *noun* 1 BEHAVIOUR, air,
aspect, bearing, conduct,
demeanour 2 STYLE, custom,
fashion, method, mode, way
3 TYPE, brand, category, form,
kind, sort, variety

mannered *adjective* AFFECTED,
artificial, pretentious, stilted

mannerism *noun* HABIT,
characteristic, foible, idiosyncrasy,
peculiarity, quirk, trait, trick

manners *plural noun* 1 BEHAVIOUR,
conduct, demeanour 2 POLITENESS,
courtesy, decorum, etiquette, p's

and q's, refinement

manoeuvre noun 1 STRATAGEM, dodge, intrigue, machination, ploy, ruse, scheme, subterfuge, tactic, trick 2 MOVEMENT, exercise, operation ♦ verb 3 MANIPULATE, contrive, engineer, machinate, pull strings, scheme, wangle (informal) 4 MOVE, deploy, exercise

mansion noun RESIDENCE, hall, manor, seat, villa

mantle noun 1 CLOAK, cape, hood, shawl, wrap 2 COVERING, blanket, canopy, curtain, pall, screen, shroud, veil

manual adjective 1 HAND-OPERATED, human, physical ♦ noun 2 HANDBOOK, bible, instructions

manufacture verb 1 MAKE, assemble, build, construct, create, mass-produce, produce, put together, turn out 2 CONCOCT, cook up (informal), devise, fabricate, invent, make up, think up, trump up ♦ noun 3 MAKING, assembly, construction, creation, production

manufacturer noun MAKER, builder, constructor, creator, industrialist, producer

manure noun COMPOST, droppings, dung, excrement, fertilizer, muck, ordure

many adjective 1 NUMEROUS, abundant, countless, innumerable, manifold, myriad, umpteen (informal), various ♦ noun 2 A LOT, heaps (informal), lots (informal), plenty, scores

mar verb SPOIL, blemish, damage, detract from, disfigure, hurt, impair, ruin, scar, stain, taint, tarnish

maraud verb RAID, forage, loot, pillage, plunder, ransack, ravage

marauder noun RAIDER, bandit, brigand, buccaneer, outlaw, plunderer

march verb 1 WALK, file, pace, parade, stride, strut ♦ noun 2 WALK, routemarch, trek 3 PROGRESS, advance, development, evolution, progression

margin noun EDGE, border, boundary, brink, perimeter, periphery, rim, side, verge

marginal adjective 1 BORDERLINE, bordering, on the edge, peripheral 2 INSIGNIFICANT, minimal, minor, negligible, slight, small

marijuana noun CANNABIS, dope (slang), grass (slang), hemp, pot (slang)

marine adjective NAUTICAL, maritime, naval, seafaring, seagoing

mariner noun SAILOR, salt, sea dog, seafarer, seaman

marital adjective MATRIMONIAL, conjugal, connubial, nuptial

maritime adjective 1 NAUTICAL, marine, naval, oceanic, seafaring 2 COASTAL, littoral, seaside

mark noun 1 SPOT, blemish, blot, line, scar, scratch, smudge, stain, streak 2 SIGN, badge, device, emblem, flag, hallmark, label, symbol, token 3 CRITERION, measure, norm, standard, yardstick 4 TARGET, aim, goal, object, objective, purpose ♦ verb 5 SCAR, blemish, blot, scratch, smudge, stain, streak 6 CHARACTERIZE, brand, flag, identify, label, stamp 7 DISTINGUISH, denote, exemplify, illustrate, show 8 OBSERVE, attend, mind, note, notice, pay attention, pay heed, watch 9 GRADE, appraise, assess, correct, evaluate

marked adjective NOTICEABLE, blatant, clear, conspicuous, decided, distinct, obvious, patent, prominent, pronounced, striking

markedly adverb NOTICEABLY, clearly, considerably, conspicuously, decidedly, distinctly, obviously, strikingly

market noun 1 FAIR, bazaar, mart ♦ verb 2 SELL, retail, vend

marketable adjective SOUGHT AFTER, in demand, saleable, wanted

marksman, markswoman noun SHARPSHOOTER, crack shot (informal), good shot

maroon verb ABANDON, desert, leave, leave high and dry (informal), strand

marriage noun WEDDING, match, matrimony, nuptials, wedlock

marry verb 1 WED, get hitched (slang), tie the knot (informal) 2 UNITE, ally, bond, join, knit, link, merge, unify, yoke

marsh noun SWAMP, bog, fen, morass, quagmire, slough

marshal verb 1 ARRANGE, align, array, deploy, draw up, group, line up, order, organize 2 CONDUCT, escort, guide, lead, shepherd, usher

marshy adjective SWAMPY, boggy, quaggy, waterlogged, wet

martial adjective MILITARY, bellicose, belligerent, warlike

martinet noun DISCIPLINARIAN, stickler

martyrdom noun PERSECUTION, ordeal, suffering

marvel verb 1 WONDER, be amazed, be awed, gape ♦ noun 2 WONDER, miracle, phenomenon, portent, prodigy

marvellous adjective 1 AMAZING, astonishing, astounding, breathtaking, brilliant, extraordinary, miraculous, phenomenal, prodigious, spectacular, stupendous 2 EXCELLENT, fabulous (informal),

fantastic (informal), great (informal), splendid, superb, terrific (informal), wonderful

masculine adjective MALE, manlike, manly, mannish, virile

mask noun 1 DISGUISE, camouflage, cover, façade, front, guise, screen, veil ♦ verb 2 DISGUISE, camouflage, cloak, conceal, cover, hide, obscure, screen, veil

masquerade noun 1 MASKED BALL, fancy dress party, revel 2 PRETENCE, cloak, cover-up, deception, disguise, mask, pose, screen, subterfuge ♦ verb 3 POSE, disguise, dissemble, dissimulate, impersonate, pass oneself off, pretend (to be)

mass noun 1 PIECE, block, chunk, hunk, lump 2 LOT, bunch, collection, heap, load, pile, quantity, stack 3 SIZE, bulk, greatness, magnitude ♦ adjective 4 LARGE-SCALE, extensive, general, indiscriminate, wholesale, widespread ♦ verb 5 GATHER, accumulate, assemble, collect, congregate, rally, swarm, throng

massacre noun 1 SLAUGHTER, annihilation, blood bath, butchery, carnage, extermination, holocaust, murder ♦ verb 2 SLAUGHTER, butcher, cut to pieces, exterminate, kill, mow down, murder, wipe out

massage noun 1 RUB-DOWN, manipulation ♦ verb 2 RUB DOWN, knead, manipulate

massive adjective HUGE, big, colossal, enormous, gigantic, hefty, immense, mammoth, monumental, whopping (informal)

master noun 1 RULER, boss (informal), chief, commander, controller, director, governor, lord, manager 2 EXPERT, ace (informal), doyen, genius, maestro, past master, virtuoso, wizard 3 <u>TEACHER</u>, guide, guru, instructor, tutor ♦ *adjective* 4 <u>MAIN</u>, chief, foremost, leading, predominant, prime, principal ♦ *verb* 5 <u>LEARN</u>, get the hang of (*informal*), grasp 6 <u>OVERCOME</u>, conquer, defeat, tame, triumph over, vanquish

masterful *adjective* 1 <u>SKILFUL</u>, adroit, consummate, expert, fine, first-rate, masterly, superlative, supreme, world-class 2 <u>DOMINEERING</u>, arrogant, bossy (*informal*), high-handed, imperious, overbearing, overweening

masterly *adjective* <u>SKILFUL</u>, adroit, consummate, crack (*informal*), expert, first-rate, masterful, supreme, world-class

mastermind *verb* 1 <u>PLAN</u>, conceive, devise, direct, manage, organize ♦ *noun* 2 <u>ORGANIZER</u>, architect, brain(s) (*informal*), director, engineer, manager, planner

masterpiece *noun* <u>CLASSIC</u>, jewel, magnum opus, *pièce de résistance*, *tour de force*

mastery *noun* 1 <u>EXPERTISE</u>, finesse, know-how (*informal*), proficiency, prowess, skill, virtuosity 2 <u>CONTROL</u>, ascendancy, command, domination, superiority, supremacy, upper hand, whip hand

match *noun* 1 <u>GAME</u>, bout, competition, contest, head-to-head, test, trial 2 <u>EQUAL</u>, counterpart, peer, rival 3 <u>MARRIAGE</u>, alliance, pairing, partnership ♦ *verb* 4 <u>CORRESPOND</u>, accord, agree, fit, go with, harmonize, tally 5 <u>RIVAL</u>, compare, compete, emulate, equal, measure up to

matching *adjective* <u>IDENTICAL</u>, coordinating, corresponding, equivalent, like, twin

matchless *adjective* <u>UNEQUALLED</u>,

incomparable, inimitable, superlative, supreme, unmatched, unparalleled, unrivalled, unsurpassed

mate *noun* 1 <u>PARTNER</u>, husband *or* wife, spouse 2 *Informal* <u>FRIEND</u>, buddy (*informal*), chum (*informal*), comrade, crony, pal (*informal*) 3 <u>COLLEAGUE</u>, associate, companion 4 <u>ASSISTANT</u>, helper, subordinate ♦ *verb* 5 <u>PAIR</u>, breed, couple

material *noun* 1 <u>SUBSTANCE</u>, matter, stuff 2 <u>INFORMATION</u>, data, evidence, facts, notes 3 <u>CLOTH</u>, fabric ♦ *adjective* 4 <u>PHYSICAL</u>, bodily, concrete, corporeal, palpable, substantial, tangible 5 <u>IMPORTANT</u>, essential, meaningful, momentous, serious, significant, vital, weighty 6 <u>RELEVANT</u>, applicable, apposite, apropos, germane, pertinent

materialize *verb* <u>OCCUR</u>, appear, come about, come to pass, happen, take shape, turn up

materially *adverb* <u>SIGNIFICANTLY</u>, essentially, gravely, greatly, much, seriously, substantially

maternal *adjective* <u>MOTHERLY</u>

maternity *noun* <u>MOTHERHOOD</u>, motherliness

matey *adjective* <u>FRIENDLY</u>, chummy (*informal*), hail-fellow-well-met, intimate, pally (*informal*), sociable, thick (*informal*)

matrimonial *adjective* <u>MARITAL</u>, conjugal, connubial, nuptial

matrimony *noun* <u>MARRIAGE</u>, nuptials, wedding ceremony, wedlock

matted *adjective* <u>TANGLED</u>, knotted, tousled, uncombed

matter *noun* 1 <u>SUBSTANCE</u>, body, material, stuff 2 <u>SITUATION</u>, affair, business, concern, event, incident, proceeding, question, subject, topic **3** *As in* **what's the matter?** PROBLEM, complication, difficulty, distress, trouble, worry ♦ *verb* **4** BE IMPORTANT, carry weight, count, make a difference, signify

matter-of-fact *adjective* UNSENTIMENTAL, deadpan, down-to-earth, emotionless, mundane, plain, prosaic, sober, unimaginative

mature *adjective* **1** GROWN-UP, adult, full-grown, fully fledged, mellow, of age, ready, ripe, seasoned ♦ *verb* **2** DEVELOP, age, bloom, blossom, come of age, grow up, mellow, ripen

maturity *noun* ADULTHOOD, experience, manhood *or* womanhood, ripeness, wisdom

maudlin *adjective* SENTIMENTAL, mawkish, overemotional, slushy (*informal*), soppy (*Brit. informal*), tearful, weepy (*informal*)

maul *verb* **1** ILL-TREAT, abuse, manhandle, molest, paw **2** TEAR, batter, claw, lacerate, mangle

maverick *noun* **1** REBEL, dissenter, eccentric, heretic, iconoclast, individualist, nonconformist, protester, radical ♦ *adjective* **2** REBEL, dissenting, eccentric, heretical, iconoclastic, individualistic, nonconformist, radical

mawkish *adjective* SENTIMENTAL, emotional, maudlin, schmaltzy (*slang*), slushy (*informal*), soppy (*Brit. informal*)

maxim *noun* SAYING, adage, aphorism, axiom, dictum, motto, proverb, rule

maximum *noun* **1** TOP, ceiling, height, peak, pinnacle, summit, upper limit, utmost, zenith ♦ *adjective* **2** GREATEST, highest, most, paramount, supreme, topmost, utmost

maybe *adverb* PERHAPS, perchance (*archaic*), possibly

mayhem *noun* CHAOS, commotion, confusion, destruction, disorder, fracas, havoc, trouble, violence

maze *noun* **1** LABYRINTH **2** WEB, confusion, imbroglio, tangle

meadow *noun* FIELD, grassland, lea (*poetic*), pasture

meagre *adjective* INSUBSTANTIAL, inadequate, measly, paltry, poor, puny, scanty, slight, small

mean[1] *verb* **1** SIGNIFY, convey, denote, express, imply, indicate, represent, spell, stand for, symbolize **2** INTEND, aim, aspire, design, desire, plan, set out, want, wish

mean[2] *adjective* **1** MISERLY, mercenary, niggardly, parsimonious, penny-pinching, stingy, tight-fisted, ungenerous **2** DESPICABLE, callous, contemptible, hard-hearted, petty, shabby, shameful, sordid, vile

mean[3] *noun* **1** AVERAGE, balance, compromise, happy medium, middle, midpoint, norm ♦ *adjective* **2** AVERAGE, middle, standard

meander *verb* **1** WIND, snake, turn, zigzag **2** WANDER, ramble, stroll ♦ *noun* **3** CURVE, bend, coil, loop, turn, twist, zigzag

meaning *noun* SENSE, connotation, drift, gist, message, significance, substance

meaningful *adjective* SIGNIFICANT, important, material, purposeful, relevant, useful, valid, worthwhile

meaningless *adjective* POINTLESS, empty, futile, inane, inconsequential, insignificant, senseless, useless, vain, worthless

meanness *noun* **1** MISERLINESS, niggardliness, parsimony, selfishness, stinginess **2** PETTINESS, disgracefulness, ignobility, narrow-mindedness, shabbiness, shamefulness

means *plural noun* **1** METHOD, agency, instrument, medium, mode, process, way **2** MONEY, affluence, capital, fortune, funds, income, resources, wealth, wherewithal **3 by all means** CERTAINLY, definitely, doubtlessly, of course, surely **4 by no means** IN NO WAY, definitely not, not in the least, on no account

meantime, meanwhile *adverb* AT THE SAME TIME, concurrently, in the interim, simultaneously

measly *adjective* MEAGRE, miserable, paltry, pathetic, pitiful, poor, puny, scanty, skimpy

measurable *adjective* QUANTIFIABLE, assessable, perceptible, significant

measure *noun* **1** QUANTITY, allotment, allowance, amount, portion, quota, ration, share **2** GAUGE, metre, rule, scale, yardstick **3** ACTION, act, deed, expedient, manoeuvre, means, procedure, step **4** LAW, act, bill, resolution, statute **5** RHYTHM, beat, cadence, metre, verse ♦ *verb* **6** QUANTIFY, assess, calculate, calibrate, compute, determine, evaluate, gauge, weigh

measured *adjective* **1** STEADY, dignified, even, leisurely, regular, sedate, slow, solemn, stately, unhurried **2** CONSIDERED, calculated, deliberate, reasoned, sober, studied, well-thought-out

measurement *noun* CALCULATION, assessment, calibration, computation, evaluation, mensuration, valuation

measure up to *verb* FULFIL THE EXPECTATIONS, be equal to, be suitable, come up to scratch (*informal*), fit *or* fill the bill, make

the grade (*informal*)

meat *noun* FLESH

meaty *adjective* **1** BRAWNY, beefy (*informal*), burly, heavily built, heavy, muscular, solid, strapping, sturdy **2** INTERESTING, meaningful, profound, rich, significant, substantial

mechanical *adjective* **1** AUTOMATIC, automated **2** UNTHINKING, automatic, cursory, impersonal, instinctive, involuntary, perfunctory, routine, unfeeling

mechanism *noun* **1** MACHINE, apparatus, appliance, contrivance, device, instrument, tool **2** PROCESS, agency, means, method, operation, procedure, system, technique

meddle *verb* INTERFERE, butt in, intervene, intrude, pry, tamper

meddlesome *adjective* INTERFERING, intrusive, meddling, mischievous, officious, prying

mediate *verb* INTERVENE, arbitrate, conciliate, intercede, reconcile, referee, step in (*informal*), umpire

mediation *noun* ARBITRATION, conciliation, intercession, intervention, reconciliation

mediator *noun* NEGOTIATOR, arbiter, arbitrator, go-between, honest broker, intermediary, middleman, peacemaker, referee, umpire

medicinal *adjective* THERAPEUTIC, curative, healing, medical, remedial, restorative

medicine *noun* REMEDY, cure, drug, medicament, medication, nostrum

mediocre *adjective* SECOND-RATE, average, indifferent, inferior, middling, ordinary, passable, pedestrian, run-of-the-mill, so-so (*informal*), undistinguished

mediocrity *noun* INSIGNIFICANCE, indifference, inferiority, ordinariness, unimportance

meditate verb 1 REFLECT, cogitate, consider, contemplate, deliberate, muse, ponder, ruminate, think 2 PLAN, have in mind, intend, purpose, scheme

meditation noun REFLECTION, cogitation, contemplation, musing, pondering, rumination, study, thought

medium adjective 1 MIDDLE, average, fair, intermediate, mean, median, mediocre, middling, midway ♦ noun 2 MIDDLE, average, centre, compromise, mean, midpoint 3 MEANS, agency, channel, instrument, mode, organ, vehicle, way 4 ENVIRONMENT, atmosphere, conditions, milieu, setting, surroundings 5 SPIRITUALIST

medley noun MIXTURE, assortment, farrago, hotchpotch, jumble, mélange, miscellany, mishmash, mixed bag (informal), potpourri

meek adjective SUBMISSIVE, acquiescent, compliant, deferential, docile, gentle, humble, mild, modest, timid, unassuming, unpretentious

meekness noun SUBMISSIVENESS, acquiescence, compliance, deference, docility, gentleness, humility, mildness, modesty, timidity

meet verb 1 ENCOUNTER, bump into, chance on, come across, confront, contact, find, happen on, run across, run into 2 CONVERGE, come together, connect, cross, intersect, join, link up, touch 3 SATISFY, answer, come up to, comply with, discharge, fulfil, match, measure up to 4 GATHER, assemble, collect, come together, congregate, convene, muster 5 EXPERIENCE, bear, encounter, endure, face, go through, suffer, undergo

meeting noun 1 ENCOUNTER, assignation, confrontation, engagement, introduction, rendezvous, tryst 2 CONFERENCE, assembly, conclave, congress, convention, gathering, get-together (informal), reunion, session

melancholy noun 1 SADNESS, dejection, depression, despondency, gloom, low spirits, misery, sorrow, unhappiness ♦ adjective 2 SAD, depressed, despondent, dispirited, downhearted, gloomy, glum, miserable, mournful, sorrowful

melee, mêlée noun FIGHT, brawl, fracas, free-for-all (informal), rumpus, scrimmage, scuffle, set-to (informal), skirmish, tussle

mellifluous adjective SWEET, dulcet, euphonious, honeyed, silvery, smooth, soft, soothing, sweet-sounding

mellow adjective 1 SOFT, delicate, full-flavoured, mature, rich, ripe, sweet ♦ verb 2 MATURE, develop, improve, ripen, season, soften, sweeten

melodious adjective TUNEFUL, dulcet, euphonious, harmonious, melodic, musical, sweet-sounding

melodramatic adjective SENSATIONAL, blood-and-thunder, extravagant, histrionic, overdramatic, overemotional, theatrical

melody noun 1 TUNE, air, music, song, strain, theme 2 TUNEFULNESS, euphony, harmony, melodiousness, musicality

melt verb 1 DISSOLVE, fuse, liquefy, soften, thaw 2 often with away DISAPPEAR, disperse, dissolve, evanesce, evaporate, fade, vanish 3 SOFTEN, disarm, mollify, relax

member noun 1 REPRESENTATIVE,

associate, fellow 2 <u>LIMB</u>, appendage, arm, extremity, leg, part

membership noun 1 <u>MEMBERS</u>, associates, body, fellows 2 <u>PARTICIPATION</u>, belonging, enrolment, fellowship

memento noun <u>SOUVENIR</u>, keepsake, memorial, relic, remembrance, reminder, token, trophy

memoir noun <u>ACCOUNT</u>, biography, essay, journal, life, monograph, narrative, record

memoirs plural noun <u>AUTOBIOGRAPHY</u>, diary, experiences, journals, life story, memories, recollections, reminiscences

memorable adjective <u>NOTEWORTHY</u>, celebrated, famous, historic, momentous, notable, remarkable, significant, striking, unforgettable

memorandum noun <u>NOTE</u>, communication, jotting, memo, message, minute, reminder

memorial noun 1 <u>MONUMENT</u>, memento, plaque, record, remembrance, souvenir ♦ adjective 2 <u>COMMEMORATIVE</u>, monumental

memorize verb <u>REMEMBER</u>, commit to memory, learn, learn by heart, learn by rote

memory noun 1 <u>RECALL</u>, recollection, remembrance, reminiscence, retention 2 <u>COMMEMORATION</u>, honour, remembrance

menace noun 1 <u>THREAT</u>, intimidation, warning 2 Informal <u>NUISANCE</u>, annoyance, pest, plague, troublemaker ♦ verb 3 <u>THREATEN</u>, bully, frighten, intimidate, loom, lour or lower, terrorize

menacing adjective <u>THREATENING</u>, forbidding, frightening, intimidating, looming, louring or lowering, ominous

mend verb 1 <u>REPAIR</u>, darn, fix, patch, refit, renew, renovate, restore, retouch 2 <u>IMPROVE</u>, ameliorate, amend, correct, emend, rectify, reform, revise 3 <u>HEAL</u>, convalesce, get better, recover, recuperate ♦ noun 4 <u>REPAIR</u>, darn, patch, stitch 5 **on the mend** <u>CONVALESCENT</u>, getting better, improving, recovering, recuperating

mendacious adjective <u>LYING</u>, deceitful, deceptive, dishonest, duplicitous, fallacious, false, fraudulent, insincere, untruthful

menial adjective 1 <u>UNSKILLED</u>, boring, dull, humdrum, low-status, routine ♦ noun 2 <u>SERVANT</u>, attendant, dogsbody (informal), drudge, flunky, lackey, skivvy (chiefly Brit.), underling

mental adjective 1 <u>INTELLECTUAL</u>, cerebral 2 Informal <u>INSANE</u>, deranged, disturbed, mad, mentally ill, psychotic, unbalanced, unstable

mentality noun <u>ATTITUDE</u>, cast of mind, character, disposition, make-up, outlook, personality, psychology

mentally adverb <u>IN THE MIND</u>, in one's head, intellectually, inwardly, psychologically

mention verb 1 <u>REFER TO</u>, bring up, declare, disclose, divulge, intimate, point out, reveal, state, touch upon ♦ noun 2 <u>ACKNOWLEDGMENT</u>, citation, recognition, tribute 3 <u>REFERENCE</u>, allusion, indication, observation, remark

mentor noun <u>GUIDE</u>, adviser, coach, counsellor, guru, instructor, teacher, tutor

menu noun <u>BILL OF FARE</u>, carte du jour, tariff (chiefly Brit.)

mercantile adjective <u>COMMERCIAL</u>, trading

mercenary *adjective* 1 GREEDY, acquisitive, avaricious, grasping, money-grubbing (*informal*), sordid, venal ◆ *noun* 2 HIRELING, soldier of fortune

merchandise *noun* GOODS, commodities, produce, products, stock, wares

merchant *noun* TRADESMAN, broker, dealer, purveyor, retailer, salesman, seller, shopkeeper, supplier, trader, trafficker, vendor, wholesaler

merciful *adjective* COMPASSIONATE, clement, forgiving, generous, gracious, humane, kind, lenient, sparing, sympathetic, tender-hearted

merciless *adjective* CRUEL, barbarous, callous, hard-hearted, harsh, heartless, pitiless, ruthless, unforgiving

mercurial *adjective* LIVELY, active, capricious, changeable, impulsive, irrepressible, mobile, quicksilver, spirited, sprightly, unpredictable, volatile

mercy *noun* 1 COMPASSION, clemency, forbearance, forgiveness, grace, kindness, leniency, pity 2 BLESSING, boon, godsend

mere *adjective* SIMPLE, bare, common, nothing more than, plain, pure, sheer

meretricious *adjective* TRASHY, flashy, garish, gaudy, gimcrack, showy, tawdry, tinsel

merge *verb* COMBINE, amalgamate, blend, coalesce, converge, fuse, join, meet, mingle, mix, unite

merger *noun* UNION, amalgamation, coalition, combination, consolidation, fusion, incorporation

merit *noun* 1 WORTH, advantage, asset, excellence, goodness, integrity, quality, strong point, talent, value, virtue ◆ *verb* 2 DESERVE, be entitled to, be worthy of, earn, have a right to, rate, warrant

meritorious *adjective* PRAISEWORTHY, admirable, commendable, creditable, deserving, excellent, good, laudable, virtuous, worthy

merriment *noun* FUN, amusement, festivity, glee, hilarity, jollity, joviality, laughter, mirth, revelry

merry *adjective* 1 CHEERFUL, blithe, carefree, convivial, festive, happy, jolly, joyous 2 *Brit. informal* TIPSY, happy, mellow, squiffy (*Brit. informal*), tiddly (*slang, chiefly Brit.*)

mesh *noun* 1 NET, netting, network, tracery, web ◆ *verb* 2 ENGAGE, combine, connect, coordinate, dovetail, harmonize, interlock, knit

mesmerize *verb* ENTRANCE, captivate, enthral, fascinate, grip, hold spellbound, hypnotize

mess *noun* 1 DISORDER, chaos, clutter, confusion, disarray, disorganization, hotchpotch, jumble, litter, shambles, untidiness 2 DIFFICULTY, deep water, dilemma, fix (*informal*), jam (*informal*), muddle, pickle (*informal*), plight, predicament, tight spot ◆ *verb* 3 often with *up* DIRTY, clutter, disarrange, dishevel, muck up (*Brit. slang*), muddle, pollute, scramble 4 often with *with* INTERFERE, fiddle (*informal*), meddle, play, tamper, tinker

mess about *or* **around** *verb* POTTER, amuse oneself, dabble, fool (about *or* around), muck about (*informal*), play about *or* around, trifle

message *noun* 1 COMMUNICATION, bulletin, communiqué, dispatch, letter, memorandum, note, tidings, word 2 POINT, idea, import, meaning, moral, purport, theme

messenger noun <u>COURIER</u>, carrier, delivery boy, emissary, envoy, errand-boy, go-between, herald, runner

messy adjective <u>UNTIDY</u>, chaotic, cluttered, confused, dirty, dishevelled, disordered, disorganized, muddled, shambolic, sloppy (informal)

metamorphosis noun <u>TRANSFORMATION</u>, alteration, change, conversion, mutation, transmutation

metaphor noun <u>FIGURE OF SPEECH</u>, allegory, analogy, image, symbol, trope

metaphorical adjective <u>FIGURATIVE</u>, allegorical, emblematic, symbolic

mete verb <u>DISTRIBUTE</u>, administer, apportion, assign, deal, dispense, dole, portion

meteoric adjective <u>SPECTACULAR</u>, brilliant, dazzling, fast, overnight, rapid, speedy, sudden, swift

method noun 1 <u>MANNER</u>, approach, mode, modus operandi, procedure, process, routine, style, system, technique, way 2 <u>ORDERLINESS</u>, order, organization, pattern, planning, purpose, regularity, system

methodical adjective <u>ORDERLY</u>, businesslike, deliberate, disciplined, meticulous, organized, precise, regular, structured, systematic

meticulous adjective <u>THOROUGH</u>, exact, fastidious, fussy, painstaking, particular, precise, punctilious, scrupulous, strict

mettle noun <u>COURAGE</u>, bravery, fortitude, gallantry, life, nerve, pluck, resolution, spirit, valour, vigour

microbe noun <u>MICROORGANISM</u>,

bacillus, bacterium, bug (informal), germ, virus

microscopic adjective <u>TINY</u>, imperceptible, infinitesimal, invisible, minuscule, minute, negligible

midday noun <u>NOON</u>, noonday, twelve o'clock

middle adjective 1 <u>CENTRAL</u>, halfway, intermediate, intervening, mean, median, medium, mid ♦ noun 2 <u>CENTRE</u>, focus, halfway point, heart, midpoint, midsection, midst

middle-class adjective <u>BOURGEOIS</u>, conventional, traditional

middling adjective 1 <u>MEDIOCRE</u>, indifferent, run-of-the-mill, so-so (informal), tolerable, unexceptional, unremarkable 2 <u>MODERATE</u>, adequate, all right, average, fair, medium, modest, O.K. or okay (informal), ordinary, passable, serviceable

midget noun <u>DWARF</u>, pygmy or pigmy, shrimp (informal), Tom Thumb

midnight noun <u>TWELVE O'CLOCK</u>, dead of night, middle of the night, the witching hour

midst noun **in the midst of** <u>AMONG</u>, amidst, during, in the middle of, in the thick of, surrounded by

midway adjective, adverb <u>HALFWAY</u>, betwixt and between, in the middle

might noun 1 <u>POWER</u>, energy, force, strength, vigour 2 **with might and main** <u>FORCEFULLY</u>, lustily, manfully, mightily, vigorously

mightily adverb 1 <u>VERY</u>, decidedly, exceedingly, extremely, greatly, highly, hugely, intensely, much 2 <u>POWERFULLY</u>, energetically, forcefully, lustily, manfully, strongly, vigorously

mighty adjective <u>POWERFUL</u>, forceful,

lusty, robust, strapping, strong, sturdy, vigorous

migrant noun 1 WANDERER, drifter, emigrant, immigrant, itinerant, nomad, rover, traveller ♦ adjective 2 TRAVELLING, drifting, immigrant, itinerant, migratory, nomadic, roving, shifting, transient, vagrant, wandering

migrate verb MOVE, emigrate, journey, roam, rove, travel, trek, voyage, wander

migration noun WANDERING, emigration, journey, movement, roving, travel, trek, voyage

migratory adjective NOMADIC, itinerant, migrant, peripatetic, roving, transient

mild adjective 1 GENTLE, calm, docile, easy-going, equable, meek, peaceable, placid 2 BLAND, smooth 3 CALM, balmy, moderate, temperate, tranquil, warm

mildness noun GENTLENESS, calmness, clemency, docility, moderation, placidity, tranquillity, warmth

milieu noun SURROUNDINGS, background, element, environment, locale, location, scene, setting

militant adjective AGGRESSIVE, active, assertive, combative, vigorous

military adjective 1 WARLIKE, armed, martial, soldierly ♦ noun 2 ARMED FORCES, army, forces, services

militate verb militate against COUNTERACT, be detrimental to, conflict with, counter, oppose, resist, tell against, weigh against

milk verb EXPLOIT, extract, pump, take advantage of

mill noun 1 FACTORY, foundry, plant, works 2 GRINDER, crusher ♦ verb 3 GRIND, crush, grate, pound, powder 4 SWARM, crowd, throng

millstone noun 1 GRINDSTONE, quernstone 2 BURDEN, affliction, albatross, encumbrance, load, weight

mime verb ACT OUT, gesture, represent, simulate

mimic verb 1 IMITATE, ape, caricature, do (informal), impersonate, parody, take off (informal) ♦ noun 2 IMITATOR, caricaturist, copycat (informal), impersonator, impressionist

mimicry noun IMITATION, burlesque, caricature, impersonation, mimicking, mockery, parody, take-off (informal)

mince verb 1 CUT, chop, crumble, grind, hash 2 As in **mince one's words** TONE DOWN, moderate, soften, spare, weaken

mincing adjective AFFECTED, camp (informal), dainty, effeminate, foppish, precious, pretentious, sissy

mind noun 1 INTELLIGENCE, brain(s) (informal), grey matter (informal), intellect, reason, sense, understanding, wits 2 MEMORY, recollection, remembrance 3 INTENTION, desire, disposition, fancy, inclination, leaning, notion, urge, wish 4 SANITY, judgment, marbles (informal), mental balance, rationality, reason, senses, wits 5 **make up one's mind** DECIDE, choose, determine, resolve ♦ verb 6 TAKE OFFENCE, be affronted, be bothered, care, disapprove, dislike, object, resent 7 PAY ATTENTION, heed, listen to, mark, note, obey, observe, pay heed to, take heed 8 GUARD, attend to, keep an eye on, look after, take care of, tend, watch 9 BE CAREFUL, be cautious, be on (one's) guard, be wary, take care, watch

mindful adjective AWARE, alert, alive to, careful, conscious, heedful, wary, watchful

mindless *adjective* STUPID, foolish, idiotic, inane, moronic, thoughtless, unthinking, witless

mine *noun* **1** PIT, colliery, deposit, excavation, shaft **2** SOURCE, abundance, fund, hoard, reserve, stock, store, supply, treasury, wealth ♦ *verb* **3** DIG UP, dig for, excavate, extract, hew, quarry, unearth

miner *noun* COALMINER, collier (*Brit.*), pitman (*Brit.*)

mingle *verb* **1** MIX, blend, combine, intermingle, interweave, join, merge, unite **2** ASSOCIATE, consort, fraternize, hang about *or* around, hobnob, rub shoulders (*informal*), socialize

miniature *adjective* SMALL, diminutive, little, minuscule, minute, scaled-down, tiny, toy

minimal *adjective* MINIMUM, least, least possible, nominal, slightest, smallest, token

minimize *verb* **1** REDUCE, curtail, decrease, diminish, miniaturize, prune, shrink **2** PLAY DOWN, belittle, decry, deprecate, discount, disparage, make light *or* little of, underrate

minimum *adjective* **1** LEAST, least possible, lowest, minimal, slightest, smallest ♦ *noun* **2** LEAST, lowest, nadir

minion *noun* FOLLOWER, flunky, hanger-on, henchman, hireling, lackey, underling, yes man

minister *noun* **1** CLERGYMAN, cleric, parson, pastor, preacher, priest, rector, vicar ♦ *verb* **2** ATTEND, administer, cater to, pander to, serve, take care of, tend

ministry *noun* **1** DEPARTMENT, bureau, council, office, quango **2** THE PRIESTHOOD, holy orders, the church

minor *adjective* SMALL, inconsequential, insignificant, lesser, petty, slight, trivial, unimportant

minstrel *noun* MUSICIAN, bard, singer, songstress, troubadour

mint *verb* MAKE, cast, coin, produce, punch, stamp, strike

minuscule *adjective* TINY, diminutive, infinitesimal, little, microscopic, miniature, minute

minute[1] *noun* MOMENT, flash, instant, jiffy (*informal*), second, tick (*Brit. informal*), trice

minute[2] *adjective* **1** SMALL, diminutive, infinitesimal, little, microscopic, miniature, minuscule, tiny **2** PRECISE, close, critical, detailed, exact, exhaustive, meticulous, painstaking, punctilious

minutes *plural noun* RECORD, memorandum, notes, proceedings, transactions, transcript

minutiae *plural noun* DETAILS, finer points, ins and outs, niceties, particulars, subtleties, trifles, trivia

minx *noun* FLIRT, coquette, hussy

miracle *noun* WONDER, marvel, phenomenon, prodigy

miraculous *adjective* WONDERFUL, amazing, astonishing, astounding, extraordinary, incredible, phenomenal, prodigious, unaccountable, unbelievable

mirage *noun* ILLUSION, hallucination, optical illusion

mire *noun* **1** SWAMP, bog, marsh, morass, quagmire **2** MUD, dirt, muck, ooze, slime

mirror *noun* **1** LOOKING-GLASS, glass, reflector ♦ *verb* **2** REFLECT, copy, echo, emulate, follow

mirth *noun* MERRIMENT, amusement,

cheerfulness, fun, gaiety, glee, hilarity, jollity, joviality, laughter, revelry

mirthful *adjective* MERRY, blithe, cheerful, cheery, festive, happy, jolly, jovial, light-hearted, playful, sportive

misadventure *noun* MISFORTUNE, accident, bad luck, calamity, catastrophe, debacle, disaster, mishap, reverse, setback

misanthropic *adjective* ANTISOCIAL, cynical, malevolent, unfriendly

misapprehend *verb* MISUNDERSTAND, misconstrue, misinterpret, misread, mistake

misapprehension *noun* MISUNDERSTANDING, delusion, error, fallacy, misconception, misinterpretation, mistake

misappropriate *verb* STEAL, embezzle, misspend, misuse, peculate, pocket

miscalculate *verb* MISJUDGE, blunder, err, overestimate, overrate, slip up, underestimate, underrate

miscarriage *noun* FAILURE, breakdown, error, mishap, perversion

miscarry *verb* FAIL, come to grief, fall through, go awry, go wrong, misfire

miscellaneous *adjective* MIXED, assorted, diverse, jumbled, motley, sundry, varied, various

miscellany *noun* ASSORTMENT, anthology, collection, hotchpotch, jumble, medley, *mélange*, mixed bag, mixture, potpourri, variety

mischance *noun* MISFORTUNE, accident, calamity, disaster, misadventure, mishap

mischief *noun* 1 TROUBLE, impishness, misbehaviour, monkey business (*informal*), naughtiness, shenanigans (*informal*), waywardness 2 HARM, damage, evil, hurt, injury, misfortune, trouble

mischievous *adjective* 1 NAUGHTY, impish, playful, puckish, rascally, roguish, sportive, troublesome, wayward 2 MALICIOUS, damaging, destructive, evil, harmful, hurtful, spiteful, vicious, wicked

misconception *noun* DELUSION, error, fallacy, misapprehension, misunderstanding

misconduct *noun* IMMORALITY, impropriety, malpractice, mismanagement, wrongdoing

miscreant *noun* WRONGDOER, blackguard, criminal, rascal, reprobate, rogue, scoundrel, sinner, vagabond, villain

misdeed *noun* OFFENCE, crime, fault, misconduct, misdemeanour, sin, transgression, wrong

misdemeanour *noun* OFFENCE, fault, infringement, misdeed, peccadillo, transgression

miser *noun* SKINFLINT, cheapskate (*informal*), niggard, penny-pincher (*informal*), Scrooge

miserable *adjective* 1 UNHAPPY, dejected, depressed, despondent, disconsolate, forlorn, gloomy, sorrowful, woebegone, wretched 2 SQUALID, deplorable, lamentable, shameful, sordid, sorry, wretched

miserly *adjective* MEAN, avaricious, grasping, niggardly, parsimonious, penny-pinching (*informal*), stingy, tightfisted, ungenerous

misery *noun* 1 UNHAPPINESS, anguish, depression, desolation, despair, distress, gloom, grief, sorrow, suffering, torment, woe 2 *Brit. informal* MOANER, killjoy, pessimist, prophet of doom, sourpuss (*informal*), spoilsport, wet blanket (*informal*)

misfire *verb* FAIL, fall through, go wrong, miscarry

misfit *noun* NONCONFORMIST, eccentric, fish out of water (*informal*), oddball (*informal*), square peg (in a round hole) (*informal*)

misfortune *noun* 1 BAD LUCK, adversity, hard luck, ill luck, infelicity 2 MISHAP, affliction, calamity, disaster, reverse, setback, tragedy, tribulation, trouble

misgiving *noun* UNEASE, anxiety, apprehension, distrust, doubt, qualm, reservation, suspicion, trepidation, uncertainty, worry

misguided *adjective* UNWISE, deluded, erroneous, ill-advised, imprudent, injudicious, misplaced, mistaken, unwarranted

mishandle *verb* MISMANAGE, botch, bungle, make a mess of, mess up (*informal*), muff

mishap *noun* ACCIDENT, calamity, misadventure, mischance, misfortune

misinform *verb* MISLEAD, deceive, misdirect, misguide

misinterpret *verb* MISUNDERSTAND, distort, misapprehend, misconceive, misconstrue, misjudge, misread, misrepresent, mistake

misjudge *verb* MISCALCULATE, overestimate, overrate, underestimate, underrate

mislay *verb* LOSE, lose track of, misplace

mislead *verb* DECEIVE, delude, fool, hoodwink, misdirect, misguide, misinform, take in (*informal*)

misleading *adjective* CONFUSING, ambiguous, deceptive, disingenuous, evasive, false

mismanage *verb* MISHANDLE, botch, bungle, make a mess of, mess up, misconduct, misdirect, misgovern

misplace *verb* LOSE, lose track of, mislay

misprint *noun* MISTAKE, corrigendum, erratum, literal, typo (*informal*)

misquote *verb* MISREPRESENT, falsify, twist

misrepresent *verb* DISTORT, disguise, falsify, misinterpret

misrule *noun* DISORDER, anarchy, chaos, confusion, lawlessness, turmoil

miss *verb* 1 OMIT, leave out, let go, overlook, pass over, skip 2 AVOID, escape, evade 3 LONG FOR, pine for, yearn for ♦ *noun* 4 MISTAKE, blunder, error, failure, omission, oversight

misshapen *adjective* DEFORMED, contorted, crooked, distorted, grotesque, malformed, twisted, warped

missile *noun* ROCKET, projectile, weapon

missing *adjective* ABSENT, astray, lacking, left out, lost, mislaid, misplaced, unaccounted-for

mission *noun* TASK, assignment, commission, duty, errand, job, quest, undertaking, vocation

missionary *noun* EVANGELIST, apostle, preacher

missive *noun* LETTER, communication, dispatch, epistle, memorandum, message, note, report

misspent *adjective* WASTED, dissipated, imprudent, profitless, squandered

mist *noun* FOG, cloud, film, haze, smog, spray, steam, vapour

mistake noun 1 ERROR, blunder, erratum, fault, faux pas, gaffe, howler (*informal*), miscalculation, oversight, slip ♦ *verb* 2 MISUNDERSTAND, misapprehend, misconstrue, misinterpret, misjudge, misread 3 CONFUSE WITH, mix up with, take for

mistaken adjective WRONG, erroneous, false, faulty, inaccurate, incorrect, misguided, unsound, wide of the mark

mistakenly adverb INCORRECTLY, by mistake, erroneously, fallaciously, falsely, inaccurately, misguidedly, wrongly

mistimed adjective INOPPORTUNE, badly timed, ill-timed, untimely

mistreat verb ABUSE, harm, ill-treat, injure, knock about *or* around, maltreat, manhandle, misuse, molest

mistress noun LOVER, concubine, girlfriend, kept woman, paramour

mistrust verb 1 DOUBT, be wary of, distrust, fear, suspect ♦ *noun* 2 SUSPICION, distrust, doubt, misgiving, scepticism, uncertainty, wariness

mistrustful adjective SUSPICIOUS, chary, cynical, distrustful, doubtful, fearful, hesitant, sceptical, uncertain, wary

misty adjective FOGGY, blurred, cloudy, dim, hazy, indistinct, murky, obscure, opaque, overcast

misunderstand verb MISINTERPRET, be at cross-purposes, get the wrong end of the stick, misapprehend, misconstrue, misjudge, misread, mistake

misunderstanding noun MISTAKE, error, misconception, misinterpretation, misjudgment, mix-up

misuse noun 1 WASTE, abuse, desecration, misapplication, squandering ♦ *verb* 2 WASTE, abuse, desecrate, misapply, prostitute, squander

mitigate verb EASE, extenuate, lessen, lighten, moderate, soften, subdue, temper

mitigation noun RELIEF, alleviation, diminution, extenuation, moderation, remission

mix verb 1 COMBINE, blend, cross, fuse, intermingle, interweave, join, jumble, merge, mingle 2 SOCIALIZE, associate, consort, fraternize, hang out (*informal*), hobnob, mingle ♦ *noun* 3 MIXTURE, alloy, amalgam, assortment, blend, combination, compound, fusion, medley

mixed adjective 1 COMBINED, amalgamated, blended, composite, compound, joint, mingled, united 2 VARIED, assorted, cosmopolitan, diverse, heterogeneous, miscellaneous, motley

mixed-up adjective CONFUSED, at sea, bewildered, distraught, disturbed, maladjusted, muddled, perplexed, puzzled, upset

mixture noun BLEND, amalgam, assortment, brew, compound, fusion, jumble, medley, mix, potpourri, variety

mix-up noun CONFUSION, mess, mistake, misunderstanding, muddle, tangle

mix up verb 1 COMBINE, blend, mix 2 CONFUSE, confound, muddle

moan noun 1 GROAN, lament, sigh, sob, wail, whine 2 *Informal* GRUMBLE, complaint, gripe (*informal*), grouch (*informal*), grouse, protest, whine ♦ *verb* 3 GROAN, lament, sigh, sob, whine 4 *Informal* GRUMBLE, bleat, carp, complain, groan, grouse, whine, whinge (*informal*)

mob noun 1 CROWD, drove, flock, horde, host, mass, multitude, pack, swarm, throng 2 *Slang* GANG, crew (*informal*), group, lot, set ♦ *verb* 3 SURROUND, crowd around, jostle, set upon, swarm around

mobile *adjective* MOVABLE, itinerant, moving, peripatetic, portable, travelling, wandering

mobilize *verb* PREPARE, activate, call to arms, call up, get *or* make ready, marshal, organize, rally, ready

mock *verb* 1 LAUGH AT, deride, jeer, make fun of, poke fun at, ridicule, scoff, scorn, sneer, taunt, tease 2 MIMIC, ape, caricature, imitate, lampoon, parody, satirize, send up (*Brit. informal*) ♦ *adjective* 3 IMITATION, artificial, dummy, fake, false, feigned, phoney *or* phony (*informal*), pretended, sham, spurious

mockery noun 1 DERISION, contempt, disdain, disrespect, insults, jeering, ridicule, scoffing, scorn 2 FARCE, apology (*informal*), disappointment, joke, letdown

mocking *adjective* SCORNFUL, contemptuous, derisive, disdainful, disrespectful, sarcastic, sardonic, satirical, scoffing

mode noun 1 METHOD, form, manner, procedure, process, style, system, technique, way 2 FASHION, craze, look, rage, style, trend, vogue

model noun 1 REPRESENTATION, copy, dummy, facsimile, image, imitation, miniature, mock-up, replica 2 PATTERN, archetype, example, ideal, original, paradigm, paragon, prototype, standard 3 SITTER, poser, subject ♦ *verb* 4 SHAPE, carve, design, fashion, form, mould, sculpt 5 SHOW OFF, display, sport (*informal*), wear

moderate *adjective* 1 MILD, controlled, gentle, limited, middle-of-the-road, modest, reasonable, restrained, steady 2 AVERAGE, fair, indifferent, mediocre, middling, ordinary, passable, so-so (*informal*), unexceptional ♦ *verb* 3 REGULATE, control, curb, ease, modulate, restrain, soften, subdue, temper, tone down

moderately *adverb* REASONABLY, fairly, passably, quite, rather, slightly, somewhat, tolerably

moderation noun RESTRAINT, fairness, reasonableness, temperance

modern *adjective* CURRENT, contemporary, fresh, new, newfangled, novel, present-day, recent, up-to-date

modernity noun NOVELTY, currency, freshness, innovation, newness

modernize *verb* UPDATE, make over, rejuvenate, remake, remodel, renew, renovate, revamp

modest *adjective* 1 UNPRETENTIOUS, bashful, coy, demure, diffident, reserved, reticent, retiring, self-effacing, shy 2 MODERATE, fair, limited, middling, ordinary, small, unexceptional

modesty noun RESERVE, bashfulness, coyness, demureness, diffidence, humility, reticence, shyness, timidity

modicum noun LITTLE, bit, crumb, drop, fragment, scrap, shred, touch

modification noun CHANGE, adjustment, alteration, qualification, refinement, revision, variation

modify *verb* 1 CHANGE, adapt, adjust, alter, convert, reform, remodel, revise, rework 2 TONE DOWN, ease, lessen, lower, moderate, qualify, restrain, soften, temper

modish *adjective* FASHIONABLE, contemporary, current, in, smart, stylish, trendy (*Brit. informal*), up-to-the-minute, voguish

modulate *verb* ADJUST, attune, balance, regulate, tune, vary

mogul *noun* TYCOON, baron, big noise (*informal*), big shot (*informal*), magnate, V.I.P.

moist *adjective* DAMP, clammy, dewy, humid, soggy, wet

moisten *verb* DAMPEN, damp, moisturize, soak, water, wet

moisture *noun* DAMP, dew, liquid, water, wetness

molecule *noun* PARTICLE, jot, speck

molest *verb* 1 ANNOY, badger, beset, bother, disturb, harass, persecute, pester, plague, torment, worry 2 ABUSE, attack, harm, hurt, ill-treat, interfere with, maltreat

mollify *verb* PACIFY, appease, calm, conciliate, placate, quiet, soothe, sweeten

mollycoddle *verb* PAMPER, baby, cosset, indulge, spoil

moment *noun* 1 INSTANT, flash, jiffy (*informal*), second, split second, trice, twinkling 2 TIME, juncture, point, stage

momentarily *adverb* BRIEFLY, for a moment, temporarily

momentary *adjective* SHORT-LIVED, brief, fleeting, passing, short, temporary, transitory

momentous *adjective* SIGNIFICANT, critical, crucial, fateful, historic, important, pivotal, vital, weighty

momentum *noun* IMPETUS, drive, energy, force, power, propulsion, push, strength, thrust

monarch *noun* RULER, emperor *or* empress, king, potentate, prince *or* princess, queen, sovereign

monarchy *noun* 1 SOVEREIGNTY, autocracy, kingship, monocracy, royalism 2 KINGDOM, empire, principality, realm

monastery *noun* ABBEY, cloister, convent, friary, nunnery, priory

monastic *adjective* MONKISH, ascetic, cloistered, contemplative, hermit-like, reclusive, secluded, sequestered, withdrawn

monetary *adjective* FINANCIAL, budgetary, capital, cash, fiscal, pecuniary

money *noun* CASH, capital, coin, currency, hard cash, legal tender, readies (*informal*), riches, silver, wealth

mongrel *noun* 1 HYBRID, cross, crossbreed, half-breed ♦ *adjective* 2 HYBRID, crossbred

monitor *noun* 1 WATCHDOG, guide, invigilator, prefect (*Brit.*), supervisor ♦ *verb* 2 CHECK, follow, keep an eye on, keep tabs on, keep track of, observe, survey, watch

monk *noun* FRIAR, brother

monkey *noun* 1 SIMIAN, primate 2 RASCAL, devil, imp, rogue, scamp ♦ *verb* 3 FOOL, meddle, mess, play, tinker

monolithic *adjective* HUGE, colossal, impenetrable, intractable, massive, monumental, solid

monologue *noun* SPEECH, harangue, lecture, sermon, soliloquy

monopolize *verb* CONTROL, corner the market in, dominate, hog (*slang*), keep to oneself, take over

monotonous *adjective* TEDIOUS, boring, dull, humdrum, mind-numbing, repetitive, tiresome, unchanging, wearisome

monotony noun TEDIUM, boredom, monotonousness, repetitiveness, routine, sameness, tediousness

monster noun 1 BRUTE, beast, demon, devil, fiend, villain 2 FREAK, monstrosity, mutant 3 GIANT, colossus, mammoth, titan ♦ adjective 4 HUGE, colossal, enormous, gigantic, immense, mammoth, massive, stupendous, tremendous

monstrosity noun EYESORE, freak, horror, monster

monstrous adjective 1 UNNATURAL, fiendish, freakish, frightful, grotesque, gruesome, hideous, horrible 2 OUTRAGEOUS, diabolical, disgraceful, foul, inhuman, intolerable, scandalous, shocking 3 HUGE, colossal, enormous, immense, mammoth, massive, prodigious, stupendous, tremendous

monument noun MEMORIAL, cairn, cenotaph, commemoration, gravestone, headstone, marker, mausoleum, shrine, tombstone

monumental adjective 1 IMPORTANT, awesome, enormous, epoch-making, historic, majestic, memorable, significant, unforgettable 2 Informal IMMENSE, colossal, great, massive, staggering

mood noun STATE OF MIND, disposition, frame of mind, humour, spirit, temper

moody adjective 1 SULLEN, gloomy, glum, ill-tempered, irritable, morose, sad, sulky, temperamental, touchy 2 CHANGEABLE, capricious, erratic, fickle, flighty, impulsive, mercurial, temperamental, unpredictable, volatile

moon noun 1 SATELLITE ♦ verb 2 IDLE, daydream, languish, mope, waste time

moor[1] noun MOORLAND, fell (Brit.), heath

moor[2] verb TIE UP, anchor, berth, dock, lash, make fast, secure

moot adjective 1 DEBATABLE, arguable, contestable, controversial, disputable, doubtful, undecided, unresolved, unsettled ♦ verb 2 BRING UP, broach, propose, put forward, suggest

mop noun 1 SQUEEGEE, sponge, swab 2 MANE, shock, tangle, thatch

mope verb BROOD, fret, languish, moon, pine, pout, sulk

mop up verb CLEAN UP, soak up, sponge, swab, wash, wipe

moral adjective 1 GOOD, decent, ethical, high-minded, honourable, just, noble, principled, right, virtuous ♦ noun 2 LESSON, meaning, message, point, significance

morale noun CONFIDENCE, esprit de corps, heart, self-esteem, spirit

morality noun 1 INTEGRITY, decency, goodness, honesty, justice, righteousness, virtue 2 STANDARDS, conduct, ethics, manners, morals, mores, philosophy, principles

morals plural noun MORALITY, behaviour, conduct, ethics, habits, integrity, manners, mores, principles, scruples, standards

morass noun 1 MARSH, bog, fen, quagmire, slough, swamp 2 MESS, confusion, mix-up, muddle, tangle

moratorium noun POSTPONEMENT, freeze, halt, standstill, suspension

morbid adjective 1 UNWHOLESOME, ghoulish, gloomy, melancholy, sick, sombre, unhealthy 2 GRUESOME, dreadful, ghastly, grisly, hideous, horrid, macabre

mordant adjective SARCASTIC, biting, caustic, cutting, incisive, pungent, scathing, stinging, trenchant

more adjective 1 EXTRA, added, additional, further, new, other, supplementary ◆ adverb 2 TO A GREATER EXTENT, better, further, longer

moreover adverb FURTHERMORE, additionally, also, as well, besides, further, in addition, too

morgue noun MORTUARY

moribund adjective DECLINING, on its last legs, stagnant, waning, weak

morning noun DAWN, a.m., break of day, daybreak, forenoon, morn (*poetic*), sunrise

moron noun FOOL, blockhead, cretin, dunce, dunderhead, halfwit, idiot, imbecile, oaf

moronic adjective IDIOTIC, cretinous, foolish, halfwitted, imbecilic, mindless, stupid, unintelligent

morose adjective SULLEN, depressed, dour, gloomy, glum, ill-tempered, moody, sour, sulky, surly, taciturn

morsel noun PIECE, bit, bite, crumb, mouthful, part, scrap, soupçon, taste, titbit

mortal adjective 1 HUMAN, ephemeral, impermanent, passing, temporal, transient, worldly 2 FATAL, deadly, death-dealing, destructive, killing, lethal, murderous, terminal ◆ noun 3 HUMAN BEING, being, earthling, human, individual, man, person, woman

mortality noun 1 HUMANITY, impermanence, transience 2 KILLING, bloodshed, carnage, death, destruction, fatality

mortification noun 1 HUMILIATION, annoyance, chagrin, discomfiture, embarrassment, shame, vexation 2 DISCIPLINE, abasement, chastening, control, denial, subjugation 3 *Medical* GANGRENE, corruption, festering

mortified adjective HUMILIATED, ashamed, chagrined, chastened, crushed, deflated, embarrassed, humbled, shamed

mortify verb 1 HUMILIATE, chagrin, chasten, crush, deflate, embarrass, humble, shame 2 DISCIPLINE, abase, chasten, control, deny, subdue 3 *Of flesh* PUTREFY, deaden, die, fester

mortuary noun MORGUE, funeral parlour

mostly adverb GENERALLY, as a rule, chiefly, largely, mainly, on the whole, predominantly, primarily, principally, usually

moth-eaten adjective DECAYED, decrepit, dilapidated, ragged, shabby, tattered, threadbare, worn-out

mother noun 1 PARENT, dam, ma (*informal*), mater, mum (*Brit. informal*), mummy (*Brit. informal*) ◆ adjective 2 NATIVE, inborn, innate, natural ◆ verb 3 NURTURE, care for, cherish, nurse, protect, raise, rear, tend

motherly adjective MATERNAL, affectionate, caring, comforting, loving, protective, sheltering

motif noun 1 THEME, concept, idea, leitmotif, subject 2 DESIGN, decoration, ornament, shape

motion noun 1 MOVEMENT, flow, locomotion, mobility, move, progress, travel 2 PROPOSAL, proposition, recommendation, submission, suggestion ◆ verb 3 GESTURE, beckon, direct, gesticulate, nod, signal, wave

motionless adjective STILL, fixed, frozen, immobile, paralysed, standing, static, stationary, stock-still, transfixed, unmoving

motivate verb INSPIRE, arouse, cause, drive, induce, move, persuade, prompt, stimulate, stir

motivation noun INCENTIVE, incitement, inducement, inspiration, motive, reason, spur, stimulus

motive noun REASON, ground(s), incentive, inducement, inspiration, object, purpose, rationale, stimulus

motley adjective 1 MISCELLANEOUS, assorted, disparate, heterogeneous, mixed, varied 2 MULTICOLOURED, chequered, variegated

mottled adjective BLOTCHY, dappled, flecked, piebald, speckled, spotted, stippled, streaked

motto noun SAYING, adage, dictum, maxim, precept, proverb, rule, slogan, watchword

mould[1] noun 1 CAST, pattern, shape 2 DESIGN, build, construction, fashion, form, format, kind, pattern, shape, style 3 NATURE, calibre, character, kind, quality, sort, stamp, type ♦ verb 4 SHAPE, construct, create, fashion, forge, form, make, model, sculpt, work 5 INFLUENCE, affect, control, direct, form, make, shape

mould[2] noun FUNGUS, blight, mildew

mouldy adjective STALE, bad, blighted, decaying, fusty, mildewed, musty, rotten

mound noun 1 HEAP, drift, pile, rick, stack 2 HILL, bank, dune, embankment, hillock, knoll, rise

mount verb 1 CLIMB, ascend, clamber up, go up, scale 2 BESTRIDE, climb onto, jump on 3 INCREASE, accumulate, build, escalate, grow, intensify, multiply, pile up, swell ♦ noun 4 BACKING, base, frame, setting, stand, support 5 HORSE, steed (literary)

mountain noun 1 PEAK, alp, fell (Brit.), mount 2 HEAP, abundance, mass, mound, pile, stack, ton

mountainous adjective 1 HIGH, alpine, highland, rocky, soaring, steep, towering, upland 2 HUGE, daunting, enormous, gigantic, great, immense, mammoth, mighty, monumental

mourn verb GRIEVE, bemoan, bewail, deplore, lament, rue, wail, weep

mournful adjective 1 SAD, melancholy, piteous, plaintive, sorrowful, tragic, unhappy, woeful 2 DISMAL, disconsolate, downcast, gloomy, grieving, heavy-hearted, lugubrious, miserable, rueful, sombre

mourning noun 1 GRIEVING, bereavement, grief, lamentation, weeping, woe 2 BLACK, sackcloth and ashes, widow's weeds

mouth noun 1 LIPS, gob (slang, especially Brit.), jaws, maw 2 OPENING, aperture, door, entrance, gateway, inlet, orifice

mouthful noun TASTE, bit, bite, little, morsel, sample, spoonful, swallow

mouthpiece noun SPOKESPERSON, agent, delegate, representative, spokesman or spokeswoman

movable adjective PORTABLE, detachable, mobile, transferable, transportable

move verb 1 GO, advance, budge, proceed, progress, shift, stir 2 CHANGE, shift, switch, transfer, transpose 3 LEAVE, migrate, pack one's bags (informal), quit, relocate, remove 4 DRIVE, activate, operate, propel, shift, start, turn 5 TOUCH, affect, excite, impress 6 INCITE, cause, induce, influence, inspire, motivate, persuade, prompt, rouse 7 PROPOSE, advocate, put forward, recommend, suggest, urge ♦ noun 8 ACTION, manoeuvre, measure, ploy, step, stratagem, stroke, turn 9 TRANSFER, relocation, removal, shift

movement noun 1 <u>MOTION</u>, action, activity, change, development, flow, manoeuvre, progress, stirring 2 <u>GROUP</u>, campaign, crusade, drive, faction, front, grouping, organization, party 3 <u>WORKINGS</u>, action, machinery, mechanism, works 4 *Music* <u>SECTION</u>, division, part, passage

movie noun <u>FILM</u>, feature, flick (*slang*), picture

moving adjective 1 <u>EMOTIONAL</u>, affecting, inspiring, pathetic, persuasive, poignant, stirring, touching 2 <u>MOBILE</u>, movable, portable, running, unfixed

mow verb <u>CUT</u>, crop, scythe, shear, trim

mow down verb <u>MASSACRE</u>, butcher, cut down, cut to pieces, shoot down, slaughter

much adjective 1 <u>GREAT</u>, abundant, a lot of, ample, considerable, copious, plenty of, sizable *or* sizeable, substantial ♦ noun 2 <u>A LOT</u>, a good deal, a great deal, heaps (*informal*), loads (*informal*), lots (*informal*), plenty ♦ adverb 3 <u>GREATLY</u>, a great deal, a lot, considerably, decidedly, exceedingly

muck noun 1 <u>MANURE</u>, dung, ordure 2 <u>DIRT</u>, filth, gunge (*informal*), mire, mud, ooze, slime, sludge

muck up verb <u>RUIN</u>, blow (*slang*), botch, bungle, make a mess of, make a pig's ear of (*informal*), mess up, muff, spoil

mucky adjective <u>DIRTY</u>, begrimed, filthy, grimy, messy, muddy

mud noun <u>DIRT</u>, clay, mire, ooze, silt, slime, sludge

muddle verb 1 <u>JUMBLE</u>, disarrange, disorder, disorganize, mess, scramble, spoil, tangle 2 <u>CONFUSE</u>, befuddle, bewilder, confound, daze, disorient, perplex, stupefy

♦ noun 3 <u>CONFUSION</u>, chaos, disarray, disorder, disorganization, jumble, mess, mix-up, predicament, tangle

muddy adjective 1 <u>DIRTY</u>, bespattered, grimy, mucky, mud-caked, soiled 2 <u>BOGGY</u>, marshy, quaggy, swampy

muffle verb 1 <u>WRAP UP</u>, cloak, cover, envelop, shroud, swaddle, swathe 2 <u>DEADEN</u>, muzzle, quieten, silence, soften, stifle, suppress

muffled adjective <u>INDISTINCT</u>, faint, muted, stifled, strangled, subdued, suppressed

mug[1] noun <u>CUP</u>, beaker, pot, flagon, tankard

mug[2] noun <u>FACE</u>, countenance, features, visage 1 <u>FOOL</u>, chump (*informal*), easy *or* soft touch (*slang*), simpleton, sucker (*slang*) ♦ verb 2 <u>ATTACK</u>, assault, beat up, rob, set about *or* upon

muggy adjective <u>HUMID</u>, clammy, close, moist, oppressive, sticky, stuffy, sultry

mug up verb <u>STUDY</u>, bone up on (*informal*), burn the midnight oil (*informal*), cram (*informal*), swot (*Brit. informal*)

mull verb <u>PONDER</u>, consider, contemplate, deliberate, meditate, reflect on, ruminate, think over, weigh

multifarious adjective <u>DIVERSE</u>, different, legion, manifold, many, miscellaneous, multiple, numerous, sundry, varied

multiple adjective <u>MANY</u>, manifold, multitudinous, numerous, several, sundry, various

multiply verb 1 <u>INCREASE</u>, build up, expand, extend, proliferate, spread 2 <u>REPRODUCE</u>, breed, propagate

multitude noun <u>MASS</u>, army, crowd,

horde, host, mob, myriad, swarm, throng

munch *verb* CHEW, champ, chomp, crunch

mundane *adjective* 1 ORDINARY, banal, commonplace, day-to-day, everyday, humdrum, prosaic, routine, workaday 2 EARTHLY, mortal, secular, temporal, terrestrial, worldly

municipal *adjective* CIVIC, public, urban

municipality *noun* TOWN, borough, city, district, township

munificence *noun* GENEROSITY, beneficence, benevolence, bounty, largesse *or* largess, liberality, magnanimousness, philanthropy

munificent *adjective* GENEROUS, beneficent, benevolent, bountiful, lavish, liberal, magnanimous, open-handed, philanthropic, unstinting

murder *noun* 1 KILLING, assassination, bloodshed, butchery, carnage, homicide, manslaughter, massacre, slaying ♦ *verb* 2 KILL, assassinate, bump off (*slang*), butcher, eliminate (*slang*), massacre, slaughter, slay

murderer *noun* KILLER, assassin, butcher, cut-throat, hit man (*slang*), homicide, slaughterer, slayer

murderous *adjective* DEADLY, bloodthirsty, brutal, cruel, cut-throat, ferocious, lethal, savage

murky *adjective* DARK, cloudy, dim, dull, gloomy, grey, misty, overcast

murmur *verb* 1 MUMBLE, mutter, whisper 2 GRUMBLE, complain, moan (*informal*) ♦ *noun* 3 DRONE, buzzing, humming, purr, rumble, whisper

muscle *noun* 1 TENDON, sinew

2 STRENGTH, brawn, clout (*informal*), forcefulness, might, power, stamina, weight ♦ *verb* 3 **muscle in** *Informal* IMPOSE ONESELF, butt in, force one's way in

muscular *adjective* STRONG, athletic, powerful, robust, sinewy, strapping, sturdy, vigorous

muse *verb* PONDER, brood, cogitate, consider, contemplate, deliberate, meditate, mull over, reflect, ruminate

mushy *adjective* 1 SOFT, pulpy, semi-solid, slushy, squashy, squelchy, squidgy (*informal*) 2 *Informal* SENTIMENTAL, maudlin, mawkish, saccharine, schmaltzy (*slang*), sloppy (*informal*), slushy (*informal*)

musical *adjective* MELODIOUS, dulcet, euphonious, harmonious, lyrical, melodic, sweet-sounding, tuneful

must *noun* NECESSITY, essential, fundamental, imperative, prerequisite, requirement, requisite, sine qua non

muster *verb* 1 ASSEMBLE, call together, convene, gather, marshal, mobilize, rally, summon ♦ *noun* 2 ASSEMBLY, collection, congregation, convention, gathering, meeting, rally, roundup

musty *adjective* STALE, airless, dank, fusty, mildewed, mouldy, old, smelly, stuffy

mutability *noun* CHANGE, alteration, evolution, metamorphosis, transition, variation, vicissitude

mutable *adjective* CHANGEABLE, adaptable, alterable, fickle, inconsistent, inconstant, unsettled, unstable, variable, volatile

mutation *noun* CHANGE, alteration, evolution, metamorphosis, modification, transfiguration, transformation, variation

mute *adjective* SILENT, dumb, mum, speechless, unspoken, voiceless, wordless

mutilate *verb* 1 MAIM, amputate, cut up, damage, disfigure, dismember, injure, lacerate, mangle 2 DISTORT, adulterate, bowdlerize, censor, cut, damage, expurgate

mutinous *adjective* REBELLIOUS, disobedient, insubordinate, insurgent, refractory, riotous, subversive, unmanageable, unruly

mutiny *noun* 1 REBELLION, disobedience, insubordination, insurrection, revolt, revolution, riot, uprising ♦ *verb* 2 REBEL, disobey, resist, revolt, rise up

mutter *verb* GRUMBLE, complain, grouse, mumble, murmur, rumble

mutual *adjective* SHARED, common, interchangeable, joint, reciprocal, requited, returned

muzzle *noun* 1 JAWS, mouth, nose, snout 2 GAG, guard ♦ *verb* 3 SUPPRESS, censor, curb, gag, restrain, silence, stifle

myopic *adjective* SHORT-SIGHTED, near-sighted

myriad *adjective* 1 INNUMERABLE, countless, immeasurable, incalculable, multitudinous, untold ♦ *noun* 2 MULTITUDE, army, horde, host, swarm

mysterious *adjective* STRANGE, arcane, enigmatic, inexplicable, inscrutable, mystifying, perplexing, puzzling, secret, uncanny, unfathomable, weird

mystery *noun* PUZZLE, conundrum, enigma, problem, question, riddle, secret, teaser

mystic, mystical *adjective* SUPERNATURAL, inscrutable, metaphysical, mysterious, occult, otherworldly, paranormal, preternatural, transcendental

mystify *verb* PUZZLE, baffle, bewilder, confound, confuse, flummox, nonplus, perplex, stump

mystique *noun* FASCINATION, awe, charisma, charm, glamour, magic, spell

myth *noun* 1 LEGEND, allegory, fable, fairy story, fiction, folk tale, saga, story 2 ILLUSION, delusion, fancy, fantasy, figment, imagination, superstition, tall story

mythical *adjective* 1 LEGENDARY, fabled, fabulous, fairy-tale, mythological 2 IMAGINARY, fictitious, invented, made-up, make-believe, nonexistent, pretended, unreal, untrue

mythological *adjective* LEGENDARY, fabulous, mythic, mythical, traditional

mythology *noun* LEGEND, folklore, lore, tradition

N n

nab verb CATCH, apprehend, arrest, capture, collar (*informal*), grab, seize, snatch

nadir noun BOTTOM, depths, lowest point, minimum, rock bottom

naevus noun BIRTHMARK, mole

naff adjective BAD, duff (*Brit. informal*), inferior, low-grade, poor, rubbishy, second-rate, shabby, shoddy, worthless

nag[1] verb 1 SCOLD, annoy, badger, harass, hassle (*informal*), henpeck, irritate, pester, plague, upbraid, worry ♦ noun 2 SCOLD, harpy, shrew, tartar, virago

nag[2] noun HORSE, hack

nagging adjective IRRITATING, persistent, scolding, shrewish, worrying

nail verb FASTEN, attach, fix, hammer, join, pin, secure, tack

naive adjective 1 GULLIBLE, callow, credulous, green, unsuspicious, wet behind the ears (*informal*) 2 INNOCENT, artless, guileless, ingenuous, open, simple, trusting, unsophisticated, unworldly

naivety, naïveté noun 1 GULLIBILITY, callowness, credulity 2 INNOCENCE, artlessness, guilelessness, inexperience, ingenuousness, naturalness, openness, simplicity

naked adjective NUDE, bare, exposed, starkers (*informal*), stripped, unclothed, undressed, without a stitch on (*informal*)

nakedness noun NUDITY, bareness, undress

namby-pamby adjective FEEBLE, insipid, sentimental, spineless, vapid, weak, weedy (*informal*), wimpish *or* wimpy (*informal*), wishy-washy (*informal*)

name noun 1 TITLE, designation, epithet, handle (*slang*), moniker *or* monicker (*slang*), nickname, sobriquet, term 2 FAME, distinction, eminence, esteem, honour, note, praise, renown, repute ♦ verb 3 CALL, baptize, christen, dub, entitle, label, style, term 4 NOMINATE, appoint, choose, designate, select, specify

named adjective 1 CALLED, baptized, christened, dubbed, entitled, known as, labelled, styled, termed 2 NOMINATED, appointed, chosen, designated, mentioned, picked, selected, singled out, specified

nameless adjective 1 ANONYMOUS, unnamed, untitled 2 UNKNOWN, incognito, obscure, undistinguished, unheard-of, unsung 3 HORRIBLE, abominable, indescribable, unmentionable, unspeakable, unutterable

namely adverb SPECIFICALLY, to wit, viz.

nap[1] noun 1 SLEEP, catnap, forty winks (*informal*), kip (*Brit. slang*), rest, siesta ♦ verb 2 SLEEP, catnap, doze, drop off (*informal*), kip (*Brit. slang*), nod off (*informal*), rest, snooze (*informal*)

nap[2] noun WEAVE, down, fibre, grain, pile

napkin noun SERVIETTE, cloth

narcissism noun EGOTISM, self-love, vanity

narcotic noun 1 DRUG, anaesthetic, analgesic, anodyne, opiate, painkiller, sedative, tranquillizer ♦ adjective 2 SEDATIVE, analgesic, calming, hypnotic, painkilling, soporific

nark verb <u>ANNOY</u>, bother, exasperate, get on one's nerves (*informal*), irritate, nettle

narrate verb <u>TELL</u>, chronicle, describe, detail, recite, recount, relate, report

narration noun <u>TELLING</u>, description, explanation, reading, recital, relation

narrative noun <u>STORY</u>, account, chronicle, history, report, statement, tale

narrator noun <u>STORYTELLER</u>, author, chronicler, commentator, reporter, writer

narrow adjective 1 <u>THIN</u>, attenuated, fine, slender, slim, spare, tapering 2 <u>LIMITED</u>, close, confined, constricted, contracted, meagre, restricted, tight 3 <u>INSULAR</u>, dogmatic, illiberal, intolerant, narrow-minded, partial, prejudiced, small-minded ♦ verb 4 <u>TIGHTEN</u>, constrict, limit, reduce

narrowly adverb <u>JUST</u>, barely, by the skin of one's teeth, only just, scarcely

narrow-minded adjective <u>INTOLERANT</u>, bigoted, hidebound, illiberal, opinionated, parochial, prejudiced, provincial, small-minded

nastiness noun <u>UNPLEASANTNESS</u>, malice, meanness, spitefulness

nasty adjective 1 <u>OBJECTIONABLE</u>, disagreeable, loathsome, obnoxious, offensive, unpleasant, vile 2 <u>SPITEFUL</u>, despicable, disagreeable, distasteful, malicious, mean, unpleasant, vicious, vile 3 <u>PAINFUL</u>, bad, critical, dangerous, serious, severe

nation noun <u>COUNTRY</u>, people, race, realm, society, state, tribe

national adjective 1 <u>NATIONWIDE</u>, countrywide, public, widespread ♦ noun 2 <u>CITIZEN</u>, inhabitant,

native, resident, subject

nationalism noun <u>PATRIOTISM</u>, allegiance, chauvinism, jingoism, loyalty

nationality noun <u>RACE</u>, birth, nation

nationwide adjective <u>NATIONAL</u>, countrywide, general, widespread

native adjective 1 <u>LOCAL</u>, domestic, home, indigenous 2 <u>INBORN</u>, congenital, hereditary, inbred, ingrained, innate, instinctive, intrinsic, natural ♦ noun 3 <u>INHABITANT</u>, aborigine, citizen, countryman, dweller, national, resident

natter verb 1 <u>GOSSIP</u>, blether, chatter, gabble, jaw (*slang*), prattle, rabbit (on) (*Brit. informal*), talk ♦ noun 2 <u>GOSSIP</u>, chat, chinwag (*Brit. informal*), chitchat, conversation, gab (*informal*), jaw (*slang*), prattle, talk

natty adjective <u>SMART</u>, dapper, elegant, fashionable, neat, snazzy (*informal*), spruce, stylish, trim

natural adjective 1 <u>NORMAL</u>, common, everyday, legitimate, logical, ordinary, regular, typical, usual 2 <u>UNAFFECTED</u>, genuine, ingenuous, open, real, simple, spontaneous, unpretentious, unsophisticated 3 <u>INNATE</u>, characteristic, essential, inborn, inherent, instinctive, intuitive, native 4 <u>PURE</u>, organic, plain, unrefined, whole

naturalist noun <u>BIOLOGIST</u>, botanist, ecologist, zoologist

naturalistic adjective <u>REALISTIC</u>, lifelike, true-to-life

naturally adverb 1 <u>OF COURSE</u>, certainly 2 <u>GENUINELY</u>, normally, simply, spontaneously, typically, unaffectedly, unpretentiously

nature noun 1 <u>CREATION</u>, cosmos, earth, environment, universe, world 2 <u>MAKE-UP</u>, character,

complexion, constitution, essence
3 KIND, category, description, sort,
species, style, type, variety
4 TEMPERAMENT, disposition,
humour, mood, outlook, temper

naughty *adjective* **1** DISOBEDIENT,
bad, impish, misbehaved,
mischievous, refractory, wayward,
wicked, worthless **2** OBSCENE,
improper, lewd, ribald, risqué,
smutty, vulgar

nausea *noun* SICKNESS, biliousness,
queasiness, retching,
squeamishness, vomiting

nauseate *verb* SICKEN, disgust,
offend, repel, repulse, revolt, turn
one's stomach

nauseous *adjective* SICKENING,
abhorrent, disgusting, distasteful,
nauseating, offensive, repugnant,
repulsive, revolting

nautical *adjective* MARITIME, marine,
naval

naval *adjective* NAUTICAL, marine,
maritime

navigable *adjective* **1** PASSABLE,
clear, negotiable, unobstructed
2 SAILABLE, controllable, dirigible

navigate *verb* SAIL, drive, guide,
handle, manoeuvre, pilot, steer,
voyage

navigation *noun* SAILING,
helmsmanship, seamanship,
voyaging

navigator *noun* PILOT, mariner,
seaman

navvy *noun* LABOURER, worker,
workman

navy *noun* FLEET, armada, flotilla

near *adjective* **1** CLOSE, adjacent,
adjoining, nearby, neighbouring
2 FORTHCOMING, approaching,
imminent, impending, in the
offing, looming, nigh, upcoming

nearby *adjective* NEIGHBOURING,

adjacent, adjoining, convenient,
handy

nearly *adverb* ALMOST,
approximately, as good as, just
about, practically, roughly,
virtually, well-nigh

nearness *noun* CLOSENESS,
accessibility, availability,
handiness, proximity, vicinity

near-sighted *adjective*
SHORT-SIGHTED, myopic

neat *adjective* **1** TIDY, orderly,
shipshape, smart, spick-and-span,
spruce, systematic, trim **2** ELEGANT,
adept, adroit, deft, dexterous,
efficient, graceful, nimble, skilful,
stylish **3** *Of alcoholic drinks*
STRAIGHT, pure, undiluted, unmixed

neatly *adverb* **1** TIDILY, daintily,
fastidiously, methodically, smartly,
sprucely, systematically
2 ELEGANTLY, adeptly, adroitly,
deftly, dexterously, efficiently,
expertly, gracefully, nimbly,
skilfully

neatness *noun* **1** TIDINESS,
daintiness, orderliness, smartness,
spruceness, trimness **2** ELEGANCE,
adroitness, deftness, dexterity,
efficiency, grace, nimbleness, skill,
style

nebulous *adjective* VAGUE,
confused, dim, hazy, imprecise,
indefinite, indistinct, shadowy,
uncertain, unclear

necessarily *adverb* CERTAINLY,
automatically, compulsorily,
incontrovertibly, inevitably,
inexorably, naturally, of necessity,
undoubtedly

necessary *adjective* **1** NEEDED,
compulsory, essential, imperative,
indispensable, mandatory,
obligatory, required, requisite,
vital **2** CERTAIN, fated, inescapable,
inevitable, inexorable, unavoidable

necessitate *verb* COMPEL, call for,

coerce, constrain, demand, force, impel, oblige, require

necessities *plural noun* ESSENTIALS, exigencies, fundamentals, needs, requirements

necessity *noun* 1 INEVITABILITY, compulsion, inexorableness, obligation 2 NEED, desideratum, essential, fundamental, prerequisite, requirement, requisite, *sine qua non*

necromancy *noun* MAGIC, black magic, divination, enchantment, sorcery, witchcraft, wizardry

necropolis *noun* CEMETERY, burial ground, churchyard, graveyard

need *verb* 1 REQUIRE, call for, demand, entail, lack, miss, necessitate, want ♦ *noun* 2 POVERTY, deprivation, destitution, inadequacy, insufficiency, lack, paucity, penury, shortage 3 REQUIREMENT, demand, desideratum, essential, requisite 4 EMERGENCY, exigency, necessity, obligation, urgency, want

needed *adjective* NECESSARY, called for, desired, lacked, required, wanted

needful *adjective* NECESSARY, essential, indispensable, needed, required, requisite, stipulated, vital

needle *verb* IRRITATE, annoy, get on one's nerves (*informal*), goad, harass, nag, pester, provoke, rile, taunt

needless *adjective* UNNECESSARY, gratuitous, groundless, pointless, redundant, superfluous, uncalled-for, unwanted, useless

needlework *noun* EMBROIDERY, needlecraft, sewing, stitching, tailoring

needy *adjective* POOR, deprived, destitute, disadvantaged, impoverished, penniless, poverty-stricken, underprivileged

ne'er-do-well *noun* LAYABOUT, black sheep, good-for-nothing, idler, loafer, loser, skiver (*Brit. slang*), wastrel

nefarious *adjective* WICKED, criminal, depraved, evil, foul, heinous, infernal, villainous

negate *verb* 1 INVALIDATE, annul, cancel, countermand, neutralize, nullify, obviate, reverse, wipe out 2 DENY, contradict, disallow, disprove, gainsay (*archaic or literary*), oppose, rebut, refute

negation *noun* 1 CANCELLATION, neutralization, nullification 2 DENIAL, contradiction, converse, disavowal, inverse, opposite, rejection, renunciation, reverse

negative *adjective* 1 CONTRADICTORY, contrary, denying, dissenting, opposing, refusing, rejecting, resisting 2 PESSIMISTIC, cynical, gloomy, jaundiced, uncooperative, unenthusiastic, unwilling ♦ *noun* 3 CONTRADICTION, denial, refusal

neglect *verb* 1 DISREGARD, disdain, ignore, overlook, rebuff, scorn, slight, spurn 2 FORGET, be remiss, evade, omit, pass over, shirk, skimp ♦ *noun* 3 DISREGARD, disdain, inattention, indifference 4 NEGLIGENCE, carelessness, dereliction, failure, laxity, oversight, slackness

neglected *adjective* 1 ABANDONED, derelict, overgrown 2 DISREGARDED, unappreciated, underestimated, undervalued

neglectful *adjective* CARELESS, heedless, inattentive, indifferent, lax, negligent, remiss, thoughtless, uncaring

negligence *noun* CARELESSNESS, dereliction, disregard, inattention, indifference, laxity, neglect, slackness, thoughtlessness

negligent *adjective* CARELESS, forgetful, heedless, inattentive, neglectful, remiss, slack, slapdash, thoughtless, unthinking

negligible *adjective* INSIGNIFICANT, imperceptible, inconsequential, minor, minute, small, trifling, trivial, unimportant

negotiable *adjective* DEBATABLE, variable

negotiate *verb* **1** DEAL, arrange, bargain, conciliate, debate, discuss, mediate, transact, work out **2** GET ROUND, clear, cross, get over, get past, pass, surmount

negotiation *noun* BARGAINING, arbitration, debate, diplomacy, discussion, mediation, transaction, wheeling and dealing (*informal*)

negotiator *noun* MEDIATOR, ambassador, delegate, diplomat, honest broker, intermediary, moderator

neighbourhood *noun* DISTRICT, community, environs, locale, locality, quarter, region, vicinity

neighbouring *adjective* NEARBY, adjacent, adjoining, bordering, connecting, near, next, surrounding

neighbourly *adjective* HELPFUL, considerate, friendly, harmonious, hospitable, kind, obliging, sociable

nemesis *noun* RETRIBUTION, destiny, destruction, fate, vengeance

nepotism *noun* FAVOURITISM, bias, partiality, patronage, preferential treatment

nerd, nurd *noun* BORE, anorak (*informal*), dork (*slang*), drip (*informal*), geek (*informal*), obsessive, trainspotter (*informal*), wonk (*informal*)

nerve *noun* **1** BRAVERY, bottle (*Brit. slang*), courage, daring, fearlessness, grit, guts (*informal*), pluck, resolution, will **2** IMPUDENCE, audacity, boldness, brazenness, cheek (*informal*), impertinence, insolence, temerity ♦ *verb* **3 nerve oneself** BRACE ONESELF, fortify oneself, steel oneself

nerveless *adjective* CALM, composed, controlled, cool, impassive, imperturbable, self-possessed, unemotional

nerve-racking *adjective* TENSE, difficult, distressing, frightening, harrowing, stressful, trying, worrying

nerves *plural noun* TENSION, anxiety, butterflies (in one's stomach) (*informal*), cold feet (*informal*), fretfulness, nervousness, strain, stress, worry

nervous *adjective* APPREHENSIVE, anxious, edgy, fearful, jumpy, on edge, tense, uneasy, uptight (*informal*), worried

nervousness *noun* ANXIETY, agitation, disquiet, excitability, fluster, tension, touchiness, worry

nervy *adjective* ANXIOUS, agitated, fidgety, jittery (*informal*), jumpy, nervous, on edge, tense, twitchy (*informal*)

nest *noun* REFUGE, den, haunt, hideaway, retreat

nest egg *noun* RESERVE, cache, deposit, fall-back, fund(s), savings, store

nestle *verb* SNUGGLE, cuddle, curl up, huddle, nuzzle

nestling *noun* CHICK, fledgling

net[1] *noun* **1** MESH, lattice, netting, network, openwork, tracery, web ♦ *verb* **2** CATCH, bag, capture, enmesh, ensnare, entangle, trap

net[2], **nett** *adjective* **1** FINAL, after taxes, clear, take-home ♦ *verb* **2** EARN, accumulate, bring in, clear, gain, make, realize, reap

nether adjective LOWER, below, beneath, bottom, inferior, under, underground

nettled adjective IRRITATED, annoyed, exasperated, galled, harassed, incensed, peeved, put out, riled, vexed

network noun SYSTEM, arrangement, complex, grid, labyrinth, lattice, maze, organization, structure, web

neurosis noun OBSESSION, abnormality, affliction, derangement, instability, maladjustment, mental illness, phobia

neurotic adjective UNSTABLE, abnormal, compulsive, disturbed, maladjusted, manic, nervous, obsessive, unhealthy

neuter verb CASTRATE, doctor (*informal*), emasculate, fix (*informal*), geld, spay

neutral adjective 1 UNBIASED, disinterested, even-handed, impartial, nonaligned, nonpartisan, uncommitted, uninvolved, unprejudiced 2 INDETERMINATE, dull, indistinct, intermediate, undefined

neutrality noun IMPARTIALITY, detachment, nonalignment, noninterference, noninvolvement, nonpartisanship

neutralize verb COUNTERACT, cancel, compensate for, counterbalance, frustrate, negate, nullify, offset, undo

never adverb AT NO TIME, not at all, on no account, under no circumstances

nevertheless adverb NONETHELESS, but, even so, (even) though, however, notwithstanding, regardless, still, yet

new adjective 1 MODERN, contemporary, current, fresh, ground-breaking, latest, novel, original, recent, state-of-the-art, unfamiliar, up-to-date 2 CHANGED, altered, improved, modernized, redesigned, renewed, restored 3 EXTRA, added, more, supplementary

newcomer noun NOVICE, arrival, beginner, Johnny-come-lately (*informal*), parvenu

newfangled adjective NEW, contemporary, fashionable, gimmicky, modern, novel, recent, state-of-the-art

newly adverb RECENTLY, anew, freshly, just, lately, latterly

newness noun NOVELTY, freshness, innovation, oddity, originality, strangeness, unfamiliarity, uniqueness

news noun INFORMATION, bulletin, communiqué, exposé, gossip, hearsay, intelligence, latest (*informal*), report, revelation, rumour, story

newsworthy adjective INTERESTING, important, notable, noteworthy, remarkable, significant, stimulating

next adjective 1 FOLLOWING, consequent, ensuing, later, subsequent, succeeding 2 NEAREST, adjacent, adjoining, closest, neighbouring ♦ adverb 3 AFTERWARDS, following, later, subsequently, thereafter

nibble verb 1 BITE, eat, gnaw, munch, nip, peck, pick at ♦ noun 2 SNACK, bite, crumb, morsel, peck, soupçon, taste, titbit

nice adjective 1 PLEASANT, agreeable, attractive, charming, delightful, good, pleasurable 2 KIND, courteous, friendly, likable or likeable, polite, well-mannered 3 NEAT, dainty, fine, tidy, trim 4 SUBTLE, careful, delicate, fastidious, fine, meticulous, precise, strict

nicely adverb **1** PLEASANTLY, acceptably, agreeably, attractively, charmingly, delightfully, pleasurably, well **2** KINDLY, amiably, commendably, courteously, politely **3** NEATLY, daintily, finely, tidily, trimly

nicety noun SUBTLETY, daintiness, delicacy, discrimination, distinction, nuance, refinement

niche noun **1** ALCOVE, corner, hollow, nook, opening, recess **2** POSITION, calling, pigeonhole (*informal*), place, slot (*informal*), vocation

nick verb **1** CUT, chip, dent, mark, notch, scar, score, scratch, snick **2** STEAL, pilfer, pinch (*informal*), swipe (*slang*) ♦ noun **3** CUT, chip, dent, mark, notch, scar, scratch

nickname noun PET NAME, diminutive, epithet, label, moniker *or* monicker (*slang*), sobriquet

nifty adjective NEAT, attractive, chic, deft, pleasing, smart, stylish

niggard noun MISER, cheapskate (*informal*), Scrooge, skinflint

niggardly adjective STINGY, avaricious, frugal, grudging, mean, miserly, parsimonious, tightfisted, ungenerous

niggle verb **1** WORRY, annoy, irritate, rankle **2** CRITICIZE, carp, cavil, find fault, fuss

niggling adjective **1** PERSISTENT, gnawing, irritating, troubling, worrying **2** PETTY, finicky, fussy, nit-picking (*informal*), pettifogging, picky (*informal*), quibbling

night noun DARKNESS, dark, night-time

nightfall noun EVENING, dusk, sundown, sunset, twilight

nightly adjective **1** NOCTURNAL,

night-time ♦ adverb **2** EVERY NIGHT, each night, night after night, nights (*informal*)

nightmare noun **1** BAD DREAM, hallucination **2** ORDEAL, horror, torment, trial, tribulation

nil noun NOTHING, love, naught, none, zero

nimble adjective AGILE, brisk, deft, dexterous, lively, quick, sprightly, spry, swift

nimbly adverb QUICKLY, briskly, deftly, dexterously, easily, readily, smartly, spryly, swiftly

nincompoop noun IDIOT, blockhead, chump, fool, nitwit (*informal*), numbskull *or* numskull, twit (*informal, chiefly Brit.*)

nip[1] verb PINCH, bite, squeeze, tweak

nip[2] noun DRAM, draught, drop, mouthful, shot (*informal*), sip, snifter (*informal*)

nipper noun Informal CHILD, baby, boy, girl, infant, kid (*informal*), tot

nippy adjective **1** CHILLY, biting, sharp **2** Informal QUICK, active, agile, fast, nimble, spry

nirvana noun PARADISE, bliss, joy, peace, serenity, tranquillity

nit-picking adjective FUSSY, captious, carping, finicky, hairsplitting, pedantic, pettifogging, quibbling

nitty-gritty noun BASICS, brass tacks (*informal*), core, crux, essentials, fundamentals, gist, substance

nitwit noun Informal FOOL, dimwit (*informal*), dummy (*slang*), halfwit, nincompoop, oaf, simpleton

no interjection **1** NEVER, nay, not at all, no way ♦ noun **2** REFUSAL, denial, negation

nob noun ARISTOCRAT, bigwig (*informal*), toff (*Brit. slang*), V.I.P.

nobble *verb* <u>BRIBE</u>, get at, influence, intimidate, win over

nobility *noun* **1** <u>INTEGRITY</u>, honour, incorruptibility, uprightness, virtue **2** <u>ARISTOCRACY</u>, elite, lords, nobles, patricians, peerage, upper class

noble *adjective* **1** <u>WORTHY</u>, generous, honourable, magnanimous, upright, virtuous **2** <u>ARISTOCRATIC</u>, blue-blooded, highborn, lordly, patrician, titled **3** <u>GREAT</u>, dignified, distinguished, grand, imposing, impressive, lofty, splendid, stately ♦ *noun* **4** <u>LORD</u>, aristocrat, nobleman, peer

nobody *pronoun* **1** <u>NO-ONE</u> ♦ *noun* **2** <u>NONENTITY</u>, cipher, lightweight (*informal*), menial

nocturnal *adjective* <u>NIGHTLY</u>, night-time

nod *verb* **1** <u>ACKNOWLEDGE</u>, bow, gesture, indicate, signal **2** <u>SLEEP</u>, doze, drowse, nap ♦ *noun* **3** <u>GESTURE</u>, acknowledgment, greeting, indication, sign, signal

noggin *noun* **1** <u>CUP</u>, dram, mug, nip, tot **2** *Informal* <u>HEAD</u>, block (*informal*), nut (*slang*)

no go *adjective* <u>IMPOSSIBLE</u>, futile, hopeless, not on (*informal*), vain

noise *noun* <u>SOUND</u>, clamour, commotion, din, hubbub, racket, row, uproar

noiseless *adjective* <u>SILENT</u>, hushed, inaudible, mute, quiet, soundless, still

noisome *adjective* **1** <u>POISONOUS</u>, bad, harmful, pernicious, pestilential, unhealthy, unwholesome **2** <u>OFFENSIVE</u>, disgusting, fetid, foul, malodorous, noxious, putrid, smelly, stinking

noisy *adjective* <u>LOUD</u>, boisterous, cacophonous, clamorous, deafening, ear-splitting, strident, tumultuous, uproarious, vociferous

nomad *noun* <u>WANDERER</u>, drifter, itinerant, migrant, rambler, rover, vagabond

nomadic *adjective* <u>WANDERING</u>, itinerant, migrant, peripatetic, roaming, roving, travelling, vagrant

nom de plume *noun* <u>PSEUDONYM</u>, alias, assumed name, nom de guerre, pen name

nomenclature *noun* <u>TERMINOLOGY</u>, classification, codification, phraseology, taxonomy, vocabulary

nominal *adjective* **1** <u>SO-CALLED</u>, formal, ostensible, professed, puppet, purported, supposed, theoretical, titular **2** <u>SMALL</u>, inconsiderable, insignificant, minimal, symbolic, token, trifling, trivial

nominate *verb* <u>NAME</u>, appoint, assign, choose, designate, elect, propose, recommend, select, suggest

nomination *noun* <u>CHOICE</u>, appointment, designation, election, proposal, recommendation, selection, suggestion

nominee *noun* <u>CANDIDATE</u>, aspirant, contestant, entrant, protégé, runner

nonaligned *adjective* <u>NEUTRAL</u>, impartial, uncommitted, undecided

nonchalance *noun* <u>INDIFFERENCE</u>, calm, composure, equanimity, imperturbability, sang-froid, self-possession, unconcern

nonchalant *adjective* <u>CASUAL</u>, blasé, calm, careless, indifferent, insouciant, laid-back (*informal*), offhand, unconcerned, unperturbed

noncombatant *noun* CIVILIAN, neutral, nonbelligerent

noncommittal *adjective* EVASIVE, cautious, circumspect, equivocal, guarded, neutral, politic, temporizing, tentative, vague, wary

non compos mentis *adjective* INSANE, crazy, deranged, mentally ill, unbalanced, unhinged

nonconformist *noun* MAVERICK, dissenter, eccentric, heretic, iconoclast, individualist, protester, radical, rebel

nonconformity *noun* DISSENT, eccentricity, heresy, heterodoxy

nondescript *adjective* ORDINARY, commonplace, dull, featureless, run-of-the-mill, undistinguished, unexceptional, unremarkable

none *pronoun* NOT ANY, nil, nobody, no-one, nothing, not one, zero

nonentity *noun* NOBODY, cipher, lightweight (*informal*), mediocrity, small fry

nonessential *adjective* UNNECESSARY, dispensable, expendable, extraneous, inessential, peripheral, superfluous, unimportant

nonetheless *adverb* NEVERTHELESS, despite that, even so, however, in spite of that, yet

nonevent *noun* FLOP (*informal*), disappointment, dud (*informal*), failure, fiasco, washout

nonexistent *adjective* IMAGINARY, chimerical, fictional, hypothetical, illusory, legendary, mythical, unreal

nonsense *noun* RUBBISH, balderdash, claptrap (*informal*), double Dutch (*Brit. informal*), drivel, gibberish, hot air (*informal*), stupidity, tripe (*informal*), twaddle

nonsensical *adjective* SENSELESS, absurd, crazy, foolish, inane, incomprehensible, irrational, meaningless, ridiculous, silly

nonstarter *noun* DEAD LOSS, dud (*informal*), lemon (*informal*), loser, no-hoper (*informal*), turkey (*informal*), washout (*informal*)

nonstop *adjective* 1 CONTINUOUS, constant, endless, incessant, interminable, relentless, unbroken, uninterrupted ♦ *adverb* 2 CONTINUOUSLY, ceaselessly, constantly, endlessly, incessantly, interminably, perpetually, relentlessly

nook *noun* NICHE, alcove, corner, cubbyhole, hide-out, opening, recess, retreat

noon *noun* MIDDAY, high noon, noonday, noontide, twelve noon

norm *noun* STANDARD, average, benchmark, criterion, par, pattern, rule, yardstick

normal *adjective* 1 USUAL, average, common, conventional, natural, ordinary, regular, routine, standard, typical 2 SANE, rational, reasonable, well-adjusted

normality *noun* 1 REGULARITY, conventionality, naturalness 2 SANITY, balance, rationality, reason

normally *adverb* USUALLY, as a rule, commonly, generally, habitually, ordinarily, regularly, typically

north *adjective* 1 NORTHERN, Arctic, boreal, northerly, polar ♦ *adverb* 2 NORTHWARD(S), northerly

nose *noun* 1 SNOUT, beak, bill, hooter (*slang*), proboscis ♦ *verb* 2 EASE FORWARD, nudge, nuzzle, push, shove 3 PRY, meddle, snoop (*informal*)

nosegay *noun* POSY, bouquet

nosey, nosy *adjective* INQUISITIVE,

curious, eavesdropping,
interfering, intrusive,
meddlesome, prying, snooping
(*informal*)

nostalgia *noun* REMINISCENCE,
homesickness, longing, pining,
regretfulness, remembrance,
wistfulness, yearning

nostalgic *adjective* SENTIMENTAL,
emotional, homesick, longing,
maudlin, regretful, wistful

nostrum *noun* MEDICINE, cure, drug,
elixir, panacea, potion, remedy,
treatment

notability *noun* FAME, celebrity,
distinction, eminence, esteem,
renown

notable *adjective* 1 REMARKABLE,
conspicuous, extraordinary,
memorable, noteworthy,
outstanding, rare, striking,
uncommon, unusual ◆ *noun*
2 CELEBRITY, big name, dignitary,
personage, V.I.P.

notably *adverb* PARTICULARLY,
especially, outstandingly, strikingly

notation *noun* SIGNS, characters,
code, script, symbols, system

notch *noun* 1 CUT, cleft, incision,
indentation, mark, nick, score
2 *Informal* LEVEL, degree, grade,
step ◆ *verb* 3 CUT, indent, mark,
nick, score, scratch

notch up *verb* REGISTER, achieve,
gain, make, score

note *noun* 1 MESSAGE, comment,
communication, epistle, jotting,
letter, memo, memorandum,
minute, remark, reminder
2 SYMBOL, indication, mark, sign,
token ◆ *verb* 3 SEE, notice, observe,
perceive 4 MARK, denote,
designate, indicate, record,
register 5 MENTION, remark

notebook *noun* JOTTER, diary,
exercise book, journal, notepad

noted *adjective* FAMOUS, acclaimed,
celebrated, distinguished,
eminent, illustrious, notable,
prominent, renowned, well-known

noteworthy *adjective* REMARKABLE,
exceptional, extraordinary,
important, notable, outstanding,
significant, unusual

nothing *noun* NOUGHT, emptiness,
nil, nothingness, nullity, void, zero

nothingness *noun* 1 OBLIVION,
nonbeing, nonexistence, nullity
2 INSIGNIFICANCE, unimportance,
worthlessness

notice *noun* 1 OBSERVATION,
cognizance, consideration, heed,
interest, note, regard 2 ATTENTION,
civility, respect 3 ANNOUNCEMENT,
advice, communication,
instruction, intimation, news,
notification, order, warning ◆ *verb*
4 OBSERVE, detect, discern,
distinguish, mark, note, perceive,
see, spot

noticeable *adjective* OBVIOUS,
appreciable, clear, conspicuous,
evident, manifest, perceptible,
plain, striking

notification *noun* ANNOUNCEMENT,
advice, declaration, information,
intelligence, message, notice,
statement, warning

notify *verb* INFORM, advise, alert,
announce, declare, make known,
publish, tell, warn

notion *noun* 1 IDEA, belief, concept,
impression, inkling, opinion,
sentiment, view 2 WHIM, caprice,
desire, fancy, impulse, inclination,
wish

notional *adjective* SPECULATIVE,
abstract, conceptual,
hypothetical, imaginary,
theoretical, unreal

notoriety *noun* SCANDAL, dishonour,
disrepute, infamy, obloquy,
opprobrium

notorious adjective INFAMOUS, dishonourable, disreputable, opprobrious, scandalous

notoriously adverb INFAMOUSLY, dishonourably, disreputably, opprobriously, scandalously

notwithstanding preposition DESPITE, in spite of

nought noun ZERO, nil, nothing

nourish verb 1 FEED, nurse, nurture, supply, sustain, tend 2 ENCOURAGE, comfort, cultivate, foster, maintain, promote, support

nourishing adjective NUTRITIOUS, beneficial, nutritive, wholesome

nourishment noun FOOD, nutriment, nutrition, sustenance

novel[1] noun STORY, fiction, narrative, romance, tale

novel[2] adjective NEW, different, fresh, innovative, original, strange, uncommon, unfamiliar, unusual

novelty noun 1 NEWNESS, freshness, innovation, oddity, originality, strangeness, surprise, unfamiliarity, uniqueness 2 GIMMICK, curiosity, gadget 3 KNICK-KNACK, bauble, memento, souvenir, trifle, trinket

novice noun BEGINNER, amateur, apprentice, learner, newcomer, probationer, pupil, trainee

now adverb 1 NOWADAYS, any more, at the moment 2 IMMEDIATELY, at once, instantly, promptly, straightaway 3 **now and then** or **again** OCCASIONALLY, from time to time, infrequently, intermittently, on and off, sometimes, sporadically

nowadays adverb NOW, any more, at the moment, in this day and age, today

noxious adjective HARMFUL, deadly, destructive, foul, hurtful, injurious, poisonous, unhealthy, unwholesome

nuance noun SUBTLETY, degree, distinction, gradation, nicety, refinement, shade, tinge

nubile adjective MARRIAGEABLE, ripe (informal)

nucleus noun CENTRE, basis, core, focus, heart, kernel, nub, pivot

nude adjective NAKED, bare, disrobed, stark-naked, stripped, unclad, unclothed, undressed, without a stitch on (informal)

nudge verb PUSH, bump, dig, elbow, jog, poke, prod, shove, touch

nudity noun NAKEDNESS, bareness, deshabille, nudism, undress

nugget noun LUMP, chunk, clump, hunk, mass, piece

nuisance noun PROBLEM, annoyance, bother, drag (informal), hassle (informal), inconvenience, irritation, pain in the neck, pest, trouble

null adjective **null and void** INVALID, inoperative, useless, valueless, void, worthless

nullify verb CANCEL, counteract, invalidate, negate, neutralize, obviate, render null and void, veto

nullity noun NONEXISTENCE, invalidity, powerlessness, uselessness, worthlessness

numb adjective 1 UNFEELING, benumbed, dead, deadened, frozen, immobilized, insensitive, paralysed, torpid ◆ verb 2 DEADEN, benumb, dull, freeze, immobilize, paralyse

number noun 1 NUMERAL, character, digit, figure, integer 2 QUANTITY, aggregate, amount, collection, crowd, horde, multitude, throng 3 ISSUE, copy, edition, imprint, printing ◆ verb 4 COUNT, account, add, calculate, compute, enumerate, include, reckon, total

numberless *adjective* <u>INFINITE</u>, countless, endless, innumerable, multitudinous, myriad, unnumbered, untold

numbness *noun* <u>DEADNESS</u>, dullness, insensitivity, paralysis, torpor

numbskull, numskull *noun* <u>FOOL</u>, blockhead, clot (*Brit. informal*), dolt, dummy (*slang*), dunce, oaf, twit (*informal*)

numeral *noun* <u>NUMBER</u>, digit, figure, integer

numerous *adjective* <u>MANY</u>, abundant, copious, plentiful, profuse, several, thick on the ground

nuncio *noun* <u>AMBASSADOR</u>, envoy, legate, messenger

nunnery *noun* <u>CONVENT</u>, abbey, cloister, house

nuptial *adjective* <u>MARITAL</u>, bridal, conjugal, connubial, matrimonial

nuptials *plural noun* <u>WEDDING</u>, marriage, matrimony

nurse *verb* **1** <u>LOOK AFTER</u>, care for, minister to, tend, treat

2 <u>BREAST-FEED</u>, feed, nourish, nurture, suckle, wet-nurse
3 <u>FOSTER</u>, cherish, cultivate, encourage, harbour, preserve, promote, succour, support

nursery *noun* <u>CRECHE</u>, kindergarten, playgroup

nurture *noun* **1** <u>DEVELOPMENT</u>, discipline, education, instruction, rearing, training, upbringing
♦ *verb* **2** <u>DEVELOP</u>, bring up, discipline, educate, instruct, rear, school, train

nut *noun* **1** *Slang* <u>MADMAN</u>, crank (*informal*), lunatic, maniac, nutcase (*slang*), psycho (*slang*)
2 *Slang* <u>HEAD</u>, brain, mind, reason, senses

nutrition *noun* <u>FOOD</u>, nourishment, nutriment, sustenance

nutritious *adjective* <u>NOURISHING</u>, beneficial, health-giving, invigorating, nutritive, strengthening, wholesome

nuzzle *verb* <u>SNUGGLE</u>, burrow, cuddle, fondle, nestle, pet

nymph *noun* <u>SYLPH</u>, dryad, girl, maiden, naiad

O o

oaf *noun* IDIOT, blockhead, clod, dolt, dunce, fool, goon, lout, moron, numbskull *or* numskull

oafish *adjective* MORONIC, dense, dim-witted (*informal*), doltish, dumb (*informal*), loutish, stupid, thick

oath *noun* 1 PROMISE, affirmation, avowal, bond, pledge, vow, word 2 SWEARWORD, blasphemy, curse, expletive, profanity

obdurate *adjective* STUBBORN, dogged, hard-hearted, immovable, implacable, inflexible, obstinate, pig-headed, unyielding

obedience *noun* RESPECT, acquiescence, compliance, docility, observance, reverence, submissiveness, subservience

obedient *adjective* RESPECTFUL, acquiescent, biddable, compliant, deferential, docile, dutiful, submissive, subservient, well-trained

obelisk *noun* COLUMN, monolith, monument, needle, pillar, shaft

obese *adjective* FAT, corpulent, gross, heavy, overweight, paunchy, plump, portly, rotund, stout, tubby

obesity *noun* FATNESS, bulk, corpulence, grossness, portliness, stoutness, tubbiness

obey *verb* CARRY OUT, abide by, act upon, adhere to, comply, conform, follow, heed, keep, observe

obfuscate *verb* CONFUSE, befog, cloud, darken, muddy the waters, obscure, perplex

object[1] *noun* 1 THING, article, body, entity, item, phenomenon 2 TARGET, focus, recipient, victim

3 PURPOSE, aim, design, end, goal, idea, intention, objective, point

object[2] *verb* PROTEST, argue against, demur, draw the line (at something), expostulate, oppose, take exception

objection *noun* PROTEST, counter-argument, demur, doubt, opposition, remonstrance, scruple

objectionable *adjective* UNPLEASANT, deplorable, disagreeable, intolerable, obnoxious, offensive, regrettable, repugnant, unseemly

objective *noun* 1 PURPOSE, aim, ambition, end, goal, intention, mark, object, target ♦ *adjective* 2 UNBIASED, detached, disinterested, dispassionate, even-handed, fair, impartial, open-minded, unprejudiced

objectively *adverb* IMPARTIALLY, disinterestedly, dispassionately, even-handedly, with an open mind

objectivity *noun* IMPARTIALITY, detachment, disinterestedness, dispassion

obligation *noun* DUTY, accountability, burden, charge, compulsion, liability, requirement, responsibility

obligatory *adjective* COMPULSORY, binding, *de rigueur*, essential, imperative, mandatory, necessary, required, requisite, unavoidable

oblige *verb* 1 COMPEL, bind, constrain, force, impel, make, necessitate, require 2 INDULGE, accommodate, gratify, please

obliged *adjective* 1 GRATEFUL, appreciative, beholden, indebted, in (someone's) debt, thankful 2 BOUND, compelled, forced, required

obliging *adjective* COOPERATIVE, accommodating, agreeable, considerate, good-natured, helpful, kind, polite, willing

oblique *adjective* **1** SLANTING, angled, aslant, sloping, tilted **2** INDIRECT, backhanded, circuitous, implied, roundabout, sidelong

obliterate *verb* DESTROY, annihilate, blot out, efface, eradicate, erase, expunge, extirpate, root out, wipe out

obliteration *noun* ANNIHILATION, elimination, eradication, extirpation, wiping out

oblivion *noun* **1** NEGLECT, abeyance, disregard, forgetfulness **2** UNCONSCIOUSNESS, insensibility, obliviousness, unawareness

oblivious *adjective* UNAWARE, forgetful, heedless, ignorant, insensible, neglectful, negligent, regardless, unconcerned, unconscious, unmindful

obloquy *noun* **1** ABUSE, aspersion, attack, blame, censure, criticism, invective, reproach, slander, vilification **2** DISCREDIT, disgrace, dishonour, humiliation, ignominy, infamy, shame, stigma

obnoxious *adjective* OFFENSIVE, disagreeable, insufferable, loathsome, nasty, nauseating, objectionable, odious, repulsive, revolting, unpleasant

obscene *adjective* **1** INDECENT, dirty, filthy, immoral, improper, lewd, offensive, pornographic, prurient, salacious **2** SICKENING, atrocious, disgusting, evil, heinous, loathsome, outrageous, shocking, vile, wicked

obscenity *noun* **1** INDECENCY, coarseness, dirtiness, impropriety, lewdness, licentiousness, pornography, smut **2** SWEARWORD, four-letter word, profanity,

vulgarism **3** OUTRAGE, abomination, affront, atrocity, blight, evil, offence, wrong

obscure *adjective* **1** VAGUE, ambiguous, arcane, confusing, cryptic, enigmatic, esoteric, mysterious, opaque, recondite **2** INDISTINCT, blurred, cloudy, dim, faint, gloomy, murky, shadowy **3** LITTLE-KNOWN, humble, lowly, out-of-the-way, remote, undistinguished, unheard-of, unknown ♦ *verb* **4** CONCEAL, cover, disguise, hide, obfuscate, screen, veil

obscurity *noun* **1** DARKNESS, dimness, dusk, gloom, haze, shadows **2** INSIGNIFICANCE, lowliness, unimportance

obsequious *adjective* SYCOPHANTIC, cringing, deferential, fawning, flattering, grovelling, ingratiating, servile, submissive, unctuous

observable *adjective* NOTICEABLE, apparent, detectable, discernible, evident, obvious, perceptible, recognizable, visible

observance *noun* HONOURING, carrying out, compliance, fulfilment, performance

observant *adjective* ATTENTIVE, alert, eagle-eyed, perceptive, quick, sharp-eyed, vigilant, watchful, wide-awake

observation *noun* **1** STUDY, examination, inspection, monitoring, review, scrutiny, surveillance, watching **2** REMARK, comment, note, opinion, pronouncement, reflection, thought, utterance

observe *verb* **1** SEE, detect, discern, discover, note, notice, perceive, spot, witness **2** WATCH, check, keep an eye on (*informal*), keep track of, look at, monitor, scrutinize, study, survey, view **3** REMARK, comment, mention, note, opine, say, state **4** <u>HONOUR</u>, abide by, adhere to, comply, conform to, follow, heed, keep, obey, respect

observer noun <u>SPECTATOR</u>, beholder, bystander, eyewitness, fly on the wall, looker-on, onlooker, viewer, watcher, witness

obsessed adjective <u>PREOCCUPIED</u>, dominated, gripped, haunted, hung up on (slang), infatuated, troubled

obsession noun <u>PREOCCUPATION</u>, complex, fetish, fixation, hang-up (informal), infatuation, mania, phobia, thing (informal)

obsessive adjective <u>COMPULSIVE</u>, besetting, consuming, gripping, haunting

obsolescent adjective <u>WANING</u>, ageing, declining, dying out, on the wane, on the way out, past its prime

obsolete adjective <u>EXTINCT</u>, antiquated, archaic, discarded, disused, old, old-fashioned, outmoded, out of date, passé

obstacle noun <u>DIFFICULTY</u>, bar, barrier, block, hindrance, hitch, hurdle, impediment, obstruction, snag, stumbling block

obstinacy noun <u>STUBBORNNESS</u>, doggedness, inflexibility, intransigence, obduracy, persistence, pig-headedness, tenacity, wilfulness

obstinate adjective <u>STUBBORN</u>, determined, dogged, inflexible, intractable, intransigent, pig-headed, refractory, self-willed, strong-minded, wilful

obstreperous adjective <u>UNRULY</u>, disorderly, loud, noisy, riotous, rowdy, turbulent, unmanageable, wild

obstruct verb <u>BLOCK</u>, bar, barricade, check, hamper, hinder, impede, restrict, stop, thwart

obstruction noun <u>OBSTACLE</u>, bar, barricade, barrier, blockage, difficulty, hindrance, impediment

obstructive adjective <u>UNCOOPERATIVE</u>, awkward, blocking, delaying, hindering, restrictive, stalling, unhelpful

obtain verb **1** <u>GET</u>, achieve, acquire, attain, earn, gain, land, procure, secure **2** <u>EXIST</u>, be in force, be prevalent, be the case, hold, prevail

obtainable adjective <u>AVAILABLE</u>, achievable, attainable, on tap (informal), to be had

obtrusive adjective <u>NOTICEABLE</u>, blatant, obvious, prominent, protruding, protuberant, sticking out

obtuse adjective <u>SLOW</u>, dense, dull, stolid, stupid, thick, uncomprehending

obviate verb <u>PRECLUDE</u>, avert, prevent, remove

obvious adjective <u>EVIDENT</u>, apparent, clear, conspicuous, distinct, indisputable, manifest, noticeable, plain, self-evident, undeniable, unmistakable

obviously adverb <u>CLEARLY</u>, manifestly, of course, palpably, patently, plainly, undeniably, unmistakably, unquestionably, without doubt

occasion noun **1** <u>TIME</u>, chance, moment, opening, opportunity, window **2** <u>EVENT</u>, affair, celebration, experience, happening, occurrence **3** <u>REASON</u>, call, cause, excuse, ground(s), justification, motive, prompting, provocation ♦ verb **4** <u>CAUSE</u>, bring about, engender, generate, give rise to, induce, inspire, lead to, produce, prompt, provoke

occasional adjective <u>INFREQUENT</u>, incidental, intermittent, irregular, odd, rare, sporadic, uncommon

occasionally *adverb* <u>SOMETIMES</u>, at times, from time to time, irregularly, now and again, once in a while, periodically

occult *adjective* <u>SUPERNATURAL</u>, arcane, esoteric, magical, mysterious, mystical

occupancy *noun* <u>TENURE</u>, possession, residence, tenancy, use

occupant *noun* <u>INHABITANT</u>, incumbent, indweller, inmate, lessee, occupier, resident, tenant

occupation *noun* 1 <u>PROFESSION</u>, business, calling, employment, job, line (of work), pursuit, trade, vocation, walk of life 2 <u>POSSESSION</u>, control, holding, occupancy, residence, tenancy, tenure 3 <u>INVASION</u>, conquest, seizure, subjugation

occupied *adjective* 1 <u>BUSY</u>, employed, engaged, working 2 <u>IN USE</u>, engaged, full, taken, unavailable 3 <u>INHABITED</u>, lived-in, peopled, settled, tenanted

occupy *verb* 1 often passive <u>TAKE UP</u>, divert, employ, engage, engross, involve, monopolize, preoccupy, tie up 2 <u>LIVE IN</u>, dwell in, inhabit, own, possess, reside in 3 <u>FILL</u>, cover, permeate, pervade, take up 4 <u>INVADE</u>, capture, overrun, seize, take over

occur *verb* 1 <u>HAPPEN</u>, befall, come about, crop up (*informal*), take place, turn up (*informal*) 2 <u>EXIST</u>, appear, be found, be present, develop, manifest itself, show itself 3 **occur to** <u>COME TO MIND</u>, cross one's mind, dawn on, enter one's head, spring to mind, strike one, suggest itself

occurrence *noun* 1 <u>INCIDENT</u>, adventure, affair, circumstance, episode, event, happening, instance 2 <u>EXISTENCE</u>, appearance,

development, manifestation, materialization

odd *adjective* 1 <u>UNUSUAL</u>, bizarre, extraordinary, freakish, irregular, peculiar, rare, remarkable, singular, strange 2 <u>OCCASIONAL</u>, casual, incidental, irregular, periodic, random, sundry, various 3 <u>SPARE</u>, leftover, remaining, solitary, surplus, unmatched, unpaired

oddity *noun* 1 <u>IRREGULARITY</u>, abnormality, anomaly, eccentricity, freak, idiosyncrasy, peculiarity, quirk 2 <u>MISFIT</u>, crank (*informal*), maverick, oddball (*informal*)

oddment *noun* <u>LEFTOVER</u>, bit, fag end, fragment, off cut, remnant, scrap, snippet

odds *plural noun* 1 <u>PROBABILITY</u>, chances, likelihood 2 **at odds** <u>IN CONFLICT</u>, at daggers drawn, at loggerheads, at sixes and sevens, at variance, out of line

odds and ends *plural noun* <u>SCRAPS</u>, bits, bits and pieces, debris, oddments, remnants

odious *adjective* <u>OFFENSIVE</u>, detestable, horrid, loathsome, obnoxious, repulsive, revolting, unpleasant

odour *noun* <u>SMELL</u>, aroma, bouquet, essence, fragrance, perfume, redolence, scent, stench, stink

odyssey *noun* <u>JOURNEY</u>, crusade, pilgrimage, quest, trek, voyage

off *adverb* 1 <u>AWAY</u>, apart, aside, elsewhere, out ♦ *adjective* 2 <u>UNAVAILABLE</u>, cancelled, finished, gone, postponed 3 <u>BAD</u>, mouldy, rancid, rotten, sour, turned

offbeat *adjective* <u>UNUSUAL</u>, eccentric, left-field (*informal*), novel, outré, strange, unconventional, unorthodox, way-out (*informal*)

off colour *adjective* <u>ILL</u>, out of sorts,

peaky, poorly (*informal*), queasy, run down, sick, under the weather (*informal*), unwell

offence noun **1** CRIME, fault, misdeed, misdemeanour, sin, transgression, trespass, wrongdoing **2** SNUB, affront, hurt, indignity, injustice, insult, outrage, slight **3** ANNOYANCE, anger, displeasure, indignation, pique, resentment, umbrage, wrath

offend verb INSULT, affront, annoy, displease, hurt (someone's) feelings, outrage, slight, snub, upset, wound

offended adjective RESENTFUL, affronted, disgruntled, displeased, outraged, piqued, put out (*informal*), smarting, stung, upset

offender noun CRIMINAL, crook, culprit, delinquent, lawbreaker, miscreant, sinner, transgressor, villain, wrongdoer

offensive adjective **1** INSULTING, abusive, discourteous, disrespectful, impertinent, insolent, objectionable, rude **2** DISAGREEABLE, disgusting, nauseating, obnoxious, odious, repellent, revolting, unpleasant, vile **3** AGGRESSIVE, attacking, invading ◆ noun **4** ATTACK, campaign, drive, onslaught, push (*informal*)

offer verb **1** BID, proffer, tender **2** PROVIDE, afford, furnish, present **3** PROPOSE, advance, submit, suggest **4** VOLUNTEER, come forward, offer one's services ◆ noun **5** BID, proposal, proposition, submission, suggestion, tender

offering noun DONATION, contribution, gift, hand-out, present, sacrifice, subscription

offhand adjective **1** CASUAL, aloof, brusque, careless, curt, glib

◆ adverb **2** IMPROMPTU, ad lib, extempore, off the cuff (*informal*)

office noun POST, function, occupation, place, responsibility, role, situation

officer noun OFFICIAL, agent, appointee, executive, functionary, office-holder, representative

official adjective **1** AUTHORIZED, accredited, authentic, certified, formal, legitimate, licensed, proper, sanctioned ◆ noun **2** OFFICER, agent, bureaucrat, executive, functionary, office bearer, representative

officiate verb PRESIDE, chair, conduct, manage, oversee, serve, superintend

officious adjective INTERFERING, dictatorial, intrusive, meddlesome, obtrusive, overzealous, pushy (*informal*), self-important

offing noun **in the offing** IN PROSPECT, imminent, on the horizon, upcoming

off-putting adjective DISCOURAGING, daunting, disconcerting, dispiriting, disturbing, formidable, intimidating, unnerving, unsettling

offset verb CANCEL OUT, balance out, compensate for, counteract, counterbalance, make up for, neutralize

offshoot noun BY-PRODUCT, adjunct, appendage, development, spin-off

offspring noun **1** CHILD, descendant, heir, scion, successor **2** CHILDREN, brood, descendants, family, heirs, issue, progeny, young

often adverb FREQUENTLY, generally, repeatedly, time and again

ogle verb LEER, eye up (*informal*)

ogre noun MONSTER, bogeyman, bugbear, demon, devil, giant, spectre

oil *verb* LUBRICATE, grease

oily *adjective* GREASY, fatty, oleaginous

ointment *noun* LOTION, balm, cream, embrocation, emollient, liniment, salve, unguent

O.K., okay *interjection* **1** ALL RIGHT, agreed, right, roger, very good, very well, yes ♦ *adjective* **2** ALL RIGHT, acceptable, adequate, fine, good, in order, permitted, satisfactory, up to scratch (*informal*) ♦ *verb* **3** APPROVE, agree to, authorize, endorse, give the green light, rubber-stamp (*informal*), sanction ♦ *noun* **4** APPROVAL, agreement, assent, authorization, consent, go-ahead (*informal*), green light, permission, sanction, say-so (*informal*), seal of approval

old *adjective* **1** SENILE, aged, ancient, decrepit, elderly, mature, venerable **2** ANTIQUE, antediluvian, antiquated, dated, obsolete, superannuated, timeworn **3** FORMER, earlier, erstwhile, one-time, previous

old-fashioned *adjective* OUT OF DATE, behind the times, dated, obsolescent, obsolete, old hat, outdated, outmoded, passé, unfashionable

omen *noun* SIGN, foreboding, indication, portent, premonition, presage, warning

ominous *adjective* SINISTER, fateful, foreboding, inauspicious, portentous, threatening, unpromising, unpropitious

omission *noun* EXCLUSION, failure, lack, neglect, oversight

omit *verb* LEAVE OUT, drop, eliminate, exclude, forget, neglect, overlook, pass over, skip

omnipotence *noun* SUPREMACY, invincibility, mastery

omnipotent *adjective* ALMIGHTY, all-powerful, supreme

omniscient *adjective* ALL-KNOWING, all-wise

once *adverb* **1** FORMERLY, at one time, long ago, once upon a time, previously **2 at once: a** IMMEDIATELY, directly, forthwith, instantly, now, right away, straight away, this (very) minute **b** SIMULTANEOUSLY, at the same time, together

oncoming *adjective* APPROACHING, advancing, forthcoming, looming, onrushing

onerous *adjective* DIFFICULT, burdensome, demanding, exacting, hard, heavy, laborious, oppressive, taxing

one-sided *adjective* BIASED, lopsided, partial, partisan, prejudiced, unfair, unjust

ongoing *adjective* EVOLVING, continuous, developing, progressing, unfinished, unfolding

onlooker *noun* OBSERVER, bystander, eyewitness, looker-on, spectator, viewer, watcher, witness

only *adjective* **1** SOLE, exclusive, individual, lone, single, solitary, unique ♦ *adverb* **2** MERELY, barely, just, purely, simply

onset *noun* BEGINNING, inception, outbreak, start

onslaught *noun* ATTACK, assault, blitz, charge, offensive, onrush, onset

onus *noun* BURDEN, liability, load, obligation, responsibility, task

onward, onwards *adverb* AHEAD, beyond, forth, forward, in front, on

ooze[1] *verb* SEEP, drain, dribble, drip, escape, filter, leak

ooze[2] *noun* MUD, alluvium, mire, silt, slime, sludge

opaque adjective CLOUDY, dim, dull, filmy, hazy, impenetrable, muddy, murky

open adjective 1 UNFASTENED, agape, ajar, gaping, uncovered, unfolded, unfurled, unlocked, yawning 2 ACCESSIBLE, available, free, public, unoccupied, unrestricted, vacant 3 UNRESOLVED, arguable, debatable, moot, undecided, unsettled 4 FRANK, candid, guileless, honest, sincere, transparent ♦ verb 5 START, begin, commence, inaugurate, initiate, kick off (informal), launch, set in motion 6 UNFASTEN, unblock, uncork, uncover, undo, unlock, untie, unwrap 7 UNFOLD, expand, spread (out), unfurl, unroll

open-air adjective OUTDOOR, alfresco

open-handed adjective GENEROUS, bountiful, free, lavish, liberal, munificent, unstinting

opening noun 1 HOLE, aperture, chink, cleft, crack, fissure, gap, orifice, perforation, slot, space 2 OPPORTUNITY, chance, look-in (informal), occasion, vacancy 3 BEGINNING, commencement, dawn, inception, initiation, launch, outset, start ♦ adjective 4 FIRST, beginning, inaugural, initial, introductory, maiden, primary

openly adverb CANDIDLY, forthrightly, frankly, overtly, plainly, unhesitatingly, unreservedly

open-minded adjective TOLERANT, broad-minded, impartial, liberal, reasonable, receptive, unbiased, undogmatic, unprejudiced

operate verb 1 WORK, act, function, go, perform, run 2 HANDLE, be in charge of, manage, manoeuvre, use, work

operation noun PROCEDURE, action, course, exercise, motion, movement, performance, process

operational adjective WORKING, functional, going, operative, prepared, ready, up and running, usable, viable, workable

operative adjective 1 IN FORCE, active, effective, functioning, in operation, operational ♦ noun 2 WORKER, artisan, employee, labourer

operator noun WORKER, conductor, driver, handler, mechanic, operative, practitioner, technician

opinion noun BELIEF, assessment, feeling, idea, impression, judgment, point of view, sentiment, theory, view

opinionated adjective DOGMATIC, bigoted, cocksure, doctrinaire, overbearing, pig-headed, prejudiced, single-minded

opponent noun COMPETITOR, adversary, antagonist, challenger, contestant, enemy, foe, rival

opportune adjective TIMELY, advantageous, appropriate, apt, auspicious, convenient, favourable, fitting, suitable, well-timed

opportunism noun EXPEDIENCY, exploitation, pragmatism, unscrupulousness

opportunity noun CHANCE, moment, occasion, opening, scope, time

oppose verb FIGHT, block, combat, counter, defy, resist, take issue with, take on, thwart, withstand

opposed adjective AVERSE, antagonistic, clashing, conflicting, contrary, dissentient, hostile

opposing adjective HOSTILE, conflicting, contrary, enemy, incompatible, opposite, rival

opposite adjective 1 FACING, fronting 2 DIFFERENT, antithetical, conflicting, contrary, contrasted, reverse, unlike ♦ *noun* 3 REVERSE, antithesis, contradiction, contrary, converse, inverse

opposition *noun* 1 HOSTILITY, antagonism, competition, disapproval, obstruction, prevention, resistance, unfriendliness 2 OPPONENT, antagonist, competition, foe, other side, rival

oppress *verb* 1 DEPRESS, afflict, burden, dispirit, harass, sadden, torment, vex 2 PERSECUTE, abuse, maltreat, subdue, subjugate, suppress, wrong

oppressed *adjective* DOWNTRODDEN, abused, browbeaten, disadvantaged, harassed, maltreated, tyrannized, underprivileged

oppression *noun* PERSECUTION, abuse, brutality, cruelty, injury, injustice, maltreatment, subjection, tyranny

oppressive *adjective* 1 TYRANNICAL, brutal, cruel, despotic, harsh, inhuman, repressive, severe, unjust 2 SULTRY, airless, close, muggy, stifling, stuffy

oppressor *noun* PERSECUTOR, autocrat, bully, despot, scourge, slave-driver, tormentor, tyrant

opt *verb*, often with *for* CHOOSE, decide (on), elect, go for, plump for, prefer

optimistic *adjective* HOPEFUL, buoyant, cheerful, confident, encouraged, expectant, positive, rosy, sanguine

optimum *adjective* IDEAL, best, highest, optimal, peak, perfect, superlative

option *noun* CHOICE, alternative, preference, selection

optional *adjective* VOLUNTARY, discretionary, elective, extra, open, possible

opulence *noun* 1 WEALTH, affluence, luxuriance, luxury, plenty, prosperity, riches 2 ABUNDANCE, copiousness, cornucopia, fullness, profusion, richness, superabundance

opulent *adjective* 1 RICH, affluent, lavish, luxurious, moneyed, prosperous, sumptuous, wealthy, well-off, well-to-do 2 ABUNDANT, copious, lavish, luxuriant, plentiful, profuse, prolific

opus *noun* WORK, brainchild, composition, creation, *oeuvre*, piece, production

oracle *noun* 1 PROPHECY, divination, prediction, prognostication, revelation 2 PUNDIT, adviser, authority, guru, mastermind, mentor, wizard

oral *adjective* SPOKEN, verbal, vocal

oration *noun* SPEECH, address, discourse, harangue, homily, lecture

orator *noun* PUBLIC SPEAKER, declaimer, lecturer, rhetorician, speaker

oratorical *adjective* RHETORICAL, bombastic, declamatory, eloquent, grandiloquent, high-flown, magniloquent, sonorous

oratory *noun* ELOQUENCE, declamation, elocution, grandiloquence, public speaking, rhetoric, speech-making

orb *noun* SPHERE, ball, circle, globe, ring

orbit *noun* 1 PATH, circle, course, cycle, revolution, rotation, trajectory 2 SPHERE OF INFLUENCE, ambit, compass, domain, influence, range, reach, scope, sweep ♦ *verb* 3 CIRCLE, circumnavigate, encircle, revolve around

orchestrate verb 1 <u>SCORE</u>, arrange
2 <u>ORGANIZE</u>, arrange, coordinate,
put together, set up,
stage-manage

ordain verb 1 <u>APPOINT</u>, anoint,
consecrate, invest, nominate
2 <u>ORDER</u>, decree, demand, dictate,
fix, lay down, legislate, prescribe,
rule, will

ordeal noun <u>HARDSHIP</u>, agony,
anguish, baptism of fire,
nightmare, suffering, test, torture,
trial, tribulation(s)

order noun 1 <u>INSTRUCTION</u>,
command, decree, dictate,
direction, directive, injunction,
law, mandate, regulation, rule
2 <u>SEQUENCE</u>, arrangement, array,
grouping, layout, line-up,
progression, series, structure
3 <u>TIDINESS</u>, method, neatness,
orderliness, organization, pattern,
regularity, symmetry, system
4 <u>DISCIPLINE</u>, calm, control, law, law
and order, peace, quiet,
tranquillity 5 <u>REQUEST</u>, application,
booking, commission, requisition,
reservation 6 <u>CLASS</u>, caste, grade,
position, rank, status 7 <u>KIND</u>, class,
family, genre, ilk, sort, type
8 <u>SOCIETY</u>, association,
brotherhood, community,
company, fraternity, guild,
organization ♦ verb 9 <u>INSTRUCT</u>, bid,
charge, command, decree,
demand, direct, require
10 <u>REQUEST</u>, apply for, book,
reserve, send away for 11 <u>ARRANGE</u>,
catalogue, classify, group,
marshal, organize, sort out,
systematize

orderly adjective 1 <u>WELL-ORGANIZED</u>,
businesslike, in order, methodical,
neat, regular, scientific, shipshape,
systematic, tidy 2 <u>WELL-BEHAVED</u>,
controlled, disciplined,
law-abiding, peaceable, quiet,
restrained

ordinarily adverb <u>USUALLY</u>, as a rule,
commonly, customarily, generally,
habitually, in general, normally

ordinary adjective 1 <u>USUAL</u>,
common, conventional, everyday,
normal, regular, routine, standard,
stock, typical 2 <u>COMMONPLACE</u>,
banal, humble, humdrum,
modest, mundane, plain,
run-of-the-mill, unremarkable,
workaday

organ noun 1 <u>PART</u>, element,
structure, unit 2 <u>MOUTHPIECE</u>,
forum, medium, vehicle, voice

organic adjective 1 <u>NATURAL</u>,
animate, biological, live, living
2 <u>SYSTEMATIC</u>, integrated,
methodical, ordered, organized,
structured

organism noun <u>CREATURE</u>, animal,
being, body, entity, structure

organization noun 1 <u>GROUP</u>,
association, body, company,
confederation, corporation,
institution, outfit (informal),
syndicate 2 <u>MANAGEMENT</u>,
construction, coordination,
direction, organizing, planning,
running, structuring
3 <u>ARRANGEMENT</u>, chemistry,
composition, format, make-up,
pattern, structure, unity

organize verb <u>ARRANGE</u>, classify,
coordinate, group, marshal, put
together, run, set up, systematize,
take care of

orgy noun 1 <u>REVEL</u>, bacchanalia,
carousal, debauch, revelry,
Saturnalia 2 <u>SPREE</u>, binge
(informal), bout, excess,
indulgence, overindulgence,
splurge, surfeit

orient verb <u>FAMILIARIZE</u>, acclimatize,
adapt, adjust, align, get one's
bearings, orientate

orientation noun 1 <u>POSITION</u>,
bearings, direction, location
2 <u>FAMILIARIZATION</u>, acclimatization,

adaptation, adjustment, assimilation, introduction, settling in

orifice noun OPENING, aperture, cleft, hole, mouth, pore, rent, vent

origin noun 1 ROOT, base, basis, derivation, fount, fountainhead, source, wellspring 2 BEGINNING, birth, creation, emergence, foundation, genesis, inception, launch, start

original adjective 1 FIRST, earliest, initial, introductory, opening, primary, starting 2 NEW, fresh, ground-breaking, innovative, novel, seminal, unprecedented, unusual 3 CREATIVE, fertile, imaginative, ingenious, inventive, resourceful ◆ noun 4 PROTOTYPE, archetype, master, model, paradigm, pattern, precedent, standard

originality noun NOVELTY, creativity, freshness, imagination, ingenuity, innovation, inventiveness, newness, unorthodoxy

originally adverb INITIALLY, at first, first, in the beginning, to begin with

originate verb 1 BEGIN, arise, come, derive, emerge, result, rise, spring, start, stem 2 INTRODUCE, bring about, create, formulate, generate, institute, launch, pioneer

originator noun CREATOR, architect, author, father or mother, founder, inventor, maker, pioneer

ornament noun 1 DECORATION, accessory, adornment, bauble, embellishment, festoon, knick-knack, trimming, trinket ◆ verb 2 DECORATE, adorn, beautify, embellish, festoon, grace, prettify

ornamental adjective DECORATIVE, attractive, beautifying, embellishing, for show, showy

ornamentation noun DECORATION, adornment, elaboration, embellishment, embroidery, frills, ornateness

ornate adjective ELABORATE, baroque, busy, decorated, fancy, florid, fussy, ornamented, overelaborate, rococo

orthodox adjective ESTABLISHED, accepted, approved, conventional, customary, official, received, traditional, well-established

orthodoxy noun CONFORMITY, authority, conventionality, received wisdom, traditionalism

oscillate verb FLUCTUATE, seesaw, sway, swing, vacillate, vary, vibrate, waver

oscillation noun SWING, fluctuation, instability, vacillation, variation, wavering

ossify verb HARDEN, fossilize, solidify, stiffen

ostensible adjective APPARENT, outward, pretended, professed, purported, seeming, so-called, superficial, supposed

ostensibly adverb APPARENTLY, on the face of it, professedly, seemingly, supposedly

ostentation noun DISPLAY, affectation, exhibitionism, flamboyance, flashiness, flaunting, parade, pomp, pretentiousness, show, showing off (informal)

ostentatious adjective PRETENTIOUS, brash, conspicuous, flamboyant, flashy, gaudy, loud, obtrusive, showy

ostracism noun EXCLUSION, banishment, exile, isolation, rejection

ostracize verb EXCLUDE, banish, cast out, cold-shoulder, exile, give (someone) the cold shoulder, reject, send to Coventry, shun

other *adjective* 1 ADDITIONAL, added, alternative, auxiliary, extra, further, more, spare, supplementary 2 DIFFERENT, contrasting, dissimilar, distinct, diverse, separate, unrelated, variant

otherwise *conjunction* 1 OR ELSE, if not, or then ♦ *adverb* 2 DIFFERENTLY, any other way, contrarily

ounce *noun* SHRED, atom, crumb, drop, grain, scrap, speck, trace

oust *verb* EXPEL, depose, dislodge, displace, dispossess, eject, throw out, topple, turn out, unseat

out *adjective* 1 AWAY, abroad, absent, elsewhere, gone, not at home, outside 2 EXTINGUISHED, at an end, dead, ended, exhausted, expired, finished, used up

outbreak *noun* ERUPTION, burst, epidemic, explosion, flare-up, outburst, rash, upsurge

outburst *noun* OUTPOURING, eruption, explosion, flare-up, outbreak, paroxysm, spasm, surge

outcast *noun* PARIAH, castaway, exile, leper, *persona non grata*, refugee, vagabond, wretch

outclass *verb* SURPASS, eclipse, excel, leave standing (*informal*), outdo, outshine, outstrip, overshadow, run rings around (*informal*)

outcome *noun* RESULT, conclusion, consequence, end, issue, payoff (*informal*), upshot

outcry *noun* PROTEST, clamour, commotion, complaint, hue and cry, hullaballoo, outburst, uproar

outdated *adjective* OLD-FASHIONED, antiquated, archaic, obsolete, outmoded, out of date, passé, unfashionable

outdo *verb* SURPASS, beat, best, eclipse, exceed, get the better of, outclass, outmanoeuvre, overcome, top, transcend

outdoor *adjective* OPEN-AIR, alfresco, out-of-door(s), outside

outer *adjective* EXTERNAL, exposed, exterior, outlying, outside, outward, peripheral, surface

outfit *noun* 1 COSTUME, clothes, ensemble, garb, get-up (*informal*), kit, suit 2 *Informal* GROUP, company, crew, organization, setup (*informal*), squad, team, unit

outgoing *adjective* 1 LEAVING, departing, former, retiring, withdrawing 2 SOCIABLE, approachable, communicative, expansive, extrovert, friendly, gregarious, open, warm

outgoings *plural noun* EXPENSES, costs, expenditure, outlay, overheads

outing *noun* TRIP, excursion, expedition, jaunt, spin (*informal*)

outlandish *adjective* STRANGE, bizarre, exotic, fantastic, far-out (*slang*), freakish, outré, preposterous, unheard-of, weird

outlaw *noun* 1 BANDIT, brigand, desperado, fugitive, highwayman, marauder, outcast, robber ♦ *verb* 2 FORBID, ban, bar, disallow, exclude, prohibit, proscribe

outlay *noun* EXPENDITURE, cost, expenses, investment, outgoings, spending

outlet *noun* 1 RELEASE, avenue, channel, duct, exit, opening, vent 2 SHOP, market, store

outline *noun* 1 SUMMARY, recapitulation, résumé, rundown, synopsis, thumbnail sketch 2 SHAPE, configuration, contour, delineation, figure, form, profile, silhouette ♦ *verb* 3 SUMMARIZE, adumbrate, delineate, draft, plan, rough out, sketch (in), trace

outlive verb SURVIVE, outlast

outlook noun 1 ATTITUDE, angle, frame of mind, perspective, point of view, slant, standpoint, viewpoint 2 PROSPECT, expectations, forecast, future

outlying adjective REMOTE, distant, far-flung, out-of-the-way, peripheral, provincial

outmoded adjective OLD-FASHIONED, anachronistic, antiquated, archaic, obsolete, out-of-date, outworn, passé, unfashionable

out-of-date adjective OLD-FASHIONED, antiquated, dated, expired, invalid, lapsed, obsolete, outmoded, outworn, passé

outpouring noun STREAM, cascade, effusion, flow, spate, spurt, torrent

output noun PRODUCTION, achievement, manufacture, productivity, yield

outrage noun 1 VIOLATION, abuse, affront, desecration, indignity, insult, offence, sacrilege, violence 2 INDIGNATION, anger, fury, hurt, resentment, shock, wrath ♦ verb 3 OFFEND, affront, incense, infuriate, madden, scandalize, shock

outrageous adjective 1 OFFENSIVE, atrocious, disgraceful, flagrant, heinous, iniquitous, nefarious, unspeakable, villainous, wicked 2 SHOCKING, exorbitant, extravagant, immoderate, preposterous, scandalous, steep (informal), unreasonable

outré adjective ECCENTRIC, bizarre, fantastic, freakish, odd, off-the-wall (slang), outlandish, unconventional, weird

outright adjective 1 ABSOLUTE, complete, out-and-out, perfect, thorough, thoroughgoing, total, unconditional, unmitigated, unqualified 2 DIRECT, definite, flat, straightforward, unequivocal, unqualified ♦ adverb 3 ABSOLUTELY, completely, openly, overtly, straightforwardly, thoroughly, to the full

outset noun BEGINNING, commencement, inauguration, inception, kickoff (informal), onset, opening, start

outshine verb OVERSHADOW, eclipse, leave or put in the shade, outclass, outdo, outstrip, surpass, transcend, upstage

outside adjective 1 EXTERNAL, exterior, extraneous, outer, outward 2 As in **an outside chance** UNLIKELY, distant, faint, marginal, remote, slight, slim, small ♦ noun 3 SURFACE, exterior, façade, face, front, skin, topside

outsider noun INTERLOPER, incomer, intruder, newcomer, odd man out, stranger

outsize adjective EXTRA-LARGE, giant, gigantic, huge, jumbo (informal), mammoth, monster, oversized

outskirts plural noun EDGE, boundary, environs, periphery, suburbia, suburbs

outspoken adjective FORTHRIGHT, abrupt, blunt, explicit, frank, open, plain-spoken, unceremonious, unequivocal

outstanding adjective 1 EXCELLENT, exceptional, great, important, impressive, special, superior, superlative 2 UNPAID, due, payable, pending, remaining, uncollected, unsettled

outstrip verb SURPASS, better, eclipse, exceed, excel, outdistance, outdo, overtake, transcend

outward adjective APPARENT, noticeable, observable, obvious, ostensible, perceptible, surface, visible

outwardly adverb OSTENSIBLY, apparently, externally, on the face of it, on the surface, seemingly, superficially, to all intents and purposes

outweigh verb OVERRIDE, cancel (out), compensate for, eclipse, prevail over, take precedence over, tip the scales

outwit verb OUTTHINK, cheat, dupe, get the better of, outfox, outmanoeuvre, outsmart (informal), put one over on (informal), swindle, take in (informal)

outworn adjective OUTDATED, antiquated, discredited, disused, hackneyed, obsolete, outmoded, out-of-date, worn-out

oval adjective ELLIPTICAL, egg-shaped, ovoid

ovation noun APPLAUSE, acclaim, acclamation, big hand, cheers, clapping, plaudits, tribute

over preposition 1 ON, above, on top of, upon 2 EXCEEDING, above, in excess of, more than ♦ adverb 3 ABOVE, aloft, on high, overhead 4 EXTRA, beyond, in addition, in excess, left over ♦ adjective 5 FINISHED, bygone, closed, completed, concluded, done (with), ended, gone, past

overact verb EXAGGERATE, ham or ham up (informal), overdo, overplay

overall adjective 1 TOTAL, all-embracing, blanket, complete, comprehensive, general, global, inclusive ♦ adverb 2 IN GENERAL, on the whole

overawe verb INTIMIDATE, abash, alarm, daunt, frighten, scare, terrify

overbalance verb OVERTURN, capsize, keel over, slip, tip over, topple over, tumble, turn turtle

overbearing adjective ARROGANT, bossy (informal), dictatorial, domineering, haughty, high-handed, imperious, supercilious, superior

overblown adjective EXCESSIVE, disproportionate, immoderate, inflated, overdone, over the top, undue

overcast adjective CLOUDY, dismal, dreary, dull, grey, leaden, louring or lowering, murky

overcharge verb CHEAT, diddle (informal), fleece, rip off (slang), short-change, sting (informal), surcharge

overcome verb 1 CONQUER, beat, defeat, master, overpower, overwhelm, prevail, subdue, subjugate, surmount, triumph over, vanquish ♦ adjective 2 AFFECTED, at a loss for words, bowled over (informal), overwhelmed, speechless, swept off one's feet

overconfident adjective BRASH, cocksure, foolhardy, overweening, presumptuous

overcrowded adjective CONGESTED, bursting at the seams, choked, jam-packed, overloaded, overpopulated, packed (out), swarming

overdo verb 1 EXAGGERATE, belabour, gild the lily, go overboard (informal), overindulge, overreach, overstate 2 **overdo it** OVERWORK, bite off more than one can chew, burn the candle at both ends (informal), overload, strain or overstrain oneself, wear oneself out

overdone adjective 1 EXCESSIVE, exaggerated, fulsome, immoderate, inordinate, overelaborate, too much, undue, unnecessary 2 OVERCOOKED, burnt, charred, dried up, spoiled

overdue *adjective* <u>LATE</u>, behindhand, behind schedule, belated, owing, tardy, unpunctual

overeat *verb* <u>OVERINDULGE</u>, binge (*informal*), gorge, gormandize, guzzle, pig out (*slang*), stuff oneself

overemphasize *verb* <u>OVERSTRESS</u>, belabour, blow up out of all proportion, make a mountain out of a molehill (*informal*), overdramatize

overflow *verb* **1** <u>SPILL</u>, brim over, bubble over, pour over, run over, well over ♦ *noun* **2** <u>SURPLUS</u>, overabundance, spilling over

overhang *verb* <u>PROJECT</u>, extend, jut, loom, protrude, stick out

overhaul *verb* **1** <u>REPAIR</u>, check, do up (*informal*), examine, inspect, recondition, restore, service **2** <u>OVERTAKE</u>, catch up with, get ahead of, pass ♦ *noun* **3** <u>CHECKUP</u>, check, examination, going-over (*informal*), inspection, reconditioning, service

overhead *adverb* **1** <u>ABOVE</u>, aloft, in the sky, on high, skyward, up above, upward ♦ *adjective* **2** <u>AERIAL</u>, overhanging, upper

overheads *plural noun* <u>RUNNING COSTS</u>, operating costs

overindulgence *noun* <u>EXCESS</u>, immoderation, intemperance, overeating, surfeit

overjoyed *adjective* <u>DELIGHTED</u>, cock-a-hoop, elated, euphoric, jubilant, on cloud nine (*informal*), over the moon (*informal*), thrilled

overload *verb* <u>OVERBURDEN</u>, burden, encumber, oppress, overtax, saddle (with), strain, weigh down

overlook *verb* **1** <u>FORGET</u>, disregard, miss, neglect, omit, pass **2** <u>IGNORE</u>, condone, disregard, excuse, forgive, make allowances for, pardon, turn a blind eye to, wink at **3** <u>HAVE A VIEW OF</u>, look over *or* out on

overpower *verb* <u>OVERWHELM</u>, conquer, crush, defeat, master, overcome, overthrow, quell, subdue, subjugate, vanquish

overpowering *adjective* <u>IRRESISTIBLE</u>, forceful, invincible, irrefutable, overwhelming, powerful, strong

overrate *verb* <u>OVERESTIMATE</u>, exaggerate, overvalue

override *verb* <u>OVERRULE</u>, annul, cancel, countermand, nullify, outweigh, supersede

overriding *adjective* <u>ULTIMATE</u>, dominant, paramount, predominant, primary, supreme

overrule *verb* <u>REVERSE</u>, alter, annul, cancel, countermand, override, overturn, repeal, rescind, veto

overrun *verb* **1** <u>INVADE</u>, occupy, overwhelm, rout **2** <u>INFEST</u>, choke, inundate, permeate, ravage, spread over, swarm over **3** <u>EXCEED</u>, go beyond, overshoot, run over *or* on

overseer *noun* <u>SUPERVISOR</u>, boss (*informal*), chief, foreman, master, superintendent

overshadow *verb* **1** <u>OUTSHINE</u>, dominate, dwarf, eclipse, leave *or* put in the shade, surpass, tower above **2** <u>SPOIL</u>, blight, mar, put a damper on, ruin, temper

oversight *noun* <u>MISTAKE</u>, blunder, carelessness, error, fault, lapse, neglect, omission, slip

overt *adjective* <u>OPEN</u>, blatant, manifest, observable, obvious, plain, public, unconcealed, undisguised

overtake *verb* **1** <u>PASS</u>, catch up with, get past, leave behind, outdistance, outdo, outstrip, overhaul **2** <u>BEFALL</u>, engulf, happen, hit, overwhelm, strike

overthrow verb 1 DEFEAT, bring down, conquer, depose, dethrone, oust, overcome, overpower, topple, unseat, vanquish ♦ noun 2 DOWNFALL, defeat, destruction, dethronement, fall, ousting, undoing, unseating

overtone noun CONNOTATION, hint, implication, innuendo, intimation, nuance, sense, suggestion, undercurrent

overture noun 1 Music INTRODUCTION, opening, prelude 2 overtures APPROACH, advance, invitation, offer, proposal, proposition

overturn verb 1 TIP OVER, capsize, keel over, overbalance, topple, upend, upturn 2 OVERTHROW, bring down, depose, destroy, unseat

overweight adjective FAT, bulky, chubby, chunky, corpulent, heavy, hefty, obese, plump, portly, stout, tubby (informal)

overwhelm verb 1 DEVASTATE, bowl over (informal), knock (someone) for six (informal), overcome, stagger, sweep (someone) off his or her feet, take (someone's) breath away 2 DESTROY, crush, cut to pieces, massacre, overpower, overrun, rout

overwhelming adjective DEVASTATING, breathtaking, crushing, irresistible, overpowering, shattering, stunning, towering

overwork verb 1 STRAIN, burn the midnight oil, sweat (informal), work one's fingers to the bone 2 OVERUSE, exhaust, exploit, fatigue, oppress, wear out, weary

overwrought adjective AGITATED, distracted, excited, frantic, keyed up, on edge, overexcited, tense, uptight (informal)

owe verb BE IN DEBT, be in arrears, be obligated or indebted

owing adjective UNPAID, due, outstanding, overdue, owed, payable, unsettled

owing to preposition BECAUSE OF, as a result of, on account of

own adjective 1 PERSONAL, individual, particular, private ♦ pronoun 2 hold one's own COMPETE, keep going, keep one's end up, keep one's head above water 3 on one's own ALONE, by oneself, independently, singly, unaided, unassisted, under one's own steam ♦ verb 4 POSSESS, be in possession of, enjoy, have, hold, keep, retain 5 ACKNOWLEDGE, admit, allow, concede, confess, grant, recognize 6 own up CONFESS, admit, come clean, make a clean breast, tell the truth

owner noun POSSESSOR, holder, landlord or landlady, proprietor

ownership noun POSSESSION, dominion, title

P p

pace *noun* **1** STEP, gait, stride, tread, walk **2** SPEED, rate, tempo, velocity ♦ *verb* **3** STRIDE, march, patrol, pound **4 pace out** MEASURE, count, mark out, step

pacifist *noun* PEACE LOVER, conscientious objector, dove

pacify *verb* CALM, allay, appease, assuage, mollify, placate, propitiate, soothe

pack *verb* **1** PACKAGE, bundle, load, store, stow **2** CRAM, compress, crowd, fill, jam, press, ram, stuff **3 pack off** SEND AWAY, dismiss, send packing (*informal*) ♦ *noun* **4** BUNDLE, back pack, burden, kitbag, knapsack, load, parcel, rucksack **5** PACKET, package **6** GROUP, band, bunch, company, crowd, flock, gang, herd, mob, troop

package *noun* **1** PARCEL, box, carton, container, packet **2** UNIT, combination, whole ♦ *verb* **3** PACK, box, parcel (up), wrap

packed *adjective* FULL, chock-a-block, chock-full, crammed, crowded, filled, jammed, jam-packed

packet *noun* **1** PACKAGE, bag, carton, container, parcel **2** *Slang* FORTUNE, bomb (*Brit. slang*), king's ransom (*informal*), pile (*informal*), small fortune, tidy sum (*informal*)

pack in *verb Brit. informal* STOP, cease, chuck (*informal*), give up *or* over, kick (*informal*)

pack up *verb* **1** PUT AWAY, store **2** *Informal* STOP, finish, give up, pack in (*Brit. informal*) **3** BREAK DOWN, conk out (*informal*), fail

pact *noun* AGREEMENT, alliance, bargain, covenant, deal, treaty, understanding

pad[1] *noun* **1** CUSHION, buffer, protection, stuffing, wad **2** NOTEPAD, block, jotter, writing pad **3** PAW, foot, sole **4** *Slang* HOME, apartment, flat, place ♦ *verb* **5** PACK, cushion, fill, protect, stuff **6 pad out** LENGTHEN, elaborate, fill out, flesh out, protract, spin out, stretch

pad[2] *verb* SNEAK, creep, go barefoot, steal

padding *noun* **1** FILLING, packing, stuffing, wadding **2** WAFFLE (*informal, chiefly Brit.*), hot air (*informal*), verbiage, verbosity, wordiness

paddle[1] *noun* **1** OAR, scull ♦ *verb* **2** ROW, propel, pull, scull

paddle[2] *verb* **1** WADE, slop, splash (about) **2** DABBLE, stir

pagan *adjective* **1** HEATHEN, idolatrous, infidel, polytheistic ♦ *noun* **2** HEATHEN, idolater, infidel, polytheist

page[1] *noun* FOLIO, leaf, sheet, side

page[2] *noun* **1** ATTENDANT, pageboy, servant, squire ♦ *verb* **2** CALL, send for, summon

pageant *noun* SHOW, display, parade, procession, spectacle, tableau

pageantry *noun* SPECTACLE, display, grandeur, parade, pomp, show, splendour, theatricality

pain *noun* **1** HURT, ache, discomfort, irritation, pang, soreness, tenderness, throb, twinge **2** SUFFERING, agony, anguish, distress, heartache, misery, torment, torture ♦ *verb* **3** HURT, smart, sting, throb **4** DISTRESS, agonize, cut to the quick, grieve, hurt, sadden, torment, torture

pained *adjective* DISTRESSED, aggrieved, hurt, injured, offended, upset, wounded

painful *adjective* 1 DISTRESSING, disagreeable, distasteful, grievous, unpleasant 2 SORE, aching, agonizing, smarting, tender 3 DIFFICULT, arduous, hard, laborious, troublesome, trying

painfully *adverb* DISTRESSINGLY, clearly, dreadfully, sadly, unfortunately

painkiller *noun* ANALGESIC, anaesthetic, anodyne, drug

painless *adjective* SIMPLE, easy, effortless, fast, quick

pains *plural noun* TROUBLE, bother, care, diligence, effort

painstaking *adjective* THOROUGH, assiduous, careful, conscientious, diligent, meticulous, scrupulous

paint *noun* 1 COLOURING, colour, dye, pigment, stain, tint ♦ *verb* 2 DEPICT, draw, picture, portray, represent, sketch 3 COAT, apply, colour, cover, daub

pair *noun* 1 COUPLE, brace, duo, twins ♦ *verb* 2 COUPLE, bracket, join, match (up), team, twin

pal *noun Informal* FRIEND, buddy (*informal*), chum (*informal*), companion, comrade, crony, mate (*informal*)

palatable *adjective* DELICIOUS, appetizing, luscious, mouthwatering, tasty

palate *noun* TASTE, appetite, stomach

palatial *adjective* MAGNIFICENT, grand, imposing, majestic, opulent, regal, splendid, stately

palaver *noun* FUSS, business (*informal*), carry-on (*informal*, chiefly Brit.*), pantomime (*informal*,

chiefly Brit.*), performance (*informal*), rigmarole, song and dance (*Brit. informal*), to-do

pale *adjective* 1 WHITE, ashen, bleached, colourless, faded, light, pallid, pasty, wan ♦ *verb* 2 BECOME PALE, blanch, go white, lose colour, whiten

pall[1] *noun* 1 CLOUD, mantle, shadow, shroud, veil 2 GLOOM, check, damp, damper

pall[2] *verb* BECOME BORING, become dull, become tedious, cloy, jade, sicken, tire, weary

pallid *adjective* PALE, anaemic, ashen, colourless, pasty, wan

pallor *noun* PALENESS, lack of colour, pallidness, wanness, whiteness

palm off *verb* FOB OFF, foist off, pass off

palpable *adjective* OBVIOUS, clear, conspicuous, evident, manifest, plain, unmistakable, visible

palpitate *verb* BEAT, flutter, pound, pulsate, throb, tremble

paltry *adjective* INSIGNIFICANT, contemptible, despicable, inconsiderable, meagre, mean, measly, minor, miserable, petty, poor, puny, slight, small, trifling, trivial, unimportant, worthless

pamper *verb* SPOIL, coddle, cosset, indulge, mollycoddle, pet

pamphlet *noun* BOOKLET, brochure, circular, leaflet, tract

pan[1] *noun* 1 POT, container, saucepan ♦ *verb* 2 SIFT OUT, look for, search for 3 *Informal* CRITICIZE, censure, knock (*informal*), slam (*slang*), tear into (*informal*)

pan[2] *verb* MOVE, follow, sweep, track

panacea *noun* CURE-ALL, nostrum, universal cure

panache *noun* STYLE, dash, élan, flamboyance

pandemonium *noun* UPROAR, bedlam, chaos, confusion, din, hullabaloo, racket, rumpus, turmoil

pander *verb* **pander to** INDULGE, cater to, gratify, play up to (*informal*), please, satisfy

pang *noun* TWINGE, ache, pain, prick, spasm, stab, sting

panic *noun* 1 FEAR, alarm, fright, hysteria, scare, terror ◆ *verb* 2 GO TO PIECES, become hysterical, lose one's nerve 3 ALARM, scare, unnerve

panic-stricken *adjective* FRIGHTENED, frightened out of one's wits, hysterical, in a cold sweat (*informal*), panicky, scared, scared stiff, terrified

panoply *noun* ARRAY, attire, dress, garb, regalia, trappings

panorama *noun* VIEW, prospect, vista

panoramic *adjective* WIDE, comprehensive, extensive, overall, sweeping

pant *verb* PUFF, blow, breathe, gasp, heave, wheeze

pants *plural noun* 1 *Brit.* UNDERPANTS, boxer shorts, briefs, drawers, knickers, panties 2 *U.S.* TROUSERS, slacks

paper *noun* 1 NEWSPAPER, daily, gazette, journal 2 ESSAY, article, dissertation, report, treatise 3 **papers: a** DOCUMENTS, certificates, deeds, records **b** LETTERS, archive, diaries, documents, dossier, file, records ◆ *verb* 4 WALLPAPER, hang

par *noun* AVERAGE, level, mean, norm, standard, usual

parable *noun* LESSON, allegory, fable, moral tale, story

parade *noun* 1 PROCESSION, array, cavalcade, march, pageant 2 SHOW, display, spectacle ◆ *verb*

3 FLAUNT, display, exhibit, show off (*informal*) 4 MARCH, process

paradigm *noun* MODEL, example, ideal, pattern

paradise *noun* 1 HEAVEN, Elysian fields, Happy Valley, Promised Land 2 BLISS, delight, felicity, heaven, utopia

paradox *noun* CONTRADICTION, anomaly, enigma, oddity, puzzle

paradoxical *adjective* CONTRADICTORY, baffling, confounding, enigmatic, puzzling

paragon *noun* MODEL, epitome, exemplar, ideal, nonpareil, pattern, quintessence

paragraph *noun* SECTION, clause, item, part, passage, subdivision

parallel *adjective* 1 EQUIDISTANT, alongside, side by side 2 MATCHING, analogous, corresponding, like, resembling, similar ◆ *noun* 3 EQUIVALENT, analogue, counterpart, equal, match, twin 4 SIMILARITY, analogy, comparison, likeness, resemblance

paralyse *verb* 1 DISABLE, cripple, incapacitate, lame 2 IMMOBILIZE, freeze, halt, numb, petrify, stun

paralysis *noun* 1 IMMOBILITY, palsy 2 STANDSTILL, breakdown, halt, stoppage

paralytic *adjective* PARALYSED, crippled, disabled, incapacitated, lame, palsied

parameter *noun* Informal LIMIT, framework, limitation, restriction, specification

paramount *adjective* PRINCIPAL, cardinal, chief, first, foremost, main, primary, prime, supreme

paranoid *adjective* 1 MENTALLY ILL, deluded, disturbed, manic, neurotic, paranoiac, psychotic 2 Informal SUSPICIOUS, fearful, nervous, worried

paraphernalia noun EQUIPMENT, apparatus, baggage, belongings, effects, gear, stuff, tackle, things, trappings

paraphrase noun 1 REWORDING, rephrasing, restatement ♦ verb 2 REWORD, express in other words or one's own words, rephrase, restate

parasite noun SPONGER (informal), bloodsucker (informal), hanger-on, leech, scrounger (informal)

parasitic, parasitical adjective SCROUNGING (informal), bloodsucking (informal), sponging (informal)

parcel noun 1 PACKAGE, bundle, pack ♦ verb 2 often with up WRAP, do up, pack, package, tie up

parch verb DRY UP, dehydrate, desiccate, evaporate, shrivel, wither

parched adjective DRIED OUT or UP, arid, dehydrated, dry, thirsty

pardon verb 1 FORGIVE, absolve, acquit, excuse, exonerate, let off (informal), overlook ♦ noun 2 FORGIVENESS, absolution, acquittal, amnesty, exoneration

pardonable adjective FORGIVABLE, excusable, minor, understandable, venial

pare verb 1 PEEL, clip, cut, shave, skin, trim 2 CUT BACK, crop, cut, decrease, dock, reduce

parent noun FATHER or MOTHER, procreator, progenitor, sire

parentage noun FAMILY, ancestry, birth, descent, lineage, pedigree, stock

pariah noun OUTCAST, exile, undesirable, untouchable

parish noun COMMUNITY, church, congregation, flock

parity noun EQUALITY, consistency, equivalence, uniformity, unity

park noun PARKLAND, estate, garden, grounds, woodland

parlance noun LANGUAGE, idiom, jargon, phraseology, speech, talk, tongue

parliament noun ASSEMBLY, congress, convention, council, legislature, senate

parliamentary adjective GOVERNMENTAL, law-making, legislative

parlour noun Old-fashioned SITTING ROOM, drawing room, front room, living room, lounge

parlous adjective Archaic or humorous DANGEROUS, hazardous, risky

parochial adjective PROVINCIAL, insular, limited, narrow, narrow-minded, petty, small-minded

parody noun 1 TAKEOFF (informal), burlesque, caricature, satire, send-up (Brit. informal), skit, spoof (informal) ♦ verb 2 TAKE OFF (informal), burlesque, caricature, do a takeoff of (informal), satirize, send up (Brit. informal)

paroxysm noun OUTBURST, attack, convulsion, fit, seizure, spasm

parrot verb REPEAT, copy, echo, imitate, mimic

parry verb 1 WARD OFF, block, deflect, rebuff, repel, repulse 2 EVADE, avoid, dodge, sidestep

parsimonious adjective MEAN, close, frugal, miserly, niggardly, penny-pinching (informal), stingy, tightfisted

parson noun CLERGYMAN, churchman, cleric, minister, pastor, preacher, priest, vicar

part noun 1 PIECE, bit, fraction,

fragment, portion, scrap, section, share **2** COMPONENT, branch, constituent, division, member, unit **3** *Theatre* ROLE, character, lines **4** SIDE, behalf, cause, concern, interest **5** often plural REGION, area, district, neighbourhood, quarter, vicinity **6 in good part** GOOD-NATUREDLY, cheerfully, well, without offence **7 in part** PARTLY, a little, in some measure, partially, somewhat ♦ *verb* **8** DIVIDE, break, come apart, detach, rend, separate, sever, split, tear **9** SEPARATE, depart, go, go away, leave, split up, withdraw

partake *verb* **1 partake of** CONSUME, eat, take **2 partake in** PARTICIPATE IN, engage in, share in, take part in

partial *adjective* **1** INCOMPLETE, imperfect, uncompleted, unfinished **2** BIASED, discriminatory, one-sided, partisan, prejudiced, unfair, unjust

partiality *noun* **1** BIAS, favouritism, preference, prejudice **2** LIKING, fondness, inclination, love, penchant, predilection, taste, weakness

partially *adverb* PARTLY, fractionally, incompletely, in part, not wholly, somewhat

participant *noun* PARTICIPATOR, contributor, member, player, stakeholder

participate *verb* TAKE PART, be involved in, join in, partake, perform, share

participation *noun* TAKING PART, contribution, involvement, joining in, partaking, sharing in

particle *noun* BIT, grain, iota, jot, mite, piece, scrap, shred, speck

particular *adjective* **1** SPECIFIC, distinct, exact, peculiar, precise, special **2** SPECIAL, especial, exceptional, marked, notable,

noteworthy, remarkable, singular, uncommon, unusual **3** FUSSY, choosy (*informal*), demanding, fastidious, finicky, pernickety (*informal*), picky (*informal*) ♦ *noun* **4** usually plural DETAIL, circumstance, fact, feature, item, specification **5 in particular** ESPECIALLY, distinctly, exactly, particularly, specifically

particularly *adverb* **1** ESPECIALLY, exceptionally, notably, singularly, uncommonly, unusually **2** SPECIFICALLY, distinctly, especially, explicitly, expressly, in particular

parting *noun* **1** GOING, farewell, goodbye **2** DIVISION, breaking, rift, rupture, separation, split

partisan *noun* **1** SUPPORTER, adherent, devotee, upholder **2** UNDERGROUND FIGHTER, guerrilla, resistance fighter ♦ *adjective* **3** PREJUDICED, biased, interested, one-sided, partial, sectarian

partition *noun* **1** SCREEN, barrier, wall **2** DIVISION, segregation, separation **3** ALLOTMENT, apportionment, distribution ♦ *verb* **4** SEPARATE, divide, screen

partly *adverb* PARTIALLY, slightly, somewhat

partner *noun* **1** SPOUSE, consort, husband *or* wife, mate, significant other (*U.S. informal*) **2** COMPANION, ally, associate, colleague, comrade, helper, mate

partnership *noun* COMPANY, alliance, cooperative, firm, house, society, union

party *noun* **1** GET-TOGETHER (*informal*), celebration, do (*informal*), festivity, function, gathering, reception, social gathering **2** GROUP, band, company, crew, gang, squad, team, unit **3** FACTION, camp, clique, coterie, league, set, side **4** *Informal* PERSON, individual, someone

pass verb 1 GO BY or PAST, elapse, go, lapse, move, proceed, run 2 QUALIFY, do, get through, graduate, succeed 3 SPEND, fill, occupy, while away 4 GIVE, convey, deliver, hand, send, transfer 5 APPROVE, accept, decree, enact, legislate, ordain, ratify 6 EXCEED, beat, go beyond, outdo, outstrip, surpass 7 END, blow over, cease, go ◆ noun 8 GAP, canyon, gorge, ravine, route 9 LICENCE, authorization, passport, permit, ticket, warrant

passable adjective ADEQUATE, acceptable, all right, average, fair, mediocre, so-so (informal), tolerable

passage noun 1 WAY, alley, avenue, channel, course, path, road, route 2 CORRIDOR, hall, lobby, vestibule 3 EXTRACT, excerpt, piece, quotation, reading, section, text 4 JOURNEY, crossing, trek, trip, voyage 5 SAFE-CONDUCT, freedom, permission, right

passageway noun CORRIDOR, aisle, alley, hall, hallway, lane, passage

pass away verb Euphemistic DIE, expire, kick the bucket (slang), pass on, pass over, shuffle off this mortal coil, snuff it (informal)

passé adjective OUT-OF-DATE, dated, obsolete, old-fashioned, old hat, outdated, outmoded, unfashionable

passenger noun TRAVELLER, fare, rider

passer-by noun BYSTANDER, onlooker, witness

passing adjective 1 MOMENTARY, brief, ephemeral, fleeting, short-lived, temporary, transient, transitory 2 SUPERFICIAL, casual, cursory, glancing, quick, short

passion noun 1 LOVE, ardour, desire, infatuation, lust 2 EMOTION, ardour, excitement, feeling, fervour, fire, heat, intensity, warmth, zeal 3 RAGE, anger, fit, frenzy, fury, outburst, paroxysm, storm 4 MANIA, bug (informal), craving, craze, enthusiasm, fascination, obsession

passionate adjective 1 LOVING, amorous, ardent, erotic, hot, lustful 2 EMOTIONAL, ardent, eager, fervent, fierce, heartfelt, impassioned, intense, strong

passive adjective SUBMISSIVE, compliant, docile, inactive, quiescent, receptive

pass off verb FAKE, counterfeit, make a pretence of, palm off

pass out verb Informal FAINT, become unconscious, black out (informal), lose consciousness

pass over verb DISREGARD, ignore, overlook, take no notice of

pass up verb Informal MISS, abstain, decline, forgo, give (something) a miss (informal), let slip, neglect

password noun SIGNAL, key word, watchword

past adjective 1 FORMER, ancient, bygone, early, olden, previous 2 OVER, done, ended, finished, gone ◆ noun 3 BACKGROUND, history, life, past life 4 **the past** FORMER TIMES, days gone by, long ago, olden days ◆ preposition 5 AFTER, beyond, later than 6 BEYOND, across, by, over

paste noun 1 ADHESIVE, cement, glue, gum ◆ verb 2 STICK, cement, glue, gum

pastel adjective PALE, delicate, light, muted, soft

pastiche noun MEDLEY, blend, hotchpotch, mélange, miscellany, mixture

pastime noun ACTIVITY, amusement, diversion, entertainment, game, hobby, recreation

pastor noun CLERGYMAN, churchman, ecclesiastic, minister, parson, priest, rector, vicar

pastoral adjective 1 RUSTIC, bucolic, country, rural 2 ECCLESIASTICAL, clerical, ministerial, priestly

pasture noun GRASSLAND, grass, grazing, meadow

pasty adjective PALE, anaemic, pallid, sickly, wan

pat verb 1 STROKE, caress, fondle, pet, tap, touch ♦ noun 2 STROKE, clap, tap

patch noun 1 REINFORCEMENT 2 SPOT, bit, scrap, shred, small piece 3 PLOT, area, ground, land, tract ♦ verb 4 MEND, cover, reinforce, repair, sew up

patchwork noun MIXTURE, hotchpotch, jumble, medley, pastiche

patchy adjective UNEVEN, erratic, fitful, irregular, sketchy, spotty, variable

patent noun 1 COPYRIGHT, licence ♦ adjective 2 OBVIOUS, apparent, clear, evident, glaring, manifest

paternal adjective FATHERLY, concerned, protective, solicitous

paternity noun 1 FATHERHOOD 2 PARENTAGE, descent, extraction, family, lineage

path noun 1 WAY, footpath, road, track, trail 2 COURSE, direction, road, route, way

pathetic adjective SAD, affecting, distressing, heart-rending, moving, pitiable, plaintive, poignant, tender, touching

pathos noun SADNESS, pitifulness, plaintiveness, poignancy

patience noun 1 FORBEARANCE, calmness, restraint, serenity, sufferance, tolerance 2 ENDURANCE, constancy, fortitude, long-suffering, perseverance, resignation, stoicism, submission

patient adjective 1 LONG-SUFFERING, calm, enduring, persevering, philosophical, resigned, stoical, submissive, uncomplaining 2 FORBEARING, even-tempered, forgiving, indulgent, lenient, mild, tolerant, understanding ♦ noun 3 SICK PERSON, case, invalid, sufferer

patriot noun NATIONALIST, chauvinist, loyalist

patriotic adjective NATIONALISTIC, chauvinistic, jingoistic, loyal

patriotism noun NATIONALISM, jingoism

patrol noun 1 POLICING, guarding, protecting, vigilance, watching 2 GUARD, patrolman, sentinel, watch, watchman ♦ verb 3 POLICE, guard, inspect, keep guard, keep watch, safeguard

patron noun 1 SUPPORTER, backer, benefactor, champion, friend, helper, philanthropist, sponsor 2 CUSTOMER, buyer, client, frequenter, habitué, shopper

patronage noun 1 SUPPORT, aid, assistance, backing, help, promotion, sponsorship 2 CUSTOM, business, clientele, commerce, trade, trading, traffic

patronize verb 1 TALK DOWN TO, look down on 2 BE A CUSTOMER or CLIENT OF, do business with, frequent, shop at 3 SUPPORT, back, fund, help, maintain, promote, sponsor

patronizing adjective CONDESCENDING, disdainful, gracious, haughty, snobbish, supercilious, superior

patter[1] verb 1 TAP, beat, pat, pitter-patter 2 WALK LIGHTLY, scurry, scuttle, skip, trip ♦ noun 3 TAPPING, pattering, pitter-patter

patter[2] noun 1 SPIEL (informal), line, pitch 2 CHATTER, gabble, jabber, nattering, prattle **3** JARGON, argot, cant, lingo (*informal*), patois, slang, vernacular ♦ *verb* **4** CHATTER, jabber, prate, rattle on, spout (*informal*)

pattern *noun* **1** DESIGN, arrangement, decoration, device, figure, motif **2** ORDER, method, plan, sequence, system **3** PLAN, design, diagram, guide, original, stencil, template ♦ *verb* **4** MODEL, copy, follow, form, imitate, mould, style

paucity *noun Formal* SCARCITY, dearth, deficiency, lack, rarity, scantiness, shortage, sparseness

paunch *noun* BELLY, pot, potbelly, spare tyre (*Brit. slang*)

pauper *noun* DOWN-AND-OUT, bankrupt, beggar, mendicant, poor person

pause *verb* **1** STOP BRIEFLY, break, cease, delay, halt, have a breather (*informal*), interrupt, rest, take a break, wait ♦ *noun* **2** STOP, break, breather (*informal*), cessation, gap, halt, interlude, intermission, interval, lull, respite, rest, stoppage

pave *verb* COVER, concrete, floor, surface, tile

paw *verb Informal* MANHANDLE, grab, handle roughly, maul, molest

pawn[1] *verb* HOCK (*informal, chiefly U.S.*), deposit, mortgage, pledge

pawn[2] *noun* TOOL, cat's-paw, instrument, plaything, puppet, stooge (*slang*)

pay *verb* **1** REIMBURSE, compensate, give, recompense, remit, remunerate, requite, reward, settle **2** GIVE, bestow, extend, grant, hand out, present **3** BENEFIT, be worthwhile, repay **4** BE PROFITABLE, make a return, make money **5** YIELD, bring in, produce, return ♦ *noun* **6** WAGES, allowance, earnings, fee, income, payment,

recompense, reimbursement, remuneration, reward, salary, stipend

payable *adjective* DUE, outstanding, owed, owing

pay back *verb* **1** REPAY, refund, reimburse, settle up, square **2** GET EVEN WITH (*informal*), get one's own back, hit back, retaliate

payment *noun* **1** PAYING, discharge, remittance, settlement **2** REMITTANCE, advance, deposit, instalment, premium **3** WAGE, fee, hire, remuneration, reward

pay off *verb* **1** SETTLE, clear, discharge, pay in full, square **2** SUCCEED, be effective, work

pay out *verb* SPEND, disburse, expend, fork out *or* over *or* up (*slang*), shell out (*informal*)

peace *noun* **1** STILLNESS, calm, calmness, hush, quiet, repose, rest, silence, tranquillity **2** SERENITY, calm, composure, contentment, repose **3** HARMONY, accord, agreement, concord **4** TRUCE, armistice, treaty

peaceable *adjective* PEACE-LOVING, conciliatory, friendly, gentle, mild, peaceful, unwarlike

peaceful *adjective* **1** AT PEACE, amicable, friendly, harmonious, nonviolent **2** CALM, placid, quiet, restful, serene, still, tranquil, undisturbed **3** PEACE-LOVING, conciliatory, peaceable, unwarlike

peacemaker *noun* MEDIATOR, arbitrator, conciliator, pacifier

peak *noun* **1** POINT, apex, brow, crest, pinnacle, summit, tip, top **2** HIGH POINT, acme, climax, crown, culmination, zenith ♦ *verb* **3** CULMINATE, climax, come to a head

peal *noun* **1** RING, blast, chime, clang, clap, crash, reverberation, roar, rumble ♦ *verb* **2** RING, chime, crash, resound, roar, rumble

peasant noun RUSTIC, countryman

peccadillo noun MISDEED, error, indiscretion, lapse, misdemeanour, slip

peck verb, noun PICK, dig, hit, jab, poke, prick, strike, tap

peculiar adjective 1 ODD, abnormal, bizarre, curious, eccentric, extraordinary, freakish, funny, offbeat, outlandish, outré, quaint, queer, singular, strange, uncommon, unconventional, unusual, weird 2 SPECIFIC, characteristic, distinctive, particular, special, unique

peculiarity noun 1 ECCENTRICITY, abnormality, foible, idiosyncrasy, mannerism, oddity, quirk 2 CHARACTERISTIC, attribute, feature, mark, particularity, property, quality, trait

pedagogue noun TEACHER, instructor, master or mistress, schoolmaster or schoolmistress

pedant noun HAIRSPLITTER, nit-picker (informal), quibbler

pedantic adjective HAIRSPLITTING, academic, bookish, donnish, formal, fussy, nit-picking (informal), particular, precise, punctilious

pedantry noun HAIRSPLITTING, punctiliousness, quibbling

peddle verb SELL, flog (slang), hawk, market, push (informal), trade

pedestal noun SUPPORT, base, foot, mounting, plinth, stand

pedestrian noun 1 WALKER, foot-traveller ♦ adjective 2 DULL, banal, boring, commonplace, humdrum, mediocre, mundane, ordinary, prosaic, run-of-the-mill, uninspired

pedigree noun 1 LINEAGE, ancestry, blood, breed, descent, extraction, family, family tree, genealogy, line, race, stock ♦ adjective 2 PUREBRED, full-blooded, thoroughbred

pedlar noun SELLER, door-to-door salesman, hawker, huckster, vendor

peek verb 1 GLANCE, look, peep ♦ noun 2 GLANCE, glimpse, look, look-see (slang), peep

peel verb 1 SKIN, flake off, pare, scale, strip off ♦ noun 2 SKIN, peeling, rind

peep[1] verb 1 PEEK, look, sneak a look, steal a look ♦ noun 2 LOOK, glimpse, look-see (slang), peek

peep[2] verb, noun TWEET, cheep, chirp, squeak

peephole noun SPYHOLE, aperture, chink, crack, hole, opening

peer[1] noun 1 NOBLE, aristocrat, lord, nobleman 2 EQUAL, compeer, fellow, like

peer[2] verb SQUINT, gaze, inspect, peep, scan, snoop, spy

peerage noun ARISTOCRACY, lords and ladies, nobility, peers

peerless adjective UNEQUALLED, beyond compare, excellent, incomparable, matchless, outstanding, unmatched, unparalleled, unrivalled

peevish adjective IRRITABLE, cantankerous, childish, churlish, cross, crotchety (informal), fractious, fretful, grumpy, petulant, querulous, snappy, sulky, sullen, surly

peg verb FASTEN, attach, fix, join, secure

pejorative adjective DEROGATORY, deprecatory, depreciatory, disparaging, negative, uncomplimentary, unpleasant

pelt[1] verb 1 THROW, batter,

bombard, cast, hurl, pepper, shower, sling, strike **2** RUSH, belt (*slang*), charge, dash, hurry, run fast, shoot, speed, tear **3** POUR, bucket down (*informal*), rain cats and dogs (*informal*), rain hard, teem

pelt[2] *noun* COAT, fell, hide, skin

pen[1] *verb* WRITE, compose, draft, draw up, jot down

pen[2] *noun* **1** ENCLOSURE, cage, coop, fold, hutch, pound, sty ♦ *verb* **2** ENCLOSE, cage, confine, coop up, fence in, hedge, shut up *or* in

penal *adjective* DISCIPLINARY, corrective, punitive

penalize *verb* PUNISH, discipline, handicap, impose a penalty on

penalty *noun* PUNISHMENT, fine, forfeit, handicap, price

penance *noun* ATONEMENT, penalty, reparation, sackcloth and ashes

penchant *noun* LIKING, bent, bias, fondness, inclination, leaning, partiality, predilection, proclivity, propensity, taste, tendency

pending *adjective* UNDECIDED, awaiting, imminent, impending, in the balance, undetermined, unsettled

penetrate *verb* **1** PIERCE, bore, enter, go through, prick, stab **2** GRASP, comprehend, decipher, fathom, figure out (*informal*), get to the bottom of, suss (out) (*slang*), work out

penetrating *adjective* **1** SHARP, carrying, harsh, piercing, shrill **2** PERCEPTIVE, acute, astute, incisive, intelligent, keen, perspicacious, quick, sharp, sharp-witted, shrewd

penetration *noun* **1** PIERCING, entrance, entry, incision, puncturing **2** PERCEPTION, acuteness, astuteness, insight, keenness, sharpness, shrewdness

penitence *noun* REPENTANCE, compunction, contrition, regret, remorse, shame, sorrow

penitent *adjective* REPENTANT, abject, apologetic, conscience-stricken, contrite, regretful, remorseful, sorry

pen name *noun* PSEUDONYM, nom de plume

pennant *noun* FLAG, banner, ensign, pennon, streamer

penniless *adjective* POOR, broke (*informal*), destitute, dirt-poor (*informal*), down and out, flat broke (*informal*), impecunious, impoverished, indigent, penurious, poverty-stricken, skint (*Brit. slang*), stony-broke (*Brit. slang*)

pension *noun* ALLOWANCE, annuity, benefit, superannuation

pensioner *noun* SENIOR CITIZEN, O.A.P., retired person

pensive *adjective* THOUGHTFUL, contemplative, dreamy, meditative, musing, preoccupied, reflective, sad, serious, solemn, wistful

pent-up *adjective* SUPPRESSED, bottled up, curbed, held back, inhibited, repressed, smothered, stifled

penury *noun* POVERTY, beggary, destitution, indigence, need, privation, want

people *plural noun* **1** PERSONS, humanity, mankind, men and women, mortals **2** NATION, citizens, community, folk, inhabitants, population, public **3** FAMILY, clan, race, tribe ♦ *verb* **4** INHABIT, colonize, occupy, populate, settle

pepper *noun* **1** SEASONING, flavour, spice ♦ *verb* **2** SPRINKLE, dot, fleck, spatter, speck **3** PELT, bombard, shower

perceive verb 1 SEE, behold, discern, discover, espy, make out, note, notice, observe, recognize, spot 2 UNDERSTAND, comprehend, gather, grasp, learn, realize, see, suss (out) (slang)

perceptible adjective VISIBLE, apparent, appreciable, clear, detectable, discernible, evident, noticeable, observable, obvious, recognizable, tangible

perception noun UNDERSTANDING, awareness, conception, consciousness, feeling, grasp, idea, impression, notion, sensation, sense

perceptive adjective OBSERVANT, acute, alert, astute, aware, percipient, perspicacious, quick, sharp

perch noun 1 RESTING PLACE, branch, pole, post ♦ verb 2 SIT, alight, balance, land, rest, roost, settle

percussion noun IMPACT, blow, bump, clash, collision, crash, knock, smash, thump

peremptory adjective 1 IMPERATIVE, absolute, binding, compelling, decisive, final, obligatory 2 IMPERIOUS, authoritative, bossy (informal), dictatorial, dogmatic, domineering, overbearing

perennial adjective LASTING, abiding, constant, continual, enduring, incessant, persistent, recurrent

perfect adjective 1 COMPLETE, absolute, consummate, entire, finished, full, sheer, unmitigated, utter, whole 2 FAULTLESS, flawless, immaculate, impeccable, pure, spotless, unblemished 3 EXCELLENT, ideal, splendid, sublime, superb, superlative, supreme 4 EXACT, accurate, correct, faithful, precise, true, unerring ♦ verb 5 IMPROVE, develop, polish, refine 6 ACCOMPLISH, achieve, carry out,

complete, finish, fulfil, perform

perfection noun 1 COMPLETENESS, maturity 2 PURITY, integrity, perfectness, wholeness 3 EXCELLENCE, exquisiteness, sublimity, superiority 4 EXACTNESS, faultlessness, precision

perfectionist noun STICKLER, precisionist, purist

perfectly adverb 1 COMPLETELY, absolutely, altogether, fully, quite, thoroughly, totally, utterly, wholly 2 FLAWLESSLY, faultlessly, ideally, impeccably, superbly, supremely, wonderfully

perfidious adjective Literary TREACHEROUS, disloyal, double-dealing, traitorous, two-faced, unfaithful

perforate verb PIERCE, bore, drill, penetrate, punch, puncture

perform verb 1 CARRY OUT, accomplish, achieve, complete, discharge, do, execute, fulfil, pull off, work 2 PRESENT, act, enact, play, produce, put on, represent, stage

performance noun 1 CARRYING OUT, accomplishment, achievement, act, completion, execution, fulfilment, work 2 PRESENTATION, acting, appearance, exhibition, gig (informal), play, portrayal, production, show

performer noun ARTISTE, actor or actress, player, Thespian, trouper

perfume noun FRAGRANCE, aroma, bouquet, odour, scent, smell

perfunctory adjective OFFHAND, cursory, heedless, indifferent, mechanical, routine, sketchy, superficial

perhaps adverb MAYBE, conceivably, feasibly, it may be, perchance (archaic), possibly

peril noun DANGER, hazard,

jeopardy, menace, risk, uncertainty

perilous *adjective* DANGEROUS, hazardous, precarious, risky, threatening, unsafe

perimeter *noun* BOUNDARY, ambit, border, bounds, circumference, confines, edge, limit, margin, periphery

period *noun* TIME, interval, season, space, span, spell, stretch, term, while

periodic *adjective* RECURRENT, cyclical, intermittent, occasional, regular, repeated, sporadic

periodical *noun* PUBLICATION, journal, magazine, monthly, paper, quarterly, weekly

peripheral *adjective* 1 INCIDENTAL, inessential, irrelevant, marginal, minor, secondary, unimportant 2 OUTERMOST, exterior, external, outer, outside

perish *verb* 1 DIE, be killed, expire, lose one's life, pass away 2 BE DESTROYED, collapse, decline, disappear, fall, vanish 3 ROT, decay, decompose, disintegrate, moulder, waste

perishable *adjective* SHORT-LIVED, decaying, decomposable

perjure *verb* **perjure oneself** *Criminal law* COMMIT PERJURY, bear false witness, forswear, give false testimony, lie under oath, swear falsely

perjury *noun* LYING UNDER OATH, bearing false witness, false statement, forswearing, giving false testimony

perk *noun Brit. informal* BONUS, benefit, extra, fringe benefit, perquisite, plus

permanence *noun* CONTINUITY, constancy, continuance, durability, endurance, finality, indestructibility, perpetuity,

stability

permanent *adjective* LASTING, abiding, constant, enduring, eternal, everlasting, immutable, perpetual, persistent, stable, steadfast, unchanging

permeate *verb* PERVADE, charge, fill, imbue, impregnate, infiltrate, penetrate, saturate, spread through

permissible *adjective* PERMITTED, acceptable, allowable, all right, authorized, lawful, legal, legitimate, O.K. *or* okay (*informal*)

permission *noun* AUTHORIZATION, allowance, approval, assent, consent, dispensation, go-ahead (*informal*), green light, leave, liberty, licence, sanction

permissive *adjective* TOLERANT, easy-going, forbearing, free, indulgent, lax, lenient, liberal

permit *verb* 1 ALLOW, authorize, consent, enable, entitle, give leave *or* permission, give the green light to, grant, let, license, sanction ♦ *noun* 2 LICENCE, authorization, pass, passport, permission, warrant

permutation *noun* TRANSFORMATION, alteration, change, transposition

pernicious *adjective Formal* WICKED, bad, damaging, dangerous, deadly, destructive, detrimental, evil, fatal, harmful, hurtful, malign, poisonous

pernickety *adjective Informal* FUSSY, exacting, fastidious, finicky, overprecise, particular, picky (*informal*)

perpendicular *adjective* UPRIGHT, at right angles to, on end, plumb, straight, vertical

perpetrate *verb* COMMIT, carry out, do, enact, execute, perform, wreak

perpetual *adjective* 1 EVERLASTING, endless, eternal, infinite, lasting, never-ending, perennial, permanent, unchanging, unending **2** CONTINUAL, constant, continuous, endless, incessant, interminable, never-ending, persistent, recurrent, repeated

perpetuate *verb* MAINTAIN, immortalize, keep going, preserve

perplex *verb* PUZZLE, baffle, bewilder, confound, confuse, mystify, stump

perplexing *adjective* PUZZLING, baffling, bewildering, complex, complicated, confusing, difficult, enigmatic, hard, inexplicable, mystifying

perplexity *noun* **1** PUZZLEMENT, bafflement, bewilderment, confusion, incomprehension, mystification **2** PUZZLE, difficulty, fix (*informal*), mystery, paradox

perquisite *noun Formal* BONUS, benefit, dividend, extra, perk (*Brit. informal*), plus

persecute *verb* **1** VICTIMIZE, afflict, ill-treat, maltreat, oppress, torment, torture **2** HARASS, annoy, badger, bother, hassle (*informal*), pester, tease

perseverance *noun* PERSISTENCE, determination, diligence, doggedness, endurance, pertinacity, resolution, tenacity

persevere *verb* KEEP GOING, carry on, continue, go on, hang on, persist, remain, stick at *or* to

persist *verb* **1** CONTINUE, carry on, keep up, last, linger, remain **2** PERSEVERE, continue, insist, stand firm

persistence *noun* DETERMINATION, doggedness, endurance, grit, perseverance, pertinacity, resolution, tenacity, tirelessness

persistent *adjective* **1** CONTINUOUS, constant, continual, endless, incessant, never-ending,

perpetual, repeated **2** DETERMINED, dogged, obdurate, obstinate, persevering, pertinacious, steadfast, steady, stubborn, tenacious, tireless, unflagging

person *noun* **1** INDIVIDUAL, being, body, human, soul **2 in person** PERSONALLY, bodily, in the flesh, oneself

personable *adjective* PLEASANT, agreeable, amiable, attractive, charming, good-looking, handsome, likable *or* likeable, nice

personage *noun* PERSONALITY, big shot (*informal*), celebrity, dignitary, luminary, megastar (*informal*), notable, public figure, somebody, V.I.P.

personal *adjective* **1** PRIVATE, exclusive, individual, intimate, own, particular, peculiar, special **2** OFFENSIVE, derogatory, disparaging, insulting, nasty

personality *noun* **1** NATURE, character, disposition, identity, individuality, make-up, temperament **2** CELEBRITY, famous name, household name, megastar (*informal*), notable, personage, star

personally *adverb* **1** BY ONESELF, alone, independently, on one's own, solely **2** IN ONE'S OPINION, for one's part, from one's own viewpoint, in one's books, in one's own view **3** INDIVIDUALLY, individualistically, privately, specially, subjectively

personification *noun* EMBODIMENT, epitome, image, incarnation, portrayal, representation

personify *verb* EMBODY, epitomize, exemplify, represent, symbolize, typify

personnel *noun* EMPLOYEES, helpers, human resources, people, staff, workers, workforce

perspective *noun* **1** OUTLOOK,

angle, attitude, context, frame of reference **2** OBJECTIVITY, proportion, relation, relative importance, relativity

perspicacious *adjective Formal* PERCEPTIVE, acute, alert, astute, discerning, keen, percipient, sharp, shrewd

perspiration *noun* SWEAT, moisture, wetness

perspire *verb* SWEAT, exude, glow, pour with sweat, secrete, swelter

persuade *verb* **1** TALK INTO, bring round (*informal*), coax, entice, impel, incite, induce, Influence, sway, urge, win over **2** CONVINCE, cause to believe, satisfy

persuasion *noun* **1** URGING, cajolery, enticement, inducement, wheedling **2** PERSUASIVENESS, cogency, force, potency, power, pull (*informal*) **3** CREED, belief, conviction, credo, faith, opinion, tenet, views **4** FACTION, camp, denomination, party, school, school of thought, side

persuasive *adjective* CONVINCING, cogent, compelling, credible, effective, eloquent, forceful, influential, plausible, sound, telling, valid, weighty

pert *adjective* IMPUDENT, bold, cheeky, forward, impertinent, insolent, sassy (*U.S. informal*), saucy

pertain *verb* RELATE, apply, befit, belong, be relevant, concern, refer, regard

pertinent *adjective* RELEVANT, applicable, apposite, appropriate, apt, fit, fitting, germane, material, proper, to the point

pertness *noun* IMPUDENCE, audacity, cheek (*informal*), cheekiness, effrontery, forwardness, front, impertinence, insolence, sauciness

perturb *verb* DISTURB, agitate,

bother, disconcert, faze, fluster, ruffle, trouble, unsettle, vex, worry

perturbed *adjective* DISTURBED, agitated, anxious, disconcerted, flustered, shaken, troubled, uncomfortable, uneasy, worried

peruse *verb* READ, browse, check, examine, inspect, scan, scrutinize, study

pervade *verb* SPREAD THROUGH, charge, fill, imbue, infuse, penetrate, permeate, suffuse

pervasive *adjective* WIDESPREAD, common, extensive, general, omnipresent, prevalent, rife, ubiquitous, universal

perverse *adjective* **1** ABNORMAL, contrary, deviant, disobedient, improper, rebellious, refractory, troublesome, unhealthy **2** WILFUL, contrary, dogged, headstrong, intractable, intransigent, obdurate, wrong-headed **3** STUBBORN, contrary, cussed (*informal*), mulish, obstinate, pig-headed, stiff-necked, wayward **4** ILL-NATURED, churlish, cross, fractious, ill-tempered, peevish, stroppy (*Brit. slang*), surly

perversion *noun* **1** DEVIATION, aberration, abnormality, debauchery, depravity, immorality, kink (*Brit. informal*), kinkiness (*slang*), unnaturalness, vice **2** DISTORTION, corruption, falsification, misinterpretation, misrepresentation, twisting

perversity *noun* CONTRARINESS, contradictoriness, intransigence, obduracy, refractoriness, waywardness, wrong-headedness

pervert *verb* **1** DISTORT, abuse, falsify, garble, misrepresent, misuse, twist, warp **2** CORRUPT, debase, debauch, degrade, deprave, lead astray ♦ *noun* **3** DEVIANT, degenerate, sicko (*informal*), weirdo (*informal*)

perverted *adjective* <u>UNNATURAL</u>, abnormal, corrupt, debased, debauched, depraved, deviant, kinky (*slang*), pervy (*slang*), sick, twisted, unhealthy, warped

pessimism *noun* <u>GLOOMINESS</u>, dejection, depression, despair, despondency, distrust, gloom, hopelessness, melancholy

pessimist *noun* <u>WET BLANKET</u> (*informal*), cynic, defeatist, killjoy, prophet of doom, worrier

pessimistic *adjective* <u>GLOOMY</u>, bleak, cynical, dark, dejected, depressed, despairing, despondent, glum, hopeless, morose

pest *noun* **1** <u>NUISANCE</u>, annoyance, bane, bother, drag (*informal*), irritation, pain (*informal*), thorn in one's flesh, trial, vexation **2** <u>INFECTION</u>, blight, bug, epidemic, pestilence, plague, scourge

pester *verb* <u>ANNOY</u>, badger, bedevil, be on one's back (*slang*), bother, bug (*informal*), harass, harry, hassle (*informal*), nag, plague, torment

pestilence *noun* <u>PLAGUE</u>, epidemic, visitation

pestilent *adjective* **1** <u>ANNOYING</u>, bothersome, irksome, irritating, tiresome, vexing **2** <u>HARMFUL</u>, detrimental, evil, injurious, pernicious **3** <u>CONTAMINATED</u>, catching, contagious, diseased, disease-ridden, infected, infectious

pestilential *adjective* <u>DEADLY</u>, dangerous, destructive, detrimental, harmful, hazardous, injurious, pernicious

pet *noun* **1** <u>FAVOURITE</u>, darling, idol, jewel, treasure ♦ *adjective* **2** <u>FAVOURITE</u>, cherished, dearest, dear to one's heart ♦ *verb* **3** <u>PAMPER</u>, baby, coddle, cosset, mollycoddle, spoil **4** <u>FONDLE</u>, caress, pat, stroke **5** *Informal* <u>CUDDLE</u>, canoodle (*slang*), kiss, neck (*informal*), smooch (*informal*), snog (*Brit. slang*)

peter out *verb* <u>DIE OUT</u>, dwindle, ebb, fade, fail, run out, stop, taper off, wane

petite *adjective* <u>SMALL</u>, dainty, delicate, elfin, little, slight

petition *noun* **1** <u>APPEAL</u>, entreaty, plea, prayer, request, solicitation, suit, supplication ♦ *verb* **2** <u>APPEAL</u>, adjure, ask, beg, beseech, entreat, plead, pray, solicit, supplicate

petrify *verb* **1** <u>TERRIFY</u>, horrify, immobilize, paralyse, stun, stupefy, transfix **2** <u>FOSSILIZE</u>, calcify, harden, turn to stone

petty *adjective* **1** <u>TRIVIAL</u>, contemptible, inconsiderable, insignificant, little, measly (*informal*), negligible, paltry, slight, small, trifling, unimportant **2** <u>SMALL-MINDED</u>, mean, mean-minded, shabby, spiteful, ungenerous

petulance *noun* <u>SULKINESS</u>, bad temper, ill humour, irritability, peevishness, pique, sullenness

petulant *adjective* <u>SULKY</u>, bad-tempered, huffy, ill-humoured, moody, peevish, sullen

phantom *noun* **1** <u>SPECTRE</u>, apparition, ghost, phantasm, shade (*literary*), spirit, spook (*informal*), wraith **2** <u>ILLUSION</u>, figment of the imagination, hallucination, vision

phase *noun* <u>STAGE</u>, chapter, development, juncture, period, point, position, step, time

phase out *verb* <u>WIND DOWN</u>, close, ease off, eliminate, pull out, remove, run down, terminate, wind up, withdraw

phenomenal *adjective* EXTRAORDINARY, exceptional, fantastic, marvellous, miraculous, outstanding, prodigious, remarkable, unusual

phenomenon *noun* **1** OCCURRENCE, circumstance, episode, event, fact, happening, incident **2** WONDER, exception, marvel, miracle, prodigy, rarity, sensation

philanderer *noun* WOMANIZER (*informal*), Casanova, Don Juan, flirt, ladies' man, lady-killer (*informal*), Lothario, playboy, stud (*slang*), wolf (*informal*)

philanthropic *adjective* HUMANITARIAN, beneficent, benevolent, charitable, humane, kind, kind-hearted, munificent, public-spirited

philanthropist *noun* HUMANITARIAN, benefactor, contributor, donor, giver, patron

philanthropy *noun* HUMANITARIANISM, almsgiving, beneficence, benevolence, brotherly love, charitableness, charity, generosity, kind-heartedness

philistine *noun* **1** BOOR, barbarian, ignoramus, lout, lowbrow, vulgarian, yahoo ◆ *adjective* **2** UNCULTURED, boorish, ignorant, lowbrow, tasteless, uncultivated, uneducated, unrefined

philosopher *noun* THINKER, logician, metaphysician, sage, theorist, wise man

philosophical, philosophic *adjective* **1** WISE, abstract, logical, rational, sagacious, theoretical, thoughtful **2** STOICAL, calm, collected, composed, cool, serene, tranquil, unruffled

philosophy *noun* **1** THOUGHT, knowledge, logic, metaphysics, rationalism, reasoning, thinking, wisdom **2** OUTLOOK, beliefs, convictions, doctrine, ideology, principles, tenets, thinking, values, viewpoint, world view **3** STOICISM, calmness, composure, equanimity, self-possession, serenity

phlegmatic *adjective* UNEMOTIONAL, apathetic, impassive, indifferent, placid, stoical, stolid, undemonstrative, unfeeling

phobia *noun* TERROR, aversion, detestation, dread, fear, hatred, horror, loathing, repulsion, revulsion, thing (*informal*)

phone *noun* **1** TELEPHONE, blower (*informal*) **2** CALL, ring (*informal, chiefly Brit.*), tinkle (*Brit. informal*) ◆ *verb* **3** CALL, get on the blower (*informal*), give someone a call, give someone a ring (*informal, chiefly Brit.*), give someone a tinkle (*Brit. informal*), make a call, ring (up) (*informal, chiefly Brit.*), telephone

phoney *Informal* ◆ *adjective* **1** FAKE, bogus, counterfeit, ersatz, false, imitation, pseudo (*informal*), sham ◆ *noun* **2** FAKE, counterfeit, forgery, fraud, impostor, pseud (*informal*), sham

photograph *noun* **1** PICTURE, photo (*informal*), print, shot, snap (*informal*), snapshot, transparency ◆ *verb* **2** TAKE A PICTURE OF, film, record, shoot, snap (*informal*), take (someone's) picture

photographic *adjective* **1** LIFELIKE, graphic, natural, pictorial, realistic, visual, vivid **2** *Of a person's memory* ACCURATE, exact, faithful, precise, retentive

phrase *noun* **1** EXPRESSION, group of words, idiom, remark, saying ◆ *verb* **2** EXPRESS, put, put into words, say, voice, word

phraseology *noun* WORDING, choice of words, expression, idiom, language, parlance, phrase, phrasing, speech, style, syntax

physical *adjective* 1 BODILY, corporal, corporeal, earthly, fleshly, incarnate, mortal 2 MATERIAL, natural, palpable, real, solid, substantial, tangible

physician *noun* DOCTOR, doc (*informal*), doctor of medicine, general practitioner, G.P., M.D., medic (*informal*), medical practitioner

physique *noun* BUILD, body, constitution, figure, form, frame, shape, structure

pick *verb* 1 SELECT, choose, decide upon, elect, fix upon, hand-pick, opt for, settle upon, single out 2 GATHER, collect, harvest, pluck, pull 3 NIBBLE, have no appetite, peck at, play *or* toy with, push the food round the plate 4 PROVOKE, incite, instigate, start 5 OPEN, break into, break open, crack, force ♦ *noun* 6 CHOICE, decision, option, preference, selection 7 THE BEST, *crème de la crème*, elect, elite, the cream

picket *noun* 1 PROTESTER, demonstrator, picketer 2 LOOKOUT, guard, patrol, sentinel, sentry, watch 3 STAKE, pale, paling, post, stanchion, upright ♦ *verb* 4 BLOCKADE, boycott, demonstrate

pickle *noun* 1 *Informal* PREDICAMENT, bind (*informal*), difficulty, dilemma, fix (*informal*), hot water (*informal*), jam (*informal*), quandary, scrape (*informal*), tight spot ♦ *verb* 2 PRESERVE, marinade, steep

pick-me-up *noun Informal* TONIC, bracer (*informal*), refreshment, restorative, shot in the arm (*informal*), stimulant

pick on *verb* TORMENT, badger, bait, bully, goad, hector, tease

pick out *verb* IDENTIFY, discriminate, distinguish, make out, perceive, recognize, tell apart

pick up *verb* 1 LIFT, gather, grasp, raise, take up, uplift 2 OBTAIN, buy, come across, find, purchase 3 RECOVER, be on the mend, get better, improve, mend, rally, take a turn for the better, turn the corner 4 LEARN, acquire, get the hang of (*informal*), master 5 COLLECT, call for, get

pick-up *noun* IMPROVEMENT, change for the better, rally, recovery, revival, rise, strengthening, upswing, upturn

picnic *noun* EXCURSION, outdoor meal, outing

pictorial *adjective* GRAPHIC, illustrated, picturesque, representational, scenic

picture *noun* 1 REPRESENTATION, drawing, engraving, illustration, image, likeness, painting, photograph, portrait, print, sketch 2 DESCRIPTION, account, depiction, image, impression, report 3 DOUBLE, carbon copy, copy, dead ringer (*slang*), duplicate, image, likeness, lookalike, replica, spitting image (*informal*), twin 4 PERSONIFICATION, embodiment, epitome, essence 5 FILM, flick (*slang*), motion picture, movie (*U.S. informal*) ♦ *verb* 6 IMAGINE, conceive of, envision, see, visualize 7 REPRESENT, depict, draw, illustrate, paint, photograph, show, sketch

picturesque *adjective* 1 PRETTY, attractive, beautiful, charming, quaint, scenic, striking 2 VIVID, colourful, graphic

piebald *adjective* PIED, black and white, brindled, dappled, flecked, mottled, speckled, spotted

piece *noun* 1 BIT, chunk, fragment, morsel, part, portion, quantity, segment, slice **2** <u>WORK</u>, article, composition, creation, item, study, work of art

piecemeal *adverb* <u>BIT BY BIT</u>, by degrees, gradually, little by little

pier *noun* **1** <u>JETTY</u>, landing place, promenade, quay, wharf **2** <u>PILLAR</u>, buttress, column, pile, post, support, upright

pierce *verb* <u>PENETRATE</u>, bore, drill, enter, perforate, prick, puncture, spike, stab, stick into

piercing *adjective* **1** *Usually of sound* <u>PENETRATING</u>, ear-splitting, high-pitched, loud, sharp, shrill **2** <u>KEEN</u>, alert, penetrating, perceptive, perspicacious, quick-witted, sharp, shrewd **3** *Usually of weather* <u>COLD</u>, arctic, biting, bitter, freezing, nippy, wintry **4** <u>SHARP</u>, acute, agonizing, excruciating, intense, painful, severe, stabbing

piety *noun* <u>HOLINESS</u>, faith, godliness, piousness, religion, reverence

pig *noun* **1** <u>HOG</u>, boar, porker, sow, swine **2** *Informal* <u>SLOB</u> (*slang*), boor, brute, glutton, swine

pigeonhole *noun* **1** <u>COMPARTMENT</u>, cubbyhole, locker, niche, place, section ♦ *verb* **2** <u>CLASSIFY</u>, categorize, characterize, compartmentalize, ghettoize, label, slot (*informal*) **3** <u>PUT OFF</u>, defer, postpone, shelve

pig-headed *adjective* <u>STUBBORN</u>, contrary, inflexible, mulish, obstinate, self-willed, stiff-necked, unyielding

pigment *noun* <u>COLOUR</u>, colouring, dye, paint, stain, tincture, tint

pile¹ *noun* **1** <u>HEAP</u>, accumulation, collection, hoard, mass, mound, mountain, stack **2** *often plural Informal* <u>A LOT</u>, great deal, ocean, quantity, stacks **3** <u>BUILDING</u>, edifice,

erection, structure ♦ *verb* **4** <u>COLLECT</u>, accumulate, amass, assemble, gather, heap, hoard, stack **5** <u>CROWD</u>, crush, flock, flood, jam, pack, rush, stream

pile² *noun* <u>FOUNDATION</u>, beam, column, pillar, post, support, upright

pile³ *noun* <u>NAP</u>, down, fibre, fur, hair, plush

pile-up *noun Informal* <u>COLLISION</u>, accident, crash, multiple collision, smash, smash-up (*informal*)

pilfer *verb* <u>STEAL</u>, appropriate, embezzle, filch, knock off (*slang*), lift (*informal*), nick (*slang, chiefly Brit.*), pinch (*informal*), purloin, snaffle (*Brit. informal*), swipe (*slang*), take

pilgrim *noun* <u>TRAVELLER</u>, wanderer, wayfarer

pilgrimage *noun* <u>JOURNEY</u>, excursion, expedition, mission, tour, trip

pill *noun* **1** <u>TABLET</u>, capsule, pellet **2 the pill** <u>ORAL CONTRACEPTIVE</u>

pillage *verb* **1** <u>PLUNDER</u>, despoil, loot, maraud, raid, ransack, ravage, sack ♦ *noun* **2** <u>PLUNDER</u>, marauding, robbery, sack, spoliation

pillar *noun* **1** <u>SUPPORT</u>, column, pier, post, prop, shaft, stanchion, upright **2** <u>SUPPORTER</u>, leader, leading light (*informal*), mainstay, upholder

pillory *verb* <u>RIDICULE</u>, brand, denounce, stigmatize

pilot *noun* **1** <u>AIRMAN</u>, aviator, flyer **2** <u>HELMSMAN</u>, navigator, steersman ♦ *adjective* **3** <u>TRIAL</u>, experimental, model, test ♦ *verb* **4** <u>FLY</u>, conduct, direct, drive, guide, handle, navigate, operate, steer

pimple *noun* <u>SPOT</u>, boil, plook (*Scot.*), pustule, zit (*slang*)

pin *verb* **1** <u>FASTEN</u>, affix, attach, fix,

join, secure **2** <u>HOLD FAST</u>, fix, hold down, immobilize, pinion

pinch *verb* **1** <u>SQUEEZE</u>, compress, grasp, nip, press **2** <u>HURT</u>, cramp, crush, pain **3** *Informal* <u>STEAL</u>, filch, knock off (*slang*), lift (*informal*), nick (*slang, chiefly Brit.*), pilfer, purloin, snaffle (*Brit. informal*), swipe (*slang*) ♦ *noun* **4** <u>SQUEEZE</u>, nip **5** <u>DASH</u>, bit, jot, mite, *soupçon*, speck **6** <u>HARDSHIP</u>, crisis, difficulty, emergency, necessity, plight, predicament, strait

pinched *adjective* <u>THIN</u>, drawn, gaunt, haggard, peaky, worn

pin down *verb* **1** <u>FORCE</u>, compel, constrain, make, press, pressurize **2** <u>DETERMINE</u>, identify, locate, name, pinpoint, specify

pine *verb* **1** often with *for* <u>LONG</u>, ache, crave, desire, eat one's heart out over, hanker, hunger for, thirst for, wish for, yearn for **2** <u>WASTE</u>, decline, fade, languish, sicken

pinion *verb* <u>IMMOBILIZE</u>, bind, chain, fasten, fetter, manacle, shackle, tie

pink *adjective* <u>ROSY</u>, flushed, reddish, rose, roseate, salmon

pinnacle *noun* <u>PEAK</u>, apex, crest, crown, height, summit, top, vertex, zenith

pinpoint *verb* <u>IDENTIFY</u>, define, distinguish, locate

pioneer *noun* **1** <u>SETTLER</u>, colonist, explorer **2** <u>FOUNDER</u>, developer, innovator, leader, trailblazer ♦ *verb* **3** <u>DEVELOP</u>, create, discover, establish, initiate, instigate, institute, invent, originate, show the way, start

pious *adjective* <u>RELIGIOUS</u>, devout, God-fearing, godly, holy, reverent, righteous, saintly

pipe *noun* **1** <u>TUBE</u>, conduit, duct, hose, line, main, passage, pipeline ♦ *verb* **2** <u>WHISTLE</u>, cheep, peep, play,

sing, sound, warble **3** <u>CONVEY</u>, channel, conduct

pipe down *verb Informal* <u>BE QUIET</u>, hold one's tongue, hush, quieten down, shush, shut one's mouth, shut up (*informal*)

pipeline *noun* <u>TUBE</u>, conduit, duct, passage, pipe

piquant *adjective* **1** <u>SPICY</u>, biting, pungent, savoury, sharp, tangy, tart, zesty **2** <u>INTERESTING</u>, lively, provocative, scintillating, sparkling, stimulating

pique *noun* **1** <u>RESENTMENT</u>, annoyance, displeasure, huff, hurt feelings, irritation, offence, umbrage, wounded pride ♦ *verb* **2** <u>DISPLEASE</u>, affront, annoy, get (*informal*), irk, irritate, nettle, offend, rile, sting **3** <u>AROUSE</u>, excite, rouse, spur, stimulate, stir, whet

piracy *noun* <u>ROBBERY</u>, buccaneering, freebooting, stealing, theft

pirate *noun* **1** <u>BUCCANEER</u>, corsair, freebooter, marauder, raider **2** <u>PLAGIARIST</u>, cribber (*informal*), infringer, plagiarizer ♦ *verb* **3** <u>COPY</u>, appropriate, crib (*informal*), plagiarize, poach, reproduce, steal

pit *noun* **1** <u>HOLE</u>, abyss, cavity, chasm, crater, dent, depression, hollow ♦ *verb* **2** <u>SCAR</u>, dent, indent, mark, pockmark

pitch *verb* **1** <u>THROW</u>, cast, chuck (*informal*), fling, heave, hurl, lob (*informal*), sling, toss **2** <u>SET UP</u>, erect, put up, raise, settle **3** <u>FALL</u>, dive, drop, topple, tumble **4** <u>TOSS</u>, lurch, plunge, roll ♦ *noun* **5** <u>SPORTS FIELD</u>, field of play, ground, park (*U.S. & Canad.*) **6** <u>LEVEL</u>, degree, height, highest point, point, summit **7** <u>SLOPE</u>, angle, dip, gradient, incline, tilt **8** <u>TONE</u>, modulation, sound, timbre **9** <u>SALES TALK</u>, patter, spiel (*informal*)

pitch-black *adjective* <u>JET-BLACK</u>, dark,

inky, pitch-dark, unlit

pitch in verb HELP, chip in (*informal*), contribute, cooperate, do one's bit, join in, lend a hand, participate

pitch into verb Informal ATTACK, assail, assault, get stuck into (*informal*), tear into (*informal*)

piteous adjective PATHETIC, affecting, distressing, harrowing, heartbreaking, heart-rending, moving, pitiable, pitiful, plaintive, poignant, sad

pitfall noun DANGER, catch, difficulty, drawback, hazard, peril, snag, trap

pith noun ESSENCE, core, crux, gist, heart, kernel, nub, point, quintessence, salient point

pithy adjective SUCCINCT, brief, cogent, concise, epigrammatic, laconic, pointed, short, terse, to the point, trenchant

pitiful adjective 1 PATHETIC, distressing, grievous, harrowing, heartbreaking, heart-rending, piteous, pitiable, sad, wretched 2 CONTEMPTIBLE, abject, base, low, mean, miserable, paltry, shabby, sorry

pitiless adjective MERCILESS, callous, cold-blooded, cold-hearted, cruel, hardhearted, heartless, implacable, relentless, ruthless, unmerciful

pittance noun PEANUTS (*slang*), chicken feed (*slang*), drop, mite, slave wages, trifle

pity noun 1 COMPASSION, charity, clemency, fellow feeling, kindness, mercy, sympathy 2 SHAME, bummer (*slang*), crying shame, misfortune, sin ◆ verb 3 FEEL SORRY FOR, bleed for, feel for, grieve for, have compassion for, sympathize with, weep for

pivot noun 1 AXIS, axle, fulcrum,

spindle, swivel 2 HUB, centre, heart, hinge, kingpin ◆ verb 3 TURN, revolve, rotate, spin, swivel, twirl 4 RELY, be contingent, depend, hang, hinge

pivotal adjective CRUCIAL, central, critical, decisive, vital

pixie noun ELF, brownie, fairy, sprite

placard noun NOTICE, advertisement, bill, poster

placate verb CALM, appease, assuage, conciliate, humour, mollify, pacify, propitiate, soothe

place noun 1 SPOT, area, location, point, position, site, venue, whereabouts 2 REGION, district, locale, locality, neighbourhood, quarter, vicinity 3 POSITION, grade, rank, station, status 4 SPACE, accommodation, room 5 HOME, abode, domicile, dwelling, house, pad (*slang*), property, residence 6 DUTY, affair, charge, concern, function, prerogative, responsibility, right, role 7 JOB, appointment, employment, position, post 8 **take place** HAPPEN, come about, go on, occur, transpire (*informal*) ◆ verb 9 PUT, deposit, install, lay, locate, position, rest, set, situate, stand, station, stick (*informal*) 10 CLASSIFY, arrange, class, grade, group, order, rank, sort 11 IDENTIFY, know, put one's finger on, recognize, remember 12 ASSIGN, allocate, appoint, charge, entrust, give

placid adjective CALM, collected, composed, equable, even-tempered, imperturbable, serene, tranquil, unexcitable, unruffled, untroubled

plagiarism noun COPYING, borrowing, cribbing (*informal*), infringement, piracy, theft

plagiarize verb COPY, borrow, crib (*informal*), lift (*informal*), pirate, steal

plague noun 1 DISEASE, epidemic, infection, pestilence 2 AFFLICTION, bane, blight, curse, evil, scourge, torment ♦ verb 3 PESTER, annoy, badger, bother, harass, harry, hassle (*informal*), tease, torment, torture, trouble, vex

plain adjective 1 CLEAR, comprehensible, distinct, evident, manifest, obvious, overt, patent, unambiguous, understandable, unmistakable, visible 2 HONEST, blunt, candid, direct, downright, forthright, frank, open, outspoken, straightforward, upfront (*informal*) 3 UNADORNED, austere, bare, basic, severe, simple, Spartan, stark, unembellished, unfussy, unornamented 4 UGLY, ill-favoured, no oil painting (*informal*), not beautiful, unattractive, unlovely, unprepossessing 5 ORDINARY, common, commonplace, everyday, simple, unaffected, unpretentious ♦ noun 6 FLATLAND, grassland, plateau, prairie, steppe, veld

plain-spoken adjective BLUNT, candid, direct, downright, forthright, frank, outspoken

plaintive adjective SORROWFUL, heart-rending, mournful, pathetic, piteous, pitiful, sad

plan noun 1 SCHEME, design, method, plot, programme, proposal, strategy, suggestion, system 2 DIAGRAM, blueprint, chart, drawing, layout, map, representation, sketch ♦ verb 3 DEVISE, arrange, contrive, design, draft, formulate, organize, outline, plot, scheme, think out 4 INTEND, aim, mean, propose, purpose

plane noun 1 AEROPLANE, aircraft, jet 2 FLAT SURFACE, level surface 3 LEVEL, condition, degree, position ♦ adjective 4 LEVEL, even, flat, horizontal, regular, smooth ♦ verb

5 SKIM, glide, sail, skate

plant noun 1 VEGETABLE, bush, flower, herb, shrub, weed 2 FACTORY, foundry, mill, shop, works, yard 3 MACHINERY, apparatus, equipment, gear ♦ verb 4 SOW, put in the ground, scatter, seed, transplant 5 PLACE, establish, fix, found, insert, put, set

plaster noun 1 MORTAR, gypsum, plaster of Paris, stucco 2 BANDAGE, adhesive plaster, dressing, Elastoplast (*Trademark*), sticking plaster ♦ verb 3 COVER, coat, daub, overlay, smear, spread

plastic adjective 1 MANAGEABLE, docile, malleable, pliable, receptive, responsive, tractable 2 PLIANT, ductile, flexible, mouldable, pliable, soft, supple

plate noun 1 PLATTER, dish, trencher (*archaic*) 2 HELPING, course, dish, portion, serving 3 LAYER, panel, sheet, slab 4 ILLUSTRATION, lithograph, print ♦ verb 5 COAT, cover, gild, laminate, overlay

plateau noun 1 UPLAND, highland, table, tableland 2 LEVELLING OFF, level, stability, stage

platform noun 1 STAGE, dais, podium, rostrum, stand 2 POLICY, manifesto, objective(s), party line, principle, programme

platitude noun CLICHÉ, banality, commonplace, truism

platoon noun SQUAD, company, group, outfit (*informal*), patrol, squadron, team

platter noun PLATE, dish, salver, tray, trencher (*archaic*)

plaudits plural noun APPROVAL, acclaim, acclamation, applause, approbation, praise

plausible adjective 1 REASONABLE, believable, conceivable, credible, likely, persuasive, possible, probable, tenable **2** <u>GLIB</u>, smooth, smooth-talking, smooth-tongued, specious

play *verb* **1** <u>AMUSE ONESELF</u>, entertain oneself, fool, have fun, revel, romp, sport, trifle **2** <u>COMPETE</u>, challenge, contend against, participate, take on, take part **3** <u>ACT</u>, act the part of, perform, portray, represent ♦ *noun* **4** <u>DRAMA</u>, comedy, dramatic piece, farce, pantomime, piece, show, stage show, tragedy **5** <u>AMUSEMENT</u>, diversion, entertainment, fun, game, pastime, recreation, sport **6** <u>FUN</u>, humour, jest, joking, lark (*informal*), prank, sport **7** <u>SPACE</u>, elbowroom, latitude, leeway, margin, room, scope

playboy *noun* <u>WOMANIZER</u>, ladies' man, lady-killer (*informal*), philanderer, rake, roué

play down *verb* <u>MINIMIZE</u>, gloss over, make light of, make little of, soft-pedal (*informal*), underplay, underrate

player *noun* **1** <u>SPORTSMAN</u> *or* <u>SPORTSWOMAN</u>, competitor, contestant, participant **2** <u>MUSICIAN</u>, artist, instrumentalist, performer, virtuoso **3** <u>PERFORMER</u>, actor *or* actress, entertainer, Thespian, trouper

playful *adjective* <u>LIVELY</u>, frisky, impish, merry, mischievous, spirited, sportive, sprightly, vivacious

playmate *noun* <u>FRIEND</u>, chum (*informal*), companion, comrade, pal (*informal*), playfellow

play on *or* **upon** *verb* <u>TAKE ADVANTAGE OF</u>, abuse, capitalize on, exploit, impose on, trade on

plaything *noun* <u>TOY</u>, amusement, game, pastime, trifle

play up *verb* **1** <u>EMPHASIZE</u>, accentuate, highlight, stress,

underline **2** *Brit. informal* <u>BE AWKWARD</u>, be disobedient, be stroppy (*Brit. slang*), give trouble, misbehave **3** *Brit. informal* <u>HURT</u>, be painful, be sore, bother, pain, trouble **4** *Brit. informal* <u>MALFUNCTION</u>, be on the blink (*slang*), not work properly

plea *noun* **1** <u>APPEAL</u>, entreaty, intercession, petition, prayer, request, suit, supplication **2** <u>EXCUSE</u>, defence, explanation, justification

plead *verb* <u>APPEAL</u>, ask, beg, beseech, entreat, implore, petition, request

pleasant *adjective* **1** <u>PLEASING</u>, agreeable, amusing, delightful, enjoyable, fine, lovely, nice, pleasurable **2** <u>NICE</u>, affable, agreeable, amiable, charming, congenial, engaging, friendly, genial, likable *or* likeable

pleasantry *noun* <u>JOKE</u>, badinage, banter, jest, quip, witticism

please *verb* <u>DELIGHT</u>, amuse, entertain, gladden, gratify, humour, indulge, satisfy, suit

pleased *adjective* <u>HAPPY</u>, chuffed (*Brit. slang*), contented, delighted, euphoric, glad, gratified, over the moon (*informal*), satisfied, thrilled

pleasing *adjective* <u>ENJOYABLE</u>, agreeable, charming, delightful, engaging, gratifying, likable *or* likeable, pleasurable, satisfying

pleasurable *adjective* <u>ENJOYABLE</u>, agreeable, delightful, fun, good, lovely, nice, pleasant

pleasure *noun* <u>HAPPINESS</u>, amusement, bliss, delectation, delight, enjoyment, gladness, gratification, joy, satisfaction

plebeian *adjective* **1** <u>COMMON</u>, base, coarse, low, lower-class, proletarian, uncultivated, unrefined, vulgar, working-class

♦ *noun* **2** <u>COMMONER</u>, common man, man in the street, pleb, prole (*derogatory slang, chiefly Brit.*), proletarian

pledge *noun* **1** <u>PROMISE</u>, assurance, covenant, oath, undertaking, vow, warrant, word **2** <u>GUARANTEE</u>, bail, collateral, deposit, pawn, security, surety ♦ *verb* **3** <u>PROMISE</u>, contract, engage, give one's oath, give one's word, swear, vow

plentiful *adjective* <u>ABUNDANT</u>, ample, bountiful, copious, generous, lavish, liberal, overflowing, plenteous, profuse

plenty *noun* **1** <u>LOTS</u> (*informal*), abundance, enough, great deal, heap(s) (*informal*), masses, pile(s) (*informal*), plethora, quantity, stack(s) **2** <u>ABUNDANCE</u>, affluence, copiousness, fertility, fruitfulness, plenitude, profusion, prosperity, wealth

plethora *noun* <u>EXCESS</u>, glut, overabundance, profusion, superabundance, surfeit, surplus

pliable *adjective* **1** <u>FLEXIBLE</u>, bendable, bendy, malleable, plastic, pliant, supple **2** <u>IMPRESSIONABLE</u>, adaptable, compliant, docile, easily led, pliant, receptive, responsive, susceptible, tractable

pliant *adjective* **1** <u>FLEXIBLE</u>, bendable, bendy, plastic, pliable, supple **2** <u>IMPRESSIONABLE</u>, biddable, compliant, easily led, pliable, susceptible, tractable

plight *noun* <u>DIFFICULTY</u>, condition, jam (*informal*), predicament, scrape (*informal*), situation, spot (*informal*), state, trouble

plod *verb* **1** <u>TRUDGE</u>, clump, drag, lumber, tramp, tread **2** <u>SLOG</u>, grind (*informal*), labour, persevere, plough through, plug away (*informal*), soldier on, toil

plot[1] *noun* **1** <u>PLAN</u>, cabal, conspiracy, intrigue, machination, scheme, stratagem **2** <u>STORY</u>, action, narrative, outline, scenario, story line, subject, theme ♦ *verb* **3** <u>PLAN</u>, collude, conspire, contrive, intrigue, machinate, manoeuvre, scheme **4** <u>DEVISE</u>, conceive, concoct, contrive, cook up (*informal*), design, hatch, lay **5** <u>CHART</u>, calculate, locate, map, mark, outline

plot[2] *noun* <u>PATCH</u>, allotment, area, ground, lot, parcel, tract

plough *verb* **1** <u>TURN OVER</u>, cultivate, dig, till **2** usually with *through* <u>FORGE</u>, cut, drive, plunge, press, push, wade

ploy *noun* <u>TACTIC</u>, device, dodge, manoeuvre, move, ruse, scheme, stratagem, trick, wile

pluck *verb* **1** <u>PULL OUT *or* OFF</u>, collect, draw, gather, harvest, pick **2** <u>TUG</u>, catch, clutch, jerk, pull at, snatch, tweak, yank **3** <u>STRUM</u>, finger, pick, twang ♦ *noun* **4** <u>COURAGE</u>, backbone, boldness, bottle (*Brit. slang*), bravery, grit, guts (*informal*), nerve

plucky *adjective* <u>COURAGEOUS</u>, bold, brave, daring, game, gutsy (*slang*), have-a-go (*informal*), intrepid

plug *noun* **1** <u>STOPPER</u>, bung, cork, spigot **2** *Informal* <u>MENTION</u>, advert (*Brit. informal*), advertisement, hype, publicity, push ♦ *verb* **3** <u>SEAL</u>, block, bung, close, cork, fill, pack, stop, stopper, stop up, stuff **4** *Informal* <u>MENTION</u>, advertise, build up, hype, promote, publicize, push **5 plug away** *Informal* <u>SLOG</u>, grind (*informal*), labour, peg away, plod, toil

plum *adjective* <u>CHOICE</u>, best, first-class, prize

plumb *verb* **1** <u>DELVE</u>, explore, fathom, gauge, go into,

penetrate, probe, unravel ♦ *noun*
2 WEIGHT, lead, plumb bob,
plummet ♦ *adverb* **3** EXACTLY, bang,
precisely, slap, spot-on (*Brit.
informal*)

plume *noun* FEATHER, crest, pinion,
quill

plummet *verb* PLUNGE, crash,
descend, dive, drop down, fall,
nose-dive, tumble

plump *adjective* CHUBBY, corpulent,
dumpy, fat, podgy, roly-poly,
rotund, round, stout, tubby

plunder *verb* **1** LOOT, pillage, raid,
ransack, rifle, rob, sack, strip
♦ *noun* **2** LOOT, booty, ill-gotten
gains, pillage, prize, spoils, swag
(*slang*)

plunge *verb* **1** THROW, cast, pitch
2 HURTLE, career, charge, dash,
jump, rush, tear **3** DESCEND, dip,
dive, drop, fall, nose-dive,
plummet, sink, tumble ♦ *noun*
4 DIVE, descent, drop, fall, jump

plus *preposition* **1** AND, added to,
coupled with, with ♦ *adjective*
2 ADDITIONAL, added, add-on,
extra, supplementary ♦ *noun*
3 *Informal* ADVANTAGE, asset,
benefit, bonus, extra, gain, good
point

plush *adjective* LUXURIOUS, de luxe,
lavish, luxury, opulent, rich,
sumptuous

ply *verb* **1** WORK AT, carry on,
exercise, follow, practise, pursue
2 USE, employ, handle,
manipulate, wield

poach *verb* ENCROACH, appropriate,
infringe, intrude, trespass

pocket *noun* **1** POUCH, bag,
compartment, receptacle, sack
♦ *verb* **2** STEAL, appropriate, filch,
lift (*informal*), pilfer, purloin, take
♦ *adjective* **3** SMALL, abridged,
compact, concise, little, miniature,
portable

pod *noun, verb* SHELL, hull, husk,
shuck

podgy *adjective* TUBBY, chubby,
dumpy, fat, plump, roly-poly,
rotund, stout

podium *noun* PLATFORM, dais,
rostrum, stage

poem *noun* VERSE, lyric, ode, rhyme,
song, sonnet

poet *noun* BARD, lyricist, rhymer,
versifier

poetic *adjective* LYRICAL, elegiac,
lyric, metrical

poetry *noun* VERSE, poems, rhyme,
rhyming

poignancy *noun* **1** SADNESS,
emotion, feeling, pathos,
sentiment, tenderness **2** SHARPNESS,
bitterness, intensity, keenness

poignant *adjective* MOVING, bitter,
distressing, heart-rending,
intense, painful, pathetic, sad,
touching

point *noun* **1** ESSENCE, crux, drift,
gist, heart, import, meaning, nub,
pith, question, subject, thrust
2 AIM, end, goal, intent, intention,
motive, object, objective,
purpose, reason **3** ITEM, aspect,
detail, feature, particular
4 CHARACTERISTIC, aspect, attribute,
quality, respect, trait **5** PLACE,
location, position, site, stage
6 FULL STOP, dot, mark, period, stop
7 END, apex, prong, sharp end,
spike, spur, summit, tip, top
8 HEADLAND, cape, head,
promontory **9** STAGE, circumstance,
condition, degree, extent,
position **10** MOMENT, instant,
juncture, time, very minute
11 UNIT, score, tally ♦ *verb*
12 INDICATE, call attention to,
denote, designate, direct, show,
signify **13** AIM, direct, level, train

point-blank *adjective* **1** DIRECT,
blunt, downright, explicit,

express, plain ♦ *adverb* **2** <u>DIRECTLY</u>, bluntly, candidly, explicitly, forthrightly, frankly, openly, plainly, straight

pointed *adjective* **1** <u>SHARP</u>, acute, barbed, edged **2** <u>CUTTING</u>, acute, biting, incisive, keen, penetrating, pertinent, sharp, telling

pointer *noun* **1** <u>HINT</u>, advice, caution, information, recommendation, suggestion, tip **2** <u>INDICATOR</u>, guide, hand, needle

pointless *adjective* <u>SENSELESS</u>, absurd, aimless, fruitless, futile, inane, irrelevant, meaningless, silly, stupid, useless

point out *verb* <u>MENTION</u>, allude to, bring up, identify, indicate, show, specify

poise *noun* <u>COMPOSURE</u>, aplomb, assurance, calmness, cool (*slang*), dignity, presence, sang-froid, self-possession

poised *adjective* **1** <u>READY</u>, all set, prepared, standing by, waiting **2** <u>COMPOSED</u>, calm, collected, dignified, self-confident, self-possessed, together (*informal*)

poison *noun* **1** <u>TOXIN</u>, bane, venom ♦ *verb* **2** <u>MURDER</u>, give (someone) poison, kill **3** <u>CONTAMINATE</u>, infect, pollute **4** <u>CORRUPT</u>, defile, deprave, pervert, subvert, taint, undermine, warp

poisonous *adjective* **1** <u>TOXIC</u>, deadly, fatal, lethal, mortal, noxious, venomous, virulent **2** <u>EVIL</u>, baleful, corrupting, malicious, noxious, pernicious

poke *verb* **1** <u>JAB</u>, dig, nudge, prod, push, shove, stab, stick, thrust ♦ *noun* **2** <u>JAB</u>, dig, nudge, prod, thrust

poky *adjective* <u>SMALL</u>, confined, cramped, narrow, tiny

pole *noun* <u>ROD</u>, bar, mast, post, shaft, spar, staff, stick

police *noun* **1** <u>THE LAW</u> (*informal*), boys in blue (*informal*), constabulary, fuzz (*slang*), police force, the Old Bill (*slang*) ♦ *verb* **2** <u>CONTROL</u>, guard, patrol, protect, regulate, watch

policeman *noun* <u>COP</u> (*slang*), bobby (*informal*), constable, copper (*slang*), fuzz (*slang*), officer

policy *noun* <u>PROCEDURE</u>, action, approach, code, course, custom, plan, practice, rule, scheme

polish *verb* **1** <u>SHINE</u>, brighten, buff, burnish, rub, smooth, wax **2** <u>PERFECT</u>, brush up, enhance, finish, improve, refine, touch up ♦ *noun* **3** <u>VARNISH</u>, wax **4** <u>SHEEN</u>, brightness, finish, glaze, gloss, lustre **5** <u>STYLE</u>, breeding, class (*informal*), elegance, finesse, finish, grace, refinement

polished *adjective* **1** <u>ACCOMPLISHED</u>, adept, expert, fine, masterly, professional, skilful, superlative **2** <u>SHINING</u>, bright, burnished, gleaming, glossy, smooth **3** <u>ELEGANT</u>, cultivated, polite, refined, sophisticated, well-bred

polite *adjective* **1** <u>MANNERLY</u>, civil, complaisant, courteous, gracious, respectful, well-behaved, well-mannered **2** <u>REFINED</u>, civilized, cultured, elegant, genteel, polished, sophisticated, well-bred

politeness *noun* <u>COURTESY</u>, civility, courteousness, decency, etiquette, mannerliness

politic *adjective* <u>WISE</u>, advisable, diplomatic, expedient, judicious, prudent, sensible

political *adjective* <u>GOVERNMENTAL</u>, parliamentary, policy-making

politician *noun* <u>STATESMAN</u>, legislator, Member of Parliament, M.P., office bearer, public servant

politics *noun* <u>STATESMANSHIP</u>, affairs of state, civics, government, political science

poll *noun* 1 <u>CANVASS</u>, ballot, census, count, sampling, survey 2 <u>VOTE</u>, figures, returns, tally, voting ♦ *verb* 3 <u>TALLY</u>, register 4 <u>QUESTION</u>, ballot, canvass, interview, sample, survey

pollute *verb* 1 <u>CONTAMINATE</u>, dirty, foul, infect, poison, soil, spoil, stain, taint 2 <u>DEFILE</u>, corrupt, debase, debauch, deprave, desecrate, dishonour, profane, sully

pollution *noun* <u>CONTAMINATION</u>, corruption, defilement, dirtying, foulness, impurity, taint, uncleanness

pomp *noun* 1 <u>CEREMONY</u>, flourish, grandeur, magnificence, pageant, pageantry, splendour, state 2 <u>SHOW</u>, display, grandiosity, ostentation

pomposity *noun* <u>SELF-IMPORTANCE</u>, affectation, airs, grandiosity, pompousness, portentousness, pretension, pretentiousness

pompous *adjective* 1 <u>SELF-IMPORTANT</u>, arrogant, grandiose, ostentatious, pretentious, puffed up, showy 2 <u>GRANDILOQUENT</u>, boastful, bombastic, high-flown, inflated

pond *noun* <u>POOL</u>, duck pond, fish pond, millpond, small lake, tarn

ponder *verb* <u>THINK</u>, brood, cogitate, consider, contemplate, deliberate, meditate, mull over, muse, reflect, ruminate

ponderous *adjective* 1 <u>DULL</u>, heavy, long-winded, pedantic, tedious 2 <u>UNWIELDY</u>, bulky, cumbersome, heavy, huge, massive, weighty 3 <u>CLUMSY</u>, awkward, heavy-footed, lumbering

pontificate *verb* <u>EXPOUND</u>, hold forth, lay down the law, preach, pronounce, sound off

pool[1] *noun* 1 <u>POND</u>, lake, mere, puddle, tarn 2 <u>SWIMMING POOL</u>, swimming bath

pool[2] *noun* 1 <u>SYNDICATE</u>, collective, consortium, group, team, trust 2 <u>KITTY</u>, bank, funds, jackpot, pot ♦ *verb* 3 <u>COMBINE</u>, amalgamate, join forces, league, merge, put together, share

poor *adjective* 1 <u>IMPOVERISHED</u>, broke (*informal*), destitute, down and out, hard up (*informal*), impecunious, indigent, needy, on the breadline, penniless, penurious, poverty-stricken, short, skint (*Brit. slang*), stony-broke (*Brit. slang*) 2 <u>INADEQUATE</u>, deficient, incomplete, insufficient, lacking, meagre, measly, scant, scanty, skimpy 3 <u>INFERIOR</u>, below par, low-grade, mediocre, no great shakes (*informal*), not much cop (*Brit. slang*), rotten (*informal*), rubbishy, second-rate, substandard, unsatisfactory 4 <u>UNFORTUNATE</u>, hapless, ill-fated, luckless, pitiable, unlucky, wretched

poorly *adverb* 1 <u>BADLY</u>, inadequately, incompetently, inexpertly, insufficiently, unsatisfactorily, unsuccessfully ♦ *adjective* 2 *Informal* <u>ILL</u>, below par, off colour, rotten (*informal*), seedy (*informal*), sick, under the weather (*informal*), unwell

pop *verb* 1 <u>BURST</u>, bang, crack, explode, go off, snap 2 <u>PUT</u>, insert, push, shove, slip, stick, thrust, tuck ♦ *noun* 3 <u>BANG</u>, burst, crack, explosion, noise, report

pope *noun* <u>HOLY FATHER</u>, Bishop of Rome, pontiff, Vicar of Christ

populace *noun* <u>PEOPLE</u>, general public, hoi polloi, masses, mob, multitude

popular *adjective* 1 <u>WELL-LIKED</u>, accepted, approved, fashionable, favourite, in, in demand, in favour, liked, sought-after

2 COMMON, conventional, current, general, prevailing, prevalent, universal

popularity noun FAVOUR, acceptance, acclaim, approval, currency, esteem, regard, vogue

popularize verb MAKE POPULAR, disseminate, give currency to, give mass appeal, make available to all, spread, universalize

popularly adverb GENERALLY, commonly, conventionally, customarily, ordinarily, traditionally, universally, usually, widely

populate verb INHABIT, colonize, live in, occupy, settle

population noun INHABITANTS, community, denizens, folk, natives, people, residents, society

populous adjective POPULATED, crowded, heavily populated, overpopulated, packed, swarming, teeming

pore[1] verb **pore over** STUDY, examine, peruse, ponder, read, scrutinize

pore[2] noun OPENING, hole, orifice, outlet

pornographic adjective OBSCENE, blue, dirty, filthy, indecent, lewd, salacious, smutty

pornography noun OBSCENITY, dirt, filth, indecency, porn (informal), smut

porous adjective PERMEABLE, absorbent, absorptive, penetrable, spongy

port noun HARBOUR, anchorage, haven, seaport

portable adjective LIGHT, compact, convenient, easily carried, handy, manageable, movable

portend verb FORETELL, augur, betoken, bode, foreshadow, herald, indicate, predict, prognosticate, promise, warn of

portent noun OMEN, augury, forewarning, indication, prognostication, sign, warning

portentous adjective **1** SIGNIFICANT, crucial, fateful, important, menacing, momentous, ominous **2** POMPOUS, ponderous, self-important, solemn

porter[1] noun BAGGAGE ATTENDANT, bearer, carrier

porter[2] noun DOORMAN, caretaker, concierge, gatekeeper, janitor

portion noun **1** PART, bit, fragment, morsel, piece, scrap, section, segment **2** SHARE, allocation, allotment, allowance, lot, measure, quantity, quota, ration **3** HELPING, piece, serving **4** DESTINY, fate, fortune, lot, luck ◆ verb **5 portion out** DIVIDE, allocate, allot, apportion, deal, distribute, dole out, share out

portly adjective STOUT, burly, corpulent, fat, fleshy, heavy, large, plump

portrait noun **1** PICTURE, image, likeness, painting, photograph, representation **2** DESCRIPTION, characterization, depiction, portrayal, profile, thumbnail sketch

portray verb **1** REPRESENT, depict, draw, figure, illustrate, paint, picture, sketch **2** DESCRIBE, characterize, depict, put in words **3** PLAY, act the part of, represent

portrayal noun REPRESENTATION, characterization, depiction, interpretation, performance, picture

pose verb **1** POSITION, model, sit **2** PUT ON AIRS, posture, show off (informal) **3 pose as** IMPERSONATE, masquerade as, pass oneself off as, pretend to be, profess to be ◆ noun **4** POSTURE, attitude, bearing, position, stance **5** <u>ACT</u>, affectation, air, façade, front, mannerism, posturing, pretence

poser noun <u>PUZZLE</u>, enigma, problem, question, riddle

posh adjective Informal <u>UPPER-CLASS</u>, classy (slang), grand, high-class, luxurious, ritzy (slang), smart, stylish, swanky (informal), swish (informal, chiefly Brit.), up-market

posit verb <u>PUT FORWARD</u>, advance, assume, postulate, presume, propound, state

position noun **1** <u>PLACE</u>, area, bearings, locale, location, point, post, situation, spot, station, whereabouts **2** <u>POSTURE</u>, arrangement, attitude, pose, stance **3** <u>ATTITUDE</u>, belief, opinion, outlook, point of view, slant, stance, view, viewpoint **4** <u>STATUS</u>, importance, place, prestige, rank, reputation, standing, station, stature **5** <u>JOB</u>, duty, employment, occupation, office, place, post, role, situation ♦ verb **6** <u>PLACE</u>, arrange, lay out, locate, put, set, stand

positive adjective **1** <u>CERTAIN</u>, assured, confident, convinced, sure **2** <u>DEFINITE</u>, absolute, categorical, certain, clear, conclusive, decisive, explicit, express, firm, real **3** <u>HELPFUL</u>, beneficial, constructive, practical, productive, progressive, useful **4** Informal <u>ABSOLUTE</u>, complete, consummate, downright, out-and-out, perfect, thorough, utter

positively adverb <u>DEFINITELY</u>, absolutely, assuredly, categorically, certainly, emphatically, firmly, surely, unequivocally, unquestionably

possess verb **1** <u>HAVE</u>, enjoy, hold, own **2** <u>CONTROL</u>, acquire, dominate, hold, occupy, seize,

take over

possessed adjective <u>CRAZED</u>, berserk, demented, frenzied, obsessed, raving

possession noun **1** <u>OWNERSHIP</u>, control, custody, hold, occupation, tenure, title **2 possessions** <u>PROPERTY</u>, assets, belongings, chattels, effects, estate, things

possessive adjective <u>JEALOUS</u>, controlling, covetous, dominating, domineering, overprotective, selfish

possibility noun **1** <u>FEASIBILITY</u>, likelihood, potentiality, practicability, workableness **2** <u>LIKELIHOOD</u>, chance, hope, liability, odds, probability, prospect, risk **3** often plural <u>POTENTIAL</u>, capabilities, potentiality, promise, prospects, talent

possible adjective **1** <u>CONCEIVABLE</u>, credible, hypothetical, imaginable, likely, potential **2** <u>LIKELY</u>, hopeful, potential, probable, promising **3** <u>FEASIBLE</u>, attainable, doable, practicable, realizable, viable, workable

possibly adverb <u>PERHAPS</u>, maybe, perchance (archaic)

post[1] noun **1** <u>MAIL</u>, collection, delivery, postal service ♦ verb **2** <u>SEND</u>, dispatch, mail, transmit **3 keep someone posted** <u>NOTIFY</u>, advise, brief, fill in on (informal), inform, report to

post[2] noun **1** <u>SUPPORT</u>, column, picket, pillar, pole, shaft, stake, upright ♦ verb **2** <u>PUT UP</u>, affix, display, pin up

post[3] noun **1** <u>JOB</u>, appointment, assignment, employment, office, place, position, situation **2** <u>STATION</u>, beat, place, position ♦ verb **3** <u>STATION</u>, assign, place, position, put, situate

poster noun NOTICE, advertisement, announcement, bill, placard, public notice, sticker

posterity noun 1 FUTURE, succeeding generations 2 DESCENDANTS, children, family, heirs, issue, offspring, progeny

postpone verb PUT OFF, adjourn, defer, delay, put back, put on the back burner (informal), shelve, suspend

postponement noun DELAY, adjournment, deferment, deferral, stay, suspension

postscript noun P.S., addition, afterthought, supplement

postulate verb PRESUPPOSE, assume, hypothesize, posit, propose, suppose, take for granted, theorize

posture noun 1 BEARING, attitude, carriage, disposition, set, stance ♦ verb 2 SHOW OFF (informal), affect, pose, put on airs

pot noun CONTAINER, bowl, pan, vessel

potency noun POWER, effectiveness, force, influence, might, strength

potent adjective 1 POWERFUL, authoritative, commanding, dominant, dynamic, influential 2 STRONG, forceful, mighty, powerful, vigorous

potential adjective 1 POSSIBLE, dormant, future, hidden, inherent, latent, likely, promising ♦ noun 2 ABILITY, aptitude, capability, capacity, possibility, potentiality, power, wherewithal

potion noun CONCOCTION, brew, dose, draught, elixir, mixture, philtre

potter verb MESS ABOUT, dabble, footle (informal), tinker

pottery noun CERAMICS, earthenware, stoneware, terracotta

pouch noun BAG, container, pocket, purse, sack

pounce verb 1 SPRING, attack, fall upon, jump, leap at, strike, swoop ♦ noun 2 SPRING, assault, attack, bound, jump, leap, swoop

pound[1] verb 1 BEAT, batter, belabour, clobber (slang), hammer, pummel, strike, thrash, thump 2 CRUSH, powder, pulverize 3 PULSATE, beat, palpitate, pulse, throb 4 STOMP (informal), march, thunder, tramp

pound[2] noun ENCLOSURE, compound, pen, yard

pour verb 1 FLOW, course, emit, gush, run, rush, spew, spout, stream 2 LET FLOW, decant, spill, splash 3 RAIN, bucket down (informal), pelt (down), teem 4 STREAM, crowd, swarm, teem, throng

pout verb 1 SULK, glower, look petulant, pull a long face ♦ noun 2 SULLEN LOOK, glower, long face

poverty noun 1 PENNILESSNESS, beggary, destitution, hardship, indigence, insolvency, need, penury, privation, want 2 SCARCITY, dearth, deficiency, insufficiency, lack, paucity, shortage

poverty-stricken adjective PENNILESS, broke (informal), destitute, down and out, flat broke (informal), impecunious, impoverished, indigent, poor

powder noun 1 DUST, fine grains, loose particles, talc ♦ verb 2 DUST, cover, dredge, scatter, sprinkle, strew

powdery adjective FINE, crumbly, dry, dusty, grainy, granular

power noun 1 ABILITY, capability, capacity, competence, competency, faculty, potential 2 CONTROL, ascendancy, authority, command, dominance, domination, dominion, influence, mastery, rule **3** AUTHORITY, authorization, licence, prerogative, privilege, right, warrant **4** STRENGTH, brawn, energy, force, forcefulness, intensity, might, muscle, potency, vigour

powerful *adjective* **1** CONTROLLING, authoritative, commanding, dominant, influential, prevailing **2** STRONG, energetic, mighty, potent, strapping, sturdy, vigorous **3** PERSUASIVE, cogent, compelling, convincing, effectual, forceful, impressive, striking, telling, weighty

powerless *adjective* **1** DEFENCELESS, dependent, ineffective, subject, tied, unarmed, vulnerable **2** HELPLESS, debilitated, disabled, feeble, frail, impotent, incapable, incapacitated, ineffectual, weak

practicability *noun* FEASIBILITY, advantage, possibility, practicality, use, usefulness, viability

practicable *adjective* FEASIBLE, achievable, attainable, doable, possible, viable

practical *adjective* **1** FUNCTIONAL, applied, empirical, experimental, factual, pragmatic, realistic, utilitarian **2** SENSIBLE, businesslike, down-to-earth, hard-headed, matter-of-fact, ordinary, realistic **3** FEASIBLE, doable, practicable, serviceable, useful, workable **4** SKILLED, accomplished, efficient, experienced, proficient

practically *adverb* **1** ALMOST, all but, basically, essentially, fundamentally, in effect, just about, nearly, very nearly, virtually, well-nigh **2** SENSIBLY, clearly, matter-of-factly, rationally, realistically, reasonably

practice *noun* **1** CUSTOM, habit, method, mode, routine, rule,

system, tradition, usage, way, wont **2** REHEARSAL, drill, exercise, preparation, repetition, study, training **3** PROFESSION, business, career, vocation, work **4** USE, action, application, exercise, experience, operation

practise *verb* **1** REHEARSE, drill, exercise, go over, go through, prepare, repeat, study, train **2** DO, apply, carry out, follow, observe, perform **3** WORK AT, carry on, engage in, pursue

practised *adjective* SKILLED, able, accomplished, experienced, expert, proficient, seasoned, trained

pragmatic *adjective* PRACTICAL, businesslike, down-to-earth, hard-headed, realistic, sensible, utilitarian

praise *verb* **1** APPROVE, acclaim, admire, applaud, cheer, compliment, congratulate, eulogize, extol, honour, laud **2** GIVE THANKS TO, adore, bless, exalt, glorify, worship ♦ *noun* **3** APPROVAL, acclaim, acclamation, approbation, commendation, compliment, congratulation, eulogy, plaudit, tribute **4** THANKS, adoration, glory, homage, worship

praiseworthy *adjective* CREDITABLE, admirable, commendable, laudable, meritorious, worthy

prance *verb* **1** DANCE, caper, cavort, frisk, gambol, romp, skip **2** STRUT, parade, show off (*informal*), stalk, swagger, swank (*informal*)

prank *noun* TRICK, escapade, jape, lark (*informal*), practical joke

prattle *verb* CHATTER, babble, blather, blether, gabble, jabber, rabbit (on) (*Brit. informal*), waffle (*informal, chiefly Brit.*), witter (*informal*)

pray *verb* **1** SAY ONE'S PRAYERS, offer a

prayer, recite the rosary 2 BEG, adjure, ask, beseech, entreat, implore, petition, plead, request, solicit

prayer noun 1 ORISON, devotion, invocation, litany, supplication 2 PLEA, appeal, entreaty, petition, request, supplication

preach verb 1 DELIVER A SERMON, address, evangelize 2 LECTURE, advocate, exhort, moralize, sermonize

preacher noun CLERGYMAN, evangelist, minister, missionary, parson

preamble noun INTRODUCTION, foreword, opening statement or remarks, preface, prelude

precarious adjective DANGEROUS, dodgy (Brit., Austral., & N.Z. informal), hazardous, insecure, perilous, risky, shaky, tricky, unreliable, unsafe, unsure

precaution noun 1 SAFEGUARD, insurance, protection, provision, safety measure 2 FORETHOUGHT, care, caution, providence, prudence, wariness

precede verb GO BEFORE, antedate, come first, head, introduce, lead, preface

precedence noun PRIORITY, antecedence, pre-eminence, primacy, rank, seniority, superiority, supremacy

precedent noun INSTANCE, antecedent, example, model, paradigm, pattern, prototype, standard

preceding adjective PREVIOUS, above, aforementioned, aforesaid, earlier, foregoing, former, past, prior

precept noun RULE, canon, command, commandment, decree, instruction, law, order, principle, regulation, statute

precinct noun 1 ENCLOSURE, confine, limit 2 AREA, district, quarter, section, sector, zone

precious adjective 1 VALUABLE, costly, dear, expensive, fine, invaluable, priceless, prized 2 LOVED, adored, beloved, cherished, darling, dear, prized, treasured 3 AFFECTED, artificial, overnice, overrefined, twee (Brit. informal)

precipice noun CLIFF, bluff, crag, height, rock face

precipitate verb 1 QUICKEN, accelerate, advance, bring on, expedite, hasten, hurry, speed up, trigger 2 THROW, cast, fling, hurl, launch, let fly ♦ adjective 3 HASTY, heedless, impetuous, impulsive, precipitous, rash, reckless 4 SWIFT, breakneck, headlong, rapid, rushing 5 SUDDEN, abrupt, brief, quick, unexpected, without warning

precipitous adjective 1 SHEER, abrupt, dizzy, high, perpendicular, steep 2 HASTY, heedless, hurried, precipitate, rash, reckless

précis noun 1 SUMMARY, abridgment, outline, résumé, synopsis ♦ verb 2 SUMMARIZE, abridge, outline, shorten, sum up

precise adjective 1 EXACT, absolute, accurate, correct, definite, explicit, express, particular, specific, strict 2 STRICT, careful, exact, fastidious, finicky, formal, meticulous, particular, punctilious, rigid, scrupulous, stiff

precisely adverb EXACTLY, absolutely, accurately, correctly, just so, plumb (informal), smack (informal), square, squarely, strictly

precision noun EXACTNESS, accuracy, care, meticulousness, particularity, preciseness

preclude *verb* PREVENT, check, debar, exclude, forestall, inhibit, obviate, prohibit, rule out, stop

precocious *adjective* ADVANCED, ahead, bright, developed, forward, quick, smart

preconceived *adjective* PRESUMED, forejudged, prejudged, presupposed

preconception *noun* PRECONCEIVED IDEA *or* NOTION, bias, notion, predisposition, prejudice, presupposition

precursor *noun* **1** HERALD, forerunner, harbinger, vanguard **2** FORERUNNER, antecedent, forebear, predecessor

predatory *adjective* HUNTING, carnivorous, predacious, raptorial

predecessor *noun* **1** PREVIOUS JOB HOLDER, antecedent, forerunner, precursor **2** ANCESTOR, antecedent, forebear, forefather

predestination *noun* FATE, destiny, foreordainment, foreordination, predetermination

predestined *adjective* FATED, doomed, meant, preordained

predetermined *adjective* PREARRANGED, agreed, fixed, preplanned, set

predicament *noun* FIX (*informal*), dilemma, hole (*slang*), jam (*informal*), mess, pinch, plight, quandary, scrape (*informal*), situation, spot (*informal*)

predict *verb* FORETELL, augur, divine, forecast, portend, prophesy

predictable *adjective* LIKELY, anticipated, certain, expected, foreseeable, reliable, sure

prediction *noun* PROPHECY, augury, divination, forecast, prognosis, prognostication

predilection *noun* LIKING, bias, fondness, inclination, leaning, love, partiality, penchant, preference, propensity, taste, weakness

predispose *verb* INCLINE, affect, bias, dispose, influence, lead, prejudice, prompt

predisposed *adjective* INCLINED, given, liable, minded, ready, subject, susceptible, willing

predominant *adjective* MAIN, ascendant, chief, dominant, leading, paramount, prevailing, prevalent, prime, principal

predominantly *adverb* MAINLY, chiefly, for the most part, generally, largely, mostly, primarily, principally

predominate *verb* PREVAIL, be most noticeable, carry weight, hold sway, outweigh, overrule, overshadow

pre-eminence *noun* SUPERIORITY, distinction, excellence, predominance, prestige, prominence, renown, supremacy

pre-eminent *adjective* OUTSTANDING, chief, distinguished, excellent, foremost, incomparable, matchless, predominant, renowned, superior, supreme

pre-empt *verb* ANTICIPATE, appropriate, assume, usurp

preen *verb* **1** *Of birds* CLEAN, plume **2** SMARTEN, dress up, spruce up, titivate **3 preen oneself (on)** PRIDE ONESELF, congratulate oneself

preface *noun* **1** INTRODUCTION, foreword, preamble, preliminary, prelude, prologue ♦ *verb* **2** INTRODUCE, begin, open, prefix

prefer *verb* LIKE BETTER, be partial to, choose, desire, fancy, favour, go for, incline towards, opt for, pick

preferable *adjective* BETTER, best, chosen, favoured, more desirable, superior

preferably adverb RATHER, by choice, first, in or for preference, sooner

preference noun 1 FIRST CHOICE, choice, desire, favourite, option, partiality, pick, predilection, selection 2 PRIORITY, favoured treatment, favouritism, first place, precedence

preferential adjective PRIVILEGED, advantageous, better, favoured, special

preferment noun PROMOTION, advancement, elevation, exaltation, rise, upgrading

pregnant adjective 1 EXPECTANT, big or heavy with child, expecting (informal), in the club (Brit. slang), with child 2 MEANINGFUL, charged, eloquent, expressive, loaded, pointed, significant, telling, weighty

prehistoric adjective EARLIEST, early, primeval, primitive, primordial

prejudge verb JUMP TO CONCLUSIONS, anticipate, presume, presuppose

prejudice noun 1 BIAS, partiality, preconceived notion, preconception, prejudgment 2 DISCRIMINATION, bigotry, chauvinism, injustice, intolerance, narrow-mindedness, unfairness ♦ verb 3 BIAS, colour, distort, influence, poison, predispose, slant 4 HARM, damage, hinder, hurt, impair, injure, mar, spoil, undermine

prejudiced adjective BIASED, bigoted, influenced, intolerant, narrow-minded, one-sided, opinionated, unfair

prejudicial adjective HARMFUL, damaging, deleterious, detrimental, disadvantageous, hurtful, injurious, unfavourable

preliminary adjective 1 FIRST, initial, introductory, opening, pilot, prefatory, preparatory, prior, test, trial ♦ noun 2 INTRODUCTION, beginning, opening, overture, preamble, preface, prelude, start

prelude noun INTRODUCTION, beginning, foreword, overture, preamble, preface, prologue, start

premature adjective 1 EARLY, forward, unseasonable, untimely 2 HASTY, ill-timed, overhasty, previous (informal), rash, too soon, untimely

premeditated adjective PLANNED, calculated, conscious, considered, deliberate, intentional, wilful

premeditation noun PLANNING, design, forethought, intention, plotting, prearrangement, predetermination, purpose

premier noun 1 HEAD OF GOVERNMENT, chancellor, chief minister, P.M., prime minister ♦ adjective 2 CHIEF, first, foremost, head, highest, leading, main, primary, prime, principal

premiere noun FIRST NIGHT, debut, opening

premise noun ASSUMPTION, argument, assertion, hypothesis, postulation, presupposition, proposition, supposition

premises plural noun BUILDING, establishment, place, property, site

premium noun 1 BONUS, bounty, fee, perk (Brit. informal), perquisite, prize, reward 2 **at a premium** IN GREAT DEMAND, hard to come by, in short supply, rare, scarce

premonition noun FEELING, foreboding, hunch, idea, intuition, presentiment, suspicion

preoccupation noun 1 OBSESSION, bee in one's bonnet, fixation 2 ABSORPTION, absent-mindedness, abstraction, daydreaming, engrossment, immersion, reverie, woolgathering

preoccupied *adjective* ABSORBED, absent-minded, distracted, engrossed, immersed, lost in, oblivious, rapt, wrapped up

preparation *noun* 1 GROUNDWORK, getting ready, preparing 2 often plural ARRANGEMENT, measure, plan, provision 3 MIXTURE, compound, concoction, medicine

preparatory *adjective* INTRODUCTORY, opening, prefatory, preliminary, primary

prepare *verb* MAKE *or* GET READY, adapt, adjust, arrange, practise, prime, train, warm up

prepared *adjective* 1 READY, arranged, in order, in readiness, primed, set 2 WILLING, disposed, inclined

preponderance *noun* PREDOMINANCE, dominance, domination, extensiveness, greater numbers, greater part, lion's share, mass, prevalence, supremacy

prepossessing *adjective* ATTRACTIVE, appealing, charming, engaging, fetching, good-looking, handsome, likable *or* likeable, pleasing

preposterous *adjective* RIDICULOUS, absurd, crazy, incredible, insane, laughable, ludicrous, nonsensical, out of the question, outrageous, unthinkable

prerequisite *noun* 1 REQUIREMENT, condition, essential, must, necessity, precondition, qualification, requisite, *sine qua non* ◆ *adjective* 2 REQUIRED, essential, indispensable, mandatory, necessary, obligatory, requisite, vital

prerogative *noun* RIGHT, advantage, due, exemption,

immunity, liberty, privilege

presage *verb* PORTEND, augur, betoken, bode, foreshadow, foretoken, signify

prescience *noun* FORESIGHT, clairvoyance, foreknowledge, precognition, second sight

prescribe *verb* ORDER, decree, dictate, direct, lay down, ordain, recommend, rule, set, specify, stipulate

prescription *noun* 1 INSTRUCTION, direction, formula, recipe 2 MEDICINE, drug, mixture, preparation, remedy

presence *noun* 1 BEING, attendance, existence, inhabitance, occupancy, residence 2 PERSONALITY, air, appearance, aspect, aura, bearing, carriage, demeanour, poise, self-assurance

presence of mind *noun* LEVEL-HEADEDNESS, calmness, composure, cool (*slang*), coolness, self-possession, wits

present[1] *adjective* 1 HERE, at hand, near, nearby, ready, there 2 CURRENT, contemporary, existent, existing, immediate, present-day ◆ *noun* 3 **the present** NOW, here and now, the present moment, the time being, today 4 **at present** JUST NOW, at the moment, now, right now 5 **for the present** FOR NOW, for the moment, for the time being, in the meantime, temporarily

present[2] *noun* 1 GIFT, boon, donation, endowment, grant, gratuity, hand-out, offering, prezzie (*informal*) ◆ *verb* 2 INTRODUCE, acquaint with, make known 3 PUT ON, display, exhibit, give, show, stage 4 GIVE, award, bestow, confer, grant, hand out, hand over

presentable *adjective* DECENT,

acceptable, becoming, fit to be seen, O.K. *or* okay (*informal*), passable, respectable, satisfactory, suitable

presentation *noun* 1 GIVING, award, bestowal, conferral, donation, offering 2 PRODUCTION, demonstration, display, exhibition, performance, show

presently *adverb* SOON, anon (*archaic*), before long, by and by, shortly

preservation *noun* PROTECTION, conservation, maintenance, safeguarding, safekeeping, safety, salvation, support

preserve *verb* 1 SAVE, care for, conserve, defend, keep, protect, safeguard, shelter, shield 2 MAINTAIN, continue, keep, keep up, perpetuate, sustain, uphold ◆ *noun* 3 AREA, domain, field, realm, sphere

preside *verb* RUN, administer, chair, conduct, control, direct, govern, head, lead, manage, officiate

press *verb* 1 FORCE DOWN, compress, crush, depress, jam, mash, push, squeeze 2 HUG, clasp, crush, embrace, fold in one's arms, hold close, squeeze 3 SMOOTH, flatten, iron 4 URGE, beg, entreat, exhort, implore, petition, plead, pressurize 5 CROWD, flock, gather, herd, push, seethe, surge, swarm, throng ◆ *noun* 6 **the press: a** NEWSPAPERS, Fleet Street, fourth estate, news media, the papers **b** JOURNALISTS, columnists, correspondents, newsmen, pressmen, reporters

pressing *adjective* URGENT, crucial, high-priority, imperative, important, importunate, serious, vital

pressure *noun* 1 FORCE, compressing, compression, crushing, squeezing, weight 2 POWER, coercion, compulsion, constraint, force, influence, sway 3 STRESS, burden, demands, hassle (*informal*), heat, load, strain, urgency

prestige *noun* STATUS, credit, distinction, eminence, fame, honour, importance, kudos, renown, reputation, standing

prestigious *adjective* CELEBRATED, eminent, esteemed, great, illustrious, important, notable, prominent, renowned, respected

presumably *adverb* IT WOULD SEEM, apparently, in all likelihood, in all probability, on the face of it, probably, seemingly

presume *verb* 1 BELIEVE, assume, conjecture, guess (*informal, chiefly U.S. & Canad.*), infer, postulate, suppose, surmise, take for granted, think 2 DARE, go so far, make so bold, take the liberty, venture

presumption *noun* 1 CHEEK (*informal*), audacity, boldness, effrontery, gall (*informal*), impudence, insolence, nerve (*informal*) 2 PROBABILITY, basis, chance, likelihood

presumptuous *adjective* PUSHY (*informal*), audacious, bold, forward, insolent, overconfident, too big for one's boots, uppish (*Brit. informal*)

presuppose *verb* PRESUME, assume, imply, posit, postulate, take as read, take for granted

presupposition *noun* ASSUMPTION, belief, preconception, premise, presumption, supposition

pretence *noun* 1 DECEPTION, acting, charade, deceit, falsehood, feigning, sham, simulation, trickery 2 SHOW, affectation, artifice, display, façade, veneer

pretend *verb* 1 FEIGN, affect, allege,

assume, fake, falsify, impersonate, profess, sham, simulate **2** MAKE BELIEVE, act, imagine, make up, suppose

pretended *adjective* FEIGNED, bogus, counterfeit, fake, false, phoney *or* phony (*informal*), pretend (*informal*), pseudo (*informal*), sham, so-called

pretender *noun* CLAIMANT, aspirant

pretension *noun* **1** CLAIM, aspiration, assumption, demand, pretence, profession **2** AFFECTATION, airs, conceit, ostentation, pretentiousness, self-importance, show, snobbery, vanity

pretentious *adjective* AFFECTED, conceited, grandiloquent, grandiose, high-flown, inflated, mannered, ostentatious, pompous, puffed up, showy, snobbish

pretext *noun* GUISE, cloak, cover, excuse, ploy, pretence, ruse, show

pretty *adjective* **1** ATTRACTIVE, beautiful, bonny, charming, comely, fair, good-looking, lovely ♦ *adverb* **2** *Informal* FAIRLY, kind of (*informal*), moderately, quite, rather, reasonably, somewhat

prevail *verb* **1** WIN, be victorious, overcome, overrule, succeed, triumph **2** BE WIDESPREAD, abound, be current, be prevalent, exist generally, predominate

prevailing *adjective* **1** WIDESPREAD, common, current, customary, established, fashionable, general, in vogue, ordinary, popular, prevalent, usual **2** PREDOMINATING, dominant, main, principal, ruling

prevalence *noun* COMMONNESS, currency, frequency, popularity, universality

prevalent *adjective* COMMON, current, customary, established, frequent, general, popular,

universal, usual, widespread

prevaricate *verb* EVADE, beat about the bush, cavil, deceive, dodge, equivocate, flannel (*Brit. informal*), hedge

prevent *verb* STOP, avert, avoid, foil, forestall, frustrate, hamper, hinder, impede, inhibit, obstruct, obviate, preclude, thwart

prevention *noun* ELIMINATION, avoidance, deterrence, precaution, safeguard, thwarting

preventive, preventative *adjective* **1** HINDERING, hampering, impeding, obstructive **2** PROTECTIVE, counteractive, deterrent, precautionary ♦ *noun* **3** HINDRANCE, block, impediment, obstacle, obstruction **4** PROTECTION, deterrent, prevention, remedy, safeguard, shield

preview *noun* ADVANCE SHOWING, foretaste, sneak preview, taster, trailer

previous *adjective* EARLIER, erstwhile, foregoing, former, past, preceding, prior

previously *adverb* BEFORE, beforehand, earlier, formerly, hitherto, in the past, once

prey *noun* **1** QUARRY, game, kill **2** VICTIM, dupe, fall guy (*informal*), mug (*Brit. slang*), target

price *noun* **1** COST, amount, charge, damage (*informal*), estimate, expense, fee, figure, rate, value, worth **2** CONSEQUENCES, cost, penalty, toll ♦ *verb* **3** EVALUATE, assess, cost, estimate, rate, value

priceless *adjective* **1** VALUABLE, costly, dear, expensive, invaluable, precious **2** *Informal* HILARIOUS, amusing, comic, droll, funny, rib-tickling, side-splitting

pricey, pricy *adjective* EXPENSIVE, costly, dear, high-priced, steep (*informal*)

prick verb 1 <u>PIERCE</u>, jab, lance, perforate, punch, puncture, stab 2 <u>STING</u>, bite, itch, prickle, smart, tingle ♦ noun 3 <u>PUNCTURE</u>, hole, perforation, pinhole, wound

prickle noun 1 <u>SPIKE</u>, barb, needle, point, spine, spur, thorn ♦ verb 2 <u>TINGLE</u>, itch, smart, sting 3 <u>PRICK</u>, jab, stick

prickly adjective 1 <u>SPINY</u>, barbed, bristly, thorny 2 <u>ITCHY</u>, crawling, scratchy, sharp, smarting, stinging, tingling

pride noun 1 <u>SATISFACTION</u>, delight, gratification, joy, pleasure 2 <u>SELF-RESPECT</u>, dignity, honour, self-esteem, self-worth 3 <u>CONCEIT</u>, arrogance, egotism, hubris, pretension, pretentiousness, self-importance, self-love, superciliousness, vanity 4 <u>GEM</u>, jewel, pride and joy, treasure

priest noun <u>CLERGYMAN</u>, cleric, curate, divine, ecclesiastic, father, minister, pastor, vicar

prig noun <u>GOODY-GOODY</u> (informal), prude, puritan, stuffed shirt (informal)

priggish adjective <u>SELF-RIGHTEOUS</u>, goody-goody (informal), holier-than-thou, prim, prudish, puritanical

prim adjective <u>PRUDISH</u>, demure, fastidious, fussy, priggish, prissy (informal), proper, puritanical, strait-laced

prima donna noun <u>DIVA</u>, leading lady, star

primarily adverb 1 <u>CHIEFLY</u>, above all, essentially, fundamentally, generally, largely, mainly, mostly, principally 2 <u>AT FIRST</u>, at or from the start, first and foremost, initially, in the beginning, in the first place, originally

primary adjective 1 <u>CHIEF</u>, cardinal, first, greatest, highest, main, paramount, prime, principal 2 <u>ELEMENTARY</u>, introductory, rudimentary, simple

prime adjective 1 <u>MAIN</u>, chief, leading, predominant, pre-eminent, primary, principal 2 <u>BEST</u>, choice, excellent, first-class, first-rate, highest, quality, select, top ♦ noun 3 <u>PEAK</u>, bloom, flower, height, heyday, zenith ♦ verb 4 <u>INFORM</u>, brief, clue in (informal), fill in (informal), notify, tell 5 <u>PREPARE</u>, coach, get ready, make ready, train

primeval adjective <u>EARLIEST</u>, ancient, early, first, old, prehistoric, primal, primitive, primordial

primitive adjective 1 <u>EARLY</u>, earliest, elementary, first, original, primary, primeval, primordial 2 <u>CRUDE</u>, rough, rudimentary, simple, unrefined

prince noun <u>RULER</u>, lord, monarch, sovereign

princely adjective 1 <u>REGAL</u>, imperial, majestic, noble, royal, sovereign 2 <u>GENEROUS</u>, bounteous, gracious, lavish, liberal, munificent, open-handed, rich

principal adjective 1 <u>MAIN</u>, cardinal, chief, essential, first, foremost, key, leading, paramount, pre-eminent, primary, prime ♦ noun 2 <u>HEAD</u> (informal), dean, headmaster or headmistress, head teacher, master or mistress, rector 3 <u>STAR</u>, lead, leader 4 <u>CAPITAL</u>, assets, money

principally adverb <u>MAINLY</u>, above all, chiefly, especially, largely, mostly, predominantly, primarily

principle noun 1 <u>RULE</u>, canon, criterion, doctrine, dogma, fundamental, law, maxim, precept, standard, truth 2 <u>MORALS</u>, conscience, integrity, probity, scruples, sense of honour 3 **in principle** <u>IN THEORY</u>, ideally, theoretically

print verb 1 PUBLISH, engrave, impress, imprint, issue, mark, stamp ♦ noun 2 PUBLICATION, book, magazine, newspaper, newsprint, periodical, printed matter 3 REPRODUCTION, copy, engraving, photo (informal), photograph, picture

prior adjective 1 EARLIER, foregoing, former, preceding, pre-existent, pre-existing, previous 2 **prior to** BEFORE, earlier than, preceding, previous to

priority noun PRECEDENCE, pre-eminence, preference, rank, right of way, seniority

priory noun MONASTERY, abbey, convent, nunnery, religious house

prison noun JAIL, clink (slang), confinement, cooler (slang), dungeon, jug (slang), lockup, nick (Brit. slang), penitentiary (U.S.), slammer (slang)

prisoner noun 1 CONVICT, con (slang), jailbird, lag (slang) 2 CAPTIVE, detainee, hostage, internee

prissy adjective PRIM, old-maidish (informal), prim and proper, prudish, strait-laced

pristine adjective NEW, immaculate, pure, uncorrupted, undefiled, unspoiled, unsullied, untouched, virginal

privacy noun SECLUSION, isolation, retirement, retreat, solitude

private adjective 1 EXCLUSIVE, individual, intimate, own, personal, reserved, special 2 SECRET, clandestine, confidential, covert, hush-hush (informal), off the record, unofficial 3 SECLUDED, isolated, secret, separate, sequestered, solitary

privilege noun RIGHT, advantage, claim, concession, due, entitlement, freedom, liberty, prerogative

privileged adjective SPECIAL, advantaged, elite, entitled, favoured, honoured

privy adjective 1 **privy to** INFORMED OF, apprised of, aware of, cognizant of, in on, in the know about (informal), wise to (slang) ♦ noun 2 LAVATORY, latrine, outside toilet

prize[1] noun 1 REWARD, accolade, award, honour, trophy 2 WINNINGS, haul, jackpot, purse, stakes ♦ adjective 3 CHAMPION, award-winning, best, first-rate, outstanding, top, winning

prize[2] verb VALUE, cherish, esteem, hold dear, treasure

probability noun LIKELIHOOD, chance(s), expectation, liability, likeliness, odds, prospect

probable adjective LIKELY, apparent, credible, feasible, plausible, possible, presumable, reasonable

probably adverb LIKELY, doubtless, maybe, most likely, perchance (archaic), perhaps, possibly, presumably

probation noun TRIAL PERIOD, apprenticeship, trial

probe verb 1 EXAMINE, explore, go into, investigate, look into, scrutinize, search 2 EXPLORE, feel around, poke, prod ♦ noun 3 EXAMINATION, detection, exploration, inquiry, investigation, scrutiny, study

problem noun 1 DIFFICULTY, complication, dilemma, dispute, predicament, quandary, trouble 2 PUZZLE, conundrum, enigma, poser, question, riddle

problematic adjective TRICKY, debatable, doubtful, dubious, problematical, puzzling

procedure noun METHOD, action, conduct, course, custom, modus operandi, policy, practice, process, routine, strategy, system

proceed verb 1 GO ON, carry on, continue, go ahead, move on, press on, progress 2 ARISE, come, derive, emanate, flow, issue, originate, result, spring, stem

proceeding noun 1 ACTION, act, deed, measure, move, procedure, process, step 2 **proceedings** BUSINESS, account, affairs, archives, doings, minutes, records, report, transactions

proceeds plural noun INCOME, earnings, gain, products, profit, returns, revenue, takings, yield

process noun 1 PROCEDURE, action, course, manner, means, measure, method, operation, performance, practice, system 2 DEVELOPMENT, advance, evolution, growth, movement, progress, progression ♦ verb 3 HANDLE, deal with, fulfil

procession noun PARADE, cavalcade, cortege, file, march, train

proclaim verb DECLARE, advertise, announce, circulate, herald, indicate, make known, profess, publish

proclamation noun DECLARATION, announcement, decree, edict, notice, notification, pronouncement, publication

procrastinate verb DELAY, dally, drag one's feet (informal), gain time, play for time, postpone, put off, stall, temporize

procure verb OBTAIN, acquire, buy, come by, find, gain, get, pick up, purchase, score (slang), secure, win

prod verb 1 POKE, dig, drive, jab, nudge, push, shove 2 PROMPT, egg on, goad, impel, incite, motivate, move, rouse, spur, stimulate, urge

♦ noun 3 POKE, dig, jab, nudge, push, shove 4 PROMPT, cue, reminder, signal, stimulus

prodigal adjective EXTRAVAGANT, excessive, immoderate, improvident, profligate, reckless, spendthrift, wasteful

prodigious adjective 1 HUGE, colossal, enormous, giant, gigantic, immense, massive, monstrous, vast 2 WONDERFUL, amazing, exceptional, extraordinary, fabulous, fantastic (informal), marvellous, phenomenal, remarkable, staggering

prodigy noun 1 GENIUS, mastermind, talent, whizz (informal), wizard 2 WONDER, marvel, miracle, phenomenon, sensation

produce verb 1 CAUSE, bring about, effect, generate, give rise to 2 BRING FORTH, bear, beget, breed, deliver 3 SHOW, advance, demonstrate, exhibit, offer, present 4 MAKE, compose, construct, create, develop, fabricate, invent, manufacture 5 PRESENT, direct, do, exhibit, mount, put on, show, stage ♦ noun 6 FRUIT AND VEGETABLES, crop, greengrocery, harvest, product, yield

producer noun 1 DIRECTOR, impresario 2 MAKER, farmer, grower, manufacturer

product noun 1 GOODS, artefact, commodity, creation, invention, merchandise, produce, work 2 RESULT, consequence, effect, outcome, upshot

production noun 1 PRODUCING, construction, creation, fabrication, formation, making, manufacture, manufacturing 2 PRESENTATION, direction, management, staging

productive adjective 1 FERTILE,

creative, fecund, fruitful,
inventive, plentiful, prolific, rich
2 USEFUL, advantageous, beneficial,
constructive, effective, profitable,
rewarding, valuable, worthwhile

productivity noun OUTPUT,
production, work rate, yield

profane adjective 1 SACRILEGIOUS,
disrespectful, godless, impious,
impure, irreligious, irreverent,
sinful, ungodly, wicked 2 CRUDE,
blasphemous, coarse, filthy, foul,
obscene, vulgar ♦ verb 3 DESECRATE,
commit sacrilege, debase, defile,
violate

profanity noun 1 SACRILEGE,
blasphemy, impiety, profaneness
2 SWEARING, curse, cursing,
irreverence, obscenity

profess verb 1 CLAIM, allege, fake,
feign, make out, pretend, purport
2 STATE, admit, affirm, announce,
assert, avow, confess, declare,
proclaim, vouch

professed adjective 1 SUPPOSED,
alleged, ostensible, pretended,
purported, self-styled, so-called,
would-be 2 DECLARED, avowed,
confessed, confirmed, proclaimed,
self-acknowledged, self-confessed

profession noun 1 OCCUPATION,
business, calling, career,
employment, office, position,
sphere, vocation 2 DECLARATION,
affirmation, assertion, avowal,
claim, confession, statement

professional adjective 1 EXPERT,
adept, competent, efficient,
experienced, masterly, proficient,
qualified, skilled ♦ noun 2 EXPERT,
adept, maestro, master, past
master, pro (informal), specialist,
virtuoso

professor noun DON (Brit.), fellow
(Brit.), prof (informal)

proficiency noun SKILL, ability,
aptitude, competence, dexterity,

expertise, knack, know-how
(informal), mastery

proficient adjective SKILLED, able,
accomplished, adept, capable,
competent, efficient, expert,
gifted, masterly, skilful

profile noun 1 OUTLINE, contour,
drawing, figure, form, side view,
silhouette, sketch 2 BIOGRAPHY,
characterization, sketch,
thumbnail sketch, vignette

profit noun 1 often plural EARNINGS,
gain, proceeds, receipts, return,
revenue, takings, yield 2 BENEFIT,
advancement, advantage, gain,
good, use, value ♦ verb 3 BENEFIT,
be of advantage to, gain, help,
improve, promote, serve 4 MAKE
MONEY, earn, gain

profitable adjective 1 MONEY-MAKING,
commercial, cost-effective, fruitful,
lucrative, paying, remunerative,
worthwhile 2 BENEFICIAL,
advantageous, fruitful, productive,
rewarding, useful, valuable,
worthwhile

profiteer noun 1 RACKETEER,
exploiter ♦ verb 2 RACKETEER,
exploit, make a quick buck (slang)

profligate adjective 1 EXTRAVAGANT,
immoderate, improvident,
prodigal, reckless, spendthrift,
wasteful 2 DEPRAVED, debauched,
degenerate, dissolute, immoral,
licentious, shameless, wanton,
wicked, wild ♦ noun 3 SPENDTHRIFT,
squanderer, waster, wastrel
4 DEGENERATE, debauchee, libertine,
rake, reprobate, roué

profound adjective 1 WISE, abstruse,
deep, learned, penetrating,
philosophical, sagacious, sage
2 INTENSE, acute, deeply felt,
extreme, great, heartfelt, keen

profuse adjective PLENTIFUL,
abundant, ample, bountiful,
copious, luxuriant, overflowing,
prolific

profusion noun ABUNDANCE, bounty, excess, extravagance, glut, plethora, quantity, surplus, wealth

progeny noun CHILDREN, descendants, family, issue, lineage, offspring, race, stock, young

prognosis noun FORECAST, diagnosis, prediction, prognostication, projection

programme noun 1 SCHEDULE, agenda, curriculum, line-up, list, listing, order of events, plan, syllabus, timetable 2 SHOW, broadcast, performance, presentation, production

progress noun 1 DEVELOPMENT, advance, breakthrough, gain, growth, headway, improvement 2 MOVEMENT, advance, course, passage, way 3 in progress GOING ON, being done, happening, occurring, proceeding, taking place, under way ♦ verb 4 DEVELOP, advance, gain, grow, improve 5 MOVE ON, advance, continue, go forward, make headway, proceed, travel

progression noun 1 PROGRESS, advance, advancement, furtherance, gain, headway, movement forward 2 SEQUENCE, chain, course, cycle, series, string, succession

progressive adjective 1 ENLIGHTENED, advanced, avant-garde, forward-looking, liberal, modern, radical, reformist, revolutionary 2 GROWING, advancing, continuing, developing, increasing, ongoing

prohibit verb 1 FORBID, ban, debar, disallow, outlaw, proscribe, veto 2 PREVENT, hamper, hinder, impede, restrict, stop

prohibition noun 1 PREVENTION, constraint, exclusion, obstruction, restriction 2 BAN, bar, boycott, embargo, injunction, interdict, proscription, veto

prohibitive adjective EXORBITANT, excessive, extortionate, steep (*informal*)

project noun 1 SCHEME, activity, assignment, enterprise, job, occupation, plan, task, undertaking, venture, work ♦ verb 2 FORECAST, calculate, estimate, extrapolate, gauge, predict, reckon 3 STICK OUT, bulge, extend, jut, overhang, protrude, stand out

projectile noun MISSILE, bullet, rocket, shell

projection noun 1 PROTRUSION, bulge, ledge, overhang, protuberance, ridge, shelf 2 FORECAST, calculation, computation, estimate, estimation, extrapolation, reckoning

proletarian adjective 1 WORKING-CLASS, common, plebeian ♦ noun 2 WORKER, commoner, man of the people, pleb, plebeian, prole (*derogatory slang, chiefly Brit.*)

proletariat noun WORKING CLASS, commoners, hoi polloi, labouring classes, lower classes, plebs, proles (*derogatory slang, chiefly Brit.*), the common people, the masses

proliferate verb INCREASE, breed, expand, grow rapidly, multiply

proliferation noun MULTIPLICATION, expansion, increase, spread

prolific adjective PRODUCTIVE, abundant, copious, fecund, fertile, fruitful, luxuriant, profuse

prologue noun INTRODUCTION, foreword, preamble, preface, prelude

prolong verb LENGTHEN, continue, delay, drag out, draw out, extend, perpetuate, protract, spin out, stretch

promenade noun 1 WALKWAY, esplanade, parade, prom 2 STROLL, constitutional, saunter, turn, walk ♦ verb 3 STROLL, perambulate, saunter, take a walk, walk

prominence noun
1 CONSPICUOUSNESS, markedness
2 FAME, celebrity, distinction, eminence, importance, name, prestige, reputation

prominent adjective 1 NOTICEABLE, conspicuous, eye-catching, obtrusive, obvious, outstanding, pronounced 2 FAMOUS, distinguished, eminent, foremost, important, leading, main, notable, renowned, top, well-known

promiscuity noun LICENTIOUSNESS, debauchery, immorality, looseness, permissiveness, promiscuousness, wantonness

promiscuous adjective LICENTIOUS, abandoned, debauched, fast, immoral, libertine, loose, wanton, wild

promise verb 1 GUARANTEE, assure, contract, give an undertaking, give one's word, pledge, swear, take an oath, undertake, vow, warrant 2 SEEM LIKELY, augur, betoken, indicate, look like, show signs of, suggest ♦ noun
3 GUARANTEE, assurance, bond, commitment, oath, pledge, undertaking, vow, word
4 POTENTIAL, ability, aptitude, capability, capacity, talent

promising adjective 1 ENCOURAGING, auspicious, bright, favourable, hopeful, likely, propitious, reassuring, rosy 2 TALENTED, able, gifted, rising

promontory noun POINT, cape, foreland, head, headland

promote verb 1 HELP, advance, aid, assist, back, boost, encourage, forward, foster, support 2 RAISE, elevate, exalt, upgrade 3 ADVERTISE, hype, plug (informal), publicize, push, sell

promotion noun 1 RISE, advancement, elevation, exaltation, honour, move up, preferment, upgrading 2 PUBLICITY, advertising, plugging (informal)
3 ENCOURAGEMENT, advancement, boosting, furtherance, support

prompt verb 1 CAUSE, elicit, give rise to, occasion, provoke 2 REMIND, assist, cue, help out ♦ adjective
3 IMMEDIATE, early, instant, quick, rapid, speedy, swift, timely
♦ adverb 4 Informal EXACTLY, on the dot, promptly, punctually, sharp

promptly adverb IMMEDIATELY, at once, directly, on the dot, on time, punctually, quickly, speedily, swiftly

promptness noun SWIFTNESS, briskness, eagerness, haste, punctuality, quickness, speed, willingness

promulgate verb MAKE KNOWN, broadcast, circulate, communicate, disseminate, make public, proclaim, promote, publish, spread

prone adjective 1 LIABLE, apt, bent, disposed, given, inclined, likely, predisposed, subject, susceptible, tending 2 FACE DOWN, flat, horizontal, prostrate, recumbent

prong noun POINT, spike, tine

pronounce verb 1 SAY, accent, articulate, enunciate, sound, speak 2 DECLARE, affirm, announce, decree, deliver, proclaim

pronounced adjective NOTICEABLE, conspicuous, decided, definite, distinct, evident, marked, obvious, striking

pronouncement noun ANNOUNCEMENT, declaration, decree, dictum, edict, judgment, proclamation, statement

pronunciation noun INTONATION, accent, articulation, diction, enunciation, inflection, speech, stress

proof noun 1 EVIDENCE, authentication, confirmation, corroboration, demonstration, substantiation, testimony, verification ♦ adjective 2 IMPERVIOUS, impenetrable, repellent, resistant, strong

prop verb 1 SUPPORT, bolster, brace, buttress, hold up, stay, sustain, uphold ♦ noun 2 SUPPORT, brace, buttress, mainstay, stanchion, stay

propaganda noun INFORMATION, advertising, disinformation, hype, promotion, publicity

propagate verb 1 SPREAD, broadcast, circulate, disseminate, promote, promulgate, publish, transmit 2 REPRODUCE, beget, breed, engender, generate, increase, multiply, procreate, produce

propel verb DRIVE, force, impel, launch, push, send, shoot, shove, thrust

propensity noun TENDENCY, bent, disposition, inclination, liability, penchant, predisposition, proclivity

proper adjective 1 SUITABLE, appropriate, apt, becoming, befitting, fit, fitting, right 2 CORRECT, accepted, conventional, established, formal, orthodox, precise, right 3 POLITE, decent, decorous, genteel, gentlemanly, ladylike, mannerly, respectable, seemly

properly adverb 1 SUITABLY, appropriately, aptly, fittingly, rightly 2 CORRECTLY, accurately 3 POLITELY, decently, respectably

property noun 1 POSSESSIONS, assets, belongings, capital, effects, estate, goods, holdings, riches, wealth 2 LAND, estate, freehold, holding, real estate 3 QUALITY, attribute, characteristic, feature, hallmark, trait

prophecy noun PREDICTION, augury, divination, forecast, prognostication, second sight, soothsaying

prophesy verb PREDICT, augur, divine, forecast, foresee, foretell, prognosticate

prophet noun SOOTHSAYER, diviner, forecaster, oracle, prophesier, seer, sibyl

prophetic adjective PREDICTIVE, oracular, prescient, prognostic, sibylline

propitious adjective FAVOURABLE, auspicious, bright, encouraging, fortunate, happy, lucky, promising

proportion noun 1 RELATIVE AMOUNT, ratio, relationship 2 BALANCE, congruity, correspondence, harmony, symmetry 3 PART, amount, division, fraction, percentage, quota, segment, share 4 **proportions** DIMENSIONS, capacity, expanse, extent, size, volume

proportional, proportionate adjective BALANCED, commensurate, compatible, consistent, corresponding, equitable, even, in proportion

proposal noun SUGGESTION, bid, offer, plan, presentation, programme, project, recommendation, scheme

propose verb 1 PUT FORWARD, advance, present, submit, suggest 2 NOMINATE, name, present, recommend 3 INTEND, aim, design, have in mind, mean, plan, scheme 4 OFFER MARRIAGE, ask for someone's hand (in marriage), pop the question (*informal*)

proposition *noun* 1 <u>PROPOSAL</u>, plan, recommendation, scheme, suggestion ♦ *verb* 2 <u>MAKE A PASS AT</u>, accost, make an improper suggestion, solicit

propound *verb* <u>PUT FORWARD</u>, advance, postulate, present, propose, submit, suggest

proprietor, proprietress *noun* <u>OWNER</u>, landlord *or* landlady, titleholder

propriety *noun* 1 <u>CORRECTNESS</u>, aptness, fitness, rightness, seemliness 2 <u>DECORUM</u>, courtesy, decency, etiquette, manners, politeness, respectability, seemliness

propulsion *noun* <u>DRIVE</u>, impetus, impulse, propelling force, push, thrust

prosaic *adjective* <u>DULL</u>, boring, everyday, humdrum, matter-of-fact, mundane, ordinary, pedestrian, routine, trite, unimaginative

proscribe *verb* 1 <u>PROHIBIT</u>, ban, embargo, forbid, interdict 2 <u>OUTLAW</u>, banish, deport, exclude, exile, expatriate, expel, ostracize

prosecute *verb Law* <u>PUT ON TRIAL</u>, arraign, bring to trial, indict, litigate, sue, take to court, try

prospect *noun* 1 <u>EXPECTATION</u>, anticipation, future, hope, odds, outlook, probability, promise 2 *sometimes plural* <u>LIKELIHOOD</u>, chance, possibility 3 <u>VIEW</u>, landscape, outlook, scene, sight, spectacle, vista ♦ *verb* 4 <u>LOOK FOR</u>, search for, seek

prospective *adjective* <u>FUTURE</u>, anticipated, coming, destined, expected, forthcoming, imminent, intended, likely, possible, potential

prospectus *noun* <u>CATALOGUE</u>, list, outline, programme, syllabus, synopsis

prosper *verb* <u>SUCCEED</u>, advance, do well, flourish, get on, progress, thrive

prosperity *noun* <u>SUCCESS</u>, affluence, fortune, good fortune, luxury, plenty, prosperousness, riches, wealth

prosperous *adjective* 1 <u>WEALTHY</u>, affluent, moneyed, rich, well-heeled (*informal*), well-off, well-to-do 2 <u>SUCCESSFUL</u>, booming, doing well, flourishing, fortunate, lucky, thriving

prostitute *noun* 1 <u>WHORE</u>, call girl, fallen woman, harlot, hooker (*U.S. slang*), loose woman, pro (*slang*), scrubber (*Brit. & Austral. slang*), streetwalker, strumpet, tart (*informal*), trollop ♦ *verb* 2 <u>CHEAPEN</u>, debase, degrade, demean, devalue, misapply, pervert, profane

prostrate *adjective* 1 <u>PRONE</u>, flat, horizontal 2 <u>EXHAUSTED</u>, dejected, depressed, desolate, drained, inconsolable, overcome, spent, worn out ♦ *verb* 3 <u>EXHAUST</u>, drain, fatigue, sap, tire, wear out, weary 4 **prostrate oneself** <u>BOW DOWN TO</u>, abase oneself, fall at (someone's) feet, grovel, kneel, kowtow

protagonist *noun* 1 <u>SUPPORTER</u>, advocate, champion, exponent 2 <u>LEADING CHARACTER</u>, central character, hero *or* heroine, principal

protect *verb* <u>KEEP SAFE</u>, defend, guard, look after, preserve, safeguard, save, screen, shelter, shield, stick up for (*informal*), support, watch over

protection *noun* 1 <u>SAFETY</u>, aegis, care, custody, defence, protecting, safeguard, safekeeping, security 2 <u>SAFEGUARD</u>, barrier, buffer, cover, guard, screen, shelter, shield

protective *adjective* <u>PROTECTING</u>, defensive, fatherly, maternal, motherly, paternal, vigilant, watchful

protector *noun* <u>DEFENDER</u>, bodyguard, champion, guard, guardian, patron

protest *noun* 1 <u>OBJECTION</u>, complaint, dissent, outcry, protestation, remonstrance ♦ *verb* 2 <u>OBJECT</u>, complain, cry out, demonstrate, demur, disagree, disapprove, express disapproval, oppose, remonstrate 3 <u>ASSERT</u>, affirm, attest, avow, declare, insist, maintain, profess

protestation *noun* <u>DECLARATION</u>, affirmation, avowal, profession, vow

protester *noun* <u>DEMONSTRATOR</u>, agitator, rebel

protocol *noun* <u>CODE OF BEHAVIOUR</u>, conventions, customs, decorum, etiquette, manners, propriety

prototype *noun* <u>ORIGINAL</u>, example, first, model, pattern, standard, type

protracted *adjective* <u>EXTENDED</u>, dragged out, drawn-out, long-drawn-out, prolonged, spun out

protrude *verb* <u>STICK OUT</u>, bulge, come through, extend, jut, obtrude, project, stand out

protrusion *noun* <u>PROJECTION</u>, bulge, bump, lump, outgrowth, protuberance

protuberance *noun* <u>BULGE</u>, bump, excrescence, hump, knob, lump, outgrowth, process, prominence, protrusion, swelling

proud *adjective* 1 <u>SATISFIED</u>, content, glad, gratified, pleased, well-pleased 2 <u>CONCEITED</u>, arrogant, boastful, disdainful, haughty, imperious, lordly, overbearing, self-satisfied, snobbish, supercilious

prove *verb* 1 <u>VERIFY</u>, authenticate, confirm, demonstrate, determine, establish, justify, show, substantiate 2 <u>TEST</u>, analyse, assay, check, examine, try 3 <u>TURN OUT</u>, come out, end up, result

proven *adjective* <u>ESTABLISHED</u>, attested, confirmed, definite, proved, reliable, tested, verified

proverb *noun* <u>SAYING</u>, adage, dictum, maxim, saw

proverbial *adjective* <u>CONVENTIONAL</u>, acknowledged, axiomatic, current, famed, famous, legendary, notorious, traditional, typical, well-known

provide *verb* 1 <u>SUPPLY</u>, cater, equip, furnish, outfit, purvey, stock up 2 <u>GIVE</u>, add, afford, bring, impart, lend, present, produce, render, serve, yield 3 **provide for** *or* **against** <u>TAKE PRECAUTIONS</u>, anticipate, forearm, plan ahead, plan for, prepare for 4 **provide for** <u>SUPPORT</u>, care for, keep, maintain, sustain, take care of

providence *noun* <u>FATE</u>, destiny, fortune

provident *adjective* 1 <u>THRIFTY</u>, economical, frugal, prudent 2 <u>FORESIGHTED</u>, careful, cautious, discreet, far-seeing, forearmed, shrewd, vigilant, well-prepared, wise

providential *adjective* <u>LUCKY</u>, fortuitous, fortunate, happy, heaven-sent, opportune, timely

provider *noun* 1 <u>SUPPLIER</u>, donor, giver, source 2 <u>BREADWINNER</u>, earner, supporter, wage earner

providing, provided *conjunction* <u>ON CONDITION THAT</u>, as long as, given

province *noun* 1 <u>REGION</u>, colony, department, district, division, domain, patch, section, zone 2 <u>AREA</u>, business, capacity, concern, duty, field, function, line, responsibility, role, sphere

provincial *adjective* 1 RURAL, country, hick (*informal, chiefly U.S. & Canad.*), homespun, local, rustic 2 NARROW-MINDED, insular, inward-looking, limited, narrow, parochial, small-minded, small-town (*chiefly U.S.*), unsophisticated ♦ *noun* 3 YOKEL, country cousin, hayseed (*U.S. & Canad. informal*), hick (*informal, chiefly U.S. & Canad.*), rustic

provision *noun* 1 SUPPLYING, catering, equipping, furnishing, providing 2 CONDITION, clause, demand, proviso, requirement, rider, stipulation, term

provisional *adjective* 1 TEMPORARY, interim 2 CONDITIONAL, contingent, limited, qualified, tentative

provisions *plural noun* FOOD, comestibles, eatables, edibles, fare, foodstuff, rations, stores, supplies, victuals

proviso *noun* CONDITION, clause, qualification, requirement, rider, stipulation

provocation *noun* 1 CAUSE, grounds, incitement, motivation, reason, stimulus 2 OFFENCE, affront, annoyance, challenge, dare, grievance, indignity, injury, insult, taunt

provocative *adjective* OFFENSIVE, annoying, galling, goading, insulting, provoking, stimulating

provoke *verb* 1 ANGER, aggravate (*informal*), annoy, enrage, hassle (*informal*), incense, infuriate, irk, irritate, madden, rile 2 CAUSE, bring about, elicit, evoke, incite, induce, occasion, produce, promote, prompt, rouse, stir

prowess *noun* 1 SKILL, accomplishment, adeptness, aptitude, excellence, expertise, genius, mastery, talent 2 BRAVERY, courage, daring, fearlessness, heroism, mettle, valiance, valour

prowl *verb* MOVE STEALTHILY, skulk, slink, sneak, stalk, steal

proximity *noun* NEARNESS, closeness

proxy *noun* REPRESENTATIVE, agent, delegate, deputy, factor, substitute

prudence *noun* COMMON SENSE, care, caution, discretion, good sense, judgment, vigilance, wariness, wisdom

prudent *adjective* 1 SENSIBLE, careful, cautious, discerning, discreet, judicious, politic, shrewd, vigilant, wary, wise 2 THRIFTY, canny, careful, economical, far-sighted, frugal, provident, sparing

prudish *adjective* PRIM, old-maidish (*informal*), overmodest, priggish, prissy (*informal*), proper, puritanical, starchy (*informal*), strait-laced, stuffy, Victorian

prune *verb* CUT, clip, dock, reduce, shape, shorten, snip, trim

pry *verb* BE INQUISITIVE, be nosy (*informal*), interfere, intrude, meddle, poke, snoop (*informal*)

prying *adjective* INQUISITIVE, curious, interfering, meddlesome, meddling, nosy (*informal*), snooping (*informal*), spying

psalm *noun* HYMN, chant

pseudo- *adjective* FALSE, artificial, fake, imitation, mock, phoney *or* phony (*informal*), pretended, sham, spurious

pseudonym *noun* FALSE NAME, alias, assumed name, incognito, nom de plume, pen name

psyche *noun* SOUL, anima, individuality, mind, personality, self, spirit

psychiatrist *noun* PSYCHOTHERAPIST, analyst, headshrinker (*slang*), psychoanalyst, psychologist, shrink (*slang*), therapist

psychic *adjective* 1 SUPERNATURAL, mystic, occult 2 MENTAL, psychological, spiritual

psychological *adjective* 1 MENTAL, cerebral, intellectual 2 IMAGINARY, all in the mind, irrational, psychosomatic, unreal

psychology *noun* 1 BEHAVIOURISM, science of mind, study of personality 2 *Informal* WAY OF THINKING, attitude, mental make-up, mental processes, thought processes, what makes one tick

psychopath *noun* MADMAN, headbanger (*informal*), headcase (*informal*), lunatic, maniac, nutcase (*slang*), nutter (*Brit. slang*), psychotic, sociopath

psychotic *adjective* MAD, certifiable, demented, deranged, insane, lunatic, mental (*slang*), *non compos mentis*, unbalanced

pub *or* **public house** *noun* TAVERN, bar, inn

puberty *noun* ADOLESCENCE, pubescence, teens

public *adjective* 1 GENERAL, civic, common, national, popular, social, state, universal, widespread 2 COMMUNAL, accessible, open, unrestricted 3 WELL-KNOWN, important, prominent, respected 4 PLAIN, acknowledged, known, obvious, open, overt, patent ◆ *noun* 5 PEOPLE, citizens, community, electorate, everyone, nation, populace, society

publication *noun* 1 PAMPHLET, brochure, issue, leaflet, magazine, newspaper, periodical, title 2 ANNOUNCEMENT, broadcasting, declaration, disclosure, notification, proclamation, publishing, reporting

publicity *noun* ADVERTISING,

attention, boost, hype, plug (*informal*), press, promotion

publicize *verb* ADVERTISE, hype, make known, play up, plug (*informal*), promote, push

public-spirited *adjective* ALTRUISTIC, charitable, humanitarian, philanthropic, unselfish

publish *verb* 1 PUT OUT, issue, print, produce 2 ANNOUNCE, advertise, broadcast, circulate, disclose, divulge, proclaim, publicize, reveal, spread

pucker *verb* 1 WRINKLE, contract, crease, draw together, gather, knit, purse, screw up, tighten ◆ *noun* 2 WRINKLE, crease, fold

pudding *noun* DESSERT, afters (*Brit. informal*), pud (*informal*), sweet

puerile *adjective* CHILDISH, babyish, foolish, immature, juvenile, silly, trivial

puff *noun* 1 BLAST, breath, draught, gust, whiff 2 SMOKE, drag (*slang*), pull ◆ *verb* 3 BLOW, breathe, exhale, gasp, gulp, pant, wheeze 4 SMOKE, drag (*slang*), draw, inhale, pull at *or* on, suck 5 usually with *up* SWELL, bloat, dilate, distend, expand, inflate

puffy *adjective* SWOLLEN, bloated, distended, enlarged, puffed up

pugilist *noun* BOXER, fighter, prizefighter

pugnacious *adjective* AGGRESSIVE, belligerent, combative, hot-tempered, quarrelsome

pull *verb* 1 DRAW, drag, haul, jerk, tow, trail, tug, yank 2 STRAIN, dislocate, rip, sprain, stretch, tear, wrench 3 EXTRACT, draw out, gather, pick, pluck, remove, take out, uproot 4 *Informal* ATTRACT, draw, entice, lure, magnetize ◆ *noun* 5 TUG, jerk, twitch, yank 6 PUFF, drag (*slang*), inhalation 7 *Informal* INFLUENCE, clout (*informal*), muscle, power, weight

pull down *verb* <u>DEMOLISH</u>, bulldoze, destroy, raze, remove

pull off *verb* <u>SUCCEED</u>, accomplish, carry out, do the trick, manage

pull out *verb* <u>WITHDRAW</u>, depart, evacuate, leave, quit, retreat

pull through *verb* <u>SURVIVE</u>, get better, rally, recover

pull up *verb* **1** <u>STOP</u>, brake, halt **2** <u>REPRIMAND</u>, admonish, bawl out (*informal*), rap over the knuckles, read the riot act, rebuke, reprove, slap on the wrist, tear (someone) off a strip (*Brit. informal*), tell off (*informal*)

pulp *noun* **1** <u>PASTE</u>, mash, mush **2** <u>FLESH</u>, soft part ♦ *verb* **3** <u>CRUSH</u>, mash, pulverize, squash ♦ *adjective* **4** <u>CHEAP</u>, lurid, rubbishy, trashy

pulsate *verb* <u>THROB</u>, beat, palpitate, pound, pulse, quiver, thump

pulse *noun* **1** <u>BEAT</u>, beating, pulsation, rhythm, throb, throbbing, vibration ♦ *verb* **2** <u>BEAT</u>, pulsate, throb, vibrate

pulverize *verb* **1** <u>CRUSH</u>, granulate, grind, mill, pound **2** <u>DEFEAT</u>, annihilate, crush, demolish, destroy, flatten, smash, wreck

pummel *verb* <u>BEAT</u>, batter, hammer, pound, punch, strike, thump

pump *verb* **1** often with *into* <u>DRIVE</u>, force, inject, pour, push, send, supply **2** <u>INTERROGATE</u>, cross-examine, probe, quiz

pun *noun* <u>PLAY ON WORDS</u>, double entendre, quip, witticism

punch[1] *verb* **1** <u>HIT</u>, belt (*informal*), bop (*informal*), box, pummel, smash, sock (*slang*), strike ♦ *noun* **2** <u>BLOW</u>, bop (*informal*), hit, jab, sock (*slang*), wallop (*informal*) **3** *Informal* <u>EFFECTIVENESS</u>, bite, drive, forcefulness, impact, verve, vigour

punch[2] *verb* <u>PIERCE</u>, bore, cut, drill, perforate, prick, puncture, stamp

punctilious *adjective* <u>PARTICULAR</u>, exact, finicky, formal, fussy, meticulous, nice, precise, proper, strict

punctual *adjective* <u>ON TIME</u>, exact, on the dot, precise, prompt, timely

punctuality *noun* <u>PROMPTNESS</u>, promptitude, readiness

punctuate *verb* **1** <u>INTERRUPT</u>, break, intersperse, pepper, sprinkle **2** <u>EMPHASIZE</u>, accentuate, stress, underline

puncture *noun* **1** <u>HOLE</u>, break, cut, damage, leak, nick, opening, slit **2** <u>FLAT TYRE</u>, flat ♦ *verb* **3** <u>PIERCE</u>, bore, cut, nick, penetrate, perforate, prick, rupture

pungent *adjective* <u>STRONG</u>, acrid, bitter, hot, peppery, piquant, sharp, sour, spicy, tart

punish *verb* <u>DISCIPLINE</u>, castigate, chasten, chastise, correct, penalize, sentence

punishable *adjective* <u>CULPABLE</u>, blameworthy, criminal, indictable

punishing *adjective* <u>HARD</u>, arduous, backbreaking, exhausting, gruelling, strenuous, taxing, tiring, wearing

punishment *noun* <u>PENALTY</u>, chastening, chastisement, correction, discipline, penance, retribution

punitive *adjective* <u>RETALIATORY</u>, in reprisal, retaliative

punt *verb* **1** <u>BET</u>, back, gamble, lay, stake, wager ♦ *noun* **2** <u>BET</u>, gamble, stake, wager

punter *noun* **1** <u>GAMBLER</u>, backer, better **2** *Informal* <u>PERSON</u>, man in the street

puny *adjective* <u>FEEBLE</u>, frail, little, sickly, stunted, tiny, weak

pupil noun <u>LEARNER</u>, beginner, disciple, novice, schoolboy or schoolgirl, student

puppet noun 1 <u>MARIONETTE</u>, doll 2 <u>PAWN</u>, cat's-paw, instrument, mouthpiece, stooge, tool

purchase verb 1 <u>BUY</u>, acquire, come by, gain, get, obtain, pay for, pick up, score (slang) ♦ noun 2 <u>BUY</u>, acquisition, asset, gain, investment, possession, property 3 <u>GRIP</u>, foothold, hold, leverage, support

pure adjective 1 <u>UNMIXED</u>, authentic, flawless, genuine, natural, neat, real, simple, straight, unalloyed 2 <u>CLEAN</u>, germ-free, sanitary, spotless, squeaky-clean, sterilized, uncontaminated, unpolluted, untainted, wholesome 3 <u>INNOCENT</u>, blameless, chaste, impeccable, modest, uncorrupted, unsullied, virginal, virtuous 4 <u>COMPLETE</u>, absolute, outright, sheer, thorough, unmitigated, unqualified, utter

purely adverb <u>ABSOLUTELY</u>, completely, entirely, exclusively, just, merely, only, simply, solely, wholly

purge verb 1 <u>GET RID OF</u>, do away with, eradicate, expel, exterminate, remove, wipe out ♦ noun 2 <u>REMOVAL</u>, ejection, elimination, eradication, expulsion

purify verb 1 <u>CLEAN</u>, clarify, cleanse, decontaminate, disinfect, refine, sanitize, wash 2 <u>ABSOLVE</u>, cleanse, redeem, sanctify

purist noun <u>STICKLER</u>, formalist, pedant

puritan noun 1 <u>MORALIST</u>, fanatic, prude, rigorist, zealot ♦ adjective 2 <u>STRICT</u>, ascetic, austere, moralistic, narrow-minded, prudish, severe, strait-laced

puritanical adjective <u>STRICT</u>, ascetic, austere, narrow-minded, proper, prudish, puritan, severe, strait-laced

purity noun 1 <u>CLEANNESS</u>, cleanliness, faultlessness, immaculateness, pureness, wholesomeness 2 <u>INNOCENCE</u>, chasteness, chastity, decency, honesty, integrity, virginity, virtue

purloin verb <u>STEAL</u>, appropriate, filch, nick (slang, chiefly Brit.), pilfer, pinch (informal), swipe (slang), thieve

purport verb 1 <u>CLAIM</u>, allege, assert, profess ♦ noun 2 <u>SIGNIFICANCE</u>, drift, gist, idea, implication, import, meaning

purpose noun 1 <u>REASON</u>, aim, idea, intention, object, point 2 <u>AIM</u>, ambition, desire, end, goal, hope, intention, object, plan, wish 3 <u>DETERMINATION</u>, firmness, persistence, resolution, resolve, single-mindedness, tenacity, will 4 **on purpose** <u>DELIBERATELY</u>, designedly, intentionally, knowingly, purposely

purposeless adjective <u>POINTLESS</u>, aimless, empty, motiveless, needless, senseless, uncalled-for, unnecessary

purposely adverb <u>DELIBERATELY</u>, consciously, expressly, intentionally, knowingly, on purpose, with intent

purse noun 1 <u>POUCH</u>, money-bag, wallet 2 <u>MONEY</u>, exchequer, funds, means, resources, treasury, wealth ♦ verb 3 <u>PUCKER</u>, contract, pout, press together, tighten

pursue verb 1 <u>FOLLOW</u>, chase, dog, hound, hunt, hunt down, run after, shadow, stalk, tail (informal), track 2 <u>TRY FOR</u>, aim for, desire, seek, strive for, work towards 3 <u>ENGAGE IN</u>, carry on, conduct, perform, practise 4 <u>CONTINUE</u>, carry on, keep on, maintain, persevere in, persist in, proceed

pursuit noun 1 PURSUING, chase, hunt, quest, search, seeking, trailing 2 OCCUPATION, activity, hobby, interest, line, pastime, pleasure

purvey verb SUPPLY, cater, deal in, furnish, provide, sell, trade in

push verb 1 SHOVE, depress, drive, press, propel, ram, thrust 2 MAKE or FORCE ONE'S WAY, elbow, jostle, move, shoulder, shove, squeeze, thrust 3 URGE, encourage, hurry, impel, incite, persuade, press, spur ♦ noun 4 SHOVE, butt, nudge, thrust 5 Informal DRIVE, ambition, dynamism, energy, enterprise, go (informal), initiative, vigour, vitality 6 the push Informal, chiefly Brit. DISMISSAL, discharge, one's cards (informal), the boot (slang), the sack (informal)

pushed adjective, often with for SHORT OF, hurried, pressed, rushed, under pressure

pushover noun 1 PIECE OF CAKE (Brit. informal), breeze (U.S. & Canad. informal), child's play (informal), cinch (slang), doddle (Brit. slang), picnic (informal), plain sailing, walkover (informal) 2 SUCKER (slang), easy game (informal), easy or soft mark (informal), mug (Brit. slang), soft touch (slang), walkover (informal)

pushy adjective FORCEFUL, ambitious, assertive, bold, brash, bumptious, obtrusive, presumptuous, self-assertive

pussyfoot verb HEDGE, beat about the bush, be noncommittal, equivocate, flannel (Brit. informal), hum and haw, prevaricate, sit on the fence

put verb 1 PLACE, deposit, lay, position, rest, set, settle, situate 2 EXPRESS, phrase, state, utter, word 3 THROW, cast, fling, heave, hurl,

lob, pitch, toss

put across or **over** verb COMMUNICATE, convey, explain, get across, make clear, make oneself understood

put aside or **by** verb SAVE, deposit, lay by, stockpile, store

put away verb 1 SAVE, deposit, keep, put by 2 COMMIT, certify, institutionalize, lock up 3 CONSUME, devour, eat up, gobble, wolf down 4 PUT BACK, replace, tidy away

put down verb 1 RECORD, enter, set down, take down, write down 2 STAMP OUT, crush, quash, quell, repress, suppress 3 usually with to ATTRIBUTE, ascribe, impute, set down 4 PUT TO SLEEP, destroy, do away with, put out of its misery 5 Slang HUMILIATE, disparage, mortify, shame, slight, snub

put forward verb RECOMMEND, advance, nominate, propose, submit, suggest, tender

put off verb 1 POSTPONE, defer, delay, hold over, put on the back burner (informal), take a rain check on (U.S. & Canad. informal) 2 DISCONCERT, confuse, discomfit, dismay, faze, nonplus, perturb, throw (informal), unsettle 3 DISCOURAGE, dishearten, dissuade

put on verb 1 DON, change into, dress, get dressed in, slip into 2 FAKE, affect, assume, feign, pretend, sham, simulate 3 PRESENT, do, mount, produce, show, stage 4 ADD, gain, increase by

put out verb 1 ANNOY, anger, exasperate, irk, irritate, nettle, vex 2 EXTINGUISH, blow out, douse, quench 3 INCONVENIENCE, bother, discomfit, discommode, impose upon, incommode, trouble

putrid adjective ROTTEN, bad, decayed, decomposed, off, putrefied, rancid, rotting, spoiled

put up *verb* **1** <u>ERECT</u>, build, construct, fabricate, raise **2** <u>ACCOMMODATE</u>, board, house, lodge, take in **3** <u>RECOMMEND</u>, nominate, offer, present, propose, put forward, submit **4 put up with** *Informal* <u>STAND</u>, abide, bear, endure, stand for, swallow, take, tolerate

puzzle *verb* **1** <u>PERPLEX</u>, baffle, bewilder, confound, confuse, mystify, stump ♦ *noun* **2** <u>PROBLEM</u>, conundrum, enigma, mystery, paradox, poser, question, riddle

puzzled *adjective* <u>PERPLEXED</u>, at a loss, at sea, baffled, bewildered, confused, lost, mystified

puzzlement *noun* <u>PERPLEXITY</u>, bafflement, bewilderment, confusion, doubt, mystification

puzzling *adjective* <u>PERPLEXING</u>, abstruse, baffling, bewildering, enigmatic, incomprehensible, involved, mystifying

Q q

quack *noun* <u>CHARLATAN</u>, fake, fraud, humbug, impostor, mountebank, phoney *or* phony (*informal*)

quaff *verb* <u>DRINK</u>, down, gulp, imbibe, swallow, swig (*informal*)

quagmire *noun* <u>BOG</u>, fen, marsh, mire, morass, quicksand, slough, swamp

quail *verb* <u>SHRINK</u>, blanch, blench, cower, cringe, falter, flinch, have cold feet (*informal*), recoil, shudder

quaint *adjective* **1** <u>UNUSUAL</u>, bizarre, curious, droll, eccentric, fanciful, odd, old-fashioned, peculiar, queer, rum (*Brit. slang*), singular, strange **2** <u>OLD-FASHIONED</u>, antiquated, old-world, picturesque

quake *verb* <u>SHAKE</u>, move, quiver, rock, shiver, shudder, tremble, vibrate

qualification *noun* **1** <u>ATTRIBUTE</u>, ability, aptitude, capability, eligibility, fitness, quality, skill, suitability **2** <u>CONDITION</u>, caveat, limitation, modification, proviso, requirement, reservation, rider, stipulation

qualified *adjective* **1** <u>CAPABLE</u>, able, adept, competent, efficient, experienced, expert, fit, practised, proficient, skilful, trained **2** <u>RESTRICTED</u>, bounded, conditional, confined, contingent, limited, modified, provisional, reserved

qualify *verb* **1** <u>CERTIFY</u>, empower, equip, fit, permit, prepare, ready, train **2** <u>MODERATE</u>, diminish, ease, lessen, limit, reduce, regulate, restrain, restrict, soften, temper

quality *noun* **1** <u>EXCELLENCE</u>, calibre, distinction, grade, merit, position, rank, standing, status **2** <u>CHARACTERISTIC</u>, aspect, attribute, condition, feature, mark, property, trait **3** <u>NATURE</u>, character, kind, make, sort

qualm *noun* <u>MISGIVING</u>, anxiety, apprehension, compunction, disquiet, doubt, hesitation, scruple, twinge *or* pang of conscience, uneasiness

quandary *noun* <u>DIFFICULTY</u>, cleft stick, dilemma, impasse, plight, predicament, puzzle, strait

quantity *noun* **1** <u>AMOUNT</u>, lot, number, part, sum, total **2** <u>SIZE</u>, bulk, capacity, extent, length, magnitude, mass, measure, volume

quarrel *noun* **1** <u>DISAGREEMENT</u>, argument, brawl, breach, contention, controversy, dispute, dissension, feud, fight, row, squabble, tiff ♦ *verb* **2** <u>DISAGREE</u>, argue, bicker, brawl, clash, differ, dispute, fall out (*informal*), fight, row, squabble

quarrelsome *adjective* <u>ARGUMENTATIVE</u>, belligerent, combative, contentious, disputatious, pugnacious

quarry *noun* <u>PREY</u>, aim, game, goal, objective, prize, victim

quarter *noun* **1** <u>DISTRICT</u>, area, locality, neighbourhood, part, place, province, region, side, zone **2** <u>MERCY</u>, clemency, compassion, forgiveness, leniency, pity ♦ *verb* **3** <u>ACCOMMODATE</u>, billet, board, house, lodge, place, post, station

quarters *plural noun* <u>LODGINGS</u>, abode, barracks, billet, chambers, dwelling, habitation, residence, rooms

quash *verb* **1** <u>ANNUL</u>, cancel, invalidate, overrule, overthrow, rescind, reverse, revoke **2** <u>SUPPRESS</u>, beat, crush, overthrow, put down, quell, repress, squash, subdue

quasi- adjective <u>PSEUDO-</u>, apparent, seeming, semi-, so-called, would-be

quaver verb **1** <u>TREMBLE</u>, flicker, flutter, quake, quiver, shake, vibrate, waver ◆ noun **2** <u>TREMBLING</u>, quiver, shake, tremble, tremor, vibration

queasy adjective **1** <u>SICK</u>, bilious, green around the gills (informal), ill, nauseated, off colour, squeamish, upset **2** <u>UNEASY</u>, anxious, fidgety, ill at ease, restless, troubled, uncertain, worried

queen noun **1** <u>SOVEREIGN</u>, consort, monarch, ruler **2** <u>IDEAL</u>, mistress, model, star

queer adjective **1** <u>STRANGE</u>, abnormal, curious, droll, extraordinary, funny, odd, peculiar, uncommon, unusual, weird **2** <u>FAINT</u>, dizzy, giddy, light-headed, queasy

quell verb **1** <u>SUPPRESS</u>, conquer, crush, defeat, overcome, overpower, put down, quash, subdue, vanquish **2** <u>ASSUAGE</u>, allay, appease, calm, mollify, pacify, quiet, soothe

quench verb **1** <u>SATISFY</u>, allay, appease, sate, satiate, slake **2** <u>PUT OUT</u>, crush, douse, extinguish, smother, stifle, suppress

querulous adjective <u>COMPLAINING</u>, captious, carping, critical, discontented, dissatisfied, fault-finding, grumbling, peevish, whining

query noun **1** <u>QUESTION</u>, doubt, inquiry, objection, problem, suspicion ◆ verb **2** <u>DOUBT</u>, challenge, disbelieve, dispute, distrust, mistrust, suspect **3** <u>ASK</u>,

inquire or enquire, question

quest noun <u>SEARCH</u>, adventure, crusade, enterprise, expedition, hunt, journey, mission

question noun **1** <u>ISSUE</u>, motion, point, point at issue, proposal, proposition, subject, theme, topic **2** <u>DIFFICULTY</u>, argument, contention, controversy, dispute, doubt, problem, query **3 in question** <u>UNDER DISCUSSION</u>, at issue, in doubt, open to debate **4 out of the question** <u>IMPOSSIBLE</u>, inconceivable, unthinkable ◆ verb **5** <u>ASK</u>, cross-examine, examine, inquire, interrogate, interview, probe, quiz **6** <u>DISPUTE</u>, challenge, disbelieve, doubt, mistrust, oppose, query, suspect

questionable adjective <u>DUBIOUS</u>, controversial, debatable, dodgy (Brit., Austral., & N.Z. informal), doubtful, iffy (informal), moot, suspect, suspicious

queue noun <u>LINE</u>, chain, file, sequence, series, string, train

quibble verb **1** <u>SPLIT HAIRS</u>, carp, cavil ◆ noun **2** <u>OBJECTION</u>, cavil, complaint, criticism, nicety, niggle

quick adjective **1** <u>FAST</u>, brisk, express, fleet, hasty, rapid, speedy, swift **2** <u>BRIEF</u>, cursory, hasty, hurried, perfunctory **3** <u>SUDDEN</u>, prompt **4** <u>INTELLIGENT</u>, acute, alert, astute, bright (informal), clever, perceptive, quick-witted, sharp, shrewd, smart **5** <u>DEFT</u>, adept, adroit, dexterous, skilful **6** <u>EXCITABLE</u>, irascible, irritable, passionate, testy, touchy

quicken verb **1** <u>SPEED</u>, accelerate, expedite, hasten, hurry, impel, precipitate **2** <u>INVIGORATE</u>, arouse, energize, excite, incite, inspire, revive, stimulate, vitalize

quickly adverb <u>SWIFTLY</u>, abruptly, apace, briskly, fast, hastily, hurriedly, promptly, pronto (*informal*), rapidly, soon, speedily

quick-tempered *adjective* <u>HOT-TEMPERED</u>, choleric, fiery, irascible, irritable, quarrelsome, ratty (*Brit. & N.Z. informal*), testy, tetchy

quick-witted *adjective* <u>CLEVER</u>, alert, astute, bright (*informal*), keen, perceptive, sharp, shrewd, smart

quiet *adjective* 1 <u>SILENT</u>, hushed, inaudible, low, noiseless, peaceful, soft, soundless 2 <u>CALM</u>, mild, peaceful, placid, restful, serene, smooth, tranquil 3 <u>UNDISTURBED</u>, isolated, private, secluded, sequestered, unfrequented 4 <u>RESERVED</u>, gentle, meek, mild, retiring, sedate, shy ◆ *noun* 5 <u>PEACE</u>, calmness, ease, quietness, repose, rest, serenity, silence, stillness, tranquillity

quieten *verb* 1 <u>SILENCE</u>, compose, hush, muffle, mute, quell, quiet, stifle, still, stop, subdue 2 <u>SOOTHE</u>, allay, appease, blunt, calm, deaden, dull

quietly *adverb* 1 <u>SILENTLY</u>, in an undertone, inaudibly, in silence, mutely, noiselessly, softly 2 <u>CALMLY</u>, mildly, patiently, placidly, serenely

quietness *noun* <u>PEACE</u>, calm, hush, quiet, silence, stillness, tranquillity

quilt *noun* <u>BEDSPREAD</u>, continental quilt, counterpane, coverlet, duvet, eiderdown

quintessence *noun* <u>ESSENCE</u>, distillation, soul, spirit

quintessential *adjective* <u>ULTIMATE</u>, archetypal, definitive, prototypical, typical

quip *noun* <u>JOKE</u>, gibe, jest, pleasantry, retort, riposte, sally, wisecrack (*informal*), witticism

quirk *noun* <u>PECULIARITY</u>, aberration, characteristic, eccentricity, foible, habit, idiosyncrasy, kink, mannerism, oddity, trait

quirky *adjective* <u>ODD</u>, eccentric, idiosyncratic, offbeat, peculiar, unusual

quit *verb* 1 <u>STOP</u>, abandon, cease, discontinue, drop, end, give up, halt 2 <u>RESIGN</u>, abdicate, go, leave, pull out, retire, step down (*informal*) 3 <u>DEPART</u>, go, leave, pull out

quite *adverb* 1 <u>SOMEWHAT</u>, fairly, moderately, rather, reasonably, relatively 2 <u>ABSOLUTELY</u>, completely, entirely, fully, perfectly, totally, wholly 3 <u>TRULY</u>, in fact, in reality, in truth, really

quiver *verb* 1 <u>SHAKE</u>, oscillate, quake, quaver, shiver, shudder, tremble, vibrate ◆ *noun* 2 <u>SHAKE</u>, oscillation, shiver, shudder, tremble, tremor, vibration

quixotic *adjective* <u>UNREALISTIC</u>, dreamy, fanciful, idealistic, impractical, romantic

quiz *noun* 1 <u>EXAMINATION</u>, investigation, questioning, test ◆ *verb* 2 <u>QUESTION</u>, ask, examine, interrogate, investigate

quizzical *adjective* <u>MOCKING</u>, arch, questioning, sardonic, teasing

quota *noun* <u>SHARE</u>, allowance, assignment, part, portion, ration, slice, whack (*informal*)

quotation *noun* 1 <u>PASSAGE</u>, citation, excerpt, extract, quote (*informal*), reference 2 *Commerce* <u>ESTIMATE</u>, charge, cost, figure, price, quote (*informal*), rate, tender

quote *verb* <u>REPEAT</u>, cite, detail, instance, name, recall, recite, recollect, refer to

R r

rabble noun <u>MOB</u>, canaille, crowd, herd, horde, swarm, throng

rabid adjective 1 <u>FANATICAL</u>, extreme, fervent, irrational, narrow-minded, zealous 2 <u>MAD</u>, hydrophobic

race[1] noun 1 <u>CONTEST</u>, chase, competition, dash, pursuit, rivalry ♦ verb 2 <u>RUN</u>, career, compete, contest, dart, dash, fly, gallop, hurry, speed, tear, zoom

race[2] noun <u>PEOPLE</u>, blood, folk, nation, stock, tribe, type

racial adjective <u>ETHNIC</u>, ethnological, folk, genealogical, genetic, national, tribal

rack noun 1 <u>FRAME</u>, framework, stand, structure ♦ verb 2 <u>TORTURE</u>, afflict, agonize, crucify, harrow, oppress, pain, torment

racket noun 1 <u>NOISE</u>, clamour, din, disturbance, fuss, outcry, pandemonium, row 2 <u>FRAUD</u>, scheme

racy adjective 1 <u>RISQUÉ</u>, bawdy, blue, naughty, near the knuckle (informal), smutty, suggestive 2 <u>LIVELY</u>, animated, energetic, entertaining, exciting, sparkling, spirited

radiance noun 1 <u>HAPPINESS</u>, delight, gaiety, joy, pleasure, rapture, warmth 2 <u>BRIGHTNESS</u>, brilliance, glare, gleam, glow, light, lustre, shine

radiant adjective 1 <u>HAPPY</u>, blissful, delighted, ecstatic, glowing, joyful, joyous, on cloud nine (informal), rapturous 2 <u>BRIGHT</u>, brilliant, gleaming, glittering, glowing, luminous, lustrous, shining

radiate verb 1 <u>SPREAD OUT</u>, branch out, diverge, issue 2 <u>EMIT</u>, diffuse, give off or out, pour, scatter, send out, shed, spread

radical adjective 1 <u>FUNDAMENTAL</u>, basic, deep-seated, innate, natural, profound 2 <u>EXTREME</u>, complete, drastic, entire, extremist, fanatical, severe, sweeping, thorough ♦ noun 3 <u>EXTREMIST</u>, fanatic, militant, revolutionary

raffle noun <u>DRAW</u>, lottery, sweep, sweepstake

ragamuffin noun <u>URCHIN</u>, guttersnipe

rage noun 1 <u>FURY</u>, anger, frenzy, ire, madness, passion, rampage, wrath 2 As in **all the rage** <u>CRAZE</u>, enthusiasm, fad (informal), fashion, latest thing, vogue ♦ verb 3 <u>BE FURIOUS</u>, blow one's top, blow up (informal), fly off the handle (informal), fume, go ballistic (slang, chiefly U.S.), go up the wall (slang), lose the plot (informal), seethe, storm

ragged adjective 1 <u>TATTERED</u>, in rags, in tatters, shabby, tatty, threadbare, torn, unkempt 2 <u>ROUGH</u>, jagged, rugged, serrated, uneven, unfinished

raging adjective <u>FURIOUS</u>, beside oneself, enraged, fuming, incensed, infuriated, mad, raving, seething

rags plural noun <u>TATTERS</u>, castoffs, old clothes, tattered clothing

raid noun 1 <u>ATTACK</u>, foray, incursion, inroad, invasion, sally, sortie ♦ verb 2 <u>ATTACK</u>, assault, foray, invade, pillage, plunder, sack

raider noun <u>ATTACKER</u>, invader, marauder, plunderer, robber, thief

railing noun FENCE, balustrade, barrier, paling, rails

rain noun 1 RAINFALL, cloudburst, deluge, downpour, drizzle, fall, raindrops, showers ◆ verb 2 POUR, bucket down (informal), come down in buckets (informal), drizzle, pelt (down), teem 3 FALL, deposit, drop, shower, sprinkle

rainy adjective WET, damp, drizzly, showery

raise verb 1 LIFT, build, elevate, erect, heave, hoist, rear, uplift 2 INCREASE, advance, amplify, boost, enhance, enlarge, heighten, inflate, intensify, magnify, strengthen 3 COLLECT, assemble, form, gather, mass, obtain, rally, recruit 4 CAUSE, create, engender, occasion, originate, produce, provoke, start 5 BRING UP, develop, nurture, rear 6 SUGGEST, advance, broach, introduce, moot, put forward

rake[1] verb 1 GATHER, collect, remove 2 SEARCH, comb, scour, scrutinize

rake[2] noun LIBERTINE, debauchee, lecher, playboy, roué

rakish adjective DASHING, dapper, debonair, devil-may-care, jaunty, natty (informal), raffish, smart

rally noun 1 GATHERING, assembly, congress, convention, meeting 2 RECOVERY, improvement, recuperation, revival ◆ verb 3 REASSEMBLE, regroup, reorganize, unite 4 GATHER, assemble, collect, convene, marshal, muster, round up, unite 5 RECOVER, get better, improve, recuperate, revive

ram verb 1 HIT, butt, crash, dash, drive, force, impact, smash 2 CRAM, crowd, force, jam, stuff, thrust

ramble verb 1 WALK, range, roam, rove, saunter, stray, stroll, wander 2 BABBLE, rabbit (on) (Brit. informal), waffle (informal, chiefly Brit.), witter on (informal) ◆ noun 3 WALK, hike, roaming, roving, saunter, stroll, tour

rambler noun WALKER, hiker, rover, wanderer, wayfarer

rambling adjective LONG-WINDED, circuitous, digressive, disconnected, discursive, disjointed, incoherent, wordy

ramification noun ramifications CONSEQUENCES, developments, results, sequel, upshot

ramp noun SLOPE, gradient, incline, rise

rampage verb 1 GO BERSERK, rage, run amok, run riot, storm ◆ noun 2 on the rampage BERSERK, amok, out of control, raging, riotous, violent, wild

rampant adjective 1 WIDESPREAD, prevalent, profuse, rife, spreading like wildfire, unchecked, uncontrolled, unrestrained 2 Heraldry UPRIGHT, erect, rearing, standing

rampart noun DEFENCE, bastion, bulwark, fence, fortification, wall

ramshackle adjective RICKETY, crumbling, decrepit, derelict, flimsy, shaky, tumbledown, unsafe, unsteady

rancid adjective ROTTEN, bad, fetid, foul, off, putrid, rank, sour, stale, strong-smelling, tainted

rancour noun HATRED, animosity, bad blood, bitterness, hate, ill feeling, ill will

random adjective 1 CHANCE, accidental, adventitious, casual, fortuitous, haphazard, hit or miss, incidental ◆ noun 2 at random HAPHAZARDLY, arbitrarily, by chance, randomly, unsystematically, willy-nilly

randy adjective Informal AROUSED,

amorous, horny (*slang*), hot,
lascivious, lustful, turned-on
(*slang*)

range *noun* 1 <u>LIMITS</u>, area, bounds,
orbit, province, radius, reach,
scope, sphere 2 <u>SERIES</u>, assortment,
collection, gamut, lot, selection,
variety ♦ *verb* 3 <u>VARY</u>, extend,
reach, run, stretch 4 <u>ROAM</u>, ramble,
rove, traverse, wander

rangy *adjective* <u>LONG-LIMBED</u>,
gangling, lanky, leggy,
long-legged

rank[1] *noun* 1 <u>STATUS</u>, caste, class,
degree, division, grade, level,
order, position, sort, type 2 <u>ROW</u>,
column, file, group, line, range,
series, tier ♦ *verb* 3 <u>ARRANGE</u>, align,
array, dispose, line up, order, sort

rank[2] *adjective* 1 <u>ABSOLUTE</u>, arrant,
blatant, complete, downright,
flagrant, gross, sheer, thorough,
total, utter 2 <u>FOUL</u>, bad, disgusting,
noisome, noxious, offensive,
rancid, revolting, stinking
3 <u>ABUNDANT</u>, dense, lush, luxuriant,
profuse

rank and file *noun* <u>GENERAL PUBLIC</u>,
majority, mass, masses

rankle *verb* <u>ANNOY</u>, anger, gall, get
on one's nerves (*informal*), irk,
irritate, rile

ransack *verb* 1 <u>SEARCH</u>, comb,
explore, go through, rummage,
scour, turn inside out 2 <u>PLUNDER</u>,
loot, pillage, raid, strip

ransom *noun* <u>PAYMENT</u>, money,
payoff, price

rant *verb* <u>SHOUT</u>, cry, declaim, rave,
roar, yell

rap *verb* 1 <u>HIT</u>, crack, knock, strike,
tap ♦ *noun* 2 <u>BLOW</u>, clout
(*informal*), crack, knock, tap
3 *Slang* <u>PUNISHMENT</u>, blame,
responsibility

rapacious *adjective* <u>GREEDY</u>,
avaricious, grasping, insatiable,

predatory, preying, voracious

rape *verb* 1 <u>SEXUALLY ASSAULT</u>, abuse,
force, outrage, ravish, violate
♦ *noun* 2 <u>SEXUAL ASSAULT</u>, outrage,
ravishment, violation
3 <u>DESECRATION</u>, abuse, defilement,
violation

rapid *adjective* <u>QUICK</u>, brisk, express,
fast, hasty, hurried, prompt,
speedy, swift

rapidity *noun* <u>SPEED</u>, alacrity,
briskness, fleetness, haste, hurry,
promptness, quickness, rush,
swiftness, velocity

rapidly *adverb* <u>QUICKLY</u>, briskly, fast,
hastily, hurriedly, in haste,
promptly, pronto (*informal*),
speedily, swiftly

rapport *noun* <u>BOND</u>, affinity,
empathy, harmony, link,
relationship, sympathy, tie,
understanding

rapprochement *noun*
<u>RECONCILIATION</u>, detente, reunion

rapt *adjective* <u>SPELLBOUND</u>, absorbed,
engrossed, enthralled, entranced,
fascinated, gripped

rapture *noun* <u>ECSTASY</u>, bliss, delight,
euphoria, joy, rhapsody, seventh
heaven, transport

rapturous *adjective* <u>ECSTATIC</u>,
blissful, euphoric, in seventh
heaven, joyful, overjoyed, over the
moon (*informal*), transported

rare *adjective* 1 <u>UNCOMMON</u>, few,
infrequent, scarce, singular,
sparse, strange, unusual 2 <u>SUPERB</u>,
choice, excellent, fine, great,
peerless, superlative

rarefied *adjective* <u>EXALTED</u>, elevated,
high, lofty, noble, spiritual,
sublime

rarely *adverb* <u>SELDOM</u>, hardly, hardly
ever, infrequently

raring *adjective As in* **raring to**
<u>EAGER</u>, desperate, enthusiastic,

impatient, keen, longing, ready

rarity noun **1** CURIO, collector's item, find, gem, treasure **2** UNCOMMONNESS, infrequency, scarcity, shortage, sparseness, strangeness, unusualness

rascal noun ROGUE, blackguard, devil, good-for-nothing, imp, ne'er-do-well, scamp, scoundrel, villain

rash[1] adjective RECKLESS, careless, foolhardy, hasty, heedless, ill-advised, impetuous, imprudent, impulsive, incautious

rash[2] noun **1** OUTBREAK, eruption **2** SPATE, flood, outbreak, plague, series, wave

rashness noun RECKLESSNESS, carelessness, foolhardiness, hastiness, heedlessness, indiscretion, thoughtlessness

rate noun **1** SPEED, pace, tempo, velocity **2** DEGREE, proportion, ratio, scale, standard **3** CHARGE, cost, fee, figure, price **4 at any rate** IN ANY CASE, anyhow, anyway, at all events ♦ verb **5** EVALUATE, consider, count, estimate, grade, measure, rank, reckon, value **6** DESERVE, be entitled to, be worthy of, merit

rather adverb **1** TO SOME EXTENT, a little, fairly, moderately, quite, relatively, somewhat, to some degree **2** PREFERABLY, more readily, more willingly, sooner

ratify verb APPROVE, affirm, authorize, confirm, endorse, establish, sanction, uphold

rating noun POSITION, class, degree, grade, order, placing, rank, rate, status

ratio noun PROPORTION, fraction, percentage, rate, relation

ration noun **1** ALLOWANCE, allotment, helping, measure, part, portion, quota, share ♦ verb **2** LIMIT, budget, control, restrict

rational adjective SANE, intelligent, logical, lucid, realistic, reasonable, sensible, sound, wise

rationale noun REASON, grounds, logic, motivation, philosophy, principle, raison d'être, theory

rationalize verb JUSTIFY, account for, excuse, vindicate

rattle verb **1** CLATTER, bang, jangle **2** SHAKE, bounce, jar, jolt, vibrate **3** Informal FLUSTER, disconcert, disturb, faze, perturb, shake, upset

raucous adjective HARSH, grating, hoarse, loud, noisy, rough, strident

raunchy adjective Slang SEXY, coarse, earthy, lusty, sexual, steamy (informal)

ravage verb **1** DESTROY, demolish, despoil, devastate, lay waste, ransack, ruin, spoil ♦ noun **2 ravages** DAMAGE, destruction, devastation, havoc, ruin, ruination, spoliation

rave verb **1** RANT, babble, be delirious, go mad (informal), rage, roar **2** Informal ENTHUSE, be mad about (informal), be wild about (informal), gush, praise

ravenous adjective STARVING, famished, starved

ravine noun CANYON, defile, gorge, gulch (U.S.), gully, pass

raving adjective MAD, crazed, crazy, delirious, hysterical, insane, irrational, wild

ravish verb **1** ENCHANT, captivate, charm, delight, enrapture, entrance, fascinate, spellbind **2** RAPE, abuse, force, sexually assault, violate

ravishing adjective ENCHANTING, beautiful, bewitching, charming, entrancing, gorgeous, lovely

raw adjective **1** UNCOOKED, fresh, natural **2** UNREFINED, basic, coarse, crude, natural, rough, unfinished, unprocessed **3** INEXPERIENCED, callow, green, immature, new **4** CHILLY, biting, bitter, cold, freezing, parky (*Brit. informal*), piercing

ray *noun* BEAM, bar, flash, gleam, shaft

raze *verb* DESTROY, demolish, flatten, knock down, level, pull down, ruin

re *preposition* CONCERNING, about, apropos, regarding, with reference to, with regard to

reach *verb* **1** ARRIVE AT, attain, get to, make **2** TOUCH, contact, extend to, grasp, stretch to **3** CONTACT, communicate with, get hold of, get in touch with, get through to ◆ *noun* **4** RANGE, capacity, distance, extension, extent, grasp, influence, power, scope, stretch

react *verb* **1** RESPOND, answer, reply **2** ACT, behave, function, operate, proceed, work

reaction *noun* **1** RESPONSE, answer, reply **2** RECOIL, counteraction **3** CONSERVATISM, the right

reactionary *adjective* **1** CONSERVATIVE, right-wing ◆ *noun* **2** CONSERVATIVE, die-hard, right-winger

read *verb* **1** LOOK AT, peruse, pore over, scan, study **2** INTERPRET, comprehend, construe, decipher, discover, see, understand **3** REGISTER, display, indicate, record, show

readable *adjective* **1** ENJOYABLE, entertaining, enthralling, gripping, interesting **2** LEGIBLE, clear, comprehensible, decipherable

readily *adverb* **1** WILLINGLY, eagerly, freely, gladly, promptly, quickly **2** EASILY, effortlessly, quickly, smoothly, speedily, unhesitatingly

readiness *noun* **1** WILLINGNESS, eagerness, keenness **2** EASE,

adroitness, dexterity, facility, promptness

reading *noun* **1** PERUSAL, examination, inspection, scrutiny, study **2** RECITAL, lesson, performance, sermon **3** INTERPRETATION, grasp, impression, version **4** LEARNING, education, erudition, knowledge, scholarship

ready *adjective* **1** PREPARED, arranged, fit, organized, primed, ripe, set **2** WILLING, agreeable, disposed, eager, glad, happy, inclined, keen, prone **3** PROMPT, alert, bright, clever, intelligent, keen, perceptive, quick, sharp, smart **4** AVAILABLE, accessible, convenient, handy, near, present

real *adjective* GENUINE, actual, authentic, factual, rightful, sincere, true, unfeigned, valid

realistic *adjective* **1** PRACTICAL, common-sense, down-to-earth, level-headed, matter-of-fact, real, sensible **2** LIFELIKE, authentic, faithful, genuine, natural, true, true to life

reality *noun* TRUTH, actuality, fact, realism, validity, verity

realization *noun* **1** AWARENESS, cognizance, comprehension, conception, grasp, perception, recognition, understanding **2** ACHIEVEMENT, accomplishment, fulfilment

realize *verb* **1** BECOME AWARE OF, comprehend, get the message, grasp, take in, understand **2** ACHIEVE, accomplish, carry out *or* through, complete, do, effect, fulfil, perform

really *adverb* TRULY, actually, certainly, genuinely, in actuality, indeed, in fact, positively, surely

realm *noun* **1** KINGDOM, country, domain, dominion, empire, land **2** SPHERE, area, branch, department, field, province, territory, world

reap verb 1 COLLECT, bring in, cut, garner, gather, harvest 2 OBTAIN, acquire, derive, gain, get

rear[1] noun 1 BACK, end, rearguard, stern, tail, tail end ♦ adjective 2 BACK, following, hind, last

rear[2] verb 1 BRING UP, breed, educate, foster, nurture, raise, train 2 RISE, loom, soar, tower

reason noun 1 CAUSE, aim, goal, grounds, incentive, intention, motive, object, purpose 2 SENSE(S), intellect, judgment, logic, mind, rationality, sanity, soundness, understanding ♦ verb 3 DEDUCE, conclude, infer, make out, think, work out 4 **reason with** PERSUADE, bring round (informal), prevail upon, talk into or out of, urge, win over

reasonable adjective 1 SENSIBLE, logical, plausible, practical, sane, sober, sound, tenable, wise 2 MODERATE, equitable, fair, fit, just, modest, O.K. or okay (informal), proper, right

reasoned adjective SENSIBLE, clear, logical, well-thought-out

reasoning noun THINKING, analysis, logic, thought

reassure verb ENCOURAGE, comfort, hearten, put or set one's mind at rest, restore confidence to

rebate noun REFUND, allowance, bonus, deduction, discount, reduction

rebel verb 1 REVOLT, mutiny, resist, rise up 2 DEFY, disobey, dissent ♦ noun 3 REVOLUTIONARY, insurgent, revolutionist, secessionist 4 NONCONFORMIST, apostate, dissenter, heretic, schismatic ♦ adjective 5 REBELLIOUS, insurgent, insurrectionary, revolutionary

rebellion noun 1 RESISTANCE, mutiny, revolt, revolution, rising, uprising 2 NONCONFORMITY, defiance, heresy, schism

rebellious adjective 1 REVOLUTIONARY, disloyal, disobedient, disorderly, insurgent, mutinous, rebel, seditious, unruly 2 DEFIANT, difficult, refractory, resistant, unmanageable

rebound verb 1 BOUNCE, recoil, ricochet 2 MISFIRE, backfire, boomerang, recoil

rebuff verb 1 REJECT, cold-shoulder, cut, knock back (slang), refuse, repulse, slight, snub, spurn, turn down ♦ noun 2 REJECTION, cold shoulder, kick in the teeth (slang), knock-back (slang), refusal, repulse, slap in the face (informal), slight, snub

rebuke verb 1 SCOLD, admonish, castigate, censure, chide, dress down (informal), give a rocket (Brit. & N.Z. informal), haul (someone) over the coals (informal), reprimand, reprove, tear (someone) off a strip (informal), tell off (informal) ♦ noun 2 SCOLDING, admonition, censure, dressing down (informal), reprimand, row, telling-off (informal)

rebut verb DISPROVE, confute, invalidate, negate, overturn, prove wrong, refute

rebuttal noun DISPROOF, confutation, invalidation, negation, refutation

recalcitrant adjective DISOBEDIENT, defiant, insubordinate, refractory, unmanageable, unruly, wayward, wilful

recall verb 1 RECOLLECT, bring or call to mind, evoke, remember 2 ANNUL, cancel, countermand, repeal, retract, revoke, withdraw ♦ noun 3 RECOLLECTION, memory, remembrance 4 ANNULMENT, cancellation, repeal, rescindment, retraction, withdrawal

recant verb WITHDRAW, disclaim, forswear, renege, repudiate, retract, revoke, take back

recapitulate verb REPEAT, outline, recap (*informal*), recount, restate, summarize

recede verb FALL BACK, abate, ebb, regress, retire, retreat, return, subside, withdraw

receipt noun 1 SALES SLIP, counterfoil, proof of purchase 2 RECEIVING, acceptance, delivery, reception

receive verb 1 GET, accept, acquire, be given, collect, obtain, pick up, take 2 EXPERIENCE, bear, encounter, suffer, sustain, undergo 3 GREET, accommodate, admit, entertain, meet, welcome

recent adjective NEW, current, fresh, late, modern, novel, present-day, up-to-date

recently adverb NEWLY, currently, freshly, lately, latterly, not long ago, of late

receptacle noun CONTAINER, holder, repository

reception noun 1 PARTY, function, levee, soirée 2 WELCOME, acknowledgment, greeting, reaction, response, treatment

receptive adjective OPEN, amenable, interested, open-minded, open to suggestions, susceptible, sympathetic

recess noun 1 ALCOVE, bay, corner, hollow, niche, nook 2 BREAK, holiday, intermission, interval, respite, rest, vacation

recession noun DEPRESSION, decline, drop, slump

recipe noun 1 DIRECTIONS, ingredients, instructions 2 METHOD,

formula, prescription, procedure, process, technique

reciprocal adjective MUTUAL, alternate, complementary, correlative, corresponding, equivalent, exchanged, interchangeable

reciprocate verb RETURN, exchange, reply, requite, respond, swap, trade

recital noun 1 PERFORMANCE, rehearsal, rendering 2 RECITATION, account, narrative, reading, relation, statement, telling

recitation noun RECITAL, lecture, passage, performance, piece, reading

recite verb REPEAT, declaim, deliver, narrate, perform, speak

reckless adjective CARELESS, hasty, headlong, heedless, imprudent, mindless, precipitate, rash, thoughtless, wild

reckon verb 1 THINK, assume, believe, guess (*informal, chiefly U.S. & Canad.*), imagine, suppose 2 CONSIDER, account, count, deem, esteem, judge, rate, regard 3 COUNT, add up, calculate, compute, figure, number, tally, total

reckoning noun 1 COUNT, addition, calculation, estimate 2 BILL, account, charge, due, score

reclaim verb REGAIN, recapture, recover, redeem, reform, retrieve, salvage

recline verb LEAN, lie (down), loll, lounge, repose, rest, sprawl

recluse noun HERMIT, anchoress, anchorite, monk, solitary

reclusive adjective SOLITARY, hermit-like, isolated, retiring, withdrawn

recognition noun 1 IDENTIFICATION, discovery, recollection, remembrance 2 ACCEPTANCE, admission, allowance, confession 3 APPRECIATION, notice, respect

recognize verb 1 IDENTIFY, know, notice, place, recall, recollect, remember, spot 2 ACCEPT, acknowledge, admit, allow, concede, grant 3 APPRECIATE, notice, respect

recoil verb 1 JERK BACK, kick, react, rebound, spring back 2 DRAW BACK, falter, quail, shrink 3 BACKFIRE, boomerang, misfire, rebound ♦ noun 4 REACTION, backlash, kick, rebound, repercussion

recollect verb REMEMBER, place, recall, summon up

recollection noun MEMORY, impression, recall, remembrance, reminiscence

recommend verb 1 ADVISE, advance, advocate, counsel, prescribe, propose, put forward, suggest 2 PRAISE, approve, commend, endorse

recommendation noun 1 ADVICE, counsel, proposal, suggestion 2 PRAISE, advocacy, approval, commendation, endorsement, reference, sanction, testimonial

recompense verb 1 REWARD, pay, remunerate 2 COMPENSATE, make up for, pay for, redress, reimburse, repay, requite ♦ noun 3 COMPENSATION, amends, damages, payment, remuneration, reparation, repayment, requital, restitution 4 REWARD, payment, return, wages

reconcile verb 1 RESOLVE, adjust, compose, put to rights, rectify, settle, square 2 REUNITE, appease, conciliate, make peace between, propitiate 3 ACCEPT, put up with (informal), resign oneself, submit, yield

reconciliation noun REUNION,

conciliation, pacification, reconcilement

recondite adjective OBSCURE, arcane, concealed, dark, deep, difficult, hidden, mysterious, occult, profound, secret

recondition verb RESTORE, do up (informal), overhaul, remodel, renew, renovate, repair, revamp

reconnaissance noun INSPECTION, exploration, investigation, observation, recce (slang), scan, survey

reconnoitre verb INSPECT, case (slang), explore, investigate, observe, scan, spy out, survey

reconsider verb RETHINK, reassess, review, revise, think again

reconstruct verb 1 REBUILD, recreate, regenerate, remake, remodel, renovate, restore 2 DEDUCE, build up, piece together

record noun 1 DOCUMENT, account, chronicle, diary, entry, file, journal, log, register, report 2 EVIDENCE, documentation, testimony, trace, witness 3 DISC, album, LP, single, vinyl 4 BACKGROUND, career, history, performance 5 **off the record** CONFIDENTIAL, not for publication, private, unofficial ♦ verb 6 WRITE DOWN, chronicle, document, enter, log, minute, note, register, set down, take down 7 TAPE, make a recording of, tape-record, video, video-tape 8 REGISTER, give evidence of, indicate, say, show

recorder noun CHRONICLER, archivist, clerk, diarist, historian, scribe

recording noun RECORD, disc, tape, video

recount verb TELL, depict, describe, narrate, recite, relate, repeat, report

recoup verb 1 REGAIN, recover, retrieve, win back 2 COMPENSATE, make up for, refund, reimburse, repay, requite

recourse noun OPTION, alternative, choice, expedient, remedy, resort, resource, way out

recover verb 1 GET BETTER, convalesce, get well, heal, improve, mend, rally, recuperate, revive 2 REGAIN, get back, recapture, reclaim, redeem, repossess, restore, retrieve

recovery noun 1 IMPROVEMENT, convalescence, healing, mending, recuperation, revival 2 RETRIEVAL, reclamation, repossession, restoration

recreation noun PASTIME, amusement, diversion, enjoyment, entertainment, fun, hobby, leisure activity, play, relaxation, sport

recrimination noun BICKERING, counterattack, mutual accusation, quarrel, squabbling

recruit verb 1 ENLIST, draft, enrol, levy, mobilize, muster, raise 2 WIN (OVER), engage, obtain, procure ♦ noun 3 BEGINNER, apprentice, convert, helper, initiate, learner, novice, trainee

rectify verb CORRECT, adjust, emend, fix, improve, redress, remedy, repair, right

rectitude noun MORALITY, decency, goodness, honesty, honour, integrity, principle, probity, virtue

recuperate verb RECOVER, convalesce, get better, improve, mend

recur verb HAPPEN AGAIN, come again, persist, reappear, repeat, return, revert

recurrent adjective PERIODIC, continued, frequent, habitual, recurring

recycle verb REPROCESS, reclaim,

reuse, salvage, save

red adjective 1 CRIMSON, carmine, cherry, coral, ruby, scarlet, vermilion 2 Of hair CHESTNUT, carroty, flame-coloured, reddish, sandy, titian 3 FLUSHED, blushing, embarrassed, florid, shamefaced ♦ noun 4 **in the red** Informal IN DEBT, in arrears, insolvent, overdrawn 5 **see red** Informal LOSE ONE'S TEMPER, blow one's top, crack up (informal), fly off the handle (informal), go ballistic (slang, chiefly U.S.), go mad (informal)

red-blooded adjective Informal VIGOROUS, lusty, robust, strong, virile

redden verb FLUSH, blush, colour (up), crimson, go red

redeem verb 1 MAKE UP FOR, atone for, compensate for, make amends for 2 REINSTATE, absolve, restore to favour 3 SAVE, deliver, emancipate, free, liberate, ransom 4 BUY BACK, reclaim, recover, regain, repurchase, retrieve

redemption noun 1 COMPENSATION, amends, atonement, reparation 2 SALVATION, deliverance, emancipation, liberation, release, rescue 3 REPURCHASE, reclamation, recovery, repossession, retrieval

red-handed adjective IN THE ACT, bang to rights (slang), (in) flagrante delicto

redolent adjective 1 REMINISCENT, evocative, suggestive 2 SCENTED, aromatic, fragrant, odorous, perfumed, sweet-smelling

redoubtable adjective FORMIDABLE, fearful, fearsome, mighty, powerful, strong

redress verb 1 MAKE AMENDS FOR, compensate for, make up for 2 PUT RIGHT, adjust, balance, correct, even up, rectify, regulate ♦ noun 3 AMENDS, atonement, compensation, payment, recompense, reparation

reduce *verb* 1 LESSEN, abate, curtail, cut down, decrease, diminish, lower, moderate, shorten, weaken 2 DEGRADE, break, bring low, downgrade, humble

redundancy *noun* UNEMPLOYMENT, joblessness, layoff, the axe (*informal*), the sack (*informal*)

redundant *adjective* SUPERFLUOUS, extra, inessential, supernumerary, surplus, unnecessary, unwanted

reek *verb* 1 STINK, pong (*Brit. informal*), smell ♦ *noun* 2 STINK, fetor, odour, pong (*Brit. informal*), smell, stench

reel *verb* 1 STAGGER, lurch, pitch, rock, roll, sway 2 WHIRL, revolve, spin, swirl

refer *verb* 1 ALLUDE, bring up, cite, mention, speak of 2 RELATE, apply, belong, be relevant to, concern, pertain 3 CONSULT, apply, go, look up, turn to 4 DIRECT, guide, point, send

referee *noun* 1 UMPIRE, adjudicator, arbiter, arbitrator, judge, ref (*informal*) ♦ *verb* 2 UMPIRE, adjudicate, arbitrate, judge, mediate

reference *noun* 1 CITATION, allusion, mention, note, quotation 2 TESTIMONIAL, character, credentials, endorsement, recommendation 3 RELEVANCE, applicability, bearing, connection, relation

referendum *noun* PUBLIC VOTE, plebiscite, popular vote

refine *verb* 1 PURIFY, clarify, cleanse, distil, filter, process 2 IMPROVE, hone, perfect, polish

refined *adjective* 1 CULTURED, civilized, cultivated, elegant, polished, polite, well-bred 2 PURE, clarified, clean, distilled, filtered, processed, purified 3 DISCERNING, delicate, discriminating, fastidious, fine, precise, sensitive

refinement *noun* 1 SOPHISTICATION, breeding, civility, courtesy, cultivation, culture, discrimination, gentility, good breeding, polish, taste 2 SUBTLETY, fine point, nicety, nuance 3 PURIFICATION, clarification, cleansing, distillation, filtering, processing

reflect *verb* 1 THROW BACK, echo, mirror, reproduce, return 2 SHOW, demonstrate, display, indicate, manifest, reveal 3 THINK, cogitate, consider, meditate, muse, ponder, ruminate, wonder

reflection *noun* 1 IMAGE, echo, mirror image 2 THOUGHT, cogitation, consideration, contemplation, idea, meditation, musing, observation, opinion, thinking

reflective *adjective* THOUGHTFUL, contemplative, meditative, pensive

reform *noun* 1 IMPROVEMENT, amendment, betterment, rehabilitation ♦ *verb* 2 IMPROVE, amend, correct, mend, rectify, restore 3 MEND ONE'S WAYS, clean up one's act (*informal*), go straight (*informal*), pull one's socks up (*Brit. informal*), shape up (*informal*), turn over a new leaf

refractory *adjective* UNMANAGEABLE, difficult, disobedient, headstrong, intractable, uncontrollable, unruly, wilful

refrain[1] *verb* STOP, abstain, avoid, cease, desist, forbear, leave off, renounce

refrain[2] *noun* CHORUS, melody, tune

refresh *verb* 1 REVIVE, brace, enliven, freshen, reinvigorate, revitalize, stimulate 2 STIMULATE, jog, prompt, renew

refreshing *adjective* 1 STIMULATING, bracing, fresh, invigorating 2 NEW, novel, original

refreshment *noun* **refreshments** FOOD AND DRINK, drinks, snacks, titbits

refrigerate *verb* COOL, chill, freeze, keep cold

refuge *noun* SHELTER, asylum, haven, hide-out, protection, retreat, sanctuary

refugee *noun* EXILE, displaced person, émigré, escapee

refund *verb* 1 REPAY, pay back, reimburse, restore, return ♦ *noun* 2 REPAYMENT, reimbursement, return

refurbish *verb* RENOVATE, clean up, do up (*informal*), mend, overhaul, repair, restore, revamp

refusal *noun* DENIAL, knock-back (*slang*), rebuff, rejection

refuse[1] *verb* REJECT, decline, deny, say no, spurn, turn down, withhold

refuse[2] *noun* RUBBISH, garbage, junk (*informal*), litter, trash, waste

refute *verb* DISPROVE, discredit, negate, overthrow, prove false, rebut

regain *verb* 1 RECOVER, get back, recapture, recoup, retrieve, take back, win back 2 GET BACK TO, reach again, return to

regal *adjective* ROYAL, kingly *or* queenly, magnificent, majestic, noble, princely

regale *verb* ENTERTAIN, amuse, delight, divert

regalia *plural noun* EMBLEMS, accoutrements, decorations, finery, paraphernalia, trappings

regard *verb* 1 CONSIDER, believe, deem, esteem, judge, rate, see, suppose, think, view 2 LOOK AT, behold, check out (*informal*), clock (*Brit. slang*), eye, gaze at, observe, scrutinize, view, watch 3 HEED, attend, listen to, mind, pay attention to, take notice of 4 **as regards** CONCERNING, pertaining to, regarding, relating to ♦ *noun* 5 HEED, attention, interest, mind, notice 6 RESPECT, care, concern, consideration, esteem, thought 7 LOOK, gaze, glance, scrutiny, stare

regarding *preposition* CONCERNING, about, as regards, in *or* with regard to, on the subject of, re, respecting, with reference to

regardless *adjective* 1 HEEDLESS, inconsiderate, indifferent, neglectful, negligent, rash, reckless, unmindful ♦ *adverb* 2 ANYWAY, in any case, in spite of everything, nevertheless

regards *plural noun* GOOD WISHES, best wishes, compliments, greetings, respects

regenerate *verb* RENEW, breathe new life into, invigorate, reawaken, reinvigorate, rejuvenate, restore, revive

regime *noun* GOVERNMENT, leadership, management, reign, rule, system

regimented *adjective* CONTROLLED, disciplined, ordered, organized, regulated, systematized

region *noun* AREA, district, locality, part, place, quarter, section, sector, territory, tract, zone

regional *adjective* LOCAL, district, parochial, provincial, zonal

register *noun* 1 LIST, archives, catalogue, chronicle, diary, file, log, record, roll, roster ♦ *verb* 2 RECORD, catalogue, chronicle, enlist, enrol, enter, list, note 3 SHOW, display, exhibit, express, indicate, manifest, mark, reveal

regress *verb* REVERT, backslide, degenerate, deteriorate, fall away *or* off, go back, lapse, relapse, return

regret *verb* **1** FEEL SORRY ABOUT, bemoan, bewail, deplore, grieve, lament, miss, mourn, repent, rue ♦ *noun* **2** SORROW, bitterness, compunction, contrition, penitence, remorse, repentance, ruefulness

regretful *adjective* SORRY, apologetic, contrite, penitent, remorseful, repentant, rueful, sad, sorrowful

regrettable *adjective* UNFORTUNATE, disappointing, distressing, lamentable, sad, shameful

regular *adjective* **1** NORMAL, common, customary, habitual, ordinary, routine, typical, usual **2** EVEN, balanced, flat, level, smooth, straight, symmetrical, uniform **3** SYSTEMATIC, consistent, constant, even, fixed, ordered, set, stated, steady, uniform

regulate *verb* **1** CONTROL, direct, govern, guide, handle, manage, rule, run, supervise **2** ADJUST, balance, fit, moderate, modulate, tune

regulation *noun* **1** RULE, decree, dictate, edict, law, order, precept, statute **2** CONTROL, direction, government, management, supervision **3** ADJUSTMENT, modulation, tuning

regurgitate *verb* VOMIT, disgorge, puke (*slang*), sick up (*informal*), spew (out *or* up), throw up (*informal*)

rehabilitate *verb* **1** REINTEGRATE, adjust **2** REDEEM, clear, reform, restore, save

rehash *verb* **1** REWORK, refashion, rejig (*informal*), reuse, rewrite ♦ *noun* **2** REWORKING, new version, rearrangement, rewrite

rehearsal *noun* PRACTICE, drill,

preparation, rehearsing, run-through

rehearse *verb* PRACTISE, drill, go over, prepare, recite, repeat, run through, train

reign *noun* **1** RULE, command, control, dominion, monarchy, power ♦ *verb* **2** RULE, be in power, command, govern, influence **3** BE SUPREME, hold sway, predominate, prevail

reimburse *verb* PAY BACK, compensate, recompense, refund, remunerate, repay, return

rein *verb* **1** CONTROL, check, curb, halt, hold back, limit, restrain, restrict ♦ *noun* **2** CONTROL, brake, bridle, check, curb, harness, hold, restraint

reincarnation *noun* REBIRTH, transmigration of souls

reinforce *verb* SUPPORT, bolster, emphasize, fortify, prop, strengthen, stress, supplement, toughen

reinforcement *noun* **1** STRENGTHENING, augmentation, fortification, increase **2** SUPPORT, brace, buttress, prop, stay **3 reinforcements** RESERVES, additional *or* fresh troops, auxiliaries, support

reinstate *verb* RESTORE, recall, re-establish, replace, return

reiterate *verb* REPEAT, do again, restate, say again

reject *verb* **1** DENY, decline, disallow, exclude, renounce, repudiate, veto **2** REBUFF, jilt, refuse, repulse, say no to, spurn, turn down **3** DISCARD, eliminate, jettison, scrap, throw away *or* out ♦ *noun* **4** CASTOFF, discard, failure, second

rejection *noun* **1** DENIAL, dismissal, exclusion, renunciation, repudiation, thumbs down, veto **2** REBUFF, brushoff (*slang*), kick in the teeth (*slang*), knock-back (*slang*), refusal

rejig *verb* REARRANGE, alter, juggle, manipulate, reorganize, tweak

rejoice *verb* BE GLAD, be happy, be overjoyed, celebrate, exult, glory

rejoicing *noun* HAPPINESS, celebration, elation, exultation, gladness, joy, jubilation, merrymaking

rejoin *verb* REPLY, answer, respond, retort, riposte

rejoinder *noun* REPLY, answer, comeback (*informal*), response, retort, riposte

rejuvenate *verb* REVITALIZE, breathe new life into, refresh, regenerate, reinvigorate, renew, restore

relapse *verb* 1 LAPSE, backslide, degenerate, fail, regress, revert, slip back 2 WORSEN, deteriorate, fade, fail, sicken, sink, weaken ♦ *noun* 3 LAPSE, backsliding, regression, retrogression 4 WORSENING, deterioration, turn for the worse, weakening

relate *verb* 1 CONNECT, associate, correlate, couple, join, link 2 CONCERN, apply, be relevant to, have to do with, pertain, refer 3 TELL, describe, detail, narrate, recite, recount, report

related *adjective* 1 AKIN, kindred 2 ASSOCIATED, affiliated, akin, connected, interconnected, joint, linked

relation *noun* 1 CONNECTION, bearing, bond, comparison, correlation, link 2 RELATIVE, kin, kinsman *or* kinswoman 3 KINSHIP, affinity, kindred

relations *plural noun* 1 DEALINGS, affairs, connections, contact, interaction, intercourse, relationship 2 FAMILY, clan, kin, kindred, kinsfolk, kinsmen, relatives, tribe

relationship *noun* 1 ASSOCIATION, affinity, bond, connection, kinship, rapport 2 AFFAIR, liaison 3 CONNECTION, correlation, link, parallel, similarity, tie-up

relative *adjective* 1 DEPENDENT, allied, associated, comparative, contingent, corresponding, proportionate, related 2 RELEVANT, applicable, apposite, appropriate, apropos, germane, pertinent ♦ *noun* 3 RELATION, kinsman *or* kinswoman, member of one's *or* the family

relatively *adverb* COMPARATIVELY, rather, somewhat

relax *verb* 1 BE *or* FEEL AT EASE, calm, chill out (*slang, chiefly U.S.*), lighten up (*slang*), rest, take it easy, unwind 2 LESSEN, abate, ease, ebb, let up, loosen, lower, moderate, reduce, relieve, slacken, weaken

relaxation *noun* LEISURE, enjoyment, fun, pleasure, recreation, rest

relaxed *adjective* EASY-GOING, casual, comfortable, easy, free and easy, informal, laid-back (*informal*), leisurely

relay *noun* 1 SHIFT, relief, turn 2 MESSAGE, dispatch, transmission ♦ *verb* 3 PASS ON, broadcast, carry, communicate, send, spread, transmit

release *verb* 1 SET FREE, discharge, drop, extricate, free, liberate, loose, unbridle, undo, unfasten 2 ACQUIT, absolve, exonerate, let go, let off 3 ISSUE, circulate, distribute, launch, make known, make public, publish, put out ♦ *noun* 4 LIBERATION, deliverance, discharge, emancipation, freedom, liberty 5 ACQUITTAL, absolution, exemption, exoneration 6 ISSUE, proclamation, publication

relegate *verb* DEMOTE, downgrade

relent verb BE MERCIFUL, capitulate, change one's mind, come round, have pity, show mercy, soften, yield

relentless adjective 1 UNREMITTING, incessant, nonstop, persistent, unrelenting, unrelieved 2 MERCILESS, cruel, fierce, implacable, pitiless, remorseless, ruthless, unrelenting

relevant adjective SIGNIFICANT, apposite, appropriate, apt, fitting, germane, pertinent, related, to the point

reliable adjective DEPENDABLE, faithful, safe, sound, staunch, sure, true, trustworthy

reliance noun TRUST, belief, confidence, dependence, faith

relic noun REMNANT, fragment, keepsake, memento, souvenir, trace, vestige

relief noun 1 EASE, comfort, cure, deliverance, mitigation, release, remedy, solace 2 REST, break, breather (informal), relaxation, respite 3 AID, assistance, help, succour, support

relieve verb 1 EASE, alleviate, assuage, calm, comfort, console, cure, mitigate, relax, soften, soothe 2 HELP, aid, assist, succour, support, sustain

religious adjective 1 DEVOUT, devotional, faithful, godly, holy, pious, sacred, spiritual 2 CONSCIENTIOUS, faithful, meticulous, punctilious, rigid, scrupulous

relinquish verb GIVE UP, abandon, abdicate, cede, drop, forsake, leave, let go, renounce, surrender

relish verb 1 ENJOY, delight in, fancy, like, revel in, savour ♦ noun 2 ENJOYMENT, fancy, fondness, gusto, liking, love, partiality, penchant, predilection, taste

3 CONDIMENT, sauce, seasoning 4 FLAVOUR, piquancy, smack, spice, tang, taste, trace

reluctance noun UNWILLINGNESS, aversion, disinclination, dislike, distaste, loathing, repugnance

reluctant adjective UNWILLING, disinclined, hesitant, loath, unenthusiastic

rely verb DEPEND, bank, bet, count, trust

remain verb 1 CONTINUE, abide, dwell, endure, go on, last, persist, stand, stay, survive 2 STAY BEHIND, be left, delay, linger, wait

remainder noun REST, balance, excess, leavings, remains, remnant, residue, surplus

remaining adjective LEFT-OVER, lingering, outstanding, persisting, surviving, unfinished

remains plural noun 1 REMNANTS, debris, dregs, leavings, leftovers, relics, residue, rest 2 BODY, cadaver, carcass, corpse

remark verb 1 COMMENT, declare, mention, observe, pass comment, reflect, say, state 2 NOTICE, espy, make out, mark, note, observe, perceive, see ♦ noun 3 COMMENT, observation, reflection, statement, utterance

remarkable adjective EXTRAORDINARY, notable, outstanding, rare, singular, striking, surprising, uncommon, unusual, wonderful

remedy noun 1 CURE, medicine, nostrum, treatment ♦ verb 2 PUT RIGHT, correct, fix, rectify, set to rights

remember verb 1 RECALL, call to mind, commemorate, look back (on), recollect, reminisce, think back 2 BEAR IN MIND, keep in mind

remembrance noun 1 MEMORY, recall, recollection, reminiscence, thought **2** SOUVENIR, commemoration, keepsake, memento, memorial, monument, reminder, token

remind verb CALL TO MIND, jog one's memory, make (someone) remember, prompt

reminisce verb RECALL, hark back, look back, recollect, remember, think back

reminiscence noun RECOLLECTION, anecdote, memoir, memory, recall, remembrance

reminiscent adjective SUGGESTIVE, evocative, similar

remiss adjective CARELESS, forgetful, heedless, lax, neglectful, negligent, thoughtless

remission noun **1** PARDON, absolution, amnesty, discharge, exemption, release, reprieve **2** LESSENING, abatement, alleviation, ebb, lull, relaxation, respite

remit verb **1** SEND, dispatch, forward, mail, post, transmit **2** CANCEL, halt, repeal, rescind, stop **3** POSTPONE, defer, delay, put off, shelve, suspend ♦ noun **4** INSTRUCTIONS, brief, guidelines, orders

remittance noun PAYMENT, allowance, fee

remnant noun REMAINDER, end, fragment, leftovers, remains, residue, rest, trace, vestige

remonstrate verb ARGUE, dispute, dissent, object, protest, take issue

remorse noun REGRET, anguish, compunction, contrition, grief, guilt, penitence, repentance, shame, sorrow

remorseful adjective REGRETFUL, apologetic, ashamed, conscience-stricken, contrite, guilty, penitent, repentant, sorry

remorseless adjective **1** PITILESS,

callous, cruel, inhumane, merciless, ruthless **2** RELENTLESS, inexorable

remote adjective **1** DISTANT, far, inaccessible, in the middle of nowhere, isolated, out-of-the-way, secluded **2** ALOOF, abstracted, cold, detached, distant, reserved, standoffish, uncommunicative, withdrawn **3** SLIGHT, doubtful, dubious, faint, outside, slender, slim, small, unlikely

removal noun **1** TAKING AWAY or OFF or OUT, dislodgment, ejection, elimination, eradication, extraction, uprooting, withdrawal **2** DISMISSAL, expulsion **3** MOVE, departure, flitting (*Scot. & Northern English dialect*), relocation, transfer

remove verb **1** TAKE AWAY or OFF or OUT, abolish, delete, detach, displace, eject, eliminate, erase, excise, extract, get rid of, wipe from the face of the earth, withdraw **2** DISMISS, depose, dethrone, discharge, expel, oust, throw out **3** MOVE, depart, flit (*Scot. & Northern English dialect*), relocate

remunerate verb PAY, compensate, recompense, reimburse, repay, requite, reward

remuneration noun PAYMENT, earnings, fee, income, pay, return, reward, salary, stipend, wages

remunerative adjective PROFITABLE, economic, lucrative, moneymaking, paying, rewarding, worthwhile

renaissance, renascence noun REBIRTH, reappearance, reawakening, renewal, restoration, resurgence, revival

rend verb TEAR, rip, rupture, separate, wrench

render verb 1 <u>MAKE</u>, cause to become, leave 2 <u>PROVIDE</u>, furnish, give, hand out, pay, present, submit, supply, tender 3 <u>PORTRAY</u>, act, depict, do, give, perform, play, represent

rendezvous noun 1 <u>APPOINTMENT</u>, assignation, date, engagement, meeting, tryst (archaic) 2 <u>MEETING PLACE</u>, gathering point, venue ♦ verb 3 <u>MEET</u>, assemble, come together, gather, join up

rendition noun 1 <u>PERFORMANCE</u>, arrangement, interpretation, portrayal, presentation, reading, rendering, version 2 <u>TRANSLATION</u>, interpretation, reading, transcription, version

renegade noun 1 <u>DESERTER</u>, apostate, defector, traitor, turncoat ♦ adjective 2 <u>REBELLIOUS</u>, apostate, disloyal, traitorous, unfaithful

renege verb <u>BREAK ONE'S WORD</u>, back out, break a promise, default, go back

renew verb 1 <u>RECOMMENCE</u>, continue, extend, reaffirm, recreate, reopen, repeat, resume 2 <u>RESTORE</u>, mend, modernize, overhaul, refit, refurbish, renovate, repair 3 <u>REPLACE</u>, refresh, replenish, restock

renounce verb <u>GIVE UP</u>, abjure, deny, disown, forsake, forswear, quit, recant, relinquish, waive

renovate verb <u>RESTORE</u>, do up (informal), modernize, overhaul, recondition, refit, refurbish, renew, repair

renown noun <u>FAME</u>, distinction, eminence, note, reputation, repute

renowned adjective <u>FAMOUS</u>, celebrated, distinguished, eminent, esteemed, notable, noted, well-known

rent[1] verb 1 <u>HIRE</u>, charter, lease, let ♦ noun 2 <u>HIRE</u>, fee, lease, payment, rental

rent[2] noun <u>TEAR</u>, gash, hole, opening, rip, slash, slit, split

renunciation noun <u>GIVING UP</u>, abandonment, abdication, abjuration, denial, disavowal, forswearing, rejection, relinquishment, repudiation

reorganize verb <u>REARRANGE</u>, reshuffle, restructure

repair verb 1 <u>MEND</u>, fix, heal, patch, patch up, renovate, restore ♦ noun 2 <u>MEND</u>, darn, overhaul, patch, restoration 3 <u>CONDITION</u>, form, shape (informal), state

reparation noun <u>COMPENSATION</u>, atonement, damages, recompense, restitution, satisfaction

repartee noun <u>WIT</u>, badinage, banter, riposte, wittiness, wordplay

repast noun <u>MEAL</u>, food

repay verb 1 <u>PAY BACK</u>, compensate, recompense, refund, reimburse, requite, return, square 2 <u>GET EVEN WITH</u> (informal), avenge, get one's own back on (informal), hit back, reciprocate, retaliate, revenge

repeal verb 1 <u>ABOLISH</u>, annul, cancel, invalidate, nullify, recall, reverse, revoke ♦ noun 2 <u>ABOLITION</u>, annulment, cancellation, invalidation, rescindment

repeat verb 1 <u>REITERATE</u>, echo, replay, reproduce, rerun, reshow, restate, retell ♦ noun 2 <u>REPETITION</u>, echo, reiteration, replay, rerun, reshowing

repeatedly adverb <u>OVER AND OVER</u>, frequently, many times, often

repel verb 1 <u>DISGUST</u>, gross out (U.S. slang), nauseate, offend, revolt, sicken 2 <u>DRIVE OFF</u>, fight, hold off, parry, rebuff, repulse, resist, ward off

repellent *adjective* **1** <u>DISGUSTING</u>, abhorrent, hateful, horrid, loathsome, nauseating, noxious, offensive, repugnant, repulsive, revolting, sickening **2** <u>PROOF</u>, impermeable, repelling, resistant

repent *verb* <u>REGRET</u>, be sorry, feel remorse, rue

repentance *noun* <u>REGRET</u>, compunction, contrition, grief, guilt, penitence, remorse

repentant *adjective* <u>REGRETFUL</u>, contrite, penitent, remorseful, rueful, sorry

repercussion *noun* **repercussions** <u>CONSEQUENCES</u>, backlash, result, sequel, side effects

repertoire *noun* <u>RANGE</u>, collection, list, repertory, stock, store, supply

repetition *noun* <u>REPEATING</u>, echo, recurrence, reiteration, renewal, replication, restatement, tautology

repetitious *adjective* <u>LONG-WINDED</u>, prolix, tautological, tedious, verbose, wordy

repetitive *adjective* <u>MONOTONOUS</u>, boring, dull, mechanical, recurrent, tedious, unchanging, unvaried

rephrase *verb* <u>REWORD</u>, paraphrase, put differently

repine *verb* <u>COMPLAIN</u>, fret, grumble, moan

replace *verb* <u>TAKE THE PLACE OF</u>, follow, oust, substitute, succeed, supersede, supplant, take over from

replacement *noun* <u>SUCCESSOR</u>, double, proxy, stand-in, substitute, surrogate, understudy

replenish *verb* <u>REFILL</u>, fill, provide, reload, replace, restore, top up

replete *adjective* <u>FULL</u>, crammed, filled, full up, glutted, gorged, stuffed

replica *noun* <u>DUPLICATE</u>, carbon copy (*informal*), copy, facsimile, imitation, model, reproduction

replicate *verb* <u>COPY</u>, duplicate, mimic, recreate, reduplicate, reproduce

reply *verb* **1** <u>ANSWER</u>, counter, reciprocate, rejoin, respond, retaliate, retort ♦ *noun* **2** <u>ANSWER</u>, counter, counterattack, reaction, rejoinder, response, retaliation, retort

report *verb* **1** <u>COMMUNICATE</u>, broadcast, cover, describe, detail, inform of, narrate, pass on, recount, relate, state, tell **2** <u>PRESENT ONESELF</u>, appear, arrive, come, turn up ♦ *noun* **3** <u>ACCOUNT</u>, communication, description, narrative, news, record, statement, word **4** <u>ARTICLE</u>, piece, story, write-up **5** <u>RUMOUR</u>, buzz, gossip, hearsay, talk **6** <u>BANG</u>, blast, boom, crack, detonation, discharge, explosion, noise, sound

reporter *noun* <u>JOURNALIST</u>, correspondent, hack (*derogatory*), journo (*slang*), pressman, writer

repose *noun* **1** <u>PEACE</u>, ease, quietness, relaxation, respite, rest, stillness, tranquillity **2** <u>COMPOSURE</u>, calmness, poise, self-possession **3** <u>SLEEP</u>, slumber ♦ *verb* **4** <u>REST</u>, lie, lie down, recline, rest upon

repository *noun* <u>STORE</u>, depository, storehouse, treasury, vault

reprehensible *adjective* <u>BLAMEWORTHY</u>, bad, culpable, disgraceful, shameful, unworthy

represent *verb* **1** <u>STAND FOR</u>, act for, betoken, mean, serve as, speak for, symbolize **2** <u>SYMBOLIZE</u>, embody, epitomize, exemplify, personify, typify **3** <u>PORTRAY</u>, denote, depict, describe, illustrate, outline, picture, show

representation *noun* <u>PORTRAYAL</u>,

account, depiction, description, illustration, image, likeness, model, picture, portrait

representative noun 1 DELEGATE, agent, deputy, member, proxy, spokesman or spokeswoman 2 SALESMAN, agent, commercial traveller, rep ♦ adjective 3 TYPICAL, archetypal, characteristic, exemplary, symbolic

repress verb 1 INHIBIT, bottle up, check, control, curb, hold back, restrain, stifle, suppress 2 SUBDUE, quell, subjugate

repression noun SUBJUGATION, constraint, control, despotism, domination, restraint, suppression, tyranny

repressive adjective OPPRESSIVE, absolute, authoritarian, despotic, dictatorial, tyrannical

reprieve verb 1 GRANT A STAY OF EXECUTION TO, let off the hook (slang), pardon 2 RELIEVE, abate, allay, alleviate, mitigate, palliate ♦ noun 3 STAY OF EXECUTION, amnesty, deferment, pardon, postponement, remission 4 RELIEF, alleviation, mitigation, palliation, respite

reprimand verb 1 BLAME, censure, dress down (informal), haul over the coals (informal), rap over the knuckles, rebuke, scold, tear (someone) off a strip (Brit. informal) ♦ noun 2 BLAME, censure, dressing-down (informal), rebuke, reproach, reproof, talking-to (informal)

reprisal noun RETALIATION, retribution, revenge, vengeance

reproach noun 1 BLAME, censure, condemnation, disapproval, opprobrium, rebuke ♦ verb 2 BLAME, censure, condemn, criticize, lambast(e), read the riot act, rebuke, reprimand, scold, upbraid

reproachful adjective CRITICAL, censorious, condemnatory, disapproving, fault-finding, reproving

reprobate noun 1 SCOUNDREL, bad egg (old-fashioned informal), blackguard, degenerate, evildoer, miscreant, ne'er-do-well, profligate, rake, rascal, villain ♦ adjective 2 DEPRAVED, abandoned, bad, base, corrupt, degenerate, dissolute, immoral, sinful, wicked

reproduce verb 1 COPY, duplicate, echo, imitate, match, mirror, recreate, repeat, replicate 2 BREED, multiply, procreate, propagate, spawn

reproduction noun 1 BREEDING, generation, increase, multiplication 2 COPY, duplicate, facsimile, imitation, picture, print, replica

reproof noun REBUKE, blame, censure, condemnation, criticism, reprimand, scolding

reprove verb REBUKE, berate, blame, censure, condemn, read the riot act, reprimand, scold, tear into (informal), tear (someone) off a strip (Brit. informal), tell off (informal)

repudiate verb REJECT, deny, disavow, disclaim, disown, renounce

repugnance noun DISTASTE, abhorrence, aversion, disgust, dislike, hatred, loathing

repugnant adjective DISTASTEFUL, abhorrent, disgusting, loathsome, nauseating, offensive, repellent, revolting, sickening, vile

repulse verb 1 DRIVE BACK, beat off, fight off, rebuff, repel, ward off 2 REBUFF, refuse, reject, snub, spurn, turn down

repulsion noun DISTASTE, abhorrence, aversion, detestation, disgust, hatred, loathing, repugnance, revulsion

repulsive *adjective* DISGUSTING, abhorrent, foul, loathsome, nauseating, repellent, revolting, sickening, vile

reputable *adjective* RESPECTABLE, creditable, excellent, good, honourable, reliable, trustworthy, well-thought-of, worthy

reputation *noun* ESTIMATION, character, esteem, name, renown, repute, standing, stature

repute *noun* REPUTATION, celebrity, distinction, eminence, fame, name, renown, standing, stature

reputed *adjective* SUPPOSED, alleged, believed, considered, deemed, estimated, held, reckoned, regarded

reputedly *adverb* SUPPOSEDLY, allegedly, apparently, seemingly

request *verb* 1 ASK (FOR), appeal for, demand, desire, entreat, invite, seek, solicit ♦ *noun* 2 ASKING, appeal, call, demand, desire, entreaty, suit

require *verb* 1 NEED, crave, desire, lack, miss, want, wish 2 DEMAND, ask, bid, call upon, command, compel, exact, insist upon, oblige, order

required *adjective* NEEDED, called for, essential, necessary, obligatory, requisite

requirement *noun* NECESSITY, demand, essential, lack, must, need, prerequisite, stipulation, want

requisite *adjective* 1 NECESSARY, called for, essential, indispensable, needed, needful, obligatory, required ♦ *noun* 2 NECESSITY, condition, essential, must, need, prerequisite, requirement

requisition *verb* 1 DEMAND, call for,

request ♦ *noun* 2 DEMAND, call, request, summons

requital *noun* RETURN, repayment

requite *verb* RETURN, get even, give in return, pay (someone) back in his *or* her own coin, reciprocate, repay, respond, retaliate

rescind *verb* ANNUL, cancel, countermand, declare null and void, invalidate, repeal, set aside

rescue *verb* 1 SAVE, deliver, get out, liberate, recover, redeem, release, salvage ♦ *noun* 2 LIBERATION, deliverance, recovery, redemption, release, salvage, salvation, saving

research *noun* 1 INVESTIGATION, analysis, examination, exploration, probe, study ♦ *verb* 2 INVESTIGATE, analyse, examine, explore, probe, study

resemblance *noun* SIMILARITY, correspondence, kinship, likeness, parallel, sameness, similitude

resemble *verb* BE LIKE, bear a resemblance to, be similar to, look like, mirror, parallel

resent *verb* BE BITTER ABOUT, begrudge, grudge, object to, take exception to, take offence at

resentful *adjective* BITTER, angry, embittered, grudging, indignant, miffed (*informal*), offended, piqued

resentment *noun* BITTERNESS, animosity, bad blood, grudge, ill feeling, ill will, indignation, pique, rancour, umbrage

reservation *noun* 1 DOUBT, hesitancy, scruple 2 CONDITION, proviso, qualification, rider, stipulation 3 RESERVE, preserve, sanctuary, territory

reserve *verb* 1 KEEP, hoard, hold, put by, retain, save, set aside, stockpile, store 2 BOOK, engage, prearrange, secure ♦ *noun* **3** <u>STORE</u>, cache, fund, hoard, reservoir, savings, stock, supply **4** <u>RESERVATION</u>, park, preserve, sanctuary, tract **5** <u>SHYNESS</u>, constraint, reservation, restraint, reticence, secretiveness, silence, taciturnity ♦ *adjective* **6** <u>SUBSTITUTE</u>, auxiliary, extra, fall-back, secondary, spare

reserved *adjective*
1 <u>UNCOMMUNICATIVE</u>, restrained, reticent, retiring, secretive, shy, silent, standoffish, taciturn, undemonstrative **2** <u>SET ASIDE</u>, booked, engaged, held, kept, restricted, retained, spoken for, taken

reservoir *noun* **1** <u>LAKE</u>, basin, pond, tank **2** <u>STORE</u>, pool, reserves, source, stock, supply

reshuffle *noun* **1** <u>REORGANIZATION</u>, change, rearrangement, redistribution, regrouping, restructuring, revision ♦ *verb* **2** <u>REORGANIZE</u>, change around, rearrange, redistribute, regroup, restructure, revise

reside *verb* <u>LIVE</u>, abide, dwell, inhabit, lodge, stay

residence *noun* <u>HOME</u>, abode, domicile, dwelling, flat, habitation, house, lodging, place

resident *noun* <u>INHABITANT</u>, citizen, local, lodger, occupant, tenant

residual *adjective* <u>REMAINING</u>, leftover, unconsumed, unused, vestigial

residue *noun* <u>REMAINDER</u>, dregs, excess, extra, leftovers, remains, remnant, rest, surplus

resign *verb* **1** <u>QUIT</u>, abdicate, give in one's notice, leave, step down (*informal*), vacate **2** <u>GIVE UP</u>, abandon, forgo, forsake, relinquish, renounce, surrender, yield **3 resign oneself** <u>ACCEPT</u>,

acquiesce, give in, submit, succumb, yield

resignation *noun* **1** <u>LEAVING</u>, abandonment, abdication, departure **2** <u>ENDURANCE</u>, acceptance, acquiescence, compliance, nonresistance, passivity, patience, submission, sufferance

resigned *adjective* <u>STOICAL</u>, compliant, long-suffering, patient, subdued, unresisting

resilient *adjective* **1** <u>TOUGH</u>, buoyant, hardy, irrepressible, strong **2** <u>FLEXIBLE</u>, elastic, plastic, pliable, rubbery, springy, supple

resist *verb* **1** <u>OPPOSE</u>, battle, combat, defy, hinder, stand up to **2** <u>REFRAIN FROM</u>, abstain from, avoid, forbear, forgo, keep from **3** <u>WITHSTAND</u>, be proof against

resistance *noun* <u>FIGHTING</u>, battle, defiance, fight, hindrance, impediment, obstruction, opposition, struggle

resistant *adjective* **1** <u>IMPERVIOUS</u>, hard, proof against, strong, tough, unaffected by **2** <u>OPPOSED</u>, antagonistic, hostile, intractable, intransigent, unwilling

resolute *adjective* <u>DETERMINED</u>, dogged, firm, fixed, immovable, inflexible, set, steadfast, strong-willed, tenacious, unshakable, unwavering

resolution *noun* **1** <u>DETERMINATION</u>, doggedness, firmness, perseverance, purpose, resoluteness, resolve, steadfastness, tenacity, willpower **2** <u>DECISION</u>, aim, declaration, determination, intent, intention, purpose, resolve

resolve *verb* **1** <u>DECIDE</u>, agree, conclude, determine, fix, intend, purpose **2** <u>BREAK DOWN</u>, analyse, reduce, separate **3** <u>WORK OUT</u>,

answer, clear up, crack, fathom
♦ *noun* **4** <u>DETERMINATION</u>, firmness,
resoluteness, resolution,
steadfastness, willpower
5 <u>DECISION</u>, intention, objective,
purpose, resolution

resonant *adjective* <u>ECHOING</u>,
booming, resounding,
reverberating, ringing, sonorous

resort *verb* **1 resort to** <u>USE</u>, employ,
fall back on, have recourse to, turn
to, utilize ♦ *noun* **2** <u>HOLIDAY CENTRE</u>,
haunt, retreat, spot, tourist centre
3 <u>RECOURSE</u>, reference

resound *verb* <u>ECHO</u>, re-echo,
resonate, reverberate, ring

resounding *adjective* <u>ECHOING</u>,
booming, full, powerful, resonant,
reverberating, ringing, sonorous

resource *noun* **1** <u>INGENUITY</u>, ability,
capability, cleverness, initiative,
inventiveness **2** <u>MEANS</u>, course,
device, expedient, resort

resourceful *adjective* <u>INGENIOUS</u>,
able, bright, capable, clever,
creative, inventive

resources *plural noun* <u>RESERVES</u>,
assets, capital, funds, holdings,
money, riches, supplies, wealth

respect *noun* **1** <u>REGARD</u>, admiration,
consideration, deference, esteem,
estimation, honour, recognition
2 <u>POINT</u>, aspect, characteristic,
detail, feature, matter, particular,
sense, way **3** <u>RELATION</u>, bearing,
connection, reference, regard
♦ *verb* **4** <u>THINK HIGHLY OF</u>, admire,
defer to, esteem, have a good *or*
high opinion of, honour, look up
to, value **5** <u>SHOW CONSIDERATION FOR</u>,
abide by, adhere to, comply with,
follow, heed, honour, obey,
observe

respectable *adjective* **1** <u>HONOURABLE</u>,
decent, estimable, good, honest,
reputable, upright, worthy
2 <u>REASONABLE</u>, ample, appreciable,

considerable, decent, fair, sizable
or sizeable, substantial

respectful *adjective* <u>POLITE</u>, civil,
courteous, deferential, mannerly,
reverent, well-mannered

respective *adjective* <u>SPECIFIC</u>,
individual, own, particular,
relevant

respite *noun* <u>PAUSE</u>, break,
cessation, halt, interval, lull,
recess, relief, rest

resplendent *adjective* <u>BRILLIANT</u>,
bright, dazzling, glorious, radiant,
shining, splendid

respond *verb* <u>ANSWER</u>, counter,
react, reciprocate, rejoin, reply,
retort, return

response *noun* <u>ANSWER</u>,
counterattack, feedback, reaction,
rejoinder, reply, retort, return

responsibility *noun* **1** <u>AUTHORITY</u>,
importance, power **2** <u>FAULT</u>, blame,
culpability, guilt **3** <u>DUTY</u>, care,
charge, liability, obligation, onus
4 <u>LEVEL-HEADEDNESS</u>,
conscientiousness, dependability,
rationality, sensibleness,
trustworthiness

responsible *adjective* **1** <u>IN CHARGE</u>,
in authority, in control **2** <u>TO BLAME</u>,
at fault, culpable, guilty
3 <u>ACCOUNTABLE</u>, answerable, liable
4 <u>SENSIBLE</u>, dependable,
level-headed, rational, reliable,
trustworthy

responsive *adjective* <u>SENSITIVE</u>, alive,
impressionable, open, reactive,
receptive, susceptible

rest[1] *noun* **1** <u>REPOSE</u>, calm, inactivity,
leisure, relaxation, relief, stillness,
tranquillity **2** <u>PAUSE</u>, break,
cessation, halt, interlude,
intermission, interval, lull, respite,
stop **3** <u>SUPPORT</u>, base, holder, prop,
stand ♦ *verb* **4** <u>RELAX</u>, be at ease,
put one's feet up, sit down, take it
easy **5** <u>BE SUPPORTED</u>, lean, lie, prop,

recline, repose, sit

rest[2] noun REMAINDER, balance, excess, others, remains, remnants, residue, surplus

restaurant noun BISTRO, café, cafeteria, diner (*chiefly U.S. & Canad.*), eatery, tearoom

restful adjective RELAXING, calm, calming, peaceful, quiet, relaxed, serene, soothing, tranquil

restitution noun COMPENSATION, amends, recompense, reparation, requital

restive adjective RESTLESS, edgy, fidgety, impatient, jumpy, nervous, on edge

restless adjective 1 MOVING, nomadic, roving, transient, unsettled, unstable, wandering 2 UNSETTLED, edgy, fidgeting, fidgety, jumpy, nervous, on edge, restive

restlessness noun 1 MOVEMENT, activity, bustle, unrest, unsettledness 2 RESTIVENESS, edginess, jitters (*informal*), jumpiness, nervousness

restoration noun 1 REPAIR, reconstruction, renewal, renovation, revitalization, revival 2 REINSTATEMENT, re-establishment, replacement, restitution, return

restore verb 1 REPAIR, fix, mend, rebuild, recondition, reconstruct, refurbish, renew, renovate 2 REVIVE, build up, refresh, revitalize, strengthen 3 RETURN, bring back, give back, hand back, recover, reinstate, replace, send back 4 REINSTATE, reintroduce

restrain verb HOLD BACK, check, constrain, contain, control, curb, curtail, hamper, hinder, inhibit, restrict

restrained adjective CONTROLLED, calm, mild, moderate, self-controlled, undemonstrative

restraint noun 1 SELF-CONTROL, control, inhibition, moderation, self-discipline, self-possession, self-restraint 2 LIMITATION, ban, check, curb, embargo, interdict, limit, rein

restrict verb LIMIT, bound, confine, contain, hamper, handicap, inhibit, regulate, restrain

restriction noun LIMITATION, confinement, control, curb, handicap, inhibition, regulation, restraint, rule

result noun 1 CONSEQUENCE, effect, end, end result, outcome, product, sequel, upshot ♦ verb 2 HAPPEN, appear, arise, derive, develop, ensue, follow, issue, spring 3 **result in** END IN, culminate in, finish with

resume verb BEGIN AGAIN, carry on, continue, go on, proceed, restart

résumé noun SUMMARY, précis, recapitulation, rundown, synopsis

resumption noun CÓNTINUATION, carrying on, re-establishment, renewal, reopening, restart, resurgence

resurgence noun REVIVAL, rebirth, re-emergence, renaissance, resumption, resurrection, return

resurrect verb REVIVE, bring back, reintroduce, renew

resurrection noun REVIVAL, reappearance, rebirth, renaissance, renewal, restoration, resurgence, return

resuscitate verb REVIVE, bring round, resurrect, revitalize, save

retain verb 1 KEEP, hold, hold back, maintain, preserve, reserve, save 2 HIRE, commission, employ, engage, pay, reserve

retainer noun 1 FEE, advance, deposit 2 SERVANT, attendant, domestic

retaliate *verb* PAY (SOMEONE) BACK, get even with (*informal*), get one's own back (*informal*), hit back, reciprocate, strike back, take revenge

retaliation *noun* REVENGE, an eye for an eye, counterblow, reciprocation, repayment, reprisal, requital, vengeance

retard *verb* SLOW DOWN, arrest, check, delay, handicap, hinder, hold back *or* up, impede, set back

retch *verb* GAG, be sick, heave, puke (*slang*), regurgitate, spew, throw up (*informal*), vomit

reticence *noun* SILENCE, quietness, reserve, taciturnity

reticent *adjective* UNCOMMUNICATIVE, close-lipped, quiet, reserved, silent, taciturn, tight-lipped, unforthcoming

retinue *noun* ATTENDANTS, aides, entourage, escort, followers, servants

retire *verb* 1 STOP WORKING, give up work 2 WITHDRAW, depart, exit, go away, leave 3 GO TO BED, hit the hay (*slang*), hit the sack (*slang*), turn in (*informal*)

retirement *noun* WITHDRAWAL, privacy, retreat, seclusion, solitude

retiring *adjective* SHY, bashful, quiet, reserved, self-effacing, timid, unassertive, unassuming

retort *verb* 1 REPLY, answer, come back with, counter, respond, return, riposte ♦ *noun* 2 REPLY, answer, comeback (*informal*), rejoinder, response, riposte

retract *verb* 1 WITHDRAW, deny, disavow, disclaim, eat one's words, recant, renege, renounce, revoke, take back 2 DRAW IN, pull back, pull in, sheathe

retreat *verb* 1 WITHDRAW, back away, back off, depart, draw back, fall back, go back, leave, pull back ♦ *noun* 2 WITHDRAWAL, departure, evacuation, flight, retirement 3 REFUGE, haven, hideaway, sanctuary, seclusion, shelter

retrench *verb* CUT BACK, economize, make economies, save, tighten one's belt

retrenchment *noun* CUTBACK, cost-cutting, cut, economy, tightening one's belt

retribution *noun* PUNISHMENT, justice, Nemesis, reckoning, reprisal, retaliation, revenge, vengeance

retrieve *verb* GET BACK, recapture, recoup, recover, redeem, regain, restore, save, win back

retrograde *adjective* DECLINING, backward, degenerative, deteriorating, downward, regressive, retrogressive, worsening

retrogress *verb* DECLINE, backslide, deteriorate, go back, go downhill (*informal*), regress, relapse, worsen

retrospect *noun* HINDSIGHT, re-examination, review

return *verb* 1 COME BACK, go back, reappear, rebound, recur, retreat, revert, turn back 2 PUT BACK, re-establish, reinstate, replace, restore 3 GIVE BACK, pay back, recompense, refund, reimburse, repay 4 REPLY, answer, respond, retort 5 ELECT, choose, vote in ♦ *noun* 6 RESTORATION, re-establishment, reinstatement 7 REAPPEARANCE, recurrence 8 RETREAT, rebound, recoil 9 PROFIT, gain, income, interest, proceeds, revenue, takings, yield 10 REPORT, account, form, list, statement, summary 11 REPLY, answer, comeback (*informal*), rejoinder, response, retort

revamp *verb* <u>RENOVATE</u>, do up (*informal*), overhaul, recondition, refurbish, restore

reveal *verb* **1** <u>MAKE KNOWN</u>, announce, disclose, divulge, give away, impart, let out, let slip, make public, proclaim, tell **2** <u>SHOW</u>, display, exhibit, manifest, uncover, unearth, unmask, unveil

revel *verb* **1** <u>CELEBRATE</u>, carouse, live it up (*informal*), make merry **2 revel in** <u>ENJOY</u>, delight in, indulge in, lap up, luxuriate in, relish, take pleasure in, thrive on ♦ *noun* **3** often plural <u>MERRYMAKING</u>, carousal, celebration, festivity, party, spree

revelation *noun* <u>DISCLOSURE</u>, exhibition, exposé, exposure, news, proclamation, publication, uncovering, unearthing, unveiling

reveller *noun* <u>CAROUSER</u>, partygoer

revelry *noun* <u>FESTIVITY</u>, carousal, celebration, fun, jollity, merrymaking, party, spree

revenge *noun* **1** <u>RETALIATION</u>, an eye for an eye, reprisal, retribution, vengeance ♦ *verb* **2** <u>AVENGE</u>, get even, get one's own back for (*informal*), hit back, repay, retaliate, take revenge for

revenue *noun* <u>INCOME</u>, gain, proceeds, profits, receipts, returns, takings, yield

reverberate *verb* <u>ECHO</u>, re-echo, resound, ring, vibrate

revere *verb* <u>BE IN AWE OF</u>, exalt, honour, look up to, respect, reverence, venerate, worship

reverence *noun* <u>AWE</u>, admiration, high esteem, honour, respect, veneration, worship

reverent *adjective* <u>RESPECTFUL</u>, awed, deferential, humble, reverential

reverie *noun* <u>DAYDREAM</u>, abstraction, brown study, woolgathering

reverse *verb* **1** <u>TURN ROUND</u>, invert, transpose, turn back, turn over, turn upside down, upend **2** <u>CHANGE</u>, annul, cancel, countermand, invalidate, overrule, overthrow, overturn, quash, repeal, rescind, revoke, undo **3** <u>GO BACKWARDS</u>, back, back up, move backwards, retreat ♦ *noun* **4** <u>OPPOSITE</u>, contrary, converse, inverse **5** <u>BACK</u>, other side, rear, underside, wrong side **6** <u>MISFORTUNE</u>, adversity, affliction, blow, disappointment, failure, hardship, misadventure, mishap, reversal, setback ♦ *adjective* **7** <u>OPPOSITE</u>, contrary, converse

revert *verb* <u>RETURN</u>, come back, go back, resume

review *noun* **1** <u>CRITIQUE</u>, commentary, criticism, evaluation, judgment, notice **2** <u>MAGAZINE</u>, journal, periodical **3** <u>SURVEY</u>, analysis, examination, scrutiny, study **4** *Military* <u>INSPECTION</u>, march past, parade ♦ *verb* **5** <u>ASSESS</u>, criticize, evaluate, judge, study **6** <u>RECONSIDER</u>, reassess, re-evaluate, re-examine, rethink, revise, think over **7** <u>LOOK BACK ON</u>, recall, recollect, reflect on, remember **8** <u>INSPECT</u>, examine

reviewer *noun* <u>CRITIC</u>, commentator, judge

revile *verb* <u>MALIGN</u>, abuse, bad-mouth (*slang, chiefly U.S. & Canad.*), denigrate, knock (*informal*), reproach, run down, slag (off) (*slang*), vilify

revise *verb* **1** <u>CHANGE</u>, alter, amend, correct, edit, emend, redo, review, rework, update **2** <u>STUDY</u>, go over, run through, swot up (*Brit. informal*)

revision *noun* **1** <u>CHANGE</u>, amendment, correction, emendation, updating **2** <u>STUDYING</u>, homework, swotting (*Brit. informal*)

revival *noun* RENEWAL, reawakening, rebirth, renaissance, resurgence, resurrection, revitalization

revive *verb* REVITALIZE, awaken, bring round, come round, invigorate, reanimate, recover, refresh, rekindle, renew, restore

revoke *verb* CANCEL, annul, countermand, disclaim, invalidate, negate, nullify, obviate, quash, repeal, rescind, retract, reverse, set aside, withdraw

revolt *noun* 1 UPRISING, insurgency, insurrection, mutiny, rebellion, revolution, rising ♦ *verb* 2 REBEL, mutiny, resist, rise 3 DISGUST, gross out (*U.S. slang*), make one's flesh creep, nauseate, repel, repulse, sicken, turn one's stomach

revolting *adjective* DISGUSTING, foul, horrible, horrid, nauseating, repellent, repugnant, repulsive, sickening, yucky *or* yukky (*slang*)

revolution *noun* 1 REVOLT, coup, insurgency, mutiny, rebellion, rising, uprising 2 TRANSFORMATION, innovation, reformation, sea change, shift, upheaval 3 ROTATION, circle, circuit, cycle, lap, orbit, spin, turn

revolutionary *adjective* 1 REBEL, extremist, insurgent, radical, subversive 2 NEW, different, drastic, ground-breaking, innovative, novel, progressive, radical ♦ *noun* 3 REBEL, insurgent, revolutionist

revolutionize *verb* TRANSFORM, modernize, reform

revolve *verb* ROTATE, circle, go round, orbit, spin, turn, twist, wheel, whirl

revulsion *noun* DISGUST, abhorrence, detestation, loathing, repugnance, repulsion

reward *noun* 1 PAYMENT, bonus, bounty, premium, prize, recompense, repayment, return, wages 2 PUNISHMENT, comeuppance (*slang*), just deserts, retribution ♦ *verb* 3 PAY, compensate, recompense, remunerate, repay

rewarding *adjective* WORTHWHILE, beneficial, enriching, fruitful, fulfilling, productive, profitable, satisfying, valuable

rhapsodize *verb* ENTHUSE, go into ecstasies, gush, rave (*informal*)

rhetoric *noun* 1 ORATORY, eloquence 2 HYPERBOLE, bombast, grandiloquence, magniloquence, verbosity, wordiness

rhetorical *adjective* ORATORICAL, bombastic, declamatory, grandiloquent, high-flown, magniloquent, verbose

rhyme *noun* 1 POETRY, ode, poem, song, verse ♦ *verb* 2 SOUND LIKE, harmonize

rhythm *noun* BEAT, accent, cadence, lilt, metre, pulse, swing, tempo, time

rhythmic, rhythmical *adjective* CADENCED, lilting, metrical, musical, periodic, pulsating, throbbing

ribald *adjective* RUDE, bawdy, blue, broad, coarse, earthy, naughty, near the knuckle (*informal*), obscene, racy, smutty, vulgar

rich *adjective* 1 WEALTHY, affluent, loaded (*slang*), moneyed, prosperous, well-heeled (*informal*), well-off, well-to-do 2 WELL-STOCKED, full, productive, well-supplied 3 ABUNDANT, abounding, ample, copious, fertile, fruitful, lush, luxurious, plentiful, productive, prolific 4 FULL-BODIED, creamy, fatty, luscious, succulent, sweet, tasty

riches *plural noun* WEALTH, affluence, assets, fortune, plenty, resources, substance, treasure

richly adverb 1 ELABORATELY, elegantly, expensively, exquisitely, gorgeously, lavishly, luxuriously, opulently, splendidly, sumptuously 2 FULLY, amply, appropriately, properly, suitably, thoroughly, well

rickety adjective SHAKY, insecure, precarious, ramshackle, tottering, unsound, unsteady, wobbly

rid verb 1 FREE, clear, deliver, disburden, disencumber, make free, purge, relieve, unburden 2 **get rid of** DISPOSE OF, dump, eject, eliminate, expel, remove, throw away or out

riddle noun PUZZLE, conundrum, enigma, mystery, poser, problem

riddled adjective FILLED, damaged, infested, permeated, pervaded, spoilt

ride verb 1 CONTROL, handle, manage 2 TRAVEL, be carried, go, move ♦ noun 3 TRIP, drive, jaunt, journey, lift, outing

ridicule noun 1 MOCKERY, chaff, derision, gibe, jeer, laughter, raillery, scorn ♦ verb 2 LAUGH AT, chaff, deride, jeer, make fun of, mock, poke fun at, sneer

ridiculous adjective LAUGHABLE, absurd, comical, farcical, funny, ludicrous, risible, silly, stupid

rife adjective WIDESPREAD, common, frequent, general, prevalent, rampant, ubiquitous, universal

riffraff noun RABBLE, hoi polloi, ragtag and bobtail

rifle verb RANSACK, burgle, go through, loot, pillage, plunder, rob, sack, strip

rift noun 1 BREACH, disagreement, division, falling out (*informal*), quarrel, separation, split 2 SPLIT, break, cleft, crack, crevice, fault, fissure, flaw, gap, opening

rig verb 1 FIX (*informal*), arrange, engineer, gerrymander, manipulate, tamper with 2 EQUIP, fit out, furnish, kit out, outfit, supply ♦ noun 3 APPARATUS, equipment, fittings, fixtures, gear, tackle

right adjective 1 JUST, equitable, ethical, fair, good, honest, lawful, moral, proper 2 CORRECT, accurate, exact, factual, genuine, precise, true, valid 3 PROPER, appropriate, becoming, desirable, done, fit, fitting, seemly, suitable ♦ adverb 4 CORRECTLY, accurately, exactly, genuinely, precisely, truly 5 PROPERLY, appropriately, aptly, fittingly, suitably 6 STRAIGHT, directly, promptly, quickly, straightaway 7 EXACTLY, precisely, squarely ♦ noun 8 CLAIM, authority, business, due, freedom, liberty, licence, permission, power, prerogative, privilege ♦ verb 9 RECTIFY, correct, fix, put right, redress, settle, sort out, straighten

right away adverb IMMEDIATELY, at once, directly, forthwith, instantly, now, pronto (*informal*), straightaway

righteous adjective VIRTUOUS, ethical, fair, good, honest, honourable, just, moral, pure, upright

righteousness noun VIRTUE, goodness, honesty, honour, integrity, justice, morality, probity, purity, rectitude, uprightness

rightful adjective LAWFUL, due, just, legal, legitimate, proper, real, true, valid

rigid adjective 1 STRICT, exact, fixed, inflexible, rigorous, set, stringent, unbending, uncompromising 2 STIFF, inflexible, unyielding

rigmarole noun PROCEDURE, bother, carry-on (*informal, chiefly Brit.*), fuss, hassle (*informal*), nonsense, palaver, pantomime (*informal*), performance (*informal*)

rigorous *adjective* STRICT, demanding, exacting, hard, harsh, inflexible, severe, stern, stringent, tough

rigour *noun* 1 STRICTNESS, harshness, inflexibility, rigidity, sternness, stringency 2 HARDSHIP, ordeal, privation, suffering, trial

rig-out *noun* OUTFIT, costume, dress, garb, gear (*informal*), get-up (*informal*), togs

rig out *verb* 1 DRESS, array, attire, clothe, costume, kit out 2 EQUIP, fit, furnish, kit out, outfit

rig up *verb* SET UP, arrange, assemble, build, construct, erect, fix up, improvise, put together, put up

rile *verb* ANGER, aggravate (*informal*), annoy, get *or* put one's back up, irk, irritate

rim *noun* EDGE, border, brim, brink, lip, margin, verge

rind *noun* SKIN, crust, husk, outer layer, peel

ring¹ *verb* 1 CHIME, clang, peal, reverberate, sound, toll 2 PHONE, buzz (*informal*), call, telephone ◆ *noun* 3 CHIME, knell, peal 4 CALL, buzz (*informal*), phone call

ring² *noun* 1 CIRCLE, band, circuit, halo, hoop, loop, round 2 ARENA, circus, enclosure, rink 3 GANG, association, band, cartel, circle, group, mob, syndicate ◆ *verb* 4 ENCIRCLE, enclose, gird, girdle, surround

rinse *verb* 1 WASH, bathe, clean, cleanse, dip, splash ◆ *noun* 2 WASH, bath, dip, splash

riot *noun* 1 DISTURBANCE, anarchy, confusion, disorder, lawlessness, strife, tumult, turbulence, turmoil,

upheaval 2 REVELRY, carousal, festivity, frolic, high jinks, merrymaking 3 PROFUSION, display, extravaganza, show, splash 4 **run riot: a** RAMPAGE, be out of control, go wild **b** GROW PROFUSELY, spread like wildfire ◆ *verb* 5 RAMPAGE, go on the rampage, run riot

riotous *adjective* 1 UNRESTRAINED, boisterous, loud, noisy, uproarious, wild 2 UNRULY, anarchic, disorderly, lawless, rebellious, rowdy, ungovernable, violent

rip *verb* 1 TEAR, burst, claw, cut, gash, lacerate, rend, slash, slit, split ◆ *noun* 2 TEAR, cut, gash, hole, laceration, rent, slash, slit, split

ripe *adjective* 1 MATURE, mellow, ready, ripened, seasoned 2 SUITABLE, auspicious, favourable, ideal, opportune, right, timely

ripen *verb* MATURE, burgeon, develop, grow ripe, season

rip-off *noun* SWINDLE, cheat, con (*informal*), con trick (*informal*), fraud, scam (*slang*), theft

rip off *verb Slang* SWINDLE, cheat, con (*informal*), defraud, fleece, rob, skin (*slang*)

riposte *noun* 1 RETORT, answer, comeback (*informal*), rejoinder, reply, response, sally ◆ *verb* 2 RETORT, answer, come back, reply, respond

rise *verb* 1 GET UP, arise, get to one's feet, stand up 2 GO UP, ascend, climb 3 ADVANCE, get on, progress, prosper 4 GET STEEPER, ascend, go uphill, slope upwards 5 INCREASE, go up, grow, intensify, mount 6 REBEL, mutiny, revolt 7 ORIGINATE, happen, issue, occur, spring ◆ *noun* 8 INCREASE, upsurge, upswing, upturn 9 ADVANCEMENT, climb, progress, promotion 10 UPWARD SLOPE, ascent, elevation, incline 11 PAY INCREASE, increment, raise (*U.S.*) **12 give rise to** CAUSE, bring about, effect, produce, result in

risk *noun* **1** DANGER, chance, gamble, hazard, jeopardy, peril, pitfall, possibility ♦ *verb* **2** DARE, chance, endanger, gamble, hazard, imperil, jeopardize, venture

risky *adjective* DANGEROUS, chancy (*informal*), dicey (*informal, chiefly Brit.*), dodgy (*Brit., Austral., & N.Z. informal*), hazardous, perilous, uncertain, unsafe

risqué *adjective* SUGGESTIVE, bawdy, blue, improper, indelicate, naughty, near the knuckle (*informal*), racy, ribald

rite *noun* CEREMONY, custom, observance, practice, procedure, ritual

ritual *noun* **1** CEREMONY, observance, rite **2** CUSTOM, convention, habit, practice, procedure, protocol, routine, tradition ♦ *adjective* **3** CEREMONIAL, conventional, customary, habitual, routine

ritzy *adjective* LUXURIOUS, de luxe, grand, high-class, luxury, plush (*informal*), posh (*informal, chiefly Brit.*), sumptuous, swanky (*informal*)

rival *noun* **1** OPPONENT, adversary, competitor, contender, contestant ♦ *adjective* **2** COMPETING, conflicting, opposing ♦ *verb* **3** EQUAL, be a match for, come up to, compare with, compete, match

rivalry *noun* COMPETITION, conflict, contention, contest, opposition

river *noun* **1** STREAM, brook, burn (*Scot.*), creek, tributary, waterway **2** FLOW, flood, rush, spate, torrent

riveting *adjective* ENTHRALLING, absorbing, captivating, engrossing, fascinating, gripping, hypnotic, spellbinding

road *noun* WAY, course, highway, lane, motorway, path, pathway, roadway, route, track

roam *verb* WANDER, prowl, ramble, range, rove, stray, travel, walk

roar *verb* **1** CRY, bawl, bay, bellow, howl, shout, yell **2** GUFFAW, hoot, laugh heartily, split one's sides (*informal*) ♦ *noun* **3** CRY, bellow, howl, outcry, shout, yell **4** GUFFAW, hoot

rob *verb* STEAL FROM, burgle, cheat, con (*informal*), defraud, deprive, dispossess, do out of (*informal*), hold up, loot, mug (*informal*), pillage, plunder, raid

robber *noun* THIEF, bandit, brigand, burglar, cheat, con man (*informal*), fraud, looter, mugger (*informal*), plunderer, raider

robbery *noun* THEFT, burglary, hold-up, larceny, mugging (*informal*), pillage, plunder, raid, rip-off (*slang*), stealing, stick-up (*slang, chiefly U.S.*), swindle

robe *noun* **1** GOWN, costume, habit ♦ *verb* **2** CLOTHE, dress, garb

robot *noun* MACHINE, android, automaton, mechanical man

robust *adjective* STRONG, fit, hale, hardy, healthy, muscular, powerful, stout, strapping, sturdy, tough, vigorous

rock[1] *noun* STONE, boulder

rock[2] *verb* **1** SWAY, lurch, pitch, reel, roll, swing, toss **2** SHOCK, astonish, astound, shake, stagger, stun, surprise

rocky[1] *adjective* ROUGH, craggy, rugged, stony

rocky[2] *adjective* UNSTABLE, rickety, shaky, unsteady, wobbly

rod *noun* STICK, bar, baton, cane, pole, shaft, staff, wand

rogue *noun* SCOUNDREL, blackguard,

crook (*informal*), fraud, rascal, scally (*Northwest English dialect*), scamp, villain

role *noun* 1 JOB, capacity, duty, function, part, position, post, task 2 PART, character, portrayal, representation

roll *verb* 1 TURN, go round, revolve, rotate, spin, swivel, trundle, twirl, wheel, whirl 2 WIND, bind, enfold, envelop, furl, swathe, wrap 3 FLOW, run, undulate 4 LEVEL, even, flatten, press, smooth 5 TUMBLE, lurch, reel, rock, sway, toss ♦ *noun* 6 TURN, cycle, reel, revolution, rotation, spin, twirl, wheel, whirl 7 REGISTER, census, index, list, record 8 RUMBLE, boom, reverberation, roar, thunder

rollicking *adjective* BOISTEROUS, carefree, devil-may-care, exuberant, hearty, jaunty, lively, playful

roly-poly *adjective* PLUMP, buxom, chubby, fat, podgy, rounded, tubby

romance *noun* 1 LOVE AFFAIR, affair, amour, attachment, liaison, relationship 2 EXCITEMENT, charm, colour, fascination, glamour, mystery 3 STORY, fairy tale, fantasy, legend, love story, melodrama, tale

romantic *adjective* 1 LOVING, amorous, fond, passionate, sentimental, tender 2 IDEALISTIC, dreamy, impractical, starry-eyed, unrealistic 3 EXCITING, colourful, fascinating, glamorous, mysterious ♦ *noun* 4 IDEALIST, dreamer, sentimentalist

romp *verb* 1 FROLIC, caper, cavort, frisk, gambol, have fun, sport 2 WIN EASILY, walk it (*informal*), win by a mile (*informal*), win hands down ♦ *noun* 3 FROLIC, caper, lark (*informal*)

room *noun* 1 CHAMBER, apartment, office 2 SPACE, area, capacity, expanse, extent, leeway, margin, range, scope 3 OPPORTUNITY, chance, occasion, scope

roomy *adjective* SPACIOUS, ample, broad, capacious, commodious, extensive, generous, large, sizable *or* sizeable, wide

root¹ *noun* 1 STEM, rhizome, tuber 2 SOURCE, base, bottom, cause, core, foundation, heart, nucleus, origin, seat, seed 3 **roots** SENSE OF BELONGING, birthplace, cradle, family, heritage, home, origins ♦ *verb* 4 ESTABLISH, anchor, fasten, fix, ground, implant, moor, set, stick

root² *verb* DIG, burrow, ferret

rooted *adjective* DEEP-SEATED, confirmed, deep, deeply felt, entrenched, established, firm, fixed, ingrained

root out *verb* GET RID OF, abolish, do away with, eliminate, eradicate, exterminate, extirpate, remove, weed out

rope *noun* 1 CORD, cable, hawser, line, strand 2 **know the ropes** BE EXPERIENCED, be an old hand, be knowledgeable

rope in *verb* PERSUADE, engage, enlist, inveigle, involve, talk into

ropey, ropy *adjective Informal* 1 INFERIOR, deficient, inadequate, of poor quality, poor, substandard 2 UNWELL, below par, off colour, under the weather (*informal*)

roster *noun* ROTA, agenda, catalogue, list, register, roll, schedule, table

rostrum *noun* STAGE, dais, platform, podium, stand

rosy *adjective* 1 PINK, red 2 GLOWING, blooming, healthy-looking, radiant, ruddy 3 PROMISING, auspicious, bright, cheerful, encouraging, favourable, hopeful, optimistic

rot *verb* 1 <u>DECAY</u>, crumble, decompose, deteriorate, go bad, moulder, perish, putrefy, spoil 2 <u>DETERIORATE</u>, decline, waste away ♦ *noun* 3 <u>DECAY</u>, blight, canker, corruption, decomposition, mould, putrefaction 4 *Informal* <u>NONSENSE</u>, claptrap (*informal*), codswallop (*Brit. slang*), drivel, garbage (*chiefly U.S.*), hogwash, poppycock (*informal*), rubbish, stuff and nonsense, trash, tripe (*informal*), twaddle

rotary *adjective* <u>REVOLVING</u>, rotating, spinning, turning

rotate *verb* 1 <u>REVOLVE</u>, go round, gyrate, pivot, reel, spin, swivel, turn, wheel 2 <u>TAKE TURNS</u>, alternate, switch

rotation *noun* 1 <u>REVOLUTION</u>, orbit, reel, spin, spinning, turn, turning, wheel 2 <u>SEQUENCE</u>, alternation, cycle, succession, switching

rotten *adjective* 1 <u>DECAYING</u>, bad, corrupt, crumbling, decomposing, festering, mouldy, perished, putrescent, rank, sour, stinking 2 <u>CORRUPT</u>, crooked (*informal*), dishonest, dishonourable, immoral, perfidious 3 *Informal* <u>DESPICABLE</u>, base, contemptible, dirty, mean, nasty 4 *Informal* <u>INFERIOR</u>, crummy (*slang*), duff (*Brit. informal*), inadequate, lousy (*slang*), poor, substandard, unsatisfactory

rotter *noun* <u>SCOUNDREL</u>, blackguard, bounder (*old-fashioned Brit. slang*), cad (*Brit. informal*), rat (*informal*)

rotund *adjective* 1 <u>ROUND</u>, globular, rounded, spherical 2 <u>PLUMP</u>, chubby, corpulent, fat, fleshy, podgy, portly, stout, tubby

rough *adjective* 1 <u>UNEVEN</u>, broken, bumpy, craggy, irregular, jagged, rocky, stony 2 <u>UNGRACIOUS</u>, blunt, brusque, coarse, impolite, rude,

unceremonious, uncivil, uncouth, unmannerly 3 <u>APPROXIMATE</u>, estimated, general, imprecise, inexact, sketchy, vague 4 <u>STORMY</u>, choppy, squally, turbulent, wild 5 <u>NASTY</u>, cruel, hard, harsh, tough, unfeeling, unpleasant, violent 6 <u>BASIC</u>, crude, imperfect, incomplete, rudimentary, sketchy, unfinished, unpolished, unrefined 7 <u>UNPLEASANT</u>, arduous, hard, tough, uncomfortable ♦ *verb* 8 **rough out** <u>OUTLINE</u>, draft, plan, sketch ♦ *noun* 9 <u>OUTLINE</u>, draft, mock-up, preliminary sketch

rough-and-ready *adjective* <u>MAKESHIFT</u>, crude, improvised, provisional, sketchy, stopgap, unpolished, unrefined

round *adjective* 1 <u>SPHERICAL</u>, circular, curved, cylindrical, globular, rotund, rounded 2 <u>PLUMP</u>, ample, fleshy, full, full-fleshed, rotund ♦ *verb* 3 <u>GO ROUND</u>, bypass, circle, encircle, flank, skirt, turn ♦ *noun* 4 <u>SPHERE</u>, ball, band, circle, disc, globe, orb, ring 5 <u>STAGE</u>, division, lap, level, period, session, turn 6 <u>SERIES</u>, cycle, sequence, session, succession 7 <u>COURSE</u>, beat, circuit, routine, schedule, series, tour

roundabout *adjective* <u>INDIRECT</u>, circuitous, devious, discursive, evasive, oblique, tortuous

round off *verb* <u>COMPLETE</u>, close, conclude, finish off

roundup *noun* <u>GATHERING</u>, assembly, collection, herding, marshalling, muster, rally

round up *verb* <u>GATHER</u>, collect, drive, group, herd, marshal, muster, rally

rouse *verb* 1 <u>WAKE UP</u>, awaken, call, rise, wake 2 <u>EXCITE</u>, agitate, anger, animate, incite, inflame, move, provoke, stimulate, stir

rousing *adjective* <u>LIVELY</u>, exciting, inspiring, moving, spirited, stimulating, stirring

rout noun 1 DEFEAT, beating, debacle, drubbing, overthrow, pasting (*slang*), thrashing ♦ *verb* 2 DEFEAT, beat, conquer, crush, destroy, drub, overthrow, thrash, wipe the floor with (*informal*)

route noun WAY, beat, circuit, course, direction, itinerary, journey, path, road

routine noun 1 PROCEDURE, custom, method, order, pattern, practice, programme ♦ *adjective* 2 USUAL, customary, everyday, habitual, normal, ordinary, standard, typical 3 BORING, dull, humdrum, predictable, tedious, tiresome

rove verb WANDER, drift, ramble, range, roam, stray, traipse (*informal*)

row[1] noun LINE, bank, column, file, range, series, string

row[2] noun 1 DISPUTE, brawl, quarrel, squabble, tiff, trouble 2 DISTURBANCE, commotion, noise, racket, rumpus, tumult, uproar ♦ *verb* 3 QUARREL, argue, dispute, fight, squabble, wrangle

rowdy adjective 1 DISORDERLY, loud, noisy, rough, unruly, wild ♦ *noun* 2 HOOLIGAN, lout, ruffian, tearaway (*Brit.*), yob or yobbo (*Brit. slang*)

royal adjective 1 REGAL, imperial, kingly, princely, queenly, sovereign 2 SPLENDID, grand, impressive, magnificent, majestic, stately

rub verb 1 POLISH, clean, scour, shine, wipe 2 CHAFE, abrade, fray, grate, scrape ♦ *noun* 3 POLISH, shine, stroke, wipe 4 MASSAGE, caress, kneading

rubbish noun 1 WASTE, garbage (*chiefly U.S.*), junk (*informal*), litter, lumber, refuse, scrap, trash 2 NONSENSE, claptrap (*informal*), codswallop (*Brit. slang*), garbage

(*chiefly U.S.*), hogwash, hot air (*informal*), rot, tommyrot, trash, tripe (*informal*), twaddle

rub out verb ERASE, cancel, delete, efface, obliterate, remove, wipe out

ructions plural noun Informal UPROAR, commotion, disturbance, fracas, fuss, hue and cry, row, trouble

ruddy adjective ROSY, blooming, fresh, glowing, healthy, radiant, red, reddish, rosy-cheeked

rude adjective 1 IMPOLITE, abusive, cheeky, discourteous, disrespectful, ill-mannered, impertinent, impudent, insolent, insulting, uncivil, unmannerly 2 VULGAR, boorish, brutish, coarse, graceless, loutish, oafish, rough, uncivilized, uncouth, uncultured 3 UNPLEASANT, abrupt, harsh, sharp, startling, sudden 4 ROUGHLY-MADE, artless, crude, inartistic, inelegant, makeshift, primitive, raw, rough, simple

rudimentary adjective BASIC, early, elementary, fundamental, initial, primitive, undeveloped

rudiments plural noun BASICS, beginnings, elements, essentials, foundation, fundamentals

rue verb REGRET, be sorry for, kick oneself for, lament, mourn, repent

rueful adjective REGRETFUL, contrite, mournful, penitent, remorseful, repentant, sorrowful, sorry

ruffian noun THUG, brute, bully, heavy (*slang*), hoodlum, hooligan, rough (*informal*), tough

ruffle verb 1 DISARRANGE, dishevel, disorder, mess up, rumple, tousle 2 ANNOY, agitate, fluster, irritate, nettle, peeve (*informal*), upset

rugged adjective 1 ROUGH, broken, bumpy, craggy, difficult, irregular, jagged, ragged, rocky, uneven

2 STRONG-FEATURED, rough-hewn, weather-beaten 3 TOUGH, brawny, burly, husky (*informal*), muscular, robust, strong, sturdy, well-built

ruin *verb* 1 DESTROY, crush, defeat, demolish, devastate, lay waste, smash, wreck 2 BANKRUPT, impoverish, pauperize 3 SPOIL, blow (*slang*), botch, damage, make a mess of, mess up, screw up (*informal*) ◆ *noun* 4 DESTRUCTION, breakdown, collapse, defeat, devastation, downfall, fall, undoing, wreck 5 DISREPAIR, decay, disintegration, ruination, wreckage 6 BANKRUPTCY, destitution, insolvency

ruinous *adjective* 1 DEVASTATING, calamitous, catastrophic, destructive, dire, disastrous, shattering 2 EXTRAVAGANT, crippling, immoderate, wasteful

rule *noun* 1 REGULATION, axiom, canon, decree, direction, guideline, law, maxim, precept, principle, tenet 2 CUSTOM, convention, habit, practice, procedure, routine, tradition 3 GOVERNMENT, authority, command, control, dominion, jurisdiction, mastery, power, regime, reign 4 as a rule USUALLY, generally, mainly, normally, on the whole, ordinarily ◆ *verb* 5 GOVERN, be in authority, be in power, command, control, direct, reign 6 BE PREVALENT, be customary, predominate, preponderate, prevail 7 DECREE, decide, judge, pronounce, settle

rule out *verb* EXCLUDE, ban, debar, dismiss, disqualify, eliminate, leave out, preclude, prohibit, reject

ruler *noun* 1 GOVERNOR, commander, controller, head of state, king *or* queen, leader, lord, monarch, potentate, sovereign 2 MEASURE, rule, yardstick

ruling *noun* 1 DECISION,

adjudication, decree, judgment, pronouncement, verdict ◆ *adjective* 2 GOVERNING, commanding, controlling, reigning 3 PREDOMINANT, chief, dominant, main, pre-eminent, preponderant, prevailing, principal

ruminate *verb* PONDER, cogitate, consider, contemplate, deliberate, mull over, muse, reflect, think, turn over in one's mind

rummage *verb* SEARCH, delve, forage, hunt, ransack, root

rumour *noun* STORY, buzz, dirt (*U.S. slang*), gossip, hearsay, news, report, talk, whisper, word

rump *noun* BUTTOCKS, backside (*informal*), bottom, bum (*Brit. slang*), buns (*U.S. slang*), butt (*U.S. & Canad. informal*), derrière (*euphemistic*), hindquarters, posterior, rear, rear end, seat

rumpus *noun* COMMOTION, disturbance, furore, fuss, hue and cry, noise, row, uproar

run *verb* 1 RACE, bolt, dash, gallop, hare (*Brit. informal*), hurry, jog, leg it (*informal*), lope, rush, scurry, sprint 2 FLEE, beat a retreat, beat it (*slang*), bolt, do a runner (*slang*), escape, leg it (*informal*), make a run for it, take flight, take off (*informal*), take to one's heels 3 MOVE, course, glide, go, pass, roll, skim 4 WORK, function, go, operate, perform 5 MANAGE, administer, be in charge of, control, direct, handle, head, lead, operate 6 CONTINUE, extend, go, proceed, reach, stretch 7 FLOW, discharge, go, gush, leak, pour, spill, spout, stream 8 MELT, dissolve, go soft, liquefy 9 PUBLISH, display, feature, print 10 COMPETE, be a candidate, contend, put oneself up for, stand, take part 11 SMUGGLE, bootleg, traffic in ◆ *noun* 12 RACE, dash, gallop, jog, rush, sprint, spurt 13 RIDE, drive, excursion, jaunt, outing, spin (*informal*), trip **14** SEQUENCE, course, period, season, series, spell, stretch, string **15** ENCLOSURE, coop, pen **16 in the long run** EVENTUALLY, in the end, ultimately

run across *verb* MEET, bump into, come across, encounter, run into

runaway *noun* **1** FUGITIVE, deserter, escapee, refugee, truant ♦ *adjective* **2** ESCAPED, fleeing, fugitive, loose, wild

run away *verb* FLEE, abscond, bolt, do a runner (*slang*), escape, fly the coop (*U.S. & Canad. informal*), make a run for it, scram (*informal*), take to one's heels

run-down *adjective* **1** EXHAUSTED, below par, debilitated, drained, enervated, unhealthy, weak, weary, worn-out **2** DILAPIDATED, broken-down, decrepit, ramshackle, seedy, shabby, worn-out

run down *verb* **1** CRITICIZE, bad-mouth (*slang, chiefly U.S. & Canad.*), belittle, decry, denigrate, disparage, knock (*informal*), rubbish (*informal*), slag (off) (*slang*) **2** REDUCE, curtail, cut, cut back, decrease, downsize, trim **3** KNOCK DOWN, hit, knock over, run into, run over **4** WEAKEN, debilitate, exhaust

run into *verb* **1** MEET, bump into, come across *or* upon, encounter, run across **2** HIT, collide with, strike

runner *noun* **1** ATHLETE, jogger, sprinter **2** MESSENGER, courier, dispatch bearer, errand boy

running *adjective* **1** CONTINUOUS, constant, incessant, perpetual, unbroken, uninterrupted **2** FLOWING, moving, streaming ♦ *noun* **3** MANAGEMENT, administration, control, direction, leadership, organization, supervision **4** WORKING, functioning, maintenance, operation, performance

runny *adjective* FLOWING, fluid, liquefied, liquid, melted, watery

run off *verb* FLEE, bolt, do a runner (*slang*), escape, fly the coop (*U.S. & Canad. informal*), make off, run away, take flight, take to one's heels

run-of-the-mill *adjective* ORDINARY, average, bog-standard (*Brit. & Irish slang*), mediocre, middling, passable, tolerable, undistinguished, unexceptional

run out *verb* BE USED UP, be exhausted, dry up, end, fail, finish, give out

run over *verb* **1** KNOCK DOWN, hit, knock over, run down **2** GO THROUGH, check, go over, rehearse, run through

rupture *noun* **1** BREAK, breach, burst, crack, fissure, rent, split, tear ♦ *verb* **2** BREAK, burst, crack, separate, sever, split, tear

rural *adjective* RUSTIC, agricultural, country, pastoral, sylvan

ruse *noun* TRICK, device, dodge, hoax, manoeuvre, ploy, stratagem, subterfuge

rush *verb* **1** HURRY, bolt, career, dash, fly, hasten, race, run, shoot, speed, tear **2** PUSH, hurry, hustle, press **3** ATTACK, charge, storm ♦ *noun* **4** HURRY, charge, dash, haste, race, scramble, stampede, surge **5** ATTACK, assault, charge, onslaught ♦ *adjective* **6** HASTY, fast, hurried, quick, rapid, swift, urgent

rust *noun* **1** CORROSION, oxidation **2** MILDEW, blight, mould, must, rot ♦ *verb* **3** CORRODE, oxidize

rustic *adjective* **1** RURAL, country, pastoral, sylvan **2** UNCOUTH, awkward, coarse, crude, rough ♦ *noun* **3** YOKEL, boor, bumpkin, clod, clodhopper (*informal*), hick

(*informal, chiefly U.S. & Canad.*),
peasant

rustle *verb* **1** CRACKLE, crinkle,
whisper ♦ *noun* **2** CRACKLE,
crinkling, rustling, whisper

rusty *adjective* **1** CORRODED,
oxidized, rust-covered, rusted
2 REDDISH, chestnut, coppery,
reddish-brown, russet,

rust-coloured **3** OUT OF PRACTICE,
stale, unpractised, weak

rut *noun* **1** GROOVE, furrow,
indentation, track, trough, wheel
mark **2** HABIT, dead end, pattern,
routine, system

ruthless *adjective* MERCILESS, brutal,
callous, cruel, harsh, heartless,
pitiless, relentless, remorseless

S s

sabotage *noun* **1** <u>DAMAGE</u>, destruction, disruption, subversion, wrecking ♦ *verb* **2** <u>DAMAGE</u>, destroy, disable, disrupt, incapacitate, subvert, vandalize, wreck

saccharine *adjective* <u>OVERSWEET</u>, cloying, honeyed, nauseating, sickly

sack¹ *noun* **1 the sack** <u>DISMISSAL</u>, discharge, the axe (*informal*), the boot (*slang*), the push (*slang*) ♦ *verb* **2** <u>DISMISS</u>, axe (*informal*), discharge, fire (*informal*), give (someone) the push (*informal*)

sack² *noun* **1** <u>PLUNDERING</u>, looting, pillage ♦ *verb* **2** <u>PLUNDER</u>, loot, pillage, raid, rob, ruin, strip

sacred *adjective* **1** <u>HOLY</u>, blessed, divine, hallowed, revered, sanctified **2** <u>RELIGIOUS</u>, ecclesiastical, holy **3** <u>INVIOLABLE</u>, protected, sacrosanct

sacrifice *noun* **1** <u>SURRENDER</u>, loss, renunciation **2** <u>OFFERING</u>, oblation ♦ *verb* **3** <u>GIVE UP</u>, forego, forfeit, let go, lose, say goodbye to, surrender **4** <u>OFFER</u>, immolate, offer up

sacrilege *noun* <u>DESECRATION</u>, blasphemy, heresy, impiety, irreverence, profanation, violation

sacrilegious *adjective* <u>PROFANE</u>, blasphemous, desecrating, impious, irreligious, irreverent

sacrosanct *adjective* <u>INVIOLABLE</u>, hallowed, inviolate, sacred, sanctified, set apart, untouchable

sad *adjective* **1** <u>UNHAPPY</u>, blue, dejected, depressed, doleful, down, low, low-spirited, melancholy, mournful, woebegone **2** <u>TRAGIC</u>, depressing, dismal, grievous, harrowing, heart-rending, moving, pathetic, pitiful, poignant, upsetting **3** <u>DEPLORABLE</u>, bad, lamentable, sorry, wretched

sadden *verb* <u>UPSET</u>, deject, depress, distress, grieve, make sad

saddle *verb* <u>BURDEN</u>, encumber, load, lumber (*Brit. informal*)

sadistic *adjective* <u>CRUEL</u>, barbarous, brutal, ruthless, vicious

sadness *noun* <u>UNHAPPINESS</u>, dejection, depression, despondency, grief, melancholy, misery, poignancy, sorrow, the blues

safe *adjective* **1** <u>SECURE</u>, impregnable, in safe hands, out of danger, out of harm's way, protected, safe and sound **2** <u>UNHARMED</u>, all right, intact, O.K. or okay (*informal*), undamaged, unhurt, unscathed **3** <u>RISK-FREE</u>, certain, impregnable, secure, sound ♦ *noun* **4** <u>STRONGBOX</u>, coffer, deposit box, repository, safe-deposit box, vault

safeguard *verb* **1** <u>PROTECT</u>, defend, guard, look after, preserve ♦ *noun* **2** <u>PROTECTION</u>, defence, guard, security

safely *adverb* <u>IN SAFETY</u>, in one piece, safe and sound, with impunity, without risk

safety *noun* **1** <u>SECURITY</u>, impregnability, protection **2** <u>SHELTER</u>, cover, refuge, sanctuary

sag *verb* **1** <u>SINK</u>, bag, dip, droop, fall, give way, hang loosely, slump **2** <u>TIRE</u>, droop, flag, wane, weaken, wilt

saga *noun* <u>TALE</u>, epic, narrative, story, yarn

sage *noun* 1 WISE MAN, elder, guru, master, philosopher ♦ *adjective* 2 WISE, judicious, sagacious, sapient, sensible

sail *verb* 1 EMBARK, set sail 2 GLIDE, drift, float, fly, skim, soar, sweep, wing 3 PILOT, steer

sailor *noun* MARINER, marine, sea dog, seafarer, seaman

saintly *adjective* VIRTUOUS, godly, holy, pious, religious, righteous, saintlike

sake *noun* 1 BENEFIT, account, behalf, good, interest, welfare 2 PURPOSE, aim, end, motive, objective, reason

salacious *adjective* LASCIVIOUS, carnal, erotic, lecherous, lewd, libidinous, lustful

salary *noun* PAY, earnings, income, wage, wages

sale *noun* 1 SELLING, deal, disposal, marketing, transaction 2 **for sale** AVAILABLE, obtainable, on the market

salient *adjective* PROMINENT, conspicuous, important, noticeable, outstanding, pronounced, striking

sallow *adjective* WAN, anaemic, pale, pallid, pasty, sickly, unhealthy, yellowish

salt *noun* 1 SEASONING, flavour, relish, savour, taste 2 **with a grain** *or* **pinch of salt** SCEPTICALLY, cynically, disbelievingly, suspiciously, with reservations ♦ *adjective* 3 SALTY, brackish, briny, saline

salty *adjective* SALT, brackish, briny, saline

salubrious *adjective* HEALTHY, beneficial, good for one, health-giving, wholesome

salutary *adjective* BENEFICIAL, advantageous, good for one, profitable, useful, valuable

salute *noun* 1 GREETING, address, recognition, salutation ♦ *verb* 2 GREET, acknowledge, address, hail, welcome 3 HONOUR, acknowledge, pay tribute *or* homage to, recognize

salvage *verb* SAVE, recover, redeem, rescue, retrieve

salvation *noun* SAVING, deliverance, escape, preservation, redemption, rescue

salve *noun* OINTMENT, balm, cream, lotion

same *adjective* 1 AFOREMENTIONED, aforesaid 2 IDENTICAL, alike, corresponding, duplicate, equal, twin 3 UNCHANGED, changeless, consistent, constant, invariable, unaltered, unvarying

sample *noun* 1 SPECIMEN, example, instance, model, pattern ♦ *verb* 2 TEST, experience, inspect, taste, try ♦ *adjective* 3 TEST, representative, specimen, trial

sanctify *verb* CONSECRATE, cleanse, hallow

sanctimonious *adjective* HOLIER-THAN-THOU, hypocritical, pious, self-righteous, smug

sanction *noun* 1 PERMISSION, approval, authority, authorization, backing, O.K. *or* okay (*informal*), stamp *or* seal of approval 2 often plural BAN, boycott, coercive measures, embargo, penalty ♦ *verb* 3 PERMIT, allow, approve, authorize, endorse

sanctity *noun* 1 SACREDNESS, inviolability 2 HOLINESS, godliness, goodness, grace, piety

sanctuary *noun* 1 SHRINE, altar, church, temple 2 PROTECTION, asylum, haven, refuge, retreat, shelter 3 RESERVE, conservation area, national park, nature reserve

sane *adjective* 1 RATIONAL, all there (*informal*), *compos mentis*, in one's right mind, mentally sound, of sound mind **2** SENSIBLE, balanced, judicious, level-headed, reasonable, sound

sanguine *adjective* CHEERFUL, buoyant, confident, hopeful, optimistic

sanitary *adjective* HYGIENIC, clean, germ-free, healthy, wholesome

sanity *noun* **1** MENTAL HEALTH, normality, rationality, reason, saneness **2** GOOD SENSE, common sense, level-headedness, rationality, sense

sap[1] *noun* **1** VITAL FLUID, essence, lifeblood **2** *Informal* FOOL, idiot, jerk (*slang, chiefly U.S. & Canad.*), ninny, simpleton, twit (*informal*), wally (*slang*)

sap[2] *verb* WEAKEN, deplete, drain, exhaust, undermine

sarcasm *noun* IRONY, bitterness, cynicism, derision, mockery, satire

sarcastic *adjective* IRONICAL, acid, biting, caustic, cutting, cynical, mocking, sardonic, sarky (*Brit. informal*), satirical

sardonic *adjective* MOCKING, cynical, derisive, dry, ironical, sarcastic, sneering, wry

Satan *noun* THE DEVIL, Beelzebub, Lord of the Flies, Lucifer, Mephistopheles, Old Nick (*informal*), Prince of Darkness, The Evil One

satanic *adjective* EVIL, black, demonic, devilish, diabolic, fiendish, hellish, infernal, wicked

satiate *verb* **1** GLUT, cloy, gorge, jade, nauseate, overfill, stuff, surfeit **2** SATISFY, sate, slake

satire *noun* MOCKERY, burlesque, caricature, irony, lampoon, parody, ridicule

satirical, satiric *adjective* MOCKING, biting, caustic, cutting, incisive,

ironical

satirize *verb* RIDICULE, burlesque, deride, lampoon, parody, pillory

satisfaction *noun* **1** CONTENTMENT, comfort, content, enjoyment, happiness, pleasure, pride, repletion, satiety **2** FULFILMENT, achievement, assuaging, gratification

satisfactory *adjective* ADEQUATE, acceptable, all right, average, fair, good enough, passable, sufficient

satisfy *verb* **1** CONTENT, assuage, gratify, indulge, pacify, pander to, please, quench, sate, slake **2** FULFIL, answer, do, meet, serve, suffice **3** PERSUADE, assure, convince, reassure

saturate *verb* SOAK, drench, imbue, souse, steep, suffuse, waterlog, wet through

saturated *adjective* SOAKED, drenched, dripping, soaking (wet), sodden, sopping (wet), waterlogged, wet through

saturnine *adjective* GLOOMY, dour, glum, grave, morose, sombre

saucy *adjective* **1** IMPUDENT, cheeky (*informal*), forward, impertinent, insolent, pert, presumptuous, rude **2** JAUNTY, dashing, gay, natty (*informal*), perky

saunter *verb* **1** STROLL, amble, meander, mosey (*informal*), ramble, roam, wander ♦ *noun* **2** STROLL, airing, amble, ramble, turn, walk

savage *adjective* **1** WILD, feral, undomesticated, untamed **2** UNCULTIVATED, rough, rugged, uncivilized **3** CRUEL, barbarous, bestial, bloodthirsty, brutal, ferocious, fierce, harsh, ruthless, sadistic, vicious **4** PRIMITIVE, rude, unspoilt ♦ *noun* **5** LOUT, boor, yahoo, yob (*Brit. slang*) ♦ *verb* **6** ATTACK, lacerate, mangle, maul

savagery noun CRUELTY, barbarity, brutality, ferocity, ruthlessness, viciousness

save verb 1 RESCUE, deliver, free, liberate, recover, redeem, salvage 2 PROTECT, conserve, guard, keep safe, look after, preserve, safeguard 3 KEEP, collect, gather, hoard, hold, husband, lay by, put by, reserve, set aside, store

saving noun 1 ECONOMY, bargain, discount, reduction ♦ adjective 2 REDEEMING, compensatory, extenuating

savings plural noun NEST EGG, fund, reserves, resources, store

saviour noun RESCUER, defender, deliverer, liberator, preserver, protector, redeemer

Saviour noun CHRIST, Jesus, Messiah, Redeemer

savoir-faire noun SOCIAL KNOW-HOW (informal), diplomacy, discretion, finesse, poise, social graces, tact, urbanity

savour verb 1 ENJOY, appreciate, delight in, luxuriate in, relish, revel in 2 often with of SUGGEST, be suggestive, show signs, smack ♦ noun 3 FLAVOUR, piquancy, relish, smack, smell, tang, taste

savoury adjective SPICY, appetizing, full-flavoured, luscious, mouthwatering, palatable, piquant, rich, tasty

say verb 1 SPEAK, affirm, announce, assert, declare, maintain, mention, pronounce, remark, state, utter, voice 2 SUPPOSE, assume, conjecture, estimate, guess, imagine, presume, surmise 3 EXPRESS, communicate, convey, imply ♦ noun 4 CHANCE TO SPEAK, voice, vote 5 INFLUENCE, authority, clout (informal), power, weight

saying noun PROVERB, adage, aphorism, axiom, dictum, maxim

scale[1] noun FLAKE, lamina, layer, plate

scale[2] noun 1 GRADUATION, gradation, hierarchy, ladder, progression, ranking, sequence, series, steps 2 RATIO, proportion 3 DEGREE, extent, range, reach, scope ♦ verb 4 CLIMB, ascend, clamber, escalade, mount, surmount 5 ADJUST, proportion, regulate

scamp noun RASCAL, devil, imp, monkey, rogue, scallywag (informal)

scamper verb RUN, dart, dash, hasten, hurry, romp, scoot, scurry, scuttle

scan verb 1 GLANCE OVER, check, check out (informal), examine, eye, look through, run one's eye over, run over, skim 2 SCRUTINIZE, investigate, scour, search, survey, sweep

scandal noun 1 CRIME, disgrace, embarrassment, offence, sin, wrongdoing 2 SHAME, defamation, discredit, disgrace, dishonour, ignominy, infamy, opprobrium, stigma 3 GOSSIP, aspersion, dirt, rumours, slander, talk, tattle

scandalize verb SHOCK, affront, appal, horrify, offend, outrage

scandalous adjective 1 SHOCKING, disgraceful, disreputable, infamous, outrageous, shameful, unseemly 2 SLANDEROUS, defamatory, libellous, scurrilous, untrue

scant adjective MEAGRE, barely sufficient, little, minimal, sparse

scanty adjective MEAGRE, bare, deficient, inadequate, insufficient, poor, scant, short, skimpy, sparse, thin

scapegoat noun WHIPPING BOY, fall guy (informal)

scar noun 1 MARK, blemish, injury,

wound ♦ *verb* **2** <u>MARK</u>, damage, disfigure

scarce *adjective* <u>RARE</u>, few, few and far between, infrequent, in short supply, insufficient, uncommon

scarcely *adverb* **1** <u>HARDLY</u>, barely **2** <u>DEFINITELY NOT</u>, hardly

scarcity *noun* <u>SHORTAGE</u>, dearth, deficiency, insufficiency, lack, paucity, rareness, want

scare *verb* **1** <u>FRIGHTEN</u>, alarm, dismay, intimidate, panic, shock, startle, terrify ♦ *noun* **2** <u>FRIGHT</u>, panic, shock, start, terror

scared *adjective* <u>FRIGHTENED</u>, fearful, panicky, panic-stricken, petrified, shaken, startled, terrified

scarper *verb Slang* <u>RUN AWAY</u>, abscond, beat it (*slang*), clear off (*informal*), disappear, flee, run for it, scram (*informal*), take to one's heels

scary *adjective* <u>FRIGHTENING</u>, alarming, chilling, creepy (*informal*), horrifying, spine-chilling, spooky (*informal*), terrifying

scathing *adjective* <u>CRITICAL</u>, biting, caustic, cutting, harsh, sarcastic, scornful, trenchant, withering

scatter *verb* **1** <u>THROW ABOUT</u>, diffuse, disseminate, fling, shower, spread, sprinkle, strew **2** <u>DISPERSE</u>, disband, dispel, dissipate

scatterbrain *noun* <u>FEATHERBRAIN</u>, butterfly, flibbertigibbet

scenario *noun* <u>STORY LINE</u>, outline, résumé, summary, synopsis

scene *noun* **1** <u>SITE</u>, area, locality, place, position, setting, spot **2** <u>SETTING</u>, backdrop, background, location, set **3** <u>SHOW</u>, display, drama, exhibition, pageant, picture, sight, spectacle **4** <u>ACT</u>, division, episode, part **5** <u>VIEW</u>, landscape, panorama, prospect,

vista **6** <u>FUSS</u>, carry-on (*informal, chiefly Brit.*), commotion, exhibition, performance, row, tantrum, to-do **7** *Informal* <u>WORLD</u>, arena, business, environment

scenery *noun* **1** <u>LANDSCAPE</u>, surroundings, terrain, view, vista **2** *Theatre* <u>SET</u>, backdrop, flats, setting, stage set

scenic *adjective* <u>PICTURESQUE</u>, beautiful, panoramic, spectacular, striking

scent *noun* **1** <u>FRAGRANCE</u>, aroma, bouquet, odour, perfume, smell **2** <u>TRAIL</u>, spoor, track ♦ *verb* **3** <u>DETECT</u>, discern, nose out, sense, smell, sniff

scented *adjective* <u>FRAGRANT</u>, aromatic, odoriferous, perfumed, sweet-smelling

sceptic *noun* <u>DOUBTER</u>, cynic, disbeliever, doubting Thomas

sceptical *adjective* <u>DOUBTFUL</u>, cynical, disbelieving, dubious, incredulous, mistrustful, unconvinced

scepticism *noun* <u>DOUBT</u>, cynicism, disbelief, incredulity, unbelief

schedule *noun* **1** <u>PLAN</u>, agenda, calendar, catalogue, inventory, list, programme, timetable ♦ *verb* **2** <u>PLAN</u>, appoint, arrange, book, organize, programme

scheme *noun* **1** <u>PLAN</u>, programme, project, proposal, strategy, system, tactics **2** <u>DIAGRAM</u>, blueprint, chart, draft, layout, outline, pattern **3** <u>PLOT</u>, conspiracy, intrigue, manoeuvre, ploy, ruse, stratagem, subterfuge ♦ *verb* **4** <u>PLAN</u>, lay plans, project, work out **5** <u>PLOT</u>, collude, conspire, intrigue, machinate, manoeuvre

scheming *adjective* <u>CALCULATING</u>, artful, conniving, cunning, sly, tricky, underhand, wily

schism *noun* <u>DIVISION</u>, breach,

break, rift, rupture, separation, split

scholar noun 1 INTELLECTUAL, academic, savant 2 STUDENT, disciple, learner, pupil, schoolboy or schoolgirl

scholarly adjective LEARNED, academic, bookish, erudite, intellectual, lettered, scholastic

scholarship noun 1 LEARNING, book-learning, education, erudition, knowledge 2 BURSARY, fellowship

scholastic adjective LEARNED, academic, lettered, scholarly

school noun 1 ACADEMY, college, faculty, institute, institution, seminary 2 GROUP, adherents, circle, denomination, devotees, disciples, faction, followers, set ♦ verb 3 TRAIN, coach, discipline, drill, educate, instruct, tutor

schooling noun 1 TEACHING, education, tuition 2 TRAINING, coaching, drill, instruction

science noun 1 DISCIPLINE, body of knowledge, branch of knowledge 2 SKILL, art, technique

scientific adjective SYSTEMATIC, accurate, controlled, exact, mathematical, precise

scientist noun INVENTOR, boffin (informal), technophile

scintillating adjective BRILLIANT, animated, bright, dazzling, exciting, glittering, lively, sparkling, stimulating

scoff[1] verb SCORN, belittle, deride, despise, jeer, knock (informal), laugh at, mock, pooh-pooh, ridicule, sneer

scoff[2] verb GOBBLE (UP), bolt, devour, gorge oneself on, gulp down, guzzle, wolf

scold verb 1 REPRIMAND, berate, castigate, censure, find fault with, give (someone) a dressing-down, lecture, rebuke, reproach, reprove, tell off (informal), tick off (informal), upbraid ♦ noun 2 NAG, shrew, termagant (rare)

scolding noun REBUKE, dressing-down (informal), lecture, row, telling-off (informal), ticking-off (informal)

scoop noun 1 LADLE, dipper, spoon 2 EXCLUSIVE, exposé, revelation, sensation ♦ verb 3 often with up LIFT, gather up, pick up, take up 4 often with out HOLLOW, bail, dig, empty, excavate, gouge, shovel

scope noun 1 OPPORTUNITY, freedom, latitude, liberty, room, space 2 RANGE, area, capacity, orbit, outlook, reach, span, sphere

scorch verb BURN, parch, roast, sear, shrivel, singe, wither

scorching adjective BURNING, baking, boiling, fiery, flaming, red-hot, roasting, searing

score noun 1 POINTS, grade, mark, outcome, record, result, total 2 GROUNDS, basis, cause, ground, reason 3 GRIEVANCE, grudge, injury, injustice, wrong 4 scores LOTS, hundreds, masses, millions, multitudes, myriads, swarms ♦ verb 5 GAIN, achieve, chalk up (informal), make, notch up (informal), win 6 KEEP COUNT, count, record, register, tally 7 CUT, deface, gouge, graze, mark, scrape, scratch, slash 8 with out or through CROSS OUT, cancel, delete, obliterate, strike out 9 Music ARRANGE, adapt, orchestrate, set

scorn noun 1 CONTEMPT, derision, disdain, disparagement, mockery, sarcasm ♦ verb 2 DESPISE, be above, deride, disdain, flout, reject, scoff at, slight, spurn

scornful adjective CONTEMPTUOUS, derisive, disdainful, haughty, jeering, mocking, sarcastic, sardonic, scathing, scoffing, sneering

scoundrel noun ROGUE, bastard (offensive), blackguard, good-for-nothing, heel (slang), miscreant, ne'er-do-well, rascal, reprobate, rotter (slang, chiefly Brit.), scally (Northwest English dialect), scamp, swine, villain

scour[1] verb RUB, abrade, buff, clean, polish, scrub, wash

scour[2] verb SEARCH, beat, comb, hunt, ransack

scourge noun 1 AFFLICTION, bane, curse, infliction, misfortune, pest, plague, terror, torment 2 WHIP, cat, lash, strap, switch, thong ♦ verb 3 AFFLICT, curse, plague, terrorize, torment 4 WHIP, beat, cane, flog, horsewhip, lash, thrash

scout noun 1 VANGUARD, advance guard, lookout, outrider, precursor, reconnoitrer ♦ verb 2 RECONNOITRE, investigate, observe, probe, recce (slang), spy, survey, watch

scowl verb 1 GLOWER, frown, lour or lower ♦ noun 2 GLOWER, black look, dirty look, frown

scrabble verb SCRAPE, claw, scramble, scratch

scraggy adjective SCRAWNY, angular, bony, lean, skinny

scram verb GO AWAY, abscond, beat it (slang), clear off (informal), get lost (informal), leave, make oneself scarce (informal), make tracks, scarper (Brit. slang), vamoose (slang, chiefly U.S.)

scramble verb 1 STRUGGLE, climb, crawl, scrabble, swarm 2 STRIVE, contend, jostle, push, run, rush, vie ♦ noun 3 CLIMB, trek 4 STRUGGLE, commotion, competition, confusion, melee or mêlée, race, rush, tussle

scrap[1] noun 1 PIECE, bit, crumb, fragment, grain, morsel, part, particle, portion, sliver, snippet 2 WASTE, junk, off cuts 3 **scraps** LEFTOVERS, bits, leavings, remains ♦ verb 4 DISCARD, abandon, ditch (slang), drop, jettison, throw away or out, write off

scrap[2] Informal ♦ noun 1 FIGHT, argument, battle, disagreement, dispute, quarrel, row, squabble, wrangle ♦ verb 2 FIGHT, argue, row, squabble, wrangle

scrape verb 1 GRAZE, bark, rub, scratch, scuff, skin 2 RUB, clean, erase, remove, scour 3 GRATE, grind, rasp, scratch, squeak 4 SCRIMP, pinch, save, skimp, stint 5 **scrape through** GET BY (informal), just make it, struggle ♦ noun 6 Informal PREDICAMENT, awkward situation, difficulty, dilemma, fix (informal), mess, plight, tight spot

scrapheap noun **on the scrapheap** DISCARDED, ditched (slang), jettisoned, put out to grass (informal), redundant, written off

scrappy adjective FRAGMENTARY, bitty, disjointed, incomplete, piecemeal, sketchy, thrown together

scratch verb 1 MARK, claw, cut, damage, etch, grate, graze, lacerate, score, scrape 2 WITHDRAW, cancel, delete, eliminate, erase, pull out ♦ noun 3 MARK, blemish, claw mark, gash, graze, laceration, scrape 4 **up to scratch** ADEQUATE, acceptable, satisfactory, sufficient, up to standard ♦ adjective 5 IMPROVISED, impromptu, rough-and-ready

scrawl verb SCRIBBLE, doodle, squiggle, writing

scrawny adjective THIN, bony, gaunt, lean, scraggy, skin-and-bones (informal), skinny, undernourished

scream verb **1** CRY, bawl, screech, shriek, yell ♦ noun **2** CRY, howl, screech, shriek, yell, yelp

screech noun, verb CRY, scream, shriek

screen noun **1** COVER, awning, canopy, cloak, guard, partition, room divider, shade, shelter, shield **2** MESH, net ♦ verb **3** COVER, cloak, conceal, hide, mask, shade, veil **4** PROTECT, defend, guard, shelter, shield **5** VET, evaluate, examine, filter, gauge, scan, sift, sort **6** BROADCAST, present, put on, show

screw verb **1** TURN, tighten, twist **2** Informal, often with out of EXTORT, extract, wrest, wring

screw up verb **1** Informal BUNGLE, botch, make a hash of (informal), make a mess of (slang), mess up, mishandle, spoil **2** DISTORT, contort, pucker, wrinkle

screwy adjective CRAZY, crackpot (informal), eccentric, loopy (informal), nutty (slang), odd, off-the-wall (slang), out to lunch (informal), round the bend (Brit. slang), weird

scribble verb SCRAWL, dash off, jot, write

scribe noun COPYIST, amanuensis, writer

scrimp verb ECONOMIZE, be frugal, save, scrape, skimp, stint, tighten one's belt

script noun **1** TEXT, book, copy, dialogue, libretto, lines, words **2** HANDWRITING, calligraphy, penmanship, writing

Scripture noun THE BIBLE, Holy Bible, Holy Scripture, Holy Writ, The Good Book, The Gospels, The Scriptures

scrounge verb Informal CADGE, beg,

blag (slang), bum (informal), freeload (slang), sponge (informal)

scrounger adjective CADGER, freeloader (slang), parasite, sponger (informal)

scrub verb **1** SCOUR, clean, cleanse, rub **2** Informal CANCEL, abolish, call off, delete, drop, forget about, give up

scruffy adjective SHABBY, ill-groomed, mangy, messy, ragged, run-down, seedy, tatty, unkempt, untidy

scrumptious adjective Informal DELICIOUS, appetizing, delectable, luscious, mouthwatering, succulent, yummy (slang)

scruple noun **1** MISGIVING, compunction, doubt, hesitation, qualm, reluctance, second thoughts, uneasiness ♦ verb **2** HAVE MISGIVINGS ABOUT, demur, doubt, have qualms about, hesitate, think twice about

scrupulous adjective **1** MORAL, conscientious, honourable, principled, upright **2** CAREFUL, exact, fastidious, meticulous, precise, punctilious, rigorous, strict

scrutinize verb EXAMINE, explore, inspect, investigate, peruse, pore over, probe, scan, search, study

scrutiny noun EXAMINATION, analysis, exploration, inspection, investigation, perusal, search, study

scuffle verb **1** FIGHT, clash, grapple, jostle, struggle, tussle ♦ noun **2** FIGHT, brawl, commotion, disturbance, fray, scrimmage, skirmish, tussle

sculpture verb SCULPT, carve, chisel, fashion, form, hew, model, mould, shape

scum noun **1** IMPURITIES, dross, film, froth **2** RABBLE, dregs of society, riffraff, trash (chiefly U.S. & Canad.)

scupper *verb Brit. slang* DESTROY, defeat, demolish, put paid to, ruin, torpedo, wreck

scurrilous *adjective* SLANDEROUS, abusive, defamatory, insulting, scandalous, vituperative

scurry *verb* **1** HURRY, dart, dash, race, scamper, scoot, scuttle, sprint ◆ *noun* **2** FLURRY, scampering, whirl

scuttle *verb* RUN, bustle, hasten, hurry, rush, scamper, scoot, scurry

sea *noun* **1** OCEAN, main, the deep, the waves **2** EXPANSE, abundance, mass, multitude, plethora, profusion **3** **at sea** BEWILDERED, baffled, confused, lost, mystified, puzzled

seafaring *adjective* NAUTICAL, marine, maritime, naval

seal *noun* **1** AUTHENTICATION, confirmation, imprimatur, insignia, ratification, stamp ◆ *verb* **2** CLOSE, bung, enclose, fasten, plug, shut, stop, stopper, stop up **3** AUTHENTICATE, confirm, ratify, stamp, validate **4** SETTLE, clinch, conclude, consummate, finalize **5** **seal off** ISOLATE, put out of bounds, quarantine, segregate

seam *noun* **1** JOINT, closure **2** LAYER, lode, stratum, vein **3** RIDGE, furrow, line, wrinkle

sear *verb* SCORCH, burn, sizzle

search *verb* **1** LOOK, comb, examine, explore, hunt, inspect, investigate, ransack, scour, scrutinize ◆ *noun* **2** LOOK, examination, exploration, hunt, inspection, investigation, pursuit, quest

searching *adjective* KEEN, close, intent, penetrating, piercing, probing, quizzical, sharp

season *noun* **1** PERIOD, spell, term, time ◆ *verb* **2** FLAVOUR, enliven, pep up, salt, spice

seasonable *adjective* APPROPRIATE, convenient, fit, opportune, providential, suitable, timely, well-timed

seasoned *adjective* EXPERIENCED, hardened, practised, time-served, veteran

seasoning *noun* FLAVOURING, condiment, dressing, relish, salt and pepper, sauce, spice

seat *noun* **1** CHAIR, bench, pew, settle, stall, stool **2** CENTRE, capital, heart, hub, place, site, situation, source **3** RESIDENCE, abode, ancestral hall, house, mansion **4** MEMBERSHIP, chair, constituency, incumbency, place ◆ *verb* **5** SIT, fix, install, locate, place, set, settle **6** HOLD, accommodate, cater for, contain, sit, take

seating *noun* ACCOMMODATION, chairs, places, room, seats

secede *verb* WITHDRAW, break with, leave, pull out, quit, resign, split from

secluded *adjective* PRIVATE, cloistered, cut off, isolated, lonely, out-of-the-way, sheltered, solitary

seclusion *noun* PRIVACY, isolation, shelter, solitude

second[1] *adjective* **1** NEXT, following, subsequent, succeeding **2** ADDITIONAL, alternative, extra, further, other **3** INFERIOR, lesser, lower, secondary, subordinate ◆ *noun* **4** SUPPORTER, assistant, backer, helper ◆ *verb* **5** SUPPORT, approve, assist, back, endorse, go along with

second[2] *noun* MOMENT, flash, instant, jiffy (*informal*), minute, sec (*informal*), trice

secondary *adjective* **1** SUBORDINATE, inferior, lesser, lower, minor, unimportant **2** RESULTANT, contingent, derived, indirect **3** BACKUP, auxiliary, fall-back, reserve, subsidiary, supporting

second-class *adjective* INFERIOR, indifferent, mediocre, second-best, second-rate, undistinguished, uninspiring

second-hand *adjective* 1 USED, hand-me-down (*informal*), nearly new ◆ *adverb* 2 INDIRECTLY

second in command *noun* DEPUTY, number two, right-hand man

secondly *adverb* NEXT, in the second place, second

second-rate *adjective* INFERIOR, low-grade, low-quality, mediocre, poor, rubbishy, shoddy, substandard, tacky (*informal*), tawdry, two-bit (*U.S. & Canad. slang*)

secrecy *noun* 1 MYSTERY, concealment, confidentiality, privacy, silence 2 SECRETIVENESS, clandestineness, covertness, furtiveness, stealth

secret *adjective* 1 CONCEALED, close, disguised, furtive, hidden, undercover, underground, undisclosed, unknown, unrevealed 2 STEALTHY, secretive, sly, underhand 3 MYSTERIOUS, abstruse, arcane, clandestine, cryptic, occult ◆ *noun* 4 MYSTERY, code, enigma, key 5 **in secret** SECRETLY, slyly, surreptitiously

secrete[1] *verb* GIVE OFF, emanate, emit, exude

secrete[2] *verb* HIDE, cache, conceal, harbour, stash (*informal*), stow

secretive *adjective* RETICENT, close, deep, reserved, tight-lipped, uncommunicative

secretly *adverb* IN SECRET, clandestinely, covertly, furtively, privately, quietly, stealthily, surreptitiously

sect *noun* GROUP, camp, denomination, division, faction, party, schism

sectarian *adjective* 1 NARROW-MINDED, bigoted, doctrinaire, dogmatic, factional, fanatical, limited, parochial, partisan ◆ *noun* 2 BIGOT, dogmatist, extremist, fanatic, partisan, zealot

section *noun* 1 PART, division, fraction, instalment, passage, piece, portion, segment, slice 2 *Chiefly U.S.* DISTRICT, area, region, sector, zone

sector *noun* PART, area, district, division, quarter, region, zone

secular *adjective* WORLDLY, civil, earthly, lay, nonspiritual, temporal

secure *adjective* 1 SAFE, immune, protected, unassailable 2 SURE, assured, certain, confident, easy, reassured 3 FIXED, fast, fastened, firm, immovable, stable, steady ◆ *verb* 4 OBTAIN, acquire, gain, get, procure, score (*slang*) 5 FASTEN, attach, bolt, chain, fix, lock, make fast, tie up

security *noun* 1 PRECAUTIONS, defence, protection, safeguards, safety measures 2 SAFETY, care, custody, refuge, safekeeping, sanctuary 3 SURENESS, assurance, certainty, confidence, conviction, positiveness, reliance 4 PLEDGE, collateral, gage, guarantee, hostage, insurance, pawn, surety

sedate *adjective* CALM, collected, composed, cool, dignified, serene, tranquil

sedative *adjective* 1 CALMING, anodyne, relaxing, soothing, tranquillizing ◆ *noun* 2 TRANQUILLIZER, anodyne, downer or down (*slang*)

sedentary *adjective* INACTIVE, desk, desk-bound, seated, sitting

sediment *noun* DREGS, deposit, grounds, lees, residue

sedition noun RABBLE-ROUSING, agitation, incitement to riot, subversion

seditious adjective REVOLUTIONARY, dissident, mutinous, rebellious, refractory, subversive

seduce verb 1 CORRUPT, debauch, deflower, deprave, dishonour 2 TEMPT, beguile, deceive, entice, inveigle, lead astray, lure, mislead

seduction noun 1 CORRUPTION 2 TEMPTATION, enticement, lure, snare

seductive adjective ALLURING, attractive, bewitching, enticing, inviting, provocative, tempting

seductress noun TEMPTRESS, enchantress, femme fatale, siren, vamp (informal)

see verb 1 PERCEIVE, behold, catch sight of, discern, distinguish, espy, glimpse, look, make out, notice, observe, sight, spot, witness 2 UNDERSTAND, appreciate, comprehend, fathom, feel, follow, get, grasp, realize 3 FIND OUT, ascertain, determine, discover, learn 4 MAKE SURE, ensure, guarantee, make certain, see to it 5 CONSIDER, decide, deliberate, reflect, think over 6 VISIT, confer with, consult, interview, receive, speak to 7 GO OUT WITH, court, date (informal, chiefly U.S.), go steady with (informal) 8 ACCOMPANY, escort, lead, show, usher, walk

seed noun 1 GRAIN, egg, embryo, germ, kernel, ovum, pip, spore 2 ORIGIN, beginning, germ, nucleus, source, start 3 OFFSPRING, children, descendants, issue, progeny 4 **go** or **run to seed** DECLINE, decay, degenerate, deteriorate, go downhill (informal), go to pot, let oneself go

seedy adjective 1 SHABBY, dilapidated, grotty (slang), grubby, mangy, run-down,

scruffy, sleazy, squalid, tatty 2 Informal UNWELL, ill, off colour, out of sorts, poorly (informal), under the weather (informal)

seeing conjunction SINCE, as, inasmuch as, in view of the fact that

seek verb 1 LOOK FOR, be after, follow, hunt, pursue, search for 2 TRY, aim, aspire to, attempt, endeavour, essay, strive

seem verb APPEAR, assume, give the impression, look

seemly adjective FITTING, appropriate, becoming, decent, decorous, fit, proper, suitable

seep verb OOZE, exude, leak, permeate, soak, trickle, well

seer noun PROPHET, sibyl, soothsayer

seesaw verb ALTERNATE, fluctuate, oscillate, swing

seethe verb 1 BE FURIOUS, be livid, fume, go ballistic (slang, chiefly U.S.), rage, see red (informal), simmer 2 BOIL, bubble, fizz, foam, froth

see through verb 1 BE UNDECEIVED BY, be wise to (informal), fathom, not fall for, penetrate 2 **see (something) through** PERSEVERE (WITH), keep at, persist, stick out (informal) 3 **see (someone) through** HELP OUT, stick by, support

segment noun SECTION, bit, division, part, piece, portion, slice, wedge

segregate verb SET APART, discriminate against, dissociate, isolate, separate

segregation noun SEPARATION, apartheid, discrimination, isolation

seize verb 1 GRAB, catch up, clutch, grasp, grip, lay hands on, snatch, take 2 CONFISCATE, appropriate, commandeer, impound, take possession of 3 CAPTURE, apprehend, arrest, catch, take captive

seizure noun **1** <u>ATTACK</u>, convulsion, fit, paroxysm, spasm **2** <u>CAPTURE</u>, apprehension, arrest **3** <u>TAKING</u>, annexation, commandeering, confiscation, grabbing

seldom adverb <u>RARELY</u>, hardly ever, infrequently, not often

select verb **1** <u>CHOOSE</u>, opt for, pick, single out ◆ adjective **2** <u>CHOICE</u>, excellent, first-class, hand-picked, special, superior, top-notch (informal) **3** <u>EXCLUSIVE</u>, cliquish, elite, privileged

selection noun **1** <u>CHOICE</u>, choosing, option, pick, preference **2** <u>RANGE</u>, assortment, choice, collection, medley, variety

selective adjective <u>PARTICULAR</u>, careful, discerning, discriminating

self-assurance noun <u>CONFIDENCE</u>, assertiveness, positiveness, self-confidence, self-possession

self-centred adjective <u>SELFISH</u>, egotistic, narcissistic, self-seeking

self-confidence noun <u>SELF-ASSURANCE</u>, aplomb, confidence, nerve, poise

self-confident adjective <u>SELF-ASSURED</u>, assured, confident, poised, sure of oneself

self-conscious adjective <u>EMBARRASSED</u>, awkward, bashful, diffident, ill at ease, insecure, nervous, uncomfortable

self-control noun <u>WILLPOWER</u>, restraint, self-discipline, self-restraint

self-esteem noun <u>SELF-RESPECT</u>, confidence, faith in oneself, pride, self-assurance, self-regard

self-evident adjective <u>OBVIOUS</u>, clear, incontrovertible, inescapable, undeniable

self-important adjective <u>CONCEITED</u>, bigheaded, cocky, full of oneself, pompous, swollen-headed

self-indulgence noun <u>INTEMPERANCE</u>, excess, extravagance

selfish adjective <u>SELF-CENTRED</u>, egoistic, egoistical, egotistic, egotistical, greedy, self-interested, ungenerous

selfless adjective <u>UNSELFISH</u>, altruistic, generous, self-denying, self-sacrificing

self-possessed adjective <u>SELF-ASSURED</u>, collected, confident, cool, poised, unruffled

self-reliant adjective <u>INDEPENDENT</u>, self-sufficient, self-supporting

self-respect noun <u>PRIDE</u>, dignity, morale, self-esteem

self-restraint noun <u>SELF-CONTROL</u>, self-command, self-discipline, willpower

self-righteous adjective <u>SANCTIMONIOUS</u>, complacent, holier-than-thou, priggish, self-satisfied, smug, superior

self-sacrifice noun <u>SELFLESSNESS</u>, altruism, generosity, self-denial

self-satisfied adjective <u>SMUG</u>, complacent, pleased with oneself, self-congratulatory

self-seeking adjective <u>SELFISH</u>, careerist, looking out for number one (informal), out for what one can get, self-interested, self-serving

sell verb **1** <u>TRADE</u>, barter, exchange **2** <u>DEAL IN</u>, handle, market, peddle, retail, stock, trade in, traffic in

seller noun <u>DEALER</u>, agent, merchant, purveyor, retailer, salesman or saleswoman, supplier, vendor

selling noun <u>DEALING</u>, business, trading, traffic

sell out verb **1** <u>DISPOSE OF</u>, be out of

stock of, get rid of, run out of **2** *Informal* BETRAY, double-cross (*informal*), sell down the river (*informal*), stab in the back

semblance *noun* APPEARANCE, aspect, façade, mask, pretence, resemblance, show, veneer

seminal *adjective* INFLUENTIAL, formative, ground-breaking, important, innovative, original

send *verb* **1** CONVEY, direct, dispatch, forward, remit, transmit **2** PROPEL, cast, fire, fling, hurl, let fly, shoot

send for *verb* SUMMON, call for, order, request

sendoff *noun* FAREWELL, departure, leave-taking, start, valediction

send-up *noun* IMITATION, parody, satire, skit, spoof (*informal*), take-off (*informal*)

send up *verb* IMITATE, burlesque, lampoon, make fun of, mimic, mock, parody, satirize, spoof (*informal*), take off (*informal*)

senile *adjective* DODDERING, decrepit, doting, in one's dotage

senility *noun* DOTAGE, decrepitude, infirmity, loss of one's faculties, senile dementia

senior *adjective* **1** HIGHER RANKING, superior **2** OLDER, elder, major (*Brit.*)

senior citizen *noun* PENSIONER, O.A.P., old age pensioner, old *or* elderly person, retired person

seniority *noun* SUPERIORITY, precedence, priority, rank

sensation *noun* **1** FEELING, awareness, consciousness, impression, perception, sense **2** EXCITEMENT, commotion, furore, stir, thrill

sensational *adjective* **1** DRAMATIC, amazing, astounding, exciting, melodramatic, shock-horror

(*facetious*), shocking, thrilling **2** *Informal* EXCELLENT, fabulous (*informal*), impressive, marvellous, mean (*slang*), mind-blowing (*informal*), out of this world (*informal*), smashing (*informal*), superb

sense *noun* **1** FACULTY, feeling, sensation **2** FEELING, atmosphere, aura, awareness, consciousness, impression, perception **3** sometimes plural INTELLIGENCE, brains (*informal*), cleverness, common sense, judgment, reason, sagacity, sanity, sharpness, understanding, wisdom, wit(s) **4** MEANING, drift, gist, implication, import, significance ♦ *verb* **5** PERCEIVE, be aware of, discern, feel, get the impression, pick up, realize, understand

senseless *adjective* **1** STUPID, asinine, crazy, daft (*informal*), foolish, idiotic, illogical, inane, irrational, mad, mindless, nonsensical, pointless, ridiculous, silly **2** UNCONSCIOUS, insensible, out, out cold, stunned

sensibility *noun* **1** often plural FEELINGS, emotions, moral sense, sentiments, susceptibilities **2** SENSITIVITY, responsiveness, sensitiveness, susceptibility

sensible *adjective* **1** WISE, canny, down-to-earth, intelligent, judicious, practical, prudent, rational, realistic, sage, sane, shrewd, sound **2** usually with *of* AWARE, conscious, mindful, sensitive to

sensitive *adjective* **1** EASILY HURT, delicate, tender **2** SUSCEPTIBLE, easily affected, impressionable, responsive, touchy-feely (*informal*) **3** TOUCHY, easily offended, easily upset, thin-skinned **4** RESPONSIVE, acute, fine, keen, precise

sensitivity *noun* SENSITIVENESS,

delicacy, receptiveness, responsiveness, susceptibility

sensual *adjective* 1 PHYSICAL, animal, bodily, carnal, fleshly, luxurious, voluptuous 2 EROTIC, lascivious, lecherous, lewd, lustful, raunchy (*slang*), sexual

sensuality *noun* EROTICISM, carnality, lasciviousness, lecherousness, lewdness, sexiness (*informal*), voluptuousness

sensuous *adjective* PLEASURABLE, gratifying, hedonistic, sybaritic

sentence *noun* 1 PUNISHMENT, condemnation, decision, decree, judgment, order, ruling, verdict ♦ *verb* 2 CONDEMN, doom, penalize

sententious *adjective* POMPOUS, canting, judgmental, moralistic, preachifying (*informal*), sanctimonious

sentient *adjective* FEELING, conscious, living, sensitive

sentiment *noun* 1 EMOTION, sensibility, tenderness 2 often plural FEELING, attitude, belief, idea, judgment, opinion, view 3 SENTIMENTALITY, emotionalism, mawkishness, romanticism

sentimental *adjective* ROMANTIC, emotional, maudlin, nostalgic, overemotional, schmaltzy (*slang*), slushy (*informal*), soft-hearted, touching, weepy (*informal*)

sentimentality *noun* ROMANTICISM, corniness (*slang*), emotionalism, mawkishness, nostalgia, schmaltz (*slang*)

sentinel *noun* GUARD, lookout, sentry, watch, watchman

separable *adjective* DISTINGUISHABLE, detachable, divisible

separate *verb* 1 DIVIDE, come apart, come away, detach, disconnect, disjoin, remove, sever, split, sunder 2 PART, break up, disunite,

diverge, divorce, estrange, part company, split up 3 ISOLATE, segregate, single out ♦ *adjective* 4 UNCONNECTED, detached, disconnected, divided, divorced, isolated, unattached 5 INDIVIDUAL, alone, apart, distinct, particular, single, solitary

separated *adjective* DISCONNECTED, apart, disassociated, disunited, divided, parted, separate, sundered

separately *adverb* INDIVIDUALLY, alone, apart, severally, singly

separation *noun* 1 DIVISION, break, disconnection, dissociation, disunion, gap 2 SPLIT-UP, break-up, divorce, parting, rift, split

septic *adjective* INFECTED, festering, poisoned, putrefying, putrid, suppurating

sepulchre *noun* TOMB, burial place, grave, mausoleum, vault

sequel *noun* 1 FOLLOW-UP, continuation, development 2 CONSEQUENCE, conclusion, end, outcome, result, upshot

sequence *noun* SUCCESSION, arrangement, chain, course, cycle, order, progression, series

serene *adjective* CALM, composed, peaceful, tranquil, unruffled, untroubled

serenity *noun* CALMNESS, calm, composure, peace, peacefulness, quietness, stillness, tranquillity

series *noun* SEQUENCE, chain, course, order, progression, run, set, string, succession, train

serious *adjective* 1 SEVERE, acute, critical, dangerous 2 IMPORTANT, crucial, fateful, grim, momentous, no laughing matter, pressing, significant, urgent, worrying 3 SOLEMN, grave, humourless, sober, unsmiling 4 SINCERE, earnest, genuine, honest, in earnest

seriously *adverb* 1 GRAVELY, acutely, badly, critically, dangerously, severely 2 SINCERELY, gravely, in earnest

seriousness *noun* 1 IMPORTANCE, gravity, significance, urgency 2 SOLEMNITY, earnestness, gravitas, gravity

sermon *noun* 1 HOMILY, address 2 LECTURE, harangue, talking-to (*informal*)

servant *noun* ATTENDANT, domestic, help, maid, retainer, skivvy (*chiefly Brit.*), slave

serve *verb* 1 WORK FOR, aid, assist, attend to, help, minister to, wait on 2 PERFORM, act, complete, discharge, do, fulfil 3 PROVIDE, deliver, dish up, present, set out, supply 4 BE ADEQUATE, answer the purpose, be acceptable, do, function as, satisfy, suffice, suit

service *noun* 1 HELP, assistance, avail, benefit, use, usefulness 2 WORK, business, duty, employment, labour, office 3 OVERHAUL, check, maintenance 4 CEREMONY, observance, rite, worship ♦ *verb* 5 OVERHAUL, check, fine tune, go over, maintain, tune (up)

serviceable *adjective* USEFUL, beneficial, functional, helpful, operative, practical, profitable, usable, utilitarian

servile *adjective* SUBSERVIENT, abject, fawning, grovelling, obsequious, sycophantic, toadying

serving *noun* PORTION, helping

session *noun* MEETING, assembly, conference, congress, discussion, hearing, period, sitting

set[1] *verb* 1 PUT, deposit, lay, locate, place, plant, position, rest, seat, situate, station, stick 2 PREPARE, arrange, lay, make ready, spread 3 HARDEN, cake, congeal, crystallize, solidify, stiffen, thicken 4 ARRANGE, appoint, decide (upon), determine, establish, fix, fix up, resolve, schedule, settle, specify 5 ASSIGN, allot, decree, impose, ordain, prescribe, specify 6 GO DOWN, decline, dip, disappear, sink, subside, vanish ♦ *noun* 7 POSITION, attitude, bearing, carriage, posture 8 SCENERY, scene, setting, stage set ♦ *adjective* 9 FIXED, agreed, appointed, arranged, decided, definite, established, prearranged, predetermined, scheduled, settled 10 INFLEXIBLE, hard and fast, immovable, rigid, stubborn 11 CONVENTIONAL, stereotyped, traditional, unspontaneous 12 **set on** *or* **upon** DETERMINED, bent, intent, resolute

set[2] *noun* 1 SERIES, assortment, batch, collection, compendium 2 GROUP, band, circle, clique, company, coterie, crowd, faction, gang

setback *noun* HOLD-UP, blow, check, defeat, disappointment, hitch, misfortune, reverse

set back *verb* HOLD UP, delay, hinder, impede, retard, slow

set off *verb* 1 LEAVE, depart, embark, start out 2 DETONATE, explode, ignite

setting *noun* BACKGROUND, backdrop, context, location, scene, scenery, set, site, surroundings

settle *verb* 1 PUT IN ORDER, adjust, order, regulate, straighten out, work out 2 LAND, alight, come to rest, descend, light 3 MOVE TO, dwell, inhabit, live, make one's home, put down roots, reside, set up home, take up residence 4 COLONIZE, people, pioneer, populate 5 CALM, lull, pacify, quell, quiet, quieten, reassure, relax, relieve, soothe 6 PAY, clear, discharge, square (up) **7** often with *on or upon* DECIDE, agree, confirm, determine, establish, fix **8** RESOLVE, clear up, decide, put an end to, reconcile

settlement *noun* **1** AGREEMENT, arrangement, conclusion, confirmation, establishment, working out **2** PAYMENT, clearing, discharge **3** COLONY, community, encampment, outpost

settler *noun* COLONIST, frontiersman, immigrant, pioneer

setup *noun* ARRANGEMENT, conditions, organization, regime, structure, system

set up *verb* **1** BUILD, assemble, construct, erect, put together, put up, raise **2** ESTABLISH, arrange, begin, found, initiate, institute, organize, prearrange, prepare

sever *verb* **1** CUT, cut in two, detach, disconnect, disjoin, divide, part, separate, split **2** BREAK OFF, dissociate, put an end to, terminate

several *adjective* SOME, different, diverse, manifold, many, sundry, various

severe *adjective* **1** STRICT, austere, cruel, drastic, hard, harsh, oppressive, rigid, unbending **2** GRIM, forbidding, grave, serious, stern, tight-lipped, unsmiling **3** INTENSE, acute, extreme, fierce **4** PLAIN, austere, classic, restrained, simple, Spartan, unadorned, unembellished, unfussy

severely *adverb* **1** STRICTLY, harshly, sharply, sternly **2** SERIOUSLY, acutely, badly, extremely, gravely

severity *noun* STRICTNESS, hardness, harshness, severeness, sternness, toughness

sex *noun* **1** GENDER **2** *Informal* (SEXUAL) INTERCOURSE, coition, coitus, copulation, fornication,

lovemaking, sexual relations

sexual *adjective* **1** CARNAL, erotic, intimate, sensual, sexy **2** REPRODUCTIVE, genital, procreative, sex

sexual intercourse *noun* COPULATION, bonking (*informal*), carnal knowledge, coition, coitus, sex (*informal*), union

sexuality *noun* DESIRE, carnality, eroticism, lust, sensuality, sexiness (*informal*)

sexy *adjective* EROTIC, arousing, naughty, provocative, seductive, sensual, sensuous, suggestive, titillating

shabby *adjective* **1** TATTY, dilapidated, mean, ragged, run-down, scruffy, seedy, tattered, threadbare, worn **2** MEAN, cheap, contemptible, despicable, dirty, dishonourable, low, rotten (*informal*), scurvy

shack *noun* HUT, cabin, shanty

shackle *noun* **1** often plural FETTER, bond, chain, iron, leg-iron, manacle ♦ *verb* **2** FETTER, bind, chain, manacle, put in irons

shade *noun* **1** DIMNESS, dusk, gloom, gloominess, semidarkness, shadow **2** SCREEN, blind, canopy, cover, covering, curtain, shield, veil **3** COLOUR, hue, tinge, tint, tone **4** DASH, hint, suggestion, trace **5** *Literary* GHOST, apparition, phantom, spectre, spirit **6 put into the shade** OUTSHINE, eclipse, outclass, overshadow ♦ *verb* **7** COVER, conceal, hide, obscure, protect, screen, shield, veil **8** DARKEN, cloud, dim, shadow

shadow *noun* **1** DIMNESS, cover, darkness, dusk, gloom, shade **2** TRACE, hint, suggestion, suspicion **3** CLOUD, blight, gloom, sadness ♦ *verb* **4** SHADE, darken, overhang, screen, shield **5** FOLLOW, stalk, tail (*informal*), trail

shadowy *adjective* 1 DARK, dim, dusky, gloomy, murky, shaded, shady 2 VAGUE, dim, dreamlike, faint, ghostly, nebulous, phantom, spectral, unsubstantial

shady *adjective* 1 SHADED, cool, dim 2 *Informal* CROOKED, disreputable, dodgy (*Brit., Austral., & N.Z. informal*), dubious, questionable, shifty, suspect, suspicious, unethical

shaft *noun* 1 HANDLE, pole, rod, shank, stem 2 RAY, beam, gleam

shaggy *adjective* UNKEMPT, hairy, hirsute, long-haired, rough, tousled, unshorn

shake *verb* 1 VIBRATE, bump, jar, jolt, quake, rock, shiver, totter, tremble 2 WAVE, brandish, flourish 3 UPSET, distress, disturb, frighten, rattle (*informal*), shock, unnerve ♦ *noun* 4 VIBRATION, agitation, convulsion, jerk, jolt, quaking, shiver, shudder, trembling, tremor

shake up *verb* 1 STIR (UP), agitate, churn (up), mix 2 UPSET, disturb, shock, unsettle

shaky *adjective* 1 UNSTEADY, faltering, precarious, quivery, rickety, trembling, unstable, weak 2 UNCERTAIN, dubious, iffy (*informal*), questionable, suspect

shallow *adjective* 1 SUPERFICIAL, empty, slight, surface, trivial 2 UNINTELLIGENT, foolish, frivolous, ignorant, puerile, simple

sham *noun* 1 PHONEY *or* PHONY (*informal*), counterfeit, forgery, fraud, hoax, humbug, imitation, impostor, pretence ♦ *adjective* 2 FALSE, artificial, bogus, counterfeit, feigned, imitation, mock, phoney *or* phony (*informal*), pretended, simulated ♦ *verb* 3 FAKE, affect, assume, feign, pretend, put on, simulate

shambles *noun* CHAOS, confusion, disarray, disorder, havoc, madhouse, mess, muddle

shame *noun* 1 EMBARRASSMENT, abashment, humiliation, ignominy, mortification 2 DISGRACE, blot, discredit, dishonour, disrepute, infamy, reproach, scandal, smear ♦ *verb* 3 EMBARRASS, abash, disgrace, humble, humiliate, mortify 4 DISHONOUR, blot, debase, defile, degrade, smear, stain

shamefaced *adjective* EMBARRASSED, abashed, ashamed, humiliated, mortified, red-faced, sheepish

shameful *adjective* 1 EMBARRASSING, cringe-making (*Brit. informal*), humiliating, mortifying 2 DISGRACEFUL, base, dishonourable, low, mean, outrageous, scandalous, wicked

shameless *adjective* BRAZEN, audacious, barefaced, flagrant, hardened, insolent, unabashed, unashamed

shanty *noun* SHACK, cabin, hut, shed

shape *noun* 1 FORM, build, configuration, contours, figure, lines, outline, profile, silhouette 2 PATTERN, frame, model, mould 3 CONDITION, fettle, health, state, trim ♦ *verb* 4 FORM, create, fashion, make, model, mould, produce 5 DEVELOP, adapt, devise, frame, modify, plan

shapeless *adjective* FORMLESS, amorphous, irregular, misshapen, unstructured

shapely *adjective* WELL-FORMED, curvaceous, elegant, graceful, neat, trim, well-proportioned

share *noun* 1 PART, allotment, allowance, contribution, due, lot, portion, quota, ration, whack (*informal*) ♦ *verb* 2 DIVIDE, assign, distribute, partake, participate, receive, split

sharp *adjective* 1 KEEN, acute, jagged, pointed, serrated, spiky 2 SUDDEN, abrupt, distinct, extreme, marked 3 CLEAR, crisp, distinct, well-defined 4 QUICK-WITTED, alert, astute, bright, clever, discerning, knowing, penetrating, perceptive, quick 5 DISHONEST, artful, crafty, cunning, sly, unscrupulous, wily 6 CUTTING, barbed, biting, bitter, caustic, harsh, hurtful 7 SOUR, acid, acrid, hot, piquant, pungent, tart 8 ACUTE, intense, painful, piercing, severe, shooting, stabbing ◆ *adverb* 9 PROMPTLY, exactly, on the dot, on time, precisely, punctually

sharpen *verb* WHET, edge, grind, hone

shatter *verb* 1 SMASH, break, burst, crack, crush, pulverize 2 DESTROY, demolish, ruin, torpedo, wreck

shattered *adjective Informal* 1 EXHAUSTED, all in (*slang*), dead beat (*informal*), done in (*informal*), drained, knackered (*slang*), ready to drop, tired out, worn out 2 DEVASTATED, crushed

shave *verb* TRIM, crop, pare, shear

shed[1] *noun* HUT, outhouse, shack

shed[2] *verb* 1 GIVE OUT, cast, drop, emit, give, radiate, scatter, shower, spill 2 CAST OFF, discard, moult, slough

sheen *noun* SHINE, brightness, gleam, gloss, lustre, polish

sheepish *adjective* EMBARRASSED, abashed, ashamed, mortified, self-conscious, shamefaced

sheer *adjective* 1 TOTAL, absolute, complete, downright, out-and-out, pure, unmitigated, utter 2 STEEP, abrupt, precipitous 3 FINE, diaphanous, gauzy, gossamer, see-through, thin, transparent

sheet *noun* 1 COAT, film, lamina, layer, overlay, stratum, surface, veneer 2 PIECE, panel, plate, slab 3 EXPANSE, area, blanket, covering, stretch, sweep

shell *noun* 1 CASE, husk, pod 2 FRAME, framework, hull, structure ◆ *verb* 3 BOMB, attack, blitz, bombard, strafe

shell out *verb* PAY OUT, fork out (*slang*), give, hand over

shelter *noun* 1 PROTECTION, cover, defence, guard, screen 2 SAFETY, asylum, haven, refuge, retreat, sanctuary, security ◆ *verb* 3 PROTECT, cover, defend, guard, harbour, hide, safeguard, shield 4 TAKE SHELTER, hide, seek refuge

sheltered *adjective* PROTECTED, cloistered, isolated, quiet, screened, secluded, shaded, shielded

shelve *verb* POSTPONE, defer, freeze, put aside, put on ice, put on the back burner (*informal*), suspend, take a rain check on (*U.S. & Canad. informal*)

shepherd *verb* GUIDE, conduct, herd, steer, usher

shield *noun* 1 PROTECTION, cover, defence, guard, safeguard, screen, shelter ◆ *verb* 2 PROTECT, cover, defend, guard, safeguard, screen, shelter

shift *verb* 1 MOVE, budge, displace, move around, rearrange, relocate, reposition ◆ *noun* 2 MOVE, displacement, rearrangement, shifting

shiftless *adjective* LAZY, aimless, good-for-nothing, idle, lackadaisical, slothful, unambitious, unenterprising

shifty *adjective* UNTRUSTWORTHY, deceitful, devious, evasive, furtive, slippery, sly, tricky, underhand

shimmer verb 1 GLEAM, glisten, scintillate, twinkle ♦ noun 2 GLEAM, iridescence

shine verb 1 GLEAM, beam, flash, glare, glisten, glitter, glow, radiate, sparkle, twinkle 2 POLISH, brush, buff, burnish 3 STAND OUT, be conspicuous, excel ♦ noun 4 BRIGHTNESS, glare, gleam, light, radiance, shimmer, sparkle 5 POLISH, gloss, lustre, sheen

shining adjective BRIGHT, beaming, brilliant, gleaming, glistening, luminous, radiant, shimmering, sparkling

shiny adjective BRIGHT, gleaming, glistening, glossy, lustrous, polished

ship noun VESSEL, boat, craft

shipshape adjective TIDY, neat, orderly, spick-and-span, trim, well-ordered, well-organized

shirk verb DODGE, avoid, evade, get out of, skive (Brit. slang), slack

shirker noun SLACKER, clock-watcher, dodger, idler, skiver (Brit. slang)

shiver[1] verb 1 TREMBLE, quake, quiver, shake, shudder ♦ noun 2 TREMBLING, flutter, quiver, shudder, tremor

shiver[2] verb SPLINTER, break, crack, fragment, shatter, smash, smash to smithereens

shivery adjective SHAKING, chilled, chilly, cold, quaking, quivery

shock verb 1 HORRIFY, appal, disgust, nauseate, revolt, scandalize, sicken 2 ASTOUND, jolt, shake, stagger, stun, stupefy ♦ noun 3 IMPACT, blow, clash, collision 4 UPSET, blow, bombshell, distress, disturbance, stupefaction, stupor, trauma, turn (informal)

shocking adjective DREADFUL, appalling, atrocious, disgraceful, disgusting, ghastly, horrifying, nauseating, outrageous, revolting, scandalous, sickening

shoddy adjective INFERIOR, poor, rubbishy, second-rate, slipshod, tawdry, trashy

shoot verb 1 HIT, blast (slang), bring down, kill, open fire, plug (slang) 2 FIRE, discharge, emit, fling, hurl, launch, project, propel 3 SPEED, bolt, charge, dart, dash, fly, hurtle, race, rush, streak, tear ♦ noun 4 BRANCH, bud, offshoot, sprig, sprout

shop noun STORE, boutique, emporium, hypermarket, supermarket

shore noun BEACH, coast, sands, seashore, strand (poetic)

shore up verb SUPPORT, brace, buttress, hold, prop, reinforce, strengthen, underpin

short adjective 1 CONCISE, brief, compressed, laconic, pithy, succinct, summary, terse 2 SMALL, diminutive, dumpy, little, petite, squat 3 BRIEF, fleeting, momentary 4 often with of LACKING, deficient, limited, low (on), scant, scarce, wanting 5 ABRUPT, brusque, curt, discourteous, impolite, sharp, terse, uncivil ♦ adverb 6 ABRUPTLY, suddenly, without warning

shortage noun DEFICIENCY, dearth, insufficiency, lack, paucity, scarcity, want

shortcoming noun FAILING, defect, fault, flaw, imperfection, weakness

shorten verb CUT, abbreviate, abridge, curtail, decrease, diminish, lessen, reduce

shortly adverb SOON, before long, in a little while, presently

short-sighted adjective 1 NEAR-SIGHTED, myopic 2 UNTHINKING, ill-advised, ill-considered, impolitic,

impractical, improvident,
imprudent, injudicious

short-tempered *adjective*
QUICK-TEMPERED, hot-tempered,
impatient, irascible, ratty (*Brit. &
N.Z. informal*), testy

shot *noun* 1 THROW, discharge, lob,
pot shot 2 PELLET, ball, bullet, lead,
projectile, slug 3 MARKSMAN,
shooter 4 *Slang* ATTEMPT, effort,
endeavour, go (*informal*), stab
(*informal*), try, turn

shoulder *verb* 1 BEAR, accept,
assume, be responsible for, carry,
take on 2 PUSH, elbow, jostle,
press, shove

shout *noun* 1 CRY, bellow, call, roar,
scream, yell ♦ *verb* 2 CRY (OUT),
bawl, bellow, call (out), holler
(*informal*), roar, scream, yell

shout down *verb* SILENCE, drown,
drown out, overwhelm

shove *verb* PUSH, drive, elbow,
impel, jostle, press, propel, thrust

shovel *verb* MOVE, dredge, heap,
ladle, load, scoop, toss

shove off *verb* GO AWAY, clear off
(*informal*), depart, leave, push off
(*informal*), scram (*informal*)

show *verb* 1 BE VISIBLE, appear
2 DISPLAY, exhibit, present 3 PROVE,
clarify, demonstrate, elucidate,
point out 4 INSTRUCT, demonstrate,
explain, teach 5 DISPLAY, indicate,
manifest, register, reveal 6 GUIDE,
accompany, attend, conduct,
escort, lead ♦ *noun*
7 ENTERTAINMENT, presentation,
production 8 EXHIBITION, array,
display, fair, pageant, parade,
sight, spectacle 9 PRETENCE,
affectation, air, appearance,
display, illusion, parade, pose

showdown *noun* CONFRONTATION,
clash, face-off (*slang*)

shower *noun* 1 DELUGE, barrage,
stream, torrent, volley ♦ *verb*

2 INUNDATE, deluge, heap, lavish,
pour, rain

showman *noun* PERFORMER,
entertainer

show-off *noun* EXHIBITIONIST,
boaster, braggart, poseur

show off *verb* 1 EXHIBIT,
demonstrate, display, flaunt,
parade 2 BOAST, blow one's own
trumpet, brag, swagger

show up *verb* 1 STAND OUT, appear,
be conspicuous, be visible 2 REVEAL,
expose, highlight, lay bare
3 *Informal* EMBARRASS, let down,
mortify, put to shame 4 *Informal*
ARRIVE, appear, come, turn up

showy *adjective* 1 OSTENTATIOUS,
brash, flamboyant, flash
(*informal*), flashy, over the top
(*informal*) 2 GAUDY, garish, loud

shred *noun* 1 STRIP, bit, fragment,
piece, scrap, sliver, tatter
2 PARTICLE, atom, grain, iota, jot,
scrap, trace

shrew *noun* NAG, harpy, harridan,
scold, spitfire, vixen

shrewd *adjective* CLEVER, astute,
calculating, canny, crafty,
cunning, intelligent, keen,
perceptive, perspicacious, sharp,
smart

shrewdness *noun* ASTUTENESS,
canniness, discernment,
judgment, perspicacity, quick
wits, sharpness, smartness

shriek *verb, noun* CRY, scream,
screech, squeal, yell

shrill *adjective* PIERCING, high,
penetrating, sharp

shrink *verb* 1 DECREASE, contract,
diminish, dwindle, grow smaller,
lessen, narrow, shorten 2 RECOIL,
cower, cringe, draw back, flinch,
quail

shrivel *verb* WITHER, dehydrate,
desiccate, shrink, wilt, wizen

shroud noun 1 <u>WINDING SHEET</u>, grave clothes 2 <u>COVERING</u>, mantle, pall, screen, veil ♦ verb 3 <u>CONCEAL</u>, blanket, cloak, cover, envelop, hide, screen, veil

shudder verb 1 <u>SHIVER</u>, convulse, quake, quiver, shake, tremble ♦ noun 2 <u>SHIVER</u>, quiver, spasm, tremor

shuffle verb 1 <u>SCUFFLE</u>, drag, scrape, shamble 2 <u>REARRANGE</u>, disarrange, disorder, jumble, mix

shun verb <u>AVOID</u>, keep away from, steer clear of

shut verb <u>CLOSE</u>, fasten, seal, secure, slam

shut down verb 1 <u>STOP</u>, halt, switch off 2 <u>CLOSE</u>, shut up

shut out verb <u>EXCLUDE</u>, bar, debar, keep out, lock out

shuttle verb <u>GO BACK AND FORTH</u>, alternate, commute, go to and fro

shut up verb 1 Informal <u>BE QUIET</u>, fall silent, gag, hold one's tongue, hush, silence 2 <u>CONFINE</u>, cage, coop up, immure, imprison, incarcerate

shy[1] adjective 1 <u>TIMID</u>, bashful, coy, diffident, retiring, self-conscious, self-effacing, shrinking 2 <u>CAUTIOUS</u>, chary, distrustful, hesitant, suspicious, wary ♦ verb 3 sometimes with off or away <u>RECOIL</u>, balk, draw back, flinch, start

shy[2] verb <u>THROW</u>, cast, fling, hurl, pitch, sling, toss

shyness noun <u>TIMIDNESS</u>, bashfulness, diffidence, lack of confidence, self-consciousness, timidity, timorousness

sick adjective 1 <u>NAUSEOUS</u>, ill, nauseated, queasy 2 <u>UNWELL</u>, ailing, diseased, indisposed, poorly (informal), under the weather 3 Informal <u>MORBID</u>, black, ghoulish, macabre, sadistic 4 sick of <u>TIRED</u>, bored, fed up, jaded, weary

sicken verb 1 <u>DISGUST</u>, gross out (U.S. slang), nauseate, repel, revolt, turn one's stomach 2 <u>FALL ILL</u>, ail, take sick

sickening adjective <u>DISGUSTING</u>, distasteful, foul, loathsome, nauseating, offensive, repulsive, revolting, stomach-turning (informal), yucky or yukky (slang)

sickly adjective 1 <u>UNHEALTHY</u>, ailing, delicate, faint, feeble, infirm, pallid, peaky, wan, weak 2 <u>NAUSEATING</u>, cloying, mawkish

sickness noun 1 <u>ILLNESS</u>, affliction, ailment, bug (informal), complaint, disease, disorder, malady 2 <u>NAUSEA</u>, queasiness, vomiting

side noun 1 <u>BORDER</u>, boundary, division, edge, limit, margin, perimeter, rim, sector, verge 2 <u>PART</u>, aspect, face, facet, flank, hand, surface, view 3 <u>PARTY</u>, camp, cause, faction, sect, team 4 <u>POINT OF VIEW</u>, angle, opinion, position, slant, stand, standpoint, viewpoint 5 Brit. slang <u>CONCEIT</u>, airs, arrogance ♦ adjective 6 <u>SUBORDINATE</u>, ancillary, incidental, lesser, marginal, minor, secondary, subsidiary ♦ verb 7 usually with with <u>SUPPORT</u>, ally with, favour, go along with, take the part of

sidelong adjective <u>SIDEWAYS</u>, covert, indirect, oblique

sidestep verb <u>AVOID</u>, circumvent, dodge, duck (informal), evade, skirt

sidetrack verb <u>DIVERT</u>, deflect, distract

sideways adverb 1 <u>OBLIQUELY</u>, edgeways, laterally, sidelong, to the side ♦ adjective 2 <u>OBLIQUE</u>, sidelong

sidle verb EDGE, creep, inch, slink, sneak, steal

siesta noun NAP, catnap, doze, forty winks (*informal*), sleep, snooze (*informal*)

sieve noun 1 STRAINER, colander
♦ verb 2 SIFT, separate, strain

sift verb 1 SIEVE, filter, separate 2 EXAMINE, analyse, go through, investigate, research, scrutinize, work over

sight noun 1 VISION, eye, eyes, eyesight, seeing 2 VIEW, appearance, perception, range of vision, visibility 3 SPECTACLE, display, exhibition, pageant, scene, show, vista 4 Informal EYESORE, mess, monstrosity 5 **catch sight of** SPOT, espy, glimpse ♦ verb 6 SPOT, behold, discern, distinguish, make out, observe, perceive, see

sign noun 1 INDICATION, clue, evidence, hint, mark, proof, signal, symptom, token 2 NOTICE, board, placard, warning 3 SYMBOL, badge, device, emblem, logo, mark 4 OMEN, augury, auspice, foreboding, portent, warning
♦ verb 5 AUTOGRAPH, endorse, initial, inscribe 6 GESTURE, beckon, gesticulate, indicate, signal

signal noun 1 SIGN, beacon, cue, gesture, indication, mark, token
♦ verb 2 GESTURE, beckon, gesticulate, indicate, motion, sign, wave

significance noun 1 IMPORTANCE, consequence, moment, relevance, weight 2 MEANING, force, implication(s), import, message, point, purport, sense

significant adjective 1 IMPORTANT, critical, material, momentous, noteworthy, serious, vital, weighty 2 MEANINGFUL, eloquent, expressive, indicative, suggestive

signify verb 1 INDICATE, be a sign of,

betoken, connote, denote, imply, intimate, mean, portend, suggest 2 *Informal* MATTER, be important, carry weight, count

silence noun 1 QUIET, calm, hush, lull, peace, stillness 2 MUTENESS, dumbness, reticence, taciturnity
♦ verb 3 QUIETEN, cut off, cut short, deaden, gag, muffle, quiet, stifle, still, suppress

silent adjective 1 QUIET, hushed, muted, noiseless, soundless, still 2 MUTE, dumb, speechless, taciturn, voiceless, wordless

silently adjective QUIETLY, inaudibly, in silence, mutely, noiselessly, soundlessly, without a sound, wordlessly

silhouette noun 1 OUTLINE, form, profile, shape ♦ verb 2 OUTLINE, etch, stand out

silky adjective SMOOTH, silken, sleek, velvety

silly adjective FOOLISH, absurd, asinine, fatuous, idiotic, inane, ridiculous, senseless, stupid, unwise

silt noun 1 SEDIMENT, alluvium, deposit, ooze, sludge ♦ verb 2 **silt up** CLOG, choke, congest

similar adjective ALIKE, analogous, close, comparable, like, resembling

similarity noun RESEMBLANCE, affinity, agreement, analogy, closeness, comparability, correspondence, likeness, sameness

simmer verb FUME, be angry, rage, seethe, smoulder

simmer down verb CALM DOWN, control oneself, cool off *or* down

simper verb SMILE COYLY, smile affectedly, smirk

simple adjective 1 EASY, clear, intelligible, lucid, plain, straightforward, uncomplicated,

understandable, uninvolved
2 PLAIN, classic, natural,
unembellished, unfussy **3** PURE,
elementary, unalloyed,
uncombined, unmixed **4** ARTLESS,
childlike, guileless, ingenuous,
innocent, naive, natural, sincere,
unaffected, unsophisticated
5 HONEST, bald, basic, direct, frank,
naked, plain, sincere, stark
6 HUMBLE, homely, modest,
unpretentious **7** FEEBLE-MINDED,
foolish, half-witted, moronic,
slow, stupid

simple-minded *adjective*
FEEBLE-MINDED, backward,
dim-witted, foolish, idiot, idiotic,
moronic, retarded, simple, stupid

simpleton *noun* HALFWIT, dullard,
fool, idiot, imbecile (*informal*),
moron, numskull *or* numbskull

simplicity *noun* **1** EASE, clarity,
clearness, straightforwardness
2 PLAINNESS, lack of adornment,
purity, restraint **3** ARTLESSNESS,
candour, directness, innocence,
naivety, openness

simplify *verb* MAKE SIMPLER, abridge,
disentangle, dumb down, reduce
to essentials, streamline

simply *adverb* **1** PLAINLY, clearly,
directly, easily, intelligibly,
naturally, straightforwardly,
unpretentiously **2** JUST, merely,
only, purely, solely **3** TOTALLY,
absolutely, completely, really,
utterly, wholly

simulate *verb* PRETEND, act, affect,
feign, put on, sham

simultaneous *adjective* COINCIDING,
at the same time, coincident,
concurrent, contemporaneous,
synchronous

simultaneously *adverb* AT THE SAME
TIME, concurrently, together

sin *noun* **1** WRONGDOING, crime,
error, evil, guilt, iniquity, misdeed,

offence, transgression ♦ *verb*
2 TRANSGRESS, err, fall, go astray,
lapse, offend

sincere *adjective* HONEST, candid,
earnest, frank, genuine, guileless,
heartfelt, real, serious, true,
unaffected

sincerely *adverb* HONESTLY,
earnestly, genuinely, in earnest,
seriously, truly, wholeheartedly

sincerity *noun* HONESTY, candour,
frankness, genuineness,
seriousness, truth

sinecure *noun* CUSHY NUMBER
(*informal*), gravy train (*slang*),
money for jam *or* old rope
(*informal*), soft job (*informal*), soft
option

sinful *adjective* GUILTY, bad, corrupt,
criminal, erring, immoral,
iniquitous, wicked

sing *verb* **1** WARBLE, carol, chant,
chirp, croon, pipe, trill, yodel
2 HUM, buzz, purr, whine

singe *verb* BURN, char, scorch, sear

singer *noun* VOCALIST, balladeer,
chorister, crooner, minstrel, soloist

single *adjective* **1** ONE, distinct,
individual, lone, only, separate,
sole, solitary **2** INDIVIDUAL,
exclusive, separate, undivided,
unshared **3** SIMPLE, unblended,
unmixed **4** UNMARRIED, free,
unattached, unwed ♦ *verb*
5 usually with *out* PICK, choose,
distinguish, fix on, pick on *or* out,
select, separate, set apart

single-handed *adverb* UNAIDED,
alone, by oneself, independently,
on one's own, solo, unassisted,
without help

single-minded *adjective*
DETERMINED, dedicated, dogged,
fixed, unswerving

singly *adverb* ONE BY ONE,
individually, one at a time,

separately

singular *adjective* **1** SINGLE, individual, separate, sole **2** REMARKABLE, eminent, exceptional, notable, noteworthy, outstanding **3** UNUSUAL, curious, eccentric, extraordinary, odd, peculiar, queer, strange

singularly *adverb* REMARKABLY, especially, exceptionally, notably, outstandingly, particularly, uncommonly, unusually

sinister *adjective* THREATENING, dire, disquieting, evil, malign, menacing, ominous

sink *verb* **1** DESCEND, dip, drop, fall, founder, go down, go under, lower, plunge, submerge, subside **2** FALL, abate, collapse, drop, lapse, slip, subside **3** DECLINE, decay, deteriorate, diminish, dwindle, fade, fail, flag, lessen, weaken, worsen **4** DIG, bore, drill, drive, excavate **5** STOOP, be reduced to, lower oneself

sink in *verb* BE UNDERSTOOD, get through to, penetrate, register (*informal*)

sinner *noun* WRONGDOER, evildoer, malefactor, miscreant, offender, transgressor

sip *verb* **1** DRINK, sample, sup, taste ♦ *noun* **2** SWALLOW, drop, taste, thimbleful

sissy *noun* **1** WIMP (*informal*), coward, jessie (*Scot. slang*), milksop, mummy's boy, namby-pamby, softie (*informal*), weakling, wet (*Brit. informal*) ♦ *adjective* **2** WIMPISH *or* WIMPY (*informal*), cowardly, effeminate, feeble, namby-pamby, soft (*informal*), unmanly, weak, wet (*Brit. informal*)

sit *verb* **1** REST, perch, settle **2** CONVENE, assemble, deliberate, meet, officiate, preside

site *noun* **1** LOCATION, place, plot, position, setting, spot ♦ *verb* **2** LOCATE, install, place, position, set, situate

situation *noun* **1** STATE OF AFFAIRS, case, circumstances, condition, plight, state **2** LOCATION, place, position, setting, site, spot **3** STATUS, rank, station **4** JOB, employment, office, place, position, post

sizable, sizeable *adjective* LARGE, considerable, decent, goodly, largish, respectable, substantial

size *noun* DIMENSIONS, amount, bulk, extent, immensity, magnitude, mass, proportions, range, volume

size up *verb* ASSESS, appraise, evaluate, take stock of

sizzle *verb* HISS, crackle, frizzle, fry, spit

skeleton *noun* FRAMEWORK, bare bones, draft, frame, outline, sketch, structure

sketch *noun* **1** DRAWING, delineation, design, draft, outline, plan ♦ *verb* **2** DRAW, delineate, depict, draft, outline, represent, rough out

sketchy *adjective* INCOMPLETE, cursory, inadequate, perfunctory, rough, scrappy, skimpy, superficial

skilful *adjective* EXPERT, able, adept, adroit, clever, competent, dexterous, masterly, practised, professional, proficient, skilled

skill *noun* EXPERTISE, ability, art, cleverness, competence, craft, dexterity, facility, knack, proficiency, skilfulness, talent, technique

skilled *adjective* EXPERT, able, masterly, professional, proficient, skilful

skim *verb* **1** SEPARATE, cream **2** GLIDE, coast, float, fly, sail, soar **3** usually with *through* SCAN, glance, run one's eye over

skimp verb STINT, be mean with, be sparing with, cut corners, scamp, scrimp

skin noun 1 HIDE, fell, pelt 2 COATING, casing, crust, film, husk, outside, peel, rind ♦ verb 3 PEEL, flay, scrape

skinflint noun MISER, meanie or meany (informal, chiefly Brit.), niggard, penny-pincher (informal), Scrooge

skinny adjective THIN, emaciated, lean, scrawny, undernourished

skip verb 1 HOP, bob, bounce, caper, dance, flit, frisk, gambol, prance, trip 2 PASS OVER, eschew, give (something) a miss, leave out, miss out, omit

skirmish noun 1 FIGHT, battle, brush, clash, conflict, encounter, fracas, scrap (informal) ♦ verb 2 FIGHT, clash, collide

skirt verb 1 BORDER, edge, flank 2 often with around or round AVOID, circumvent, evade, steer clear of

skit noun PARODY, burlesque, sketch, spoof (informal), takeoff (informal)

skittish adjective LIVELY, excitable, fidgety, highly strung, jumpy, nervous, restive

skive verb SLACK, idle, malinger, shirk, swing the lead

skulduggery noun Informal TRICKERY, double-dealing, duplicity, machinations, underhandedness

skulk verb LURK, creep, prowl, slink, sneak

sky noun HEAVENS, firmament

slab noun PIECE, chunk, lump, portion, slice, wedge

slack adjective 1 LOOSE, baggy, lax, limp, relaxed 2 NEGLIGENT, idle, inactive, lax, lazy, neglectful, remiss, slapdash, slipshod 3 SLOW, dull, inactive, quiet, slow-moving,

sluggish ♦ noun 4 ROOM, excess, give (informal), leeway ♦ verb 5 SHIRK, dodge, idle, skive (Brit. slang)

slacken verb, often with off LESSEN, abate, decrease, diminish, drop off, moderate, reduce, relax

slacker noun LAYABOUT, dodger, idler, loafer, shirker, skiver (Brit. slang)

slag off verb Slang CRITICIZE, abuse, deride, insult, malign, mock, slander, slate

slake verb SATISFY, assuage, quench, sate

slam verb BANG, crash, dash, fling, hurl, smash, throw

slander noun 1 DEFAMATION, calumny, libel, scandal, smear ♦ verb 2 DEFAME, blacken (someone's) name, libel, malign, smear

slanderous adjective DEFAMATORY, damaging, libellous, malicious

slant verb 1 SLOPE, bend, bevel, cant, heel, incline, lean, list, tilt 2 BIAS, angle, colour, distort, twist ♦ noun 3 SLOPE, camber, gradient, incline, tilt 4 BIAS, angle, emphasis, one-sidedness, point of view, prejudice

slanting adjective SLOPING, angled, at an angle, bent, diagonal, inclined, oblique, tilted, tilting

slap noun 1 SMACK, blow, cuff, spank ♦ verb 2 SMACK, clap, cuff, spank

slapdash adjective CARELESS, clumsy, hasty, hurried, messy, slipshod, sloppy (informal)

slap-up adjective LUXURIOUS, lavish, magnificent, splendid, sumptuous, superb

slash verb 1 CUT, gash, hack, lacerate, rend, rip, score, slit 2 REDUCE, cut, drop, lower ♦ noun

3 CUT, gash, incision, laceration, rent, rip, slit

slate verb Informal CRITICIZE, censure, rebuke, scold, tear into (informal)

slaughter verb **1** MURDER, butcher, kill, massacre, slay ♦ noun **2** MURDER, bloodshed, butchery, carnage, killing, massacre, slaying

slaughterhouse noun ABATTOIR

slave noun **1** SERVANT, drudge, serf, skivvy (chiefly Brit.), vassal ♦ verb **2** TOIL, drudge, slog

slavery noun ENSLAVEMENT, bondage, captivity, servitude, subjugation

slavish adjective **1** SERVILE, abject, base, cringing, fawning, grovelling, obsequious, submissive, sycophantic **2** IMITATIVE, second-hand, unimaginative, unoriginal

slay verb KILL, butcher, massacre, mow down, murder, slaughter

sleaze noun CORRUPTION, bribery, dishonesty, extortion, fraud, unscrupulousness, venality

sleazy adjective SORDID, disreputable, low, run-down, seedy, squalid

sleek adjective GLOSSY, lustrous, shiny, smooth

sleep noun **1** SLUMBER(S), doze, forty winks (informal), hibernation, nap, siesta, snooze (informal), zizz (Brit. informal) ♦ verb **2** SLUMBER, catnap, doze, drowse, hibernate, snooze (informal), take a nap

sleepless adjective WAKEFUL, insomniac, restless

sleepy adjective DROWSY, dull, heavy, inactive, lethargic, sluggish

slender adjective **1** SLIM, lean, narrow, slight, willowy **2** FAINT, poor, remote, slight, slim,

tenuous, thin **3** MEAGRE, little, scant, scanty, small

sleuth noun DETECTIVE, private eye (informal), (private) investigator

slice noun **1** SHARE, cut, helping, portion, segment, sliver, wedge ♦ verb **2** CUT, carve, divide, sever

slick adjective **1** GLIB, plausible, polished, smooth, specious **2** SKILFUL, adroit, deft, dexterous, polished, professional ♦ verb **3** SMOOTH, plaster down, sleek

slide verb SLIP, coast, glide, skim, slither

slight adjective **1** SMALL, feeble, insignificant, meagre, measly, minor, paltry, scanty, trifling, trivial, unimportant **2** SLIM, delicate, feeble, fragile, lightly-built, small, spare ♦ verb **3** SNUB, affront, disdain, ignore, insult, scorn ♦ noun **4** SNUB, affront, insult, neglect, rebuff, slap in the face (informal), (the) cold shoulder

slightly adverb A LITTLE, somewhat

slim adjective **1** SLENDER, lean, narrow, slight, svelte, thin, trim **2** SLIGHT, faint, poor, remote, slender ♦ verb **3** LOSE WEIGHT, diet, reduce

slimy adjective **1** VISCOUS, clammy, glutinous, oozy **2** OBSEQUIOUS, creeping, grovelling, oily, servile, smarmy (Brit. informal), unctuous

sling verb **1** THROW, cast, chuck (informal), fling, heave, hurl, lob (informal), shy, toss **2** HANG, dangle, suspend

slink verb CREEP, prowl, skulk, slip, sneak, steal

slinky adjective FIGURE-HUGGING, clinging, close-fitting, skintight

slip verb **1** FALL, skid **2** SLIDE, glide, skate, slither **3** SNEAK, conceal, creep, hide, steal **4** sometimes with up MAKE A MISTAKE, blunder, err, miscalculate **5 let slip** GIVE AWAY, disclose, divulge, leak, reveal ♦ *noun* **6** MISTAKE, blunder, error, failure, fault, lapse, omission, oversight **7 give (someone) the slip** ESCAPE FROM, dodge, elude, evade, get away from, lose (someone)

slippery *adjective* **1** SMOOTH, glassy, greasy, icy, slippy (*informal or dialect*), unsafe **2** DEVIOUS, crafty, cunning, dishonest, evasive, shifty, tricky, untrustworthy

slipshod *adjective* CARELESS, casual, slapdash, sloppy (*informal*), slovenly, untidy

slit *noun* **1** CUT, gash, incision, opening, rent, split, tear ♦ *verb* **2** CUT (OPEN), gash, knife, lance, pierce, rip, slash

slither *verb* SLIDE, glide, slink, slip, snake, undulate

sliver *noun* SHRED, fragment, paring, shaving, splinter

slobber *verb* DROOL, dribble, drivel, salivate, slaver

slobbish *adjective* MESSY, slovenly, unclean, unkempt, untidy

slog *verb* **1** WORK, labour, plod, plough through, slave, toil **2** TRUDGE, tramp, trek **3** HIT, punch, slug, sock (*slang*), strike, thump, wallop (*informal*) ♦ *noun* **4** LABOUR, effort, exertion, struggle **5** TRUDGE, hike, tramp, trek

slogan *noun* CATCH PHRASE, catchword, motto

slop *verb* SPILL, overflow, slosh (*informal*), splash

slope *noun* **1** INCLINATION, gradient, incline, ramp, rise, slant, tilt ♦ *verb* **2** SLANT, drop away, fall, incline, lean, rise, tilt **3 slope off** SLINK AWAY, creep away, slip away

sloping *adjective* SLANTING, inclined, leaning, oblique

sloppy *adjective* **1** CARELESS, messy, slipshod, slovenly, untidy **2** SENTIMENTAL, gushing, mawkish, slushy (*informal*), soppy (*Brit. informal*)

slot *noun* **1** OPENING, aperture, groove, hole, slit, vent **2** *Informal* PLACE, opening, position, space, time, vacancy ♦ *verb* **3** FIT IN, fit, insert

sloth *noun* LAZINESS, idleness, inactivity, inertia, slackness, sluggishness, torpor

slothful *adjective* LAZY, idle, inactive, indolent, skiving (*Brit. slang*), workshy

slouch *verb* SLUMP, droop, loll, stoop

slovenly *adjective* CARELESS, disorderly, negligent, slack, slapdash, slipshod, sloppy (*informal*), untidy

slow *adjective* **1** PROLONGED, gradual, lingering, long-drawn-out, protracted **2** UNHURRIED, dawdling, lackadaisical, laggard, lazy, leisurely, ponderous, sluggish **3** LATE, backward, behind, delayed, tardy **4** STUPID, braindead (*informal*), dense, dim, dozy (*Brit. informal*), dull-witted, obtuse, retarded, thick ♦ *verb* **5** often with *up or down* REDUCE SPEED, brake, decelerate, handicap, hold up, retard, slacken (off)

slowly *adverb* GRADUALLY, leisurely, unhurriedly

sludge *noun* SEDIMENT, mire, muck, mud, ooze, residue, silt, slime

sluggish *adjective* INACTIVE, dull, heavy, indolent, inert, lethargic, slothful, slow, torpid

slum *noun* HOVEL, ghetto

slumber *verb* SLEEP, doze, drowse, nap, snooze (*informal*), zizz (*Brit. informal*)

slump verb 1 FALL, collapse, crash, plunge, sink, slip 2 SAG, droop, hunch, loll, slouch ♦ noun 3 FALL, collapse, crash, decline, downturn, drop, reverse, trough 4 RECESSION, depression

slur noun INSULT, affront, aspersion, calumny, innuendo, insinuation, smear, stain

slut noun Offensive TART, scrubber (Brit. & Austral. slang), slag (Brit. slang), slapper (Brit. slang), trollop

sly adjective 1 CUNNING, artful, clever, crafty, devious, scheming, secret, shifty, stealthy, subtle, underhand, wily 2 ROGUISH, arch, impish, knowing, mischievous ♦ noun 3 on the sly SECRETLY, covertly, on the quiet, privately, surreptitiously

smack verb 1 SLAP, clap, cuff, hit, spank, strike ♦ noun 2 SLAP, blow ♦ adverb 3 Informal DIRECTLY, exactly, precisely, right, slap (informal), squarely, straight

small adjective 1 LITTLE, diminutive, mini, miniature, minute, petite, pygmy or pigmy, teeny, teeny-weeny, tiny, undersized, wee 2 UNIMPORTANT, insignificant, minor, negligible, paltry, petty, trifling, trivial 3 PETTY, base, mean, narrow 4 MODEST, humble, unpretentious

small-minded adjective PETTY, bigoted, intolerant, mean, narrow-minded, ungenerous

small-time adjective MINOR, insignificant, of no account, petty, unimportant

smarmy adjective Informal OBSEQUIOUS, crawling, ingratiating, servile, smooth, suave, sycophantic, toadying, unctuous

smart adjective 1 NEAT, chic, elegant, natty (informal), snappy, spruce, stylish, trim 2 CLEVER,

acute, astute, bright, canny, ingenious, intelligent, keen, quick, sharp, shrewd 3 BRISK, lively, quick, vigorous ♦ verb 4 STING, burn, hurt ♦ noun 5 STING, pain, soreness

smart aleck noun Informal KNOW-ALL (informal), clever-clogs (informal), smarty pants (informal), wise guy (informal)

smarten verb TIDY, groom, put in order, put to rights, spruce up

smash verb 1 BREAK, crush, demolish, pulverize, shatter 2 COLLIDE, crash 3 DESTROY, lay waste, ruin, trash (slang), wreck ♦ noun 4 DESTRUCTION, collapse, downfall, failure, ruin 5 COLLISION, accident, crash

smashing adjective Informal EXCELLENT, awesome (slang), brilliant (informal), cracking (Brit. informal), fabulous (informal), fantastic (informal), great (informal), magnificent, marvellous, mean (slang), sensational (informal), super (informal), superb, terrific (informal), wonderful

smattering noun MODICUM, bit, rudiments

smear verb 1 SPREAD OVER, bedaub, coat, cover, daub, rub on 2 DIRTY, smudge, soil, stain, sully 3 SLANDER, besmirch, blacken, malign ♦ noun 4 SMUDGE, blot, blotch, daub, splotch, streak 5 SLANDER, calumny, defamation, libel

smell verb 1 SNIFF, scent 2 STINK, pong (Brit. informal), reek ♦ noun 3 ODOUR, aroma, bouquet, fragrance, perfume, scent 4 STINK, fetor, pong (Brit. informal), stench

smelly adjective STINKING, fetid, foul, foul-smelling, malodorous, noisome, reeking

smirk noun SMUG LOOK, simper

smitten adjective 1 AFFLICTED, laid

low, plagued, struck **2** INFATUATED, beguiled, bewitched, captivated, charmed, enamoured

smooth *adjective* **1** EVEN, flat, flush, horizontal, level, plane **2** SLEEK, glossy, polished, shiny, silky, soft, velvety **3** EASY, effortless, well-ordered **4** FLOWING, regular, rhythmic, steady, uniform **5** SUAVE, facile, glib, persuasive, slick, smarmy (*Brit. informal*), unctuous, urbane **6** MELLOW, agreeable, mild, pleasant ♦ *verb* **7** FLATTEN, iron, level, plane, press **8** CALM, appease, assuage, ease, mitigate, mollify, soften

smother *verb* **1** SUFFOCATE, choke, stifle, strangle **2** SUPPRESS, conceal, hide, muffle, repress, stifle

smoulder *verb* SEETHE, boil, fume, rage, simmer

smudge *verb* **1** SMEAR, daub, dirty, mark, smirch ♦ *noun* **2** SMEAR, blemish, blot

smug *adjective* SELF-SATISFIED, complacent, conceited, superior

smuggler *noun* TRAFFICKER, bootlegger, runner

smutty *adjective* OBSCENE, bawdy, blue, coarse, crude, dirty, indecent, indelicate, suggestive, vulgar

snack *noun* LIGHT MEAL, bite, refreshment(s)

snag *noun* **1** DIFFICULTY, catch, complication, disadvantage, downside, drawback, hitch, obstacle, problem ♦ *verb* **2** CATCH, rip, tear

snap *verb* **1** BREAK, crack, separate **2** CRACKLE, click, pop **3** BITE AT, bite, nip, snatch **4** SPEAK SHARPLY, bark, jump down (someone's) throat (*informal*), lash out at ♦ *noun* **5** CRACKLE, pop **6** BITE, grab, nip ♦ *adjective* **7** INSTANT, immediate, spur-of-the-moment, sudden

snappy *adjective* **1** IRRITABLE, cross, edgy, ratty (*Brit. & N.Z. informal*), testy, tetchy, touchy **2** SMART, chic, dapper, fashionable, natty (*informal*), stylish

snap up *verb* SEIZE, grab, pounce upon, take advantage of

snare *noun* **1** TRAP, gin, net, noose, wire ♦ *verb* **2** TRAP, catch, entrap, net, seize, wire

snarl *verb,* often with *up* TANGLE, entangle, entwine, muddle, ravel

snarl-up *noun* TANGLE, confusion, entanglement, muddle

snatch *verb* **1** SEIZE, clutch, grab, grasp, grip ♦ *noun* **2** BIT, fragment, part, piece, snippet

sneak *verb* **1** SLINK, lurk, pad, skulk, slip, steal **2** SLIP, smuggle, spirit **3** *Informal* INFORM ON, grass on (*Brit. slang*), shop (*slang, chiefly Brit.*), tell on (*informal*), tell tales ♦ *noun* **4** INFORMER, telltale

sneaking *adjective* **1** NAGGING, persistent, uncomfortable, worrying **2** SECRET, hidden, private, undivulged, unexpressed, unvoiced

sneaky *adjective* SLY, deceitful, devious, dishonest, double-dealing, furtive, low, mean, shifty, untrustworthy

sneer *noun* **1** SCORN, derision, gibe, jeer, mockery, ridicule ♦ *verb* **2** SCORN, deride, disdain, jeer, laugh, mock, ridicule

snide *adjective* NASTY, cynical, disparaging, hurtful, ill-natured, malicious, sarcastic, scornful, sneering, spiteful

sniff *verb* INHALE, breathe, smell

snigger *noun, verb* LAUGH, giggle, snicker, titter

snip *verb* **1** CUT, clip, crop, dock, shave, trim ♦ *noun* **2** *Informal* BARGAIN, giveaway, good buy, steal (*informal*) **3** <u>BIT</u>, clipping, fragment, piece, scrap, shred

snipe *verb* <u>CRITICIZE</u>, carp, denigrate, disparage, jeer, knock (*informal*), put down

snippet *noun* <u>PIECE</u>, fragment, part, scrap, shred

snivel *verb* <u>WHINE</u>, cry, grizzle (*informal, chiefly Brit.*), moan, sniffle, whimper, whinge (*informal*)

snob *noun* <u>ELITIST</u>, highbrow, prig

snobbery *noun* <u>ARROGANCE</u>, airs, pretension, pride, snobbishness

snobbish *adjective* <u>SUPERIOR</u>, arrogant, patronizing, pretentious, snooty (*informal*), stuck-up (*informal*)

snoop *verb* <u>PRY</u>, interfere, poke one's nose in (*informal*), spy

snooper *noun* <u>NOSY PARKER</u> (*informal*), busybody, meddler, snoop (*informal*)

snooze *verb* **1** <u>DOZE</u>, catnap, nap, take forty winks (*informal*) ♦ *noun* **2** <u>DOZE</u>, catnap, forty winks (*informal*), nap, siesta

snub *verb* **1** <u>PUT DOWN</u>, cold-shoulder, cut (*informal*), humiliate, rebuff, slight ♦ *noun* **2** <u>INSULT</u>, affront, put-down, slap in the face

snug *adjective* <u>COSY</u>, comfortable, comfy (*informal*), warm

snuggle *verb* <u>NESTLE</u>, cuddle, nuzzle

soak *verb* **1** <u>WET</u>, bathe, damp, drench, immerse, moisten, saturate, steep **2** <u>PENETRATE</u>, permeate, seep **3** **soak up** <u>ABSORB</u>, assimilate

soaking *adjective* <u>SOAKED</u>, drenched, dripping, saturated, sodden, sopping, streaming, wet through, wringing wet

soar *verb* **1** <u>ASCEND</u>, fly, mount, rise, wing **2** <u>RISE</u>, climb, escalate, rocket, shoot up

sob *verb* <u>CRY</u>, howl, shed tears, weep

sober *adjective* **1** <u>ABSTINENT</u>, abstemious, moderate, temperate **2** <u>SERIOUS</u>, composed, cool, grave, level-headed, rational, reasonable, sedate, solemn, staid, steady **3** <u>PLAIN</u>, dark, drab, quiet, sombre, subdued

sobriety *noun* **1** <u>ABSTINENCE</u>, abstemiousness, moderation, nonindulgence, soberness, temperance **2** <u>SERIOUSNESS</u>, gravity, level-headedness, solemnity, staidness, steadiness

so-called *adjective* <u>ALLEGED</u>, pretended, professed, self-styled, supposed

sociable *adjective* <u>FRIENDLY</u>, affable, companionable, convivial, cordial, genial, gregarious, outgoing, social, warm

social *adjective* **1** <u>COMMUNAL</u>, collective, common, community, general, group, public ♦ *noun* **2** <u>GET-TOGETHER</u> (*informal*), gathering, party

socialize *verb* <u>MIX</u>, fraternize, get about *or* around, go out

society *noun* **1** <u>MANKIND</u>, civilization, humanity, people, the community, the public **2** <u>ORGANIZATION</u>, association, circle, club, fellowship, group, guild, institute, league, order, union **3** <u>UPPER CLASSES</u>, beau monde, elite, gentry, high society **4** <u>COMPANIONSHIP</u>, company, fellowship, friendship

sodden *adjective* <u>SOAKED</u>, drenched, saturated, soggy, sopping, waterlogged

sofa *noun* <u>COUCH</u>, chaise longue, divan, settee

soft *adjective* **1** <u>PLIABLE</u>, bendable, elastic, flexible, malleable, mouldable, plastic, supple

2 YIELDING, elastic, gelatinous, pulpy, spongy, squashy **3** VELVETY, downy, feathery, fleecy, silky, smooth **4** QUIET, dulcet, gentle, murmured, muted, soft-toned **5** PALE, bland, light, mellow, pastel, subdued **6** DIM, dimmed, faint, restful **7** MILD, balmy, temperate **8** LENIENT, easy-going, indulgent, lax, overindulgent, permissive, spineless **9** OUT OF CONDITION, effeminate, flabby, flaccid, limp, weak **10** *Informal* EASY, comfortable, cushy (*informal*), undemanding **11** KIND, compassionate, gentle, sensitive, sentimental, tenderhearted, touchy-feely (*informal*)

soften *verb* LESSEN, allay, appease, cushion, ease, mitigate, moderate, mollify, still, subdue, temper

softhearted *adjective* KIND, charitable, compassionate, sentimental, sympathetic, tender, tenderhearted, warm-hearted

soggy *adjective* SODDEN, dripping, moist, saturated, soaked, sopping, waterlogged

soil[1] *noun* **1** EARTH, clay, dirt, dust, ground **2** LAND, country

soil[2] *verb* DIRTY, befoul, besmirch, defile, foul, pollute, spot, stain, sully, tarnish

solace *noun* **1** COMFORT, consolation, relief ♦ *verb* **2** COMFORT, console

soldier *noun* FIGHTER, man-at-arms, serviceman, squaddie *or* squaddy (*Brit. slang*), trooper, warrior

sole *adjective* ONLY, alone, exclusive, individual, one, single, solitary

solely *adverb* ONLY, alone, completely, entirely, exclusively, merely

solemn *adjective* **1** FORMAL, ceremonial, dignified, grand, grave, momentous, stately

2 SERIOUS, earnest, grave, sedate, sober, staid

solemnity *noun* **1** SERIOUSNESS, earnestness, gravity **2** FORMALITY, grandeur, impressiveness, momentousness

solicitous *adjective* CONCERNED, anxious, attentive, careful

solicitude *noun* CONCERN, anxiety, attentiveness, care, consideration, regard

solid *adjective* **1** FIRM, compact, concrete, dense, hard **2** STRONG, stable, sturdy, substantial, unshakable **3** SOUND, genuine, good, pure, real, reliable **4** RELIABLE, dependable, trusty, upright, upstanding, worthy

solidarity *noun* UNITY, accord, cohesion, concordance, like-mindedness, team spirit, unanimity, unification

solidify *verb* HARDEN, cake, coagulate, cohere, congeal, jell, set

solitary *adjective* **1** UNSOCIABLE, cloistered, isolated, reclusive, unsocial **2** SINGLE, alone, lone, sole **3** LONELY, companionless, friendless, lonesome **4** ISOLATED, hidden, out-of-the-way, remote, unfrequented

solitude *noun* ISOLATION, loneliness, privacy, retirement, seclusion

solution *noun* **1** ANSWER, explanation, key, result **2** *Chemistry* MIXTURE, blend, compound, mix, solvent

solve *verb* ANSWER, clear up, crack, decipher, disentangle, get to the bottom of, resolve, suss (out) (*slang*), unravel, work out

sombre *adjective* **1** DARK, dim, drab, dull, gloomy, sober **2** GLOOMY, dismal, doleful, grave, joyless, lugubrious, mournful, sad, sober

somebody *noun* CELEBRITY,

dignitary, household name, luminary, megastar (*informal*), name, notable, personage, star

someday *adverb* <u>EVENTUALLY</u>, one day, one of these (fine) days, sooner or later

somehow *adverb* <u>ONE WAY OR ANOTHER</u>, by fair means or foul, by hook or (by) crook, by some means or other, come hell or high water (*informal*), come what may

sometimes *adverb* <u>OCCASIONALLY</u>, at times, now and then

song *noun* <u>BALLAD</u>, air, anthem, carol, chant, chorus, ditty, hymn, number, psalm, tune

soon *adverb* <u>BEFORE LONG</u>, in the near future, shortly

soothe *verb* 1 <u>CALM</u>, allay, appease, hush, lull, mollify, pacify, quiet, still 2 <u>RELIEVE</u>, alleviate, assuage, ease

soothing *adjective* <u>CALMING</u>, emollient, palliative, relaxing, restful

soothsayer *noun* <u>PROPHET</u>, diviner, fortune-teller, seer, sibyl

sophisticated *adjective* 1 <u>CULTURED</u>, cosmopolitan, cultivated, refined, urbane, worldly 2 <u>COMPLEX</u>, advanced, complicated, delicate, elaborate, intricate, refined, subtle

sophistication *noun* <u>SAVOIR-FAIRE</u>, finesse, poise, urbanity, worldliness, worldly wisdom

soporific *adjective* 1 <u>SLEEP-INDUCING</u>, sedative, somnolent, tranquillizing ♦ *noun* 2 <u>SEDATIVE</u>, narcotic, opiate, tranquillizer

soppy *adjective Informal* <u>SENTIMENTAL</u>, overemotional, schmaltzy (*slang*), slushy (*informal*), weepy (*informal*)

sorcerer *noun* <u>MAGICIAN</u>, enchanter, necromancer, warlock, witch, wizard

sorcery *noun* <u>BLACK MAGIC</u>, black art, enchantment, magic, necromancy, witchcraft, wizardry

sordid *adjective* 1 <u>DIRTY</u>, filthy, foul, mean, seedy, sleazy, squalid, unclean 2 <u>BASE</u>, debauched, degenerate, low, shabby, shameful, vicious, vile 3 <u>MERCENARY</u>, avaricious, covetous, grasping, selfish

sore *adjective* 1 <u>PAINFUL</u>, angry, burning, inflamed, irritated, raw, sensitive, smarting, tender 2 <u>ANNOYING</u>, severe, sharp, troublesome 3 <u>ANNOYED</u>, aggrieved, angry, cross, hurt, irked, irritated, pained, resentful, stung, upset 4 <u>URGENT</u>, acute, critical, desperate, dire, extreme, pressing

sorrow *noun* 1 <u>GRIEF</u>, anguish, distress, heartache, heartbreak, misery, mourning, regret, sadness, unhappiness, woe 2 <u>AFFLICTION</u>, hardship, misfortune, trial, tribulation, trouble, woe ♦ *verb* 3 <u>GRIEVE</u>, agonize, bemoan, be sad, bewail, lament, mourn

sorrowful *adjective* <u>SAD</u>, dejected, dismal, doleful, grieving, miserable, mournful, sorry, unhappy, woebegone, woeful, wretched

sorry *adjective* 1 <u>REGRETFUL</u>, apologetic, conscience-stricken, contrite, penitent, remorseful, repentant, shamefaced 2 <u>SYMPATHETIC</u>, commiserative, compassionate, full of pity, moved 3 <u>WRETCHED</u>, deplorable, mean, miserable, pathetic, pitiful, poor, sad

sort *noun* 1 <u>KIND</u>, brand, category, class, ilk, make, nature, order, quality, style, type, variety ♦ *verb* 2 <u>ARRANGE</u>, categorize, classify, divide, grade, group, order, put in order, rank

sort out verb 1 <u>RESOLVE</u>, clarify, clear up 2 <u>ORGANIZE</u>, tidy up

soul noun 1 <u>SPIRIT</u>, essence, life, vital force 2 <u>PERSONIFICATION</u>, embodiment, epitome, essence, quintessence, type 3 <u>PERSON</u>, being, body, creature, individual, man or woman

sound[1] noun 1 <u>NOISE</u>, din, report, reverberation, tone 2 <u>IMPRESSION</u>, drift, idea, look ♦ verb 3 <u>RESOUND</u>, echo, reverberate 4 <u>SEEM</u>, appear, look 5 <u>PRONOUNCE</u>, announce, articulate, declare, express, utter

sound[2] adjective 1 <u>PERFECT</u>, fit, healthy, intact, solid, unhurt, unimpaired, uninjured, whole 2 <u>SENSIBLE</u>, correct, logical, proper, prudent, rational, reasonable, right, trustworthy, valid, well-founded, wise 3 <u>DEEP</u>, unbroken, undisturbed, untroubled

sound[3] verb <u>FATHOM</u>, plumb, probe

sound out verb <u>PROBE</u>, canvass, pump, question, see how the land lies

sour adjective 1 <u>SHARP</u>, acetic, acid, bitter, pungent, tart 2 <u>GONE OFF</u>, curdled, gone bad, turned 3 <u>ILL-NATURED</u>, acrimonious, disagreeable, embittered, ill-tempered, peevish, tart, ungenerous, waspish

source noun 1 <u>ORIGIN</u>, author, beginning, cause, derivation, fount, originator 2 <u>INFORMANT</u>, authority

souvenir noun <u>KEEPSAKE</u>, memento, reminder

sovereign noun 1 <u>MONARCH</u>, chief, emperor or empress, king or queen, potentate, prince, ruler ♦ adjective 2 <u>SUPREME</u>, absolute, imperial, kingly or queenly, principal, royal, ruling 3 <u>EXCELLENT</u>, effectual, efficacious, efficient

sovereignty noun <u>SUPREME POWER</u>, domination, kingship, primacy, supremacy

sow verb <u>SCATTER</u>, implant, plant, seed

space noun 1 <u>ROOM</u>, capacity, elbowroom, expanse, extent, leeway, margin, play, scope 2 <u>GAP</u>, blank, distance, interval, omission 3 <u>TIME</u>, duration, interval, period, span, while

spacious adjective <u>ROOMY</u>, ample, broad, capacious, commodious, expansive, extensive, huge, large, sizable or sizeable

spadework noun <u>PREPARATION</u>, donkey-work, groundwork, labour

span noun 1 <u>EXTENT</u>, amount, distance, length, reach, spread, stretch 2 <u>PERIOD</u>, duration, spell, term ♦ verb 3 <u>EXTEND ACROSS</u>, bridge, cover, cross, link, traverse

spank verb <u>SMACK</u>, cuff, slap

spar verb <u>ARGUE</u>, bicker, row, scrap (informal), squabble, wrangle

spare adjective 1 <u>EXTRA</u>, additional, free, leftover, odd, over, superfluous, surplus, unoccupied, unused, unwanted 2 <u>THIN</u>, gaunt, lean, meagre, wiry ♦ verb 3 <u>HAVE MERCY ON</u>, be merciful to, go easy on (informal), leave, let off (informal), pardon, save from 4 <u>AFFORD</u>, do without, give, grant, let (someone) have, manage without, part with

spare time noun <u>LEISURE</u>, free time, odd moments

sparing adjective <u>ECONOMICAL</u>, careful, frugal, prudent, saving, thrifty

spark noun 1 <u>FLICKER</u>, flare, flash, gleam, glint 2 <u>TRACE</u>, atom, hint, jot, scrap, vestige ♦ verb 3 often with off <u>START</u>, inspire, precipitate, provoke, set off, stimulate, trigger (off)

sparkle verb 1 GLITTER, dance, flash, gleam, glint, glisten, scintillate, shimmer, shine, twinkle ♦ noun 2 GLITTER, brilliance, flash, flicker, gleam, glint, twinkle 3 VIVACITY, dash, élan, life, spirit, vitality

sparse adjective SCATTERED, few and far between, meagre, scanty, scarce

spartan adjective AUSTERE, ascetic, disciplined, frugal, plain, rigorous, self-denying, severe, strict

spasm noun 1 CONVULSION, contraction, paroxysm, twitch 2 BURST, eruption, fit, frenzy, outburst, seizure

spasmodic adjective SPORADIC, convulsive, erratic, fitful, intermittent, irregular, jerky

spate noun FLOOD, deluge, flow, outpouring, rush, torrent

speak verb 1 TALK, articulate, converse, express, pronounce, say, state, tell, utter 2 LECTURE, address, declaim, discourse, hold forth

speaker noun LECTURER, orator, public speaker, spokesman or spokeswoman, spokesperson

speak out or **up** verb SPEAK ONE'S MIND, have one's say, make one's position plain

spearhead verb LEAD, head, initiate, launch, pioneer, set in motion, set off

special adjective 1 EXCEPTIONAL, extraordinary, important, memorable, significant, uncommon, unique, unusual 2 PARTICULAR, appropriate, distinctive, individual, precise, specific

specialist noun EXPERT, authority, buff (informal), connoisseur, consultant, master, professional

speciality noun FORTE, bag (slang), métier, pièce de résistance, specialty

species noun KIND, breed, category, class, group, sort, type, variety

specific adjective 1 PARTICULAR, characteristic, distinguishing, special 2 DEFINITE, clear-cut, exact, explicit, express, precise, unequivocal

specification noun REQUIREMENT, condition, detail, particular, qualification, stipulation

specify verb STATE, define, designate, detail, indicate, mention, name, stipulate

specimen noun SAMPLE, example, exemplification, instance, model, pattern, representative, type

speck noun 1 MARK, blemish, dot, fleck, mote, speckle, spot, stain 2 PARTICLE, atom, bit, grain, iota, jot, mite, shred

speckled adjective FLECKED, dappled, dotted, mottled, spotted, sprinkled

spectacle noun 1 SIGHT, curiosity, marvel, phenomenon, scene, wonder 2 SHOW, display, event, exhibition, extravaganza, pageant, performance

spectacular adjective 1 IMPRESSIVE, dazzling, dramatic, grand, magnificent, sensational, splendid, striking, stunning (informal) ♦ noun 2 SHOW, display, spectacle

spectator noun ONLOOKER, bystander, looker-on, observer, viewer, watcher

spectre noun GHOST, apparition, phantom, spirit, vision, wraith

speculate verb 1 CONJECTURE, consider, guess, hypothesize, suppose, surmise, theorize, wonder 2 GAMBLE, hazard, risk, venture

speculation noun 1 GUESSWORK, conjecture, hypothesis, opinion, supposition, surmise, theory 2 GAMBLE, hazard, risk

speculative adjective HYPOTHETICAL, academic, conjectural, notional, suppositional, theoretical

speech noun 1 COMMUNICATION, conversation, dialogue, discussion, talk 2 TALK, address, discourse, homily, lecture, oration, spiel (informal) 3 LANGUAGE, articulation, dialect, diction, enunciation, idiom, jargon, parlance, tongue

speechless adjective 1 MUTE, dumb, inarticulate, silent, wordless 2 ASTOUNDED, aghast, amazed, dazed, shocked

speed noun 1 SWIFTNESS, haste, hurry, pace, quickness, rapidity, rush, velocity ◆ verb 2 RACE, career, gallop, hasten, hurry, make haste, rush, tear, zoom 3 HELP, advance, aid, assist, boost, expedite, facilitate

speed up verb ACCELERATE, gather momentum, increase the tempo

speedy adjective QUICK, express, fast, hasty, headlong, hurried, immediate, precipitate, prompt, rapid, swift

spell[1] verb INDICATE, augur, imply, mean, point to, portend, signify

spell[2] noun 1 INCANTATION, charm 2 FASCINATION, allure, bewitchment, enchantment, glamour, magic

spell[3] noun PERIOD, bout, course, interval, season, stretch, term, time

spellbound adjective ENTRANCED, bewitched, captivated, charmed, enthralled, fascinated, gripped, mesmerized, rapt

spend verb 1 PAY OUT, disburse, expend, fork out (slang) 2 PASS, fill, occupy, while away 3 USE UP, consume, dissipate, drain, empty, exhaust, run through, squander, waste

spendthrift noun 1 SQUANDERER, big spender, profligate, spender, waster ◆ adjective 2 WASTEFUL, extravagant, improvident, prodigal, profligate

spew verb VOMIT, disgorge, puke (slang), regurgitate, throw up (informal)

sphere noun 1 BALL, circle, globe, globule, orb 2 FIELD, capacity, department, domain, function, patch, province, realm, scope, territory, turf (U.S. slang)

spherical adjective ROUND, globe-shaped, globular, rotund

spice noun 1 SEASONING, relish, savour 2 EXCITEMENT, colour, pep, piquancy, zest, zing (informal)

spicy adjective 1 HOT, aromatic, piquant, savoury, seasoned 2 Informal SCANDALOUS, hot (informal), indelicate, racy, ribald, risqué, suggestive, titillating

spike noun 1 POINT, barb, prong, spine ◆ verb 2 IMPALE, spear, spit, stick

spill verb 1 POUR, discharge, disgorge, overflow, slop over ◆ noun 2 FALL, tumble

spin verb 1 REVOLVE, gyrate, pirouette, reel, rotate, turn, twirl, whirl 2 REEL, swim, whirl ◆ noun 3 REVOLUTION, gyration, roll, whirl 4 Informal DRIVE, joy ride (informal), ride

spine noun 1 BACKBONE, spinal column, vertebrae, vertebral column 2 BARB, needle, quill, ray, spike, spur

spine-chilling adjective FRIGHTENING, bloodcurdling, eerie, horrifying, scary (informal), spooky (informal), terrifying

spineless adjective WEAK, cowardly, faint-hearted, feeble, gutless (informal), lily-livered, soft, weak-kneed (informal)

spin out verb PROLONG, amplify, delay, drag out, draw out, extend, lengthen

spiral noun 1 COIL, corkscrew, helix, whorl ♦ adjective 2 COILED, helical, whorled, winding

spirit noun 1 LIFE FORCE, life, soul, vital spark 2 FEELING, atmosphere, gist, tenor, tone 3 TEMPERAMENT, attitude, character, disposition, outlook, temper 4 LIVELINESS, animation, brio, energy, enthusiasm, fire, force, life, mettle, vigour, zest 5 COURAGE, backbone, gameness, grit, guts (informal), spunk (informal) 6 ESSENCE, intention, meaning, purport, purpose, sense, substance 7 GHOST, apparition, phantom, spectre 8 **spirits** MOOD, feelings, frame of mind, morale ♦ verb 9 with away or off REMOVE, abduct, abstract, carry, purloin, seize, steal, whisk

spirited adjective LIVELY, active, animated, energetic, feisty (informal, chiefly U.S. & Canad.), mettlesome, vivacious

spiritual adjective SACRED, devotional, divine, holy, religious

spit verb 1 EJECT, expectorate, splutter, throw out ♦ noun 2 SALIVA, dribble, drool, slaver, spittle

spite noun 1 MALICE, animosity, hatred, ill will, malevolence, spitefulness, spleen, venom 2 **in spite of** DESPITE, (even) though, notwithstanding, regardless of ♦ verb 3 HURT, annoy, harm, injure, vex

spiteful adjective MALICIOUS, bitchy (informal), ill-natured, malevolent, nasty, vindictive

splash verb 1 SCATTER, shower, slop, spatter, spray, sprinkle, wet 2 PUBLICIZE, broadcast, tout, trumpet ♦ noun 3 DASH, burst, patch, spattering, touch 4 Informal DISPLAY, effect, impact, sensation, stir

splash out verb Informal SPEND, be extravagant, push the boat out (Brit. informal), spare no expense, splurge

splendid adjective 1 EXCELLENT, cracking (Brit. informal), fantastic (informal), first-class, glorious, great (informal), marvellous, wonderful 2 MAGNIFICENT, costly, gorgeous, impressive, lavish, luxurious, ornate, resplendent, rich, sumptuous, superb

splendour noun MAGNIFICENCE, brightness, brilliance, display, glory, grandeur, pomp, richness, show, spectacle, sumptuousness

splinter noun 1 SLIVER, chip, flake, fragment ♦ verb 2 SHATTER, disintegrate, fracture, split

split verb 1 BREAK, burst, come apart, come undone, crack, give way, open, rend, rip 2 SEPARATE, branch, cleave, disband, disunite, diverge, fork, part 3 SHARE OUT, allocate, allot, apportion, distribute, divide, halve, partition ♦ noun 4 CRACK, breach, division, fissure, gap, rent, rip, separation, slit, tear 5 DIVISION, breach, break-up, discord, dissension, estrangement, rift, rupture, schism ♦ adjective 6 DIVIDED, broken, cleft, cracked, fractured, ruptured

split up verb SEPARATE, break up, divorce, part

spoil verb 1 RUIN, damage, destroy, disfigure, harm, impair, injure, mar, mess up, trash (slang), wreck 2 OVERINDULGE, coddle, cosset, indulge, mollycoddle, pamper

3 GO BAD, addle, curdle, decay, decompose, go off (*Brit. informal*), rot, turn

spoils *plural noun* BOOTY, loot, plunder, prey, swag (*slang*)

spoilsport *noun* KILLJOY, damper, dog in the manger, misery (*Brit. informal*), wet blanket (*informal*)

spoken *adjective* SAID, expressed, oral, told, unwritten, uttered, verbal, viva voce, voiced

spokesperson *noun* SPEAKER, mouthpiece, official, spin doctor (*informal*), spokesman *or* spokeswoman, voice

spongy *adjective* POROUS, absorbent

sponsor *noun* **1** BACKER, patron, promoter ♦ *verb* **2** BACK, finance, fund, patronize, promote, subsidize

spontaneous *adjective* UNPLANNED, impromptu, impulsive, instinctive, natural, unprompted, voluntary, willing

spoof *noun* PARODY, burlesque, caricature, mockery, satire, send-up (*Brit. informal*), take-off (*informal*)

spooky *adjective* EERIE, chilling, creepy (*informal*), frightening, scary (*informal*), spine-chilling, uncanny, unearthly, weird

sporadic *adjective* INTERMITTENT, irregular, occasional, scattered, spasmodic

sport *noun* **1** GAME, amusement, diversion, exercise, pastime, play, recreation **2** FUN, badinage, banter, jest, joking, teasing ♦ *verb* **3** *Informal* WEAR, display, exhibit, show off

sporting *adjective* FAIR, game (*informal*), sportsmanlike

sporty *adjective* ATHLETIC, energetic, outdoor

spot *noun* **1** MARK, blemish, blot, blotch, scar, smudge, speck, speckle, stain **2** PIMPLE, pustule, zit (*slang*) **3** PLACE, location, point, position, scene, site **4** *Informal* PREDICAMENT, difficulty, hot water (*informal*), mess, plight, quandary, tight spot, trouble ♦ *verb* **5** SEE, catch sight of, detect, discern, espy, make out, observe, recognize, sight **6** MARK, dirty, fleck, mottle, smirch, soil, spatter, speckle, splodge, splotch, stain

spotless *adjective* CLEAN, flawless, gleaming, immaculate, impeccable, pure, shining, unblemished, unstained, unsullied, untarnished

spotlight *noun* **1** ATTENTION, fame, limelight, public eye ♦ *verb* **2** HIGHLIGHT, accentuate, draw attention to

spotted *adjective* SPECKLED, dappled, dotted, flecked, mottled

spouse *noun* PARTNER, consort, husband *or* wife, mate, significant other (*U.S. informal*)

spout *verb* STREAM, discharge, gush, shoot, spray, spurt, surge

sprawl *verb* LOLL, flop, lounge, slouch, slump

spray[1] *noun* **1** DROPLETS, drizzle, fine mist **2** AEROSOL, atomizer, sprinkler ♦ *verb* **3** SCATTER, diffuse, shower, sprinkle

spray[2] *noun* SPRIG, branch, corsage, floral arrangement

spread *verb* **1** OPEN (OUT), broaden, dilate, expand, extend, sprawl, stretch, unfold, unroll, widen **2** PROLIFERATE, escalate, multiply **3** CIRCULATE, broadcast, disseminate, make known, propagate ♦ *noun* **4** INCREASE, advance, development, dispersal, dissemination, expansion, proliferation **5** EXTENT, span, stretch, sweep

spree noun <u>BINGE</u> (*informal*), bacchanalia, bender (*informal*), carousal, fling, orgy, revel

sprightly adjective <u>LIVELY</u>, active, agile, brisk, energetic, nimble, spirited, spry, vivacious

spring verb 1 <u>JUMP</u>, bounce, bound, leap, vault 2 often with *from* <u>ORIGINATE</u>, arise, come, derive, descend, issue, proceed, start, stem 3 often with *up* <u>APPEAR</u>, develop, mushroom, shoot up ♦ noun 4 <u>JUMP</u>, bound, leap, vault 5 <u>ELASTICITY</u>, bounce, buoyancy, flexibility, resilience

springy adjective <u>ELASTIC</u>, bouncy, buoyant, flexible, resilient

sprinkle verb <u>SCATTER</u>, dredge, dust, pepper, powder, shower, spray, strew

sprinkling noun <u>SCATTERING</u>, dash, dusting, few, handful, sprinkle

sprint verb <u>RACE</u>, dart, dash, hare (*Brit. informal*), shoot, tear

sprite noun <u>SPIRIT</u>, brownie, elf, fairy, goblin, imp, pixie

sprout verb <u>GROW</u>, bud, develop, shoot, spring

spruce adjective <u>SMART</u>, dapper, natty (*informal*), neat, trim, well-groomed, well turned out

spruce up verb <u>SMARTEN UP</u>, tidy, titivate

spry adjective <u>ACTIVE</u>, agile, nimble, sprightly, supple

spur noun 1 <u>STIMULUS</u>, impetus, impulse, incentive, incitement, inducement, motive 2 <u>GOAD</u>, prick 3 **on the spur of the moment** <u>ON IMPULSE</u>, impromptu, impulsively, on the spot, without planning ♦ verb 4 <u>INCITE</u>, animate, drive, goad, impel, prick, prod, prompt, stimulate, urge

spurious adjective <u>FALSE</u>, artificial, bogus, fake, phoney or phony (*informal*), pretended, sham, specious, unauthentic

spurn verb <u>REJECT</u>, despise, disdain, rebuff, repulse, scorn, slight, snub

spurt verb 1 <u>GUSH</u>, burst, erupt, shoot, squirt, surge ♦ noun 2 <u>BURST</u>, fit, rush, spate, surge

spy noun 1 <u>UNDERCOVER AGENT</u>, mole, nark (*Brit., Austral., & N.Z. slang*) ♦ verb 2 <u>CATCH SIGHT OF</u>, espy, glimpse, notice, observe, spot

squabble verb 1 <u>QUARREL</u>, argue, bicker, dispute, fight, row, wrangle ♦ noun 2 <u>QUARREL</u>, argument, disagreement, dispute, fight, row, tiff

squad noun <u>TEAM</u>, band, company, crew, force, gang, group, troop

squalid adjective <u>DIRTY</u>, filthy, seedy, sleazy, slummy, sordid, unclean

squalor noun <u>FILTH</u>, foulness, sleaziness, squalidness

squander verb <u>WASTE</u>, blow (*slang*), expend, fritter away, misspend, misuse, spend

square adjective 1 <u>HONEST</u>, above board, ethical, fair, genuine, kosher (*informal*), on the level (*informal*), straight ♦ verb 2 <u>EVEN UP</u>, adjust, align, level 3 sometimes with *up* <u>PAY OFF</u>, settle 4 often with *with* <u>AGREE</u>, correspond, fit, match, reconcile, tally

squash verb 1 <u>CRUSH</u>, compress, distort, flatten, mash, press, pulp, smash 2 <u>SUPPRESS</u>, annihilate, crush, humiliate, quell, silence

squashy adjective <u>SOFT</u>, mushy, pulpy, spongy, yielding

squawk verb <u>CRY</u>, hoot, screech

squeak verb <u>PEEP</u>, pipe, squeal

squeal noun, verb <u>SCREAM</u>, screech, shriek, wail, yell

squeamish *adjective* 1 DELICATE, fastidious, prudish, strait-laced 2 SICK, nauseous, queasy

squeeze *verb* 1 PRESS, clutch, compress, crush, grip, pinch, squash, wring 2 CRAM, crowd, force, jam, pack, press, ram, stuff 3 HUG, clasp, cuddle, embrace, enfold 4 EXTORT, milk, pressurize, wrest ♦ *noun* 5 HUG, clasp, embrace 6 CRUSH, congestion, crowd, jam, press, squash

squint *adjective* CROOKED, askew, aslant, awry, cockeyed, skew-whiff (*informal*)

squirm *verb* WRIGGLE, twist, writhe

stab *verb* 1 PIERCE, impale, jab, knife, spear, stick, thrust, transfix, wound ♦ *noun* 2 WOUND, gash, incision, jab, puncture, thrust 3 TWINGE, ache, pang, prick 4 **make** *or* **have a stab at** *Informal* ATTEMPT, endeavour, have a go, try

stability *noun* FIRMNESS, solidity, soundness, steadiness, strength

stable *adjective* 1 FIRM, constant, established, fast, fixed, immovable, lasting, permanent, secure, sound, strong 2 STEADY, reliable, staunch, steadfast, sure

stack *noun* 1 PILE, heap, load, mass, mound, mountain ♦ *verb* 2 PILE, accumulate, amass, assemble, heap up, load

staff *noun* 1 WORKERS, employees, personnel, team, workforce 2 STICK, cane, crook, pole, rod, sceptre, stave, wand

stage *noun* POINT, division, juncture, lap, leg, level, period, phase, step

stagger *verb* 1 TOTTER, lurch, reel, sway, wobble 2 ASTOUND, amaze, astonish, confound, overwhelm, shake, shock, stun, stupefy 3 OVERLAP, alternate, step

stagnant *adjective* STALE, quiet, sluggish, still

stagnate *verb* VEGETATE, decay, decline, idle, languish, rot, rust

staid *adjective* SEDATE, calm, composed, grave, serious, sober, solemn, steady

stain *verb* 1 MARK, blemish, blot, dirty, discolour, smirch, soil, spot, tinge ♦ *noun* 2 MARK, blemish, blot, discoloration, smirch, spot 3 STIGMA, disgrace, dishonour, shame, slur

stake[1] *noun* POLE, pale, paling, palisade, picket, post, stick

stake[2] *noun* 1 BET, ante, pledge, wager 2 INTEREST, concern, investment, involvement, share ♦ *verb* 3 BET, chance, gamble, hazard, risk, venture, wager

stale *adjective* 1 OLD, decayed, dry, flat, fusty, hard, musty, sour 2 UNORIGINAL, banal, hackneyed, overused, stereotyped, threadbare, trite, worn-out

stalk *verb* PURSUE, follow, haunt, hunt, shadow, track

stall *verb* PLAY FOR TIME, hedge, temporize

stalwart *adjective* STRONG, staunch, stout, strapping, sturdy

stamina *noun* STAYING POWER, endurance, energy, force, power, resilience, strength

stammer *verb* STUTTER, falter, hesitate, pause, stumble

stamp *noun* 1 IMPRINT, brand, earmark, hallmark, mark, signature ♦ *verb* 2 TRAMPLE, crush 3 IDENTIFY, brand, categorize, label, mark, reveal, show to be 4 IMPRINT, impress, mark, print

stampede *noun* RUSH, charge, flight, rout

stamp out *verb* ELIMINATE, crush, destroy, eradicate, put down, quell, scotch, suppress

stance noun 1 ATTITUDE, position, stand, standpoint, viewpoint 2 POSTURE, bearing, carriage, deportment

stand verb 1 BE UPRIGHT, be erect, be vertical, rise 2 PUT, mount, place, position, set 3 EXIST, be valid, continue, hold, obtain, prevail, remain 4 TOLERATE, abide, allow, bear, brook, countenance, endure, handle, put up with (*informal*), stomach, take ♦ *noun* 5 STALL, booth, table 6 POSITION, attitude, determination, opinion, stance 7 SUPPORT, base, bracket, dais, platform, rack, stage, tripod

standard noun 1 BENCHMARK, average, criterion, gauge, grade, guideline, measure, model, norm, yardstick 2 often plural PRINCIPLES, ethics, ideals, morals 3 FLAG, banner, ensign ♦ *adjective* 4 USUAL, average, basic, customary, normal, orthodox, regular, typical 5 ACCEPTED, approved, authoritative, definitive, established, official, recognized

standardize verb BRING INTO LINE, institutionalize, regiment

stand by verb 1 BE PREPARED, wait 2 SUPPORT, back, be loyal to, champion, take (someone's) part

stand for verb 1 REPRESENT, betoken, denote, indicate, mean, signify, symbolize 2 *Informal* TOLERATE, bear, brook, endure, put up with

stand-in noun SUBSTITUTE, deputy, locum, replacement, reserve, stopgap, surrogate, understudy

stand in for verb BE A SUBSTITUTE FOR, cover for, deputize for, represent, take the place of

standing adjective 1 PERMANENT, fixed, lasting, regular 2 UPRIGHT, erect, vertical ♦ *noun* 3 STATUS, eminence, footing, position, rank,

reputation, repute 4 DURATION, continuance, existence

standoffish adjective RESERVED, aloof, cold, distant, haughty, remote, unapproachable, unsociable

stand out verb BE CONSPICUOUS, be distinct, be obvious, be prominent

standpoint noun POINT OF VIEW, angle, position, stance, viewpoint

stand up for verb SUPPORT, champion, defend, stick up for (*informal*), uphold

staple adjective PRINCIPAL, basic, chief, fundamental, key, main, predominant

star noun 1 HEAVENLY BODY 2 CELEBRITY, big name, luminary, main attraction, megastar (*informal*), name ♦ *adjective* 3 LEADING, brilliant, celebrated, major, prominent, well-known

stare verb GAZE, gape, gawk, gawp (*Brit. slang*), goggle, look, watch

stark adjective 1 HARSH, austere, bare, barren, bleak, grim, hard, plain, severe 2 ABSOLUTE, blunt, downright, out-and-out, pure, sheer, unmitigated, utter ♦ *adverb* 3 ABSOLUTELY, altogether, completely, entirely, quite, utterly, wholly

start verb 1 BEGIN, appear, arise, commence, issue, originate 2 SET ABOUT, embark upon, make a beginning, take the first step 3 SET IN MOTION, activate, get going, initiate, instigate, kick-start, open, originate, trigger 4 JUMP, flinch, jerk, recoil, shy 5 ESTABLISH, begin, create, found, inaugurate, initiate, institute, launch, pioneer, set up ♦ *noun* 6 BEGINNING, birth, dawn, foundation, inception, initiation, onset, opening, outset 7 ADVANTAGE, edge, head start, lead 8 JUMP, convulsion, spasm

startle verb SURPRISE, frighten, make (someone) jump, scare, shock

starving adjective HUNGRY, famished, ravenous, starved

state noun **1** CONDITION, circumstances, position, predicament, shape, situation **2** FRAME OF MIND, attitude, humour, mood, spirits **3** COUNTRY, commonwealth, federation, government, kingdom, land, nation, republic, territory **4** CEREMONY, display, glory, grandeur, majesty, pomp, splendour, style ◆ verb **5** EXPRESS, affirm, articulate, assert, declare, expound, present, say, specify, utter, voice

stately adjective GRAND, august, dignified, lofty, majestic, noble, regal, royal

statement noun ACCOUNT, announcement, communication, communiqué, declaration, proclamation, report

state-of-the-art adjective LATEST, newest, up-to-date, up-to-the-minute

static adjective STATIONARY, fixed, immobile, motionless, still, unmoving

station noun **1** HEADQUARTERS, base, depot **2** PLACE, location, position, post, seat, situation **3** POSITION, post, rank, situation, standing, status ◆ verb **4** ASSIGN, establish, install, locate, post, set

stationary adjective MOTIONLESS, fixed, parked, standing, static, stock-still, unmoving

statuesque adjective WELL-PROPORTIONED, imposing, Junoesque

stature noun IMPORTANCE, eminence, prestige, prominence, rank, standing

status noun POSITION, condition, consequence, eminence, grade, prestige, rank, standing

staunch[1] adjective LOYAL, faithful, firm, sound, stalwart, steadfast, true, trusty

staunch[2] verb STOP, check, dam, halt, stay, stem

stay verb **1** REMAIN, abide, continue, halt, linger, loiter, pause, stop, tarry, wait ◆ noun **2** VISIT, holiday, sojourn, stop, stopover **3** POSTPONEMENT, deferment, delay, halt, stopping, suspension

steadfast adjective FIRM, faithful, fast, fixed, intent, loyal, resolute, stalwart, staunch, steady, unswerving, unwavering

steady adjective **1** FIRM, fixed, safe, stable **2** SENSIBLE, balanced, calm, dependable, equable, level-headed, reliable, sober **3** CONTINUOUS, ceaseless, consistent, constant, incessant, nonstop, persistent, regular, unbroken, uninterrupted ◆ verb **4** STABILIZE, brace, secure, support

steal verb **1** TAKE, appropriate, embezzle, filch, lift (informal), misappropriate, nick (slang, chiefly Brit.), pilfer, pinch (informal), purloin, thieve **2** SNEAK, creep, slink, slip, tiptoe

stealth noun SECRECY, furtiveness, slyness, sneakiness, stealthiness, surreptitiousness, unobtrusiveness

stealthy adjective SECRET, furtive, secretive, sneaking, surreptitious

steep[1] adjective **1** SHEER, abrupt, precipitous **2** Informal HIGH, exorbitant, extortionate, extreme, overpriced, unreasonable

steep[2] verb **1** SOAK, drench, immerse, macerate, marinate (Cookery), moisten, souse, submerge **2** SATURATE, fill, imbue, infuse, permeate, pervade, suffuse

steer verb DIRECT, conduct, control,

guide, handle, pilot

stem[1] *noun* **1** STALK, axis, branch, shoot, trunk ♦ *verb* **2 stem from** ORIGINATE IN, arise from, be caused by, derive from

stem[2] *verb* STOP, check, curb, dam, hold back, staunch

stench *noun* STINK, foul smell, pong (*Brit. informal*), reek, whiff (*Brit. slang*)

step *noun* **1** FOOTSTEP, footfall, footprint, pace, print, stride, track **2** STAGE, move, phase, point **3** ACTION, act, deed, expedient, means, measure, move **4** DEGREE, level, rank ♦ *verb* **5** WALK, move, pace, tread

step in *verb* INTERVENE, become involved, take action

step up *verb* INCREASE, intensify, raise

stereotype *noun* **1** FORMULA, pattern ♦ *verb* **2** CATEGORIZE, pigeonhole, standardize, typecast

sterile *adjective* **1** GERM-FREE, aseptic, disinfected, sterilized **2** BARREN, bare, dry, empty, fruitless, unfruitful, unproductive

sterilize *verb* DISINFECT, fumigate, purify

sterling *adjective* EXCELLENT, fine, genuine, sound, superlative, true

stern *adjective* SEVERE, austere, forbidding, grim, hard, harsh, inflexible, rigid, serious, strict

stick[1] *noun* **1** CANE, baton, crook, pole, rod, staff, twig **2** *Brit. slang* ABUSE, criticism, flak (*informal*)

stick[2] *verb* **1** POKE, dig, jab, penetrate, pierce, prod, puncture, spear, stab, thrust, transfix **2** FASTEN, adhere, affix, attach, bind, bond, cling, fix, glue, hold, join, paste, weld **3** with *out, up, etc.* PROTRUDE, bulge, extend, jut, obtrude, poke, project, show **4** *Informal* PUT, deposit, lay, place,

set **5** STAY, linger, persist, remain **6** *Slang* TOLERATE, abide, stand, stomach, take **7 stick up for** *Informal* DEFEND, champion, stand up for, support

stickler *noun* PERFECTIONIST, fanatic, fusspot (*Brit. informal*), purist

sticky *adjective* **1** TACKY, adhesive, clinging, gluey, glutinous, gooey (*informal*), gummy, viscid, viscous **2** *Informal* DIFFICULT, awkward, delicate, embarrassing, nasty, tricky, unpleasant **3** HUMID, clammy, close, muggy, oppressive, sultry, sweltering

stiff *adjective* **1** INFLEXIBLE, firm, hard, inelastic, rigid, solid, taut, tense, tight, unbending, unyielding **2** AWKWARD, clumsy, graceless, inelegant, jerky (*informal*), ungainly, ungraceful **3** DIFFICULT, arduous, exacting, hard, tough **4** SEVERE, drastic, extreme, hard, harsh, heavy, strict **5** UNRELAXED, constrained, forced, formal, stilted, unnatural

stiffen *verb* **1** BRACE, reinforce, tauten, tense **2** SET, congeal, crystallize, harden, jell, solidify, thicken

stifle *verb* **1** SUPPRESS, check, hush, repress, restrain, silence, smother, stop **2** SUFFOCATE, asphyxiate, choke, smother, strangle

stigma *noun* DISGRACE, dishonour, shame, slur, smirch, stain

still *adjective* **1** MOTIONLESS, calm, peaceful, restful, serene, stationary, tranquil, undisturbed **2** SILENT, hushed, quiet ♦ *verb* **3** QUIETEN, allay, calm, hush, lull, pacify, quiet, settle, silence, soothe ♦ *conjunction* **4** HOWEVER, but, nevertheless, notwithstanding, yet

stilted *adjective* STIFF, constrained, forced, unnatural, wooden

stimulant noun PICK-ME-UP (*informal*), restorative, tonic, upper (*slang*)

stimulate verb AROUSE, encourage, fire, impel, incite, prompt, provoke, rouse, spur

stimulating adjective EXCITING, exhilarating, inspiring, provocative, rousing, stirring

stimulus noun INCENTIVE, encouragement, fillip, goad, impetus, incitement, inducement, spur

sting verb 1 HURT, burn, pain, smart, tingle, wound 2 *Informal* CHEAT, defraud, do (*slang*), fleece, overcharge, rip off (*slang*), swindle

stingy adjective MEAN, miserly, niggardly, parsimonious, penny-pinching (*informal*), tightfisted, ungenerous

stink noun 1 STENCH, fetor, foul smell, pong (*Brit. informal*) ◆ verb 2 REEK, pong (*Brit. informal*)

stint verb 1 BE MEAN, be frugal, be sparing, hold back, skimp on ◆ noun 2 SHARE, period, quota, shift, spell, stretch, term, time, turn

stipulate verb SPECIFY, agree, contract, covenant, insist upon, require, settle

stipulation noun SPECIFICATION, agreement, clause, condition, precondition, proviso, qualification, requirement

stir verb 1 MIX, agitate, beat, shake 2 STIMULATE, arouse, awaken, excite, incite, provoke, rouse, spur ◆ noun 3 COMMOTION, activity, bustle, disorder, disturbance, excitement, flurry, fuss

stock noun 1 GOODS, array, choice, commodities, merchandise, range, selection, variety, wares 2 SUPPLY, fund, hoard, reserve, stockpile, store 3 PROPERTY, assets, capital, funds, investment 4 LIVESTOCK, beasts, cattle, domestic animals ◆ adjective 5 STANDARD, conventional, customary, ordinary, regular, routine, usual 6 HACKNEYED, banal, overused, trite ◆ verb 7 SELL, deal in, handle, keep, supply, trade in 8 PROVIDE WITH, equip, fit out, furnish, supply 9 **stock up** STORE (UP), accumulate, amass, gather, hoard, lay in, put away, save

stocky adjective THICKSET, chunky, dumpy, solid, stubby, sturdy

stodgy adjective 1 HEAVY, filling, leaden, starchy 2 DULL, boring, fuddy-duddy (*informal*), heavy going, staid, stuffy, tedious, unexciting

stoical adjective RESIGNED, dispassionate, impassive, long-suffering, philosophic, phlegmatic, stoic, stolid

stoicism noun RESIGNATION, acceptance, forbearance, fortitude, impassivity, long-suffering, patience, stolidity

stolid adjective APATHETIC, dull, lumpish, unemotional, wooden

stomach noun 1 BELLY, abdomen, gut (*informal*), pot, tummy (*informal*) 2 INCLINATION, appetite, desire, relish, taste ◆ verb 3 BEAR, abide, endure, swallow, take, tolerate

stony adjective COLD, blank, chilly, expressionless, hard, hostile, icy, unresponsive

stoop verb 1 BEND, bow, crouch, duck, hunch, lean 2 **stoop to** SINK TO, descend to, lower oneself by, resort to ◆ noun 3 SLOUCH, bad posture, round-shoulderedness

stop verb 1 HALT, cease, conclude, cut short, desist, discontinue, end, finish, pause, put an end to, quit, refrain, shut down, terminate

2 PREVENT, arrest, forestall, hinder, hold back, impede, repress, restrain **3** PLUG, block, obstruct, seal, staunch, stem **4** STAY, lodge, rest ♦ *noun* **5** END, cessation, finish, halt, standstill **6** STAY, break, rest **7** STATION, depot, terminus

stopgap *noun* MAKESHIFT, improvisation, resort, substitute

stoppage *noun* STOPPING, arrest, close, closure, cutoff, halt, hindrance, shutdown, standstill

store *verb* **1** PUT BY, deposit, garner, hoard, keep, put aside, reserve, save, stockpile ♦ *noun* **2** SHOP, market, mart, outlet **3** SUPPLY, accumulation, cache, fund, hoard, quantity, reserve, stock, stockpile **4** REPOSITORY, depository, storeroom, warehouse

storm *noun* **1** TEMPEST, blizzard, gale, hurricane, squall **2** OUTBURST, agitation, commotion, disturbance, furore, outbreak, outcry, row, rumpus, strife, tumult, turmoil ♦ *verb* **3** ATTACK, assail, assault, charge, rush **4** RAGE, bluster, rant, rave, thunder **5** RUSH, flounce, fly, stamp

stormy *adjective* WILD, blustery, inclement, raging, rough, squally, turbulent, windy

story *noun* **1** TALE, account, anecdote, history, legend, narrative, romance, yarn **2** REPORT, article, feature, news, news item, scoop

stout *adjective* **1** FAT, big, bulky, burly, corpulent, fleshy, heavy, overweight, plump, portly, rotund, tubby **2** STRONG, able-bodied, brawny, muscular, robust, stalwart, strapping, sturdy **3** BRAVE, bold, courageous, fearless, gallant, intrepid, plucky, resolute, valiant

stow *verb* PACK, bundle, load, put away, stash (*informal*), store

straight *adjective* **1** DIRECT, near, short **2** LEVEL, aligned, even, horizontal, right, smooth, square, true **3** UPRIGHT, erect, plumb, vertical **4** HONEST, above board, accurate, fair, honourable, just, law-abiding, trustworthy, upright **5** FRANK, blunt, bold, candid, forthright, honest, outright, plain, straightforward **6** SUCCESSIVE, consecutive, continuous, nonstop, running, solid **7** UNDILUTED, neat, pure, unadulterated, unmixed **8** ORDERLY, arranged, in order, neat, organized, shipshape, tidy **9** *Slang* CONVENTIONAL, bourgeois, conservative ♦ *adverb* **10** DIRECTLY, at once, immediately, instantly

straight away *adverb* IMMEDIATELY, at once, directly, instantly, now, right away

straighten *verb* NEATEN, arrange, order, put in order, tidy (up)

straightforward *adjective* **1** HONEST, candid, direct, forthright, genuine, open, sincere, truthful, upfront (*informal*) **2** EASY, easy-peasy (*slang*), elementary, routine, simple, uncomplicated

strain[1] *verb* **1** STRETCH, distend, draw tight, tauten, tighten **2** OVEREXERT, injure, overtax, overwork, pull, sprain, tax, tear, twist, wrench **3** STRIVE, bend over backwards (*informal*), endeavour, give it one's best shot (*informal*), go for it (*informal*), knock oneself out (*informal*), labour, struggle **4** SIEVE, filter, purify, sift ♦ *noun* **5** STRESS, anxiety, burden, pressure, tension **6** EXERTION, effort, force, struggle **7** INJURY, pull, sprain, wrench

strain[2] *noun* **1** BREED, ancestry, blood, descent, extraction, family, lineage, race **2** TRACE, streak, suggestion, tendency

strained *adjective* **1** FORCED, artificial, false, put on, unnatural **2** TENSE, awkward, difficult, embarrassed, stiff, uneasy

strait noun **1** often plural CHANNEL, narrows, sound **2** **straits** DIFFICULTY, dilemma, extremity, hardship, plight, predicament

strait-laced adjective STRICT, moralistic, narrow-minded, prim, proper, prudish, puritanical

strand noun FILAMENT, fibre, string, thread

stranded adjective **1** BEACHED, aground, ashore, grounded, marooned, shipwrecked **2** HELPLESS, abandoned, high and dry

strange adjective **1** ODD, abnormal, bizarre, curious, extraordinary, peculiar, queer, uncommon, weird, wonderful **2** UNFAMILIAR, alien, exotic, foreign, new, novel, unknown, untried

stranger noun NEWCOMER, alien, foreigner, guest, incomer, outlander, visitor

strangle verb **1** THROTTLE, asphyxiate, choke, strangulate **2** SUPPRESS, inhibit, repress, stifle

strap noun **1** BELT, thong, tie ♦ verb **2** FASTEN, bind, buckle, lash, secure, tie

strapping adjective WELL-BUILT, big, brawny, husky (informal), powerful, robust, sturdy

stratagem noun TRICK, device, dodge, manoeuvre, plan, ploy, ruse, scheme, subterfuge

strategic adjective **1** TACTICAL, calculated, deliberate, diplomatic, planned, politic **2** CRUCIAL, cardinal, critical, decisive, important, key, vital

strategy noun PLAN, approach, policy, procedure, scheme

stray verb **1** WANDER, drift, err, go astray **2** DIGRESS, deviate, diverge, get off the point ♦ adjective **3** LOST, abandoned, homeless, roaming,

vagrant **4** RANDOM, accidental, chance

streak noun **1** BAND, layer, line, slash, strip, stripe, stroke, vein **2** TRACE, dash, element, strain, touch, vein ♦ verb **3** SPEED, dart, flash, fly, hurtle, sprint, tear, whizz (informal), zoom

stream noun **1** RIVER, bayou, beck, brook, burn (Scot.), rivulet, tributary **2** FLOW, course, current, drift, run, rush, surge, tide, torrent ♦ verb **3** FLOW, cascade, flood, gush, issue, pour, run, spill, spout

streamlined adjective EFFICIENT, organized, rationalized, slick, smooth-running

street noun ROAD, avenue, lane, roadway, row, terrace

strength noun **1** MIGHT, brawn, courage, fortitude, muscle, robustness, stamina, sturdiness, toughness **2** INTENSITY, effectiveness, efficacy, force, potency, power, vigour **3** ADVANTAGE, asset, strong point

strengthen verb **1** FORTIFY, brace up, consolidate, harden, invigorate, restore, stiffen, toughen **2** REINFORCE, augment, bolster, brace, build up, buttress, harden, intensify, support

strenuous adjective DEMANDING, arduous, hard, laborious, taxing, tough, uphill

stress noun **1** STRAIN, anxiety, burden, pressure, tension, trauma, worry **2** EMPHASIS, force, significance, weight **3** ACCENT, accentuation, beat, emphasis ♦ verb **4** EMPHASIZE, accentuate, dwell on, underline

stretch verb **1** EXTEND, cover, put forth, reach, spread, unroll **2** PULL, distend, draw out, elongate, expand, strain, tighten ♦ noun **3** EXPANSE, area, distance, extent, spread, tract 4 PERIOD, space, spell, stint, term, time

strict adjective 1 SEVERE, authoritarian, firm, harsh, stern, stringent 2 EXACT, accurate, close, faithful, meticulous, precise, scrupulous, true 3 ABSOLUTE, total, utter

strident adjective HARSH, discordant, grating, jarring, raucous, screeching, shrill

strife noun CONFLICT, battle, clash, discord, dissension, friction, quarrel

strike verb 1 WALK OUT, down tools, mutiny, revolt 2 HIT, beat, clobber (slang), clout (informal), cuff, hammer, knock, punch, slap, smack, thump, wallop (informal) 3 COLLIDE WITH, bump into, hit, run into 4 ATTACK, assail, assault, hit 5 OCCUR TO, come to, dawn on or upon, hit, register (informal)

striking adjective IMPRESSIVE, conspicuous, dramatic, noticeable, outstanding

string noun 1 CORD, fibre, twine 2 SERIES, chain, file, line, procession, row, sequence, succession

stringent adjective STRICT, inflexible, rigid, rigorous, severe, tight, tough

stringy adjective FIBROUS, gristly, sinewy, tough

strip[1] verb 1 UNDRESS, disrobe, unclothe 2 PLUNDER, despoil, divest, empty, loot, pillage, ransack, rob, sack

strip[2] noun PIECE, band, belt, shred

strive verb TRY, attempt, bend over backwards (informal), break one's neck (informal), do one's best, give it one's best shot (informal), go all out (informal), knock oneself out (informal), labour, make an all-out effort (informal), struggle, toil

stroke verb 1 CARESS, fondle, pet, rub ♦ noun 2 APOPLEXY, attack, collapse, fit, seizure 3 BLOW, hit, knock, pat, rap, thump

stroll verb 1 WALK, amble, promenade, ramble, saunter ♦ noun 2 WALK, breath of air, constitutional, promenade, ramble

strong adjective 1 POWERFUL, athletic, brawny, burly, hardy, lusty, muscular, robust, strapping, sturdy, tough 2 DURABLE, hard-wearing, heavy-duty, sturdy, substantial, well-built 3 PERSUASIVE, compelling, convincing, effective, potent, sound, telling, weighty, well-founded 4 INTENSE, acute, deep, fervent, fervid, fierce, firm, keen, vehement, violent, zealous 5 EXTREME, drastic, forceful, severe 6 BRIGHT, bold, brilliant, dazzling

stronghold noun FORTRESS, bastion, bulwark, castle, citadel, fort

stroppy adjective Slang AWKWARD, bloody-minded (Brit. informal), difficult, obstreperous, quarrelsome, uncooperative

structure noun 1 BUILDING, construction, edifice, erection 2 ARRANGEMENT, configuration, construction, design, form, formation, make-up, organization ♦ verb 3 ARRANGE, assemble, build up, design, organize, shape

struggle verb 1 STRIVE, exert oneself, give it one's best shot (informal), go all out (informal), knock oneself out (informal), labour, make an all-out effort (informal), strain, toil, work 2 FIGHT, battle, compete, contend, grapple, wrestle ♦ noun 3 EFFORT, exertion, labour, pains, scramble, toil, work 4 FIGHT, battle, brush, clash, combat, conflict, contest, tussle

strut verb SWAGGER, parade, peacock, prance

stub *noun* **1** BUTT, dog-end (*informal*), end, remnant, stump, tail, tail end **2** COUNTERFOIL

stubborn *adjective* OBSTINATE, dogged, headstrong, inflexible, intractable, obdurate, persistent, pig-headed, recalcitrant, tenacious, unyielding

stubby *adjective* STOCKY, chunky, dumpy, short, squat, thickset

stuck *adjective* **1** FASTENED, cemented, fast, fixed, glued, joined **2** *Informal* BAFFLED, beaten, stumped

stuck-up *adjective* SNOBBISH, arrogant, bigheaded (*informal*), conceited, haughty, proud, snooty (*informal*), toffee-nosed (*slang, chiefly Brit.*)

stud *verb* ORNAMENT, bejewel, dot, spangle, spot

student *noun* LEARNER, apprentice, disciple, pupil, scholar, trainee, undergraduate

studied *adjective* PLANNED, conscious, deliberate, intentional, premeditated

studio *noun* WORKSHOP, atelier

studious *adjective* SCHOLARLY, academic, assiduous, bookish, diligent, hard-working, intellectual

study *verb* **1** CONTEMPLATE, consider, examine, go into, ponder, pore over, read **2** LEARN, cram (*informal*), mug up (*Brit. slang*), read up, swot (up) (*Brit. informal*) **3** EXAMINE, analyse, investigate, look into, research, scrutinize, survey ♦ *noun* **4** LEARNING, application, lessons, reading, research, school work, swotting (*Brit. informal*) **5** EXAMINATION, analysis, consideration, contemplation, inquiry, inspection, investigation, review, scrutiny, survey

stuff *noun* **1** THINGS, belongings, effects, equipment, gear, kit, objects, paraphernalia, possessions, tackle **2** SUBSTANCE, essence, matter **3** MATERIAL, cloth, fabric, textile ♦ *verb* **4** CRAM, crowd, fill, force, jam, pack, push, ram, shove, squeeze

stuffing *noun* FILLING, packing, wadding

stuffy *adjective* **1** AIRLESS, close, frowsty, heavy, muggy, oppressive, stale, stifling, sultry, unventilated **2** *Informal* STAID, dreary, dull, pompous, priggish, prim, stodgy

stumble *verb* **1** TRIP, fall, falter, lurch, reel, slip, stagger **2** *with across, on or upon* DISCOVER, chance upon, come across, find

stump *verb* BAFFLE, bewilder, confuse, flummox, mystify, nonplus, perplex, puzzle

stumpy *adjective* STOCKY, dumpy, short, squat, stubby, thickset

stun *verb* OVERCOME, astonish, astound, bewilder, confound, confuse, overpower, shock, stagger, stupefy

stunning *adjective* WONDERFUL, beautiful, dazzling, gorgeous, impressive, lovely, marvellous, sensational (*informal*), spectacular, striking

stunt *noun* FEAT, act, deed, exploit, trick

stunted *adjective* UNDERSIZED, diminutive, little, small, tiny

stupefy *verb* ASTOUND, amaze, daze, dumbfound, shock, stagger, stun

stupendous *adjective* **1** WONDERFUL, amazing, astounding, breathtaking, marvellous, overwhelming, sensational (*informal*), staggering, superb **2** HUGE, colossal, enormous, gigantic, mega (*slang*), vast

stupid *adjective* 1 UNINTELLIGENT, brainless, dense, dim, half-witted, moronic, obtuse, simple, simple-minded, slow, slow-witted, thick 2 FOOLISH, asinine, daft (*informal*), idiotic, imbecilic, inane, nonsensical, pointless, rash, senseless, unintelligent 3 DAZED, groggy, insensate, semiconscious, stunned, stupefied

stupidity *noun* 1 LACK OF INTELLIGENCE, brainlessness, denseness, dimness, dullness, imbecility, obtuseness, slowness, thickness 2 FOOLISHNESS, absurdity, fatuousness, folly, idiocy, inanity, lunacy, madness, silliness

stupor *noun* DAZE, coma, insensibility, stupefaction, unconsciousness

sturdy *adjective* 1 ROBUST, athletic, brawny, hardy, lusty, muscular, powerful 2 WELL-BUILT, durable, solid, substantial, well-made

stutter *verb* STAMMER, falter, hesitate, stumble

style *noun* 1 DESIGN, cut, form, manner 2 MANNER, approach, method, mode, technique, way 3 ELEGANCE, chic, élan, flair, panache, polish, smartness, sophistication, taste 4 TYPE, category, genre, kind, sort, variety 5 FASHION, mode, rage, trend, vogue 6 LUXURY, affluence, comfort, ease, elegance, grandeur ♦ *verb* 7 DESIGN, adapt, arrange, cut, fashion, shape, tailor 8 CALL, designate, dub, entitle, label, name, term

stylish *adjective* SMART, chic, dressy (*informal*), fashionable, modish, trendy (*Brit. informal*), voguish

suave *adjective* SMOOTH, charming, courteous, debonair, polite, sophisticated, urbane

subconscious *adjective* HIDDEN, inner, intuitive, latent, repressed, subliminal

subdue *verb* 1 OVERCOME, break, conquer, control, crush, defeat, master, overpower, quell, tame, vanquish 2 MODERATE, mellow, quieten down, soften, suppress, tone down

subdued *adjective* 1 QUIET, chastened, crestfallen, dejected, downcast, down in the mouth, sad, serious 2 SOFT, dim, hushed, muted, quiet, subtle, toned down, unobtrusive

subject *noun* 1 TOPIC, affair, business, issue, matter, object, point, question, substance, theme 2 CITIZEN, national, subordinate ♦ *adjective* 3 SUBORDINATE, dependent, inferior, obedient, satellite 4 **subject to: a** LIABLE TO, exposed to, in danger of, open to, prone to, susceptible to, vulnerable to **b** CONDITIONAL ON, contingent on, dependent on ♦ *verb* 5 PUT THROUGH, expose, lay open, submit, treat

subjective *adjective* PERSONAL, biased, nonobjective, prejudiced

subjugate *verb* CONQUER, enslave, master, overcome, overpower, quell, subdue, suppress, vanquish

sublime *adjective* NOBLE, elevated, exalted, glorious, grand, great, high, lofty

submerge *verb* IMMERSE, deluge, dip, duck, engulf, flood, inundate, overflow, overwhelm, plunge, sink, swamp

submission *noun* 1 SURRENDER, assent, capitulation, giving in, yielding 2 PRESENTATION, entry, handing in, tendering 3 MEEKNESS, compliance, deference, docility, obedience, passivity, resignation

submissive *adjective* MEEK, accommodating, acquiescent, amenable, compliant, docile, obedient, passive, pliant, tractable, unresisting, yielding

submit verb 1 SURRENDER, accede, agree, capitulate, comply, endure, give in, succumb, tolerate, yield 2 PUT FORWARD, hand in, present, proffer, table, tender

subordinate adjective 1 LESSER, dependent, inferior, junior, lower, minor, secondary, subject ♦ noun 2 INFERIOR, aide, assistant, attendant, junior, second

subordination noun INFERIORITY, inferior or secondary status, servitude, subjection

subscribe verb 1 DONATE, contribute, give 2 SUPPORT, advocate, endorse

subscription noun 1 MEMBERSHIP FEE, annual payment, dues 2 DONATION, contribution, gift

subsequent adjective FOLLOWING, after, ensuing, later, succeeding, successive

subsequently adverb LATER, afterwards

subservient adjective SERVILE, abject, deferential, obsequious, slavish, submissive, sycophantic

subside verb 1 DECREASE, abate, diminish, ease, ebb, lessen, quieten, slacken, wane 2 SINK, cave in, collapse, drop, lower, settle

subsidence noun 1 SINKING, settling 2 DECREASE, abatement, easing off, lessening, slackening

subsidiary adjective LESSER, ancillary, auxiliary, minor, secondary, subordinate, supplementary

subsidize verb FUND, finance, promote, sponsor, support

subsidy noun AID, allowance, assistance, grant, help, support

substance noun 1 MATERIAL, body, fabric, stuff 2 MEANING, essence, gist, import, main point, significance 3 REALITY, actuality, concreteness 4 WEALTH, assets, estate, means, property, resources

substantial adjective BIG, ample, considerable, important, large, significant, sizable or sizeable

substantiate verb SUPPORT, authenticate, confirm, establish, prove, verify

substitute verb 1 REPLACE, change, exchange, interchange, swap, switch ♦ noun 2 REPLACEMENT, agent, deputy, locum, proxy, reserve, sub, surrogate ♦ adjective 3 REPLACEMENT, alternative, fall-back, proxy, reserve, second, surrogate

substitution noun REPLACEMENT, change, exchange, swap, switch

subterfuge noun TRICK, deception, dodge, manoeuvre, ploy, ruse, stratagem

subtle adjective 1 SOPHISTICATED, delicate, refined 2 FAINT, delicate, implied, slight, understated 3 CRAFTY, artful, cunning, devious, ingenious, shrewd, sly, wily

subtlety noun 1 SOPHISTICATION, delicacy, refinement 2 CUNNING, artfulness, cleverness, craftiness, deviousness, ingenuity, slyness, wiliness

subtract verb TAKE AWAY, deduct, diminish, remove, take from, take off

subversive adjective 1 SEDITIOUS, riotous, treasonous ♦ noun 2 DISSIDENT, fifth columnist, saboteur, terrorist, traitor

subvert verb OVERTURN, sabotage, undermine

succeed verb 1 MAKE IT (informal), be successful, crack it (informal), flourish, make good, make the grade (informal), prosper, thrive, triumph, work **2** FOLLOW, come next, ensue, result

success noun **1** LUCK, fame, fortune, happiness, prosperity, triumph **2** HIT (informal), celebrity, megastar (informal), sensation, smash (informal), star, winner

successful adjective THRIVING, booming, flourishing, fortunate, fruitful, lucky, profitable, prosperous, rewarding, top, victorious

successfully adverb WELL, favourably, victoriously, with flying colours

succession noun **1** SERIES, chain, course, cycle, order, progression, run, sequence, train **2** TAKING OVER, accession, assumption, inheritance

successive adjective CONSECUTIVE, following, in succession

succinct adjective BRIEF, compact, concise, laconic, pithy, terse

succour noun **1** HELP, aid, assistance ◆ verb **2** HELP, aid, assist

succulent adjective JUICY, luscious, lush, moist

succumb verb **1** SURRENDER, capitulate, give in, submit, yield **2** DIE, fall

sucker noun Slang FOOL, dupe, mug (Brit. slang), pushover (slang), victim

sudden adjective QUICK, abrupt, hasty, hurried, rapid, rash, swift, unexpected

suddenly adverb ABRUPTLY, all of a sudden, unexpectedly

sue verb Law TAKE (SOMEONE) TO COURT, charge, indict, prosecute, summon

suffer verb **1** UNDERGO, bear, endure, experience, go through, sustain **2** TOLERATE, put up with (informal)

suffering noun PAIN, agony, anguish, discomfort, distress, hardship, misery, ordeal, torment

suffice verb BE ENOUGH, be adequate, be sufficient, do, meet requirements, serve

sufficient adjective ADEQUATE, enough, satisfactory

suffocate verb CHOKE, asphyxiate, smother, stifle

suggest verb **1** RECOMMEND, advise, advocate, prescribe, propose **2** BRING TO MIND, evoke **3** HINT, imply, indicate, intimate

suggestion noun **1** RECOMMENDATION, motion, plan, proposal, proposition **2** HINT, breath, indication, intimation, trace, whisper

suggestive adjective SMUTTY, bawdy, blue, indelicate, provocative, racy, ribald, risqué, rude

suit noun **1** OUTFIT, clothing, costume, dress, ensemble, habit **2** LAWSUIT, action, case, cause, proceeding, prosecution, trial ◆ verb **3** BE ACCEPTABLE TO, do, gratify, please, satisfy **4** BEFIT, agree, become, go with, harmonize, match, tally

suitability noun APPROPRIATENESS, aptness, fitness, rightness

suitable adjective APPROPRIATE, apt, becoming, befitting, fit, fitting, proper, right, satisfactory

suite noun ROOMS, apartment

suitor noun Old-fashioned ADMIRER, beau, young man

sulk verb BE SULLEN, be in a huff, pout

sulky adjective HUFFY, cross, disgruntled, in the sulks, moody, petulant, querulous, resentful, sullen

sullen adjective MOROSE, cross, dour,

glowering, moody, sour, surly, unsociable

sully *verb* <u>DEFILE</u>, besmirch, disgrace, dishonour, smirch, stain, tarnish

sultry *adjective* **1** <u>HUMID</u>, close, hot, muggy, oppressive, sticky, stifling **2** <u>SEDUCTIVE</u>, provocative, sensual, sexy (*informal*)

sum *noun* <u>TOTAL</u>, aggregate, amount, tally, whole

summarize *verb* <u>SUM UP</u>, abridge, condense, encapsulate, epitomize, précis

summary *noun* <u>SYNOPSIS</u>, abridgment, outline, précis, résumé, review, rundown

summit *noun* <u>PEAK</u>, acme, apex, head, height, pinnacle, top, zenith

summon *verb* **1** <u>SEND FOR</u>, bid, call, invite **2** often with *up* <u>GATHER</u>, draw on, muster

sumptuous *adjective* <u>LUXURIOUS</u>, gorgeous, grand, lavish, opulent, splendid, superb

sum up *verb* <u>SUMMARIZE</u>, put in a nutshell, recapitulate, review

sunburnt *adjective* <u>TANNED</u>, bronzed, brown, burnt, peeling, red

sundry *adjective* <u>VARIOUS</u>, assorted, different, miscellaneous, several, some

sunken *adjective* **1** <u>HOLLOW</u>, drawn, haggard **2** <u>LOWER</u>, buried, recessed, submerged

sunny *adjective* **1** <u>BRIGHT</u>, clear, fine, radiant, summery, sunlit, unclouded **2** <u>CHEERFUL</u>, buoyant, cheery, happy, joyful, light-hearted

sunrise *noun* <u>DAWN</u>, break of day, cockcrow, daybreak

sunset *noun* <u>NIGHTFALL</u>, close of (the) day, dusk, eventide

super *adjective Slang* <u>EXCELLENT</u>, cracking (*Brit. informal*), glorious, magnificent, marvellous, outstanding, sensational (*informal*), smashing (*informal*), superb, terrific (*informal*), wonderful

superb *adjective* <u>SPLENDID</u>, excellent, exquisite, fine, first-rate, grand, magnificent, marvellous, superior, superlative, world-class

supercilious *adjective* <u>SCORNFUL</u>, arrogant, contemptuous, disdainful, haughty, lofty, snooty (*informal*), stuck-up (*informal*)

superficial *adjective* **1** <u>HASTY</u>, casual, cursory, desultory, hurried, perfunctory, sketchy, slapdash **2** <u>SHALLOW</u>, empty-headed, frivolous, silly, trivial **3** <u>SURFACE</u>, exterior, external, on the surface, slight

superfluous *adjective* <u>EXCESS</u>, extra, left over, redundant, remaining, spare, supernumerary, surplus

superhuman *adjective* **1** <u>HEROIC</u>, phenomenal, prodigious **2** <u>SUPERNATURAL</u>, paranormal

superintendence *noun* <u>SUPERVISION</u>, charge, control, direction, government, management

superintendent *noun* <u>SUPERVISOR</u>, chief, controller, director, governor, inspector, manager, overseer

superior *adjective* **1** <u>BETTER</u>, grander, greater, higher, surpassing, unrivalled **2** <u>SUPERCILIOUS</u>, condescending, disdainful, haughty, lofty, lordly, patronizing, pretentious, snobbish **3** <u>FIRST-CLASS</u>, choice, de luxe, excellent, exceptional, exclusive, first-rate ♦ *noun* **4** <u>BOSS</u> (*informal*), chief, director, manager, principal, senior, supervisor

superiority *noun* <u>SUPREMACY</u>, advantage, ascendancy, excellence, lead, predominance

superlative *adjective* OUTSTANDING, excellent, supreme, unparalleled, unrivalled, unsurpassed

supernatural *adjective* PARANORMAL, ghostly, hidden, miraculous, mystic, occult, psychic, spectral, uncanny, unearthly

supersede *verb* REPLACE, displace, oust, supplant, take the place of, usurp

supervise *verb* OVERSEE, control, direct, handle, look after, manage, run, superintend

supervision *noun* SUPERINTENDENCE, care, charge, control, direction, guidance, management

supervisor *noun* BOSS (*informal*), administrator, chief, foreman, inspector, manager, overseer

supplant *verb* REPLACE, displace, oust, supersede, take the place of

supple *adjective* FLEXIBLE, limber, lissom(e), lithe, pliable, pliant

supplement *noun* 1 ADDITION, add-on, appendix, extra, insert, postscript, pull-out ♦ *verb* 2 ADD, augment, extend, reinforce

supplementary *adjective* ADDITIONAL, add-on, ancillary, auxiliary, extra, secondary

supplication *noun* PLEA, appeal, entreaty, petition, prayer, request

supply *verb* 1 PROVIDE, contribute, endow, equip, furnish, give, grant, produce, stock, yield ♦ *noun* 2 STORE, cache, fund, hoard, quantity, reserve, source, stock 3 usually plural PROVISIONS, equipment, food, materials, necessities, rations, stores

support *verb* 1 BEAR, brace, buttress, carry, hold, prop, reinforce, sustain 2 PROVIDE FOR, finance, fund, keep, look after, maintain, sustain 3 HELP, aid, assist,

back, champion, defend, second, side with 4 BEAR OUT, confirm, corroborate, substantiate, verify ♦ *noun* 5 HELP, aid, assistance, backing, encouragement, loyalty 6 PROP, brace, foundation, pillar, post 7 SUPPORTER, backer, mainstay, prop, second, tower of strength 8 UPKEEP, keep, maintenance, subsistence, sustenance

supporter *noun* FOLLOWER, adherent, advocate, champion, fan, friend, helper, patron, sponsor, well-wisher

supportive *adjective* HELPFUL, encouraging, sympathetic, understanding

suppose *verb* 1 PRESUME, assume, conjecture, expect, guess (*informal, chiefly U.S. & Canad.*), imagine, think 2 IMAGINE, conjecture, consider, hypothesize, postulate, pretend

supposed *adjective* 1 PRESUMED, accepted, alleged, assumed, professed 2 usually with *to* MEANT, expected, obliged, required

supposedly *adverb* ALLEGEDLY, hypothetically, ostensibly, presumably, theoretically

supposition *noun* GUESS, conjecture, hypothesis, presumption, speculation, surmise, theory

suppress *verb* 1 STOP, check, conquer, crush, overpower, put an end to, quash, quell, subdue 2 RESTRAIN, conceal, contain, curb, hold in *or* back, repress, silence, smother, stifle

suppression *noun* ELIMINATION, check, crushing, quashing, smothering

supremacy *noun* DOMINATION, mastery, predominance, primacy, sovereignty, supreme power, sway

supreme *adjective* HIGHEST, chief,

foremost, greatest, head, leading, paramount, pre-eminent, prime, principal, top, ultimate

supremo *noun* HEAD, boss (*informal*), commander, director, governor, leader, master, principal, ruler

sure *adjective* 1 CERTAIN, assured, confident, convinced, decided, definite, positive 2 RELIABLE, accurate, dependable, foolproof, infallible, undeniable, undoubted, unerring, unfailing 3 INEVITABLE, assured, bound, guaranteed, inescapable

surely *adverb* UNDOUBTEDLY, certainly, definitely, doubtlessly, indubitably, unquestionably, without doubt

surface *noun* 1 OUTSIDE, covering, exterior, face, side, top, veneer ♦ *verb* 2 APPEAR, arise, come to light, come up, crop up (*informal*), emerge, materialize, transpire

surfeit *noun* EXCESS, glut, plethora, superfluity

surge *noun* 1 RUSH, flood, flow, gush, outpouring 2 WAVE, billow, roller, swell ♦ *verb* 3 RUSH, gush, heave, rise, roll

surly *adjective* ILL-TEMPERED, churlish, cross, grouchy (*informal*), morose, sulky, sullen, uncivil, ungracious

surmise *verb* 1 GUESS, conjecture, imagine, presume, speculate, suppose ♦ *noun* 2 GUESS, assumption, conjecture, presumption, speculation, supposition

surpass *verb* OUTDO, beat, eclipse, exceed, excel, outshine, outstrip, transcend

surpassing *adjective* SUPREME, exceptional, extraordinary, incomparable, matchless, outstanding, unrivalled

surplus *noun* 1 EXCESS, balance, remainder, residue, surfeit ♦ *adjective* 2 EXCESS, extra, odd, remaining, spare, superfluous

surprise *noun* 1 SHOCK, bombshell, eye-opener (*informal*), jolt, revelation 2 AMAZEMENT, astonishment, incredulity, wonder ♦ *verb* 3 AMAZE, astonish, stagger, stun, take aback 4 CATCH UNAWARES *or* OFF-GUARD, discover, spring upon, startle

surprised *adjective* AMAZED, astonished, speechless, taken by surprise, thunderstruck

surprising *adjective* AMAZING, astonishing, extraordinary, incredible, remarkable, staggering, unexpected, unusual

surrender *verb* 1 GIVE IN, capitulate, give way, submit, succumb, yield 2 GIVE UP, abandon, cede, concede, part with, relinquish, renounce, waive, yield ♦ *noun* 3 SUBMISSION, capitulation, relinquishment, renunciation, resignation

surreptitious *adjective* SECRET, covert, furtive, sly, stealthy, underhand

surrogate *noun* SUBSTITUTE, proxy, representative, stand-in

surround *verb* ENCLOSE, encircle, encompass, envelop, hem in, ring

surroundings *plural noun* ENVIRONMENT, background, location, milieu, setting

surveillance *noun* OBSERVATION, inspection, scrutiny, supervision, watch

survey *verb* 1 LOOK OVER, contemplate, examine, inspect, observe, scan, scrutinize, view 2 ESTIMATE, appraise, assess, measure, plan, plot, size up ♦ *noun* 3 EXAMINATION, inspection, scrutiny 4 STUDY, inquiry, review

survive *verb* REMAIN ALIVE, endure,

last, live on, outlast, outlive

susceptible adjective 1 usually with to LIABLE, disposed, given, inclined, prone, subject, vulnerable 2 IMPRESSIONABLE, receptive, responsive, sensitive, suggestible

suspect verb 1 BELIEVE, consider, feel, guess, speculate, suppose 2 DISTRUST, doubt, mistrust ♦ adjective 3 DUBIOUS, doubtful, iffy (informal), questionable

suspend verb 1 HANG, attach, dangle 2 POSTPONE, cease, cut short, defer, discontinue, interrupt, put off, shelve

suspense noun UNCERTAINTY, anxiety, apprehension, doubt, expectation, insecurity, irresolution, tension

suspension noun POSTPONEMENT, abeyance, break, breaking off, deferment, discontinuation, interruption

suspicion noun 1 DISTRUST, doubt, dubiety, misgiving, mistrust, qualm, scepticism, wariness 2 IDEA, guess, hunch, impression, notion 3 TRACE, hint, shade, soupçon, streak, suggestion, tinge, touch

suspicious adjective 1 DISTRUSTFUL, doubtful, sceptical, unbelieving, wary 2 SUSPECT, dodgy (Brit., Austral., & N.Z. informal), doubtful, dubious, fishy (informal), questionable

sustain verb 1 MAINTAIN, continue, keep up, prolong, protract 2 KEEP ALIVE, aid, assist, help, nourish 3 WITHSTAND, bear, endure, experience, feel, suffer, undergo 4 SUPPORT, bear, uphold

sustained adjective CONTINUOUS, constant, nonstop, perpetual, prolonged, steady, unremitting

swagger verb SHOW OFF (informal), boast, brag, parade

swallow verb GULP, consume, devour, drink, eat, swig (informal)

swamp noun 1 BOG, fen, marsh, mire, morass, quagmire, slough ♦ verb 2 FLOOD, capsize, engulf, inundate, sink, submerge 3 OVERWHELM, flood, inundate, overload

swap, swop verb EXCHANGE, barter, interchange, switch, trade

swarm noun 1 MULTITUDE, army, crowd, flock, herd, horde, host, mass, throng ♦ verb 2 CROWD, flock, mass, stream, throng 3 TEEM, abound, bristle, crawl

swarthy adjective DARK-SKINNED, black, brown, dark, dark-complexioned, dusky

swashbuckling adjective DASHING, bold, daredevil, flamboyant

swathe verb WRAP, bundle up, cloak, drape, envelop, shroud

sway verb 1 LEAN, bend, rock, roll, swing 2 INFLUENCE, affect, guide, induce, persuade ♦ noun 3 POWER, authority, clout (informal), control, influence

swear verb 1 CURSE, be foul-mouthed, blaspheme 2 DECLARE, affirm, assert, attest, promise, testify, vow

swearing noun BAD LANGUAGE, blasphemy, cursing, foul language, profanity

swearword noun OATH, curse, expletive, four-letter word, obscenity, profanity

sweat noun 1 PERSPIRATION 2 Informal LABOUR, chore, drudgery, toil 3 Informal WORRY, agitation, anxiety, distress, panic, strain ♦ verb 4 PERSPIRE, glow 5 Informal WORRY, agonize, fret, suffer, torture oneself

sweaty adjective PERSPIRING, clammy, sticky

sweep verb 1 CLEAR, brush, clean, remove 2 SAIL, fly, glide, pass, skim, tear, zoom ♦ noun 3 ARC, bend, curve, move, stroke, swing 4 EXTENT, range, scope, stretch

sweeping adjective 1 WIDE-RANGING, all-embracing, all-inclusive, broad, comprehensive, extensive, global, wide 2 INDISCRIMINATE, blanket, exaggerated, overstated, unqualified, wholesale

sweet adjective 1 SUGARY, cloying, saccharine 2 CHARMING, agreeable, appealing, cute, delightful, engaging, kind, likable or likeable, lovable, winning 3 MELODIOUS, dulcet, harmonious, mellow, musical 4 FRAGRANT, aromatic, clean, fresh, pure ♦ noun 5 usually plural CONFECTIONERY, bonbon, candy (*U.S.*) 6 DESSERT, pudding

sweeten verb 1 SUGAR 2 MOLLIFY, appease, pacify, soothe

sweetheart noun LOVER, beloved, boyfriend or girlfriend, darling, dear, love

swell verb 1 EXPAND, balloon, bloat, bulge, dilate, distend, enlarge, grow, increase, rise ♦ noun 2 WAVE, billow, surge

swelling noun ENLARGEMENT, bulge, bump, distension, inflammation, lump, protuberance

sweltering adjective HOT, boiling, burning, oppressive, scorching, stifling

swerve verb VEER, bend, deflect, deviate, diverge, stray, swing, turn, turn aside

swift adjective QUICK, fast, hurried, prompt, rapid, speedy

swiftly adverb QUICKLY, fast, hurriedly, promptly, rapidly, speedily

swiftness noun SPEED, promptness, quickness, rapidity, speediness, velocity

swindle verb 1 CHEAT, con, defraud, do (*slang*), fleece, rip (someone) off (*slang*), skin (*slang*), sting (*informal*), trick ♦ noun 2 FRAUD, con trick (*informal*), deception, fiddle (*Brit. informal*), racket, rip-off (*slang*), scam (*slang*)

swindler noun CHEAT, con man (*informal*), fraud, rogue, shark, trickster

swing verb 1 SWAY, oscillate, rock, veer, wave 2 usually with *round* TURN, curve, pivot, rotate, swivel 3 HANG, dangle, suspend ♦ noun 4 SWAYING, oscillation

swingeing adjective SEVERE, drastic, excessive, harsh, heavy, punishing, stringent

swipe verb 1 HIT, lash out at, slap, strike, wallop (*informal*) 2 *Slang* STEAL, appropriate, filch, lift (*informal*), nick (*slang, chiefly Brit.*), pinch (*informal*), purloin ♦ noun 3 BLOW, clout (*informal*), cuff, slap, smack, wallop (*informal*)

swirl verb WHIRL, churn, eddy, spin, twist

switch noun 1 CHANGE, reversal, shift 2 EXCHANGE, substitution, swap ♦ verb 3 CHANGE, deflect, deviate, divert, shift 4 EXCHANGE, substitute, swap

swivel verb TURN, pivot, revolve, rotate, spin

swollen adjective ENLARGED, bloated, distended, inflamed, puffed up

swoop verb 1 POUNCE, descend, dive, rush, stoop, sweep ♦ noun 2 POUNCE, descent, drop, lunge, plunge, rush, stoop, sweep

swop see SWAP

swot verb Informal STUDY, cram (*informal*), mug up (*Brit. slang*), revise

sycophant noun CRAWLER, bootlicker (*informal*), fawner, flatterer, toady, yes man

sycophantic *adjective* OBSEQUIOUS, crawling, fawning, flattering, grovelling, ingratiating, servile, smarmy (*Brit. informal*), toadying, unctuous

syllabus *noun* COURSE OF STUDY, curriculum

symbol *noun* SIGN, badge, emblem, figure, image, logo, mark, representation, token

symbolic *adjective* REPRESENTATIVE, allegorical, emblematic, figurative

symbolize *verb* REPRESENT, denote, mean, personify, signify, stand for, typify

symmetrical *adjective* BALANCED, in proportion, regular

symmetry *noun* BALANCE, evenness, order, proportion, regularity

sympathetic *adjective* 1 CARING, compassionate, concerned, interested, kind, pitying, supportive, understanding, warm

2 LIKE-MINDED, agreeable, companionable, compatible, congenial, friendly

sympathize *verb* 1 FEEL FOR, commiserate, condole, pity 2 AGREE, side with, understand

sympathizer *noun* SUPPORTER, partisan, well-wisher

sympathy *noun* 1 COMPASSION, commiseration, pity, understanding 2 AGREEMENT, affinity, fellow feeling, rapport

symptom *noun* SIGN, expression, indication, mark, token, warning

symptomatic *adjective* INDICATIVE, characteristic, suggestive

synthetic *adjective* ARTIFICIAL, fake, man-made

system *noun* 1 METHOD, practice, procedure, routine, technique 2 ARRANGEMENT, classification, organization, scheme, structure

systematic *adjective* METHODICAL, efficient, orderly, organized

T t

table *noun* **1** <u>COUNTER</u>, bench, board, stand **2** <u>LIST</u>, catalogue, chart, diagram, record, register, roll, schedule, tabulation ◆ *verb* **3** <u>SUBMIT</u>, enter, move, propose, put forward, suggest

tableau *noun* <u>PICTURE</u>, representation, scene, spectacle

taboo *noun* **1** <u>PROHIBITION</u>, anathema, ban, interdict, proscription, restriction ◆ *adjective* **2** <u>FORBIDDEN</u>, anathema, banned, outlawed, prohibited, proscribed, unacceptable, unmentionable

tacit *adjective* <u>IMPLIED</u>, implicit, inferred, undeclared, understood, unexpressed, unspoken, unstated

taciturn *adjective* <u>UNCOMMUNICATIVE</u>, quiet, reserved, reticent, silent, tight-lipped, unforthcoming, withdrawn

tack[1] *noun* **1** <u>NAIL</u>, drawing pin, pin ◆ *verb* **2** <u>FASTEN</u>, affix, attach, fix, nail, pin **3** <u>STITCH</u>, baste **4 tack on** <u>APPEND</u>, add, attach, tag

tack[2] *noun* <u>COURSE</u>, approach, direction, heading, line, method, path, plan, procedure, way

tackle *verb* **1** <u>DEAL WITH</u>, attempt, come *or* get to grips with, embark upon, get stuck into (*informal*), have a go at (*informal*), set about, undertake **2** <u>CONFRONT</u>, challenge, grab, grasp, halt, intercept, seize, stop ◆ *noun* **3** <u>CHALLENGE</u>, block **4** <u>EQUIPMENT</u>, accoutrements, apparatus, gear, paraphernalia, tools, trappings

tacky[1] *adjective* <u>STICKY</u>, adhesive, gluey, gummy, wet

tacky[2] *adjective Informal* <u>VULGAR</u>, cheap, naff (*Brit. slang*), seedy, shabby, shoddy, sleazy, tasteless, tatty

tact *noun* <u>DIPLOMACY</u>, consideration, delicacy, discretion, sensitivity, thoughtfulness, understanding

tactful *adjective* <u>DIPLOMATIC</u>, considerate, delicate, discreet, polite, politic, sensitive, thoughtful, understanding

tactic *noun* **1** <u>POLICY</u>, approach, manoeuvre, method, move, ploy, scheme, stratagem **2 tactics** <u>STRATEGY</u>, campaigning, generalship, manoeuvres, plans

tactical *adjective* <u>STRATEGIC</u>, cunning, diplomatic, shrewd, smart

tactician *noun* <u>STRATEGIST</u>, general, mastermind, planner

tactless *adjective* <u>INSENSITIVE</u>, impolite, impolitic, inconsiderate, indelicate, indiscreet, thoughtless, undiplomatic, unsubtle

tag *noun* **1** <u>LABEL</u>, flap, identification, mark, marker, note, slip, tab, ticket ◆ *verb* **2** <u>LABEL</u>, mark **3 with** *along or on* <u>ACCOMPANY</u>, attend, follow, shadow, tail (*informal*), trail

tail *noun* **1** <u>EXTREMITY</u>, appendage, end, rear end, tailpiece **2 turn tail** <u>RUN AWAY</u>, cut and run, flee, retreat, run off, take to one's heels ◆ *verb* **3** *Informal* <u>FOLLOW</u>, shadow, stalk, track, trail

tailor *noun* **1** <u>OUTFITTER</u>, clothier, costumier, couturier, dressmaker, seamstress ◆ *verb* **2** <u>ADAPT</u>, adjust, alter, customize, fashion, modify, mould, shape, style

taint *verb* **1** <u>SPOIL</u>, blemish, contaminate, corrupt, damage, defile, pollute, ruin, stain, sully, tarnish ◆ *noun* **2** <u>STAIN</u>, black mark, blemish, blot, defect, demerit, fault, flaw, spot

take verb 1 CAPTURE, acquire, catch, get, grasp, grip, obtain, secure, seize 2 ACCOMPANY, bring, conduct, convoy, escort, guide, lead, usher 3 CARRY, bear, bring, convey, ferry, fetch, haul, transport 4 STEAL, appropriate, misappropriate, pinch (*informal*), pocket, purloin 5 REQUIRE, call for, demand, necessitate, need 6 TOLERATE, abide, bear, endure, put up with (*informal*), stand, stomach, withstand 7 HAVE ROOM FOR, accept, accommodate, contain, hold 8 SUBTRACT, deduct, eliminate, remove 9 ASSUME, believe, consider, perceive, presume, regard, understand

take in verb 1 UNDERSTAND, absorb, assimilate, comprehend, digest, get the hang of (*informal*), grasp 2 DECEIVE, cheat, con (*informal*), dupe, fool, hoodwink, mislead, swindle, trick

takeoff noun 1 DEPARTURE, launch, liftoff 2 *Informal* PARODY, caricature, imitation, lampoon, satire, send-up (*Brit. informal*), spoof (*informal*)

take off verb 1 REMOVE, discard, peel off, strip off 2 LIFT OFF, take to the air 3 *Informal* DEPART, abscond, decamp, disappear, go, leave, slope off 4 *Informal* PARODY, caricature, imitate, lampoon, mimic, mock, satirize, send up (*Brit. informal*)

takeover noun MERGER, coup, incorporation

take up verb 1 OCCUPY, absorb, consume, cover, extend over, fill, use up 2 START, adopt, become involved in, engage in

taking adjective 1 CHARMING, attractive, beguiling, captivating, enchanting, engaging, fetching (*informal*), likable *or* likeable, prepossessing ♦noun 2 **takings** REVENUE, earnings, income, proceeds, profits, receipts, returns, take

tale noun STORY, account, anecdote, fable, legend, narrative, saga, yarn (*informal*)

talent noun ABILITY, aptitude, capacity, flair, genius, gift, knack

talented adjective GIFTED, able, brilliant

talisman noun CHARM, amulet, fetish, lucky charm, mascot

talk verb 1 SPEAK, chat, chatter, communicate, converse, gossip, natter, utter 2 NEGOTIATE, confabulate, confer, parley 3 INFORM, blab, give the game away, grass (*Brit. slang*), let the cat out of the bag, tell all ♦noun 4 SPEECH, address, discourse, disquisition, lecture, oration, sermon

talkative adjective LOQUACIOUS, chatty, effusive, garrulous, gossipy, long-winded, mouthy, verbose, voluble, wordy

talker noun SPEAKER, chatterbox, conversationalist, lecturer, orator

talking-to noun REPRIMAND, criticism, dressing-down (*informal*), lecture, rebuke, reproach, reproof, scolding, telling-off (*informal*), ticking-off (*informal*)

tall adjective 1 HIGH, big, elevated, giant, lanky, lofty, soaring, towering 2 *As in* **tall story** *Informal* IMPLAUSIBLE, absurd, cock-and-bull (*informal*), exaggerated, far-fetched, incredible, preposterous, unbelievable 3 *As in* **tall order** DIFFICULT, demanding, hard, unreasonable, well-nigh impossible

tally verb 1 CORRESPOND, accord, agree, coincide, concur, conform, fit, harmonize, match, square ♦noun 2 RECORD, count, mark, reckoning, running total, score, total

tame *adjective* **1** DOMESTICATED, amenable, broken, disciplined, docile, gentle, obedient, tractable **2** SUBMISSIVE, compliant, docile, manageable, meek, obedient, subdued, unresisting **3** UNINTERESTING, bland, boring, dull, humdrum, insipid, unexciting, uninspiring, vapid ♦ *verb* **4** DOMESTICATE, break in, house-train, train **5** DISCIPLINE, bring to heel, conquer, humble, master, subdue, subjugate, suppress

tamper *verb* INTERFERE, alter, fiddle (*informal*), fool about (*informal*), meddle, mess about, tinker

tangible *adjective* DEFINITE, actual, concrete, material, palpable, perceptible, positive, real

tangle *noun* **1** KNOT, coil, entanglement, jungle, twist, web **2** CONFUSION, complication, entanglement, fix (*informal*), imbroglio, jam, mess, mix-up ♦ *verb* **3** TWIST, coil, entangle, interweave, knot, mat, mesh, ravel **4** often with *with* COME INTO CONFLICT, come up against, contend, contest, cross swords, dispute, lock horns

tangled *adjective* **1** TWISTED, entangled, jumbled, knotted, matted, messy, snarled, tousled **2** COMPLICATED, complex, confused, convoluted, involved, knotty, messy, mixed-up

tangy *adjective* SHARP, piquant, pungent, spicy, tart

tantalize *verb* TORMENT, frustrate, lead on, taunt, tease, torture

tantamount *adjective* EQUIVALENT, commensurate, equal, synonymous

tantrum *noun* OUTBURST, fit, flare-up, hysterics, temper

tap[1] *verb* **1** KNOCK, beat, drum, pat, rap, strike, touch ♦ *noun* **2** KNOCK, pat, rap, touch

tap[2] *noun* **1** VALVE, stopcock **2 on tap: a** *Informal* AVAILABLE, at hand, in reserve, on hand, ready **b** ON DRAUGHT ♦ *verb* **3** LISTEN IN ON, bug (*informal*), eavesdrop on **4** DRAW OFF, bleed, drain, siphon off

tape *noun* **1** STRIP, band, ribbon ♦ *verb* **2** RECORD, tape-record, video **3** BIND, seal, secure, stick, wrap

taper *verb* **1** NARROW, come to a point, thin **2 taper off** LESSEN, decrease, die away, dwindle, fade, reduce, subside, wane, wind down

target *noun* **1** GOAL, aim, ambition, end, intention, mark, object, objective **2** VICTIM, butt, scapegoat

tariff *noun* **1** TAX, duty, excise, levy, toll **2** SCHEDULE, menu

tarnish *verb* **1** STAIN, blacken, blemish, blot, darken, discolour, sully, taint ♦ *noun* **2** STAIN, blemish, blot, discoloration, spot, taint

tart[1] *noun* PIE, pastry, tartlet

tart[2] *adjective* SHARP, acid, bitter, piquant, pungent, sour, tangy, vinegary

tart[3] *noun* SLUT, call girl, floozy (*slang*), prostitute, trollop, whore

task *noun* **1** JOB, assignment, chore, duty, enterprise, exercise, mission, undertaking **2 take to task** CRITICIZE, blame, censure, reprimand, reproach, reprove, scold, tell off (*informal*), upbraid

taste *noun* **1** FLAVOUR, relish, savour, smack, tang **2** BIT, bite, dash, morsel, mouthful, sample, soupçon, spoonful, titbit **3** LIKING, appetite, fancy, fondness, inclination, partiality, penchant, predilection, preference **4** REFINEMENT, appreciation, discernment, discrimination, elegance, judgment,

sophistication, style ◆ *verb*
5 <u>DISTINGUISH</u>, differentiate, discern,
perceive **6** <u>SAMPLE</u>, savour, sip, test,
try **7** <u>HAVE A FLAVOUR OF</u>, savour of,
smack of **8** <u>EXPERIENCE</u>, encounter,
know, meet with, partake of,
undergo

tasteful *adjective* <u>REFINED</u>, artistic,
cultivated, cultured,
discriminating, elegant, exquisite,
in good taste, polished, stylish

tasteless *adjective* **1** <u>INSIPID</u>, bland,
boring, dull, flat, flavourless, mild,
thin, weak **2** <u>VULGAR</u>, crass, crude,
gaudy, gross, inelegant, naff (*Brit.
slang*), tacky (*informal*), tawdry

tasty *adjective* <u>DELICIOUS</u>, appetizing,
delectable, full-flavoured, luscious,
palatable, savoury, scrumptious
(*informal*), toothsome

tatters *noun* **in tatters** <u>RAGGED</u>,
down at heel, in rags, in shreds,
ripped, tattered, threadbare, torn

tatty *adjective* <u>RAGGED</u>, bedraggled,
dilapidated, down at heel,
neglected, run-down, scruffy,
shabby, threadbare, worn

taunt *verb* **1** <u>TEASE</u>, deride, insult,
jeer, mock, provoke, ridicule,
torment ◆ *noun* **2** <u>JEER</u>, derision,
dig, gibe, insult, provocation,
ridicule, sarcasm, teasing

taut *adjective* <u>TIGHT</u>, flexed, rigid,
strained, stressed, stretched, tense

tavern *noun* <u>INN</u>, alehouse
(*archaic*), bar, hostelry, pub
(*informal, chiefly Brit.*), public
house

tawdry *adjective* <u>VULGAR</u>, cheap,
gimcrack, naff (*Brit. slang*),
tacky (*informal*), tasteless, tatty,
tinselly

tax *noun* **1** <u>CHARGE</u>, duty, excise,
levy, tariff, tithe, toll ◆ *verb*
2 <u>CHARGE</u>, assess, rate **3** <u>STRAIN</u>,
burden, exhaust, load, stretch,
test, try, weaken, weary

taxing *adjective* <u>DEMANDING</u>,
exacting, onerous, punishing,
sapping, stressful, tiring, tough,
trying

teach *verb* <u>INSTRUCT</u>, coach, drill,
educate, enlighten, guide, inform,
show, train, tutor

teacher *noun* <u>INSTRUCTOR</u>, coach,
educator, guide, lecturer, master
or mistress, mentor,
schoolteacher, trainer, tutor

team *noun* **1** <u>GROUP</u>, band, body,
bunch, company, gang, line-up,
set, side, squad ◆ *verb* **2** often with
up <u>JOIN</u>, band together, cooperate,
couple, get together, link, unite,
work together

teamwork *noun* <u>COOPERATION</u>,
collaboration, coordination, esprit
de corps, fellowship, harmony,
unity

tear *verb* **1** <u>RIP</u>, claw, lacerate,
mangle, mutilate, pull apart, rend,
rupture, scratch, shred, split
2 <u>RUSH</u>, bolt, charge, dash, fly,
hurry, race, run, speed, sprint,
zoom ◆ *noun* **3** <u>HOLE</u>, laceration,
rent, rip, rupture, scratch, split

tearaway *noun* <u>HOOLIGAN</u>,
delinquent, good-for-nothing,
rowdy, ruffian

tearful *adjective* <u>WEEPING</u>,
blubbering, crying, in tears,
lachrymose, sobbing, weepy
(*informal*), whimpering

tears *plural noun* **1** <u>CRYING</u>,
blubbering, sobbing, wailing,
weeping **2** **in tears** <u>CRYING</u>,
blubbering, distressed, sobbing,
weeping

tease *verb* <u>MOCK</u>, goad, lead on,
provoke, pull someone's leg
(*informal*), tantalize, taunt,
torment

technical *adjective* <u>SCIENTIFIC</u>,
hi-tech *or* high-tech, skilled,
specialist, specialized,

technological

technique noun 1 METHOD, approach, manner, means, mode, procedure, style, system, way 2 SKILL, artistry, craft, craftsmanship, execution, performance, proficiency, touch

tedious adjective BORING, drab, dreary, dull, humdrum, irksome, laborious, mind-numbing, monotonous, tiresome, wearisome

tedium noun BOREDOM, drabness, dreariness, dullness, monotony, routine, sameness, tediousness

teeming[1] adjective FULL, abundant, alive, brimming, bristling, bursting, crawling, overflowing, swarming, thick

teeming[2] adjective POURING, bucketing down (informal), pelting

teenager noun YOUTH, adolescent, boy, girl, juvenile, minor

teeter verb WOBBLE, rock, seesaw, stagger, sway, totter, waver

teetotaller noun ABSTAINER, nondrinker

telepathy noun MIND-READING, sixth sense

telephone noun 1 PHONE, handset, line ♦ verb 2 CALL, dial, phone, ring (chiefly Brit.)

telescope noun 1 GLASS, spyglass ♦ verb 2 SHORTEN, abbreviate, abridge, compress, condense, contract, shrink

television noun TV, small screen (informal), telly (Brit. informal), the box (Brit. informal), the tube (slang)

tell verb 1 INFORM, announce, communicate, disclose, divulge, express, make known, notify, proclaim, reveal, state 2 INSTRUCT, bid, call upon, command, direct, order, require, summon 3 DESCRIBE, chronicle, depict, narrate, portray, recount, relate, report 4 DISTINGUISH, differentiate, discern, discriminate, identify 5 CARRY WEIGHT, count, have or take effect, make its presence felt, register, take its toll, weigh

telling adjective EFFECTIVE, considerable, decisive, forceful, impressive, influential, marked, powerful, significant, striking

telling-off noun REPRIMAND, criticism, dressing-down (informal), lecture, rebuke, reproach, reproof, scolding, talking-to, ticking-off (informal)

tell off verb REPRIMAND, berate, censure, chide, haul over the coals (informal), lecture, read the riot act, rebuke, reproach, scold

temerity noun BOLDNESS, audacity, chutzpah (U.S. & Canad. informal), effrontery, front, impudence, nerve (informal), rashness, recklessness

temper noun 1 RAGE, bad mood, fury, passion, tantrum 2 IRRITABILITY, hot-headedness, irascibility, passion, petulance, resentment, surliness 3 SELF-CONTROL, calmness, composure, cool (slang), equanimity 4 FRAME OF MIND, constitution, disposition, humour, mind, mood, nature, temperament ♦ verb 5 MODERATE, assuage, lessen, mitigate, mollify, restrain, soften, soothe, tone down 6 STRENGTHEN, anneal, harden, toughen

temperament noun 1 NATURE, bent, character, constitution, disposition, humour, make-up, outlook, personality, temper 2 EXCITABILITY, anger, hot-headedness, moodiness, petulance, volatility

temperamental adjective 1 MOODY, capricious, emotional, excitable, highly strung, hypersensitive,

irritable, sensitive, touchy, volatile
2 UNRELIABLE, erratic, inconsistent, inconstant, unpredictable

temperance noun **1** MODERATION, continence, discretion, forbearance, restraint, self-control, self-discipline, self-restraint **2** TEETOTALISM, abstemiousness, abstinence, sobriety

temperate adjective **1** MILD, calm, cool, fair, gentle, moderate, pleasant **2** SELF-RESTRAINED, calm, composed, dispassionate, even-tempered, mild, moderate, reasonable, self-controlled, sensible

tempest noun GALE, cyclone, hurricane, squall, storm, tornado, typhoon

tempestuous adjective **1** STORMY, blustery, gusty, inclement, raging, squally, turbulent, windy **2** VIOLENT, boisterous, emotional, furious, heated, intense, passionate, stormy, turbulent, wild

temple noun SHRINE, church, sanctuary

temporarily adverb BRIEFLY, fleetingly, for the time being, momentarily, pro tem

temporary adjective IMPERMANENT, brief, ephemeral, fleeting, interim, momentary, provisional, short-lived, transitory

tempt verb ENTICE, allure, attract, coax, invite, lead on, lure, seduce, tantalize

temptation noun ENTICEMENT, allurement, inducement, lure, pull, seduction, tantalization

tempting adjective ENTICING, alluring, appetizing, attractive, inviting, mouthwatering, seductive, tantalizing

tenable adjective SOUND, arguable, believable, defensible, justifiable, plausible, rational, reasonable, viable

tenacious adjective **1** FIRM, clinging, forceful, immovable, iron, strong, tight, unshakable **2** STUBBORN, adamant, determined, dogged, obdurate, obstinate, persistent, resolute, steadfast, unswerving, unyielding

tenacity noun PERSEVERANCE, application, determination, doggedness, obduracy, persistence, resolve, steadfastness, stubbornness

tenancy noun LEASE, occupancy, possession, renting, residence

tenant noun LEASEHOLDER, inhabitant, lessee, occupant, occupier, renter, resident

tend[1] verb **1** BE INCLINED, be apt, be liable, gravitate, have a tendency, incline, lean **2** GO, aim, bear, head, lead, make for, point

tend[2] verb TAKE CARE OF, attend, cultivate, keep, look after, maintain, manage, nurture, watch over

tendency noun INCLINATION, disposition, leaning, liability, proclivity, proneness, propensity, susceptibility

tender[1] adjective **1** GENTLE, affectionate, caring, compassionate, considerate, kind, loving, sympathetic, tenderhearted, warm-hearted **2** VULNERABLE, immature, impressionable, inexperienced, raw, sensitive, young, youthful **3** SENSITIVE, bruised, inflamed, painful, raw, sore

tender[2] verb **1** OFFER, give, hand in, present, proffer, propose, put forward, submit, volunteer ♦ noun **2** OFFER, bid, estimate, proposal, submission **3** As in **legal tender** CURRENCY, money, payment

tenderness noun **1** GENTLENESS,

affection, care, compassion, consideration, kindness, love, sentimentality, sympathy, warmth 2 SORENESS, inflammation, pain, sensitivity

tense *adjective* 1 NERVOUS, anxious, apprehensive, edgy, jumpy, keyed up, on edge, on tenterhooks, strained, uptight (*informal*) 2 STRESSFUL, exciting, nerve-racking, worrying 3 TIGHT, rigid, strained, stretched, taut ♦ *verb* 4 TIGHTEN, brace, flex, strain, stretch

tension *noun* 1 SUSPENSE, anxiety, apprehension, hostility, nervousness, pressure, strain, stress, unease 2 TIGHTNESS, pressure, rigidity, stiffness, stress, stretching, tautness

tentative *adjective* 1 EXPERIMENTAL, conjectural, indefinite, provisional, speculative, unconfirmed, unsettled 2 HESITANT, cautious, diffident, doubtful, faltering, timid, uncertain, undecided, unsure

tenuous *adjective* SLIGHT, doubtful, dubious, flimsy, insubstantial, nebulous, shaky, sketchy, weak

tepid *adjective* 1 LUKEWARM, warmish 2 HALF-HEARTED, apathetic, cool, indifferent, lukewarm, unenthusiastic

term *noun* 1 WORD, expression, name, phrase, title 2 PERIOD, duration, interval, season, span, spell, time, while ♦ *verb* 3 CALL, designate, dub, entitle, label, name, style

terminal *adjective* 1 DEADLY, fatal, incurable, killing, lethal, mortal 2 FINAL, concluding, extreme, last, ultimate, utmost ♦ *noun* 3 TERMINUS, depot, end of the line, station

terminate *verb* END, abort, cease, close, complete, conclude, discontinue, finish, stop

termination *noun* ENDING, abortion, cessation, completion, conclusion, discontinuation, end, finish

terminology *noun* LANGUAGE, jargon, nomenclature, phraseology, terms, vocabulary

terminus *noun* END OF THE LINE, depot, garage, last stop, station

terms *plural noun* 1 CONDITIONS, particulars, provisions, provisos, qualifications, specifications, stipulations 2 RELATIONSHIP, footing, relations, standing, status

terrain *noun* GROUND, country, going, land, landscape, topography

terrestrial *adjective* EARTHLY, global, worldly

terrible *adjective* 1 SERIOUS, dangerous, desperate, extreme, severe 2 *Informal* BAD, abysmal, awful, dire, dreadful, poor, rotten (*informal*) 3 FEARFUL, dreadful, frightful, horrendous, horrible, horrifying, monstrous, shocking, terrifying

terribly *adverb* EXTREMELY, awfully (*informal*), decidedly, desperately, exceedingly, seriously, thoroughly, very

terrific *adjective* 1 GREAT, enormous, fearful, gigantic, huge, intense, tremendous 2 *Informal* EXCELLENT, amazing, brilliant, fantastic (*informal*), magnificent, marvellous, outstanding, sensational (*informal*), stupendous, superb, wonderful

terrified *adjective* FRIGHTENED, alarmed, appalled, horrified, horror-struck, panic-stricken, petrified, scared

terrify *verb* FRIGHTEN, alarm, appal, horrify, make one's hair stand on end, scare, shock, terrorize

territory noun DISTRICT, area, country, domain, land, patch, province, region, zone

terror noun 1 FEAR, alarm, anxiety, dread, fright, horror, panic, shock 2 SCOURGE, bogeyman, bugbear, devil, fiend, monster

terrorize verb OPPRESS, browbeat, bully, coerce, intimidate, menace, threaten

terse adjective 1 CONCISE, brief, condensed, laconic, monosyllabic, pithy, short, succinct 2 CURT, abrupt, brusque, short, snappy

test verb 1 CHECK, analyse, assess, examine, experiment, investigate, put to the test, research, try out ◆ noun 2 EXAMINATION, acid test, analysis, assessment, check, evaluation, investigation, research, trial

testament noun 1 PROOF, demonstration, evidence, testimony, tribute, witness 2 WILL, last wishes

testify verb BEAR WITNESS, affirm, assert, attest, certify, corroborate, state, swear, vouch

testimonial noun TRIBUTE, commendation, endorsement, recommendation, reference

testimony noun 1 EVIDENCE, affidavit, deposition, statement, submission 2 PROOF, corroboration, demonstration, evidence, indication, manifestation, support, verification

testing adjective DIFFICULT, arduous, challenging, demanding, exacting, rigorous, searching, strenuous, taxing, tough

tether noun 1 ROPE, chain, fetter, halter, lead, leash 2 at the end of one's tether EXASPERATED, at one's wits' end, exhausted ◆ verb 3 TIE, bind, chain, fasten, fetter, secure

text noun 1 CONTENTS, body

2 WORDS, wording

texture noun FEEL, consistency, grain, structure, surface, tissue

thank verb SAY THANK YOU, show one's appreciation

thankful adjective GRATEFUL, appreciative, beholden, indebted, obliged, pleased, relieved

thankless adjective UNREWARDING, fruitless, unappreciated, unprofitable, unrequited

thanks plural noun 1 GRATITUDE, acknowledgment, appreciation, credit, gratefulness, recognition 2 thanks to BECAUSE OF, as a result of, due to, owing to, through

thaw verb MELT, defrost, dissolve, liquefy, soften, unfreeze, warm

theatrical adjective 1 DRAMATIC, Thespian 2 EXAGGERATED, affected, dramatic, histrionic, mannered, melodramatic, ostentatious, showy, stagy

theft noun STEALING, embezzlement, fraud, larceny, pilfering, purloining, robbery, thieving

theme noun 1 SUBJECT, idea, keynote, subject matter, topic 2 MOTIF, leitmotif

theological adjective RELIGIOUS, doctrinal, ecclesiastical

theoretical adjective ABSTRACT, academic, conjectural, hypothetical, notional, speculative

theorize verb SPECULATE, conjecture, formulate, guess, hypothesize, project, propound, suppose

theory noun SUPPOSITION, assumption, conjecture, hypothesis, presumption, speculation, surmise, thesis

therapeutic adjective BENEFICIAL, corrective, curative, good, healing, remedial, restorative, salutary

therapist noun <u>HEALER</u>, physician

therapy noun <u>REMEDY</u>, cure, healing, treatment

therefore adverb <u>CONSEQUENTLY</u>, accordingly, as a result, ergo, hence, so, then, thence, thus

thesis noun 1 <u>DISSERTATION</u>, essay, monograph, paper, treatise 2 <u>PROPOSITION</u>, contention, hypothesis, idea, opinion, proposal, theory, view

thick adjective 1 <u>WIDE</u>, broad, bulky, fat, solid, substantial 2 <u>DENSE</u>, close, compact, concentrated, condensed, heavy, impenetrable, opaque 3 Informal <u>STUPID</u>, brainless, dense, dopey (informal), moronic, obtuse, slow, thickheaded 4 Informal <u>FRIENDLY</u>, close, devoted, familiar, inseparable, intimate, pally (informal) 5 <u>FULL</u>, brimming, bristling, bursting, covered, crawling, packed, swarming, teeming 6 **a bit thick** <u>UNFAIR</u>, unjust, unreasonable

thicken verb <u>SET</u>, clot, coagulate, condense, congeal, jell

thicket noun <u>WOOD</u>, brake, coppice, copse, covert, grove

thickset adjective <u>WELL-BUILT</u>, bulky, burly, heavy, muscular, stocky, strong, sturdy

thief noun <u>ROBBER</u>, burglar, embezzler, housebreaker, pickpocket, pilferer, plunderer, shoplifter, stealer

thieve verb <u>STEAL</u>, filch, nick (slang, chiefly Brit.), pilfer, pinch (informal), purloin, rob, swipe (slang)

thin adjective 1 <u>NARROW</u>, attenuated, fine 2 <u>SLIM</u>, bony, emaciated, lean, scrawny, skeletal, skinny, slender, slight, spare, spindly 3 <u>MEAGRE</u>, deficient, scanty, scarce, scattered, skimpy, sparse, wispy

4 <u>DELICATE</u>, diaphanous, filmy, fine, flimsy, gossamer, sheer, unsubstantial 5 <u>UNCONVINCING</u>, feeble, flimsy, inadequate, lame, poor, superficial, weak

thing noun 1 <u>OBJECT</u>, article, being, body, entity, something, substance 2 Informal <u>OBSESSION</u>, bee in one's bonnet, fetish, fixation, hang-up (informal), mania, phobia, preoccupation 3 **things** <u>POSSESSIONS</u>, belongings, clobber (Brit. slang), effects, equipment, gear, luggage, stuff

think verb 1 <u>BELIEVE</u>, consider, deem, estimate, imagine, judge, reckon, regard, suppose 2 <u>PONDER</u>, cerebrate, cogitate, contemplate, deliberate, meditate, muse, reason, reflect, ruminate

thinker noun <u>PHILOSOPHER</u>, brain (informal), intellect (informal), mastermind, sage, theorist, wise man

thinking noun 1 <u>REASONING</u>, conjecture, idea, judgment, opinion, position, theory, view ♦ adjective 2 <u>THOUGHTFUL</u>, contemplative, intelligent, meditative, philosophical, rational, reasoning, reflective

think up verb <u>DEVISE</u>, come up with, concoct, contrive, create, dream up, invent, visualize

thirst noun 1 <u>THIRSTINESS</u>, drought, dryness 2 <u>CRAVING</u>, appetite, desire, hankering, keenness, longing, passion, yearning

thirsty adjective 1 <u>PARCHED</u>, arid, dehydrated, dry 2 <u>EAGER</u>, avid, craving, desirous, greedy, hungry, itching, longing, yearning

thorn noun <u>PRICKLE</u>, barb, spike, spine

thorny adjective <u>PRICKLY</u>, barbed, bristly, pointed, sharp, spiky, spiny

thorough adjective 1 <u>CAREFUL</u>,

assiduous, conscientious, efficient, exhaustive, full, in-depth, intensive, meticulous, painstaking, sweeping 2 COMPLETE, absolute, out-and-out, outright, perfect, total, unmitigated, unqualified, utter

thoroughbred adjective PUREBRED, pedigree

thoroughfare noun ROAD, avenue, highway, passage, passageway, street, way

thoroughly adverb 1 CAREFULLY, assiduously, conscientiously, efficiently, exhaustively, from top to bottom, fully, intensively, meticulously, painstakingly, scrupulously 2 COMPLETELY, absolutely, downright, perfectly, quite, totally, to the hilt, utterly

though conjunction 1 ALTHOUGH, even if, even though, notwithstanding, while ◆ adverb 2 NEVERTHELESS, for all that, however, nonetheless, notwithstanding, still, yet

thought noun 1 THINKING, brainwork, cogitation, consideration, deliberation, meditation, musing, reflection, rumination 2 IDEA, concept, judgment, notion, opinion, view 3 CONSIDERATION, attention, heed, regard, scrutiny, study 4 INTENTION, aim, design, idea, notion, object, plan, purpose 5 EXPECTATION, anticipation, aspiration, hope, prospect

thoughtful adjective 1 CONSIDERATE, attentive, caring, helpful, kind, kindly, solicitous, unselfish 2 WELL-THOUGHT-OUT, astute, canny, prudent 3 REFLECTIVE, contemplative, deliberative, meditative, pensive, ruminative, serious, studious

thoughtless adjective INCONSIDERATE, impolite, insensitive, rude, selfish, tactless, uncaring, undiplomatic, unkind

thrash verb 1 BEAT, belt (informal), cane, flog, give (someone) a (good) hiding (informal), scourge, spank, whip 2 DEFEAT, beat, crush, drub, rout, run rings around (informal), slaughter (informal), trounce, wipe the floor with (informal) 3 THRESH, flail, jerk, toss and turn, writhe

thrashing noun 1 BEATING, belting (informal), flogging, hiding (informal), punishment, whipping 2 DEFEAT, beating, drubbing, hammering (informal), hiding (informal), rout, trouncing

thrash out verb SETTLE, argue out, debate, discuss, have out, resolve, solve, talk over

thread noun 1 STRAND, fibre, filament, line, string, yarn 2 THEME, direction, drift, plot, story line, train of thought ◆ verb 3 PASS, ease, pick (one's way), squeeze through

threadbare adjective 1 SHABBY, down at heel, frayed, old, ragged, scruffy, tattered, tatty, worn 2 HACKNEYED, commonplace, conventional, familiar, overused, stale, stereotyped, tired, trite, well-worn

threat noun 1 WARNING, foreboding, foreshadowing, omen, portent, presage, writing on the wall 2 DANGER, hazard, menace, peril, risk

threaten verb 1 INTIMIDATE, browbeat, bully, lean on (slang), menace, pressurize, terrorize 2 ENDANGER, imperil, jeopardize, put at risk, put in jeopardy, put on the line 3 FORESHADOW, forebode, impend, portend, presage

threatening adjective 1 MENACING, bullying, intimidatory 2 OMINOUS, forbidding, grim, inauspicious, sinister

threshold noun 1 <u>ENTRANCE</u>, door, doorstep, doorway 2 <u>START</u>, beginning, brink, dawn, inception, opening, outset, verge 3 <u>MINIMUM</u>, lower limit

thrift noun <u>FRUGALITY</u>, carefulness, economy, parsimony, prudence, saving, thriftiness

thrifty adjective <u>ECONOMICAL</u>, careful, frugal, parsimonious, provident, prudent, saving, sparing

thrill noun 1 <u>PLEASURE</u>, buzz (*slang*), kick (*informal*), stimulation, tingle, titillation ♦ verb 2 <u>EXCITE</u>, arouse, electrify, move, stimulate, stir, titillate

thrilling adjective <u>EXCITING</u>, electrifying, gripping, riveting, rousing, sensational, stimulating, stirring

thrive verb <u>PROSPER</u>, boom, develop, do well, flourish, get on, grow, increase, succeed

thriving adjective <u>PROSPEROUS</u>, blooming, booming, burgeoning, flourishing, healthy, successful, well

throb verb 1 <u>PULSATE</u>, beat, palpitate, pound, pulse, thump, vibrate ♦ noun 2 <u>PULSE</u>, beat, palpitation, pounding, pulsating, thump, thumping, vibration

throng noun 1 <u>CROWD</u>, crush, horde, host, mass, mob, multitude, pack, swarm ♦ verb 2 <u>CROWD</u>, congregate, converge, flock, mill around, pack, swarm around

throttle verb <u>STRANGLE</u>, choke, garrotte, strangulate

through preposition 1 <u>BETWEEN</u>, by, past 2 <u>BECAUSE OF</u>, by means of, by way of, using, via 3 <u>DURING</u>, in, throughout ♦ adjective 4 <u>FINISHED</u>, completed, done, ended ♦ adverb **5 through and through** <u>COMPLETELY</u>, altogether, entirely, fully, thoroughly, totally, utterly, wholly

throughout adverb <u>EVERYWHERE</u>, all over, from start to finish, right through

throw verb 1 <u>HURL</u>, cast, chuck (*informal*), fling, launch, lob (*informal*), pitch, send, sling, toss 2 *Informal* <u>CONFUSE</u>, astonish, baffle, confound, disconcert, dumbfound, faze ♦ noun 3 <u>TOSS</u>, fling, heave, lob (*informal*), pitch, sling

throwaway adjective <u>CASUAL</u>, careless, offhand, passing, understated

throw away verb <u>DISCARD</u>, dispense with, dispose of, ditch (*slang*), dump (*informal*), get rid of, jettison, reject, scrap, throw out

thrust verb 1 <u>PUSH</u>, drive, force, jam, plunge, propel, ram, shove ♦ noun 2 <u>PUSH</u>, drive, lunge, poke, prod, shove, stab 3 <u>MOMENTUM</u>, impetus

thud noun, verb <u>THUMP</u>, clunk, crash, knock, smack

thug noun <u>RUFFIAN</u>, bruiser (*informal*), bully boy, gangster, heavy (*slang*), hooligan, tough

thump noun 1 <u>CRASH</u>, bang, clunk, thud, thwack 2 <u>BLOW</u>, clout (*informal*), knock, punch, rap, smack, wallop (*informal*), whack ♦ verb 3 <u>STRIKE</u>, beat, clobber (*slang*), clout (*informal*), hit, knock, pound, punch, smack, wallop (*informal*), whack

thunder noun 1 <u>RUMBLE</u>, boom, crash, explosion ♦ verb 2 <u>RUMBLE</u>, boom, crash, peal, resound, reverberate, roar 3 <u>SHOUT</u>, bark, bellow, roar, yell

thunderous adjective <u>LOUD</u>, booming, deafening, ear-splitting, noisy, resounding, roaring, tumultuous

thunderstruck *adjective* AMAZED, astonished, astounded, dumbfounded, flabbergasted (*informal*), open-mouthed, shocked, staggered, stunned, taken aback

thus *adverb* **1** THEREFORE, accordingly, consequently, ergo, for this reason, hence, on that account, so, then **2** IN THIS WAY, as follows, like this, so

thwart *verb* FRUSTRATE, foil, hinder, obstruct, outwit, prevent, snooker, stymie

tick[1] *noun* **1** MARK, dash, stroke **2** TAPPING, clicking, ticktock **3** *Brit. informal* MOMENT, flash, instant, minute, second, split second, trice, twinkling ♦ *verb* **4** MARK, check off, indicate **5** TAP, click, ticktock

tick[2] *noun* CREDIT, account, the slate (*Brit. informal*)

ticket *noun* **1** VOUCHER, card, certificate, coupon, pass, slip, token **2** LABEL, card, docket, marker, slip, sticker, tab, tag

tide *noun* **1** CURRENT, ebb, flow, stream, tideway, undertow **2** TENDENCY, direction, drift, movement, trend

tidy *adjective* **1** NEAT, clean, methodical, orderly, shipshape, spruce, well-kept, well-ordered **2** *Informal* CONSIDERABLE, ample, generous, goodly, handsome, healthy, large, sizable *or* sizeable, substantial ♦ *verb* **3** NEATEN, clean, groom, order, spruce up, straighten

tie *verb* **1** FASTEN, attach, bind, connect, join, knot, link, secure, tether **2** RESTRICT, bind, confine, hamper, hinder, limit, restrain **3** DRAW, equal, match ♦ *noun* **4** BOND, affiliation, allegiance, commitment, connection, liaison, relationship **5** FASTENING, bond, cord, fetter, knot, ligature, link **6** DRAW, dead heat, deadlock, stalemate

tier *noun* ROW, bank, layer, level, line, rank, storey, stratum

tight *adjective* **1** STRETCHED, close, constricted, cramped, narrow, rigid, snug, taut **2** *Informal* MISERLY, grasping, mean, niggardly, parsimonious, stingy, tightfisted **3** CLOSE, even, evenly-balanced, well-matched **4** *Informal* DRUNK, inebriated, intoxicated, paralytic (*informal*), plastered (*slang*), tipsy, under the influence (*informal*)

tighten *verb* SQUEEZE, close, constrict, narrow

till[1] *verb* CULTIVATE, dig, plough, work

till[2] *noun* CASH REGISTER, cash box

tilt *verb* **1** SLANT, heel, incline, lean, list, slope, tip ♦ *noun* **2** SLOPE, angle, inclination, incline, list, pitch, slant **3** *Medieval history* JOUST, combat, duel, fight, lists, tournament **4 (at) full tilt** FULL SPEED, for dear life, headlong

timber *noun* WOOD, beams, boards, logs, planks, trees

timbre *noun* TONE, colour, resonance, ring

time *noun* **1** PERIOD, duration, interval, season, space, span, spell, stretch, term **2** OCCASION, instance, juncture, point, stage **3** *Music* TEMPO, beat, measure, rhythm ♦ *verb* **4** SCHEDULE, set

timeless *adjective* ETERNAL, ageless, changeless, enduring, everlasting, immortal, lasting, permanent

timely *adjective* OPPORTUNE, appropriate, convenient, judicious, propitious, seasonable, suitable, well-timed

timetable *noun* SCHEDULE, agenda, calendar, curriculum, diary, list, programme

timid *adjective* <u>FEARFUL</u>, apprehensive, bashful, coy, diffident, faint-hearted, shrinking, shy, timorous

timorous *adjective* <u>TIMID</u>, apprehensive, bashful, coy, diffident, faint-hearted, fearful, shrinking, shy

tinge *noun* 1 <u>TINT</u>, colour, shade 2 <u>BIT</u>, dash, drop, smattering, sprinkling, suggestion, touch, trace ♦ *verb* 3 <u>TINT</u>, colour, imbue, suffuse

tingle *verb* 1 <u>PRICKLE</u>, have goose pimples, itch, sting, tickle ♦ *noun* 2 <u>QUIVER</u>, goose pimples, itch, pins and needles (*informal*), prickling, shiver, thrill

tinker *verb* <u>MEDDLE</u>, dabble, fiddle (*informal*), mess about, play, potter

tint *noun* 1 <u>SHADE</u>, colour, hue, tone 2 <u>DYE</u>, rinse, tincture, tinge, wash ♦ *verb* 3 <u>DYE</u>, colour

tiny *adjective* <u>SMALL</u>, diminutive, infinitesimal, little, microscopic, miniature, minute, negligible, petite, slight

tip[1] *noun* 1 <u>END</u>, extremity, head, peak, pinnacle, point, summit, top ♦ *verb* 2 <u>CAP</u>, crown, finish, surmount, top

tip[2] *noun* 1 <u>GRATUITY</u>, gift 2 <u>HINT</u>, clue, pointer, suggestion, warning ♦ *verb* 3 <u>REWARD</u>, remunerate 4 <u>ADVISE</u>, caution, forewarn, suggest, warn

tip[3] *verb* 1 <u>TILT</u>, incline, lean, list, slant 2 <u>DUMP</u>, empty, pour out, unload ♦ *noun* 3 <u>DUMP</u>, refuse heap, rubbish heap

tipple *verb* 1 <u>DRINK</u>, imbibe, indulge (*informal*), quaff, swig, tope ♦ *noun* 2 <u>ALCOHOL</u>, booze (*informal*), drink, liquor

tirade *noun* <u>OUTBURST</u>, diatribe, fulmination, harangue, invective, lecture

tire *verb* 1 <u>FATIGUE</u>, drain, exhaust, wear out, weary 2 <u>BORE</u>, exasperate, irk, irritate, weary

tired *adjective* 1 <u>EXHAUSTED</u>, drained, drowsy, fatigued, flagging, jaded, sleepy, weary, worn out 2 <u>BORED</u>, fed up, sick, weary 3 <u>HACKNEYED</u>, clichéd, corny (*slang*), old, outworn, stale, threadbare, trite, well-worn

tireless *adjective* <u>ENERGETIC</u>, indefatigable, industrious, resolute, unflagging, untiring, vigorous

tiresome *adjective* <u>BORING</u>, dull, irksome, irritating, tedious, trying, vexatious, wearing, wearisome

tiring *adjective* <u>EXHAUSTING</u>, arduous, demanding, exacting, laborious, strenuous, tough, wearing

titbit *noun* <u>DELICACY</u>, dainty, morsel, snack, treat

titillate *verb* <u>EXCITE</u>, arouse, interest, stimulate, tantalize, tease, thrill

titillating *adjective* <u>EXCITING</u>, arousing, interesting, lurid, provocative, stimulating, suggestive, teasing

title *noun* 1 <u>NAME</u>, designation, handle (*slang*), moniker *or* monicker (*slang*), term 2 <u>CHAMPIONSHIP</u>, crown 3 <u>OWNERSHIP</u>, claim, entitlement, prerogative, privilege, right

titter *verb* <u>LAUGH</u>, chortle (*informal*), chuckle, giggle, snigger

toady *noun* 1 <u>SYCOPHANT</u>, bootlicker (*informal*), crawler (*slang*), creep (*slang*), flatterer, flunkey, hanger-on, lackey, minion, yes man ♦ *verb* 2 <u>FLATTER</u>, crawl, creep, cringe, fawn on, grovel, kowtow to, pander to, suck up to (*informal*)

toast[1] *verb* <u>WARM</u>, brown, grill, heat, roast

toast[2] *noun* **1** <u>TRIBUTE</u>, compliment, health, pledge, salutation, salute **2** <u>FAVOURITE</u>, darling, hero *or* heroine ♦ *verb* **3** <u>DRINK TO</u>, drink (to) the health of, salute

together *adverb* **1** <u>COLLECTIVELY</u>, as one, hand in glove, in concert, in unison, jointly, mutually, shoulder to shoulder, side by side **2** <u>AT THE SAME TIME</u>, at one fell swoop, concurrently, contemporaneously, simultaneously ♦ *adjective* **3** *Informal* <u>WELL-ORGANIZED</u>, composed, well-adjusted, well-balanced

toil *noun* **1** <u>HARD WORK</u>, application, drudgery, effort, elbow grease (*informal*), exertion, graft (*informal*), slog, sweat ♦ *verb* **2** <u>WORK</u>, drudge, graft (*informal*), labour, slave, slog, strive, struggle, sweat (*informal*), work one's fingers to the bone

toilet *noun* <u>LAVATORY</u>, bathroom, convenience, gents (*Brit. informal*), ladies' room, latrine, loo (*Brit. informal*), privy, urinal, water closet, W.C.

token *noun* **1** <u>SYMBOL</u>, badge, expression, indication, mark, note, representation, sign ♦ *adjective* **2** <u>NOMINAL</u>, hollow, minimal, perfunctory, superficial, symbolic

tolerable *adjective* **1** <u>BEARABLE</u>, acceptable, allowable, endurable, sufferable, supportable **2** <u>FAIR</u>, acceptable, adequate, all right, average, O.K. *or* okay (*informal*), passable

tolerance *noun* **1** <u>BROAD-MINDEDNESS</u>, forbearance, indulgence, open-mindedness, permissiveness **2** <u>ENDURANCE</u>, fortitude, hardiness, resilience, resistance, stamina, staying power, toughness

tolerant *adjective* <u>BROAD-MINDED</u>, catholic, forbearing, liberal, long-suffering, open-minded, understanding, unprejudiced

tolerate *verb* <u>ALLOW</u>, accept, brook, condone, endure, permit, put up with (*informal*), stand, stomach, take

toleration *noun* <u>ACCEPTANCE</u>, allowance, endurance, indulgence, permissiveness, sanction

toll[1] *verb* **1** <u>RING</u>, chime, clang, knell, peal, sound, strike ♦ *noun* **2** <u>RINGING</u>, chime, clang, knell, peal

toll[2] *noun* **1** <u>CHARGE</u>, duty, fee, levy, payment, tariff, tax **2** <u>DAMAGE</u>, cost, loss, penalty

tomb *noun* <u>GRAVE</u>, catacomb, crypt, mausoleum, sarcophagus, sepulchre, vault

tombstone *noun* <u>GRAVESTONE</u>, headstone, marker, memorial, monument

tomfoolery *noun* <u>FOOLISHNESS</u>, buffoonery, clowning, fooling around (*informal*), horseplay, shenanigans (*informal*), silliness, skylarking (*informal*), stupidity

tone *noun* **1** <u>PITCH</u>, inflection, intonation, modulation, timbre **2** <u>CHARACTER</u>, air, attitude, feel, manner, mood, spirit, style, temper **3** <u>COLOUR</u>, hue, shade, tinge, tint ♦ *verb* **4** <u>HARMONIZE</u>, blend, go well with, match, suit

tone down *verb* <u>MODERATE</u>, play down, reduce, restrain, soften, subdue, temper

tongue *noun* <u>LANGUAGE</u>, dialect, parlance, speech

tonic *noun* <u>STIMULANT</u>, boost, fillip, pick-me-up (*informal*), restorative, shot in the arm (*informal*)

too *adverb* **1** <u>ALSO</u>, as well, besides, further, in addition, likewise, moreover, to boot **2** <u>EXCESSIVELY</u>, extremely, immoderately, inordinately, overly, unduly, unreasonably, very

tool noun 1 IMPLEMENT, appliance, contraption, contrivance, device, gadget, instrument, machine, utensil 2 PUPPET, cat's-paw, creature, flunkey, hireling, lackey, minion, pawn, stooge (*slang*)

top noun 1 PEAK, apex, crest, crown, culmination, head, height, pinnacle, summit, zenith 2 FIRST PLACE, head, lead 3 LID, cap, cover, stopper ♦ *adjective* 4 LEADING, best, chief, elite, finest, first, foremost, head, highest, pre-eminent, principal, uppermost ♦ *verb* 5 COVER, cap, crown, finish, garnish 6 LEAD, be first, head 7 SURPASS, beat, better, eclipse, exceed, excel, outstrip, transcend

topic noun SUBJECT, issue, matter, point, question, subject matter, theme

topical adjective CURRENT, contemporary, newsworthy, popular, up-to-date, up-to-the-minute

topmost adjective HIGHEST, dominant, foremost, leading, paramount, principal, supreme, top, uppermost

topple verb 1 FALL OVER, collapse, fall, keel over, overbalance, overturn, totter, tumble 2 OVERTHROW, bring down, bring low, oust, overturn, unseat

topsy-turvy adjective CONFUSED, chaotic, disorderly, disorganized, inside-out, jumbled, messy, mixed-up, upside-down

torment verb 1 TORTURE, crucify, distress, rack 2 TEASE, annoy, bother, harass, hassle (*informal*), irritate, nag, pester, vex ♦ *noun* 3 SUFFERING, agony, anguish, distress, hell, misery, pain, torture

torn adjective 1 CUT, lacerated, ragged, rent, ripped, slit, split

2 UNDECIDED, in two minds (*informal*), irresolute, uncertain, unsure, vacillating, wavering

tornado noun WHIRLWIND, cyclone, gale, hurricane, squall, storm, tempest, typhoon

torpor noun INACTIVITY, apathy, drowsiness, indolence, laziness, lethargy, listlessness, sloth, sluggishness

torrent noun STREAM, cascade, deluge, downpour, flood, flow, rush, spate, tide

torrid adjective 1 ARID, dried, parched, scorched 2 PASSIONATE, ardent, fervent, intense, steamy (*informal*)

tortuous adjective 1 WINDING, circuitous, convoluted, indirect, mazy, meandering, serpentine, sinuous, twisting, twisty 2 COMPLICATED, ambiguous, convoluted, devious, indirect, involved, roundabout, tricky

torture verb 1 TORMENT, afflict, crucify, distress, persecute, put on the rack, rack ♦ *noun* 2 AGONY, anguish, distress, pain, persecution, suffering, torment

toss verb 1 THROW, cast, fling, flip, hurl, launch, lob (*informal*), pitch, sling 2 THRASH, rock, roll, shake, wriggle, writhe ♦ *noun* 3 THROW, lob (*informal*), pitch

tot[1] noun 1 INFANT, baby, child, mite, toddler 2 MEASURE, dram, finger, nip, shot (*informal*), slug, snifter (*informal*)

tot[2] verb ADD UP, calculate, count up, reckon, tally, total

total noun 1 WHOLE, aggregate, entirety, full amount, sum, totality ♦ *adjective* 2 COMPLETE, absolute, comprehensive, entire, full, gross, thoroughgoing, undivided, utter, whole ♦ *verb* 3 AMOUNT TO, come to, mount up to, reach 4 ADD UP, reckon, tot up

totalitarian adjective DICTATORIAL, authoritarian, despotic, oppressive, tyrannous, undemocratic

totality noun WHOLE, aggregate, entirety, sum, total

totally adverb COMPLETELY, absolutely, comprehensively, entirely, fully, one hundred per cent, thoroughly, utterly, wholly

totter verb STAGGER, falter, lurch, reel, stumble, sway

touch verb 1 HANDLE, brush, caress, contact, feel, finger, fondle, stroke, tap 2 MEET, abut, adjoin, be in contact, border, contact, graze, impinge upon 3 AFFECT, disturb, impress, influence, inspire, move, stir 4 EAT, consume, drink, partake of 5 MATCH, compare with, equal, hold a candle to (informal), parallel, rival 6 **touch on** REFER TO, allude to, bring in, cover, deal with, mention, speak of ♦ noun 7 FEELING, handling, physical contact 8 TAP, brush, contact, pat, stroke 9 BIT, dash, drop, jot, small amount, smattering, soupçon, spot, trace 10 STYLE, manner, method, technique, trademark, way

touch and go adjective RISKY, close, critical, near, nerve-racking, precarious

touching adjective MOVING, affecting, emotive, pathetic, pitiable, poignant, sad, stirring

touchstone noun STANDARD, criterion, gauge, measure, norm, par, yardstick

touchy adjective OVERSENSITIVE, irascible, irritable, querulous, quick-tempered, testy, tetchy, thin-skinned

tough adjective 1 RESILIENT, durable, hard, inflexible, leathery, resistant, rugged, solid, strong, sturdy 2 STRONG, hardy, seasoned, stout, strapping, sturdy, vigorous 3 ROUGH, hard-bitten, pugnacious, ruthless, violent 4 STRICT, firm, hard, merciless, resolute, severe, stern, unbending 5 DIFFICULT, arduous, exacting, hard, laborious, strenuous, troublesome, uphill 6 Informal UNLUCKY, lamentable, regrettable, unfortunate ♦ noun 7 RUFFIAN, bruiser (informal), bully, hooligan, roughneck (slang), thug

tour noun 1 JOURNEY, excursion, expedition, jaunt, outing, trip ♦ verb 2 VISIT, explore, go round, journey, sightsee, travel through

tourist noun TRAVELLER, excursionist, globetrotter, holiday-maker, sightseer, tripper, voyager

tournament noun COMPETITION, contest, event, meeting, series

tow verb DRAG, draw, haul, lug, pull, tug

towards preposition 1 IN THE DIRECTION OF, en route for, for, on the way to, to 2 REGARDING, about, concerning, for, with regard to, with respect to

tower noun COLUMN, belfry, obelisk, pillar, skyscraper, steeple, turret

towering adjective HIGH, colossal, elevated, imposing, impressive, lofty, magnificent, soaring, tall

toxic adjective POISONOUS, deadly, harmful, lethal, noxious, pernicious, pestilential, septic

toy noun 1 PLAYTHING, doll, game ♦ verb 2 PLAY, amuse oneself, dally, fiddle (informal), fool (about or around), trifle

trace verb 1 FIND, detect, discover, ferret out, hunt down, track, unearth 2 COPY, draw, outline, sketch ♦ noun 3 TRACK, footmark, footprint, footstep, path, spoor, trail 4 <u>BIT</u>, drop, hint, shadow, suggestion, suspicion, tinge, touch, whiff 5 <u>INDICATION</u>, evidence, mark, record, remnant, sign, survival, vestige

track *noun* 1 <u>PATH</u>, course, line, orbit, pathway, road, trajectory, way 2 <u>TRAIL</u>, footmark, footprint, footstep, mark, path, spoor, trace, wake 3 <u>LINE</u>, permanent way, rails ♦ *verb* 4 <u>FOLLOW</u>, chase, hunt down, pursue, shadow, stalk, tail (*informal*), trace, trail

track down *verb* <u>FIND</u>, dig up, discover, hunt down, run to earth *or* ground, sniff out, trace, unearth

tract[1] *noun* <u>AREA</u>, district, expanse, extent, plot, region, stretch, territory

tract[2] *noun* <u>TREATISE</u>, booklet, dissertation, essay, homily, monograph, pamphlet

tractable *adjective* <u>MANAGEABLE</u>, amenable, biddable, compliant, docile, obedient, submissive, tame, willing, yielding

traction *noun* <u>GRIP</u>, friction, pull, purchase, resistance

trade *noun* 1 <u>COMMERCE</u>, barter, business, dealing, exchange, traffic, transactions, truck 2 <u>JOB</u>, business, craft, employment, line of work, métier, occupation, profession ♦ *verb* 3 <u>DEAL</u>, bargain, do business, have dealings, peddle, traffic, transact, truck 4 <u>EXCHANGE</u>, barter, swap, switch

trader *noun* <u>DEALER</u>, merchant, purveyor, seller, supplier

tradesman *noun* 1 <u>CRAFTSMAN</u>, artisan, journeyman, workman 2 <u>SHOPKEEPER</u>, dealer, merchant, purveyor, retailer, seller, supplier, vendor

tradition *noun* <u>CUSTOM</u>, convention, folklore, habit, institution, lore, ritual

traditional *adjective* <u>CUSTOMARY</u>, accustomed, conventional, established, old, time-honoured, usual

traffic *noun* 1 <u>TRANSPORT</u>, freight, transportation, vehicles 2 <u>TRADE</u>, business, commerce, dealings, exchange, peddling, truck ♦ *verb* 3 <u>TRADE</u>, bargain, deal, do business, exchange, have dealings, peddle

tragedy *noun* <u>DISASTER</u>, adversity, calamity, catastrophe, misfortune

tragic *adjective* <u>DISASTROUS</u>, appalling, calamitous, catastrophic, deadly, dire, dreadful, miserable, pathetic, sad, unfortunate

trail *noun* 1 <u>PATH</u>, footpath, road, route, track, way 2 <u>TRACKS</u>, footprints, marks, path, scent, spoor, trace, wake ♦ *verb* 3 <u>DRAG</u>, dangle, draw, haul, pull, tow 4 <u>LAG</u>, dawdle, follow, hang back, linger, loiter, straggle, traipse (*informal*) 5 <u>FOLLOW</u>, chase, hunt, pursue, shadow, stalk, tail (*informal*), trace, track

train *verb* 1 <u>INSTRUCT</u>, coach, drill, educate, guide, prepare, school, teach, tutor 2 <u>EXERCISE</u>, prepare, work out 3 <u>AIM</u>, direct, focus, level, point ♦ *noun* 4 <u>SEQUENCE</u>, chain, progression, series, set, string, succession

trainer *noun* <u>COACH</u>, handler

training *noun* 1 <u>INSTRUCTION</u>, coaching, discipline, education, grounding, schooling, teaching, tuition 2 <u>EXERCISE</u>, practice, preparation, working out

traipse *verb* <u>TRUDGE</u>, drag oneself, footslog, slouch, trail, tramp

trait *noun* <u>CHARACTERISTIC</u>, attribute, feature, idiosyncrasy, mannerism, peculiarity, quality, quirk

traitor *noun* <u>BETRAYER</u>, apostate,

back-stabber, defector, deserter, Judas, quisling, rebel, renegade, turncoat

trajectory noun PATH, course, flight path, line, route, track

tramp verb 1 HIKE, footslog, march, ramble, roam, rove, slog, trek, walk 2 TRUDGE, plod, stump, toil, traipse (*informal*) ♦ *noun* 3 VAGRANT, derelict, down-and-out, drifter 4 HIKE, march, ramble, slog, trek 5 TREAD, footfall, footstep, stamp

trample verb CRUSH, flatten, run over, squash, stamp, tread, walk over

trance noun DAZE, abstraction, dream, rapture, reverie, stupor, unconsciousness

tranquil adjective CALM, peaceful, placid, quiet, restful, sedate, serene, still, undisturbed

tranquillity noun CALM, hush, peace, placidity, quiet, repose, rest, serenity, stillness

tranquillize verb CALM, lull, pacify, quell, quiet, relax, sedate, settle one's nerves, soothe

tranquillizer noun SEDATIVE, barbiturate, bromide, downer (*slang*), opiate

transaction noun DEAL, bargain, business, enterprise, negotiation, undertaking

transcend verb SURPASS, eclipse, exceed, excel, go beyond, outdo, outstrip, rise above

transcendent adjective UNPARALLELED, consummate, incomparable, matchless, pre-eminent, sublime, unequalled, unrivalled

transcribe verb WRITE OUT, copy out, reproduce, take down, transfer

transcript noun COPY, duplicate, manuscript, record, reproduction, transcription

transfer verb 1 MOVE, change, convey, hand over, pass on, relocate, shift, transplant, transport, transpose ♦ *noun* 2 MOVE, change, handover, relocation, shift, transference, translation, transmission, transposition

transfix verb 1 STUN, engross, fascinate, hold, hypnotize, mesmerize, paralyse 2 PIERCE, impale, puncture, run through, skewer, spear

transform verb CHANGE, alter, convert, remodel, revolutionize, transmute

transformation noun CHANGE, alteration, conversion, metamorphosis, revolution, sea change, transmutation

transgress verb OFFEND, break the law, contravene, disobey, encroach, infringe, sin, trespass, violate

transgression noun OFFENCE, contravention, crime, encroachment, infraction, infringement, misdeed, misdemeanour, sin, trespass, violation

transgressor noun OFFENDER, criminal, culprit, lawbreaker, miscreant, sinner, trespasser, villain, wrongdoer

transient adjective TEMPORARY, brief, ephemeral, fleeting, impermanent, momentary, passing, short-lived, transitory

transit noun MOVEMENT, carriage, conveyance, crossing, passage, transfer, transport, transportation

transition noun CHANGE, alteration, conversion, development, metamorphosis, passing, progression, shift, transmutation

transitional adjective CHANGING,

developmental, fluid,
intermediate, passing, provisional,
temporary, unsettled

transitory *adjective* SHORT-LIVED,
brief, ephemeral, fleeting,
impermanent, momentary,
passing, short, temporary,
transient

translate *verb* INTERPRET, construe,
convert, decipher, decode,
paraphrase, render

translation *noun* INTERPRETATION,
decoding, paraphrase, rendering,
rendition, version

transmission *noun* 1 TRANSFER,
conveyance, dissemination,
sending, shipment, spread,
transference 2 BROADCASTING,
dissemination, putting out,
relaying, sending, showing
3 PROGRAMME, broadcast, show

transmit *verb* 1 PASS ON, bear,
carry, convey, disseminate, hand
on, impart, send, spread, transfer
2 BROADCAST, disseminate, radio,
relay, send out

transparency *noun* 1 CLARITY,
clearness, limpidity, pellucidness,
translucence 2 PHOTOGRAPH, slide

transparent *adjective* 1 CLEAR,
crystalline, diaphanous, limpid,
lucid, see-through, sheer,
translucent 2 PLAIN, evident,
explicit, manifest, obvious, patent,
recognizable, unambiguous,
undisguised

transpire *verb* 1 EMERGE, become
known, come out, come to light
2 *Informal* HAPPEN, arise, befall,
chance, come about, occur, take
place

transplant *verb* TRANSFER, displace,
relocate, remove, resettle, shift,
uproot

transport *verb* 1 CONVEY, bear,
bring, carry, haul, move, take,
transfer 2 EXILE, banish, deport

3 ENRAPTURE, captivate, delight,
enchant, entrance, move, ravish
♦ *noun* 4 VEHICLE, conveyance,
transportation 5 TRANSFERENCE,
conveyance, shipment,
transportation 6 ECSTASY, bliss,
delight, enchantment, euphoria,
heaven, rapture, ravishment

transpose *verb* INTERCHANGE, alter,
change, exchange, move, reorder,
shift, substitute, swap, switch,
transfer

trap *noun* 1 SNARE, ambush, gin,
net, noose, pitfall 2 TRICK, ambush,
deception, ruse, stratagem,
subterfuge, wile ♦ *verb* 3 CATCH,
corner, enmesh, ensnare, entrap,
snare, take 4 TRICK, ambush,
beguile, deceive, dupe, ensnare,
inveigle

trappings *plural noun* ACCESSORIES,
accoutrements, equipment,
finery, furnishings, gear, panoply,
paraphernalia, things, trimmings

trash *noun* 1 NONSENSE, drivel,
hogwash, moonshine, poppycock
(*informal*), rot, rubbish, tripe
(*informal*), twaddle 2 LITTER, dross,
garbage, junk (*informal*), refuse,
rubbish, waste

trashy *adjective* WORTHLESS, cheap,
inferior, rubbishy, shabby,
shoddy, tawdry

trauma *noun* SUFFERING, agony,
anguish, hurt, ordeal, pain, shock,
torture

traumatic *adjective* SHOCKING,
agonizing, damaging, disturbing,
hurtful, injurious, painful, scarring,
upsetting, wounding

travel *verb* 1 GO, journey, move,
progress, roam, tour, trek,
voyage, wander ♦ *noun* 2 usually
plural WANDERING, excursion,
expedition, globetrotting,
journey, tour, trip, voyage

traveller *noun* WANDERER, explorer,

globetrotter, gypsy, holiday-maker, tourist, voyager, wayfarer

travelling *adjective* MOBILE, itinerant, migrant, nomadic, peripatetic, roaming, roving, touring, wandering, wayfaring

traverse *verb* CROSS, go over, span, travel over

travesty *noun* 1 MOCKERY, burlesque, caricature, distortion, lampoon, parody, perversion ♦ *verb* 2 MOCK, burlesque, caricature, distort, lampoon, make a mockery of, parody, ridicule

treacherous *adjective* 1 DISLOYAL, deceitful, double-dealing, duplicitous, faithless, false, perfidious, traitorous, unfaithful, untrustworthy 2 DANGEROUS, deceptive, hazardous, icy, perilous, precarious, risky, slippery, unreliable, unsafe, unstable

treachery *noun* BETRAYAL, disloyalty, double-dealing, duplicity, faithlessness, infidelity, perfidy, treason

tread *verb* 1 STEP, hike, march, pace, stamp, stride, walk 2 TRAMPLE, crush underfoot, squash ♦ *noun* 3 STEP, footfall, footstep, gait, pace, stride, walk

treason *noun* DISLOYALTY, duplicity, lese-majesty, mutiny, perfidy, sedition, traitorousness, treachery

treasonable *adjective* DISLOYAL, mutinous, perfidious, seditious, subversive, traitorous, treacherous

treasure *noun* 1 RICHES, cash, fortune, gold, jewels, money, valuables, wealth 2 DARLING, apple of one's eye, gem, jewel, nonpareil, paragon, pride and joy ♦ *verb* 3 PRIZE, adore, cherish, esteem, hold dear, idolize, love, revere, value

treasury *noun* STOREHOUSE, bank, cache, hoard, repository, store, vault

treat *verb* 1 HANDLE, act towards, behave towards, consider, deal with, look upon, manage, regard, use 2 ATTEND TO, care for, nurse 3 ENTERTAIN, lay on, provide, regale, stand (*informal*) ♦ *noun* 4 ENTERTAINMENT, banquet, celebration, feast, gift, party, refreshment 5 PLEASURE, delight, enjoyment, fun, joy, satisfaction, surprise, thrill

treatise *noun* ESSAY, dissertation, monograph, pamphlet, paper, study, thesis, tract, work

treatment *noun* 1 CARE, cure, healing, medication, medicine, remedy, surgery, therapy 2 HANDLING, action, behaviour, conduct, dealing, management, manipulation

treaty *noun* PACT, agreement, alliance, compact, concordat, contract, convention, covenant, entente

trek *noun* 1 JOURNEY, expedition, hike, march, odyssey, safari, slog, tramp ♦ *verb* 2 JOURNEY, footslog, hike, march, rove, slog, traipse (*informal*), tramp, trudge

tremble *verb* 1 SHAKE, quake, quiver, shiver, shudder, totter, vibrate, wobble ♦ *noun* 2 SHAKE, quake, quiver, shiver, shudder, tremor, vibration, wobble

tremendous *adjective* 1 HUGE, colossal, enormous, formidable, gigantic, great, immense, stupendous, terrific 2 *Informal* EXCELLENT, amazing, brilliant, exceptional, extraordinary, fantastic (*informal*), great, marvellous, sensational (*informal*), wonderful

tremor *noun* 1 SHAKE, quaking, quaver, quiver, shiver, trembling, wobble 2 EARTHQUAKE, quake (*informal*), shock

trench *noun* DITCH, channel, drain, excavation, furrow, gutter, trough

trenchant *adjective* 1 INCISIVE, acerbic, caustic, cutting, penetrating, pointed, pungent, scathing 2 EFFECTIVE, energetic, forceful, potent, powerful, strong, vigorous

trend *noun* 1 TENDENCY, bias, current, direction, drift, flow, inclination, leaning 2 FASHION, craze, fad (*informal*), mode, rage, style, thing, vogue

trendy *adjective* FASHIONABLE, in fashion, in vogue, modish, stylish, voguish, with it (*informal*)

trepidation *noun* ANXIETY, alarm, apprehension, consternation, disquiet, dread, fear, nervousness, uneasiness, worry

trespass *verb* 1 INTRUDE, encroach, infringe, invade, obtrude ♦ *noun* 2 INTRUSION, encroachment, infringement, invasion, unlawful entry

trespasser *noun* INTRUDER, interloper, invader, poacher

trial *noun* 1 HEARING, litigation, tribunal 2 TEST, audition, dry run (*informal*), experiment, probation, test-run 3 HARDSHIP, adversity, affliction, distress, ordeal, suffering, tribulation, trouble

tribe *noun* RACE, clan, family, people

tribunal *noun* HEARING, court, trial

tribute *noun* 1 ACCOLADE, commendation, compliment, eulogy, panegyric, recognition, testimonial 2 TAX, charge, homage, payment, ransom

trick *noun* 1 DECEPTION, fraud, hoax, manoeuvre, ploy, ruse, stratagem, subterfuge, swindle, trap, wile 2 JOKE, antic, jape, leg-pull (*Brit.*

informal), practical joke, prank, stunt 3 SECRET, hang (*informal*), knack, know-how (*informal*), skill, technique 4 MANNERISM, characteristic, foible, habit, idiosyncrasy, peculiarity, practice, quirk, trait ♦ *verb* 5 DECEIVE, cheat, con (*informal*), dupe, fool, hoodwink, kid (*informal*), mislead, swindle, take in (*informal*), trap

trickery *noun* DECEPTION, cheating, chicanery, deceit, dishonesty, guile, jiggery-pokery (*informal, chiefly Brit.*), monkey business (*informal*)

trickle *verb* 1 DRIBBLE, drip, drop, exude, ooze, run, seep, stream ♦ *noun* 2 DRIBBLE, drip, seepage

tricky *adjective* 1 DIFFICULT, complicated, delicate, knotty, problematic, risky, thorny, ticklish 2 CRAFTY, artful, cunning, deceitful, devious, scheming, slippery, sly, wily

trifle *noun* 1 KNICK-KNACK, bagatelle, bauble, plaything, toy ♦ *verb* 2 TOY, dally, mess about, play

trifling *adjective* INSIGNIFICANT, measly, negligible, paltry, trivial, unimportant, worthless

trigger *verb* SET OFF, activate, cause, generate, produce, prompt, provoke, spark off, start

trim *adjective* 1 NEAT, dapper, natty (*informal*), shipshape, smart, spruce, tidy, well-groomed 2 SLENDER, fit, shapely, sleek, slim, streamlined, svelte, willowy ♦ *verb* 3 CUT, clip, crop, even up, pare, prune, shave, tidy 4 DECORATE, adorn, array, beautify, deck out, dress, embellish, ornament ♦ *noun* 5 DECORATION, adornment, border, edging, embellishment, frill, ornamentation, piping, trimming 6 CONDITION, fettle, fitness, health, shape (*informal*), state 7 CUT, clipping, crop, pruning, shave, shearing, tidying up

trimming noun **1** <u>DECORATION</u>, adornment, border, edging, embellishment, frill, ornamentation, piping **2 trimmings** <u>EXTRAS</u>, accessories, accompaniments, frills, ornaments, paraphernalia, trappings

trinity noun <u>THREESOME</u>, triad, trio, triumvirate

trinket noun <u>ORNAMENT</u>, bagatelle, bauble, knick-knack, toy, trifle

trio noun <u>THREESOME</u>, triad, trilogy, trinity, triumvirate

trip noun **1** <u>JOURNEY</u>, errand, excursion, expedition, foray, jaunt, outing, run, tour, voyage **2** <u>STUMBLE</u>, fall, misstep, slip ♦ verb **3** <u>STUMBLE</u>, fall, lose one's footing, misstep, slip, tumble **4** <u>CATCH OUT</u>, trap **5** <u>SKIP</u>, dance, gambol, hop

triple adjective **1** <u>THREEFOLD</u>, three-way, tripartite ♦ verb **2** <u>TREBLE</u>, increase threefold

trite adjective <u>UNORIGINAL</u>, banal, clichéd, commonplace, hackneyed, stale, stereotyped, threadbare, tired

triumph noun **1** <u>JOY</u>, elation, exultation, happiness, jubilation, pride, rejoicing **2** <u>SUCCESS</u>, accomplishment, achievement, attainment, conquest, coup, feat, victory ♦ verb **3** often with over <u>WIN</u>, overcome, prevail, prosper, succeed, vanquish **4** <u>REJOICE</u>, celebrate, crow, exult, gloat, glory, revel

triumphant adjective <u>VICTORIOUS</u>, celebratory, cock-a-hoop, conquering, elated, exultant, jubilant, proud, successful, winning

trivia plural noun <u>MINUTIAE</u>, details, trifles, trivialities

trivial adjective <u>UNIMPORTANT</u>, incidental, inconsequential, insignificant, meaningless, minor, petty, small, trifling, worthless

triviality noun <u>INSIGNIFICANCE</u>, meaninglessness, pettiness, unimportance, worthlessness

trivialize verb <u>UNDERVALUE</u>, belittle, laugh off, make light of, minimize, play down, scoff at, underestimate, underplay

troop noun **1** <u>GROUP</u>, band, body, company, crowd, horde, multitude, squad, team, unit **2 troops** <u>SOLDIERS</u>, armed forces, army, men, servicemen, soldiery ♦ verb **3** <u>FLOCK</u>, march, stream, swarm, throng, traipse (informal)

trophy noun <u>PRIZE</u>, award, booty, cup, laurels, memento, souvenir, spoils

tropical adjective <u>HOT</u>, steamy, stifling, sultry, sweltering, torrid

trot verb **1** <u>RUN</u>, canter, jog, lope, scamper ♦ noun **2** <u>RUN</u>, canter, jog, lope

trouble noun **1** <u>DISTRESS</u>, anxiety, disquiet, grief, misfortune, pain, sorrow, torment, woe, worry **2** <u>DISEASE</u>, ailment, complaint, defect, disorder, failure, illness, malfunction **3** <u>DISORDER</u>, agitation, bother (informal), commotion, discord, disturbance, strife, tumult, unrest **4** <u>EFFORT</u>, care, exertion, inconvenience, labour, pains, thought, work ♦ verb **5** <u>WORRY</u>, bother, disconcert, distress, disturb, pain, perturb, plague, sadden, upset **6** <u>TAKE PAINS</u>, exert oneself, make an effort, take the time **7** <u>INCONVENIENCE</u>, bother, burden, disturb, impose upon, incommode, put out

troublesome adjective **1** <u>WORRYING</u>, annoying, demanding, difficult, inconvenient, irksome, taxing, tricky, trying, vexatious **2** <u>DISORDERLY</u>, rebellious, rowdy, turbulent, uncooperative, undisciplined, unruly, violent

trough *noun* 1 MANGER, water trough 2 CHANNEL, canal, depression, ditch, duct, furrow, gully, gutter, trench

trounce *verb* THRASH, beat, crush, drub, give a hiding (*informal*), hammer (*informal*), rout, slaughter (*informal*), wipe the floor with (*informal*)

troupe *noun* COMPANY, band, cast

truancy *noun* ABSENCE, absence without leave, malingering, shirking, skiving (*Brit. slang*)

truant *noun* ABSENTEE, malingerer, runaway, shirker, skiver (*Brit. slang*)

truce *noun* CEASEFIRE, armistice, cessation, let-up (*informal*), lull, moratorium, peace, respite

truculent *adjective* HOSTILE, aggressive, bellicose, belligerent, defiant, ill-tempered, obstreperous, pugnacious

trudge *verb* 1 PLOD, footslog, lumber, slog, stump, traipse (*informal*), tramp, trek ♦ *noun* 2 HIKE, footslog, march, slog, traipse (*informal*), tramp, trek

true *adjective* 1 CORRECT, accurate, authentic, factual, genuine, precise, real, right, truthful, veracious 2 FAITHFUL, dedicated, devoted, dutiful, loyal, reliable, staunch, steady, trustworthy 3 EXACT, accurate, on target, perfect, precise, spot-on (*Brit. informal*), unerring

truism *noun* CLICHÉ, axiom, bromide, commonplace, platitude

truly *adverb* 1 CORRECTLY, authentically, exactly, factually, genuinely, legitimately, precisely, rightly, truthfully 2 FAITHFULLY, devotedly, dutifully, loyally, sincerely, staunchly, steadily 3 REALLY, extremely, greatly,

indeed, of course, very

trumpet *noun* 1 HORN, bugle, clarion ♦ *verb* 2 PROCLAIM, advertise, announce, broadcast, shout from the rooftops, tout (*informal*)

trump up *verb* FABRICATE, concoct, contrive, cook up (*informal*), create, fake, invent, make up

truncate *verb* SHORTEN, abbreviate, curtail, cut short, dock, lop, pare, prune, trim

truncheon *noun* CLUB, baton, cudgel, staff

trunk *noun* 1 STEM, bole, stalk 2 CHEST, box, case, casket, coffer, crate 3 BODY, torso 4 SNOUT, proboscis

truss *verb* 1 TIE, bind, fasten, make fast, secure, strap, tether ♦ *noun* 2 *Medical* SUPPORT, bandage 3 JOIST, beam, brace, buttress, prop, stanchion, stay, strut, support

trust *verb* 1 BELIEVE IN, bank on, count on, depend on, have faith in, rely upon 2 CONSIGN, assign, commit, confide, delegate, entrust, give 3 EXPECT, assume, hope, presume, suppose, surmise ♦ *noun* 4 CONFIDENCE, assurance, belief, certainty, conviction, credence, credit, expectation, faith, reliance

trustful, trusting *adjective* UNWARY, credulous, gullible, naive, unsuspecting, unsuspicious

trustworthy *adjective* HONEST, dependable, honourable, principled, reliable, reputable, responsible, staunch, steadfast, trusty

trusty *adjective* FAITHFUL, dependable, reliable, solid, staunch, steady, strong, trustworthy

truth *noun* TRUTHFULNESS, accuracy, exactness, fact, genuineness, legitimacy, precision, reality, validity, veracity

truthful *adjective* <u>HONEST</u>, candid, frank, precise, sincere, straight, true, trustworthy

try *verb* 1 <u>ATTEMPT</u>, aim, endeavour, have a go, make an effort, seek, strive, struggle 2 <u>TEST</u>, appraise, check out, evaluate, examine, investigate, put to the test, sample, taste ♦ *noun* 3 <u>ATTEMPT</u>, crack (*informal*), effort, go (*informal*), shot (*informal*), stab (*informal*), whack (*informal*)

trying *adjective* <u>ANNOYING</u>, bothersome, difficult, exasperating, hard, stressful, taxing, tiresome, tough, wearisome

tubby *adjective* <u>FAT</u>, chubby, corpulent, obese, overweight, plump, portly, stout

tuck *verb* 1 <u>PUSH</u>, fold, gather, insert ♦ *noun* 2 <u>FOLD</u>, gather, pinch, pleat 3 *Informal* <u>FOOD</u>, grub (*slang*), nosh (*slang*)

tuft *noun* <u>CLUMP</u>, bunch, cluster, collection, knot, tussock

tug *verb* 1 <u>PULL</u>, jerk, wrench, yank ♦ *noun* 2 <u>PULL</u>, jerk, yank

tuition *noun* <u>TRAINING</u>, education, instruction, lessons, schooling, teaching, tutelage, tutoring

tumble *verb* 1 <u>FALL</u>, drop, flop, plummet, stumble, topple ♦ *noun* 2 <u>FALL</u>, drop, plunge, spill, stumble, trip

tumbledown *adjective* <u>DILAPIDATED</u>, crumbling, decrepit, ramshackle, rickety, ruined

tumour *noun* <u>GROWTH</u>, cancer, carcinoma (*Pathology*), lump, sarcoma (*Medical*), swelling

tumult *noun* <u>COMMOTION</u>, clamour, din, hubbub, pandemonium, riot, row, turmoil, upheaval, uproar

tumultuous *adjective* <u>WILD</u>, boisterous, excited, noisy, riotous, rowdy, turbulent, unruly, uproarious

tune *noun* 1 <u>MELODY</u>, air, song, strain, theme 2 <u>PITCH</u>, concord, consonance, euphony, harmony ♦ *verb* 3 <u>ADJUST</u>, adapt, attune, harmonize, pitch, regulate

tuneful *adjective* <u>MELODIOUS</u>, catchy, euphonious, harmonious, mellifluous, melodic, musical, pleasant

tuneless *adjective* <u>DISCORDANT</u>, atonal, cacophonous, dissonant, harsh, unmusical

tunnel *noun* 1 <u>PASSAGE</u>, burrow, channel, hole, passageway, shaft, subway, underpass ♦ *verb* 2 <u>DIG</u>, burrow, excavate, mine, scoop out

turbulence *noun* <u>CONFUSION</u>, agitation, commotion, disorder, instability, tumult, turmoil, unrest, upheaval

turbulent *adjective* <u>AGITATED</u>, blustery, choppy, foaming, furious, raging, rough, tempestuous, tumultuous

turf *noun* 1 <u>GRASS</u>, sod, sward 2 **the turf** <u>HORSE-RACING</u>, racing, the flat

turmoil *noun* <u>CONFUSION</u>, agitation, chaos, commotion, disarray, disorder, tumult, upheaval, uproar

turn *verb* 1 <u>CHANGE COURSE</u>, move, shift, swerve, switch, veer, wheel 2 <u>ROTATE</u>, circle, go round, gyrate, pivot, revolve, roll, spin, twist, whirl 3 <u>CHANGE</u>, alter, convert, mould, mutate, remodel, shape, transform 4 <u>SHAPE</u>, fashion, frame, make, mould 5 <u>GO BAD</u>, curdle, go off (*Brit. informal*), sour, spoil, taint ♦ *noun* 6 <u>ROTATION</u>, circle, cycle, gyration, revolution, spin, twist, whirl 7 <u>SHIFT</u>, departure, deviation 8 <u>OPPORTUNITY</u>, chance, crack (*informal*), go, stint, time, try 9 <u>DIRECTION</u>, drift, heading, tendency, trend **10** *As in* **good turn** ACT, action, deed, favour, gesture, service

turncoat *noun* TRAITOR, apostate, backslider, defector, deserter, renegade

turn down *verb* **1** LOWER, lessen, muffle, mute, quieten, soften **2** REFUSE, decline, rebuff, reject, repudiate, spurn

turn in *verb* **1** GO TO BED, go to sleep, hit the sack (*slang*) **2** HAND IN, deliver, give up, hand over, return, submit, surrender, tender

turning *noun* JUNCTION, bend, crossroads, curve, side road, turn, turn-off

turning point *noun* CROSSROADS, change, crisis, crux, moment of truth

turn off *verb* STOP, cut out, put out, shut down, switch off, turn out, unplug

turn on *verb* **1** START, activate, ignite, kick-start, start up, switch on **2** ATTACK, assail, assault, fall on, round on **3** *Informal* EXCITE, arouse, attract, please, stimulate, thrill, titillate

turnout *noun* ATTENDANCE, assembly, audience, congregation, crowd, gate, number, throng

turnover *noun* **1** OUTPUT, business, productivity **2** MOVEMENT, change, coming and going

turn up *verb* **1** ARRIVE, appear, attend, come, put in an appearance, show one's face, show up (*informal*) **2** FIND, dig up, disclose, discover, expose, reveal, unearth **3** COME TO LIGHT, crop up (*informal*), pop up **4** INCREASE, amplify, boost, enhance, intensify, raise

tussle *noun* **1** FIGHT, battle, brawl, conflict, contest, scrap (*informal*), scuffle, struggle ◆ *verb* **2** FIGHT,

battle, grapple, scrap (*informal*), scuffle, struggle, vie, wrestle

tutor *noun* **1** TEACHER, coach, educator, guardian, guide, guru, instructor, lecturer, mentor ◆ *verb* **2** TEACH, coach, drill, educate, guide, instruct, school, train

twaddle *noun* NONSENSE, claptrap (*informal*), drivel, garbage (*informal*), gobbledegook (*informal*), poppycock (*informal*), rubbish, waffle (*informal, chiefly Brit.*)

tweak *verb, noun* TWIST, jerk, pinch, pull, squeeze

twig *noun* BRANCH, shoot, spray, sprig, stick

twilight *noun* DUSK, dimness, evening, gloaming (*Scot. or poetic*), gloom, half-light, sundown, sunset

twin *noun* **1** DOUBLE, clone, counterpart, duplicate, fellow, likeness, lookalike, match, mate ◆ *verb* **2** PAIR, couple, join, link, match, yoke

twine *noun* **1** STRING, cord, yarn ◆ *verb* **2** COIL, bend, curl, encircle, loop, spiral, twist, wind

twinge *noun* PAIN, pang, prick, spasm, stab, stitch

twinkle *verb* **1** SPARKLE, blink, flash, flicker, gleam, glint, glisten, glitter, shimmer, shine ◆ *noun* **2** FLICKER, flash, gleam, glimmer, shimmer, spark, sparkle

twirl *verb* **1** TURN, pirouette, pivot, revolve, rotate, spin, twist, wheel, whirl, wind ◆ *noun* **2** TURN, pirouette, revolution, rotation, spin, twist, wheel, whirl

twist *verb* **1** WIND, coil, curl, screw, spin, swivel, wrap, wring **2** DISTORT, contort, screw up ◆ *noun* **3** WIND, coil, curl, spin, swivel **4** DEVELOPMENT, change, revelation, slant, surprise, turn, variation

5 <u>CURVE</u>, arc, bend, meander, turn, undulation, zigzag **6** <u>DISTORTION</u>, defect, deformation, flaw, imperfection, kink, warp

twit noun <u>FOOL</u>, ass, chump (*informal*), halfwit, idiot, nincompoop, numbskull *or* numskull, prat (*slang*), twerp *or* twirp (*informal*)

twitch verb **1** <u>JERK</u>, flutter, jump, squirm ♦ noun **2** <u>SPASM</u>, flutter, jerk, jump, tic

two-faced adjective <u>HYPOCRITICAL</u>, deceitful, dissembling, duplicitous, false, insincere, treacherous, untrustworthy

tycoon noun <u>MAGNATE</u>, baron, capitalist, fat cat (*slang, chiefly U.S.*), financier, industrialist, mogul, plutocrat

type noun <u>CATEGORY</u>, class, genre, group, kind, order, sort, species, style, variety

typhoon noun <u>STORM</u>, cyclone, squall, tempest, tornado

typical adjective <u>CHARACTERISTIC</u>, archetypal, average, model, normal, orthodox, representative, standard, stock, usual

typify verb <u>SYMBOLIZE</u>, characterize, embody, epitomize, exemplify, illustrate, personify, represent, sum up

tyrannical adjective <u>OPPRESSIVE</u>, authoritarian, autocratic, cruel, despotic, dictatorial, domineering, high-handed, imperious, overbearing, tyrannous

tyranny noun <u>OPPRESSION</u>, absolutism, authoritarianism, autocracy, cruelty, despotism, dictatorship, high-handedness, imperiousness

tyrant noun <u>DICTATOR</u>, absolutist, authoritarian, autocrat, bully, despot, martinet, oppressor, slave-driver

U u

ubiquitous *adjective* EVERYWHERE, ever-present, omnipresent, pervasive, universal

ugly *adjective* 1 UNATTRACTIVE, homely (*chiefly U.S.*), ill-favoured, plain, unlovely, unprepossessing, unsightly 2 UNPLEASANT, disagreeable, distasteful, horrid, objectionable, shocking, terrible 3 OMINOUS, baleful, dangerous, menacing, sinister

ulcer *noun* SORE, abscess, boil, gumboil, peptic ulcer, pustule

ulterior *adjective* HIDDEN, concealed, covert, secret, undisclosed

ultimate *adjective* 1 FINAL, end, last 2 SUPREME, extreme, greatest, highest, paramount, superlative, utmost

ultimately *adverb* FINALLY, after all, at last, eventually, in due time, in the end, sooner or later

umpire *noun* 1 REFEREE, arbiter, arbitrator, judge ♦ *verb* 2 REFEREE, adjudicate, arbitrate, judge

unabashed *adjective* UNEMBARRASSED, blatant, bold, brazen

unable *adjective* INCAPABLE, impotent, ineffectual, powerless, unfit, unqualified

unabridged *adjective* UNCUT, complete, full-length, unexpurgated, whole

unacceptable *adjective* UNSATISFACTORY, displeasing, objectionable

unaccompanied *adjective* 1 ALONE, by oneself, lone, on one's own, solo, unescorted 2 *Music* A CAPPELLA

unaccountable *adjective* 1 INEXPLICABLE, baffling, mysterious, odd, puzzling, unexplainable, unfathomable 2 NOT ANSWERABLE, exempt, not responsible

unaccustomed *adjective* 1 UNFAMILIAR, new, strange, unwonted 2 **unaccustomed to** NOT USED TO, inexperienced at, unfamiliar with, unused to

unaffected[1] *adjective* NATURAL, artless, genuine, plain, simple, sincere, unpretentious

unaffected[2] *adjective* IMPERVIOUS, proof, unmoved, unresponsive, untouched

unafraid *adjective* FEARLESS, daring, dauntless, intrepid

unalterable *adjective* UNCHANGEABLE, fixed, immutable, permanent

unanimity *noun* AGREEMENT, accord, assent, concord, concurrence, consensus, harmony, like-mindedness, unison

unanimous *adjective* AGREED, common, concerted, harmonious, in agreement, like-minded, united

unanimously *adverb* WITHOUT EXCEPTION, nem. con., with one accord

unanswerable *adjective* CONCLUSIVE, absolute, incontestable, incontrovertible, indisputable

unanswered *adjective* UNRESOLVED, disputed, open, undecided

unappetizing *adjective* UNPLEASANT, distasteful, off-putting (*Brit. informal*), repulsive, unappealing, unattractive, unpalatable

unapproachable *adjective* 1 UNFRIENDLY, aloof, chilly, cool, distant, remote, reserved, standoffish 2 INACCESSIBLE, out of reach, remote

unarmed *adjective* <u>DEFENCELESS</u>, exposed, helpless, open, unprotected, weak

unassailable *adjective* <u>IMPREGNABLE</u>, invincible, invulnerable, secure

unassuming *adjective* <u>MODEST</u>, humble, quiet, reserved, retiring, self-effacing, unassertive, unobtrusive, unpretentious

unattached *adjective* 1 <u>FREE</u>, independent 2 <u>SINGLE</u>, available, not spoken for, unengaged, unmarried

unattended *adjective* 1 <u>ABANDONED</u>, unguarded, unwatched 2 <u>ALONE</u>, on one's own, unaccompanied

unauthorized *adjective* <u>ILLEGAL</u>, unlawful, unofficial, unsanctioned

unavoidable *adjective* <u>INEVITABLE</u>, certain, fated, inescapable

unaware *adjective* <u>IGNORANT</u>, oblivious, unconscious, uninformed, unknowing

unawares *adverb* 1 <u>BY SURPRISE</u>, off guard, suddenly, unexpectedly 2 <u>UNKNOWINGLY</u>, accidentally, by accident, inadvertently, unwittingly

unbalanced *adjective* 1 <u>BIASED</u>, one-sided, partial, partisan, prejudiced, unfair 2 <u>SHAKY</u>, lopsided, uneven, unstable, wobbly 3 <u>DERANGED</u>, crazy, demented, disturbed, eccentric, insane, irrational, mad, *non compos mentis*, not all there, unhinged, unstable

unbearable *adjective* <u>INTOLERABLE</u>, insufferable, too much (*informal*), unacceptable

unbeatable *adjective* <u>INVINCIBLE</u>, indomitable

unbeaten *adjective* <u>UNDEFEATED</u>, triumphant, victorious

unbecoming *adjective* 1 <u>UNSIGHTLY</u>, unattractive, unbefitting, unflattering, unsuitable 2 <u>UNSEEMLY</u>, discreditable, improper, offensive

unbelievable *adjective* <u>INCREDIBLE</u>, astonishing, far-fetched, implausible, impossible, improbable, inconceivable, preposterous, unconvincing

unbending *adjective* <u>INFLEXIBLE</u>, firm, intractable, resolute, rigid, severe, strict, stubborn, tough, uncompromising

unbiased *adjective* <u>FAIR</u>, disinterested, equitable, impartial, just, neutral, objective, unprejudiced

unblemished *adjective* <u>SPOTLESS</u>, flawless, immaculate, impeccable, perfect, pure, untarnished

unborn *adjective* <u>EXPECTED</u>, awaited, embryonic

unbreakable *adjective* <u>INDESTRUCTIBLE</u>, durable, lasting, rugged, strong

unbridled *adjective* <u>UNRESTRAINED</u>, excessive, intemperate, licentious, riotous, unchecked, unruly, wanton

unbroken *adjective* 1 <u>INTACT</u>, complete, entire, whole 2 <u>CONTINUOUS</u>, constant, incessant, uninterrupted

unburden *verb* <u>CONFESS</u>, confide, disclose, get (something) off one's chest (*informal*), reveal

uncalled-for *adjective* <u>UNJUSTIFIED</u>, gratuitous, needless, undeserved, unnecessary, unwarranted

uncanny *adjective* 1 <u>WEIRD</u>, mysterious, strange, supernatural, unearthly, unnatural 2 <u>EXTRAORDINARY</u>, astounding, exceptional, incredible, miraculous, remarkable, unusual

unceasing *adjective* <u>CONTINUAL</u>,

constant, continuous, endless, incessant, nonstop, perpetual

uncertain adjective 1 UNPREDICTABLE, doubtful, indefinite, questionable, risky, speculative 2 UNSURE, dubious, hazy, irresolute, unclear, unconfirmed, undecided, vague

uncertainty noun DOUBT, ambiguity, confusion, dubiety, hesitancy, indecision, unpredictability

unchangeable adjective UNALTERABLE, constant, fixed, immutable, invariable, irreversible, permanent, stable

unchanging adjective CONSTANT, continuing, enduring, eternal, immutable, lasting, permanent, perpetual, unvarying

uncharitable adjective UNKIND, cruel, hardhearted, unfeeling, ungenerous

uncharted adjective UNEXPLORED, strange, undiscovered, unfamiliar, unknown

uncivil adjective IMPOLITE, bad-mannered, discourteous, ill-mannered, rude, unmannerly

uncivilized adjective 1 PRIMITIVE, barbarian, savage, wild 2 UNCOUTH, boorish, coarse, philistine, uncultivated, uneducated

unclean adjective DIRTY, corrupt, defiled, evil, filthy, foul, impure, polluted, soiled, stained

unclear adjective 1 INDISTINCT, blurred, dim, faint, fuzzy, hazy, obscure, shadowy, undefined, vague 2 DOUBTFUL, ambiguous, indefinite, indeterminate, vague

uncomfortable adjective 1 AWKWARD, cramped, painful, rough 2 UNEASY, awkward, discomfited, disturbed, embarrassed, troubled

uncommitted adjective UNINVOLVED,

floating, free, neutral, nonaligned, not involved, unattached

uncommon adjective 1 RARE, infrequent, novel, odd, peculiar, queer, scarce, strange, unusual 2 EXTRAORDINARY, distinctive, exceptional, notable, outstanding, remarkable, special

uncommonly adverb 1 RARELY, hardly ever, infrequently, occasionally, seldom 2 EXCEPTIONALLY, particularly, very

uncommunicative adjective RETICENT, close, reserved, secretive, silent, taciturn, tight-lipped, unforthcoming

uncompromising adjective INFLEXIBLE, firm, inexorable, intransigent, rigid, strict, tough, unbending

unconcern noun INDIFFERENCE, aloofness, apathy, detachment, lack of interest, nonchalance

unconcerned adjective INDIFFERENT, aloof, apathetic, cool, detached, dispassionate, distant, uninterested, unmoved

unconditional adjective ABSOLUTE, complete, entire, full, outright, positive, total, unlimited, unqualified, unreserved

unconnected adjective 1 SEPARATE, detached, divided 2 MEANINGLESS, disjointed, illogical, incoherent, irrelevant

unconscious adjective 1 SENSELESS, insensible, knocked out, out, out cold, stunned 2 UNAWARE, ignorant, oblivious, unknowing 3 UNINTENTIONAL, accidental, inadvertent, unwitting

uncontrollable adjective WILD, frantic, furious, mad, strong, unruly, violent

uncontrolled adjective UNRESTRAINED, rampant, riotous, unbridled, unchecked, undisciplined

unconventional *adjective* <u>UNUSUAL</u>, eccentric, individual, irregular, nonconformist, odd, offbeat, original, outré, unorthodox

unconvincing *adjective* <u>IMPLAUSIBLE</u>, dubious, feeble, flimsy, improbable, lame, questionable, suspect, thin, unlikely, weak

uncooperative *adjective* <u>UNHELPFUL</u>, awkward, difficult, disobliging, obstructive

uncoordinated *adjective* <u>CLUMSY</u>, awkward, bungling, graceless, lumbering, maladroit, ungainly, ungraceful

uncouth *adjective* <u>COARSE</u>, boorish, crude, graceless, ill-mannered, loutish, oafish, rough, rude, vulgar

uncover *verb* 1 <u>REVEAL</u>, disclose, divulge, expose, make known 2 <u>OPEN</u>, bare, show, strip, unwrap

uncritical *adjective* <u>UNDISCRIMINATING</u>, indiscriminate, undiscerning

undecided *adjective* 1 <u>UNSURE</u>, dithering (*chiefly Brit.*), hesitant, in two minds, irresolute, torn, uncertain 2 <u>UNSETTLED</u>, debatable, iffy (*informal*), indefinite, moot, open, unconcluded, undetermined

undefined *adjective* 1 <u>UNSPECIFIED</u>, imprecise, inexact, unclear 2 <u>INDISTINCT</u>, formless, indefinite, vague

undeniable *adjective* <u>CERTAIN</u>, clear, incontrovertible, indisputable, obvious, sure, unquestionable

under *preposition* 1 <u>BELOW</u>, beneath, underneath 2 <u>SUBJECT TO</u>, governed by, secondary to, subordinate to ♦ *adverb* 3 <u>BELOW</u>, beneath, down, lower

underclothes *plural noun* <u>UNDERWEAR</u>, lingerie, undergarments, undies (*informal*)

undercover *adjective* <u>SECRET</u>, concealed, covert, hidden, private

undercurrent *noun* 1 <u>UNDERTOW</u>, riptide 2 <u>UNDERTONE</u>, atmosphere, feeling, hint, overtone, sense, suggestion, tendency, tinge, vibes (*slang*)

underdog *noun* <u>OUTSIDER</u>, little fellow (*informal*)

underestimate *verb* <u>UNDERRATE</u>, belittle, minimize, miscalculate, undervalue

undergo *verb* <u>EXPERIENCE</u>, bear, endure, go through, stand, suffer, sustain

underground *adjective* 1 <u>SUBTERRANEAN</u>, buried, covered 2 <u>SECRET</u>, clandestine, covert, hidden ♦ *noun* 3 **the underground: a** <u>THE RESISTANCE</u>, partisans **b** <u>THE TUBE</u> (*Brit.*), the metro, the subway

undergrowth *noun* <u>SCRUB</u>, bracken, briars, brush, underbrush

underhand *adjective* <u>SLY</u>, crafty, deceitful, devious, dishonest, furtive, secret, sneaky, stealthy

underline *verb* 1 <u>UNDERSCORE</u>, mark 2 <u>EMPHASIZE</u>, accentuate, highlight, stress

underlying *adjective* <u>FUNDAMENTAL</u>, basic, elementary, intrinsic, primary, prime

undermine *verb* <u>WEAKEN</u>, disable, sabotage, sap, subvert

underprivileged *adjective* <u>DISADVANTAGED</u>, deprived, destitute, impoverished, needy, poor

underrate *verb* <u>UNDERESTIMATE</u>, belittle, discount, undervalue

undersized *adjective* <u>STUNTED</u>, dwarfish, miniature, pygmy *or* pigmy, small

understand *verb* 1 <u>COMPREHEND</u>, conceive, fathom, follow, get, grasp, perceive, realize, see, take in 2 BELIEVE, assume, gather, presume, suppose, think

understandable *adjective* REASONABLE, justifiable, legitimate, natural, to be expected

understanding *noun* 1 PERCEPTION, appreciation, awareness, comprehension, discernment, grasp, insight, judgment, knowledge, sense 2 INTERPRETATION, belief, idea, judgment, notion, opinion, perception, view 3 AGREEMENT, accord, pact ♦ *adjective* 4 SYMPATHETIC, compassionate, considerate, kind, patient, sensitive, tolerant

understood *adjective* 1 IMPLIED, implicit, inferred, tacit, unspoken, unstated 2 ASSUMED, accepted, taken for granted

understudy *noun* STAND-IN, replacement, reserve, substitute

undertake *verb* AGREE, bargain, contract, engage, guarantee, pledge, promise

undertaking *noun* 1 TASK, affair, attempt, business, effort, endeavour, enterprise, operation, project, venture 2 PROMISE, assurance, commitment, pledge, vow, word

undertone *noun* 1 MURMUR, whisper 2 UNDERCURRENT, hint, suggestion, tinge, touch, trace

undervalue *verb* UNDERRATE, depreciate, hold cheap, minimize, misjudge, underestimate

underwater *adjective* SUBMERGED, submarine, sunken

under way *adjective* BEGUN, going on, in progress, started

underwear *noun* UNDERCLOTHES, lingerie, undergarments, underthings, undies (*informal*)

underweight *adjective* SKINNY,

emaciated, half-starved, puny, skin and bone (*informal*), undernourished, undersized

underworld *noun* 1 CRIMINALS, gangland (*informal*), gangsters, organized crime 2 NETHER WORLD, Hades, nether regions

underwrite *verb* 1 FINANCE, back, fund, guarantee, insure, sponsor, subsidize 2 SIGN, endorse, initial

undesirable *adjective* OBJECTIONABLE, disagreeable, distasteful, unacceptable, unattractive, unsuitable, unwanted, unwelcome

undeveloped *adjective* POTENTIAL, immature, latent

undignified *adjective* UNSEEMLY, improper, indecorous, inelegant, unbecoming, unsuitable

undisciplined *adjective* UNCONTROLLED, obstreperous, unrestrained, unruly, wayward, wild, wilful

undisguised *adjective* OBVIOUS, blatant, evident, explicit, open, overt, patent, unconcealed

undisputed *adjective* ACKNOWLEDGED, accepted, certain, indisputable, recognized, unchallenged, undeniable, undoubted

undistinguished *adjective* ORDINARY, everyday, mediocre, run-of-the-mill, unexceptional, unimpressive, unremarkable

undisturbed *adjective* 1 QUIET, tranquil 2 CALM, collected, composed, placid, sedate, serene, tranquil, unfazed (*informal*), unperturbed, untroubled

undivided *adjective* COMPLETE, entire, exclusive, full, solid, thorough, undistracted, united, whole

undo *verb* 1 OPEN, disentangle, loose, unbutton, unfasten, untie

2 REVERSE, annul, cancel, invalidate, neutralize, offset **3** RUIN, defeat, destroy, overturn, quash, shatter, subvert, undermine, upset, wreck

undoing noun DOWNFALL, collapse, defeat, disgrace, overthrow, reversal, ruin, shame

undone adjective UNFINISHED, left, neglected, omitted, unfulfilled, unperformed

undoubted adjective CERTAIN, acknowledged, definite, indisputable, indubitable, sure, undisputed, unquestioned

undoubtedly adverb CERTAINLY, assuredly, definitely, doubtless, surely, without doubt

undress verb **1** STRIP, disrobe, shed, take off one's clothes ♦ noun **2** NAKEDNESS, nudity

undue adjective EXCESSIVE, extreme, improper, needless, uncalled-for, unnecessary, unwarranted

unduly adverb EXCESSIVELY, overly, unnecessarily, unreasonably

undying adjective ETERNAL, constant, deathless, everlasting, infinite, permanent, perpetual, unending

unearth verb **1** DISCOVER, expose, find, reveal, uncover **2** DIG UP, dredge up, excavate, exhume

unearthly adjective EERIE, ghostly, phantom, spectral, spooky (informal), strange, supernatural, uncanny, weird

uneasiness noun ANXIETY, disquiet, doubt, misgiving, qualms, trepidation, worry

uneasy adjective **1** ANXIOUS, disturbed, edgy, nervous, on edge, perturbed, troubled, twitchy (informal), uncomfortable, worried **2** AWKWARD, insecure, precarious, shaky, strained, tense, uncomfortable

uneconomic adjective UNPROFITABLE,

loss-making, nonpaying

uneducated adjective **1** IGNORANT, illiterate, unschooled, untaught **2** LOWBROW, uncultivated, uncultured

unemotional adjective IMPASSIVE, apathetic, cold, cool, phlegmatic, reserved, undemonstrative, unexcitable

unemployed adjective OUT OF WORK, idle, jobless, laid off, redundant

unending adjective PERPETUAL, continual, endless, eternal, everlasting, interminable, unceasing

unendurable adjective UNBEARABLE, insufferable, insupportable, intolerable

unenthusiastic adjective INDIFFERENT, apathetic, half-hearted, nonchalant

unenviable adjective UNPLEASANT, disagreeable, uncomfortable, undesirable

unequal adjective **1** DIFFERENT, differing, disparate, dissimilar, unlike, unmatched, varying **2** DISPROPORTIONATE, asymmetrical, ill-matched, irregular, unbalanced, uneven

unequalled adjective INCOMPARABLE, matchless, paramount, peerless, supreme, unparalleled, unrivalled

unequivocal adjective CLEAR, absolute, certain, definite, explicit, incontrovertible, indubitable, manifest, plain, unambiguous

unerring adjective ACCURATE, exact, infallible, perfect, sure, unfailing

unethical adjective DISHONEST, disreputable, illegal, immoral, improper, shady (informal), unprincipled, unscrupulous, wrong

uneven adjective **1** ROUGH, bumpy **2** VARIABLE, broken, fitful, irregular, jerky, patchy, spasmodic

3 UNBALANCED, lopsided, odd
4 UNEQUAL, ill-matched, unfair

uneventful *adjective* HUMDRUM, boring, dull, ho-hum (*informal*), monotonous, routine, tedious, unexciting

unexceptional *adjective* ORDINARY, commonplace, conventional, mediocre, normal, pedestrian, run-of-the-mill, undistinguished, unremarkable

unexpected *adjective* UNFORESEEN, abrupt, chance, fortuitous, sudden, surprising, unanticipated, unlooked-for, unpredictable

unfailing *adjective* 1 CONTINUOUS, boundless, endless, persistent, unflagging 2 RELIABLE, certain, dependable, faithful, loyal, staunch, sure, true

unfair *adjective* 1 BIASED, bigoted, one-sided, partial, partisan, prejudiced, unjust 2 UNSCRUPULOUS, dishonest, unethical, unsporting, wrongful

unfaithful *adjective* 1 FAITHLESS, adulterous, two-timing (*informal*), untrue 2 DISLOYAL, deceitful, faithless, false, traitorous, treacherous, untrustworthy

unfamiliar *adjective* STRANGE, alien, different, new, novel, unknown, unusual

unfashionable *adjective* PASSÉ, antiquated, dated, obsolete, old-fashioned, old hat

unfasten *verb* UNDO, detach, let go, loosen, open, separate, untie

unfathomable *adjective* 1 BAFFLING, deep, impenetrable, incomprehensible, indecipherable, inexplicable, profound 2 IMMEASURABLE, bottomless, unmeasured

unfavourable *adjective* 1 ADVERSE, contrary, inauspicious, unfortunate, unlucky,
unpropitious 2 HOSTILE, inimical, negative, unfriendly

unfeeling *adjective* 1 HARDHEARTED, apathetic, callous, cold, cruel, heartless, insensitive, pitiless, uncaring 2 NUMB, insensate, insensible

unfinished *adjective* 1 INCOMPLETE, half-done, uncompleted, undone 2 ROUGH, bare, crude, natural, raw, unrefined

unfit *adjective* 1 INCAPABLE, inadequate, incompetent, no good, unqualified, useless 2 UNSUITABLE, inadequate, ineffective, unsuited, useless 3 OUT OF SHAPE, feeble, flabby, in poor condition, unhealthy

unflappable *adjective* IMPERTURBABLE, calm, collected, composed, cool, impassive, level-headed, self-possessed

unflattering *adjective* 1 BLUNT, candid, critical, honest 2 UNATTRACTIVE, plain, unbecoming

unflinching *adjective* DETERMINED, firm, immovable, resolute, staunch, steadfast, steady, unfaltering

unfold *verb* 1 OPEN, expand, spread out, undo, unfurl, unravel, unroll, unwrap 2 REVEAL, disclose, divulge, make known, present, show, uncover

unforeseen *adjective* UNEXPECTED, accidental, sudden, surprising, unanticipated, unpredicted

unforgettable *adjective* MEMORABLE, exceptional, impressive, notable

unforgivable *adjective* INEXCUSABLE, deplorable, disgraceful, shameful, unpardonable

unfortunate *adjective* 1 DISASTROUS, adverse, calamitous, ill-fated 2 UNLUCKY, cursed, doomed, hapless, unhappy, unsuccessful, wretched 3 REGRETTABLE, deplorable, lamentable, unsuitable

unfounded *adjective* GROUNDLESS, baseless, false, idle, spurious, unjustified

unfriendly *adjective* 1 HOSTILE, aloof, chilly, cold, distant, uncongenial, unsociable 2 UNFAVOURABLE, alien, hostile, inhospitable

ungainly *adjective* AWKWARD, clumsy, inelegant, lumbering, ungraceful

ungodly *adjective* 1 *Informal* UNREASONABLE, dreadful, intolerable, outrageous, unearthly 2 WICKED, corrupt, depraved, godless, immoral, impious, irreligious, profane, sinful

ungracious *adjective* BAD-MANNERED, churlish, discourteous, impolite, rude, uncivil, unmannerly

ungrateful *adjective* UNAPPRECIATIVE, unmindful, unthankful

unguarded *adjective* 1 UNPROTECTED, defenceless, undefended, vulnerable 2 CARELESS, heedless, ill-considered, imprudent, incautious, rash, thoughtless, unthinking, unwary

unhappiness *noun* SADNESS, blues, dejection, depression, despondency, gloom, heartache, low spirits, melancholy, misery, sorrow, wretchedness

unhappy *adjective* 1 SAD, blue, dejected, depressed, despondent, downcast, melancholy, miserable, mournful, sorrowful 2 UNLUCKY, cursed, hapless, ill-fated, unfortunate, wretched

unharmed *adjective* UNHURT, intact, safe, sound, undamaged, unscathed, whole

unhealthy *adjective* 1 HARMFUL, detrimental, insalubrious, insanitary, unwholesome 2 SICK, ailing, delicate, feeble, frail, infirm, invalid, sickly, unwell

unheard-of *adjective* 1 UNPRECEDENTED, inconceivable, new, novel, singular, unique 2 SHOCKING, disgraceful, outrageous, preposterous 3 OBSCURE, unfamiliar, unknown

unhesitating *adjective* 1 INSTANT, immediate, prompt, ready 2 WHOLEHEARTED, resolute, unfaltering, unquestioning, unreserved

unholy *adjective* EVIL, corrupt, profane, sinful, ungodly, wicked

unhurried *adjective* LEISURELY, easy, sedate, slow

unidentified *adjective* UNNAMED, anonymous, nameless, unfamiliar, unrecognized

unification *noun* UNION, alliance, amalgamation, coalescence, coalition, confederation, federation, uniting

uniform *noun* 1 OUTFIT, costume, dress, garb, habit, livery, regalia, suit ♦ *adjective* 2 UNVARYING, consistent, constant, even, regular, smooth, unchanging 3 ALIKE, equal, like, same, similar

uniformity *noun* 1 REGULARITY, constancy, evenness, invariability, sameness, similarity 2 MONOTONY, dullness, flatness, sameness, tedium

unify *verb* UNITE, amalgamate, combine, confederate, consolidate, join, merge

unimaginable *adjective* INCONCEIVABLE, fantastic, impossible, incredible, unbelievable

unimaginative *adjective* UNORIGINAL, banal, derivative, dull, hackneyed, ordinary, pedestrian, predictable, prosaic, uncreative, uninspired

unimportant *adjective*

INSIGNIFICANT, inconsequential, irrelevant, minor, paltry, petty, trifling, trivial, worthless

uninhabited *adjective* DESERTED, barren, desolate, empty, unpopulated, vacant

uninhibited *adjective*
1 UNSELFCONSCIOUS, free, liberated, natural, open, relaxed, spontaneous, unrepressed, unreserved 2 UNRESTRAINED, free, unbridled, unchecked, unconstrained, uncontrolled, unrestricted

uninspired *adjective* UNIMAGINATIVE, banal, dull, humdrum, ordinary, prosaic, unexciting, unoriginal

unintelligent *adjective* STUPID, braindead (*informal*), brainless, dense, dull, foolish, gormless (*Brit. informal*), obtuse, slow, thick

unintelligible *adjective* INCOMPREHENSIBLE, inarticulate, incoherent, indistinct, jumbled, meaningless, muddled

unintentional *adjective* ACCIDENTAL, casual, inadvertent, involuntary, unconscious, unintended

uninterested *adjective* INDIFFERENT, apathetic, blasé, bored, listless, unconcerned

uninteresting *adjective* BORING, drab, dreary, dry, dull, flat, humdrum, monotonous, tedious, unexciting

uninterrupted *adjective* CONTINUOUS, constant, nonstop, steady, sustained, unbroken

union *noun* 1 JOINING, amalgamation, blend, combination, conjunction, fusion, mixture, uniting 2 ALLIANCE, association, coalition, confederacy, federation, league 3 AGREEMENT, accord, concord, harmony, unanimity, unison, unity

unique *adjective* 1 SINGLE, lone,

only, solitary 2 UNPARALLELED, incomparable, inimitable, matchless, unequalled, unmatched, unrivalled

unison *noun* AGREEMENT, accord, concert, concord, harmony, unity

unit *noun* 1 ITEM, entity, whole 2 PART, component, constituent, element, member, section, segment 3 SECTION, detachment, group 4 MEASURE, measurement, quantity

unite *verb* 1 JOIN, amalgamate, blend, combine, couple, fuse, link, merge, unify 2 COOPERATE, ally, band, join forces, pool

united *adjective* 1 COMBINED, affiliated, allied, banded together, collective, concerted, pooled, unified 2 IN AGREEMENT, agreed, of one mind, of the same opinion, unanimous

unity *noun* 1 WHOLENESS, entity, integrity, oneness, singleness, union 2 AGREEMENT, accord, assent, concord, consensus, harmony, solidarity, unison

universal *adjective* WIDESPREAD, common, general, total, unlimited, whole, worldwide

universally *adverb* EVERYWHERE, always, invariably, without exception

universe *noun* COSMOS, creation, macrocosm, nature

unjust *adjective* UNFAIR, biased, one-sided, partial, partisan, prejudiced, wrong, wrongful

unjustifiable *adjective* INEXCUSABLE, indefensible, outrageous, unacceptable, unforgivable, unpardonable, wrong

unkempt *adjective* 1 UNCOMBED, shaggy, tousled 2 UNTIDY, dishevelled, disordered, messy, scruffy, slovenly, ungroomed

unkind *adjective* CRUEL, harsh, malicious, mean, nasty, spiteful, uncharitable, unfeeling, unfriendly, unsympathetic

unknown *adjective* 1 HIDDEN, concealed, dark, mysterious, secret, unrevealed 2 STRANGE, alien, new 3 UNIDENTIFIED, anonymous, nameless, uncharted, undiscovered, unexplored, unnamed 4 OBSCURE, humble, unfamiliar

unlawful *adjective* ILLEGAL, banned, criminal, forbidden, illicit, outlawed, prohibited

unleash *verb* RELEASE, free, let go, let loose

unlike *adjective* DIFFERENT, dissimilar, distinct, diverse, not alike, opposite, unequal

unlikely *adjective* 1 IMPROBABLE, doubtful, faint, remote, slight 2 UNBELIEVABLE, implausible, incredible, questionable

unlimited *adjective* 1 INFINITE, boundless, countless, endless, extensive, great, immense, limitless, unbounded, vast 2 COMPLETE, absolute, full, total, unqualified, unrestricted

unload *verb* EMPTY, discharge, dump, lighten, relieve, unpack

unlock *verb* OPEN, release, undo, unfasten, unlatch

unlooked-for *adjective* UNEXPECTED, chance, fortuitous, surprising, unanticipated, unforeseen, unpredicted

unloved *adjective* NEGLECTED, forsaken, loveless, rejected, spurned, unpopular, unwanted

unlucky *adjective* 1 UNFORTUNATE, cursed, hapless, luckless, miserable, unhappy, wretched 2 ILL-FATED, doomed, inauspicious, ominous, unfavourable

unmarried *adjective* SINGLE, bachelor, maiden, unattached, unwed

unmask *verb* REVEAL, disclose, discover, expose, lay bare, uncover

unmentionable *adjective* TABOO, forbidden, indecent, obscene, scandalous, shameful, shocking, unspeakable

unmerciful *adjective* MERCILESS, brutal, cruel, hard, implacable, pitiless, remorseless, ruthless

unmistakable *adjective* CLEAR, certain, distinct, evident, manifest, obvious, plain, sure, unambiguous

unmitigated *adjective* 1 UNRELIEVED, intense, persistent, unalleviated, unbroken, undiminished 2 COMPLETE, absolute, arrant, downright, outright, sheer, thorough, utter

unmoved *adjective* UNAFFECTED, cold, impassive, indifferent, unimpressed, unresponsive, untouched

unnatural *adjective* 1 STRANGE, extraordinary, freakish, outlandish, queer 2 ABNORMAL, anomalous, irregular, odd, perverse, perverted, unusual 3 FALSE, affected, artificial, feigned, forced, insincere, phoney *or* phony (*informal*), stiff, stilted

unnecessary *adjective* NEEDLESS, expendable, inessential, redundant, superfluous, unneeded, unrequired

unnerve *verb* INTIMIDATE, demoralize, discourage, dishearten, dismay, faze, fluster, frighten, psych out (*informal*), rattle (*informal*), shake, upset

unnoticed *adjective* UNOBSERVED, disregarded, ignored, neglected, overlooked, unheeded, unperceived, unrecognized, unseen

unobtrusive *adjective*
INCONSPICUOUS, low-key, modest,
quiet, restrained, retiring,
self-effacing, unassuming

unoccupied *adjective* EMPTY,
uninhabited, vacant

unofficial *adjective* UNAUTHORIZED,
informal, private, unconfirmed

unorthodox *adjective*
UNCONVENTIONAL, abnormal,
irregular, off-the-wall (*slang*),
unusual

unpaid *adjective* 1 VOLUNTARY,
honorary, unsalaried 2 OWING, due,
outstanding, overdue, payable,
unsettled

unpalatable *adjective* UNPLEASANT,
disagreeable, distasteful, horrid,
offensive, repugnant,
unappetizing, unsavoury

unparalleled *adjective* UNEQUALLED,
incomparable, matchless,
superlative, unique, unmatched,
unprecedented, unsurpassed

unpardonable *adjective*
UNFORGIVABLE, deplorable,
disgraceful, indefensible,
inexcusable

unperturbed *adjective* CALM, as
cool as a cucumber, composed,
cool, placid, unfazed (*informal*),
unruffled, untroubled, unworried

unpleasant *adjective* NASTY, bad,
disagreeable, displeasing,
distasteful, horrid, objectionable

unpopular *adjective* DISLIKED,
rejected, shunned, unwanted,
unwelcome

unprecedented *adjective*
EXTRAORDINARY, abnormal, new,
novel, original, remarkable,
singular, unheard-of

unpredictable *adjective*
INCONSTANT, chance, changeable,
doubtful, erratic, random,
unforeseeable, unreliable, variable

unprejudiced *adjective* IMPARTIAL,
balanced, fair, just, objective,
open-minded, unbiased

unprepared *adjective* 1 TAKEN OFF
GUARD, surprised, unaware,
unready 2 IMPROVISED, ad-lib, off
the cuff (*informal*), spontaneous

unpretentious *adjective* MODEST,
humble, plain, simple,
straightforward, unaffected,
unassuming, unostentatious

unprincipled *adjective* DISHONEST,
amoral, crooked, devious,
immoral, underhand, unethical,
unscrupulous

unproductive *adjective* 1 USELESS,
fruitless, futile, idle, ineffective,
unprofitable, unrewarding, vain
2 BARREN, fruitless, sterile

unprofessional *adjective*
1 UNETHICAL, improper, lax,
negligent, unprincipled
2 AMATEURISH, cowboy (*informal*),
incompetent, inefficient, inexpert

unprotected *adjective* VULNERABLE,
defenceless, helpless, open,
undefended

unqualified *adjective* 1 UNFIT,
ill-equipped, incapable,
incompetent, ineligible,
unprepared 2 TOTAL, absolute,
complete, downright, outright,
thorough, utter

unquestionable *adjective* CERTAIN,
absolute, clear, conclusive,
definite, incontrovertible,
indisputable, sure, undeniable,
unequivocal, unmistakable

unravel *verb* 1 UNDO, disentangle,
free, separate, untangle, unwind
2 SOLVE, explain, figure out
(*informal*), resolve, work out

unreal *adjective* 1 IMAGINARY,
dreamlike, fabulous, fanciful,
illusory, make-believe, visionary
2 INSUBSTANTIAL, immaterial,
intangible, nebulous 3 FAKE,

artificial, false, insincere, mock, pretended, sham

unrealistic *adjective* IMPRACTICAL, impracticable, improbable, romantic, unworkable

unreasonable *adjective* **1** EXCESSIVE, extortionate, immoderate, undue, unfair, unjust, unwarranted **2** BIASED, blinkered, opinionated

unrelated *adjective* **1** DIFFERENT, unconnected, unlike **2** IRRELEVANT, extraneous, inapplicable, inappropriate, unconnected

unreliable *adjective* **1** UNDEPENDABLE, irresponsible, treacherous, untrustworthy **2** UNCERTAIN, deceptive, fallible, false, implausible, inaccurate, unsound

unrepentant *adjective* IMPENITENT, abandoned, callous, hardened, incorrigible, shameless, unremorseful

unreserved *adjective* **1** TOTAL, absolute, complete, entire, full, unlimited, wholehearted **2** OPEN, demonstrative, extrovert, free, outgoing, uninhibited, unrestrained

unresolved *adjective* UNDECIDED, doubtful, moot, unanswered, undetermined, unsettled, unsolved, vague

unrest *noun* DISCONTENT, agitation, discord, dissension, protest, rebellion, sedition, strife

unrestrained *adjective* UNCONTROLLED, abandoned, free, immoderate, intemperate, unbounded, unbridled, unchecked, uninhibited

unrestricted *adjective* **1** UNLIMITED, absolute, free, open, unbounded, unregulated **2** OPEN, public

unrivalled *adjective* UNPARALLELED, beyond compare, incomparable, matchless, supreme, unequalled, unmatched, unsurpassed

unruly *adjective* UNCONTROLLABLE, disobedient, mutinous, rebellious, wayward, wild, wilful

unsafe *adjective* DANGEROUS, hazardous, insecure, perilous, risky, unreliable

unsatisfactory *adjective* UNACCEPTABLE, deficient, disappointing, inadequate, insufficient, not good enough, not up to scratch (*informal*), poor

unsavoury *adjective* **1** UNPLEASANT, distasteful, nasty, obnoxious, offensive, repellent, repulsive, revolting **2** UNAPPETIZING, nauseating, sickening, unpalatable

unscathed *adjective* UNHARMED, safe, unhurt, uninjured, unmarked, whole

unscrupulous *adjective* UNPRINCIPLED, corrupt, dishonest, dishonourable, immoral, improper, unethical

unseat *verb* **1** THROW, unhorse, unsaddle **2** DEPOSE, dethrone, displace, oust, overthrow, remove

unseemly *adjective* IMPROPER, inappropriate, indecorous, unbecoming, undignified, unsuitable

unseen *adjective* UNOBSERVED, concealed, hidden, invisible, obscure, undetected, unnoticed

unselfish *adjective* GENEROUS, altruistic, kind, magnanimous, noble, selfless, self-sacrificing

unsettle *verb* DISTURB, agitate, bother, confuse, disconcert, faze, fluster, perturb, ruffle, trouble, upset

unsettled *adjective* **1** UNSTABLE, disorderly, insecure, shaky, unsteady **2** RESTLESS, agitated, anxious, confused, disturbed, flustered, restive, shaken, tense **3** CHANGING, inconstant, uncertain, variable

unshakable adjective FIRM, absolute, fixed, immovable, staunch, steadfast, sure, unswerving, unwavering

unsightly adjective UGLY, disagreeable, hideous, horrid, repulsive, unattractive

unskilled adjective UNPROFESSIONAL, amateurish, cowboy (informal), inexperienced, unqualified, untrained

unsociable adjective UNFRIENDLY, chilly, cold, distant, hostile, retiring, unforthcoming, withdrawn

unsolicited adjective UNREQUESTED, gratuitous, unasked for, uncalled-for, uninvited, unsought

unsophisticated adjective 1 NATURAL, artless, childlike, guileless, ingenuous, unaffected 2 SIMPLE, plain, uncomplicated, unrefined, unspecialized

unsound adjective 1 UNHEALTHY, ailing, defective, diseased, ill, unbalanced, unstable, unwell, weak 2 UNRELIABLE, defective, fallacious, false, flawed, illogical, shaky, specious, weak

unspeakable adjective 1 INDESCRIBABLE, inconceivable, unbelievable, unimaginable 2 DREADFUL, abominable, appalling, awful, heinous, horrible, monstrous, shocking

unspoiled, unspoilt adjective 1 PERFECT, intact, preserved, unchanged, undamaged, untouched 2 NATURAL, artless, innocent, unaffected

unspoken adjective TACIT, implicit, implied, understood, unexpressed, unstated

unstable adjective 1 INSECURE, precarious, shaky, tottering, unsettled, unsteady, wobbly 2 CHANGEABLE, fitful, fluctuating,

inconstant, unpredictable, variable, volatile 3 UNPREDICTABLE, capricious, changeable, erratic, inconsistent, irrational, temperamental

unsteady adjective 1 UNSTABLE, infirm, insecure, precarious, shaky, unsafe, wobbly 2 CHANGEABLE, erratic, inconstant, temperamental, unsettled, volatile

unsuccessful adjective 1 USELESS, failed, fruitless, futile, unavailing, unproductive, vain 2 UNLUCKY, hapless, luckless, unfortunate

unsuitable adjective INAPPROPRIATE, improper, inapposite, inapt, ineligible, unacceptable, unbecoming, unfit, unfitting, unseemly

unsure adjective 1 UNCONFIDENT, insecure, unassured 2 DOUBTFUL, distrustful, dubious, hesitant, mistrustful, sceptical, suspicious, unconvinced

unsuspecting adjective TRUSTING, credulous, gullible, trustful, unwary

unswerving adjective CONSTANT, firm, resolute, single-minded, staunch, steadfast, steady, true, unwavering

unsympathetic adjective HARD, callous, cold, cruel, harsh, heartless, insensitive, unfeeling, unkind, unmoved

untangle verb DISENTANGLE, extricate, unravel, unsnarl

untenable adjective UNSUSTAINABLE, groundless, illogical, indefensible, insupportable, shaky, unsound, weak

unthinkable adjective 1 IMPOSSIBLE, absurd, out of the question, unreasonable 2 INCONCEIVABLE, implausible, incredible, unimaginable

untidy adjective MESSY, chaotic,

cluttered, disarrayed, disordered, jumbled, littered, muddled, shambolic, unkempt

untie verb UNDO, free, loosen, release, unbind, unfasten, unlace

untimely adjective 1 EARLY, premature 2 ILL-TIMED, awkward, inappropriate, inconvenient, inopportune, mistimed

untiring adjective TIRELESS, constant, determined, dogged, persevering, steady, unflagging, unremitting

untold adjective 1 INDESCRIBABLE, inexpressible, undreamed of, unimaginable, unthinkable, unutterable 2 COUNTLESS, incalculable, innumerable, myriad, numberless, uncountable

untouched adjective UNHARMED, intact, undamaged, unhurt, uninjured, unscathed

untoward adjective 1 ANNOYING, awkward, inconvenient, irritating, troublesome, unfortunate 2 UNLUCKY, adverse, inauspicious, inopportune, unfavourable

untrained adjective AMATEUR, green, inexperienced, raw, uneducated, unqualified, unschooled, unskilled, untaught

untroubled adjective UNDISTURBED, calm, cool, peaceful, placid, tranquil, unfazed (informal), unperturbed, unworried

untrue adjective 1 FALSE, deceptive, dishonest, erroneous, inaccurate, incorrect, lying, mistaken, wrong 2 UNFAITHFUL, deceitful, disloyal, faithless, false, inconstant, treacherous, untrustworthy

untrustworthy adjective UNRELIABLE, deceitful, devious, dishonest, disloyal, false, slippery, treacherous, tricky

untruth noun LIE, deceit, falsehood, fib, pork pie (Brit. slang), porky (Brit. slang), story

untruthful adjective DISHONEST, deceitful, deceptive, false, lying, mendacious

unusual adjective EXTRAORDINARY, curious, different, exceptional, odd, queer, rare, remarkable, singular, strange, uncommon, unconventional

unveil verb REVEAL, disclose, divulge, expose, make known, uncover

unwanted adjective UNDESIRED, outcast, rejected, uninvited, unneeded, unsolicited, unwelcome

unwarranted adjective UNNECESSARY, gratuitous, groundless, indefensible, inexcusable, uncalled-for, unjustified, unprovoked

unwavering adjective STEADY, consistent, determined, immovable, resolute, staunch, steadfast, unshakable, unswerving

unwelcome adjective 1 UNWANTED, excluded, rejected, unacceptable, undesirable 2 DISAGREEABLE, displeasing, distasteful, undesirable, unpleasant

unwell adjective ILL, ailing, sick, sickly, under the weather (informal), unhealthy

unwholesome adjective 1 HARMFUL, deleterious, noxious, poisonous, unhealthy 2 WICKED, bad, corrupting, degrading, demoralizing, evil, immoral

unwieldy adjective 1 AWKWARD, cumbersome, inconvenient, unmanageable 2 BULKY, clumsy, hefty, massive, ponderous

unwilling adjective RELUCTANT, averse, disinclined, grudging, indisposed, loath, resistant, unenthusiastic

unwind verb 1 UNRAVEL, slacken, uncoil, undo, unroll, untwine, untwist 2 RELAX, loosen up, take it easy, wind down

unwise *adjective* <u>FOOLISH</u>, foolhardy, improvident, imprudent, inadvisable, injudicious, rash, reckless, senseless, silly, stupid

unwitting *adjective* **1** <u>UNINTENTIONAL</u>, accidental, chance, inadvertent, involuntary, unplanned **2** <u>UNKNOWING</u>, ignorant, innocent, unaware, unconscious, unsuspecting

unworldly *adjective* **1** <u>SPIRITUAL</u>, metaphysical, nonmaterialistic **2** <u>NAIVE</u>, idealistic, innocent, unsophisticated

unworthy *adjective* **1** <u>UNDESERVING</u>, not fit for, not good enough **2** <u>DISHONOURABLE</u>, base, contemptible, degrading, discreditable, disgraceful, disreputable, ignoble, shameful **3 unworthy of** <u>UNBEFITTING</u>, beneath, inappropriate, unbecoming, unfitting, unseemly, unsuitable

unwritten *adjective* **1** <u>ORAL</u>, vocal **2** <u>CUSTOMARY</u>, accepted, tacit, understood

unyielding *adjective* <u>FIRM</u>, adamant, immovable, inflexible, obdurate, obstinate, resolute, rigid, stiff-necked, stubborn, tough, uncompromising

upbeat *adjective Informal* <u>CHEERFUL</u>, cheery, encouraging, hopeful, optimistic, positive

upbraid *verb* <u>SCOLD</u>, admonish, berate, rebuke, reprimand, reproach, reprove

upbringing *noun* <u>EDUCATION</u>, breeding, raising, rearing, training

update *verb* <u>REVISE</u>, amend, bring up to date, modernize, renew

upgrade *verb* <u>PROMOTE</u>, advance, better, elevate, enhance, improve, raise

upheaval *noun* <u>DISTURBANCE</u>, disorder, disruption, revolution, turmoil

uphill *adjective* **1** <u>ASCENDING</u>, climbing, mounting, rising **2** <u>ARDUOUS</u>, difficult, exhausting, gruelling, hard, laborious, strenuous, taxing, tough

uphold *verb* <u>SUPPORT</u>, advocate, aid, back, champion, defend, endorse, maintain, promote, sustain

upkeep *noun* **1** <u>MAINTENANCE</u>, keep, repair, running, subsistence **2** <u>OVERHEADS</u>, expenditure, expenses, running costs

uplift *verb* **1** <u>RAISE</u>, elevate, hoist, lift up **2** <u>IMPROVE</u>, advance, better, edify, inspire, raise, refine ♦ *noun* **3** <u>IMPROVEMENT</u>, advancement, edification, enhancement, enlightenment, enrichment, refinement

upper *adjective* **1** <u>HIGHER</u>, high, loftier, top, topmost **2** <u>SUPERIOR</u>, eminent, greater, important

upper-class *adjective* <u>ARISTOCRATIC</u>, blue-blooded, highborn, high-class, noble, patrician

upper hand *noun* <u>CONTROL</u>, advantage, ascendancy, edge, mastery, supremacy

uppermost *adjective* **1** <u>TOP</u>, highest, loftiest, topmost **2** <u>SUPREME</u>, chief, dominant, foremost, greatest, leading, main, principal

uppity *adjective Informal* <u>CONCEITED</u>, bumptious, cocky, full of oneself, impertinent, self-important, uppish (*Brit. informal*)

upright *adjective* **1** <u>VERTICAL</u>, erect, perpendicular, straight **2** <u>HONEST</u>, conscientious, ethical, good, honourable, just, principled, righteous, virtuous

uprising *noun* <u>REBELLION</u>, disturbance, insurgence, insurrection, mutiny, revolt, revolution, rising

uproar noun COMMOTION, din, furore, mayhem, noise, outcry, pandemonium, racket, riot, turmoil

uproarious adjective **1** HILARIOUS, hysterical, killing (*informal*), rib-tickling, rip-roaring (*informal*), side-splitting, very funny **2** LOUD, boisterous, rollicking, unrestrained

uproot verb **1** PULL UP, dig up, rip up, root out, weed out **2** DISPLACE, exile

upset adjective **1** SICK, ill, queasy **2** DISTRESSED, agitated, bothered, dismayed, disturbed, grieved, hurt, put out, troubled, worried **3** DISORDERED, chaotic, confused, disarrayed, in disarray, muddled **4** OVERTURNED, capsized, spilled, upside down ◆ *verb* **5** TIP OVER, capsize, knock over, overturn, spill **6** MESS UP, change, disorder, disorganize, disturb, spoil **7** DISTRESS, agitate, bother, disconcert, disturb, faze, fluster, grieve, perturb, ruffle, trouble ◆ *noun* **8** REVERSAL, defeat, shake-up (*informal*) **9** ILLNESS, bug (*informal*), complaint, disorder, malady, sickness **10** DISTRESS, agitation, bother, disturbance, shock, trouble, worry

upshot noun RESULT, culmination, end, end result, finale, outcome, sequel

upside down adjective **1** INVERTED, overturned, upturned **2** *Informal* CONFUSED, chaotic, disordered, higgledy-piggledy (*informal*), muddled, topsy-turvy

upstanding adjective HONEST, ethical, good, honourable, incorruptible, moral, principled, upright

upstart noun SOCIAL CLIMBER, arriviste, *nouveau riche*, parvenu

uptight adjective *Informal* TENSE, anxious, edgy, on edge, uneasy,

wired (*slang*)

up-to-date adjective MODERN, current, fashionable, in vogue, stylish, trendy (*Brit. informal*), up-to-the-minute

upturn noun RISE, advancement, improvement, increase, recovery, revival, upsurge, upswing

urban adjective CIVIC, city, metropolitan, municipal, town

urbane adjective SOPHISTICATED, courteous, cultivated, cultured, debonair, polished, refined, smooth, suave, well-bred

urchin noun RAGAMUFFIN, brat, gamin, waif

urge noun **1** IMPULSE, compulsion, desire, drive, itch, longing, thirst, wish, yearning ◆ *verb* **2** BEG, beseech, entreat, exhort, implore, plead **3** ADVOCATE, advise, counsel, recommend, support **4** DRIVE, compel, force, goad, impel, incite, induce, press, push, spur

urgency noun IMPORTANCE, extremity, gravity, hurry, necessity, need, pressure, seriousness

urgent adjective CRUCIAL, compelling, critical, immediate, imperative, important, pressing

usable adjective SERVICEABLE, available, current, functional, practical, utilizable, valid, working

usage noun **1** USE, control, employment, handling, management, operation, running **2** PRACTICE, convention, custom, habit, method, mode, procedure, regime, routine

use verb **1** EMPLOY, apply, exercise, exert, operate, practise, utilize, work **2** TAKE ADVANTAGE OF, exploit, manipulate **3** CONSUME, exhaust, expend, run through, spend ◆ *noun* **4** USAGE, application, employment, exercise, handling,

operation, practice, service
5 GOOD, advantage, avail, benefit,
help, point, profit, service,
usefulness, value **6** PURPOSE, end,
object, reason

used *adjective* SECOND-HAND, cast-off,
nearly new, shopsoiled

used to *adjective* ACCUSTOMED TO,
familiar with

useful *adjective* HELPFUL,
advantageous, beneficial,
effective, fruitful, practical,
profitable, serviceable, valuable,
worthwhile

usefulness *noun* HELPFULNESS,
benefit, convenience,
effectiveness, efficacy, practicality,
use, utility, value, worth

useless *adjective* **1** WORTHLESS,
fruitless, futile, impractical,
ineffectual, pointless,
unproductive, vain, valueless
2 *Informal* INEPT, hopeless,
incompetent, ineffectual, no good

use up *verb* CONSUME, absorb, drain,
exhaust, finish, run through

usher *noun* **1** ATTENDANT,
doorkeeper, doorman, escort,
guide ♦ *verb* **2** ESCORT, conduct,
direct, guide, lead

usual *adjective* NORMAL, common,
customary, everyday, general,
habitual, ordinary, regular,
routine, standard, typical

usually *adverb* NORMALLY, as a rule,

commonly, generally, habitually,
mainly, mostly, on the whole

usurp *verb* SEIZE, appropriate,
assume, commandeer, take, take
over, wrest

utility *noun* USEFULNESS, benefit,
convenience, efficacy, practicality,
serviceableness

utilize *verb* USE, avail oneself of,
employ, make use of, put to use,
take advantage of, turn to account

utmost *adjective* **1** GREATEST, chief,
highest, maximum, paramount,
pre-eminent, supreme **2** FARTHEST,
extreme, final, last ♦ *noun*
3 GREATEST, best, hardest, highest

Utopia *noun* PARADISE, bliss, Eden,
Garden of Eden, heaven,
Shangri-la

Utopian *adjective* PERFECT, dream,
fantasy, ideal, idealistic,
imaginary, romantic, visionary

utter[1] *verb* EXPRESS, articulate,
pronounce, say, speak, voice

utter[2] *adjective* ABSOLUTE, complete,
downright, outright, sheer,
thorough, total, unmitigated

utterance *noun* SPEECH,
announcement, declaration,
expression, remark, statement,
words

utterly *adverb* TOTALLY, absolutely,
completely, entirely, extremely,
fully, perfectly, thoroughly

V v

vacancy *noun* <u>JOB</u>, opening, opportunity, position, post, situation

vacant *adjective* **1** <u>UNOCCUPIED</u>, available, empty, free, idle, unfilled, untenanted, void **2** <u>VAGUE</u>, absent-minded, abstracted, blank, dreamy, idle, inane, vacuous

vacate *verb* <u>LEAVE</u>, evacuate, quit

vacuous *adjective* <u>UNINTELLIGENT</u>, blank, inane, stupid, uncomprehending, vacant

vacuum *noun* <u>EMPTINESS</u>, gap, nothingness, space, vacuity, void

vagabond *noun* <u>BEGGAR</u>, down-and-out, itinerant, rover, tramp, vagrant

vagrant *noun* **1** <u>TRAMP</u>, drifter, hobo (*U.S.*), itinerant, rolling stone, wanderer ♦ *adjective* **2** <u>ITINERANT</u>, nomadic, roaming, rootless, roving, unsettled, vagabond

vague *adjective* <u>UNCLEAR</u>, hazy, ill-defined, imprecise, indefinite, indeterminate, indistinct, loose, nebulous, uncertain, unspecified

vain *adjective* **1** <u>PROUD</u>, arrogant, conceited, egotistical, narcissistic, self-important, swaggering **2** <u>FUTILE</u>, abortive, fruitless, idle, pointless, senseless, unavailing, unprofitable, useless, worthless ♦ *noun* **3 in vain** <u>TO NO AVAIL</u>, fruitless(ly), ineffectual(ly), unsuccessful(ly), useless(ly), vain(ly)

valiant *adjective* <u>BRAVE</u>, bold, courageous, fearless, gallant, heroic, intrepid, lion-hearted

valid *adjective* **1** <u>LOGICAL</u>, cogent, convincing, good, sound, telling, well-founded, well-grounded **2** <u>LEGAL</u>, authentic, bona fide, genuine, lawful, legitimate, official

validate *verb* <u>CONFIRM</u>, authenticate, authorize, certify, corroborate, endorse, ratify, substantiate

validity *noun* **1** <u>SOUNDNESS</u>, cogency, force, power, strength, weight **2** <u>LEGALITY</u>, authority, lawfulness, legitimacy, right

valley *noun* <u>HOLLOW</u>, dale, dell, depression, glen, vale

valour *noun* <u>BRAVERY</u>, boldness, courage, fearlessness, gallantry, heroism, intrepidity, spirit

valuable *adjective* **1** <u>PRECIOUS</u>, costly, dear, expensive, high-priced **2** <u>USEFUL</u>, beneficial, helpful, important, prized, profitable, worthwhile ♦ *noun* **3 valuables** <u>TREASURES</u>, heirlooms

value *noun* **1** <u>IMPORTANCE</u>, advantage, benefit, desirability, merit, profit, usefulness, utility, worth **2** <u>COST</u>, market price, rate **3 values** <u>PRINCIPLES</u>, ethics, (moral) standards ♦ *verb* **4** <u>EVALUATE</u>, appraise, assess, estimate, price, rate, set at **5** <u>RESPECT</u>, appreciate, cherish, esteem, hold dear, prize, regard highly, treasure

vandal *noun* <u>HOOLIGAN</u>, delinquent, rowdy, yob *or* yobbo (*Brit. slang*)

vanguard *noun* <u>FORERUNNERS</u>, cutting edge, forefront, front line, leaders, spearhead, trailblazers, trendsetters, van

vanish *verb* <u>DISAPPEAR</u>, dissolve, evanesce, evaporate, fade (away), melt (away)

vanity *noun* <u>PRIDE</u>, arrogance, conceit, conceitedness, egotism, narcissism

vanquish *verb Literary* <u>DEFEAT</u>, beat,

conquer, crush, master, overcome, overpower, overwhelm, triumph over

vapid *adjective* <u>DULL</u>, bland, boring, flat, insipid, tame, uninspiring, uninteresting, weak, wishy-washy (*informal*)

vapour *noun* <u>MIST</u>, exhalation, fog, haze, steam

variable *adjective* <u>CHANGEABLE</u>, flexible, fluctuating, inconstant, mutable, shifting, temperamental, uneven, unstable, unsteady

variance *noun* **at variance** <u>IN DISAGREEMENT</u>, at loggerheads, at odds, at sixes and sevens (*informal*), conflicting, out of line

variant *adjective* 1 <u>DIFFERENT</u>, alternative, divergent, modified ♦ *noun* 2 <u>VARIATION</u>, alternative, development, modification

variation *noun* <u>DIFFERENCE</u>, change, departure, deviation, diversity, innovation, modification, novelty, variety

varied *adjective* <u>DIFFERENT</u>, assorted, diverse, heterogeneous, miscellaneous, mixed, motley, sundry, various

variety *noun* 1 <u>DIVERSITY</u>, change, difference, discrepancy, diversification, multifariousness, variation 2 <u>RANGE</u>, array, assortment, collection, cross section, medley, miscellany, mixture 3 <u>TYPE</u>, brand, breed, category, class, kind, sort, species, strain

various *adjective* <u>DIFFERENT</u>, assorted, disparate, distinct, diverse, miscellaneous, several, sundry, varied

varnish *noun, verb* <u>POLISH</u>, glaze, gloss, lacquer

vary *verb* <u>CHANGE</u>, alter, differ, disagree, diverge, fluctuate

vast *adjective* <u>HUGE</u>, boundless, colossal, enormous, gigantic, great, immense, massive, monumental, wide

vault[1] *noun* 1 <u>STRONGROOM</u>, depository, repository 2 <u>CRYPT</u>, catacomb, cellar, charnel house, mausoleum, tomb, undercroft

vault[2] *verb* <u>JUMP</u>, bound, clear, hurdle, leap, spring

vaulted *adjective* <u>ARCHED</u>, cavernous, domed

veer *verb* <u>SWERVE</u>, change course, change direction, sheer, shift, turn

vegetate *verb* <u>STAGNATE</u>, deteriorate, go to seed, idle, languish, loaf

vehemence *noun* <u>FORCEFULNESS</u>, ardour, emphasis, energy, fervour, force, intensity, passion, vigour

vehement *adjective* <u>STRONG</u>, ardent, emphatic, fervent, fierce, forceful, impassioned, intense, passionate, powerful

vehicle *noun* 1 <u>TRANSPORT</u>, conveyance, transportation 2 <u>MEDIUM</u>, apparatus, channel, means, mechanism, organ

veil *noun* 1 <u>COVER</u>, blind, cloak, curtain, disguise, film, mask, screen, shroud ♦ *verb* 2 <u>COVER</u>, cloak, conceal, disguise, hide, mask, obscure, screen, shield

veiled *adjective* <u>DISGUISED</u>, concealed, covert, hinted at, implied, masked, suppressed

vein *noun* 1 <u>BLOOD VESSEL</u> 2 <u>SEAM</u>, course, current, lode, stratum, streak, stripe 3 <u>MOOD</u>, mode, note, style, temper, tenor, tone

velocity *noun* <u>SPEED</u>, pace, quickness, rapidity, swiftness

velvety *adjective* <u>SMOOTH</u>, delicate, downy, soft

vendetta *noun* <u>FEUD</u>, bad blood, quarrel

veneer noun MASK, appearance, façade, front, guise, pretence, semblance, show

venerable adjective RESPECTED, august, esteemed, honoured, revered, sage, wise, worshipped

venerate verb RESPECT, adore, esteem, honour, look up to, revere, reverence, worship

vengeance noun REVENGE, reprisal, requital, retaliation, retribution

venom noun 1 MALICE, acrimony, bitterness, hate, rancour, spite, spleen, virulence 2 POISON, bane, toxin

venomous adjective 1 MALICIOUS, hostile, malignant, rancorous, savage, spiteful, vicious, vindictive 2 POISONOUS, mephitic, noxious, toxic, virulent

vent noun 1 OUTLET, aperture, duct, opening, orifice ◆ verb 2 EXPRESS, air, discharge, emit, give vent to, pour out, release, utter, voice

venture noun 1 UNDERTAKING, adventure, endeavour, enterprise, gamble, hazard, project, risk ◆ verb 2 RISK, chance, hazard, speculate, stake, wager 3 DARE, hazard, make bold, presume, take the liberty, volunteer 4 GO, embark on, plunge into, set out

verbal adjective SPOKEN, oral, unwritten, word-of-mouth

verbatim adverb EXACTLY, precisely, to the letter, word for word

verbose adjective LONG-WINDED, circumlocutory, diffuse, periphrastic, prolix, tautological, windy, wordy

verbosity noun LONG-WINDEDNESS, loquaciousness, prolixity, verboseness, wordiness

verdant adjective GREEN, flourishing, fresh, grassy, leafy, lush

verdict noun DECISION, adjudication, conclusion, finding, judgment, opinion, sentence

verge noun 1 BORDER, boundary, brim, brink, edge, limit, margin, threshold ◆ verb 2 **verge on** BORDER, approach, come near

verification noun PROOF, authentication, confirmation, corroboration, substantiation, validation

verify verb CHECK, authenticate, bear out, confirm, corroborate, prove, substantiate, support, validate

vernacular noun DIALECT, idiom, parlance, patois, speech

versatile adjective ADAPTABLE, adjustable, all-purpose, all-round, flexible, multifaceted, resourceful, variable

versed adjective KNOWLEDGEABLE, acquainted, conversant, experienced, familiar, practised, proficient, seasoned, well informed

version noun 1 FORM, design, model, style, variant 2 ACCOUNT, adaptation, interpretation, portrayal, rendering

vertical adjective UPRIGHT, erect, on end, perpendicular

vertigo noun DIZZINESS, giddiness, light-headedness

verve noun ENTHUSIASM, animation, energy, gusto, liveliness, sparkle, spirit, vitality

very adverb 1 EXTREMELY, acutely, decidedly, deeply, exceedingly, greatly, highly, profoundly, uncommonly, unusually ◆ adjective 2 EXACT, precise, selfsame

vessel noun 1 SHIP, boat, craft 2 CONTAINER, pot, receptacle, utensil

vest verb, with in or with PLACE, bestow, confer, consign, endow, entrust, invest, settle

vestibule noun HALL, anteroom, foyer, lobby, porch, portico

vestige noun TRACE, glimmer, indication, remnant, scrap, suspicion

vet verb CHECK, appraise, examine, investigate, review, scrutinize

veteran noun 1 OLD HAND, old stager, past master, warhorse (*informal*) ◆ adjective 2 LONG-SERVING, battle-scarred, old, seasoned

veto noun 1 BAN, boycott, embargo, interdict, prohibition ◆ verb 2 BAN, boycott, disallow, forbid, prohibit, reject, rule out, turn down

vex verb ANNOY, bother, distress, exasperate, irritate, plague, trouble, upset, worry

vexation noun 1 ANNOYANCE, chagrin, displeasure, dissatisfaction, exasperation, frustration, irritation, pique 2 PROBLEM, bother, difficulty, hassle (*informal*), headache (*informal*), nuisance, trouble, worry

viable adjective WORKABLE, applicable, feasible, operable, practicable, usable

vibrant adjective ENERGETIC, alive, animated, dynamic, sparkling, spirited, vigorous, vivacious, vivid

vibrate verb SHAKE, fluctuate, judder (*informal*), oscillate, pulsate, quiver, reverberate, sway, throb, tremble

vibration noun TREMOR, judder (*informal*), oscillation, pulsation, quiver, reverberation, shake, throbbing, trembling

vicarious adjective INDIRECT, delegated, substituted, surrogate

vice noun 1 WICKEDNESS, corruption, depravity, evil, immorality, iniquity, sin, turpitude 2 FAULT, blemish, defect, failing, imperfection, shortcoming, weakness

vice versa adverb CONVERSELY, contrariwise, in reverse, the other way round

vicinity noun NEIGHBOURHOOD, area, district, environs, locality, neck of the woods (*informal*), proximity

vicious adjective 1 VIOLENT, barbarous, cruel, ferocious, savage, wicked 2 MALICIOUS, cruel, mean, spiteful, venomous, vindictive

victim noun CASUALTY, fatality, martyr, sacrifice, scapegoat, sufferer

victimize verb PERSECUTE, discriminate against, have it in for (someone) (*informal*), pick on

victor noun WINNER, champion, conqueror, prizewinner, vanquisher

victorious adjective WINNING, champion, conquering, first, prizewinning, successful, triumphant, vanquishing

victory noun WIN, conquest, success, triumph

vie verb COMPETE, contend, strive, struggle

view noun 1 sometimes plural OPINION, attitude, belief, conviction, feeling, impression, point of view, sentiment 2 SCENE, landscape, outlook, panorama, perspective, picture, prospect, spectacle, vista 3 VISION, sight ◆ verb 4 REGARD, consider, deem, look on

viewer noun WATCHER, observer, onlooker, spectator

vigilance noun WATCHFULNESS, alertness, attentiveness, carefulness, caution, circumspection, observance

vigilant *adjective* <u>WATCHFUL</u>, alert, attentive, careful, cautious, circumspect, on one's guard, on the lookout, wakeful

vigorous *adjective* <u>ENERGETIC</u>, active, dynamic, forceful, lively, lusty, powerful, spirited, strenuous, strong

vigorously *adverb* <u>ENERGETICALLY</u>, forcefully, hard, lustily, strenuously, strongly

vigour *noun* <u>ENERGY</u>, animation, dynamism, forcefulness, gusto, liveliness, power, spirit, strength, verve, vitality

vile *adjective* **1** <u>WICKED</u>, corrupt, degenerate, depraved, evil, nefarious, perverted **2** <u>DISGUSTING</u>, foul, horrid, nasty, nauseating, offensive, repugnant, repulsive, revolting, sickening

vilify *verb* <u>MALIGN</u>, abuse, berate, denigrate, disparage, revile, slander, smear

villain *noun* **1** <u>EVILDOER</u>, blackguard, criminal, miscreant, reprobate, rogue, scoundrel, wretch **2** <u>ANTIHERO</u>, baddy (*informal*)

villainous *adjective* <u>WICKED</u>, bad, cruel, degenerate, depraved, evil, fiendish, nefarious, vicious, vile

villainy *noun* <u>WICKEDNESS</u>, delinquency, depravity, devilry, iniquity, turpitude, vice

vindicate *verb* **1** <u>CLEAR</u>, absolve, acquit, exculpate, exonerate, rehabilitate **2** <u>JUSTIFY</u>, defend, excuse

vindication *noun* **1** <u>EXONERATION</u>, exculpation, rehabilitation **2** <u>JUSTIFICATION</u>, defence, excuse

vindictive *adjective* <u>VENGEFUL</u>, implacable, malicious, resentful, revengeful, spiteful, unforgiving, unrelenting

vintage *adjective* <u>BEST</u>, choice, classic, prime, select, superior

violate *verb* **1** <u>BREAK</u>, contravene, disobey, disregard, encroach upon, infringe, transgress **2** <u>DESECRATE</u>, abuse, befoul, defile, dishonour, pollute, profane **3** <u>RAPE</u>, abuse, assault, debauch, ravish

violation *noun* **1** <u>INFRINGEMENT</u>, abuse, breach, contravention, encroachment, infraction, transgression, trespass **2** <u>DESECRATION</u>, defilement, profanation, sacrilege, spoliation

violence *noun* **1** <u>FORCE</u>, bloodshed, brutality, cruelty, ferocity, fighting, savagery, terrorism **2** <u>INTENSITY</u>, abandon, fervour, force, severity, vehemence

violent *adjective* <u>DESTRUCTIVE</u>, brutal, cruel, hot-headed, murderous, riotous, savage, uncontrollable, unrestrained, vicious

V.I.P. *noun* <u>CELEBRITY</u>, big name, luminary, somebody, star

virgin *noun* **1** <u>MAIDEN</u>, girl ♦ *adjective* **2** <u>PURE</u>, chaste, immaculate, uncorrupted, undefiled, vestal, virginal

virginity *noun* <u>CHASTITY</u>, maidenhood

virile *adjective* <u>MANLY</u>, lusty, macho, manlike, masculine, red-blooded, strong, vigorous

virility *noun* <u>MASCULINITY</u>, machismo, manhood, vigour

virtual *adjective* <u>PRACTICAL</u>, essential, in all but name

virtually *adverb* <u>PRACTICALLY</u>, almost, as good as, in all but name, in effect, in essence, nearly

virtue *noun* **1** <u>GOODNESS</u>, integrity, morality, probity, rectitude, righteousness, uprightness, worth **2** <u>MERIT</u>, advantage, asset, attribute, credit, good point, plus (*informal*), strength

virtuosity noun MASTERY, brilliance, craft, expertise, flair, panache, polish, skill

virtuoso noun MASTER, artist, genius, maestro, magician

virtuous adjective GOOD, ethical, honourable, incorruptible, moral, praiseworthy, righteous, upright, worthy

virulent adjective POISONOUS, deadly, lethal, pernicious, toxic, venomous

viscous adjective THICK, gelatinous, sticky, syrupy

visible adjective APPARENT, clear, discernible, evident, in view, manifest, observable, perceptible, unconcealed

vision noun 1 SIGHT, eyesight, perception, seeing, view 2 IMAGE, concept, conception, daydream, dream, fantasy, idea, ideal 3 HALLUCINATION, apparition, chimera, delusion, illusion, mirage, revelation 4 FORESIGHT, discernment, farsightedness, imagination, insight, intuition, penetration, prescience

visionary adjective 1 PROPHETIC, mystical 2 IMPRACTICAL, idealistic, quixotic, romantic, speculative, starry-eyed, unrealistic, unworkable, utopian ♦noun 3 PROPHET, mystic, seer

visit verb 1 CALL ON, drop in on (informal), look (someone) up, stay with, stop by ♦noun 2 CALL, sojourn, stay, stop

visitation noun 1 INSPECTION, examination, visit 2 CATASTROPHE, blight, calamity, cataclysm, disaster, ordeal, punishment, scourge

visitor noun GUEST, caller, company

vista noun VIEW, panorama, perspective, prospect

visual adjective 1 OPTICAL, ocular, optic 2 OBSERVABLE, discernible, perceptible, visible

visualize verb PICTURE, conceive of, envisage, imagine

vital adjective 1 ESSENTIAL, basic, fundamental, imperative, indispensable, necessary, requisite 2 IMPORTANT, critical, crucial, decisive, key, life-or-death, significant, urgent 3 LIVELY, animated, dynamic, energetic, spirited, vibrant, vigorous, vivacious, zestful

vitality noun ENERGY, animation, exuberance, life, liveliness, strength, vigour, vivacity

vitriolic adjective BITTER, acerbic, caustic, envenomed, sardonic, scathing, venomous, virulent, withering

vivacious adjective LIVELY, bubbling, ebullient, high-spirited, sparkling, spirited, sprightly, upbeat (informal), vital

vivacity noun LIVELINESS, animation, ebullience, energy, gaiety, high spirits, sparkle, spirit, sprightliness

vivid adjective 1 BRIGHT, brilliant, clear, colourful, glowing, intense, rich 2 LIFELIKE, dramatic, graphic, memorable, powerful, realistic, stirring, telling, true to life

vocabulary noun WORDS, dictionary, glossary, language, lexicon

vocal adjective 1 SPOKEN, oral, said, uttered, voiced 2 OUTSPOKEN, articulate, eloquent, expressive, forthright, frank, plain-spoken, strident, vociferous

vocation noun PROFESSION, calling, career, job, mission, pursuit, trade

vociferous adjective NOISY, clamorous, loud, outspoken, strident, uproarious, vehement, vocal

vogue noun **1** FASHION, craze, custom, mode, style, trend, way **2** *As in* **in vogue** POPULARITY, acceptance, currency, favour, prevalence, usage, use

voice noun **1** SOUND, articulation, tone, utterance **2** SAY, view, vote, will, wish ♦ verb **3** EXPRESS, air, articulate, declare, enunciate, utter

void noun **1** EMPTINESS, blankness, gap, lack, space, vacuity, vacuum ♦ adjective **2** INVALID, ineffective, inoperative, null and void, useless, vain, worthless **3** EMPTY, bare, free, tenantless, unfilled, unoccupied, vacant ♦ verb **4** INVALIDATE, cancel, nullify, rescind **5** EMPTY, drain, evacuate

volatile adjective **1** CHANGEABLE, explosive, inconstant, unsettled, unstable, unsteady, variable **2** TEMPERAMENTAL, erratic, fickle, mercurial, up and down (*informal*)

volition noun FREE WILL, choice, choosing, discretion, preference, will

volley noun BARRAGE, blast, bombardment, burst, cannonade, fusillade, hail, salvo, shower

voluble adjective TALKATIVE, articulate, fluent, forthcoming, glib, loquacious

volume noun **1** CAPACITY, compass, dimensions **2** AMOUNT, aggregate, body, bulk, mass, quantity, total **3** BOOK, publication, title, tome, treatise

voluminous adjective LARGE, ample, capacious, cavernous, roomy, vast

voluntarily adverb WILLINGLY, by choice, freely, off one's own bat, of one's own accord

voluntary adjective UNFORCED, discretionary, free, optional, spontaneous, willing

volunteer verb OFFER, step forward

voluptuous adjective **1** BUXOM, ample, curvaceous (*informal*), enticing, seductive, shapely **2** SENSUAL, epicurean, hedonistic, licentious, luxurious, self-indulgent, sybaritic

vomit verb BE SICK, disgorge, emit, heave, regurgitate, retch, spew out *or* up, throw up (*informal*)

voracious adjective **1** GLUTTONOUS, greedy, hungry, insatiable, omnivorous, ravenous **2** AVID, hungry, insatiable, rapacious, uncontrolled, unquenchable

vortex noun WHIRLPOOL, eddy, maelstrom

vote noun **1** POLL, ballot, franchise, plebiscite, referendum, show of hands ♦ verb **2** ELECT, cast one's vote, opt

voucher noun TICKET, coupon, token

vouch for verb **1** GUARANTEE, answer for, certify, give assurance of, stand witness, swear to **2** CONFIRM, affirm, assert, attest to, support, uphold

vow noun **1** PROMISE, oath, pledge ♦ verb **2** PROMISE, affirm, pledge, swear

voyage noun JOURNEY, crossing, cruise, passage, trip

vulgar adjective CRUDE, coarse, common, impolite, indecent, ribald, risqué, rude, tasteless, uncouth, unrefined

vulgarity noun CRUDENESS, bad taste, coarseness, indelicacy, ribaldry, rudeness, tastelessness

vulnerable adjective **1** WEAK, sensitive, susceptible, tender, thin-skinned **2** EXPOSED, accessible, assailable, defenceless, unprotected, wide open

W w

wad noun MASS, bundle, hunk, roll

waddle verb SHUFFLE, sway, toddle, totter, wobble

wade verb 1 WALK THROUGH, ford, paddle, splash 2 **wade through** PLOUGH THROUGH, drudge at, labour at, peg away at, toil at, work one's way through

waffle verb 1 PRATTLE, blather, jabber, prate, rabbit (on) (Brit. informal), witter on (informal) ♦ noun 2 VERBOSITY, padding, prolixity, verbiage, wordiness

waft verb CARRY, bear, convey, drift, float, transport

wag verb 1 WAVE, bob, nod, quiver, shake, stir, vibrate, waggle, wiggle ♦ noun 2 WAVE, bob, nod, quiver, shake, vibration, waggle, wiggle

wage noun 1 Also **wages** PAYMENT, allowance, emolument, fee, pay, recompense, remuneration, reward, stipend ♦ verb 2 ENGAGE IN, carry on, conduct, practise, proceed with, prosecute, pursue, undertake

wager noun 1 BET, flutter (Brit. informal), gamble, punt (chiefly Brit.) ♦ verb 2 BET, chance, gamble, lay, risk, speculate, stake, venture

waggle verb WAG, flutter, oscillate, shake, wave, wiggle, wobble

waif noun STRAY, foundling, orphan

wail verb 1 CRY, bawl, grieve, howl, lament, weep, yowl ♦ noun 2 CRY, complaint, howl, lament, moan, weeping, yowl

wait verb 1 REMAIN, hang fire, hold back, linger, pause, rest, stay, tarry ♦ noun 2 DELAY, halt, hold-up, interval, pause, rest, stay

waiter, waitress noun ATTENDANT, server, steward or stewardess

wait on or **upon** verb SERVE, attend, minister to, tend

waive verb SET ASIDE, abandon, dispense with, forgo, give up, relinquish, remit, renounce

wake[1] verb 1 AWAKEN, arise, awake, bestir, come to, get up, rouse, stir 2 ACTIVATE, animate, arouse, excite, fire, galvanize, kindle, provoke, stimulate, stir up ♦ noun 3 VIGIL, deathwatch, funeral, watch

wake[2] noun SLIPSTREAM, aftermath, backwash, path, track, trail, train, wash, waves

wakeful adjective 1 SLEEPLESS, insomniac, restless 2 WATCHFUL, alert, alive, attentive, observant, on guard, vigilant, wary

waken verb AWAKEN, activate, arouse, awake, rouse, stir

walk verb 1 GO, amble, hike, march, move, pace, step, stride, stroll 2 ESCORT, accompany, convoy, take ♦ noun 3 STROLL, hike, march, promenade, ramble, saunter, trek, trudge 4 GAIT, carriage, step 5 PATH, alley, avenue, esplanade, footpath, lane, promenade, trail 6 **walk of life** PROFESSION, calling, career, field, line, trade, vocation

walker noun PEDESTRIAN, hiker, rambler, wayfarer

walkout noun STRIKE, industrial action, protest, stoppage

walkover noun PUSHOVER (slang), breeze (U.S. & Canad. informal), cakewalk (informal), child's play (informal), doddle (Brit. slang), picnic (informal), piece of cake (informal)

wall noun 1 PARTITION, enclosure,

screen **2** BARRIER, fence, hedge, impediment, obstacle, obstruction

wallet *noun* HOLDER, case, pocketbook, pouch, purse

wallop *verb* **1** HIT, batter, beat, clobber (*slang*), pound, pummel, strike, thrash, thump, whack ♦ *noun* **2** BLOW, bash, punch, slug, smack, thump, thwack, whack

wallow *verb* **1** REVEL, bask, delight, glory, luxuriate, relish, take pleasure **2** ROLL ABOUT, splash around

wan *adjective* PALE, anaemic, ashen, pallid, pasty, sickly, washed out, white

wand *noun* STICK, baton, rod

wander *verb* **1** ROAM, drift, meander, ramble, range, rove, stray, stroll **2** DEVIATE, depart, digress, diverge, err, go astray, swerve, veer ♦ *noun* **3** EXCURSION, cruise, meander, ramble

wanderer *noun* TRAVELLER, drifter, gypsy, nomad, rambler, rover, vagabond, voyager

wandering *adjective* NOMADIC, itinerant, migratory, peripatetic, rootless, roving, travelling, vagrant, wayfaring

wane *verb* **1** DECLINE, decrease, diminish, dwindle, ebb, fade, fail, lessen, subside, taper off, weaken ♦ *noun* **2 on the wane** DECLINING, dwindling, ebbing, fading, obsolescent, on the decline, tapering off, weakening

wangle *verb* CONTRIVE, arrange, engineer, fiddle (*informal*), fix (*informal*), manipulate, manoeuvre, pull off

want *verb* **1** DESIRE, covet, crave, hanker after, hope for, hunger for, long for, thirst for, wish, yearn for **2** NEED, call for, demand, lack, miss, require ♦ *noun* **3** WISH, appetite, craving, desire, longing, need, requirement, yearning **4** LACK, absence, dearth, deficiency, famine, insufficiency, paucity, scarcity, shortage **5** POVERTY, destitution, neediness, penury, privation

wanting *adjective* **1** LACKING, absent, incomplete, missing, short, shy **2** INADEQUATE, defective, deficient, faulty, imperfect, poor, substandard, unsound

wanton *adjective* **1** UNPROVOKED, arbitrary, gratuitous, groundless, motiveless, needless, senseless, uncalled-for, unjustifiable, wilful **2** PROMISCUOUS, dissipated, dissolute, immoral, lecherous, libidinous, loose, lustful, shameless, unchaste

war *noun* **1** FIGHTING, battle, combat, conflict, enmity, hostilities, struggle, warfare ♦ *verb* **2** FIGHT, battle, campaign against, clash, combat, take up arms, wage war

warble *verb* SING, chirp, trill, twitter

ward *noun* **1** ROOM, apartment, cubicle **2** DISTRICT, area, division, precinct, quarter, zone **3** DEPENDANT, charge, minor, protégé, pupil

warden *noun* KEEPER, administrator, caretaker, curator, custodian, guardian, ranger, superintendent

warder, wardress *noun* JAILER, custodian, guard, prison officer, screw (*slang*)

ward off *verb* REPEL, avert, avoid, deflect, fend off, parry, stave off

wardrobe *noun* **1** CLOTHES CUPBOARD, closet **2** CLOTHES, apparel, attire

warehouse *noun* STORE, depository, depot, stockroom, storehouse

wares *plural noun* GOODS, commodities, merchandise, produce, products, stock, stuff

warfare noun <u>WAR</u>, arms, battle, combat, conflict, fighting, hostilities

warily adverb <u>CAUTIOUSLY</u>, carefully, charily, circumspectly, distrustfully, gingerly, suspiciously, vigilantly, watchfully, with care

warlike adjective <u>BELLIGERENT</u>, aggressive, bellicose, bloodthirsty, hawkish, hostile, martial, warmongering

warlock noun <u>MAGICIAN</u>, conjuror, enchanter, sorcerer, wizard

warm adjective 1 <u>HEATED</u>, balmy, lukewarm, pleasant, sunny, tepid, thermal 2 <u>AFFECTIONATE</u>, amorous, cordial, friendly, hospitable, kindly, loving, tender ♦ verb 3 <u>HEAT</u>, heat up, melt, thaw, warm up

warmonger noun <u>HAWK</u>, belligerent, militarist, sabre-rattler

warmth noun 1 <u>HEAT</u>, hotness, warmness 2 <u>AFFECTION</u>, amorousness, cordiality, heartiness, kindliness, love, tenderness

warn verb <u>NOTIFY</u>, advise, alert, apprise, caution, forewarn, give notice, inform, make (someone) aware, tip off

warning noun <u>CAUTION</u>, advice, alarm, alert, notification, omen, sign, tip-off

warp verb 1 <u>TWIST</u>, bend, contort, deform, distort ♦ noun 2 <u>TWIST</u>, bend, contortion, distortion, kink

warrant noun 1 <u>AUTHORIZATION</u>, authority, licence, permission, permit, sanction ♦ verb 2 <u>CALL FOR</u>, demand, deserve, excuse, justify, license, necessitate, permit, require, sanction 3 <u>GUARANTEE</u>, affirm, attest, certify, declare, pledge, vouch for

warranty noun <u>GUARANTEE</u>, assurance, bond, certificate, contract, covenant, pledge

warrior noun <u>SOLDIER</u>, combatant, fighter, gladiator, man-at-arms

wary adjective <u>CAUTIOUS</u>, alert, careful, chary, circumspect, distrustful, guarded, suspicious, vigilant, watchful

wash verb 1 <u>CLEAN</u>, bathe, cleanse, launder, rinse, scrub 2 <u>SWEEP AWAY</u>, bear away, carry off, move 3 Informal <u>BE PLAUSIBLE</u>, bear scrutiny, be convincing, carry weight, hold up, hold water, stand up, stick ♦ noun 4 <u>CLEANING</u>, cleansing, laundering, rinse, scrub 5 <u>COAT</u>, coating, film, layer, overlay 6 <u>SWELL</u>, surge, wave

washout noun <u>FAILURE</u>, disappointment, disaster, dud (informal), fiasco, flop (informal)

waste verb 1 <u>MISUSE</u>, blow (slang), dissipate, fritter away, lavish, squander, throw away 2 **waste away** <u>DECLINE</u>, atrophy, crumble, decay, dwindle, fade, wane, wear out, wither ♦ noun 3 <u>MISUSE</u>, dissipation, extravagance, frittering away, prodigality, squandering, wastefulness 4 <u>RUBBISH</u>, debris, dross, garbage, leftovers, litter, refuse, scrap, trash 5 **wastes** <u>DESERT</u>, wasteland, wilderness ♦ adjective 6 <u>UNWANTED</u>, leftover, superfluous, supernumerary, unused, useless, worthless 7 <u>UNCULTIVATED</u>, bare, barren, desolate, empty, uninhabited, unproductive, wild

wasteful adjective <u>EXTRAVAGANT</u>, lavish, prodigal, profligate, spendthrift, thriftless, uneconomical

waster noun <u>LAYABOUT</u>, good-for-nothing, idler, loafer, ne'er-do-well, shirker, skiver (Brit. slang), wastrel

watch verb 1 <u>LOOK AT</u>, contemplate, eye, observe, regard, see, view

2 GUARD, keep, look after, mind, protect, superintend, take care of, tend ♦ *noun* 3 WRISTWATCH, chronometer, timepiece 4 LOOKOUT, observation, surveillance, vigil

watchdog *noun* 1 GUARD DOG 2 GUARDIAN, custodian, monitor, protector, scrutineer

watchful *adjective* ALERT, attentive, observant, on the lookout, suspicious, vigilant, wary, wide awake

watchman *noun* GUARD, caretaker, custodian, security guard

watchword *noun* MOTTO, battle cry, byword, catch phrase, catchword, maxim, rallying cry, slogan

water *noun* 1 LIQUID, H_2O ♦ *verb* 2 MOISTEN, dampen, douse, drench, hose, irrigate, soak, spray

water down *verb* DILUTE, thin, water, weaken

waterfall *noun* CASCADE, cataract, fall

watertight *adjective* 1 WATERPROOF 2 FOOLPROOF, airtight, flawless, impregnable, sound, unassailable

watery *adjective* 1 WET, aqueous, damp, fluid, liquid, moist, soggy 2 DILUTED, runny, thin, washy, watered-down, weak

wave *verb* 1 SIGNAL, beckon, direct, gesticulate, gesture, indicate, sign 2 FLAP, brandish, flourish, flutter, oscillate, shake, stir, swing, wag ♦ *noun* 3 RIPPLE, billow, breaker, ridge, roller, swell, undulation 4 OUTBREAK, flood, rash, rush, stream, surge, upsurge

waver *verb* 1 HESITATE, dither (*chiefly Brit.*), falter, fluctuate, hum and haw, seesaw, vacillate 2 TREMBLE, flicker, quiver, shake, totter, wobble

wax *verb* INCREASE, develop, enlarge, expand, grow, magnify, swell

way *noun* 1 METHOD, fashion, manner, means, mode, procedure, process, system, technique 2 STYLE, custom, habit, manner, nature, personality, practice, wont 3 ROUTE, channel, course, direction, path, pathway, road, track, trail 4 JOURNEY, approach, march, passage 5 DISTANCE, length, stretch

wayfarer *noun* TRAVELLER, gypsy, itinerant, nomad, rover, voyager, wanderer

wayward *adjective* ERRATIC, capricious, inconstant, ungovernable, unmanageable, unpredictable, unruly

weak *adjective* 1 FEEBLE, debilitated, effete, fragile, frail, infirm, puny, sickly, unsteady 2 UNSAFE, defenceless, exposed, helpless, unguarded, unprotected, vulnerable 3 UNCONVINCING, feeble, flimsy, hollow, lame, pathetic, unsatisfactory 4 TASTELESS, diluted, insipid, runny, thin, watery

weaken *verb* 1 LESSEN, diminish, dwindle, fade, flag, lower, moderate, reduce, sap, undermine, wane 2 DILUTE, thin out, water down

weakling *noun* SISSY, drip (*informal*), wet (*Brit. informal*), wimp (*informal*)

weakness *noun* 1 FRAILTY, decrepitude, feebleness, fragility, infirmity, powerlessness, vulnerability 2 FAILING, blemish, defect, deficiency, fault, flaw, imperfection, lack, shortcoming 3 LIKING, fondness, inclination, partiality, passion, penchant, soft spot

wealth *noun* 1 RICHES, affluence, capital, fortune, money, opulence, prosperity 2 PLENTY, abundance, copiousness, cornucopia, fullness, profusion, richness

wealthy *adjective* RICH, affluent, flush (*informal*), moneyed, opulent, prosperous, well-heeled (*informal*), well-off, well-to-do

wear *verb* 1 BE DRESSED IN, don, have on, put on, sport (*informal*) 2 SHOW, display, exhibit 3 DETERIORATE, abrade, corrode, erode, fray, grind, rub ♦ *noun* 4 CLOTHES, apparel, attire, costume, dress, garb, garments, gear (*informal*), things 5 DAMAGE, abrasion, attrition, corrosion, deterioration, erosion, wear and tear

weariness *noun* TIREDNESS, drowsiness, exhaustion, fatigue, languor, lassitude, lethargy, listlessness

wearing *adjective* TIRESOME, exasperating, fatiguing, irksome, oppressive, trying, wearisome

wearisome *adjective* TEDIOUS, annoying, boring, exhausting, fatiguing, irksome, oppressive, tiresome, troublesome, trying, wearing

wear off *verb* SUBSIDE, decrease, diminish, disappear, dwindle, fade, peter out, wane

weary *adjective* 1 TIRED, done in (*informal*), drained, drowsy, exhausted, fatigued, flagging, jaded, sleepy, worn out 2 TIRING, arduous, laborious, tiresome, wearisome ♦ *verb* 3 TIRE, drain, enervate, fatigue, sap, take it out of (*informal*), tax, tire out, wear out

weather *noun* 1 CLIMATE, conditions ♦ *verb* 2 WITHSTAND, brave, come through, endure, overcome, resist, ride out, stand, survive

weave *verb* 1 KNIT, braid, entwine, interlace, intertwine, plait 2 CREATE,

build, construct, contrive, fabricate, make up, put together, spin 3 ZIGZAG, crisscross, wind

web *noun* 1 SPIDER'S WEB, cobweb 2 NETWORK, lattice, tangle

wed *verb* 1 MARRY, get married, take the plunge (*informal*), tie the knot (*informal*) 2 UNITE, ally, blend, combine, interweave, join, link, merge

wedding *noun* MARRIAGE, nuptials, wedlock

wedge *noun* 1 BLOCK, chunk, lump ♦ *verb* 2 SQUEEZE, cram, crowd, force, jam, lodge, pack, ram, stuff, thrust

wedlock *noun* MARRIAGE, matrimony

weed out *verb* ELIMINATE, dispense with, eradicate, get rid of, remove, root out, uproot

weedy *adjective* WEAK, feeble, frail, ineffectual, namby-pamby, puny, skinny, thin

weep *verb* CRY, blubber, lament, mourn, shed tears, snivel, sob, whimper

weigh *verb* 1 HAVE A WEIGHT OF, tip the scales at (*informal*) 2 CONSIDER, contemplate, deliberate upon, evaluate, examine, meditate upon, ponder, reflect upon, think over 3 MATTER, carry weight, count

weight *noun* 1 HEAVINESS, load, mass, poundage, tonnage 2 IMPORTANCE, authority, consequence, impact, import, influence, power, value ♦ *verb* 3 LOAD, freight 4 BIAS, load, slant, unbalance

weighty *adjective* 1 IMPORTANT, consequential, crucial, grave, momentous, portentous, serious, significant, solemn 2 HEAVY, burdensome, cumbersome, hefty (*informal*), massive, ponderous

weird *adjective* STRANGE, bizarre,

creepy (*informal*), eerie, freakish, mysterious, odd, queer, spooky (*informal*), unnatural

welcome *verb* 1 GREET, embrace, hail, meet, receive ♦ *noun* 2 GREETING, acceptance, hospitality, reception, salutation ♦ *adjective* 3 ACCEPTABLE, agreeable, appreciated, delightful, desirable, gratifying, pleasant, refreshing 4 FREE, under no obligation

weld *verb* JOIN, bind, bond, connect, fuse, link, solder, unite

welfare *noun* WELLBEING, advantage, benefit, good, happiness, health, interest, prosperity

well[1] *adverb* 1 SATISFACTORILY, agreeably, nicely, pleasantly, smoothly, splendidly, successfully 2 SKILFULLY, ably, adeptly, adequately, admirably, correctly, efficiently, expertly, proficiently, properly 3 PROSPEROUSLY, comfortably 4 SUITABLY, fairly, fittingly, justly, properly, rightly 5 INTIMATELY, deeply, fully, profoundly, thoroughly 6 FAVOURABLY, approvingly, glowingly, highly, kindly, warmly 7 CONSIDERABLY, abundantly, amply, fully, greatly, heartily, highly, substantially, thoroughly, very much ♦ *adjective* 8 HEALTHY, fit, in fine fettle, sound 9 SATISFACTORY, agreeable, fine, pleasing, proper, right, thriving

well[2] *noun* 1 HOLE, bore, pit, shaft ♦ *verb* 2 FLOW, gush, jet, pour, spout, spring, spurt, surge

well-known *adjective* FAMOUS, celebrated, familiar, noted, popular, renowned

well-off *adjective* RICH, affluent, comfortable, moneyed, prosperous, wealthy, well-heeled (*informal*), well-to-do

well-to-do *adjective* RICH, affluent, comfortable, moneyed, prosperous, wealthy, well-heeled (*informal*), well-off

well-worn *adjective* STALE, banal, commonplace, hackneyed, overused, stereotyped, trite

welt *noun* MARK, contusion, streak, stripe, wale, weal

welter *noun* JUMBLE, confusion, hotchpotch, mess, muddle, tangle, web

wet *adjective* 1 DAMP, dank, moist, saturated, soaking, sodden, soggy, sopping, waterlogged, watery 2 RAINY, drizzling, pouring, raining, showery, teeming 3 *Informal* FEEBLE, effete, ineffectual, namby-pamby, soft, spineless, timorous, weak, weedy (*informal*) ♦ *noun* 4 RAIN, drizzle 5 *Informal* WEAKLING, drip (*informal*), weed (*informal*), wimp (*informal*) 6 MOISTURE, condensation, damp, dampness, humidity, liquid, water, wetness ♦ *verb* 7 MOISTEN, dampen, douse, irrigate, saturate, soak, spray, water

whack *verb* 1 STRIKE, bang, belt (*informal*), clobber (*slang*), hit, smack, thrash, thump, thwack, wallop (*informal*) ♦ *noun* 2 BLOW, bang, belt (*informal*), hit, smack, stroke, thump, thwack, wallop (*informal*) 3 *Informal* SHARE, bit, cut (*informal*), part, portion, quota 4 *As in* have a whack ATTEMPT, bash (*informal*), crack (*informal*), go (*informal*), shot (*informal*), stab (*informal*), try, turn

wharf *noun* DOCK, jetty, landing stage, pier, quay

wheedle *verb* COAX, cajole, entice, inveigle, persuade

wheel *noun* 1 CIRCLE, gyration, pivot, revolution, rotation, spin, turn ♦ *verb* 2 TURN, gyrate, pirouette, revolve, rotate, spin, swing, swivel, twirl, whirl

wheeze verb 1 GASP, cough, hiss, rasp, whistle ♦ noun 2 GASP, cough, hiss, rasp, whistle 3 Brit. slang TRICK, idea, plan, ploy, ruse, scheme, stunt

whereabouts noun POSITION, location, site, situation

wherewithal noun RESOURCES, capital, funds, means, money, supplies

whet verb 1 As in **whet someone's appetite** STIMULATE, arouse, awaken, enhance, excite, kindle, quicken, rouse, stir 2 SHARPEN, hone

whiff noun SMELL, aroma, hint, odour, scent, sniff

whim noun IMPULSE, caprice, fancy, notion, urge

whimper verb 1 CRY, moan, snivel, sob, weep, whine, whinge (informal) ♦ noun 2 SOB, moan, snivel, whine

whimsical adjective FANCIFUL, curious, eccentric, freakish, funny, odd, playful, quaint, unusual

whine noun 1 CRY, moan, sob, wail, whimper 2 COMPLAINT, gripe (informal), grouch (informal), grouse, grumble, moan

whinge Informal ♦ verb 1 COMPLAIN, bleat, carp, gripe (informal), grouse, grumble, moan ♦ noun 2 COMPLAINT, gripe (informal), grouch, grouse, grumble, moan, whine

whip noun 1 LASH, birch, cane, cat-o'-nine-tails, crop, scourge ♦ verb 2 LASH, beat, birch, cane, flagellate, flog, scourge, spank, strap, thrash 3 Informal DASH, dart, dive, fly, rush, shoot, tear, whisk 4 BEAT, whisk 5 INCITE, agitate, drive, foment, goad, spur, stir, work up

whirl verb 1 SPIN, pirouette, revolve, roll, rotate, swirl, turn, twirl, twist 2 FEEL DIZZY, reel, spin ♦ noun

3 REVOLUTION, pirouette, roll, rotation, spin, swirl, turn, twirl, twist 4 BUSTLE, flurry, merry-go-round, round, series, succession 5 CONFUSION, daze, dither (chiefly Brit.), giddiness, spin

whirlwind noun 1 TORNADO, waterspout ♦ adjective 2 RAPID, hasty, quick, short, speedy, swift

whisk verb 1 FLICK, brush, sweep, whip 2 BEAT, fluff up, whip ♦ noun 3 FLICK, brush, sweep, whip 4 BEATER

whisper verb 1 MURMUR, breathe 2 RUSTLE, hiss, sigh, swish ♦ noun 3 MURMUR, undertone 4 Informal RUMOUR, gossip, innuendo, insinuation, report 5 RUSTLE, hiss, sigh, swish

white adjective PALE, ashen, pallid, pasty, wan

white-collar adjective CLERICAL, nonmanual, professional, salaried

whiten verb PALE, blanch, bleach, fade

whitewash noun 1 COVER-UP, camouflage, concealment, deception ♦ verb 2 COVER UP, camouflage, conceal, gloss over, suppress

whittle verb 1 CARVE, cut, hew, pare, shape, shave, trim 2 **whittle down** or **away** REDUCE, consume, eat away, erode, wear away

whole adjective 1 COMPLETE, entire, full, total, unabridged, uncut, undivided 2 UNDAMAGED, in one piece, intact, unbroken, unharmed, unscathed, untouched ♦ noun 3 TOTALITY, ensemble, entirety 4 **on the whole: a** ALL IN ALL, all things considered, by and large **b** GENERALLY, as a rule, in general, in the main, mostly, predominantly

wholehearted adjective SINCERE, committed, dedicated, determined, devoted, enthusiastic, unstinting, zealous

wholesale *adjective* **1** EXTENSIVE, broad, comprehensive, far-reaching, indiscriminate, mass, sweeping, wide-ranging ♦ *adverb* **2** EXTENSIVELY, comprehensively, indiscriminately

wholesome *adjective* **1** BENEFICIAL, good, healthy, nourishing, nutritious, salubrious **2** MORAL, decent, edifying, improving, respectable

wholly *adverb* COMPLETELY, altogether, entirely, fully, in every respect, perfectly, thoroughly, totally, utterly

whopper *noun* **1** GIANT, colossus, crackerjack (*informal*), jumbo (*informal*), leviathan, mammoth, monster **2** BIG LIE, fabrication, falsehood, tall story (*informal*), untruth

whopping *adjective* GIGANTIC, big, enormous, giant, great, huge, mammoth, massive

whore *noun* PROSTITUTE, call girl, streetwalker, tart (*informal*)

wicked *adjective* **1** BAD, corrupt, depraved, devilish, evil, fiendish, immoral, sinful, vicious, villainous **2** MISCHIEVOUS, impish, incorrigible, naughty, rascally, roguish

wide *adjective* **1** BROAD, expansive, extensive, far-reaching, immense, large, sweeping, vast **2** SPACIOUS, baggy, capacious, commodious, full, loose, roomy **3** EXPANDED, dilated, distended, outspread, outstretched **4** DISTANT, off course, off target, remote ♦ *adverb* **5** FULLY, completely **6** OFF TARGET, astray, off course, off the mark, out

widen *verb* BROADEN, dilate, enlarge, expand, extend, spread, stretch

widespread *adjective* COMMON, broad, extensive, far-reaching, general, pervasive, popular, universal

width *noun* BREADTH, compass, diameter, extent, girth, scope, span, thickness

wield *verb* **1** BRANDISH, employ, flourish, handle, manage, manipulate, ply, swing, use **2** *As in* **wield power** EXERT, exercise, have, maintain, possess

wife *noun* SPOUSE, better half (*humorous*), bride, mate, partner

wiggle *verb, noun* JERK, jiggle, shake, shimmy, squirm, twitch, wag, waggle, writhe

wild *adjective* **1** UNTAMED, feral, ferocious, fierce, savage, unbroken, undomesticated **2** UNCULTIVATED, free, natural **3** UNCIVILIZED, barbaric, barbarous, brutish, ferocious, fierce, primitive, savage **4** UNCONTROLLED, disorderly, riotous, rowdy, turbulent, undisciplined, unfettered, unmanageable, unrestrained, unruly, wayward **5** STORMY, blustery, choppy, raging, rough, tempestuous, violent **6** EXCITED, crazy (*informal*), enthusiastic, hysterical, raving ♦ *noun* **7** **wilds** WILDERNESS, back of beyond (*informal*), desert, middle of nowhere (*informal*), wasteland

wilderness *noun* DESERT, jungle, wasteland, wilds

wiles *plural noun* TRICKERY, artfulness, chicanery, craftiness, cunning, guile, slyness

wilful *adjective* **1** OBSTINATE, determined, headstrong, inflexible, intransigent, obdurate, perverse, pig-headed, stubborn, uncompromising **2** INTENTIONAL, conscious, deliberate, intended, purposeful, voluntary

will *noun* **1** DETERMINATION, purpose, resolution, resolve, willpower **2** WISH, desire, fancy, inclination,

mind, preference, volition
3 TESTAMENT, last wishes ♦ *verb*
4 WISH, desire, prefer, see fit, want
5 BEQUEATH, confer, give, leave, pass on, transfer

willing *adjective* READY, agreeable, amenable, compliant, consenting, game (*informal*), inclined, prepared

willingly *adverb* READILY, by choice, cheerfully, eagerly, freely, gladly, happily, of one's own accord, voluntarily

willingness *noun* INCLINATION, agreement, consent, volition, will, wish

willowy *adjective* SLENDER, graceful, lithe, slim, supple, svelte, sylphlike

willpower *noun* SELF-CONTROL, determination, drive, grit, resolution, resolve, self-discipline, single-mindedness

wilt *verb* **1** DROOP, sag, shrivel, wither **2** WEAKEN, fade, flag, languish, wane

wily *adjective* CUNNING, artful, astute, crafty, guileful, sharp, shrewd, sly, tricky

wimp *noun Informal* WEAKLING, coward, drip (*informal*), mouse, sissy, softy *or* softie

win *verb* **1** TRIUMPH, come first, conquer, overcome, prevail, succeed, sweep the board **2** GAIN, achieve, acquire, attain, earn, get, land, obtain, procure, secure ♦ *noun* **3** VICTORY, conquest, success, triumph

wince *verb* **1** FLINCH, blench, cower, cringe, draw back, quail, recoil, shrink, start ♦ *noun* **2** FLINCH, cringe, start

wind[1] *noun* **1** AIR, blast, breeze, draught, gust, zephyr **2** BREATH, puff, respiration **3** FLATULENCE, gas **4** TALK, babble, blather, bluster, boasting, hot air, humbug **5** *As in*

get wind of HINT, inkling, notice, report, rumour, suggestion, warning, whisper

wind[2] *verb* **1** COIL, curl, encircle, loop, reel, roll, spiral, twist **2** MEANDER, bend, curve, ramble, snake, turn, twist, zigzag

windfall *noun* GODSEND, bonanza, find, jackpot, manna from heaven

wind up *verb* **1** END, close, conclude, finalize, finish, settle, terminate, wrap up **2** END UP, be left, finish up **3** *Informal* EXCITE, put on edge, work up

windy *adjective* BREEZY, blowy, blustery, gusty, squally, stormy, wild, windswept

wing *noun* **1** FACTION, arm, branch, group, section ♦ *verb* **2** FLY, glide, soar **3** WOUND, clip, hit

wink *verb* **1** BLINK, bat, flutter **2** TWINKLE, flash, gleam, glimmer, sparkle ♦ *noun* **3** BLINK, flutter

winkle out *verb* EXTRACT, dig out, dislodge, draw out, extricate, force out, prise out

winner *noun* VICTOR, champ (*informal*), champion, conqueror, master

winning *adjective* **1** VICTORIOUS, conquering, successful, triumphant **2** CHARMING, alluring, attractive, cute, disarming, enchanting, endearing, engaging, likable *or* likeable, pleasing

winnings *plural noun* SPOILS, gains, prize, proceeds, profits, takings

winnow *verb* SEPARATE, divide, select, sift, sort out

win over *verb* CONVINCE, bring *or* talk round, convert, influence, persuade, prevail upon, sway

wintry *adjective* COLD, chilly, freezing, frosty, frozen, icy, snowy

wipe *verb* **1** CLEAN, brush, mop, rub,

sponge, swab **2** ERASE, remove
♦ *noun* **3** RUB, brush

wipe out *verb* DESTROY, annihilate,
eradicate, erase, expunge,
exterminate, massacre, obliterate

wiry *adjective* LEAN, sinewy, strong,
tough

wisdom *noun* UNDERSTANDING,
discernment, enlightenment,
erudition, insight, intelligence,
judgment, knowledge, learning,
sense

wise *adjective* SENSIBLE, clever,
discerning, enlightened, erudite,
intelligent, judicious, perceptive,
prudent, sage

wisecrack *noun* **1** JOKE, jest, jibe,
quip, witticism ♦ *verb* **2** JOKE, jest,
jibe, quip

wish *verb* **1** WANT, aspire, crave,
desire, hanker, hope, long, yearn
♦ *noun* **2** DESIRE, aspiration, hope,
intention, urge, want, whim, will

wispy *adjective* THIN, attenuated,
delicate, fine, flimsy, fragile, frail

wistful *adjective* MELANCHOLY,
contemplative, dreamy, longing,
meditative, pensive, reflective,
thoughtful

wit *noun* **1** HUMOUR, badinage,
banter, drollery, jocularity, raillery,
repartee, wordplay **2** HUMORIST,
card (*informal*), comedian, joker,
wag **3** CLEVERNESS, acumen, brains,
common sense, ingenuity,
intellect, sense, wisdom

witch *noun* ENCHANTRESS, crone,
hag, magician, sorceress

witchcraft *noun* MAGIC,
enchantment, necromancy,
occultism, sorcery, the black art,
voodoo, wizardry

withdraw *verb* REMOVE, draw back,
extract, pull out, take away, take
off

withdrawal *noun* REMOVAL,
extraction

withdrawn *adjective*
UNCOMMUNICATIVE, distant,
introverted, reserved, retiring, shy,
taciturn, unforthcoming

wither *verb* WILT, decay, decline,
disintegrate, fade, perish, shrivel,
waste

withering *adjective* SCORNFUL,
devastating, humiliating, hurtful,
mortifying, snubbing

withhold *verb* KEEP BACK, conceal,
hide, hold back, refuse, reserve,
retain, suppress

withstand *verb* RESIST, bear, cope
with, endure, hold off, oppose,
stand up to, suffer, tolerate

witless *adjective* FOOLISH,
halfwitted, idiotic, inane, moronic,
senseless, silly, stupid

witness *noun* **1** OBSERVER, beholder,
bystander, eyewitness, looker-on,
onlooker, spectator, viewer,
watcher **2** TESTIFIER, corroborator
♦ *verb* **3** SEE, note, notice, observe,
perceive, view, watch **4** SIGN,
countersign, endorse

wits *plural noun* INTELLIGENCE,
acumen, brains (*informal*),
cleverness, comprehension,
faculties, ingenuity, reason, sense,
understanding

witter *verb* CHATTER, babble, blather,
chat, gabble, jabber, prate,
prattle, waffle (*informal, chiefly
Brit.*)

witticism *noun* QUIP, bon mot,
one-liner (*slang*), pun, riposte

witty *adjective* HUMOROUS, amusing,
clever, droll, funny, piquant,
sparkling, waggish, whimsical

wizard *noun* MAGICIAN, conjuror,
magus, necromancer, occultist,
shaman, sorcerer, warlock, witch

wizardry *noun* MAGIC, sorcery,
voodoo, witchcraft

wizened *adjective* <u>WRINKLED</u>, dried up, gnarled, lined, shrivelled, shrunken, withered

wobble *verb* 1 <u>SHAKE</u>, rock, sway, teeter, totter, tremble ♦ *noun* 2 <u>UNSTEADINESS</u>, shake, tremble, tremor

wobbly *adjective* <u>UNSTEADY</u>, rickety, shaky, teetering, tottering, uneven

woe *noun* <u>GRIEF</u>, agony, anguish, distress, gloom, misery, sadness, sorrow, unhappiness, wretchedness

woeful *adjective* 1 <u>SAD</u>, deplorable, dismal, distressing, grievous, lamentable, miserable, pathetic, tragic, wretched 2 <u>PITIFUL</u>, abysmal, appalling, bad, deplorable, dreadful, feeble, pathetic, poor, sorry

woman *noun* <u>LADY</u>, female, girl

womanizer *noun* <u>PHILANDERER</u>, Casanova, Don Juan, lady-killer, lecher, seducer

womanly *adjective* <u>FEMININE</u>, female, ladylike, matronly, motherly, tender, warm

wonder *verb* 1 <u>THINK</u>, conjecture, meditate, ponder, puzzle, query, question, speculate 2 <u>BE AMAZED</u>, be astonished, gape, marvel, stare ♦ *noun* 3 <u>PHENOMENON</u>, curiosity, marvel, miracle, prodigy, rarity, sight, spectacle 4 <u>AMAZEMENT</u>, admiration, astonishment, awe, bewilderment, fascination, surprise, wonderment

wonderful *adjective* 1 <u>EXCELLENT</u>, brilliant, fabulous (*informal*), fantastic (*informal*), great (*informal*), magnificent, marvellous, outstanding, superb, terrific, tremendous 2 <u>REMARKABLE</u>, amazing, astonishing, extraordinary, incredible, miraculous, phenomenal, staggering, startling, unheard-of

wonky *adjective* <u>SHAKY</u>, unsteady, wobbly

woo *verb* <u>COURT</u>, cultivate, pursue

wood *noun* 1 <u>TIMBER</u> 2 <u>WOODLAND</u>, coppice, copse, forest, grove, thicket

wooded *adjective* <u>TREE-COVERED</u>, forested, sylvan (*poetic*), timbered, tree-clad

wooden *adjective* 1 <u>WOODY</u>, ligneous, timber 2 <u>EXPRESSIONLESS</u>, deadpan, lifeless, unresponsive

wool *noun* <u>FLEECE</u>, hair, yarn

woolly *adjective* 1 <u>FLEECY</u>, hairy, shaggy, woollen 2 <u>VAGUE</u>, confused, hazy, ill-defined, indefinite, indistinct, muddled, unclear

word *noun* 1 <u>TERM</u>, expression, name 2 <u>CHAT</u>, confab (*informal*), consultation, discussion, talk, tête-à-tête 3 <u>REMARK</u>, comment, utterance 4 <u>MESSAGE</u>, communiqué, dispatch, information, intelligence, news, notice, report 5 <u>PROMISE</u>, assurance, guarantee, oath, pledge, vow 6 <u>COMMAND</u>, bidding, decree, mandate, order ♦ *verb* 7 <u>EXPRESS</u>, couch, phrase, put, say, state, utter

wording *noun* <u>PHRASEOLOGY</u>, language, phrasing, terminology, words

wordy *adjective* <u>LONG-WINDED</u>, diffuse, prolix, rambling, verbose, windy

work *noun* 1 <u>EFFORT</u>, drudgery, elbow grease (*facetious*), exertion, industry, labour, sweat, toil 2 <u>EMPLOYMENT</u>, business, duty, job, livelihood, occupation, profession, trade 3 <u>TASK</u>, assignment, chore, commission, duty, job, stint, undertaking 4 <u>CREATION</u>, achievement, composition, handiwork, opus, piece, production ♦ *verb* 5 <u>LABOUR</u>, drudge, exert oneself, peg away, slave, slog (away), sweat, toil **6** BE EMPLOYED, be in work **7** OPERATE, control, drive, handle, manage, manipulate, move, use **8** FUNCTION, go, operate, run **9** CULTIVATE, dig, farm, till **10** MANIPULATE, fashion, form, knead, mould, shape

workable *adjective* VIABLE, doable, feasible, possible, practicable, practical

worker *noun* EMPLOYEE, artisan, craftsman, hand, labourer, tradesman, workman

working *adjective* **1** EMPLOYED, active, in work **2** FUNCTIONING, going, operative, running

workman *noun* LABOURER, artisan, craftsman, employee, hand, journeyman, mechanic, operative, tradesman, worker

workmanship *noun* SKILL, artistry, craftsmanship, expertise, handiwork, technique

work out *verb* **1** SOLVE, calculate, figure out, find out **2** HAPPEN, develop, evolve, result, turn out **3** EXERCISE, practise, train, warm up

works *plural noun* **1** FACTORY, mill, plant, workshop **2** WRITINGS, canon, *oeuvre*, output **3** MECHANISM, action, machinery, movement, parts, workings

workshop *noun* STUDIO, factory, mill, plant, workroom

world *noun* **1** EARTH, globe **2** MANKIND, everybody, everyone, humanity, humankind, man, the public **3** SPHERE, area, domain, environment, field, realm

worldly *adjective* **1** EARTHLY, physical, profane, secular, temporal, terrestrial **2** MATERIALISTIC, grasping, greedy, selfish **3** WORLDLY-WISE, blasé, cosmopolitan, experienced, knowing, sophisticated, urbane

worldwide *adjective* GLOBAL, general, international, omnipresent, pandemic, ubiquitous, universal

worn *adjective* RAGGED, frayed, shabby, tattered, tatty, the worse for wear, threadbare

worn-out *adjective* **1** RUN-DOWN, on its last legs, ragged, shabby, threadbare, used-up, useless, worn **2** EXHAUSTED, all in (*slang*), done in (*informal*), fatigued, fit to drop, spent, tired out, weary

worried *adjective* ANXIOUS, afraid, apprehensive, concerned, fearful, frightened, nervous, perturbed, tense, troubled, uneasy

worry *verb* **1** BE ANXIOUS, agonize, brood, fret **2** TROUBLE, annoy, bother, disturb, perturb, pester, unsettle, upset, vex ♦ *noun* **3** ANXIETY, apprehension, concern, fear, misgiving, trepidation, trouble, unease **4** PROBLEM, bother, care, hassle (*informal*), trouble

worsen *verb* **1** AGGRAVATE, damage, exacerbate **2** DETERIORATE, decay, decline, degenerate, get worse, go downhill (*informal*), sink

worship *verb* **1** PRAISE, adore, exalt, glorify, honour, pray to, revere, venerate **2** LOVE, adore, idolize, put on a pedestal ♦ *noun* **3** PRAISE, adoration, adulation, devotion, glory, honour, regard, respect, reverence

worth *noun* **1** VALUE, cost, price, rate, valuation **2** EXCELLENCE, goodness, importance, merit, quality, usefulness, value, worthiness

worthless *adjective* **1** USELESS, ineffectual, rubbishy, unimportant, valueless **2** GOOD-FOR-NOTHING, contemptible, despicable, vile

worthwhile *adjective* USEFUL,

beneficial, constructive, expedient, helpful, productive, profitable, valuable

worthy adjective PRAISEWORTHY, admirable, creditable, deserving, laudable, meritorious, valuable, virtuous, worthwhile

would-be adjective BUDDING, self-appointed, self-styled, unfulfilled, wannabe (*informal*)

wound noun 1 INJURY, cut, gash, hurt, laceration, lesion, trauma (*Pathology*) 2 INSULT, offence, slight ♦ verb 3 INJURE, cut, gash, hurt, lacerate, pierce, wing 4 OFFEND, annoy, cut (someone) to the quick, hurt, mortify, sting

wrangle verb 1 ARGUE, bicker, contend, disagree, dispute, fight, quarrel, row, squabble ♦ noun 2 ARGUMENT, altercation, bickering, dispute, quarrel, row, squabble, tiff

wrap verb 1 COVER, bind, bundle up, encase, enclose, enfold, pack, package, shroud, swathe ♦ noun 2 CLOAK, cape, mantle, shawl, stole

wrapper noun COVER, case, envelope, jacket, packaging, wrapping

wrap up verb 1 GIFTWRAP, bundle up, pack, package 2 *Informal* END, conclude, finish off, polish off, round off, terminate, wind up

wrath noun ANGER, displeasure, fury, indignation, ire, rage, resentment, temper

wreath noun GARLAND, band, chaplet, crown, festoon, ring

wreck verb 1 DESTROY, break, demolish, devastate, ruin, shatter, smash, spoil ♦ noun 2 SHIPWRECK, hulk

wreckage noun REMAINS, debris, fragments, pieces, rubble, ruin

wrench verb 1 TWIST, force, jerk, pull, rip, tear, tug, yank 2 SPRAIN,

rick, strain ♦ noun 3 TWIST, jerk, pull, rip, tug, yank 4 SPRAIN, strain, twist 5 BLOW, pang, shock, upheaval 6 SPANNER, adjustable spanner

wrest verb SEIZE, extract, force, take, win, wrench

wrestle verb FIGHT, battle, combat, grapple, scuffle, struggle, tussle

wretch noun SCOUNDREL, good-for-nothing, miscreant, rascal, rogue, swine, worm

wretched adjective 1 UNHAPPY, dejected, depressed, disconsolate, downcast, forlorn, hapless, miserable, woebegone 2 WORTHLESS, inferior, miserable, paltry, pathetic, poor, sorry

wriggle verb 1 TWIST, jerk, jiggle, squirm, turn, waggle, wiggle, writhe 2 CRAWL, slink, snake, worm, zigzag 3 As in **wriggle out of** MANOEUVRE, dodge, extricate oneself ♦ noun 4 TWIST, jerk, jiggle, squirm, turn, waggle, wiggle

wring verb TWIST, extract, force, screw, squeeze

wrinkle noun 1 CREASE, corrugation, crinkle, crow's-foot, crumple, fold, furrow, line ♦ verb 2 CREASE, corrugate, crumple, fold, furrow, gather, pucker, rumple

writ noun SUMMONS, court order, decree, document

write verb RECORD, draft, draw up, inscribe, jot down, pen, scribble, set down

writer noun AUTHOR, hack, novelist, penpusher, scribbler, scribe, wordsmith

writhe verb SQUIRM, jerk, struggle, thrash, thresh, toss, twist, wiggle, wriggle

writing noun 1 SCRIPT, calligraphy, hand, handwriting, penmanship, scrawl, scribble 2 DOCUMENT, book, composition, opus, publication, work

wrong *adjective* **1** INCORRECT, erroneous, fallacious, false, inaccurate, mistaken, untrue, wide of the mark **2** BAD, criminal, dishonest, evil, illegal, immoral, sinful, unjust, unlawful, wicked, wrongful **3** INAPPROPRIATE, incongruous, incorrect, unacceptable, unbecoming, undesirable, unseemly, unsuitable **4** DEFECTIVE, amiss, askew, awry, faulty ◆ *adverb* **5** INCORRECTLY, badly, erroneously, inaccurately, mistakenly, wrongly **6** AMISS, askew, astray, awry ◆ *noun* **7** OFFENCE, crime, error, injury, injustice, misdeed, sin, transgression, wickedness ◆ *verb* **8** MISTREAT, abuse, cheat, dishonour, harm, hurt, malign, oppress, take advantage of

wrongdoer *noun* OFFENDER, criminal, culprit, delinquent, lawbreaker, miscreant, sinner, villain

wrongful *adjective* IMPROPER, criminal, evil, illegal, illegitimate, immoral, unethical, unjust, unlawful, wicked

wry *adjective* **1** IRONIC, droll, dry, mocking, sarcastic, sardonic **2** CONTORTED, crooked, twisted, uneven

X x   Y y   Z z

Xmas *noun* <u>CHRISTMAS</u>, Noel, Yule (*archaic*), Yuletide (*archaic*)

X-rays *plural noun* <u>RÖNTGEN RAYS</u> (*old name*)

yank *verb, noun* <u>PULL</u>, hitch, jerk, snatch, tug, wrench

yardstick *noun* <u>STANDARD</u>, benchmark, criterion, gauge, measure, par, touchstone

yarn *noun* 1 <u>THREAD</u>, fibre 2 *Informal* <u>STORY</u>, anecdote, cock-and-bull story (*informal*), fable, tale, tall story

yawning *adjective* <u>GAPING</u>, cavernous, vast, wide

yearly *adjective* 1 <u>ANNUAL</u> ♦ *adverb* 2 <u>ANNUALLY</u>, every year, once a year, per annum

yearn *verb* <u>LONG</u>, ache, covet, crave, desire, hanker, hunger, itch

yell *verb* 1 <u>SCREAM</u>, bawl, holler (*informal*), howl, screech, shout, shriek, squeal ♦ *noun* 2 <u>SCREAM</u>, cry, howl, screech, shriek, whoop

yelp *verb* <u>CRY</u>, yap, yowl

yen *noun* <u>LONGING</u>, ache, craving, desire, hankering, hunger, itch, passion, thirst, yearning

yes man *noun* <u>SYCOPHANT</u>, bootlicker (*informal*), crawler (*slang*), minion, timeserver, toady

yet *conjunction* 1 <u>NEVERTHELESS</u>, however, notwithstanding, still ♦ *adverb* 2 <u>SO FAR</u>, as yet, thus far, until now, up to now 3 <u>STILL</u>, besides, in addition, into the bargain, to boot 4 <u>NOW</u>, just now, right now, so soon

yield *verb* 1 <u>PRODUCE</u>, bear, bring forth, earn, generate, give, net, provide, return, supply 2 <u>SURRENDER</u>, bow, capitulate, give in, relinquish, resign, submit, succumb ♦ *noun* 3 <u>PROFIT</u>, crop, earnings, harvest, income, output, produce, return, revenue, takings

yielding *adjective* 1 <u>SUBMISSIVE</u>, accommodating, acquiescent, biddable, compliant, docile, flexible, obedient, pliant 2 <u>SOFT</u>, elastic, pliable, spongy, springy, supple, unresisting

yob, yobbo *noun* <u>THUG</u>, hooligan, lout, roughneck (*slang*), ruffian

yokel *noun* <u>PEASANT</u>, (country) bumpkin, countryman, hick (*informal, chiefly U.S. & Canad.*), hillbilly, rustic

young *adjective* 1 <u>IMMATURE</u>, adolescent, callow, green, infant, junior, juvenile, little, youthful 2 <u>NEW</u>, early, fledgling, recent, undeveloped ♦ *plural noun* 3 <u>OFFSPRING</u>, babies, brood, family, issue, litter, progeny

youngster *noun* <u>YOUTH</u>, boy, girl, juvenile, kid (*informal*), lad, lass, teenager

youth *noun* 1 <u>IMMATURITY</u>, adolescence, boyhood, girlhood, salad days 2 <u>BOY</u>, adolescent, kid (*informal*), lad, stripling, teenager, young man, youngster

youthful *adjective* <u>YOUNG</u>, boyish, childish, girlish, immature, inexperienced, juvenile

zany *adjective* <u>COMICAL</u>, clownish, crazy, eccentric, goofy (*informal*), madcap, wacky (*slang*)

zeal *noun* <u>ENTHUSIASM</u>, ardour, eagerness, fanaticism, fervour, gusto, keenness, passion, spirit, verve, zest

zealot *noun* <u>FANATIC</u>, bigot, enthusiast, extremist, militant

zealous *adjective* ENTHUSIASTIC, ardent, devoted, eager, fanatical, fervent, impassioned, keen, passionate

zenith *noun* HEIGHT, acme, apex, apogee, climax, crest, high point, peak, pinnacle, summit, top

zero *noun* **1** NOTHING, nil, nought **2** BOTTOM, nadir, rock bottom

zest *noun* **1** ENJOYMENT, appetite, gusto, keenness, relish, zeal **2** FLAVOUR, charm, interest, piquancy, pungency, relish, spice, tang, taste

zip *noun* **1** *Informal* ENERGY, drive, gusto, liveliness, verve, vigour, zest ♦ *verb* **2** SPEED, flash, fly, shoot, whizz (*informal*), zoom

zone *noun* AREA, belt, district, region, section, sector, sphere

zoom *verb* SPEED, dash, flash, fly, hurtle, pelt, rush, shoot, whizz (*informal*)